Jim Murray's

WHISKY BIBLE
2010

**This 2010 edition of the Whisky Bible is dedicated to the memory
of my beloved Borat
&
celebrates a whiskey legend's 90th birthday and 60 continuous years
in the bourbon industry, a joint milestone achieved by
my treasured friend Elmer T Lee**

This edition first published 2009 by Dram Good Books Ltd

10 9 8 7 6 5 4 3 2 1

The "Jim Murray's" logo and the "Whisky Bible" logo are trade marks of Jim Murray.

For information regarding using tasting notes from Jim Murray's Whisky Bible contact:
Dram Good Books Ltd, 21 Park Road, Wellingborough, Northamptonshire, UK NN8 4PW
Tel: 44 (0)1933 279709. Or contact us via www.whiskybible.com

ISBN: 978-0-9554729-4-7

Printed in England by Stanley L Hunt (Printers) Ltd. Rushden, Northamptonshire
www.stanleylhunt.co.uk

Written and Edited by: Jim Murray
Design: Jim Murray, Darren Jordan, James Murray
Maps: James Murray
Production: James Murray, David Rankin, Billy Jeffrey, David Wilson, Mike Leaman
Sample Research: David Rankin, Ali Newton, Edna Mycawka, Julia Nourney

Author's Note
I have used the spelling "whiskey" or "whisky" depending on how the individual distillers
prefer. All Scotch is "whisky". So is Canadian. All Irish, these days, is "whiskey", though
that was not always the case. In Kentucky, bourbon and rye are spelt "whiskey", with the
exception of the produce of the early Times/Old Forester Distillery and Maker's Mark which they
bottle as "whisky". In Tennessee, it is a 50-50 split: Dickel is "whisky", while Daniel's is "whiskey".

Jim Murray's

WHISKY BIBLE
2010

*The world's leading whisky guide from
the world's foremost whisky authority*

DRAM GOOD BOOKS

Contents

Introduction

So here we go again. Seatbelts on, armrests down and enjoy the ride: you are heading off on a voyage of discovery of nearly 1,000 brand new whiskies. On top of the other 2,900 already there.

The actual astonishing number of newbies falls a few glasses short of 950, a small fraction down on last year's record-breaking four-figure total. This year's annual edition, the 7th, enjoys a greatly improved European section, a massively growing area which needs and deserves the expanded coverage we have given it

But of course the vast majority of this year's bottlings have come from Scotland, the usual mixed bunch in style and quality, but considering the economic turbulence – or is it closer to being in the doldrums? – it is truly wonderful to still see these brands flying off the bottling lines and onto the shelves. Whether they are then moved off those shelves by customers quite as fast as they have done in the past is another matter. But the marketing spirit of the whisky distiller is an indomitable one and I hope some kind of ghost of me is still hanging about in a 100 years time. I'd like to see the faces of historians re-visiting this period of our history trying to match what is considered the biggest economic downturn in 80 or 100 years, depending on who you believe, with all the new entries in Jim Murray's Whisky Bible 2010...

As ever, all the whiskies have been nosed and evaluated by myself alone without fear or favour. Even so, there was something mildly pleasing that my World Whisky of the Year has been awarded to an entirely different type of whiskey style this time round, vividly underlining the vastness of choice that whisky drinker enjoys. American Rye whiskey fell out of favour following prohibition by which time north American palates became used to blander fare. In a way it is Kentucky's version of peated whisky. Not that it is in any way smoky. Quite the opposite: it is enormously fruity. But the way in which the flavours are intense, rich and in the best cases almost onion-esque in its multi-layering make the two diverse types strangely linked. Hopefully, the much deserved award given to the compelling Sazerac Rye 18-years-old will help encourage American distillers to push this style further around the globe and back it up with stock to allow it to become mainstream once again.

On the subject of the US we know many people there were disappointed they didn't get their copies of last year's Bible by Christmas. It was out and selling rapidly elsewhere around the world, but the supply chain was just not good enough. We have tried to rectify this, but with limited success. Of the five possible distributers we spoke to, only one came back to us with an offer which meant we didn't actually lose money of up to 80 cents on each Bible sold! If you have noticed a withering number of British books from the small independent publishers in North American bookstores of late you should not be too surprised. Of the one possible distributor, no deal could be reached before going to press. So if you do have problems getting further copies of Jim Murray's Whisky Bible 2010, you can order online from whiskybible.com and we will send a copy, signed if required, to any part of the world. However, we continue our programme of selling Jim Murray's Whisky Bible through American and Canadian – and, indeed, world – liquor stores. Even with the North American problems, we are down to the last couple of boxes of Bibles 2009 here so we thank you for helping us remain the world's biggest-selling whisky book.

Yet again I cannot thank the distillers and bottlers enough for sending their samples in. Though I'd like to remind one or two that, unlike various spirit competitions, we very strictly don't accept money for their entry or advertising or sponsorship. Entry into the Bible is free: send the sample, I taste it...and in it goes, for better or for worse.

We have not been blind to the need to highlight more vividly the really great whiskies which can be found out there. So, from now on, all whiskies scoring 94 points or more will automatically gain the **Jim Murray's Whisky Bible Liquid Gold Award**. Distillers can, if they wish, use a special logo with points attained to help attract you to the whiskies I feel are the very finest to be found in the world. Naturally, the World Whisky of the Year and all other awards will continue. Good luck in your search for them....

Jim Murray
The Tasting Room
Wellingborough, August 2009

How to Read The Bible

The whole point of this book is for the whisky lover – be he or she an experienced connoisseur or, better fun still, simply starting out on the long and joyous path of discovery – to have ready access to easy-to-understand information about as many whiskies is possible. And I mean a lot. Thousands.

This book does not quite include every whisky on the market ... just by far and away the vast majority. And those that have been missed this time round – either through accident, logistics or design – will appear in later editions once we can source a sample.

Whisky Scoring

The marking for this book is tailored to the consumer and scores run out just a little higher than I use for my own personal references. But such is the way it has been devised it has not affected my order of preference.

Each whisky is given a rating out of 100. Twenty-five marks are given to each of four factors: nose **(n)**, taste **(t)**, finish **(f)**, balance and overall complexity **(b)**. That means that 50% of the marks are given for flavour alone and 25% for the nose, often an overlooked part of the whisky equation. The area of balance and complexity covers all three previous factors and a usually hidden one besides:

Nose: this is simply the aroma. Often requires more than one inspection as hidden aromas can sometimes reveal themselves after time in the glass, increased contact with air and changes in temperature. The nose very often tells much about a whisky, but – as we shall see – equally can be quite misleading.

Taste: this is the immediate arrival on the palate and involves the flavour profile up to, and including, the time it reaches maximum intensity and complexity.

Finish: often the least understood part of a tasting. This is the tail and flourish of the whisky's signature, often revealing the effects of ageing. The better whiskies tend to finish well and longer without too much oak excess. It is on the finish, also, that certain notes which are detrimental to the whisky may be observed. For instance, a sulphur-tarnished cask may be fully revealed for what it is by a dry, bitter residue on the palate which is hard to shake off. It is often worth waiting a few minutes to get the full picture of the finish before having a second taste of a whisky.

Balance: This is the part it takes a little experience to appreciate but it can be mastered by anyone. For a whisky to work well on the nose and palate, it should not be too one-sided in its character. If you are looking for an older whisky, it should have evidence of oak, but not so much that all other flavours and aromas are drowned out. Likewise, a whisky matured or finished in a sherry butt must offer a lot more than just wine alone and the greatest Islay malts, for instance, revel in depth and complexity beyond the smoky effects of peat

Each whisky has been analysed by me without adding water or ice. I have taken each whisky as it was poured from the bottle and used no more than warming in an identical glass to extract and discover the character of the whisky. To have added water would have been pointless: it would have been an inconsistent factor as people, when pouring water, add different amounts at varying temperatures. The only constant with the whisky you and I taste will be when it has been poured directly from the bottle.

Even if you and I taste the same whiskies at the same temperature and from identical glasses – and even share the same values in whisky – our scores may still be different. Because a factor that is built into my evaluation is drawn from expectation and experience. When I sample a whisky from a certain distillery at such-and-such an age or from this type of barrel or that, I would expect it to offer me certain qualities. It has taken me 30 years to acquire this knowledge (which I try to add to day by day!) and an enthusiast cannot be expected to learn it overnight. But, hopefully, Jim Murray's Whisky Bible will help...!

Score chart

Within the parentheses () is the overall score out of 100.

0–50.5 Nothing short of absolutely diabolical.

51–64.5 Nasty and well worth avoiding.

65–69.5 Very unimpressive indeed.

70–74.5 Usually drinkable but don't expect the earth to move.

75–79.5 Average and usually pleasant though sometimes flawed.

80–84.5 Good whisky worth trying.

85–89.5 Very good to excellent whiskies definitely worth buying.

90–93.5 Brilliant.

94–97.5 Superstar whiskies that give us all a reason to live.

98–100 Better than anything I've ever tasted!

Key to Abbreviations & Symbols

% Percentage strength of whisky measured as alcohol by volume. **b** Overall balance and complexity. **bott** Date of bottling. **db** Distillery bottling. In other words, an expression brought out by the owners of the distillery. **dist** Date of distillation or spirit first put into cask. **f** Finish. **n** Nose. **nc** Non-coloured. *ncf* Non-chill-filtered. *sc* Single cask. **t** Taste. ∴ New entry for 2010. ⊙ Retasted – no change. ⊙⊙ Retasted and re-evaluated. **v** Varient

Finding Your Whisky

Worldwide Malts: Whiskies are listed alphabetically throughout the book. In the case of single malts, the distilleries run A–Z style with distillery bottlings appearing at the top of the list in order of age, starting with youngest first. After age comes vintage. After all the "official" distillery bottlings are listed, next come other bottlings, again in alphabetical order. Single malts without a distillery named (or perhaps named after a dead one) are given their own section, as are vatted malts.

Worldwide Blends: These are simply listed alphabetically, irrespective of which company produce them. So "Black Bottle" appears ahead of "White Horse" and Japanese blends begin with "Ajiwai Kakubin" and ends with "Za". In the case of brands being named after companies or individuals the first letter of the brand will dictate where it is listed. So William Grant, for instance, will be found under "W" for William rather than "G" for Grant.

Bourbon/Rye: One of the most confusing types of whiskey to list because often the name of the brand bears no relation to the name of the distillery that made it. Also, brands may be sold from one company to another, or shortfalls in stock may see companies buying bourbons from another. For that reason all the brands have been listed alphabetically with the name of the bottling distiller being added at the end.

Irish Whiskey: There are four types of Irish whiskey: (i) pure pot still; (ii) single malt; (iii) single grain and (iv) blended. Some whiskies may have "pure pot still" on the label, but are actually single malts. So check both sections.

Bottle Information

As no labels are included in this book I have tried to include all the relevant information you will find on the label to make identification of the brand straightforward. Where known I have included date of distillation and bottling. Also the cask number for further recognition. At the end of the tasting notes I have included the strength and, if known, number of bottles (sometimes abbreviated to btls) released and in which markets.

Price of Whisky

You will notice that Jim Murray's Whisky Bible very rarely refers to the cost of a whisky. This is because the book is a guide to quality and character rather than the price tag attached. Also, the same whiskies are sold in different countries at varying prices due to market forces and variations of tax, so there is a relevance factor to be considered. Equally, much depends on the size of an individual's pocket. What may appear a cheap whisky to one could be an expensive outlay to another. With this in mind prices are rarely given in the Whisky Bible.

Bible Thumping
Bring Every Dram Into Judgment

Whisky is a numbers game.

Pick any distillery you like, anywhere in the world. Just so long as it hosts visitors, pop along and you will see exactly what I mean. Among the first snippets you are likely to glean will be how many years the old place has stood. Then more digits will be hurled at you in dizzying succession.

It will begin like a lonely snowflake at first, develop into a blizzard and finally you will be buried under an avalanche...of numbers. Numbers of tons of grain processed, how many times boiling water is poured over the grist, the temperatures of that water, the quantity of fermenters there are and their capacities; whether the whisky is distilled twice or thrice, the number of litres or gallons each still holds, the percentage of alcohol of the spirit produced, the numbers of casks filled each day. How many years they are left to mature; the age of oldest in the warehouse, even the age of the oldest warehouse. The number of warehouses they mature in and the cask height to which they are stacked; how much whisky is lost to the angels. And for good measure you might be told how many countries the whisky can be found in, cases sold, the exact thousands of visitors who follow in your footsteps each year as a result and, naturally and triumphantly, the number of awards collected for the excellence of the product.

Numbers, numbers, numbers. Big ones, small ones, medium-sized ones. Everywhere. In the whisky game, you can't escape the things.

So I have always found it just a little curious that the main number quite a few distilling companies tend not to be too happy about is the one given for the perceived quality of their whisky. This is not a new phenomenon. In the days Jim Murray's Whisky Bible was just a gleam in a then still 20/20 visioned eye, I remember what must have been dozens of distillery and marketing managers trot out almost exactly the same view, something along the lines of: "don't get me wrong, Jim. I like Michael's book. But I don't like the fact he scores the whisky. That's wrong. Much prefer your books where you just give an opinion."

Depending where I was or how well I knew the host, or the depth of my energy and jetlag, I would either ask them to tell me why. Or simply nod politely, unwilling to spoil an agreeable visit and appear an ungracious guest. But all the time I would be thinking: "Wait 'til you see my Bible..." When I did ask, the majority of the answers were a touch incoherent. Or perhaps I should say the numbers in the argument didn't quite add up. For instance, I remember one marketing guy telling me that they were aware that batches of their whisky could perhaps alter in quality very slightly from bottling to bottling. Not enough to affect the marks in a five star system, or even possibly out of ten. But with a numerical rating system out of 100, however, you probably could see the slight shift in quality, either for the better or worse – or both over time. And that wasn't good for the product, I was told. Or the consumer, who would be confused by it.

I never got that last bit. Surely, I would argue (and still vehemently do), if a consumer buys a whisky and notices a difference from one bottling to the next, it helps him to see that someone else has spotted the change: that he or she is not alone. Rather than confusing the consumer, it simply underlines what he believed and gives him confidence. So I have always been a massive advocate of the scoring system. Because let's face it: we spend our entire life judging things. Whether we are aware of it or not, we give marks and grades, be it which baker in town makes the best bread, which beer we prefer, which player we rate over another at left back in our football team, the next car we are going to buy. Grading, grading, grading. One big decision after another based on a hundred small ones. For all our life our brain is judging, measuring, adding, subtracting, dividing: sorting the wheat from the chaff. We do it so often and for so long, we are not even aware that it is happening. But we do.

For instance, a lady or gentleman meets some those of the opposite sex for the first time at a dinner party. None are spoken for. The evening is spent by weighing up personalities, charm, humour, intelligence, looks, figure, charisma, natural warmth, kindness, a little naughtiness.... a million little things. Then the numbers are added. And....well, of course there is something else as well. There is natural instinct; it encompasses that indefinable thing which you sense and though it doesn't fall under any of the normal headings above, you still add on a few extra marks here and there if something is stirred.

Just as we do with our whisky.

I imagine it is the same with speed-dating, only there the adding has to be done so much faster, the chances of getting the sums wrong so much easier. Ditto again with whisky: spend time over a glass and you make a more considered assessment. You can check those numbers over again. Whizz through them, mistakes are made.

So it was quite amusing when a few people appeared startled last year when I began using half points within the scoring system. They could not fathom the logic. Well, had they sat with me and tasted over 1,000 whiskies I think they might well have understood better. And possibly have begging for a move towards quarter points.

Because whisky is the most complex drink in the world: that is why you are reading this book. It has affected you to the extent that you have been moved and intrigued enough to find out more about it, possibly from someone who may be able to help back your judgment; to see if your numbers tally. And there are such myriad aspects to it that a half point here and there – even over a 100 point total system - becomes quite important. It means, as you spot the odd character that had been masked first time round, you can trim or add half a point here and there. The whisky, using my nose, taste, finish and balance scoring system can move up or down as much as two points as you fine tune. By the end of the scoring you feel you have much better represented that whisky than before.

Which is why I have problems in getting my head around five star awards: talk about painting with a broad brush. In truth, I don't have time to see what others have made of a whisky: as I taste every one in this book a minimum three times over as long a period as possible, I hardly have enough hours in the day to sort my own scores, let alone other people's. But one of the research team here, while double checking a brand's spelling, had noticed that someone online had given exactly the same number of stars to two whiskies, one I had scored in the low 90s, the other about 70. Of course everyone has the right to mark as they see fit, and offer those views to others. That is what free speech and democracy is all about. However, where does that one leave the consumer or even liquor store buyer when that person giving the scores presents themselves as an expert? Of those two whiskies, one was a staggering cask, still fresh but displaying the first signs of the onset of antiquity and needed a good half hour of contemplation to enjoy to its fullest: it was non-coloured, non-chillfiltered, non-sulphured and a celebration of all you would seek and expect from that distillery. The other had a sulphury flaw which not even heavy chill filtration had been able to cure. Yet, according to this system, they are equals. Ridiculous. And irresponsible, in my view, when it costs so much to invest in a whisky. Also, it has to be said, a bit cowardly, too.

Michael Jackson used to score out of 100. Good for him. My old buddie John Hansell still does. Excellent fellows ready to stick their heads above the parapet, rather than shrinking behind the blanket covering of stars or the relatively wide-scoped scores out of 10. In the wine world Robert Parker gets a fair bit of buffeting for his rankings. But he cannot be accused of hiding, or being wishy-washy.

I fully accept that some people find the star-scoring system perfectly adequate for their needs and does the job every bit as well as a total out of a 100. But I have to say that that has never been the case for me. For example, a score of three and half stars out of five means what exactly? Taking that three stars equals a score of 60 (or thereabouts) and four stars equals something in the region of 80, does that means that three and half stars is equal to the whisky getting 70 points? Or anything between 66 and 74? Who knows? I would personally think that one at the lower end of the scale would be bordering rubbish, the one at the other end drinkable. It is totally open to interpretation, or should I say confusion. But certainly it offers less chance of upsetting the distiller or bottler.

Now I'm not saying that my scoring is perfect: it isn't. For a start, I am not a computer, so I am apt to err. That said, for all the machines which may get invented to tell what flavours and aromas a whisky may possess, it is unlikely any in our lifetimes will be human enough to have a perceptual understanding and appreciation of what is in the glass, let alone an emotional reaction to it. It may tell you that 9.894 per cent of the aroma is honey-based, 4.673 is salt and so on. What it can never tell you is if, when combined, they harmonise.

Also I have been accused of marking too highly. And I can understand why some think that. But there is logic, I believe, to the way my scoring works. For instance, we worked out the number of whiskies scoring 95 or over – a pretty high score – in this year's Bible. Of the 950 or so new whiskies added it works out at somewhere in the region of 5%. Now that sounds about right to me. That really does represent the cream of the cream rising to the top.

It also means that those scoring 90 and above aren't too shoddy, either. I like to think that those who are producing very good whisky have something they can beat their chests about and their efforts are not going unrecognised. Because let's be honest here: there is some very ordinary whisky about. And with the effects of sulphur casks now endemic in both malts and blends – and not just in Scotland – I have had to slightly alter the marks to face the fact that things are not what they were: a lot of whiskies which would have scored low 70s six or seven years ago get a slightly higher mark now. Because the goalposts have moved; the whisky landscape has changed. We are back again to the dinner table and constantly, constantly calculating and re-calculating. Having said that, the higher up the scale you go, there is less movement and as soon as you cross the rubicon at 90 absolutely none at all. For instance, when I give tastings around the world I use only whiskies which have scored 89 or over. I have done that from my own scoring system for the last two decades. Whiskies which score lower tend to be somewhat overshadowed by the others in the line-up. And anyone who has been to my tastings over that time will vouchsafe that the quality of those whiskies on display are as high now as any time in the past.

Perhaps only in the US has scoring remained exactly the same. Because there the laws surrounding what constitutes bourbon, rye and corn whiskey have not changed and distillers work within confines that makes the judging so much easier: the fact they cannot add colouring and have to mature the spirit in virgin oak casks has safeguarded the DNA. So the scores and values in the Bible now are absolutely identical to when I gave the first notes in 2003. No moving goalposts, no change in the landscape. A wonderful constant.

So does that mean that the scores for different countries in this book are different from each other? Yes...and no. For a start, I treat all whiskies as equals, but judge them to their style, taking into account the type of still, the whiskies I have tasted from there at varying ages before and so on. It is a very complex procedure. Perhaps the best way of looking at it is like this. You are a reporter and go to cover Manchester United versus Real Madrid in front of 70,000 in the European Cup and asked to give each player's scores out of ten. After a dull 0-0 draw, you might find that of the 22 which started the game, four get nine, eight get eight, eight get seven and two get six. The following week you are sent to cover the part-timers of Banbury United against mighty Dashley in the English Zamaretto Southern Premier League, attendance, 317 And a dog It's a cracker and Banbury scrape home 4-3 with a goal in the third minute of injury time after being 3-0 down with twenty minutes to play due, mainly, to some inspired managerial substitutions. Two players get nine, nine get eight, six get seven, four get six and one gets five. Right, every player who played in the Manchester United game is an international. At Banbury only three had ever been full time professional in their careers. Does that mean that the Banbury player who got nine is a better player than a Real Madrid player who got seven? Of course not. But what he did do was contribute to the enjoyment in a more telling way, performed better than was expected of him and overall gave a more satisfying performance. Everything is relative. And when you are judging whisky it is the same, even if the comparison is very rarely quite that stark.

But again, it has to be said once the scoring in the Bible gets around the 90 mark, you have to be that good. Very good. The whisky is making the statement: I am among the best in world. I am among the top echelon of my peers.

This football analogy above helps to explain why the scoring even for the Scotch has moved fractionally. For three consecutive years the amount of sulphur detectable has risen. This year I lost many days tasting after my tastebuds had been nullified. Almost imperceptibly, the character and quality of the average Scotch whisky is changing. And, as an average, it will not improve until the sulphur-tainted casks have been used up, which may be a little way down the line. The Excellent whiskies, those scoring, 89 onwards and the Great, those of 93 plus, remain just that. So don't panic. There are still plenty of truly enjoyable whiskies of every sort to go round.

Thousands of them...

Review of the Whisky Year

The picture you get of the whisky industry is one usually of tranquility. Lonely glens in Scotland; a deer nibbling on a tuft of grass while a Golden Eagle soars on a thermal overhead. A benign sea lapping gently at the feet of an ancient Hebridean distillery. Warm, peaceful, dusty warehouses in America where both the barrel and warehouseman doze. A gallery of images to bring the blood pressure down a bit and get you reaching for a glass.

The reality in the market place has been a little different of late.

At the beginning of the year I received a phone call from the marketing director of one of the decent-sized Scotch companies. His voice was not its usual bright, upbeat self. In fact, it was a little irritated and breathless.

"Are the guys from the other companies still telling you everything's hunky dory out there and the market's fine?"

"More or less."

"Do you believe them?"

"No."

"Good. Because I'm telling you, Jim. It's a f****** slaughterhouse out there. There's blood all over the place. I've been in this game a long time and I've never known anything like it. It's brutal. And if you want to do any selling out there you've got to be prepared to f****** maim and kill if need be."

His call had not exactly surprised me. When I was in Moscow last November I caught up with a bunch of whisky marketing chaps in a hotel bar and asked how things were going. Lots of smiles in reply. And some cheerful umming and arring. But not great eye contact. Anyone who has been a fan of that wonderful old panel game Call My Bluff will get some idea of the situation.

So after years of blue skies and sales projection charts being extended onto the ceiling, the building of new distilleries and the opening of fresh markets, a new generation of whisky people are having to face up to how much of the industry felt in the 1980s. Insecure. Totally unsure of the thickness of the ice they have been happily skating on for the last 15 years.

It has meant that farm leaders in Scotland have been demanding that the industry tell them just how much malting barley they require so farmers can make maximum use of their land. And, understandably, the distillers are telling them that this is the one time when they have the least idea. Because the sticky problem with whisky production is that you are not requiring wheat to produce bread for the next day. You need barley for a market every year from three to 25 years time. It is a pity farmers can't grow crystal balls. So there has to be massive sympathy with the industry.

But one distilling company that appears fresh out of sympathy is Diageo. The biggest distilling company in the world, which traces its line back to the old Scottish Malt Distillers company, have spectacularly succeeded in turning their home nation against them by announcing the closure of the Kilmarnock bottling plant which had been the home of Johnnie Walker longer than anyone now living. And on the same day they also announced that they were closing the old Port Dundas grain distillery in Glasgow. Together, the two closures total 900 lost jobs, an absolutely massive hit for the workforce of the Scotch whisky industry.

Even though one can understand that a company, whether it makes wine gums, widgets or whisky, has to plan for the future and ensure that it is run as efficiently as possible and return an excellent dividend for its shareholders, there appears to be something genuinely cold-blooded and worryingly detached about their decision to close their bottling plant in Hill Street, Kilmarnock. A sobering 700 jobs will go.

It is the town where in the 1820s a certain John Walker from his grocery shop began selling whisky which eventually not only became an international brand, but through its success with Johnnie Walker Red Label and Johnnie Walker Black Label in particular the cornerstone of the whisky arm of the Diageo Empire. The same Diageo which in February 2009 posted a first half profit of no less than £1.63 billion.

It might be a little over the top to make out Diageo as some kind of evil empire in this, as they have been painted since the announcement of the closure was made on July 1st. They can with genuine justification claim that these redundancies will go some way towards being able to create 500 jobs elsewhere in Scotland and continue the efficiency of the company which will keep them at the very top of their tree. Yet somewhere along the way here a vital touch of humanity has been lost. In the days of John Walker and his son Alexander, at the height of Victorian philanthropy, the businessman who became startlingly rich upon the toils of his workforce would often do something for them in return. He would build a library, or a theatre, or fund a park. Anything, so long as it furthered the wellbeing of the townspeople that brought him his fortune. It appears that in Kilmarnock a loyalty dating back to the 1860s will be rewarded with about 1.6 per cent of the population being made redundant and all the hardship that ensues.

Such has been the uproar to this news there was the unprecedented spectacle of some 20,000 people marching through the Ayrshire town in protest. At the head of them, predictably, came the high-ranking politicians showing a solidarity with the town-folk that was truly touching and a sense of outrage and indignation which was fearsome. Anyone would have thought there was an election in the offing. Oh, hang on a minute, there is. Because, unless I'm very much mistaken, Port Dundas distillery is found within the Glasgow North East constituency of former Commons Speaker Michael Martin who is standing down as an MP. So a by-election is due there any time.

I am sure I was not alone wondering when I saw Scotland's First Minister Alex Salmond and Labour heavyweight and Kilmarnock MP Des Browne at the head of the anti-Diageo procession where exactly they were when Allied Distillers closed down Dumbarton grain distillery a few years back, arguably a bigger blow to the town of Dumbarton than Port Dundas is to Glasgow. The same thought probably crossed the mind of bewildered Diageo management whom I very much doubt had seen this hostility towards them coming.

After all, in recent memory we have seen Perth emptied of Bells and the White Horse operation disappear and many other closures besides. Where was the wailing and gnashing of teeth then; or when distilleries, once noisy places with a busy workforce, once a community of their own right, became one or two man operations where there is more tour guides than distillery operatives? So Diageo could have been forgiven for thinking that after a union-inspired hubbub, things would quieten down and the industry would carry on its streamlining undisturbed. Perhaps they made a miscalculation in announcing two closures simultaneously, rather than phasing them. Or perhaps the company has moved so far away from its Scottish roots that it has lost the last of the common touch it had and empathy with the people who are at the grass roots of their vast fortune. The fact that earlier in the year The Guardian newspaper published a story that ownership of many of their whisky brands, including Johnnie Walker, had been transferred from a British company to a Dutch one and Diageo refused to discuss it is certainly a worrying development. It makes the severing of historic connections like those in Kilmarnock all that easier to make.

First, what is required is to find a senior Diageo director with a social conscience. Their managing director for their operation in Scotland, Bryan Donnaghey, might be a start as at least he was quoted as saying: "I am sorry that the impact this announcement will have on our employees and families in Kilmarnock and Glasgow and the difficulty this will cause in Kilmarnock where we are a major employer." So at least he is alive to the workers' plight. And he needs to be surrounded by others of similar moral persuasion. But ones who also realize that you cannot have it both ways by selling a brand by linking it to history - "Born 1820 and still going strong"- and then ditching that historical link for financial expediency. If half year profits of over £1.5 billion are being posted in the teeth of a recession, perhaps they should think of doing what Johnnie Walker and his son Alexander might of. Thank their workforce properly for playing their part. Perhaps by giving them job security.

For at the moment it appears that all the thanks for generation upon generation of dedicated work from these good people is to see the Striding Man keep on striding...right out of town. And that, surely, cannot be right.

~

In Kentucky, 2009 proved a vintage year for distillery takeovers. In early April Wild Turkey parted company with Pernod Ricard and became a part of the ever-expanding Campari whisky empire. The sum that changed hands was $575 million. Normally that kind of money only passes between French and Italian banks when a football player is being sold. This, though, catapults Campari into the senior whisky players in the world. It had been one of the worst kept secrets in the industry that Pernod were looking for hard cash and the wonderfully evocative Wild Turkey, perched on a cliff top above the Kentucky River and Lawrenceburg was being hung out as bait.

The Italians are renowned for having a little bit of style. And there is 101 proof here with the acquisition of one of the world's greatest distilleries. It comes on top of them having set up a Scotch whisky arm at Glen Grant, another distillery which rightfully enjoys a high reputation.

Just a week or so earlier, Sazerac, owners of another top-ranking bourbon distillery, Buffalo Trace, doubled the number of Kentucky distilleries in their portfolio by taking over Constellation Brands, owners of the Barton Distillery in Bardstown in a £334 million deal. Barton was immediately re-named the Tom Moore distillery but at the moment remains the ugly duckling of all Kentucky's bourbon outposts, having been proudly geared 100 per cent towards production rather than any form of tourism. The vast majority of the whisky produced there was sold at a relatively young age. But its older stock was capable of holding its head high, though rarely given the chance. It will be interesting to see what Sazerac do with the distillery and its many brands which include Kentucky Tavern, Very Old Barton, Ten High and, of course, Tom Moore.

And in a busy period for Sazerac they also raided Jim Beam to sign their famous old brand Old Taylor. The whisky used to be made just a mile from my home at Millville, near Frankfort. But production was moved to the Beam's main distilleries at Clermont and Boston and the historic old distillery was abandoned. Part of the deal includes the purchase of stocks from Beam, presumably to buy time to mature spirit either at Buffalo Trace or Tom Moore and create the iconic brand in its old image. I have some old bottles of the stuff made at Millville, if they want to start planning...

My one sorrow is that the man who fought to retain the name and history of Old Taylor, Cecil Withrow, by buying the plant from Beam, is no longer with us to see this day. Somehow I could see the vast frame of my much loved and missed friend ambling in the direction of Buffalo Trace CEO Mark Brown's office to offer daily advice whether he wanted it or not. Cecil died at a tragically young age a few years back putting up a Christmas tree with his grand-daughter – Taylor – by his side. The news that a company had taken over Old Taylor and was intending to re-launch and eventually build the name back into a major bourbon brand has made me realize something after all these years. There must be a Father Christmas after all.

Jim Murray's Whisky Bible Award Winners 2010

It could have been the Whisky Olympics. The eight finalists lined up together, nations from all corners of the earth represented; the very finest specimens of their respective race. The lesser mortals had fallen by the wayside, so much hope and expectation dashed: we were down to the super elite.

And, just as is so often the case, it was an American claiming gold. Breasting the tape fractionally ahead of many's favourite, with a surprise outsider coming in third. Just behind, missing out on the biggest medals, was a much-loved veteran most judges thought would never have the stamina to complete the course, let alone come so close to glory. All in all, the battle for supremacy was a classic.

From a personal point of view - and of course judging these and some thousand other whiskies single handedly it was about as personal as you could possibly get - it was a great moment for me to finally find a whiskey representing probably my own favourite style that had lorded it above all other challangers. There is something about rye whiskey which has ticked my boxes for the last 35 years. But, until now, there had always been an individual bourbon or Scotch or Japanese which had been better. However the Fall 2008 bottling of Sazerac 18-year-old rye was simply uncatchable. The Ardbeg Supernova, Amrut Fusion and Glenfiddich 50-years-old each tested the Sazerac to its limits and the Ballantines 17 with its understated sophistication also made a quiet though searching enquiry, but the rye endured

What made it unbeatable was its startling performance: it reminded me of a jazz band in which all the individual musicians and instruments get their five minutes to perform solo, but then return together for a long final burst of breathtaking harmony. You are left with no choice other than to applaud each dazzling piece of virtuosity and then offer a five minute standing ovation when the overall piece ends. It just blows you away.

The Ardbeg, by contrast, was a conjuring trick. Somehow it made 100 parts per million phenols disappear for a while before slowly returning to the palate. Magic? Or smoke and mirrors? Well, certainly smoke. It has countless "Wow! How does it do that?" moments.

But the biggest surprise package, well at least for those who have never tasted the malt from this distillery before, was the whisky from Bangalore. It is not normally the first place you think of when giving a list of Premier League distilleries. But Amrut is up there all right. However, this new version, Fusion, surprised even myself and I have long banged the gong for underdog distilleries. It is one of those which commands a big mouthful, a chair with a headrest...and silence. You will chew for seemingly hours and never quite get to the bottom of its mystical complexity. It is massive whisky, but its genius is that you get the feeling that there is some almost invisible element keeping the malt together so the proportions are never less than perfect. Let us hope they can keep future bottlings up to this improbable standard, but it is a very tall ask.

The same goes for the Glenfiddich 50, launched to the hype you would expect for a whisky costing £10,000 a bottle. Is it worth it? If you have a bank account worth the gold reserves of a small Latin American country, unquestionably. If you don't, then you could do worse and splash out the relative shrapnel of just £150 for the newly released Gordon and Macphail Glen Grant 1958 which had the Single Malt Scotch 41 Years and Over Award sewn up....until Glenfiddich unleashed their spectacular new offering in the final moments of this book being written: at the end of the marathon, a sprint finish. In so doing they denied Glen Grant a hat-trick of awards in Whisky Bible 2010. But in the true Olympian spirit, these awards are not about money.

They are about quality and achievement. And there can be no doubt that, as should be the case, quality won through in the end.

The Whisky Bible Award Winners 2010
2010 World Whisky of the Year
Sazerac Rye 18 Years Old (Fall 2008)

Second Finest Whisky in the World 2010
Ardbeg Supernova
Third Finest Whisky in the World 2010
Amrut Fusion

SCOTCH

Scotch Whisky of the Year
Ardbeg Supernova
Single Malt of the Year (Multiple Casks)
Ardbeg Supernova
Single Malt of the Year (Single Cask)
Glenfarclas 1962 (3rd Release)
Best Scotch New Brand
Glenmorangie Sonnalta PX
Scotch Blend of the Year
Ballantine's 17 Years Old
Scotch Grain of the Year
Duncan Taylor North British 1978
Scotch Vatted Malt of the Year
Johnnie Walker Green Label

Single Malt Scotch
No Age Statement (Multiple Casks)
Ardbeg Supernova
No Age Statement (Runner Up)
Glenmorangie Sonnalta PX
10 Years & Under (Multiple Casks)
Octomore 5 Year Old
10 Years & Under (Single Cask)
SMWS 77.17 (Glen Ord)
11-15 Years (Multiple Casks)
Tomintoul 14 Year Old
11-15 Years (Single Cask)
Isle of Arran Sherry 353
16-21 Years (Multiple Casks)
Glen Grant 1992
16-21 Years (Single Cask)
Glendronach 1992 Cask 401
22-27 Years (Multiple Casks)
Brora 25 Year Old 7th Release
22-27 Years (Single Cask)
Cadenhead's Benriach 23 YO
28-34 Years (Multiple Casks)
Highland Park 30 Year Old
28-34 Years (Single Cask)
Douglas Laing Glencadam 32 YO
35-40 Years (Multiple Casks)
Glenglassaugh 40 Year Old
35-40 Years (Single Cask)
Whisky Fair Glen Grant 36 YO
41 Years & Over (Multiple Casks)
Glenfiddich 50 Year Old
41 Years & Over (Single Cask)
Glenfarclas 1962 Release III

Blended Scotch
No Age Statement (Standard)
Ballantine's Finest

No Age Statement (Premium)
The Last Drop
5-12 Years
Johnnie Walker Black Label
13-18 Years
Ballantine's 17 Years Old
18 Years & Over
Chivas Regal 25 Year Old

IRISH WHISKEY
Irish Whiskey of the Year
Redbreast Aged 12 Years

AMERICAN WHISKEY
Bourbon of the Year
George T Stagg (144.8)
Rye of the Year
Sazerac 18 Years Old (Fall 2008)

Bourbon
No Age Statement (Multiple Barrels)
Parker's Golden Anniversary
No Age Statement (Single Barrel)
Blanton's Single Barrel 316
9 Years & Under
Jim Beam Black Aged 8 Years
10-12 years
Wild Turkey Russell's Reserve
13-17 Years (Multiple Barrels)
George T Stagg (144.8)
13-17 Years (Single Barrel)
Buffalo Trace Experimental Course Grain
18 Years & Over
Evan Williams 23 Year Old

Rye
10 Years & Younger
Jim Beam Rye
11 Years & Over
Sazerac 18 Years Old (Fall 2008)

CANADIAN WHISKY
Canadian Whisky of the Year
Wiser's Red Letter

JAPANESE WHISKY
Japanese Whisky of the Year
SMWS 116.14 (Yoichi)

EUROPEAN WHISKY
European Whisky of the Year
Santis Malt Highlander Dreifaltaigkeit
European Single Cask Whisky of the Year
Penderyn Port Wood Single Cask

WORLD WHISKIES
Indian Whisky of the Year
Amrut Fusion

*Overall age category winners are presented in **bold**.*

The Whisky Bible Liquid Gold Awards (97.5-94)

This year Jim Murray's Whisky Bible is delighted to make a point of celebrating the very finest whiskies you can find in the world. So we salute the distillers who have maintained or even furthered the finest traditions of whisky making and taken their craft to the very highest levels. And the bottlers who have brought some of them to us.

After all, there are nearly 4,000 different brands and expressions listed in this guide and from every corner of the planet. Those which score 94 and upwards represents only a very small fraction of them. These whiskies are, in my view, the elite: the finest you can currently find on the whisky shelves of the world. Rare and precious, they are Liquid Gold.

So it is our pleasure to announce that all those scoring 94 and upwards will from now on automatically qualify for the Jim Murray's Whisky Bible Liquid Gold Award. Congratulations!

97.5

Scotch Single Malt
Ardbeg Uigedail
American Straight Rye
Sazerac Rye 18 Years Old (Fall 08)

97

Scotch Single Malt
Ardbeg 10 Years Old
Ardbeg Supernova
Brora 30 Years Old
Glenfiddich 50 Years Old
Whisky Doris Strathisla Aged 35 Years
The Ileach Single Islay Malt Cask Strength
Blended Scotch
Old Parr Superior 18 Years Old
Japanese Single Malt
The Cask of Yamazaki 1990 Sherry Butt
Nikka Whisky Single Coffey Malt 12 Years

96.5

Scotch Single Malt
Ardbeg Corryvreckan
Port Charlotte PC6
Old & Rare Glencadam Aged 32 Years
Glenfarclas 1962 The Family Cask (3rd Release)
Glenfarclas 1979 The Family Cask (3rd Release)
Gordon & MacPhail Rare Vintage Glen Grant 1958
Glenmorangie Sonnalta PX
Old Malt Cask Glenury Aged 32 Years
Cadenhead's Royal Brackla Aged 16 Years
Blended Scotch
Ballantine's 17 Years Old
The Last Drop
Bourbon
Blanton's Single Barrel Silver No. 316
Blanton's Uncut/Unfiltered
George T Stagg
Parker's Heritage Collection 3rd Edition 2009 Golden Anniversary
Japanese Single Malt
SMWS Cask 116.14 Aged 25 Years (Yoichi)

Swiss Single Malt
Säntis Malt Swiss Highlander Edition Dreifaltigkeit

96

Scotch Single Malt
Connoisseurs Choice Aberfeldy 1989
Aberlour a'bunadh Batch No. 23
Ardbeg 1974 Single Cask No. 3151
Ardbeg 1977
Ardbeg Kildalton 1980
Ardbeg Provenance 1974
Queen of the Moorlands Rare Cask Bowmore 1991 Edition XVIII
Brora 25 Year Old
Octomore 5 Years Old
The Whisky Agency Bunnahabhain 34 Years Old
Glendronach Single Cask 1992
Glenfarclas 105 40th Anniversary Limited Edition 40 Years Old
The Whisky Fair Glenfarclas 40 Years Old
Duncan Taylor Collection Glengarioch 1988 Aged 19 Years
Glenglassaugh 40 Year Old
Old & Rare Glen Grant Aged 31 Years
The Whisky Fair Glen Grant 36 Year Old
Rarest of the Rare Glenlochy 1980
Glenmorangie Truffle Oak
Glen Moray 1986 Commemorative Bottling
Cadenhead's Authentic Collection Glenrothes Aged 16 Years
Scotch Malt Whisky Society Cask 93.30 Aged 16 Years (Glen Scotia)
Rarest of the Rare Inverleven 1979
The Arran Malt Amarone Finish
Lagavulin 21 Years Old
Parkers Whisky Port Ellen 1982 "Pert mELLon" Bottling
Rosebank 25 Years Old
Cadenhead's Rosebank Aged 20 Years
The Whisky Fair Springbank Aged 35 Years
Old Malt Cask Tactical Aged 18 Years
Master of Malt Tomatin 19 Years Old Cask Strength

The Whisky Fair Tullibardine 1976 Dark Sherry

The Whisky Agency Speyside Single Malt 39 Years Old

Single Grain Scotch

Duncan Taylor Collection Port Dundas 1973

Blended Scotch

Ballantine's Finest

Johnnie Walker Gold Label The Centenary Blend 18 Years Old

Irish Pot Still

Redbreast Aged 12 Years

Irish Blended

Jameson Rarest 2007 Vintage Reserve

American Single Malt

McCarthy's Aged 3 Years

Stranahan's Colorado Whiskey Batch No. 11

Bourbon

Buffalo Trace Experimental Course Grain Oak

George T. Stagg

Wild Turkey Rare Breed

Single Malt Rye

Old Potrero Single Malt Hotaling's Whiskey Aged 11 Years Essay MCMVI-MMVI

Old Potrero Single Malt Hotaling's Whiskey Aged 12 Years Essay MCMVI-MMVII

Straight Rye

Rittenhouse Rye Single Barrel 23 Year Old

Rittenhouse Very Rare Single Barrel 21 Years Old Barrel no. 28

Japanese Single Malt

The Cask of Hakushu 1993 Heavily Peated King of Diamonds 1988

Finnish Single Malt

Old Buck Second Release

Swedish Single Malt

Mackmyra Privus 03 Rökning Tillåten

Welsh Single Malt

Penderyn Cask Strength Rich Madeira

Penderyn Port Wood Edition

95.5

Scotch Single Malt

The BenRiach Curiositas Aged 10 Years Single Peated Malt

The BenRiach 1976

Cadenhead's Benriach Aged 23 Years

Bruichladdich Redder Still 1984

Caol Ila 'Distillery Only'

Glenfarclas 1990 The Family Malt Collection

Norse Cask Selection Glen Grant 1993 Aged 16 Years

Glenmorangie 25 Years Old

Scotch Malt Whisky Society Cask 77.17 Aged 9 Years (Glen Ord)

Highland Park Aged 18 Years

Highland Park Aged 30 Years

Scotch Malt Whisky Society Cask 4.126

Aged 9 Years (Highland Park)

Scotch Malt Whisky Society Cask 122.16 Aged 15 Years (Croftengea)

Scotch Malt Whisky Society Cask 7.51 Aged 24 Years (Longmorn)

Duncan Taylor Collection Macallan 1988

Berrys' Own Selection Port Ellen 1982

Dewar Rattray Cask Collection Port Ellen Aged 24 Years

Berry's Own Selection St. Magdalene 1982 Longrow C.V

Old Malt Cask Tamnavulin Aged 20 Years

Tomintoul Aged 12 Years Oloroso Sherry Finish Limited Edition

Scotch Vatted Malt

Compass Box Flaming Hart

Blended Scotch

Johnnie Walker Black Label 12 Years Old

Irish Single Malt

The Tyrconnell Single Cask

American Single Malt

Stranahan's Colorado Whiskey Batch No. 3

Stranahan's Colorado Whisky Batch No. 17

Bourbon

Blanton's Single Barrel No. 349

Evan Williams 23 Years Old

Straight Rye

Sazerac 18 Years Old (bott fall 07)

German Single Malt

Blaue Maus Single Malt 25 Jahre

95

Scotch Single Malt

Aberlour a'bunadh Batch No. 19

Aberlour a'bunadh Batch No. 26

Ardbeg Airigh Nam Beist Ltd 1990 Release

Ardbeg Mor

Cadenhead's Ardbeg Aged 14 Years

Cadenhead's Ardbeg Aged 15 Years

Scotch Malt Whisky Society Cask 33.68 Aged 9 Years (Ardbeg)

The Single Malts of Scotland Aultmore 1990 Aged 16 Years

Scotch Malt Whisky Society Cask 3.148 Aged 9 Years (Bowmore)

Connoisseurs Choice Braes of Glenlivet 1975

Old & Rare Brora Aged 30 Years

Bruichladdich 16 Years Old

Bruichaladdich 1970 Anniversary Bott 125th

Port Charlotte Evolution PC5 Cask Strength

Chieftain's Bruichladdich 19 Years Old

Old Masters Bruichladdich Aged 20 Years

Cadenhead's Convalmore 30 Years Old

Duncan Taylor Collection Dallas Dhu 1981

The Dalmore 62 Years Old

Adelphi Dalmore 1990 Aged 17 Years

Dalwhinnie 15 Years Old

Glencadam Aged 10 Years

Montgomerie's Glencadam 1975
Old Malt Cask Glencadam Aged 21 Years
Glendronach Aged 33 Years
Glenfarclas 15 Years Old
Glenfarclas 1960 The Family Casks
Glenfarclas 1966 The Family Casks
Glenfarclas 1994 The Family Casks
Whisky Fair Single Speyside Malt Aged 40
Glenfiddich 18 Years Old
Glenglassaugh 1973 Family Silver
Glengoyne 1997 11 Year Old Single Cask
Duncan Taylor Collection Glen Grant 1970
Old Malt Cask Glen Grant Aged 30 Years
Rarest of the Rare Glen Mhor 1975
Scotch Malt Whisky Society Cask 125.1
Aged 13 Years (Glenmorangie)
Glen Ord 25 Years Old
The Glenrothes 1979 Single Cask No. 3808
The Glenrothes 1979
Berry's Own Selection Glen Scotia 1992
Cadenhead's Glenturret Aged 20 Years
Murray McDavid Highland Park 1989
Duncan Taylor Collection Knockando 1980
Laphroaig 1/4 Cask
Cadenhead's Longmorn Aged 18 Years
The Macallan 1949 (53 Years Old)
The Macallan 1970 (32 Years Old)
Duncan Taylor Collection Macallan 1987
Rarest of the Rare North Port 1981
Scott's Selection North Port 1980
Port Ellen 4th Release Aged 25 Years
Old & Rare Port Ellen Aged 25 Yrs (07 bott)
Old & Rare Port Ellen Aged 25 Yrs (08 bott)
Old Pulteney Aged 17 Years
Rosebank Aged 12 Years
Scott's Selection The Speyside 1991
Da Mhile Organic "New Born" Springbank
Premium Scotch Importers Springbank
1998
Talisker Aged 20 Years
Talisker 57 Degrees North
Secret Stills Isle of Skye 1955
Old Malt Cask Tamdhu Aged 18 Years
Tomintoul Aged 14 Years
Tullibardine 1986 John Black Selection
Secret Stills Highland 6.1 1988
Auld Reekie Islay Malt
Master of Malt Speyside 50 Years Old
Special Reserve

Scotch Vatted Malt
Celtique Connexion Sauternes Finish Aged
13 Years
Johnnie Walker Green Label 15 Years Old
Norse Cask Selection Vatted Islay 1992
Aged 16 Years
Vintner's Choice Island 10 Years Old
Wild Scotsman Aged 15 Years Vatted Malt

Scottish Grain
The Clan Denny Dumbarton Aged 43 Years

Duncan Taylor Collection North British
1978

Blended Scotch
The Bailie Nicol Jarvie (B.N.J)
Chivas Regal 25 Years Old
Duncan Taylor Collection Black Bull Deluxe
Blend Aged 30 Years
The Famous Grouse Scottish Oak Finish
William Grant's 25 Years Old

Irish Pure Pot Still
Midleton 1973 Pure Pot Still

Irish Single Malt
The Tyrconnell Aged 10 Yrs Madeira Finish
Bushmills Select Casks Aged 12 Years
Bushmills Rare Aged 21 Years

Irish Blended
Jameson

American Single Malt
McCarthy's Oregon Single Malt Aged 3
Years
Stranahan's Colorado Whiskey Batch No. 1
Stranahan's Colorado Whiskey Batch No. 23

Bourbon
Ancient Ancient Age 10 Years Old
Cougar Bourbon Aged 5 Years
Woodford Reserve Master's Four Grain

Straight Rye
Cougar Rye
Rathskeller Rye

Canadian Blended
Alberta Premium 25 Years Old
Danfield's Limited Edition Aged 21 Years
Wiser's Red Letter

Japanese Single Malt
The Hakushu Single Malt Whisky Aged 15
Years Cask Strength
Hakushu 1984
The Cask of Yamazaki 1993 Heavily Peated
Yoichi Key Malt Aged 12 Yrs "Peaty & Salty"
Yoichi 20 Years Old
Yoichi Nikka Single Cask Malt Whisky 1991

Japanese Vatted Malt
Pure Malt Black

Japanese Single Grain
Nikka Single Cask Coffey Grain 1992

Japanese Blended
Royal Aged 15 Years

Swedish Single Malt
Mackmyra Privus 04 Ratta Virket

Welsh Single Malt
Penderyn June 2007

Indian Single Malt
Amrut Two Continents Limited Edition

Australian Single Malt
Sullivans Cove Single Malt Whisky 6 Yrs Old

94.5

Scotch Single Malt
Aberlour a'bunadh Batch No. 20

Balblair 1975

Scotch Malt Whisky Society Cask 26.55 Aged 8 Years (Clynelish)

Glenfarclas 1995 45° The Heritage Malt

Whisky Doris Ballindalloch

Glenfiddich 15 Years Old

Glen Grant Cellar Reserve 1992

Duncan Taylor Collection Glen Grant 1972

Gordon & MacPhail Rare Vintage Glen Grant 1962

Kingsbury's Finest & Rarest Glenlivet 1978

Murray McDavid Mission Glenlivet 1977 Aged 30 Years

The Arran Malt Bourbon Single Cask 1998

The Arran Malt Sherry Single Cask 1996

The Arran Malt Sherry Single Cask 1998

Lagavulin 12 Years Old

Laphroaig 27 Years Old

Cadenhead's Authentic Collection Strathisla Aged 21 Years

Mackillop's Choice Tomintoul 1989

John McDougall's Selection Islay Malt 1993

Blended Scotch

Highland Dream 12 Years Old

American Single Malt

McCarthy's

Stranahan's Colorado Whiskey Batch No. 22

Bourbon

Parker's Heritage Collection

Straight Rye

Thomas H Handy Sazerac Straight Rye

Canadian Blended

Alberta Premium

Crown Royal Special Reserve

Japanese Single Malt

Ace of Diamonds Hanyu 1986

Welsh Single Malt

Penderyn (bott Jul 08)

Australian Single Malt

Sullivans Cove Cask Strength

94

ScotchSingle Malt

Aberlour 10 Years Old

Aberlour a'bunadh Batch 14

Scott's Selection Ardbeg 1992

The Whisky Fair Ardbeg Aged 15 Years

Ardmore 100th Anniversary 12 Years Old

Distillery Malt Ardmore 1991

Old Malt Cask Auchroisk Aged 33 Years

The Balvenie Roasted Malt Aged 14 Years

Bladnoch Aged 10 Years

Bowmore 30 Years Old

Exclusive Casks Bowmore 1998 Aged 10 Years

Murray McDavid Bowmore 1998 Agd 8 Yrs

Scotch Malt Whisky Society Cask 3.135 Aged 7 Years

Cadenhead's Authentic Collection The

Braes of Glenlivet Aged 17 Years

Bruichladdich 1989

Bruichladdich 1991 Aged 16 Years

Bruichladdich 1993

Bruichladdich Full Strength Special Edition Int Malt Whisky Festival, Gent 2008

Bruichladdich Infinity

Bruichladdich Infinity Second Edition

Port Charlotte First Cut

Berry's' Own Selection Bruichladdich 1991 Aged 15 Years

Cadenhead's Authentic Collection Bruichladdich Aged 15 Years

The Queen of the Moorlands Rare Cask Bruichladdich 1991 "The Anniversary Bott"

Berry's' Own Selection Caol Ila 1996 Aged 10 Years

Old Masters Caol Ila Aged 25 Years

The Scotch Single Malt Circle Caol Ila 1982

Duncan Taylor Collection Caperdonich 1972

Duncan Taylor Collection Dallas Dhu 1981 Aged 14 Years

Old Malt Cask Dalmore Aged 32 Years

Scotch Malt Whisky Society Cask 104.10 Aged 33 Years (Glencraig)

Glenfarclas 1954 The Family Casks

Glenfarclas 1970 The Family Casks

Glenfarclas 1987 Limited Rare Bottling Edition No. 13

Glenfarclas 1989 The Family Casks

Glenfarclas 1990 The Family Casks

Glenfarclas 1992 The Family Malt

Glenfiddich 1973 Vintage

Duncan Taylor Collection Glen Garioch 1988

Glenglassaugh 21 Years Old

Old Malt Cask Glen Grant Aged 32 Years

John Milroy Selection Glenlivet 1975 Aged 30 Years

Old Malt Cask Glenlivet Aged 30 Years

Glenmorangie 10 Years Old

Glenmorangie Nectar D'or Sauternes Fnsh

Glen Moray 1962 Very Rare Vintage Aged 42 Years

Glen Moray 1991 Mountain Oak Malt The Final Release

Scotch Malt Whisky Society Cask 63.22 Aged 18 Years (Glentauchers)

Duncan Taylor Collection Glenugie 1981

Kingsbury Handwriting Highland Park 15 Years Old

Oklahoma Single Malt Lovers Highland Park Single Cask Aged 27 Years

Scotch Malt Whisky Society Cask 4.133 Aged 13 Years (Highland Park)

Cadenhead's Dumbarton (Inverleven Stills) 18 Years Old

The Arran Malt Pineau des Charentes Cask Finish

Cadenhead's Authentic Collection Arran Aged 11 Years

Kilchoman New Spirit

Knockdhu 23 Years Old

Laphroaig Aged 18 Years

Laphroaig Aged 25 Years

Laphroaig Aged 30 Years

Laphroaig Aged 40 Years

Croftengea Heavily Peated Cask No.1 Distillery Select

Old Malt Cask Lochside Aged 14 Years

Montgomeries Longmorn 1975

The Macallan 1989

The Macallan Easter Elchies Seasonal Cask Selection Winter Choice 14 Years Old

The Macallan Fine Oak 15 Years Old

Gordon & MacPhail Speymalt Macallan 1938

Heiko Thieme's 1974 Macallan 65th Birthday Bottling

Rarest of the Rare Mosstowie 1975

Port Ellen 27 Years Old

Old Malt Cask Port Ellen Aged 24 Years

The Whisky Fair Port Ellen Aged 25 Years

Longrow Aged 18 Years

Strathisla Distillery Edition 15 Years Old

Talisker Aged 18 Years

Old Malt Cask Tactical Aged 18 Years

Old & Rare Tamdhu Aged 19 Years

Master of Malt Tomatin 19 Years Old

Old Malt Cask Tomatin Aged 31 Years

Tomintoul With A Peaty Tang

Tullibardine 1966

Old Malt Cask Probably Speyside's Finest Aged 41 Years

Scotch Vatted Malt

Clan Denny

The Famous Grouse 30 Years Old Malt

Scottish Grain

Clan Denny Grain Caledonian 40 Years Old

Kingsbury Finest & Rarest Carsebridge 41 Years Old 1964

Duncan Taylor Collection Invergordon 1965

Loch Lomond 2000 Cask No. 37700 Aged in Organic French Wine Hogshead

Blended Scotch

Black Grouse

Duncan Taylor Collection Rarest of the Rare Deluxe Blend 33 Years Old

Irish Single Malt

Connemara Cask Strength

Cadenhead's World Whiskies Cooley Agd 15

Knappogue Castle 1992

The Whisky Fair Connemara Aged 15 Years

Irish Blended

Bushmills 1608

American Single Malt

Edgefield Hogshead

Stranahan's Colorado Whiskey Batch No. 8

Triple 8 Notch

Bourbon

Blanton's Single Barrel No. 477

Cadenhead's World Whisky Heaven Hill Aged 10 Years

George T. Stagg

Jim Beam Black Aged 8 Years

Old Forester Birthday Bourbon

Old Taylor Aged 6 Years (old bottling)

Wild Turkey Russell's Reserve 10 Year Old

Single Malt Rye

Old Potrero Single Malt Straight Rye Whiskey Essay 10 SRW ARM E

Straight Rye

Pappy Van Winkle's Family Reserve Rye 13 Years Old

Rittenhouse 100 Proof Bottled in Bond

Rittenhouse Very Rare Single Barrel 21 Years Old Barrel No. 14

Rittenhouse Very Rare Single Barrel 21 Years Old Barrel No. 21

Rittenhouse Very Rare Single Barrel 21 Years Old Barrel No. 23

Rittenhouse Very Rare Single Barrel 21 Years Old Barrel No. 27

Japanese Single Malt

Suntory Pure Malt Hakushu Aged 20 Years

Karuizawa 1971

Karuizawa 1979 Aged 24 Years

Karuizawa 1986 Aged 17 Years

Shirakawa 32 Years Old Single Malt

The Yamazaki Single Malt Whisky Aged 15 Years Cask Strength

Yamazaki 1984

Nikka Whisky Yoichi 1986 20 Years Old

Japanese Blended

Nikka Master Blend Blended Whisky 12 Years Old 70th Anniversary

Nikka Whisky Tsuru Aged 17 Years

Special Reserve 10 Years Old

German Single Malt

Sloupisti 4 Years Old Cask Strength

Lichtenstein Single Malt

Telsington

Swedish Single Malt

Mackmyra Privus 02 Näsa För Sprit

Swiss Single Malt

Edition Kaser Castle One Single Malt

Swissky Exklusiv Abfüllung

Welsh Single Malt

Penderyn Jan 08

Australian Single Malt

Bakery Hill Classic Malt Cask Strength

Indian Single Malt

Amrut Peated

Amrut Peated Cask Strength Ltd Edition

Stillman's Dram Single Malt Ltd Edition

Scottish Malts

For those of you deciding to take the plunge and head off into the labyrinthine world of Scotch malt whisky, a piece of advice. And that is, be careful who you take your advice from. Because, too often, I hear that you should leave the Islays until you have tackled the featherlight Speysiders and the bolder, weightier Highlanders. This is just complete, patronising nonsense. The only time that rings true is if you are tasting a number of whiskies in one day. Then leave the smoky ones to last, so the lighter chaps get a fair hearing.

I know many people who didn't like whisky until they got a Talisker from Skye inside them, or a Lagavulin to swamp their tastebuds with oily iodine. The fact is, you can take your map of malt whisky, start at any point and head in whichever direction you feel. There are no hard and fast rules. Certainly with over 2,000 tasting notes for Scottish malts here you should have some help in picking where this journey of a lifetime begins.

It is also worth remembering not to be seduced by age. It is true that some of the highest scores are given to big-aged whiskies. But they are the exception rather than the rule: the truth is that the majority of malts, once they have lived beyond 20 years or so, suffer from oak influence rather than benefit. Part of the fun of discovering whiskies is to see how malts from different distilleries perform to age and type of cask.

Happy discovering.

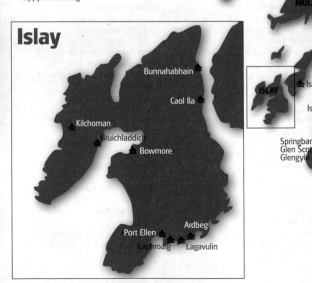

ORKNEY
ISLANDS
Highland Park
Scapa

Pultney

Clynelish
Brora

Balblair
Dalmore
Teaninich
Glenmorangie
Invergordon
Glenglassaugh
Banff†
Macduff

Glen Ord
Inverness
Glen Albyn
Glen Mhor
Millburn†
Royal Brackla
Tomatin
Knockdhu
Glendronach
Glenugie
Ardmore

Speyside see page 24

Speyside Distillery

Royal Lochnagar

Glen
Garioch

Aberdeen

Dalwhinnie

Glenury Royal
Fettercairn

Ben Nevis
Fort William
Glenlochy

Blair Athol
Edradour
Glencadam
North Port
Lochside
Glenesk†

Aberfeldy

Dundee

Glenturret
Perth
Daftmill

Tullibardine
Cameronbridge

Deanston

ch Lomond
Dumbarton
Inverleven
†Littlemill
hentoshan
Glengoyne
Rosebank
St. Magdelene
Glenkinchie
Edinburgh
North British
Glasgow
Strathclyde
Port Dundas

Girvan
Ailsa Bay
Ladyburn†

Bladnoch

Key

● Major Town or City
▲ Single Malt Distillery
▲ (Italics) Grain Distillery
† Dead Distillery

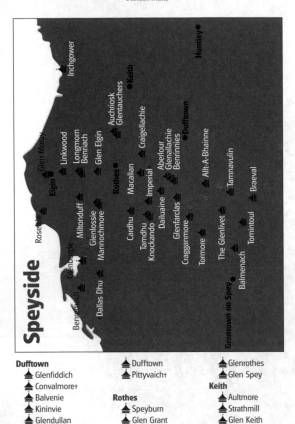

Speyside

Dufftown
- Glenfiddich
- Convalmore†
- Balvenie
- Kininvie
- Glendullan
- Mortlach

- Dufftown
- Pittyvaich†

Rothes
- Speyburn
- Glen Grant
- Caperdonich†

- Glenrothes
- Glen Spey

Keith
- Aultmore
- Strathmill
- Glen Keith
- Strathisla

Single Malts
ABERFELDY

Highlands (Perthshire), 1898. John Dewar & Sons. Working.

Aberfeldy Aged 12 Years bott no. A44103 db **(88.5) n22.5** the signature honey aroma is still there and intact but a subtle smokiness appears to have developed adding extra depth; **t23** busy delivery with the mildly waxy barley having much to say: spice prickle early on followed by some early chocolate toffee; **f21** luxuriant mouthfeel, the honey now tends towards the honeycomb variety and then Canadian, but still plenty of toffee which hushes proceedings; **b22** a lovely whisky which could be improved overnight to true brilliance by simply increasing the strength to the 46% that malt lovers these days expect and a reduction in the colour. A non-chill filtered, non-coloured policy would see this become a Premiership dram in the time it takes to brew the coffee for the marketing meeting which decides it.... 40%.

Aberlour 12 Years Old Sherry Cask Matured db **(88) n23** dry sherry and make no mistake; **t22** silky, juicy delivery; cramped slightly by a background bitterness; spices take their time but arrive eventually; **f21** double dry finale thanks to both big oak and the sherry influence; **b22** could do with some very delicate extra balancing sweetness to take it to the next level. Sophisticated nonetheless. 40%

Aberfeldy Aged 21 Years db **(91) n22** exotic fruit, under-ripe crushed ground cherry and some honey – what else..? **t23.5** sensual delivery that would be recognized and wholly appreciated by fans of Highland Park thanks to the busy honey and semi-hidden waves of smoke; a few oaky touches appear early but enhance in a toasty rather than life-threatening way; the spices rave early on then settle; **f22.5** a gentlemanly exit with its honeyed head held high to the last; no oaky screaming and shouting, just a few bitter-sweet farewells; **b23** a much improved dram which is far truer to the Aberfeldy style than earlier bottlings. Very high class malt which confidently underlines this distillery's excellence. 40%

Aberfeldy Aged 25 Years db **(85) n24 t21 f19 b21.** Just doesn't live up to the nose. When Tommy Dewar wrote, "We have a great regard for old age when it is bottled," as quoted on the label, I'm not sure he had as many as 25 years in mind. 40%. 150 bottles to mark opening of Dewar's World of Whisky.

Connoisseurs Choice Aberfeldy 1989 (96) n24 breathtaking: an amalgam of feisty and laid-back barley with a sub-strata of something much more fruity. Wonderful balance; **t24** again the barley is dual- edged and takes the lead with a ripe sultana and apples follow through; juicy and showing a very healthy sweetness and a slow gathering of delicate spice; **f24** a mildly coppery, estery lushness fuses kindly with the vanilla; long, not even a hint of tiredness and effortlessly elegant; **b24** the nose captures vividly the essence of this outstanding distillery and what follows very much continues in the same vein. A genuine must-have cracker from G&M and probably the best independent Aberfeldy bottling of all time. Long have I been waiting for a bottling to crack this outstanding distillery – and this one's done it with aplomb. One of the bottlings of the year. 43%. Gordon & MacPhail.

Connoisseurs Choice Aberfeldy 1989 Aged 18 Years refill sherry hogshead, dist Sep 1989, bott Oct 2007 **(89) n22** fruit candy and barley sugar **t22.5** some trademark honey edges to this, alongside the usual spice-oak network found here ; **f22** long and well oaked, though it performs the trick of never over indulging the drier, more bitter notes. Instead the barley sees it home all the way through, with a mildly burnt custard tart accompaniment; **b22.5** a very good distillery in excellent voice. 43%. Gordon & MacPhail

⌐ **Old Malt Cask Aberfeldy Aged 14 Years** refill hogshead, dist Jun 94, bott Mar 09 **(86) n21 t21.5 f22 b21.5.** Unusual to see Teldy in such an aggressive mood. And, as it happens, this is pretty enjoyable fare if occasionally on the thin side. The semi-thick malt really zaps into the tastebuds but the harsh vanilla has the most profound words. 50%. Douglas Laing. 338 bottles.

ABERLOUR
Speyside, 1826. Chivas Bros. Working.

Aberlour 10 Years Old bott 07 db **(94) n24** the grape is fresh, succulent and sultana-studded; the bourbon element is, well....bourbony, with some lovely liquorice and honey phrases somehow finding a perfect balance with the sherry; **t24** the body is shapely and dying to be caressed with a silky, skimpy grapiness barely covering the naked liquorice-honey beneath; the spiced oak slaloms around the palate without coming to grief showing a balance and poise which astounds; **f22.5** some toffee notes creep in from somewhere and reduce the shine but the vanilla-barley fade is still rather charming; **b23.5** this has been a malt changing slightly in style each time I come to taste a dram of it – which is quite often, as it happens. However, this bottling is about as good as it gets, with the marriage between bourbon and sherry cask as harmonious and angst-free as you are likely to find. The best rendition of this original old distillery bottling I have tasted, without any doubt. Forget all the PR, hype and egos: bottlings like this confirm that this distillery now stands above all others as Chivas' finest. 43%

Aberlour 10 Years Old Sherry Cask Finish db **(85) n21 t21 f21 b22.** Bipolar and bitter-sweet with the firmness of the grain in vivid contrast to the gentle grape. 43%

Aberlour 12 Years Old Double Cask Matured db **(88.5) n22** pretty unsubtle grape but sweet and attractive; **t22.5** serious juice at first drowns the barley but the oaky-spice heralds its return; **f22** delicate barley remnants; **b22** voluptuous and mouth-watering in some areas, firmer and less expansive in others. Pretty tasty in all of them. 43%

Aberlour 13 Years Old sherry cask, hand fill db **(84) n21 t22 f20 b21.** Skimps on the complexity. 58.8%

Aberlour 15 Year Old Double Cask Matured db **(84) n23 t22 f19 b20.** Brilliant nose full of vibrant apples and spiced sultana, but then, after a complex, chewy, malt-enriched kick-off, falls surprisingly flat on its face. 40%

Aberlour 15 Years Cuvee Marie d'Ecosse db **(91) n22** fresh sherry trace with kumquats and lime for extra zest; **t24** beautifully ethereal with the malt drifting in all directions while the fruit offers no weight at all; **f22** light vanilla apologetically drifts into the picture. The smoke of old has gone; **b23** this always was a deceptive lightweight, and it's got lighter still. It is sold primarily in France, and one can assume only that this is God's way of making amends for that pretentious, over-rated, caramel-ridden rubbish called Cognac they've had to endure. 43%

Aberlour 15 Year Old Sherry Finish db **(91) n24** exceptionally clever use of oak to add a drier element to the sharper boiled cooking apple. And a whiff of the fermenting vessel, too. Love it! **t22** the sharp fruit of the nose is magnified here ten times for one of the strangest mouth arrivals I've ever come across: the roof of the mouth won't know what's hit it; **f23** wave upon wave of malt concentrate; **b22** quite unique: freaky, even. Really a whisky to be discovered and ridden. Once you acclimatize, you'll adore it. *43%*

Aberlour 16 Years Old Double Cask Matured bott 2008/01/14 db **(93.5) n23.5** from the Aberlour 10 school of brilliant noses: the quality of the sherry butts used is as good as you'll find today with their clean, almost inspirational gently spiced clarity offering sufficient permeability to allow both barley and oak to breath and prosper; **t23.5** mouth-cleansing delivery with the clean Sauternes-esque grape polishing every tastebud; the decent weight is just about perfect for its style; again the spices are no more than a distant rumble and the barley breaks out for the relaxed stroll; **f23** remains delicate for all the weight; the mild treacle and waxed honey finale satisfies; **b23.5** another expression which has been greatly enhanced of late and this one to the . The most improved distillery in terms of house bottlings across the board in recent years? There is a very good case for it. *43%*

Aberlour 18 Years Old db **(91) n22** thick milkshake with various fruits and vanilla; **t22** immediate fresh juice which curdles beautifully as the vanilla is added; **f24** wonderful fruit-chocolate fudge development: long, and guided by a gentle oiliness; **b23** another high performance distillery age-stated bottling. *43%*

Aberlour 100 Proof db **(91) n23** beneath this sherried, volcanic start there is something rather sweet and honied. One of the most two-toned noses you'll find in a long while; **t23** sweet to begin and honied, too. The maltiness keeps its shape for some time. Between the middle and end an ebulliient spiciness takes hold **f22** massively long and fruity; **b23** stunning, sensational whisky, the most extraordinary Speysider of them all ...which it was when I wrote those official notes for the bottling back in '97, I think. Other malts have superseded it now, but on re-tasting I stand by those original notes, though I disassociate myself entirely with the rubbish: "In order to savour Aberlour 100 at its best add 1/3 to 1/2 pure water. *57.1%*

Aberlour a'bunadh Batch No. 13 db **(88) n23** very similar in style to the 15-y-o Sherry Wood Finish; **t23** lively, fresh fruit and mouthwatering malt: not for the squeamish; **f21** thin-ish; cream toffee; **b22** the dull-ish finish apart, this is sheer entertainment and one for late, cold nights. *59.8%*

Aberlour a'bunadh Batch No. 14 db **(94) n23** slightly earthy but the grape is genuinely clean, intense and spicy; **t25** truly glorious, actually quite perfect, delivery of balance between the unimpeachable grape and malt concentrate that gathers on the palate and bores into the tastebuds like a tornado into a Midwest town. One of the great moments of Speyside whisky drinking; **f22** relatively short, but the shock waves continue amid some toffee; **b24** it would be easy to pass this off as just another whisky from first time of trying, probably because of the relative ordinariness of the finish. But instinct should tell you to try again and watch. Try and find if there is a fault in the quality of the distillate or cask; find a winner between bitter and sweet. You will be amazed! *59.5%*

Aberlour a'bunadh Batch No. 15 db **(84) n20 t20 f23 b21**. A rogue lightly sulphured cask has taken the edge of this one. A shame. No: bloody annoying!! *59.6%. ncf.*

Aberlour a'bunadh Batch No. 16 db **(87) n21** I don't believe it: sulphur again. Someone is becoming a bit careless here. Fortunately, the blinding brilliance of some of the other sherry butts have helped limit the damage; **t23** the intense kumquat/orange tang to the sherry-trifle grape is pure joy and helps take the mind off the furry-interference of that single sulphur cask. Chewy...and so could have been a champion; **f22** the odd, telling off-note remains but you can't entirely suppress the fruit; **b21** for this to happen once is bad for a world-great dram. Twice in a row is close to being the stuff of nightmares. The real shame is that this could so easily have been 2007 Whisky Bible Whisky of the Year, because some of the other casks still bear the hallmark of greatness...I could weep. *59.6%. ncf.*

Aberlour a'bunadh Batch No. 17 db **(88) n22** enough thick oloroso on the nose here to make for a shortage in Jerez: the distant rumble of spice, like thunder in the air, is the one thing to edge this away from being too one-dimensional; **t23** almost immediately those stormclouds break and spices rain down on the tastebuds in torrents; first though the sherry gathers in further clean intensity; **f21** a fluffy, chalky finish – perhaps through a slight blemish – with grape lingering and some late toffee apple; **b22** if you don't like sherried whiskies, give this one a miss. *60.2%*

Aberlour a'bunadh Batch No. 19 db **(95) n24** de rigueur big sherry but of exemplary cleanness of butt, entirely blemish free and showing just enough lightness of touch for some barley and a bourbon-esque honeycomb to pass through the juicy grape. Exceptional... **t24** sublime spices launch themselves on defenceless tastebuds tattooing oloroso indelibly into them; some background honeycomb represents the oak; **f23** long, chewy, some lovely natural toffees to go with the grape and general slightly overcooked fruitcake effect; **b24** it is a sherried malt such as this that makes my daily encounter with sulphur-ruined dross entirely worthwhile. 99.9%

Aberlour a'bunadh Batch No. 20 db **(94.5) n23** quite magnificent sherry: sweet, clean, viscous even on the nose, ebullient, proud and teasingly spiced; **t24.5** a perfect translation onto the palate, except for the added bonus of the spices being even more forthcoming and the grapiness having something of the noble rot: outstanding... **f23.5** chocolate raisin; **b23.5** absolutely all that can be asked of a sherry-matured single malt. 60.5%

Aberlour a'bunadh Batch No. 22 db **(83.5) n20 t21 f21.5 b21.** thick grape but a docile mustiness acts as a straightjacket; overall, plenty to get on with, but never sparkles. And such is the high stall Aberlour has set itself in recent years, nothing but the best will do.... 59.3%. ncf. Chivas Bros, Italian market.

⁖ **Aberlour a'bunadh Batch No. 23** db **(96) n24.5** honeycomb, molasses – almost demerara rum style - and that even before we start getting to the myriad layers of sherry. This, in your mind's eye, is how you dream a sherry cask whisky to be: clean, vaguely spiced grape, offering a delicate texture, lightness of touch and yet unfathomable depth...and not a sulphur molecule in sight: well not many, anyway...; **t24.5** fabulous double whammy of intense, well-aged bourbon and chunky fruit, both shrill and demanding, colliding head on like two express trains on the same track; the resulting explosion is both enormous and yet seemingly soft, as if in slow motion; burnt raisins abound - the usual fruitcake stuff - and yet the saliva glands are stirred into overdrive by the most gorgeous clean fruit crescendo; **f23** long, a slow dissipation of spices, loads of chewy fudge and a very slight sulphur pick up which knocks a mark off.... **b24** my word: just so close to being the perfect whisky. There are one or two sherry butts used in this bottling which, individually, must be verging on perfect. Even taking into account my total inability to accept anything sulphurous, I have to say this is a masterpiece of a malt and possibly one less than perfect cask away from being among the top three bottles of Speyside whisky I've ever come across. There is no doubting in my mind that this brand has now become the most eagerly anticipated of not just all Speyside's regular bottlings but the world's. Perhaps part of the fun is that there is a degree of uncertainty to just how good it will be. But when on song this is a whisky searching every liquor store you can to find. This one was just so close to being a world champion... 60.2%

⁖ **Aberlour a'bunadh Batch No. 25** db **(82.5) n21.5 t20.5 f20 b20.5** Oh dear. One or two less than brilliant casks have sneaked in and spoiled the usual party. 60.4%

⁖ **Aberlour a'bunadh Batch No. 26** db **(95) n24.5** bizarre and stunning: picking this up and sniffing absent-mindedly, I genuinely thought it was pot still demerara rum....!!! Absolutely caked in molassed and fruity esters. Sniff deeper and there is a montage of juicy dates and plums ripe enough to explode; on another level we have the ultra rich marriage of Dundee cake and Bakewell Tart. Non-peated malt whisky noses don't get much thicker than this...; **t23** oddly, nothing like as towering as the nose: the easily identifiable juicy barley actually does a good job of thinning out the bigger fruit though for a while there is a slight off-key squabble; only towards the middle is balance re established as milk-chocolate notes begin to have a calming effect; **f24** brilliant....from the most huge nose to something of a civil war on delivery the story ends with a charmingly elegant chocolate mousse and plum pudding mix...; **b23.5** another fabulous and enthralling adventure from now one of the truly great brands that is always one of the highlights of the whisky-tasting year to discover. 60.6%

⁖ **Berry's Own Selection Aberlour 1995** bott 09 **(85) n21 t22 f21 b21.** Plenty of fresh barley and the odd wave of tannin. 46%. Berry Bros & Rudd.

Cadenhead's Authentic Collection Aberlour Aged 12 Years port hogshead, dist 95, bott Sep 07 **(92.5) n23** outwardly light but the true intensity of the grape slowly unravels; something of the Noble Rot and cobwebby about this; **t23** serious fruit plastering every tastebud; thick, chewy and lush barley refuses to hide; **f23.5** black cherries dipped in cocoa; **b23** a real treat of a Speysider making full use of its bruising, big fruity strength. Everything you could ask of such a cask. 58.2%. 252 bottles.

Cadenhead's Authentic Collection Aberlour Aged 18 Years sherry hogshead, matured in oak cask, dist 89, bott Jun 08 **(91) n22** a curiously salty nip to the barley and jackfruit; **t23.5** salivating, intense almost petulant barley refuses to play second fiddle to the fruit, which is on a slow burn; shards of honey pepper the proceedings **f22.5** back to some salty notes with fabulous vanilla-fruit layering: the elegance is enough to make one swoon; **b23** quite simply: wonderful! And for Aberlour fans, a bottling which shows the distillery in a subtly different light. 58%. 255 bottles.

Duncan Taylor The NC2 Range Aberlour Aged 11 Years dist 95, bott 07 **(84.5) n21 t22.5 f21 b20.** A brief flowering of charming, sweet, gristy malt gives a fascinating insight into Aberlour thanks to an older cask. 46%. nc ncf.

Old Malt Cask Aberlour Aged 17 Years refill hogshead, cask no. 4275, dist Nov 90, bott May 08 **(85.5) n21 t21.5 f22 b21.** Even the odd shard of rich barley cannot entirely overcome the tiredness on this. Still mouth-watering and attractive, though, and for those who prefer their martinis dry. *50%. Douglas Laing. 335 bottles.*

Old Malt Cask Aberlour Aged 21 Years refill hogshead, cask no. 3933, dist Oct 86, bott Oct 07 **(90) n22** a must-nose malt – in the grapey sense! **t23** salivating statement of rich clean barley and apparent grape; **f22.5** soft, satisfying fruit and oils; **b22.5** an ultra-friendly well-mannered malt with not a single degree of aggression. *50%. nc ncf. Douglas Laing. 277 bottles.*

⋅≈⋅ **Old Malt Cask Aberlour Aged 22 Years** refill hogshead, dist Oct 86, bott Dec 08 **(87) n21** docile and shows little of its age. A sprig of ginger and mint offsets the otherwise conservative nose; **t22.5** mouth-watering and barley laden; **f22** long-ish with a touch of burnt toast bittering up the sugars; a spicy buzz completes the score; **b21.5** tasted blind, I'd never have recognised this as Aberlour, except for the sprig o' mint on the nose, perhaps. Composed and steady stuff. *50%. Douglas Laing. 295 bottles.*

Provenance Aberlour Aged 12 Years refill hogshead, cask no. 4254, dist Spring 96, bott Spring 08 **(83) n22 t21 f20 b20.** Malty, firm blending fodder. *46%. nc ncf. Douglas Laing.*

Scott's Selection Aberlour 1990 bott 07 **(86) n21.5 t22 f21 b21.5.** A sprig o' mint on the nose sets off a familiar Aberlour, crisp malty, bitter-sweet style. *51.1%*

Wilson & Morgan Barrel Selection Aberlour 1992 Marsala Finish bott 2007 **(77) n20 t19 f19 b19.** Decent, but never finds its legs or direction. Bottled at the wrong point in finishing. *46%*

ALLT-A-BHAINNE
Speyside, 1975. Chivas Bros. Working.

Cadenhead's Authentic Collection Allt-a-Bhainne Aged 14 Years bourbon, dist 92, bott May 07 **(86) n21 t21 f23 b21.** A handsome malt full of sweet barley and vim. Hoping Cadenhead's can supply me with another from this distillery soon. *56.2%. 216 bottles.*

⋅≈⋅ **Chester Whisky & Liquer Co. Allt-A-Bhainne Aged 12 Years** dist 96 **(78.5) n19 t21 f19 b19.5.** One of the weirder whiskies of the year, almost worth collecting in its own right for its oddity alone. Nosed and tasted blind I would have sworn this was from a Holstein still in Germany. Even so, sweet and drinkable but nothing like I would have expected from this distillery. *54.3%*

Deerstalker Allt-A-Bhainne Aged 12 Years (88) n22 soft barley and toffee fudge; a pleasant ice-cream vanilla touch; **t22.5** juicy, lively delivery with a pleasant sugar coating; thickens towards the middle as the oils, vanilla and caramel congregate; **f21.5** dogged caramel stalks the tastebuds and hunts down the barley; **b22** even though uncoloured, caramel, one presumes naturally extracted from the wood, plays a large part here, especially at the fade. *46%. nc ncf. Aberko.*

Duncan Taylor The NC2 Range Alt-a-Bhainne 14 Years Old (87) n20 ungainly and slightly thin; **t23** ample compensation with the barley in full flow showing gristy sweetness, a grassy juiciness and the oak adding peppery spices to the side of the tongue; **f22** good vanilla follow through aided by soft, oaky salts; **b22** works impressively from the moment it hits the tastebuds. *46%. nc ncf.*

Forbes Ross Allt-A-Bhainne 1992 Aged 15 Years dist 92, bott 07 **(84) n22 t22 f20 b20.** The fun is all up-front on the charming nose and sweet barley delivery. *43%. Forbes Ross & Co.*

Harry's No. 5 All-a-Bhainne Aged 14 Years cask no. 40657, dist 1993, bott 2007 **(87) n21** the sharp barley is concreted on; **t22** blistering barley of the rock-hard, juicy variety; **f22** good spice and coffee fade; **b22** solid whisky in every respect. *56.4%. James MacArthur & Co Ltd for Sweden.*

Old Malt Cask Allt-A-Bhainne Aged 17 Years (79) n21 t22 f18 b18. Something distinctly virginal about this 17 year old: it's certainly never seen any wood worth mentioning.... *50%*

⋅≈⋅ **Old Malt Cask Allt-A-Bhaine Aged 17 Years** refill hogshead, dist Jun 91, bott Dec 08 **(84.5) n19.5 t23 f21 b21.** For all the evidence of fading glory and slightly over enthusiastic oak, there is much on the punchy, spicy, bourbon-sweetened delivery to celebrate. Almost diametrically opposed to the last Original Malt Cask 17 I tasted from this distillery!! *50%. Douglas Laing. 283 bottles*

Old Masters Allt-A-Bhainne Aged 11 Years cask no. 107158, dist 96, bott 08 **(60.5) n17.5 t18 f17 b18.** Not even the mega barley and spice can save it from the sulphur. *56.9%. James MacArthur & Co. Ltd.*

Provenance Allt-A-Bhainne Aged 11 Years refill hogshead no. 4186, dist Autumn 96, bott Spring 08 **(79.5) n19 t20 f21 b20.** Incredible barley, but starkly immature for its age with almost zero oak input. *46%. Douglas Laing.*

ARDBEG

Islay, 1815. Glenmorangie Plc. Working.

Ardbeg 10 Years Old db **(97) n24** more complex, citrus-led and sophisticated than recent bottlings, though the peat is no less but now simply displayed in an even greater elegance; a beautiful sea salt strain to this; **t24** gentle oils carry on them a lemon-lime edge, sweetened by barley and a weak solution of golden syrup; the peat is omnipotent, turning up in every crevice and wave, yet never one once overstepping its boundary; **f24** stunningly clean, the oak offers not a bitter trace but rather a vanilla and butterscotch edge to the barley. Again the smoke wafts around in a manner unique in the world of whisky when it comes to sheer élan and adroitness; **b25** like when you usually come across something that goes down so beautifully and with such a nimble touch and disarming allure, just close your eyes and enjoy.... 46%

Ardbeg 17 Years Old earlier bottlings db **(92) n23 t22 f23 b24.** OK, I admit I had a big hand in this, creating it with the help of Glenmorangie Plc's John Smith. It was designed to take the weight off the better vintages of Ardbeg whilst ensuring a constant supply around the world. Certainly one of the more subtle expressions you are likely to find, though criticised by some for not being peaty enough. As the whisky's creator, all I can say is they are missing the point. 40%

Ardbeg 17 Years Old later bottlings db **(90) n22 t23 f22 b23.** The peat has all but vanished and cannot really be compared to the original 17-year-old: it's a bit like tasting a Macallan without the sherry: fascinating to see the naked body underneath, and certainly more of a turn on. Peat or no peat, great whisky by any standards. 40%

Ardbeg Guaranteed 30 Years Old db **(91) n24 t23 f21 b23.** An unsual beast, one of the last ever bottled by Allied. The charm and complexity early on is enormous, but the fade rate is surprising. That said, still a dram of considerable magnificence. 40%

Ardbeg 1972 Single Cask No. 2738 db **(92) n23 t23 f23 b23.** Charming. Evocative of a storm-lashed Scottish coastal village with peat reek on the wind and enough lightning and thunder to show this is still alive and kicking. 53.1%

Ardbeg 1974 Single Cask No. 3151 db **(96) n24** some concentrated lime has been brought in to lighten the peaty load; the oak is pretty full on, yet plays to the Ardbeg rules of not interrupting the complexity of the smoke; **t24** the delivery borders on perfection with the oil being no more than a hint, the smoke offering myriad possibilities and the citrus yo-yoing between sweet and sharp: it is impossible not to close your eyes in pleasure with this one... **f23.5** some oil arrives at last to give a gliding effect to the more demonstrative themes; smoky butterscotch is to the fore while a few honey notes begin to gain momentum; **b24.5** you cannot find fault with a whisky of this calibre: everything is in order, the intensities are large but never booming or vaguely out of control. There are no off notes, nothing dominates yet every single element found within the malt seems to be effortless: maximum in any other whisky...but not here. It is, quite simply, a dram to die for... 47.7%

Ardbeg 1974 Single Cask No. 3160 db **(92.5) n23.5** surging oak, but the peat runs at varying bitter-sweet levels to compensate. Plenty of saline, coastal notes to remind you of its provenance; **t23.5** delicately sweet with - and this is highly unusual – the barley being clearly detached in its juiciness to the rumbling smoke; **f23** dries and does so with aplomb as the oak begin to take hold; vanilla and almost a bready, doughy, yeasty attack. The oaks carry on regardless, but the smoke picks up some of the lighter citrus notes to try and maintain balance; **b23** brilliant, but the oaky signature shows that the flag to this great Ardbeg is just beginning to be lowered. 49%

Ardbeg 1974 Single Cask No. 3524 db **(93) n24** a malt which appears to lie: this doesn't seem to be anything like in its mid thirties simply because the oak is not just genteel but adds only a further depth to the peat rather than working against it; lots of the house citrus and – and here's a curious trick – breath in deeply through the nose a few moments after you have had your proboscis in the glass for a while and the fabulous sensation of fresh grist greets you; **t22.5** almost tame on delivery and the slow build up of the smoke and lemon with barley and vanilla getting in on the act; **f23** a short, sharp burst of spice and a dull throb of smoke; the vanillas are quite astounding; **b23.5** Ardbeg is, by nature, an understated malt. This almost overstates the understatement... 44.9%

Ardbeg 1974 Single Cask No. 3528 db **(93.5) n23.5** now starting to head into bourbon territory despite the smoke: even so, it's citrus that is leading the way with some fragments of mothballs; the smoke drifts around, trying to impose, allowing the toast and honey to develop pleasantly; **t23** again, and quite improbably for its age, it's citrus on the delivery with the smoke both making a weighty entrance and then again drifting off into a lighter mode; soft salty, oaky notes underscore the age but amid the many layers are some near weightless marmalade and butterscotch tones; **f23** long with pastel shades of all the usual Ardbeg suspects, except late on there's an earthier resonance as the peats congregate; **b24** ridiculously delicate for its age. Wonderful. *44.3%*

Ardbeg 1975 Single Cask No. 1375 db **(84) n22 t21 f20 b21.** Some delightful aspects but something doesn't quite click here the way you'd think a sherry butt would. Some lovely sweet, fruity elements but... *54.4%*

Ardbeg 1975 Single Cask No. 1378 db **(77) n19 t20 f19 b19.** When Ardbeg re-opened ten years ago there was the odd cask from this vintage I put to one side with a recommendation to blend them off as I thought they were not quite right,. I wondered where they had got to... *53.8%*

Ardbeg 1975 Single Cask No. 4699 db **(92) n23** the weightlessness of the fine and moderate smoke helps amplify the oak, but the balance remains excellent; **t23** again, soufflé light and then a slow, growling peat presence. Detectable barley sweetness sees off any oak; **f23** perhaps a shade tired with some dryness accentuated by cocoa and spices but the freshness of the delicate grape is wonderful; **b23** I had to come back to this cask three times, as the palate has to be spot- on to get the story here. At first I thought it was over-oaked; on second tasting got a different reading. These third and fourth times my palate has been free of a slight blocked nose etc and the patience has paid dividends. Yes, it is on the aged side, but the shades of subtlety astound. *40.9%. 121 bottles.*

Ardbeg 1977 db **(96) n25 t24 f23 b24.** When working through the Ardbeg stocks, I earmarked '77 a special vintage, the sweetest of them all. So it has proved. Only the '74 absorbed that extra oak that gave greater all-round complexity. Either way, the quality of the distillate is beyond measure: simply one of the greatest experiences – whisky or otherwise – of your life. *46%*

Ardbeg 1978 db **(91) n23 t24 f22 b22.** An Ardbeg on the edge of losing it because of encroaching oak, hence the decision made by John Smith and I to bottle this vintage early alongside the 17-year-old. Nearly ten years on, still looks a pretty decent bottling, though slightly under strength! *43%*

Ardbeg Airigh Nam Beist Limited 1990 Release bott 06 db **(95) n24 t24 f23 b24** There is only one distillery on earth that could make something so gigantic, yet so delicate. And mind-blowingly complex. Smoky sophistication. *46%. ncf.*

⋅∷⋅ **Ardbeg 1998 Single Cask No. 1189** db **(87) n22.5** so dense, hard to make neither head nor tail of it. You can peel away the layers, first with the salty crust, next to something vaguely kumquatish and so on. The trouble is, as lovely as this may be, the smoke is rather clumped together; **t22** tangy fruit entangled in salt and mocha; again the peat is kind of lumpy; f21 light oils and a light sprinkling of dark sugars; **b21.5** this has been a vintage year for very odd new bottlings of Ardbeg. Yes, I've warmed it and reduced with water (anything!); and yes it is enjoyable. But just not up to snuff on the Ardbeg front for me... *54%*

Ardbeg Almost There 3rd release dist 98, bott 07 db **(93) n23** fabulous peat and coal-gas mix with a citrus thinning and strimming things out; **t24** marauding barley and orange peel combine for a grassy, mouth-watering delivery, but with the peat riding a gently oiled wave; enormous and you'll keep chewing until your jaw drops off...; **f23** long, quite big smoke but some oils help disguise some of the more complex final moments; **b23** further proof that a whisky doesn't have to reach double figures in age to enter the realms of brilliance... *54.1%. ncf.*

Ardbeg Blasda db **(90.5) n23.5** distant kumquat and lime intertwine with gentle butterscotch tart; it's all about the multi-layered barley and the most vague smokiness imaginable which adds a kind of almost invisible weight; the overall clarity is like that found swimming off a Pacific atoll; **t22.5** sharp barley hits home to almost mouth-watering effect; again there is the most pathetic hint of something smoky (like the SMWS cask, perhaps from the local water and warehouse air), but it does the trick and adds just the right ballast; **f22** soft spices arrive apologetically, but here it could do with being at 46% just to give it some late lift; **b22.5** a beautiful, if slightly underpowered malt, which shows Ardbeg's naked self to glowing effect. Overshadowed by some degree in its class by the SMWS bottling, but still something to genuinely make the heart flutter. *40%.*

Ardbeg Corryvreckan db **(96.5) n23** excellent, thick, not entirely un-penetrable – but close – nascent smoke and a vignette of salty, coastal references save the day; **t24.5** amazing: here we have Ardbeg nutshelled. Just so many layers of almost uncountable personalities with perhaps the citrus leading the way in both tart and sweet form and then meaningful speeches from those saline-based, malty sea-spray refreshed barley notes with the oak, in vanilla form, in close proximity. The peat, almost too dense to be seen on the nose, opens out with a fanfare of phenols. It is slumping-in-the-chair stuff, the enormity of the peat taking on the majesty of Cathedral-esque proportions, the notes reverberating around the hollows and recesses and reaching dizzying heights; such is its confidence, this is a malt which says: "I know where I'm going...!" ; **f24** long, outwardly laconic but on further investigation just brimming with complexity. Some brown sugary notes help the barley to come up trumps late on but it's the uniquely salty shield to the mocha which sets this apart. Simply brilliant and unique in its effortless enormity...even by Ardbeg standards; **b25** as famous writers – including the occasional genius film director (stand up wherever you are my heroes Powell and Pressburger) – appear to be attracted to Corryvreckan, the third most violent whirlpool found in the world and just off Islay, to boot, - I selected this as my 1,500th whisky tasted for the historic Jim Murray Whisky Bible 2009. I'm so glad I did because many have told me they thought Blasda ahead of this. To me, it's not even a contest. Currently I have only a sample. Soon I shall have a bottle. I doubt if even the feared whirlpool is this deep and perplexing. *57.1%. 5000 bottles.*

Ardbeg Kildalton 1980 bott 04 db **(96) n23 t24 f24 b25**. Many years back, when I helped get Ardbeg back on the road, I selected certain years as vintages and created the 17-year-old by using this unpeated version as the heart, with some overly old but highly peated casks to ensure the Ardbeg style flourished and equilibrium was maintained. The one and only recommendation I made that was not carried out, though, was to launch Kildalton as a malt in its own right, showing – uniquely – the inner working of Ardbeg in much the same way as a bourbon cask version does to Macallan. Now, at very long last, they have got around to it. This is better now than when it was 17 years old, and a degree of unbalanced freshness remained (to confirm my suspicions, I have tasted it against the samples I took then). It has developed extra fruit and complexity, making it a breathtaking treat – a masterpiece map of Ardbeg – that no true whisky connoisseur can afford to miss... and proof positive that Ardbeg doesn't need peat to bring complexity, balance and Scotch whisky to their highest peaks.... *57.6%*

Ardbeg Lord of the Isles bott autumn 06 db **(85) n20 t22 f22 b21**. A version of Ardbeg I have never really come to terms with. This bottling is of very low peating levels and shows a degree of Kildalton-style fruitiness. No probs there. More, it's a fact that some of the casks are leaching a soft soapy character noticeable on the nose. Enjoyable enough, but a bit frustrating. *46%*

Ardbeg Mor db **(95) n24** coastal to the point of sea spray showering you, with the smell of salt all the way home until you reach the peat fire. Evocative, sharp with elements of vinegar to the iodine; **t24** one of the biggest deliveries from Ardbeg for yonks; the peat appears way above the normal 50%, thickset and gloriously bitter-sweet, the steadying vanillas carried on the soft oils; **f23** mocha enters the fray with a raspberry jam fruitiness trying to dampen the continuing smoke onslaught; **b24** quite simply Mor the merrier... *57.5%*

Ardbeg Provenance 1974 bott 99 db **(96) n24 t25 f23 b24**. This is an exercise in subtlety and charisma, the beauty and the beast drawn into one. Until I came across the 25-year-old OMC verson during a thunderstorm in Denmark, this was arguably the finest whisky I had ever tasted: I opened this and drank from it to see in the year 2000. When I went through the Ardbeg warehouse stocks In 1997 I earmarked the '74 and '77 vintages as something special. This bottling has done me proud. *55.6%*

Ardbeg Renaissance db **(92) n22.5** sharp and punchy smoke with more than a hint of coke dust, too; the citrus is there but is partially hiding while the phenol level, usually appearing less than it actually is, makes no great secret of its enormity; **t22.5** a stunning delivery both reflecting the sharpness on the nose yet also couched in a light oiliness which aborts all but the first few shockwaves; **f23.5** long, already the vanilla is beginning to bristle and the smoke is moving towards a praline-brushed finale; the bitter-sweet finish could not be better-balanced and just sighs Ardbeg... **b23.5** how fitting that the 1,200th (and almost last) new-to-market whisky I have tasted for the 2009 Bible should be Renaissance...because that's what I need after tasting that lot....!! This is an Ardbeg that comes on strong, is not afraid to wield a few hefty blows and yet, paradoxically, the heavier it gets the more delicate, sophisticated and better-balanced it becomes. Enigmatically Ardbegian. *55.9%*.

Ardbeg Still Young dist 98, 2nd release bott 06 db **(93) n24** still the sizzling smoky bacon, with perhaps a salty-buttered Arbroath Smoky for company; even a touch of the dentists...; **t24** if this was any more delicate or highly strung, my tastebuds would have a breakdown. The peats are enormous, but simply hover and then land like butterflies; the barley offers moisture; **f22** even at this age the oak begin to have an input, drying and adding a vanilla pod to the sweeter peats. Lengthy and lip-smacking; **b23** a couple of generations back – maybe even less – this would not have been so much "Still Young" as "Getting on a Bit." This is a very good natural age for an Ardbeg as the oak is making a speech, but refuses to let it go on too long. Stylish – as one might expect. And, in my books, should be a regular feature. Go on. Be bold. Be proud say it: Ardbeg Aged 8 Years. Get away from the marketing straightjacket of old age... *56.2%. ncf.*

⁘ **Ardbeg Supernova** db **(97) n24.5** moody, atmospheric; hints and threats; Lynchian in its stark black and white forms, it's meandering plot, it's dark and at times indecipherable message and meaning...; **t24** at first a wall of friendly phenols but only when you stand back and see the overall picture you can get an idea just how mammoth that wall is; there are intense sugary gristy notes, then this cuts away slightly towards something more mouth-fillingly smoky but now with a hickory sweetness; a light oil captures the long, rhythmic waves, a pulse almost; **f24** gentle, sweetening cocoa notes evolve while the peat pulses... again...and again... **b24.5** apparently this was called "Supernova" in tribute of how I once described a very highly peated Ardbeg. This major beast, carrying a phenol level in excess of 100ppm, isn't quite a Supernova...much more of a Black Hole. Because once you get dragged into this one, there really is no escaping... 58.9%

Ardbeg Uigeadail db **(97.5) n25** quite simple: perfect. The smoke is dry, something akin to the ash from a cold peat fire; there are hints, though no more, of fruit, possibly sherry. There are hints, though no more, of slightly overdone roasted potato. There are hints, though no more, of coffee-stained old Demerara rum. There are hints, though no more, of sweet grist falling from the mill. There are no hints of perfection: that is stated loud and clear.... **t24.5** from the utter silky brilliance of the delivery to the multi-layered middle this simply oozes complexity, and on a level only a handful of distilleries in the world can even dream of reaching; a molecule or two of over enthusiastic oak takes this away from a full mark, but I am being harsh; the fruit and barley are in an embrace that only the purest of lovers would know... **f23.5** some serious caramel from the cask, and a fruity follow through, perhaps robs the whisky of some of its more intricate notes, but again I am being ultra picky. An unusual oiliness for Ardbeg, though only slight, helps further the finale and encourages some mocha to develop; **b24.5** massive yet tiny. Loud yet whispering. Seemingly ordinary from the bottle, yet unforgettable. It is snowing outside my hotel room in Calgary, yet the sun, in my soul at least, is shining. I came across this bottling while lecturing the Liquor Board of British Columbia in Vancouver on May 6th 2008, so one assumes it is a Canadian market bottling. It was one of those great moments in my whisky life on a par with tasting for the first time the Old Malt Cask 1975 at a tasting in Denmark. There is no masking genius.The only Scotch to come close to this one is another from Ardbeg, Corryvreckan. That has more oomph and lays the beauty and complexity on thick....it could easily have been top dog. But this particular Uigeadail (for I have tasted another bottling this year, without pen or computer to hand and therefore unofficially, which was a couple of points down) offers something far more restrained and cerebral. Believe me: this bottling will be going for thousands at auction in the very near future, I wager. 54.2%

Ardbeg Uigeadail db **(89) n25** awesome package of intense peat reek amid complex fruitcake and leather notes. Everything about this nose is broadside-big yet the massive oak never once oversteps its mark. A whiff of engine oil compliments the kippers. Perfection; **t22** begins with a mind-blowing array of bitter-sweet oaky notes and then a strangely fruity peat entry; real scattergun whisky; **f20** very odd finish with an off-key fruit element that flattens the usual Ardbeg grand finale; **b22** a curious Ardbeg with a nose to die for. Some tinkering - please guys, as the re-taste is not better - regarding the finish may lift this to being a true classic 54.1%

Cadenhead's Authentic Collection Ardbeg Aged 13 Years bourbon hogshead, dist 1994, bott May 07 **(91) n23** big, wedges of enormous peat; **t23** spiced, massive peat delivery with a big, upfront maltiness; **f22** a procession of fruits, including citrus; **b23** a chewy emphatic Ardbeg not much caring for airs nor graces. 58%. 300 bottles.

Cadenhead's Authentic Collection Ardbeg Aged 13 Years bourbon hogshead, dist 1994, bott May 07 **(92) n24** soft, delicate, citrussy peat; **t23** fabulous meeting point of lively spices, varied vanillas and sweet barley; **f22** lethargic, understated smoke with soft oils amplifying the gristy barley sweetness; **b23** most probably a very close relation to Cadenhead's other Ardbeg 1994 bottling, but here everything is just little more laid back and relaxed. 58.4%. 318 bottles.

Cadenhead's Ardbeg Aged 14 Years dist 93, bott Feb 08 **(95) n22** big display of citrus and natural caramels as well as the deft smoke; **t24** dreamy, sexy, lush delivery; just bursts at the seems with the juiciest citrus and barley mix; the peat somehow offers both base and higher notes as the complexity of the structure goes through the roof; **f24.5** think the delivery was good? Just close your eyes and now allow a perfectly weighted, sublimely spiced finale to serenade you for six or seven minutes: tasting notes are pointless... **b24.5** the type of cask which silently sets out why Ardbeg is different to any other whisky in the world. 57.2%. 207 bottles.

Cadenhead's Ardbeg Aged 14 Years dist 93, bott Feb 08 **(91.5) n22** pretty tight by Ardbeg standards with the peat in firm and sharp profile; **t23** no less firm delivery, but the magic of the distillery begins to ensure that as it softens, more and more delicate and complex notes are recognisable, especially the juicy, citric ones; **f23.5** now a 180 degree turn as the finale offers soft smoke and even softer cocoa. Long, bitter-sweet and pulsing with class; **b23** just as one would expect from an Ardbeg. *57.5%. 288 bottles.*

⋅⋅⋅ **Cadenhead's Ardbeg Aged 15 Years** cask no. 1056, dist 94, bott 09 **(92.5) n23** quiet, warm, seaweedy rock pools; orange blossom on the wind... **t23.5** melt-in-the-mouth barley, sweet, juicy and then legions of delicate peat notes marching through...; **f23** silky with a little touch of raspberry preserve to the smoke and vanilla; **b23** typically understated Ardbeg, where everything first appears big, but when analysed is just so delicate and almost coy. Wonderful. *58.1%*

⋅⋅⋅ **Cadenhead's Ardbeg Aged 15 Years** cask no. 1057, dist 94, bott 09 **(95) n23** quiet, warm, seaweedy rock pools which have dried up a bit; spilt pepper on the wind; **t24** melt-in-the-mouth barley, sweet, juicy, then legions of spiced up peat notes march through; **f23.5** silky with a few liberal shakes of the pepper pot on a vague fruity note plus smoke and vanilla; **b24.5** virtually peas in a pod, are casks 1056/7. Except this is a spicier cove. And doesn't suffer for it, for those tiny differences add up to a lot. *573%*

Connoisseurs Choice Ardbeg 1979 (93) n24 that uniquely Ardbegian mixture of brain-explodingly complex peat and orangey citrus tones, only here the balance and denouement are as near as damn it perfect; **t23** light to the point that the molecules virtually fall apart on the palate; again it's citrus leading the line and the peat showing restraint to the point of good old fashioned manners; **f22** dry vanilla; **b24** quite beautiful malt but at 43% compared to every man and his dog bringing out Ardbeg at full strength – and at at least 46% by the owners themselves – this does at first appear underpowered. But as the strands of complexity unravel... *43%. Gordon & MacPhail.*

⋅⋅⋅ **Connoisseurs Choice Ardbeg 1991 (93.5) n24.5** unmistakably Ardbeg. a unique combination of salt and smoke, this time in a fruity shell, which boasts a weight and balance that nature has a hard job to explain, but is way beyond the ability of man; **t23.5** light, intrinsically malty and gristy sweet, and then a slow build up of smoke; **f22.5** remains on the sweet side and has to be to see off some rather burnt toasty oakiness; **b23** a superb whisky unable to live up to the supernatural nose by being merely excellent on the palate. *43%. Gordon & MacPhail.*

The Exclusive Malts Ardbeg Aged 7 Years cask no. 107, dist Apr 00 **(78.5) n18.5 t21.5 f19 b19.5.** This is Ardbeg? How disappointing. *55.7%. The Creative Whisky Co. 380 bottles.*

⋅⋅⋅ **Hart Brothers Ardbeg Aged 17 Years** dist Feb 91, bott Mar 08 **(92) n23.5** dry, salty, earthy and a little spice nip and some curious background juniper; **t23** a slight orangey note to open followed by a sweeter blossoming of barley; the peat operates on two levels, both as rich background note and also to offer shape and substance, **f22.5** a tad more bitter, with some mocha on the fade; **b23** a busy and engaging Ardbeg. *46%. Hart Brothers Limited.*

⋅⋅⋅ **Old & Rare Ardbeg Aged 36 Years** dist Mar 73, bott Apr 09 **(76) n19 t20 f18 b19.** Some serious cowshed moments on the nose: fruity, too. But, frankly, to nose and taste as uniquely weird as any Ardbeg I've come across in over 25 years of worshipping the stuff. Can't help thinking that this might become the stuff of legend in some parts of northern Germany... *44.7%. Douglas Laing. 78 bottles.*

Old Malt Cask Ardbeg 15 Years Old dist Mar 91, bott Mar 06 **(92) n23** heady, pungent peats battle orange peel, sultanas and even a touch of liquorice head on. The thing is, just how many layers are there?; **t23** big and rich, the grapey theme continues until unseated by a hickory/peat stand; well spiced early but fades; **f23** long, more hickory and Fishermen's Friend cough sweet with the sweetness holding sway throughout and the return of spice is perfect; **b23** a dram that threatens to run amok but a sweet malty theme pervades. *50%. 341 bottles.*

Old Malt Cask Ardbeg 15 Years Old rum finish, dist Mar 91, bott Jul 06 **(82) n20 t22 f20 b20.** Austere and lacking in the usual Ardbegian grace and elegance: I'm not sure this has been bottled at a time when the Ardbeg and rum were on the best speaking terms. *50%. Douglas Laing. 378 bottles.*

Old Malt Cask Ardbeg Aged 15 Years dist Mar 91, bott Oct 06 **(86) n22 t22 f21 b21.** Some OTT oils clip the wings of the higher-flying notes. Attractive but limited by Ardbeg standards. *50%. Douglas Laing. 358 bottles.*

Old Malt Cask Ardbeg Aged 15 Years Rum Finish dist Mar 91, bott Oct 06 **(90) n23** rock-hard smoke with a shell of sugar; **t23** brittle barley with the peat coming in silver sugar-sweetened strata; an unmistakable rum character offers another dimension **f22** melts at last but the recently released oils contains the complexity slightly; **b22** wonderful stuff but underscoring that sugary sheen often found in rum finishes. Not normally a bad thing, but perhaps restrictive when it comes to something so labyrinthine as Ardbeg. *50%. nc ncf. Douglas Laing. 312 bottles.*

Old Malt Cask Ardbeg Aged 16 Years rum cask no. 3719, dist 91, bott Jun 07 **(88.5) n21.5** slightly more ajar than previous rum-finished Ardbegs, this one showing some green shoots of smoke of varying intensity if not complexity; **t22** much more delicate than other rum-shaped Ardbegs with an immediate sweetness gained from both barley and barrel; the smoke appears to be clogged up at times but releases in attractive puffs; **f23** at last we see some real Ardbeg at work! Cocoa forms a backdrop but the iodiney punctuation is clever and full of coastal treats; the oak and barley forms a mutual admiration society; **b22** pretty bitty by Ardbeg standards, with the rum still causing all kinds of unusual dead ends to the norm. But here we do have Ardbeg in recognisable, if unique, form. *50%. 346 bottles.*

Old Malt Cask Ardbeg Aged 16 Years rum cask no. 3883, dist May 91, bott Sep 07 **(87) n22** a tight nose: the peat is peculiarly sharp and angular; **t22** again closed and hard, almost rummy in its delivery with hard, chiselled edges where normally there are curves and layers; **f21** again, a strange sugary coating that cuts down on development though there is a decent chocolate flourish; **b22** on the sample bottle there was no mention of it, but I have just noticed it was from a rum cask: hand on heart, I didn't know when tasting (in fact, I see there are three of these). But I could think of no other explanation as to why you'd want to finish Ardbeg in rum, well.... *50%. nc ncf. Douglas Laing. 334 bottles.*

Old Malt Cask Ardbeg Aged 16 Years rum cask no. 3893, dist Mar 91, bott Sep 07 **(81.5) n20 t22 f20 b19.5.** Ardbeg in a straightjacket: somehow all the peat and complexity has been locked away inside a flinty wall and simply can't escape. The bitterness on the finish doesn't help either. Drinkable, decent malt....but knowing it's Ardbeg...!! Memo to self (cc Glenmorangie Ltd): never mature Ardbeg in rum casks... *50%. Douglas Laing. 335 bottles.*

❖ **Old Malt Cask Ardbeg Aged 17 Years** refill hogshead, finished in rum cask, dist Mar 91, bott Oct 08 **(86.5) n21.5 t22 f22 b21.** Enjoyable, juicy, candy-crisp sweet and spicy but relatively flat for an Ardbeg with the higher notes cropped by the rum. *50%. Douglas Laing. 316 bottles.*

❖ **Old Malt Cask Ardbeg Aged 17 Years** refill hogshead, dist Mar 91, bott Aug 08 **(90.5) n23.5** brilliant bitter-sweetness on the smoke; a touch of the farm byre about this, too; **t22.5** despite some very early dissolving sugars, remains on the dryish side with a slow-motion development of smoke; the vanilla arrives early and quite sternly; **f22** the oak and smoke continue to trade positions of supremacy; **b22.5** a whispering Ardbeg... *50%. Douglas Laing. 226 bottles.*

❖ **Old Malt Cask Ardbeg Aged 18 Years** refill hogshead, dist Mar 91, bott Apr 09 **(86.5) n21.5 t23 f21 b21**. A very different kind of Ardbeg with the oils really showing to maximum effect. Helps the intensity of the delivery, but perhaps not the unveiling of the more complex notes further down the line. Very pleasant, but ordinary by Ardbegian standards. 50%. Douglas Laing. *357 bottles.*

The Queen of the Moorlands Edition XXII Ourbeg Aged 6 Years cask no. 29, dist 01, bott 07 **(84) n22 t21 f22 b19.** A charming toddler of a malt still trying to find its feet. The sweet peats and oak are delicately displayed but the balance just aint there. Enjoyable and entertaining, as toddlers tend to be, this one was plucked slightly at the wrong time. *58.7%. nc ncf. Wine Shop The Leek and Congleton. 196 bottles.*

Scotch Malt Whisky Society Cask 33.68 Aged 9 Years 1st fill barrel, dist May 98 **(95) n23.5** just the lightest dusting of smoke makes for a virtually un-peated malt by Ardbeg standards, though distinctly more smoky than their true unpeated bottlings. What stands out are the rockpools and ozone which transports you immediately to a craggy Hebridean shoreline; elsewhere soft grists tantalise and seduce; **t23.5** brilliant delivery: the mouthfeel and weight are absolutely faultless. Also, the cask was a good 'un as the support of the oak offers a sweetness as well as depth; again the smoke is just ghostly stuff, perhaps from the local water and/or the environment of the warehouse or perhaps there was a small – and I mean very small – dose of peat added to the fire; **f24** long, complex and meticulously weighted: golden syrup in diluted form mixes with the saline-crusted barley; the oak offers both dry and sweetness in even measures; **b24** in bottled form this is perhaps the best example I have seen yet of why Ardbeg makes the greatest whisky in the world. Here there's no peat to talk of, so you get a clear view of the mechanics of the malt. It is like looking at the inner workings of a Rolex, only here time stands still... *57.4%*

❖ **Scotch Malt Whisky Society Cask 33.74 Aged 10 Years** sherry gorda, dist May 98 **(73.5) n18 t20 f17.5 b18.** Great whisky filled into an absolute rubbish barrel. More like, Good Gorda, What The Hell Was That....??? Or more to the point: Why? *56.6%*

❖ **Scotch Malt Whisky Society Cask 33.75 Aged 7 Years** 1st fill barrel, dist Sep 01 **(90.5) n23.5** the background is lightly sugared custard; the foreground is peat – not always the way Ardbeg comes across, preferring, usually, to let those phenols gang up on you. But here the peat is, quite literally, thrust in your face. Still magic, though...; **t23.5** multi-layers of citrus offer the juiciest of starts; the peat begins as a murmur, forms into a rumble and finally crashes upon the tastebuds like a line delivered by James Robertson-Justice; **f21.5** bits and bobs of weak tannin and smoke and natural caramels...in a bit of a maturation no-man's land; **b22** this is a fascinating whisky. It shows, as vividly as can be imagined, the effects of the last two useless, rainy, freezing British summers on maturing whisky stocks: they have taken their toll, for this should be much further advanced after seven years in first fill bourbon. But, that said, not a bad way to bring up my 900th new whisky tasted for Jim Murray's Whisky Bible 2010. 61.5%

Scott's Selection Ardbeg 1992 bott 07 **(94) n24** a wonderful interplay of salt and peat makes this coastal in a way peated malts from elsewhere cannot come close to matching; overtly dry but the famous counterbalance of delicate, semi-hidden sweetness is there to find; **t23** the delivery begins, obtusely, with citrus and then pans out into quite massive smoke; the barley somehow detaches itself for a juicy, sweetish yield; **f23.5** now fans out for all manner of the usual complexities with the peat appearing at various levels from delicately dry and cocoa-dusted to quite weighty and intense; **b23.5** an exceptionally fine cask, dryer than usual, showing the distillery carried on making a uniquely complex spirit even at a time when massive doubts hang over its future. 51.6%

The Whisky Fair Ardbeg Aged 15 Years bourbon hogshead, dist 1991, bott 07 **(94) n24** dry, gristy peat: clean, oil-free and displaying a salty-iodine coastal quality to die for; **t23** massive delivery with the peats ganging up like sweet, smoky thugs ready to bash the living daylights out of the tastebuds only to caress them instead with molasses-tinged sweetness; remains salty and islandy; **f23** the salts continue but an intense gristy sweetness prevents an oaky charge; **b24** a substantial Ardbeg, absolutely brimming with malice and front but, on reflection, showing nothing but restraint and breeding. 54.4%. Germany.

The Whisky Fair "Still Very Young Islay Single Malt" (Ardbeg) refill sherry, dist 00, bott 07 **(90) n24** gorgeous dusty, old ash of a coal and peat fire; **t22** oily sweet peat; **f22** sweat peat at first, dries to a dust; **b22** very sweet peat. But the nose is legendary. 62.6%. Germany.

ARDMORE

Speyide, 1899. Fortune Brands. Working.

Ardmore 100th Anniversary 12 Years Old dist 86, bott 99 db **(94) n24 t23.5 f22.5 b24.** I cannot believe there are still bottles of this still around. It was going to be removed from my guide for having been included for too long, until I was informed that it was still to be had. So I re-tasted it using my new scoring system....and still came to an identical result...!!! Even if by a slightly different route. OK: let's summarise this one more time. Brilliant. Absolutely stunning, with the peat almost playing games on the palate. Had they not put caramel in this bottling, it most likely would have been an award winner. So, by this time next year, I fully expect to see every last bottle accounted for... 40%

Ardmore Fully Peated Quarter Casks db **(89) n21** the most un-Ardmore-ish nose of all time due to the thumping American oak tones. Those, plus a touch of caramel have to a degree flattened the peat-smoke so celebrated on the label; still, a rare example of where bourbon meets soft peat... **t23** a surprisingly dull, toffee-led initial entry is compensated for by an astonishing degree of development towards the middle where the smoke battles through the double-sweet sword of intense bourbon and barley sugar, helped along the way by an unusual oiliness; something to really chew on... **f23** the barley-fruit touch that has developed lingers for a while, as do those big, sweet tannins; soft oils continue and the smoke tries to be heard above the oaky noise and excellent, balancing spices. A touch of returning caramel flattens it out; **b22** this is an astonishingly brave attempt by the new owners of Ardmore who, joy of all joys, are committed to putting this distillery in the public domain. Anyone with a 2004 copy of the Whisky Bible will see that my prayers have at last been answered. However, this bottling is for Duty Free and, due to the enormous learning curve associated with this technique, a work in progress. They have used the Quarter Cask process which has been such a spectacular success at its sister distillery Laphroaig. Here I think they have had the odd slight teething problem. Firstly, Ardmore has rarely been filled in ex-bourbon and that oak type is having an effect on the balance and smoke weight; also they have unwisely added caramel, which has flattened things further. I don't expect the caramel to be in later bottlings and, likewise, I think the bourbon edge might be purposely blunted a little. But for a first attempt this is seriously big whisky that shows enormous promise. When they get this right, it could – and should – be a superstar. Now I await the more traditional vintage bottlings... 46%. ncf.

Ardmore Traditional Cask db **(88.5) n21.5 t22 f23 b22.** (For general tasting notes, see above) Not quite what I expected. "Jim. Any ideas on improving the flavour profile?" asked the nice man from Ardmore distillery when they were originally launching the thing. "Yes. Cut out the caramel." "Ah, right...." So what do I find when the next bottling comes along? More caramel. It's good to have influence... Actually, I can't quite tell if this is a result of natural caramelization from the quarter casking or just an extra dollop of the stuff in the bottling hall. The result is pretty similar: some of the finer complexity is lost. My guess, due to an extra fraction of sweetness and spice, is that it is the former. All that said, the overall experience remains quite beautiful. And this remains one of my top ten distilleries in the world. *46%. ncf.*

Cask Strength Ardmore 1991 (89) n22 rather plodding, oily, but never less than attractive; **t23** enormous sweet punch to this one with the lighty peated oils apparently bolstering the natural sugars and citrus notes; **f22** the smoke has been hiding somewhat but fully reveals itself towards the finale; **b22** a much less smoky version with an astonishing sweetness. The quality is unquestionable, though. *57.9%.*

Distillery Malt Ardmore 1991 (94) n23 Ardmore at one of its highest peating levels – certainly more than the normal 9-14ppm. Even so, there is room for lovely profusion of vanilla and grist. Just so delicate for all its weight; **t24** quite stunning: the weight of the peat is telling but the soft oils help both propel and even out the smokiness. Chewy yet juicy: quite fabulous; **f23** lightens towards a smoky custard but very long with a delicate barley sugar towards the end; **b24** this is simply brilliant whisky that no whisky lover can afford to be without. Startling. *43%. Gordon & MacPhail.*

The Exclusive Malts Ardmore Aged 13 Years cask no. 335, dist Sep 94 **(89.5) n21.5** smoky bacon crisps; **t23** massive peat delivery, much closer to 35ppm phenols than the usual barely double figures Ardmore reaches: they must have sent it some of Laphroaig's malt by mistake...; the old barrel also helps to ensure a massively mouth-watering dram; **f22.5** some mocha tries to make inroads into the smoke; **b22.5** this is the most enormously peated Ardmore I've ever come across: the phenols plus the tired cask and unusual saltiness makes this pretend to be an 8-year-old Islay. You don't think that once upon a time there was a leaking Laphroaig cask and they emptied it into an old Ardmore cask and forgot to re-mark it Laphroaig and....no, such things don't happen...do they....? *52.5%. The Creative Whisky Company. 324 bottles.*

Gordon & MacPhail Ardmore Aged 16 Years dist 91, bott 07 **(87) n22** brittle barley is flanked by no more than a shadow of smoke; **t21.5** the delivery is rock hard, a shortage of normal smoke means the barley clatters onto the tastebuds; **f22** one of the flintiest Ardmores for a while, even as the cocoa arrives; **b21.5** Hardmore – with a silent "H". Lovely stuff – but every bit lacking in smoke as the previous vintage was groaning with it. *43%*

Old Malt Cask Ardmore Aged 30 Years dist Apr 77, bott Apr 07 **(90) n22** delicate peat is little more than a wisp in a fruity breeze; **t23** a passionate delivery, full of busy spice and silky barley; the fruit element is fuzzy but never less than juicy; the smoke offers little more than a haze; **f22** excellent muscovado sugar and vanilla sign off; **b23** a real sweetie. Elegance and understanding are key here. *50%. 595 bottles.*

⋅⋅⋅ **Old Malt Cask Ardmore Aged 12 Years** refill hogshead, dist Mar 96, bott Sep 08 **(85.5) n22.5 t20.5 f21.5 b21.** Billowing smoke, with an earthy, bonfire quality; chewy, malty, pleasantly sweet in part; peppery and gristy. *50%. Douglas Laing. 348 bottles.*

⋅⋅⋅ **Provenance Ardmore Aged 11 Years** refill hogshead, dist autumn 96, bott summer 08 **(80) n21 t20 f20 b19.** I'd like to say this is a third-fill cask. Except it appears to have done the rounds at least once more than that. Pleasant smoke, though. *46%. Douglas Laing.*

Scotch Malt Whisky Society Cask 66.24 Aged 22 Years refill hogshead, dist Mar 85 **(86) n22 t22 f21 b21.** Busy oak on the smoke and while quick dose of honey helps overcome the over-vigorous wood it's all rather too much for true greatness. *52.7%*

AUCHENTOSHAN
Lowlands, 1800. Morrison Bowmore. Working.

Auchentoshan 10 Years Old db **(81) n22 t21 f19 b19.** Much better, maltier, cleaner nose than before. But after the initial barley surge on the palate it shows a much thinner character. *40%*

Auchentoshan 12 Years Old db **(85) n20 t23 f21 b21.** Thicker and more chewy malt than is the norm for a 'Toshan. But don't get this one confused with the astonishing peaty number that was 43%!! The finish is OK, but the delivery is superb. *40%*

Auchentoshan 18 Years Old db **(84) n19 t21 f22.5 b2.51.** A stretched malt, struggling to find development from the basic barley. Helped and hindered by a curious oiliness to this: hinders as it arrests development early on. Helps because the finish lasts much longer than the standard 'Toshan and allows the vanillas to balance out well. *43%*

Auchentoshan 21 Years Old db **(93) n23.5** the most unblemished, desirable and surprising of all the distillery-bottled 'Toshan noses: a sprig of mint buried in barely warmed peat, all with an undercoat of the most delicate honeys; **t23** velvety and waif-like, the barley-honey theme is played out is hushed tones and unspoiled elegance; **f23** the smoke deftly returns as the vanillas and citrus slowly rise but the gentle honey-barley plays to the end, despite the shy introduction of cocoa; **b23.5** one of the finest Lowland distillery bottlings of our time. A near faultless masterpiece of astonishing complexity to be cherished and discussed with deserved reverence. So delicate, you fear that sniffing too hard will break the poor thing...! *43%*

Auchentoshan 1976 Aged 28 Years cask no. 1115 db **(91) n23.5** quite beautiful in its lofty elegance: there are certain toasty ginger cake aromas vying to be top dog amid the citrus and sultana. It succeeds. Softly spiced and vibrant, it grows markedly in stature as it warms in the glass; **t22.5** sweet, brown sugar attack recedes as the tannins kick in; the middle offers a metallic coppery sheen which appears to weld the two styles together; **f22** simple and gentle with natural toffee and butterscotch; some late jammy fruitiness bids adieu; **b23** great to see Auchentoshan hit this kind of heights: it is not the most common of phenomena. Works well in nearly every respect and few Lowlanders reach this degree of excellence when so grey bearded. *47.5%. 156 bottles exclusively for CSN, Calgary.*

Auchentoshan Classic db **(80) n19 t20 f21 b20.** Classic what exactly...? Some really decent barley, but goes little further. *40%*

Auchentoshan Select db **(85) n20 t21.5 f22 b21.5.** Has changed shape of late, if not quality. Much more emphasis on the enjoyable juicy barley sharpness these days. *40%*

Auchentoshan Three Wood db **(76) n20 t18 f20 b18.** Takes you directly into the rough. Refuses to harmonise, except maybe for some late molassed sugar. *43%*

⋙ **A.D. Rattray Auchentoshan 1990** cask no. 17285 **(86.5) n21 t23 f21 b21.5** A messy nose and confused, vanilla-clad finish is rescued in magnificent fashion by a startlingly bright delivery full of lilting, juicy barley notes.

Berrys' Own Selection Auchentoshan 1991 cask no. 481, bott 07 **(62) n17 t17 f13 b15.** Gruesomely off key....almost worth getting just for the horror show!!! *46%*

Cadenhead's Authentic Collection Auchentoshan Aged 16 Years bourbon barrel, dist 90, bott Feb 07 **(92) n22** pure Canadian or pure grain scotch....this is malt...?!?!? **t24** the bizarre nose is followed by a similar Canadian theme on the delivery – then whoosh!!! The barley turns up in force and at its most thick, juicy and chewy and stuns the tastebuds with its uncompromising beauty; **f23** long, lingering vanilla and a gentle breakdown of something Canadian blessed with sweet malt. To call it charming hardly does it justice... **b23** 'Toshan at its very best.... In fact one of the finest I've come across from this distillery for a very long time. Tasted blind I'd never have recognised it! *59.2%. Cadenhead's. 204 bottles.*

Cadenhead's Authentic Collection Auchentoshan Aged 17 Years bourbon, dist 90, bott Sep 07 **(80.5) n21 t19 f20.5 b20.** Soars above the distillery bottling 18-y-o on nose, but at times viciously hot. *59.2%. 252 bottles.*

Dewar Rattray Individual Cask Bottling Auchentoshan 1991 Aged 15 Years cask no. 478, dist Feb 91, bott May 06 **(83) n19 t22 f21 b21.** It's not often you get a slightly feinty triple distilled whisky... but you have one here. On the plus side there is enough body here for you to get your tongue around... *59%. 390 bottles.*

Duncan Taylor Collection Auchentoshan 1999 cask no. 800003, dist Mar 99, bott Mar 06 **(73) n21 t21 f15 b16.** After textbook nose and delivery, falls apart alarmingly and bitterly as the balance with oak is lost. *43%. 430 bottles.*

⋙ **Duthies Auchentoshan 19 Years** Old **(86) n21.5 t22 f21 b21.5.** Mouth-watering, juicy and boasting a lot of natural toffee. *46%. Cadenhead's for Germany.*

Kingsbury Celtic Series Auchentoshan 21 Years Old 1984 (86.5) n21 t21 f22.5 b22. Robust, crisp and mega-malt intense. A bit hot, as 'Toshan can oft be, but generates enough crystalline barley towards the end to win the heart over twice-fold. Overall, much younger than its years with the oak barely making a noise. *55.4%. nc ncf. Japan Import System Co. Ltd.*

Milroy's of Soho Auchentoshan 1990 hogshead, cask no. 17284, dist 14 Dec 90, bott 23 Feb 07 **(84) n20 t22 f21 b21.** Not your standard Auchentoshan, this. Much more oily and displaying bigger natural caramels than usual. A competent dram. *46%. 329 bottles.*

⋙ **Milroy's of Soho Selection Number One 1991 Auchentoshan Aged 16 Years** refill butt, cask no. 485, dist Feb 91, bott Nov 07 **(86) n21 t22 f22 b21.** Competent, attractive and on it's best ultra malty behaviour. With nearly 3,000 bottles from this cask, designated exclusively for miniatures, one assumes, but nothing petit about this bottling. *40%. Milroy's of Soho, 2880 bottles.*

Murray McDavid Auchentoshan 1992 (77) n19 t20 f19 b19. Creamy, fruity...but somehow not on the ball. *46%.*

Murray McDavid Auchentoshan 1999 Aged 8 Years bourbon/mourvedre **(86) n21 t21 f22 b22.** One of the few whiskies in the world I suggest you take with water. Not to improve the flavour. Just to save you from dehydration...Sophisticated, though. *46%*

∴ **Old Malt Cask Auchentoshan Aged 13 years** refill hogshead, dis Dec 95, bott Feb 09 **(86.5) n21 t22 f21.5 b22.** Genuinely enjoyable and showing a deft touch to the barley component. The spices are located where you want them to help counter the juicy onslaught, but also not to an extent that would shut out that source of entertainment. The degree of sweetness if also spot on. Always good to come across a 'Toshan of this calibre. *50%. Douglas Laing. 365 bottles.*

Old Malt Cask Auchentoshan Aged 17 Years refill hogshead no. 4217, dist Aug 90, bott Mar 08 **(94) n23.5** freakishly identical in aroma to the distillery 21-year-old!! If anything, has a suggestion of bourbon the other lacks; **t23.5** sweet, brown sugar candy with a wonderful injection of spice; excellent mouthfeel and balance; the eye-watering succulence makes you purr; **f23** long, with the spices countering the thick barley intensity; gentle waves of vanilla offer the required dryness; **b24** if casks of such brilliance can be located in the 'Toshan warehouses – and they must be in there somewhere – the distillery can do worse than to find them and follow Douglas Laing's lead to up the distillery's profile. A legendary bottling. *50%. Douglas Laing. 295 bottles.*

∴ **Provenance Auchentoshan Aged 12 Years** refill hogshead, dist winter 96, bott spring 09 **(73) n18 t20 f17 b18.** Thin, mildly off key. *46%. Douglas Laing.*

Scotch Malt Whisky Society Cask 5.22 Aged 9 Years 1st fill barrel, dist Mar 99 **(92) n22** lemon curd tart with a lively fresh oak buzz; **t23.5** serious impact of fresh, resounding barley; oilier than you might expect with major bourbony-liquorice-edged weight; the salivameter goes berserk; **f23** long, with fingers of drier oak grasping the ever-surging barley; late mocha rounds it off wonderfully; **b23.5** 'Toshan at arguably its best age from this kind of cask. Droolingly brilliant. *60.0%*

∴ **Scotch Malt Whisky Society Cask 5.25 Aged 9 Years** refill barrel, dist Jun 99 **(88.5) n22.5** barley bounces around the glass; clean, a tad gristy and very green; **t22.5** every bit as juicy as the nose heralds; a delicate nuttiness combines well with the malt concentrate and soft oil; spicy; **f21.5** remains sweet and delicate, still with a nutty outline to the dominant barley; dries and bitters very slightly as the (improbable) oak intrudes; **b22** a fine, hugely enjoyable example of a (probably) 2nd fill cask allowing a relatively young malt to do its own thing. *57.8%*

∴ **Old Malt Cask Auchentoshan Aged 18 Years** refill hogshead, dist Aug 90, bott Nov 08 **(83.5) n22 t22 f19.5 b20.** At times unashamedly throat-ripping but plenty of ginger-led fun for those who want to go for the white knuckle ride. *50%. Douglas Laing. 335 bottles.*

Whisky Galore Auchentoshan 1999 (78.5) n19 t21 f19.5 b19. Raw, unrefined and eye-watering. But what fun!! *46%. Duncan Taylor.*

AUCHROISK

Speyside, 1974. Diageo. Working.

Auchroisk Aged 10 Years db **(84) n20 t22 f21 b21.** Tangy orange on the nose, the malt amplified by a curious saltiness on the palate. *43%. Flora and Fauna.*

Chieftain's Auchroisk Aged 11 Years Medoc Finish (79) n20 t22 f18 b19. Salivating but thin. *43%. Ian Macleod.*

Chieftain's Auchroisk 13 Years Old American/Spanish oak, dist Feb 94 **(84.5) n21 t21 f21.5 b21.** An honest Speysider teaming with lively barley. *43%. nc ncf. Ian Macleod.*

Connoisseurs Choice Auchroisk 1993 (78) n19 t21 f19 b19. Simplistic malt essay of few words. *43%. Gordon & MacPhail.*

Dun Bheagan Auchroisk 17 Year Old port finish, dist Sep 90 **(69) n18 t17 f17 b17.** If ever there was a case to colour and chill-filter, this might be it... *43%. nc ncf. Ian Macleod.*

Kingsbury Celtic Series Auchroisk 15 Years Old 1990 (83.5) n21 t20 f21.5 b21. Even at this massive strength, pretty threadbare in terms of complexity and impact although the clarity of the barley late on impresses. *62.8%. nc ncf. Japan Import System Co. Ltd.*

Mackillop's Choice Auchroisk cask no. 15576, dist Oct 92, bott May 07 **(87) n22 t22 f21.5; b21.5** Pavlovian responses usually mean I shudder at the prospect of a single cask Auckroisk of this kind of age. This is above the norm in every respect. *46%. ncf. Iain Mackillop*

Murray McDavid Auchroisk 1992 Aged 14 Years bourbon/guigal cotes rotie syrah **(76) n19 t19 f19 b19.** Time for me to have a little whine... *46%*

Old Malt Cask Auchroisk Aged 16 Years (81) n21 t20 f20 b20. Pear drops and barley. *50%. Douglas Laing.*

Old Malt Cask Auchroisk Aged 33 Years (94) n22.5 somehow the malt clings on to be the main shareholder with some waves of oak-based fruitiness starting to stir; a few bourbony strands begin to become entangled; **t24** a real surprise mouthful because the body of this is far fuller, richer and oilier than it was when distilled all those years ago. Fabulous, light coating of golden syrup which comfortably sees off the background oak; **f23.5** long, beautifully textured with oaky sinews amid the rich barley; chalky towards the finish but keeps on track; **b24** just a few weeks back I attended the memorial dinner for former J&B Blender Jim Milne, who was in charge when Auchroisk first came on stream. He was always a little disappointed with the frailty and lightness of this malt and had to work punishingly hard to get it up to scratch for when he first unveiled it as a single malt. This stunning OMC is the oldest bottling of this malt I have ever seen, and I am so sorry I did not have a bottle to hand to celebrate his life with his fellow friends. Because had it shown all those qualities and depth 22 years ago, a lot of his problems would have been solved. *47.2%. Douglas Laing.*

Scotch Malt Whisky Society Cask 95.6 Aged 21 Years refill hogshead, dist Mar 85 **(81) n20 t22 f19 b20.** Sharp, malty and bigger-bodied than more recent expressions. But there is still something rather hot and hostile about this. *54.6%*

⌘ **Scotch Malt Whisky Society Cask 95.9 Aged 18 Years** refill barrel, dist Sep 90 **(79) n18 t19 f22 b20.** An emaciated malt with some oaky ribs showing. Juicy in part, though. *59.4%*

Scott's Selection Auchroisk 1989 bott 07 **(83) n20.5 t21.5 f23 b19.** If this were art, which I suppose it is, then as a painting it is the equivalent of hurling paint at a fresh canvas. Neither rhyme nor reason to this, but the honey edge to the barley, especially late on, does impress when given a chance. The finish, seemingly against the odds, does have a certain resonance and spontaneity. *54.7%*

Secret Stills Lowland 1989 distillery no. 3 release no. 2 **(86) n19 t22 f23 b22.** A very sweet rendition of one of Scotland's most temperamental malts. Just to add to the confusion there is even a degree of smoke to this one. *45%. Gordon & MacPhail.*

AULTMORE

Speyside, 1896. John Dewar & Son. Working.

Aultmore 12 Years Old db **(86) n22 t22 f20 b22.** Do any of you remember the old DCL distillery bottling of this from, what, 25 years ago? Well, this is nothing like it. *40%*

Cadenhead's Authentic Collection Aultmore Aged 17 Years bourbon barrel, dist 89, bott Feb 07 **(86) n21 t23 f21 b21.** some delightful moments, especially when it comes to the intense bourbon middle. Lovely cocoa-clad finish but at times runs a little hot. *54.4%. 186 bottles.*

Connoisseurs Choice Aultmore 1995 (92.5) n24 I know there is no such thing as an exact definition of a Speyside aroma: historically it was lightly smoked and today more are going back to that style. However, if you ask a blender how he would think in terms of a "Speysider", this would just about be it: not just clean and malty, but with a distinctive lemon jam sponge sweetness and freshness. And, for its age, laced with just the correct amount of vanilla. Oh, and for no extra cost, some over-ripe greengages, too... **t23.5** all that barley juice promised on the nose just drips from every tastebud; next come those fruitier notes – pretty hard to make out what exactly – just fruity... but it's all so clean and damned yummy... **f22.5** dries with a dusting of cocoa; **b22.5** Aultmore up to its usual brilliant but simple tricks. *43%. Gordon & MacPhail.*

Dun Bheagan Aultmore Aged 15 Years (76) n19 t19 f19 b19. A bit dense, monosyllabic and bitter. *43%. Ian Macleod.*

⌘ **Norse Cask Selection Aultmore 1992 Aged 16 Years** barrel no. 3839, dist 92, bott 08 **(91) n23** toffee apples...and those apples are pretty damned green..! **t24** tastebuds...we have lift-off...!!!! What a delivery! Spices abound, but while they explode there is no collateral damage, with the barley free to roam unmolested and a natural toffee molasses ensuring a delicate sweetness keeps things in order; **f21.5** perhaps over enthusiastic caramels now as complexity levels minimalise; **b22.5** what a treat to find Aultmore in this kind of mood. Great fun! *56.8%. Qualityworld for WhiskyOwner.com, Denmark.*

⌘ **Old Malt Cask Aultmore Aged 12 Years** sherry butt, dist Jan 96, bott Sep 08 **(79) n20 t21 f18.5 b19.5.** Ferociously hot on delivery, you will hunt the grape in vain. Plenty of malt, though. *50%. Douglas Laing. 687 bottles.*

Old Malt Cask Aultmore Aged 16 Years sherry finish dist May 90, bott Feb 07 **(66) n14 t19 f16 b17.** scuppered by the dreaded "S" word... *50%. 742 bottles.*

⌘ **Old Malt Cask Aultmore Aged 18 Years** dist Sep 90, bott Jul 09 **(89) n21** threatening oak...could go either way... **t23** selects the spicy, juicy route...and what spices...what juice!! Salivating barley with a touch of bourbony sweet liquorice **f22** settles towards a tongue-tickling spice exit, but with plenty of butterscotch to enjoy en-route; **b23** a fizzing beaut! *50%. Douglas Laing.*

⌘ **Provenance Aultmore Aged 11 Years** sherry butt, dist autumn 96, bott summer 08 **(86) n22.5 t21.5 f21 b21.** Perplexing in style, with loads of crystalised brown sugar ensuring a solidity you would hardly expect. The malt is deliciously flinty; crunchy almost. *46%. Douglas Laing.*

Provenance Aultmore Aged 13 Years sherry butt, dist winter 96, bott winter 09 **(77.5)** n19 t21 f19 b18.5. Tangy with the odd distinctive unhappy note. The colour is excellent but the oak somehow doesn't quite gel. *46%. Douglas Laing.*

Scotch Malt Whisky Society Cask 73.30 Aged 15 Years refill barrel, dist May 92 **(86.5)** n22 t21 f22 b21.5. For a malt with a viperous 60% alcohol after 15 years, this is an incredibly well-mannered dram and not without some bourbon pretensions. Lots of lip-smacking qualities. *60.1%*

Scotch Malt Whisky Society Cask 73.31 Aged 16 Years refill barrel, dist Mar 92 **(91.5)** n22.5 magnificent blood orange – bourbon mix; t23.5 a serious leap in the bourbon feel with honey-vanilla present on entry; the barley is there in big enough tones to make for a major segment of the experience; f22 spices, first apparent from about the fifth wave in, continue to buzz and fizz; the tapering of the barley is in line with the oak fade: excellent stuff... b23.5 in shape and style, a twin brother of 70.30, only in execution this is just so much further ahead. A better cask and extra time has moved it on a bit further allowing the oak to have a slightly louder say. Often the time factor can go either way but, in this case, it is a development very much for the better. Make no mistake: this guy is huge and Aultmore at its finest. *9.2%*

Scotch Malt Whisky Society Cask 73.34 Aged 16 Years refill barrel, dist Mar 92 **(81)** n19 t20 f22 b20. Ye Gods! This is hot stuff. Gluey, slightly bourbony nose is followed by a searing delivery. Only when the intense malt and natural caramels settle on the finish does it begin to relax. *58.9%*

Scott's Selection Aultmore 1987 bott 07 **(88)** n22.5 quintessential clean Speyside aroma, very little the worse for wear considering its age; t22 ultra-intense malt where a dab of orange peel goes a long way in adding sharpness; attractive oils throughout; f21.5 bitters out with an uncertain cocoa finale; b22 it's been some time since I've seen Aultmore bottled at this age. The above average oiliness helps with the length and mouthfeel for this very decent dram. *55.8%*

The Single Malts of Scotland Aultmore 1992 Aged 15 Years small batch, bott Sep 07 **(90.5)** n23 engaging citrus fits perfectly with clean barley and restrained oak; t22 juicy, teasing multi-layered barley. A coating of sweetish, barley-rich oil keeps out the oak; lemon-curd tart and butterscotch helps it on its way; f23 pleasing complexity in what proves to be a long finale: genuine structure here as the cocoa adds weight to the re-emerging citrus and confident barley; b22.5 a sublime, outwardly simplistic, cleverly understated dram. *46%. Speciality Drinks.*

The Single Malts of Scotland Aultmore 1990 Aged 16 Years (95) n24 crushed Crunchy bars – it's honeycomb and chocolate all the way, except for a slight puff of peat smoke; t23 lush delivery with the accent on honey, though the oak ensures bitter-sweet harmony; a tad oily; f24 at first seems oak-riddled and bitter. By the third mouthful the honey has permeated so deeply that balance is restored and also some juicier barley tones radiate impressively until the cocoa arrives to give a virtuoso display; b24 at first taste I thought this was all nose with the oak doing damage further down the line. Then, slowly, you realise you are in the company of greatness and your palate has been caressed by genius. Magnificent whisky. *58.8%. sc. Speciality Drinks, UK.*

BALBLAIR
Highlands (Northern), 1872. Inver House. Working.

Balblair 10 Years Old db **(86)** n21 t22 f22 b21. Such an improved dram away from the clutches of caramel. *40%*

Balblair Aged 16 Years db **(84)** n22 t22 f20 b20. Definitely gone up a notch in the last year. The lime on the nose has been replaced by dim Seville oranges; the once boring finish reveals elements of fruit and spice. It's the barley- rich middle that shines, though, and some more work will belt this up into the high 90s where this great distillery belongs. *40%*

Balblair 1975 db **(94.5)** n24.5 one of the most complex noses in the Highlands with just about everything you can think of making a starring, or at least guest, appearance at some time. That's not a taster's get-out. Nose it and then defy me...For starters, watch the clever bourbon edge alongside the crème brulee and ground cherry topping...hunt the smoke down, also... t23.5 silk. No, wait....it could be velvet. No, definitely silk. The barley descends in the most gentle manner possible but this does not detract from the intensity: wave upon wave of barley melts upon the tastebuds, varying only in their degree of sweetness; f23 a few more bitter oak noises, but it remains barley all the way, even at this age. Amazing....; b23.5 essential Balblair. *46%*

Balblair 1989 db **(91)** n23 a sprinkle of salt has maximised the bourbon intensity; the soft oak benefits, too. But it is the clarity of the barley that makes the hairs stand on end; t23 superb delivery, with the ultra rich barley showing superb intent; the body is firm and the weight is perfect while the vanilla enters bang on cue; f22.5 above medium length but hangs on the sweeter elements of the barley longer than anticipated; the soft buttery oak is a wonderful foil; **b22.5** don't expect gymnastics on the palate or the pyrotechnics of the Cadenhead 18: in many ways a simple malt, but one beautifully told. Almost Cardhu-esque in the barley department. *43%*

Balblair Vintage 1979 dist 79, bott 07 db **(84) n21 t22 f20 b21.** A pretty whisky, but one which refuses to open out entirely despite the barley-rich prompting. *46%. nc.*

Balblair Vintage 1989 dist 89, bott 07 db **(89) n22** custard powder mixed into barley grist; **t23** plate-cleansing from the off with the barley surging in gigantic waves; the oak is hardly shy but very much kept in check; **f22** soft, juicy barley-fruit re-enters the fray as the oaks do their best to dry with that European-fruit distillate bitterness (wild cherries, to be precise) that seems to be a part of this distillery's latter-day character; **b22** the key to this malt is its refreshing qualitiy: the way the oak come on board but the barley wins the day. An excellent journey. *43%. nc.*

Balblair Vintage 1997 dist 97, bott 07 db **(88) n23** an exceptionally confident nose. bursting out of the bottle with kumquats and jazzed-up barley. Just so intense and fresh; **t22** again the fruits pile in, both a mixture of something citrussy and barley-related. Big yet refined with the house-style light bitterness towards the middle as the oaks absorb easily; **f21** a delicate and rather simple fade pepped up by the lightest of spices; **b22** this is the way I've been wanting to see Balblair at this age for a long, long time. Easily the most true to character distillery bottling for the last 20 years. *43%. nc.*

Cadenhead's Authentic Collection Balblair Aged 17 Years bourbon, dist 90, bott Sep 07 **(87.5) n22** strident bourbon complete with the leather armchair bit... **t22.5** softly oiled barley soon morphs into something found somewhere between Canada and Kentucky as a waxy liquorice and natural toffee dovetail; **f21** slightly on the bitter side; **b22** one assumes a first full cask at work here with all those neo bourbon notes around. *56.6%. 192 bottles.*

Cadenhead's Balblair Aged 18 Years bourbon wood, matured in oak cask, dist 90, bott Jun 08 **(92.5) n22** blood orange concentrate; a little sap but the salted barley makes amends; **t25** masterful: the barley is delivered as a controlled explosion, a touch fiery but as malt-intense as anything you will taste this year. Truly fantastic....and faultless! **f22.5** settles down with lots of natural caramels making a creamy entrance; **b23** a sublime cask which shows just what this outstanding distillery is capable of. *55.9%. 252 bottles.*

The Creative Whisky Company Balblair 1975 Aged 29 Years (93 .5) n24 almost a twin of the official distillery bottling, complete with sexy smoke nose; just a little lighter with a touch of citrus; **t22.5** oaky and aged, but the silkiness and gentle smoke is bang in line **f24** really relaxes now as the oak is reduced to a vanilla subtext and the barley takes up the reins. A touch of fading citrus cuts through the gentle peat...so classy.... **b23** almost an off-cut of the original distillery bottling. Very similar, except this is a tad lighter in colour and nature and with a fraction more apparent oak and age. Glorious. *46.2%*

⋰⋱ **Old Distillery Label Balblair Aged 10 Years (92) n22** oozes class from every pore... and pour: lots of bourbon-cask and barley and a breezy citrus, too; **t23.5** juicy and beautifully busy. Almost impossible to spit, so faultlessly distinctive is the rich barley-bourbon tapestry; **f23** loads of chocolate on the finale with plenty of zingy zestiness and spice to keep the juices flowing despite the move towards a digestive biscuity dryness; some lovely soft oils at the death ensures good length; **b23.5** I'm a sucker for these juicy, big-malted flawless numbers. And this one certainly leaves you sucking hard as you pucker up. A top-notch thirst-quencher. *43%. Gordon & MacPhail.*

Old Malt Cask Balblair Aged 17 Years refill butt 3930, dist Apr 90, bott Oct 07 **(77.5) n19 t19 f20 b19.5.** Not quite the finest oak ever selected for maturation. *50%. nc ncf. Douglas Laing. 743 bottles.*

BALMENACH
Speyside, 1824. Inver House. Working.

Balmenach Aged 25 Years Golden Jubilee db **(89) n21 t23 f22 b23.** What a glorious old charmer this is! An essay in balance despite the bludgeoning nature of the beast early on. Takes a little time to get to know and appreciate: persevere with this belter because it is classic stuff for its age. *58%. Around 800 decanters.*

Cadenhead's Authentic Collection Balmenach-Glenlivet Aged 17 Years bourbon hogshead, dist 89, bott Sep 06 **(90) n23 t22 f22 b23.** In many ways simplistic, but has that certain something that picks it out above the norm. *53.1%. 312 bottles.*

⋰⋱ **The Cärn Mör Vintage Collection Braes of Balmenach 2001** barrel, cask no. 800412, dist 01, bott 09 **(85.5) n20.5 t22 f21.5 b21.5.** Light, crisp, sweetly malted and a pleasing spiciness. *46%. The Scottish Liqueur Centre.*

Chieftain's Balmenach 15 Years Old Hogshead (77) n19 t21 f18 b19. Fruity and pleasant, but a fraction too over-oaked. *43%. Ian MacLeod.*

⋰ **Connoisseurs Choice Balmenach Aged 18 Years** first fill sherry butt, dist 90, bott 08 **(76) n19 t20.5 f18 b18.5.** Sufficient sulphur to take the shine from the experience. *43%. Gordon & MacPhail.*

Connoisseurs Choice Balmenach 1975 (92) n24 wonderful oloroso theme: clean and with a distinctive "cream sherry" lead-in to the roasty and very lightly smoked barley; **t23** age is immediately apparent but such is the intensity and clarity of the sherry the balance is maintained; lovely barley sub strata; **f22** soft toffee apple and vanilla **b23** what a great little malt, showing just how a sherry cask should influence, and marking clearly the gap between the quality of latter -day sherry butts and the pre-sulphured hey-days of over 30 years ago. *43%. Gordon & MacPhail.*

⋰ **Connoisseurs Choice Balmenach 1991 (88) n22** sweetened oakiness and the vaguest hint of smoke; **t22** chewy, big, busty and lusty with a big oak tang; **f22** various sorts of chocolate confirms the maturity; **b22** firm, steady-as-she-goes malt which would not have improved with further aging. A musty-have though for those who prefer their dram spiced up and chunky. *43%. Gordon & MacPhail.*

Deerstalker Balmenach Aged 10 Years (90) n22.5 green, young, a fraction gristy, a fraction spent wash: it smells like a distillery... **t22.5** fresh, gently oiled and then a charming build up of barley; **f22** soft vanillas mingle with the malt; **b23** you've nosed the dull Deerstalker 12; you've tasted the mildly dented Deerstalker 18: now get your laughing gear around the best of the lot, the brand-spanking new 10-year-old. Really does show the distillery in a straw-coloured and quite wonderful light...and would do it better still at 46%. *40%. Aberko.*

Deerstalker Balmenach Aged 18 Years (85.5) n22 t21 f21.5 b21. Huge sherry but not exactly faultless: blood oranges and chocolate malt leap at you. A must have for those who prefer their sherried dram of the ancient Macallan silky variety, but a pity about the vague sulphur traces. *46%. ncf. Aberko.*

⋰ **Deerstalker Balmenach Aged 18 Years (86) n22.5 t22 f21 b21.** Not quite in the same sparkling mode as many previous Deerstalkers, though the fruitiness does have a spicy tang. *46%. Aberko.*

⋰ **Old Malt Cask Balmenach Aged 18 Years** dist Oct 90, bott Jul 09 **(87.5) n21** an interesting array of mildly tired oak notes and grassy barley; **t24** a bucking bronco of a kick as far as the barley is concerned: enormous. Takes you through all layers from style and intensity, though the starring roles go to those malt notes tinged with golden syrup: quite wonderful; **f21** altogether more moribund and plain once the oak gains control; **b21.5** excellently weighted and shows some fine touches. *50%. Douglas Laing.*

⋰ **Provenance Balmenach Aged 8 Years** refill hogshead, dist winter 99, bott autumn 08 **(86) n21 t22 f21.5 b21.5.** Clean, simplistic but delightfully malty. *46%. Douglas Laing.*

Scotch Malt Whisky Society Cask 48.12 Aged 8 Years 1st fill barrel, dist Sep 99 **(86.5) n21 t22 f21.5 b22.** Warming, spiced, tangy with clipped, firm barley. Quite flawless in its own precise way. *60.6%*

⋰ **Scotch Malt Whisky Society Cask 48.15 Aged 9 Years** 1st fill barrel, dist Sep 99 **(84) n20 t21 f22 b21.** A big, rousing dram where the barley dominates despite the caramelised biscuit sheen. Perhaps short on complexity, but doesn't stint a jot on effect. When the alcohol burn subsides, and the vanillas shine rather than glow, the quality of the cask is fully evident. *61.3%*

⋰ **Scotch Malt Whisky Society Cask 48.16 Aged 8 Years** 1st fill barrel, dist Oct 00 **(90) n21** slightly ungainly with the oak not quite in alignment with the barley and under-ripe pear; **t23.5** classy, if mildly abrasive, pear drop delivery. Soon gets into a divine malty-mocha stride and the dark sugars build in intensity and suavity; **f22.5** beautifully long and sculpted with the barley re-emerging unscathed while a touch of manuka honey enriches the vanilla; **b23** a beautiful multi-textured dram which at times threatens towards a bitter course but stays on track with a refined, juicy intensity. *58.5%*

THE BALVENIE
Speyside, 1892. William Grant & Sons. Working.

The Balvenie Aged 10 Years Founders Reserve db **(90) n23** astonishing complexity: the fruit is relaxed, crushed sultanas and malty suet. A sliver of smoke and no more: everything is hinted and nudged at rather than stated. Superb; **t24** here we go again: threads of malt binding together barely detectable nuances. Thin liquorice here, grape there, smoke and vanilla somewhere else; **f20** Light muscovado-toffee flattens out the earlier complexity. The bitter-sweet balance remains brilliant to the end; **b23** just one of those all-time-great standard 10-year-olds from a great distillery – pity they've decided to kill it off. *40%*

The Balvenie Double Wood Aged 12 Years db **(80.5) n22 t20.5 f19 b19**. OK. So here's the score: Balvenie is one of my favourite distilleries in the world, I confess. I admit it. The original Balvenie 10 is a whisky I would go to war for. It is what Scotch malt whisky is all about. It invented complexity; or at least properly introduced me to it. But I knew that it was going to die, sacrificed on the altar of ageism. So I have tried to get to love Double Wood. And I have tasted and/or drunk it every month for the last couple of years to get to know it and, hopefully fall in love. But still I find it rather boring company. We may have kissed and canoodled. But still there is no spark. No romance whatsoever. 40%

The Balvenie Signature Aged 12 Years batch no 001 db **(93) n25** dried dates and walnuts with a touch of truffle oil. The Melton Mowbray Hunt fruit cake is massaged by demerara while shy strands of liquorice, ginger and chocolate malt add to the brilliance. If anyone wants to know just what a true master blender can do when allowed to get on with it, stick your snout in this and learn.... **t23** watery and delicate, there is a diffused, almost drowned, noble rot feel to this; bolstered by the most delicate spices – again of the fruitcake variety – the malt makes a pretty speech before the custard tart takes over; **f21** disappointing, as it appears to fade just too quickly leaving some vanilla tidemarks; **b24** this whisky was created by Grant's blender David Stewart and bottled to mark his 45 years in the industry. For my money, he's now the best in the business and has been for a little while. But it is a great shame that the marketing guys didn't insist on this being an apposite 45% because, for all the subtle wizardry going on here and the fact that the nose should immediately become the stuff of whisky legend, this is dreadfully underpowered. 40%

Balvenie Rum Wood Aged 14 Years db **(88) n22** excitable malt; lively almost piercing sugars; **t23** incredible spice delivery, seriously warming and increasingly sensual as the malt fights back; **f21** lots of toffee-barley; **b22** tasted blind I would never have recognized the distillery: I'm not sure if that's a good thing. 471%

The Balvenie Roasted Malt Aged 14 Years (90) n21 a European style of aroma often found in the smaller distilleries being in some ways closed, offering a hard edge and, on another level, showing attractive bitter-sweet conflict; **t23** it's the sweet element that shows the more powerful hand, especially with a delicious barley rush, though rabid peppers soon gather all the attention **f22** dry at first, a little sinewy but the gradual build up of mocha is sublime **b24** Balvenie very much as you've never seen it before: it takes time to settle, but when it does it becomes an absolute, mouth-filling cracker! 471%

The Balvenie Roasted Malt Aged 14 Years dist 92 db **(94) n23** thick, sweet, intense, vaguely floral, even more vaguely bourbony but very, very different; **t25** salivating for all the enormity. The fruitiness is in barley concentrate form and offers a delivery as memorable as it is unique; the barley juice appears to seep into the palate in equal spurts. Breathtaking and nigh-on perfect; **f23** warming spices develop while the oak tries to gain a foothold into the silky barley; a tad thin towards the end; **b23** having beaten the drum for this distillery longer than any independent observer breathing, it is so rewarding to find a bottling that so encapsulates Balvenie's brilliance. To do so, though, they have used a percentage of malt briefly germinated before being massively roasted in the style of a stout beer. The result is not unlike some European mainland malt whisky styles but fortified with the usual Balvenie complexity and weight. For the first 25 seconds on the palate it is, quite frankly, probably as good as anything you are likely to taste for many years and only the quick-ish finish robs it of a certain Bible Award. 471%. ncf

⁖ **Balvenie 14 Years Old Cuban Selection** db **(86) n20 t22 f22.5 b21.5**. Unusual malt and tasted blind you wouldn't recognise the distillery in a million years. No great fan of the nose but the roughness of the delivery grows on you, there is a jarring, tongue-drying quality which actually works quite well and the development of the inherent sweetness is almost in slow motion. Some sophistication here, but also the odd note which, on the nose especially, is a little out of tune. 43%

⁖ **Balvenie 14 Years Old Golden Cask** db **(91) n23.5** mildly tart: rhubarb and custard, with a vague sprinkling of brown sugar; bourbon notes, too; **t23** mouth-watering and zingy spice offer up a big delivery, but settles towards the middle towards a more metallic barley-rich sharpness; **f22** soft spices peddle towards the finish and a wave or three of gathering oak links well with the sweetened barley strands; **b22.5** a confident, elegant malt which doesn't stint one iota on complexity. Worth raiding the Duty Free shops for this little gem alone. 47.5%

⁖ **Balvenie 17 Years Old Rum Cask** db **(88.5) n22** green bananas and oak: curious... **t22.5** initially dry with the oak elbowing in first; several levels of barley battle back while some fudge enters the middle ground; **f22** remains fudgy, with a touch of oily butterscotch tart, but the emphasis is on the dryer, flaky tart; **b22** for all the best attentions of the rum cask at times this feels all its 17 years, and perhaps a few summers more. Impossible not to love, however. *43%*

The Balvenie Aged 15 Years Single Barrel db **(90.5) n22** candy fruit and barley sugar; **t23.5** juicy delivery where the barley leads the way and is soon backed up by sweet enforcements; a powder-dry oakiness ghosts around and a soft fruitiness can likewise be detected; **f22.5** long with a clever and astonishingly slow spice development. When it finally arrives, it really lets you know....! **b23** sadly, unable to discover which cask this was from or for which market. So one takes this as a generic Balvenie at its new strength. *478%*

Balvenie New Wood Aged 17 Years db **(85) n23 t22 f19 b21.** A naturally good age for Balvenie; the nose is lucid and exciting, the early delivery is thick with rich malt. This, though, has sucked out lots of caramel from the wood to leave an annoyingly flat finish. *40%*

The Balvenie 17 Year Old Sherry Oak db **(88) n23** glorious grape with no off notes: just sherry trifle sweetness with the odd spice kick for good measure; **t22.5** superbly clean grape even offers an early noble rot flourish; the oaks ensure ballast; **f21** long, dry and a touch bitter; **b21.5** clean as a nut. High-class sherry it may be but the price to pay is a flattening out of the astonishing complexity one normally finds from this distillery. Bitter-sweet in every respect. *43%*

The Balvenie Aged 21 Years Port Wood db **(88.5) n22** unusual aroma for a wine-finished whisky: here we are getting distinct ye olde oake signs that are leaning towards the exotic fruitiness of old bourbon casks; **t22** salivating and on the money malt-wise with the juicy chewiness appearing a lot fresher than the nose would have you believe; **f22.5** busy, multi-layered with some lovely praline amid the soft grape; **b22** beautiful, subtle malt. But the fruit element has been reduced considerably, as if the original Port pipes are being used a second or third time round. *40%*

The Balvenie Thirty Aged 30 Years db **(92) n24** has kept its character wonderfully, with a real mixture of varied fruits. Again the smoke is apparent, as is the panting oak. Astonishing that the style should have been kept so similar to previous bottlings; **t23** big, full delivery first of enigmatic, thick barley, then a gentle eruption of controlled, warming spices; **f22** much more oaky involvement but such is the steadiness of the barley, its extraordinary confidence, no damage is done and the harmony remains; **b23** rarely have I come across a bottling of a whisky of these advanced years which is so true to previous ones. Amazing. *473%*

Balvenie 1972 Vintage cask no. 14811 db **(82) n20 t22 f20 b20.** A tiring, exotic fruited effort which glows rather than shines. *473%*

The Balvenie 1993 Port Wood (89) n21 well-weighted but a trifle stifled; **t23** much busier arrival, with a lovely roastiness playing off the wine; the spices buzz gorgeously; **f22** finds a light-roast Java element; **b23** oozes class without getting too flash about it: the secret is in the balance. *40%*

BANFF
Speyside, 1863–1983. Demolished.

Cadenhead's Banff 29 Years Old (73) n19 t19 f18 b17. Too heavily oaked: should have been bottled at 25. *52%*

⁘ **Cadenhead's Banff Aged 32 Years** dist 76, bott 09 **(85) n22.5 t21 f20.5 b21.** Valiantly offers all the barley it can muster, and even a touch of defiant sweet grassiness, but the passing years and accumulated oak have the biggest say. *471%*

⁘ **Celtic Heartlands Banff 1975** bott 08 **(93) n23** sturdy, solid barley fortified with vanilla-oak (and a bit of sap) and citrus; the most delicate drift of smoke; **t23.5** big mouth-feel thanks to the suave oils; strawberry jam and cream-Victoria sponge feel; **f23** a move towards muscovado-sweetened mocha but elegant with those soft oils ensuring a lengthy tail off; **b23.5** pure, unambiguous quality. 48.1%. *Bruichladdich Ltd. 449 bottles.*

Old & Rare Banff Aged 37 Years dist Mar 71, bott Mar 08 **(74) n19 t18 f19 b18.** A strange malt: like finding an old piece of music written by Delius, or someone, and finding the whole thing out of key. *53%. ncf. Douglas Laing. 271 bottles.*

Old Malt Cask Banff Aged 32 Years dist May 74, bott Apr 07 **(86) n20 t23 f21 b22.** Beautifully honeyed and silky. *478%. Douglas Laing. 272 bottles.*

⁘ **Old Malt Cask Banff Aged 32 Years** refill hogshead, dist Nov 75, bott Aug 08 **(89) n22** oak shavings stirred into custard powder and a tablespoon full of acacia honey for good measure; **t23** wonderful layers of sugar-tipped barley head towards an oaky core; **f21.5** dries but the threatened oaks don't really overpower and unbalance the malty theme; **b22.5** funny how age works on some distilleries and not others. Technically, this probably has too much oak. Yet such is the overall richness and class of this enchanting dram, you can easily forgive its weaknesses. *48.7%. Douglas Laing. 164 bottles.*

Old Malt Cask Banff Aged 36 Years refill butt no. 3188, dist Mar 71, bott Sep 07 **(88) n22.5** thin exotic fruit, kippers frying next door; **t21** well oiled, with sharper citrus; a dose of over-enthusiastic oak; **f22.5** steadies and rights itself as the barley-oils take hold; vague, distant smoke returns. Delicate citrus enters at the endgame. **b22** has as many grey hairs as me. But just as sexy. A hint of something smoky on the nose; citrus seeing off the intruding oak on the palate. *50%. Douglas Laing. 451 bottles.*

Rarest of the Rare Banff 1975 cask no. 3416 **(91) n23** friendliest oak imaginable, with some ginger and crushed pine nuts sweetened by profuse honey; **t22** perfect delivery of honeyed barley which rides the oaky, softly spiced waves with nonchalance; **f23** gentle and chalky with enough spicy verve to keep it interesting; **b23** again Banff shows itself to be an outstanding old-timer. The continuing shards of honey radiate brilliance despite the oak's best attentions. *42.2%. Duncan Taylor.*

BEN NEVIS
Highland (Western), 1825. Nikka. Working.

Ben Nevis 10 Years Old db **(88) n21** enormously chunky and weighty: for a 10-y-o the oak is thick, but sweetened medley of ripe fruits; **t22** an almost syrupy mouth feel: a tad cloying but the malt is something you can so get your teeth into; **f23** long with traces of liquorice and hickory; **b22** a massive malt that has steadied itself in recent bottlings, but keep those knives and forks to hand! *46%*

Ben Nevis 14 Years Old Single Sherry Cask dist Sep 92, bott Jan 07 db **(88.5) n21** ooops! A distinctive off note here but the grape and malt are pretty intense and do their best to paper over the cracks; **t22.5** incredible thickness to the grape and when you get through that there appears to be a wall of malt to overcome; some sulphur does its best to screw up the experience but the malt and grape, though bloodied, sees it off; **f22** the sweetness really pushes through now and at several levels; from standard rich barley to denser acacia honey; **b22.5** talk about brinkmanship! This sherry butt has been introduced to sulphur. Luckily, its acquaintance was a passing one only, otherwise the marks would have tumbled frighteningly; but they shook hands sufficiently for five or six points to be lost here. That said, the integrity of the actual distillate is so high it comes through as a serious dram to savour. Mind you, I know a few Germans who would do anything for this kind of malt...well almost... *46%. 815 bottles.*

Ben Nevis 1997 Single Cask double wood matured, dist Feb 97, bott Jul 07 db **(91) n20** not entirely without charm but generally uncomfortable and a bit sulphurous-rubbery threatening: odd! **t23.5** mouth-watering and juicy with some stunning spices all couched in a sweet grapey sheen; **f24** longer, with some serious moves towards a chocolaty character; in the end the marriage between sweet grape and natural sugars plus the oaky cocoa makes something of a classic; **b23.5** from the colour, it appears to have been matured with cherries: I have never seen any whisky this ruddy colour in my life. But it tastes a whole lot better than it looks and even appears to see off a sulphurous threat that appears on the nose. Very different and, if in Sweden, worth hunting down. *Borders on the mad genius. 46%. ncf. 697 bottles. For Sweden.*

Battlehill Ben Nevis Aged 8 Years (80.5) n20.5 t22 f19 b19. A butch, nutty delivery. The malt and oak are barely on speaking terms. *43%. Duncan Taylor.*

⋰ **Berry's Own Selection Ben Nevis 1996** bott 09 **(86.5) n21.5 t21 f22.5 b21.5.** One of those almost impenetrably dense malty affairs this distillery conjours up from time to time, this one showing some fabulous sweet touches to the barley late on. Serve with a spoon. *56.9%. Berry Bros & Rudd.*

Cadenhead's Authentic Collection Ben Nevis Aged 16 Years butt, dist 90, bott May 07 **(83) n19 t22 f21 b21.** the odd butt-induced flaw, but this is one of the biggest malts of the year with the power of the barley giving the taste buds a salivating workover. *66%. 720 bottles.*

Duncan Taylor The NC2 Range Ben Nevis 1990 Aged 16 Years (75) n18.5 t20 f18 b18.5. A bitter-sweet affair with the emphasis on the bitter. *46%*

⋰ **Milroy's of Soho Ben Nevis 1996** refill sherry butt, cask no. 1670, dist Oct 96, bott Jul 08 **(90.5) n21.5** toasty, for all the hints of fruit; **t22** better delivery than the nose heralds with a confident malt thrust into the building grape; **f24** plateaus superbly with that preserve and toast on the nose now coming through as juicy fig jam with a prickly sweetness reflecting off the stunning oak-fruit sheen: just wonderful... **b23** hard not to be seduced by the rich and silkily-textured finish. A malt of great character. *46%. 198 bottles.*

Murray McDavid Ben Nevis 1999 Aged 8 Years bourbon/fortified grenache blanc **(82) n19 t20 f22 b21.** Excellent finish of soft-centre chocolate with superb squidgy fruit fondant. *46%*

⋰ **Old Masters Ben Nevis Aged 10 Years** cask no. 172, dist 98, bott 08 **(86) n22 t22.5 f20.5 b21.** Typical Nevis thick barley soupiness with the sharpness of the malt and bourbony nose. A real early delight. *57.9%. James MacArthur & Co. Ltd.*

Provenance Ben Nevis Aged 10 Years Gabriel Meffre wine cask no. 3686 **(84.5) n21 t21 f21.5 b21.** A thin vin fin. 46%. Douglas Laing.

Provenance Ben Nevis Aged 10 Years refill butt no. 3941, dist winter 97, bott autumn 07 **(81) n18.5 t22 f20.5 b20.** The big, juicy malt sweetness on arrival does its best to overcome some sub-standard oak. 46%. Douglas Laing.

Provenance Ben Nevis Aged 11 Years sherry finish butt no. 4236, dist winter 96, bott spring 08 **(86.5) n21.5 t22 f22 b21.** Much more like the full-bodied Ben Nevis we know and love. The grape has done a good job adding extra weight. Sweet if borderline cloying. 46%. nc ncf. Douglas Laing.

Scotch Malt Whisky Society Cask 78.37 Aged 9 Years sherry gorda, dist Dec 97 **(63) n14 t17 f16 b16.** A sherry gorda, eh? Good Gorda, more like. Completely wrecked by sulphur. 56.3%

BENRIACH

Speyside, 1898. The BenRiach Distillery Co. Working.

The BenRiach db **(86) n21 t22 f21.5 b21.5.** The kind of soft malt you could wean nippers on, as opposed to Curiositas, which would be kippers. Unusually for a BenRiach there is a distinct toffee-fudge air to this one late on, but not enough to spoil that butterscotch-malt charm. No colouring added, so a case of the oak being a bit naughty. 40%

The BenRiach Curiositas Aged 10 Years Single Peated Malt db **(95.5) n23.5** a wonderful buttery quality to the smoke, though curiously drier than previous bottlings; **t24** thickly cut chunks of peat are dunked into a softly oiled barley-citrus body: just eye-rollingly stunning; **f24** long, with a build up of liquorice to compliment the dogged but elegant smoke; the vanillas are mounting to ice-cream intensity; **b24** I have always compared over-smoked Arbroath Smokies to this. A few months back I had one – well two, actually – for breakfast, and that reminded me of this malt. The two, obviously, are synonymous. And this a malt which just gets better and better... 46%

The BenRiach Aged 12 Years db **(78.5) n21.5 t20 f18 b19.** White peppers on the nose, then goes uncharacteristically quiet and shapeless. 43%

The BenRiach Aged 12 Years Matured in Sherry Wood db **(90.5) n22.5** bitter-sweet grape with a chalky, sober dryness; **t23.5** a celebration of velvety fruit offers succulence and unusual clarity; there is enough room for the barley and a delightful latte development; **f22** medium length, continuing on the coffeed theme; even the late custard powder-vanilla oaky influx charms; **b22.5** a treat of a sherried malt: not a single off note and a real depth to the grape. 46%

The BenRiach Aged 13 Years Maderensis Fumosus Heavily Peated finished in Madeira barrels db **(87.5) n23** dry peat laid on with a trowel but particularly attractive due to the unusual layering of intensity; found hiding amongst these strata is a faint grapiness; **t21.5** no hiding the fruit now as it takes on the smoke for supremacy: a bit of an untidy battle; **f22** settles, possible due to exhaustion. Excellent vanilla calms the squabbling elements and even a touch of liquorice and molasses dives in at the death; **b21** a sharp and wild experience. 46%. nc ncf.

The BenRiach Aged 16 Years db **(83.5) n21.5 t21 f20 b21.** Pleasant malt but now without the dab of peat which gave it weight; also a marked reduction of the complexity that once gave this such a commanding presence. Doubtless next time I come across this it'll be back to its brilliant old self. 43%

The BenRiach Aged 16 Years Sauternes Wood Finish db **(93) n22.5** nutty, marzipan, rolled dough, sultanas; **t24** sublime delivery with the confident, clean sweetness being kept in check by some raging spices and thickening vanilla; deft for all its strong-arm stuff but it's the superb body-feel which really works; **f23** some major oak, but the dry, burnt toast aspect works ridiculously well with the waves of spice and fruit which have little intention of ending; **b23.5** a malt which works amazingly well despite the obvious cantankerousness of the oak. Macho stuff seduced by the allure of the silky fruit. A real late night dram for consenting adults. 46%

The BenRiach Aged 20 Years db **(88) n22** an oaky underscore to the toffee-honey barley; **t22** this one's all about the slow development in the intensity of the acacia honey; there are cream toffee elements to it also, but the malt, for all the years and thickness of flavour, remains intact; **f22** ultra soft and refusing at first to acknowledge its oaky inheritance. Again a burnt toffee statement is made; **b22** a 20-year-old that tries to act something five years younger with the oak being ganged up on. The intensity in itself means picking out characteristics is difficult: not unlike the very old fashioned whiskies which were married in barrel for a very long time before bottling. 43%

The BenRiach Aged Over 12 Years "Arumaticus Fumosus" richly peated style, ex-dark rum barrels db **(91) n23** cracklingly-hard peat; embers of a crofter's fire; **t23** big entry yet always controlled; the peat is shackled by something non-gristy yet sweet but comes and comes again in waves; the tingling spices are well harnessed; **f22** a Java/Indian medium roast coffee mix with a touch of demerara to lighten it...and the smoke, of course; **b23** very often finishing in rum can sharpen the mouthfeel yet at the same time add a sugary sheen. This little gem is no exception. 46%

The BenRiach Aged Over 12 Years "Heredotus Fumosus" richly peated style, ex-pedro ximinez sherry butt db **(84) n20 t22 f21 b21.** Perfectly respectable, perfectly drinkable, highly enjoyable and pretty more-ish. But if any whisky was to convince me that latter-day sherry butts and peat make entirely happy bedfellows...this wouldn't be it. 46%

The BenRiach Aged Over 12 Years "Importanticus Fumosus" richly peated style, ex-port hogshead db **(87) n22** the phenols are hard enough to still be embedded in a New Pitsligo peat stack; **t22** some grudging fruitiness attempts to make inroads into the solid peat base; **f21** some spices chisel their way into the malt; **b22** spill some of this on your foot and you'll break a toe. Hardicus asius Nailsus. 46%

The BenRiach Aged 15 Years Dark Rum Wood Finish db (86) **n21 t22 f22 b21.** Some malts, when put into a dark rum cask, have a propensity to become enjoyable but pretty sweet. This is one such example. 46%. nc ncf.

The BenRiach 1975 Vintage Single Cask Campaign No. 4 ex port pipe, cask no. 4451, bott Jun 07 db **(91) n23** highly complex fruit salad ranging from wild strawberries to boiled rhubarb. Very earthy, too; **t23** boiled candy: a mixture of fruit and cough ones. Gorgeous texture, though, and the gristiness excels; **f22** sawdusty oak pokes through; a touch of something smoky and a slightly thin finale; **b23** the Port has certainly breathed life into this old 'un. The complexity and enormity of the experience means it takes about 20 minutes to even begin to fathom this one out. 53.9%. 650 bottles.

The BenRiach 1976 hogshead, cask no. 2014, dist 19 Mar 76, bott Jul 08 db **(95.5) n24** no doubting its great age for supposedly one of the lighter Speysiders, but the way the butterscotch, rice pudding with a dollop of honey and physalis congregate, oh, and some very light smoke, too, you cannot be other than transfixed; **t24** sharp, juicy barley; some oaky extremes are brought under control by varying levels of non-specific juicy, vaguely exotic, fruit and the lightest layer of smoke; **f23.5** long, soft custard notes which sit well with the fruit; some late spices confirm the oak and smoke involvement; b24 a classic with memorable barley at its very richest. 50.3%. 200 bottles.

The BenRiach 1976 Vintage Single Cask Campaign No. 4 ex port pipe, cask no. 4469, bott Jun 07 db **(90) n22** ribald and rollicking – a real spiced- up ultra fruity treat; **t22** grip your chair as the spices scorch in! Prisoners slaughtered to order here as the white peppers rip through the tangy, salivating fruits; a soft echo of barley can just about be heard; **f23** fabulously long and the most extraordinary thing: it really does have the taste of straw to accompany the barley and fading fruit; **b23** good grief! Another BenRiach that is almost redefining cask finishes. This one works a treat, though! 55.5%. 750 bottles.

The BenRiach 1977 Muscatel wine barrel, cask no. 1029, dist 15 Apr 77, bott Jul 08 db **(80) n22.5 t20 f19 b18.5.** Superb nose, but on delivery I find this type of malt simply too overpowered by wine with the balance compromised. Doubtless, though, there will wine finish fundamentalists who will drool over it. Good luck to them. 54.9%. 313 bottles.

The BenRiach 1977 hogshead, cask no. 7186, dist 30 Jun 77, bott Jul 08 db **(88) n21.5** mixed messages here: not overly impressive oak but the varying citrus notes delight; **t23.5** fabulously sharp and alive; the barley fans out in all directions, taking a rich malty theme on one hand and also a massively active citric shape on another: breathtakingly beautiful...! **f21** bitter orange and...bitter; **b22** some signs of a cask that was unloved before being filled. Nothing wrong with the spirit which entered into it, though. 51.3%. 237 bottles.

The BenRiach 1978 Muscatel wine barrel, cask no. 4412, dist 20 Feb 78, bott Jul 08 db **(77) n21 t20 f17.5 b18.5.** One massive grape impact: for those who like some whisky notes in their wine. 50%. 274 bottles.

The BenRiach 1978 Vintage Single Cask Campaign No. 4 ex moscatel, cask no. 4413, bott Jun 07 db **(81) n22 t21 f20 b18.** My lack of fondness for certain finishes is well documented. Where does this sit in the pantheon of finishes? Very hard to say. Certainly it aint a rip-roaring success. But on the other hand the odd succulence drifts over the palate...but not enough to make it entirely work, sadly. 52.5%. 198 bottles.

The BenRiach 1978 Vintage Single Cask Campaign No. 4 ex tokaji, cask no. 4416, bott Jun 07 db **(88) n23** buzzing spices and even a touch of tequila about this one; the fruits sits pretty and the barley is entirely relaxed; **t21** a bit messy as the wine and barley fight; the red hot spices have to be tasted to be believed; **f22** a mouth-watering denouement with the wine still calling the shots; **b22** exceptionally rare for this wine style to work with whisky. But here it pulls it off. 52.7%. 246 bottles.

The BenRiach 1979 bourbon barrel, cask no. 10771, dist 5 Dec 79, bott Jul 08 db **(92.5)** **n23.5** pear drops, sherbet lemons, wooden floors, freshly waxed leather; more pear drops; **t24** stunningly fresh: the barley leaps out at you almost three dimensionally alerting every tastebud alive; more pear drop and shapes itself towards a vague honeycomb note near the middle; **f22** vanilla, butterscotch and custard ensure a degree of conventionality; **b23** I just adore slightly older bourbon casks which give the malt the freedom to express itself. *51.2%. 169 bottles.*

The BenRiach 1980 Limited Release Cask Bottling virgin oak cask no. 2535, bott Jun 06 db **(88) n24 t23 f20 b21.** The nose is the stuff of dreams, the mouth arrival is the most classic of drams, then some real problems fending off the tannins. But some moments of genius here. *52%. nc ncf. 236 bottles.*

The BenRiach 1984 Tawny port hogshead, cask no. 4046, dist 10 Oct 84, bott Jul 08 db **(91) n23** the peat and grape crash into each other with gay abandon; **t23** good grief.... the tastebuds don't stand much of a chance as thick wine notes and muscular peat slam relentlessly into them; **f22** tries to calm down a bit, showing at first a sharp, angular grapiness then kinder smoke; from start to finish there is a sharpness which is semi-eye-watering; **b23** being slugged around the kisser with a giant kipper and a bottle of port wouldn't have much more effect than a mouthful or two of this. Seriously, head-shaking stuff... *52.4%. 306 bottles.*

The BenRiach 1984 Vintage Single Cask Campaign No. 4 ex port hogshead, cask no. 4049, bott Jun 07 db **(83) n21 t20 f22 b20.** Another weird assembly of peat and port. I've yet to be entirely convinced this combination works for the best. Certainly no shortage of entertainment value but the wear and tear on the tastebuds is enormous. No wonder why they call it Campaign Number 4. Because this is one hell of a battle... *54.3%. 276 bottles.*

The BenRiach 1985 Vintage Single Cask Campaign No. 4 ex oloroso butt, cask no. 3766, bott Jun 07 db **(76) n19 t20 f18 b19.** The oloroso and gristy, smoky malt never quite find the right stride together. Pleasantish, haphazard and very dry. *54.6%. 672 bottles.*

The BenRiach 1988 new wood oak barrel, cask no. 4020, dist 12 Oct 88, bott Jul 08 db **(87) n20** big oak and vague sugars but not exactly great... **t23** huge delivery which arrives in a bit of a tangle but unfolds to reveal the most complex array of sugars I have tasted in a long time; for all that a bitter-sweet affair; **f22** various tannins and spices pitch into the muddle **b22** what can you quite make of this? If whisky is a work of art, this is pure abstract. *53.6%. 314 bottles.*

The BenRiach 1991 claret wine barrel, cask no. 6903, dist 19 Aug 91, bott Jul 08 db **(87)** **n22** spiced, pungent and sharp; **t20.5** thumping wine hits home: the malt takes a while to find its bearings; **f23** settles, relaxes and balances at last; **b21.5** blimey! A French wine barrel and not an atom of sulphur to be had anywhere: I must be dreaming. The wine still perhaps over-dominates in places. *52.8%. 311 bottles.*

The BenRiach 1994 new wood oak barrel, cask no. 4022, dist 2 Mar 94, bott Jul 08 db **(92.5)** **n23.5** vanilla pods and tannin fuse attractively with the maple syrup and natural caramel; some blood orange gets to work in there, too, as it stretches out to embrace a bourbony style; **t23.5** superb interplay between firm malt and softened, enveloping, honeyed oak; no shortage of brown sugars at work; **f22.5** the barley holds out against the oaky surge – just..!! **b23** at this age this has to be the way to go if you want to give your malt a big rich kick and stay away from the shark-infested waters that is today's sherry butt. Major stuff. *54%. 317 bottles.*

The BenRiach 1994 Vintage Single Cask Campaign No. 4 ex port hogshead, cask no. 26, bott Jun 07 db **(88) n22** absolutely unique: you'll either love it or hate it. I'm still not sure which...but I'm marking up for sheer entertainment value...it's like nothing on this planet: peat as you've never nosed it before; **t21** a faltering start as the port and peat jarringly and quarrelsomely collide; massive spice blast and then, suddenly, we are past the industrial grime and into open countryside where everything is beautiful and natural; **f24** fantastic finish entirely out of keeping with the outbreak of World War Three which preceded it. The peat is now sweet and swarthy and the gentleness of the gristiness is sublime; **b21** good grief....!!! Those of a nervous disposition had better give this one a miss. It's like tasty TNT.... *55.7%. 300 bottles.*

⬩⬩⬩ **Birnie Moss Heavily Peated** db **(93) n23.5** peat (dry and sweet); **t24** peat (mainly sweet); **f23** peat (oily, sweet, but some dryness, too) **b22.5** no chance of them being done under the Trade Descriptions Act.... *48%*

⬩⬩⬩ **Cadenhead's Benriach Aged 23 Years** dist 86, bott 09 **(95.5) n24** extravagantly salty barley and oak with a wonderful mulchy, floral sub-strata: a complex aroma to keep your nose occupied for a good half hour; **t24** mouth-watering and fresh, honey-crusted barley making a mockery of the passing years. The salt remains visible and works wonders with the slow butterscotch development; **f23.5** long with lingering vanilla and absolutely no oak burnt out; **b24** how blenders for so long considered this very much a second rate distillery is entirely beyond me. 53.3%

Chieftain's Benriach 14 Years Old Medoc finish, dist Sep 93 **(89) n22** a firm, pithy fruitiness forms sturdy barriers with the malt; **t22.5** firm, crisper than normal Benriach full of all kinds of juicy, fruity nuances; **f22** tangy marmalade and growing vanilla; **b22.5** a gifted wine finish which works well in every respect. 43%. nc ncf. Ian Macleod.

⁙ **Connoisseurs Choice Benriach 1987 (82.5) n20 t22 f20 b20.5.** Pretty oak-laden, even for its age. Attractive barley sugar attack, though. 43%. Gordon & MacPhail.

Dewar Rattray Benriach 1990 cask no. 1779, dist Feb 90, bott Nov 07 **(83.5) n22 t20.5 f21 b20.** Delightful, mountainous malt, but complexity at a minimum. 61.5%

Dun Bheagan BenRiach Aged 10 Years (86) n21 t22 f21 b22. A delicate, delicious and youthful Benriach in full blending colours. 43%. Ian Macleod.

Duncan Taylor Collection Benriach 1968 cask no. 2597 **(91) n23** exotic fruit and ginger **t23** busy oak but there remain loads of barley still to get your teeth into. The warming ginger does impress; **f22** dries towards a toasty finale but enough barley survives for the requisite sweetness; **b23** hard to believe that a Speyside can live this long in the cask and come out guns blazing. Wonderful. 48.6%. Duncan Taylor.

⁙ **Duncan Taylor The NC2 Range Benriach Aged 12 Years** dist 96, bott 08 **(85.5) n22 t21 f21.5 b21.** Has soaked up no shortage of oak in its dozen years, but the barley and spice fizz, topped with plain chocolate, evens things out. 46%

The Exclusive Malts Benriach Aged 11 Years cask no. 30608, dist Mar 96 **(90.5) n22** uncomplicated, highly attractive malt; **t22.5** puckeringly sharp barley; **f23.5** the barleyfest continues with a wonderful, tapering sweetness; **b22.5** an exceptionally lively and clean version with the barley in highly concentrated form: stunning and one for the purists. 55.9%. The Creative Whisky Company. 317 bottles.

Old Malt Cask Benriach Aged 18 Years refill hogshead cask no. 4278, dist Feb 90, bott May 08 **(84.5) n20.5 t22 f21 b21.** Elegant, malty and some fine mocha but certainly showing some grey hairs. 50%. Douglas Laing. 204 bottles.

⁙ **Old Malt Cask Benriach Aged 19 Years** refill hogshead, dist Feb 90, bott Apr 09 **(83.5) n20 t22 f20 b20.5.** It's all about the malty delivery: exceptional balance to the sweetness. Light latte, too. 50%. Douglas Laing. 235 bottles.

Provenance Benriach Aged 11 Years refill hogshead no. 4074, dist 96, bott 07 **(90) n22.5** a seemingly simple barley character rarely becomes more elegant than this; **t23** mouth-watering and full, this ticks every box you could demand from a Speyside-style malt: just so clean and juicy with heaps of sexy spice; **f22** remains outwardly simplistic but the barley remains on slow burn; **b22.5** for as much as I love their peated style, this is a way in which I adore to see Benriach. When I say this is sublime blending malt, I don't mean that as a put down – quite the opposite. The clarity of barley, the subtlety of the sweetness and extra, manageable, complexity offered by the spice are the kind of things blenders quietly purr about. Also, most likely, from a high quality second fill bourbon cask – which helps. 46%. nc ncf. Douglas Laing.

The Single Malts of Scotland Benriach 1984 Aged 22 Years bott Sep 07 **(90.5) n23** thick, curiously coastal peat, considering it's a Benriach! Wonder where the cask has been sitting all these years...; **t22.5** wonderful muscovado sugar kick to the smoke; **f22.5** lots of flinty citrus amid the smoke; **b22.5** a quite lovely cask. 53.2%. Speciality Drinks.

⁙ **Whisky Doris Benriach 12 Year Old** cask no. 45757, dist Mar 96, bott Oct 08 **(88) n22 t22 f23 b21.5.** See 52.1% below. Works very fractionally better at this strength as the honey just gets a slightly higher profile and there is less jarring. On the minus side, there is much less character and is a little too suave. 46%

⁙ **Whisky Doris Benriach 12 Year Old** cask no. 45757, dist Mar 96, bott Oct 08 **(87.5) n22** a surprising hint of pine and spearmint amid the citrus; a touch of honey lightens it; **t21** useful honeyed barley-rich delivery cracks quickly under the oak and then re-asserts itself briefly; **f23** really does gather in momentum and intensity to with a rich, oily barley theme. Softens noticeably; **b21.5** bit of a stop-start merchant, never quite finding a rhythm. That said, the goods parts really are excellent...! 52.1%

⁙ **The Whisky Fair Benriach 33 Year Old** dist 76, bott 09 **(84.5) n21.5 t21.5 f21 b21.** Has all the exotic fruit flourishes to mark the years - and a touch of coppery sheen on the palate, but perhaps a fair few splinters, too. 46.2%. The Whisky Fair, Germany.

⁙ **The Whisky Fair Benriach 33 Year Old** dist 76, bott 09 **(84.5) n21.5 t21.5 f21 b21.** The absolute twin of the 46.2% version, other than a quick, briefly passing explosion of juicy barley. 47.4%. The Whisky Fair, Germany.

BENRINNES

Speyside, 1826. Diageo. Working.

Benrinnes Aged 15 Years db **(70) n16 t19 f17 b18.** What a shame that in the year the independent bottlers at last get it right for Benrinnes, the actual owners of the distillery make such a pig's ear of it. Sulphured and sicklysweet, this bottling has little to do with the very good whisky made there day in day out by its talented team. Depressing. *43%. Flora and Fauna.*

Cadenhead's Authentic Collection Benrinnes Aged 18 Years bourbon hogshead, dist 88, bott Sep 06 **(92) n23 t24 f22 b23.** A magnificent Speysider. This distillery is, at last, coming out of the shadows. *55.9%. 246 bottles.*

⸭⸭ **The Càrn Mòr Vintage Collection Braes of Benrinnes 2002** hogshead, cask no. 5, dist 02, bott 09 **(80) n19 t21 f20 b20.** An entirely competent example of sweet, malty blending fodder untroubled by oak. *46%. The Scottish Liqueur Centre.*

Connoisseurs Choice Benrinnes 1991 (78) n17 t23 f19 b19. Forget the very poor nose and the indifferent, frugal and ultimately bitter finish. It's all about the lip-smacking freshness of the ultra- intense barley on delivery. *43%. Gordon & MacPhail.*

D&M Aficionados' Club Bottling Benrinnes Aged 18 Years cask no. 2858, dist Oct 88 **(78) n20 t20 f19 b19.** A malty, simplistic offering which shows signs of tiring towards the finish. *54.2%. sc ncf. US by Angus Dundee Distillers.*

Old Malt Cask Benrinnes Aged 14 Years sherry cask no. 4428, dist 94, bott Jun 08 **(81) n16 t21 f22.5 b21.5.** Some whiskies just leave you speechless: after the disaster of a nose I feared the worst. Yet the delivery on the palate and follow through is relative bliss. Get past the nose and be charmed! *50%. Douglas Laing. 661 bottles.*

⸭⸭ **Old Malt Cask Benrinnes Aged 21 Years** refill hogshead, dist Mar 88, bott May 09 **(91.5) n23** a light coating of fried banana and almonds really does lift the barley; **t23** beautiful texture on delivery with the oak offering perfect vanilla on the barley sugar; the malt simply melts on the tongue and a vague saltiness intensifies the sharpness of the grain... **f22.5** long, subtly oiled with almonds and remains remarkably intact and sweet to the end; **b23** heart-warming to see Benrinnes in this outstanding nick and so clean on nose and delivery. A distillery classic. *50%. Douglas Laing. 276 bottles.*

Provenance Benrinnes Aged 10 Years bourbon finished barrel no. 3940 **(84) n22 t20 f21 b21.** Exceptionally light, thought the squeeze of lemon really lifts it. *46%. Douglas Laing.*

Scotch Malt Whisky Society Cask 36.39 Aged 11 Years refill hogshead, dist Apr 96 **(68) n15 t16 f19 b18.** I'd put my house on this being a dud barrel even before spirit was put into it. Rarely do such poor casks slip through the SMWS net. Some decent cocoa on the finish tries to salvage a little pride. *60.8%*

⸭⸭ **Scotch Malt Whisky Society Cask 36.42 Aged 15 Years** sherry butt, dist Feb 93 **(83.5) n20 t22.5 f20 b21.** For the all less than subtle fruit involvement – classic early '90s United Distillers style – and stomping spices really it is the big natural caramels which steal the show. *57%*

⸭⸭ **Scotch Malt Whisky Society Cask 36.43 Aged 9 Years** 1st fill barrel, dist Sep 99 **(86) n20.5 t23 f21 b21.5.** One for those with a penchant for sweet, eye-wateringly sharp barley. Excellent oak for age, too, though the massive natural caramels flatten the nose somewhat. *59.9%*

⸭⸭ **Scotch Malt Whisky Society Cask 36.44 Aged 20 Years** refill butt, dist May 88 **(74.5) n18.5 t19 f18 b19.** Lively, tangy, some interesting cocoa but with its many flaws really would have been better suited to a blend. *60.5%*

BENROMACH

Speyside, 1898. Gordon & MacPhail. Working.

⸭⸭ **Benromach 21 Years Old** db **(91.5) n22** some exotic fruit and green banana is topped off with a splodge of maple syrup; **t23.5** excellent interplay between the sweeter, barley-rich components and the elegant, spiced oaky backbone; virtually no bite and softened further by an unfurling of vanilla on the middle; **f23** long, oak-edged with a slow, tapering dryness which does nothing to confront the sugared backnotes or even the suggesting of the most delicate smoke; **b23** an entirely different, indeed lost, style of malt from the old, now gone, big stills. The result is an airier whisky which has embraced such good age with a touch of panache and grace. The sweetness has been underlined in the last few seconds by attracting a tiny fruit fly which, whilst writing these notes, has chosen this to dive into and drown in. What a way to go: you could hardly wish for a classier end... *43%*

Benromach 22 Years Old Finished in Port Pipes db **(86) n22 t23 f20 b21.** Slightly Jekyll and Hyde. *45%. 3500 bottles.*

Benromach 25 Years Old db **(92) n24** seriously sexy with spices interplaying with tactile malt: the bitter-sweet balance is just so.There is even the faintest flicker of peat-smoke to underscore the pedigree; **t22** an early, surprising, delivery of caramel amongst the juicy barley; **f23** lots of gentle spices warm the enriched barley and ice-creamy vanilla; **b23** a classic old-age Speysider, showing all the quality you'd hope for. *43%*

Benromach Classic 55 Years Old dist 49, bott 04 db **(93) n24 t23 f22 b24.** Only distillery owners G&M could come up with something like this. Scotland had a King in those far off days. In fact, so did the British Empire – and there was still an Empire (just) in 1949. And this has to be a king of aged whiskies because it bears virtually no scars of time. Charlie Hewitt was back as manager of recently relegated Millwall; my parents were in their first year of marriage; Surrey were on the cusp of forming a cricket team to dominate the English game for the next decade and some guy in Scotland, possibly long dead and his name lost to history, laid down one cask that a generation and a half on would delight and astound a lucky few. That's whisky for you. *42.4%. 83 bottles.*

Benromach Cask Strength 1981 db **(91) n21.5** a day out at Margate, only crushed grapes for fish 'n' chips...; **t23** the sherry dives in head first, leaving little doubt about its fruity intent; although less coastal on the palate, there is still a touch of brine to the grape; **f23.5** long, with a soft barley tune being heard just above the grapey symphony; **b23** really unusual with that seaweedy aroma awash with salt: stunningly delicious stuff. *54.2%*

Benromach Latitude 57° cask no. 580 db **(73.5) n18.5 t19 f18 b18.** I'm afraid with that sulphur evident it shows the wrong kind of latitude altogether... *57%. 330 bottles.*

❖ **Benromach Madeira Wood** db **(92) n22** some rolling smoke and chunky dried fruits almost cancel each other out...almost...; **t24** voluptuous body displaying soft oils which coat the mouth with a spot on peat which is at once full and chewy yet light enough to allow the layered fruits full reign; the bitter-sweet balance just couldn't be better; **f23** long with some touches of almost Jack Daniel hickory amid the circling smoke and juiced up fruit; mind-boggling complexity to this for so long... **b23** good grief! If you want a boring, safe, timid malt, stay well away from this one. Fabulous: you are getting the feeling that the real Benromach is now beginning to stand up. *45%*

❖ **Benromach Marsala Wood** db **(86.5) n21.5 t22 f22 b21.** Solid, well made, enjoyable malt, which in some ways is too solid: the imperviousness of both the peat and grape appears not to allow much else get through. Not a dram to say no to, however, and the spices in particular are a delight. *45%*

Benromach Organic db **(91) n23** massive oak input and the freshest oak imaginable. But sits comfortably with the young pulsing malts. Wow!!; **t23** oak arrives first again, but has enough deftness of touch to allow the rich, mouthwatering malts to prosper; **f22** plenty of vanillins and natural, sweet toffee; **b23** young and matured in possibly first fill bourbon or, more likely, European (even Scottish) oak; you cannot do other than sit up and take notice of this guns-blazing big 'un. An absolute treat! *43%. nc ncf.*

Benromach Origins db **(84.5) n20 t22 f21 b21.5.** You'd think after tasting over 1,250 whiskies in the space of a few months you'd have nosed and tasted it all. But no: here is something very different. Discordant noises from nose to finish, it is saved by the extraordinary richness of the coppery input and a vague smoky richness finishing with cold latte. Very different, indeed. *50%*

Benromach Peat Smoke db **(88) n21** very clean and sweet; the smoke isn't big yet dominates...; **t23** a wonderful, clean, gristy feel – even a touch of drinking the mash about this; **f22** minimal oak interference as the smoke gently simmers down; the sweetness holds well; **b22** nothing overly complex about this. Just wonderfully distilled and sympathetically matured malt. *46%*

Benromach Peat Smoke Aged 6 Years 2nd edition 1st fill bourbon barrel, dist 02, bott 08 db **(92) n22.5** beautiful, sweet, flakey smoke with hickory amid the phenols; **t23.5** intense, soft, complex delivery but the accent very much of a sweet, controlled evolution of refined barley; **f23** medium length and smoky; the oak kicks in with aplomb and sympathy with just the right degree of weight and dryness; **b23** this is Benromach getting it right at every turn, including bottling at such tender years. Proof that excellence can be achieved with first class wood selection and fine work in the still house, rather than simply summers spent in the warehouse. *46%*

Benromach Sassicaia Wood Finish bott 07 db **(86) n23 t20 f22 b21.** Benromach in very different clothing here – in fact, there is no other malt with the elements so portrayed. Particularly pleasing is the beauty of the balance between the soft smoke and the varied oaky tones – very European. The arrival is a little confused (a touch of the Italian tantrums at one point) but it eventually pans out into an attractively sweet, and again softly peated, little charmer. Unique. *45%*

❖ **Benromach Traditional** db **(89) n24** hard not to adore: young, vibrant, elegantly smoky; gooseberry jam and Arbroath Smokies on a Aberdeenshire breakfast table. Stunning for all its youth; **t22** clean, relentlessly youth barley with no shortage of peat: chewy yet fresh; **f21** thins out not least because of lack of oak but enough around to ensure a chalky vanilla death; **b22** some will regard this way too young. It is just that reason, though, that this malt is such a treat, soaring on the nose and delivery with abandon. Just lovely. And very well made, too. 40%

Bevmo Benromach Single Cask No 704 dist 4/Oct/99 bott Jul 07 db **(74) n17 t20 f19 b18.** Young - very young! Some feints on the nose and a touch of smoke, too. Some grappling caramel also on the finish. Plenty to chew over, but minimal harmony. 43%

BLADNOCH
Lowland, 1817. Working.

⋯ **Berry's Own Selection Bladnoch 1990** bott 09 **(89) n23** the house style of boiling gooseberries at their pippiest; **t22** light, ultra-clean grassy barley with no more than a hint of vanilla; **f22** one of cleanest finishes you'll find with the barley still dominating, leading with that green fruity, grassy edge; the excellent barley-sugar sees off any threat of bitterness from the oak; **b22** some people will be disappointed with this as an 18-year-old, as it doesn't actually do much. And they might have a point. But on the other hand, how can you not be charmed by something so crystalline. 43%. Berry Bros & Rudd.

Bladnoch Aged 6 Years Bourbon Matured db **(91) n21.5** young, yes. But the soft feints have nothing to do with that; **t22.5** a youthful, oily delivery, not exactly a picture of harmony, gives way to a brutal coup d'etat of ultra intense prisoner-slaughtering barley; **f24** I'm in barley heaven: intense barley-concentrate oils offer a perplexing array of sweet, grassy tones; you simply chew and chew until the jaw aches. Cocoa at last arrives, all with a spiced buzz and a smearing of vanillas. Meanwhile your tongue explores the mouth, wondering what the hell is going on... **b23** ignore the mildly feinty nose and delivery. The fun starts with the late middle, where those extra oils congregate and the taste buds are sent rocking. Great to see a Lowlander bottled at an age nearer its natural best and even the smaller cut, in a roundabout way, ensures a mind-blowing dram. 57.3%

Bladnoch Aged 6 Years Lightly Peated db **(93) n23** a peat fire just bursting into life; **t23** firm, bitter-sweet; the layering of the peat is awesome, with the youth of the malt adding an extra dimension; some citrus notes help lighten the load; **f23.5** smoky hickory; the vanillas make a feeble entry, a gentle oiliness persists; **b23.5** the peat has nothing to do with the overall score here: this is a much better-made whisky with not a single off-note and the cut is spot on. And although it claims to be lightly peated, that is not exactly true: such is the gentle nature of the distillate, the smoke comes through imperiously and on several levels. "Spirit of the Lowlands" drones the label. Since when has outstanding peated malt been associated with that part of the whisky world...?? 58.5%

Bladnoch Aged 6 Years Sherry Matured db **(73.5) n18 t19 f18.5 b18.** A sticky, lop-sided malt where something, or a group of somethings, conjures up a very unattractive overture. Feints on the palate but no excellent bourbon cask to the rescue here. 56.9%

Bladnoch Aged 10 Years db **(94) n23** lemon and lime, marmalade on fresh-sliced flour-topped crusty bread; **t24** immensely fruity and chewy, lush and mouthwatering and then the most beguiling build-up of spices: the mouthfeel is full and faultless; **f23** long, remains mildly peppery and then a dryer advance of oak. The line between bitter and sweet is not once crossed; **b24** this is probably the ultimate Bladnoch, certainly the best I have tasted in over 25 years. This Flora and Fauna bottling by then owners United Distillers should be regarded as the must-get-at-all-costs Bladnoch. If the new owner can create something even to hang on to this one's coat-tails then he has excelled himself. For those few of us lucky enough to experience this, this dram is nothing short of a piece of Lowland legend and folklore. 43%. *For those of you with a nervous disposition, the author would like to point out that not a single drop of this whisky was spat out during the creation of these tasting notes.*

Bladnoch Aged 15 Years db **(91) n22.5** remnants of zest and barley sit comfortably with the gentle oaks; **t22.5** excellent delivery and soon gets into classic Bladnoch citric stride; **f23** wonderfully clean barley belies the age and lowers the curtain so delicately you hardly notice; **b23** quite outstanding Lowland whisky which, I must admit, is far better than I would have thought possible at this age. 55%.

Bladnoch Aged 15 Years sherry cask no. 1056 db **(81) n17 t22 f21 b21.** Perhaps not the best sherry influence of all time here but the juicy malt experience on the palate compensates for the nose. 46%. ncf.

Bladnoch Aged 15 Years sherry butt no. 2615, dist Jul 92, bott Feb 08 db **(86.5) n19 t23 f22.5 b22.** Maybe not the greatest-ever butt to be filled with Scotch, but there is no denying that the challenge of the enormous delivery and finish makes for some serious and hugely enjoyable dramming. There is something of the thick chocolate mousse late on, and then only after a sherry trifle opening. Have a fork and dessertspoon beside your glass when you pour this monster! And forget the nose – just add this to your collection: it's a rather delicious education... *55%. 550 bottles.*

Bladnoch Aged 16 Years "Spirit of the Lowlands" db **(88) n22** vaguely salty, digestive biscuit; very firm and attractive with pleasing barley edge; **t22** salivating and entire: the age doesn't detract from the richness of the barley one iota; **f22** continues in the same vein though the oak does dry things out; **b22** really lovely whisky and unusual to see a Lowlander quite this comfortable at such advanced age. *46%. ncf.*

⁙ **Bladnoch 18 Years Old** db **(88.5) n21** dulled with oak; **t23.5** fabulous balance between juicy fruit and juicy barley. The gooseberries are green, fat and splitting at the sides...; **f22** vanilla and a trail of light oil allows the barley an extended stay **b22** the juiciness and clarity to the barley, and especially the big gooseberry kick, early on makes this a dram well worth finding. *55%*

Cadenhead's Bladnoch Aged 15 Years dist 92, bott Feb 08 **(87.5) n22** lively, sharp barley with the faintest squeeze of lemon; **t21.5** a succession of malty waves; **f22** from malty to salty as a little oak bites, but some citrus lightens it wonderfully, **b22** a charming dram that gets better the longer it stays in the palate. *53.5%. 320 bottles.*

⁙ **Cadenhead's Bladnoch Aged 17 Years** dist 92, bott 09 **(92.5) n23.5** doesn't come much cleaner with the accent on barley and a sherbet citrus buzz; **t23.5** eye-wateringly salivating: this is 3-D barley; **f22.5** a touch of vanilla and mocha rounds off the fun; **b23** an exceptional cask full of charisma and quality. *55.1%*

Cadenhead's Authentic Collection Bladnoch Aged 18 Years bourbon barrel, dist 1989, bott May 07 **(90) n23** some Ancient Age 10 years old...no perhaps more of a 12-y-o Wild turkey, or somewhere between the two...no, hang on, there is some barley in there, too...; **t22** yet, it really is malt but that slips in gently from a sandwich of sweet bourbon notes; **f23** loads of honey and a hint of liquorice – the bourbon-barley fun continues; **b22** one assumes this is from first fill bourbon because there is more Kentucky here than Wigtown. Lovely stuff. *478%. 156 bottles.*

⁙ **John McDougall's Selection Bladnoch 1990** cask no. CM101, dist 90 **(83.5) n22 t21 f20 b20.5.** Clean and crammed with big malt. But on the hot and thin side. *54.2%. House of Macduff. 260 bottles.*

⁙ **John McDougall's Selection Bladnoch 1990** cask no. CM124, dist 90 **(92) n23.5** gooseberries – and pretty plump, splitting ones, at that; a beautiful vanilla and citrus backdrop, all rounded off by the most unexpected and barely audible smoke; **t23** mouth-watering and intensely malty; the excellent oils help crank up the richness and spices yet allow the brighter, more citrusy notes, to shine; **f22.5** dries out with vanilla and cocoa aplenty and a very slight nod to that mysterious distant phenol; **b23** just wonderful malt, showing Bladnoch in a clear and excellent light. The structure and layering is sublime. *53.3%. House of Macduff. 240 bottles.*

Old Malt Cask Bladnoch Aged 15 Years refill hogshead no. 4241, dist Jul 92, bott Apr 08 **(86) n21.5 t22.5 f21 b21.** Even and refreshing with some chewy natural caramel at the death. *50%. nc ncf. Douglas Laing. 364 bottles.*

Old Malt Cask Bladnoch Aged 16 Years refill hogshead, cask no. 4446, dist Mar 92, bott Jun 08 **(86.5) n21.5 t22 f21.5 b21.5.** Lovely malt in so many ways. Yet you do get the feeling that it is reaching the limit of its range at this kind of age. *50%. Douglas Laing. 295 bottles.*

Private Cellar's Selection Bladnoch 1993 bott 07 **(86.5) n22 t23 f20 b21.5.** Soft, sensual, a little syrupy, perhaps, but seriously sexy. *43%*

Scotch Malt Whisky Society Cask 50.33 Aged 17 Years refill barrel, dist Jul 90 **(83.5) n20 t21 f21.5 b21.** Malt and citrus aplenty. A bit hot. *55.9%*

⁙ **Scotch Malt Whisky Society Cask 50.38 Aged 16 Years** refill hogshead, dist Oct 92 **(78.5) n20 t20 f18.5 b19.** Technically decent, refreshing distillate, but the evidence points towards a cask left out in the rain too long between fillings. *54.4%*

⁙ **Scotch Malt Whisky Society Cask 50.39 Aged 16 Years** refill hogshead, dist Oct 92 **(89) n22** crisp barley with a mildly starchy, cassava undertone; **t23** gorgeous, salivating malt is stretched even further by a vague saltiness and that wonderfully distinctive cassava; the lightest oil carries with it a gentle throb of spice; **f22** dries, but not with a hint of over-oakiness. Chalky but dusted with sweetened vanilla; **b22** fascinating: same distillate as 50.38, but not denigrated by a sub-standard cask. Here the malt is given perfect support and the difference is spell-binding. By comparing the two, what a great way for whisky students to discover the negative impact of dodgy cask on very good malt. *56.1%*

Scott's Selection Bladnoch 1993 bott 07 **(87) n21** spiced custard tart; **t23** under-ripe gooseberries by the bowlful early on then clean-as-a-whistle barley radiating in all directions; **f21** a bit thin and stilted but the cocoa's a bonus; **b22** honest and no frills. *59.5%.*

Signatory Vintage Bladnoch 14 Years Old 1992 (86) n21 t21 f22 b22. A steady-Eddie of a dram that is delightfully clean and grows in riches despite the attention of a pretty tired cask. *46%. ncf. USA.*

⋯ **Wilson & Morgan Barrel Selection Bladnoch Aged 18 Years** rum finish, dist 90, bott 08 **(93) n22.5** dense, barely penetrable with the sugar and barley combining to offer toffee apple and jelly babies; **t24** whoosh...!!! The barley is so concentrated and firm, the sugars so crisp and brittle, you feel your teeth are in danger of being chipped; thick, almost gloopy but the barley is sharp and juicy enough to offer a salivating arm which nigh makes the eyes water... **f23** long, very long and wonderfully sweet. The barley really does appear polished and crisp to the very last; **b23.5** a glittering malt whose delivery is nothing short of sublime. *51%*

BLAIR ATHOL
Highlands (Perthshire), 1798. Diageo. Working.
Blair Athol Aged 12 Years db **(77) n18 t19 f21 b19.** Thick, fruity, syrupy and a little sulphury and heavy. The finish has some attractive complexity among the chunkyness. *43%. Flora and Fauna range.*

Duncan Taylor Collection Blair Atholl 1977 cask no. 36853D **(84) n21 t20 f22 b21.** made at the distillery when it was churning the stuff out for Bells as if there was no tomorrow. Evidenced through a distinctive hotness and lack of body but there have been compensations from the oak over the years, especially when the gristy sweetness begins to take shape around the vanilla and custard powder. A mixed bag, but enjoyable nonetheless. *54.4%*

⋯ **Old & Rare Blair Athol Aged 32 Years** dist Jun 76, bott Aug 08 **(86.5) n22 t22.5 f21 b21.** Belies its years in any number of ways, not least in how the oak is so easily accommodated. Hugely enjoyable, especially on the lightly smoked, gingerbread nose and early Parkin Cake delivery, and even though not one to exactly raise the pulse there is a very agreeable degree of complexity. *55.4%. Douglas Laing. 119 bottles.*

⋯ **Old Malt Cask Blair Athol Aged 9 Years** sherry butt, dist Sep 99, bott Mar 09 **(81) n19 t20 f21 b21** Sweet, warming and clean. *46%. Douglas Laing.*

⋯ **Old Malt Cask Blair Athol Aged 10 Years** sherry butt, dist Dec 98, bott Jul 09 **(73) n18 t20 f17 b18** More Blair Witch. *50%. Douglas Laing.*

Old Malt Cask Blair Athol Aged 18 Years (89.5) n21.5 tinned tangerines and salmon sandwiches...it must be a Sunday afternoon in the 60s... **t22** huge malt sweetens by the second with only a trace of the salty edge to the nose; **f23.5** unravels with some barley sugar but it's the perfect texture to the oils which wins the day... **b22.5** borders on cloying and over-indulgent – gets away with it. As sweet and malty as this distillery gets. And, to be honest, seriously enjoyable. *50%. Douglas Laing.*

Premier Barrel Blair Athol Aged 9 Years sherry cask **(77) n19 t20 f19 b19.** Curious whisky: it is rare to find one that does so little. An old cask means the oak aint around while the abundance of light malt yields minimal complexity. *46%. Douglas Laing. 776 bottles.*

⋯ **Premier Barrel Blair Athol Aged 10 Years** sherry cask **(78) n18 t20 f20 b20.** A very sweet and simple barley-fest. The oak is mainly conspicuous by its absence. *46%. Douglas Laing. 651 bottles.*

⋯ **Provenance Blair Athol Aged 10 Years** sherry butt, dist autumn 99, bott autumn 08 **(85) n20 t22 f21.5 b21.5.** Beautifully spiced, chewy and juicy for all its weight. *46%. Douglas Laing.*

Provenance Blair Athol Aged 11 Years Sherry Butt 3937, dist 95, bott 07 **(74.5) n19.5 t19 f18 b18.** Not great. *46%. nc ncf. Douglas Laing.*

Provenance Blair Athol Aged 12 Years sherry butt, dist Jul 95, bott 08 **(86.5) n22 t21.5 f21.5 b22.** Lots of biscuity moments on nose and palate with fruit shortcake taking the leading role. *46%. nc ncf. Douglas Laing.*

BOWMORE
Islay, 1779. Suntory. Working.
Bowmore 12 Years Old db **(91) n22.5** light peats, the air of a room with a man sucking cough sweets; sweet pipe smoke; **t23.5** soft, beautiful delivery of multi-layered peats; lots of effervescent spices and molassed sugars; spices abound; **f22.5** much drier with sharper berries and barley; the peat still rumbles onwards, but has no problems with the light, sawdusty oaks; **b23.5** this new bottling still proudly carries the Fisherman's Friend cough sweet character, but the coastal, saline properties here are a notch or three up: far more representative of Islay and the old distillery style. Easily by far the truest Bowmore I have tasted in a long while with myriad complexity. Even going back more than a quarter of a century, the malt at this age rarely showed such relaxed elegance. Most enjoyable. *40%*

Bowmore 12 Years Old Enigma db **(82) n19 t22 f20 b21.** Sweet, molassed and with that tell-tale Fisherman's Friend tang representing the light smoke. This Enigma hasn't quite cracked it, though. *40%. Duty Free.*

Bowmore 15 Years Old Darkest db **(74) n18 t18 f19 b19.** An improvement on the dreadful original. Just. *43%.*

Bowmore 15 Years Old Mariner db **(79) n19 t21 f19 b20.** There are two ways of looking at this. As a Bowmore. Which is how I have marked it. Or a something to throw down your neck for pure fun. Which is probably worth another seven or eight points. Either way, there is something not entirely right here. *43%. Duty Free.*

Bowmore Aged 16 Years Limited Edition oloroso sherry, dist 90, bott 06 db **(89) n24 t22 f21 b22.** It has peat. And fruit. And never the two do meet. But the battle for supremacy is engrossing. *53.8%. ncf.*

Bowmore 18 Years Old db **(79) n20 t21 f19 b19.** Pleasant, drinkable Fisherman's Friend style – like every Bowmore it appears around this age. But why so toffee-dull? *43%.*

Bowmore 25 Years Old db **(86) n21 t22 f21 b22.** Not the big, chunky guy of yore: the age would surprise you if tasted blind. *43%*

Bowmore 30 Years Old db **(94) n23** intense burnt raisin amid the intense burnt peat; a deft rummy sweetness strikes an improbable chord with the sweetened lime; the oak is backward coming forward but binds beautifully with both peat and fruit; **t24** near flawless delivery showing a glimpse of Bowmore in a form similar to how I remember it some 25 years ago. The peat, though intense - much bigger than you will find today - does have a hint of the Fisherman's Friend about it, but not so upfront as today. For all the peat this is clean whisky, showing by a craftsman into how a truly great Islay should be; **f23** dries sublimely as the oak contains the peat and adds a touch of coffee to it in unsugared form. Gentle oils cling tightly to the roof of the mouth but it is at once gentle yet enormous; **b24** frankly, a Bowmore that no Islay scholar should be without. Shows the distillery at its most intense yet delicate; an essay in balance and how great oak, peat and fruit can combine for those special moments in life. Unquestionably one of the best Bowmores bottled this century. *43%*

Bowmore 1971 Vintage 34 Years Old sherry cask db **(86) n23 t22 f20 b21.** Loses it on the finish. But one for those who like their whisky big and with splinters aplenty. *51%. 960 bottles.*

Bowmore Legend db **(88) n22** big peat fire; dry, but really attractively so; **t22.5** Ok, Fisherman's Friend cough sweet maybe, but the countering barley and brown sugar sweetness appears to dissipate the worst of the effect: the result is big peat, very evenly spread; **f22** gentle finale with a vanilla flourish; **b22.5** not sure what has happened here, but it has gone through the gears dramatically to offer a substantial dram with both big peat and excellent balancing molasses. Major stuff. *40%*

⋰ **A.D. Rattray Bowmore 1991** sherry butt, cask no. 2060, bott Nov 08 **(85.5) n21 t22.5 f20.5 b21.5** Dry, ashy, sooty, with an excellent thick, fruity swirl and flourish; but ultimately over bitters out. *56.2%*

⋰ **Alchemist Bowmore Aged 9 Years** dist Apr 98, bott Aug 07 **(75.5) n18.5 t19 f19 b19.** Sweet and slightly off centre. *46%. nc, ncf.*

⋰ **Berry's Own Selection Bowmore 1989** bott 08 **(89) n22** very light peat plays hide-and-seek amid the honey and butterscotch; **t23** superbly weighted: golden syrup with a few pinches of peat stirred into it. Add some salt and zingy vanilla and your tastebuds are really worked over; **f22** bittering vanilla but the peat now enters a spicy mode; **b22** technically, Berry's 1994 bottling is a superior whisky. But here you just have to admire the structure and complexity. *53.5%. Berry Bros & Rudd.*

⋰ **Berry's Own Selection Bowmore 1994** bott 08 **(86.5) n21 t22.5 f21.5 b21.5.** A must for those looking for something very sweet and moderately smoky yet exceptionally clean. *53.5%. Berry Bros & Rudd.*

Berry's Own Selection Bowmore Aged 11 Years (84) n20 t23 f21 b20. To see Bowmore like this from a second- (or even third) - filled bourbon cask makes for interesting tasting: such is the mouthwatering malt intensity, and so retiring is the peat, this could almost pass for lightly smoked Speyside. *56.2%. Berry Bros & Rudd..*

Cadenhead's Authentic Collection Bowmore Aged 14 Years bourbon, dist 93, bott Sep 07 **(86.5) n22 t21.5 f21.5 b21.5.** Entertaining and energetic, the peat is out of the traps in double quick time, followed by liquorice. Do look out for the chocolate on the nose. Delicious, even if the oak isn't entirely at home. *63.9%. 162 bottles*

Cadenhead's Bowmore Aged 15 Years dist 92, bott Feb 08 **(87) n22.5** lovely mixture of coal and peat ash; **t21** a tad hot; **f22** simmers down for a long barley-smoke fade; sweetens considerably; **b21.5** slightly aggressive at times but a real treat. *54.4%. 333 bottles.*

Cadenhead's Bowmore Aged 15 Years dist 92, bott Feb 08 **(84.5) n21 t21 f21.5 b21.** Bit of a hothead for all its charming and beguiling ways. *55%. 343 bottles.*

The Coopers Choice Bowmore Aged 12 Years dist 94, bott 07 **(87) n21** a crofter's fire; **t22** sweet barley followed by sumptuous waves of soft peat: simplistic but attractive; **f22** vanilla brushed with smoke; **b22** a good, honest Islay. *46%. The Vintage Malt Whisky Co.*

The Coopers Choice Bowmore 1990 Aged 16 Years (79) n20 t20 f19 b20. Well oaked and some sweet barley residue. But you'd hope for more. *46%. sc ncf. The Vintage Malt Whisky Co.*

The Creative Whisky Company Exclusive Malts Bowmore Aged 10 Years cask no. 60105, dist Apr 97 **(89.5) n21** hickory and cough sweet amid the smoke; **t23** full frontal and immediately bitter-sweet with the oaks striking earlier than the norm for the age; the spices work beautifully with the chocolaty peat; **f22.5** some soft oils heal the wounds from the semi-savage attack; some mocha absorbs the brown sugars; **b23** hugely enjoyable, teeth-baring, malt that has been very well made. *56.9%.*

Dewar Rattray Bowmore Aged 17 Years cask no. 2058, dist Jul 91, bott Sep 08 **(89) n22** well!! Farmyards, yes. Fruits, yes. Brown sugar yes. Peat, why – naturally. Does it try and mingle happily? Not really. Enjoyable and memorable? You bet.... **t23** here we go again: the delivery is all about rock-hard influences chiselling into the tastebuds. The peat zooms in and out as main player and then background; complex and entirely unconventional; it's all about effect with scant regard to structure and direction...but who cares....? **f21.5** the Achilles heel by comparison with a bitterness confirming that all is not entirely ticketyboo. But the sugary smoke does its best to compensate; **b22.5** not the kind of whisky you want to land on your desk when you are desperately trying to finish a book: this isn't a tale that can be unravelled in a few minutes. There isn't a single element of this malt which is straightforward. From nose to finish something is not right about this. Yet, so much of it works so well that you can forgive it its trespasses. It's as if cognac, rum and sherry cask have all been at work on this one, each leaving unfinished business. If I had £100 for every Bowmore I'd tasted over the years I'd be a pretty wealthy guy. But I have never come across anything with a signature like this. *55.9%. Bottled for the West Coast Whisky Society, Canada. 585 bottles.*

Dewar Rattray Individual Cask Bottling Bowmore 1989 Aged 17 Years sherry cask no. 1095, dist Feb 89, bott May 06 **(66) n15 t18 f16 b17.** From a sherry cask, apparently. But the nose and finish suggests something metallic got into that cask and given it a strange, seriously flawed personality. A shame. *49.6%. 180 bottles.*

Dewar Rattray Bowmore 1990 cask no. 261, dist Feb 90, bott Jun 07 **(86.5) n20 t22 f22.5 b22.** For those who prefer their peat sweet and a bit nippy. Excellent cocoa on the finale. *54.1%*

Duncan Taylor Collection Bowmore 1968 cask no. 3827 **(86) n22 t21 f22 b21.** Thanks to the exotic fruit, the peat is so scarce that it's just oak, fruit and barley all the way. *42.7%.*

⠿ **Duncan Taylor Collection Bowmore 1982** cask no. 85030 **(82) n20.5 t20 f21 b20.5.** Had to laugh when I lined up this latest bunch of DT Bowmores. Talk about déjà vous...!! It was like opening up a packet of Fisherman's Friends, that cough sweet style unique for a while at this distillery. And I thought: didn't DT do something like this last year? Well, on consulting my notes, yes they did. And here a half a dozen more or so from the same batch – peas from the same pod. The thing is, you can't not like them. Nor do they blow you away: they simply offer a quite different whisky style, one that no other distillery has done before or since. *50.1%*

⠿ **Duncan Taylor Collection Bowmore 1982** cask no. 85031 **(86.5) n21.5 t23 f21 b21.** By far and away one of the best casks in the set: everything is a tad sharper and more intense. The barley is truly salivating and there is even a thread of honey woven through the smoke and liquorice. Lovely. *52.1%*

⠿ **Duncan Taylor Collection Bowmore 1982** cask no. 85032 **(83) n20 t21 f21 b21.** A bit of a hot-head, this. The nose is a dullard, but a bit of zip on the palate compensates and really cranks out the cough sweet side of things. *53.7%*

⠿ **Duncan Taylor Collection Bowmore 1982** cask no. 85057 **(86) n23 t22 f20 b21.** We have moved on a few casks and the whisky has moved on in style, slightly, too. To nose, some real butterscotch on the cereals and smoke ensure a touch of class and there is shades of demerara and liquorice on delivery before the finish bitters and flattens. *53.5%*

Duncan Taylor Collection Bowmore 1982 cask no. 85059 **(83) n21 t21 f20 b21.** A 25-year-old cough sweet...!! Some delicious sweet elements, but there is just something about this house style of the time... *56.7%*

Duncan Taylor Collection Bowmore 1982 cask no. 85060 **(83.5) n21 t21 f20.5 b21.** Pure, unadulterated Fisherman's Friend cough sweet. *55.4%*

Duncan Taylor Collection Bowmore 1982 cask no. 85062 **(85.5) n20.5 t22 f21.5 b21.5.** Some bourbony liquorice and redcurrant. Oh, and Fisherman's Friend. *57.1%*

Duncan Taylor Collection Bowmore 1982 cask no. 85063 **(77.5) n19.5 t22 f17.5 b18.5.** Cough sweet. But the oak really does it some damage. *55.8%*

⠿ **Duncan Taylor Collection Bowmore 1982** cask no. 85064 **(84) n21 t22.5 f20 b20,5.** Slightly in the style of 85032 but with a touch of extra citrus and finesse. *54.9%*

⠿ **Duncan Taylor Collection Bowmore 1982** cask no. 85068 **(84) n21 t21 f21 b21.** A fleet of Fishermen's Friends: sweet, but absolutely uncompromising in the cough sweet department. *53.8%*

⠿ **Duncan Taylor Collection Bowmore 1982** cask no. 85072 **(83.5) n20 t21.5 f21 b21.** A bit of a softie, but sticks to the cough sweet script for all the best vanilla-led intentions. *50.4%*

Duncan Taylor Collection Bowmore 1987 cask no. 18027, dist Oct 87, bott Apr 06 **(81) n21 t22 f18 b20.** Distinctly pungent and peppery in that uniquely and un-unnervingly fresh Bowmore style; just runs out of legs at the finish. *58.1%. 252 bottles.*

Duncan Taylor Collection Bowmore 1987 cask no. 18052 **(84) n21 t21 f21 b21.** Steady as she goes with the distillery's unmistakable peat character. But there is no fourth gear. *52.1%*

Duncan Taylor Collection Bowmore 1987 cask no. 18054 **(80) n20 t19 f21 b20.** Enjoyable, but with more natural toffee which makes for a duller, less integrated and characterful version of the 18052 (above). *54.3%*

Duncan Taylor Collection Bowmore 1987 cask no. 18053 **(83) n20.5 t21.5 f20 b21.** Pretty limited beyond the bizarre cough sweet characteristic of that period. *52.4%*

⠿ **Exclusive Casks Bowmore 1998 Aged 10 Years** American oak **(94) n24** now this is a charmer: amid the heather there is that familiar hint of Fishermen's Friend cough sweet, but it appears to have been calmed by honey: noses don't come any healthier than this... and certainly one not to be sneezed at; **t23.5** mouth-watering and stunningly fresh: the vanilla from the cask melts into the phenols while the barley sugar offers perfect weight and balance; **f23** hickory and unbelievably mellow smoke drift off towards a chocolaty finale; **b23.5** a gold nugget of a cask that is worth a trip to the walled city for alone... *52.7%. Chester Whisky & Liqueur Co.*

⠿ **The Golden Cask Bowmore 1992** dist 92, bott 02 **(89) n22.5** allotment bonfires and Rupp cheese rubbed in with salt; **t23.5** brilliant delivery: absolutely bang on muscovado sweetness, helped along by a coppery sheen, sits perfectly with the fizzing spice and silky smoke; **f21** after a soft smoky winding down, threatens to get a bit too bitter –and then does, **b22** pretty damned good! *55%*

John Milroy Selection Bowmore 1996 Aged 10 Years (76) n19 t20 f18 b19. Decent sweetness but some tobacco notes and unhelpful bitterness towards the end. Yet another Bowmore that disappoints. *46%*

⠿ **Hart Brothers Bowmore Aged 10 Years** dist Apr 98, bott Jun 08 **(85) n21.5 t21 f21.5 b21.** Sweet, simplistic but with a pleasing degree of peat ash. *46%. Hart Brothers Limited.*

⠿ **Hart Brothers Bowmore Aged 11 Years** dist Apr 97, bott Oct 08 **(77) n20 t20 f18 b19.** Interesting farm yard nose. But, overall, a bitter experience. *46%. Hart Brothers Limited.*

⠿ **Hart Brothers Bowmore Aged 18 Years** dist May 90, bott Jun 08 **(86.5) n22 t22 f21 b21.5.** Very pleasing malt with a distinctively fresh, fruity edge to the smoke. *46%. Hart Brothers Limited.*

⠿ **Kingsbury's 'The Selection' Bowmore 7 Years Old** dist 01, bott 07 **(82) n20.5 t21 f20 b20.5.** Docile, sweet and very clean. Could have done with being at cask strength. *43%. Japan Import System.*

⠿ **Kingsbury's Single Cask Bowmore Aged 19 Years** dist Dec 87, bott Aug 07 **(85.5) n21 t21.5 f22 b21.** Right out of the Fisherman's Friend school of Bowmore, but in crisp, attractive form. *46%. Japan Import System.*

⠿ **Master of Malt Bowmore 26 Years** Old bott 09 **(88) n21.5** uniquely Bowmore: a hickory-sweetened mixture of Fisherman's Friends and kippers; **t21** weird: there is no other word for it. The cough sweet peat appears to be drowned in a tidal wave of sweet, nondescript fruit. For a moment there is silence on the palate...then spices break out... **f23.5**...and at last we have serious whisky. Beautiful texture to the oaky vanilla and phenols materialise in various degrees of intensity and sweetness and dryness: a fabulous fade.... **b22** now that's something completely different: the nose and early delivery has you checking the paper for the date: nope, it really isn't April 1st. Where the hell is all that sweetness coming from...? Then it starts to settle towards something recognisable as very good whisky and from then onwards you are served up a minor treat. *53.4%. Master of Malt.*

Murray McDavid Bowmore 1995 bourbon/guigal condrieu viognier **(92) n22** tight, almost crisp peat, entirely kept in place by even tighter, crisper fruit; **t23** the veneer of fruit is eroded away by wave upon wave of peat, which splendidly grows in intensity; **f24** a grapey return which is completely at one with the smoke: muscular but delicate and, late on, quite spicy; **b23** not normally a fan of peat and fruit. This, though, works wonders. *46%*

Murray McDavid Bowmore 1998 Aged 8 Years bourbon/quart de chaume chenin blank **(94) n23** firm grape does its best to outshine the peat-shed earthiness. And fails...; **t23** smoked malt is first to arrive then builds into something altogether sweeter with the green grape oozing juice; **f24** becomes a much more delicate, thoughtful creature towards the end; **b24** wonderful Bowmore which shows so brilliantly when not trying to impersonate a particular brand of cough candy. A genuine treat that does the reputation of Bowmore no harm whatsoever. *46%*

Norse Cask Selection Bowmore 1985 Aged 21 Years hogshead ref. QW7023, dist 85, bott 07 **(89) n23** spikey peat and crushed gorse: pretty floral; **t23** beautifully full on the palate with immediate spices battling against a honeyed barley thread: a chewy mouthfiller; **f21** toffees out annoyingly as the oak intercedes and makes for a dull fade; **b22** beautiful, curiously fruitless malt for all the barley flying about. The peat offers an unmistakable Bowmore fingerprint. *57.5%. WhiskyOwner.com, Denmark. 293 bottles.*

Norse Cask Selection Bowmore 1989 Aged 17 Years sherry hogshead, cask no. 1096 **(91) n24** perfect, clean, intact, thick and intense sherry face-to-face with chunky peat; **t23** again, perfect delivery with the sherry revealing its juicy nature and then peat, in that mega Fisherman's Friend style unique to this distillery, rampages about; **f22** more FF; **b22** I fall prostrate in awe before this unvilified sherry butt. But I cock a withering snook at the unsubtle FF. Works, though! *52.8%. WhiskyOwner.com, Denmark.*

Old Malt Cask Bowmore Aged 15 Years refill hogshead no. 3972, dist Mar 92, bott Nov 07 **(88) n21.5** light, heathery, gently peated; **t22.5** gristy and mouth-watering at first before the irritating FF arrives. Some wonderful liquorice sees off the hickory and the brown sugars arrive with light barley riding shotgun; **f22** gentle, smoky, deft; **b22** plenty of cough sweet. But here there's so much more.... *50%. Douglas Laing. 357 bottles.*

Old Malt Cask Bowmore Aged 18 Years refill hogshead no. 4237, dist Oct 89, bott Apr 08 **(90) n23** almost like being in the distillery: fresh, pungent but with subtle, sea-swept clarity; **t22** sweet, molassed and then myriad peat notes; **f22** liquorice, burnt toast, cremated raisin and... no, I can't say it.... **b23** truly glorious Bowmore with any number of twists and turns. Not exactly textbook, but there are so many brilliant asides... *50%. nc ncf. Douglas Laing. 318 bottles.*

⬧ **Old Malt Cask Bowmore Aged 21 Years** refill hogshead, dist Jun 87, bott Sep 08 **(88) n21.5** some surprising gristiness for one so old; gentle smoke and mildly floral; **t23** delicate in the extreme though the peat does get chunkier as the oak gathers weight; **f21.5** bitter marmalade and a light, silky smoke; **b22** a cask taken as far as it dare go but the light radiation of peat is lovely. *50%. Douglas Laing. 229 bottles.*

Old Malt Cask Bowmore Aged 25 Years refill hogshead, dist Mar 83, bott Mar 08 **(75) n18.5 t18 f19.5 b19.** Twentyfive years????? All that cough sweet and bugger all else...???.... nooooooooooool!!!! *50%. nc ncf. Douglas Laing. 259 bottles.*

Old Masters Bowmore Aged 12 Years cask no. 20100, dist 94, bott 06 **(83) n20 t21 f22 b20.** Decent, delicate whisky for those who prefer their peat toned down a little. *57.8%.*

⬧ **Old Malt Cask A Fine Cigar's Pleasure Bowmore Aged 9 Years** refill hogshead **(84) n21 t21 f22 b21.** Lots of natural caramel wrapped in chocolate. *50%. Douglas Laing. 354 bottles.*

⬧ **Premier Barrel Bowmore Aged 9 Years (83.5) n21.5 t22 f20 b20.** Pleasantly sweet before running out of legs. *46%. Douglas Laing. 302 bottles.*

Premier Barrel Bowmore Aged 9 Years (89) n22.5 soft evening garden perfumes amid the delicate smoke; **t23** sweet malt and smoke delivery which soon conjours up something fuller yet teasing and controlled; the molassed sweetness really does strike a cord with the peat; **f21.5** some oils enter the fray; **b22** a beautiful, creaseless malt. *46%. Douglas Laing. 383 bottles.*

Premier Barrel Bowmore Aged 10 Years (78.5) n19 t20.5 f19 b19. If it's a Premier barrel then it must be non-league spirit...*46%. nc ncf. Douglas Laing. 382 bottles.*

Provenance Bowmore Aged 8 Years hogshead no. 3866-3887, dist winter 98, bott autumn 07 **(89) n23** clean, punchy peat: beautifully salty with a dab of honey; **t22.5** mouth-watering barley; the smoke wanders in as an afterthought; **f21.5** drier, a little spice prickle amid the vanilla; **b22** an untaxing but complex malt. Lovely stuff. *46%. Douglas Laing.*

Provenance Bowmore Aged 8 Years Gabriel Meffre wine cask no. 3895, dist winter 98, bott autumn 07 **(82) n21 t21 f20 b20.** What an interesting one-off (one-hopes) experiment! *46%. Douglas Laing.*

Provenance Bowmore Aged 9 Years hogshead cask nos. 4109, 4110 dist winter 98, bott winter 08 **(88.5) n22 t23 f22 b21.5.** Minimal input from the cask maximizes the malt. And this is pretty good stuff, even if much younger than the age suggests. Refreshing. Sweet. Fun. Absolutely love it!! *46%. nc ncf. Douglas Laing.*

Provenance Bowmore Aged 10 Years dist spring 97, bott spring 07 **(89) n22** crisp barley and firm peat; a lovely controlled sweetness; **t23** mouth filling with a real gristy freshness and even an echo of new make; **f22** clean sherbet sweetness to the prevailing oak and citrus-juicy barley; **b22** an honest dram that delivers on the sweet-peat front. Much closer to the 10 year old Bowmores of 25 years ago. *46%. Douglas Laing.*

Queen of the Moorlands Rare Cask Bowmore 1991 Edition XVIII (96) n24 layers of pugnacious, spicy peat of varied intensity attempt to knock the crap out of layers of high quality sherry of equally contrasting hues: it's an honourable draw; **t25** so massive my palate sends out for extra tastebuds: a deluge of opaque sherry carries with it that wondrous peat – and spice. For a Bowmore of this age it simply cannot be bettered; **f23** by the standards of before just a fraction tame, but the bitter-sweet balance remains true and some molassed burnt raisin really does help calm things; **b24** an exceptional shock to the system. By the third mouthful you know you are experiencing a true Islay moment never to be forgotten. And by the fifth I'd given up spitting...The 400th new whisky for the 2008 Bible... and what a way to celebrate! *57.7%. nc ncf. Available at The Wine Shop, Leek & Congleton, and Islay Whisky Shop.*

Scotch Malt Whisky Society Cask 3.127 Aged 10 Years refill hogshead, dist Mar 97 **(88) n22 t23 f22 b21** The cough sweet peat has gone (thank heavens!) and a crisper, more Islay-defined dram has taken its place. *59%*

Scotch Malt Whisky Society Cask 3.135 Aged 7 Years 1st fill barrel, dist Oct 00 **(94) n24 t23.5 f23 b23.5** As some of us in the game have long suspected: if it can be this good at 7 years – the kind of age preferred by our forefathers – why let it get into a greybeard stage? Keep these kinds of bottlings coming, guys!!! *58%*

Scotch Malt Whisky Society Cask 3.138 Aged 10 Years refill butt, dist Feb 98 **(89) n23 t23 f21 b22** Oh, what might have been had this been filled into a top quality cask? *57.2%*

Scotch Malt Whisky Society Cask 3.139 Aged 10 Years refill butt, dist Feb 98 **(83) n22 t21.5 f19 b20.5.** Sharp and awkward, what would have been a very good dram – the spirit is excellent – has been limited by a so-so cask. *56.5%*

Scotch Malt Whisky Society Cask 3.140 Aged 10 Years refill butt, dist Feb 98 **(85.5) n22.5 t22 f20 b21.** Some wonderful peaty touches. But again the cask has spoken. And not wisely. *56.4%*

⋅∷⋅ **Scotch Malt Whisky Society Cask 3.146 Aged 9 Years** refill hogshead, dist Feb 99 **(78) n19 t21 f19 b19.** Prepare to be underwhelmed. *60.1%*

⋅∷⋅ **Scotch Malt Whisky Society Cask 3.147 Aged 10 Years** refill hogshead, dist Feb 98 **(85) n20 t21.5 f21.5 b22.** A spiced up bottling which really gets the tastebuds tingling. The peat conjures up some hickory and cocoa amid the sweeter demerara. *57.3%*

⋅∷⋅ **Scotch Malt Whisky Society Cask 3.148 Aged 9 Years** refill hogshead, dist Feb 99 **(95) n23.5** now this is a classy nose: some lavender amid the soft peat and a touch of bourbon for good measure; **t24** thick and chewy, the smoke arrives as the very best peaty malts tend to: slowly and with a build up that allows the other sides of its personality to shine. Bourbony liquorice and cocoa haunt the middle ground; **f23.5** long, with that smoky cocoa hanging onto an oily slick; some velvety muscovado balances out the drier vanillas **b24** the kind of excellent and intrinsically structured malt which will re-assert where this distillery was 30 years ago...this is actually a twin sister cask to 3.146, being one cask number along. It is worth getting both to see how the line between success and failure can be so fine... *59.8%*

⋅∷⋅ **Scotch Malt Whisky Society Cask 3.149 Aged 10 Years** dist Feb 98 **(86.5) n22 t23 f20.5 b21.** An up and down, no frills bottling. The oak has intervened enough only to as act as a gentle foil to the clean, softly honeyed peat which though bigger than many Bowmores is entirely non aggressive. *56.4%*

⋅∷⋅ **Scotch Malt Whisky Society Cask 3.150 Aged 18 Years** refill hogshead, dist Aug 90 **(91.5) n22** some knotty oak is unpicked by lemon-zesty smoke; **t23.5** light and juicy. The mouth-watering freshness embraces the hickory-tipped smoked with ease; **f23** long, much drier with vanilla replacing the citrus within the delicate smoke; **b23** charming and delicate with just the right dose of sweetness where needed. *54.5%*

⋅∷⋅ **Scotch Malt Whisky Society Cask 3.151 Aged 18 Years** refill hogshead, dist Aug 90 **(84) n20 t20.5 f22.5 b21.** Sharp, malty, zesty, sometimes bracing. *56.2%*

Scott's Selection Bowmore 1990 bott 07 **(86.5) n21.5 t22 f21.5 b21.5.** Sweet, at times nutty, with pretty decent peat for a Bowmore. Pussycat malt and what it loses on lack of complexity it makes up for with style, clarity and confidence. Enjoy. *52%*

Whisky-Doris Bowmore Aged 16 Years bourbon cask, dist 24 Apr 90, bott 1 Feb 07 **(88)** **n22** buttered kipper; emptied coal sacks; **t23** lively, punchy smoke with reserves of sweet barley; **f21** enough oil for the Pentagon to get interested; **b22** disappointing end to a lovely malt. *58.4%. ncf. Germany. 88 bottles.*

Whisky-Doris Bowmore 1994 The Dram (86.5) n21.5 t22 f21.5 b21.5. Lots of sweet barley on the gently oiled delivery; a tad bitter from the oak. *46%*

⌖ **The Whisky Fair Bowmore 10 Year** Old dist 98, bott 09 **(93)** **n23** beautiful mocha attached to the chunky, salty malt; **t24.5** mouth filling: every sinew of the sweet barley can be tasted and chewed. But the malt and cocoa fill the middle ground with unblemished brilliance; **f22.5** slows down as the vanilla takes a firmer grip but still that smoky, sugared cocoa has a long way to go; **b23** simply and beautifully made whisky matured in a cask which gives full view to the malt. *59.8%. The Whisky Fair, Germany.*

Wilson & Morgan Barrel Selection Bowmore 1997 Extra Strength bott 07 **(89)** **n22** apologetic peat on clean barley; still weighty, though; **t23** spot-on delivery with exceptional weight; bit of a confused middle but the soft oils and touches of honey delight; **f22** long, still a touch oily but a good chew; **b22** peaty, despite the nose. *50%*

BRAEVAL
Speyside, 1974. Chivas. Silent.

Cadenhead's Authentic Collection The Braes of Glenlivet Aged 17 Years sauterne hogshead, dist 89, bott Feb 07 **(94)** **n22** an odd twosome of bourbony notes and over-ripe fruit. Strange...; **t25** Gadzooks! No-one could possibly expect such a confused nose to come up with something so confident and vivid! Remains bipolar, with amazingly intense wine in one corner and a rip-roaring roasty barley in the other, with spices and high cocoa content chocolate somewhere in between. Sublime...faultless; **f23** enormously long and uncompromising. The oak does fade towards a sultana sweetness and the barley gathers oils as well as more cocoa. But it's a long, long fade...and just as well; **b24** simply stupendous and quite enormous whisky by any standards. *55.9%. 276 bottles.*

⌖ **Connoisseurs Choice Braes of Glenlivet 1975 (95) n23.5** the antiquity of the malt has pointed it in the direction of a mild exotic fruitiness, but never to the extent that the oak even thinks about dominating, so the barley gets a fair hearing. Diluted lemon helps keep the aroma fresh and keen; **t24.5** spit.....???? Not likely: not when a malt of this age absolutely refuses to show wrinkles and sprints around the tastebuds in a lemon-yeasty tracksuit; the barley and vanilla harmonise effortlessly in its wake; **f23.5** how can a malt so light carry on for so long? Obviously the chocolaty oak has something to do with it, as well as the growing spice. But delicate oils appear to also keep the show going, with not an off or bitter note to be had. What a charmer..... **b23.5** an astonishing time capsule of a dram. We are tasting a malt made within months of the distillery being opened, nearly 35 years on. The result is one of the malts of the year: how it has survived so flawlessly should keep connoisseurs in heated debate for a very long time. Spectacularly elegant and beautiful. And an all time Braes classic, never to be forgotten. *43% Gordon & MacPhail*

⌖ **The Cärn Mör Vintage Collection Braes of Glenlivet 1989** hogshead, cask no. 997, dist 89, bott 09 **(88) n22.5** beautiful clean barley with the lightest speck of smoke; **t22** juicy, crisp barley and light spices; **f21.5** oily, slightly sweet vanilla; **b22** charming, simplistic but beautifully made malt. *46%. The Scottish Liqueur Centre.*

Deerstalker Braeval Aged 10 Years bott 18.09.07 **(92) n23** breathtaking: those gooseberries remain and, if anything ,are slightly fatter and less hairy; **t23.5** few Speysiders, or any Highlander come to that, manage to hit the button so consistently when it comes to extreme, unfettered intensity of the barley; this is from the bitter-sweet school which induces mouth-watering on a Niagara scale; the white peppers weave in and out while a sauternes-style sweetness (which it isn't, of course) adds to the barley's richness; **f22.5** much more vanilla stacked but the barley continues to pulse; **b23** for Speyside lovers, this bottling (see details above) is an absolute must. A hard distillery to find, Deerstalker has the habit of bottling it at this age in near perfect fettle. A backwater blinder. *40%. Aberko.*

Deerstalker Braeval Aged 15 Years (83) n20.5 t22 f20 b20.5. By contrast to the 10-y-0, this is flat and uninspiring. It could be the extra oak, there might be a touch of toffee. Dazzles briefly on delivery. *46%. ncf. Aberko.*

⌖ **Dun Bheagan Braeval Aged 13 Years** Manzanilla sherry butt, dist Jun 95 **(83) n20 t23 f20 b20.** One of those curious malts which needs some serious adjustments of the tastebuds to help come to terms with the uncompromising character. The dishevelled nose puts you on guard and it needs possibly four of five mouthfuls to really get into this one. At first the character again appears all over the shop, and of no particular style, but the richer fruits to guarantee a sumptuous and divinely bitter-sweet backbone. The fade is just too bitter, though. *46%. Ian Macleod Distillers Ltd.*

Duncan Taylor Collection Braes of Glenlivet 1989 cask no. 1070 **(91) n22.5** has shrugged off the years with a mighty malty cloak; no shortage of butterscotch, either; **t23** brilliantly crisp and erudite in its malty qualities; salivating and lively before the drier middle approaches; **f22.5** shows a more austere timbre, but the finesse remains beyond doubt; **b23** quietly complex and classy. *50.3%*

⋯ **Old Malt Cask Braeval Aged 12 Years** sherry butt, dist Jul 96, bott Sep 08 **(88) n20** a tad thin and uncertain; **t23** made its mind up now...going for it big time with a huge battering ram of juicy, crusty barley and crisped sugars **f22.5** outstanding follow-through of gentle spices and ever sweetening barley; light fruity edges support the late oak; **b22.5** makes the nose something of a liar. An ultimately fine dram with a tale to tell. *50%. Douglas Laing. 665 bottles.*

⋯ **Provenance Braeval Aged 10 Years** sherry butt, dist summer 98, bott autumn 08 **(73) n18 t19 f18 b18.** Some grand barley does its best to negate the lightly sulphured flaws. *46%. Douglas Laing.*

BRORA

Highland (northern), 1819–1983. Diageo. Closed.

⋯ **Brora 25 Year Old 7th release,** bott 08 db **(96) n24** even with the lowest peating levels you ever have nosed from this distillery, the aura of beauty is unmistakable: the soft phenol molecules appears to be perfectly matched with the oak ones. Meanwhile fragile citrus ensures a youthful charm; somewhere there is a hint of bourbon; **t24.5** superb barley kick off, absolute waves of juices running about the palate, and still the smoke holds back, no more than a background murmur; as the middle fills, that bourbon on the nose become more pronounced with shades of honeyed liquorice; **f23.5** long, with the sugars hanging in there allowing the vanillas to form very slowly; **b24** as the distillery closed in March 1983, if memory serves me correctly, this must be coming to the end of the road for the true 25-year-old. Those looking for the usual big peat show might be disappointed. Others, in search of majesty, sophistication and timeless grace, will be blown away. *56.3%*

Brora 30 Years Old Special Releases 2006 db **(92) n23 t24 f22 b23.** Showing a degree of age decay but even so the sheer beauty of this malt leaves you gasping. *55.7%*

Brora 30 Years Old Special Releases 2007 db **(88.5) n21.5** smoke, hickory and some tired oak notes; **t23.5** excellent arrival of sweet peat and almost sweeter oak; lush, not overly complex but does what it can with minimum fuss and maximum effect; **f21.5** the soft oils and smoke can't entirely blot out the unwelcome off-oak notes; **b22** not in the highest echelons of old Broras with a degree of lactic being milked from the oak. But close your eyes, concentrate on the more delicate smoke tones – especially on arrival – and still be amazed. *55.7%. 2,958 bottles.*

Brora 30 Years Old db **(97) n24** that stunning Brora farmyard again, perhaps with a touch of extra fruit this time round. Beautiful structure, layering and harmony; **t25** Gosh! Perfect or what? How can something be this old yet offer such a gristy sweetness? Chewy, smoky, barely oaky but 100 okay-dokey; **f24** some late peat spice buzz adds a bit of bite to the smoke-fuelled serenity of this dram. A touch of something citrus helps thin out the layers; **b24** here we go again! Just like last year's bottling, we have something of near unbelievable beauty with the weight perfectly pitched and the barley-oak interaction the stuff of dreams. And as for the peat: an entirely unique species, a giant that is so gentle. Last year's bottling was one of the whiskies of the year. This even better version is the perfect follow-up. *56.4%*

⋯ **Chieftain's Brora 26 Years Old** oloroso sherry butt, dist Dec 81 **(92.5) n24** deep, sweet peak reek and cloves: pure dentist's surgery. All the sweeter notes are of a classic bourbony character; **t22** a discordant battle between well-muscled oak and the sweeter barley notes trying to hold their ground make for an early mess. The middle though settles as the smoke re-asserts itself; **f23.5** long and some really outstanding intertwining between the late ashy peat and the demerara notes; the light mocha fade glistens with the late oils; **b23** on delivery there is a fear that the great nose of the work will be undone. But hang on in there: the ending is a happy one. *48%. Ian Macleod Distillers Ltd.*

Connoisseurs Choice Brora 1982 (86) n21 t22 f22 b21. A curiously tight Brora where the peat gets up to sing and only a squeak is heard. Some decent buttery-oaky waves, but something is muffled here. The odd fruity spark and a fabulous range of complex smoky notes, yet an unfulfilled pleasure. *43%. Gordon & MacPhail.*

Dun Bheagan Brora Aged 23 Years sherry butt **(86) n22 t23 f20 b21.** Some uncommonly good sherry influence at work here. *48%. Ian Macleod.*

Duncan Taylor Collection Brora 1981 cask no. 1424 **(92) n22.5** one of the most peat-less Brora noses of all time; makes up for it with a lovely mixture of foresty, floral tones, honey and maple syrup; **t23** as soft and delicate as this can ever get: the barley flows around the palate on a wave of nectar; **f22.5** ridiculous clarity for a malt so old: barley and soft sugars link convivially with the vanilla; **b23** graceful, charming, entirely unexpected. That's why I love this job so much... *54.5%*

⋰∴⋱ **Chieftain's Brora 26 Years Old** oloroso sherry butt, dist Dec 81 **(92.5) n24** deep, sweet peak reek and cloves: pure dentist's surgery. All the sweeter notes are of a classic bourbony character; **t22** a discordant battle between well-muscled oak and the sweeter barley notes trying to hold their ground make for an early mess. The middle though settles as the smoke re-asserts itself; **f23.5** long and some really outstanding intertwining between the late ashy peat and the demerara notes; the light mocha fade glistens with the late oils; **b23** on delivery there is a fear that the great nose of the work will be undone. But hang on in there: the ending is a happy one. *48%. Ian Macleod Distillers Ltd.*

Old & Rare Brora Aged 30 Years dist Oct 76, bott Sep 07 **(87) n22** the smoke is working overtime to keep out the oak; **t22** delicate both on the gristy front and vanillas; **f21.5** a gentle send off; **b21.5** for all the strength, it refuses to be anything other than a lullaby dram. *55.1%. ncf. Douglas Laing. 104 bottles.*

Old & Rare Brora Aged 30 Years dist Oct 76, bott Apr 07 **(95) n23** strumming smoke in perfect tune; **t24** enormous delivery with the silkiest peat imaginable, oaky dry at first then sweetening out as a beyond- the- grave gristiness kicks in; **f24** the usual molassed finale, except it's not quite that simple with the layering oscillating between spice and honey, oak and smoke; **b24** once more a dram from a distillery that leaves you spellbound. No descriptors entirely do justice. And as I am just completing this edition and space is at a premium, I'll not even try. *57.5%. Douglas Laing. 109 bottles.*

Signatory Vintage Brora 1981 24 Years Old Cask Strength (88) n22 salty and oaky, the peat needs some persuading to make its mark; **t22** genuinely warming experience as the cough sweet peat makes sweetly-molassed home runs; **f22** loads of hickory and roasty bourbon **b22** quite different from the norm: for those who like a Bowmore style of malt. *60.1%. USA.*

BRUICHLADDICH
Islay, 1881. Bruichladdich Ltd, Working.

Bruichladdich 10 Years Old db **(90) n22** beautifully clean and zesty, the malt is almost juvenile; **t23** sweet, fruity then malty charge along the tastebuds that geets the mouth salivating; **f23** the usual soft vanilla and custard but a bigger barley kick in the latter stages; **b22** more oomph than previous bottlings, yet still retaining its fragile personality. Truly great stuff for a standard bottling. *46%*

Bruichladdich 12 Years Old 2nd Edition db **(88) n23** big barrage of fruit; crisp barley beautifully integrates with oak; **t22** an uneven, mildly uncertain, delivery due to the grape being out of sync with the big barley; give it about eight-ten seconds and they have found a delicious degree of harmony; **f22** long with the intense, chiselled flavours still slightly at odds, but calming down with some oils; **b21** a similar type of wine involvement to "Waves", but this is oilier in the old-fashioned 'Laddie style and lacks a little of the sparkle. The fruit on the finish is outstanding, though, and I don't think you or I would turn down a third glass... *46%*

Bruichladdich 15 Years Old 2nd Edition db **(86) n22 t23 f20 b21.** Delicious, as usual, but something, possibly fruity, appears to be holding back the show. *46%*

⋰∴⋱ **Bruichladdich 16 Years Old** bourbon cask db **(89) n22.5** sweet barley hangs from sturdy oak beams; **t22.5** remains firm yet sweet with a charming honeyed streak; again the oak plays a major role but its obvious dry input remains contained; **f22** dries further, with vanilla replacing the honey; some superb spices; **b22** plucked from the cask in the nick of time. In this state rather charming, but another summer or two might have seen the oak take a more sinister turn. *46%*

⋰∴⋱ **Bruichladdich 16 Years Old** bourbon/Chateau d'Yquem cask db **(95) n24** if you've got a good half an hour to spend, try using it intelligently by sticking your nose in this for a while: the grape is sweet and sultana juicy; the understated spices somehow hit just the right point to satisfy grape, oak and barley in one hit: some achievement... **t23.5** sweet, as the nose suggests, but the arrival is not all about grape. That sweetness also contains pristine barley.... **f23.5** just so soft and subtle with the vanillas offering a discreet escort to the barley-grape marriage; **b24** possibly the most delicate and understated of all the truly great whiskies of the year. Not one for the ice and water brigade. *46%*

Bruichladdich 18 Years Old bourbon/cognac cask db **(84.5) n23.5 t21 f20 b20.** Big oak-spice buzz but thin. Sublime grapey nose, for sure, but pays a certain price, ultimately, for associating with such an inferior spirit... 46%

Bruichladdich 18 Years Old bourbon/opitz cask db **(80.5) n19 t22 f19.5 b20.** Dry, complex; at times oak-stretched. 46%

⋅≫⋅ **Bruichladdich 18 Years Old 2nd Edition** bourbon/jurancon db **(86) n22 t21.5 f21 b21.5.** Plenty of fruit, including medium ripe greengages and slightly under-ripe grape. Juicy and sweet in the right places. 46%

Bruichladdich Flirtation Aged 20 Years 2nd Edition db **(86) n21 t22 f22 b21.** Hi sugar! A Laddie for those with a sweet tooth. 46%

Bruichaladdich 1970 Anniversary Bottling 125th bourbon cask, mature enhanced in zind humbrecht selection de grains noble pinot gris alsace white wine casks db **(95) n24** Good grief!! You don't sniff many aromas like this during the course of a year...decade... lifetime...!!! Initially you think: aha! loads of passion fruit and other exotics = great age. Then you think. hang on a mo... what's all that vaguely paprika-esque spice doing? Then you start detecting the most delicate of smoke notes and then spices, boiled plums and stewed apples and even something peculiarly boiled-crab- like. I kid you not...see for yourself... **t24** think of the softest delivery you ever tasted in your life...then multiply that softness by a factor of about 1.5. Silk doesn't do this justice, nor does the simple descriptor of varied, lightly spiced Pacific fruits. There is a distinctive boubony edge to this as if Kentucky's finest has galloped in to town. An absolute treat; **f23** incredibly light with just a smattering of roasty over-the-top oak, but it's so refined it sits very comfortably amid the bourbon, fruit and barley; **b24** an unbelievably complex malt that defies time. A must-experience malt. 40.1%

⋅≫⋅ **Bruichladdich "Golder Still" 1984** bourbon cask, db **(88.5) n22 t23 t22 b21.5.** A huge amount of natural caramels leached from the oak does the joint job of ensuring extraordinary softness and eroding the higher notes. Still, there is enough eye-rolling honey and spice to keep anyone happy and the rich bourbony character on delivery really is dreamy stuff. 51%

Bruichladdich Blacker Still 1986 sherry cask db **(87) n21** a not entirely un-flawed cask but before treatment this must have been a peach of a butt as the intensity of the sherry makes your hairs stand on end; **t22** again ribbons of something that shouldn't quite be there, yet such is the totality of the grape and spice that you cannot do other than be entertained with its sweet and juicy brilliance; **f22** that nagging S word continues, but now a gorgeous hickory tone wades in and stirs the pot; **b22** mildly flawed but you can forgive it its trespasses on account of its utterly juicy deliciousness. 50.7%

⋅≫⋅ **Bruichladdich "DNA" 37 Years Old** 80% bourbon/20% sherry cask, aged in Le Pin wine casks db **(87) n23.5** a beautiful, if potentially dodgy, counter between some gray-haired oak and pre-pubescent grape; **t22** nothing is settled with this one: the oak charges about in one direction, grapey waves soothes in another. A real flavour factory, especially with some light mocha in the middle ground, but don't look for a story here; **f20.5** a bit bitter, furry and nibbling; **b21** balance..? What balance...? Actually, somehow, this crazy thing does find some kind of equilibrium... 41%

Bruichladdich 1989 bourbon/tempranillo db **(94) n23** not dissimilar to African violet petals crushed in the fingers, though this is no shrinking violet. Floral, fruity but very firm; **t24** cracking delivery: crisp and mouth-watering with an excellent involvement of barley sugar and soft fruit juices; the spices are weighted with rare diligence; **f23** a light silver sugar sprinkling over gorgeous custard and coffee; and still those playful spices persist; **b24** stunning structure: a malt that feels as if it has been carved into shape by the most gifted of hands. Wonderful. 46%. Scanlines, Denmark.

Bruichladdich 1989 db **(75.5) n20 t19 f17.5 b19.** Ouch! 52.9%. Special bottling for Alberta.

Bruichladdich 1990 Aged 18 Years db **(85.5) n22.5 t21 f21 b21.** Enlivened by citrus and emboldened by soft salt. 46%

Bruichladdich 1990 Aged 18 Years cognac cask db **(81.5) n20.5 t21 f20 b20.** Wouldn't be a far greater benefit to the spirit world if Cognac was matured in a Bruichladdich cask...? 46%. Canada.

Bruichladdich Ghost Ship Valinch 1990 db **(92) n23** on the surface a drier than most Laddie cask with almost a background touch of Riesling; the balance and charm never waver; **t24** part-dissolves on the palate with barley just pulsing through, building in sweetness and chewability: one of the best deliveries of the year. Of its type, absolutely amazing... **f22** a little more conventional with its mocha fade once the oak digs in but the sheer class cannot be diluted; **b23** what an honest and wonderful cask this came from. Some moments offered are to die for. 54.5%. Available exclusively from distillery where drawn directly from cask.

Bruichladdich 1991 Aged 16 Years Chat Margaux finish db **(94) n23** fingers of grape essence tease and play with the crisp malt; there is almost a frailty to the spices; **t25** quite simply one of the finest deliveries of any non-peated Islay I have ever encountered; or any other whisky, come to that. The perfection of the juicy grape, the élan, as it glides over the barley is something you are likely never to forget; words, I'm afraid, could simply never do it justice; **f22.5** dries and reverts to a spiced attack as the vanilla gets little more than a foothold; **b23.5** a true Premier Cru malt...I have been almost certainly the most outspoken critic of whisky finishes: trust me, if they were all like this, you would never hear the merest clack of a dissenting typing key from me again... 46%

Bruichladdich 1993 db **(94) n23.5** softer than the Arran, mildly herbal and dry. There is a sweeter fruit sub-stratum, but very faint; **t24** orgasmico! So much for the Italians being great lovers: straight in – and bam!!! All at once there is rush of head-exploding spices, fruit and barley...then slower, less intense waves of gentle sugars; **f23** thins out elegantly to allow wafer-dry oak tones to tease the grape; **b23.5** as far as I can remember, or am aware, I had never tasted a Sassicaia-finished whisky before. And, as luck would have it, I have now tasted two in one day. On this evidence it would be entirely fair to argue that these tastebud-exploding finishes are Italy's greatest contribution to the whisky world....!! 50.2%. Special bottling for Alberta.

Bruichladdich 1994 db **(87) n22** butterscotch and barley; decent oak spices; **t22** mouth-wateringly sharp delivery; vanilla follow through; **f21.5** long and bitter-sweet; **b21.5** bravo to Bruichladdich for demonstrating to the Taiwanese that you don't have to have your whisky coloured to death to experience a very substantial dram. 54.9%. Taiwan.

Bruichladdich 1994 Full Strength db **(90) n21.5** gristy barley and layers of herbs and vanilla; **t23** massive delivery with stunning head-rocking spice; fat and fruity, topped out with mocha; **f22** more of the same, except a degree of two quieter...and with more emphasis on the mocha which thinks about entering overdrive; **b23.5** not dissimilar to the stunning Sassicaia, except a tad fatter. Just brilliant! 56.5%

Bruichladdich 1994 bourbon/PX sherry db **(78) n19 t20 f19 b20.** Love the distillery. Love the shop. Just don't particularly love this bottling. Sorry. 59.7%. Special Bottling for Potstill, Austria.

⁙ **Bruichladdich Valinch Blandola 1994** bourbon/Chateau d'Yquem casks, dist Sep 94 db **(87) n21.5** musty, dusty grape; **t22.5** a confused early delivery but pans out with a really complex fruit-toffee delivery with a touch of coffee and, finally, juicy barley; **f21** vanilla and a dry, furry grapiness; **b22** a bit muddled here and there but, like the distillery and staff, no shortage of personality. 55.3%. Available only from Bruichladdich's distillery shop.

Bruichladdich 1998 db **(89) n22** is manzanilla a wine or a cheese...? Because there is a distinctive cheese puff element to this. Tied in with the overt barley and soft grape, it works charmingly, too...; **t22.5** puckering, firm grape grips the roof of the mouth, elsewhere lighter, more vanilla-clad notes can be heard; **f22.5** long, sharp barley and a sensual mouthfeel; **b22** a truly unique signature to this but absolute class in a glass. 46%

⁙ **Bruichladdich 1998** bourbon/oloroso cask, dist 98 db **(87.5) n22.5** splatted grape shows a fresh, juicy character; **t22.5** two or three waves of tart grape crash against the tastebuds before a more delicate spicy shadow forms, followed by richer barley; **f21** a lazy, custard cream biscuit sweetness dwindles towards a remarkably dry finale; **b21.5** surprisingly conservative. But, joy of joys, not an atom of sulphur to be found...!! 46%

⁙ **Bruichladdich 1998** bourbon/Manzanilla cask, dist 98 db **(82.5) n21 t21 f20 b20.5.** Fruity. But bitter where it should be sweet. 46%

Bruichladdich Full Strength Special Edition - The International Malt Whisky Festival, Gent 2008 db **(94) n23** if all noses were this dense, this outrageously unpickable when it comes to unlocking just what is going on in there, this book would never get finished. Thick, enlivened with some of the most intense pith notes I've ever comes across, almost too rich oak...everything is there...you just need a week or two to unravel the mystery; **t23.5** mouth-filling, tooth melting, gum stroking...every sensation as the tastebuds are blitzed with concentrated malt concentrate, that's been concentrated a bit more for good measure; can't make its mind up if sweet or dry, so is both, sometimes taking turns, often together; the spices buzz but never distract; **f23** a lovely denouement of the laziest smoke, slightly more energetic cocoa, plenty of barley, of course, and then various other members of the oak fraternity; **b24.5** the only thing more beautiful than this I came across for the first time at Gent was the girl selling my books. Both are enough to dive you inSanne with desire. 56.5%. nc, ncf.

Bruichladdich Infinity Second Edition bourbon/rioja db **(94) n24** Jesus H....a nose to both rock you back in your chair and getting you springing to your feet at the same moment. Cured bacon (though there was probably nothing wrong with it) and peppered kippers; barley grist and roasted oatmeal: staggering bitter-sweet combination with no imbalance at all. Simply a wondrous nose... **t24** A spicier affair than the first edition with just a little extra oil to coat the mouth, not quite Caol Ila style but getting there. The fruit also plays a big part with those blatant spices; but it's juicy also and ultra chewy; **f23** real smokiness to the finish which dries in the same way as when you swallow the fumes of your cottage's peat fire; mildly dusty towards the finish...and classy; **b23** Wasn't it Daffy Duck who used to put on his cape and shout: "Infinity and Beyond" ? Oh, no... it was Buzz Lightyear. Anyways, he must have been thinking of this. And there's certainly nothing dethspicable about this one... *52.5%*

Bruichladdich "Kosher" 1994 Aged 12 Years db **(85.5) n22 t21 f21 b21.5.** Clean. What else, my dear? *46%*

Bruichladdich Legacy Series 3 Aged 35 Years db **(91) n22** the old Exotic Fruit School of Aged Whisky in early evidence: just starting to go through the wood but some Kentucky notes ride to the rescue; **t22.5** such a charming display of soft, velvety sweet – almost sugared – citrus tones; the barley refuses to shrink, however, and adds a juicy nuance to the gathering vanilla; **f23.5** a spice buzz and attractive bourbony notes with the liquorice and honeycomb in full, sexy attendance; **b23** so they managed to find a whisky exactly the same age as Ladie distiller Jim. *40.7%*

Bruichladdich Links "Carnoustie" 14 Years Old db **(78) n19 t20 f19 b20.** Hits some unexpected rough. *46%*

Bruichladdich Links K Club Ireland "16th Hole" 14 Years Old bourbon/syrah, dist 92, bott 07 db **(93) n23 t23 f23 b24.** I quite like this, though as hard as I try I can't quite love it. The spices offer great entertainment value and the juiciness on delivery is astonishing, but..... My tongue is investigating every crevice in my mouth with some urgency, so I know it's complex – and very unusual, but..... It's gossamer light. It kind of teases you. It's playful. But it's not beautiful. Is it...? Third mouthful in and I'm getting hooked. Oh, sod it! I've just upped it from a 86 to 93. What can I do? I'm in love... *46%. nc ncf. 12,000 bottles.*

Bruichladdich Links "Torrey Pines" 15 Years Old db **(89.5) n23** the clarity of the fruit is almost glacial; **t22.5** fine delineation between the fruit and grain at first, then they mould together; **f22** vanilla advances with the spice; **b22** as clean as the perfect tee shot from the 15th... *46%*

Bruichladdich Redder Still 1984 db **(95.5) n23.5** fascinating, ultra complex aroma: old, long un-opened wardrobes mixed with a fresher, fruitier element, mainly based on waxy apple; distant kumquat and a bag of boiled fruit candy add to the mix; **t24** helped along by a welcome and very marked lack or anything overly oily, it gives the palate a chance to see just how complex this is: the barley actually manages to find a voice, dishing out a salivating salvo and then heading into a pleasing latte and demerara middle; **f23.5** as dry finales go, this is about as good as it gets: the vanillas are there to be admired, but the gentle, white coffee effect continues longer than most. Just a sprinkle of the most delicate spices, evident and slightly more intense from pretty early on, continues to the milky end; **b24.5** now it's finding whiskies like this that I became the world's first-full time whisky for. I dreamed of discovering drams which stretched my tastebuds and spoke to me with eloquence, charisma and unmistakable class. This is one such whisky: the style is highly unusual; the cleverness of the layering almost unique. This is the kind of near flawless whisky for which we were given tastebuds. Oh, and a nose... *50.4%*

⠿ **Bruichladdich "The Resurrection"** bourbon cask, dist 01 db **(90) n23** sharp, striking, salty oak and a light yet firm smokiness: beautifully coastal; **t22.5** sweet, soft and the peat simply glides over the buds; **f22** some chocolate mint to keep the smoke company; **b22.5** from the distillery that brings orgasms (see PC6), no doubt about the surrection here... *46%*

Bruichladdich Rocks db **(82) n19 t22 f20 b21.** Perhaps softer than you'd imagine something called "rocks"! Beautiful little malty charge on entry. *46%*

Bruichladdich 3D Third Edition a marriage of Bruichladdich, Port Charlotte & Octomore, bourbon/madeira db **(91) n23** a Bowmore-ish style of sherry-kippery peat, perhaps exaggerated by a certain youthful trait; the phenols are prickly and at times attractively stark; as near as damn it like sticking your head into the pagoda as the smoke from the densest, darkest peat is wafting through; **t22** soft, sweet delivery with a deliberate ramping up of the smoke yet the barley is still there to add a juicy dimension; **f23** superb balance at the finish with that thick knot of smoke now evening out allowing fruit, barley and mild hickory tones to play off the light spices. Charming; **b23** an incredibly old-fashioned style of high-class Islay malt... taking me back to my first-ever visits to the island over 25 years ago. In fact, about the time I first met the Norrie Campbell, peat cutter extraordinaire and now, sadly, lost to us...So, those of you who taste this – or any other Islay, come to that – please share with me a smoky toast to his memory. *46%. Norrie Campbell Tribute.*

⇌ **Bruichladdich 16 Years Old** bourbon/Chateau Haut Brion cask db **(81.5) n21 t21.5 f19 b20.** fruity and busy for sure. But just not the kind of wine barrel effect that does much for me, I'm afraid, not least because of the background buzz on the palate. 46%

⇌ **Bruichladdich 16 Years Old** bourbon/Chateau Lafite cask db **(89) n24** yet another nose where the grape appears almost three dimensional in its ability to offer the cleanest of fruits...and somehow sharpen the barley element for all those years in cask; **t22.5** absolutely melt-in-the-mouth: deliveries rarely come softer or so dripping in grape. The spices which form belatedly towards the middle are of a servile nature; **f21.5** perhaps too soft here, as the grape, though delicate, somehow appears to dominate and desired late complexity doesn't materialise; **b21.5** ridiculously soft. Could just do with an injection of something to propel it into greatness. 46%

⇌ **Bruichladdich 16 Years Old** bourbon/Chateau Lafleur cask db **(92.5) n23** a real floral dustiness to the grape; delicate spice prickle; **t23.5** barley tries to make a brief statement before the microphone is snatched away by bristling fruit; the mouthfeel is a bit like a dissolving sugar candy; **f23** some oak gets a word in, but can barely make itself heard against the barley; **b23** so luminous on the palate, it's positively Lafleurescent... 46%

⇌ **Bruichladdich 16 Years Old** bourbon/Chateau Latour cask db **(84.5) n21 t21.5 f21 b21.** Enjoyable. But there is a strange aggression to the spice which doesn't altogether sit as comfortably as it might. The fruit heads off into not just grapey but citrus territory, but there is a always a but about the direction it takes... 46%

⇌ **Bruichladdich 16 Years Old** bourbon/Chateau Margaux cask db **(78.5) n20.5 t20 f19 b19.** Not 1st Cru Bruichladdich, I'm afraid. 46%

⇌ **Bruichladdich 21 Years Old** oloroso sherry cask db **(76.5) n18.5 t21 f18 b19.** Oops! 46%
Bruichladdich WMD II - The Yellow Submarine 1991 db **(75) n20 t19 f18 b18.** This one just doesn't have the balance and sinks. 46%

⇌ **Bruichladdich X4** db **(82) n18 t22 f21 b21.** Frankly, like no new make I have ever come across in Scotland before. Thankfully, the taste is sweet, malty and compact: far, far better than the grim, cabbage water nose. Doesn't really have the X-Factor yet, though. 50%

Bruichladdich X4 2007 db **(86.5) n18 t23 f23.5 b22.** So here we have it: a quadruple-distilled malt. In flavour style, not dissimilar to certain efforts from Mackmyra in Sweden. Except it lacks the overall balance, especially on the nose-punching aroma and layering of flavour. This stuff is distilled up to 92% abv, though here it is served at a mincing 65.4% - pathetic! However, it is on the palate – or palette, as the 'Laddie website calls it, obviously convinced that this is a work of art, that the real fun begins. It is distinctly herbal with the fruits I had been promised in very short supply to the point of non-existence. The oak and cocoa tones provide an almost erotic massage of the tastebuds. Some people will love it, others hate it. Had it not been for the nose, this would have scored much more highly. Personally, I love it: absolutely adore it. Taste slowly with the eyes closed and just let that silky-soft oil coat the palate/palette until you find yourself giving an involuntary whimper. That's what happens when your tastebuds are being seduced and screwed by something of naked, bold beauty. And at 65.4% even the outwardly ugly can be beautiful... 65.4%. 2008 festival bottling.

⇌ **Octomore 5 Years Old** db **(96) n23.5** seeing how Octomore is actually a farm on Islay, it is rather fitting that the massive peat here yields a distinctly farm-yardy aroma. Yet this is curiously low on peat reek for a dram boasting phenomenal phenols at 131 parts per million – Ardbeg is about 50; the much smokier PC7 is just 40. That said, obviously peaty, yet an age-related lemon lightness, too...and a herd of cattle...; **t24.5** the oils are absolutely perfect, as is the slow unfurling of the myriad strata of peat; those youthful, zesty, citrus notes have been enriched with a perfect degree of golden syrup; a near-perfect sprinkling of spice enriches further...; **f24** a wonderful array of vanillas lighten not just the peat but the sweetened mocha which is now making its mark. Long, relaxed and very assured for a malt so young... **b24** forget about the age. Don't be frightened by the phenol levels. Great whisky is not about numbers. It is about excellent distillation and careful maturation. And here you have a memorable combination of both... 63.5%

Port Charlotte Evolution PC5 Cask Strength db **(95) n24** enormously heavy going with the thick grape and the 40ppm peat (actually, it seems a lot bigger than that) arm-wrestling for control. Perhaps the peat wins, but only after it has spent ten minutes oxidizing in the glass... **t23** a spice kick on the nose is no less evident on delivery where again the sherry and peat arrive in one massive and very sharp tangle. Only with the introduction of a touch of oak do matters become a little clearer and less confused; **f24** wonderful denouement as finally the palate finds space to make sense of it all. The grape thins out sufficiently to at last add colour to the haze of the peat smoke while the phenols begin to grasp gently the custard tart oakiness to help lighten and sweeten the load; **b24** a bit like a David Lynch movie: you are caught in the dazzling genius of it all, not exactly knowing what is going on, yet never doubting that you are experiencing something very special; and only at the very end does the plot make any sense at all. One thing is for certain: even the most experienced peat whisky lovers are unlikely to have encountered anything quite like this....simply because Port Charlotte offers a style of peating different from any other not only on Islay but in the world. 63.5%. 6,000 bottles.

Port Charlotte First Cut 27/05/07 bourbon cask no. 007, dist 28 May 01, bott May 07 db **(94) n23** dry, clumpy peat; a sweet pipe tobacco balances things slightly; an entirely different peat-reek aroma from any other whisky on this planet: there is an intensity to this that borders on the manic; **t24** big: a slow dissolving of thick peat on the palate; always sweet and mildly gristy; given the conditions, spices are expected – and arrive in force; **f24** a light involvement of vanilla helps and at last the intensity softens to something much more delicate and even sophisticated. But it is never less than a white knuckle ride...; **b23** great whisky, even if it does, through youth, struggle slightly to get its legs and balance. For best results, leave in the glass to settle and oxidise for a while before tasting. A malt for extremists. 61.5%

Port Charlotte PC6 db **(96.5) n24.5** ohhhhhh... arrrrrrrrhh..... mmmmmmmmmmm..... oh, the peat, the peat...., vesssssss , oh my god......mmmmmmmm..... ohhhhhhhhh.... **t24** first you get the smoky... ooooohhhhhhh... arrrrrrrrr.... then the sweeter.... mmmmmmmmm..... arrrrooooohhhh.... **f24** it finishes with a more gentle arghoooo...... mmmmmmmm..... oooophhhhhh..... arrrrrrrrr.... **b24** not many whiskies have a truly unmistakable nose.... and....., but this is, this........ is....... this..... mmmmmmmm..., arrrrrhh. Ohhhhhhhhh........ 61.6%

⋰⋱ **Port Charlotte PC7** dist 01 db **(93.5) n24** dry. The most profound peat fire ashes: not for peaty amateurs... **t24** a few drops of sweetness added; a liquorice/molassed melt to the massive smoke: the phenols seems a lot higher than the 40ppm they talk about; **f22** drops down a gear or two as some bitterness creeps in, as does a secondary fizz to the spice; **b22.5** not quite as orgasmic as last year, sadly. But should still be pretty stimulating... 60.5%

Berrys' Own Selection Bruichladdich 1988 cask no. 1879, bott 07 **(84.5) n21 t22 f20.5 b21.** The kind of neat and tidy cask which blenders used to enjoy for its powers of simply malty persuasion. 56.4%. Berry Bros & Rudd.

Berry's' Own Selection Bruichladdich 1991 Aged 15 Years (94) n24 greengages, honey, salt and a vague smokiness combine for something rather wonderful; **t24** a stunning honey thread weaves through the crystal-clear barley; threatens to be mouthwatering, but prevented at the last minute by drier vanilla. The weight and delicacy of the sweetness defy the odds. 'Laddie, you feel, unplugged...; **f23** raspberry jam raps itself around that renegade peat; **b23** unexpected little gems like this make you feel so lucky to do this job... 46%.

Cadenhead's Authentic Collection Bruichladdich Aged 15 Years bourbon hogshead, dist 92, bott Sep 07 **(94) n23** multi shades of vanilla with flecks of meringue and scented garden; a gentle crust of salt ups the intensity, **t23.5** massive barley with the flavours honed to the sharpest edge imaginable by both the intensity and those helping salts; in the background balancing sugars flit lightly about; **f23.5** back to the vanilla, only now topped with gentle cocoa; long with a most elegant fade with soft, pulsing spices; **b24** exemplary 'Laddie with such clever sweetness that for not a single moment is the balance lost on either nose or palate. 55.5%. 286 bottles.

Cadenhead's Bruichladdich Aged 15 Years bourbon, dist 1991, bott May 07 **(86) n23 t22 f20 b21.** A detailed tapestry of gently salted barley notes and varying shades of oak make this a dram to take your time over. 46%. 312 bottles.

Chieftain's Bruichladdich 19 Years Old hogshead, dist Apr 89 **(95) n23.5** rarely does malt of this age and oak dovetail with such compatibility: banana milkshake offers the most delicate of sweetnesses, the barley is more biscuity; the oak is everywhere, but so lightly coated that it just needs that faint hint of lemon to counter any semblance of imbalance; the most distant of smoke notes can just be detected; **t24** just about the perfect mouthfeel: a touch of oil, but no more – just enough to form a gossamer-light coating – and then successive waves of citrus, each of varying intensity; **f23.5** dries towards a powdery oakiness but there is enough zest to keep everything perfectly fresh; the late smoke on the nose is repeated here; **b24** weirdly enough, although this doesn't come from the distillery, I'd choose this cask as being perhaps the closest thing I could find to the absolute textbook 'Laddie. A must-have Islay. 50%. nc ncf. Ian Macleod Distillers.

Eidora 9 Port Charlotte 6 Years Old bourbon cask, dist 01, bott 07 **(86.5) n21 t23.5 f21.5 b20.5.** Certainly enjoyable and worth the ride for the ultra intense peat and shock factor alone. However, here is a malt bottled at the wrong time, when the oaks and the malt were not quite in sync and, therefore, the vital balance had been compromised. The same can't be said for the PC6, which has been masterfully engineered. All that said, still well worth the experience: nose, taste a decent mouthful and hold on tight... 66.5%. Slowdrink, Germany.

⠿ **The Golden Cask Bruichladdich 1992** cask no. CM114 **(93)** n23.5 barley dipped in runny honey; **t24** more honey on delivery, this time engulfing strands of coconut; the spices arrive early and are consistent; the cocoa arrives later and is beautifully controlled and met in the middle with a hint of molasses; **f22.5** much drier finish with the odd sign of a tiring cask. But that is mere detail: the vanillas, remaining strands of honey and lightly pulsing spice are good enough; **b23** a quite truly golden cask... 54.2%. 223 bottles.

Japan Import System Bruichladdich Classic (83.5) n22 t20.5 f21 b20. Thick, oily almost Caol Ila in style; sweet, delicate but niggardly in complexity. 46%

Murray McDavid Bruichladdich 1989 sherry **(93)** n23 like opening a bag of fresh organic sultanas; wonderful fruit and a tang of something spiced; **t23** mmm! Juicy! Outstanding meeting of yielding barley and less yielding fruit; the spices on the nose quickly translate to something more substantial on the palate; **f23** comfortable layers of oak add weight and counter dryness in the boiled candy grape; **b24** when I moan at the front of the Bible about the lack of decent sherry bottlings – this isn't one I have in mind! Excellent. 46%

Old Malt Cask Bruichladdich Aged 13 Years refill hogshead, cask no. 3700, dist Nov 93, bott Jun 07 **(89)** n22 "Nice" coconut biscuit, extracted from a tin of Lemon Puffs; **t22** juicy barley, fresh green grass, drier vanillas and a distant hint of smoke; **f22.5** much drier but still subtle and complex with the oak toying with the gentle barley; **b22.5** the kind of whisky you could drink all day every day: dangerous stuff! 50%. nc ncf. Douglas Laing. 345 bottles.

Old Malt Cask Bruichladdich Aged 14 Years refill hogshead no. 3826, dist Nov 93, bott Dec 07 **(89)** n22 massive malt concentrate: think American drugstore malt-shake – only without anything milky...; **t22.5** exactly as it says on the nose: the richest malt imaginable, slightly biscuity with mounting sugars; **f22.5** vanilla and salt is gradually stirred in; **b22** there isn't a blender in Scotland who wouldn't give his left nostril for a malt of this unerring intensity. Not exactly shabby as a single malt, either. Finishes? Who needs 'em...? 50%. nc ncf. Douglas Laing . 352 bottles.

⠿ **Old Malt Cask Bruichladdich Aged 15 Years** refill hogshead, dist Nov 93, bott Nov 08 **(91)** n22.5 huge citrus lead: the barley is clean and delicate; **t23** lively lemon energises the barley and salty oaks; **f22.5** delicate barley, more citrus and some wonderful chocolate mint on the fade; **b23** very similar to the old Invergordon bottlings at this age. 50%. Douglas Laing. 353 bottles.

⠿ **Old Malt Cask Bruichladdich Aged 18 Years** refill hogshead, dist Nov 89, bott Aug 08 **(76)** n20 t21 f17 b18. Sweet, fat and juicy early on. But never gets into a stride and the finish is rather inevitable. 50%. Douglas Laing. 350 bottles.

Old Malt Cask Bruichladdich Aged 19 Years refill hogshead, cask no. 3839, dist Feb 88, bott Aug 07 **(84)** n21 t21.5 f21.5 b20. Clean, juicy malt: that's the start and end of it. 50%. nc ncf. Douglas Laing. 328 bottles.

Old Malt Cask Bruichladdich Aged 20 Years refill hogshead 4065, dist Feb 88, bott Feb 08 **(86)** n21 t22.5 f21 b21.5. Charming whisky which ramps up the barley big time. Perhaps a shade oversweet in part but the tongue is puckered to the utmost. 50%. nc ncf. Douglas Laing. 341 bottles.

Old Masters Bruichladdich Aged 19 Years cask no. 1882 dist 88, bott 08 **(86.5)** n21 **t22.5 f21 b22.** Softly oiled in the classic 'Laddie style and a natural step on from the original old 10-year-old which graced the distillery and island for so many years. 54%. James MacArthur & Co. Ltd.

⠿ **Old Masters Bruichladdich Aged 20 Years** cask no. 1883, dist 88, bott 08 **(95)** n24 classic 'Laddie of the old school: big, salty malt style; **t23.5** unusually viscous but the malts carry on pressing home that salty, malty theme and not without an attractive early sweetness. Chewy and just lightest hint of burnt fudge; **f23.5** long, still persistently oily and the fudge just keeps on amassing a bigger molassed style; **b24** a beautiful version of the old-fashioned peatless Bruichladdich 10, which was once the most popular malt on the island. Twice as old and twice as intense. An indisputable must-have malt for the Islayphile, whether you are peathead or not, for this is one of the true classic Islays of the year. 52.6%. James MacArthur & Co. Ltd.

Provenance Bruichladdich Aged 11 Years refill hogshead no. 3870, dist autumn 95, bott autumn 07 **(92.5)** n23 stick your head in a mash tun and you might get an idea...fabulous clarity to the malt which is delicately peated and salivatingly green...; **t23** sweet grist (surprise, surprise!) with the juiciest, lightly smoked malt imaginable; **f23.5** spices up as some timid vanilla arrive, but the charm of the malt just goes on; **b23** such an unusual malt: rarely does anything come on the market so clean and refreshing. It is as though the mash has been injected with alcohol without any of that yeasty stuff reducing its fresh sweetness. A brilliant one off! 46%.

The Queen of the Moorlands Rare Cask Bruichladdich 1991 "The Anniversary Bottling" (94) n22 an old-fashioned traditional Laddie nose with a light, attractively salty edge; **t24**

powering barley with breathtaking integrity; the oak acts only as a foil to the tidal waves of juicy grist; lovely fruit notes help complete mouth-watering deliciousness; **f24** coffee cake, drying towards a more chocolately finale. Long and just wonderful; **b24** a quite stunning bottling very much in the style that made this the islanders' choice. A light viscosity holding the most delicate sweetness makes for an unmistakable fingerprint. Glorious and in part near faultless. I'm blown away... *52.8%. nc ncf. Available at The Wine Shop, Leek, and Islay Whisky Shop.*

Scotch Malt Whisky Society Cask 23.59 Aged 14 Years refill hogshead, dist Apr 93 **(83) n20 t21 f21 b21.** The tobacco smoke nose warns of an unusual 'Laddie, and so it proves with a real sharpness to the barley that is mildly out of character. *52.1%*

⊹ **Scotch Malt Whisky Society Cask 23.61 Aged 7 Years** refill butt, dist Nov 01 **(77) n18 t20.5 f18.5 b20.** A very odd cask of whisky. The strength is pretty weird, for a start. But there is something, some kind of off note, on the nose I don't exactly recognise (pretty unusual), but every sinew of my instinct tells me it's not quite right. There is also a suspicion that the powering spirit perhaps helps mask other off notes. The phenols are attractive to taste in a plain, girl-next-door way while ugly to sniff; but the warning lights come on again for the finish. *68.2%*

Scott's Selection Bruichladdich 1990 bott 07 **(80) n21 t21 f19 b19.** Pretty coarse from nose to finish. There are some rich seams of barley concentrate but a real bruiser, this. *57.4%. Speyside Distillers*

The Whisky Fair Bruichladdich Aged 17 Years bourbon hogshead, dist 90, bott 07 **(92) n23** wonderful interplay between lemon, kumquats and sweet custard...just so damn yummy!! **t23.5** clean to the point of hearing the malt squeak; just so many juicy, grassy notes and breathtaking layering of bitter-sweet; **f22.5** becalmed by a charming degree of vanilla; **b23** now this is exactly how a bourbon cask Bruichladdich should be. Not at this age, perhaps, but who gives a toss? *57.9%. The Whisky Fair.*

BUNNAHABHAIN
Islay, 1881. Burn Stewart. Working.
Bunnahabhain Aged 12 Years db **(84.5) n22.5 t21 f20 b21.** I thought I noticed it when I tasted it late last year and earlier this, in two different places. "Where's that bracing, mildly tart, eye-watering Bunna that I so adore?" I wondered. Thankfully no sign of the sulphur that caused so many problems for so long. But something, I thought, was missing. Right: now having spent a good 45 minutes with it, I can report there is no shortage of charm and the earliest barley belt on the palate rocks. But the fire has been doused, most probably by caramel. Something has got in there and flattened the development and finale, its very soul. A quarter of a century ago I would stand at the door of my holiday cottage above the distillery, the fearsome Atlantic storms driving stinging rain horizontally into my face, and I would drink this most enlivening of drams to amplify nature's propensity for drama, to revert. If only momentarily, to something in my nature more basic and primeval. It was, frankly, one of the greatest experiences of my life as for ten, maybe fifteen minutes the rain, the wind, the stark Paps of Jura, invisible in the storm but whose brooding presence you could feel a few hundred yards away, the frothing, swirling cauldron of the Sound of Islay below me and all my heightened senses would be one....then, when my glass was long empty, I would open my eyes, wonder what the hell I was doing getting drenched and scuttle back inside and shiver meekly by the peat fire. With this bottling it would be hard to repeat such a sensation, when the spark of life zapped into every sense, every apparent nerve-ending both inside and outside the body. If ever there was a case for a malt to strip back down to the essentials, to be more basic and primeval, this'd be it. Bourbon barrel. 46%. Seeping with saline. Natural colour. A mouthful....close your eyes...and then dare nature, itself the father of this usually awesome dram, to do its worst.... *40%*

⊹ **Bunnahabhain Aged 16 Years Manzanilla Sherry Wood Finish** db **(87) n20.5** big, fruity and ungainly; **t23** eye-watering stuff: a wave of salty grape-juice comes hurtling at you and right behind comes a second wave of sweeter barley which thumps you with equal force; **f21.5** definitely an off-key note, but there is so much happening with the grape, ultra dry vanilla and soft cocoa tones...oh, and salt...you hardly get a chance to notice; **b22** the kind of undisciplined but fun malt which just makes it up as it goes along... *53.2%*

Bunnahabhain Aged 18 Years db **(85.5) n22.5 t22 f20 b21.** Much better nose than of old, but still the malt dies an unnatural death at an earlier stage of its life than it should. Again caramel appears to be a suspect as the early, juicy delivery, after a few citrus circuits, vanishes with nothing to take its place. *43%*

Bunnahabhain XXV Aged 25 Years db **(93) n22** some serious coastal saltiness here...and grape; **t24** big saline kick as the oak offers some early latte; mouthwatering barley also impresses, topped off with brown sugar and damson tart; **f23** more milky coffee with an oatcake side dish; **b24** a fruity Bunna, but jam-packed with all the big barley-salt notes which set this distillery apart. One of the few bottlings around at the moment that us Bunna Old Timers can hold up and say: "Yeah, this is the business." Quite superb. 43%

Bunnahabhain 1971 Aged 35 Years 125th Anniversary bott Oct 06 db **(94)** n25 t24 f22 **b23**. When I stayed at the distillery on holiday in both 1983 and 1984 – long before I let on the secret of it being a must-experience whisky destination – the 12 year-old Bunna that sat on my table before the peat fire came from sister casks of what we are tasting here. Previous owners Highland lost the plot with Bunna when they strangled it with sherry, often sulphured, and though the grape shapes the malt here, there is enough of the old clean signature to take me back to those wonderful days. Frankly, it is doubtful if this great distillery's anniversary could have been celebrated in finer style. 44.9%. ncf. 750 bottles.

Cadenhead's Chairman's Stock Bunnahabhain Aged 28 Years bourbon hogshead, dist 79, bott Sep 07 **(86)** n22 t22.5 f20 b21.5. Salty and tangy with some startling orangey notes. A tad furry, too. 45.8%. 168 bottles.

⸬ **Celtic Heartlands Bunnahabhain 1973** bott 08 **(91)** n20 a touch of lactic coming through... **t24** wow..!! didn't expect that...!!! Near perfect delivery with the intense malt funnelled directly into the tastebuds through the sexy oils which accompany this. A gossamer delivery of accompanying sugars is then overtaken by sea salt...; **f23.5** the complexity doesn't even begin to diminish, though now we have a touch of mocha landing and an upping of the molasses to counter the intrusion of the saltier, drier oak...and then, bizarrely, a quick flash of orangey citrus.... **b23.5** the tired, slightly through-the-wood nose warns you of the worst...then the delivery blows you away....!! 46.1%. Bruichladdich Ltd. 669 bottles.

Chieftain's Bunnahabhain 10 Years Old cask no. 3207, dist Sep 97 **(89)** n22.5 soft, sensual, citrus-tinged smoke; **t22** sweet barley, then a slow, mounting intensity of gristy peat; **f22** drier, a touch of salt and cocoa...but the gentle peat continues on its meandering course; **b22.5** the new look Bunna in its most naked form: and pretty tasty, too! 46%. nc ncf. Ian Macleod Distillers. Danish Market.

Chieftain's Bunnahabhain Aged 10 Years Sherry Finish (79) n20 t21 f19 b19. Bit of a half-way house with the sherry seemingly scrubbing out much of the bourbon complexity, but not quite imparted enough of its own character. 46%.

Chieftain's Bunnahabhain Peated 10 Years Old hogshead, dist Sep 97 **(92)** n22.5 salty and sharp, the peat is quite two-toned in its cocoa-smoky character; **t23.5** splendid delivery and mouthfeel: sweet with lashings of muscovado and honeycomb and deep with the smoke biting with spice and a saline thrust; **f23** fabulous layers of mocha and smoke; **b23** enough to make Edvard Munch scream in ecstasy....historic, really, because with this bottling Bunna has indubitably arrived as a top-rank Islay peated malt...!! 56.1%. nc ncf. Ian Macleod Distillers. Norwegian market.

Dun Bheagan Bunnahabhain Aged 10 Years Manzanilla Finish (86) n22 t22 f20 b22. Distinctive fruity bite to this. 46%. Ian Macleod.

Duncan Taylor Collection Bunnahabhain 1966 cask no. 4878 (80) n22 t21 f18 b19. Interesting. Not true whisky, apparently, if the strength is correct. I would have been tempted to vat this off because, for all its fruity promise, on its own there is not quite enough depth to see off the oak. 39.9%. Duncan Taylor.

Duncan Taylor Collection Bunnahabhain 1970 cask no. 4073 (79) n21 t21 f18 b19. Hanging on for grim life to any last vestiges of its old self. Curious to think: it was malt from this vintage of Bunna that made up the 12-y-o stuff I used to drink at the distillery when I first stayed there. Let's just say it was then in its prime... 40.3%

⸬ **Duncan Taylor Collection Bunnahabhain 1970** cask no. 4075 **(81)** n20.5 t20 f20.5 **b20**. Clung like a limpet to retain its whisky life. In so doing has taken on nougat and honey clothing with just enough depth and sharpness to the barley to see off the mounting resin. Yet, for all its best effort, unwieldy and inelligent. 40.2%

The MacPhail's Collection Bunnahabhain 1991 (86) n22 t21 f22 b21. Bunna in reflective, barley-rich mood with a shake of salt making an interesting contrast to the gentle raspberry preserve at the death. Deliciously curious. 43%. Gordon & MacPhail.

Murray McDavid Mission Bunnahabhain 1966 oloroso sherry **(86)** n21 t23 f20 b22. Creaks a fair bit, but never goes snap... 40.3%. 500 bottles.

⸬ **Old & Rare Bunnahabhain Aged 34 Years** dist May 74, bott Sep 08 **(93.5)** n23 the real deal with sherry: a mixture of burst sultana with suet sprinkled with salt and vanilla; **t23** oak takes little time to show, but is roundly seen off by a real old juicy fruitcake, in which liquorice and molasses have been added with abandon; **f24** long and stunningly weighted with this beauty getting sweeter by the moment as the oak, astonishingly, abates, allowing the sultana to return with gristy barley and a wonderful interplay of salt and peppers: one of the finest Bunna finishes for a while; **b23.5** ah, pride of my heart, my own love.... 58.3%. Douglas Laing. 333 bottles.

Old Malt Cask Bunnahabhain Aged 11 Years refill hogshead no. 3699, dist Jun 96, bott Jun 07 **(70.5) n17 t19 f17 b17.5.** Matured in a dreadful, stale cask. 50%. nc ncf. Douglas Laing. 340 bottles.

Old Malt Cask Bunnahabhain Aged 11 Years refill hogshead no. 3936, dist Sep 96, bott Oct 07 **(81.5) n18 t22.5 f20 b21.** Malty, almost yeasty in places. 50%. Douglas Laing. 320 bottles.

Old Malt Cask Bunnahabhain Aged 12 Years (80.5) n20 t21 f19 b20.5. A knackered old cask hasn't done much to add to the attractive early barley kick. 50%

◌·ː· **Old Malt Cask Bunnahabhain Aged 19 Years** dist Feb 90, bott Jul 09 **(73.5) n18 t19 f18 b18.5.** Typical Bunna sherry cask of the era. Alas. 50%. Douglas Laing.

◌·ː· **Old Malt Cask Bunnahabhain Aged 30 Years** refill butt, dist Dec 78, bott Apr 09 **(87) n23.5** if you can imagine an old sherry butt sitting in a Jerez bodega just inches from the sea and drinking in salty air for three decades...well, there you have it... **t20.5** dry and angular with burnt raisin and toast making heavy going of it; **f22** blossoms deliciously as the sweeter barley notes emerge and some sultanas chip in; **b21** ground to a halt on delivery just through old age, but there's still some fabulous life to be found. 50%. Douglas Laing. 566 bottles

Provenance Bunnahabhain Aged 7 Years Gabriel Meffre wine cask no. 3706, dist winter 99, bott summer 07 **(84.5) n21 t21.5 f21 b21.** Rosy, rounded and spiced. 46%. Douglas Laing.

Provenance Bunnahabhain Aged 8 Years refill hogshead cask no. 4073, dist 99, bott 07 **(89) n22.5** wonderful coastal kick: salty, sharp and bracing. No idea what warehouse it's come from – could have been one inland, who knows? But real Bunna character here; **t22.5** outstanding delivery with the malt fresh, and chiselled, it seems, from granite; salt and pepper follow through; **f22** more vanilla and early natural caramel, **b22** beautiful, lively, malt. 46%. nc ncf. Douglas Laing.

◌·ː· **Provenance Bunnahabhain Aged 9 Years** refill hogshead, dist winter 99, bott winter 08 **(79.5) n18.5 t20 f21 b20.** I have spent many a summer at Bunna. And from the early '80s got to know its whisky uncommonly well, at all ages and in all casks. It was never like this, though; a mixture of sweet, sticky barley and an assortment of vague off notes. 46%. Douglas Laing.

◌·ː· **Scotch Malt Whisky Society Cask 10.66 Aged 11 Years** refill hogshead, dist Aug 97 **(91) n23.5** a light, bonfire-esque smoky bacon signature leaves little doubt about the use of peat; still delicate enough for the subtly oaky backbone of liquorice and toasted hazelnut; **t23** sweet, malty, mildly olly and youthful delivery with a slow build up of smoky kippers; **f22** half-hearted spices make little impression of the peat and oak-led cocoa; **b22.5** this 10.66 is one in the eye for those who don't like smoky Bunnas: altogether now: "Westering Home with peat in the air...." 573%

◌·ː· **Scotch Malt Whisky Society Cask 10.67 Aged 11 Years** refill hogshead, dist Aug 97 **(82) n20.5 t20.5 f21 b20.** Another example of an indifferent cask doing nothing to help the malt. Thin, with only the peat holding this one together as the oak involvement is woefully sketchy. 59.9%

Signatory Vintage Peated Bunnahabhain 1997 cask no. 5355, dist 04 Dec 97, bott 04 Feb 08 **(69) n14 t19 f18 b18.** An escapee. A reject which got away, surely? The nose is a crash site. But the intensity of the peat makes for something palatable at least and compensates... at times impressively. 46%. 852 bottles.

The Single Malts of Scotland Bunnahabhain 1979 Aged 27 Years (76) n21 t19 f18 b18. A peculiarly furry beast with a good nose. 46%. sc. Speciality Drinks, UK.

◌·ː· **The Whisky Agency Bunnahabhain 32 Year Old** fino cask, dist 76, bott 08 **(92.5) n23** dry, nutty: mainly marzipan. Elegant, delicate; **t24** beautiful crystalline and delicate sweetness frames the salty barley; **f22.5** dries as the oak invades and the nuttiness returns; **b23** this is one very sophisticated dram. 53.7%. The Whisky Agency, Germany.

◌·ː· **The Whisky Agency Bunnahabhain 34 Year Old** dist 74, bott 08 **(96) n24** a salty coffee surround, but the core of the aroma is deepest, cleanest, oldest oloroso; **t24.5** the nose in flavour form: absolutely identical...but of glorious intensity; **f23.5** more oak here, as to be expected, and the coffee moves up a gear...as to be expected; pure textbook old oloroso matured; **b24** as magnificent and mighty as The Paps which looked down upon this whisky being made and matured... 59.3%. The Whisky Agency, Germany.

◌·ː· **The Whisky Agency Bunnahabhain 35 Year Old** dist 73, bott 08 **(78) n17 t21 f19 b21.** Tastes better than its noses, which is hardly difficult. 50.1%. The Whisky Agency, Germany.

The Whisky Fair Bunnahabhain Aged 29 Years bourbon hogshead, dist 77, bott 07 **(85) n23 t19 f22 b21.** Salt 'n' honey nose offers exceptional poise and charm but an uncomfortable landing on the palate with the oak not entirely in sync. 53%. Germany.

The Whisky Fair Bunnahabhain Aged 30 Years Artist Edition Bourbon hogshead, dist 77, bott 07 **(82.5) n21.5 t22 f19 b20.** An exotic fruit merchant. Short changes you on the complexity, though. *43%. Germany.*

CAOL ILA
Islay, 1846. Diageo. Working.

Caol Ila (Highland) 8 Years Old dist 97 db **(87) n22** massive oak injection for something so relatively young with the malt coming into a world of dry toast and cardboard dust. Good spices; **t22** mouth-filling barley of decent, juicy intensity at first; then surprisingly dry; **f21** the oils I had expected don't materialise and instead the spices zing; **b22** I remember tasting this when new make and being impressed and hopeful (both for its development and that they wouldn't make unpeated malt at Caol Ila too often!). Perhaps hasn't quite complexed out the way I had hoped. But no faulting its structure and depth. Scores higher on novelty than genuine thrills – but entirely enjoyable malt. *59.8%*

Caol Ila Aged 8 Years Unpeated Style dist 99, bott 07 db **(93.5) n23** beautifully delicate with the gentle chirruping of lemon so comfortable with the soft barley; **t24** magnificent delivery again with two distinct camps; rich barley and citrus. The two dovetail and pepper the tastebuds with eye watering freshness and a sharp, brittle character wonderfully devoid of the usual lumbering oils; **f23** long, with sly, complex ultra-high quality interplay between citrus, fresh barley and vanilla; **b23.5** oh well, here goes my reputation...honest opinion: on this evidence (backed by other samples over the years) Caol Ila makes better straight malt than it does the peated stuff. Sorry, peat lovers. This should be a, if not the, mainstay of the official Caol Ila portfolio. *64.9%*

⸬ **Caol Ila Aged 8 Years Unpeated Style** 1st fill bourbon, dist 00, bott 08 db **(91.5) n23** a touch maltier than the previous bottling; salty digestive biscuit; **t23** beautifully refreshing with a real puckering, salty tartness to the barley; I seem to remember citrus here last year. But this time we have butterscotch and toffee; **f22.5** long, very delicately oiled with the vanillas and toffee in decent harmony; **b23** a bit more of a pudding than last year's offering, but delicious dramming all the way. *64.2%*

Caol Ila Aged 12 Years db **(89) n23** a coastal, salty biting tang (please don't tell me this has been matured on the mainland!) with hints of rockpools and visions of rock pipits and oystercatchers among the seaweed; **t23** enormously oily, coating the palate with a mildly subdued smokiness and then a burst of gristy malt; **f21** caramel and oil; **b22** a telling improvement on the old 12-y-o with much greater expression and width. *43%*

Caol Ila Aged 18 Years db **(80) n21 t20 f19 b20.** Another improvement on the last bottling, especially with the comfortable integration of citrus. But still too much oil spoils the dram, particularly at the death. *43%*

Caol Ila 25 Years Old dist 78 db **(90) n24 t23 f21 b22.** A wonderful Caol Ila in so many respects: truly great. Yet another, like most it has to be said, that noses better than it tastes because of the massive oiliness. Still some genuine quality here, make no mistake. *59.4%*

Caol Ila 1979 db **(74) n20 t19 f17 b18.** So disappointing. I could go on about tropical fruit yada, yada, yada. Truth is, it just conks out under the weight of the oak. Too old. Simple as that. *58.6%*

Caol Ila Distillery Bottling bott May 07 db **(88) n24** a curious inflection to the nose makes for an un-Caol Ila-ish aroma. Something of the south-east coast to this one: both at once oily and dry. Strange...and rather beautiful... **t22** some thumping spices; the peat is a dry force trying to overcome the early sweet barley dominance; **f20** runs out of steam slightly balance-wise and bitters out as the oak and peat go their different ways; **b22** like most bottlings from this distillery, it's a dram that refuses to run a natural path. Never lives up to the nose, but still enough to delight Islay lovers. *58.4%*

⸬ **Caol Ila 'Distillery Only'** bott 07 **(95.5) n24** one of those coal dust and peat reek versions; **t24** gooseberries? With peat...? Wasn't sure if it was possible: trust me...it is! **f23.5** so long, so sweet, so wonderfully peated and the gristy barley gathers in intensity as the spices gather pace; **b24** Caol Ila is the third hardest distillery to get to in Scotland: however should you do so some time soon you can reward yourself by picking up a bottle of this. I can say honestly that the journey will be very much worthwhile... *58.4%. 5,000 bottles. Available only from the Caol Ila Distillery shop.*

Adelphi Caol Ila Aged 13 Years cask no. 9154, dist 93, bott 07 **(85) n23 t21 f20 b21.** Perhaps a touch too heavily oaked for total comfort. But the nose has the refined earthiness of a dank Surrey bluebell wood. *59.4%. Adelphi Distillery Ltd. 282 bottles.*

⸬ **A.D. Rattray Caol Ila 1995** cask no. 10035 **(92) n24** breathtakingly attractive and complex:delicate portions of salt, smoke and apple blossom mix charmingly; **t23.5** absolutely brilliant: not a hint of oil on delivery, allowing the gristier barley notes to shine; the smoke is almost a distant rumble of thunder; **f21.5** the oak begins to bitter out; late oils form and the vanilla punctuates the smoke frequently; **b23** the nose and delivery is pure textbook. 60.4%

⫶ **Alchemist Caol Ila Aged 10 Years** dist Oct 96, bott Sep 07 **(85) n21.5 t21 f21.5 b21.** Silky and lazily smoked, appears even younger than its relatively tender years. 46%. nc, ncf. The Alchemist Beverage Co.

Berrys' Own Selection Caol Ila 1982 cask nos. 727/8 **(85) n21 t22 f21 b21.** Deliciously sweet, fat... and a little flat maybe. 46%

Berry's Own Selection Caol Ila 1991 cask nos. 486/487, bott 07 **(93) n23** that rare beast: a Caol Ila that's multi-stratum in the peat department: excellent complexity; **t23** hard and hot with enough late, citrussy sharpness to the barley to make for rounded experience; **f23** long and well layered coffee and smoke and even a spoonful of demerara to keep it going; **b24** one of the few Caol Ilas this year to really get my pulse racing. 51.8%.

Berry's Own Selection Caol Ila 1991 bott 07 **(88) n21** attractive smoke fails to cover the thinness of the malt; **t23** entirely different on delivery with a honeyed thread helping to add weight as well as charm to the rich smoke and butterscotch middle; wonderful layering; **f22** more of the same but dries with a sawdusty, bourbony-vanilla charm; **b22** some serious lustre to this bottling. 46%

⫶ **Berry's Own Selection Caol Ila 1995** bott 08 **(93) n23** anthracite and peat mix in an ash-dry heavenly manner; **t24** really outstanding weight to the delivery: the smoke has a lot to say, but doesn't shout; the sub-barley notes are of the juiciest variety and the oak offers some red liquorice to the table: a real soup of malt with the dryness and sweetness inter-twining to magnificent effect; **f23** gentle, oily smoky butterscotch; dries as the ashes return and the vanillas kick in; **b23** now that's the way a Caol Ila of this age should behave... 58.9%. Berry Bros & Rudd.

Berry's' Own Selection Caol Ila 1996 Aged 10 Years (94) n23 with its hints of apple and celery, this pretty subtle by Caol Ila standards; even a touch of the gristy Port Ellens about it. Spooky; **t24** beautifully delivered peat on a base of sugared black pepper. This is so big for this distillery, but also just so mercurial; **f23** long, remains lush and the slow development of the cocoa is pure tease; **b24** so often the malt from this distillery passes my heart by. Excellent blending malt, usually, but a bit of a plodder in the glass. Here Dougie McIvor has pulled a stunner out of the hat. A must have collector's item for those who want to wallow in ultra delicate and complex Islays. 57%. Berry Bros & Rudd.

Bladnoch Forum Range Caol Ila Aged 16 Years hogshead, cask no. 3869, dist 11 Mar 91, bott 28 Jun 07 **(86.5) n21.5 t22.5 f21 b21.5.** From the farmyard school of peaty whisky this is big stuff eschewing the normal oily style but boasting an almost rummy sugary-flintiness at times. 59%. ncf. Bladnoch Forum.

Cadenhead's Caol Ila Aged 16 Years bourbon, dist 91, bott May 07 **(84) n20 t22 f21 b21.** Another Caol Ila this season which hasn't quite got its all-round act together. Plenty of smoke but lacking fire when it comes to complexity. 46%. 360 bottles.

Cadenhead's Caol Ila Aged 17 Years dist 91, bott Feb 08 **(85.5) n22 t22.5 f19.5 b21.5.** Dry, rasping malt. Excellent complexity but a less than sympathetic cask has curtailed the class. 53.4%. 338 bottles.

Cadenhead's Caol Ila Aged 17 Years dist 91, bott Feb 08 **(89) n22** very similar to the 53.4% bottling – doubtless twins – but perhaps an almost imperceptible fraction of extra body and honey; **t23** sweet, honeyed start with the peat arriving in elegant waves; **f22** some toffee notes mingle comfortably with the peat; **b22** it is amazing what a good quality cask can do to a whisky. Taste this beside Cadenhead's 53.4% and see what I mean... 55.4%. 361 bottles.

Cadenhead's Authentic Collection Caol Ila Aged 22 Years bourbon hogshead, dist 84, bott Feb 07 **(92) n22** drier than the Bible belt of America... **t24** bursts into an immediate sweet rhapsody that entirely defies the nose; the smoke is shovelled on thick, but the barley retains the upper hand; **f23** long, lovely mocha and reverting to dry; **b23** ultra complex? Hardly. Something I've never come across before? Most probably not. A genuinely well made whisky that has matured as well as might be expected for its age and makes all the right noises? Most certainly. 55.5%. Cadenhead's. 246 bottles.

Cadenhead's Authentic Collection Caol Ila Aged 23 Years bourbon hogshead, dist 84, bott Sep 07 **(89) n22.5** peaty but no hint of ostentation and the drier oaks make their mark; **t22.5** an immediate wave of spice arrives with the smoke, but it's all well-balanced, gentle stuff; varying vanillas try to gain control but back down as the malt re-emerges; **f22** custardy with waves of cocoa and spiced smoke; **b22** delicate and boasting some impressive strata, this is the other side of the coin to the Whisky Society's 23-y-o for example. 56.3%. 258 bottles.

Cask Strength Caol Ila 1995 (77) n19 t21 f18 b19. Strangely lethargic and a pinch of bitterness on nose and finish. 57.6%. Gordon & MacPhail

Chester Whisky & Liqueur Co. Caol Ila Aged 13 Years dist 95 **(84) n22 t21.5 f20 b20.5.** Excellent ashy dryness to the smoky nose and soft oils on delivery. *50.6%*

Chieftain's Caol Ila Aged 12 Years hogshead **(77) n19 t20 f19 b19.** Pleasant and plodding in its own way, but has little to say. *43%. Ian Macleod.*

Chieftain's Caol Ila 12 Years Old Rum Finish (83) n22 t20 f20 b21. Slightly too oily and thick to fully take advantage of the proffered rum influence. But the peat is more polished than it might be. *46%. Ian Macleod.*

Chieftain's Caol Ila 17 Years Old Chateau la Nerthe finish, dist April 90 **(86.5) n21 t23 f21 b21.5.** Whenever a whisky plops into your glass showing a strange orangey-pink hue, the Pavlovian gene in me starts to twitch and goes on sulphur alert. Here, though, my fears were ill-founded. This is pretty good stuff with the fruits at times finding it difficult to find a home, but the overall mouth-watering qualities are delightful in tandem with the un-oiled peat. *48%. nc ncf. Ian Macleod.*

Chieftain's Caol Ila 24 Years Old hogshead, dist Apr 84 **(89.5) n24** brilliant! A wonderful mixture of very deeply cut, high density peat reek offers that farmyard manure edge, sweetened by a light gristiness; **t23** punchy, juicy, spicy and big; the sweetness is of the sugared rather than honeyed variety; **f21** vanilla and fading smoke; **b22.5** the guys at Ian Macleod must have been sitting on this one with a little smile on their faces. Great mischief and fun on nose and delivery. By the way: anyone who has ever made or cleared out a peat fire will be touched by this one. *48%. nc ncf. Ian Macleod Distillers.*

Connoisseurs Choice Caol Ila 1993 (81) n21 t20 f21 b19. The nip and bite to the nose is hardly matched by the supine, oily delivery to the palate. *40%.*

Connoisseurs Choice Caol Ila 1994 (72) n17 t19 f18 b18. Misses the target: just never feels right either on nose or palate. *40%. Gordon & MacPhail.*

Connoisseurs Choice Caol Ila 1995 (91.5) n23.5 gristy, excellent sweet-dry balance to the smoke; **t22** touches of citrus help break up the peaty dominance; **f23** clean, minimal oils and chalky oaks; still the citrus-peat combination works superbly; **b23** I have been drinking Connoisseurs Choice Caol Ila since the days when the stuff in the bottle came from the original distillery which, I'm afraid, rather dates me. But I have to say, that this brand always seems to get the most out of this malt. Another excellent bottling. *40%. Gordon & MacPhail.*

The Coopers Choice Caol Ila 1991 Aged 16 Years (85) n21 t22 f21 b21. Clean, pleasant and surprisingly undemanding for a 16-y-o. Good gristy sweetness throughout. *46%. sc ncf. The Vintage Malt Whisky Co.*

Demijohn Caol Ila 1991 Single Malt (91) n23 superb and unlikely balance between the deftest vanilla and dolloped-on peat; **t23** stilted sweetness, first heading towards grist, then thicker oiled and back to much softer grist again; **f22** long, a touch lethargic; **b23** tip top Caol Ila at its gristiest. *46%. Demijohn Ltd, UK.*

Dewar Rattray Caol Ila 1984 cask no. 1358, dist Mar 84, bott Nov 07 **(89.5) n23** some people swear blind this is a low to middle ranking malt in peat intensity. Yeah? Nose this, then... **t23.5** wall to wall peat, helped along by a massive Demerara kick; the oils join later than usual; **f21** delicate, if a little oily; **b22** oiled up and full of big, chewy, personality. Excellent stuff. *58%*

Dewar Rattray Cask Collection Caol Ila Aged 22 Years cask no. 6264, dist 12 Dec 84, bottled 25 Jun 07 **(89.5) n24** peat reek and coal cinders; a genuinely impressive marriage between oak vanilla and smoke with none of the usual obscuring by oil which often blights this distillery as a single malt. Excellent; **t21** the oak is not slow to come forward but is slowly driven off by the sweet citrusy barley: juicy with the peat present but not all-powerful; **f22.5** Swiss roll-type jam reveals the age and some late oils turn up at the death; **b22** an above average Caol Ila which offers much more complexity than you might expect from this distillery. A true gentle giant which does show a touch of creaking age, but more than compensated for by the brilliance of the nose. *57.7%. 221 bottles for Willow Park, Calgary.*

Dun Bheagan Caol Ila Aged 15 Years hogshead, dist Jun 93 **(86.5) n22.5 t22 f21 b21.** From the slightly slithery, oily school of Caol Ila. The dry nose and sharp delivery are a treat, though. *50%. Ian Macleod Distillers Ltd.*

Dun Bheagan Caol Ila 16 Years Old Medoc finish, dist March 91 **(82) n20 t21 f20 b21.** Pleasant and easy going, but, if anything, rather too clean and sanitised. What's up, Medoc..? *46%. nc ncf. Ian Macleod.*

Duncan Taylor Collection Caol Ila 1981 cask no. 2932 **(91) n22.5** clinker and peat ash mix; **t23** eye-closingly delightful delivery of sweet, gristy peat and ultra-intense barley; spices slowly stack up as the oak invades; **f22.5** long, wonderfully oil-free with a fabulous denouemont of kumquat and lemon amid the soft mocha and smoke; **b23** this year has seen the best releases for a long time of lightly- or un-oiled Caol Ila and this is among the finest. *53.8%*

⁜ **Duncan Taylor Collection Caol Ila 1982** cask no. 2736 **(91) n22** evening primroses amid the peat; **t23** the fabulous sweet and lush phenols counter the drier oaks with aplomb; **f22.5** spicy, soft and with some excellent custard tart to balance the ashier peats; **b23.5** very complex and excellently balanced. 55.4%

⁜ **Duncan Taylor Collection Caol Ila 1982** cask no. 2741 **(84) n20.5 t21 f21.5 b21.** Full-flavoured. But never less than sharp and hot. 55.9%

⁜ **Duthies Caol Ila 13 Years Old (90.5) n23** ridiculously young and gristy: even a touch of the Port Ellens at 10 years old here, but without the body; **t23** sweeter and smokier than a smoked sweet thing; **f22** makes the most of the gentle oils to further the cause of lightly smoked sugar cane; **b22.5** young and green (in every sense) for its age. But a sweet, refreshing delight. 46%. Springbank Distillers for Germany.

⁜ **Exclusive Casks Caol Ila 1980 Aged 28 Years** American oak **(92) n23.5** for its age, exceptional: wonderful, earthy, evening hedgerows and garden. There really is cowslip and farmyards at play: pastoral; **t24** excellent sweet and sharp delivery, some really astonishing clarity to the juicy barley for a malt of this age; oils up for the middle; **f22** vanilla and cocoa slip through the oiliness; **b22.5** you never quite know what you are going to get from this distillery. This one's a winner. 50.5%. Chester Whisky & Liqeur Co

⁜ **Hart Brothers Caol Ila Aged 11 Years** dist Aug 96, bott Jun 08 **(84.5) n21.5 t21 f21 b21.** A quiet dram, happy to rumble along with gentle peat and dry vanilla. 46%. Hart Brothers Limited.

Kingsbury Celtic Series Caol Ila 22 Years Old 1984 (91) n23.5 t23 f21.5 b23. An unusual style of CI with the emphasis almost entirely on the dry peat, something not often found today. Confession time: in the summer of 1984, I actually made love on the hills just above the distillery, breathing in the steam from the mash that floated up above and drinking the malt that had been made at the previous distillery before it had been rebuilt. Forever the romantic, I wondered, just as a father wonders about his child yet to be born, how the whisky below with its new stills would fare. Now I know... 55.1%. nc ncf. Japan Import System Co. Ltd.

⁜ **Kingsbury's Caol Ila 1984 24 Years** Old Cask Strength **(92) n23.5** outstandingly clean nose for its age: wonderful coke and peat mix to the smoke but still retaining green shoots of sweet barley; the oak is specific and shows great clarity on the vanilla; **t23.5** beautifully bitter-sweet, showing just the right amount of oaky age-wear. The peat is deft and very lightly oiled; **f23** strains of butterscotch accompany the long delicately smoked finale; **b22.5** classy little cask. 53.2% Japan Import System.

⁜ **Kingsbury's Finest & Rarest Caol Ila 1982 (90.5) n23** smoky bacon crisps; a wonderfully nagging nip to the phenols; **t23** assertive and sharp. The barley appears to send short, sweet blasts of grassiness independently of the rampaging smoke: some trick; **f22** salivating to the end, for all the best attention of drying vanillas; **b22.5** another tip-top Caol Ila from Kingbury. 58.9%. Japan Import System.

Kingsbury "The Selection" Caol Ila 6 Years Old 2000 (85) n21 t22 f21.5 b21.5. Not as peaty as you might expect, allowing the grassy citrusy notes full voice. Charming. And perhaps one of the most refreshing drams of the year! 43.0%. nc ncf. Japan Import System Co. Ltd.

Murray McDavid Mission Caol Ila 1984 gold series, bourbon/grenache Vincent Le Grand **(91) n24** perhaps the ultimate seaside rock pool experience in a whisky glass. You half expect to see a starfish and sea urchin in the glass; **t22** as is so often the case with wine casks, the peat is backed into a corner and shy; mainly fruit, the smoke is tight and nervous; **f23** relaxes as the fruit recedes, the vanillas shine and the peat returns in respectable but, crucially, un-oiled waves; **b22** the big question is: is it an Islay or a French rock pool? I'm sure this is near the Singing Sands... 54.1%

Murray McDavid Caol Ila 1991 Aged 16 Years bourbon/mourvedre **(70) n17 t18 f17 b18.** Really a mess. The dreaded S word at work, it appears. 46%

Norse Cask Selection Caol Ila 1991 Aged 16 Years hogshead cask no. 3871, dist 91, bott Aug 07 **(93) n23** dry, dusty peat ash with some of the inherent lemon notes drifting through; **t24** salty, sharp citrus kick, then a slow smoky development; some stunning mocha is about for the middle but first has to overcome some stinging spice; **f22.5** dry and wonderfully well weighted with more cocoa notes dominating; **b23.5** one of the best Caol Ilas I have come across for a long time. Devoid of that limiting oiliness which usually does it so much damage on the complexity front, this has enough about it for the real Caol Ila to come through, citrus and all. Wonderful. 59.2%. nc ncf. Qualityworld, Denmark. 288 bottles.

Old & Rare Caol Ila Aged 28 Years dist Feb 79, bott Sep 07 **(90) n22** much more coal smoke than peat on this; **t23** massive spice on delivery, a real sweet, buzzing intro to the barley and then a few waves of citrus; the sweetness is diluted golden syrup and lightly smoked barley grist; **f22** fades to good effect, but a touch of toffee smothers things a little;

b23 this was my 900th whisky for this edition and it hasn't let me down, finish apart. Loads of character from a relatively lightly peated version. *54.2%. Douglas Laing, exclusively for The Whisky Shop, Edinburgh. 261 bottles.*

Old & Rare Caol Ila Aged 28 Years dist Feb 79, bott Mar 07 **(93) n24** salty but the peats have structure and variations. Complex; **t23** big spice delivery and uplifting citrus notes abound. None of the usual oils, so the gristy nature is unearthed; the vanillas complement, the spices attack like Port Askaig hotel midges.; **f22** medium length with spices and smoked vanilla; **b24** great to see a CA with this kind of attitude. One of the rare un-oily versions and worth investigating for its delicate but unrestricted beauty. A recent Caol Ila classic. *54.6%. Douglas Laing. 272 bottles.*

⋰ **Old Malt Cask Caol Ila Aged 12 Years** dist Sep 96, bott Jul 09 **(88) n22** pepper, smoky style; **t22** soft at first, then ker-pow-fizz...!! Those peppers on the nose bite... **f22** smoky and sweet; **b22** sweet, but with attitude. *50%. Douglas Laing.*

Old Malt Cask Caol Ila Aged 12 Years refill butt no. 4104, dist Sep 95, bott Jan 08 **(86) n21.5 t22 f21 b21.5.** Lots of smoke and gristy sweetness but limited oak balance for its age. *50%. Douglas Laing. 743 bottles.*

Old Malt Cask Caol Ila Aged 12 Years refill hogshead, cask no. 4445, dist Feb 96, bott Jun 08 **(91) n23** one of the rare occasions when I picked up a CI and thought, absent-mindedly, that this was from the original old distillery rather than the rebuild: dry, a little cranky and brimming with pagoda-roofed possibilities....; **t22.5** sweet delivery on one level, much drier and bounding with silky peat on a deeper; the two meet towards the middle as the complexity starts to take off; **f22** gentle undulations of smoke and oak; **b23.5** oh, if only all Caol Ilas were like this! *50%. Douglas Laing. 340 bottles.*

Old Malt Cask Caol Ila Aged 17 Years dist Mar 90, bott Mar 07 **(83) n20 t22 f20 b21.** Some grizzle and attitude, but just a shade on the oily side. *50%. 365 bottles.*

Old Malt Cask Caol Ila Aged 17 Years rum barrel no. 3807, dist Mar 90, bott Aug 07 **(86) n21 t23 f21 b21.** Very drinkable with the peat clear, crisp and clean. Lovely stuff. *50%. Douglas Laing. 243 bottles.*

Old Malt Cask Caol Ila Aged 17 Years rum barrel, cask no. 3898, dist Mar 90, bott Sep 07 **(84.5) n20 t22 f21.5 b21.** Well spiced, clean, standard fare. *50%. Douglas Laing. 182 bottles.*

Old Malt Cask Caol Ila Aged 17 Years claret wine barrel, cask no. 4055, dist Mar 90, bott Dec 07 **(73) n18 t20 f17 b18.** It's not that often you get sulphur bringing down massive peat...!! *44.1%. Douglas Laing.*

⋰ **Old Malt Cask Caol Ila Aged 19 Years** claret finish, bott 09 **(82) n20 t21 f21.5 b20.5** For a cask finish, especially wine, to work well, the barley, oak and fruit have to somehow integrate to reach a harmony. It is always more much difficult when big peat is thrown in the mix. This one shows you just how difficult it can be. *50%. Douglas Laing.*

Old Malt Cask Caol Ila Aged 21 Years dist Apr 85, bott Jan 07 **(84) n21 t22 f20 b21.** The oak has leapt in here and made some bitter marmalade statements. A touch of salt and docile smoke: seems older than its 21 years. *50%. Douglas Laing. 327 bottles.*

⋰ **Old Malt Cask Caol Ila Aged 25 Years** refill hogshead, dist Jan 84, bott Apr 09 **(84) n21.5 t22 f20 b20.5.** Attractively floral in part and well weighted. But showing distinct sign of fatigue. *50%. Douglas Laing. 309 bottles.*

Old Malt Cask Caol Ila Aged 27 Years bourbon barrel, cask no. 3896, dist Nov 79, bott Sep 07 **(86) n22 t22.5 f20 b21.5.** Quite lovely malt, not least because it heroically does its best to overcome the creaking of the cask. One of the few Caol Ilas around to show a sea-weedy, coastal quality, but time catches up with it in the end. *50%. nc ncf. Douglas Laing. 240 bottles.*

⋰ **Old Malt Cask Caol Ila Aged 29 Years** refill hogshead, dist Feb 79, bott Aug 08 **(93) n24** a rare case of where delicate smoke and exotic fruit combine; the label offers age and the nose dishes it out but showing style every step of the way; **t23.5** every bit as soft as the nose, possibly more so; those exotic fruits are persistent early on before the ashy phenols make their mark; some elegant liquorice adds weight and age; **f22.5** now really has dried out but remains intact with no negative notes from the assembling oak **b23** melts on the nose and mouth and shows that even big Islays like this can be purring, graceful pussycats even after the best part of three decades. A classic. *50%. Douglas Laing. 238 bottles.*

Old Masters Caol Ila Aged 12 Years dist 95, bott Jul 08 **(87.5) n22.5** bulldozing peat; **t22** the smoke thumps home without too much thought...wonderful! **f21.5** house-style oils arrive and spread a bit of sweetness before the bitter oak cuts in; **b21.5** about as subtle as a punch in the chops. If you are looking for structure and delicate tendencies, forget it. If it's peat you want... *59.8%. James MacArthur & Co. Ltd.*

⋰ **Old Masters Caol Ila Aged 13 Years** cask no. 10046, dist 95, bott 08 **(92) n23.5** wonderful sweet/dry sibling battle on the peaty side; **t22.5** the sugars arrive first making a friendly landing site for the weighty ashy smoke which follows; **f23** long, peat-laden vanilla and still those playful sweet-drier notes interplay; **b23** a quite beautifully constructed malt. 59.8%. James MacArthur & Co. Ltd.

Old Masters Caol Ila Aged 25 Years cask no. 731, dist 82, bott 07 **(94) n23** an avalanche of smoke with much oak caught in its path; **t23** buzzing, zippy spices that enliven the peat but fall respectfully quiet when the coffee and flecks of raspberry jam arrive; the subtlety of the sweetness is divine; **f24** glorious finish with layer upon layer of complex oak showing its feminine side: the coffee remains soft, the smoke understated and the texture is textbook; **b24** this is Caol Ila at its very best. 55.5%.

⋙ **Old Masters Caol Ila Aged 26 Years** cask no. 733, dist 82, bott 08 **(86) n22.5 t21.5 f21 b21.** Some lovely lavender mingles charmingly with the smoke on the nose, but a big thrust of natural caramel limits the complexity of the salty but gentle palate. 55.2%. James MacArthur & Co. Ltd.

Premier Barrel Caol Ila Aged 9 Years (84.5) n21.5 t22 f21 b20. Enjoyable, ultra simplistic malt from a well used cask. Might have profited from being cask strength in order to really pump up and exploit those juicier notes. 46%. Douglas Laing.

Provenance Caol Ila Aged 8 Years dist winter 98, bott winter 07 **(88) n20** hmmm: not great but the uninterrupted, oakless smoke lets you know you are in for something unusual...; **t23** quite gorgeous arrival with spot on oils helping to fix the salivating barley to every quarter of the palate; the smoke builds and builds in weight; **f23** very long, with nothing quite so boring as oak to get in the way: just the slow disappearance of smoke into the horizonless background; **b22** another warts-and-all bottling from a well used cask (to put it mildly) — and you can only applaud its naked beauty. 46%. Douglas Laing.

Provenance Caol Ila Aged 10 Years refill barrel no. 4297, dist spring 98, bott spring 08 **(86.5) n20 t22.5 f22 b22.** Plenty of chocolate to keep the smoke company. A bit flat in part, nose especially, but a chewy cove that'll entertain the tastebuds more than enough. Decent sweetness throughout. 46%. nc ncf. Douglas Laing.

⋙ **Provenance Caol Ila Aged 11 Years** dist Sep 97, bott Jul 09 **(89.5) n23** clean and in perfectly smoky order; **t22** simplistic maybe, but the sweetness to smoke ratio is superb; **f22.5** the lack of usual oils from this distillery allow the vanilla, citrus and smoke each to have separate personalities; **b22** a spot on cask. 46%. Douglas Laing.

⋙ **Provenance Caol Ila Aged 11 Years** refill hogshead, dist summer 97, bott winter 09 **(88) n23** wonderful complexity to the smoke alone· works on both sweet and dry levels; **t22** a touch of oil, but enough to ensure the barley has a say in proceedings and the slightly sugary word is spread; **f21** bitters out slightly; **b22** sweet and delicious 46%. Douglas Laing.

Scotch Malt Whisky Society Cask 53.104 Aged 13 Years refill butt, dist Jul 93 **(86) n22 t21 f22 b21.** Faultless Caol Ila, clean, decently peated, sweet and a tad gristy. Lovely, but perhaps missing that vital spark. 61.3%

Scotch Malt Whisky Society Cask 53.113 Aged 11 Years refill hogshead, dist Mar 96 **(88) n22 t23 f21 b22** Rather excellent despite having enough oil for Bush to send the troops in to secure the distillery from perceived tyrannical forces... 60.7%

⋙ **Scotch Malt Whisky Society Cask 53.128 Aged 19 Years** refill hogshead, dist Dec 89 **(91) n22.5** attractive, but some oak nip unsettles the otherwise embedded peat; **t23** big custard tart and the inevitable silky smoke and gentle bite: a very handsome combination; **f22.5** the sweetness continues with some intriguing marzipan getting in amid the chocolate-smoke; **b23** a high quality malt that is confident and comfortable with itself. 56.1%

⋙ **Scotch Malt Whisky Society Cask 53.129 Aged 19 Years** refill hogshead, dist Dec 89 **(88.5) n23.5** fabulous quasi-bourbony depth to the smoke; the profound saltiness also lifts this above the norm; **t22** again the oaks punch hard, but the silky oils act as a buffer; delicate sweet, grassy barley thread to the smoke; some cocoa in towards the late middle; **f21** bitters out a little too enthusiastically; **b22** doesn't quite end with the same panache as it starts, but still a good 'un. 55.2%

⋙ **Scotch Malt Whisky Society Cask 53.130 Aged 9 Years** refill hogshead, dist Nov 99 **(90) n23.5** much more flaky smoke: drier, less oily, more ashy than the old Caol Ila style; **t21.5** nips and bites, not least because of the extraordinary alcoholic strength, but the peat is always to the fore (not always the case with this distillery) and accentuated; **f22.5** one of the driest Caol Ila finishes I have encountered in bottled form. Invariably there is a cocoa powder dusting to this; **b22.5** Caol Ila. But few of you would recognise it if tasted blind. The peated George T Stagg of the whisky world.... 68.2%

⋙ **Scotch Malt Whisky Society Cask 53.131 Aged 9 Years** refill hogshead, dist Nov 99 **(83) n21 t20 f21 b21.** Take away the big alcohol kick and it's just a little too plain and ordinary: not a patch on it's twin cask 53.130. 67.9%

⠿ **The Scotch Single Malt Circle Caol Ila 1982** cask no. 2724, dist Apr 82, bott Oct 08 **(94) n23.5** two pronged: from one side comes a distinctly, grey, ashy, dead peat fire; from the other a fizzing barley, sweet, salivating monster...; **t24** eye-watering delivery, and it's not about the strength: the barley is sharp and piercing: first blood to the monster. The waves are sweet and relentless until the middle is reached. Milky Way candy bar meets that ashy element and all is sweetness and dust; **f23** elegant, peaceful and refined it may be, but by comparison with what's gone before this, relatively drab as the peated vanillas fade; **b23.5** hardly one for those with a heart condition. Big, rousing. Beautifully made and matured.And bloody delicious. *62.7%. German market.*

⠿ **Scott's Selection Caol Ila 1982** bott 08 **(86) n23 t21.5 f21 b21.** The nose gets top billing where the smoke churns out with a sweet, Madeira cake twist. The remainder, though, is reduced by tired, burnt, toasty oak. *60.6%. Speyside Distillers.*

⠿ **Scott's Selection Caol Ila 1982** bott 08 **(76.5) n20 t19.5 f18 b19.** Oily and austere, despite the smoke and strength. *61.2%. Speyside Distillers.*

Scott's Selection Caol Ila 1984 bott 07 **(78) n18 t22 f17 b19.** The nose baffled me for a bit: it was something I had come across before. Then it clicked – rainy or wet patches in a leaking Islay warehouse. Not exactly how things should be and the finish confirms that not all is tickety-boo. *54.1%*

The Single Malts of Scotland Caol Ila 1991 Aged 16 Years bott Sep 07 **(90) n23** dry peat with diced plain chocolate added into it; **t23** seriously big with the peat threatening early, as does the oil, but both back off to allow a salty, vanilla and citrus sub-plot to develop; **f22.5** the cocoa promised on the nose arrives in style; **b22.5** complex, genuinely well balanced and enticing. *57.5%. Speciality Drinks.*

The Single Malts of Scotland Caol Ila 1991 Aged 16 Years (90) n22 clean, softly oiled peat, nosing a lot younger than its age; **t23** attractive early oak involvement restricted to thick vanilla, soon overcome but soon met head on by a wonderful injection of juicy barley; **f22** gorgeous barley continues, with some unfurling butterscotch on the smoke; **b23** way above average for this distillery thanks, mainly, to its lightness of touch with the salivating barley. *57.9%.*

The Single Malts of Scotland Caol Ila 1982 Aged 25 Years bott Sep 07 **(91.5) n20.5** exhausted in part: only the peat is keeping this intact; **t23.5** just hold on...whoa...! I was expecting a sappy greeting. Instead I am met at the door by gloriously courteous citrus and peats, neither of which are happy to entirely take the lead, but the smoke does eventually through weight alone; the oak offers a vanilla backdrop while some natural caramels provide the chewy extra depth; **f23** long, with some buzzing spice and cocoa; the sweetness develops through a maple syrup link and lasts to the death; **b25** astounding: rarely do you get a nose which sends out such clear signals, then an experience on the palate which contradicts almost completely. This is great Caol Ila. But for the nose, a possible award-winner. *54.7%. Speciality Drinks.*

⠿ **The Whisky Agency Caol Ila 26 Year Old** dist 82, bott 09 **(85.5) n21 t22 f21 b21.5.** Softly oiled, lightly smoked and very pleasant without ever bothering about complexity. *63%. The Whisky Agency, Germany.*

⠿ **The Whisky Agency Caol Ila 27 Year Old** dist 82, bott 09 **(87) n21** sooty: as much coal dust as there is peat reek; **t23** sharp, eye-watering, juicy barley pierces the softer, sleepier smoke; **f21** a slight off note towards the finish, as though the oak isn't too happy; **b22** this one was probably on the way down and was plucked from the cask in the nick of time. Some great moments, but a few dodgy ones too. *62.4%. The Whisky Agency, Germany.*

⠿ **The Whisky Agency Caol Ila 27 Year Old** Rum Finish dist 82, bott 09 **(80.5) n20 t21 f19.5 b20.** A disappointingly tart, closed and very average bottling from this normally first-class bottler. *50%. The Whisky Agency, Germany.*

Whisky-Doris Caol Ila Aged 16 Years bourbon cask, dist 15 Jan 91, bott 1 Feb 07 **(88) n21** big, yet thin: strange... **t23** juicy malt with some serious bite amid the lemon curd tart and smoke; **f22** long, silky and still that lingering touch of citrus to the smoke; **b22** beautifully made, big-hearted Islay. *57.4%. Germany. 115 bottles.*

⠿ **Whisky Doris Caol Ila 1992** dist 92, bott 09 **(85.5) n22 t21 f21.5 b21.** A very pleasant, medium- sweet and safe Caol Ila which doesn't overly depend on its natural oils and accentuates some gristy qualities. *46%*

The Whisky Fair Caol Ila Aged 22 Years sherry hogshead, dist 84, bott 07 **(73) n19 t19 f17 b18.** Sometimes sherry (especially poor sherry) and peat don't mix. Like here. Not bad farmyardy nose, though. *55.9%. Germany.*

The Whisky Fair Caol Ila Aged 23 Years bourbon, dist 84, bott 07 **(92) n23** dry peat, beautifully crisp with a touch of hickory; **t23** seriously intense, again dry with the peat showing full respect to the oaky vanilla; clean and with a seriously appealing bitter-sweet personality; **f22** a touch of coffee and demerara sugar to the lingering smoke and oak **b24** an excellent bottling devoid of the usual spoiling oiliness. Not overly complex in variety of flavours, but certainly in the way they are delivered. *55.9%. Germany.*

The Whisky Fair Caol Ila 26 Year Old bourbon hogshead, dist May 79 **(88) n22 t23 f22 b21.** A remarkable malt: my guess is that you have a barely used first-fill bourbon barrel at work here. The results are near unique. *57.2%. Germany. 212 bottles.*

The Whisky Society Caol Ila 1984 Aged 23 Years bott Sep 07 **(84.5) n21.5 t22 f20 b21.** Enjoyable dramming, but really doesn't show or even begin to hint at the great age it has achieved. *57%. Speciality Drinks.*

Wilson & Morgan Barrel Selection Caol Ila 18 Years Old Cask Strength dist 89, bott 07 **(85) n21 t22 f21 b21.** A pleasant if perfunctory Islay showing the occasional neat touch. *53.2%*

⋄⋅⋅ **Wilson & Morgan Barrel Selection Caol Ila Aged 20 Years** dist 88, bott 08 **(76) n19 t20 f18 b19.** You know that grating sound when the bagpipes first start up? Yep, as off key as that... *46%*

Wilson & Morgan Barrel Selection Caol Ila 23 Years Old dist 84, bott 07 **(82) n21 t21.5 f19 b20.5** Hard not to believe that this isn't related in some way to the Whisky Society bottling of the same age. Not quite so sweet. *46%*

⋄⋅⋅ **Wilson & Morgan barrel Selection Caol Ila 1995** refill butt, bott 08 **(87) n22** floral with trace smoke at the most delicate, almost puniest level; **t22.5** the phenols, bizarrely, are the first to show, offering a hint of camp coffee; salty; **f21** rather typically fades and bitters as the oak takes command; **b21.5** for those who like their peat to tease them.. *46%*

Wilson & Morgan Barrel Selection Caol Ila 1996 bott 08 **(79.5) n20.5 t21 f19 b19.** A old cask filled for blending has somehow turned up as a single malt. *48%*

Wilson & Morgan Barrel Selection Caol Ila 1996 Limited Edition bott 07 **(86) n21 t23 f20 b22.** A sleepy and docile nose is rocked back by the fabulously explosive delivery. The bitter finish is out of keeping but hold on to something tightly when you take your first, fantastic, mouthful! *48%*

CAPERDONICH
Speyside, 1898. Chivas. Silent.

Cadenhead's Chairman's Stock Caperdonich Aged 27 Years bourbon hogshead, dist 80, bott Jun 08 **(76.5) n20 t20 f18.5 b18.** Something of the wallpaper glue about this one. *56.8%. 264 bottles.*

Duncan Taylor Collection Caperdonich 1968 cask no. 2608 **(86.5) n22 t22 f21 b21.5.** I don't believe it! 56% at 40-years-old! Well, yes it's true. And this Victor Meldrew of a malt, curmudgeonly, cantankerous and fiery despite having one foot in the grave, still has some style, albeit bourbony, despite the flat cap-ing finale. *56%*

Duncan Taylor Collection Caperdonich 1968 cask no. 2616 **(89) n22** polished oak with hints of hickory and crisp barley; **t23** mountainous oak, but scaled sublimely by the most deft malt fashioned with a touch of barley sugar; **f22** the soft sugars remain, keeping at bay the encroaching burnt, toasty oak. All played out with a degree of sophistication; **b22** a touch of quiet class. *56.3%.*

⋄⋅⋅ **Duncan Taylor Collection Caperdonich 1970** cask no. 4376 **(84.5) n22 t21.5 f21 b20.** A drowsy ride along barley sewn on oaky ground. *42.3%*

⋄⋅⋅ **Duncan Taylor Collection Caperdonich 1970** cask no. 4377 **(86.5) n21.5 t22.5 f21.5 b21.** Punchier, weightier, tellingly more intense than 4376 and for a while a real malty treat. But still the complexity is at a premium and we are finding Caper at its most simplistic and undemanding, taking into account the whisky's great age. Some flakes of chocolate do help at the end. *45.9%*

⋄⋅⋅ **Duncan Taylor Collection Caperdonich 1970** cask no. 4381 **(82.5) n20 t21 f21.5 b20.** Some sharp barley and waxy vanilla, but you get the feeling this was once a hot whisky, which may explain the limited development on its sister casks. *46.8%*

Duncan Taylor Collection Caperdonich 1972 cask no. 3246 **(94) n24** a Pacific fruit cocktail with a small shake of oaky allspice on the mashed banana and passion fruit; **t23** busy delivery with the oak threatening then lying low as the barley garners all the eclectic fruit it can find; **f24** really classy with a vanilla drying out the barley; quite sawdusty in places but the juicy instincts of the barley continue; liquorice and burned honeycomb completes one enormous experience... **b23** any number of distilleries reach the "exotic fruit" stage of old age, but none seem to master the genre with such panache as Caper. What a treat! *46.5%*

Duncan Taylor Collection Caperdonich 1972 cask no. 6712 **(85) n20 t22.5 f21.5 b21.5.** Some quite lovely movements to this old classic, especially in the exotic fruit department, but ultimately closer in style to 7435 than 3246, alas. *51.3%*

⸬ **Duncan Taylor Collection Caperdonich 1972** cask no. 7421 **(87) n22.5** rhubarb and custard with an extra big dollop of vanilla; **t22.5** massive delivery. The sweet malt and silky fruits are backed to the hilt by aggressive, OTT, spiced-out oaks. You know that its too old and too much – but the effect is so, well, kapowering!!, you are happy to let it go; **f21** dries to a toasty desert; **b21** Oooh, so borderline!! I have given this one the benefit of the doubt. The march of the oak towards the late middle and finish is relentless. *55.6%*

⸬ **Duncan Taylor Collection Caperdonich 1972** cask no. 7422 **(94) n23.5** has moved from rhubarb to a much more exotic style befitting its age; leathery and bourbony, too: a much more intense and classy nose than its sister cask; **t24** held on the palate, you are immediately aware of the depth of flavours here: again there is a spicy, bourbony thrust, fattened out by molasses and a hint of liquorice then as the middle approaches the barley saunters through; **f23** so very long: chewy and muttering dark sugars and burned honeycomb. The vanillas are no more than decoration; **b23.5** tasted against its sister cask, 7421, here is a display of how one barrel can absorb the years and come out positively gleaming, while the other is tarnished and hanging on to its fading beauty grimly. This is truly stunning malt. *54.8%*

Duncan Taylor Collection Caperdonich 1972 cask no. 7435 **(84) n22 t22 f19 b21.** So many good things to say about this, especially in the buttery, spiced butterscotch department. But, ultimately, just a shade too old. *55.6%*

⸬ **Lonach Caperdonich 1969 (83.5) n22 t21 f20 b20.5.** Curious. Nothing like the famed ancient Caper fruitfest I imagined I'd get. Instead, we have a malt which has been submerged in oak, but has retained enough oxygen in the form of barley to keep alive. Just. *42.4%. Duncan Taylor.*

Lonach Caperdonich 1969 (89.5) n22 barley aplenty and even outweighs the south Pacific fruit...which is a good sign thing... **t23** plenty of integrity on the malt which makes a cushioned impact: superb... **f22.5** melted vanilla ice cream over pears and butterscotch tart; **b22** a beautiful Speysider which has withstood the ravages of time: wonderful. *40.6%. Duncan Taylor.*

Lonach Caperdonich 1969 bott 08 **(80) n20.5 t20.5 f19 b20.** Malty but fading fast. *44.7%. Duncan Taylor.*

Lonach Caperdonich 1970 (78.5) n21 t20 f18.5 b19. You can almost hear the fingernails screeching as this malt tries to grip frantically on to the right side of the aging process. God, it has my sympathy... *43.3%. Duncan Taylor.*

Old Malt Cask Caperdonich Aged 34 Years refill hogshead, cask no. 4296, dist Dec 73, bott May 08 **(77.5) n21 t19.5 f18 b19.** Does its best to start brightly but soon becomes evident this is pretty shagged out (very lightly smoked) whisky. *41.5%. Douglas Laing. 267 bottles.*

Old Malt Cask Caperdonich Aged 40 Years refill hogshead, cask no. 3920, dist Feb 67, bott Oct 07 **(74.5) n18.5 t18 f19 b19.** It's strange how 40-year-old sounds older than 1968 vintage: a message for us all there, I think. However, this one simply does feel older... *42.9%. Douglas Laing. 133 bottles.*

Provenance Caperdonich Aged 11 Years hogshead, cask no. 4200, dist summer 96, spring 08 **(73.5) n18.5 t18 f19 b18.** Excessively thin, malty. Yep, Caperdonich all right... *46%. Douglas Laing.*

⸬ **Provenance Caperdonich Aged 12 Years** refill hogshead, dist spring 96, bott winter 08 **(81.5) n22 t20.5 f20 b19.** An uncommon Caper at this age, but a good example of a malt which flatters to deceive – and why the owners despaired so. The under-ripe greengage nose is attractive but the thinness of the body underwhelms. *46%. Douglas Laing.*

Scotch Malt Whisky Society Cask 38.16 Aged 12 Years refill hogshead, dist May 94 **(74) n19 t18 f19 b18.** Hot, harsh, thin and pretty unforgiving: so not bad for a Caper of this age.. *58.7%*

⸬ **Whisky Doris Caperdonich 36 Year Old** bourbon hogshead, cask no. 7425, dist Nov 72, bott Feb 09 **(89.5) n22** no shortage of oak, but the honey is big enough to see it off; **t22.5** beautiful mouthfeel and weight. Again the oak really does try to shout as loudly as possible, but those acacia honey notes succeed in intervening; **f23** at its best now with the drier oak involvement settling for a subtler, more chocolaty approach which works well with that persistent honey; **b22** a must for lovers of Crunchie bars or just those with a sweet tooth who like to chew the toothpicks. *54.4%*

⸬ **The Whisky Fair Caperdonich 1972** refill sherry hogshead, dist Nov 72, bott Aug 08 **(93.5) n22.5** the usual exotic fruit, except now with a faint ginger incursion; **t24** there we go: a mixture of youthful Caperdonich's fire and brimstones alongside the mature whisky-of-the-world Caperdonich's ability to strike a suave, intelligent lushness embracing those juicy fruits, titillating spices and, again, a hint of something gingery; **f23** back to the vanilla, but the light trickle of barley oils ensures a balanced finale; **b24** just fantastic... *48.3%. Duncan Taylor for The Whisky Fair.*

CARDHU
Speyside, 1824. Diageo. Working.

Cardhu 12 Years Old db **(90) n23** just about the cleanest, most uncluttered, pure, sweet malt you will ever find, a touch of apple, perhaps, giving an extra dimension; **t24** again the malt is pure and rich, just a thread of oak adding some dryness and depth; **f21** vanilla and malt; **b22** a classic: welcome back! 40% (see also Cardhu Pure Malt)

CLYNELISH
Highlands (Northern), 1968. Diageo. Working.

Clynelish Aged 15 Years "The Distillers Edition" double matured in oloroso-seco casks Cl-Br: 169-1f, bott code L6264CM000 03847665, dist 91, bott 06 db **(79) n20 t20 f19 b20.** Big in places, distinctly oily in others but the overall feel is of a potentially brilliant whisky matured in unsympathetic barrels. 46%

Cadenhead's Authentic Collection Clynelish Aged 17 Years bourbon, dist 90, bott Sep 07 **(86.5) n22 t21 f22 b21.5.** Hugely intense malt which is blemish-free and improves wave upon wave. 51.2%. 204 bottles.

∵ **The Cárn Mór Vintage Collection Clynelish 2003** hogshead, cask no. 2223, dist 03, bott 09 **(78.5) n22 t20 f18 b18.5.** Lovely nose but all the signs of a cask that would add little in 60 years, let alone six... 46%. The Scottish Liqueur Centre.

Chieftain's Clynelish 14 Years Old hogshead, cask no. 15103, dist Nov 92 **(85.5) n22 t21.5 f21 b21.** Big malt though playing down the normal sweetness. 46%. nc ncf. Ian Macleod. Danish Market.

The Clydesdale Clynelish 14 Years Old cask nos. 0264/7164, dist May 92, bott Sep 06 **(92) n23 t22 f24 b23.** Genuinely well-made malt from an excellent bourbon cask. Ultra-subtle bitter-sweet balance here. A malt that repays a search for finer detail. 60.4%. nc ncf. Blackadder International.

The Creative Whisky Company Clynelish 1994 Aged 11 Years ex-sherry **(64) n16 t17 f15 b16.** Entirely jiggered by sulphur. 53.3%

Dun Bheagan Clynelish 13 Years Old hogshead **(79) n20 t21 f19 b19.** Some pleasant shards of honey and butterscotch cannot disguise the relatively hot nature of this one. 46%. Ian Macleod.

∵ **Dun Bheagan Clynelish Aged 17 Years** butt, dist Dec 90 **(89) n23.5** subtle peat smoke drifts around the glass and mingles sublimely with the clean grape and healthy barley. Very high quality; **t23** typical Clynelish silk when in this top mode with the malt melting and diffusing about the palate with those same smoky/grapey notes harmonising without breaking sweet; **f21** some spices which gain ground in the middle fizz about until the finish, though the background becomes relatively drier and more austere, even bitter; **b22.5** there is no silencing a fine distillery and here it crows effortlessly. Beautiful. 46%. Ian Macleod Distillers Ltd.

Duncan Taylor The NC2 Range Clynelish 1993 (88.5) n21.5 like sticking your head in a florist's; **t23** wonderful build up of ultra clean barley sugar and muscovado, **f22** barley remains crisp and neat; **b22** simple yet high quality malt. 46%

Duncan Taylor The NC2 Range Clynelish 1994 (87.5) n22.5 mown grass and haylofts; **t22** firm, juicy barley; **f21.5** you know that toffee you get in the middle of Everton mints... **b21.5** a strange one this: has all the scaffolding for a exceptional malt, but not quite enough Brix. 46%

∵ **Gordon & MacPhail Cask Strength Clynelish 1997 (91.5) n23** the barley is stark but the fruity punchiness is something to get your nose round. The coal dust adds just-so weight; **t22.5** crisp and juicy on one level, abounding with spice and oak on another; **f23** dipped in cocoa powder for a drying finish to the long barley-rich theme; **b23** plenty of class and more age than you would expect. 59.7%

John Milroy Selection Clynelish 1992 (87) n21 clean with a hint of smoke? Lightly spiced; **t23** juiced- up barley that flies off the salivameter. Lots of marmalade and a dash of spice; **f21** soft landing for the barley, helped by the sawdust; **b22** a close relation to the Boisdale, except this one has 240 volts of barley running through it! 46%

Lombard's Jewels of Scotland Clynelish 1982 Aged 21 Years (88) n21 clean, surprisingly fresh barley for its age with a sliver or two of ginger, pine nut and diced, unripe yam; **t23** a real juiceball of a malt with waves of salivating barley helped along by big oaky spice; **f22** remains a real spicefest; **b22** a busy and quite joyous bottling. 50% Lombard Brands.

Murray McDavid Clynelish 1995 Aged 11 Years bourbon/port **(86) n21 t21 f22 b22.** Highly unusual both as a Clynelish and Port finish. The port is offering a slightly restrained character and the Clynelish has none of its usual honeyed charm. Enjoyable and attractive to those who prefer their malts dry enough to be stirred but not shaken. 46%

⌁ **Norse Cask Selection Clynelish 1995 Aged 12 Years** sherry butt no. 12773, dist Dec 95, bott Nov 08 **(69) n17.5 t18.5 f16 b17.** Sulphured. *57.3%. Qualityworld for WhiskyOwner. com, Denmark.*

⌁ **Old Malt Cask Clynelish Aged 20 Years** bott 09 **(92.5) n22** typically honeyed and lightly fruited; t23 fine delivery with a real richness to the radiating malt; **f24** continues on this theme for ever and a day, perhaps with some natural caramels turning up, too. Juicy with the final fade is just so beautifully estery; **b23.5** an excellent must-have example of typically classy from this great distillery. *50%. Douglas Laing.*

Old Malt Cask Clynelish Aged 23 Years dist Apr 83, bott Dec 06 **(88) n21 t22 f23 b22.** A malt which becomes more content with itself as it develops. The exotic fruitiness hints at decay and the arrival reinforces this, but there is enough strength in depth to see it home as an elderly statesman rather than a clapped-out journeyman. *50%. Douglas Laing. 303 bottles.*

Old Malt Cask Clynelish Aged 24 Years dist Apr 83, bott May 07 **(88) n22** celery and linseed; **t23** wonderful deftness to the lush barley **f21** vanilla wafer; late spice; **b22** elegant and clean. *50%. Douglas Laing. 305 bottles.*

Old Malt Cask Clynelish Aged 36 Years refill hogshead, cask no. 3913, dist Mar 71, bott Sep 07 **(83) n22 t20.5 f20 b20.5.** Bruised and battered by some severe oaky beatings, there is just enough pep in the barley for a final sweet, malty hurrah. *44.6%. nc ncf. 191 bottles.*

⌁ **Old Malt Cask Clynelish Aged 38 Years** refill hogshead, dist Mar 71, bott Mar 09 **(91.5) n23** stylish to the point of being quietly majestic: the anthracite smoke really does offer a beautiful backdrop to the surprisingly clear barley and murkier citrus; the complexity, though, and in particular the weight is fabulous.. **t23.5** brilliant delivery which falls somewhere between silk on one hand and intensely lively barley on the other. There is the odd oaky phrase which announces an unmistakable tiredness from age (the odd bit of exotic fruit here and there), but countering it is that juicy barley thrust and, just like the nose, the most subtle of not necessarily peaty smoke; **f22** plenty of vanilla custard as a sweetness begins to outweigh those signs of age; finally dries to a chalky dustiness; **b23** an absolute class act which grows on you with every single, ultra-complex mouthful. Unusually, the obvious age wrinkles somehow add to the charm. *47.9%. Douglas Laing. 145 bottles.*

Old Masters Clynelish Aged 10 Years dist 97, bott May 08 **(86.5) n21.5 t22 f22 b21.** Not the usual honeyed style, but every bit as mouth-watering as it should be with an attractive soft cocoa finale. *57.8%. James MacArthur & Co. Ltd.*

Private Collection Clynelish 1969 (82) n20 t21 f21 b20. Just hangs onto its integrity by the width of an oak's bark; enough mocha-themed fruit and spicy complexity and charm to see it through some dodgy moments. *45%. G&M*

Provenance Clynelish Aged 10 Years dist 96, bott 07 **(86) n22 t21.5 f21.5 b21.** A dram closer to 10 months than 10-years in style: a cask that's seen much of life has contributed minimally, except for the filtering out of some of the more volatile qualities. That said, they certainly don't come much more mouth-watering or barley-laden than this. *46%. Douglas Laing, exclusively for Edinburgh University Water of Life Society. 240 bottles.*

Provenance Clynelish Aged 11 Years hogshead, cask no. 4187 & 4188, dist autumn 96, bott spring 08 **(88) n22** grassy with coal gas and lime; **t22.5** every bit as juicy as the nose suggests: malt at its cleanest; **f22** straight-laced barley with a smidgeon of vanilla and butterscotch; **b21.5** Clynelish at its most simple, clean, elegant and malty. *46%. Douglas Laing.*

Scotch Malt Whisky Society Cask 26.55 Aged 8 Years 1st fill barrel, dist Nov 99 **(94.5) n24 t24 f23 b23.5** Almost an exact imprint of how you imagine the finest Clynelish to be. Both spooky and spanking and the blueprint by which all other such bottlings should be measured. A serious contender for young whisky of the year. *62.4%*

Scotch Malt Whisky Society Cask 26.56 Aged 8 Years refill barrel, dist Nov 99 **(90.5) n22.5 t23 f22.5 b22.5** A wonderful dram, if lacking the sparkle, devilment and indisputable élan of the 26.55. Amazing the difference a cask can make. *61.8%*

⌁ **Scotch Malt Whisky Society Cask 26.61 Aged 25 Years** refill hogshead, dist May 83 **(92) n23.5** exquisite soft smoke and honey makes for what, nosed blind, appears a low voltage Highland Park; **t24** even better delivery with a spicy fizz helping to seriously ramp up the soft acacia honey notes and playful phenols. Fabulous mouthfeel with the oak steady and sturdy, but on very best behaviour; **f22** cocoa dependent; **b22.5** at times simply irresistible and with a sprig of heather this could be top-notch HP. *55%*

⌁ **The Scotch Single Malt Circle Clynelish 1995** cask no. 12780, dist Sep 95, bott Aug 08 **(88) n21** barley concentrate and vanilla; **t23** big early barley and honey mix, then a slow, irreversable penetration of bourbony-sweet, spiced oak; **f22** much drier as the oaky element takes control; **b22** impressive, well-made malt with a particularly well-balanced entry. *60.6%. German market.*

The Single Malts of Scotland Clynelish 1992 Aged 15 Years bott Sep 07 **(84) n21.5 t21.5 f20 b21.** Just so much natural caramel! 46%. *Speciality Drinks.*

The Single Malts of Scotland Clynelish 1972 Aged 34 Years small batch **(83) n20 t22 f21 b20.** Such is the honeyed grace before it is crushed under the weight of oak, that this must have been a stunner ten years ago. *50.5%. Speciality Drinks, UK.*

⌐⋅ **The Whisky Agency Clynelish 27 Year Old** dist 82, bott 09 **(90) n22** serious heather honey; **t22.5** firm barley-oak delivery, with pulsing, spiced honey arriving in nearby waves; **f22** long with vanilla and salt; **b22.5** holds its age stupendously: like a Highland Park without the peat. *53.9%. The Whisky Agency, Germany.*

Whisky-Doris Clynelish 1997 dist 97, bott 07 **(86.5) n21.5 t22 f21.5 b21.5.** Thickset and malty, the usual freshness is missing. That said, this is wonderful stuff, especially if you like an American malt shake-style whisky. *59%*

The Whisky Society Clynelish 1992 Aged 15 Years bott Sep 07 **(89) n23 t23 f21 b22.** A kind of sophisticated, handsome brother to the Single Malts bottling. *58.5%. Speciality Drinks.*

Wilson & Morgan Barrel Selection Clynelish 1992 Sherry Finish bott 07 **(79) n20 t21 f19 b19.** Unusually flat for a Clynelish. Jam tarty in part, but you get the feeling the sherry finish has done the complexity no favours. *46%*

⌐⋅ **Wilson & Morgan Barrel Selection Clynelish Aged 12 Years** marsala finish, dist 96, bott 08 **(84.5) n23 t21.5 f19 b21.** Wow...!! Well, that's different. This is quite massive with about as much prickle as you might find at a porcupine convention. There has been a touch of sulphur involved somewhere, but the sulphur stick must have passed through like and an express as the damage is manageable. The nose is just one salivating chorus of sultana fruitcake and the intensity on the palate is something else besides. The marauding chocolate later on is pretty telling, too. For those who never detect sulphur, or perhaps even like it, you might mark this one well in the 90s... *58.6%*

⌐⋅ **Wilson & Morgan Barrel Selection Clynelish 1996** bott 08 **(79.5) n20.5 t20 f19 b20.** Dry, occasionally to the point of austerity, and locates far too many cul-de-sacs. *46%*

COLEBURN
Speyside, 1897–1985. Diageo. Closed.

Connoisseurs Choice Coleburn 1981 (81) n21 t21 f19 b20. Usual thin, hot stuff from Coleburn but benefits from a big malt kick. Way above the norm. *43%*

Connoisseurs Choice Coleburn 1981 (74) n20 t19 f17 b18. The barley is sparse and stretched thinly over the hot body 43%. *Gordon & MacPhail.*

Old Malt Cask Coleburn Aged 25 Years dist Feb 80, bott Aug 05 **(68) n20 t17 f15 b16.** Best Coleburn nose in years, but spectacularly disintegrates on the palate as is its wont. *50%. Douglas Laing. 661 bottles.*

⌐⋅ **The Whisky Agency Coleburn 26 Year Old** dist 83, bott 09 **(88.5) n22** light, clean, citrusy malt: the epitome of Speyside style; **t23** juicy, clean, salivating barley sees off the growing oaky attention with a sugar candy barley-sugar, chocolate lime infusion; **f21.5** cocoa and vanilla...the oaky bitterness is expected, threatens and then is headed off... **b22** Coleburn is a rare whisky. A thoroughly enjoyable Coleburn is rarer still. So here's one you've just got to go and track down... *49.5%. The Whisky Agency, Germany.*

CONVALMORE
Speyside, 1894–1985. Closed.

Convalmore 1977 bott 05 db **(91) n23 t23 f22 b23.** Must be blended with Botox, as there is no detrimental ageing to either nose or delivery. A quite lovely and charming whisky to remember this lost – and extremely rare - distillery by. *57.9%. 3900 bottles.*

Cadenhead's Convalmore 30 Years Old dist 77, bott Sep 07 **(95) n23.5** some over-ripe oranges – even slightly mouldy – plus footplate coal dust and elderberry flower. Not exactly a day-to-day common or garden Speyside combo... **t24** mouth-watering with a slow dissolving of barley and kumquats in about equal measure; the spices aren't - it's alcohol kick...and then a succession of vanilla waves; **f23.5** long duration with vanilla and cream /ice cream mixed, topped by something playfully smoky; **b24** the strength for the age is unbelievable: this appears a throwback, to a time 25 years ago when I was tasting this at full strength and full of vitality. It's been a ling time since I was hit by Convalmore like this; thinking about it, I really cannot remember this distillery showing to such near perfection in the past at all. Just amazing. *61.6%. 240 bottles.*

⌐⋅ **Connoisseurs Choice Convalmore 1984 (88.5) n23** the house style, curiously plasticy and fruity, still intact: delicate and unusual hint of fried yam and softened passion fruit all slightly confused by coke smoke; **t22** juicy, outwardly thin and missing meat in the middle but compensated by beautiful, bitter-sweet layering of clean malt; **f21** cocoa powder and peppers compensate for the vanishing sweetness and body; **b22.5** one of the younger Convanmores to have found its way on the market of late, having been distilled shortly before its fatal closure. This is crisper than older expressions, yet celebrates the finesse so often found from the older versions. An historic treat. *43%. Gordon & MacPhail.*

Old Malt Cask Convalmore Aged 30 Years dist Oct 76, bott Apr 07 **(88) n23** plasticine, gooseberries, custard; so light..; **t22** early barley juice augmented by something fruity; dries and spices up slightly; **f21** sawdusty; **b22** a charming and unusual expression of this rare malt. *44.1%. Douglas Laing. 192 bottles.*

Old Malt Cask Convalmore Aged 32 Years refill hogshead, cask no. 4246, dist Oct 75, bott Apr 08 **(89.5) n23** tangerines and barley for a simple but wonderfully effective duo; **t22.5** silky, malty, more citrus to ensure a fresh, lively element seeing off the vanilla; **f22** runs out of gas slightly and retires meekly but with no little elegance; **b22** almost too charming to be true. *50%. nc ncf. Douglas Laing. 202 bottles.*

Scott's Selection Convalmore 1975 bott 07 **(91) n22** sugar-dusted mallow and citrus; **t23** emphatic barley which layers beautifully but stubbornly refuses to delve much further. Some oak bitters and a sprinkle of spice; **f23** more oak and vanilla, but always with an almost gristy dusting of barley; almost defiantly the honey grows from being background noise to the final hurrah, boosted along the way by that gathering spice **b23** a malt determined to keep its head below the parapet. But once you make the effort to notice it, its quiet but unmistakable quality is there to admire. *46%*

CRAGGANMORE
Speyside, 1870. Diageo. Working.
⁘ **Cragganmore Aged 12 Years** db **(81.5) n20 t21 f20 b20.5.** I have a dozen bottles of Cragganmore in my personal cellar dating from the early 90s when the distillery was first bottled as a Classic Malt. Their astonishing dexterity and charm, their naked celebration of all things Speyside, casts a sad shadow over this drinkable but drab and instantly forgettable expression. *40%.*

⁘ **Cragganmore Aged 14 Years** The Distillers Edition finished in port casks, dist 93, bott 07 db **(85) n22 t21 f21 b21.** The tightly closed fruit on the palate doesn't quite match the more expansive and complex nose. *40%.*

Cadenhead's Authentic Collection Cragganmore Aged 18 Years sherry butt, dist 89, bott Sep 07 **(88) n21.5** oak threatens but kept in line by a thin layer of grape and barley; **t22.5** big barley sugar kick; sublime body with excellent light oil texture; **f22** the oaks do their best to take over, sawdust dryness but lightened by the grape-grain combo; **b22** a malt battling with old age very effectively. *58.5%. 594 bottles.*

⁘ **Duthies Cragganmore 15 Years Old (84) n20.5 t22 f20.5 b21.** Does its best in a tight cask. *46%. Cadenhead's for Germany.*

⁘ **Kingsbury's Cragganmore 1989 18 Years Old** Cask Strength **(84.5) n21.5 t23 f20 b20.** Big, intense barley with massive early maple syrup kick. Fades as the bitter-ish oak takes charge. *54.8%. Japan Import System.*

⁘ **Kingsbury's Single Cask Cragganmore Aged 17 Years** dist Sep 89, bott Aug 07 **(75.5) n19 t20 f17.5 b19.** Lots of "Nourishment" chocolate energy drink. But a few flaws along the way, especially at the brutal death. *46%. Japan Import System.*

Kingsbury Celtic Series Cragganmore 14 Years Old 1989 (84.5) n21 t21.5 f21 b21. Puffing a bit and creaking with oak. The barley though ensures a soft centre. *58.9%. nc ncf. Japan Import System Co. Ltd.*

Murray McDavid Mission Cragganmore 1985 Aged 21 Years bourboun/syrah enhanced in Guigal Côte Rôtie **(82) n23 t21 f19 b19.** When they say bourbon, they aren't kidding: parts of this is pure Kentucky, especially on the glorious nose. But the truth is that it's gone through the wood and after the brain-blowing entry, things slip downhill. *56.5%. nc ncf. 665 bottles.*

Norse Cask Selection Cragganmore 1993 Aged 14 Years hogshead, cask no. 001979, dist 93, bott Dec 07 **(89) n22** charming, fragile with a light and tender sweetness; **t23** top rate delivery with the barley at maximum power; scorching spices add to the density; **f21.5** mildly sappy but a touch of sweetening bourbon helps; **b22.5** wonderful to see this distillery on such great form. *60.5%. nc ncf. Qualityworld, Denmark. 276 bottles.*

Scotch Malt Whisky Society Cask 37.38 Aged 16 Years refill barrel, dist Apr 92 **(85.5) n21.5 t21 f21.5 b21.5.** At times delicate and complex...but tired, also. Would love to have tasted this six years ago... *55.7%*

⁘ **Scotch Malt Whisky Society Cask 37.43 Aged 15 Years** sherry butt, dist Mar 93 **(83.5) n20 t20.5 f22 b21.** A big, ungamely clodhopping brute of a malt. Even so, the marriage between bourbon and grape makes for some (mildly sulphured) nose. Once past the at times entertaining mess of a delivery excellent blood orange notes emerge. *60.4%*

CRAIGELLACHIE

Speyside, 1891. Dewar's. Working.

Berrys' Own Selection Craigellachie 1994 cask no. 1057, bott 07 **(84) n20 t21 f22 b21.** Distinct similarities between this and SMWS bottling 44.36. There is a sulphury element to the nose and early delivery which has nothing to do with casks - and then, after a confused start, a much more harmonious, slightly cocoa-infused finale. However, here the cask is a little more worn and allows the barley a clearer say. *56.4%. Berry Bros & Rudd.*

Cadenhead's Authentic Collection Craigellachie-Glenlivet Aged 12 Years bourbon hogshead, dist 94, bott May 07 **(80) n19 t21 f20 b20.** Big barley and biscuity fare. *58.3%.*

⋰ **Cadenhead's Craigellachie Aged 14 Years** dist 94, bott 09 **(91) n23** always love it when I see that old Craigellachie peat smoke molecule signature – and there it is... accompanied by kumquats and crème brule; **t24** absolutely brilliant arrival: as top notch as I've ever experienced from this distillery at this age even in blending samples, **f21.5** a catch: bitters out late on with a shade too much enthusiasm; **b22.5** can't have it all: the indifferent, though not unpleasant, finish is the devil's trade off for some earlier heaven. *56.5%*

Connoisseurs Choice Craigellachie 1990 (86) n21 t22 f21 b22. Enjoyable dual personality being at once lush and barley rich and on another plane firm and crisp. Clean and well-balanced. *43%. Gordon & MacPhail.*

Dewar Rattray Craigellachie 1991 cask no. 6924, dist Aug 91, bott Sep 07 **(91) n24** absolutely everything I could ask for: barley concentrate, a variation on an orangey theme and a smattering of a few smoky molecules; **t23** mouth-watering before the soft oils emerge; barley rarely comes this intense yet controlled and the strength helps fan the malty flames; **f22.5** long, a movement towards cocoa but the gently oiled, mildly nutty barley makes it through to the end; **b22.5** helps confirm my suspicions that the spirit made here in the early 90s tailed off slightly in quality as the decade progressed. This is just brimming with the character that made me fall slightly in love with this distillery back in the early 80s. A treasure. *60.7%*

Provenance Craigellachie Aged 11 Years refill hogshead, cask no. 4256, dist Autumn 96, bott Spring 08 **(85) n21 t22 f21 b21.** Sharp, clean malt softly oil-coated and spiced. *46%. nc ncf. Douglas Laing.*

Scotch Malt Whisky Society Cask 44.36 Aged 14 Years refill hogshead, dist Feb 94 **(85) n21 t19 f23.5 b21.5.** One of those malts you'll either love or hate. Though most probably both during the space of about three minutes. Fractious and ill-disciplined for the most part, there are still some wonderfully garbled cocoa notes at the finish which are quite superb. *59.1%*

⋰ **Scotch Malt Whisky Society Cask 44.39 Aged 15 Years** refill barrel, dist Aug 93 **(91) n22.5** Finest Kentucky....like a young bourbon achieving sweet-vanilla maturity; **t23** a beautiful balance on delivery between juicy barley and intense vanilla; a dollop of molasses ensures a fine sweetness; a charming soft lemon freshness also hits the right note; **f22.5** long, oaky butterscotch and red liquorice flourish combine effortlessly with the fudgy sugars; **b23** some serious bourbon notes to this, from first nosing right through to the dying embers of oak on the finish. *58.1%*

⋰ **Scotch Malt Whisky Society Cask 44.40 Aged 9 Years** refill butt, dist Aug 99 **(89.5) n22** circles planet bourbon in a grapey capsule; **t23.5** almost oafishly intense, duffing up the tastebuds with a blistering bourbony-oak attack; some juicy barley-sultana enters as a sub plot; **f22** a major cocoa incident; **b22** as mouth-watering as you might expect from a malt of this age, and the odd zingy injection. But grapey remnants and a big vanilla surge minimally limit the range of the higher notes and complexity. *58.5%*

DAILUAINE

Speyside, 1854. Diageo. Working.

Dailuaine Aged 16 Years bott lot no. L4334 db **(79) n19 t21 f20 b19.** Syrupy, almost grotesquely heavy at times; the lighter, more considered notes of previous bottlings have been lost under an avalanche of sugary, over-ripe tomatoes. Definitely one for those who want a massive dram. *43%*

Berry's' Own Selection Dailuaine 1974 Aged 31 Years (83) n23 t21 f19 b20. Sparkling, salivating bitter-sweet barley at first then a heavy oak portcullis shuts off the fun. *46%. Berry Bros & Rudd.*

Chieftain's Dailuaine Aged 10 Years (88) n21 the barley and oak barely gel; **t23** rock-solid malt: no compromising at all!; **f22** barley sugar and mallows; **b22** hard-nosed malt, takes time to unravel. Ignore the occasional flat bit. *43%.*

Connoisseurs Choice Dailuaine 1991 (78) n21 t20 f18 b19. Another Dailuaine felled by oak. 43%. Gordon & MacPhail.

Connoisseurs Choice Dailuaine 1993 (82) n21 t22 f19 b20. Some attractive touches that show this distillery in its more expansive and barley-sugary light. Not too bad at all. 43%. Gordon & MacPhail.

⋅⋅⋅ **Hart Brothers Dailuaine Aged 11 Years** dist Mar 97, bott Jun 08 **(74) n16 t20 f19 b19.** Typically feinty, though some of the oils do have a scarred attractiveness. 46%

John Milroy Selection Dailuaine 1996 Aged 10 Years (72) n17 t19 f18 b18. Good Dailuaines are pretty rare – and this ain't one of them. Cloying at best, the feinty nose is especially worth avoiding. 46%

Norse Cask Selection Dailuaine 1989 Aged 14 Years (79) n20 t19 f21 b19. Diamond-hard and revealing exactly why this is such good blending malt. 60.4%. Quality World, Denmark.

Old Malt Cask Dailuaine Aged 34 Years refill hogshead, cask no. 3976, dist Nov 73, bott Dec 07 **(89.5) n23.5** exotically fruity with a scoop of blancmange; the molten Demerara and vague smoke is, kind of literally, the icing... **t22** wonderful glitter and sheen to the barley for all its years; the vanilla punches quickly and hard but the sweetness and pliability of the barley wins through; **f22** soft vanillas and a late infusion of delicate spice; **b22** some malts just don't work at this age...this one very clearly does. Lovely! 50%. Douglas Laing. 238 bottles.

Old Malt Cask Dailuaine Aged 35 Years dist Dec 71, bott Apr 07 **(79) n19 t20 f20 b20.** Tangy. The oils keep the gathering oaks at bay. 45.6%. Douglas Laing. 152 bottles.

⋅⋅⋅ **Provenance Dailuaine Aged 9 Years** sherry butt, dist autumn 99, bott autumn 08 **(67) n15 t19 f16 b17.** Badly made and matured. 46%. Douglas Laing.

DALLAS DHU
Speyside, 1899–1983. Closed. Now a museum.

Cadenhead's Chairman's Stock Dallas Dhu Aged 27 Years bourbon hogshead, dist 79, bott May 07 **(89) n23** shortbread and oaky, roasted barley; **t22** the oak gathers like storm clouds but the palate explodes with barley sugar, butterscotch and manuka honey...then the oaks rain in; **f22** the storm clears to leave a dusty, burnt toasty finale. But just enough barley-led sweetness to even the scores; **b22** this distillery never fails to amaze me. Yes, the oak is a little too emboldened but such is the chemistry of the barley and butterscotch foreground, you have to be impressed. 59.2%. 198 bottles.

Dun Bheagan Dallas Dhu 26 Years Old sherry butt, dist April 81 **(92) n24** doing the biz in so many departments: mainly it's the rich bourbon (and yes, I know this is from a sherry butt!) aided by a soupcon of manuka honey; prunes lead the fruits; **t23.5** immediate oaky awareness, but this first fades as the honeyed, bourbony barley glides in, then returns with some toastier notes; **f22** the gentle patter of minor spices elongate the finale; **b22.5** delightful stuff. Not exactly textbook as it lurches about the palate, but the messages sent are lovely ones. 50%. nc ncf. Ian Macleod.

⋅⋅⋅ **Duncan Taylor Collection Dallas Dhu 1981** cask no. 389 **(90) n21.5** a curious mixture of acacia honey and dry, mildly soaped pummace stone; **t21.5** honeyed silk - and then a screeching delivery of nippy spices; settles in the middle to something more comfortably vanilla and cocoa; **f24** now really comes into its own as the barley finds a foothold to ensure a charming complexity to the vanilla and mocha. Sheer class; **b23** until the finale, it's difficult to know where this one is going. Or even that it is Dallas Dhu, as this is a much wilder, kick ass version than most... 55.1%

Duncan Taylor Collection Dallas Dhu 1981 cask no. 419 **(95) n24 t24 f23 b24.** It's almost as if this old distillery is sending a message: forget about me being a bloody museum...just fire up my stills again!!! Just marvellous...incredible...a thing of total beauty! 57.9%

Duncan Taylor Collection Dallas Dhu 1981 cask no. 421 **(91) n22** barley leads the vanilla; **t23.5** beautiful, sharp barley retains some unblemished youth; **f22.5** remains mouth-watering but the vanilla slowly invades; **b23** another outstanding malt from this lost distillery. 55.8%

Duncan Taylor Collection Dallas Dhu 1981 cask no. 422, dist Apr 81 **(85.5) n20.5 t22 f21.5 b21.5.** Clean and delightful, but an extra dose of natural caramel reduces the brightness. 53.3%

Duncan Taylor Collection Dallas Dhu 1981 cask no. 432 **(90) n22 t23 f22 b23.** The notes for cask 421 will just about do for this. Rare as hen's teeth do two barrels play so similar a tune after all these years, even when sitting side by side. This is a tad duller thanks to the fractionally stronger vanillins and caramel. But still you wouldn't say no to a fourth glass... 55.7%

Old Malt Cask Dallas Dhu Aged 36 Years refill hogshead, cask no. 4106, dist Apr 71, bott Jan 08 **(89.5) n23** lemon drizzle cake; **t22.5** an invasion of mildly furry oaky notes, but the barley appears to take it in its stride; **f21.5** thins out but sweetens; **b22.5** few Speysiders appear to embrace old age with such open arms as DD. 46.2%. Douglas Laing. 151 bottles.

Old Malt Cask Dailas Dhu Aged 36 Years refill hogshead, cask no. 3802, dist Mar 71, bott Aug 07 **(82) n21 t20.5 f20 b20.5.** Heads in the direction of exotic fruit, but doesn't quite have the legs to get there. 42.3%. nc ncf. Douglas Laing. 181 bottles.

Old Malt Cask Dailas Dhu Aged 37 Years refill hogshead, cask no. 3927, dist Apr 70, bott Nov 07 **(93) n24** such a sexy, teasing aroma: everything in perfect proportions and caressing the nose. Orange blossom and orchids: get in touch with your feminine side...and enjoy! **t23.5** powering barley, or at least powering by the sedate nature of the vanilla-rich body; **f22.5** gentle, under-stated but keeping to the barley-vanilla theme; **b23** a malt which simply defies its enormous age. Just how much longer we'll be able to find gems like this from the distillery is anyone's guess. 50%. nc ncf. 109 bottles. Douglas Laing.

DALMORE
Highand (northern), 1839. Whyte and Mackay. Working.

The Dalmore 12 Years Old db **(90) n22** mixed dates: both dry and juicy, **t23** fat, rich delivery with a wonderful dovetailing of juicy barley and thick, rumbling fruit; **f22.5** lots of toffee on the finish, but gets away with it thanks to the sheer depth to the barley and the busy sherry sub-plot; **b22.5** has changed character of late yet remains underpowered and with a shade too much toffee. But such is the quality of the malt in its own right it can overcome any hurdles placed before it to ensure a real mouth-filling, rumbustious dram. 40%

The Dalmore 15 Years Old db **(83.5) n21 t21 f20.5 b21.** Another pleasant Dalmore that coasts along the runway but simply fails to get off the ground. The odd off note here and there, but it's the blood orange which shines brightest. 40%

The Dalmore 21 Years Old db **(87) n22** just how many citrus notes can we find here? Answers on a postcard ... on second thoughts, don't. Just beautifully light and effervescent for its age: a genuine delight; **t23** again, wonderfully fruity though this time the malt pushes through confidently to create its own chewy island: fabulous texture; **f20** simplifies towards toffee slightly too much in the interests of great balance. A lovely coffee flourish late on; **b22** bottled elegance. 43%

The Dalmore Forty Years Old db **(82) n23 t20 f19 b20.** Doubtless my dear friend Richard Paterson will question whether I have the ability to spot a good whisky if it ran me over in a ten ton truck. But I have to say here that we have a disappointing malt: I had left this too late on in writing this year's (2008) Bible as a treat. But it wasn't to be. A soft delivery: but of what? Hard to exactly pin down what's going on here as there is so much toffee and fruit that the oak and barley have been overwhelmed. Pleasant, perhaps, but it's all rather dull and passionless. I like going through the motions with an old lover. Adore the sherry-trifle/toffee mousse nose, though... 40%

The Dalmore 50 Years Old db **(88) n21** buxom and bourbony, the oak makes no secret of the antiquity; **t19** oak again arrives first and without apology, some salty malt creaking in later. Ripe cherries offer a mouthwatering backdrop; **f25** comes into its own as harmony is achieved as the oak quietens to allow a beautiful malt-cherry interplay. Spices arrive for good measure in an absolutely has-it-all, faultless finish: really as much a privilege to taste as a delight; **b23** takes a while to warm up, but when it does becomes a genuinely classy and memorable dram befitting one of the world's great and undervalued distilleries. 52%

The Dalmore 62 Years Old db **(95) n23** PM or REV marked demerara potstill rum, surely? Massive coffee presence, clean and enormous, stunning, topdrawer peat just to round things off; **t25** this is brilliant: pure silk wrapping fabulous moist fruitcake soaked in finest oloroso sherry and then weighed with peat which somehow has defied nature and survived in cask all these years. I really cannot fault this: I sit here stunned and in awe; **f24** perfect spices with flecks of ginger and lemon rind; **b24** if I am just half as beautiful, elegant and fascinating as this by the time I reach 62, I'll be a happy man. Somehow I doubt it. A once-in-a-lifetime whisky – something that comes around every 62 years, in fact. Forget Dalmore Cigar Malt – even I might be tempted to start smoking just to get a full bottle of this. 40.5%

The Dalmore 1263 King Alexander III db **(86) n22 t22.5 f20 b21.5.** Starts brightly with all kinds of barley sugar, fruit and decent age and oak combinations, plus some excellent spice prickle. So far, so good...and obviously thoughtfully and complexly structured. But then vanishes without trace on finish. 40%

The Dalmore 1974 db **(83.5) n22 t21 f20 b20.5.** Extremely odd whisky: on one hand there is a big fruity thrust, presumably from sherry, on the other is over-tired oak. It's a bit of a mess as balance is never quite attained. There are enough highlights in this muddle to make for an interesting experience. Definitely different. 42%

The Dalmore 1980 db **(81.5) n19 t21 f20.5 b21.** Wonderful barley intensity on delivery does its best to overcome the so-so nose and finale. 40%

The Dalmore Cabernet Sauvignon db **(79) n22 t19 f19 b19.** Too intense and soupy for its own good. *45%*

Dalmore The Gran Reserva db **(78.5) n22 t19.5 f18 b19.** Pleasantish, but after tasting this against the Adelphi bottling...well, it's a bit of a miss-match to put it politely. Writing this on the men's Final's Day at Wimbledon, it is like pitting Roger Federer against Baldrick. As for the finish...well, is there one...? *40%*

Adelphi Dalmore 1990 Aged 17 Years sherry butt, cask no. 7327, dist 90, bott 07 **(95) n24** oh, you fruity thing....this must have been one hell of a sweet sherry because it's a kind of sauternes, spicy number with under-ripe greengages. And some sherry there, too... **t24** perfect sherry cask delivery: the grape is there in force, but so clean that the barley has no problem poking through. Spices arrive the very first instant, but exactly as might be expected from a high grade sweet sherry; there are some early signs of cocoa as the age makes a statement; **f23** long, beautifully sprinkled with cocoa and still the grape has much to say even at this stage; **b24** truly magnificent, un-sulphur-blemished sherried whiskies are now so rare, that when one like this turns up it automatically hits classic status. One of the finest sherry bottlings I have come across in a very long time. I feel the hand of Gonzalez Byass at work here, and somehow one of their very finest got away... *59.7%. 590 bottles.*

Berrys' Own Selection Dalmore 1997 cask nos. 16634/16635, bott 07 **(88.5) n22** barley grist; **t22.5** plenty of sugars on the grist: clean, a touch of youthful lemon drop; **f22** lazy barley, sugar edged and salivating to the last drop, despite the onset of cocoa; **b22** about as sweet as you can take - a very good whisky. *46%. Berry Bros & Rudd.*

⠿ **Chester Whisky & Liquer Co. Dalmore Aged 10 Years** dist 99 **(84) n21.5 t21.5 f21 b20.** Evidence of feints backed up by the oiliness and near black hole-like mass of this blighter. Prisoners barely taken as the molten Rollo toffee/chocolate sticks to all corners of the palate. Enjoyable and fun, but not without its flaws and hardly one for the purest. *54.8%*

Chieftain's Dalmore Aged 10 Years hogshead **(78) n19 t21 f19 b19.** A bit of a sweaty armpit nose and the malt meanders aimlessly, if sweetly and fruitily, around the palate. *58%.*

⠿ **Connoisseurs Choice Dalmore 1992 (81) n20 t21 f20 b20.** Sweet, sticky and spiced, without offering much in the way of form or format. Not the distillery at its finest. *40%. Gordon & MacPhail.*

Duncan Taylor Collection Dalmore 1990 Aged 17 Years cask no. 7325 **(93) n22.5** pulped under-ripe gooseberry, crushed green leaf, bread dough; **t24** lively, prickly delivery but with the most glorious sweetness attached to the rotund malt; a touch green for its age, but the salivating qualities are almost immeasurable; **f23** remains gristy and fresh to the death with regular guest appearances from citrus and tannin; **b23.5** enough to make you swoon. Genuinely underlines the greatness of the Dalmore in a way the distillery bottlings sadly, these days, very rarely do. *55.5%*

Duncan Taylor Collection Dalmore 1990 Aged 17 Years cask no. 7328 **(89) n23** a gooseberry-bourbon combo with the accent firmly on the hickory-honey; **t22** big fanfare but actually quite dry in its early intensity; the barley takes time to slip its marker; **f22** relatively closed, yet enough charm and guile to impress. The late fruits, especially in the shape of citrus, really do entertain; **b22** slightly tight but, as we know, that can mean some serious pleasure along the way.... *56.9%*

⠿ **Duncan Taylor Collection Dalmore 1990** cask no. 7329 **(87) n22** gosh! Now there's a nose: a fleck of lavender further invigorates the weighty oiled and sugared vanilla; **t23** sweetly spiced; again the oils from a generous, shall we say daring, cut give this malt a real wide body, allowing the malt to stick to the palate for a real chew; **f20.5** the downside to the slight feints kick in with the odd, flawed wobble on the barley; **b21.5** brimming with esters and quite a few acceptable feints and spice this is absolutely enormous whisky which might equally appeal to rum freaks. *56.7%*

Old Malt Cask Dalmore Aged 15 Years dist May 91, bott Feb 07 **(86) n21 t22 f21 b22.** Quite simplistic despite – or maybe because of – its barley-concentrate character. Decent spices and a touch of mocha at the death. *50%. Douglas Laing. 357 bottles.*

⠿ **Old Malt Cask Dalmore Aged 19 Years** dist Apr 90, bott Jul 09 **(83) n20 t22 f21 b20.** Pleasant but perhaps over sweet. *50%. Douglas Laing.*

⠿ **Old Malt Cask Dalmore Aged 32 Years** refill hogshead dist Dec 76, Apr 09 **(94) n23** nutty, green fig and fresh boxwood: soft, sublime and even boasting a whiff of smoke; **t24** brilliant delivery of the highest standard: the malt is thick but delicate enough to show its fresh, juicy colours; soft spices intermingle with the muscovado sugars; mildly overcooked butterscotch tart; **f23** natural caramels abound, but in no way interfere with the further development of that now very crisp barley; **b24** quite a triumph of age over probability. Oh, if only the distillery bottlings were regularly this fresh and breathtaking. *50%. Douglas Laing. 306 bottles.*

⟐ **Old Masters Dalmore Aged 12 Years** cask no. 5603, dist 97, bott 09 **(90) n22** minty with huge clean, intense barley and leather back up; **t23** salivating and deliciously sharp on delivery it then heads off on many quieter paths including liquorice-honey, muscovado sugar and something involving mocha with a sprig of mint; **f22.5** chocolate mint chip; **b22.5** if they were to make a Scottish Mint Julip... *59.8%. James MacArthur & Co. Ltd.*

Scotch Malt Whisky Society Cask 13.41 Aged 11 Years refill butt, dist Dec 96 **(62) n16 t16.5 f14 b15.5.** I absolutely dread to think how bad the sulphur must have been first time round...one can assume only that the chairman of the panel was getting "citrus"... *62.4%*

DALWHINNIE
Highlands (central), 1898. Diageo. Working.

Dalwhinnie 15 Years Old db **(95) n24** sublime stuff: a curious mixture of coke smoke and peat-reek wafts teasingly over the gently honied malt. A hint of melon offers some fruit but the caressing malt stars; **t24** that rarest of combinations: at once silky and malt intense, yet at the same time peppery and tin-hat time for the tastebuds, but the silk wins out and a sheen of barley sugar coats everything, soft peat included; **f23** some cocoa and coffee notes, yet the pervading slightly honied sweetness means that there is no bitterness that cannot be controlled; **b24** a malt it is hard to decide whether to drink or bath in: I suggest you do both. One of the most complete mainland malts of them all. Know anyone who reckons they don't like whisky? Give them a glass of this – that's them cured. Oh, if only the average masterpiece could be this good. *43%*

Dalwhinnie Aged 17 Years Distiller's Edition finished in oloroso casks, dist 90, bott 07 db **(83.5) n23 t21 f19.5 b20.** Yes, very pleasant and all that. And the nose really does radiate some finer, deftly smoked, honey tones. But the oloroso does a pretty thorough job of flattening out the development on the palate. Enjoyable, certainly. But I'd just love to know what this was like had the grape not become involved. *43%*

Old Malt Cask Dufftown Aged 30 Years refill hogshead, dist Mar 77, bott Apr 07 **(82) n22 t21 f20 b20.** A bit on the hot side it may be, but one can only admire how it's kept its truculent attitude after all these years. *50%. Douglas Laing. 303 bottles.*

DEANSTON
Highland (Perthshire), 1966. Burn Stewart. Working.

Deanston 6 Years Old db **(83) n20 t21 f22 b20.** Great news for those of us who remember how good Deanston was a decade or two ago: it's on its way back. A delightfully clean dram with its trademark honey character restored. A little beauty slightly undermined by caramel. *40%*

Deanston 12 Years Old db **(74) n18 t19 f18.5 b18.5.** It is quite bizarre how you can interchange this with Tobermory in style; or, rather, at least the faults are the same. *46%. ncf.*

Deanston 1967 casks 1051-2, filled Friday 31st Mar 67 db **(90) n23** the very faintest hint of peat rubs shoulders with high fluting honey and polished pine floors; **t23** the loud oak influence is perfectly tempered by rich barley concentrate. Sweet towards the middle with hints of honey and peat; **f21** spiced and softening towards vanilla; **b23** the oak is full on but there is so much class around that cannot gain control. A Perthshire beauty. *50.7%*

⟐ **Deanston Aged 12 Years Un-Chill Filtered** db **(84.5) n21 t21.5 f21 b21** A decent, attractive Deanston which is a definite step in the right direction. Nutty for sure, but some attractive barley sweetness flits about the palate. A wide cut at work here, one feels, but plenty to chew on. *46.3%*

Old Malt Cask Deanston Aged 12 Years refill hogshead, cask no. 4422, dist Mar 86, bott Jun 08 **(75.5) n18.5 t20 f18.5 b18.5.** A rare chance at commercial level to analyse a single cask of a malt not remotely happy with itself. The delightful, sweet malt fanfare on delivery apart, it groans its off-key discontent at every chance. *50%. Douglas Laing. 327 bottles.*

⟐ **Old Malt Cask Deanston Aged 16 Years** refill hogshead, dist Dec 92, bott Mar 09 **(90) n21.5** honey scraped onto pencil shavings; **t23.5** hick honey mingles superbly with spices and marmalade; juicy and pulsing with sweet barley; **f22.5** good length, the oils calming and soft butterscotch drifts off with the vanillas; **b23** distinctly a cut above for this distillery of late: indeed, much more what this place was about 20-odd years ago. *50%. Douglas Laing. 330 bottles.*

DUFFTOWN
Speyside, 1898. Diageo. Working.

Singleton of Dufftown 12 Years Old db **(71) n18 t18 f17 b18.** A roughhouse malt that's finesse-free. For those who like their tastebuds Dufft up a bit... *40%*

Cadenhead's Dufftown Aged 19 Years sherry butt, dist 88, bott Feb 08 **(86) n21.5 t22 f21 b21.5.** Dufftown at its friendliest. Enough sugar to give a an area the size of Wales diabetes, perhaps. But by this distillery's usually duff standards, there is something enjoyable here, especially on the bourbony nose, an impressive theme it keeps going to the very last. A must-get bottling. *53.5%. 243 bottles.*

∴ **Cadenhead's Dufftown Aged 31 Years** dist 78, bott 09 **(84) n21.5 t21.5 f21 b20.** No surprise about the syrupy fruit. Behaves itself to offer a pleasant chewy dram. *48.6%*

Murray McDavid Dufftown 1993 Aged 14 Years bourbon/guigal St. Joseph syrah **(79) n20 t19 f20 b20.** Big malt that lumbers about the palate rather slobbishly. Dufftown is rarely known for finesse and you'll do well to find any here, despite the best efforts of some pretty decent casks. *46%*

Murray McDavid Dufftown 1997 bourbon/syrah **(76) n18 t19 f20 b19.** My poor 'ol tastebuds! Having just been duffed-up for the second time in 20 minutes by a Dufftown, I can hear them pining for a non ex-Bell's behemoth. *46%*

∴ **Old Malt Cask Collection Dufftown Aged 14 Years** refill butt, dist Aug 94, bott Oct 08 **(84.5) n19 t22 f21.5 b21.** Syrupy and spicy. Faintly trashy and certainly not one to take home to your parents, but some nice curves in some of the right places and a sweet heart. *50%. Douglas Laing. 714 bottles.*

∴ **Old Malt Cask Collection Dufftown Aged 28 Years** sherry cask, dist May 80, bott Oct 08 **(80) n18 t22 f21 b19.** An outrageous dram. Rumbustious, rollicking, uncouth, more oak than a Henry VIII battleship and a few more explosions, too. And dirtier than the filthiest Jolly Jack Tar. But for its myriad faults, it's fun, by gum! 50%. Douglas Laing. *302 bottles.*

Old Malt Cask Dufftown Aged 30 Years dist Mar 77, bott Apr 07 **(76) n18 t20 f19 b19.** There is an unwritten law that says that malts that are a bit rubbish when they are young (Fettercairn, Littlemill, Caperdonich et al) can be quite brilliant when older. Here is a syrupy exception. *50%. Douglas Laing. 303 bottles.*

∴ **Private Cellar Dufftown 1985** bott 07 **(88.5) n23** gracious me...!! Really attractive kumquat and apricot in a wonderful anthracite smog. How appealing...no, really, it is...!! **t23** usual soupy delivery, but here there appears to be shape and form, again with the fruits really lumping it out and that coke-smoke somewhere nearby. Barley big time, but some juicier, slowly melting sugars help out, too; **f20.5** becomes a tad too syrupy and shapeless, as is this distillery's want, and a bit dry, too; **b22** OK, it's happened: a Dufftown I like. I'll turn a blind eye to the rough landing; but eually I can't praise the nose and delivery highly enough. Good stuff!! *43%. Speyside Distillers.*

Provenance Dufftown Aged 12 Years Sherry Finish dist winter 95, bott winter 07 **(86) n21 t22 f21 b22.** From a distillery that is so often a dud, this has more than its fair share of charming, even delicate, moments with a very attractive clean barley theme – despite the sherry intervention. And it's not often you can say that – with or without the sherry! *46%.*

EDRADOUR

Highland (Perthshire), 1837. Signatory. Working.

Edradour Aged 10 Years db **(79) n18 t20 f22 b19.** A dense, fat malt that tries offer something along the sherry front but succeeds mainly in producing a whisky cloyingly sweet and unfathomable. Some complexity to the finish compensates. *43%*

Edradour Ballachin #1 The Burgundy Casks db **(63) n17 t16 f15 b15.** A bitter disappointment in every sense. Were the Burgundy casks sulphur treated? I'd say so. Something completely off-key here. A shocker. *46%*

Edradour Ballachin #2 Madeira Matured db **(89) n22** stonking peat which takes absolutely no prisoners; **t22** if there was any fruit there it is soon crushed by the intense smoke; **f23** a fleeting degree of something fruity; **b22** on the nose and entry I didn't quite get the point here: putting a massively peated malt like this in a Madeira cask is a bit like putting Stan Laurel into bed with Marilyn Monroe. Thankfully doesn't come out a fine mess and the Madeira certainly has a vital say towards the beautifully structured finale. It works! I feel the hand of a former Laphroaig man at work here. *46%*

FETTERCAIRN

Highland (Eastern), 1824. Whyte and Mackay. Working.

Fettercairn 12 Year Old db **(66) n14 t19 f16 b17.** If the nose doesn't get you, what follows probably will...Grim doesn't quite cover it. *40%*

Fettercairn 1824 db **(69) n17 t19 f16 b17.** By Fettercairn standards, not a bad offering. Relatively free from its inherent sulphury and rubbery qualities, this displays a sweet nutty character not altogther unattractive – though caramel plays a calming role here. Need my arm twisting for a second glass, though. *40%*

Cadenhead's Authentic Collection Fetercairn Aged 13 Years bourbon hogshead, dist 93, bott May 07 **(78) n19 t19 f20 b20.** Hot and boiled candy but more barley than rubber this time. 59%. 318 bottles.

Old Malt Cask Fettercairn Aged 33 Years (85.5) n19 t23 f22 b21.5. Funny how some malts get better as they reach their Darby and Joan years. Some 23 years ago, I probably would not have much enjoyed the experience, sampling this as a 10-year-old. And whilst this has some distinctly weird and rough edges, it also now possesses serious character, too. Certainly, there is a charming fruitiness and silky delivery which is worth the entrance fee alone. As are the spices and balancing sweetness. 50%

❖ **The Whisky Agency Fettercairn 34 Year Old** dist 75, bott 09 **(75.5) n18 t17.5 f21 b19.** The sweet, nutty finish helps compensate for some of the earlier crimes against the tastebuds. 57%. The Whisky Agency, Germany.

GLEN ALBYN
Highland (Northern) 1846–1983. Demolished.

Old Malt Cask Glen Albyn 35 Years Old dist 26 Sep 69, bott Jul 05 **(90) n24** a star-studded aroma for something this ancient: the oak weaves delicate vanilla patterns around the apple-honey-barley lead. As aromas go, a veritable gold nugget for its age; **t23** early barley absolutely rips through the tastebuds helped along the way by a glossy sweetness and a puff of smoke and cocoa; **f21** the drying oak lays claim with tolerable force; **b22** understandable signs of longevity, but overall this is simply wonderful. 50%. Douglas Laing. 229 bottles.

Rarest of the Rare Glen Albyn 1979 cask no. 3960, dist Dec 79, bott Mar 06 **(91) n23** melon and barley play host to a clever, nose-nipping spiciness. So relaxed: supreme confidence here; **t23** the incredibly fresh, salivating barley intertwines with glorious vanilla to give a drier tier to the delicately sweet malt; **f22** some chalky vanilla and mocha but the barley holds true; **b23** of Scotland's disappearing malts, this is going with flourish. 57.3%. Duncan Taylor. 244 bottles.

GLENALLACHIE
Speyside, 1968. Chivas. Working.

Glenallachie 15 Years Old Distillery Edition db **(81) n20 t21 f19 b19.** Real battle between nature and nurture: an exceptional sherry butt has silk gloves and honied marzipan, while a hot-tempered bruiser lurks beneath. 58%

Cadenhead's Authentic Collection Glenallachie Aged 17 Years bourbon hogshead, dist 89, bott Feb 07 **(88) n22** distinct tangerine thread amid the firm oak and deft barley. A delightful surprise as the balance is lovely **t23** the charm offensive continues as the rich barley counters the usual hotness to deliver an impassioned maltiness; **f21** good length and a biscuity delivery before the natural caramels and bitterness intervene; **b22** the best Glenallachie bottled? Certainly I have never tasted a superior expression and for once I have to say this is a malt that unquestionably delights. 58.5%. Cadenhead's. 240 bottles.

❖ **The Carn Mòr Vintage Collection Braes of Glenallachie 1992** barrel, cask no. 587, dist 92, bott 09 **(82) n20 t21 f21 b20.** Thin and malty in the typical house style. No off notes, but no real development, either. 46%. The Scottish Liqueur Centre.

Connoisseurs Choice Glenallachie 1992 (69) n16 t19 f17 b17. Scotch malt whisky's version of Dickensian gruel. And badly made gruel at that... 43%. Gordon & MacPhail.

Connoisseurs Choice Glenallachie 1992 (67) n18 t17 f16 b16. Sweaty armpits: this really isn't Scotland's finest distillery, is it. 46%. Gordon & MacPhail.

Dewar Rattray Glenallachie 1995 cask no. 1258, dist Mar 95, bott Nov 07 **(85.5) n21 t22 f21.5 b21.** I'm as shocked every bit as much as I'm impressed. A year or two back the distillery manager of Glenallachie told me that he thought it was capable of producing pretty decent whisky. The look I gave him was the kind of double take Laurel and Hardy stooge James Finlayson would have been proud of. Well, just as Stan Laurel once famously did, perhaps its time for me to eat my hat. 'Cos this aint half bad. Not great, just not bad. I thought tasting this at 60% abv would see me rushed to hospital with my throat ripped out. Not a bit of it: the malt is intense and clean and although asking for complexity on top might be taking the piss, you just can't deny that this is one enjoyable, ultra malty dram. Half eaten hats off to Glenallachie. 60.7%

Dun Bheagan Glenallachie Aged 13 Years sherry finish **(68) n19 t18 f15 b16.** Just dreadful. Further confirmation, hardly that it's needed, that here is a distillery which should rarely be bottled. 43%. Ian Macleod.

Duncan Taylor The NC2 Range Glenallachie 1995 (82.5) n21 t20 f21.5 b20. Fortune favours the brave, obviously!! I had thought about the prospects of suing DT for the likely disintegration of my teeth on tasting this bottling. But instead I found a genuinely friendly malt, not the usual jet fuel one associates with this distillery, which clearly basks in its simplistic role as a pure maltfest. *46%*

⁘ **Old Malt Cask Glenallachie Aged 38 Years** dist Feb 71, bott May 09 **(72) n20 t17 f17.5 b17.5.** I don't think they had quite got to grips with the stills 38 years ago, or the casks: typical of the period in being spectacularly off key almost to the point of vulgarity. *50%. Douglas Laing.*

⁘ **Provenance Glenallachie Aged 9 Years** refill hogshead, dist spring 99, bott autumn 08 **(79) n20.5 t20.5 f19 b19.** Clean, malty, gristy, slightly yeasty, well made, under-matured (from the point of view of being in an over-aged cask) blending fodder. *46%. Douglas Laing.*

GLENBURGIE
Speyside, 1810. Chivas. Working.

Glenburgie Aged 15 Years bott code L00/129 db **(84) n22 t23 f19 b20.** Doing so well until the spectacularly flat, bitter finish. Orangey citrus and liquorice had abounded. *46%*

Duncan Taylor The NC2 Range Glenburgie 1996 Aged 11 Years (86.5) n22 t22 f21.5 b21. Youthful, slightly raw, ultra-clean...the barley appears to be gleaming on both nose and palate. Superficial development, perhaps, but as a good old fashioned slap around the tastebuds...well, it doesn't come much better! *46%*

⁘ **Gordon & MacPhail Distillery Label Glenburgie 10 Years Old (77) n20 t20 f18 b19.** Sweet, toffeed and dull. *40%*

⁘ **Gordon & MacPhail Rare Vintage Glenburgie 1963 (86) n20.5 t22 f22.5 b21.5.** For all its chewiness and enormity, as lovely as the spiced fruit and liquorice is: you can't get over the fact that just a too much oak has entered the system. Still, those lingering coffee and walnut cake notes are a delight. *43%*

⁘ **Old Malt Cask Glenburgie Aged 20 Years** dist May 89, bott Jul 09 **(91) n22** butterscotch, but with a touch of the antique about it.. **t23** supremely juicy with a huge charge of barley rolling back the years; a grassy, sugary sweetness compliments perfectly; **f22.5** drier, spicier, subtler; **b22.5** hardly a gray hair...! *50%. Douglas Laing.*

⁘ **Provenance Glenburgie Aged 12 Years** refill hogshead, dist spring 96, bott autumn 08 **(81) n20.5 t21.5 f19 b19.** Pear-drops, anyone? *46%. Douglas Laing.*

GLENCADAM
Highland (Eastern), 1825. Angus Dundee. Working.

⁘ **Glencadam Aged 10 Years** db **(95) n24** crystal clarity to the sharp, ultra fresh barley. Clean, uncluttered by excessive oak, the apparent lightness is deceptive; the intensity of the malt carries its own impressive weight and the citrus note compliments rather than thins. Enticing; **t24** immediately zingy and eye-wateringly salivating with a fabulous layering of sweet barley. Equally delicate oak chimes in to ensure a lightly spiced balance and a degree of attitude; **f23** longer than the early barley freshness would have you expecting, with soft oils ensuring an extended, tapering, malty edge to the gentle, clean oak; **b24** sophisticated, sensual, salivating and seemingly serene, this malt is all about juicy barley and balance. Just bristles with character and about as puckeringly elegant as single malt gets....and even thirst-quenching. My God: the guy who put this one together must be a genius, or something... *46%*

⁘ **Glencadam Aged 15 Years** db **(90.5) n22.5** soft kumquats mingle with the even softer barley. A trace of drier mint and chalk dust points towards the shy oak. Harmonious and dovetails beautifully; **t23** sharp, juicy barley - almost fruity - fuses with sharper oak. The mouth-watering house style appears to fatten out as gentle oils emerge and then give way for a spicy middle; **f22** long, with those teasing, playful spices pepping up the continued barley theme. Dries as a 15 year old ought but the usual bitterness is kept in check by the prevailing malt; **b23** the spices keep the taste buds on full alert but the richness and depth of the barley defies the years. Another exhibition of Glencadam's understated elegance. Some more genius malt creation.... *46%*

Glencadam Aged 15 Years db **(84) n19 t22 f22 b21.** The first distillery-bottled Glencadam I can remember thanks to new owners and the brakes are never taken off. The middle and early finale are really quite sublime with that glorious malt-intense signature that offers the kind of irresistible drive and style to the tastebuds that Frank Lampard gives to Chelsea...and it's worth getting just for that. But something, a roasty caramel maybe, is holding back on the start and finish: oh, what might have been! Delicious all the same! *40%*

⁘ **Glencadam 25 Years Old Single Cask** cask no. 1002, dist Apr 83, bott Dec 08 db **(76.5) n20.5 t21 f16 b19.** One of those "oh what might have been" casks. Or, if you are German or Swiss, one of the best experiences you will have for a very long time. Those who can't pick up sulphur will have a new love in their lives. The rest of us will continue to sob quietly.... *46%*

Cadenhead's Authentic Collection Glencadam Aged 25 Years bourbon hogshead, dist 82, bott Sep 07 **(87.5) n22** has a curious kind of rum cask gloss to the barley; **t23** big, bracing, rather salty delivery with the barley cascading onto the tastebuds; **f21** massive natural caramel from the barley quietens things; **b21.5** starts beautifully but naturally tails off. A lovely experience, though. *51.2%. 150 bottles.*

⋅∵⋅ **Connoisseurs Choice Glencadam 1987 (87.5) n23** fulsome and fruity with a distinctive blood orange and grape theme; **t22** silky delivery with malt and fruit dished out in equal measures; the house spice kicks in playfully and enlivens the chalky middle; **f21** lots of spice still, but lightly duller at the death as the cocoa bites; **b21.5** charming and fruity. *43%. Gordon & MacPhail.*

Dewar Rattray Glencadam 1990 cask no. 5981, dist Oct 90, bott Nov 07 **(86.5) n21.5 t22 f21.5 b21.5.** Hot whisky from some charmless oak. But, oddly enough, the fire and brimstone personality works amazingly well with the barley. *59.6%*

Dun Bheagan Glencadam 20 Years Old Hogshead (80) n20 t19 f21 b20. For all its age it remains hot stuff. The honey influence will win friends, though. *48%*

Montgomerie's Glencadam 1975 (95) n23.5 clear as a bell with the oak standing far enough back for the barley sugar and fruit candy to get on with it unhampered; **t23.5** textbook delivery for a malt half its age with the barley-fruit resonance helped along by the precise oak; **f24** long, very softly spiced with now a wonderful intermingling of tingling, earthier oak and that improbable crisp barley; **b24** a gem of a malt: compact and defies the years like a film star. Possesses the clarity of a 10-year-old choirboy and the body of 32-year-old nymph. *46%. Montgomery & Co. Ltd.*

⋅∵⋅ **Montgomerie's Glencadam 1990** cask no. 5990, dist Aug 89, bott Mar 08 **(87) n24.5** sweet gooseberry, even a distant echo of lychee, provides a shimmering, fruity edge to the faultless and crystal crisp barley. The proportions of one to the other is perfect. Outrageously sexy and sophisticated; **t21.5** soft delivery full of semi-sweet barley promise; the bitter oak is a worry; **f20** does bitter out as feared, with maybe the vaguest hint of marmalade to compensate; **b21** taste-wise, the oak has gone through the barley. But the nose is simply exceptional, one of the best malts of the year, and the delivery is no mug, either. *43%. Montgomerie & Co. Ltd.*

⋅∵⋅ **Old & Rare Glencadam Aged 32 Years** dist Apr 77, bott Jul 09 **(96.5) n25** bulging with yielding bourbon: all those gorgeous brown sugar, liquorice and antique furniture notes are just soft watercolours, but together form something tangible and magnificent; so delicate it is nigh-on perfect...actually, with that crushed Malteser chocolate candy to boot, it is perfect...25 points it is; **t24** again the delivery is at once soft yet profound: a nanosecond of barley and then we are engulfed by a gently rolling river of light...well...everything.. !! Honeycomb dipped in milk chocolate, barley which is almost three dimensional in its delicate sharpness; molten demerara; molten praline....; **f23.5** not so much short as just fades away. Where does the middle end and the start begin...? A bit like a massive orgasm, you are not sure where the beginning, middle and end exactly is...you know it's just something special you immerse into and you don't want it to go away...it's a thing that 32-year-olds have a tendency to do to you.. **b25** from Brechin to Bardstown in 32 years: brilliant! Worth getting just to nose alone... *58.6%. Douglas Laing.*

Old Malt Cask Glencadam Aged 21 Years dist Jun 85, bott Apr 07 **(95) n24** super-complex: butterscotch, marzipan with apricot filling, lightly salted barley.....and so much more; **t24** those apricots deliver on arrival then a wave of vanilla-led barley; spices sweep in...as they must!! **f23** drier but with the fruits and barley still haggling for presence; excellent pepper tingle; **b24** a true gem of a cask with a nose that, alone, could seduce a eunuch. *50%. Douglas Laing. 311 bottles.*

Provenance Glencadam Aged 11 Years hogshead, cask no. 3938, dist winter 95, bott autumn 07 **(76.5) n18 t19.5 f20 b19.** You know when you find an interesting whisky....well, you won't here... *46%. Douglas Laing.*

The Whisky Fair Glencadam Aged 32 Years sherry wood, dist 74, bott 07 **(83) n22 t22 f19 b20.** Some lovely red berry fruits are crushed latterly under oak. *57.3%.*

GLENCRAIG

Speyside, 1958. Allied. Silent.

Rarest of the Rare Glencraig 1974 cask no. 2923 **(89) n22.5** the fruitiness suggests very good age; but also clean and delicate with the barley offering little more than sweetness: a curious old and new feel to this; **t22** immediate firm barley followed by clean vanilla: for its age simple and elegant, with just enough citrus to ensure freshness; **f22.5** quite estery with a metallic, coppery edge to the barley; plenty of natural caramels represent the oak; **b22** such an elegant dram which feels very at home with its age. After all these years, a bottling worth waiting for. 40.9%. Duncan Taylor.

⋅≣⋅ **Rarest of the Rare Glencraig 1974** cask no. 2929 **(89.5) n22.5** very similar to its sister cask bottled by DT with a fruitiness suggesting that we are entering the autumn of the cask. But attractive every step of the way; **t23** fabulous arrival with the barley and natural caramels herding together. The lightest hint of liquorice and hickory ensures a deft sweetness; **f22** long, still intact with absolutely no negative oak and even a few spasms of spice for good measure; **b22** Rarest of the Rare, alright; the smallest sample I have ever been sent for the Whisky Bible. Must have gone out on April 1st. Come on guys: give me – and the whisky – a chance!! 40.8%. Duncan Taylor.

Scotch Malt Whisky Society Cask 104.10 Aged 33 Years refill barrel, dist Jun 74 **(94) n24 t23 f23.5 b23.5** I chose this to be the 1,000th whisky tasted for the 2009 edition simply because this really is one of the rarest whiskies in the world. Indeed, the first new commercial bottling I have tasted for five years. So you hope against hope that it will be a classic. And it most certainly is. For God's sake, re-install them stills...!!!! 45%

⋅≣⋅ **Scotch Malt Whisky Society Cask 104.12 Aged 34 Years** refill barrel, dist Jun 74 **(91) n22.5** school custard with a high sugar content; the surprisingly pleasant aroma of distant slightly rotting tangerines; **t23.5** wow!! The barley is still making a stand after all these years, with a brittle barley-sugar theme successfully preventing the oak from getting too aggressive; natural caramels and a small cocktail of exotic fruit; the dissolving mouth-feel also makes for a spot-on malt; **f22** finally the oak has its say, but a lingering muscovado sweetness sees off any bitter excesses; **b23** not quite in the same league as 104.10, but confirms what a fabulous make this was. 48.4%

GLENDRONACH
Highlands, 1826. BenRiach Distillers. Working.

⋅≣⋅ **Glengarioch 1797 Founders Reserve** db **(87.5) n21** fruit toffee fudge; **t22** some fizz on delivery followed by a rampaging barley juiciness; much lighter and softer than the strength indicates; **f22.5** excellent mocha accompanies the fruit with aplomb; **b22** impressively fruity and chewy: some serious flavour profiles in there. 48%

Glendronach Original Aged 12 Years Double Matured db **(88) n23** dense, ripe plummy fruit: serious touches of fruitcake, complete with brown sugars. Oak does give a vanilla topping but barley also punches through. Some coal smoke buzzes around, too. Needs some time to get the full story; **t21** some serious infighting here, some of it off-key, between grape and grain. The grape wins but is not entirely unbloodied as the mouthwatering barley has some juicy moments; **f22** the lull after the storm; much more measured doses of bitter marmalade and vanilla, softening towards a gentle spice within the cocoa. Very different; **b22** vastly improved from the sulphur-tainted bottling of last year. In fact, their most enjoyable standard distillery bottling I've had for many years. But forget about the whisky: the blurb on the back is among the most interesting you likely to find anywhere. And I quote: "Founder James Allardice called the original Glendronach, 'The Guid Glendronach'. But there's no need to imitate his marketing methods. The first converts to his malt were the 'ladies of the night' in Edinburgh's Canongate!" Fascinating. And as a professional whisky taster I am left wondering: did they swallow or spit... 40%

⋅≣⋅ **Glendronach 12 Years Old** db **(92) n22** some pretty juicy grape in there; **t24** silky delivery with the grape teaming with the barley to produce the sharpest delivery and follow through you can imagine: exceptionally good weight with just enough oils to make full use of the delicate sweetness and the build towards spices and cocoa in the middle ground is a wonderful tease; **f22.5** dries and heads into bitter marmalade country; **b23.5** an astonishingly beautiful malt despite the fact that a rogue sherry butt has come in under the radar. But for that, this would have been a mega scorer: potentially an award-winner. Fault or no fault, seriously worth discovering this bottling of this too long undiscovered great distillery 43%

⋅≣⋅ **Glendronach 15 Years Old** db **(77.5) n19 t18.5 f20 b20.** The really frustrating thing is, you can hear those amazingly brilliant sherry butts screaming to be heard in their purest voice. Those alone, and you could, like the 12-y-o, have a score cruising over 95 mark. I can't wait for the next bottling. 46%

Glendronach 15 Years Old db **(83) n20 t22 f20 b21.** Chocolate fudge and grape juice to start then tails off towards a slightly bitter, dry finish. 40%

⋅≣⋅ **Glendronach 18 Years Old** db **(87) n22** rhubarb and custard – both the sweet and candy; this is underpinned by a real resonance to the oak, and undermined by a subtle evidence of a less than helpful sherry butt; **t21.5** a dry delivery with the sweet grape taking its time to get a grip; **f22** lightly overdone toast and fruit preserve...smoothed over with a knife that had previously dipped into the pot of chocolate spread; **b21.5** apart from those dead few seconds on delivery and the obvious mild flaw, this is really lovely stuff – just so good to see this distillery back in harness. But you know that even better is to come... *46%*

Glendronach Aged 33 Years oloroso sherry db **(95) n24** it's as if your head is stuck in a sherry butt still in the bodega; be transported back in time to when soft, very gently smoked malt still had the wherewithal to link with the grape and offer something teasing yet profound, ripe yet beautifully fresh. Majestic...; **t24** sublime sherry arrival with a wonderful toffee-apple, honeycomb and leather (almost very old bourbon) theme; the malt is almost thick enough to cut, and the softest smoke imaginable combines to add extra weight to the fruit; **f23** the oak now arrives, but offering layers of vanilla to complement the fruit; still the smoke drifts and this adds further to the near bitter-sweet perfection; **b24** want to know what sherry should really nose like: invest in a bottle of this. This is a vivid malt boasting spellbinding clarity and charm. A golden nugget of a dram, which would have been better still at 46% *40%*

The Glendronach 1968 db **(92) n23** nuts, clean sherry of the highest order; **t22** exceptionally together with the most vibrant oloroso: not a single off note; **f23** astonishing depth, with more than a touch of pot still Demerara (PM mark to be precise); **b24** an almost extinct style of sherry that is faultless in its firmness and clarity. This was bottled in 1993 – I remember it well. Astonishingly, some bottles have just turned up in Whisky of the World Duty Free in UK and this is how it tastes now. Grab while you can. *43%*

⋯ **Glendronach Single Cask 1992** cask no. 401 db **(96) n24** more than a hint of Demerara rum to the rich, sherried nose. Molasses sweeten the high roast Java while the barley screams to make itself heard; the oak has a slightly unusual, mossy earthiness adding to the overall enormity; **t23.5** the palate is swamped in luxuriant, lush sugar-coated burnt raisins: wave upon wave of spice explode on the back of the tongue and roof of the mouth. A big, sugary coating gives a distinct crispness to the rigid malt; **f24.5** the coffee, so well defined on the nose, returns here with even more molasses to sweeten it up. Excellent soft oils coat the roof of the mouth, ensuring a long fade as busy spices continue their lively assault. The juicy barley finale offers a welcome lightness and balance; **b24** ultra distinctive with that firm sheen offering a very unusual dimension. However, the unmistakable rum character on a sherry theme really makes for a memorable and massive malt which never quite tastes the same twice and alters in weight and complexity considerably depending on heat and time applied. Outrageously excellent. The distillery at its most complex. *60.2%*. *BenRiach Distillers exclusively for Parkers Whisky.*

⋯ **Glendronach Single Cask 1994** cask no. 2311 db **(91.5) n21.5** almost playfully light; fragile barley embraces the oak and the two fuse so that after a while it is difficult to distinguish where one note starts and the other ends. A lazy nuttiness perfectly compliments the bitter-sweet tone; **t23** mouthwatering barley pounds the tastebuds relentlessly from the start, bringing with it delicate oaky shades for extra weight and depth. A lively character with a fiery temperament when cool but at body temperature relaxes allowing the barley to reach searing levels of intensity. The biting, salivating sharpness of the malt nigh brings tears to the eyes; **f23.5** there is a minty chocolate edge to this, as well as hazelnuts and vanilla. For all the obvious lightness there is considerable length with the barley dovetailing comfortably with the oak, as ever, for the final say; **b23.5** about the closest I have ever tasted to the long defunct 12-year-old bourbon cask Glendronach, a legendary single malt in the old Allied armoury. A malt which really needs to be warmed to body temperature to see it in its full glory and form, one quite unique to this little-known distillery. Fascinating and fabulous. *59.4%*. *BenRiach Distillers exclusively for Parkers Whisky.*

⋯ **Duncan Taylor Collection Glendronach 1975** cask no. 706 **(87.5) n22.5** brittle barley on the nose, encased by sugar, sprinkled Bakewell tart crust; **t22** almost crystalline in its delivery: the barley is rock hard while the myriad sugar notes seep out offering varying intensity; **f22** vanilla and caramelised ice cream cones; **b21.5** maybe at 25 years you might be looking for a touch more variance. But on the other hand, what it does it does very well... *51.4%*

GLENDULLAN (see also below)
Speyside, 1972. Diageo. Working.

Glendullan Aged 8 Years db **(89) n20** fresh, gingery, zesty; **t22** distinctly mealy and malty. **f24** brilliant – really stunning grassy malt powers through. Speyside in a glass – and a nutshell; **b23** this is just how I like my Speysiders: young fresh and uplifting. A charming malt.

Singleton of Glendullan 12 Years Old db **(87) n22** significant oak hides some of the Jamaican ginger; **t22** a gutsier barley character with stifled honey and the oak dives in again; **f21** dry with a slight return of ginger; **b22** much more age than is comfortable for a 12-y-o. *40%*

Connoisseurs Choice Glendullan 1993 (88) n22 fresh barley and smidgeon of smoke; **t22** mouth-watering at first, then a slow building of oils; **f22** attractively bitter-sweet as the oak makes a polite entrance; **b22** usually, because of the wood policy, you never quite know what you are going to get from this distillery. Pretty decent cask yet you have very pleasant, untaxing up and downer simply because of the extra oil on the body. *43%. Gordon & MacPhail.*

Murray McDavid Glendullan 1993 Aged 14 Years bourbon/rioja **(79) n21 t19 f20 b19.** Weird, eh? I adore Glendullan. I have a house in Kentucky, such is my love for bourbon. And my wine of the season I had served in any football boardroom during 05/06 was a Rioja at Coventry City. Yet put these together...works in part, but too bitty. Though I love the chocolate finale. *46%*

⠿ **Old Masters Glendullan Aged 12 Years** cask no. 5059, dist 97, bott 09 **(85) n21.5 t22 f20.5 b21.** Decent, thoroughly enjoyable, simplistic malt with a good, refreshing zing to the barley delivery. *56.1%. James MacArthur & Co. Ltd.*

⠿ **Provenance Glendullan Aged 12 Years** refill hogshead, dist summer 96, bott autumn 08 **(80.5) n21.5 t20 f19 b20.** Very happy to steer a malty course, causing minimum wake. *46%. Douglas Laing.*

⠿ **Scotch Malt Whisky Society Cask 84.11 Aged 11 Years** refill hogshead, dist Sep 97 **(89) n21** dry, oak dominated; **t22** excellent, juicy delivery which makes a lie of the nose: resounding barley notes are thick and subtly sweetened; the middle has an oaky threat but soft mocha's to the rescue; **f23.5** beautiful chocolate mint, soft spice, and a reprise of the juicy barley...fabulous; **b22.5** after such an ordinary nose the complex beast which follows simply stuns. *58.6%*

GLENDULLAN (see also above)
Speyside, 1898–1985. Closed.

Glendullan 1978 Rare Malt db **(88) n23** exceptional piquancy to this with the quietness of the oak shattered by a lemon-citrus shrill. Genuinely wonderful; **t22** a lovely, tart start with that citrus making a crashing entry but the oak barges in soon after and coffee is soon on the menu; **f21** more coffee and lemon cake, though it by now a very small slice; **b22** Sherlock Holmes would have loved this one: he would have found it lemon-entry. *56.8%*

GLEN ELGIN
Speyside, 1900. Diageo. Working.

Glen Elgin Aged 12 Years db **(89) n23** blistering, mouthwatering fruit of unspecified origin. The intensity of the malt is breathtaking; **t24** stunning fresh malt arrival, salivating barley that is both crisp and lush: then a big round of spice amid some squashed, over-ripe plums. Faultless mouthfeel; **f20** the spice continues as does the intense malt but is devalued dramatically by a bitter-toffee effect; **b22** absolutely murders Cragganmore as Diageo's top dog bottled Speysider. The marks would be several points further north if one – rightly or wrongly – didn't get the feeling that some caramel was weaving a derogatory spell. Brilliant stuff nonetheless. States Pot Still on label – not to be confused with Irish Pot Still. This is 100% malt... and it shows! *43%*

⠿ **Cadenhead's Glen Elgin Aged 30 Years** dist 78, bott 09 **(92) n23** no doubting the age. Suet pudding and curiously salted bread pudding provide the curious complexity; **t24** ginger and honey really beef up the cut glass barley. Layer upon layer of delicious stuff with always a thread of sweetness to be found in every one; **f22** bitters slightly as the oak interjects but still retains a juicy freshness to the last; **b23** worthy of this excellent distillery. *49.1%*

Connoisseurs Choice Glen Elgin 1995 (91) n22.5 gloriously layered barley ranging from crisp to yielding and a small puff of smoke for good measure; **t23** mouth-filling chewy, lively barley that again reaches out at many levels; **f22.5** spices up pleasantly as the drier, flaky oaks arrive; **b23** an essential Glen Elgin: textbook excellence. If only this malt could be more easily found. *46%. Gordon & MacPhail.*

Duncan Taylor The NC2 Range Glen Elgin 1991 (72) n17 t18 f17 b17. A United Distillers' sherry "butt", one assumes. Say no more... *46%*

Old Malt Cask Glen Elgin Aged 16 Years refill hogshead no. 3927, dist Jun 91, bott Oct 07 **(88) n22** a barley only club; **t22** distinctive coppery sheen adds lustre to the malt; **f22** some late apples join in; warms up on the palate; **b22** fair degree of complexity. *50%. Douglas Laing. 287 bottles.*

⠿ **Old Malt Cask Glen Elgin Aged 24 Years** dist May 85, bott Jul 09 **(83) n21.5 t21 f20 b20.5.** One of my favourite Speyside distilleries here feels the oaky pace. Pleasant natural caramels. *44.9%. Douglas Laing.*

Old Masters Glen Elgin Aged 17 Years cask no. 2598 dist 91, bott 08 **(91.5) n23.5** ultra-clean sherry coats every aspect of this lightly spiced nose; **t23.5** lush, freshly-crushed grape moving on to lightly spiced sultana. There is a barley sub-plot here; **f22** slightly bitter burnt toast; **b22.5** benefits from an unusually beautiful sherry influence. How rare is that these days...? 54.6%. James MacArthur & Co. Ltd.

GLENESK

Highland (Eastern), 1897–1985. Closed.

Hillside 25 Years Old Rare Malts Selection db **(83) n20 t23 f20 b20.** Hot as Hades, but for a Glenesk this gets off to a cracking start and is let down only by the paucity of the finale. Plenty to enjoy though, with some really top-rate malt-honey notes. 62%

Connoisseurs Choice Glenesk 1982 (68) n17 t18 f16 b17. Poorley made whisky. Not at all pleasant. 40%. Gordon & Macphail

Connoisseurs Choice Glenesk 1984 (83) n19 t21 f21 b22. A very rare malt this, but the style is consistent. Here the sweetness is down slightly and hangs together and harmonises much, much better than in many previous bottlings. An attractive, surprise package. 43%. Gordon & MacPhail.

Duncan Taylor Collection Glenesk 1981 cask no. 932 **(57) n14 t15 f14 b14.** I say! Sulphur, anyone? 54.3%

Duncan Taylor Collection Glenesk 1981 cask no. 933 **(84) n22 t20 f21 b21.** I say! Sherry anyone? 56.9%

⁖ **Duncan Taylor Collection Glenesk 1983** cask no. 4930 **(89.5) n22** chugging, thick, two-tone fruit – one mildly nondescript, the other offering physalis while the barley is fit and healthy; **t23** now that is rather lovely. Hot, perhaps, but in its way it helps accentuate the depth to the barley while allowing the more juicy, tangy notes free reign; **f22** some lovely latte towards the finish, a touch creamy; **b22.5** by far the best Glen Esk I've tasted in years. Perhaps not the most complex, but the liveliness and clarity are a treat. 52.1%

Duncan Taylor Rare Auld Glenesk 26 Years Old sherry cask, dist Feb 81, bott Dec 07 **(82.5) n20.5 t21 f20.5 b20.5.** I say! Sherry and sulphur, anyone..? 56.9%. Whisky-Doris.

GLENFARCLAS

Speyside, 1836. J&G Grant. Working.

Glenfarclas 8 Years Old db **(86) n21 t22 f22 b21.** Less intense sherry allows the youth of this malt to stand out. Mildly quirky as a Glenfarclas and enormous entertainment. 40%

Glenfarclas 10 Years Old db **(80) n19 t20 f22 b19.** Always an enjoyable malt, but for some reason this version never seems to fire on all cylinders. There is a vague honey sheen which works well with the barley, but struggles for balance and the nose is a bit sweaty. Still has distinctly impressive elements but an odd fish. 40%

Glenfarclas 105 Cask Strength 10 Years Old db **(91) n22** perfect fresh sherry influence; clean, intense, charismatic, fruity and precise; **t23** rather confusing as the might of the malt and sherry battle for supremacy: takes time to settle and the drier oak helps enormously to accentuate the honied qualities of the malt; **f23** a fine, layered oak seeing off the sweeter honeycomb theme for a distinguished finale; **b23** this, for various reasons, has been a regular dram of mine for over 20 years. It has been at its very best in recent bottlings, though the nose here doesn't quite hit the heights. 60%

Glenfarclas 12 Years Old db **(89) n22** oops! Nothing like its usual near brilliant self early on, but some golden strands of honey compensate handsomely; **t23** recovers superbly to offer lashings of the trademark honeycomb amid a riot of gentle oaky spice; the light sprinkling of muscovado sugar is sublime, as is the crushed raisins; **f22** more burned honeycomb and some subtle extra oak offers dry vanilla; **b23** from this sample just the odd cask has tarnished the usual brilliance, but it's still good enough to offer moments of Speyside most glorious. 43%

Glenfarclas 15 Years Old db **(95) n23** such is the intensity of the fruit and sugar-rich barley, there is an element of medium ester Jamaican pot still rum to this, a feeling intensified by an orangey-oak influence that seems greater than 15 years. The top-shelf sherry, though, is of a classical type rarely found these days, though common 30 years ago; **t24** succulent and stupendous. Barley sugar shows first then a sherry input that borders on intense but dissipates as the spicy oak digs in; **f24** long, chewy, a tad oily and fades with a wonderful coffee-vanilla combination and a late surge of something bourbony; **b24** Eureka!!! The 15-y-o back to how I can remember it in the past. Some of you may have been scared away by some less than impressive recent bottlings. It's safe to come back because now it has been returned to its position as one of Scotland's most sublime malts. The quality of the sherry is astonishing; its interaction with the barley is a wondrous joy. Go find and get... 46%

Glenfarclas 17 Years Old db **(93) n23** just so light and playful: custard powder lightens and sweetens, sultana softens, barley moistens, spice threatens...; **t23** the relaxed sherry influence really lets the honey deliver; delightfully roasty and well spiced towards the middle; **f23** when I was a kid there was a candy – pretend tobacco, no less! – made from strands of coconut and sweetened with a Demerara syrup. My, this takes me back...; **b24** an excellent age for this distillery, allowing just enough oak in to stir up the complexity. A stupendous addition to the range. *40%*

Glenfarclas 21 Years Old db **(83) n20 t23 f19 b21.** A chorus of sweet, honied malt and mildly spiced, teasing fruit on the fabulous mouth arrival and middle compensates for the blips. *43%*

Glenfarclas 25 Years Old db **(88) n22** a heavy, impervious nose with the sherry and oak providing a cleanly-built wall; **t23** much softer with an immediate mouthwatering delivery full of prime, sweet barley and then toasted raisins; **f21** soft vanilla; fruitcake and cream; **b22** an distinct improvement on previous bottlings with the finish here having much more to say. *43%*

Glenfarclas 30 Years Old db **(85) n20 t22 f21 b22.** Flawed yet juicy. *43%*

Glenfarclas 40 Years Old Millennium Edition db **(92) n23 t23 f23 b23.** An almost immaculate portrayal of an old-fashioned, high-quality malt with unblemished sherry freshness and depth. The hallmark of quality is the sherry's refusal to dominate the spicy, softly peated malt. The oak offers a bourbony sweetness but ensures a rich depth throughout. Quite outstanding for its age. *nc ncf.*

Glenfarclas 50 Years Old db **(92) n24** Unique. Almost a marriage between 20-y-o bourbon and intense, old-fashioned sherry. Earthy, weighty stuff that repays time in the glass and oxidization because only then does the subtlety become apparent and a soft peat-reek reveal itself; **t23** an unexpected sweet – even mouthwatering - arrival, again with a touch of peat to add counter ballast to the intense richness of the sherry. The oak is intense from the middle onwards, but of such high quality that it merely accompanies rather then dominates; **f22** warming black peppers ping around the palate; some lovely cocoa oils coat the mouth for a bitter-sweet, warming and very long finish; **b23** Most whiskies cannot survive such great age. This one really does bloom in the glass and the earthy, peaty aspect makes it all the more memorable. It has taken 50 years to reach this state. Give a glass of this at least an hour's inquisition, as I have. Your patience will be rewarded many times over. *44.4%*

Glenfarclas 1952 The Family Casks cask no. 1712, plain hogshead db **(78) n21** papaya fruit and crushed cherry stone; **t19** the oak has taken over, leaving enough for a Fisherman's Friend sweetness; **f19** cough sweet. Or, a sweet that makes you cough... **b19** perfectly drinkable. Quite enjoyable. But this is old whisky. And tastes like it. *56.5%. 110 bottles.*

⋰ **Glenfarclas 1952 The Family Casks (3rd Release)** plain hogshead, cask no. 1713 db **(81) n20.5 t20 f20.5 b20.** For a curious moment there is an almost hoppy bitterness to this one: a dram for the Campaign For Real Whisky. Just too much oak for greatness, I'm afraid. *473%*

Glenfarclas 1953 The Family Casks cask no. 1678, sherry butt db **(87) n23** fruit spirit: cherry and raspberry brandy softened by burnt honeycomb; **t21** excellent malt delivery then a sinus-attacking wave of oak; **f22** recovers superbly for a tangy grapey finale; **b21** myriad battles are fought to keep the oak in check. Most are won. *53.7%. 480 bottles.*

Glenfarclas 1954 The Family Casks cask no. 444, sherry butt db **(94) n22** more oak than an Elizabethan man-of-war. Except this is far from sunk... **t24** oak scorches into the back and roof of the mouth; countering muscovado tries to douse the flames. The ensuing battle is fabulous.. **f24** long, ultimately on the dry and mildly bitter side, but not before some mocha and Melton cake have made their fabulous marks, as well as marmalade and cherry preserve; **b24** simply defies time and belief. Carries the scars of 52 summers, for sure. But with the same pride a legionnaire would wear his trophies of combat. *52.6%. 406 bottles.*

Glenfarclas 1955 The Family Casks cask no. 2211, sherry butt db **(88) n23** medium roast Brazilian and crushed hazelnuts adds complexity to dried dates; **t21** big oak start, off balance slightly but stabilised by a pinch of Demerara; **f22** recovers for an impressive finale with outstanding vanilla camp coffee; **b22** a proud dram gallantly hanging on to its last sweet traces. *46.1%. 545 bottles.*

Glenfarclas 1956 The Family Casks cask no. 1758, sherry butt db **(83) n24** amazingly similar to the '58 but with a shot of extra oak; **t21** short oloroso blast, soft oils and spice; dries quickly; **f19** pretty well oaked and bitters up; **b19** great nose but relentless oak. *473%. 435 bottles.*

Glenfarclas 1957 The Family Casks cask no. 2111, sherry hogshead db **(91) n23** a hickory/Java coffee combo, only not so camp; the fruit is almost opaque; **t23** the inside of your mouth puckers as your tastebuds try to negotiate the minefield laid by the massive oak and the intense, sharp sherry; **f22** traces of molassed barley filter through, as does sherry concentrate; bitter fruit stones abound; **b23** I left this as the last whisky before finishing the tasting notes to the 2008 edition (this is the 811th and final brand new dram fresh to market to be included this year, and exactly the 950th to be tasted in all). I was born in 1957. And in four and half months I shall be celebrating (?) my 50th birthday. So it had to be. Great whisky. Unquestionably: if you have the balls to take a fourth or fifth mouthful. Enjoyable? Hugely. Providing you strap yourself into your chair first. Ladies and gentlemen. The tasting notes for 2008 are finished. *54%. 158 bottles.*

Glenfarclas 1957 The Family Casks (2nd Release) cask no. 2115, bott 10 Oct 07 db **(88) n24** a swamp of a nose with massive sherry: reminds me of the Glenrothes I spotted in Fleet Street back in the 80s, except this has more peppery resonance, all to bring out the richer textures and exploding over-ripe French greengages; a touch of basil for good measure and off it goes.... **t22** much sweeter than the nose suggests, but the sherry coats everything it touches; **f21** some bitter coffee; **b21** you really can get too much of a good thing. For its age, remarkable. But spend as much time on the nose as you can. *46.5%. 116 bottles.*

⋰ **Glenfarclas 1957 The Family Casks (3rd Release)** sherry hogshead, cask no. 2 db **(91.5) n25** the perfect oldie nose: medium roast, un-ground Blue Mountain coffee beans merging blissfully with a super-rich Dundee cake magnificently beyond its sell by date and all topped with what first appears to be sherry trifle, but on further inspection is old, nutty oloroso of the highest order; **t22.5** improbable, sweet, mouth-watering delivery for a second or two but then the oak rushes in....and some. There is a spicy counter, but the middle ground dries and thinks about offering a eucalyptus layer or three; **f22** some molasses help dispel the more fundamental oaky themes and we are left with a kind of slightly burned honeycomb and spice; **b22** to mark my 50th birthday in 2007, I had planned on buying a cask of Glenfarclas 1957 and bottling it. Sadly, I was simply too busy to make it happen; had I done so this might possibly have been the cask I chose. It is a couple of summers past its best – well, probably more. But back in '07, I might just have been able to prevent some of the oaky excess. Then again, maybe not. What cannot be denied is that the nose would probably be Nose of the Year for this Bible, were there such an award. And that even though, like the rest of us from that vintage, it has seen better days, there is no denying that this is less a whisky but more of a life experience. And it is certainly as good and privileged a way I can think of wrapping up all my new whiskies for 2010, this being something like number 920 (actually I have lost count – we'll have to do a final tally by computer), because astonishing whiskies like this don't grow on trees: they simply mature in bits of them....if they are very, very lucky... *46.2%*

Glenfarclas 1958 The Family Casks cask no. 2245, sherry butt db **(88) n24** outrageous aroma for its age: walnut oil coated on ripe greengage and mildly burnt Dundee cake and sprinkled with demerara...swoon!..; **t22** lush, juicy delivery then, after about ten seconds, in comes the oak. With a vengeance... **f20** brown sugars try to head off the oak's excesses; **b22** keeps its head above the oaky water - just. *51.6%. 455 bottles*

Glenfarclas 1959 The Family Casks cask no. 1816, sherry hogshead db **(83) n22 t21 f20 b20.** The nose with its fabulous array of latte coffee, saves this one. The delivery is as searingly oaked as you'll find. *52.5%. 194 bottles.*

⋰ **Glenfarclas 1959 The Family Casks (3rd Release)** sherry hogshead, cask no. 3227 db **(79.5) n23 t20 f17.5 b19.** Huge gooseberry and grape. But appears to have suffered from a little renovation work. *50.9%*

Glenfarclas 1960 The Family Casks cask no. 1767, sherry hogshead db **(95) n23** thumping blood orange, grape and a sliver of bourbon; **t25** enormous delivery but absolutely sublime in the honeycomb and molassed mix to the barley and fruitcake, chewy and a touch salty; **f23** Mysore medium roast coffee under-sprinkled with molassed sugar; long and bitters out; **b24** yes, there is no doubting the oak is present. The trick is making it sing, which it does almost without a crack'd note. The secret is warming it right up to body temp. Simply marvellous whisky. *52.4%. 228 bottles*

Glenfarclas 1960 The Family Casks (2nd Release) cask no. 1773, bott 10 Oct 07 db **(91) n24** like standing outside a coffee roaster: sweet oat stout and demerara rum figure in there somewhere, too; **t22** more tired than the nose but cherry juice and allspice offer a welcome deviation; **f23** more settled and back with the coffee, if slightly on the bitter side; **b22** certainly not lacking in character, let alone style. The way it stays intact and entertains as it does so is truly brilliant. *43.8%. 157 bottles.*

⋰ **Glenfarclas 1960 The Family Casks (3rd Release)** sherry hogshead, cask no. 1768 db **(91) n24** attractively stewed oak with the sherry offering both lighter juice and depth; the odd big, ripe cherry moment, too; **t23** puckering sharpness to the fruitcake; somewhere in the recipe are a few spoonfuls of molasses and again those cherries; **f21.5** predictably tires at the end, though the odd milk-coffee note sympathises; **b22.5** retains a fabulous degree of life for its age. *44.6%*

Glenfarclas 1961 The Family Casks cask no. 4913, sherry hogshead db **(79) n19 t21 f19 b20.** A '61 vintage yet appears to have vague, weird sulphur-type traces....nah, must be my imagination. Something very bitty about it, though. *46%. 159 bottles.*

∵ **Glenfarclas 1961 The Family Cask (3rd Release)** sherry hogshead, cask no. 1322 db **(79) n20 t23 f17.5 b19.** Fat and full with the grape leading from the front though the bitterness does seem rather over rampant and not entirely oak related: a touch of déjà vous... *52.2%*

Glenfarclas 1962 The Family Casks cask no. 2645, sherry hogshead db **(91) n23** clean demi-sec oloroso keeps the oak honest; **t23** warming oloroso: soft grape counters the stinging oak; **f22** some major age here plus liquorice-lime to balance; **b23** another summer may have broken this one. *54.8%. 166 bottles.*

∵ **Glenfarclas 1962 The Family Casks (3rd Release)** sherry hogshead, cask no. 2647 db **(96.5) n25** good grief...!!! Had this been marked a 25-year-old Demerara Pot Still rum, I would have believed them. The fruit and oak have fused together to form one rich, semi-sweet, breathtakingly spiced, coffee-enriched, marmalade-lightened thing of brain-exploding beauty. Nose-wise: perfection... **t24** the oaks make all the running, being of the big toasty nature you would expect. But those rich and still juicy fruits also play a magnificent part in forming the early balance and high-class flourish; **f23.5** when those sweeter notes dissolve you are left with a big burnt toast and torched raisin wedge of oak; **b24** the age takes its toll late on, which is to be expected. But up until the finish you nose this one until your nostrils bleed and close your eyes and swallow something a little special. Do I normally advocate spitting...? Not this time.... *52%*

Glenfarclas 1963 The Family Casks cask no. 4098, sherry butt db **(87) n24** stunningly floral with crushed, dank petals, marzipan and hickory...phew!! **t22** dry and spiced for all the grape; **f19** a tad too oaked; bitter; **b22** borderline. The oak really is big, but the grape holds out – just. The nose is a different matter. *56.7%. 420 bottles.*

Glenfarclas 1964 The Family Casks cask no. 4717, sherry butt db **(92) n23** signs of creaking oak but clean, sweetish oloroso stands firm; **t24** juicy, tangy marmalade and spice; **f22** gentle, refined finale with grape in hand; **b23** a gentleman dram which speaks quietly despite the obvious power at hand. *53.1%. 415 bottles.*

Glenfarclas 1965 The Family Casks cask no. 3861, sherry butt db **(86) n22 t21 f22 b21.** No shortage of active, tangy oak. A non-phenol version of Fisherman's Friend. *60%. 417 bottles.*

Glenfarclas 1966 The Family Casks cask no. 4177, sherry butt db **(95) n25** faultless. Exactly how you dream a 40 year old sherry butt should be. Curves everywhere, not a jagged edge, just caresses, hints, whispers and innuendoes. A king – or perhaps queen - among casks; **t23** surprising lightness with some raspberry amid the juicy grape; **f23** soft honey and spice. Absolutely no evidence of oaky deterioration; **b24** how fitting this whisky is the same colour as Alan Ball's hair. Because there is no greater way of toasting the memory of the man who was 1966. *51.5%. 514 bottles.*

Glenfarclas 1967 The Family Casks cask no. 5118, sherry hogshead db **(90) n23** wonderful fino-style dryness; bite and freshness; **t22** oaky incursions met by chocolate and grape; **f22** remains fresh and fruit salady mouth-watering; **b23** diced plain chocolate on the plummy nose; a fruity mishmash on delivery. Tasty, though. *58.5%. 181 bottles.*

Glenfarclas 1967 The Family Casks (2nd Release) cask no. 5117, bott 11 Oct 07 db **(89.5) n23** first-class grape radiates from the glass, bringing a decent amount of oak and linseed with it; **t22** puckeringly dry thanks to the age but the grape fights back to muster some juice **f22.5** better balanced at the death with some wonderful roast Java moments; **b22** teetering on the edge, this one, but excellence of the sherry wins the day. *58.7%. 138 bottles.*

Glenfarclas 1968 The Family Casks cask no. 1316, sherry butt db **(84) n21 t20 f22 b21.** Despite the massive strength for its age, has a slightly metallic resonance. *65.1%. 483 bottles.*

Glenfarclas 1969 The Family Casks cask no. 3184, sherry hogshead db **(89) n22** knots of oak and sweetish liquorice; **t22** a real battle between the dry oak and honeycomb; **f23** increasingly dry and oaky...then those rich rays of golden syrup breaking through the oaky cloud – unbelievable. Especially when it looked as though age had won; **b22** bravo this brave and proud cask. Fights back from the brink with absolute class. *56.2%. 148 bottles.*

Glenfarclas 1969 The Family Casks (2nd Release) cask no. 3185, bott 11 Oct 07 db **(65) n18 t16 f15 b16.** One can assume only that this was "rounded off" in some present days butt(s). I could almost weep. *56.5%. 121 bottles.*

∵ **Glenfarclas 1969 The Family Casks (3rd Release)** sherry hogshead, cask no. 3188 db **(92.5) n22.5** such intensity, this really needs a few minutes in the glass to breath and unravel. Eventually a mega thick, nutty, almost primeaval oloroso emerges: the barley has vanished but some toasty, flakey oak guarantees some serious dryness; for a moment there even appears to be a kind of mild sulphur whiff – it's a 1969, so surely can't be...can it...? **t24** a sherry/oak duo is dolloped on delivery, but the salivating grapey raisiny notes begin to spread and thin and eventually an initial bitter-dryness is evened out; wonderful demarara, mocha and hickory fill the middle ground as a quasi-bourbony character momentarily takes hold; **f22.5** a gentle dark sugared sweetness pervades while burnt raisin offer a fruity edge to the vanilla; bitters out...strange.... **b23.5** even taking into account what appears a minor fault, this is not a dram you can knock back in a couple of minutes. Treat this malt as you would a first growth Bordeaux and you will be amply rewarded. 55.6%

Glenfarclas 1970 The Family Casks cask no. 566, sherry butt db **(94) n24** Jamaica Ginger Cake doused in beautifully clean oloroso; **t23** massively mouth-filling with heavyweight fruit punctuated by lazy spice; **f23** back to the moist ginger again with black peppers and molassed sugar in equal measures; **b24** seriously elegant and complex malt that shows not a single blemish despite the extraordinary great age. A Glenfarclas Great. 53.6%. 497 bottles.

Glenfarclas 1971 The Family Casks cask no. 140, sherry butt db **(93) n24** Demerara rummy with enormous depth: bitter-sweet heaven with slow build up of big fruit; **t24** sandalwood, toffee and berry fruit; **f22** thins quite fast, allowing in the vanilla; **b23** a noble dram. 57.1%. 459 bottles.

Glenfarclas 1972 The Family Casks cask no. 3546, sherry butt db **(83) n21 t21 f21 b20.** Dry, a tad dull and much more natural toffee here. 51.1%. 645 bottles.

Glenfarclas 1973 The Family Casks cask no. 2578, sherry butt db **(92) n24** ginger and honeycomb; **t22** soft, yielding grape; usual spices abound; **f23** vanilla stirs up the complexity; **b23** a more gentle expression than most from the mid 70s: one for the faint hearted. 58.8%. 457 bottles.

Glenfarclas 1974 The Family Casks cask no. 5786, sherry butt db **(93) n23** salty and seasoned; **t23** wonderful orangey-grapey-spicy infusion; Warming spices become positively vicious; **f23** some old citrus sinks deeply into the vanilla; the pugilistic spices are positively puckering; **b24** what a real brawling dram! A kind of Oliver Reed of malts; shows that touch of class despite those rough diamond edges. 60.8%. 555 bottles.

Glenfarclas 1975 The Family Casks cask no. 5038, refill hogshead db **(92) n23** chunky marmalade with the oak at full throttle; **t22** dry yet salivating. Only a wonderful stratum of juicy grape absorbs the blows; **f24** so long, so spicy: so get stuck in...!! **b23** dry yet balances wonderfully. Another spicy number. 51.4%. 187 bottles.

Glenfarclas 1976 The Family Casks cask no. 3111, refill butt db **(92) n23** wallows in a Dundee cake fruit richness, complete with nuts and perhaps with a curl of butter; **t23** melts on impact to leave a grapey residue. Burnt raisin and plump sultana dominate; **f23** dries with a suety dryness but barley water and a sprinkle of silver sugar maintains the balance; **b23** no whisky that's 30 years old has any right to be this juicy and fresh. A malt to take your time over. 49.4%.

Glenfarclas 1977 The Family Casks cask no. 61, refill butt db **(90) n22** slight, crushed sultana; **t23** wonderful amalgam of barley sugar and grape juice: light, but on a waxy body; **f22** delicate banana custard; **b23** a class, understated act from nose to finale. 59%. 582 bottles.

Glenfarclas 1978 The Family Casks cask no. 587, refill hogshead db **(85) n21 t21 f22 b21.** Chewy and fat. Not a hint of bitterness on the well-oiled grape. 50.3%. 251 bottles.

⋯ **Glenfarclas 1978 The Family Casks (3rd Release)** plain hogshead, cask no. 626 db **(88) n22** attractive rhubarb and custard topped with barley sugar; **t21.5** fizzing barley and fizzier oak; **f23.5** settles down majestically for a really classy display of boiled sweets and low sugared chocolate with the malt really gathering a head of steam; **b22** the oak grabs hard early on but lets go gently to allow the barley to escape unscathed. 57.6%

Glenfarclas 1979 The Family Casks cask no. 146, plain hogshead db **(92) n22** sherbet lemon; lively vanillas; **t23** eye-watering, mouth-watering sharpness that reveals the distillery's grassy, Speyside roots; **f24** continues in the same manner with the barley frothing about the palate, light spices teasing and weak golden syrup balancing out the drier oaks; **b23** for its age, a real surprise cask. Has more life than I do, that's for sure... Sheer class. 52.8%. 225 bottles.

⋯ **Glenfarclas 1979 The Family Casks (3rd Release)** plain hogshead, cask no. 2216 db **(96.5) n24.5** the oak makes all kind of fruity noises not unlike a Grenadian breakfast table and is bolstered further by honey roast nut and trifle sans sherry; of it's style, not far off perfect... **t24** dissolves on impact: soft but not to the point of subjugation as there are firmer, ultra clean, juicy barley notes springing forward to develop a malty theme, but one which is caked in delicate honey; the oak is always showing but refuses steadfastly to cross the line of good taste and manners; **f24** an unbelievably civilised winding down. Full of gentle, sweet, cocoa notes, the oak certainly has a bigger role, but one it carries off with aplomb; **b24** proof, not that it was ever needed, that this quite brilliant distillery does not need sherry to bolster its quality. On this evidence, there could be an argument put forward that sherry actually detracts from the greatness of the distillate. At 30 years there appears to be a marriage forged in heaven between the honey-rich barley and the oak. But to achieve this kind of style and depth, it is the raw spirit which must stand up and be counted. Game set and match against those who reckon Glenfarclas a one trick pony: if this isn't proof that the foundations of complexity aren't laid by the make, then I have no idea what is. *50.6%*

Glenfarclas 1980 The Family Casks cask no. 1942, refill sherry butt db **(80) n19 t21 f20 b20.** Soft toffee apple, but not entirely flawless. *50.1%. 681 bottles.*

Glenfarclas 1981 The Family Casks cask no. 29, refill sherry hogshead db **(86) n20 t22 f22 b22.** Enjoyable, especially the explosive delivery. *52.4%. 234 bottles.*

Glenfarclas 1982 Vintage db **(90) n22** fat sultanas and fresh-cut grass; **t22** immensely sweet by Glenfarclas standards with a big barley rush; **f23** stunningly layered with delicate vanilla found with varying levels of toastiness; **b23** a good choice for the market as there is extraordinary youth for a malt so old. Just so clean and quietly sophisticated. *43%. Spain Market.*

Glenfarclas 1982 The Family Casks cask no. 2213, refill sherry hogshead db **(82) n19 t21 f21 b21.** Silky, lush, toffeed and well spiced. *58.3%. 258 bottles.*

Glenfarclas 1983 The Family Casks cask no. 50, refill hogshead db **(88) n20** tight, a tad untidy; **t22** firm barley which slowly blossoms into a wonderful, bitter-sweet spicefest; **f24** better balance as the barley shines and muscovado sugar sorts out the oak; **b22** a sunshine after a rainy afternoon malt *56%. 302 bottles.*

Glenfarclas 1984 The Family Casks cask no. 6028, plain hogshead db **(93) n23** citrus!! What's all this about? Nostrils-full of barley....; **t23** more citrus on delivery with soft, mildly chalky oak dovetailing with the grassy, mouth-watering barley; **f23** lemon then a light dusting of cocoa; **b24** at first I thought I had been poured malt from the wrong distillery until I saw the cask type. By no means the first non-sherry Glenfarclas, but perhaps the most lemony-fresh and palate-cleansing at this age. So, so lovely! *51.3%. 267 bottles.*

Glenfarclas 1985 The Family Casks cask no. 2826, refill sherry hogshead db **(91) n23** apple crumble and near cinnamon; **t23** lush, warmed plum pudding on a caramel base; **f22** custard pie and light spice; **b23** what a tart! And a fruity one at that... *46.3%. 329 bottles.*

Glenfarclas 1986 The Family Casks cask no. 3434, refill sherry puncheon db **(87) n22** fruity, but with nip and bite; **t22** the spices initially rise above the laid-back sherry-toffee theme; some honeycomb notes counter the drier oaks; **f21** genuinely lethargic finale with very light oak; **b22** the fight on the nose and delivery isn't matched by the sleepy follow through. *56.5%. 521 bottles.*

Glenfarclas 1987 The Family Casks cask no. 1010, refill sherry hogshead db **(90) n22** floral with violets et al; **t23** lovely silky delivery with restrained spices but no shyness to the stewed plum and toffee; **f22** more caramel trifle; **b23** an honest to goodness cask with not a hint of a fault. *55.1%. 262 bottles.*

⋯ **Glenfarclas 1987 The Family Casks (3rd Release)** sherry butt, cask no. 3826 db **(92) n22** not unattractive: steady, over-ripened grape keeps the barley in place; **t24** at first the clean, sweet grape sends the senses heading towards a state of dormantsy; then all hell breaks lose as the spices arrive. Big, salivating stuff as the barley escapes its oaky confines to run riot, then a bitter cocoa nod towards the oak; **f23** settles, though that cocoa is now met by some light coffee tones as it bitters out; the barley still makes some juicy waves; **b23** I can so see why this butt was selected: it wasn't for the relatively plane Jane nose, that's for sure. Someone obviously took a mouthful of this and thought: "bloody hell!!". Massive in a breathtaking kind of way. *53.2%*

⋯ **Glenfarclas 1987 Limited Rare Bottling - Edition No. 13** cask no. 6806 - 6809, dist Dec 87, bott Sep 08 db **(94) n24** ultra clean grape mixes beautifully with polished wooden floors; there is also a wonderful walk on part of botanicals sans juniper; **t23.5** lush, sharp delivery; a hint of blood orange and some momentarily raging spice; vanilla holds the middle ground; **f23.5** that classy fruit/barley/oak balance continues to the end with a hint of very late hickory; **b23** the grape grazes serenely around the tastebuds without a single note of discord. Simply delicious malt whisky which brings the major elements into play without any major conflict. *46%. German market. 1,200 bottles.*

Glenfarclas 1988 The Family Casks cask no. 7033, sherry butt db **(85) n21 t21 f22 b21.** Clean, if a tad soapy. Significantly oily. But good barley richness. *56.3%. 572 bottles.*

⋯ **Glenfarclas 1988 Quarter Casks** cask no. 251 - 261, dist Jan 88, bott Feb 08 db **(91) n23** soft, juicy grape is hemmed in by friendly oak; custard tart, too; **t23.5** beautiful delivery with a spot on degree of treacle to counter those firmer oak notes and spices; the mouthfeel is exemplary; **f22** nutty but the fruit continues its journey; some late cocoa; **b22.5** chocolate fruit and nut bar lovers will be happy with this one, as will devotees of unspoiled sherry casks. *46.1%. German market. 1,478 bottles.*

Glenfarclas 1989 The Family Casks cask no. 11721, sherry butt db **(94) n23** almost identical to the 1990 bottling; **t24** see 1990 **f23** slight change here with more of a molassed, old bourbon accent here, otherwise identical; **b24** the 1989 and 1990 could be twins born a year apart – astonishing! *60%. 600 bottles.*

Glenfarclas 1990 The Family Casks cask no. 9246, sherry butt db **(94) n23** big thickish, faultless sherry well padded with oak; **t24** another fruit 'n' spice blitz with oloroso oozing into every pore; **f23** long, lush, sensibly spiced and that house chocolate style coming through loud and clear; **b24** this is how every sherry butt should be. It almost brings a tear to the eye. *58.9%. 617 bottles.*

Glenfarclas 1990 The Family Malt Collection bott Mar 06 db **(95.5) n23.5** dry and cream oloroso mixed with all its attendant spices pulsing at you; this is a serious, entirely flawless aroma for the sherry lover... but only if you do the following: when first poured there is a slight sulphur problem. Allow to sit in the glass for at least 45 minutes before nosing and tasting. In that time that slight mark will vanish and you will be left with a sherry butt as nature intended; **t24** near perfect mouth-feel with only outline oil helping to spread the sherried word; the grape arrives cleanly and with wonderful bitter-sweet harmonisation; **f24** again the cream sherry softness just oozes from every molecule; almost unbelievable balance between sweet and dry; **b24** I really found myself swallowing here when I should have spit, But sherry bottlings of this distinction just don't come along that often. As gems go, 24 carat. I've always said that Spain should be sent our sulphured bottlings as a thank you for services rendered. Instead, our lucky amigos get this...!!! There's just no bloody justice in the world... *43%. Spain.*

Glenfarclas 1991 The Family Casks cask no. 5623, sherry butt db **(92) n24** exemplary display of highly complex fruit and toffee tones; some over-ripe cherry, a touch salty and some crushed pine nut; **t23** mildly aggressive arrival, mainly thanks to early spices; again complexity rules and the brief raspberry stratum is a treat; **f22** simplifies out with the natural toffee; **b23** an entrancing malt which has your tastebuds on full alert. *57.9%. 613 bottles.*

Glenfarclas 1992 The Family Casks cask no. 264, sherry butt db **(89) n23** wonderful marmalade and botanicals; **t22** the fruit is voluptuous, the body curvy and soft; **f22** long, traces of cocoa and massive chewing power; **b22** big, gutsy, oily stuff. *55.5%. 669 bottles.*

Glenfarclas 1992 The Family Malt Collection bott Mar 06 db **(94) n24** just love that smoke which drifts rights across the richly sherried torso; fruit and nuts add to the excellent weight; **t24** more of the same on delivery; refreshing and belies its 14 years by at least a couple. The grape at times exhibits something of the noble rot about it and that light smoke just keeps on drifting... **f22** dulls out slightly with a touch of caramel getting in on the act. But soft spices and a certain dryness suggest some Fino at work here at least in part; **b24** coming across whiskies like this with such finesse and grace makes what is a harder job than some might imagine, entirely worthwhile. A malt to restore my faith in sherried whiskies in general...! *43%. Spain.*

Glenfarclas 1993 The Family Casks cask no. 11, sherry butt db **(77) n19 t20 f19 b19.** The three Ss: sherry, spice and sul****. Shame. *58.9%. 592 bottles.*

⠿ **Glenfarclas 1993 Premium Edition Limited Rare Bottling** oloroso sherry casks, cask no. 29 & 30 distilled Feb 93, bott Dec 08 db **(75.5) n18 t20 f18.5 b19.** Lots of grape and chocolate. But one of these casks just wasn't right to begin with. *46%. German market. 3,600 bottles.*

Glenfarclas 1994 The Family Casks cask no. 2935, sherry butt db **(95) n24** an orangey on a warm, sunny day; beautifully botanical; **t24** staggeringly complex from first arrival with the fruit and barley hamming it up and harmonising to the nth degree; **f23** lively spices rumble on as the cocoa goes crackers; **b24** a fabulous cask choice which appears perfectly to encapsulate the excellence of the distillery. *59.6%. 628 bottles.*

Glenfarclas 1994 The Family Malt Collection bott Mar 06 db **(84.5) n21.5 t22 f20 b21** Pretty toffeed in character. Tries to take off but never quite finds its wings. *43%. Spain.*

Glenfarclas 1995 45° The Heritage Malt Collection sherry cask, dist Nov 95, bott Sep 06 db **(94.5) n24** blood orange, teasing spice, vanilla pods and even a touch of barley: who could ask for more...? **t23.5** salivating and fresh, the grape pulses with ripeness; **f23.5** long with much more barley apparent, though the grape never loses its sheen; a touch of toffee with a hint of mocha; **b23.5** exceptional. Absolutely everything you could demand from a sherried malt of this age. Not a single off note and the freshness of comparative youth and complexity of years in the cask are in perfect harmony. *45%. Spain.*

⠿ **Glenfarclas 1996 Premium Edition** matured in sherry casks, cask no. 678 & 679 dist Feb 96, bott Sep 08 db **(75) n17.5 t20 f18.5 b19.** Plenty of excellent grape. But spoiled by the obvious fault. I am told that quite a number of Germans actually enjoy sulphured casks. Then this should be right up their strasse. 46%. German market.

⁖ **Glenfarclas 1997 Cask Strength Premium Edition** matured in sherry casks, cask no. 642 - 648, dist Feb 97, bott Mar 09 db **(77.5) n18.5 t20 f19.5 b19.5.** In their defence, the quality of some of the casks that have gone into this are so good, it may have been possible to have missed the obvious problem. But it is there, and unmistakably so 55.5%. German market.

Glenfarclas 105 40th Anniversary Limited Edition 40 Years Old dist 68, bott 08 db **(96) n24** hickory, basil and any number of thick ye olde bourbony notes collide head on with faultless fruit; **t24** this is massive: you have to count to three to get your breath back and only then can you start getting to grips with the complexities that have been delivered on your palate: again lots of bourbony tones and some countering middle-aged and old notes. The sherry is surprising down at heel to the rich molasses and honeycomb....and there's that basil again...; **f24** just so long with all that had gone on before winding down like a clock. A memorable experience... **b24** I have had quite a few 105s over 33 of those 40 years. And not a single one was quite like this. Quite magnificent! 60%

Cadenhead's Authentic Collection Glenfarclas Aged 18 Years bourbon hogshead, dist 88, bott May 06 **(87) n20** not entirely happy with itself: some farmyardy notes confuse the rich barley; **t23** big, semi-thuggish malt offers countless waves of salivating complexity; the oak plays a clever, restrained and spicy part; **f22** oak to the fore; the barley refuses to secede; **b22** firebrand malt that for all its rawness delivers intense quality by the mouthful... 55.2%. 276 btls.

Cadenhead's Glenfarclas Aged 19 Years bourbon, dist 88, bott May 07 **(86) n21 t21 f22 b22.** An attractive malt offering light – almost green – grape and a radiance to the pulsing barley. 46%. 306 bottles.

Cadenhead's Chairman's Stock Glenfarclas Aged 34 Years bourbon hogshead, dist 73, bott Sep 07 **(84) n21 t22 f20 b21.** Big oak character. 43.7%. 198 bottles.

⁖ **Old Malt Cask Glenfarclas Aged 42 Years** dist Jun 66, bott 08 **(92) n23** familiar hickory-bourbony flag is waved; **t22.5** early oak threatens dominance but the oloroso springs back into play with lusty and wonderfully clean fruitiness; **f23** for a while there is a hint of barley, but this is soon lost in a vanilla-led onslaught of fruity-bourbony notes which provide a softness beyond belief for such great age; **b23.5** another beautiful Glenfarclas which absolutely defies the years. 48.8%. Douglas Laing.

Scotch Malt Whisky Society Cask 1.137 Aged 14 Years refill hogshead, dist Sep 93 **(85) n21.5 t21 f21.5 b21.** Barley concentrate in concentrated form. Pretty hot stuff. 58%

⁖ **Scotch Malt Whisky Society Cask 1.144 Aged 15 Years** refill hogshead, dist Sep 93 **(86.5) n22 t22.5 f20 b22.** Plenty of malty biff about the nose and the sharp delivery equally warms and entertains. 57.6%

Whisky Doris Ballindalloch dark sherry cask, dist 66, bott 07 db **(94.5) n24** minimal age damage as the vibrant oaky notes are massaged by the freshest grape you could pray for such a vintage; nutty and rounded with a molassed-honey mix; **t24** beautiful mouthfeel even before delivery is complete: the intensity and clarity of the wine is second to none; the slow build up of honey is a treat; **f23** lots of natural caramels begin to fudge up the issue, but the barley-grape fade is almost beyond its reach; **b23.5** a sherry butt to make even a perfectionist swoon. 51.3%

⁖ **The Whisky Fair Glenfarclas 40 Years Old** oloroso sherry cask, dist 66, bott 07 **(96) n23.5** hickory, burnt cherries and raisins; mildly over baked Melton Hunt cake; a real old bourbony edge to this; **t24.5** the sweetness on delivery is a surprising contrast to the nose, except it perhaps carries on with the Melton cake theme with lashings of Demerara sugar, though now slightly undercooked. Figs and apricot add to the raisin and there is a lovely build up of latte towards the middle; **f24** more frappe in character to the coffee now (though of course at body temp, but you'll see what I mean) **b24** a type of cask and style lost to us. Tasted blind you really wouldn't be able to tell between the oloroso or a near faultless 20-year-old bourbon. A magnificent experience. And probably this organisation's greatest ever bottling. 52.4%. The Whisky Fair, 150 bottles.

The Whisky Fair Single Speyside Malt Aged 40 Years oloroso sherry, dist 66, bott 07 **(95) n24** roasty-oaked but perfectly matched with grape; **t24** fabulous sweet delivery allows the barley top billing; more wonderful roasty elements, including coffee and molasses; **f23** long, more coffee, slightly less sugar, gorgeous burnt fudge...sigh... **b24** well: 1966 must have been one hell of a bloody year at the Glenfarclas distillery...!! 52.4%. Germany.

The Whisky Fair Single Speyside Malt Aged 41 Years sherry wood, dist 65, bott 07 **(85) n21 t21 f22 b21.** Heaps of character and attitude. But a bit tight and remarkably similar in cough-sweet style to the distillery's own '65 vintage. 53.5%

GLENFIDDICH
Speyside, 1887. William Grant & Sons. Working.

Glenfiddich 12 Years Old db **(79) n20 t21 f19 b19**. Attractively malty in part, but caramel dulls a dram already struggling to come to terms with the oaky imbalance. A real 40 watt bulb. 40%

Glenfiddich 12 Years Old Toasted Oak Reserve (92.5) n22.5 the oaky building blocks to this are firm and substantial; just enough natural sweet caramel and spice to balance; traces of apple, pear and other soft fruit; **t23.5** much softer delivery than you might imagine from the nose with barley – which was invisible on the nose – making the first impression; again there is a soft fruit moment followed by a wonderful oak development which is at once dry and spicy but by no means out of sync with its surrounds; **f22.5** much drier with rhubarb tart (unsweetened) offering the background notes to that wonderful barley and custard finale; **b24** another bottling to confound the critics of Glenfiddich. This is as fine an essay in balance, charm and sophistication as you are likely to find in the whole of Speyside this year. Crack open a bottle...but only when you have a good hour to spend. 40%

Glenfiddich Aged 12 Years Special Reserve (see Glenfiddich 12 Years Old)

Glenfiddich 15 Years Old db **(94.5) n23** such a deft intermingling of the softer fruits and bourbon notes...with barley in there to remind you of the distillery; **t23** intense and big yet all the time appearing delicate and light; the most apologetic of spices help spotlight the barley sweetness and delicate fruits; **f24.5** just so long and complex; something of the old fashioned fruit salad candy about this but with a small degree of toffee just rounding off the edges; **b24** if an award were to be given for the most consistently beautiful dram in Scotland, this would win more often than not. This under-rated distillery has won more friends with this masterpiece than probably any other brand. 40%

Glenfiddich Aged 15 Years Cask Strength db **(85.5) n20 t23 f21 b21.5**. Improved upon the surprisingly bland bottlings of old, especially on the fabulously juicy delivery. Still off the pace due to an annoying toffee-ness towards the middle and at the death. 51%

Glenfiddich Aged 15 Years Solera Reserve (see Glenfiddich 15 Years Old)

Glenfiddich 18 Years Old db **(95) n23.5** the smoke, which for long marked this aroma, appears to have vanished. But the usual suspects of blood orange and various other fruit appear to thrive in the lightly salted complexity; **t24.5** how long are you allowed to actually keep the whisky held on the palate before you damage your teeth? One to really close your eyes and study because here we have one of the most complex deliveries Speyside can conjour: the peat may have gone, but there is coal smoke around as the juicy barley embeds with big fat sultanas, plums, dates and grapes. Despite the distinct lack of oil, the mouthfeel is entirely yielding to present one of the softest and most complete essays on the palate you can imagine, especially when you take the bitter-sweet ratio and spice into balance; **f23** long, despite the miserly 40% offered, with plenty of banana-custard and a touch of pear; **b24** at the moment, the ace in the Glenfiddich pack. If this was bottled at 46%, unchilfiltered etc, I dread to think what the score might be... 40%

Glenfiddich 21 Years Old db **(86) n21 t23 f21 b21**. A much more uninhibited bottling with loads of fun as the mouth-watering barley comes rolling in. But still falls short on taking the hair-raisingly rich delivery forward and simply peters out. 40%

Glenfiddich 30 Years Old db **(91.5) n23.5** the usual custard trifle but with a bit of extra bourbon tipped on for good measure; **t23.5** again a big early dose of rich honey-hickory bourbon then softer fruits including blackberries; **f21.5** a tad tired; chalky and dry; **b23** one assumes this is a new vatting because, finale apart, here everything appears to be just that much sharper and cleaner than the last version I officially tasted. 40%

Glenfiddich Rare Collection 40 Years Old db **(86.5) n22.5 t23 f20 b21**. A quite different version to the last with the smoke having all but vanished, allowing the finish to show the full weight of its considerable age. The nose and delivery are superb, though. The barley sheen on arrival really deserves better support. 43.5%

Glenfiddich 50 Years Old db **(97) n25** we are talking 50 years, and yet we are still talking fresh barley, freshly peeled grape and honey. Not ordinary honey. Not the stuff you find in jars. But the pollen that attracts the bees to the petunia; and not any old petunia: not the white or the red or pink or yellow. But the two-toned purple ones. For on the nose at least this is perfection; this is nectar.... **t24** a silky delivery: silky barley with silky, watered down maple syrup. The middle ground, in some previous Glenfiddich 50-year-olds a forest of pine and oak, is this time filled with soft, grassy barley and the vaguest hint of a distant smoke spice; **f24** long, long, long, with the very faintest snatch of something most delicately smoked: a distant puff of peat reek carried off on the persistent Speyside winds, then a winding-down of vanillas, dropping through the gears of sweetness until the very last traces are chalky dry; **b24** for the record, my actual words, after tasting my first significant mouthful, were: "fuck! This is brilliant." It was an ejaculation of genuine surprise, as any fly on the wall of my Tasting Room at 1:17am on Tuesday 4th August would testify. Because I have tasted many 50-year-old whiskies over the years, quite possibly as many as anyone currently drawing breath. For not only have I tasted those which have made it onto the whisky shelves, but, privately, or as a consultant, an untold number which didn't: the heroic but doomed oak-laden failures. This, however, is a quite different animal. We were on the cusp of going to press when this was released, so we hung back. William Grant blender David Stewart, whom I rank above all other blenders on this planet, has known me long and well enough to realise that the surrounding hype, with this being the most expensive whisky ever bottled at £10,000 a go or a sobering £360 a pour, would bounce off me like a pebble from a boulder. "Honestly, David," he told my chief researcher with a timorous insistence, "please tell Jim I really think this isn't too oaky." He offered almost an apology for bringing into the world this 50-year-old babe. Well, as usual David Stewart, doyen of the blending lab and Ayr United season ticket holders, was absolutely spot on. And, as is his want, he was rather understating his case. For the record, David, next time someone asks you how good this whisky is, just for once do away with the Ayeshire niceness installed by generations of very nice members of the Stewart family and tell them: "Actually, it's bloody brilliant if I say so myself! And I don't give a rat's bollocks what Murray thinks." *46.1%*

Glenfiddich 1955 Vintage cask no. 4221 db **(93) n23** pumped up oak, but deflated somewhat by the subtle nuances of the barley which, somehow, have enough breeziness to breathe a doughy freshness into the proceedings; **t23** brilliant, entirely schizophrenic, delivery of honey-oak and big spice, all on a base of a coppery sheen: very much the sma' still character to this one; **f23** long, lush with drying, oak-vanilla and still that wonderful barley/ coppery gloss. Oh, and a dribble of smoke bleeding into the late honey; **b24** a real surprise package, because even without sherry or peat to hide behind there is enough complexity and, at times, utter brilliance to dazzle the most demanding of commentators. And, believe me; this is one sample I didn't spit.... Over 50 years old and quite majestic. Truly classic stuff. *52.6%*

Glenfiddich 1958 Vintage cask no. 8642 db **(78) n23 t18 f18 b19.** Oak can be such an unforgiving master. Fabulous old oloroso nose, though. *46.3%*

Glenfiddich 1959 Vintage cask no. 3934 db **(89) n23** big age here: this one is creaking with oak and oloroso but the harmony is excellent. Pans out with spiced toffee apple and dates: superb; **t22** stunning delivery with big fruit at first then several layers of spice over the burned fudge; the oak is less than discreet but does limited damage; **f22** long, toasty and a fade of cremated raisins; some lovely esters last the pace; **b22** from the year Jacky Cox led Ayr United to the old Scottish Second Division Championship, something equally as rare! Glenfiddich showing something of a rummy side to its character with lots of copper and ester in the mix. The oak is profound, but sits comfortably in the scheme of things. One for late at night, closed eyes and memories of long-lost days at Somerset Park. *48.1%*

Glenfiddich 1964 Vintage cask no. 13430 db **(80) n22 t22 f17 b19.** The nose is pure bourbon – and very old bourbon at that. Wobbles a bit in both aroma and delivery but for all its oaky over- zestfulness – and even a touch of the soaps (especially on the finish) – you still cannot help but enjoy this one. To say it is a character is something of an understatement...!! *45.6%*

Glenfiddich 1973 Vintage cask no. 9874 db **(94) n23** citrus - made from concentrate: hard as nails nose really pumps out the barley-fruit marriage; **t23** mouth-filling, luxuriously mouthwatering and barley, fruit and spice all at full throttle; **f24** the oak is driven like a stake through the barley, but there is a fabulous molassed edge to it. The late viscosity carries a delightful hint of liquorice. Wow!; **b24** I've been tasting these special casks from this distillery since before my hair went grey. I've sampled some good 'uns. This is possibly the best of the lot. *48.1%*

Glenfiddich Vintage Reserve 1973 cask no. 9874 **(92) n23** very few Glenfiddich casks of this age stand quite so tall: wonderful hot-cross bun theme, even with a sliver of salted butter; the fruit-barley element excels; **t23** exquisite delivery and mouth-feel: the oak is pounding at the door but that glorious fruit/bourbon/barley core refuses to budge; some wonderful strands of smoke disappear into the middle's demerara depths **f22** appears for a while to be sliding under the oak, then bucks up as the honey-barley breathes fresh life back into it; **b24** whisky picked at its very ripest! The juices are still flowing despite a massive oak threat. But such is the sheer élan and fruit and sweet edges that an astounding and beautiful experience is assured. *46.5%*

Glenfiddich 1976 cask no. 16389 bott 07 db **(87) n23.5** apricots and pears, all under a dollop of custard, sees off the encroaching oaks; finely tuned and finely balanced, the bitter-sweet ratio is just about spot on and the clarity at body temp is excellent; look close enough and you might even find the most delicate flicker of smoke; **t22** a few splinters early on are overcome by intense barley and vanilla; mouth-watering at first, and a tad spicy; the middle sees the oak gaining ground fast; **f20** just a shade too oaky for its own good, but some fruit does counter; **b21.5** bottled in the nick of time. The vast majority of Glenfiddichs crash and burn by this age: it is not a malt, peaking in age as it does in the 15 to 18 region, that can usually stand up to great years in the cask. Here it manages it, just, and for good measure offers a truly memorable nose. 47.4%. *Exclusively for Willow Park, Calgary*

Glenfiddich Vintage Reserve 1976 cask no. 516, bott 07 db **(93.5) n23** a few creaks, splinters and grumbles but rice pudding and spiced prune juice really wins the day; **t24** I could almost cry: Glenfiddich, naked and without the unflattering bodice of caramel covering its superb body; juicy and salivating to a ridiculous degree for a malt this age, the barley is vibrant and squeaky clean; light, dusty oaky notes give a tap on the shoulder just to remind you of the vintage; **f23** pretty long with a slow glow of spice; the barley-oak balance is spot on, **b23.5** I still say that Glenfiddich is not naturally disposed to old age. However, the odd ancient gem crops up...and this is one. 51.9%. 549 bottles.

Glenfiddich Caoran Reserve Aged 12 Years db **(89) n22.5** barley breezes in and there is a "did I really see that?" flicker of smoke, too..; **t22** sweet, buzzing malts and some vanilla lashed oak; **f21.5** traces of muscovado sugar balance the soft spice and custardy finale; b23 has fizzed up a little in the last year or so with some salivating charm from the barley and a touch of cocoa from the oak. A complex little number. 40%

Glenfiddich Toasted Oak Reserve Aged 12 Years (89) n22 toasty alright, but with a butterscotch spread and a dollop of bourbon extract; **t23** cleverly sweet with delicate bourbon-style honies blending beautifully with the fatted-up barley; **f22** again a toasty bite to the finale which balances well with the persistent sweetness of the barley and butterscotch; **b22** an elegant, bourbony, not overly complex, malt for those with a slightly sweet tooth. 40%

GLEN GARIOCH
Highland (Eastern), 1798. Suntory. Working.

Glen Garioch 8 Years Old db **(85.5) n21 t22 f21 b21.5.** A soft, gummy, malt – not something one would often write about a dram of this or any age from Geary! However, this may have something to do with the copious toffee which swamps the light fruits which try to emerge. 40%

Glen Garioch 10 Years Old db **(80) n19 t22 f19 b20.** Chunky and charming, this is a malt that once would have ripped your tonsils out. Much more sedate and even a touch of honey to the rich body. Toffeed at the finish. 40%

Glen Garioch 12 Years Old db **(88.5) n22** gooseberries and fudge....and a touch of smoke...!!!!; **t23** mouth filling with a delicious degree of sharp maltiness; **f21.5** toffees out, though a little smoke drifts back in; **b22** a significant improvement on the complexity front. The return of the smoke after a while away was a surprise and treat. 43%

Glen Garioch 15 Years Old db **(86.5) n20.5 t22 f22 b22.** In the a bottling I sampled last year the peat definitely vanished. Now it's back again, though in tiny, if entertaining, amounts. 43%

Glen Garioch 21 Years Old db **(91) n21** a few wood shavings interrupt the toasty barley; **t23** really good bitter-sweet balance with honeycomb and butterscotch leading the line; pretty juicy, busy stuff; **f24** dries as it should with some vague spices adding to the vanilla and hickory; **b23** an entirely re-worked, now smokeless, malt that has little in common with its predecessors. Quite lovely, though. 43%

Glen Garioch 1958 db **(90) n24** what a brilliant, heady, almost eccentric mix of once chunky peat, once vivid malt and now beautifully varnished oak; **t21** loses its early balance but settles on a waxy honey thread to complement the slowly reasserting peat; **f23** elegance in abundance as the oak plays lip-service to the sweet, chewy malt. Just so charming! **b22** the distillery in its old clothes: and quite splendid it looks! 43%. 328 bottles.

Duncan Taylor Collection Glengarioch 1988 cask no. 1557 **(87) n21** flour and biscuits sweetened with maple syrup **t22** sugar-coated barley **f22** a dash of vanilla and some rapidly drying oak **b22** a pussy cat of a Glengarioch, much sweeter than the norm and with the customary fires completely doused. Highly attractive. 52.8%

Duncan Taylor Collection Glengarioch 1988 Aged 19 Years cask no. 1559 **(96) n24.5** the complexity is almost silly: mocha, dates, basil, vanilla (of course), molasses (naturally), varying shades of barley (well, it is a malt...)...oh, just go and discover it for yourself!! **t24** those extraordinary strands on the nose do their utmost to recreate the sensations on delivery. Except here there is more kumquat and spice; **f23.5** back to the vanilla, but more citrus and the barley has the last say with some late dissolving grist... **b24** I knew there must have been a reason I got up this morning...it was to discover this irresistible, slightly feisty, sublimely-structured malt!!! Oh, joy! 55.4%

Duncan Taylor Collection Glengarioch 1988 cask no. 1560 **(86) n22 t22 f21 b21.** Seriously enjoyable, long and some insanely rich barley. But by comparison to its twin – cask 1559 – just rather flat and docile. Such is the difference a cask can make. 55.5%

⁖ **Duncan Taylor Collection Glen Garioch 1988** cask no. 1988 **(94) n23** sexy peat is understated yet, despite a fruity presence, offers the lead and background: intriguing... **t24** pure old-fashioned Geary in the way the peat pulses through, but the final delivery is near orgasmic as the sultana fruits and smoke combine with an irresistable rough edge and bite: mind-blowing... **f23** long, slick, for all the nip and bite and wave upon wave of ever-sweetening smoke; ultimately a slightly over-burned fruit cake; **b24** glorious whisky with attitude. A must get malt: simple as that! 54.4%

Lonach Glengarioch 1989 cask no. 8426 **(89.5) n22** the vanillas are lost amid delicate gristy-sweet tones; **t23.5** near perfect mouthfeel: no oil to speak of, allowing the barley to fizz and zip around, landing soft and/or thumping blows to different taste buds; **f22** a gentlemanly fade with the barley and vanilla taking turns to lead the way; **b22** another wonderful Geary! 53.3%. Duncan Taylor.

⁖ **Mackillop's Choice Glen Garioch 1990** cask no. 10291, dist Dec 90, bott Jan 07 **(84) n21 t22 f21 b20.** Usual 'Geary bite, passion and fun . But the fruity notes and the trace peat don't somehow gel with the oak in a way you hope it might. 57.1%. Iain Mackillop & Co. Ltd.

Murray McDavid Glen Garioch 1993 bourbon/banyuls grenache rouge **(80) n19 t19 f22 b20.** Pleasant, if limited in complexity. 46%

Old Masters Glen Garioch Aged 19 Years cask no. 1536 dist 88, bott 08 **(93) n23** outstanding toffee apple and burnt raisin aroma; spotted dog pudding and custard; **t24** firm barley arrives first with multi-layers of brown molasses and dried dates; never less than huge, yet always controlled; **f23** long and refined: it is like picking very old fruitcake from between the teeth; **b23** Old Master by name and nature! 53.1%. James MacArthur & Co. Ltd.

Provenance Glen Garioch Aged 11 Years refill hogshead 1880, dist autumn 94, bott winter 06 **(85) n20 t22 f21 b22.** The refreshing fruits of a Garioch matured in a clapped-out third-fill cask, I assume. Not instantly recognizable as malt from this distillery, a burst of smoke gives some clue. Deliciously light...in every sense. 46%. nc ncf. McGibbon's.

Provenance Glen Garioch Aged 12 Years refill hogshead, cask no. 4072, dist 95, bott 07 **(87.5) n22** the gentle, probably accidental, smoke reminds me of the days when I drank a now sadly lost Geary style from another era; **t22** superb grist and citrus: totally refreshing; **f21.5** some burnt toast as the oak invades; **b22** there is an older generation who will appreciate certain aspects of this one. 46%. nc ncf. Douglas Laing.

GLENGLASSAUGH
Speyside, 1875. Scaent Group. Silent since 1986.

⁖ **Glenglassaugh 21 Year Old** db **(94) n23.5** elegant and adroit, the lightness of touch between the citrus and barley is nigh on mesmeric: conflicting messages of age in that it appears younger and yet you feel something has to be this kind of vintage to hit this degree of aloofness. Delicate and charming...; **t24.5** again we have all kinds of messages on delivery: the spices fizz around announcing oaky intentions and then the barley sooths and sweetens even with a degree of youthful juiciness. The tastebuds are never more than caressed, the sugar-sweetened citrus ensuring neither the barley or oak form any kind of advantage; impeccably weighted, a near perfect treat for the palate; **f22.5** white chocolate and vanilla lead the way as the oak begins to offer a degree of comparative austerity; **b23.5** a malt which simply sings on the palate and a fabulous benchmark for the new owners to try to achieve in 2030...!! 46%

⁖ **Glenglassaugh 30 Year Old** db **(89) n23** the grape of noble rot stands haughtily beside the oak without blot; **t23** fruity, silky, if in some places a little flat. Lots of dried dates, demerara, chocolate raisins, a little of this, a little of that... **f21** against every wish, drifts away incoherently, mumbling something coffee-ish; **b22** sheer poetry. Or not... 43.1%

⁖ **Glenglassaugh 40 Year Old** db **(96) n24.5** the kind of oak you'd expect at this age – if you are uncommonly lucky or have access to some of the most glorious-nosing ancient casks in all Scotland - but there is so much else on the fruity front besides: grape, over-ripe yam, fat cherries...And then there is a bourbony element with molassed hickory and sweetened vanilla: wake me, I must be dreaming...on second thoughts, don't; **t24.5** pure silk on delivery. All the flavours arrive in one rich wave of consummate sweetness, a tapestry celebrating the enormity of both the fruit and oak, yet condensed into a few inches rather than feet; plenty of soft medium roast Jamaican Blue Mountain and then at times mocha; on the fruity front there is juicy dates mulched with burned raisin; **f23** the relative Achilles heel as the more bitter, nutty parts of the oak gather; **b24** it is as if this malt has gone through a 40-year marrying process: the interlinking of flavours and styles is truly beyond belief. One of the great world whiskies for 2010 44.6%

❖ **Glenglassaugh 'The Spirit Drink'** db **(85) n20 t22 f21.5 b21.5.** A pretty wide margin taken on the cut here, it seems, so there is plenty to chew over. Richly flavoured and a tad oily, as is to be expected, which helps the barley to assert itself in midstream. The usual new make chocolaty element at work here, too, late on. Just great to see this distillery back in harness after all these years. And a great idea to get the new spirit out to the public, something I have been encouraging distilleries to do since my beard was still blue. Look forward to seeing another version where a narrower cut has been made. 50%. 8,160 bottles.

❖ **Glenglassaugh 'The Spirit Drink That Blushes to Speak Its Name'** db **(85) n22 t21.5 f21 b21.** Not whisky, of course. New make matured for a few months in wine barrels. The result is a Rose-looking spirit. Actually takes me back to my early childhood – no, not the tasting of new make spirit. But the redcurrant aroma which does its best to calm the new make ruggedness. Tasty and fascinating, though the wine tries to minimalise the usual sweetness you find in malt spirit. 50%

Glenglassaugh 1973 Family Silver db **(95) n23** fruity and exceptionally complex: quite coastal with something vaguely citrussy, orange in particular; **t24** melt-in-the-mouth malt that intensifies by the second. Never becomes either too sweet or vaguely woody. There is a soft hint of peat around the spices; **f24** virtually without a blemish as the malt continues on its rich and merry way. Some sublime marmalade follows through on the spice; **b24** from first to last this whisky caresses and teases. It is old but shows no over-ageing. It offers what appears a malt veneer but is complexity itself. Brilliant. And now, sadly, almost impossible to find. Except, possibly, at the Mansefield Hotel, Elgin. 40%

Berrys' Own Selection Glenglassaugh 1983 bott 07 **(89.5) n22** custard tart with a butterscotch side-dish. A peat fire went out a few days back; **t22** buzzing spice punctuates the molten sugar and barley; **f23** greater balance as drier vanillas interject; **b22.5** drag off the shelf and buy: it's a diamond. 46%. Berry Bros & Rudd.

Cadenhead's Authentic Collection Glenglassaugh Aged 23 Years sherry butt, dist 84, bott Sep 07 **(79) n19 t21.5 f19 b19.5.** At its better moments much closer to Demerara pot still rum in style than malt. One assumes the sherry butt is authentically from the old distillery owners, taking into account its obvious 's' fault. 52.5%. 612 bottles.

Dewar Rattray Glenglassaugh 1986 cask no. 162, dist Mar 86, bott Jun 07 **(75.5) n18 t21 f18 b18.5.** Sulphur all over this one like a rash. Massive injection of orangey citrus tries to compensate. Memo to new owners: don't put your spirit into sulphur-screwed sherry butts. 53.4%

Milroy's of Soho Glenglassaugh 1976 ex bourbon hogshead, cask no. 2373, dist 17 Dec 76, bott 7 Dec 06 **(89) n23** the most playful puff of smoke adds excellent weight to the potpourri of floral tones that sits so well with the maple syrup; **t23** gorgeous, pouting malt makes a seductive sweet of the tastebuds; the weight and mouth-feel as good as a 30-year-old gets but perhaps thins out too readily towards the middle; **f21** surprisingly lazy with the soft oak holding sway; **b22** another charming and very high class malt from beyond the grave. 46%. 318 bottles.

Murray McDavid Mission Glenglassaugh 1978 Aged 28 Years fresh sherry/syrah, bott 06 **(86) n24 t20 f23 b19.** What balance? One of the challenges of cask finishing is that you never know when it will get better or worse: the nature of the beast there is nothing with which you can compare the whisky. This works and fails on two massive levels, but it is worth experiencing for the astonishing nose and charming finale alone. 46.6%. nc ncf. 500 bottles.

Wilson & Morgan Barrel Selection Glenglassaugh 23 Years Old dist 84, bott 07 **(91.5) n23** an attractive waft of peat ensures the grape doesn't over elaborate: superb interplay, weight and complexity; a hint of sulphur, but it is beaten to death by the enormity of the main players; **t23** big, sweet fruity stance, a spice kick then a succession of juicy notes including greengages and dates; **f22.5** long, vanilla clad but the grape hangs on in; **b23** the best 'Glassaugh for a little while and even able to overcome a minor glitch. A real gentle giant, which is more of a giant than it is gentle. 46%

GLENGOYNE
Highlands (Southwest), 1833. Peter Russell. Working.

Glengoyne 10 Years Old db **(90) n22** beautifully clean despite coal-gas bite. The barley is almost in concentrate form with a marmalade sweetness adding richness; **t23** crisp, firm arrival with massive barley surge, seriously chewy and textbook bitter-sweet balance; but now some oils have tucked in to intensify and lengthen; **f22** incredibly long and refined for such a light malt. The oak, which made soft noises in the middle now intensifies, but harmonises with the intense barley; an added touch of coffee signals some extra oak in recent bottlings; **b23** proof that to create balance you do not have to have peat at work. The secret is the intensity of barley intermingling with oak. Not a single negative note from first to last and now a touch of oil and coffee has upped the intensity further. *40%*

Glengoyne 12 Years Old Cask Strength db **(79) n18 t22 f19 b20.** Not quite the happiest Glengoyne I've ever come across with the better notes compromised. *57.2%. nc ncf.* ☉☉

Glengoyne 17 Years Old db **(86) n21 t23 f21 b21.** Some of the guys at Glengoyne think I'm nuts. They couldn't get their head around the 79 I gave it last time. And they will be shaking my neck not my hand when they see the score here...Vastly improved but there is an off sherry tang which points to a naughty butt or two somewhere. Elsewhere mouth-watering and at times fabulously intense. *43%*

Glengoyne 21 Years Old db **(90) n21** closed and tight for the most part as Glengoyne sometimes has a tendency to be nose-wise, with the emphasis very much on coal gas; **t22** slow to start with a few barley heads popping up to be seen; then spices arrive with the oak for a slightly bourbony feel. Gentle butterscotch and honey add a mouth-watering edge to the drier oaks; **f24** a stupendous honey thread is cross-stitched through the developing oak to deliver near perfect poise and balance at finish; **b23** a vastly improved dram where the caramel has vanished and the tastebuds are constantly assailed and questioned. A malt which builds in pace and passion to delivery a final, wonderful coup-de-grace. Moments of being quite cerebral stuff. *43%*

Glengoyne 21 Years Old Sherry Edition db **(93) n22** heavy, nutty oily, slightly sweaty and not entirely faultless. When warmed the full, brooding oloroso gamut comes into play. Seriously big, if somewhat cumbersome; **t24** much sweeter arrival than you might have thought possible from the nose, and less sticky too. The richness of the oloroso coats every crevice and a playful spice teases while a mollased, toasted oaky/barley sub plot develops delightfully; **f23** not dissimilar to an excellent Demerara rum on the finish with no shortage of coffee-tinted roasty notes on the death. A real chew; **b24** the nose at first is not overly promising, but it settles at it warms and what follows on the palate is at times glorious. Few whiskies will match this for its bitter-sweet depth which is pure textbook. Glengoyne as few will have seen it before. *43%*

Glengoyne 33 Years Old 1972 Single Cask Limited Edition db **(87) n23** egg custard tart, seasoned and with a fruity side-dish; **t21** soft landing but the accent is on spice; **f22** back to fruit again and more vanilla-custard; **b21** the cask may be from somewhere near Rotorua, but the fruity, simplistic qualities are disarming. *50%. Exclusive for Taiwan.*

Glengoyne 34 Years Old 1972 Single Cask Limited Edition db **(92) n24** unspoiled fruit is complemented by soft cinnamon and sweet barley tones; **t23** mouth-watering delivery that astounds for its age: how can barley remain so beautifully fresh for so long? The oaks are omnipresent but reveal themselves only in spice form; **f22** medium length finale, concentrating mainly on spice and vanilla and interplay between simple malt and something juicier; **b23** one of those lovely whiskies that you just have to spend a little time alone with... *55%. Exclusive for Taiwan.*

Glengoyne 1986 20 Year Old Single Cask Spanish oak, sherry butt, cask no. 1384 db **(78.5) n20 t20 f19 b19.5.** Massive grape. But taken down a peg or three by you-know-what. *54.2%*

Glengoyne 1988 19 Year Old Single Cask Pedro Ximinex butt, cask no.718 db **(92) n23** stunning spices are radiated with grapey abandon; **t21.5** a soup of a delivery: thick, oily and very un-Glengoyne in mouthfeel; **f24.5** a mix of juicy and dried dates; crushed sultanas sprinkled with demerara; seemingly continues forever, even with barley and vanilla making guest appearances; **b23** the delivery is a bit too glutinous, but on the finish the story can be told: and in what detail!! A whisky to smear over your partner's body. Or anyone consenting you fancy, really... *58.3%. German Market.*

Glengoyne 1989 Single Cask Billy's Choice Amontillado hogshead, cask no. 1202 db **(65.5) n15 t17 f16.5 b17.** You genuinely shudder with this one. Seriously, sulphurously grim. *54.1%*

Glengoyne 1989 Single Cask Robbie's Choice ruby port hogshead, cask no. 328 db **(89) n21.5** sandalwood and crushed petal (yes, really....!!); **t22** proud grape struts its stuff; sweet and spicy; **f23** genuinely sophisticated with bitter cocoa putting the final touches to the oily juices; **b22.5** Robbie 1, Billy 0. *55.1%*

Glengoyne 1990 17 Year Old Single Cask Amontillado butt, cask no. 1523 db **(63) n14 t17.5 f15.5 b16.** The grape fights bravely against the sulphur, but it's a bloodbath. *56.3%. German Market.*

⬩⬩ **Glengoyne 1992 16 Year Old Single Cask** refill hogshead, cask no. 2078, dist Sep 92 db **(87) n21** a strange one: both generous and niggardly at the same time, the rich barley being kept down by some sharp, unhelpful oak notes; **t22** not quite a faultless delivery but there are all kinds of sugar-spangled barley themes going on. Light shards of almond found amid the growing spice; sharp, at times eye-watering; **f21.5** dries allowing a few cracks to show. But those sweeter elements keep out the worst; **b22.5** have to admit: than the nose suggests: at times a sugar sprinkled (mildly flawed) charmer... *52.3%*

Glengoyne 1993 14 Year Old Single Cask American oak, sherry hogshead, cask no. 832 db **(90) n23** I have just been buried alive under an avalanche of juicy-dribbling, over-ripe grape....; **t22** fresh grape concentrate and all the associated spices make for a plush delivery and middle; **f22.5** strands of malt, a dusting of cocoa and....grape....!!! **b22.5** I suppose a curmudgeon would grumble about there being too much sherry. Perhaps. But then I would counter argue that in this day and age to find a cask so not screwed by sulphur is in itself something to truly celebrate. *59.6%*

Glengoyne 1993 14 Year Old Single Cask Pedro Ximinex hogshead, cask no. 876 db **(91.5) n23.5** having just dug my way out of the grape that engulfed my nose on the sherry hogshead cask (above), I find myself now entombed in a larger grape-slide, this time with extra oaky weight pinning me down; **t23** the spices which blossom on the nose show no hesitation on coming forward as the oak and thick grape plaster themselves to the tastebuds; **f22.5** sweeter, more genteel now with strands of vanilla and marmalade coming into play; **b22.5** for those of us who are rapidly losing confidence in whisky held in sherry (and from what I understand I am by no means alone), here is something to restore your faith. Well, a little bit, anyway.... *57.9%. German Market.*

⬩⬩ **Glengoyne 1993 15 Year Old Single Cask** oloroso sherry hogshead, cask no. 845, dist Apr 93 db **(92.5) n24** unmistakable oloroso mixed with blood orange, dense with a fudge border; **t22.5** juicy, winey arrival and then a slow leaking of spices; even becomes a bit sharp and semi-aggressive; **f23** some barley actually gets a word in as the camp coffee begins to melt into the burnt raisin; **b23** sherry as it used to be and a strange choice for the Germans, as they appear to be the one nation that can cope with the sulphur with minimum fuss. *55.5%. German market.*

Glengoyne 1996 11 Year Old Single Finish Cask La Nerthe cask finish db **(88) n21.5** Malteaser candy and pistachio; **t21.5** immediate malt surge crashes into the more bitter fruit element **f22.5** levels out with a return to the chocolate-malt candy with the softest trace elements of fruit; **b22.5** beautifully textured and weighted: a real delight. *52.5%. German Market.*

⬩⬩ **Glengoyne 1997 11 Year Old Single Cask** European oak sherry hogshead, cask no. 2692, dist Jun 97 db **(93) n24** huge, and I mean gigantic, sherry. Almost something of the old fashioned nut brown ale to this one, except this is also dripping with noble rot grape. Of the barley you cannot hear a squeak; **t23** sherry, anyone? For the first few waves that's all that can be found, as it crashes with a feather-light softness against the tastebuds; the early sweetness is slowly replaced by a much more down to earth spice and a bit of a salty edge, too; **f24** a glorious sherry-led sunset, but now the grape has thinned to allow all manner of spices and demerara-sweetened mocha notes to show; the body changes too, from silk to a pleasant bit of rough; **b23** I bet you 20 years ago I might have given this a 89 or so. However, such has been the damage done by the influx of sulphur-ruined or -damaged sherry butts into the industry, and so wide their rotting net, that you just have to give the rare, wonderful specimens such as this a standing ovation. The first two or three mouthfuls are overwhelming: when your tastebuds adjust you will be in for a rare treat. *56.3%*

⬩⬩ **Glengoyne 1997 11 Year Old Single Cask** bourbon hogshead, cask no. 2725, dist Jun 97 db **(95) n24** absolutely cracking first-fill bourbon cask thumping out zesty vanilla, red liquorice and barley as though its life depends on it; **t24.5** you almost swoon, such is the piled high, unrelenting intensity to the barley: this is concentrated barley concentrate. To the power of ten. Wonderful golden syrup-dipped strands of oak tie in beautifully; **t23** long, delicately spiced, with a light oiliness further expounding the virtues of liquorice-led bourbony notes; **b23.5** taking into account that Norway has to be the most expensive place on this planet, this still will have been worth twice whatever price was asked for it. *56.5%. Bottled for the Oslo Whisky Festival*

Glengoyne 1999 Single Cask Deek's Choice refill hogshead, cask no. 16 db **(83.5) n20.5 t21.5 f21 b21.** Crisp, juicy barley and emerging vanilla. Some bitter orange, too. *60.9%*

Glengoyne 'Glen Guin' 16 Year Old Shiraz Finish db **(79) n18.5 t20 f19.5 b20.** Some oily depth here. *48%*

Glengoyne Burnfoot db **(84) n21 t21 f21.5 b21.** A clodhopping bruiser of a malt. Good honey, though. *40%. Duty Free Market.*

⸭ **The Cärn Mör Vintage Collection Glengoyne 2000** hogshead, cask no. 438, dist 00, bott 09 **(76.5) n18.5 t18.5 f19.5 b19.** Even taking into account its age, there should be a lot more offered than this. Settles only when the natural caramels kick in late on. *46%. The Scottish Liqueur Centre.*

⸭ **Hart Brothers Glengoyne Aged 12 Years** dist Jun 95, bott May 08 **(85.5) n22 t22 f20.5 b21.** Magnificently clean and malty. But too much a straight bat and the finish is smothered by natural caramel. *46%. Hart Brothers Limited.*

Old Malt Cask Glengoyne Aged 10 Years Gabriel Meffre wine cask no. 3686, dist Dec 96, bott Jun 07 **(75.5) n18 t20 f19.5 b18.** Sweet in part, but simply doesn't gel. *50%. Douglas Laing. 303 bottles.*

Old Malt Cask Glengoyne Aged 11 Years Bourbon Finish dist Jun 96, **(83) n21 t21 f20 b21.** Intense barley sugar, though a bit of a fuzzy note. Even, so, in a different league to the Wine Finish. *50%. Douglas Laing.*

⸭ **Provenance Glengoyne Aged 10 Years** refill hogshead, dist autumn 97, bott summer 08 **(82.5) n19 t22.5 f21 b20.** Soaring, intense barley. Given a better cask, and this would have been some dram. *46%. Douglas Laing.*

GLEN GRANT
Speyside, 1840. Campari. Working.

Glen Grant db **(87) n21.5** young barley, new-mown grass and a smudge of toffee; **t23** huge flavour explosion led by juicy, young malt. Soft spices reveal an oaky interest, too; **f21** over-laced with caramel; **b21.5** this is a collector's malt for the back label alone: truly one of the most bizarre I have ever seen. "James Grant, 'The Major'" it cheerfully chirrups, "was only 25 when he set about achieving his vision of a single malt with a clear colour. The unique flavour and appearance was due to the purifiers and the tall slender stills he designed and the decision to retain its natural colour...." Then underneath is written: "Farven Justeter Med Karamel/Mit Farbstoff"" Doh! Or, as they say in German: "Doh!" Need any more be said about the nonsense, the pure insanity, of adding colouring to whisky. *40%*

Glen Grant 5 Years Old db **(89) n22.5** dry and herbal with crushed celery, grist, agave, a sprinkle of pepper; **t22** crisp, firm barley with the sweetness handcuffed by a quick spurt of vanilla; semi-serious spice; **f21.5** clean, late oils and warming peppers; **b23** elegant malt which has noticeably grown in stature and complexity of late. *40%*

Glen Grant 10 Years Old db **(88.5) n22 t22 f22 b22.** ...And on re-taste it appears a honey and spice element has been upped slightly. *40%*

Glen Grant 15 Years Old Cask Strength Limited Edition Cask no.17163 dist Feb 92, bott Sep 07 db **(86) n20 t23.5 f21 b21.5.** Such a frustrating bottling: thumping caramel makes its mark on both the nose and finish. Glen Grant is, for me, unquestionably one of the truly great distilleries of Scotland. And this should have been a cask soaring into the 90s score-wise because elsewhere the stunning oak-spice and layered bourbon-esque honey is truly brilliant. But caramel, either added, or naturally leaking from the cask, has flattened the beginning and end, leaving memories of those fabulous waves of rich, sweet barley to haunt you. *59.9%. ncf. 378 bottles.*

⸭ **Glen Grant Cellar Reserve 1992** bottled 08 db **(94.5) n23** a beguiling array of crisp barley and crystalised sugary notes; if a nose can be crunchy and brittle, then this really is it; **t24** the tastebuds virtually swoon under this glorious bathing of barley and sugar; unbelievably juicy and mouth-watering for its age, the oak is there to ensure backbone and fair play and does nothing to subtract from the most graceful notes, except perhaps to pep up slightly with a teasing spiciness; **f24** long, with more playful spices and a chocolate fudge lending weight to the glassy barley edge; one to close the eyes to and be consumed by; **b23.5** one of the great world distilleries being revealed to the us in its very finest colours. They tend to be natural, with no colourings added, therefore allowing the extraordinary kaleidoscope of subtle sweetnesses to be deployed and enjoyed to their fullest. I defy you not to be blown away by this one, especially when you realise there is not a single big base note to be heard.... *46% nc, ncf*

Adelphi Glen Grant 1985 Aged 22 Years bourbon hogshead, cask no. 10184, dist 85, bott 08 **(87.5) n20** just dull, dull, dull... **t23** just exciting, exciting, exciting...the delivery is caked in muscovado sugar and light, fruity barley. But the 62.1 abv ensures that the impact maximises the effect; **f22.5** long, aided by the most gentle of oils and burned fudge; **b22** a classic example of a dull nose leading you up the garden path....which is quite apposite seeing as it's Glen Grant... *62.1%. 167 bottles.*

Berrys' Own Selection Glen Grant 1973 cask no. 6643, bott 07 **(83.5) n20.5 t21.5 f21 b20.5.** No shortage of signs of life as the marmalade-fruit cuts a sharp figure on the palate.

Decently honeyed, too, but just a few signs of oaky degradation reveal that the game was up for this cask in terms of possible improvement. 46%. Berry Bros & Rudd.

Berrys' Own Selection Glen Grant 1993 cask no. 121908, bott 07 **(88.5) n21** slightly green and immature; **t23** youthful with bitter-sweet barley; amazingly lively and energetic on the palate; the peppers really nip and bite while the saliva glands struggle to handle the freshness of the barley as the flavour profile goes nuts; **f22.5** myriad barley tones helped by non GG-style soft oils; **b22** unusually fat and weighty for a GG. But really clean, delicious fun! 53.8%. Berry Bros & Rudd.

Cadenhead's Authentic Collection Glen Grant-Glenlivet Aged 18 Years bourbon barrel, dist 89, bott May 07 **(90) n22** for a bourbon barrel, the degree of soft grape with the barley effect is astonishing; **t23** big, booming barley, unusually yielding in places but a firmness to the malty sheen; **f22** those gentle fruit notes resurface with the vanilla; sharp and eye watering; **b23** beautiful malt that is much fruitier than it has any right to be. 60.8%. 204 bottles

·:⬧· **Cärn Mör Glen Grant 1993** hogshead, cask no. 121910, dist 93, bott 09 **(87.5) n22** clean, intense malt; **t23.5** the lightest, cleanest, grassiest, juiciest of barley: **f20.5** the usual old cask bitter-ish pay off... **b21.5** to be honest, I would have been willing, just from the nose alone, to have bet that this would be a tired, bitter finish. From this kind of third-time around cask you are unlikely to get much else. But the virgin freshness to the barley on both nose and delivery is worth the compromise. 46%. The Scottish Liqueur Centre.

The Coopers Choice Glen Grant 1977 Sherry Wood Aged 30 Years (91) n22 clean, faultless oloroso – almost too clean and faultless as the barley battles to stake a claim; **t23** amazingly sweet for a sherry butt with lashings of molassed sugar amid the juicy mildly toasted raisin; **f23** long, a hint of spice; a touch of barley on the grape helps integrate the oak; **b23** quite beautiful whisky. 46%. sc ncf. The Vintage Malt Whisky Co.

Distillery Malt Glen Grant 1990 (88) n22 apple blossom and Chinese pears amid the barley; **t23** firm, beautifully structured with the malt arriving in layers of varying sweetness and tempered slightly by an oaky-vanilla and mildly spiced weightiness; **f21** a touch of toffee and bitters while the deft spices continue; **b22** only a slight bitterness to the finale detracts from an otherwise excellent malt. 40%. Gordon & MacPhail.

Duncan Taylor Collection Glen Grant 1970 cask no. 818 **(95) n24 t23 f24 b24.** Where demerara meets oloroso. But for all the enormity of the sherry, the trick is that it is complex enough to allow full development of the juicy barley, too... as well as oak. Simply gorgeous. 53.6%. Duncan Taylor.

Duncan Taylor Collection Glen Grant 1970 cask no. 3490 **(89) n20.5** a few splinters in the barley, the vaguest hint of peat; **t21.5** sharp, piercing barley with a staccato rat-a-tat-tat of spices piercing through the gathering oak; again a soupcon of smoke; **f23.5** some honeyed threads further enliven the thickening malt; the oaky vanilla weaves delightful contours while a sprinkling of cocoa tries to further balance the honey: truly wonderful; **b23** the nose and delivery leaves you thinking this is a malt for the scrapyard. But the fabulous recovery leaves you gasping. 49.7%

·:⬧· **Duncan Taylor Collection Glen Grant 1970** cask no. 3494 **(88) n21** a real sprig of heather and distant peat among the dominant oaks; **t22.5** a sweeter delivery than the nose heralds, emphasising the intensity and clean-cut nature of the barley. Some butterscotch reinforces the middle segment; **f22** long, spiced, vaguely smoked and dries with a genuine nod towards elegance; **b22.5** only exceptionally well made spirit can absorb oak with such seemingly effortless aplomb. Classy stuff. 49.9%

Duncan Taylor Collection Glen Grant 1970 cask no. 3496 **(84.5) n20.5 t20 f22.5 b21.5.** Charming old buffer of a dram, showing great age and, from the lack of backbone, infirmity. Knows its way around the palate, though, and enough citrus-lined barley gathers for a delicious middle and finish. 44%

Duncan Taylor Collection Glen Grant 1972 cask no. 1641 **(85) n21 t22 f21 b21.** A decent, honest malt that has seen the odd summer too many, but the big oaks still – just – play second fiddle to the bustling barley. 53.5%

Duncan Taylor Collection Glen Grant 1972 cask no. 1643 **(83.5) n19 t21 f22 b21.5.** Improves markedly after an uncomfortable start on the nose and delivery. The middle veritably hums with ultra-intense barley. 53.4%

Duncan Taylor Collection Glen Grant 1972 cask no. 3890 **(94.5) n23.5** yessirree! That's one fine, tootin' single malt we have here: even if it does have all the attributes of a stunning bourbon. Honey, soft liquorice – you name it – it's there.... **t24** close your eyes and just allow your tastebuds to wallow in this enormous celebration of intense barley out-intensified by the lush, silky cocoa-crusted honeycomb and liquorice; **f23.5** gentle embers of hickory with Demerara and barley; **b23.5** I know people who swear blind they loathe bourbon. Hate the stuff with a passion. And then eulogise over top-quality ancient single malts. I'd love to be there when they taste this.... *57.7%*

⟡ **Duncan Taylor Collection Glen Grant 1972** cask no. 8948 **(85.5) n21.5 t22.5 f20.5 b21.** Barley and gooseberries fight off the spicy oaks. Almost. *46.2%*

⟡ **Duncan Taylor Collection Glen Grant 1972** cask no. 8950 **(88) n22** gooseberries being boiled; elsewhere a jam tart is being baked; **t23** beautifully soft delivery with the oils really coming to the fore to ensure the softest of landings for the butterscotch malt; salivating and mildly supine; **f21.5** chalky vanilla as the oak takes a gentle hand; **b21.5** the barley and oak have reached a pleasant understanding. *45%*.

⟡ **Duncan Taylor Collection Glen Grant 1974** cask no. 16574 **(86.5) n21 t22 f22.5 b21.** At times a seeringly hot, though by no means unpleasant. Massively malty, sharp and no shrinking violet. *55.6%*.

⟡ **Duncan Taylor Collection Glen Grant 1974** cask no. 16576 **(85) n22 t21 f21 b21.** Malty, clean, juicy, vanilla-flecked but ultimately runs out of ideas. *48.4%*.

⟡ **Duncan Taylor Collection Glen Grant 1974** cask no. 16577 **(81) n21 t19 f21 b20.** Vaguely similar in style to cask 16574, but thinner, hotter and generally lacking its all round charisma. *54.5%*.

⟡ **Duncan Taylor Collection Glen Grant 1974** cask no. 16578 **(82.5) n21 t20 f21.5 b20.** A cheery, unsophisticated dram which slaps the barley on as paste might be brushed onto wallpaper. Thin, but some buttery notes help out at the death. *52.2%*.

⟡ **Duthies Glen Grant 13 Years Old (74.5) n18 t21.5 f17 b18.** Sparkles on the palate for a few moments, but the remainder is hard work. A style which might be appreciated by certain sections of the German whisky market. But in pure technical terms, a real disappointment. *46%.* Cadenhead's for Germany.

⟡ **Gordon & MacPhail Distillery Label Glen Grant 25 Years Old (93) n24.5** the type of nose it takes hours to fully measure: a soupcon of smoke helps entangle one of the most complex noses of the year even further, making for a dense undergrowth of creamed rice, over-ripened greengages. A pithy orangey note and, above all, a thickness to the barley attained usually only by sticking your head in a mash tun. Beyond glorious... **t23** silky and sweet, the usual brittleness takes a little time to develop, so until then enjoy the porridge and molten brown sugar... **f22.5** long, prickly and spiced with the oaks showing an aging dryness plus a hint of medium roast Mysore coffee; **b23** the type of malt us long-in-the-tooth whisky specialists dream off, but too rarely find. The nose, though, defies belief. *43%*

Gordon & MacPhail Glen Grant 1948 rare vintage range **(91) n24** something to be experienced, with a nod towards exotic fruit, a distant smokiness and a shake of salt. Changes countless times through temperature and oxidisation in the glass: a real moving target; **t22** the arrival is silk, what follows is warming oak in spicy form and kept honest by a very gentle and delicious smokiness; just a dab or two of light molasses for good measure; **f22** bitter-sweet with just a hint of marmalade before the oak and delicate smoke dry proceedings; **b23** The guys at G&M did exactly right bottling this now, rather than waiting until it reached 60. I'm not convinced there was another summer in this one to keep the peaty structure intact. Genuinely inspiring malt. *40%*

Gordon & MacPhail Glen Grant 1953 rare vintage range **(92) n23** just a catch of smoke attached to the faultless sherry. The oak lets everyone know its about; **t24** excellent weight to the oloroso and the spices are spot on; particular wonderful is the interplay between the grape and honeycomb sweetnesses; again a wisp of smoke towards the middle; **f22** shows a degree of oaky stress but there is enough weight and finesse to see it through to a sultana-rich finale; **b23** same age as my brother, David, this; except has worn better and, because it doesn't ceaselessly drone on and on and on about bloody Chelsea, has a lot more interesting things to say...One of the great super oldies of the last few years. The whisky, I mean. Not my brother... *48%*

⟡ **Gordon & MacPhail Rare Vintage Glen Grant 1958 (96.5) n24** it's as though a blender – one of those noisy things you find in a kitchen, as opposed to a quiet, saintly soul located in a whisky lab - has been deployed to hurtle together in microscopic form a pot peuri of mashed, sun-kissed fruit and a complex array of vanilla notes. The result is curiously light if intense, if that makes sense: but that is exactly what you will find. The oak is controlled and elegant, the degree of sweetness to dryness absolute textbook stuff; **t24** if you want an essay in finesse, then just take a small mouthful of this: the rich, plummy fruits have been liberally doused in muscovado sugar and the vanillas have a toasty edge. The results is a delivery which frankly defies years as well as description. Astonishing. **f24** you might expect this to be the Achilles heel: sure this dram must have a flaw somewhere, and the build up of oak at the death has to be where you find it. Right? Wrong! Here we have the oaks collecting for sure, but they have been so well impregnated with those stunningly sweet fruity tones, any bitterness is entirely eradicated. Long, lush and lasting... **b24.5** virtually no grey hairs on this 50-year-old which has embraced half a century with an unbelievable degree of finesse and grace. One of the truly great Glen Grants – indeed, Speyside malts – of recent years, this is textbook stuff as to regard how to showcase enormous age with virtually no blemishes to speak of. One of the all time great Old Timers. And if you can't afford Glenfiddich 50-year-old at £10,000 a throw, then settle for this one that is just half a point and £9,850 behind... *40%*

⬧ **Gordon & MacPhail Rare Vintage Glen Grant 1962 (94.5) n22.5** overcooked fruitcake with oak where the almonds should be; **t24** oh, my word!! Pure silk and near perfection on delivery as the intense barley gets caught up in some sumptuous treacled spice; the majestic middle makes no secret of the age, but such is lightness of touch and the quiet benevolence of the liquid fruit makes one almost purr out loud...; **f24** long, lingering, deft, raisiny and sugared barley but with vanilla aplenty; **b24** almost faultlessly weighted and a wonderful example of where great oak is used to add nothing but a positive slant. A stunner. And cements my belief, along with the amazing 1958 vintage, that G&M understand this distillery in a way the more recent blender(s) of the previous owners never came close to. *40%*

Gordon & MacPhail Glen Grant 1964 rare vintage range **(89) n22** spotted dick pudding; heavily toasted raisins; **t23** vibrant fruit and barley very much in tandem; **f22** a decent viscosity and sweetness to the fruit sees off the oak; **b22** has stood up to time with uncanny depth. What a treat!! *48%*

Gordon & MacPhail Glen Grant 1966 rare vintage range **(88) n23** French toast, a touch of salt and toffee apples; **t22** stupendously well balanced delivery with barley and fruit profound and in sync; a touch of over-eager oak towards the bitter-coffee middle **f21** again the oak pushes a little too hard but enough firm malt in reserve to see off the worst; **b22** yes, there are a few cracks showing here, but for such age the overall picture is a pretty one. *40%*

Gordon & MacPhail Glen Grant 1967 rare vintage range **(86) n23 t22 f20 b21.** Curious how this works far better on the nose than the '68, yet, for all the lovely honey apparent, tires much more quickly. Funny ol' game, this whisky lark. *40%*

Gordon & MacPhail Glen Grant 1968 rare vintage range **(89) n21** a mild hint of sap; exotic fruit on oxidisation; **t23** such beautiful barley: the oak is around but the structure of the malt is propped up by several layers of lightly coated maple syrup; **f22** long, beautifully gentle with the accent return to the barley; **b23** one whiff of the nose suggests a possible problem, but the palate confounds. *40%*

⬧ **Harris Whisky Co. Glen Grant Aged 35 Years** cask no. 6650, dist Jul 73, bott Sep 08 **(87) n20.5** heavily oaked but some golden syrup tries to rescue the situation; **t22** an incredible transformation on the nose; yes, the oak is there in stave-loads, but the delivery is almost explosive as the spiced sugars erupt immediately on delivery; surprisingly malty and juicy middle, considering; **f22** some better behaved and more sensible mocha calms things down; **b21.5** an injection of sugar concentrate helps negate the overenthusiastic oak. Not one for those looking for a sedate dram... *57.5%. 100 bottles.*

John Milroy Selection Glen Grant 1984 Aged 22 Years (83) n20 t22 f20 b21. Unusually sweet. Raisin concentrate. *46%*

⬧ **Kingsbury's Single Cask Glen Grant Aged 12 Years** dist Jul 96, bott Jul 08 **(84) n21.5 t22 f20 b20.5.** Hard nosed and hard arsed. Little give but the crunchy barley offers some juicy sweetness. *46%. Japan Import System.*

Kingsbury "The Selection" Glen Grant 11 Years Old 1996 (87.5) n22 spiced up celery and vanilla; **t22.5** an explosion of barley which takes with it some early spice, but the juicy malt settles with a soothing sweetness; **f21** medium but the barley and soft vanilla intensifies; **b22** the delicate sweetness of the intense malt ticks every box. *43.0%. nc ncf. Japan Import System Co. Ltd.*

Lonach Glen Grant 31 Years Old (84) n21 t22 f21 b20. Exceptionally firm barley for its age; enjoys a sugar-coated lustre and good depth. *42.3%.*

Lonach Glen Grant 35 Years Old (83) n20 t21 f21 b21. Creaks a bit, but some lovely barley sugar and liquorice. *41.8%. Duncan Taylor.*

Lonach Glen Grant 1969 (83) n20 t19.5 f23 b20.5. One small sip for man; one giant leap for oak-kind. *52.3%. Duncan Taylor.*

⬧ **Lonach Glen Grant 1969 (87) n21** the exotic fruit shows age, but some niggardly oak refuses to allow it an elegant flourish; **t21** juicy, fruity but with splinters everywhere; **f23** at last evens out with a stunning fanning out of soft Java coffee notes and glorious spices; silky, beautifully textured and rich...and goes on and on...and on... **b22** talk about an over-aged malt. Far too old. Yet such is the enormity of the fruit and barley character, it somehow sees off the excesses of the oak which spoils the start and offers instead a very late alternative. A rare style, indeed. *51.7%. Duncan Taylor.*

Montgomerie's Glen Grant 1990 (84.5) n21.5 t22 f20 b21. Another well used cask allowing the malt a pretty open platform. *46%. Montgomery & Co. Ltd.*

Norse Cask Selection Glen Grant 1965 Aged 40 Years (84) n22 t22 f20 b20. The nose is a mildly drier version of the G&M '66; enough early sweetness but dries big time. *52.5%. WhiskyOwner.com, Denmark.*

⸪ **Norse Cask Selection Glen Grant 1993 Aged 16 Years** hogshead cask no. 121914, dist 93, bott May 09 **(95.5) n23.5** beautiful custard poured over barley pie; not a single hint of an off note. Pure gold...literally... **t25** just about the perfect – no, sod it!!! - absolutely perfect latter-day non-sherried Speyside delivery: the most intense, complete, perfectly sweetened, juicy and gloriously dense malt massages the tastebuds, adding just a pinch of salt and spice to ensure all is on full alert. It can hardly get better... **f23** all that went on before, but now in nostalgic sepia tones with an extra squirt of vanilla from the oak for good measure... **b24** a truly great cask from a great distillery: this, surely, is what drinking single malt Scotch should be about... *57.8%. Qualityworld for WhiskyOwner.com, Denmark.*

Old Malt Cask Glen Grant Aged 12 Years Gabriel Meffre wine cask no. 3899, dist Jun 95, bott Sep 07 **(92) n22** quiet, save a threatening spice; a nose that is all about hinted potential; **t23** the firm bite of the barley sits well with rounder fruit; **f23.5** now some real complexity with a cocoa bitterness interlinking with the soft barley and grape: seductive and teasing; **b23.5** OK, I admit it: a wine cask which works....and a French one at that!! No sulphur. No grapey flatness. A flimsily clad comtesse of a dram beckoning you towards an evening of elegance and pleasure. *50%. nc ncf. Douglas Laing. 300 bottles.*

Old Malt Cask Glen Grant Aged 18 Years sherry butt no. 4280, dist Mar 90, bott May 08 **(84.5) n21.5 t22 f219 b21.** Juicy for its age with a degree of bite, too. The odd blemish, however. *50%. nc ncf. Douglas Laing. 665 bottles.*

Old Malt Cask Glen Grant Aged 22 Years bourbon barrel no. 4242, dist Sep 85, bott Apr 08 **(92) n23.5** superb, ultra-complex combo of browning brown toast, freshly crushed Demerara sugar, custard tart and ripped-sandpaper...oh, and barley....; **t22.5** biting, pawing, snapping barley with sensuous layers of sugared vanilla; **f23** the sugared coating thins slightly as the vanillas gain a foothold. Toasty again, but the sweet-dry balance is exceptional; **b23** a contented cask which gleefully celebrates its Kentucky origins. Sweet, but the panache of the oaky fight-back leaves you drooling. *50%. nc ncf. Douglas Laing. 265 bottles.*

Old Malt Cask Glen Grant Aged 30 Years sherry hogshead no. 3745, dist Dec 76, bott Jul 07 **(90) n22** excellent sherry sees off the tiring cask...just and in a rummy kind of way; **t23** beautiful delivery of silky grape spiced up with aging oak and crisp barley; **f22.5** the oak threatens, then thinks better of it as stunningly deft grape returns; **b22.5** what was once a classic butt has been singed by age, but the brilliance still exudes. *50%. Douglas Laing. 228 bottles.*

Old Malt Cask Glen Grant Aged 30 Years sherry butt no. 4295, dist May 78, bott May 08 **(95) n23.5** ancient oak but with a honeycomb theme; **t24** wow!! Was I right about the honeycomb on the nose...!! Pure Crunchie candy bar. Burnt honey, some wonderful cocoa, a touch of spice and then barley in the most concentrated form imaginable. A real bourbony theme now with red liquorice...astonishing... **f23.5** a warm finale with a cough sweet edge indicating more ancient oak; a hint of hickory and molasses...genius!! **b24** have to admit, on first nose though, this was a gonner. But given the chance to breathe, it comes back to life...and how..!! A blueprint for how great 30-year-old and over whiskies should be. *45.9%. nc ncf. Douglas Laing. 341 bottles.*

⸪ **Old Malt Cask Glen Grant Aged 32 Years** sherry butt, dist Dec 76, bott Mar 09 **(94) n23.5** dismisses its age with contemptuous ease, helped along the way by the slickest, cleanest oloroso imaginable; a background wisp of smoke helps bump up the already considerable complexity; **t24** exactly as the nose heralds: clean, thick, grape with some wonderful spicy talons; a touch of bourbony liquorice is also present. It is as if a younger and older top rate cask have been vatted together; **f23** the spices gently pulse as the fade is a slow de-intensification of the oloroso; some natural caramel also comes into play; **b23.5** an old school sherry butt. And just like old schools, tends to be far more correct and exacting in standards. The flavour of a nearly lost world. *50%. Douglas Laing. 266 bottles.*

Old & Rare Glen Grant Aged 31 Years sherry cask, dist Dec 76, bott Feb 08 **(96) n24** weighty with a spec of smoke amid the grizzled grape; burnt raisins and nutty fruitcake left twenty minutes too long in the oven: fantastic!! **t23.5** melt-in-the-mouth barley somehow appears ahead of the onrushing grape. The oak offers a toasty countenance but somehow the fruit juices explode into action, making for one of the most salivating 31-year-olds you'll ever find; **f24** perfectly roasty, as it should be, ensuring the bitter-sweet complexity such a great whisky demands; the oaky dryness is the perfect foil to the chewy, juicy succulence; the mocha mocks the crisp barley; roasted cherries top the fruitcake effect; **b24.5** a near impeccable cask, even after all these years. Few distilleries did sherry as well as Glen Grant during this period. A contender for Scotch of the Year without question. *58.6%. nc ncf. Douglas Laing. 196 bottles.*

Provenance Glen Grant Aged 11 Years hogshead no. 4133, dist autumn 96, bott winter 08 **(84.5) n21 t21 f21.5 b21.** Absolutely clean, juicy straight down the line GG with not an oaky deviation. *46%. Douglas Laing.*

⸬ **Provenance Glen Grant Aged 12 Years** refill hogshead, dist autumn 96, bott winter 08 **(86) n20 t22 f22 b22.** Recovers spectacularly from a dodgy nose to a real clean barley salvo. Lots of spice and barley sugar. *46%*

Scotch Malt Whisky Society Cask 9.44 Aged 11 Years refill hogshead, dist Apr 97 **(85.5) n22.5 t21 f21 b21.** Attractively malty but makes a point of not making a point. *59.4%*

The Single Malts of Scotland Glen Grant 1972 Aged 35 Years bott Sep 07 **(86) n22 t21 f22 b21.** Big, sweet, intense whisky staying just on the right side of stodgy. The barley-sugar concentrate on the nose delights. *54.9%. Speciality Drinks.*

⸬ **The Whisky Fair Glen Grant 36 Year Old** sherry hogshead, dist 72, bott 09 **(96) n24** not so much that the oloroso here is huge, but it is the overall shape and impact that really takes the breath away. Faultlessly clean: sherry from the old school which embraces the oak with dignity; **t24** a mirror image of the nose on delivery, except perhaps there is more juicy fruit than you might expect. This moves in the middle ground first towards an eggy fruitcake and then one accompanied by milky coffee; **f24** long, sweetening as the molasses and raisin gets to work; **b24** this, in a bottle, is the very point of sherried malt whisky. *56.3%. The Whisky Fair, Germany.*

GLEN KEITH

Speyside, 1957. Chivas. Silent.

Glen Keith 10 Years Old db **(80) n22 t21 f18 b19.** A malty if thin dram that finishes with a whimper after an impressively refreshing, grassy start. *43%*

⸬ **Old Malt Cask Glen Keith Aged 18 Years** refill barrel, dist Mar 90, bott Dec 08 **(93.5) n23** distant peat secures a thicker back note than you might normally expect and a touch of extra marmaladey sweetness, too: quite lovely; **t24** brilliant delivery, with a real mixed bag of sweets for beginners. A wonderful blending of molassed, fudgy sugars is lightened by a thinner, honeyed edge. All this is almost perfectly integrated with the thickest sweet barley imaginable. Fabulous; **f23** long, medium weighted and absorbs the developing oak with open arms; in the background a ghost of a smoky trace ensures a light spice and subtle weight; **b23.5** this has never been one of the sexy Speysiders, but now and again a superb bottling rears its head – and here's the best of the lot. Occasionally a peated version was produced here by Chivas. Though this isn't peaty, as such, there is a subtle, smoky echo to this one which does it no harm whatsoever. A distillery classic and must have. *50%. Douglas Laing. 259 bottles.*

Old Malt Cask Glen Keith Aged 33 Years dist Jun 73, bott Mar 07 **(83) n21 t22 f20 b20.** A tendency towards thinness and a hot nature, but just enough barley juice to stir the adrenalin. Some deft exotic fruit via the oak also weighs in a large early on. A pretty attractive if raw proposition. *50%. Douglas Laing.*

GLENKINCHIE

Lowland, 1837. Diageo. Working.

Glenkinchie 12 Years Old db **(66) n16 t19 f18 b18.** The nose is a disaster with more off notes than I can begin to count. Never have I come across a more sorry Classic Malt since the range was launched. Luckily - or unluckily for the market – this is from a bottling for Canada with half the label in French. One for the guillotine. *43%*

⸬ **Glenkinchie Aged 15 Years** The Distillers Edition finished in Amontillado casks, dist 92, bott 07 db **(94) n23.5** clean, creamy, unhindered grape; **t24** soft delivery, but the slow-motion evolvement of spice is almost something to marvel at; **f23** returns to a creamier place, drier, nuttier, chewier... **b23.5** now this is absolutely top class wine cask finishing. One of my last whiskies of the night, and one to take home with me. Sophisticated, intelligent and classy. *46%*

Glenkinchie 20 Years Old db **(85.5) n21 t22 f21.5 b21.** When I sampled this, I thought: "hang on, haven't I tasted this one before?" When I checked with my tasting notes for one or two independents who bottled around this age a year or two ago, I found they were nigh identical to what I was going to say here. Well, you can't say its not a consistent dram. The battle of the citrus-barley against the welling oak is a rich and entertaining one. *58.4%*

Cadenhead's Authentic Collection Glenkinchie Aged 19 Years bourbon hogshead, dist 87, bott May 07 **(84) n20 t23 f20 b21.** A magnificent show by the barley against the oaky odds. At times the mouth-watering elements offer an unexpected citrus joy. *54.8%. 234 bottles.*

⠐ **Cadenhead's Glenkinchie Aged 21 Years** dist 87, bott 09 **(89) n22** pine fresh; **t23** bristling oak kept in place by muscovado sugar-almonded barley; **f22** long, assisted with a soft oil which keeps the vanilla moving; **b22** has no right to be excellent whisky, yet somehow is... *51.6%*

Old Malt Cask Glenkinchie Aged 27 Years (83) n22 t21 f20 b20. Feels the strain from carrying the oak, but the nose of salty fish with rosemary and citrus makes for a good aperitif; *50%. nc ncf. Douglas Laing. Miniature bottle.*

Secret Stills Lowland 5.1 1987 (86.5) n22 t22 f21.5 b21. Certainly a secret in seeing the distillery in this light: unquestionably a first. Rich and full nose and delivery balances fruit and floral attractively. Though seeing off the age, the growing fruity, coppery edge, flattens somewhat. *45%. Gordon & MacPhail.*

THE GLENLIVET
Speyside 1824. Chivas. Working.

The Glenlivet Aged 12 Years db **(83) n22.5 t21 f20 b19.5.** Wonderful nose and very early development but then flattens out towards the kind of caramel finish you just wouldn't traditionally associate with this malt. *40%*

The Glenlivet Aged 12 Years Old First Fill Matured db **(90.5) n22.5** unmistakable oak influence, edging the light barley towards a soft, red liquorice, Kentuckian feel. Gentle but never docile and the malty freshness exuberates; **t22.5** a real barrel-full of apples early on with a gathering sweet edge. Always the barley is in control, though the oaky influence is never far behind; **f22.5** long, with an almost apologetic build up of spices again underlying the barrel type. The barley remains true but it is the elegance of the delivery which raises the hairs; **b23** a quite wonderful whisky, far truer to The Glenlivet than the standard 12 and one which really every malt whisky lover should try once in their journey through the amber stuff. Forget the tasting notes on the bottle, which are unhelpful and bear little relation to what is inside. A gem of a dram. *40%*

The Glenlivet 15 Years of Age db **(80) n19 t21 f20 b20.** There is an undeniable charm to the countless waves of malt and oak. But don't expect much in the way of complexity or charisma. *40%*

The Glenlivet Nadurra 16 Years Old db **(94) n22** caramelised ginger wrapped in bitter chocolate; **t24** enveloping, spellbinding, shocking...an immediate outbreak of Demerara sugar before the tastebuds are crept upon by stealthy malt and coshed by a voluptuous attack of Fox's ginger chocolate biscuits; the middle arrival of faintly chilli-ish spice combines beautifully with the warming ginger; **f24** lengthier and with more ginger than a very lengthy gingery thing; **b24** in some respects one of the sweetest single malts of all time. It would be too sweet altogether except for a balancing ginger-led spice attack that drags the oak into action. The closest thing to a liqueur whisky you will ever find: pure entertainment, sheer class and immeasurable fun. *48%*

⠐ **The Glenlivet Nadurra 16 Year** Old batch no. 1007D, bott Oct 07 db **(84) n21.5 t22 f20.5 b20.** Somehow, the sample we have been sent through seems untypical of the Nadurras I have been encountering around the world. This is flat and heavily toffeed, almost as if caramel has been added – though the whole point of this brand is that it is Nadurra (the Gaelic for "natural"). Others I have encountered have been far more full of fun and mischief and belting out a malty message. Mark this one down as an aberration. *57.7%*

The Glenlivet 18 Years Old db **(83.5) n21 t22 f20.5 b21.** Honey and spice by the bucket load. On first couple of tastes what appears to be caramel flattens all before it. But some persistence pays with the overall intensity making an enjoyable mark. *43%*

⠐ **The Glenlivet Archive 21 Years Old** batch no. 0508B bott 2008/11/17 db **(87.5) n22** weighty and fibrous. Thick layers of honeyed fruit: not what I was expecting or how I remember it. Lumbering but attractive despite the odd flaw; **t23.5** fabulous arrival and mouthfeel: arguably the silkiest on the market. Soupy but you can't not love the interplay between barley and deep honeycomb while the spices set it all off beautifully; some liquorice notes fill the middle; **f20** the degree of flattening caramel – be it added or natural – is quite a shock and the building bitterness doesn't help, either; **b22** forget the nondescript finish: just settle down and be royally entertained by the enormity and panache of the big honey arrival. *43%*

The Glenlivet XXV 25 Years Old db **(91) n24** blindfolded, I might have marked this down as a bourbon with a gender crisis: on the one hand hairy and blokey with muscular oaks, on the other showing feminine nimbleness of grain and mature fruits. Superb... **t22** some real grapey signs on delivery and again this is a super-soft show, but one that bitters out towards the middle; **f22** low key with lots of rumbling toffee and spice; **b23** the nose sends this into superstar status, though for all its brilliance it's a bit like driving a Mercedes E320 with the engine of a Ford Anglia. *43%*

Adelphi Glenlivet 1978 Aged 29 Years bourbon hogshead, cask no. 13503 **(89.5) n22** the very first molecules of the tell-tale exotic fruit are just beginning to form....; **t22.5** soft mouthfeel on delivery, some immediate oak spice but the barley sparkles as some toast is buttered (healthy non-salt, by the way); **f22.5** long with those fruity molecules that also formed on impact now vanishing slightly towards the finish as the barley somehow begins to intensify with a stylish flourish; **b22.5** a real touch of class. *52.1%. 193 bottles.*

Berrys' Own Selection Glenlivet 1971 cask no. 6450, bott 07 **(77) n18 t20.5 f19 b19.5.** Some old casks work. Some don't. This one cannot for the life of it make up its mind as to whether it wants to or not. *46%. Berry Bros & Rudd.*

Berry's' Own Selection Glenlivet 1972 Aged 32 Years (86) n19 t23 f22 b22. A fascinating cask which cherishes its vitality. *46%. Berry Bros & Rudd.*

Berrys' Own Selection Glenlivet 1974 Aged 32 Years (84) n19 t22 f21 b22. A well-mannered dram offering barley-sugar in all the right places. But has a few bags under the eyes. *46%.*

⋯ **Berry's Own Selection Glenlivet 1975** bott 08 **(87.5) n22** barley juice led; **t23** excellent sharpness to the barley, salivating and mildly spiced; a glossy metallic sheen and light demerara sweetness; **f21** happy to embrace vanilla when you want it to do a little more; **b21.5** typically non-committal, as this distillery has a tendency to be, but has that little touch of class. *46%. Berry Bros & Rudd.*

⋯ **Berry's Own Selection Glenlivet 1977** bott 08 **(85) n21 t21 f22 b21.** Very even: silky-soft with massive vanilla. *46%. Berry Bros & Rudd.*

Cadenhead's Glenlivet Aged 19 Years port, dist 88, bott Feb 08 **(85) n19 t23.5 f21 b21.5.** As Port accented casks goes, this is unique. The nose is all over the place, the finish feels like a dreary caramel convention but the fruity, spicy delivery is eye-closingly superb. Very, very strange. *56.7%. 269 bottles.*

⋯ **Celtic Heartlands Glenlivet 1975** bott 08 **(85) n21.5 t21.5 f21 b21.** oak in as many guises as you can imagine here. Bit OTT on that front, to be honest, but you cannot be blown away by some aspects of the bourbony intensity. *51.2%. Bruichladdich Ltd. 450 bottles.*

D&M Aficionados' Club Bottling Glenlivet Aged 27 Years cask no. 6097, dist Mar 79 **(91) n21** a touch lazy, but sandpaper and barley make an interesting mix; **t24** absolutely top-of-the-range arrival with an intensity to the sweet malt that has to be tasted to be believed; hints of Demerara and leather sit comfortably with the natural fudge. The spongy mouth-feel orbits perfection; **f23** a really classy fade-out with hints of honey balancing out the gathering oak; **b23** a corker of a dram whose arrival on the palate is as profound as it is beguiling. *43%. nc ncf. US*

Distillery Malt Glenlivet Aged 21 Years (92) n23 serious complexity with fresh, newly exposed oak teaming up perfectly with a fruitier, citrussy lead. Lovely; **t24** light, delicate malt with varying layers of thickening oak but the emphasis on diluted maple sugar; **f22** oak-rich; takes on some late, controlled bitterness; **b23** a very feminine dram full of curves, elegance and grace. *40%. Gordon & MacPhail.*

Duncan Taylor Collection Glenlivet 1968 cask no. 5246, bott 08 **(86) n20 t23 f21.5 b21.5.** Rolls its sleeves up to reveal oaky muscles from the very first sniff. And splinters and sawdust are flying in the fray that follows. But the enormity of the compensating honey is mind-blowing, as are the spices. If you are going to go down, it might as well be fighting... *53.6%*

Duncan Taylor Collection Glenlivet 1968 cask no. 6199 **(87) n23** clean grape given an oaky boost; **t22** signs of wear and tear but the climax of the oloroso is a sexy diversion; **f21** showing the oaky strain, but some Java helps the cause, **b21** hangs on in there....just! *52.1%*

Duncan Taylor Collection Glenlivet 1968 cask no.7601 **(90.5) n23** marzipan and lemon jelly; **t22.5** crunching oak soon dissipates as the fabulously sweet barley evolves; so mouth-watering....!!! **f22.5** the clean juices, which make a mockery of the 40 passing years cling the cocoa-dusted end; **b23** allow to settle in the glass for a good 20 minutes and the rewards are wonderful. *49.9%*

Duncan Taylor Collection Glenlivet 1968 cask no. 8227, dist Dec 68 **(73) n19 t19 f17 b18.** Once mighty sherry sinks beneath the oaky waves. *50.9%*

⋯ **Duncan Taylor Collection Glenlivet 1970** cask no. 2009 **(83.5) n21 t21 f21.5 b20.** Eye-watering oak offers ample evidence of a few summers too far. The middle, though, broadens out as some bitter-sweet barley counters beautifully, before crushed without pity by the wooden weight at the death. *52.6%*

Duncan Taylor Collection Glenlivet 1970 cask no. 2020 **(88) n22.5** effortlessly complex. And by that I mean it's a bit lazy...; **t22** sharp, mouth-watering, punchy barley; **f22** soft oils stretch out the toffee- sweetness; **b21.5** beautiful whisky, but never appears to break sweat. *53.6%*

∵ **Gordon & MacPhail Distillery Label Glenlivet 21 Years Old (88.5) n22** almost thick with fruit, crushed juicy sultana in particular; **t23** spiced sherry trifle-type fruitiness but with some fudgy caramel keeping development relatively muted; silky and revels in its age; **f21.5** lots of natural caramel but surprisingly lacking ambition after the outstanding start; **b22** always merits a refill. *43%*

∵ **Gordon & MacPhail Rare Vintage Glenlivet 1965 (87) n22.5** textbook "oldie" nose with spicy splinters but a countering blancmange sweetness; vanilla dominates as the malt oxidizes in the glass; **t21.5** lush delivery with soft barley and hints of blood orange and then a gradual heaping on of the oak, at times a touch bitter; **f22** delicate maple syrup sweetness blends in with the most parched oakiness to charming effect; **b21** takes the oak to the limit but somehow works. *40%*

Gordon & MacPhail Station Series Duirinish Glenlivet 1991 refill sherry hogshead 48288, bott Feb 07 **(86.5) n21 t22 f22 b21.5.** Thick malt backed up by ultra soft fruit. Some oaky indulgence, but all very well mannered. *46.0%. nc ncf. Japan Import System Co. Ltd.*

John Milroy Selection Glenlivet 1975 Aged 30 Years (94) n24 fizzy spice punctuates the intense oloroso; a stream of soft molasses and figs helps make for real complexity; sublimely weighted; **t23** graceful delivery: sheer velvet as the sherry slides to every point on the palate; the barley-sultana sweetness mocks the oak which fails to get a real foothold; **f23** long, no less complex and a touch of latte to complete the job; **b24** style and class by the bodega-load... *46%*

∵ **Kingsbury's Finest & Rarest Glenlivet 1978 (94.5) n23.5** a dusting of molasses on a vague fruitiness which hints at that exotic style old malts crave for...but hasn't quite reached; some definite papaya, though; however it is the improbable gristy, fresh malt which wins hearts and minds; **t24** succulent, soft, silky landing on the palate. The malts are at the vanguard, but in many guises. Again a light molassed sheen appears to be attached but after 29 years still the malts are improbably salivating; a faint milky cocoa notes floats towards the middle as do some simmering oaky spices; **f23** still long, clean and elegant. The vanillas are now out in force, offering a milky-custard fade and light flecks of cassava. Effortlessly graceful to the very end of the tapering finish; **b24** does and says all the right things for its age. Premier class malt. *52.6%. Japan Import System.*

∵ **Kingsbury's Single Cask Glenlivet Aged 15 Years** dist May 93, bott Jun 08 **(79) n21 t20 f18 b18.** Bitter-sweet. But mainly bitter: certainly not as the distiller intended... *46%. Japan Import System.*

Lonach Glenlivet 37 Years Old (86) n21 t21 f22 b22. Chic and fruity. *43.1%*

Lonach Glenlivet 1968 (83) n21.5 t21 f20 b20.5. A malt on the periphery of exhaustion craves some understanding and indulgence here. It deserves it for its big malt statement alone. *40.1%. Duncan Taylor.*

Lonach Glenlivet 1968 bott 08 **(85.5) n23 t21.5 f20 b21.** Some lovely molassed sugar helps save it from the oaky trap door. It's all about the gorgeous nose, though. *41.4%. Duncan Taylor.*

Lonach Glenlivet 1968 (90.5) n22.5 bourbony; red liquorice; **t23** really nubile delivery: unsugared gooseberry and raspberry, tart up the stroking barley; **f22** custard cream biscuits with some faint, oily citrus; **b23** by far and away the star turn of the three new Lonach Glenlivets. Belies its age impeccably. *44.8%. Duncan Taylor.*

Lonach Glenlivet 1968 (90) n22 touches of guava and passion fruit; **t22** any softer and it'd never quite land on the palate; the barley really is almost too light for belief; **f23** vanilla and red liquorice **b23** at first it seems it doesn't quite have the legs. By the third mouthful you review things a little... *41.7%. Duncan Taylor.*

Murray McDavid Mission Glenlivet 1977 Aged 30 Years bott 07 **(94.5) n24.5** faint, swoon...!! Here we go: one of the great Glenlivet noses thanks to this obviously coming from that wonderful old pile of butts used by the distillery at various periods throughout the 1970s: this must be one of the very last. Sultana concentrate with a near perfect degree of oak added for weight – doubtless from the bourbon cask; such other delights such as ginger and over-ripe pears are there for those bothered to look; **t23** a real fruitfest with glorious raisins and honey-liquorice; an immediate spice implosion, with it staying controlled and haughty; **f23.5** settles down for a complex and very long finale: some creaking oak from time to time but the marriage between fruit and unspoiled, manuka-honey-driven oak is something to behold; **b23.5** now here's a conundrum. The label says

"Cask Type: Bourbon". Yet I have tasted enough Glenlivets over the years to put my house on this once being filled into a first fill sherry. My guess is that it was then transferred at some stage into bourbon, possibly because the butt was needed elsewhere, or to stop it from tiring. If this really has matured for 30 years in a bourbon cask and come out like this, then we have a new type of whisky on our hands....I look into my crystal ball and see a long chat with Jim McEwan.... And on the subject of crystal, this is a gem for collectors everywhere. *51.7%. 270 bottles exclusively for Willow Park, Calgary.*

Old Malt Cask Glenlivet Aged 16 Years dist May 90, bott Feb 07 **(84) n22 t22 f19 b21.** A beautiful ginger nose. Some fierce oak at times. *50%. Douglas Laing. 742 bottles.*

⁖ **Old Malt Cask Glenlivet Aged 17 Years** bourbon cask, dist Apr 92, bott Jul 09 **(90.5) n23** hints of ginger in plain chocolate; some flatter oaky notes, too, but comfortably controlled; **t23** caramelised ginger again, but superbly supported by lively malt. Excellent spice prickle; **f22** vanillas out, but the barley sweetness lingers; **b22.5** amazing how lovely this distillery can be in the right cask and with no colouring. Grab this dazzler if you see it. *50%. Douglas Laing.*

⁖ **Old Malt Cask Glenlivet Aged 18 Years** rum cask, dist Sep 90, bott Sep 08 **(85) n20 t22 f21.5 b21.5.** Well made and delivers on the maltiness. *50%. Douglas Laing. 272 bottles.*

Old Malt Cask Glenlivet Aged 27 Years dist Apr 80, bott Apr 07 **(82) n20 t22 f20 b20.** Makes the right noises early on, but somehow doesn't set the pulse racing. *50%. Douglas Laing. 277 bottles.*

Old Malt Cask Glenlivet Aged 27 Years refill hogshead 3842, dist Apr 80, bott Aug 07 **(83.5) n21 t21.5 f21 b20.** Oak-tanged but quite gentle for all the obvious wear and tear. *50%. nc ncf. Douglas Laing. 222 bottles.*

⁖ **Old Malt Cask Glenlivet Aged 30 Years** refill hogshead, dist Jun 78, bott Apr 09 **(94) n23** dull yet intriguing pulsing of oak and barley. Clean and sophisticated in its lightness of touch; **t24** the distillery's traditional mixture of vanilla and barley are in force. But here with a degree of oiliness and weight no longer found in Glenlivet, alas. It means that not only does the barley flex its juicy muscles to the max, but the sugary layers never get out of control; **f23** eye-watering elegance as the barley intensity decreases notch by notch, allowing the drier, chalkier vanillas the final word; teasing spices wrap up a job superbly done; **b24** from the days when The Glenlivet had body enough to cope with 30 years with nothing more than a shrug. Glorious. *50%. Douglas Laing. 205 bottles.*

Old Masters Glenlivet Aged 10 Years cask no. 906680, dist 96, bott 07 **(88) n21** thin barley; stretched by vanilla **t23** more voluptuous and pounding with clean, beautifully rich malt; **f22** the sugared gloss slowly vanishes as delicate, chalky vanilla drives home; late natural toffee; **b22** shows more signs of age than you might expect but the barley impact is a scorcher. *57.6%. James MacArthur for Milan Fair 2007. Italy only.*

⁖ **Old Masters Glenlivet Aged 12 Years** cask no. 906680, dist 96, bott 08 **(82) n22 t21 f19 b20.** Sharp, tasty barley but the feeling is that not all is well with the cask *57.8%. James MacArthur & Co. Ltd.*

⁖ **Old Masters Glenlivet Aged 30 Years** cask no. 1975, dist 78, bott 08 **(85) n22 t22 f20.5 b20.5.** A malt of two halves: the nose shows signs of enormous age with its hints of exotic fruit, but works pleasantly, as does the juicy malt arrival with its delightful, eye-watering zinginess. After that the splinters are harder to remove though some praline does ensure the overall experience is an enjoyable one. *57.6%. James MacArthur & Co. Ltd.*

Scotch Malt Whisky Society Cask 2.72 Aged 22 Years refill hogshead, dist Aug 85 **(89) n21 t24 f21.5 b22.5** Showing the first signs of grey hairs: wisely bottled in time. *56.9%*

⁖ **Scotch Malt Whisky Society Cask 2.74 Aged 15 Years** refill hogshead, dist May 93 **(89.5) n22.5** a neo-bourbon displaying forests of sweet oak and thick barley: if it was sitting on a fence, it'd be an oaky one....; **t22.5** fat, tart and juicy with waves of hickory-led oaky influence; **f22** much more subtle: rhubarb and custard with minimum sugar; **b22.5** attractively shaped and curves in all the right places. *57.2%*

Scott's Selection Glenlivet 1971 bott 07 **(85) n19 t23.5 f21 b22.** The serious wrinkles on the nose are flattened out on the palate to a pretty decent degree. For a few glorious moments we are treated to a fanfare of honeycombe concentrate, but it's all pretty knife-edge stuff. *55%*

Scott's Selection Glenlivet 1977 bott 07 **(86.5) n21 t22 f22 b21.5.** Wholly enjoyable with stout barley tendencies; sweet and chewy. *50.8%*

⁖ **Wilson & Morgan Barrel Selection Glenlivet Aged 30 Years** cask no. 13501, dist 78, bott 08 **(84.5) n21 t22 f20.5 b21.** Very much in the Glenlivet mould for older bottlings: starts off at a cracking pace on the barley and soft fruits and then flags as the vanillas drive home. *46%. Wilson & Morgan.*

GLENLOCHY

Highland (Western), 1898–1983. Closed.

Rarest of the Rare Glenlochy 1980 cask no. 2454 **(96) n24** verging on the perfect nose for a malt of this age: honey on several levels, mainly acacia, but some manuka creeps in; there are friendly polished oak floors, a dab of smoke, toasting mallows and orange peel.... mmmm...!! **t24.5** followed by the near perfect delivery: the sweetness is governed by the sharpness of the barley which still has the most important lines; even the spices are two-toned, one definitely of an oaky hue, the other, one suspects, having some kind of smoky root; **f23.5** a mixture of soft fruit and barley has no problems with the mallow-like vanilla finale; **b24** this does what it says on the tin: this really is the rarest of the rare. I do not often see this stuff either in bottled form or privately through a whisky year. It makes hen's teeth look pretty two-a-penny. But then one must ask the question: why? Any distillery capable of making malt this good should still be working, rather than being turned into a small hotel. (Jim Murray and all at Dram Good Books Ltd would like to assure readers of a nervous disposition that no whisky was spat out during the tasting of this sample.) *54.8%. Duncan Taylor.*

Scotch Malt Whisky Society Cask 62.15 Aged 26 Years refill hogshead, dist May 80 **(91) n23** heads towards exotic fruit but tempered by honey; excellent weight aided by a dab of the most distant smoke; **t23** perfect delivery belying the years: barley arrives first with a gooseberry backup; textures changes from dry to oily back to dry as the spices evolve; **f22** dry toast and barley water; **b23** there's exotic fruit and exotic fruit. Some work. Others don't. This does. There are many worse ways to discover this lost distillery. *59.2%*

GLENLOSSIE

Speyside, 1876. Diageo. Working.

Cadenhead's Glenlossie Aged 14 Years port, dist 93, bott Feb 08 **(91.5) n22.5** one of the most coastal aromas of any Speysider I've ever found: seaweed and rockpools everywhere; even distant peat reek from a seaside cottage; **t23.5** good grief: you are left gasping as the magnificent delivery hurls the sharpest barley at you. The much gentler fruit and lazy smoke tries to soothe and sweet-tale the battered tastebuds; **f22.5** elegant, rich, multilayered finale; **b23** colossal Lossie...!! The 777th whisky specially tasted for this book...and my word, did it take off!! *576%. 267 bottles.*

⠐ **The Cärn Mör Vintage Collection Glenlossie 1984** sherry butt, cask no. 2537, dist 84, bott 09 **(73) n18 t19 f18 b18.** Sulphur-affected cask. *46%. The Scottish Liqueur Centre.*

Duncan Taylor The NC2 Range Glenlossie 1993 (79) n21 t21 f18 b19. This one must have smoked 30 a day, spent its summers in the sun without cream, been a Millwall supporter, or been a whisky writer some time in its life because, my word, it has aged way beyond its years... *46%. nc ncf.*

Scotch Malt Whisky Society Cask 46.17 Aged 15 Years refill barrel, dist Sep 92 **(83.5) n20 t22 f20.5 b21.** A refreshing wallpaper paste / lemon drop combo. *53.5%*

Scotch Malt Whisky Society Cask 46.18 Aged 15 Years refill barrel, dist Sep 92 **(86) n21 t21 f22.5 b21.5.** Outwardly a light, delicate malt but one which eventually glows with intensity. *51.6%*

The Spirit Safe Cask Glenlossie Vintage 1993 Aged 13 Years hogshead no. 1168, bott 07 **(87) n21.5** real heavyweight stuff for a Lossie: as thought the spirit safe was still holding some feints when the swivel arm was moved... **t22** good grief! A real fatty with lush oils holding all kind of vaguely honeyed barley notes, but no shortage of notes that reveal early distillate that usually go around the still one more time... **f22** long, waxy honey and...feints... **b21.5** really unusual stuff this: a Lossie the like of which you will find rarely. For all its obvious shortcomings, a flip side to a feinty dram is that you can often get some real complexity in there, too. I could either have marked it low as a purist or thought: what the hell...enjoy! Guess which I chose... *46%. nc ncf. Celtic Whisky Compagnie. 383 bottles.*

GLEN MHOR

Highland (Northern), 1892–1983. Demolished.

Glen Mhor 1976 Rare Malt db **(93) n23** pure barley sugar but any excess sweetness is trimmed by a luxuriant oaky-vanilla thread that is dipped in honeydew melon; **t24** the delivery on palate edges close to perfection as the natural barley lushness is pricked by oak-induced spice. Oak is very often a detracting factor in an old malt: here it adds depth to the effortless elegance and adds sophistication to the sweetness; **f22** long, lithe and lengthened by a surprising puff of peat popping up from nowhere; **b24** you just dream of truly great whisky sitting in your glass from time to time. But you don't expect it, especially from such an old cask. This was the best example from this distillery I've tasted in 30 years....until the

Glenkeir version was unleashed! If you ever want to see a scotch that has stretched the use of oak as far it will go without detriment, here it is. What a pity the distillery has gone because the Mhor the merrier... *52.2%*

Duncan Taylor Collection Glen Mhor 1975 cask no. 4037 **(77) n21 t20 f17 b19.** Rich and voluptuous to start and no little fruit but I'm still picking the splinters out of my taste buds. *41.8%*

⚬ **Gordon & MacPhail Distillery Label Glen Mhor 1980 (77) n19 t21 f18 b19.** A lesser Mhor. *43%*

Old Malt Cask Glen Mhor Aged 32 Years refill hogshead no. 4208, dist Dec 75, bott Mar 08 **(85.5) n22 t21 f21 b21.5.** Lovely whisky for its age with the barley having to be at its sharpest to keep out the oak. None of the peat that helps make the RoR the true classic, it has but sufficient charisma and malty depth to ensure a lush and lovely experience. *44.1%. Douglas Laing. 137 bottles.*

Rarest of the Rare Glen Mhor 1975 cask no. 4031 **(76) n20 t20 f17 b19.** More or less ditto the Duncan Taylor version above. *42.6%. Duncan Taylor.*

Rarest of the Rare Glen Mhor 1975 cask no. 4034 **(95) n24.5** sublime little waves of peat help counter the onset of oaky tiredness; barley still thrives as do minor fruity notes; complex, subtle something of the exhibitionist martyr about this; **t24** beautifully soft from arrival to middle with the barley entirely in control; soft smoke adds perfect ballast and the oak is restricted to gentle custardy notes; **f22** much drier but a beautiful hint of muscovado in the mocha works wonderfully with those most gentle of peat notes; **b23.5** Mhor or less a miracle it has survived intact after so many years. A great way by which to remember the distillery, as this really is priceless stuff in terms of both scarcity and excellence. I can imagine this changing hands for lots of money in the not too distant... *43.5%. Duncan Taylor.*

⚬ **Rarest of the Rare Glen Mhor 1975** cask no. 4035 **(85) n21 t22 f21 b21.** Exceptionally gentle to the point of being docile. At one stage, threatens to go down the dramatic olde worlde exotic fruit road, decides against it and, a few spice prickles apart, glides to the finish line. *40.2%*

⚬ **Rarest of the Rare Glen Mhor 1975** cask no. 4041 **(85.5) n21 t21.5 f22 b21.** Never quite know what you are going to get from this batch of casks. They can be ordinary or stupendous. Here we have something of a halfway house, though tending towards the Mhor ordinaire. Wallpaper pasty in part but the crystal brown sugar edge to the barley is quite a treat. Very drinkable and for its age in pretty good nick. Just don't expect to be blown away by the complexity. *40.6%*

GLENMORANGIE

Highland (Northern), 1843. Glenmorangie plc. Working.

Glenmorangie 10 Years Old db **(94) n24** perhaps the most enigmatic aroma of them all: delicate yet assertive, sweet yet dry, young yet oaky: a malty tone poem; **t22** flaky oakiness throughout but there is an impossibly complex toastiness to the barley which seems to suggest the lightest hint of smoke; **f24** amazingly long for such a light dram, drying from the initial sweetness but with flaked almonds amid the oakier, rich cocoa notes; **b24** you might find the occasional "orange variant", where the extra degree of oak, usually from a few too many first-fill casks, has flattened out the more extreme peaks and toughs of complexity (scores about 89). But these are pretty rare – almost a collector's item – and overall this remains one of the great single malts: a whisky of uncompromising aesthetic beauty from the first enigmatic whiff to the last teasing and tantalising gulp. Complexity at its most complex. *40%*

Glenmorangie 15 Years Old db **(90.5) n23** chunky and fruity: something distinctly sugar candy about this one; the barley's no slouch, either; and, just to raise the eyebrows, just the faintest waft of something smoky...; **t23** silky, a tad sultry, and serious interplay between oak and barley; a real, satisfying juiciness to this one; **f22** dries towards the oaky side of things, but just a faint squeeze of liquorice adds extra weight; **b22.5** exudes quality. *43%*

Glenmorangie 15 Years Old Sauternes Wood Finish db **(68) n16 t18 f17 b17.** I had hoped – and expected – an improvement on the sulphured version I came across last time. Oh, whisky! Why are you such a cruel mistress.....? *46%*

Glenmorangie 18 Years Old db **(87.5) n22** freshly sliced lime, mildly under-ripe gooseberry...and malt; **t22.5** beautiful, almost crisp delivery of barley tinged with sharp fruit; **f21** duller vanillas and a soft latte flourish; **b22** much more like it! The citrus has made a welcome and much needed return. *43%*

Glenmorangie 25 Years Old db **(95.5) n24** it's strap yourself in time: this is a massive nose with more layers, twists and turns than you can shake a thief at. Soft, mildly lush Lubec marzipan is sandwiched between fruit bonbons and myriad barley tones. Worth taking half an hour over this one, and no kidding... **t24** the clarity on the nose is matched here. Every single wave of flavour is there in crystal form, starting, naturally, with the barley but this is soon paired with various unidentified fruits. The result is salivation. Towards the middle the oak shows form and does so in various cocoa-tinged ways; every nuance is delicately carved, almost fragile, but the overall picture is one of strength; **f23.5** medium length with the cocoa heading towards medium roast Java **b24** every bit as statesmanlike and elegant as a whisky at this age from such a blinding distillery should be. Ticks every single box for a 25-year-old and is Morangie's most improved malt by the distance of Tain to Wellingborough. There is a hint of genius with each unfolding wave of flavours with this one: a whisky that will go in 99/100 whisky lover's top 50 malts of all time. And that includes the Peatheads. *43%*

Glenmorangie Quarter Century 25 Years Old db (**92**) **n23** complex, multi-layered oak segmented by barley of varying sweetness; **t23** massive delivery with a threat of OTT oak dispelled by nuggets of lightly sweetened cocoa and a soft barley serenade; **f23** chocolate honeycomb that must have taken every bee in Scotland to produce, as this goes on for a very long time; **b23** one of those great whiskies where the genius that shaped the picture becomes clear only on fifth or six time of viewing. *43%*

Glenmorangie 30 Years Old db (**72**) **n17 t18 f19 b18.** From the evidence in the glass the jury is out on whether it has been spruced up a little in a poor sherry cask – and spruce is the operative word: lots of pine on this wrinkly. *44.1%*

Glenmorangie 1977 db (**92**) **n24** you know that saying about the oranges in 'Morangie....? **t23** beautifully soft, and sweet with a breathtaking build- up of ever-sweetening malt – and spices to guarantee balance; salivating; **f22** spices remain and the barley bows out slowly as vanilla arrives; **b23** excellent, but a trifle underpowered....what would this have been like at 46%...??? Shows little of its great age as the oak is always subservient to the sweet barley and citrus. *43%. Exclusively at Harrods.*

Glenmorangie Artisan Casks db (**93**) **n23** the evening flowers that marked this brand's nose for so long is out. Earthy, dank and cool bluebell woods are in. You can almost hear the jays cackling. For all the extra weight, strands of citrus provide the light entertainment; **t23.5** quite lovely: the barley almost throbs with intensity backed by teeming, busy oak notes; **f23** more greatly weighted than last year, thanks not least to some late spices and a return to a soft earthy feel; **b23.5** if whisky could be sexed, this would be a woman. Every time I encounter Morangie Artisan, it pops up with a new look, a different perfume. And mood. It appears not to be able to make up its mind. But does it know how to pout, seduce and win your heart...? Oh yes. *46%*

Glenmorangie Astar db (**88**) **n21** it is as though someone has got hold of the grist, picked out all the sugary bits and added it to an oaky dough; **t23** rarely does spice arrive so early or with such force; doesn't last that long as a massive sugary avalanche hits the palate; **f22.5** bitters out as the oak takes hold; only at the death is barley injected – and then with some concentration – into the proceedings; **b22** decidedly strange malt: for quite a while it is as if someone has extracted the barley and left everything else behind. A star is born? Not yet, perhaps. But perhaps a new breed of single malt. *57.1%*

Glenmorangie Burgundy Wood Finish db (**72**) **n17.5 t19.5 f18 b18.** Sulphured whisky de table. *43%*

Glenmorangie Burr Oak Reserve db (**92**) **n24** burr by name and nature: prickly, nipping, biting but enormous and not without a passing resemblance to a very high quality bourbon; **t24** capow!! The enormity of the oak-thrusted malt leaves little to the imagination: the mouth is coated in its radiance and the bitter-sweet richness positively glows; could easily mistake this for a bourbon; **f22** relatively bitter and twisted, but a bourbony liquorice-cocoa character; **b22** fades on the finish as a slightly spent force, but nose and arrival are simply breathtaking. Wouldn't be out of place in Kentucky. *56.3%*

Glenmorangie Cellar 13 Ten Years Old db (**88.5**) **n22** the richer bourbon note of old has been replaced by much finer, drier layers of oak thanks mainly to a shyer deployment of barley; **t22.5** no less delicate on delivery: the thing feels as though it is about to crumble and fall at any second; **f22** gosh...it hardly seems possible but it is getting even more delicate still: again it is wafer-thin oak that dictates with an almost apologetic honey-butterscotch sub-plot; **b22** oh, if only I could lose weight as efficiently as this appears to have done... *43%*

Glenmorangie Elegance db (**92**) **n22** quite herbal and soothing; **t24** the thinnest layer of icing sugar coats the silk-soft malt; every bit as gentle as the nose suggests; **f22** medium to short with some attractive rolling vanilla; **b24** a surprise package that is not entirely dissimilar to the Golden Rum, only a tad sweeter. *43%*

Glenmorangie Lasanta Sherry Finish db **(79)** n19 t21 f19 b20. Bugger. Some sulphur has crept in here. Not a lot. Some may even struggle to find it. But there is enough working behind the scenes to completely throw the show and flatten the experience. *46%*

Glenmorangie Madeira Wood Finish db **(78)** n19.5 t20.5 f19 b19. One of the real problems with wine finishes is getting the point of balance right when the fruit, barley and oak are in harmony. Here it is on a par with me singing in the shower, though frankly my aroma would be a notch or two up. *43%*

Glenmorangie Margaux Cask Finish db **(88)** n22 dark, a bit moody and the odd vinegar note. But, overall, impressive; **t22** soft with a soupy barley-grape feel; **f22** sweet at first, bitters up; **b22** even taking every whisky with an open mind, I admit this was better than my subconscious might have considered. Certainly better than the near undrinkable Ch. Margaux '57 I used to bring out for my birthday each year some 20-odd years ago... *46%*

Glenmorangie Nectar D'or Sauternes Finish db **(94)** n23 delicate cinnamon on toast and a drizzle of greengage and sultana; **t24** equally refreshing and dense on the palate as the bitter-sweet battle goes into overdrive; excellent weight and body; **f23** remains clean and precise, allowing some custard onto the apple strudel finale; **b24** great to see French casks that actually complement a whisky – so rare! This has replaced the Madeira finish. But there are some similar sweet-fruit characteristics. An exercise in outrageously good sweet-dry balancing. *46%*

Glenmorangie Quinta Ruban Port Finish db **(92)** n24 typical Morangie complexity, but the grape notes added act almost like a prism to show their varied hues; **t23** fruit and spice about as the oak goes in search of glory: barley stands in its way; **f22** light, deftly sweetened and juicy to the end; **b23** this replacement of the original Port finish shows a genuine understanding of the importance of grape-oak balance. Both are portrayed with clarity and confidence. This is a form of cask finishing that has progressed from experimentation to certainty. *46%*

Glenmorangie Sherry Wood Finish db **(84)** n23 t21 f20 b20. Stupendous clean sherry nose, then disappoints with a somewhat bland display on the palate. *43%*

Glenmorangie Signet db **(93)** n23 huge oak, doubtless coming from the virgin casks but it works wonderfully, as, rather than overpower, it appears to fuse with the malt. The result is thick, toasty bitter-sweet, with almost a marmalade hit; **t23.5** oooophh!! One hell of a hit with again the oak storming in as if about to wallop you, then holding back becalmed by a chocolate malt insurgence; unquestionably oilier than usual allowing all the elements a platform to stick around; **f23** lengthy, with chocolate now the main theme, both, it appears, from the oak and barley. Genuinely delicious...a bit like praline spread on toast... **b23.5** as there is a Morangie Traditional, then this has to be Morangie Untraditional. An entirely different direction for this malt with an oiliness for a Glenmorangie the like of which I have never seen before and a thick oak intensity unique not just to the distillery but any other Highland malt I can think of. And a tip: drink at cask strength, a fraction above room and not quite body temp...and after it has breathed in the glass for about 20 minutes. Then, believe me, you are in for one hell of a show!! *46%*

⊰⊱ **Glenmorangie Sonnalta PX** db **(96.5)** n24.5 now this works: that heavy-handed feel of a sweet sherry butt (or five) at work here, usually the kiss of death for so many whiskies. But an adroit praline sub-plot really does the trick. So with the malt evident, too, we have a three-pronged attack which somehow meshes in to one. And not even the merest hint of an off-note...goodness gracious: a new experience...!!! **t23** Neanderthal grape drags its knuckles along the big vanilla floor before a really subtle light Columbian coffee kick puts us back on course; sharper vanillas from some awkward oak threatens to send us off course again but somehow it finds a settled, common ground; **f25** now goes into orgasmic overdrive as Demerara sugar is tipped into some gorgeous, cream-lightened mocha. This is obviously to wash down the Melton Hunt cake which is resplendent in its grape and roast nut finery...phew!!! It is, unquestionably, the perfect whisky finish... **b24** this one passed me by. If they told me anything about this chap, I'd forgotten. It absolutely groans from the lucid sweet grape and I discover it's actually Pedro Ximinez. Brave. Foolhardy, even. Because over the last decade of studying whiskies matured in that sugary beast the experience has usually ended in tears. Not here, though. This is a gamble that has handsomely paid off: Glenmorangie as you've never seen it before. Probably Scotch malt as you've never seen before. But after buying one bottle, you'll be wanting to see it again. A giant among the tall stills. *46%*

Glenmorangie Traditional db **(90.5)** n22 orange blossom, barley sugar and chalk dust; **t23** delicate delivery revelling in gentle complexity: really playful young-ish malt makes for a clean start and middle; **f22.5** soft mocha notes play out a quiet finish; **b23** an improved dram with much more to say, but does so quietly. *57.1%*

Glenmorangie Truffle Oak db **(96) n24** a significant aroma: big, powering oak yet controlled with no sign of bitterness or tiredness. Some golden syrup on the barley is toned down by age. If you can find a flaw or off-note, e-mail me; **t24** bloody hell!!! Now the golden syrup comes out to play, but the intensity of that plus the barley fair takes the breath away. Something very breakfast- cerealy about this experience. But for grown ups...; **f25** burning embers of honey-nut cereal last forever. Keeping them company are varying shades of golden to molassed sugar. One of the longest un-peated finishes you'll ever find; **b23** the Glenmorangie of all Glenmorangies. I really have to work hard and deep into the night to find fault with it. If I am going to be hyper-critical, I'll dock it a mark for being so constantly sweet, though in its defence I have to say that the degree of sweetness alters with astonishing dexterity. Go on, it's Truffle oak: make a pig of yourself...!! 60.5%

Glenmorangie Vintage 1975 db **(89) n23** clementines! It must be Christmas...; **t23** improbably clean malt for something so aged, then a layer or three of fruit and spiced vanilla; **f21** bitters out as an oaky trench is found; **b22** a charming, fruity and beautifully spiced oldie. 43%

Glenmorangie Warehouse Three Reserve db **(92) n22** dry, yet effervescent malt offers a fruity barley thrust; **t23** slightly oily perhaps, it's all about thrusting barley and a mouth-puckering sharpness; **f23** excellent arrival of light oak adding a touch of extra class and charisma to the finale. Lovely cocoa notes radiate warmly; **b24** another genuinely outstanding expression, a cathartic catalogue of complexity, from a distillery that shows its greatness when allowed. 40%. Glenmorangie for Asda.

Scotch Malt Whisky Society Cask 125.1 Aged 13 Years designer hogshead, dist May 93 **(95) n24 t23 f24 b24.** Just a peach of a cask that re-defines fruitiness as far as whisky is concerned. 51.2%

Scotch Malt Whisky Society Cask 125.2 Aged 11 Years designer hogshead, dist Jun 95 **(90) n21 t23 f23 b23.** Very sweet but countered by wonderful spice. Another chance to see the distillery in a light it has rarely been seen in before. 53.5%

Scotch Malt Whisky Society Cask 125.11 Aged 11 Years (84) n22 t21 f20 b21. A curious one: for all its very obvious barley-led charm missing the normal Glenmorangie complexity on the nose or typical orangie lightness. A bit of a pudding in places with a pleasant sprinkling of something a little sweet. 57%

Scotch Malt Whisky Society Cask 125.13 Aged 12 Years 1st fill barrel, dist Jun 95 **(90.5) n22.5 t23 f22.5 b22.5** It helps when you get a really well-made spirit, then many things are possible. Here it absorbs the oak comfortably and milks it for all it is worth. 55.9%

⋯ **Scotch Malt Whisky Society Cask 125.19 Aged 13 Years** 1st fill hogshead, dist Jun 95 **(86.5) n21.5 t23.5 f20 b21.5.** What can you say? Glenmorangie owns the SMWS. So therefore one would assume that this, with all the casks available, would be the pinnacle of Glenmorangie's 13-y-o whiskies. Somehow I don't think so. Certainly an attractive dram, well made from a noble family and having enjoyed a privileged upbringing in a top quality cask. There is spice. There is malt – lots of malt, in fact. There is oak. There is a well-balanced sweet-dry interchange...but. And the but is the butt, or the cask to be precise. It is too good. Too much for 13 years because the massive degree of natural caramels have started to wear the edges off the finer notes you would expect to find from this wonderful distillery. So there is a rumbling dullness in the undergrowth where the higher notes should be singing from the top branches. Lovely stuff. But not lovely enough... 56.3%

⋯ **Scotch Malt Whisky Society Cask 125.20 Aged 13 Years** 1st fill hogshead, dist Jun 95 **(91) n22.5** predominantly oaky notes, a variety of them and the majority of them keeping the barley at bay. But the odd few are uplifting and gently sweetened in a custardy manner, too... **t23** another silk-soft delivery from a 'Morangie, but that's due mainly to that custard tendency to dictate things; some fabulously juicier barley notes also up the flavour amps; some spiffing spices really get going; **f22.5** reverts to a more conservative cocoa-rich haven, but still bangs out a decent barley theme; **b23** many of the points made about 125.19 could apply here, except a trilling sweetness takes it up several extra notches and the complexity enters another stratosphere. 56.2%

⋯ **Scotch Malt Whisky Society Cask 125.21 Aged 13 Years** 1st fill hogshead, dist Jun 95 **(86) n22 t22 f21 b21.** Part of any performer's art is to know when to milk the silence: it can be so much more effective than just saying something because you are there. And so, too, with whisky casks. Here we have a great cask, but too much of it: we need the silence, just as in 125.19, to make the piece work to its fullest potential. Good whisky? Certainly. Enjoyable? undoubtedly. Annoying? Massively. Now here's an idea. Three casks. All from the same distillery. And same age. What if I, and other whisky lovers, had been able to monitor a first fill bourbon against a second fill and then third fill and listen to the effect those silences would have had. Now that would have been fun... 56.4%

GLEN MORAY

Speyside, 1897. La Martiniquaise. Working.

Glen Moray Classic 8 Years Old db **(86) n20 t22 f21 b23.** A vast improvement on previous bottlings with the sluggish fatness replaced by a thinner, barley-rich, slightly sweeter and more precise mouthfeel. *40%*

Glen Moray 12 Years Old db **(90) n22.5** gentle malt of varying pitch and intensity; **t22** a duller start than it should be with the vanilla diving in almost before the barley but the juicy, grassy notes arrive in good time; **f23** long, back on track with intense malt and the custardy oak is almost apologetic but enlivened with a dash of lime: mmmmm... pure Glen Moray! **b22.5** I have always regarded this as the measuring stick by which all other malty and clean Speysiders should be tried and tested. It is still a fabulous whisky, full of malty intricacies. Something has fallen off the edge, perhaps, but minutely so. Still think a trick or two is being missed by bottling this at 40%: the natural timbre of this malt demands 46% and no less.... *40%*

Glen Moray 16 Years Old db **(74) n19 t19 f18 b19.** A serious dip in form. Drab. *40%*

Glen Moray 16 Years Old Chenin Blanc Mellowed in Wine Barrels db **(85) n20 t22 f22 b21.** A fruity, oak-shaded dram just brimming with complexity. *40%*

Glen Moray 20 Years Old db **(80) n22 t22 f18 b18.** With so much natural cream toffee, it is hard to believe that this has so many years on it. After a quick, refreshing start it pans out, if anything, a little dull. *40%*

Glen Moray 30 Years Old db **(92.5) n23.5** it's probably the deftness of the old-fashioned Speyside smoke in tandem with the structured fruits that makes this so special; **t23.5** for a light Speysider, the degree of barley to oak is remarkable: soft, oil-gilde d barley is met by a wonderful, if brief, spice prickle; **f22.5** deft layering of vanilla and cocoa; a sprinkle of muscovado sugar repels any darker oak notes; **b23** for all its years, this is comfortable malt, untroubled by time. There is no mistaking quality. *43%*

Glen Moray 1959 Rare Vintage db **(91) n25 t23 f21 b22.** They must have been keeping their eyes on this one for a long time: a stunning malt that just about defies nature. The nose reaches absolute perfection. *50.9%*

Glen Moray 1962 Very Rare Vintage Aged 42 Years db **(94) n23** the thick oak offers something of the farmyard, but there is a hint of apple, rhubarb and citrus to thin it out a little; **t24** the orangey/citrussy notes defy the years as the malt delivers some early and surprising blows for youth; by the time the middle arrives the oak has caught up and we have a mishmash of liquorice, bitter chocolate and beautifully controlled spices; **f23** some banana milkshake and a very late surge of a vague orangey fruitiness as well; **b24** the first temptation is to think that this has succumbed to age, but a second and a third tasting reveal that there is much more complexity, integrity and balance to this than first meets the tastebuds. The last cask chosen by the legendary Ed Dodson before his retirement from the distillery: a pretty perceptive choice. A corker! *50.9% sc*

Glen Moray 1984 db **(83) n20 t22 f20 b21.** Mouthwatering and incredibly refreshing malt for its age. *40%*

Glen Moray 1986 Commemorative Bottling cask 4698 db **(96) n25** take your time over this: like a week or so! The bourbon notes are unmistakable (nosing blind I might have plumped for Kentucky!) with a series of rich and sharp blood orange/kumquat notes interlaced with dark chocolate. A peculiarly coastal saltiness has also crept in. Amid all this can be found a sharp maltiness. Just one of the great noses of this and many other years; **t24** spectacular bitter-sweet arrival on the palate shows a glorious harmony between the malt and bourbony oak. Beyond this gentle spices about, as do mouthwatering, candy-fruit riches; **f23** one of the longest non-peaty fade-outs since "Hotel California"...the ripeness of the malt, enriched by the most fabulous of bitter-sweet molasses lasts until finally replaced by a toasty vanilla; **b24** Ed Dodson hand-picked this cask from the warehouse to mark the opening of the distillery's visitor centre in late 2004. Ed has now retired but – and this bottling proves the point entirely – he should be brought back to the distillery, as Elmer T. Lee has at Buffalo Trace, and be given his own named brand. You simply cannot buy the experience and natural feel Ed has for Glen Moray. This astonishing single cask proves the point with a delicious and unforgettable eloquence. *64.4%. ncf.*

Glen Moray 1989 db **(86) n23 t22 f20 b21.** Doesn't quite live up to the fruit smoothie nose but I'm being a little picky here. *40%*

Glen Moray 1991 Mountain Oak Malt The Final Release dist 15 Mar 91, bott 5 Feb 07 db **(94) n24** a wonderful liquorice/kumquat mix with diluted maple syrup toning down the honey; **t24** again that syrup/honey combo is first out of the blocks then we are back to barley – well spiced – and a myriad of vanillins; **f23** lots of oaky notes, some bitter, but now encased in soft oils which contain a balancing sweetness; **b23** another Scotch malt masquerading as bourbon. Massive and quite beautiful. Until the 1986 edition was released, the previous Mountain Oak was the best Glen Moray I had ever happened upon – and if memory serves me correctly that had a decidly bourbony bent, too. This is up there among the distillery's best ever. 58.6%. 1,158 bottles.

Glen Moray 1992 Single Cask No 1441 sherry butt db **(74)** n17 t21 f18 b18. Oops! Didn't anyone spot the sulphur ...? 59.6%

Glen Moray 1995 Single Sherry Cask sherry butt db **(56)** n15 t14 f13 b14. So stunned was I about the abject quality of this bottling, I even looked on the Glen Moray website to see if they had said anything about it. Apparently, if you add water you find on the nose "the lingering soft sulphury smoke of a struck match." Well, here's the news: you don't need water. Just open the bottle and there's Rotorua in all it's stink bomb finery. And errr...hullo, guys...some further news: that means it's a bloody faulty, useless cask. And has no right to be put anywhere near a bottling hall let alone set loose in a single bottling. This, quite frankly, is absolutely rank whisky, the type of which makes my blood boil. I mean, is this really the best cask that could be found in the entire and considerable estate of Glen Moray..????? Am I, or is it the whisky world going mad...? 59.6%

Glen Moray Classic db **(86.5)** n22 t21.5 f21.5 b21.5. I once rather witheringly described this as being short of ideas if memory serves me correctly... (having just dived in to the 2008 Bible, I see my memory has, indeed, served me correctly). Now the idea appears to be to give it a fruity outer coat and it works well. The nose is the star with a wonderful, clean barley-fruit tandem, but what follows cannot quite match its sure-footed wit. 40%

Glen Moray Mountain Oak Final Release dist 91 db **(82)** n23.5 t21 f18.5 b19. A malt which reminds me of the sequel to the film Elizabeth: you look forward to something of distinctly high class for a very long time and then, when it arrives, you can only look on aghast as your dreams are dashed. No, this whisky doesn't have anything quite so ludicrously ridiculous as the dramatically mountainous Scottish backdrop to Fotheringhay castle, Mary's prison for days, not years as the film depicts and which was in reality set on the very flattest Northamptonshire countryside heading towards the Fens; or outlandish age issues such as good Queen Bess discussing having children by which time, historically, she was in her mid 50s. But for those who enjoyed the much tighter, historically true first Elizabeth, you will know what I mean. There was something truer, tighter, less fanciful about the first bottling, with the bourbon edge filtering down in perfect synchronization. Here the bourbony nose is sublime. But once it hits the palate it's all imagery and OTT. This should sell well in Hollywood. 58.6%

Cadenhead's Glen Moray Aged 15 Years sauternes wood, dist 92, bott Jun 08 **(92.5)** n22.5 spicy sultana: spotted dog...with plenty of spots **t24** near perfection the delivery: mouth-feel soft yet firm: perfect; barley loud but cloistered; spices lively but entirely in keeping with the fruit and barley; **f23** pretty long and almost ridiculously clean; the oak is almost apologetic in its vanilla approach **b23** I am slowly coming to the conclusion that a non-sulphured sauternes cask, with all spice and oak-defeating sweetness that is so elegantly offered, is about as good as any wine cask you'll find for whisky maturation. This is an object lesson in exactly how it should be done. 46%. 320 bottles.

Cadenhead's Authentic Collection Glen Moray-Glenlivet Aged 16 Years bourbon hogshead, dist 91, bott May 07 **(81)** n20 t21 f20 b20. Leached so much toffee and tannin out of the oak, it's more like Canadian. 57.1%. 258 bottles

Duncan Taylor The NC2 Range Glen Moray 1991 Aged 16 Years (86) n22 t22 f21 b21. Ultra pleasant malt, entirely untaxing and plays upon the most simple of barley themes. 46%

⫸ **Kingsbury's 'The Selection' Glen Moray 7 Years Old** hogshead, cask no. 56 & 57, dist Mar 01, bott Jun 08 **(82)** n19 t22 f21 b20. The third-fill cask allows the malt full, though not entirely unblemished scope. Would have been more effective at full strength, though. 43%. Japan Import System. 870 bottles.

Mackillop's Choice Glen Moray cask no. 4065, dist Sep 92, bott Jul 07 **(78.5)** n21 t19.5 f19 b19. A bitter-sweet experience in every sense. The over-used cask allows the barley some early play, but some of the more bitter components of the oak are heard a touch too loudly. 43%. Iain Mackillop & Co. Ltd.

Murray McDavid Glen Moray 1992 bourbon/madeira **(88)** n23 dig deep and be patient enough and you'll find some marzipan and apricots here; **t20** at first a bit bitter and untidy, early vanilla; **f22** balances better here, and now some interplay between malt and grape; a well integrated finish; **b23** the rich malt canvas of the Glen Moray gives the Madeira an unrestricted medium to do its stuff. 46%

Old Malt Cask Glen Moray Aged 16 Years (85.5) n22 t22.5 f20 b21. Both the nose and delivery are swamped with superb malt, though the finish is on the bitter side. 50%

Old Malt Cask Glen Moray Aged 16 Years refill hogshead 4068, dist Nov 91, bott Dec 07 **(85) n22 t21.5 f20.5 b21.** Huge malt à la Glen Moray house style. *50%. nc ncf. Douglas Laing. 340 bottles.*

Scotch Malt Whisky Society Cask 35.23 Aged 10 Years 1st fill barrel, dist Mar 98 **(87) n21.5 t22 f22 b21.5** Good, enjoyable rather simple malt which, knowing the what the Society has to choose from regarding this distillery, must be seen as something of a slight disappointment. *59.8%*

⫶ **Scotch Malt Whisky Society Cask 35.26 Aged 10 Years** 1st fill barrel, dist Mar 98 **(90) n22** slightly ungainly, not least because the oak is trying to take a big chunk out of the malt...and fails; distinctive soft cedar wood and vanilla combine attractively; **t23** the malt is layered and offers itself in flimsy gossamer form through to thick concentrate; balances well between sweet and sharp; **f22.5** moves back towards a more bourbony edge with shimmering dark sugared coating and a late touch of leather; **b22.5** where bourbon and malt collide... *58.8%*

⫶ **Scotch Malt Whisky Society Cask 35.27 Aged 10 Years** 1st fill hogshead, dist Mar 98 **(81.5) n21 t20 f21.5 b19.** Warming, with the usual big malt theme. But, compared to 35.26, the impact of the oak is far less benign and only a gentle butter-toffee quality helps soften the experience. *58.4%*

GLEN ORD

Highland (Northern) 1838. Diageo. Working.

Glen Ord Aged 12 Years db **(81) n20 t23 f18 b20.** Just when you thought it safe to go back....for a while Diageo ditched the sherry-style Ord. It has returned. Better than some years ago, when it was an unhappy shadow of its once-great self, but without the sparkle of the vaguely-smoked bottling of a year or two back. Nothing wrong with the rich arrival, but the finish is a mess. I'll open the next bottling with trepidation... *43%*

Glen Ord 25 Years Old dist 78 db **(95) n24** the most narrow seams of peat offer backbone to deeply impressive arrays of fruits, including kumquats, unripe figs and greengages. The oak is firm, as is the malt; **t24** nectar-plus!! The astonishing mouthfeel is matched only by the perfectly presented fruit, mainly a citrussy affair, that battles for supremacy against grassy malt and spiced oak. Waiting in the wings is wonderfully gentle smoke. A faultlessly choreographed production; **f23** slightly more simplistic here thanks to some caramel being sucked from the oak, but the spices continue as does a fruity tang; **b24** some stupendous vatting here. cask selection at its very highest to display Ord in all its far too rarely seen magnificence. *58.3%*

Glen Ord 28 Years Old db **(90) n22** malt and mint bound together by soft liquorice and dark fudge; **t23** delightful barley-sugar theme that forms a stupendously rigid middle with the most delicate hints of smoke and coffee. The body weight is perfect; **f22** amazingly long finale with lashings of cocoa to go with the mollassed sugar and powering barley; **b23** this is mega whisky showing slight traces of sap, especially on the nose, but otherwise a concentrate of many of the qualities I remember from this distillery before it was bottled in a much ruined form. Blisteringly beautiful. *58.3%.*

Glen Ord 30 Years Old db **(87) n22** shaped by oak, there is a peppery element to the floral thrust; **t21** molten barley spearheads the arrival before a cumbersome oakiness interferes. Plenty of spice and underpinning sweetness; **f23** settles down for a really long and delightful finish with a glorious interaction between delicate, velvety barley and vanilla. Charming; **b21** creaking with oak, but such is the polish to the barley some serious class is on show. *58.8%*

Singleton of Glen Ord 12 Years Old db **(83) n21 t22 f20 b20.** Pleasant with some attractive blood orange notes. But, overall, it's all rather flat and fails to take off the way it should. *40%*

Cadenhead's Authentic Collection Ord Aged 12 Years bourbon hogshead, matured in oak cask, dist 96, bott Jun 08 **(91.5) n22.5** clean, gristy, young for age; **t24** faultless malt delivery: clean, crisp, salivating with outstanding degree of a maple syrup sweetness; a shadow of something smoky, too; **f22.5** even gristy at the death with the vaguest hint of salt; **b22.5** massive malty: perfect for blending, superb as a singleton. *58.2%. 210 bottles.*

⫶ **The Càrn Mòr Vintage Collection Glen Ord 2004** hogshead, cask no. 55, bott 09 **(84) n22 t21.5 f20 b20.5.** Beautiful citrus and barley though always new makey. *46%. The Scottish Liqueur Centre.*

Old Malt Cask Glen Ord Aged 18 Years sherry finish dist Jan 89, bott Feb 07 **(90) n24** multiple layers of barley and sultana dovetail with lemon-ginger and oak. Sublime; **t23** more mouth-watering on delivery than any 18-year-old has a right to be; again it's the barley and grape at full play, with the very lightest wisps of smoke. The oak crashes in mid stream;

f21 lots more oak, this time with a natural toffee/dried date edge **b22** just shows how stupendous this distillery can be when left to its own devices. *50%. 808 bottles.*

⋯ **Provenance Glen Ord Aged 11 Years** dist mar 98, bott Jul 09 **(83) n21 t21.5 f20.5 b20.** Attractive, simple malty but standard Ordie for an oft recycled cask. *46%. Douglas Laing.*

Provenance Glen Ord Aged 12 Years refill hogshead no. 4243, dist Spring 96, bott Spring 08 **(84.5) n21.5 t22 f20 b21.** Pure grist with a squirt of lemon juice. *46%. nc ncf. Douglas Laing.*

Signatory Vintage Glen Ord 1998 8 Years Old (86) n21.5 t22 f21 b21.5. Lots of banana milkshake and barley with this simple but very attractive number. Suffers a little from reduced strength. *43%. USA.*

⋯ **Scotch Malt Whisky Society Cask 77.16 Aged 21 Years** refill hogshead, dist Aug 87 **(84) n20.5 t23 f20 b20.5.** Hmmm. Either we have a malt which boasts juniper on the nose. Or this was bottled after some gin was and someone didn't change the filters. Some attractive celery notes, too. Sweet and malty early on; bland at the death. *55.8%*

⋯ **Scotch Malt Whisky Society Cask 77.17 Aged 9 Years** refill hogshead, dist Mar 00 **(95.5) n24** beauty without a blemish: diced green pear freshens the oak; the most distant speck of smoke and acacia honey of the thinnest most delicate kind; **t24** didn't expect that: surely the taste can't be as pure as the aroma...it is!! Again, one is soothed with a beautiful acacia honey coating to the gristy barley; again there appears a semi-hidden hint of something vaguely smoked; **f23.5** custard tart with a spot-on degree of white sugar; the oak offers nothing more than weight and a balancing dryness; **b24** just one of those unspoiled drams that offers everything with crystal clarity: not a mark, an off note or blemish. Almost virginal in its delivery. *53.6%*

⋯ **Singleton of Glen Ord 32 Year Old** db **(91) n23.5** some dreamy, creamy sherry...and very little evidence of age decline; **t23** sharp and juicy punch with toasty oak making its move soon after; plenty of marmalade going round; **f22** sweetens slightly with a touch of barley entering the fray, then oak and finally a furry, orangey feel; **b22.5** delicious. But if ever a malt has screamed out to be at 46%, this is it. *40%*

GLENROTHES
Speyside, 1878. Edrington. Working.

The Glenrothes 1978 dist Nov 78, bott 08 db **(90.5) n23** over-ripe gooseberries mixed with dry tobacco; suet pudding and vanilla pods: attractively intriguing; **t23** relaxed, lush barley coats the mouth with a muscovado sugar edge; **f22** mushy sultana and toasty oak; **b22.5** sheer – and delicious – entertainment. *43%*

The Glenrothes 1979 Single Cask No. 3808 db **(95) n24** a near faultless nose with the clarity of the fruit, presumably sherry (though maybe not first fill), is enough to bring a tear to the eye: a sweet nougat kick is matched by rich, spiced sultana, the most elegant wisp of smoke and a polished, leathery edge that is not entirely like a well-aged bourbon: absolutely something for everyone... **t23** the malt dissolves on impact letting in several shockwaves of spice; almost brutally fruity yet the honeyed seam is a thick one; **f24** long, the most playful vanillas and with a confidence bordering on arrogance as the spices re-ignite, as if telling you that it'll end when it feels like it...not when it theoretically should...meanwhile, the very lightly smoked honey and burned fudge just go on and on and on... **b24** a pearl of a malt that has me scratching my head in wonder. Although from a single cask, there are elements in this which are pure bourbon and others which are pure sherry – in every sense. In the end, it doesn't much matter because the tastebuds are almost too overwhelmed to take in all that is on offer. Stunning. *55.2%*

The Glenrothes 1979 Single Cask No. 13458 db **(68) n18 t19 f15 b16.** Wrecked by sulphur. In whisky terms, tragic. *57%*

The Glenrothes 1979 Single Cask No. 13459 db **(75) n20 t20 f17 b18.** This twin cask to 13458 has also seen a sulphur stick at work, but it wasn't kept inside anything to lie so long. Even so, enough damage to the finish undoes the promising big fruit start. *56.6%*

The Glenrothes 1979 cask no. 13470 db **(95) n24** a basket of toffee apples sitting under a spice rack. Awesome; **t24** massive spice and hickory start, sweetened with mollased sugar and honeycomb; **f23** long, with the spices remaining playful and the vanilla intervention soft and empathic; **b24** that's what you call a sherry cask: big, yet everything just-so. Classic. *57.5%. sc.*

The Glenrothes 1994 dist Oct 94, bott 07 db **(77) n19 t20 f19 b19.** The citrus appears as promised on the label, but sadly a few unadvertised sulphured butt-related gremlins are present also. *43%*

The Glenrothes Select Reserve db **(80) n17.5 t22 f20.5 b21.** Flawed in the usual Glenrothes sherry places, but the brilliance of the sharp barley wins your heart. *40%*

Adelphi Glenrothes 2000 Aged 8 Years sherry hogshead, cask no. 2414, dist 00, bott 08 **(71) n16 t19 f18 b18.** A crying shame because I suspect this was a decent butt before being fatally treated with the S-word. *58%. 309 bottles.*

Cadenhead's Authentic Collection Glenrothes Aged 16 Years rum butt, dist 90, bott Feb 07 **(96) n24** weird sherry-type aroma, with a weird Demerara-style kick and weird burnt raisin without the bitterness, probably because of barley...beautiful in its very own very weird and slightly bourbony-rummy way... **t23** entirely off-key delivery steadies itself quite quickly with the aid of in-rushing spices. Loads of burnt fruit and toasty barley abound; **f25** Java coffee by the teaspoonful, embracing spices and then the coffee sweetened by Demerara sugar. Good grief... **b24** you don't many of these to the dozen. A very different shape and delivery from most malts with the balance at times slipping and sliding like a one-legged man on a skate... and then suddenly everything falls wondrously into shape. A malt that shows that the line between madness and genius is so very thin...and genius this genuinely is... *57.3%. 588 bottles.*

Cadenhead's Glenrothes Aged 17 Years sherry butt, dist 90, bott Feb 08 **(82.5) n19.5 t20 f22 b21.** The faintest of sulphur traces makes for some moments of awkwardness, but the tightness of the grain and grape are at times truly extraordinary. *57.7%. 395 bottles.*

Chieftain's Glenrothes 7 Years Old sherry hogshead **(78) n19 t20 f21 b18.** Mon sherry!! The grape has drowned out any evidence of whisky on the nose and delivery or any semblance of balance. But the complexity of the coffee-led fightback is wonderful. Puckeringly dry, though. *53.1%. nc ncf. Ian Macleod Distillers.*

D&M Aficionados' Club Bottling Glenrothes Aged 20 Years cask no. 100107, dist May 87 **(88.5) n20** some milky notes dumb down the barley; **t23** spices and barley do enough to make for a pleasant and juicy ride with a quite surprising intensity; **f23** now zips into complex overdrive with the malty richness going up a further notch: remarkable... **b22.5** At first I gave this a so-so score: the traces of lactic on the nose didn't endear me. But it is simply one of those drams that demands further and further research. Until you have to at last admit; damn it, this is superb stuff!! *46%. nc ncf. US by Angus Dundee.*

Dun Bheagan Glenrothes 12 Years Old sherry finish **(79) n20 t21 f19 b19.** A cleanish, sound sherry cask but short changes in the complexity department. *43%. Ian Macleod.*

Duncan Taylor Collection Glenrothes 1968 cask no.13498 **(79.5) n20.5 t22 f18 b19.** The creosotey finish confirms perhaps a little too much has been asked of the cask. But its early answer is bright and honeyed. *48.2%*

Duncan Taylor Collection Glenrothes 1969 cask no. 381, dist Jan 69 **(73) n19 t19 f17 b18.** This doesn't need water...just a Zimmer. *40.7%*

Duncan Taylor Collection Glenrothes 1969 cask no. 383, dist Jan 69 **(80) n21 t21 f19 b19.** It may be the twin to cask 381 (above), but this one is still breathing. Collapses at the end but does a neat barley-honey shuffle before the oxygen mask is applied. *41.5%*

·:·· **Duncan Taylor Collection Glenrothes 1969** cask no. 12889 **(88.5) n22.5** am I in Kentucky, sticking my head into some 12-year-old samples? It kind of appears that way as liquorice and Demerara out-manoeuvre the more problematic piny oak notes; **t21.5** early signs aren't encouraging as some big oak punches come raining in. But the barley has stature enough to recover; **f22.5** remains juicy and now gathers a Fox's party Rings-type biscuity sweetness; some late hickory takes us back to Kentucky; **b22** Very similar to 12890, except here, on the nose and sometimes elsewhere, this has managed to find a bourbony edge to the oak encroachment. Because of this the body feels fuller and healthier. *46.5%*

·:·· **Duncan Taylor Collection Glenrothes 1969** cask no. 12890 **(85.5) n21 t21 f22.5 b21** Fascinating to compare this to the DTC 1970 I have just tasted. So many similarities that they appear closely related. But here the oak has delved deeper and upset the vital balance. Pleasant and thoroughly enjoyable and the muscovado-sweetened mocha finish is quite lovely. But you know this cask has crossed the Rubicon. Just. *45.5%*

·:·· **Duncan Taylor Collection Glenrothes 1970** cask no. 10557 **(93) n23.5** barley-enriched apricot; **t23** like dipping into a bag of mixed boiled sweets with the odd eye-watering sharp one among them: a vague fruitiness meets the sharp barley head on; **f23.5** more salivating over the barley until late on; the vanilla arrives apologetically; **b23** always endearing to find a malt some 40-year-old with this kind of playful persona and so little bothered about oak. Charismatic and full of mouth-watering fun. A minor classic of its type. *42.3%*

Mackillop's Choice Glenrothes cask no. 100107, dist May 87, bott Jul 07 For tasting notes see D&M Aficionados Club bottling. Presumably this has come from a split cask. *46%. ncf. Iain Mackillop & Co. Ltd.*

The MacPhail's Collection Glenrothes 1965 (83) n20 t22 f20 b21. A distinctively bourbony air to this one with no little liquorice amid the honey. Good spice, too. But maybe the odd splinter too many. *43%.*

Old & Rare Glenrothes Aged 22 Years dist Feb 85, bott Aug 07 **(91.5) n24.5** just so tantalising and complex: the toasted hazelnuts sits so beautifully with the orange rind and polished floors. Bitter-sweet-dry aroma par excellence; take at least five minutes over the nose before tasting; **t22.5** intense and muddled at first; then takes off on a massive honeycomb surge; soft oils and droplets of orangey citrus; **f22** much drier as the toasty, cocoa-note crips in; **b22.5** as good as it is on the palate, it has a problem living up to the astonishing nose. But, there again, so would about 99% of all known whiskies. *56%. Douglas Laing. 277 bottles.*

Old Malt Cask Glenrothes Aged 10 Years Gabriel Meffre wine cask no. 3705, dist Nov 96, bott Jun 07 **(88) n21** grape sprinkled with coal dust; **t23** warming – very warming! – arrival with a slow fanning out of the maltier elements; **f22** delicate despite the spicy buzz with gathering oak; **b22** not a totally dissimilar animal to the OMC Glen Grant 12. Only less finesse and lot more spice. *50%. Douglas Laing. 348 bottles.*

⋅⋅⋅ **Old Malt Cask Glenrothes Aged 12 Years** refill butt, dist May 96, bott Feb 08 **(77) n19 t20 f19 b19.** Give me a prod when something happens....zzzz. *50%. Douglas Laing. 657 bottles.*

⋅⋅⋅ **Old Malt Cask Glenrothes Aged 14 Years** red wine cask, bott 09 **(88) n21** even before knowing this was from a red wine cask, there was a threatening red wine thinness to the barley; complex, though; **t22.5** and the wine is confirmed on the palate with the thin, shaky start. Then it all takes off: the grape and barley at last fuse and harmony is achieved –and some impressive weight; **f22.5** no problems here with a light, sweet juicy element to the cocoa and swirl of smoke; **b22** begins jerkily a bit like a train in a shunting yard before heading off on a frictionless journey. *50%. Douglas Laing.*

Old Malt Cask Glenrothes Aged 16 Years Rum Finish dist Nov 90, bott Mar 07 **(92) n23** for all the obvious rum involvement it is probably the bourbon oakiness that holds sway; excellent weight and balance – slightly Jamaican in style; **t22** warm, biting and at once bracing delivery with a massive barley surge that battles against the peppers; **f24** settles down for something a little special with a glorious marriage of coffee and spice which only sets the scene for the delicate but distinctive echoes of rum and real – or imaginary Jackfruit. Beautifully oiled and quite superb; **b23** a malt that lives long on the finish and in the memory. Wonderful! *50%. Douglas Laing. 318 bottles.*

⋅⋅⋅ **Old Malt Cask Glenrothes Aged 18 Years** refill hogshead, dist Nov 90, bott Apr 09 **(84) n18 t21.5 f22.5 b22.** The broken nose is compensated by the fine, if slightly fizzy, malty recovery. Delicious Maltesers at the death. *50%. Douglas Laing. 295 bottles.*

Old Malt Cask Glenrothes 27 Years Old wine finish, dist Apr 79, bott Jul 06 **(66) n17 t18 f15 b16.** Suicide or murder? Was the sulphur there with an early sherry butt or was it the wine cask that did it? *50%. Douglas Laing. 363 bottles.*

Old Malt Cask Glenrothes Aged 28 Years sherry finished butt 3901, dist Apr 79, bott Sep 07 **(92) n23.5** scrummy, highly intense, stand-your-fork-in-it oloroso that has not even a hint of a blemish; **t23** fruit cake quality with ribbons of sweet barley running through it; some pretty ripe greengages abound, too; **f23** raisins and chocolate; some late big age oak bitterness; **b22.5** now that's how a sherried Glenrothes should be...!! *50%. nc ncf. Douglas Laing. 311 bottles.*

⋅⋅⋅ **Old Malt Cask Glenrothes Aged 32 Years** refill hogshead, dist Dec 75, bott Aug 08 **(92) n24** stick your beak in this one for a good fifteen minutes: changes colours so many times but at its best a sublime citrus note dovetails with vanilla which has set up camp in a field of honeyed barley; **t22.5** beautiful weight; seemingly light but the barley begins to gather intensity; a slight salty tinge sharpens things up further; **f22.5** the most pleasant vanilla fade you'll taste for a while; some natural fudgy caramels add a chewy quality; **b23** first class bottling just dripping with quiet dignity. *50%. Douglas Laing. 253 bottles.*

Old Masters Glenrothes Aged 12 Years Old cask no. 826089, dist 94, bott 07 **(91) n23** very clean and rich sherry with a honeyed, plummy aside; **t23** outstanding oloroso effect with an immediate build up of spice; the oak then suggests something a lot older; **f22** almost a bourbony-style vanilla alongside grape; **b23** bit of an oddity this: begins life as uncompromising and rare unspoiled sherry... and finishes as something from Kentucky! Fabulous. *51.9%. James MacArthur for USA only.*

Private Cellar's Selection Glenrothes 1986 bott 07 **(93) n22** the clarity of the honeyed barley is rather simplistic, but for those of us who can read the signs...it promises much.... **t23.5** ...and there is no disappointment here as the myriad sweet and spicy tones to the malt absolutely explode on impact. Even as the oaky vanilla is welcomed aboard, the barley still sings the sweetest of songs; **f24** wonderful layering of intense barley, even to the death; the vanillas gather but serve only to redistribute the charming sweetness. Wonderful.. **b23.5** a real, honest-to-goodness gem of a dram. And not a sherry butt in sight...!!! *43%*

Provenance Glenrothes Aged 11 Years refill hogshead 4075, dist 96, bott 07 **(85.5) n21.5 t22 f21 b21.** Pleasant, grassy, untaxing Speyside fare. *46.0%. nc ncf. Douglas Laing.*

Provenance Glenrothes Aged 12 Years refill hogshead, dist autumn 96, bott autumn 08 (85.5) n20 t21 f23 b21.5. Elegant if simple malt where somehow less is more: the clean barley delivery mutates into a light custard tart and bourbon biscuit as if in slow motion. 46%. Douglas Laing.

Provenance Glenrothes Aged 12 Years sherry finished butt no. 3808, dist summer 95, bott summer 07 (89) n22.5 unmistakable wisps of peat reek drift over the clean barley; t21.5 soft coating of smoke over the oilier-textured body; f22.5 vanilla and gentle oils continue to paint a picture of the Sound of Islay....; b22.5 Smoky Glenrothes! Whatever next! Tasted blind, I would have sworn this to be a Caol Ila. 46%. Douglas Laing.

Scotch Malt Whisky Society Cask 30.55 Aged 15 Years refill hogshead, dist Jul 92 (86.7) n21.5 t22 f21.5 b21.5. An enjoyable workaday malt with a blue collar. Honest Joe feel to it. 57.5%

Scotch Malt Whisky Society Cask 30.59 Aged 16 Years refill hogshead, dist Jul 92 (90) n22 simplistic, faultless, clean barley in a healthy oak surround; t23 more of the same, especially on delivery where soft vanilla notes merge gracefully with the much bigger sweet malts; the middle ground fills with butterscotch and butter shortbread; f22.5 very long, using the limited soft oils to full capacity. Again it's malt all the way, enlivened with a light spice prickle, and delicate vanillas; b22.5 now this is how I remember Glenrothes all those years ago before it was launched as a single malt and went all sherryfied (and not always for the better). A high quality, big malty number perfect for blending and when in this form a well made, if untaxing, dram. 55.1%

Scott's Selection Glenrothes 1986 bott 08 (84) n21.5 t19.5 f22 b21. Decidedly on the hot side, but otherwise solid and occasionally sweet with a generous late middle barley development. 52.2%. Speyside Distillers.

GLEN SCOTIA
Campbeltown, 1832. Loch Lomond Distillers. Working.

Berry's Own Selection Glen Scotia 1992 bott 08 (95) n24 a heavy, weighty plug of dry peat: almost certainly the moss here was cut from very deep in the trench. An acrid acidic bite to the peat should not be confused with any off notes from the cask – of which there are none. This is a rare, natural state and one once found sometimes with Ardbeg samples from the 1960s in particular; t24 a to-die-for delivery: the sweetness proffers a wonderful sharpness; natural caramels are light and attracts rich barley...and then, of course, that dull, throbbing smoke; f23.5 spices which had formed in the middle ground have a louder say and the deftly sweetened vanilla sees us out; b23.5 from among the earliest days of smoked Scotia (well since World War II, certainly), here's a peaty nugget. I bet Berry's very own Dougie McIvor made a pact with the devil for his beloved Charlton to be relegated to their natural place in the third tier of English football in exchange for getting hold of a cask like this. A good bit of business, Dougie, my son...see you soon at The Valley!! 55.7%. Berry Bros & Rudd.

Glen Scotia 1999 heavily peated, cask no. 518, dist 23 Jul 99 db (92) n22 moist marzipan adds a sweet, nutty element to the pre-pubescent, vaguely Bowmore-style peat. Deliciously young; t23 fresh, enormously sweet and surprisingly oily for this distillery: but, for all this, it is stunningly balanced and charismatic; f23 dries very impressively; there is an imperious flourish to the peaty signature; b24 this is pretty big and quite beautifully made malt. Forget the age. Enjoy a touch of class. 45%

Glen Scotia 1999 heavily peated, cask no. 525, dist 23 Jul 99 db (85) n21 t22 f22 b20. Tasty, but relatively blunt, nothing like so together or complex as cask 518. 45%

Glen Scotia Aged 12 Years db (81) n23 t21 f18 b19. What a whisky· you could write a book about it, a thriller. It'd be called "Murder by Caramel." The early signs on the nose and palate arrival are genuinely awesome. But then...then.....!!! I can't say for sure if it's natural from the oak, or has been added. Unmolested, this malt would be in the very high 80s, possibly low 90s: there is something wondrous in there, not least the richness of the diced apple and honey on the nose: you don't have to hunt too hard to see what I mean. Let's hope I'll be able to give it that score next year. 40%

Glen Scotia Cask No. 78 american oak, dist 31 May 99, bott 24 Apr 07 db (85) n22 t22 f20 b21. Juicy and chewy; perhaps a slight conflict when the oak gets close and personal. 45%.

Glen Scotia Cask No. 337 dist 23 Jul 99, bott 25 Apr 07 db (86.5) n21 t22 f22 b21.5. The thin smoke has almost a tobacco feel. Decent, but you have the feeling it is underperforming a little. 45%. nc ncf. 325 bottles.

Glen Scotia Cask No. 404 american oak, dist 18 Jul 01, bott 23 Apr 07 db (89) n23 though so young there is a distinct touch of the bourbons here amid the clean, intense malt; t22 further evidence that a malt can sing on the palate even at these tender years with wonderful waves of unrushing sweet barley sugar; **f22** lovely spices abound; **b22** remarkable isn't it? Put some people into a distillery who know how to make whisky and...hey presto!! A five-year-old beauty! 45%. 410 bottles.

Glen Scotia Cask No. 511 american oak, dist 23 Jul 99, bott 26 Apr 07 db **(90) n22** a sprig of mint lightens the peat; **t23** the lightness of the body allows the smoke to show bigger than it might; so delicate for a peaty guy with the sweetness of the barley not afraid to show itself; **f22** remains light with spices suffusing into the building vanilla; **b23** not every cylinder fires here, but enough to make for a pretty profound and unforgettable dram. 45%. 360 bottles.

Glen Scotia Cask No. 546 american oak, dist 23 Jul 99, bott 25 Apr 07 db **(84) n21 t22 f21 b20.** Considering this is from the same distillate as 511, we have chalk and cheese here. In this bottling the oak is rather niggardly and closed. Very pleasant but... 45%. 325 btls.

Cadenhead's Authentic Collection Glen Scotia Aged 15 Years sherry hogshead, dist 91, bott Feb 07 **(87) n22** Any heavier and it'd have a heart attack; really dense oloroso; meaty; **t23** punchy delivery with the big thick malt in cahoots with the big thick sherry; **f21** bitters out with burnt raisin; **b21** about as subtle as a poke in the eye, but equally as noticeable. 57.8%. Cadenhead's. 210 bottles.

∴ **Duthies Glen Scotia 17 Years Old (80.5) n20 t21 f19 b20.5.** Busy, mouth-watering...and yet. Definitely not quite the best wood a spirit has ever been filled into. 46%. Cadenhead's for Germany.

The Exclusive Malts Glen Scotia Aged 15 Years cask no. 424, dist Jan 92 **(90) n22** sharp, big barley with a vanilla topping; **t23** big. No, make that massive. Huge barley in bitter-sweet mood. Very faint oils, and more vanilla towards the middle; **f22.5** long. Just the right buzz to keep the interest going and a late mocha fade; **b22.5** truly delightful stuff. 53.4%. The Creative Whisky Company. 241 bottles.

∴ **Exclusive Malts Glen Scotia 1992** Aged 16 Years dist 92 **(89.5) n20** less than flawless; some rough edges and technically unsound...yet attractive in a gritty kind of way; **t24** hot-ish, hard as granite and yet reaches the middle having exploded all kinds of malt bombs around the palate and winning you over in the process; some flinty fruity notes, too; salivating and intensely satisfying; **f23** more blandly defined fruit and barley sugar, sprinkled with some oaky cocoa; b22.5 an imposing malt impossible not to love: a real rough diamond... 52.1%. Chester Whisky & Liqueur Co.

Kingsbury Single Cask Series Glen Scotia 14 Years Old 1992 dist Mar 92, bott Jun 06 **(87.5) n21.5 t23 f21.** Smoke drifts back in with natural toffee; **b22** a malt which caresses. 46.0%. nc ncf. Japan Import System Co. Ltd.

∴ **Kingsbury's Glen Scotia 1992 (86.5) n21 t22.5 f21.5 b21.5.** Something of the Sugar Frosties about this: a sweet, malty cereal feel – and a bit crunchy, too. But the most impressive quality is its intense Kentucky kick, perhaps due to the heady mix of muscovado and soft cocoa. 66.2%. Japan Import System

The MacPhail's Collection Glen Scotia 1991 (72) n19 t18 f17 b18. The distillery not quite at its co-ordinated best. 43%. Gordon & MacPhail.

The MacPhail's Collection Glen Scotia 1992 Aged 15 Years dist 92, bott 07 **(75) n18 t20 f18.5 b18.5.** Around this period Scotia were at times having all kinds of problems with their distillate and, to boot, were filling into poor casks. Here's proof. 43%. Gordon & MacPhail.

Old Malt Cask Glen Scotia Aged 15 Years sherry butt 4080, dist Mar 92, bott Dec 07 **(76.5) n19 t19.5 f19 b19.** Pretty flat. 50%. nc ncf. Douglas Laing. 707 bottles.

Old Malt Cask Glen Scotia Aged 16 Years refill hogshead, cask no. 4436, dist Mar 92, bott Jun 08 **(90.5) n23.5** big, bourbony overture: powering burnt honey and leather but the malt's in there, too...; **t22.5** superb intensity: the malt really does come alive; **f22** settles with crème caramel with a barley/muscovado sugar sprinkling; **b22.5** a delight from first to last. 50%. nc ncf. Douglas Laing. 257 bottles.

∴ **Old Malt Cask Glen Scotia Aged 17 Years** bott 09 **(92.5) n23** gloriously anarchic; **t23.5** typically lively with booming bourbony notes; rips into your throat with glee; **f23** a few spices liven up the vanillas **b23** fabulous fun: if this doesn't shake some life into your tastebuds, nothing will. 50%. Douglas Laing.

Scotch Malt Whisky Society Cask 93.30 Aged 16 Years refill barrel, dist Mar 92 **(96) n23** fizzing barley with myriad oaky side roads and even the vaguest hint of smoke; **t24.5** simply perfection on delivery with an almost aggressive, explosive countenance on one hand and then a bed of barley-straw on the other; bipolar in personality but there are very few malts in the world which manage to extract so much out of the barley: spicy, gently phenoled, gripping, brain and palate-teasing... **f24** molassed chocolate and still the barley just continues to rumble onwards; **b24.5** I think if someone had asked me to describe or create in the glass exactly how I would envisage the very best malt from this distillery made during that period of its history and put it into concentrated form, I'd have to say this would just about be it exactly. Rarely does a whisky come up, to the nearest nuance, how it sits in your mind. A strange and wonderful experience. One of the whiskies of the year and from what most would consider an unlikely source. 64.5%

Scotch Malt Whisky Society Cask 93.31 Aged 16 Years refill barrel, dist Mar 92 **(92) n22.5** beautifully bourbony; **t23.5** big barley; **f23** classic cocoa; **b23** superb, seductive whisky in its own right but shows and Lord Mayors come to mind. 65.5%

⠶ **Scotch Malt Whisky Society Cask 93.34 Aged 16 Years** refill butt, dist Mar 92 **(93) n24** oatmeal stout meets nut brown ale....it's like the bottle skip of an old boozer in the '70s with a few emptied cream sherries for good measure; **t23.5** sweet 'n' spicy delivery from the off with more than a hint of those brown Liquorice Allsorts towards the middle; malty despite all the lumpenly sherried razzamatazz; **f22.5** much more sober and sensible – though still pretty extrovert – with a lovely sweet lilt to the malty, stouty burnt fudge fade; **b23** not the kind of dram you happen upon too often in a year. Or career. Technically a mess, as the flavours never conform to either type or a set pattern. But this helter-skelter ride is pure fun. Hold on to your hats...and this gloriously idiosyncratic malt's coat-tails... 55.1%

⠶ **Scotch Malt Whisky Society Cask 93.35 Aged 17 Years** refill hogshead, dist Apr 91 **(81.5) n19.5 t21 f21 b20.** Abrasive and never quite happy with the oaky environment in which it has been held for the last 17 years. The malt, once past the hot gluey notes, is huge, though, and the finish displays loads of natural caramels. 58.9%

Scott's Selection Glen Scotia 1992 bott 07 **(75) n19 t18 f20 b18.** Hot and fractured in part; the finish has its odd decent cocoa-rich moment. 57.2%. *Speyside Distillers.*

GLEN SPEY
Speyside, 1885. Diageo. Working.

Glen Spey Aged 12 Years db **(90) n23** the kind of firm, busy malt you expect from this distillery plus some lovely spice; **t22** mouthwatering and fresh, a layer of honey makes for an easy three or four minutes; **f22** drier vanilla, but the pulsing oak is controlled and stylish; **b23** very similar to the first Glen Spey I can remember in this range, the one before the over-toffeed effort of two years ago. Great to see it back to its more natural, stunningly beautiful self. 43%. *Flora and Fauna range.*

Cadenhead's Authentic Collection Glen Spey Aged 13 Years bourbon hogshead, dist 95, bott Jun 08 **(84.5) n20 t22 f21.5 b21.** Identical nose to the Dewar Rattray bottling of same year, but this is glossier on the palate and homed in a better cask. 58.8%. 246 bottles.

Connoisseurs Choice Glen Spey 1995 (76) n19 t19 f19 b19. Vapid blending fodder. 43%. *Gordon & MacPhail.*

Dewar Rattray Glen Spey 1995 cask no. 422, dist Apr 95, bott Mar 07 **(81) n20 t21.5 f19.5 b20.** A bantamweight packing a big punch. 59%

Murray McDavid Glen Spey 1996 Aged 11 Years bourbon/madeira **(78) n20 t20 f19 b19.** The wafer-thin malt appears to buckle under the weight of the fruit. Not at all unpleasant, but appears to find balance hard to come by. 46%

Old Malt Cask Glen Spey Aged 17 Years bourbon finished barrel 3900, dist Feb 90, bott Sep 07 **(85) n20.5 t21 f22 b21.5.** Juicy malt leads the way. Safe whisky. 50%. nc ncf. *Douglas Laing.* 293 bottles.

Norse Cask Selection Glen Spey 1995 Aged 11 Years hogshead cask no. 421 **(79) n18 t21 f20 b20.** Glen Spey has always, traditionally, been one of the lightest and cleanest of the Speyside malts. This, though pleasant, is hardly representative. 59.7% whiskyowner.com, Denmark.

Norse Cask Selection Glen Spey 1995 Aged 11 Years cognac finish hogshead cask no. 421 **(84) n20 t22 f21 b21.** A fascinating experiment: part of exactly the same cask which failed above has been finished in Cognac. The result is sweeter, cleaner malt all round. Though, for all its added charms, still falls a little short of excellence. 59.7%. WhiskyOwner.com, Denmark.

GLENTAUCHERS
Speyside, 1898. Chivas. Working.

⠶ **The Cärn Mör Vintage Collection Glentauchers 2006** barrel, cask no. 9, dist 06, bott 09 **(85) n22 t21 f21 b21.** A three year-old still in its new make nappies thanks to absolute minimum oak input. Shows the high quality malty distillate at its most naked. And refreshing. 46%. *The Scottish Liqueur Centre.*

⠶ **Dun Bheagan Glentauchers Aged 15 Years** hogshead, dist Sep 92 **(85) n22 t22 f20 b21.** Some really wonderful barley and citrus touches to this but a bitter finish undermines some of the good work. No doubt a better cask would have produced a sparkling gem. 43%. *Ian Macleod Distillers Ltd.*

Duncan Taylor Collection Glentauchers 1990 cask no. 14435 **(91) n22.5** boiled gooseberries...and easy on the sugar; **t23** sublime malt/fruit interplay. Ridiculously lively with those gooseberries backed by citrus and grape; **f22.5** soft, wave upon wave of slightly spiced barley; **b23** odd; when I first nosed this against the DT 46%, I thought it'd get slaughtered. But slow consideration and a few mouthfuls later, and there really is no contest. And the malt floored by a devastating knockout blow....is the 46%....Taste this and, like me, wonder why the hell this has never been brought out as a regular top-quality single malt. *576%*

Duncan Taylor The NC2 Range Glentauchers 1990 Aged 16 Years (85.5) n22 t21 f21 b21.5. A soft, malt-dominated bottling with enough soft fruit nuances to keep it alive and ticking. *46%*

⋰ **Gordon & MacPhail Distillery Label Glentauchers 1991 (83) n21 t22.5 f19.5 b20.** Hardly does this under-rated distillery justice: the nose is lagged down by a vague lactic note from some exhausted oak while the finish is thin and unhappy. Yet the show is saved by a genuinely vivid barley dash on delivery. *43%*

Old Malt Cask Glentauchers Aged 12 Years dist Nov 94, bott Feb 07 **(88) n22** clean, cement-hard barley softened by oak **t23** juiced-up barley attack with a sweetish, gristy edge; **f21** oakier, making just the right drier noises **b22** fabulous blending whisky that doubles up as an unerring single malt of crisp substance. *50%. 354 bottles.*

⋰ **Old Malt Cask Glentauchers Aged 13 Years** refill hogshead, dist Nov 95, bott Feb 09 **(87) n22** gristy malt with a squeeze of lemon; **t22** the citrus-barley combo keeps the salivating going; **f21.5** a dab of vanilla and scorched toast; **b21.5** simple, clean, elegant and very drinkable. *50%. Douglas Laing. 334 bottles.*

Scotch Malt Whisky Society Cask 63.20 Aged 18 Years refill barrel, dist Dec 89 **(88) n21.5 t22.5 f22 b22** From an entirely underrated distillery that usually thanks you for bottling at a younger age, comes a malt of serious distinction...and one that probably thanks you for even bottling in at all. *54.7%*

⋰ **Scotch Malt Whisky Society Cask 63.22 Aged 18 Years** refill barrel, dist Dec 89 **(94) n22.5** woodworking sheds: a sawdusty quality dries the sharp, scratchy barley; **t24** for a malt so brittle, rarely is a delivery quite as soft as this: on one hand the barley is hard enough to chip at your teeth, on another the understated lush sweetness appears to graft itself to the salivating, juices; mild peppers spice matters up further while some custard and sugared rice pudding invade the middle ground; **f23.5** medium to long in length but it's barley and chewy hay all the way with a mildly overcooked vanilla still having the sugary wherewithal to see off any oak; **b24** a minor gem from Speyside which does much to show the subtle but incisive qualities of this wonderful distillery. The first to third tastings won't do the trick on this one: only after the fourth or fifth mouthful can you really unravel the intricate plot. What a treat!! *53.8%*

GLENTURRET

Highlands (Perthshire), 1775. Edrington. Working.

Glenturret Aged 8 Years db **(88) n21** some sma' still randomness; **t22** silky honey, a few feinty oils perhaps, but attractive; **f23** honey overdrive with spice; **b22** technically no prizewinner. But the dexterity of the honey is charming, as this distillery has a tendency sometimes to be. *40%*

The Glenturret Aged 10 Years db **(76) n19 t18 f20 b19.** Lots of trademark honey but some less than impressive contributions from both cask and the stillman. *40%*

The Glenturret Aged 15 Years db **(87) n21 t22 f22 b22.** A beautifully clean, small-still style dram that would have benefitted from being bottled at a fuller strength. A discontinued bottling now: if you see it, it is worth the small investment. *40%*

Glenturret 1991 Aged 15 Years cask no. 638 db **(82) n20 t21 f21 b20.** Honeycomb and chocolate: liquid fruit jelly. Heavyweight stuff and at times a little stodgy. *55.3%*

Glenturret 1992 Aged 14 Years cask no. 855 db **(72) n18 t19 f17 b18.** A tad feinty and never quite finds the right key despite the best efforts of the honey and spice. *59.7%*

Glenturret 1993 cask no. 840 db **(83.5) n21 t20 f21.5 b21.** I'm afraid the heat on this one isn't simply down to the giant strength. This is hot whisky but with some attractively sharp notes. *59.5%*

Cadenhead's Glenturret Aged 20 Years dist 87, bott Feb 08 **(95) n24** I'm on my knees: soft smoke, soft honey, soft barley, the gentle sea-breezy salt of Scottish rock-pools that the Oystercatcher rather likes for its crabs... **t24** big saline barley kick, then a succession of honeyed waves topped with a hefty dollop of spice topped with soft cocoa; **f23** now the honey goes into whimpering mode playing hide and seek with the vanilla: complex, subtle, beautifully formed and balanced; **b24** brilliant: absolutely bloody brilliant!! Why can't the distillery bottling be this damn good!!! *51.6%. 229 bottles.*

Cadenhead's Authentic Collection Glenturret Aged 20 Years bourbon hogshead, dist 86, bott Feb 07 **(83) n21 t21 f20 b21.** Starts with great promise and just the right degree of honey and bourbon-esque influence. *50.3%. 222 bottles.*

The MacPhail's Collection Glenturret Aged 10 Years dist 97, bott 07 **(83.5) n20 t19 f23 b21.5.** After a rocky, off-balanced start settles down to impart that rich, rather attractive copper-honey sharpness which appears unique to this distillery. *40%. Gordon & MacPhail.*

⫶⫶ **Old Malt Cask Glenturret Aged 19 Years** refill hogshead, dist Sep 89, bott Mar 09 **(91) n23** slivers of honey attach to nutty, barley notes: coppery, light and delicate; **t23.5** mouth-watering, intense barley again shows that vein of honey; the usual metallic tingle is there, but there is also some unexpected pomegranate juice, too; **f22** long, with the usual small still metallic edge usually found on Glenturret, but also slightly pithy with a lime-vanilla fade; **b22.5** one of the few bottlings of late which shows off the Glenturret character to its fullest degree. And at the higher quality found in the early 1990s. A must get malt. *50%. Douglas Laing. 298 bottles.*

Old Masters Glenturret Aged 14 Years cask no. 188 dist 93, bott 07 **(90) n22** grassy, gristy, fresh; **t23** both soft and firm barley head off in grassy and honeyed directions; touches of custard tart, too, but the honey makes a return towards the middle, this time with a richer, more confident stance; **f22.5** biscuity (a touch of Nice and coffee) as drier, oakier tunes are whistled. A late hurrah of muscovado sugar is a delicate and elegant touch; **b22.5** Ah-ha! A Glenturret just like what I remember from the good ol' days! Honey by the hive-load. *56.9%. James MacArthur & Co. Ltd.*

⫶⫶ **Provenance Glentauchers Aged 8 Years** sherry butt, dist summer 00, dist autumn 08 **(85.5) n21.5 t22 f21 b21.** Another 'Tauchers bottling struggling against indifferent oak. Thankfully there is enough of the trademark low-key complexity and biscuity barley to ensure a pleasant time. *46%*

Signatory Vintage Glenturret 1992 13 Years Old sherry butt **(74) n19 t19 f18 b18.** Sulpher. *43%. USA.*

GLENUGIE
Highland (Eastern). 1834–1983. Closed.

Duncan Taylor Collection Glenugie 1981 cask no. 5158 **(94) n23** butterscotch embedded with ginger and lemon-juiced pancakes: genuinely deep, fun and fascinating **t23** despite the age the malt still offers juice and grist and fizzing spices which accentuate the vanilla; the sugar types are varied and plentiful and perfectly counter the oak; **f24** long with the vaguest hint of smoke and now the gristiness dries at last. But never is there a hint of bitterness to be found· this is near perfectly balanced whisky and a miracle for its age; **b24** sightings of Glenugie are about as common as instances of Gordon Brown leaving those around him in helpless mirth. But, unlike politicians, this distillery never seems to let you down. The rule of thumb is: find a bottle of Glenugie and you'll find liquid gold. This is no exception. In fact, it's probably the best of the lot! *51.5%*

Old & Rare Glenugie Aged 26 Years dist Mar 82, bott Mar 08 **(87.5) n22** weird, slapped on sherry; the barley and oak combines to find a way through and mostly fails... **t22** eye-watering stuff from this hot-head. The saving grace is the ultra intense sweet malt sandwiched between the flame-throwing delivery and the white-hot spices which follow **f22** some gentle malts meander through, but you are probably too busy counting your teeth to notice... **b21.5** distilled towards the last days in the life of this distillery. By then it was getting a reputation for making hot whisky, and a mouthful of this is enough to give third degree burns to your oesophagus for a year or two. But if you can ride it, and overcome the OTT sherry, then you can enjoy some history. *58%. Douglas Laing. 117 bottles.*

⫶⫶ **Old Malt Cask Glenugie Aged 26 Years** bourbon cask, dist Mar 82, bott Oct 08 **(92.5) n23.5** that nagging hint of ginger – a kind of unofficial Glenugie Trademark – enlivens the thin citrus. Beautifully understated and absolutely zero over encroachment of the oak; **t23.5** another old Trademark, the oils, arrive in force, allowing the bold barley to stick benignly to the palate; the sweetness is of almost perfect weight; **f22.5** an enchanting ending with light spices making their mark on the vanilla; **b23** it is possible I have tasted more bottled versions of Glenugie over the years as anyone else out there. And although it has made many of its usual statements, the manner in which they have been delivered opens new ground; the softest Glenugie and possibly most elegant of them all. *50%. Douglas Laing. 265 bottles.*

⫶⫶ **Old Malt Cask Glenugie Aged 27 Years** bourbon cask, dist Mar 82, bott Mar 09 **(86) n21.5 t21 f22.5 b21.** Pleasantly and intensely malty. A tad thin for the real Glenugie purists and showing a hot streak, too. But seriously enjoyable from first to last, especially last. *50%. Douglas Laing. 216 bottles.*

GLENURY ROYAL
Highland (Eastern), 1868–1985. Demolished.

Glenury Royal 36 Years Old db **(89) n22** sawdusty and spiced: a busy nose where the barley offers little more than a shadow; **t23.5** improbably juicy and mouth-watering with barley sugar concentrate; the clarity of the malt appears to bring out the best in the brown sugar accompaniment; the middle gets a bit overly dry, though; **f21.5** the barley lingers sweetly – and has to: the oak is pretty toasty and profound; soft, slightly burnt fudge notes go well with the overcooked butterscotch tart; the final fade is almost that of pot still Demerara rum; **b22** with so much dark, threatening oak around, the delivery defies belief or logic. Cracking stuff!! *57.9%*

Glenury Royal 36 Years Old db **(89) n21** oak interference damages the fruit balance; **t23** starts worryingly dull then takes off to fabulous heights on fresh, beautifully textured barley; **f22** begins to fall out of sync as some heavyweight hickory is driven home, but lightens with a succession of gentle waves of cocoa; **b23** an undulating dram, hitting highs and lows. The finish, in particular, is impressive: just when it looks on its last legs, it revives delightfully. The whole package, though far from perfect, is pretty astounding. *50.2%*

Glenury Royal 50 Years Old dist 53 db **(91) n23** marvellous freshness to the sherry butt; this had obviously been a high quality cask in its day and the intensity of the fruit sweetened slightly by the most delicate marzipan and old leather oozes class; a little mint reveals some worry lines; **t24** the early arrival is sweet and nimble with the barley, against the odds, still having the major say after all these years. The oak is waiting in the wings and with a burst of soft liquorice and velvety, understated spice beginning to make an impression; the sweetness is very similar to a traditional British child's candy of "tobacco" made from strands of coconut and sugar; **f22** masses of oak yet, somehow, refuses to go over the top and that slightly molassed sweetness sits very comfortably with the mildly oily body; **b22** I am always touched when sampling a whisky like this from a now departed distillery. *42.8%*

Gordon & MacPhail Rare Old Glenury Royal 1972 (90) n22 there is little doubting the 30-odd years on the clock here but some molassed fruitcake ensures the wrinkles don't show; **t23** sublime delivery with a velvet caress as it stokes the tastebuds; lovely burnt fudge takes me back to my earliest childhood and a touch of liquorice, too; **f22** molasses see off the oak to leave a languid finale; **b23** a thumping malt showing good age but wears it effortlessly. Just beautiful. *40%*

⁂ **Gordon & MacPhail Rare Old Glenury Royal 1984 (95.5) n25** playful coal and peat smoke drifts around the astonishing fruit soup of greengage, physalis and kiwifruit: mind-blowing in the most subtle and understated way possible...it is hard to imagine it getting much better than this flawless display; **t24** the velvet-clad delivery couches burnished barley, gleaming on the palate with the honey radiating a controlled sweetness and lightly fizzing smoke and oak; **f23** dries with the odd burnt toast twinge; **b23.5** Royal and Ancient...another lost distillery comes back to haunt those with the wrecking ball. *43%*

⁂ **Old Malt Cask Glenury Aged 32 Years** refill hogshead, dist Mar 76, bott Oct 08 **(96) n23.5** tense, marriage between thickset barley and confident oak; a squeeze of lime relieves the pressure; elsewhere there is a sweet, diluted Port Ellen style smokiness which adds to the beauty; **t23.5** melt-in-the-mouth barley leaves in its wake a smouldering chocolatey smokiness; the middle ground is mainly oak, but in such a wonderfully docile form that you feel like applauding; meanwhile the barley spreads, as does that chocolate; **f24.5** long, sweet in just the right muscovado manner and still that chocolate mousse-type cocoa lingers; **b24.5** imagine a night of passion consisting solely of long fingernails running over your body and little else, except maybe your head being massaged at the same time. Teasing, beautiful, delectable; impossible not to release a sigh of pleasure when nosing and tasting - and a serious contender for World Whisky of the Year. *50%. Douglas Laing. 37 bottles.*

Rarest of the Rare Glenury Royal 1984 cask no. 3047 **(86.5) n22 t22 f21 b21.5.** Loads of custardy notes on nose and finish. The body is pretty thin for its age, with the oaks offering a gentlemanly hand and not much more until the dry finale. The sugars are like those which melt on hot porridge. Elegant, delicate and refuses, point blank, to say boo to a goose. *49.3%. Duncan Taylor.*

HAZELBURN (see Springbank)

HIGHLAND PARK
Highland (Island–Orkney), 1795. Edrington. Working.

Highland Park 8 Years Old db **(87) n22** firm young, honied malt with food coke/peat smoke; **t22** silky honey and excellent complexity for a malt so young; **f22** complex layers of vanilla and soft peat at first then caramel grabs hold: shame; **b21** a journey back in time for some of us: this is the orginal distillery bottling of the 70s and 80s, bottles of which are still doing the rounds in obscure Japanese bars and specialist outlets such as the Whisky Exchange. 40%

Highland Park Aged 12 Years db **(91) n22.5** a lighter version than the last few I've enjoyed this year: less honey with more barley to the fore. Almost younger in style though the soft smoke does add the weight demanded; **t23.5** here it comes into its own with a style unlike any other malt in the world: first you get the silky coating. Just as you purr from that and you settle into the malty attack, from nowhere a subtle honey edge descends. An unusual, brief sharpness retreats, allowing room for the most delicate of smoke; **f22** only half-serious vanilla and lazy citrus continue to give the feel of a younger than normal malt; **b23** no heather. The lightest sprinkling of peat. A youthfulness hangs to it. Disappointing HP? Not a bit of it!! Because the complexity still keeps you mesmerised. 40%

Highland Park Aged 15 Years db **(92) n23** nosed blind, and at this relatively unusual age, there could be only one distillery: the honey-smoke balance and intensity is unique; **t22.5** soft, dissolving honey finds a mint humbuggy kind of middle to offer toffee and spice; **f23.5** some real length to this finale with the usual myriad honey notes going through their repertoire but a further polishing with Demerara and smoke and then buffed with lime, appears to up the charm; **b23** immeasurably better than the last time I came face to face with this. 40%

Highland Park 16 Years Old db **(88) n23** softly softly strains of oranges, honey and vanilla; **t23** mouthwatering and delightfully weighted barley with soft nuances of liquorice and smoke; **f20** toffee-vanilla: just a little too quiet; **b22** I tasted this the day it first came out at one of the Heathrow whisky shops. I thought it a bit flat and uninspiring. This sample, maybe from another bottling, is more impressive and showing true Highland Park colours, the finish apart. 40% *Exclusively available in Duty Free/Travel Retail.*

Highland Park Aged 18 Years db **(95.5) n23.5** a thick dollop of honey spread across a layer of salted butter; in the background the ashes of a peat fire are emptied; **t24** eye closing beauty: immediate glossy impact of rich, vaguely metallic honey but upped in the complexity stakes by the subtle intense marbling of peat; the muscular richness, aided by the softness of the oil ensures that maximum intensity is not only reached but maintained; **f24** long continuation of those elements found in the delivery but now radiating soft spices and hints of marzipan; **b24** if familiarity breeds contempt, then it has yet to happen between myself and HP 18. This is a must-have dram. I show it to ladies the world over to win their hearts, minds and tastebuds when it comes to whisky. And the more time I spend with it, the more I become aware and appreciative of its extraordinary consistency. The very latest bottlings have been astonishing, possibly because colouring has now been dropped, and wisely so. Why in any way reduce what is one of the world's great whisky experiences? Such has been the staggering consistency of this dram I have thought of late of promoting the distillery into the world's top three: only Ardbeg and Buffalo Trace have been bottling whisk(e)y of such quality over a wide range of ages in such metronomic fashion. Anyway, enough: a glass of something honeyed and dazzling calls... 43% ☉

⋰ **Highland Park 21 Years Old** db **(85.5) n22 t21.5 f21 b21** Massively honeyed. But also the feeling that there is a fair bit of stuff way beyond the 21 mark here, such is the magnitude of the oaky impact. Enjoy at this strength for now; in future will be at 40%, their guys tell me. 47.5%

Highland Park Aged 25 Years db **(79) n20 t21 f19 b19.** I had to look twice at the sample here. And pour twice. The flattest HP 25 of all time. The sherry is dull and mainly lifeless and if caramel has been kicked out of the brand, some of the charmless variety must have made it from the cask. Also a strange bitterness descends....Pleasant-ish. But easily one of the most disappointing versions of this I have come across anywhere. 48%

Highland Park Aged 30 Years db **(95.5) n23.5** a very different nose to before with now the emphasis on a gamut of pastel shades of citrus, pink grapefruit and lime at the fore. But, of course, there are the soft shades of smoke and honey...; **t23** the gentle embers of smoke add further weight to the metallic, coppery sharpness which shows this dram is still alive and kicking; **f24.5** busy, ever more intense layering of vanilla and cocoa (indeed, not entirely unlike the milky chocolate you could find on lollies in the 1980s) , but the smoke and honey simply cannot be repressed; **b24.5** one of the whiskies of the year: embarrasses the 25-year-old with its astonishing balance and near perfect shape in every department. A whisky for the gods...but only if they are worthy... 48% ☉

Highland Park 40 Years Old db **(90.5) n20.5** tired and over-oaked but the usual HP traits are there in just enough force to save it from failing with an extra puff of something smoky diving in to be on the safe side, **t22.5** even after 40 years, pure silk Like a 40-year-old woman who has kept her figure and looks, and now only satin stands in the way between you and so much beauty and experience...and believe me: she's spicy...; **f24** amazing layering of peat caresses you at every level; the oak has receded and now barley and traces of golden syrup balance things; **b23.5** I have to admit to picking splinters from my nose with this one. Some of the casks used here have obviously choked on oak, and I feared the worst. But such is the brilliance of the resilience by being on the money with the honey, you can say only that it has pulled off an amazing feat with the peat. Sheer poetry... *48%*

Highland Park Ambassador's Cask 3 db cask no. 9035, dist 74 **(84) n22 t21 f21 b20.** At times in the realms of Caperdonich-esque exotic fruit maturity. But Caper was a nothing malt finding an aristocratic bent in very old age. This is from a great distillery where the unique style is obscured. There is a difference. Needs warming to release latent smoke. *45%*

⁖ **Cadenhead's Highland Park Aged 17 Years** dist 92, bott 09 **(87) n23** a beautiful salty lilt to the standard honey and vague smoke; **t22.5** controlled honeyed sweetness to delivery; **f20** a touch of cask tang and bitterness; **b21.5** nose and delivery are the essence of HP. *64%*

Cask Strength Highland Park 1995 (89) n22 spiced up nougat, a dab of smoke; **t22** you don't often see HP this creamy-textured; mouth-watering for all its heavy weight with an early move towards cocoa while the spices ping and zip with gusto; **f22** serious complexity here as fruity, smoke and mocha notes harmonise; **b23** not immediately recognisable as from Orkney. What is genuinely amazing is that here we have a not entirely spotless cask, yet despite the odd trace of it, we still have a true corker. *57.2%. G & M.*

D&M Aficionados' Club Bottling Highland Park Aged 22 Years cask no. 369, dist Feb 85 **(76.5) n18 t20 f19.5 b19.** The stillman must have dozed off when he'd reached the cut off point.... *43%. nc ncf. US by Angus Dundee.*

Duncan Taylor Collection Highland Park 1968 cask no. 3466 **(76) n19.5 t19 f18 b19.5.** The poor old chap just faded away... *40.9%*

Duncan Taylor Collection Highland Park 1986 cask no. 2251 **(82.5) n19 t22.5 f20 b21.** The tiredness on the nose and finish is compensated for by the exemplary HP character on delivery. *53.3%*

Duncan Taylor Collection Highland Park 1986 cask no. 2252 **(86) n22 t22.5 b20.5 f21.** Oh brother!! This sister cask also reveals different degrees of wear and tear but the spicy injection and the thicker layering of honey appears to see off the worst excesses. *55.7%*

⁖ **Duncan Taylor Collection Highland Park 1986** cask no. 2254 **(89.5) n21** a touch of pine amid the citrus; **t23** early oak makes you fear the worst, but the honey/lemon-barley recovery is outstanding; big delivery and has no hesitation to shout its points when need be; **f23** really takes off here as some very belated, and laid back, phenols dovetail with the mocha sweetened by honeycomb; the spice buzz is relentless; **b22.5** bit of a Lazarus malt, this... *55.7%*

⁖ **Duncan Taylor Collection Highland Park 1987** cask no. 1529 **(86.5) n21.5 t22.5 f21 b21.5.** Enjoyable, for sure. But you can't get past the fact the oak has too big a toe hold here. Even so, the shinier edges on the first delivery certainly do reveal some talented honey and there is a good smoke-cocoa element, too. *50.4%*

⁖ **Duncan Taylor Collection Highland Park 1991** cask no. 8088 **(91) n21.5** smoke apart, natural caramels even out some of the hoped-for complexity; **t23** stunning, lush body with loads of spice prickle and then an ever-waxier feel to the smoked honey malt; **f23.5** chewy barley with first class bitter-sweet layering and strands of cocoa to show a touch of age; long and one to slump back in the armchair and relish; **b23** a stand up and be counted malt with much to say about itself. *55.2%*

⁖ **Duncan Taylor Collection Highland Park 1991** cask no. 8089 **(83.5) n21 t20.5 f21 b21.** A hotter, sharper version of cask 8089 where the murderous natural caramels have disposed of the smoky body. *54.6%*

Kingsbury Handwriting Highland Park 15 Years Old (94) n23.5 HP at its thickest: as though bourbon concentrate has been stirred into the honey; **t24.5** one of the most honeyed of all single casks this year: traces of smoke infiltrate into the manuka mix, the considerable weight of which is supported by timber; **f22.5** vanilla at first, then drier oak to counter the sweeter grains; **b23.5** memorable, magnificent malt for those who prefer theirs distilled by bees. *61.5%. nc ncf. Japan Import System Co. Ltd.*

Lonach Highland Park 1984 (88) n22 vanilla, honey and smoke; **t22** honey, smoke and vanilla; **f22** vanilla, smoke and...honey...**b22** not the most complex HP, but is, delightfully, exactly what it says on the tin... *50.9%. Duncan Taylor.*

⁖ **Mackillop's Choice Highland Park 1973** cask no. 8395, dist Jun 73, bott Jun 07 **(94.5) n24** even after 34 years the smoke somehow offers the perfect accompaniment to the honey...as astonishing as it is improbable; **t22.5** silk all the way – even when some tangibly more ragged oak appears. But such is the sheen to the soft honey tones you can forgive anything...;

f24 sublime complexity as the smoke regroups and brings with it a wonderful milk chocolate depth...dreamy... **b24** just so wonderfully HP...!!! *43%. Iain Mackillop & Co. Ltd.*

Montgomerie's Highland Park 1992 (91) n23 a healthy waft of smoke forms a haze over the spiced honey; **t23** for a 46 percenter, this has a pretty explosive entry with fine immediate interplay between barley, smoke and honey; **f22.5** very comfortable, even a tad copper-rich, with all the complex noises you'd expect; **b22.5** this wonderful distillery nutshelled. *46%. Montgomery & Co. Ltd.*

Murray McDavid Highland Park 1989 sherry/port **(95) n23** complex, well-weighted and possessing a pleasant chalkiness to counter the fruit; the most gentle waft of smoke reminds you of the distillery at the centre of this experience; **t24** black and red Jelly Babies send the palate into salivation overdrive. Some HP character finally arrives towards the middle with a swathe of honey cutting through the barley-fruit proceedings. Good grief...! **f24** an improbably long finale with the honey hanging on for dear life, the fruits trying to edge their way back into pole position (and failing) and the smoke bringing some gravity to proceedings; **b24** my tastebuds, having recovered from the unpleasant shock of having to analyse not one but two Dufftowns, have been amply rewarded by this truly magnificent malt. Stunningly haphazard, but everything – through either luck or design – falls into place gloriously. *46%*

Oklahoma Single Malt Lovers Highland Park Single Cask Aged 27 Years cask No 8294 **(94) n23.5** truly outstanding HP which ticks every box: all the trademark heather-honey peat are there in alchemists' proportions. Bananas and even a hint of pot still rum add to the heady mix, though there is the suggestion that the oak is just beginning to dominate. One to linger over for a long time before committing to taste; **t23.5** serious spice oomph from the start but the early fruits dissipate as some improbably juicy malt moves in for the kill; **f24** long with the smoke offering little more than an echo. So much fruitcake and burnt fudge battle to the death. Wonderful. B23 a HP that stuns the senses. A real coup by the Oklahoma club. I suggest you join up today!! *56.1%*

Old & Rare Highland Park Aged 29 Years sherry finish dist 1978, bott 07 **(90) n22** burnt fruitcake softened by a puff of peat; **t22** thick oak but the splinters are individually coated in honeycomb; **f23** soft latte again detracts from the oak while the late smoke does wonders; **b23** creakier than a sinking ship, but somehow rides the tidal waves of time. *56.7%. Douglas Laing. 328 bottles.*

⬧ **Old & Rare Highland Park Aged 30 Years** dist Mar 78, bott Aug 08 **(74.5) n19 t19 f18.5 b18**. A real shame. There appears to be an astonishing degree of honey to this. But something has crept in to spoil the party. Any guesses what....? *55.1%. Douglas Laing. 302 bottles.*

Old Malt Cask Highland Park Aged 11 Years refill hogshead 3975, dist Feb 96, bott Nov 07 **(87) n21.5** much more tender than its years; **t22** juicy malt, a slow smoke development; **f21.5** honey and smoke in pinch-measured amounts; **b22** doesn't try to be anything other than soufflé light, despite the peat. *50%. Douglas Laing. 367 bottles.*

Old Malt Cask Highland Park Aged 11 Years (81) n19 t21.5 f20.5 b20. Some great honey-intense moments are undermined by sub standard wood. *50%. Douglas Laing.*

Old Malt Cask Highland Park Aged 11 Years dist Feb 96, bott Feb 07 **(87) n21** clean barley sugar; **t22** juicy, pulsing barley with that honey-tinged sweetness unique to HP; **f22** the usual cocoa-smoke finale; **b22** Douglas Laing are cornering the market in eminently drinkable third filled casks by the looks of it. *50%. Douglas Laing. 362 bottles.*

⬧ **Old Malt Cask Highland Park Aged 15 Years** dist Feb 94, bott Jul 09 **(88) n21.5** a wisp of smoke rescues some stretched oak; **t22** sharp barley and a big salt kick; some bite and light oils here, too; **f22.5** a few friendly, sweeter notes tie up the moodier, meaner elements: excellent complexity; **b22** lovely stuff with just the right degree of attitude. *50%. Douglas Laing.*

Old Malt Cask Highland Park Aged 21 Years sherry **(92) n22** caramel wafers and dank sultana; **t23** lively delivery but is becalmed by waves of softening honey; **f23** the spice picks up beautifully and goes hand-in-hand with the juicy malt and wispy smoke; **b24** a not dissimilar bottling to the Glenkeir expression. A really big HP to take as much time as you like over. *54.1%. Exclusively for Vintage House.*

Old Malt Cask Highland Park Aged 23 Years refill butt no. 3805, dist May 84, bott Aug 07 **(93) n23.5** just how subtle can a nose get? Oak aplenty but such is the sensuality of the citrus touch, and the elegant nuances of the honey, it is as though the entire thing is being played out in slow motion; **t23** smoke engulfs the mild honey delivery; the barley is busy forming puckering juiciness, and playful spice reminds you of the advancing years; **f23** long, beautifully toasted with latte and hazelnut; **b23.5** solid for all its softness, beautifully crafted and charming. 70cl of pure elegance. *50%. Douglas Laing. 655 bottles.*

Old Malt Cask Highland Park Aged 30 Years refill butt no. 4190, dist Mar 78, bott Mar 08 **(85.5) n21 t22 f21 b21.5.** No doubting here about the vintage. As ever, honey dives in to the rescue. And the smoke helps with the camouflage. *50%. Douglas Laing. 477 bottles.*

⋅⋅⋅ **Private Cellar Highland Park 1988** bott 07 **(86.5) n22 t22 f21.5 b21.** No shortage of honey and slightly more body to this than the common or garden HP. But the smoke fails to really make itself heard to give us the usual, recognisable distillery character. That said, effortlessly drinkable and delicious. *43%. Speyside Distillers.*

Provenance Highland Park Aged 10 Years (91) n22 busy, prickly malt; fruit candy – pear drops in particular; **t24** now that is stunning....the delivery has near perfect doses of clean, sweet malt, acacia honey lightened with maple syrup (or is it the other way round...?), more pear drops and the perfect counter of no more than a shadow of softly oiled smoke; **f22.5** oils up, though continues its delicate course; natural caramel towards the finish; **b22.5** a slightly usual view of a great distillery. *46%. Douglas Laing.*

⋅⋅⋅ **Provenance Highland Park Aged 10 Years** refill hogshead, dist autumn 98, bott autumn 08 **(87) n22** the lightness of the oak gives the peat a clear road; **t21.5** lively and bracing with a salty tang; **f22** long, sweetens and really comes into its own as the smoke re-emerges; late vanilla and soft chalk; **b21.5** good, delicate malt, for all the smokiness. *46%. Douglas Laing.*

⋅⋅⋅ **Provenance Highland Park Aged 10 Years** dist Sep 98, bott Jul 09 **(89) n21.5** distant, dank peat reek on a cold, rainy Scottish day; well, any day in Scotland, really... **t23** quintessential HP with the smoke and heather really in just-so proportions. But the delicate honey plays the starring role, as is often the case; **f22** a light spice buzz alongside the salty vanilla; **b22.5** a common and garden HP treat. *46%. Douglas Laing.*

Scotch Malt Whisky Society Cask 4.119 Aged 8 Years 1st fill barrel, dist Apr 99 **(87) n22 t22 f21 b22** Anybody remember back a quarter of a century ago and more when HP was available at 8? From G&M, I think. Bit more devil about this one. *60.2%*

Scotch Malt Whisky Society Cask 4.124 Aged 8 Years 1st fill barrel, dist Apr 99 **(93.5) n23.5 f22.5 b24** It is a sad fact that my grey beard testifies to the fact that I have been around long enough to remember the days when Highland Park came only as an 8 year old. It was pretty spectacular, as 8 year olds went, though some caramel on the finale did it few favours. Never, though, did it present itself in this mind-boggling and truly awesome manner: this is the kind of 8 year old that other distilleries loathe: how can they expect to pack so much depth into so few years? This is a malt to savour from a distillery that has somehow begun to improve on its long established highest standards...and remind you, in the most glorious fashion possible, that a malt doesn't have to be a greybeard to achieve true brilliance. *59.8%*

Scotch Malt Whisky Society Cask 4.126 Aged 9 Years 1st fill barrel, dist Apr 99 **(95.5) n23.5** a rare and genuine case of locating the heather amongst the honey and smoke: it really is there!! Indescribable in form, but there nonetheless... **t24.5** now we are into the honey phase. And when I say honey, I mean bees and bleedin' millions of them! A malt suffering from hives in the most delicious way possible with the acacia style foremost; a little smoke wanders about aimlessly and a little lost and I'm not surprised: it's found itself involved with something beyond the norm. This is legendary for its age; **f23.5** long, much older than its age suggests thanks to the complexity of the layering with the barley now having a major say as the vanilla and custard; the smoke reappears for a curtain call and then makes way for the starring honey again; **b24** there can't be that many of us grizzled old grey-beard sods left who can remember when the only HP you could find was not a million miles from this timeless bottling. Every bottling and tasting note of HP you find these days bangs on about the heather. Often you feel that the way people see it is 1% reality 99% cliché. How many people have actually nosed and tasted the stuff, I wonder? Well, for a start not that many HP bottlings these days have the heather there to be found, simply because of the enormity of the age and these degree of oak or sherry influence. This one does, just like it once usually did – it is much easier to indentify when younger. And how many people have actually nosed and tasted heather, as I and a (very) few others I know have (or had, for those now departed) done? Again, not that many, I would pretty safely guess. So always take HP tasting notes from people you have barely heard of with a pinch of salt...and heather. You can take it from me, though, that this is a classic of our time....and of times past. *60.7%*

Scotch Malt Whisky Society Cask 4.127 Aged 19 Years sherry butt, dist Nov 88 **(84.5) n21 t21 f21.5 b21.** HP 9-y-o bourbon cask 1; HP 19-y-o sherry butt 0. Game abandoned due to total mis-match in quality....and this is pretty decent, if overly sweet. *58.1%*

⋅⋅⋅ **Scotch Malt Whisky Society Cask 4.131 Aged 20 Years** sherry butt, dist Nov 88 **(93.5) n23.5** a deeply enjoyable fug of smoke and weighty grape; the oak is a bit more than a bystander; **t24** what a clever boy: a big delivery, but those chunky notes are somehow fed to the tastebuds in bite-size nibbles; the grape is pure sultana and when the barley kicks in becomes just so salivating...; **f23** Cadbury's Fruit and Nut candy bar....but without the nut; **b23** heavy-handed grape gets the better of the gentle smoke throughout. The result is a light fug both on nose and palate. The sharper barley notes, touched by liquorice, do help allow fresher tones to develop. Big and chewy. And fantastic...! 60%

⋄⋄ **Scotch Malt Whisky Society Cask 4.132 Aged 13 Years** refill hogshead, dist Nov 95 **(78.5) n21.5 t20 f18 b19.** Malty, a tad smoky but hot and showing wear and tear from an unsympathetic cask. Pretty niggardly fare. Surprised it was picked. 57.6%

⋄⋄ **Scotch Malt Whisky Society Cask 4.133 Aged 13 Years** refill hogshead, dist Nov 95 **(94) n23** lime juice sprinkled over grassy barley and the most delicate, semi-erotic peat imaginable....what a tease!.... **t24** a graceful delivery with the malt landing in sweet, mildly juicy waves before there is a warming, biting spice sensation; light peat dots itself around the palate like sentries on duty and light liquorice mingles with watered manuka honey; **f23.5** the elegance continues with a slow fade of smoke and a build up of butterscotch. All is concluded in slow motion and with near perfect sweet-dry ratio between barley and oak with not a single hint of bitterness **b23.5** now that's much more like it!

Scott's Selection Highland Park 1986 bott 07 **(91) n21** dank sugar and freshly emptied barrel! A tad soapy; **t24** a near perfect dual soft/hard landing on the palate, the barley is in playful, rich mood with an intensity to the sweetness which hit the g spot; **f23** light oak shavings amid that barley stream and developing cocoa and honeycomb – real Crunchie candy stuff; **b23** some quite wonderful moments of intensity 54.5%

The Whisky Fair Highland Park Aged 19 Years bourbon hogshead, dist 88, bott 07 **(89) n22** honey...surprise, surprise!! **t23** lush and sparkling in its barley-rich intensity, the acacia honey and butterscotch break through slowly, then triumphantly; **f22** buzzing spice, soft vanilla and some burnt toast, **b22** if this is from the same cask as the 46% version, here is proof positive how extra strength helps. The oily intensity of the honey is sufficient to see off the budding oak bitterness, And how....!!!! 55.7%. Germany.

The Whisky Fair Highland Park Aged 19 Years Artist Edition bourbon hogshead, dist 88, bott 07 **(85) n21.5 t22 f20 b21.5.** All the usual honeyed suspects, but a tad oak bitter. 46%. Germany.

IMPERIAL
Speyside, 1897. Chivas. Silent.

Imperial Aged 15 Years "Special Distillery Bottling" db **(69) n17 t18 f17 b17.** At least one very poor cask, hot spirit and overly sweet. Apart from that it's wonderful. 46%

Battlehill Imperial 1998 (86.5) n22 t21.5 f21.5 b21.5. Lovely stuff, full of natural caramels – a bit like a Tunnocks with a kick. Perfect blending malt which shows attractively as a single. Impressed. 43%. Duncan Taylor.

Berry's' Own Selection Imperial 1976 Aged 29 Years (91) n23 tight little nose, excellent firm honey edge. Shows virtually no sign of wear and tear; **t23** again there is a clipped and polished element to the barley, steadfastly refusing to allow the oak to get too dominant; lovely hints of melon on the soft manuka honey; **f22** some toasty notes show that this whisky does doff its cap, if only briefly, to advancing years; **b23** unbelievably comfortable in old age; in human terms you'd have expected this to have had the full nip and tuck treatment. A wonderful cask. 46%. Berry Bros & Rudd.

Cadenhead's Chairman's Stock Imperial-Glenlivet Aged 29 Years bourbon hogshead, dist 1977, bott May 07 **(92) n22** excellent weight; the oak-barley interaction is spot- on; **t24** beautiful, near perfect delivery with masses of barley offering excellent variations of sweetness; the spices arrive on cue as does a touch of latte; **f23** the oak adds a drier touch, as it should after 30 years, but the toastiness fits well with the barley lead; **b23** Imperial by name and nature. 54.7%. 228 bottles.

Duncan Taylor Collection Imperial 1990 cask no. 352 **(88) n21** crisp, clean barley underscored by the dry custard powder; **t22** mouth-watering and again barley- rich with decent oils and oak buzz; **f22** delicious mocha fade; **b23** A juicy, sparkling Speysider with few pretensions and excellent overall style. 55.7%

Duncan Taylor Collection Imperial 1990 cask no. 353 **(75.5) n19 t20 f18 b18.5.** Uninspiring blending fodder. 53.9%

Duncan Taylor Collection Imperial 1990 cask no. 357 **(88.5) n22** a touch of gnarled oak but it can't dampen the malty intensity, soft bourbon tones drift around; **t23** fabulous – everything you could ask of a well aged Speysider rarely known for its complexity; **f21.5** Farley's Rusks and slow vanilla development; **b22** much more like it! The malt is thick and clean while the cask has contributed positively with soft peppers: this may be related to cask 353, but this is from another planet quality-wise. 53.4%

Duncan Taylor Collection Imperial 1990 cask no. 358 **(93) n23** red liquorice and toasted oak barrel with a cocoa and grist topping; **t23** seriously wonderful barley reveals rare clarity for its age, but is not content just to slip down, but attacks on the way; the middle shows a perfect bitter-sweet rendezvous; **f23.5** back to waves of barley assisted by some bourbony liquorice burnt honey; **b23.5** a bit of an edge to this one: some nip and bite and a wave or three of charming bourbon. My kind of malt. And the best Imperial bottled this year by a significant margin. *52.2%*

Duncan Taylor Collection Imperial 1990 cask no. 359 **(84.5) n20 t22.5 f21 b21.** Complexity? Forget it: just go for the ultra-malty ride. *53.1%*

⋄⋄⋄ **Duncan Taylor Collection Imperial 1990** cask no. 443 **(92) n22.5** custard powder on butterscotch. All on a bed of rich barley... **t23.5** simply caresses the tastebuds with long fingernails coated in honey-sweetened barley; spices fizz around to ensure a degree of belligerence to what could be simply too relaxing; **f23** long, with the barley melting into the vanilla in many improbable shades of sweetness; **b23** a superbly made malt. Imperial often gets a bad press for its quality and occasionally perceived blandness. Nonsense! I have always rated this distillery, and here you can see why. This is simply fabulous. *55%*

⋄⋄⋄ **Duncan Taylor Collection Imperial 1990** cask no. 445 **(91) n23** eyebrows raise as you immediately spot you are in for a treat: real depth to the clean malt; **t23** a wonderful gooseberry phase to this adds the perfect light fruit edge to the barley; **f22.5** thins as the vanilla arrives, but that lightly sweetened, vaguely fruity malt hangs about to the end with a touch of cocoa and butterscotch at the death; **b22.5** quite adorable. *53.1%. Duncan Taylor.*

⋄⋄⋄ **Duncan Taylor Collection Imperial 1990** cask no. 446 **(86) n21.5 t22 f21.5 b21.** A sharper, thinner, but no less malty version of cask 443. *53.7%*

⋄⋄⋄ **Duncan Taylor Collection Imperial 1990** cask no. 448 **(88.5) n22.5** a touch gluey but the barley is crisp with a sugared edge; bourbony; **t23** lilting barley goes through the sweetness gears without so much as a judder; eye-watering sharp, refreshing and salivating; **f21** the oak bites quickly as the body quickly thins; **b22** fades too quickly. Otherwise, a malty charmer. *55.7%*

⋄⋄⋄ **Duncan Taylor Collection Imperial 1990** cask no. 449 **(86.5) n21.5 t22 f21.5 b21.5.** Excellent barley theme and tense, at times, too. Plus a fine bourbony skit at the finish. A tad hot here and there, maybe. *53.4%. Duncan Taylor.*

Duncan Taylor The NC2 Range Imperial 1994 (84.5) n22 t22 f20 b20.5. Starts brightly with all kinds of clean, attractive Speysider phrases, but steadfastly refuses to open up. *46%*

Duncan Taylor The NC2 Range Imperial 1994 (86) n21 t22 f21 b22. just the right sprinkling of muscovado sugar accentuates the clean barley. Simple, clean and charming. *46%. nc ncf.*

Duncan Taylor The NC2 Range Imperial 1996 dist 96, bott 07 **(85) n21.5 t22 f20.5 b21.** Typical Imperial of its type: loads of wonderful, salivating barley to start and then no further development. Even so, charmingly attractive. *46%. nc ncf.*

Platinum Imperial Aged 25 Years dist 81, bott 07 **(67) n17 t17 f16 b17.** Another one from the sulphur mines of Jerez. *57.2%. Douglas Laing. 270 bottles.*

⋄⋄⋄ **Provenance Imperial Aged 12 Years** refill hogshead, dist summer 96, bott spring 09 **(84.5) n22 t21.5 f20 b21.** Light, airy, malty. Juicy barley early on delivery. *46%. Douglas Laing.*

⋄⋄⋄ **Provenance Imperial Aged 12 Years** refill barrel, dist spring 96, bott winter 08 **(88) n22** a shapely body with some toasty, soft smoke elements; **t23** some pulsing, salivating malt assisted by a clever sweetness carried on the oils; **f21.5** dryer with vanilla substituting for the barley; a touch bitter late on **b21.5** tasting this and another Prov. Imp. 12 together, the difference a good cask can make is clearly defined. *46%. Douglas Laing.*

Whisky-Doris Imperial 8 Years Old dist 18 Dec 98, bott 19 Oct 07 **(83) n20.5 t22.5 f20 b20.** Pleasantly malted but no special awards to the oak. *55.1%. Whisky-Doris.*

INCHGOWER
Speyside, 1872. Diageo. Working.

Cadenhead's Inchgower Aged 18 Years dist 89, bott Feb 08 **(76) n20 t19 f18 b19.** Evidence of peat on the nose but this mess of a malt never comes close to finding any rhythm or balance. Not an entirely hopeless case as there are some attractive, sharper elements to this but please don't look for anything inspiring; really for those who like a bit of rough. *57.6%. 290 bottles.*

⋄⋄⋄ **Connoisseurs Choice Inchgower 1993 (87.5) n21** a touch dirty, but some non specific phenols and grizzled malt ensures something interesting; **t22** chewy with the malt arriving in varying degrees of sweetness; excellent weight and flavour waves come thick and fast; **f22.5** long with some fudgy, maple syrup sweetness topping the more bitter oak very pleasantly, indeed; **b22** finding decent Inchgowers has been far from an easy task in recent years. Good ol' G&M have come to the rescue here, though, with a bottling bursting with character. *43%. Gordon & MacPhail.*

Demijohn Inchgower 1980 Single Cask (84) n20 t22 f21 b21. Inchgower at its most quarrelsome: a touch rubbery and swimming in spicy and mildly sulphured fighting sherry. That said there is a honeyed glow that compensates deliciously. *59.9%. Demijohn, UK.*

Duncan Taylor Collection Inchgower 1969 cask no. 6129 **(88) n23** Melted moist ginger cake. Weird, bizarre...unique; **t20** falls about slapstick style as the sweetness tries to outdo the oak: little shape or rhythm... but still works; **f23** now comes back into line with a return of the ginger, liberally sprinkled with moscovado sugar: fabulous... **b22** if, like me and my sons, you have a penchant for Jamaican ginger cake, here's a malt that will leave you aghast. Question is, was this whisky baked or distilled...? *46.2%.*

Duncan Taylor The NC2 Range Inchgower 1992 Aged 15 Years (86.5) n21 t22 f22 b21.5 Inchgower at its most respectable with lashings of clean, often sweet malt. Zero complexity, but you can't have everything: if you see the bottle, just buy the bloody thing because you might not get one in this delightful form again for a while. *46%*

Old Malt Cask Inchgower Aged 21 Years refill hogshead 3434, dist Jun 86, bott Dec 07 **(80.5) n22 t21 f18 b19.5.** The cask isn't the greatest, which is a shame because whilst decent malt from this distillery is getting increasingly more difficult to chance across, there was enough honey on the nose and delivery to hope-against-hope that I might just have found one. *50%. nc ncf. Douglas Laing. 240 bottles.*

◈ **Old Malt Cask Inchgower Aged 34 Years** dist Sep 74, bott Jul 09 **(91) n23** a balmy evening garden with honeysuckle sweetening the damp earthiness; violets and bluebells, too; **t22** chunky, lightly smoked, sweet and sprightly spiced; some liquorice amid the mushy cashews; **f23** chewy dates; lightly molassed; **b23** dating from the days when the distillery was in its pomp. And it shows. *50%. Douglas Laing*

Scotch Malt Whisky Society Cask 18.26 Aged 23 Years refill hogshead, dist Feb 85 **(76.5) n18 t19 f20 b19.5.** Some decent malty blows, but just so uninspiring and at times reveals itself as a not particularly well made whisky. *48.3%*

INVERLEVEN

Lowland, 1938–1991. Demolished.

Cadenhead's Dumbarton (Inverleven Stills) 18 Years Old (94) n22 old parchment and barley water; **t25** beautiful, intact malt that starts confidently but with a dozen graceful, mouthwatering sweeps of the palate becomes something intense and glorious. With a charming citric and barley fruitiness, too, this is sheer perfection as far as an 18-year-old Lowlander goes; **f23** the vanilla never overdoes it, though the barley backs off with the same grace with which it initially sweeps the palate; unsalted butter coats toasted fresh bread; **b24** while the label might be somewhat confusing, what isn't is the élan of this glorious bottling. Often the malt from this distillery was too light to withstand too long an inquisition from the oak; here it has not only survived but thrived. Not just stunning. But also outranked only by an exceptional Rosebank as Scottish Lowlander of the year. *57.9%*

◈ **Gordon & MacPhail Distillery Label Inverleven 1990 (87) n20** oddball stuff. Butyric, lemon-zesty, a touch of something juniper-ish...and in the background the faintest sound of smoke... **t23** the early malty delivery melts away towards the no less juicy citrus. As the middle approaches a phenolic element is introduced, a background weight which appears to see off the worst of any off notes the nose suggests might be on their way and offers an understated spicy buzz; **f22** long, vaguely smoked; light yet still plenty to chew over; more, lasting, hints of a jenever; **b22** absolutely unique version from this lost distillery: if I was a gambling man I'd say that this was filled into an old Laphroaig or Ardbeg cask, for there is a delicate smoky element that was never intended during mashing. Odd, also because the nose reveals a mild, butyric flaw...as well as unmistakable hints of gin/jenever. But as soon as it hits the tastebuds...my, oh my..!!! *40%.*

Rarest of the Rare Inverleven 1978 cask no. 1878, bott 08 **(90.5) n22.5** crushed grapefruit and orange pith: just so clean; **t23** soft barley at first, still showing those fruity elements, then a slow building on firmer, oakier foundations; **f22.5** long, sensual, almost perfectly weighted with exquisite bitter-sweet qualities; **b22.5** Inverleven never, ever, showed this kind of balls when younger and still alive. If it had, the distillery still might be standing. Hang on a minute... Allied...maybe not. *45.5%. Duncan Taylor.*

Rarest of the Rare Inverleven 1979 cask no. 5662 **(84) n20 t21 f22 b21.** Gravelled well in time. Won't trouble you so far as complexity is concerned. But you cannot be other than impressed with its sweet, malty confidence. A really charming Lowlander sadly lost to us. *53.7%. Duncan Taylor.*

⣿ **Rarest of the Rare Inverleven 1979** cask no. 5666 **(96) n23.5** more than an element of Kentucky as the sweeter oak notes sing freely. Lightened by clean citrus and mashed barley; **t24** spellbinding delivery: clean with a sublime concert of sweet-dry notes as the oak and barley harmonize with astonishing clarity for all the big age; there is even a wonderfully soft oil to help the flavours glide along; **f24.5** one of the most elegant finishes of the year: rather than simply fade and die like any good Lowland malt should do, this one actually comes to a crescendo, with all the aspects found on the early delivery now being delivered in heightened, concentrated form. Even when it does decide enough is enough, the final fade is as long as a Scottish midsummer evening... **b24** easily one of the best lowlanders I've come across in the last five years oozing nothing but sheer class. Beautifully made, wonderfully casked and no less than stunning in the glass. *56.2%. Duncan Taylor.*

Rarest of the Rare Inverleven 1979 cask no. 5667 **(88) n21.5** respectable oak involvement: the barley holds together well; **t22.5** salivating, prickly barley; clean with slow oaky vanilla leak; **f22** long, oils up gently but the barley refuses to cede to the drying, mocha-flaked vanilla; **b22** simply splendid stuff. *57%. Duncan Taylor.*

ISLE OF ARRAN
Highland (Island–Arran), 1995. Isle of Arran Distillers. Working.

The Arran Malt Under 10 Years Old db **(89) n22** limp, lush barley of the butterscotch variety; **t23** those stunning soft oils are working overtime to spread the sweet barley; **f22** long, biscuity and balanced; **b22** this one's kicked its shoes and socks off... *43%*

The Arran Malt Aged 10 Years L140206 db **(93) n23** charming, delicate; varying citrus notes hand-in-hand with rich, butterscotch-barley; the odd youthful note thins things out; t24 the palate coated in caressing oils, to which stick the cleanest and most profound barley. You can chew your jaw off here; **f23** developing vanillas dovetail with some of those younger new-makish notes but still cannot escape the clutches of the fat barley. Some fizzing spice decides to make an appearance; **b23** at last! The distillery feels confident enough to put an age statement to their malt, although it's been good enough to do that for the last four or five years. This bottling of some of Arran's first casks entertains and delight. It won't be long before the world's malt connoisseurs add Arran to their list of must haves. Because if it's character and quality you want, it's here by the malt shiel load. *46%. ncf.*

⣿ **The Arran Malt 12 Years Old** db **(85) n21.5 t22 f20.5 b21** Hmmmm. Surprise one, this. There must be more than one bottling already of this. The first I tasted was perhaps slightly on the oaky side but otherwise intact and salt-honeyed where need be. This one has a bit of a tang: very drinkable, but definitely a less than brilliant cask around. *46%*

The Arran Malt 100° Proof L210806 db **(91) n23** complex not just in aroma but weight: both firm yet soft; the barley offers varying degrees of intensity. Youthful and deeply desirable; **t23** just so barley rich! That lovely hint of youth embracing something older and more oakily complex as it develops; the early barley offers a fruit edge, some natural toffees and then cocoas develop; **f22** much drier, though with enough moistening barley, and waves of mocha; **b23** different, intriguing, style of Arran; some excellent use of bourbon cask allows a relaxed meeting of barley and oak. Sheer class. *57%. ncf.*

The Arran Malt Amarone Finish db **(96) n24** perhaps the best Arran nose of all time: dry rose-petaly Turkish Delight moistened with grape and toasted almond...then it starts getting really complex...! **t23** melt-in-the-mouth arrival with succulent grape and bitter-sweet apricot and nuts; **f24** beautiful chocolate and latte mix as the soft fruit tantalises even further; so long your tastebuds will be tested like they have never been tested before... **b25** a true gold nugget of a bottling. I'm astonished at its total brilliance. Trust the Italians to have a hand in something of such style. The Whisky Gentlemen of Verona will be very proud. *55%*

⣿ **The Arran Malt Ambassador's Choice** db **(87.5) n22** attractive, if a touch too dense as there seems little air for the barley fruit and oak to breathe; **t22** the tightness on the aroma is not part of your imagination: delivery is also claustrophobic, thanks mainly to the vastness of the tannins; **f21.5** barley, liquorice and a light hint of apricot; **b22** so heavy with oak I was amazed I could pick the nosing glass up... *46%*

The Arran Malt Bordeaux Finish db **(90) n22** awkward and cumbersome, though the salty element appeals; **t23** wonderful delivery on gently fruited malt, but then it unravels clumsily and falls apart to reveal its intricate workings; **f22** the eclectic style here continues with a burnt raisin and chocolate finale; **b23** bloody hell! I'm exhausted after that lot. Whatever balance it has is by fluke rather than design. Never settles down and the palate can't quite get a grip. Yet we have a slapdash masterpiece. Arran has gone all French with its Calvados, Bordeaux and Cognac finishes. This is probably the most intriguing of the lot. And the unconventional colour should appeal in San Francisco, Soho and Sydney.... *59.6%.*

The Arran Bourbon Cask 1996 cask no. 2125 dist Dec 96, bott Jun 07 db **(91.5) n23** the intensity of the barley forms a fruity front; **t22.5** trademark Arran soft oil and then that barley again goes into overdrive; **f23** the simplistic develops into complexity as vanilla and citrus add their charms **b23** all you could ask from a bourbon cask – plus a dollop of something extra. 53.8%. 205 bottles.

⋄ **The Arran Malt Bourbon Single Cask 1998** cask no. 671 db **(94.5) n24** superb tangerine topping to the oak-thickened malt: sublime... **t24** weight of malt and mouth delivery rarely gets better than this: just a soupcon of oil coats the tastebuds allowing this perfect sharp'n'sweet barley a perfect footing. The oak has arrived in just the right numbers to both add a drier element and a spicy base line; **f23** lightens as the citrus notes reappear and thin the vanilla; **b23.5** my gut instinct is that Arran is just about at its best at 10-11 years in bourbon cask, and here is a bottling which does little to change my mind. Brilliantly made malt in a very fine bourbon cask. What a superstar. 58%

⋄ **The Arran Malt Bourbon Single Cask 1998** cask no. 675 db **(85.5) n22 t20.5 f22 b21.** Similar, beautifully made malt to 671 (above) but the cask is more fragile and offers flattening caramels where the livelier citrus ought to be... 57.5%

⋄ **The Arran Malt Bourbon Single Cask 1998** cask no. 682 db **(88.5) n22** soft vanilla, a hint of marmalade and plenty of natural caramel and barley; **t21.5** busy delivery with early spices and some sharp barley; the middle slips into neutral; **f23** readjusts as some drier oak notes arrive, somehow engaging the sharper barley tones in the process. Long and intriguingly complex; **b22** at times conservative, there is enough life in the cask to lift the barley. 46%

The Arran Malt Bourgogne Finish db **(74) n18 t19 f18 b19.** Arran Malt Vinegar more like... 56.4%

The Arran Malt Chianti Classico Riserva Cask Finish db **(85) n19 t23 f21 b22.** Mamma mia; there eeza poco zolfo ina mia malto!! Butta chicco d'uva, ee eez eccellente! 55%

The Arran Malt Fino Sherry Cask Finish db **(82.5) n21 t20 f21 b20.5.** Pretty tight with the bitterness not being properly compensated for. 50%

The Arran Malt Fontalloro Wine Cask Finish db **(84.5) n20 t22 f21.5 b21.** For a wine cask, the malt really does sing. 55%

The Arran Malt Grand Cru Champagne Finish db **(87) n21** dry; **t22** bitter-sweet winey-oak then a breakthrough of trad Arran; **f22** that barley oiliness continues with the fruitiness all but lost, other than a late dry soft wine echo; **b22** recognisable as Arran. And the ghost of champagnes past hang unmistakably on the palate. 58.9%

The Arran Malt Lepanto PX Brandy Finish db **(85) n22 t22 f20 b21.** Tight, unusually thin for an Arran, but some lovely sweet fruit amid the confusion. Pretty oaky, too. 59%

⋄ **The Arran Malt Madeira Wine Cask Finish** db **(77.5) n19 t21 f18.5 b19.** The odd exultant moment but generally flat, flaky and bitter. 50%

The Arran Malt Moscatel Cask Finish db **(87) n22** immensely dense with the barley drowned out by lush grape; **t21.5** big delivery, a touch stodgy with a real mushy grape feel to this, sweet with the faintest barley SOS visible; **f22** pretty stretched grape with a degree of warming spices; **b21.5** Arran is pretty full bodied stuff when just left to its own devices. In this kind of finish it heads towards an almost syrupy texture. Luckily, the grape effect works fine. 55%

⋄ **The Arran Malt Pineau des Charentes Cask Finish** db **(94) n22.5** wispy barley clouds in a bright, sweet-grapey sky; **t24** succulent and spicy. Delivery is first class, allowing full weight to the grassy barley before those fuller, fruitier notes close in. The spices are fabulously subtle and mildly puckering; **f23.5** a real chocolate dessert helped by the slow build up of soft oils; **b24** I may not be the greatest fan of cask finishes, but when one comes along like this, exhibiting such excellence, I'll be the first to doff my hat. 55%

⋄ **The Arran Malt Pinot Noir Cask Finish** db **(73.5) n18 t19 f18 b18.5.** A less than efficient cask from the Germans who produced it. Plenty of off key moments on nose and taste, but it does enjoy a too brief, barely redeeming Bird's Angel Delight chocolaty moment. 50%

⋄ **The Arran Malt Pomerol Cask Finish Bordeux wine casks** db **(86.5) n20 t23 f22 b21.5.** Although the cask is very marginally flawed, the relentlessness of the sweet, juicy grape and barley is a sheer delight. The odd cocoa note does no harm either. 50%

The Arran Malt Premier Cru Bourgogne Cask Finish db **(86) n21 t22 f21 b22.** An entertaining dram which some would do somersaults for, but marks docked because we have lost the unique Arran character. 56.4%

⋄ **The Arran Malt Robert Burns 250 Years Anniversary Edition** db **(91.5) n22.5** mainly floral with just a light touch from the barley; **t23.5** unusually light and flighty in body: most unArran...!! A dusting of castor sugar softens the vanilla even further: juicy, a touch spicy and quite wonderful; **f22.5** a few oils had formed towards the middle and follow through to the end. Again it is barley dominant with a squeeze of something citrussy; **b23** curiously, not that far away from the light Lowland style of malt produced in the 60s and 70s in Burns' native Lowlands. Not the usual Arran, but shows that it can change personality now and again and still be a total charmer. *43%*

∴ **The Arran Malt St. Emilion Cask Finish** Grand Cru Classé wine casks db **(89) n24** huge aroma: thick grape and big fruitcake. The vanillas have a toasted feel to them; crisped hazelnut, too; **t22** almost too big and busy as the intensity of the grape and the roastiness of the oak clash. But a fabulous river of sweet barley flows freely enough once it gets past the early dam; **f21.5** muscovado and grapey sugars see off some threatening bitterness but it is still a bit on the heavy side; **b21.5** not the best balanced whisky you'll ever pour. But such is the sheer force of flavours, you have to doff your beret... *50%*

The Arran Malt Sassicaia Wine Cask Finish db **(92.5) n22.5** gin-like botanicals only minus the juniper; **t23.5** crisp and initially oil-free for an Arran with wonderful, expressive strata of citrus and spice; amazingly sharp and lively; **f23** a curiously smoky note develops as the barley softens and opens up towards a mocha, oaky fade. The spices, if anything, become pricklier; **b23.5** unquestionably one of Arran's better wine finishes. *55%*

The Arran Malt Sauternes Finish db **(84) n21 t22 f20 b21.** Strap yourself in for this one: eye-watering sultana and 240 volts of spice. Choked with oak, though. *56%*

The Arran Malt Sherry Single Cask cask no. 1860, dist 27 Nov 96 bott Jan 08 db **(94.5) n23** brown and black liquorice allsorts; spiced grape; **t23.5** rich, lightly oiled delivery, the grape building in intensity allows good barley-vanilla penetration; beautifully balanced and complex; **f24** delicate, drying confidently; tantalising mocha and custard; **b24** blazingly beautiful: outwardly big sherry but in fact just so delicate....one of the great Arrans. *56.2%. 233 bottles. Bottled for The Nectar, Belgium.*

The Arran Malt Single Bourbon Cask 1996 ex-bourbon barrel cask no. 2092 db **(71) n17 t19 f17 b18.** Not the greatest cask ever to grace Arran. *54.4%*

The Arran Malt Single Bourbon Cask 1996 ex-bourbon barrel cask no. 2125 db **(91) n24** stunning barley-oak interaction: rarely comes more delicate from this distillery; the subtle degree of sweetness borders perfection; **t22.5** immediately juicy, then an oaky spice buzz; the complexity lessens as soft oils arrive; **f22** natural caramels and vanilla; **b22.5** beautifully constructed whisky which cranks up the barley complexity up to max. *53.8%*

The Arran Malt Single Sherry Cask 1996 ex-sherry butt cask no. 1760 db **(85) n22 t20.5 f21.5 b21.** Pretty too heavy with the malt having to battle through the grape. Lots of liquorice, though. *573%*

The Arran Single Sherry Cask 1998 cask no. 24 dist Jan 98, bott Feb 07 db **(88) n22** firm, almost solid barley with gentle fruit accompaniment; **t22** the trademark Arran oil silts up every tastebud with barley; the fruit happens along as an afterthought; **f22** cocoa by the warehouseload; **b22** a wonderful example of how very good whisky is made. *58.7%. 669 bottles.*

The Arran Malt Single Sherry Cask 1998 ex-sherry butt cask no. 89 db **(89) n23** whatever sherry this was from, it was dry... **t23** sexy, super-spiced grape from the off; vanilla soon develops; **f21** fattens; **b22** clean and classy. *56.9%*

The Arran Malt Single Sherry Cask 1998 ex-sherry butt cask no. 84 db **(72) n18.5 t19 f16.5 b18.** Nope...! *56%*

∴ **The Arran Malt Single Sherry Cask 1998** cask no. 724 db **(73) n17 t20 f18 b18.** Massive – and what otherwise would certainly have been outstanding - sweet grape juice tries to fight off the worst of the sulphur excesses. But it is asking too much. *573%*

∴ **The Arran Malt Single Sherry Cask 1998** cask no. 353 db **(94.5) n25** made and matured in Grenada...? Ginger and allspice at the double...; kiwi fruit and papaya add to the tropical theme. But somehow there is room for honey in there, too: light, watered manuka and soft toasted honeycomb...one of the noses of the year, for sure; **t23.5** much more bite and spite on the delivery than the silky nose, but then there had to be. Early delivery really juicy with the barley – which hardly features as an aroma – making an early statement before the countless waves of soft, diced fruit cocktail take hold; an annoying bitterness creeps in slightly upsetting the papaya cart; **f22.5** that bitterness continues but still cannot entirely dampen the lush, fruitier tones which fade gracefully; **b23.5** oh, it is just so rare to come across sherry butts unspoiled by sulphur these days I could weep for joy when I find one like this. I immediately nosed its partner (724) afterwards and could thrash myself with a thorned twig because it is a complete negative of it. *53%*

The Arran Malt Single Sherry Cask 1998 ex-sherry butt cask no. 450 db **(91.5) n22.5** pretty well oaked for age; the grape is fat and fulsome; **t23** big, thumping fruit; just like cask 89 the spices go into overdrive; slowly citrus follows through; **f23** rhubarb tart and custard; the lightest sprinkling of muscovado sugar; **b23** absolutely top-notch. Just underlines this distillery's class. *53.6%*

The Arran Malt Tokaji Aszu Wine Cask Finish db **(83) n20 t21.5 f21 b20.5.** Pleasant enough, but the wine dulls the more interesting edges. *55%*

Isle of Arran 'Jons Utvalgte' Aged 7 Years db **(87) n22** intense malt with trace vanilla; t21.5 tangy malt thickens; **f22** a touch of spiced butterscotch and vanilla adds relief to the full on barley; **b21.5** The clean intensity of the malt is soup-like. *46%. Norway.*

⋯ **A.D. Rattray Arran 1996** cask no. 723 **(71.5) n17.5 t18 f18 b18.** Oops. A dodgy, sulphury, cask has slipped through the very early Arran net. *55.7%*

Berrys' Own Selection Arran 1996 cask no. 462, bott 07 **(77) n18 t21 f19 b19.** I'd put any money on this cask having sat empty in the sun and rain for a few months before being filled. A pity as the malt itself is/was complex. *54.6%. Berry Bros & Rudd.*

Berrys' Own Selection Arran 1996 cask no. 1507, bott 07 **(85) n21 t22 f21 b21.** Simple malt. *46%. Berry Bros & Rudd.*

Cadenhead's Authentic Collection Arran Aged 11 Years fino sherry hogshead, dist 96, bott May 07 **(94) n23** unsmoked bacon sizzling beside grits and grapes; **t24** perfect barley with the most sublime and varied sweet tones imaginable; almost Warholesque the way the malt is painted in so many shades; **f23** long with a scaled down version, except now some spice and vanilla; **b24** Arran can always be relied on for beauty, though not always complexity. This has both – and in buckets. *56%. 330 bottles.*

Connoisseurs Choice Arran 1998 (88) n21 lime squeezed over barley; **t23** that big Arran malt kick; **f22** a trickle of custard into the barley; **b22** not the most complex Arran, but no faulting its barley breeze *43%. Gordon & MacPhail.*

Duncan Taylor The NC2 Range Isle of Arran db **(80) n20 t21 f19 b20.** Clunks around a bit for all the heavy oils. *56%. nc ncf.*

Master of Malt Arran 12 Years Old Cask Strength (91.5) n22 thick briny malt; **t22** exactly the same effect on the palate, except here there is much more citrus, albeit hiding behind the barley; **f24** now really comes into its own as the delicate sweetness helps envelope the palate with the malt, leading to a cocoa-rich fanfare; **b23.5** this, certainly towards the finish, is exactly how I imagine whisky from this distillery should be. Uncanny. *55%. Master of Malt, UK.*

Norse Cask Selection Arran 1996 cask no. 2108 **(73.5) n17.5 t20 f18 b18.** Hot whisky thanks to a very poor cask. *58.3%. Qualityworld, Denmark.*

Norse Cask Selection Arran 1996 Aged 11 Years puncheon cask no. 1637, dist 96, bott Sep 07 **(82.5) n21 t21 f20 b20.** Sharp and juicy but not helped by poor oak. *56.5%. nc ncf. 577 bottles. Qualityworld, Denmark.*

Old Malt Cask Arran Aged 11 Years refill hogshead no. 3931, dist Dec 95, bott Oct 07 **(87.5) n22** crisp barley; softly gristy; **t21** sweet, soft oils; **f22.5** long with furthering oils and the barley getting into concentrate proportions; **b22** pretty simplistic, but just works wonderfully. *50%. nc ncf. Douglas Laing. 355 bottles.*

Old Malt Cask Arran Aged 11 Years dist Nov 95, bott Feb 07 **(91) n22** clean, buzzy malt; **t23** sparkling, spicy then usual thick maltfest middle; faultlessly intense and so delicious... **f23** an endless strand of barley intertwines with the peppery fade; **b23** if this whisky was a person, it'd be that bloke who puts you to shame because he's so damned nice... *50%. Douglas Laing. 422 bottles.*

⋯ **Old Malt Cask Arran Aged 12 Years** refill puncheon, dist Sep 96, bott Dec 08 **(73) n18 t19 f18 b18.** Furry, flat and out of sorts. *50%. Douglas Laing. 687 bottles.*

⋯ **Premier Barrel Arran Aged 12 Years (81) n22 t21 f19 b19.** Fine, malty nose and a juicy delivery but the cask cracks rather. *46%. Douglas Laing. 369 bottles.*

Provenance Arran Aged 9 Years sherry hogshead no. 4271, dist autumn 98, bott spring 08 **(84.5) n21.5 t21 f21 b21.** Light, malty and clean. *46%. nc ncf. Douglas Laing.*

⋯ **Provenance Arran Aged 10 Years** refill hogshead, dist summer 98, bott autumn 08 **(90) n22** simple yet ultra-attractive sweet malt with just the right amount of custard powdered on; **t23** the barley sugar really is so attractive; intense and not a single note out of place; **f22.5** a touch of oil lengthens matters and helps the malt and vanilla gel; **b22.5** this distillery appears to manage excellence effortlessly. *46%. Douglas Laing.*

Provenance Arran Aged 10 Years Sherry Finish dist spring 97, bott spring 07 **(91) n23** more rum than sherry; **t23** again the influence appears to be from a sweet, high quality rum cask as the varying sugars collide; **f22** vanilla cream; **b23** for a sherry- casked whisky, this is as rummy as it gets. Beautiful malt. *46%. Douglas Laing.*

⋯ **Provenance Arran Aged 11 Years** refill hogshead, dist spring 97, bott winter 09 **(87) n21** a tad light this by Arran standards, with the oak ensuring bite; **t22** fizzy, lively delivery with the oak having a real go at the barley's dominance; **f22.5** for a while that threatened, austere oak wins, but then comes a final and irresistible cavalry charge of rich barley.... **b21.5** not the distillery's finest hour, but enough in there to enjoy and savour. *46%. Douglas Laing.*

Scotch Malt Whisky Society Cask 121.19 Aged 9 Years refill butt, dist Jan 98 **(92) n22 t24 f23 b23** One of the most intensely malty island drams you are ever likely to unearth. 57.4%

Scotch Malt Whisky Society Cask 121.20 Aged 9 Years refill butt, dist Jan 98 **(91) n23 t23 f22 b23** I must be going mad: but there really are some curry oils attached to the finish here, too. Don't let the owners of Whyte and MacKay get hold of this, or bang goes Arran's independence....!! 56.5%

⋄⋄⋄ **Scotch Malt Whisky Society Cask 121.28 Aged 11 Years** refill butt, dist Jan 98 **(91.5) n23** sublime light fruitcake; a kind of mix between a cherry Madeira and undercooked Dundee... **t23.5** enormous delivery of malt with a real cocoa and dark cherry back up; there is a superb spice fizz which helps accentuate the lightness of the vanilla against the backdrop of raisins and prunes. This is Arran at its most absorbing and delicious... **f22** the late honeycomb fade is a very unusual aspect of this distillery, and one that sits well with the richness of body; yet more cherry cake...with plenty of cherries and the molassed excellence of a Melton Hunt cake; **b23** were this not for the very slightest of sulphury tangs on both nose and finish in particular this might have been one of the best Arrans yet. Even despite the blemish the delicate sophistication of the sherry is monumentally impressive. 53.3%

⋄⋄⋄ **Victoria Single Malt Club Arran 10 Years Old** sherry refill, cask no. 374, dist 98, bott 08 **(94) n23.5** although from refill sherry, there is almost a bourbony character to this, with substantial oaky toffee and spice and a dab of red liquorice; the grape appears in top toffee-apple guise; **t24** the malt cascades in the juiciest form, giving just a cursory nod to some soft fruit; vanilla arrives early for a 10-year-old and that playful bourbony feel starts again... **f23** long, a little sharp and still able to keep the saliva buds on full alert; **b23.5** always one of the better experiences of whisky tasting when you come across an in-form Arran like this. 55.8%. Canada.

ISLE OF JURA

Highland (Island–Jura), 1810. Whyte and Mackay. Working.

Isle of Jura 5 Years Old 1999 db **(83) n19 t23 f21 b20.** Absolutely enormously peated, but has reached that awkward time in its life when it is massively sweet and as well balanced as a two-hour-old foal. 46% The Whisky Exchange

Isle of Jura 10 Years Old db **(80.5) n19 t21 f20 b20.5.** For a distillery located pretty close to the startling Paps of Jura, how can anything be this flat....? 40% ⊙⊙

⋄⋄⋄ **Isle of Jura Mountain of Gold 15 Years Old** Pinot Noir cask finish db **(67.5) n15 t18 f17 b17.5.** Not for the first time a Jura seriously hamstrung by sulphur - for all its honeyed sweetness and promise: there are some amazingly brilliant casks in there tragically wasted. And my tastebuds partially crocked because of it. Depressing. 46%. 1366 bottles.

⋄⋄⋄ **Isle of Jura Mountain of Sound 15 Years Old** Cabernet Sauvignon finish db **(81) n20 t21.5 f19.5 b20.** Pretty quiet. 43%

⋄⋄⋄ **Isle of Jura The Sacred Mountain 15 Years Old** Barolo finish db **(89.5) n21.5** tight, not exactly on song but enough salty, sultry, sherry-esque notes to keep you amused; **t24** good grief...! Didn't expect to be confronted by this beauty...the entire mouth is engaged from kick off with the fresh grape appearing to really attack the roof. The barley and spice intermingle firstly among themselves and then interweave with the salty wine effect. The result is clean, juicy, a textbook balance of sugars to oak, and, overall, is absolutely first class; **f21.5** dulls down as toffee creeps in but not without a fight from the (very late on furry) grape, spice and deft mocha: after all the excitement it's all over too quickly...I believe some people will recognise that feeling... **b22.5** hoo-bloody-rah! One of the three from this series has actually managed to raise my pulse. Not, it must be said, without the odd fault here and there. But there really is a stunning interaction between the grape and barley that sets the nerves twitching: at its height this is about as entertaining a malt as I've come across for some time and should be on everyone's list for a jolly jaunt for the taste buds. Just when I was beginning to lose faith in this distillery... 43%

Isle of Jura 16 Years Old db **(78.5) n19 t20.5 f19 b20.** I had hoped that this dram would have moved on from the last few lacklustre glasses I quaffed here and there. Nope. Still flatters to deceive with the odd honeyed turn, but nowhere near enough breeziness to pull itself away from the doldrums. The odd feint doesn't help, either. 40% ⊙⊙

Isle of Jura 21 Years Old Cask Strength db **(92) n22** something hard and grainy against the ultra-clean fruit; **t24** fabulous mouth arrival, just such a brilliant fruit-spice combo held together in a malty soup; **f23** long and intensely malty; **b23** every mouthful exudes class and quality. A must-have for Scottish Island collector ... or those who know how to appreciate a damn fine malt 58.1%

⋄⋄⋄ **Isle of Jura 30 Years Old** db **(89) n22.5** a touch of orange peel and mildly overcooked yam: soft, intriguing and pepped up further by the beginnings of a few sweet bourbony notes; **t22.5** the delivery flutters onto the palate. It's a pretty delicate encounter, perhaps softened by a touch of cream toffee but there is enough life in the juicy citrus and layered barley to get the tongue exploring; spices soon begin to pop around the palate as some vanilla encroaches; **f22** chewy, toffeed, fat and still a touch of spicy feistiness; **b22** a relaxed dram with the caramel dousing the higher notes just as they started to get very interesting. If there is a way of bringing down these presumably natural caramels – it is a 30 years old, so who in their right mind would add colouring? – this would score very highly, indeed. *40%*

Isle of Jura 40 Years Old finished in Oloroso sherry wood db **(90) n23** a different species of Jura from anything you are likely to have seen before: swamped in sherry, there is a vague, rather odd smokiness to this. Not to mention salty, sea-side rockpools. As a pairing (sherry and smoke), the odd couple... which works and doesn't work at the same time. Strange... **t22** syrupy sweet delivery with thick waves of fruit and then an apologetic 'ahem' from the smoke, which drifts in nervously. Again, everything is awkward... **f22** remains soft and velvety, though now strands of bitter, salty oak and molasses drift in and out; **b23** throw the Jura textbooks away. This is something very different. Completely out of sync in so many ways, but... *40%*

Isle of Jura 1974 db **(87.5) n23** big, clean molassed fruit and polished floor overture; **t22.5** every bit as silky on delivery with oak increasing in intensity with each flavour wave...then stops... **f20.5** curiously vanishes off the palate: no oak coming through...just seems to disappear save some echoes of vanilla and toffeed barley... **b21.5** stick your nose in this and enjoy those very first outstanding moments on delivery. *42%*

Jura Elements "Air" db **(76) n19.5 t19 f18.5 b19.** Initially, I thought this was earth: there is something strangely dirty and flat about both nose and delivery. Plenty of fruits here and there but just doesn't get the pulse racing at all. *45%*

Jura Elements "Earth" db **(89) n23.5** peat at you from all directions: thick and earthy, as the name implies. A unique style and intensity with something of the farmyard and a strange kind of off-note which somehow works. The spirit looks pretty young to me and this ruggedness has worked in its favour; **t22** massive juicy barley is stalked by menacing peat; there are laid-back ultra soft spices but a dullness has arrived towards the middle; **f21.5** smoked caramel tops the shy vanillas; **b22** I haven't spoken to blender Richard Paterson about these whiskies yet. No doubt I'll be greeted with a knee on the nuts for declaring two of these as duds. My guess is that this is the youngest of the quartet by a distance and that is probably why it is the best. The peat profile is very different and challenging. I'd still love to see this in its natural plumage as the caramel really does put the brakes on the complexity and development. Otherwise we could have had an elementary classic. *45%*

Jura Elements "Fire" db **(86.5) n22.5 t21.5 f21 b21.5.** Pleasant fare, the highlight coming with the vaguely Canadian-style nose thanks to a classic toffee-oak mix well known east of the Rockies. Some botanicals also there to be sniffed at while a few busy oaky notes pep up the barley-juiced delivery, too. Sadly, just a shade too toffee dependent. *45%*

Jura Elements "Water" db **(73.5) n18.5 t19 f18 b18.** What a shame. Oranges by the box-full trying to get out but the mouth is sent into puckering spasm by the same sulphur which spoils the nose. *50%*

Jura Superstition db **(86) n21 t22 f20 b23.** A rare case of where the whole is better than the parts. A malt that wins through because of a superb balance between peat and sweeter barley. Distinctive to the point of being almost unique. *45%*

⋅⋅⋅ **Jura Superstition** db **(75) n18 t21.5 f17.5 b18.** The last time I had Superstition it was still at 45% and a pretty enjoyable dram...with a few flaws but a hell of a lot of character. Then this.....THIS...!!! First you have to come to terms with a nose uniquely blended from feints and peat; then for a few glorious moments on delivery it threatens to burst out into a honeyed, vaguely smoky rhapsody in gold. But instead of taking me on a thrilling journey, we are shunted off into a multi-story car park....with the exit barriers stuck. This is a dead end whisky. If it's flavour and excitement you are looking for, forget Superstition and try some Super Stilton (white, of course) with Dickenson and Morris Pork Pie (made at Melton only, naturally) and a pint of Grainstore Cooking or (if you must have your dose of caramel) Phipps IPA. Now that is what your taste buds are really for.... *43%*

Connoisseurs Choice Jura 1992 (89) n23 delicate and complex: pecan nut on butterscotch tart; the background noise is floral (with a distant hint of lavender) plus a dash of citrus; **t22.5** intense barley going through the gears of sweetness; **f21.5** clean vanilla with a pulse of spice; **b22** if only all Jura were this expressive and clean. *43%. Gordon & MacPhail*

Old Malt Cask Jura Aged 15 Years (89) n22.5 a lemon sherbet effervescence and uncluttered barley; **t23** divine delivery: massive malt fizzing and foaming on the palate; **f21.5** bitter oak intervenes but still the malt bustles on; **b22** just shows what Jura sans caramel can do: absolutely brimming with life, vitality and charm. *50%. Douglas Laing.*

Old Malt Cask Jura Aged 16 Years refill hogshead no. 3841, dist Feb 91, bott Aug 07 **(79.5) n19 t21 f19.5 b20.** Plenty of barley and sugars in there do battle with the oak. *50%. nc ncf. Douglas Laing. 332 bottles.*

⟐ **Old Malt Cask Jura Aged 16 Years** refill barrel, dist Oct 92, bott Apr 09 **(91.5) n24** absolutely beautiful malt: clean, the very lightest trace of sweet peat and seasoned with salt and a dab of allspice; **t23.5** salivating and juiced up, the barley reveals a wonderful clarity while the smoke drifts around lightly stroking the tastebuds. The most subtle oils makes a gentle experience softer still... **f22** touches of vanilla and still that lazy phenol; a hint of bitterness is the evidence of a cask under any stress; **b22** ah...if only more Juras were like this... *50%. Douglas Laing. 323 bottles.*

Old Masters Isle of Jura Aged 15 Years cask no. 1934, dist 92, bott 07 **(88.5) n22 t23 f21 b22.5** Just about an action replay of the OMC 15 above. I can't believe the two aren't closely related and for a while warehouse mates. *53.9%. James MacArthur & Co. Ltd.*

Provenance Jura Aged 11 Years refill hogshead, cask no. 3710, dist Nov 95, bott summer 07 **(80.5) n19 t21 f20.5 b20.** Ultra sweet barley. *46%. nc, ncf. Douglas Laing.*

⟐ **Scotch Malt Whisky Society Cask 31.18 Aged 20 Years** refill hogshead, dist Apr 88 **(89) n21.5** under-ripe gooseberry crushed in the fingers; **t23** some wonderful elements to this, especially the coarseness to the malt and salty oak which battle viciously at times for supremacy; at other times tight and restricted in direction; **f22.5** big late, delicious chocolate surge; **b22** a Jekyll and Hyde distillery at the best of times and here you get a feel of that in just one bottle. A fine, salty tang, though; like taking a mouthful of the Atlantic. *56.2%*

Scott's Selection Isle of Jura 1989 bott 07 **(90) n22.5** almost like a sweetened corn oil; **t23** mouth-filling, barley-packed, juicy and just all-round yummy; **f22** heads towards vanilla and Jaffa cake; **b22.5** now that was an enjoyable Jura!! *59.6%*

KILCHOMAN
Islay, 2006. Working.
Kilchoman New Spirit bourbon cask, dist 27.7.07 bott 24.9.07 db **(93.5) n23.5 t24 f23 b23.** Not whisky at all, of course, as that has to spend three years in cask. So I have marked this as new(ish) spirit, complete with slight yellowing. And following on from the last first-class sample I tasted, confirmation that there is no doubting this malt will be an excellent addition to the Islay family. Superb stuff. *63.5%.*

Kilchoman New Spirit bourbon/sherry, dist 6 Dec 06 db **(94) n23 t24 f23 b24.** Not whisky at all, but new make that has, I understand, spent a few weeks in wood and is for sale at the distillery. And there is no doubting: this is quite beautifully – and, technically, faultlessly - made spirit, far better than the owner could possibly have hoped for, and which, if this is an average sample of this new Islay make, bodes exceptionally well for the future. *63.5%*

KILKERRAN
Campbeltown, 2004. J&A Mitchell & Co. Working.
Kilkerran Single Malt db **(80) n19** very young, slightly Shredded Wheaty, a touch of tobacco leaf, mint and some heavy oils; **t20** ungainly arrival with big barley, big oils, big natural caramel; **f21** settles towards a light, slightly sweeter and gristier fade; **b20** Glyngyle's first offering doesn't rip up any trees. And maybe the odd flaw to its character that you won't see when the distillery is fine-tuned. But this is the first-ever bottling from this brand new Campbeltown distillery and therefore its chances of being a worldbeater as an untried and untested 3-y-o were pretty slim. I will be watching its development with relish. And with heart pounding... *46%. Available exclusively from distillery direct from cask.*

Kilkerran Single Malt bott 22 May 07 db **(84) n20** bit of an oily, vaguely feinty beast with the odd note that is a bit rowdy and coarse. But the malt intensity cannot be denied; **t21** massive delivery of barley aided and abetted by puffed-up oils and a delightful coppery sharpness unique to new stills; **f22** better balance with the very first signs of oak intrusion in the barley which is showing some sugary teeth; **b21** sadly, I was out of the country and couldn't attend the Coming of Age of Kilkerran, when its first casks turned three and became whisky. Very kindly, they sent me a bottle as if I was there and, therefore, these are the notes of the very first bottling handed out to visitors. Interestingly, there is a marked similarity in distillery style to the 46% bottling in that the malt offers a crescendo of quality. This is only three year old whisky, of course, and its fingerprints will alter as it spends longer in the cask. *62%. nc ncf.*

⟐ **Kilkerran 'Work in Progress'** db **(88) n22.5** youthful, malty and a pinch of salt creeping into this one.. **t22** a simple malty delivery is the prologue to a simple, barley-rich tale. Dries to a surprising degree after the initial quick burst of barley sugar with the vanillas kicking hard, followed even by some spice; **f21.5** lots of natural caramel with the malt; **b22** doing very well. *46%*

KNOCKANDO

Speyside, 1898. Diageo. Working.

Knockando 1994 Aged 12 Years db **(86) n22 t22 f21 b21.** An usually light bottling for Diageo. Here you get full exploration of the attractive, malty skeleton. But Knockando has a tendency towards dryness and the casks here oblige rather too well. A delicate dram all the same. *43%*

⫶ **Knockando Aged 12 Years** dist 95 db **(71.5) n16 t19 f18 b18.5.** If there was an award for Worst Nose of the Year, this must be somewhere in the running. *43%*

Knockando Aged 18 Years sherry casks, dist 87 db **(77) n19 t21 f18 b19.** Bland and docile. Someone wake me up. *43%*

Knockando 1990 db **(83) n21 t22 f20 b20.** The most fruity Knockando I've come across with some attractive salty notes. Dry, but a little extra malty sweetness these days. *40%*

Duncan Taylor Collection Knockando 1980 cask no. 1910 **(95) n24** now we are talking connoisseur stuff: that's not to put down the newcomers to whisky, because that is the last thing I'll ever do and everything against what I'm about. But you've had to have been around a bit to appreciate the rarity of barley-oak balance here. Trust me: this kind of delicate horse-trading between the elements is a one in 250 event... **t23.5** the delivery is a scaled down version of the nose with the barley at first all juice and sweetness and then bristling, drier oaks dry to dominate; the remainder is balance and counter-balance...; the odd citrus note can be detected from time to time; **f23.5** slightly salty as the vanillas dig deep with a toasty dryness. But some muscovado sugar is lurking, nectarish and to the rescue...; **b24** the one reservation I have always held about this malt is its degree of dryness. Here is a rare example of the barley offering sufficient sweetness to see it into great age. Now this really is sophistication. *49.1%*

Duncan Taylor Collection Knockando 1980 cask no. 1911 **(84.5) n21.5 t22 f20 b21.** Relatively dull except for the odd juicy moment. Not bad but very much the poorer relation. *46.7%*

Duncan Taylor Collection Knockando 1980 cask no. 1912, dist Jul 80 **(81) n21 t21 f19 b20.** Sharp and exotically bitter. *46%.*

⫶ **Old Malt Cask Knockando Aged 14 Years** bourbon barrel, dist Sep 94, bott Jan 09 **(83.5) n19 t22.5 f21 b21.** Very sweet for a Knockando with a big barley sugar theme, despite the misfiring nose. *50%. Douglas Laing. 357 bottles.*

KNOCKDHU

Speyside, 1894. Inver House. Working.

AnCnoc 12 Year Old db **(90) n22** an aggressive pepperiness bites deep into the usual grassy maltiness and coal smoke. Excellent depth and complexity, though slightly more aggressive, if younger, in style than of old; **t23** absolutely fabulous, near-perfect, malt arrival, perhaps the most clean, yet intense of any in Scotland. The complexity is staggering with not only multi-layers of malt but a distant peat and oak infusion; **f22** deliciously spicy; **b23** if there is a more complete 12-year-old Speyside malt on the market, I have yet to find it. A malt that should adorn a shelf in every whisky-drinking home.

AnCnoc 13 Year Old Highland Selection db **(85) n21 t23 f20 b21.** A big Knockdhu, but something is dulling the complexity. *46%*

AnCnoc 16 Years Old db **(90.5) n22** a comfortable marriage of gentle, zesty barley and softer oak-induced liquorice and vanilla; as it warms and oxidizes a move towards bourbon is detected with some toast and honey in evidence; **t23** luxurious, deftly oiled delivery with the bourbon effect really taking hold: liquorice and hickory give extra depth to the soft brown sugars; **f22.5** decent length with more sugared barley and spice develops before unwelcome toffee takes up valuable space and reduces the complexity, drier vanillas are allowed to take full control; **b23** ignore the tasting notes on the label: it is a much better whisky than it suggests... *46%. nc ncf.*

AnCnoc 26 Years Old Highland Selection db **(89) n23** profound. Everything is big, but perfectly proportioned: massive grapey fruit and malt concentrate; **t22** pure Knockdhu: intense malt carrying some beautiful spices and an obscure but refreshing fruit; **f23** the lull after a minor storm: rich vanilla and echoes of malt; **b21** there is a little flat moment between the middle and finish for which I have chipped off a point or two. That apart, superb. *48.2%*

AnCnoc 30 Years Old db **(85) n21** pipe smoke, old leather armchairs and a sprig of mint: this seems older than its years, **t23** wonderfully thick malt, beefed up in intensity by drawing in as much oak as it comfortably can; the honeycomb and molassed sweetness adds a lovely touch; **f19** big natural caramel and some pretty rough-stuff oak; **b22** seat-of-the-pants whisky that is just on the turn. Still has a twinkle in the eye, though. 49%

An Cnoc 1993 db **(89) n22** butterscotch on shortbread pastry and barley sugar interweaves attractively with the trademark soft honey note and the very lightest whiff of something vaguely smoky; **t21** surprising oak charge arrives early, bringing with it spices and soft oils; **f24** it's the finish that makes this one with a late – and highly unusual – intervention of citrus to help lighten the oaky load and emphasise the richness of the barley; **b22** quite an odd one this. I have tasted it a couple of times with different samples and there is a variance. This one takes an oakier path and then invites the barley to do its stuff. Delicious, but underscores the deft touch of the standard 12-year-old. 46%

AnCnoc 1994 db **(88.5) n22.5** yessiree, some real ol' Kentuck' in that thar nose...but the barley is full on, too; **t22.5** toffee apple delivery with some juicy barley and lazy spice; **f21.5** crème brulee and butterscotch, helped along with vanilla: dessert anyone...? **b22** coasts through effortlessly, showing the odd flash of brilliance here and there. Just get the feeling that it never quite gets out of third gear... 46%. ncf.

Knockdhu 23 Years Old db **(94) n23 t24 f23 b24.** Pass the smelling salts. This is whisky to knock you out. A malt that confirms Knockdhu as not simply one of the great Speysiders, but unquestionably among the world's elite. 57.4%

Harrods Knockdhu Aged 12 Years (84) n19 t23 f21 b21. One can assume only that caramel (or an exceptional dull sherry cask) has been added here because it is otherwise impossible to find such a flat nose from a Knockdhu. However, the arrival on the palate is bliss, with dates combining with glossy honey and marzipan, but again the finish is only a dull echo of what it should be. Shackled greatness. 40%.

LAGAVULIN
Islay, 1816. Diageo. Working.

Lagavulin 12 Years Old 7th release, bott 07 db **(92.5) n23** there is almost a tenderness to the peat smoke – almost...; a wisp of something citrussy lightens the intensity further. Though an intensity not to be confused with this distillery's 12-y-o of a decade ago; **t23** blemish-free and beautifully constructed, the delivery holds a delicate oiliness which boosts the unusually dry peat; every segment of the experience appears to be structured and in tune with the custardy oak; **f23** a hint and nip of spice here and there, a faint degree of juniper on the smoke and a sprinkle of cocoa; **b23.5** brooding, enigmatic and just pulsing with quiet sophistication. A dram to drink quietly so all can be heard in the glass... 56.4%

⋅⋅⋅⋅ **Lagavulin 12 Year Old** 8th release, bott 08 db **(94.5) n24** heady mixture of coal dust and peat reek, quite dry but not without some fried banana sweetness in the most delicate terms possible; **t24.5** a lightly oiled landing allows the peats to glide around the palate with minimal friction; a light dusting of hickory powder works well with the big, but by no means brooding phenols; the sweetness levels are just about perfect; **f22.5** surprisingly short with a dull toffee flourish to the smoke; **b23.5** sensational malt: simply by doing all the simple things rather brilliantly. 56.4%

Lagavulin Aged 16 Years db **(95) n24 t24 f23 b24.** Much more like the Lagavulin of old with unfettered development and delivery. Befitting the great distillery this unquestionably is. Forget some previous disappointing bottlings: this is the real thing! 43%

Lagavulin Aged 16 Years The Distillers Edition Pedro Ximenez cask, dist 91, bott 07 db **(83) n22 t21 f20 b20.** I have oft stated that peat and sherry are uncomfortable bed-fellows. Here, the two, both obviously from fine stock and not without some individual attraction, manage to successfully cancel each other out. One is hard pressed to imagine any Lagavulin this dull. 43%

Lagavulin 21 Years Old bott 07 db **(96) n24.5** the aroma is pure distillery: just emptied washbacks; the kiln being cleaned of its peat and coke ash; a musty, dank warehouse, especially one where a few sherry butts are hanging around... **t24** no prisoners taken as a semi-sweet grapiness slides directly into a huge wall of peat and biscuity barley: the shockwaves reverberate around the tastebuds with a big bitter-sweet whack with spices heading off on various tangents; **f23** long with much bigger, thicker peat than the 12-y-o seeing off a succession of grapey-vanilla enquiries. That dry ashy taste only those of us who have cleaned out myriad peat fires on a regular basis will appreciate, is there in force; although drying in waves there is enough fruit and barley to keep the sweetness at desired levels; **b24.5** this is rough and ready malt of extraordinary character. It would be easy to dismiss this as off-key and unbalanced. To be honest, I did on the first to third tastings. But something about it bothered me: I was being too pedantic and failing to see the whisky for what exactly it is. So I tried again, clearing my mind in the process. I was rewarded handsomely. This is not a malt that is for those looking for a handsome time of it: this is

Islay malt warts and all and almost brought me back to where I came in over a quarter of a century ago. It somehow encapsulates the stormy disposition of the island and its closeness to nature. For those of you who have struggled with this, let me show you my first notes before I twigged what this was all about and tuned in on the right wavelength. It shows what happens when you are tired and you are hunting on the wrong frequency.... (80) n19 t20 f22 b19 Big peat and grape rarely work comfortably together and here we a have malt which struggles from the nose to finish to make some kind of sense of itself. There will be some Islayphiles who will doubtless drool at this and while certain aspects of the finish are quite excellent the balance never appears to come into focus. *56.5%*

Lagavulin 30 Years Old special releases 06, dist 76 db **(91) n22 t23 f23 b23.** A malt that at first sniff appears a shade past its best repays closer inspection. *52.6%*

LAPHROAIG

Islay, 1820. Fortune Brands. Working.

Laphroaig 10 Years Old db **(91) n22** less intense smoke; **t24** much silkier delivery than usual with the sweetness all up front as the peat dovetails in and out of the barley – more complex; **f22** a drier finale with a shade more caramel; **b23** I discovered these 20cl 43% bottlings just after it was announced they were to be phased out. I also noticed that the whisky inside them had a slightly different character from the standard bottlings... *43%* ⊙

Laphroaig 10 Years Old Original Cask Strength (with UK Government's Sensible Drinking Limits boxed on back label) db **(92) n22** a duller nose than usual: caramel reducing the normal iodine kick; **t24** recovers supremely for the early delivery with some stunning black peppers exploding all over the palate leaving behind a trail of peat smoke; the controlled sweetness to the barley is sublime; **f23** again there is a caramel edge to the finish, but this does not entirely prevent a fizzing finale: **b23** caramel apart. this is much truer to form than one or two or more recent bottlings, aided by the fresh, gristy sweetness and explosive spices. Wonderful! *55.7%*

Laphroaig Aged 15 Years db **(79) n20 t20 f19 b20.** A hugely disappointing, lacklustre dram that is oily and woefully short on complexity. Not what one comes to expect either from this distillery or age. *43%*

⠿ **Laphroaig 18 Years Old** db **(94) n24** multi-layered smokiness: there are soft, flightier, sweeter notes and a duller, earthier peat ingrained with salt and leather; **t23.5** perhaps it's the big leg-up from the rampant hickory, but the peat here offers a vague Fisherman's Friend cough sweet quality far more usually associated with Bowmore, except here it comes in a milder, Demerara-sweetened form with a few strands of liquorice helping that hickory to a gentler level; **f23** soft oils help keep some late, slightly juicy barley notes on track while the peat dances off with some spices to niggle the roof of the mouth and a few odd areas of the tongue; **b23.5** this is Laphroaig's replacement to the woefully inadequate and gutless 15-year-old. And talk about taking a giant step in the right direction. Absolutely brimming with character and panache, from the first molecules escaping the bottle as you pour to the very final ember dying on the middle of your tongue. This is as noisily Islay as a sky-blackening invasion of White-fronted Geese or rain pelting against your cottage windows. Relentlessly first class. *48%*

Laphroaig Aged 25 Years db **(94) n23** the clean - almost prim and proper - fruit appears to have somehow given a lift to the iodine character and accentuated it to maximum effect. The result is something much younger than the label demands and not immediately recognisable as Islay, either. But no less dangerously enticing... **t24** the grapes ensure the peat is met by a salivating palate; particularly impressive is the way the sweet peat slowly finds its footing and spreads beautifully; **f23.5** no shortage of cocoa: a kind of peaty fruit and nut chocolate bar... **b23.5** like the 27-y-o, an Islay which doesn't suffer for sherry involvement. Very different from a standard, bourbon barrel-aged Laphroaig with much of the usually complexity reined in, though its development is first class. This one's all about effect - and it works a treat! *40%*

Laphroaig 27 Years Old sherry cask, dist 80, bott 07 db **(94.5) n24** the sherry is ridiculously clean considering the vintage yet neither fruit nor smoke cloud the way of the other – a fabulous freak of its type, perhaps, but more likely to be the result of great distilling and cask selection... **t23.5** again, a collector's item to find sherry of this age coming across so fresh and intense, especially with such major peat to deal with; the result is clear bright and rich and just full of that unique Melton Hunt Cake roasty fruitiness; wonderfully spiced throughout; **f23** delicate viscosity clinging to every crevice in your mouth. Dark coffee, though never bitters out and moves into mocha mode: a real chewy dram; **b24** one of the better examples of big sherry and big peat working in close harmony without the usual bristling stand off. A real class act. *57.4%. nc. 972 bottles.*

Laphroaig Aged 30 Years db **(94) n24 t23 f23 b24.** The best Laphroaig of all time? Nope, because the 40-y-o is perhaps better still... just. However, Laphroaig of this subtlety and charm gives even the very finest Ardbeg a run for its money. A sheer treat that should be bottled at greater strength. *43%*

Laphroaig Aged 40 Years db **(94) n23 t24 f23 b24.** Mind-blowing. A malt that defies all logic and theory to be in this kind of shape at such enormous age. The Jane Fonda of Islay whisky. *43%*

Laphroaig 1994 Islay Festival of Malt and Music 2006 db **(90) n22 t23 f22 b23.** A beautifully complex malt and one not depending on peat alone for charm and charisma. A pleasant touch, this coming from casks filled (as an apprentice) and emptied by new distillery manager John Campbell. *56%. 600 bottles.*

Laphroaig 1/4 Cask db **(95) n22** burning embers of peat in a crofter's fireplace; sweet intense malt and lovely, refreshing citrus as well; **t24** mouthwatering, mouth-filling and mouth-astounding: the perfect weight of the smoke has no problems filling every crevice of the palate; builds towards a sensationally sweet maltiness at the middle; **f24** really long, and dries appropriately with smoke and spice. Classic Laphroaig: **b25** a great distillery back to its awesome, if a little sweet, self. Layer upon layer of sexed-up peatiness, this is the closest to how I remember it some 30 years ago! *48%* ☉

⟐ **A.D. Rattray Laphroaig 1996** cask no. 7290 **(81) n19.5 t21 f20.5 b20.** Long finish, but should have quit whilst it was ahead... *60.3%*

⟐ **Berry's Own Selection Laphroaig 1990** bott 08 **(73) n17 t20 f18 b18.** Both nose and finish are disasters. Though there is a brief sweet peated revival on delivery, it is not enough to save this from being a rare Berry's dud. *55.6%. Berry Bros & Rudd.*

⟐ **Berry's Own Selection Laphroaig 1998** bott 09 **(87) n21.5** dry, spluttering peat fires; **t22** finely tuned peat-liquorice combo; **f21.5** reverts to drier self through the late signature of weak golden syrup; **b22** simple but effective. *58.7%. Berry Bros & Rudd.*

Chieftain's Laphroaig 1997 chateau la Nethe finish, dist Oct 97 **(77) n19 t20 f19 b19.** Dull and off key. The nose even has a weird stale beer touch to it... I really fail to see how a classic distillery such as this needs the help of an obscure French vineyard..... ! An irritating way to mark the 800th new whisky of the book. *46%. nc ncf. Ian Macleod.*

The Creative Whisky Company Exclusive Malts Laphroaig 1998 Aged 8 Years cask no. 103, dist Dec 98 **(90) n22 t23 f22.5 b22.5.** A bruiser for its age. *53.7%.*

⟐ **Exclusive Casks Laphroaig 1996 Aged 12 Years (79.5) n22 t20 f18.5 b19.** The charming nose gives a subtle hint of the impending fire waters to be overcome. This is bloody hot stuff...! *52.4%. Chester Whisky & Liqueur Co.*

⟐ **Hart Brothers Laphroaig Aged 18 Years** dist Apr 90, bott Jun 08 **(90.5) n23.5** salty, cindery peat; a butterscotch flourish; **t23** superb delivery with excellent degree of citrussy sweetness to vanilla and smoke: classy layering; **f22** long, dries, back with a salty tang, a touch of liquorice but the malt remains intact; **b22.5** high quality whisky with effortless complexity. *46%. Hart Brothers Limited.*

⟐ **Kingsbury's Laphroaig 1990 18 Years Old** Cask Strength **(86) n22 t21.5 f21.5 b21.** The tight, ashy nose – with circling light citrus - is followed by the most cramped of deliveries where the hot barley grunts firm peat. Only towards the finish, where some natural caramels soften and sweeten, is there any room for complexity; but in finding it, a slight bitter oak note is revealed, too. *53.9%. Japan Import System.*

Montgomerie's Laphroaig 1990 (86.5) n22 t22 f21 b21.5. Laphroaig can from cask to cask be a touch lethargic. Here is one such dram. Loads of citrus and grist, this would have made decent blending fodder. But for those not looking to be shaken to their boots and want to be charmed instead, here you go. *46%. Montgomery & Co. Ltd.*

⟐ **Montgomerie's Laphroaig 1990** cask no. M586, dist Oct 90, bott Jun 07 **(86) n22 t22 f20.5 b21.5.** Sweet, buxom smoky malt softly oiled and spiced in the right places. *46%.*

Norse Cask Selection Laphroaig 1987 Aged 18 Years hogshead ref. DL1763 **(92) n24** peat and acacia honey have rarely gone so fittingly hand in hand...dank bluebell woods for good measure; **t23** how cruel: the brain is immediately engaged by that honey first spotted on the nose then...kaboom!! An explosion of spices of legendary dimensions; **f22** still tingling and warming, though things settle for the peat to have a louder say; **b23** someone dropped a jar of honey into this cask...! *48.3%. WhiskyOwner.com, Denmark.*

⟐ **Old Malt Cask Laphroaig Aged 12 Years** refill hogshead, dist Oct 96, bott Feb 09 **(76.5) n18 t20.5 f19 b19.** What little influence the cask has is not particularly positive. *50%.*

Old Malt Cask Laphroaig Aged 13 Years refill hogshead, dist Sep 94, bott Nov 07 **(87) n22** sweetish oily smoke; **t22** smoky, oily and sweet; **f21** oily sweet smoke; **b22** a dram not in the mood for complexity.... *50%. nc ncf. Douglas Laing. 370 bottles.*

Old Malt Cask Laphroaig Aged 13 Years refill hogshead, cask no. 4419, dist Sep 94, bott Jun 08 **(88.5) n23** dry, sooty; **t22** reluctantly sweeter at first, then the malty sugars blossom; **f21.5** dries, vanilla; **b22** clean, delicate and undemanding. *50%. nc ncf. Douglas Laing. 333 bottles.*

Old Malt Cask Laphroaig Aged 15 Years refill butt no. 3701, dist Apr 92, bott Jun 07 **(82) n21 t22 f19 b20.** Big peat but the bitterness reveals the end of a cask. *50%. Douglas Laing. 688 bottles.*

Old Malt Cask Laphroaig Aged 15 Years refill hogshead, cask no. 4066, dist 92, bott Dec 07 **(84.5) n21.5 t21.5 f20.5 b21.5.** Fragile oak but the complex peats are a treat. *50%. Douglas Laing.*

Old Malt Cask Laphroaig Aged 15 Years refill hogshead no. 3932, dist Apr 92, bott Oct 07 **(85) n20 t21.5 f22 b21.5.** Attractive, softly oiled and negotiates some less than perfect oak with complex aplomb. *50%. nc ncf. Douglas Laing. 343 bottles.*

·❧· **Old Malt Cask Laphroaig Aged 15 Years** refill hogshead, dist Mar 93, bott Aug 08 **(90) n22.5** busy with a decent peat prickle; **t23** beautiful oils link the sweeter gristy notes with the more lavish honeyed oak; beautifully paced and balanced; **f22** liquorice and a touch of hickory dry proceedings and add the required ballast; **b22.5** a malt which benefits from a good quality cask to match the even higher distilling: a delightful and complex experience. What a shame the distillery's own 15-y-o could not match this. *50%. Douglas Laing. 352 bottles.*

·❧· **Old Malt Cask Laphroaig Aged 16 Years** refill butt, dist Apr 92, bott Jan 09 **(75) n17 t19.5 f19.5 b19.** Sweet, fat, rather shapeless and never quite gets its act together. *50%. Douglas Laing. 691 bottles.*

Old Malt Cask Laphroaig Aged 18 Years refill hogshead no. 3974, dist Nov 89, bott Nov 07 **(88.5) n23** pure peat ash; **t21.5** sweet, gristy but some really wonderful citrus moments; **f22** long, entirely non-oiled so the fade is down to the complex inter-play between smoke and gristy barley; **b22** a lightweight in some ways but the seduction is wonderful. *50%. nc ncf. Douglas Laing. 288 bottles.*

Old Malt Cask Laphroaig Aged 18 Years (84.5) n21 t22 f20.5 b21. Pleasant, light, gristy malt. Does its best not to be noticed. *50%. Douglas Laing*

Old Malt Cask Laphroaig Aged 18 Years (89) n22.5 dry, ashy, tight: fabulous...! **t22** firm barley is backed by a tat-a-tat strafing of spices on the tastebuds; some citrus lightens things; **f22** the spice grumbles on, as do those sharp, almost fresh-cut grassy, notes; **b22.5** hard to believe the age of this guy. Take the one away and you'd believe it: absolutely no oak spoiling the show. *50%. Douglas Laing.*

·❧· **Old Malt Cask Laphroaig Aged 18 Years** refill hogshead, dist Nov 89, bott Aug 08 **(92.5) n23.5** beautifully interlaced sweetness and dryness to the peat: a sprig of lavender and a small cube of chocolate fudge helps lighten the earthier backbone; **t23.5** quite beautiful delivery with the peat a constant, a regular full but not over demanding presence; again the sweet-dry delicate liquorice delivery pushes all the right buttons; **f22.5** a very even fade, again with the peat taking the lead and pulsing gently to the finish; a few delicate dark sugars balance the vanillas: technically spot on for the age; **b23** classic for age and distillery. *50%. Douglas Laing. 229 bottles.*

Old Malt Cask Laphroaig Aged 19 Years rum barrel no. 3804, dist Mar 88, bott Aug 07 **(90) n23** sharp, precise sugars home in on the decadent peats: you can only wonder what happens next... **t22** the sugars take over the asylum for a while; the delivery is sweet and delicate while the peats appear to be in a sulk; **f22.5** some spices suggest a peaty fight-back, vanillas try to dry matters but still those nectarish notes are heard loudest; **b22.5** rum finishes do have curious ability to kick things around and produce attitude. No exception here with this very different slant on sweet peat. A one-off classic. *50%. Douglas Laing. 324 bottles.*

·❧· **Old Malt Cask Laphroaig Aged 20 Years** sherry hogshead, dist Mar 89, bott Apr 09 **(91) n23** a liberal dose of cream sherry gives the aroma real weight especially with the oak not willing to be outperformed, **t22** thick grape-smoke delivery, though perhaps missing rhythm early on; **f23.5** re-settles superbly for the best part of the experience with all three major players – grape, smoke and oak – interacting with a degree of suavity; **b22.5** weighty yet works with an improbable degree of harmony given the major players looking for top billing. *50%. Douglas Laing.259 bottles.*

·❧· **Old Malt Cask Laphroaig Aged 21 Years** refill hogshead, dist Nov 87, bott Jan 09 **(77.5) n20.5 t20 f18 b19.** Aggressive in part despite the sugary mask. *50%. Douglas Laing. 439 bottles.*

·❧· **Old Malt Cask Laphroaig Aged 21 Years** rum barrel, dist Mar 88, bott Apr 09 **(84) n21 t20.5 f21.5 b21.** Very sharp, very sweet and very brittle, the smoke gets lost somewhere along the way, re-emerging late on....very. *50%. Douglas Laing. 311 bottles.*

⁘ **Premier Barrel Laphroaig Aged 7 Years** dist May 01, bott Feb 09 **(83.5) n23.5 t21 f19 b20.** Despite the tired, bitter cask finish, this is one to simply stick your snout in. *46%. Douglas Laing. 366 bottles.*

⁘ **Premier Barrel Laphroaig Aged 7 Years (85.5) n20.5 t22 f22 b21.** From an unprepossessing nose comes a malt with a lot to say for itself. The peat is orderly and the fudge on the finish is a smoky delight. *46%. Douglas Laing. 370 bottles.*

Premier Barrel Laphroaig Aged 8 Years (85.5) n22 t21.5 f21 b21. Decent, gristy fare. *46.0%. nc ncf. Douglas Laing. 374 bottles.*

Premier Barrel Laphroaig Aged 8 Years (86) n21 t22 f22 b21. Sparkling, gently spiced and lazily peated. *46%. Douglas Laing. 371 bottles.*

Premier Barrel Laphroaig Aged 9 Years (89.5) n23 textbook powdery peat and delicate coastal qualities: stick your beak in this for a while... **t23** small peaty explosions at first then a huge wave of juicy young barley; **f21.5** oily and closed to development; **b22** some of the elements which make this up are pure, unadulterated joy....and I think the age is the key. *46%. Douglas Laing.*

Provenance Laphroaig Aged 8 Years refill hogshead no. 3868-3869, dist autumn 98, bott autumn 07 **(88) n22.5** seriously floral with a few pot still tequila notes thrown in; **t23** clean, sweet, gristy with a touch of attitude to the smoke; **f21** vanillas and smoke; **b21.5** bit of a mixed up kid but really lovely. *46%. Douglas Laing.*

Provenance Laphroaig Aged 8 Years refill hogshead no. 4203, dist summer 99, bott spring 08 **(88) n22** plenty of peat fire ash and agave; **t22.5** gristy, young with tender citrus; **f22** gentle, vanilla and delicate smoke; **b21.5** very similar to the previous Prov Laphroaig. Quality identical, characteristics similar but reaches same point from slightly different direction. *46%. nc ncf. Douglas Laing.*

Provenance Laphroaig Aged 8 Years dist autumn 98, bott winter 07 **(90) n22** defies belief just how downy-soft peat can sometimes be; **t23** grassy barley and dissolving peat on entry. Like being caressed in your half-sleep; **f23** long, softly smoked with green, almost limey tinge to the peat; **b22** distilling and maturation of the top order allowing the true charisma of the distillery to shine. *46%. Douglas Laing.*

⁘ **Provenance Laphroaig Aged 8 Years** refill hogshead, dist spring 01, bott spring 09 **(88) n21** non-committal but delicate; **t23** deft integration of muscovado sugars and smoke with a stunning liquorice follow through; **f22** a slow rising of spices adds an edge to the dusty but sweet smoke; **b22** lots of whisky to get your tastebuds round despite the limited oak influence. But clean and compelling throughout with just the right amount of oomph. *46%.*

⁘ **Provenance Laphroaig Aged 10 Years** refill hogshead, dist autumn 98, bott winter 09 **(87.5) n21** is there a cleaner, lighter Laphroaig...? **t22.5** the entire outline of the malt is bounded by sweet, gristy sugars; the inner notes are pillow-soft peat; **f22** stays on its most gentle course despite the vanillas getting a bit frantic; **b22** a real pussycat. *46%. Douglas Laing.*

Robert Burns Laphroaig 9 Years Old (90.5) n24 quite superb; lots of peat apparently cut from deeper parts of the bog; huge salt kick, too; **t22.5** youthful delivery with as much citrus as there is smoke; **f22** soft vanilla, caressing smoke and developing hickory; **b22** a whisky beyond its years. *53.6%. TasTToe, Belgium. 87 bottles.*

Scotch Malt Whisky Society Cask 29.66 Aged 18 Years refill butt, dist Nov 89 **(83.5) n21.5 t20 f21 b21.** Hmmm! Nothing like the quality I'd expect...Overly aggressive. *53.7%*

Scotch Malt Whisky Society Cask 29.67 Aged 16 Years refill butt, dist Oct 91 **(84) n21 t23 f19 b21.** Appears to be some grape flouncing about with the massive peat. Not exactly a marriage in heaven, but the shear enormity of it all makes for a tale to tell over dinner. Oh, some gooseberry pops up from time to time, by the way... off-key off-beat and actually at times unpleasant; this most likely is a faulty cask. "Love it or hate it..." their advertising blurb went (without crediting or paying me, the swine!). In this case, like me, you'll probably do both. Whoever is choosing the Laphroaig casks needs a kick up the arse. *53.5%*

Scotch Malt Whisky Society Cask 29.68 Aged 18 Years refill butt, dist Nov 89 **(90.5) n22.5 t23 f22.5 b22.5** The balance between sweet and dry is rarely better. There is no mistaking this distillery's fingerprint of excellence. *54%*

⁘ **Scotch Malt Whisky Society Cask 29.74 Aged 18 Years** refill hogshead, dist Oct 90 **(85) n21 t22 f21 b21.** Pleasant, sweet, lightly peated and a tad monotonous. *51.5%*

⁘ **Scotch Malt Whisky Society Cask 29.75 Aged 18 Years** refill hogshead, dist Oct 90 **(90.5) n21.5** salty, lightly smoked and teasingly unbalanced; **t23.5** absolutely jives on the palate with a lively flurry of nibbling, sharp peaty notes partnered by a sweet muscovado-barley theme. Surprisingly salivating; **f22.5** even the old-grand-dad vanillas have a spring to their step; **b23** top rank entertainment from a cask which is the antitheses of its fuddy-duddy stay-at-home sister 29.74. *51.5%*

⬙ **Scotch Malt Whisky Society Cask 29.76 Aged 18 Years** refill hogshead, dist Oct 90 **(84.5) n21.5 t21.5 f21 b20.5.** Rotund, sweet and caramel-clad. *51.3%*

⬙ **The Whisky Agency Laphroaig 8 Year Old** dist 01, bott 09 **(89) n22** a Highland hearth; **t23** crisp barley at first, sweet smoke with a light salty tang; **f22** oils out slightly while the phenols take their time to disperse; **b22** exactly the kind of young, near flawless dram you should have in your hand at a ceilidh...and in the other, a woman of a similar description. *59.1%. The Whisky Agency, Germany.*

⬙ **The Whisky Agency Laphroaig 12 Year Old** dist 96, bott 09 **(81) n23 t21 f18 b19.** Superb nose with all kinds of complex ashy possibilities. But the cask errs on the unfriendly side with a disappointing degree of bitterness. *56.9%. The Whisky Agency, Germany.*

⬙ **The Whisky Agency Laphroaig 18 Year Old** dist 90, bott 08 **(88) n22** clean barley, clean smoke and good balance between oils and ash; **t22** again, more battles between bitter-sweet and oils and ash...beautifully made malt, that's for sure; **f22** the oils win as the vanillas are absorbed; **b22** not entirely complex of the flavour front, but certainly in composition and structure. *56%. The Whisky Agency, Germany.*

The Whisky Fair Laphroaig Aged 9 Years refill sherry butt, dist 88, bott 07 **(92) n24** nose just about identical to the Tasttoe bottling; **t23** now though it really digs deep on the palate; the peats are thick. Mildly cough sweetie and spiced; **f22.5** camp coffee and hickory; **b22.5** a kind of bigger more full-on version of Tasttoe. Wonderful. *56.7%. The Whisky Fair.*

⬙ **The Whisky Fair Laphroaig 1998** bott 09 **(82) n21 t20 f21 b20.** Peaty and pleasant. But far too fat, oily, sweet and graceless for greatness. *57.1%. The Whisky Fair, Germany.*

LINKWOOD
Speyside, 1820. Diageo. Working.

Linkwood 12 Years Old db **(79) n21 t22 f17 b19.** Not a patch on previous bottlings, with the usual clarity lost to a very confused fruit-caramel theme. Especially on the finish. *43%*

⬙ **Linkwood 26 Year Old** Port Finish dist 81, bott 08 db **(85) n20 t24 f20.5 b20.5.** Can't say that either nose or finish do it for me. But the delivery is brilliant: the enormity and luxurious sweetness of the grape leaves you simply purring and rolling your eyes in delight. *56.9%*

⬙ **Linkwood 26 Year Old** Rum Finish dist 81, bott 08 db **(89.5) n23.5** sharp, flinty; enticing nose prickle; **t23.5** lots of juice, then a touch of spruce as the oak kicks in; the sweetness is delicate and softer on development than many rum finishes; **f21** becomes dependent on cream toffee; **b21.5** a real touch of the rum toffee raisin candy to this one. *56.5%*

⬙ **Linkwood 26 Year Old** Sweet red Wine dist 81, bott 08 db **(89) n22.5** punchy, salty and lively; distinct sherry-custard trifle; wine and oak together spin out the spice; **t23** perky delivery, again with spice to the fore; juicy grape and a lively layering of oak; **f21** dulls out slightly as it sweetens, again with a cream toffee softness; **b22** juicy, spicy: doesn't stint on complexity. *56.5%*

Linkwood 1974 Rare Malt db **(79) n20 t21 f19 b19.** Wobbles about the palate in search of a story and balance. Finds neither but some of the early moments, though warming, offer very decent malt. The best bit follows a couple of seconds after – and lasts as long. *55%*

⬙ **A.D. Rattray Linkwood 1983** cask no. 5711 **(86) n21 t22.5 f21.5 b21.** Very sweet. white sugar cubes dropped into a whisky toddy. Pleasant and well spiced. *53%*

Berry's Own Selection Linkwood 1985 casks no. 4545/4546, bott 07 **(87) n21** floral and fresh, the clean grassiness of the barley charms; **t22** typically hot for the distillery, but the palate is cooled by the intense maltiness aided by soft citrus; drying oaks also have a gentle part to play earlier than normal, **f22** wonderfully biscuity with an oat-meal dryness amid the barley; **b22** delicate and simplistic malt at first with a heavy emphasis on barley. But the richness of the malt, coupled with the gradual build up of prickly spices cannot do other than impress. Really charming stuff. *46%.*

⬙ **Berry's Own Selection Linkwood 1993** bott 07 **(83) n20.5 t21 f21 b20.5.** Malty, if standard, stuff. *46%. Berry Bros & Rudd.*

Cadenhead's Authentic Collection Linkwood Aged 18 Years sherry butt, dist 88, bott Feb 07 **(64) n17 t16 f15 b16.** The kind of sulphur taint that made this a distillery worth avoiding for so long. *58.7%. 660 bottles.*

Cask Strength Linkwood 1991 (86) n22 t21 f22 b21. There is a difference between spicy and hot whisky: this is hot. Even so, there is an intriguing and wholly delicious clump of peat attached to this – very unusual for Linkwood. Flawed in its making but you cannot but love its attitude or its odd brush with genius. A must experience malt. *52.5%. Gordon & MacPhail.*

Chieftain's Linkwood Aged 13 Years French oak **(72) n19 t18 f17 b18.** Overly sweet and latterly furry. *43%. Ian Macleod.*

Chieftain's Linkwood 15 Years Old fino sherry finish, dist Oct 92 **(71) n19 t18 f19 b19.** The incongruous strands of peat appear only to make this an even more muddled dram than usual. 46%. nc ncf. Ian Macleod Distillers.

Dewar Rattray Linkwood 1996 cask no. 3982, dist May 96, bott Mar 07 **(73) n18 t18 f19 b18.** Yet another dud from Linkwood. When are the Independents going to give younger malts from this distillery the widest berth possible? 57.7%

Dun Bheagan Linkwood 1993 14 Years Old bourbon cask no. 4702, dist April 93, bott 07 **(76) n18 t20 f19 b19.** If all the whiskies I tasted were this sweet I wouldn't have any teeth left by the time I'd finished writing the book... 56.1%. Ian Macleod Distillers. 300 bottles. Norwegian market.

Dun Bheagan Linkwood 1993 14 Years Old bourbon cask no. 4704, dist April 93, bott 07 **(84.5) n21 t21 f21 b21.5.** Distinctly more malt punching through the sugars. Attractively spiced, too. 56.6%. Ian Macleod Distillers. 306 bottles.

Gordon & MacPhail Linkwood 1972 (87) n22 burnt raisin, crisped barley; **t22** juicy fruit and barley mix: salivating but remains rock-hard; **f21** sharp, flinty, metallic at death; **b22** no yield to this hard-as-nails but fun bottling. 43%. Rare Vintage range.

⋅⋅⋅❖⋅⋅ **Hart Brothers Linkwood Aged 10 Years** dist Feb 98, bott Mar 08 **(91.5) n23** sprightly clean barley of the grassiest sweetest kind... **t22.5** mouth-watering if simplistically sweet and malt-driven; **f23** now some serious complexity as the oak wakes up and begins to create butterscotch and salt patterns...so the salivation continues... **b23** I had almost given up hope of seeing a Linkwood as good as this again. A ray of malty sunshine. 46%. Hart Brothers Limited.

Kingsbury Finest & Rarest Linkwood 32 Years Old 1973 bourbon cask **(92.5) n24** a surprise guest appearance by soft peat keeps the lid on a fruity, at times ethereal, number; wonderfully complex with the oak well manicured; **t23** silky, buzzing spices, a wave or three of big oak but again recedes as the juicy, rounded malts occupy the middle; **f22.5** dries as according to plan and another barely detectable wave of peat rumbles through; **b23** absolutely charming old malt at the limit of its powers. 49.5%. nc ncf. Japan Import System Co. Ltd.

Northern Light Linkwood 1995 Cask Strength port finish cask no. Q8311 **(77) n18.5 t19 f20 b19.5.** The nose is straight from the sweaty armpit school; the cloying sweetness takes some time to unravel. 51.2%. Qualityworld, Denmark.

Old Malt Cask Linkwood Aged 10 Years refill hogshead DL3539, dist Dec 1996, bott Apr 2007 **(75.5) n19 t19 f18.5 b19.** Not a bad dram. No off notes, other than the actual Linkwood persona. Just doesn't really say or do anything. 50%. nc ncf. Douglas Laing.

Old Malt Cask Linkwood Aged 18 Years dist May 88, bott Jan 07 **(85) n21 t21 f22 b21.** Too hot off the still ever to be a classic, but you can't but help loving the crushed Maltesers. 50%. Douglas Laing. 336 bottles.

Old Masters Linkwood Aged 18 Years cask no. 2011 dist 89, bott 07 **(86) n21 t22 f21.5 b21.5.** If in search of a decent, pretty unspoiled Linkwood, you could do a lot worse than this. Still oversweet and shapeless, but that's Linkwood for you. 50.1%. James MacArthur & Co. Ltd.

⋅⋅⋅❖⋅⋅ **Old Malt Cask Linkwood Aged 25 Years** refill hogshead, dist Apr 83, bott Oct 08 **(84.5) n22 t21.5 f21 b20.** Proof that whiskies can be too sweet. This one is like molten sugar bedeviled by spice. Have to say its enjoyable, but you can get too much of a good thing...!! 50%.

Provenance Linkwood Aged 10 Years dist winter 96, bott spring 07 **(84) n21 t21 f21 b21.** Clean, malty fare. Perfect for blending. 46%. Douglas Laing.

⋅⋅⋅❖⋅⋅ **Provenance Linkwood Aged 11 Years** bourbon barrel, dist spring 97, bott autumn 08 **(81.5) n20 t21 f20.5 b20.** Sugared almonds. Untaxing. 46%. Douglas Laing.

Scotch Malt Whisky Society Cask 39.65 Aged 11 Years refill barrel, dist May 96 **(82.5) n20 t22 f20 b20.5.** Malty, clean, sweet, citric, simple: the stuff of blends. 54.6%

⋅⋅⋅❖⋅⋅ **Scotch Malt Whisky Society Cask 39.69 Aged 26 Years** refill hogshead, dist Oct 82 **(87.5) n21.5** sharp barley; sharper oak; **t22** delightfully juicy, salivating and clean; **f22** attractive dusting of latte **b22** easy going and delicate. 55.8%

⋅⋅⋅❖⋅⋅ **Scotch Malt Whisky Society Cask 39.70 Aged 26 Years** refill hogshead, dist Oct 82 **(83) n20.5 t21.5 f21 b20.5.** Typical Linkwood maltiness; typical Linkwood unsympathetic cask. 55.9%

The Single Malts of Scotland Linkwood 1990 Aged 16 Years (78) n19 t21 f19 b19. Tired and unemotional stuff. 58.7%. sc cs. Speciality Drinks, UK.

LITTLEMILL

Lowland, 1772. Demolished.

Littlemill Aged 8 Years db **(84) n20 t22 f21 b21.** Aged 8 Years, claims the neck of the dumpy bottle, which shows a drawing of a distillery that no longer exists, as it has done for the last quarter of a century. Well, double that and you'll be a lot closer to the real age of this deliciously sweet, chewy and increasingly spicy chap. And it is about as far removed from the original 8-y-o fire-water it once was as is imaginable. 40%.

Littlemill 1964 db **(82) n21 t20 f21 b20.** A soft-natured, bourbony chap that shows little of the manic tendencies that made this one of Scotland's most-feared malts. Talk about mellowing with age... 40%

Berrys' Best Lowland Littlemill 12 Years Old (71) n17 t19 f17 b18. Astonishingly tame by Littlemill standards. But, though bad form to speak ill of the dead, pretty naff. 43%

Connoisseurs Choice Littlemill 1991 (73.5) n19 t18 f18.5 b18. Remind me never to wallpaper a room when I have a bottle of this with me. A momentary lapse of concentration could be disastrous for my insides...and the plaster. Yep: pure Littlemill! 43%. Gordon & MacPhail.

Dun Bheagan Littlemill Aged 21 Years Sherry Finish (74) n20 t19 f17 b18. Mutton dressed as lamb. 46%. Ian Macleod.

⊰⊱ **Hart Brothers Littlemill Aged 16 Years** dist Feb 92, bott Dec 08 **(81) n18 t21.5 f21 b20.5.** After all these years, and still the feints keep coming. This is probably worth buying, as it is history in a bottle: it shows you just how utterly inept they were at making Scotch style whisky at this distillery: this is pure European Holstein still malt. Actually, some of the oils caught up in this inject a pleasing chocolate note, so no question of it not being moderately enjoyable. 46%.

Murray McDavid Littlemill 1991 Aged 16 lot 07-1700 **(76.5) n18 t20 f19 b19.5.** The aroma gleefully strips all living flesh – and hair – from your nostrils. The big barley back up works for a while. 46%. Norway. 480 bottles.

Old Malt Cask Littlemill Aged 16 Years refill hogshead no. 4064, dist Oct 91, bott Jan 08 **(80.5) n18 t20.5 f21 b21.** Anorexic, naked barley. Relatively friendly and embracing by Littlemill standards. 50%.

Old Malt Cask Littlemill Aged 16 Years refill hogshead no. 3840, dist Mar 91, bott Aug 07 **(77) n18 t19 f20.5 b19.5.** Douglas Laing must be employing a Littlemill tamer among their staff. Another, clean, malty inoffensive if strictly limited bottling. 50%. Douglas Laing. 332 bottles.

Old Malt Cask Littlemill Aged 16 Years (89) n22 a rum, surely? **t23** no, the fist-fighting barley confirms the distillery, though the juiciness of the barley is a shock; **f21** thins down in house style but none of the usual rough edges; **b23** Littlemill as never been before. It is passed the hell-fire days of its youth that brought its demise. But there is enough attitude to jab through the barley-rum theme to land some delicious punches. A little cracker. Had only the distillery bottled such malt when still standing. 50%. Douglas Laing.

⊰⊱ **Old Malt Cask Littlemill Aged 17 Years** refill hogshead, dist Mar 92, bott Mar 09 **(72) n18 t19 f16 b17.** Sweet barley but the finish is bitter. the kind of badly produced malt this distillery was once a byword for. 50%. Douglas Laing. 320 bottles.

⊰⊱ **Old & Rare Littlemill Aged 19 Years** dist Mar 90, bott Mar 09 **(76) n19 t20 f18 b19.** Some of the old distilled-from-razors faults are there, but the extra zeal on the barley has helped iron out the worst of the kinks over the years. 55.4%. Douglas Laing. 333 bottles.

Scotch Malt Whisky Society Cask 97.11 Aged 18 Years 1st fill barrel, dist Mar 90 **(76.5) n18.5 t19 f19 b19.** Thin, hot, a little jammy fruitiness at the death. But there goes the last of my enamel: a barium meal of a malt. 56%

Scotch Malt Whisky Society Cask 97.13 Aged 18 Years 1st fill barrel, dist Mar 90 **(78.5) n18.5 t19 f20 b20.** Morbidly pleasantish concentrated barley sweetness: the perfect malt for fire-eaters fresh out of matches. 55.6%

⊰⊱ **Scotch Malt Whisky Society Cask 97.16 Aged 18 Years** 1st fill barrel, dist Mar 90 **(83.5) n19.5 t22 f21 b21.** Much better cask than the norm, allowing the barley to churn out some juicy notes and no little natural caramel and vanilla. But still a traditional Littlemill viciousness to the bite. 56.4%

⊰⊱ **Scotch Malt Whisky Society Cask 97.17 Aged 19 Years** 1st fill barrel, dist Feb 90 **(88.5) n21** sabre-toothed and fair warning of what is coming; **t23.5** barley in its most explosive and concentrated form, even offering a degree of citrus and sweetness; the bite is more entertaining than damaging but hold on to your seats, this is some ride...; **f22** some tight and mildly bitter oak but the huge barley hangs on in there; **b22** what great fun!! Almost like a long-lost old baddie we have come to love. Massive entertainment for the palate. 58.7%

Scott's Selection Littlemill 1990 bott 07 **(77.5) n18 t19 f21 b19.5.** For those who like chillied barley. How many ways are there of describing paint stripper? 57%

LOCH LOMOND
Highland (Southwestern), 1966. Loch Lomond Distillers. Working.

Craiglodge sherry wood cask 139, dist 26 Mar 98 db **(72) n17 t19 f18 b18.** Cloying, off-key, rough...and they're the good points. The nose of sherry and smoke don't gel and it never recovers. 45%

Craiglodge Peated Cask No.137 Distillery Select sherry hogshead, dist 26 Mar 98, bott 9 May 07 db **(85) n18 t24 f21 b22.** Good grief!! Have you even been run over and then re-trampled on by a sherry-peat steam roller? Well, now I know for a fact I have. I've been in this game a long, long time. But I haven't, ever, encountered anything quite like this.... The sherry (oloroso presumably) must still have been slightly sloshing around the bottom of the butt when the big, smoky whisky was filled into it. The result is a nose that defies description but demands witnesses so the tale can be passed on to future generations and an arrival to the palate which at once amazes, charms and, ultimately, mugs. To be honest, the sheer gloss on the arrival is stunning and unquestionably beautiful but there are many issues left unresolved on the madcap (iron in the spirit-style) finish. There are only 150 bottles of this. Get one. Because you will have something to discuss at dinner parties for the rest of your life... 45%. 150 bottles.

Croftengea cask no. 24, dist 22 Jan 97 db **(87) n22** pungent young peat, bracing, clean and even mildly salty; **t22** refreshing barley with coffee/smoke double act; **f21** vanilla and dry toast; **b22** what a difference a cask makes: entirely together and charming. 45%

Croftengea American Oak Cask No. 32 dist Jan 97, bott Jun 07 db **(91) n21.5** feinty but the peats are fine; **t23.5** enormous delivery: oiled, rich, biscuity, smoked, dabbed with Golden Syrup...you just can't lose..!! **f23** long, a slow unravelling of the plot now with more vanilla concentrate; peaty ashes ensure a certain dryness at the death; **b23** a tad off key, but the enormity of the sweet oils and peat just wins your heart. This is big, mildly flawed, but stunningly enjoyable whisky. 45%. 410 bottles.

Croftengea Heavily Peated Cask No.1 Distillery Select sherry butt, dist 3 Mar 03, bott 10 May 07 db **(94) n23 t24 f23 b24** Fabulous knife and fork malt that doesn't even try to look pretty on the plate....let alone the palate. 45%. 885 bottles.

Glen Douglas Cask No. 1 Distillery Select madeira puncheon, dist 23 Sep 02, bott 08 May 07 db **(89) n22** busy, slightly sweaty sock but the uppercuts of barley and grape are a knockout; **t21** soft, well structured delivery but runs into a flat in a few seconds. Recovers as some light vanilla adds weight to the barley; **f23** really beautiful finish with spicy grape showing a delicate touch amid the cocoa; very vaguely mouth-watering; **b23** not exactly firing on all cylinders, with the odd note way out of tune. But very different... and delicious. 45%. 910 bottles.

Inchfad 2001 Heavily Peated cask no. 665 dist 14 Feb 01 db **(80) n20 t21 f19 b20.** Pretty atypical of this particular malt. Missing the fruity ester kick that comes with the big peat. In fact, what big peat? An underwhelming example. 45%

Inchfad 2001 Heavily Peated cask no. 666, dist 14 Feb 01 db **(87) n22** a real youngster, but with all the charm a child can bring. Smokey, though to call it heavily peated stretches the imagination somewhat; **t23** sweet, gristy, soft esters and a wonderful barley rounding. High quality distillate; **f21** the oak grabs far too large a hold and the balance is compromised; **b21** one cask on and so much more in tune. From the same distillate, but an excellent example of how a better quality cask can allow the malt to thrive. Perhaps the cask numbers are the wrong way round...!! 45%

Inchfad Cask No. 27 Distillery Select American oak, dist 15 Mar 01, bott 3 May 07 db **(90) n22** chopped raw, under-ripe hazelnut with a vanilla-barley twist; **t23** fat and full bodied, the malty element in this totally fills the mouth; beyond that is a wonderful structure of vanilla and muscovado sugar and even the most distant echo of smoke; **f22** spices up attractively as the body slims; **b23** a beautiful malt that shows stunning maturity; very individualistic. 45%. 375 bottles.

Inchfad Cask No. 4359 Distillery Select freshly charred American oak, dist 18 Dec 02, bott 2 May 07 db **(83) n20 t22 f20 b21.** A tad new- makey though the barley is slapped on thick and to eye watering effect. 45%. 445 bottles.

Inchmurrin Madeira puncheon cask no. 1, dist May 02, bott Apr 07 db **(78.5) n17.5 t21 f20 b20.** A brave and almost successful attempt to disguise that Inchmurrin is by far the worst of the Loch Lomond styles. 45%. 685 bottles.

Inchmurrin American oak cask no. 414, dist Jan 03, bott Apr 07 db **(68.5) n16.5 t18 f17 b17.** The last time I saw I saw a nose this badly broken I was covering boxing in Nigeria over 30 years ago. Hardly a knockout. 45%. 450 bottles

Inchmurrin Aged 12 Years db **(80) n19 t21 f20 b20.** Peas from the same pod as the 10-year-old. A tad more citrus, though. 40%

Inchmurrin Cask No. 1 Distillery Select Madeira puncheon, dist May 02, bott Apr 07 db **(86) n20 t22 f22 b22.** Some lovely oils paint a chewy, beautifully well-balanced malt. The nose drops it down a few points, but worth a go for the curvy body alone. Look forward to seeing a second cask of this one day. 45%. 685 bottles.

Inchmurrin Organic Cask No. 3946 Distillery Select organic French oak, dist 28 Jul 00, bott 01 May 07 db **(74) n19 t19 f18 b18.** Another poor French cask accounts for a promising malt. In terms of whisky, they should be outlawed. 45%. 410 bottles.

Duncan Taylor The NC2 Range Rhosdhu 1995 Aged 11 Years (79.5) n18 t21 f20 b20.5 The feinty nose is compensated for somewhat, and logically, by the enormity of the body and corresponding oils. 46%

Loch Lomond Gavin's Single Highland Malt dist 96, bott 07 db **(90.5) n23** stunning mix of bourbony notes and thick barley with a small blob of maple syrup for good order: dense and dreamy; **t23** the oak makes no secret of its quest for power with an early, mildly bitter attack. But the ester-led barley snuffs out the threat and heads off towards burnt sugar; **f22.5** long, with excellent weight to both oak and barley which battle it out to the very last; **b22** ester-fuelled and fabulous. 45%. nc ncf.

Scotch Malt Whisky Society Cask 122.16 Aged 15 Years (Croftengea) refill barrel, dist Sep 92 **(95.5) n24.5** kappow!!! About as good as it gets in Scotland on the peated front away from Islay. The depth, the varying levels to be precise, to the peat is on the boundary of description. I can imagine a number of people out there forgetting to taste, having become entranced by this most complex and, frankly, sexy and seductive, of noses. **t24** the sweet-dry complexity on the nose develops immediately on delivery. The peat is enormous – well over the 35ppm phenol mark – yet the dexterity almost puts the brain into meltdown. Varying sugars are played out superbly against the drier vanillas and mounting ash; **f23** soft, gristy – from extremely heavily peated malt, that is – and dries comfortably from outstanding quality oak; **b24** now this Croftengea is the kind of stuff I work with in the lab. And it is sublime....the finest I think Loch Lomond produces on the malt front. In fact, in this form forget just the distillery: there aren't many malts on earth which can touch this. 59.4%

LOCHSIDE
Highland (Eastern), 1957–1992. Closed.
Cadenhead's Authentic Collection Lochside Aged 24 Years dist 81, bott Sep 05 **(75) n17 t21 f18 b19.** There is something not quite 100% clean on nose or palate with this one, as if from poor sherry rather than a bourbon cask. But there is just enough versatility and fruit on the barley to make for an interesting dram. 59.1%. 276 bottles.

⋯ Connoisseurs Choice Lochside 1991 refill bourbon barrel, dist 91, bott 08 **(68) n18 t19 f15 b16.** Sweet delivery and nutty at first. Then nasty. 43%. Gordon & MacPhail.

Old Malt Cask Lochside Aged 14 Years dist Oct 90 **(94) n24** bedazzling with a rare firmness to the barley and lucid grassy presence which suggests a whisky considerably younger; **t23** every bit as mouthwatering and charming as the nose suggests with a delicate digression from the barley towards a neat cocoa influx; **f23** really beautifully balanced with a light infusion of vanilla and toast – and a dash of marmalade? – to make for a serene finale; **b24** when a distillery capable of making whisky this good is lost to us for ever, I could almost weep. 50%.

LONGMORN
Speyside, 1895. Chivas. Working.
Longmorn 15 Years Old db **(93) n23** curiously salty and coastal for a Speysider, really beautifully structured oak but the malt offers both African violets and barley sugar; **t24** your mouth aches from the enormity of the complexity, while your tongue wipes grooves into the roof of your mouth. Just about flawless bitter-sweet balance, the intensity of the malt is enormous, yet – even after 15 years – it maintains a cut grass Speyside character; **f22** long, acceptably sappy and salty with chewy malt and oak. Just refuses to end; **b24** these latest bottlings are the best yet: previous ones had shown just a little too much oak but this has hit a perfect compromise. An all-time Speyside great. 45%

Longmorn 16 Years Old db **(84.5) n20.5 t22 f21 b21.** This was one of the disappointments of the 2008 edition, thanks to the lacklustre nose and finish. This time we see a cautious nudge in the right direction: the colour has been dropped fractionally and the nose celebrates with a sharper barley kick with a peppery accompaniment. The non-existent (caramel apart) finale of yore now offers a distinct wave of butterscotch and thinned honey...and still some spice. Only the delivery has dropped a tad...but a price worth paying for the overall improvement. Still a way to go before the real Longmorn 16 shines in our glasses for all to see and fall deeply in love with. Come on lads in the Chivas lab: we know you can do it.... 48%

Longmorn Aged 16 Years bott 07 db **(78) n19** dull and characterless. No off notes, but... **t23** hurrah..!! There is life there as the barley piles in and the spice is not too far behind; some lovely fruit elements, too. But thickens and ultimately chokes up on toffee; **f18** what the heck is all that about? Caramel? Dull sherry? I don't know for sure: but what is certain is that the malt and complexity are stopped dead in their tracks; the malt bemused...amazed...non-plussed: ultimately hugely disappointed in this expression. Let's make no bones here: Longmorn is one of the great distilleries of the world. No argument. So why a distillery bottling that is so bland when they must have such outstanding stocks of it? Yes, this is drinkable whisky with a good early delivery. But one that has undergone a charisma bypass. And as for the nose and finish...dear, oh dear. This shouldn't be just good whisky – it should be bloody great whisky of the very top order. The label talks a great game but it's back to the drawing board, I'm afraid. Because this is one of the great disappointments of the year. A bit like meeting the most beautiful woman in the bar and expecting the shag of your life...but ending up with a gum-chewer constantly checking her watch. 48%. ncf.

Berrys' Own Selection Longmorn 1992 cask no. 62551, bott 07 **(87.5) n21.5** egg custard, but light on sugar; **t22** some early but distinctive signs of age but the barley compensates; **f22** bitter-sweet with a toasted mallow sweetness countered by burnt toast and peppers; **b22** caught in the nick of time this malt really has some brinkmanship complexity going on...! 46%. Berry Bros & Rudd.

❄ **Berry's Own Selection Longmorn 1996** bott 08 **(91.5) n22** the waft of smoke is an eye-opener so far as in bottled form. The barley and oak share equal billing backstage; **t22.5** delicate barley and vanilla with light peat and cocoa gaining ground towards the middle; **f23.5** lightly oiled finale ensures excellent length and that delicate smoke just teases away. The controlled degree of sweetness is spot on.. **b23.5** now that Benriach is no longer a part of Chivas, will we be seeing more delightfully smoked Longmorns like this, only officially? 56.7%. Berry Bros & Rudd.

Cadenhead's Longmorn Aged 18 Years bourbon wood, matured in oak cask, dist 90, bott Jun 08 **(95) n24** hints of Kentucky as the liquorice and boiled fruit candy collide; honeysuckle and mallows; and butterscotch spread on American sweet bread: astonishing! **t24** stunning delivery with the mouthfeel offering just a hint of oils. The barley is firm yet malleable, the oaks behaved and always in proportion; **f23** long with a succession of brown sugar waves and a touch of hickory to return to the Kentucky theme; **b24** this has obviously matured in one hell of a cask. A triumph. 58.3%. 186 bottles.

❄ **Cärn Mör Vintage Collection Longmorn 1996** hogshead, cask no. 156794, bott 09 **(82.5) n20 t21 f21.5.** Malty, gristy almost, and exceptionally young in style for its age. Not entirely representative of this distillery's usually excellent output. **b20** 46%. The Scottish Liqueur Centre.

Chieftain's Longmorn 13 Years Old white port finish, dist April 94 **(88) n22** rich wine, a touch of sulphur but disguised to a significant degree by a waft of peat; **t22.5** gosh! The wine really does have a cleansing effect on the palate, then a gradual build up of sweet, slightly chocolaty peat; **f21** dries and a hint of something rather too dry and off-key; **b22** I hadn't read that this was a Port finish before nosing and nearly fell off my chair when I first stuck my nose in this. There appears to be something very un-Longmornish in its smokiness, too, so this really is a collectors' item. Juicy, clean and a bit off the wall. 43%. nc ncf. Ian Macleod.

Dun Bheagan Longmorn Aged 11 Years Madeira Finish (82) n21 t22 f19 b20. A pretty whisky but, for all its mildly fruity make-up, lacks personality. 43%.

Duncan Taylor Collection Longmorn 1973 cask no. 8916 **(82.5) n21.5 t21 f19.5 b20.5.** Some lovely barley-sugar, citrus-minty moments cannot disguise a malt that is getting a stitch. Even so, there is the odd phrase of advanced complexity here, on the nose especially. 46.9%

❄ **Kingsbury's Finest & Rarest Longmorn 1980 (89) n21.5** showing some major woodiness but butterscotch compensates; **t23.5** superb delivery with a spicy edge to the layered honey; **f22** natural caramels and vanillas fill in the oaky cavities; **b22** the big oak is well contained in this chunky, stylish bottling. 52.6%. Japan Import System.

❄ **Montgomeries Longmorn 1975** cask no. 3967, dist Mar 75, bott Jul 08 **(94) n23** peaches and honeydew melon served with a custard topping; **t23** a few pine nuts tend to point towards good age, as does the fruit element which is a little more exotic than the nose; the spices freshen things up and the silk to the barley is divine; **f24** for all the obvious oak, this holds out with consummate ease: the vanillas are chattering and busy but the barley enriched latte is sweetened with a lump of Demerara; **b24** this is exactly how you want to find your old whisky: showing age but the grey hairs are confined to the temples and the sophistication is effortless. 46%. Montgomerie's & Co. Ltd.

Murray McDavid Longmorn 1994 bourbon/tempranillo **(79) n19 t21 f19 b20.** Is this the way to Tempranillo, so that I can weep in my pillow; screaming dreams of Tempranillo, and sweet Longmorn who waits for me...This whisky could easily be a number one with some undoubted catchy notes. But, for us purists, there is just something that you can't put your finger on that is so bloody annoying about it. *46%*

⁘ **Old Malt Cask Longmorn Aged 14 Years** refill hogshead, dist Oct 94, bott Dec 08 **(83) n20 t23 f19 b21.** The thin, unpromising nose is reflected in the stingy finish. However, it is impossible not to be amazed by the beauty of the rich malt delivery which is far more in keeping with the distillery's hallmark. *50%. Douglas Laing.352 bottles.*

Old Malt Cask Longmorn Aged 15 Years dist Oct 91, bott Feb 07 **(86) n22 t22 f21 b21.** Celery on the nose and intense barley on the delivery. Fades just a little too easily towards the growling oak. *50%. Douglas Laing. 299 bottles.*

⁘ **Old Masters Longmorn Aged 12 Years** cask no. 156777, dist 96, bott 08 **(85) n22 t21.5 f20.5 b21.** Natural caramels have a big say on this otherwise malty affair. *60.1%. James MacArthur & Co. Ltd.*

⁘ **Old Malt Cask Longmorn Aged 19 Years** refill hogshead, dist Apr 89, bott Sep 08 **(88) n22** butterscotch with a lemon drizzle: beautifully clean; **t23** just as juicy as the nose suggests with multi-layered barley offering a degree of sharpness, too; **f21** lots of vanilla; bitters out; **b22** there is sometimes no keeping an excellent distillery down. *50%. Douglas Laing. 313 bottles.*

⁘ **Provenance Longmorn Aged 10 Years** bott 09 **(79) n20 t20 f19 b20** Pleasant. Sweet but surprisingly dull. *46%. Douglas Laing.*

Provenance Longmorn Aged 11 Years hogshead DMG ref. 3963, dist 96, bott 07 **(75) n18 t19 f19 b19.** Not sure about some of the cask policy at this time. More dud wood. *46%. nc ncf. Douglas Laing.*

Provenance Longmorn Aged 12 Years hogshead no. 4199, dist autumn 95, bott spring 08 **(88) n22** pineapple and citrus; **t22** clean barley but just a light degree of oak; **f22** elegant with the oaks offering a slightly chalky countenance but the barley still chimes in; **b22** a well-made, fresh malt where barley remains king. *46%. Douglas Laing.*

Scotch Malt Whisky Society Cask 7.44 Aged 23 Years refill hogshead, dist Oct 84 **(90) n22 t24 f21.5 b22.5** Now this really is how to grow old gracefully... *57.3%*

Scotch Malt Whisky Society Cask 7.45 Aged 23 Years refill hogshead, dist Oct 84 **(86) n21.5 t22 f21 b21.5.** Hugely enjoyable, exceptionally well spiced to the point of being hit, but lacks the vital spark that took otherwise similar 7.44 to greatness. *57.7%*

⁘ **Scotch Malt Whisky Society Cask 7.51 Aged 24 Years** refill hogshead, dist Oct 84 **(95.5) n24** the oak involvement is considerable though controlled, giving a decidedly bourbon slant to the still firm barley; **t24.5** that same bourbon character announces its arrival early: a leathery-liquorice edge to the muscovado sugars which prime and prep the thick, dogged malt; for all the complexity, remains refreshingly juicy; **f23.5** wonderfully long with many a fudge note and dried date for good measure; **b23.5** brilliant whisky from one of the great distilleries. The malt is entirely intact despite the obvious bourbony intentions of the oak. Very much the best of both worlds. *57.4%*

⁘ **Scotch Malt Whisky Society Cask 7.52 Aged 18 Years** refill hogshead, dist Sep 90 **(75.5) n17.5 t20.5 f18.5 b19.** A gruesome nose. And, considering the distillery and age, pretty sweet and anaemic on the palate, too. *56.4%*

The Spirit Safe Cask Longmorn Aged 11 Years dist 95 **(89) n21** suety; **t23** massive – and I mean massive – malt: soft honey theme balances out the chalky oak; **f22** a soft oil has formed to stretch out the malty theme, accompanied now with delicate spice; **b23** a malt which will thank you enormously for allowing to breathe in the glass for about 20 minutes before nosing and drinking. *46%. Celtic Whisky Compagnie.*

The Whisky Fair Longmorn Aged 31 Years bourbon, dist 76, bott 07 **(87) n22** big barley, a touch of boiled apple and a vague hint of elderly Longpond Jamaican rum; **t22** quite a thick mixture once the oak gets stirred in **f21** just sweet enough; **b22** hangs on until the nails bleed. *54.1%. Germany.*

THE MACALLAN

Speyside, 1824. Edrington. Working.

The Macallan 7 Years Old db **(89) n23** beautifully clean sherry, lively, salty, gentle peppers; **t23** mouth-filling and slightly oily. Some coffee tones intertwine with deep barley and fruit; **f21** unravels to reveal very soft oak and lingering fruity spice; **b22** an outstanding dram that underlines just how good young malts can be. Fun, fabulous and in recent bottlings has upped the clarity of the sherry intensity to profound new heights. *40%*

The Macallan 10 Years Old db **(91) n23** oloroso appears to be the big noise here, but clever, almost meaty, incursions of spice offer an extra dimension; fruity, yet bitter-sweet: dense yet teasingly light in places; **t23** chewy fruit and the old Macallan silk is back: creamy cherries and mildly under-ripe plum ensures a sweet-sour style; **f21.5** traces of vanilla and barley remind us of the oak and barley, but the fruit reverberates for some while, as does some annoying caramel; **b23.5** for a great many of us, it is with the Mac 10 our great Speyside odyssey began. It has to be said that in recent years it has been something of a shadow of its former great self. However, this is the best version I have come across for a while. Not perhaps in the same league as those bottlings in the 1970s which made us re-evaluate the possibilities of single malt. But fine enough to show just how great this whisky can be when the butts have not been tainted and, towards the end, the balance between barley and grape is a relatively equal one. *40%*

The Macallan 10 Years Old Cask Strength db **(85) n20 t22 f22 b21.** Enjoyable and a would give chewing gum a run for its money. But over-egged the sherry here and not a patch on the previous bottling. *58.8%. Duty Free.*

The Macallan 12 Years Old db **(88) n22.5** classic Macallan nose, taking off on a one way sherried flight; **t22.5** a sweeter, fresher sherry delivery than of recent times with an almost PX kick to this early on; lots of toffee nougat fills towards the middle; **f21** the sherry and caramel become confused; **b22** great to see a Macallan so clean. Really enjoyable, but the development is too stunted to make this a true classic. *40%*

The Macallan 12 Years Old Sherry Oak Elegancia db **(86) n23 t22 f20 b21.** Promises, but delivers only to an extent. *40%*

The Macallan 18 Years Old db **(87) n24** near perfection as to regard the sherry: soft, oloroso led, the most playful spice prickle with the balance of sweet and dry almost faultless: stick your nose in this and abide a while... **t22** soft, silky...but without backbone. Limited development and caramel appears to outwit the malt; **f20** pretty dull and lifeless, caramel apart: I really can't get my head around this... **b21** an entirely underpowered dram. The body doesn't even come close to matching the nose which builds up the expectancy to enormous levels and, by comparison to the Independents, this at 43% appears weak and unrepresentative. Why this isn't at 46% at the very least and unambiguously uncoloured, I have no idea. *43%*

The Macallan 25 Years Old db **(84.5) n22 t21 f20.5 b21.** Dry with an even drier oloroso residue; blood orange adds to the fruity mix. Something, though, is not entirely right about this and one fears from the bitter tang at the death that a rogue butt has gained entry to what should be the most hallowed of dumping troughs. *43%*

The Macallan 30 Years Old db **(93) n22.5** a few notes from the lactic-forming, tired parts of butt but these are comprehensively outweighed by the rich sherry and busy spices; **t23.5** lavish, peppy-spiced oloroso thumps headfirst into every tastebud going; as it settles towards the vanilla-clad middle, the grapes take on a much cleaner, juicier form; **f23** long, honey and liquorice add up towards a rich bourbon-esque finale which gamely counters the thick fruit; the late chocolate topping is almost too good to be true; **b24** a grizzled and weary malt it may outwardly appear, on much closer and more time-consuming inspection there is no questioning its lineage: Macallan at its most traditional. And brilliant! *43%*

The Macallan 40 Years Old dist 10 May 61, bott 9 Sep 05 db **(90) n23** no shortage of oak, as you might expect. But nutty, too (chestnut pure, to be precise). The scope is broadened with a distracted smokiness while oak maximizes the longer it stays in the glass; **t23** soft and yielding, with a lovely dovetailing of vanillins and delicate sherry. The grape appears to gain control with a sweet barley sidekick before the oak recovers; **f22** soft oils formulate with some laite and slightly salted, Digestive-style biscuit. Gentle spices delight; **b22** very well-rounded dram that sees off advancing years with a touch of grace and humour. So often you think the oak will take control, but each time an element intervenes to win back the balance. It is as if the dram is teasing you. Wonderful entertainment. *43%*

The Macallan 50 Years Old dist 29 Mar 52, bott 21 Sep 05 db **(90) n25** we all have pictures in our minds of the perfect grandmother: perhaps grey-haired and knitting in her rocking-chair. Or grandfather: kindly, gentle, quietly wise, pottering about in the shed with some gadget he has just made for you. This, then, is the cliched nose of the perfect 50-year-old malt: time-defying intensity and clarity; attractive demerara (rum and sugar!) sweetened coffee, a tantalizing glimpse at something smoky and sensationally rich grape and old fruit cake. So that the sweetness and dryness don't cancel each other out, but complement each other and between them tell a thousand tales. Basically, there's not much missing here... and absolutely all you could wish to find in such an ancient Speysider...; **t23** dry delivery with the oak making the early running. But slowly the grape and grain fights back to gain more than just a foot-hold; again telling wisps of smoke appear to lay down a sound base and some oily barley; **f19** now the oak has taken over. There is a burnt-toast and burnt raisin bitterness, lessened in effect marginally by a sweeter vanilla add-on; **b23** loses it at the end, which is entirely excusable. But until then it has been one fabulous experience full of passion and complexity. I nosed and tasted this for over an hour. It was one very rewarding, almost touching, experience. 46%

The Macallan 55 Years Old Lalique II db **(90.5) n23.5** a plume of ancient smoke settles over sawdust and grist steeped in molasses; great age is apparent, but you'd never for one moment think that this was distilled in another world; **t21** a touch prickly in the oak department with some tell-tale bitterness but still there is enough malt and peat around to overcome those woody hurdles; **f23.5** brilliant and quite improbably so. Now that smoke has evened out and the oak overcome, the layering of the soft sugars and hints of juicy barley are bedazzling; **b22.5** even after all these years, whisky never loses its ability to amaze me. It is the norm that smoke in a malt tends to bale out regarding its intensity as the years pass. And that as the oak increases during that time it becomes impossible to delineate or recognize the forms and characters that give a particular whisky a style or shape. Here neither has happened to a degree where you cannot recognise this for exactly what it is: a classic post war Macallan, complete with all its peaty zest and articulation. Remember, when this was distilled, Elizabeth II had still to become Queen, Winston Churchill was Prime Minister and the very year this was put into cask director David Lean was making films about breaking the sound barrier, let alone man reaching the moon. This is liquid history: a bygone style of Speyside from a bygone age - a gem of a wrinkly. 40.1%

⋯ **The Macallan 1824** db **(88) n24** welcome to the true, traditional nose of Macallan. Oloroso, ladies and gentlemen. But not just any old oloroso: this is more or less exactly how I remember it form the mid-70s, radiating the rind of kumquats and blood orange juice in pretty equal measure; and as well as grape we have greengages absolutely bursting from their skins. There is a 'but', a very slight mustiness...but it is so far outweighed by the grapey symphony, it is to be contemptuously ignored **t23.5** not surprisingly, the delivery and first five or six waves are of grape in varying forms of juiciness, sweetness, weight and brilliance... but there is, eventually, a bitterness, too...; **f19** that background noise on the nose cannot be ignored any longer...it is now biting deep into the finish; **b21.5** absolutely magnificent whisky, in part. But there are times my job is depressing...and this is one of them.. 48%

The Macallan 1851 Inspiration db **(77) n19.5 t19.5 f19 b19.** Flat and uninspirational in 2008. 41%

The Macallan 1937 bott 69 db **(92) n23** an outline of barley can eventually be made in the oaky mist; becomes better defined as a honeyed sweetness cuts in. Fingers of smoke tease. When nosing in the glass hours later the fresh, smoky gristiness is to die for ... and takes you back to the mill room 67 years ago; **t22** pleasantly sweet start as the barley piles in – even a touch of melon in there; this time the oak takes second place and acts as a perfect counter, **f24** excellent weight with soft peat softening the oak; **b23** a subtle if not overly complex whisky where there are few characters but each play its part exceptionally well. One to get out with a DVD of Will Hay's sublime Oh Mr Porter which was being made in Britain at the same time as this whisky and as Laurel and Hardy were singing about a Lonesome Pine on the other side of the pond; or any Pathe film of Millwall's FA Cup semi-final with Sunderland. 43%

The Macallan 1937 bott 74 db **(83) t19 t24 f20 b20.** It's all about the superb, silky initial mouth impact. 43%.

The Macallan 1938 bott 73 db **(90) n21** hint of apple blossoms on oak; **t23** stupendous balance and poise as the barley rolls, wave after wave over the palate bringing with it a sweet sugar-almond biscuity quality; **f23** fabulous finish of great length. Spices dovetail with an almost perfect barley-oak charm; **b23** no hint of tiredness here at all: a malt that has all the freshness and charisma yet old-world charm and mystery of Hitchcock's The Lady Vanishes, which was made at the same time as this whisky. 43%

The Macallan 1938 (31 Years Old) dist 38, first bott 69, re-bottled 02 db **(83) n20 t22 f20 b21.** Some wonderful trills of barley early on but the oak dominates. 43%.

The Macallan 1939 bott 79 db **(90) n23** pleasing peaty edges to the thick malt; a touch of hickory for extra weight and Highland Park-esque heather-honey; **t22** spot on barley gives an unmolested mouthwatering performance; the oak tags on reluctantly drying towards cocoa at the middle; **f22** the integrity is kept as the oak backs off and little wisps of smoke re-surface; some brown sugar keeps the bitter-sweet pot boiling; **b23** enormous complexity confidence to a whisky distilled at a time of uncertainty; one to accompany the original Goodbye Mr Chips, though the whisky seems nothing like so faded. 43%

The Macallan 1940 bott 75 db **(83) n20 t22 f21 b20.** Easily the most modern style discernible from this distillery; a Macallan recogisable as an ancestor of today's famous dram, even with one or two warts apparent. 43%

The Macallan 1940 (37 Years Old) dist 40, first bott 77, re-bottled 02 db **(91) n22** not dissimilar to an old sherried Irish of this era with the barley having a firm, crisp, almost abrasive quality. Rather lovely especially with the most subtle wisps of peat imaginable; **t23** bracing, full-on barley where the flintiness from the nose is transferred perfectly to the palate; a touch of spice and hint of smoke towards the middle; **f23** clean, long finale where the barley pulsates its rock hard message; **b23** blind-tasting I would have declared this Irish, though slightly mystified by the distant hints of peat. Hard to believe that something so sublime could have been made by a nation under siege. Obviously nothing can distract a Scotsman from making great whisky ... 43%

The Macallan 1945 (56 Years Old) cask 262, bott 02 db **(89) n22** extraordinary to the point of improbability: the sherry is fresh and keeping at bay logjams of chunky oak, though the fruitiness burns off the longer it remains in the glass; the smoke hovers and soars like pin-prick eagles on the wing; **t23** battling oak fizzes against the sweeter, mouthwatering barley; the fruit is subtle though there is a pineapple sharpness amid the still lush grape; **f22** really impressive, slow development of peat that offers no spice but a smoky overlay to the oak; **b22** how can a whisky retain so much freshness and character after so long in the cask? This game never ceases to amaze me. 51.5%

The Macallan 1946 Select Reserve db **(93) n25** does peat arrive any more delicately than this? The sherry, barley and oak offer perfect harmony: perfect and faultless; **t23** teasingly mouthwatering and fruity. Crushed sultanas cruise with the peat; **f22** the oak makes inroads at the expense of the barley. Remains chewy and tantalisingly smoky, though; **b23** I have never found a finer nose to any whisky. Once-in-a-lifetime whisky. 40%

The Macallan 1946 (56 Years Old) cask 46/3M, bott 02 db **(84) n21 t21 f20 b22.** The most peat-free '46 I've come across yet 44.3%

The Macallan 1948 (53 Years Old) cask 609, bott 02 db **(77) n18 t21 f19 b19.** Drinkable, but showing some major oaky cracks. 45.3%

The Macallan 1948 Select Reserve db **(75) n22 t19 f17 b17.** What a fabulous nose! Sadly the package trails behind the '46. 40%

The Macallan 1949 (53 Years Old) cask 136, bott 02 db **(95) n23** wonderfully lively fruit interwoven with waxy, polished wooden floors and acacia honey; a touch of salt sharpens it further; **t24** nothing extinct about this old Scottish volcano as oak-led spices assert their grip on the tastebuds while soft, sultry sherry tries to act as placator; **f24** oaky-cocoa/liquorice and intense barley; remains mouthwatering yet spicy for seemingly hours; **b24** hold on to your trilbies: this punchy malt knows exactly where it is going. What a year: Carol Reed makes the incomparable The Third Man and Macallan can come up with something like this. Oh, to swap Orson Welles for H. G. Wells and his time machine. Sheer, unrepeatable class. 49.8%

The Macallan 1949 (52 Years Old) cask 935, bott 02 db **(82) n23 t21 f19 b19.** Faded and slightly tired, it has problems living up to the heaven-made nose. 41.1%

The Macallan 1950 (52 Years Old) cask 598, bott 02 db **(83) n22 t22 f18 b21.** Charmingly delicate peat but probably about two or three summers past being a truly excellent whisky. 46.7%

The Macallan 1950 (52 Years Old) cask no. 600, bott 02 db **(91) n20** the early fruit quickly evaporates to leave a clear path for the oak; **t24** stunning sherry: the grape absolutely sparkles yet is soft enough to allow through a tidal wave of malt, on which peat is sensuously surfing; **f23** spices from the middle carry through as does the chewy peat. Some fabulous undercurrents of burnt raisin and healthy malt continue; **b24** only two casks apart, but this is almost a mirror image of the first, in the sense that everything is the other way round... 51.3%

The Macallan 1951 (51 Years Old) cask 644, bott 02 db **(93) n23** a minor fruitfest with withering grapes and raisins the main attraction but over-ripe greengages and raspberries bulk up the sub-plot: needs this to see off the firm oak. A gentle, barely discernible peatiness drifts over it all with absolutely no signs of over-aging; **t24** fascinating detail to the barley: it is fresh and still mildly gristy at first but the sherry builds a dark path towards it. All the time the sherry remains clean and in harmony; some confident peat weaves a delicious path through the complexity; **f23** unrefined brown sugar digs in with the barley to see off the encroaching oak; the most delicate wafts of peat imaginable caress the senses; **b23** a malt instantly recognisable to Macallan lovers of the last two decades. Simply outstanding. 52.3%

The Macallan 1952 (50 Years Old) cask no. 627, bott 02 db **(80) n20 t20 f21 b19.** Good, clean sherry but it all seems a little detached 50.8%

The Macallan 1952 (49 Years Old) cask 1250, bott 02 db **(74) n19 t19 f18 b18.** Ye olde weirde Macallane. 48%

The Macallan 1953 (49 Years Old) cask no. 516, bott 02 db **(92) n22** a shade meaty with the oak offering a big counter to the thumping sherry and delicate smoke; **t24** full sherry alert as the fruitcake richness goes into overdrive, as do the spices; **f23** some medium roast Santos lightens the oak while enrichening the barley; **b23** deliciously big and unflinching in its Christmas pudding intensity. *51%*

The Macallan 1954 (47 Years Old) cask 1902, bott 02 db **(77) n19 t18 f21 b19.** The line between success and failure is thin: outwardly the '53 and 54 are similar but the 53 controls the oak much tighter. I love the coffee finale on this, though. *50.2%*

The Macallan 1955 (46 Years Old) cask 1851 49, bott 02 db **(88) n21** more burnt raisins and apples; **t22** the tastebuds get a good spicy peppering as the barley rootles about the palate; the sherry is clear and intact; **f23** amazingly long with the oak falling short of its desired palate domination; **b22** close call: one more Speyside August and this dram would have been matchwood. *45.9%*

The Macallan 1958 (43 Years Old) cask 2682, bott 02 db **(86) n17 t22 f24 b23.** One fears the worst from the sappy nose but the taste is sheer Highland Park in its honey depth. *52.9%*

The Macallan 1959 (43 Years Old) cask 360, bott 02 db **(79) n19 t21 f19 b20.** The oak is giving the malt a good hiding but it just hangs on to a delicious sub-plot. *46.7%*

The Macallan 1964 (37 Years Old) cask 3312, bott 02 db **(86) n24 t22 f20 b20.** butterscotch and honey: a real chewing whisky if ever there was one. *58.2%*

The Macallan 1965 (36 Years Old) cask 4402, bott 02 db **(91) n22** pretty well oaked but wonderful balance from blood oranges; **t23** again lovely mouthfeel as the fabulously balanced and lush barley hits the palate; fruit and oak are dished out in even measures with the spice: this is top notch whisky; **f22** after the big bust comes the ample arse: heaps of chewy barley fortified by sultanas and raisins; **b24** if this was a woman it would be Marilyn Monroe. *56.3%*

The Macallan 1966 (35 Years Old) cask 7878, bott 02 db **(83) n21 t22 f20 b20.** a malt which never quite works out where it is going but gives a comfortable ride all the same. *55.5%*

The Macallan 1967 (35 Years Old) cask 1195, bott 02 db **(93) n23** top notch uncompromised sherry with some lovely nutty touches; **t24** the sherry deftly flicks each individual tastebud while the burnt fudge offers a bitter-sweet distraction; **f23** coffee ice cream but a whole lot warmer as the spices pop about the mouth. Vanilla and raisins gather around the spicy centrepiece; some lovely salt towards the finale; **b23** this is what happens when you get a great sherry cask free of sulphur and marauding oak: whisky the way God intended. Unquestionably classic Macallan. *55.9%*

The Macallan 1968 (34 Years Old) cask 2875, bott 02 db **(92) n23** lemon curd tart and barley; **t23** full frontal barley with a grape chaperone; **f22** continues to mouthwater now with late cocoa adding depth and finesse; **b24** possibly the most sophisticated and delicate malt in the pack despite the strength. *51%*

The Macallan 1968 (33 Years Old) cask 5913, bott 02 db **(84) n17 t23 f22 b22.** Flawed genius: how can a whisky with such a poor nose produce the goods like this? *46.6%*

The Macallan 1969 cask 9369 db **(75) n19 t18 f20 b18.** One of those ungainly sherry butts that swamps everything in sight. *52.7%*

The Macallan 1969 (32 Years Old) cask no. 10412, bott 02 db **(76) n18 t20 f18 b20.** One small sip for man, one ordinary vintage for Macallan. Splinters. anybody? *59%*

The Macallan 1970 (32 Years Old) cask no. 241, bott 02 db **(95) n23** another heavyweight but this time with some honey and ripe fig to offer complexity; passable impersonation of ancient bourbon blended with old Demerara rum; **t24** quite massive with strands of brown sugar bringing out the best of the grape; **f23** very long and so subtle: the barley and vanilla stretch a long distance with some natural toffee rounding things off; **b25** Brazil win the World Cup with the finest team and performance of all time, my girlfriend born there soon after and Macallan receive a butt from Heaven via Jerez. 1970 was some year ... *54.9%*

The Macallan 1970 (31 Years Old) cask no. 9033, bott 02 db **(81) n20 t20 f22 b19.** A butt bottled on its way down. *52.4%*

The Macallan 1971 (30 Years Old) cask no. 4280, bott 02 db **(86) n21 t22 f22 b21.** Imagine the trusty 10 years old from about 1980 with a grey beard ... *56.4%*

The Macallan 1971 (30 Years Old) cask 7556, bott 02 db **(91) n22** delicate salt helps develop the barley; **t22** vivid barley with rather soft sherry and then spice; **f24** lengthy, subtle end with waves of rich sherry carrying a Demerara sweetness and coffee; **b23** a complex dram that is comfortable with its age. *55.9%*

The Macallan 1972 (29 Years Old) cask no. 4041, bott 02 db **(92) n23** hell's teeth!!! This is probably what an explosion in a bodega would smell like. The most awesomely powerful sherry I can probably ever remember on a whisky, much more one dimensional than cask

4043, though; **t24** that trademark coffee-ness is there (in this case something of a heavy roast Costa Rican) then some tomato and burnt raisin; **f22** bitter and slightly nutty as the oak begins to gain some control; **b23** once, I would have hated this type of malt. But I have come across so many sulphur-tainted casks over recent years that I have learned to have fun with monsters like this. Snatched from an awesome clutch of butts. 49.2%

The Macallan 1972 29 Years Old cask 4043, bott 02 db **(93) n25** well, it has to be said: a quite faultless nose. The spices are entirely in true with the perfect sherry-oak balance. This is big stuff, but perfectly proportioned: seems almost a shame to drink it ...; **t24** stupendous spice-plum-giant-boiled-Italian-tomato: enormous with a waft of smoke through the middle; **f21** slightly bitter as the oak nibbles but still lots of complexity; **b23** the sherry butt used for this was a classic: the intensity of the whisky memorable. If, as Macallan claim, the sherry accounts for only 5% of the flavour, I'd like to know what happened to the other 95.... 58.4%

The Macallan 1973 (30 Years Old) cask 6098, bott 03 db **(93) n23** the grape is brittle and nestles behind barley and honey; some ripe pears add to the freshness; **t24** the honey is at the vanguard of a brilliant display of intense, sugarcoated barley; **f23** the sweetness vanishes to leave the more mouthwatering, grassy malt elements; **b23** a superbly chosen cask for those with a sweet tooth in particular. If you know any women who claim not to like whisky, seduce them with this. 60.9%

The Macallan 1989 cask no 552 db **(94) n23** stunningly clean sherry with wonderful nuttiness amid spice and oak; moist Melton Hunt cake at its most subtle; **t23** explosive entrance with spices and a superbly full-on oakiness that bathes in the luxuriant, simply flawless, leathery sherry; the sweetness is not entirely unlike Demerara rum; **f24** calms down for wave upon wave of chocolate fruit and nut... only without the excessive sweetness; **b24** there are countless people out there who cut their whisky teeth 20 years ago on Macallan. Battle to get a bottle of this and the grey hairs will return to black, the eyesight will improve and your clothes will fit more easily. This is timewarp Macallan at its most dangerously seductive. 59.2%

Macallan Cask Strength db **(82) n20 t20 f22 b20.** I could weep. What could have been an absolute classic is just one less-than-perfect cask away from greatness. Even so, an enjoyable and memorable ride for the most part. 57.8%. Canada.

Macallan Cask Strength db **(94) n22** cranked up, sweet, clean sherry; **t24** absolutely spot on delivery with grape concentrate, thickened further by intense barley. Wonderful spices arrive on cue; **f24** long, with the tastebuds storm-lashed by juicy sherry for some time. And still those spices rock....; **b24** one of those big sherry babies; it's like surfacing a massive wave of barley-sweetened sherry. Go for the ride. 58.6%. USA.

The Macallan Easter Elchies Summer Selection 2006 Aged 8 Years (88) n21 musty, dusty bookshelves; **t23** beautiful symphony of varied barley tones, each caressed by the lightest touch of fruit; **f22** softly furred fruit with a sprinkling of cocoa; **b22** perhaps not every cask here is faultless but the whole really does remind you how deliciously entertaining is a mere 8-year-old can be. Good for Macallan for showing the way. 45.2%

The Macallan Easter Elchies Seasonal Cask Selection Winter Choice 14 Years Old db **(94) n24** you can almost picture the butt before it was filled: large, dripping with dampness inside and smelling as sweet as a nut. Nothing has changed in 14 years, except some exquisite marmalade and honeycomb has been added; **t24** sizzling spices cut rapier-like through the intense grape; juicy barley seeps through the wounds; **f23** lilting, rich-textured natural caramel and vanilla; **b23** from a faultless cask and one big enough to have its own Postcode... 54%. Exclusive to visitor centre.

The Macallan Easter Elchies Winter Selection 2006/07 Aged 15 Years db **(90) n23** the mahogany tinged with punk-orange colour is a worry, but relief is at hand at first sniff: one of the few sherry noses around these days without even a hint of sulphur. And here we are talking mega-sherry. Perhaps too one-tricked to be great, but a delight; **t23** grape sloshes juicily around, sharply at times, but even as the oak tries to get a word in everything is so clean; **f22** pretty long; bitter as oloroso hangs about and a late, intriguing dash of Fisherman's Friend; **b22** Some 20 years ago I would have marked this down as over-the-top sherry. But so rare these days to find faultless butts – and this really is faultless – that I've marked it up for its ability to take you back to another era. Brings a tear to the eye of those who lament a lost whisky world... 58.5%

⌁ **The Macallan Estate Reserve** db **(84) n22 t22 f20 b20.** Doh! So much juice lurking about, but so much bitterness, too. ....grrrrr!!!! 45.7%

The Macallan Fine Oak 8 Years Old db **(82.5) n20.5 t22 f20 b20.** A slight flaw has entered the mix here. Even so, the barley fights to create a distinctive sharpness. However, a rogue sherry butt has put paid to any hopes the honey and spice normally found in this brand. *40%*

The Macallan Fine Oak 10 Years Old db **(90) n23** finely tuned and balanced: everything on a nudge-nudge basis with neither fruit nor barley willing to come out and lead: really take your time over this to maximise the entertainment; **t22.5** brimming with tiny, delicate oak notes which just brush gently, almost erotically, against the clean barley; **f21.5** drier, chewier and no less laid-back; **b22** much more on the ball than the last bottling of this I came across. Malts really come as understated or clever than this. *40%*

The Macallan Fine Oak 12 Years Old db **(92.5) n24** moist dates and quartered lime; gristy barley perfectly countered by roasted hazelnut and sweetened cocoa: an aromatic triumph; **t23** thin acacia honey brushed over the emboldened malt; lightweight at first and gradually more chewy; still, though, it is a fine gristiness which prevails; **f22.5** a touch of bitterness as the oak clears its throat but the dexterity of the vanilla allows the sweet a clear path to the finish; **b23** a star of a malt, altered in style slightly since its launch, offering such clever nuances as the picture, always on a theme, changes from moment to moment. It's the ultra complex nose, though, which takes star billing. *40%*

The Macallan Fine Oak 15 Years Old db **(94) n24** vanilla holds the key here, with the oak bridging the gap between the myriad soft fruit notes and the angular barley; surprisingly, a deft trail of something smoky is also evident; the first time I have seen this in the F015 since the very first bottlings; **t24.5** ye Gods! Not quite perfection, but its going for it big time: the molten brown sugars simply melt into the gentle fruit while the deft oils carry the barley; some rising spice may indicate very distant smoke, **f22** unquestionably a duller finale than when first launched; there is now a telling degree of treacle caramel seeping in from somewhere which is trampling and flattening all around it; **b23.5** the finish may have knocked it down a point. But considering that the last time I came across this, in Canada I think, the bottling had been sulphur ruined, this rates as the best and most exciting comeback since Queen of the South's heroic and unforgettable effort in the Scottish Cup Final against Rangers this year. Remains a quite stunning dram; a Queen of the Speyside. *43%*

The Macallan Fine Oak 17 Years Old db **(84) n21 t21 f21 b21.** A curious, pleasant but not entirely convincing addition to the Fine Oak family, having neither the 15-year-old's outrageous complexity or the deftness of the 18. An expression too far? *43%*

The Macallan Fine Oak 18 Years Old db **(84) n20 t23 f20 b21.** The surprisingly bland nose and finish is partly compensated for by the intensity of the honey barley on delivery. Some non-firing cylinders are evident. *43%*

The Macallan Fine Oak 21 Years Old db **(82.5) n21 t22 f19.5 b20.** How dull! No off notes. No sulphur. Granted. But just no character, either. Get past the lovely, honeyed energetic barley on delivery and then there is a void. Unrecognisable from the excellence of previous bottlings. *43%*

The Macallan Fine Oak 25 Years Old db **(90) n22** coal dusty: the plate of old steam engines; a speckle of raisin and fruitcake; **t23.5** despite the early signs of juicy grape, it takes only a nanosecond or two for a much drier oak-spiced spine to take shape; the weight is never less than ounce perfect, however; **f22** puckering, aged oak leaves little doubt that this is a malt of advanced years, but a few liquorice notes ensure a degree of balance; **b22.5** the first time I tasted this brand a few years back I was knocked off my perch by the peat reek which wafted about with cheerful abandon. Here the smoke is tighter, more shy and of a distinctly more anthracitic quality. Even so, the sweet juiciness of the grape juxtaposes gamely with the obvious age to create a malt of obvious class. *43%*

The Macallan Fine Oak 30 Years Old db **(91) n22** oak. And lots of it. Leaves of barley makes the canopy a lot more attractive; **t23** big oak delivery, but just like the nose there is a pause before much sweeter elements arrive. Here some honeycomb works wonders; **f22.5** a natural fire-break occurs and a Demerara-burnt fudge sweetness sees the malt reach a comfortable conclusion; **b23.5** a malt once famed for its refusal to take the oaky path has now led us into a forest. Thankfully, there are enough nuances to the barley to ensure complexity and balance; satisfies pretty high expectation. *43%*

The Macallan Fine Oak Master's Edition db **(91) n23** one of the most delicate of all Macallan's house noses, depending on a floral scented theme with a sweetish malty tinge to the dank bracken and bluebells; **t23** so salivating and sensual! The tastebuds are caressed with sugar-coated oaky notes that have a devilish buzz about them; **f22** more malt and now vanilla with a bitter cocoa death... **b23** adorable. *42.8%*

The Macallan Fine Oak Whisky Maker's Selection db **(92) n22** good age with the oak determining a dry course; the barley carries delicate grape; **t23** distinctively Speyside-style with an early avalanche of spice; there is a barley-juiced fruitiness and perhaps a fino touch, too; **f23** long, with all the vanilla you'd expect from such a well oaked dram; the clean-ness of the barley and grape is stunning, as is the light oily sheen that carries the dim sweetness; **b24** those who cannot see Macallan in anything other than chestnut oloroso will be having sleepless nights: this is a dram of exquisite sophistication. The ultimate pre-prandial dram with it's coy, mildly cocoaed dryness, set against just enough barley and fruit sweetness here and there to see off any hints of austerity. Some great work has gone on in the lab to make this happen: fabulous stuff, chaps! *42.8%. Duty Free.*

Macallan Gran Reserva Aged 12 Years db **(92) n23** massive cream sherry background with well matured fruit cake to the fore: big, clean, luxurious in a wonderfully old-fashioned way. Oh, and a sprinkling of crushed sultana just in case the grapey message didn't get across... **t24** a startlingly unusual combination on delivery: dry yet juicy! The ultra fruity lushness is dappled with soft spices; oak arriving early-ish does little to alter the path of the sweetening fruit; just a hint of hickory reveals the oak's handiwork towards the middle; **f22** dry, as oloroso does, with a vaguely sweeter edge sparked by notes of dried date; the delicate but busy spices battle through to the toffeed end; **b23** well, you don't get many of these to the pound. A real throwback. The oloroso threatens to overwhelm but there is enough intrigue to make for a quite lovely dram which, as all good whiskies should, never quite tells the story the same way twice. Not entirely without blemish, but I'm being picky. A Macallan soaked in oloroso which traditionalists will swoon over. *45.6%*

The Macallan Gran Reserva 1981 db **(90) n23 t22 f22 b23.** Macallan in a nutshell. Brilliant. But could do with being at 46% for full effect. *40%*

The Macallan Gran Reserva 1982 db **(82) n21 t22 f20 b19.** Big, clean, sweet sherry influence from first to last but doesn't open up and sing like the '81 vintage. *40%*

The Macallan Millennium 50 Years Old (1949) db **(90) n23 t22 f22 b23.** Magnificent finesse and charm despite some big oak makes this another Macallan to die for. *40%*

⋙ **The Macallan Select Oak** db **(83) n23 t21 f19 b20.** Exceptionally dry and tight; and a little furry despite the early fruitiness. *40%*

⋙ **The Macallan Whisky Makers Edition** db **(76) n19 t20 f18 b19.** Distorted and embittered by the horrific "S" element... *42.8%*

The Macallan Woodlands Limited Edition Estate Bottling db **(86) n21 t23 f21 b21.** Toffee towards the finish brings a premature halt to a wonderfully mollased early delivery. *40%*

Adelphi Macallan Aged 16 Years cask no. 14995, dist 90, bott 07 **(79) n19 t22 f19 b19.** Gatecrashed by a surprising degree of oak. *57.4%. 399 bottles.*

⋙ **Alchemist Macallan Aged 10 Years** bourbon barrel, dist Oct 97, bott Oct 07 **(83.5) n20 t21.5 f21 b21.** A malty haze. Sweet, grassy but supine. *46%. Alchemist Beverage Co.*

Cadenhead's Authentic Collection Macallan Aged 19 Years sherry butt, dist 87, bott Sep 07 **(78) n18.5 t21 f19 b19.5.** Honey and grape strains against the sulphur input. Pity: it would have been a classic. *52.5%. 672 bottles.*

Cadenhead's Authentic Collection Macallan-Glenlivet Aged 19 Years sherry butt, dist 87, bott May 07 **(71) n17 t19 f17 b18.** A good example of sulphur influence. *56.2%. 576 bottles.*

Duncan Taylor Collection Macallan 1969 cask no. 6846 **(88) n21 t22.5 f22 b22.5** Oak bangs on the door like the Grim Reaper. Just creeps over the line in terms of both strength and quality. Balances beautifully considering the big oak threat which never quite goes away. The late syrup and mocha is almost taking the piss. *40.4%*

Duncan Taylor Collection Macallan 1969 cask no. 8373 **(90) n22** heads in direction of exotic fruit; **t22** flat delivery: takes time to wake up and overcome the oak but then a slow spreading of rich and pretty sweet barley; **f23** takes forever: the barley somehow becomes even softer with gentle, doughy, vanilla; **b23** few malts at this age show such control and poise. *44.6%.*

Duncan Taylor Collection Macallan 1987 cask no. 2561 **(91) n21** pithy; crushed fruit stones; a touch of citrus; **t23** superb delivery: this could scratch a diamond, so hard is the barley; mouth-watering, grassy, fluty notes dazzle; **f23** unrealistically long and with a mind-blowing build up of cocoa and spice; **b24** Macallan at its most refreshing. *55.3%.*

Duncan Taylor Collection Macallan 1987 cask no. 9795 **(95) n24** classic blood-orange sherry notes – so clean they almost squeak; **t24** lumbering fruit at first then an explosion of pure, mouth-watering barley that is beyond description; **f23** the vanilla and milk gums make an interesting combo; roasted raisins mixed with fresh, juicy ones abound; **b24** I know those who are no great fans of Macallan: try this glass of genius, guys..!! *57.7%*

Duncan Taylor Collection Macallan 1987 cask no. 9796 **(91.5) n23** one of the spotted dog style. Ahhh, just so sensual....**t23** spicy kick off with a quick, vague, quirky barley-grape delivery; sharp copper-rich malt towards the middle; **f22.5** a few layers of toffee and cocoa thicken the grapey appeal; **b23** wonderful Macallan revealing some pretty deep insights into its rich personality. *57.4%*

Duncan Taylor Collection Macallan 1988 cask no. 8426 **(95.5) n24.5** there you have it: arguably the perfect Macallan nose. The sherry pulses oloroso, the clarity like a lone church bell on a chill winter's morn; the oak is there to support rather than crush; the barley embraces the fruit rather than fights it. Breathtaking.... **t24.5** oh, oh, my...here we go again. Perfection in delivery with the bodyweight being just right to caress the tastebuds rather than engulf. The crystal clear grape shows first and reveals itself in several dimensions, especially in terms of sweetness; juicy with a countering drying vanilla blast and even an echo of something lightly smoked; **f23** perhaps shorter than it should be considering the genius of nose and delivery but there is no denying the finesse of the grape; even so, relatively long and lush by other mortal whiskies' standards with not a single quiver to its voice; **b23.5** unquestionably one of the great Macallans of recent times. Grab a bottle and defend to the death... 53.3%

Duncan Taylor Collection Macallan 1989 cask no. 3025 **(90.5) n24** wafer-light, biscuity with the most seductive ripple of fruit: spellbindingly complex; **t23** juiced-up, sexed-up barley that salivates and teases; soft melted cherry cake fills in the background noise; **f21.5** relatively thin with vanilla and soft oil; **b22** if a whisky ever says less to say more, this is it. 48.7%

⇒ **Duncan Taylor Collection Macallan 1990** cask no. 18222 **(87.5) n22** sweetened ginger nut biscuit with light fruits; **t23** silky, malty start. The oils kick in, as does a more aggressive oakiness; **f21** the sugars are leeched out and soften the leaden, oak-vanilla impact; **b21.5** quite a confused and confusing malt, not quite sure what it wants to be, or where it wants to go. Luckily, it works out attractively. 54.1%

⇒ **Duncan Taylor Collection Macallan 1991** cask no. 21437 **(92.5) n23** a real butterscotch-marzipan mix; **t23.5** the barley goes on a sugary spree, helped by the lightest of oils...and more butterscotch; **f23** the wonderful barley clarity on the palate continues even as slightly salty vanilla begins to creep in; **b23** no doubting the quality on offer. 52.8%

⇒ **Duncan Taylor Collection Macallan 1991** cask no. 21439 **(86) n22 t21 f22 b21.** Acacia honey escorts the barley and the interaction with the oak on the finish is pleasing, as is the intensity. But at times a little on the hot side. 55.1%

Duncan Taylor The NC2 Range Macallan 1990 (82.5) n21 t21.5 f20 b20. No shortage of natural caramels follow the banana-vaguely smoked lead. 46%

Duncan Taylor The NC2 Range Macallan 1995 (87) n22 freshly printed colour magazine; **t22** freshly crushed barley; **f21** freshly sprinkled vanilla; **b22** fresh. 46%

Gordon & MacPhail Speymalt Macallan 1938 (94) n25 can this really be over 65-years of age? How, after all these years, does the dynamic of the millroom fit so comfortably with pulped citrus and lavender? And, lurking at the very back, almost wishing not to be noticed, a waft of the softest peat imaginable. I have spent over half an hour nosing this. I cannot fault it. True legend...; **t22** an oaky barrage doesn't anger well, but soon it runs out of ammunition. It doesn't take long for accompanying spices and following barley-sugar and burnt honeycomb to unite and link with the pithy orange which has kept the oak in check from the off; **f23** amazingly, the oak remains on the retreat and now we get to the real serious bit. Soft peats return to offer little more than a smoky echo but the sweetness continues for dozens more waves. There is a lingering dryness, totally in sympathy with the leading malt but, most of all, the tangy orange remains sharp and delicious; **b24** when a malt is bottled at this near unbelievable age you expect the worst. And, even if it doesn't come, you have to be hyper-critical because such whisky doesn't come cheap and tasting notes written in awe of age rather than giving a true, honest assessment of its quality is not worth the ink used to print it. So, I have taken a long time to study this. And to find fault. Naturally, there are faults: every whisky has them, and at this age is expected to have more than most. But was it the quality of the wood they used in those days, or the peat involvement? Somehow, this malt has come through the best part of seven decades without any fatal flaws. The nose, in fact, is perfect. And although it wobbles on the palate on the start of its journey, by the end you cannot but be astounded. This is nature-defying whisky, very much like the 62-year-old Dalmore. Few people will be lucky enough ever to taste this. But those that do will be one of the truly privileged. And that includes me. 41.4%

Gordon & MacPhail Speymalt Macallan 1950 (91) n24 a swirl of peat beds down into the firm barley; the fruit is masterful with blood orange lightened by plums and juicy sultana. Oak is present but refuses to unbalance the delightful tranquillity and weight; **t22** wonderfully fruity pulse but there is still a gristy youth hanging on in there, allowing a subtle touch of peat to weave into the fabric. Again the oak holds back from doing any damage and the off wave of tangy kumquat is there to be found, **f22** does it's best to take an oaky route, but hasn't the heart to do it. Instead, light barley recovers to mingle playfully with the vanilla. Dry and sawdusty, but always in tune and balanced; **b23** I always taste these ultra-ancient whiskies with trepidation. Nature suggests that they should not be that good as barley – even with the aid of sherry – can see off only so much oak. But fortified with a delightful touch of peat, this holds itself together like an old Shakespeare first in original buckskin. It creaks. It's delicate. But take the time and handled carefully, this will amaze you. 43%

Gordon & MacPhail Speymalt Macallan 1967 (93) n23 fruitcake fortified, curiously, with a dash of rum; **t24** stunningly soft delivery of mixed fruits – especially sultana – and almost gristy barley; **f22** just the right sprinkling of chalky oak to counter the rising spice and suet; **b24** a mighty classy malt which has withstood the years with aplomb. 40%

Gordon & MacPhail Speymalt Macallan 1998 (73.5) n18.5 t19 f18 b18. The off key sulphur notes say rather more than it should about stocks of maturing Speyside malt right now... 43%

Gordon & MacPhail Station Series Kyle of Lochalsh Macallan 1996 refill sherry hogshead no. 11069, bott Feb 07 **(92) n22.5** lively and fresh, there is almost a brilliance to the sparkle of the barley; **t23.5** just glorious!!! The malt offers just the perfect degree of sweetness yet allows a soft vanilla and spice to muscle in; **f23** long, remains improbably clean and the sma' still oiliness kicks in to spread the fun further – and longer...; **b23** exactly how you dream a Macallan to be when un-molested by a poor sherry butt – or sherry at all, come to that. Should you ever be passing Tokyo... 46%. nc ncf. Japan Import System Co. Ltd. 377 bottles.

⌁ **The Golden Cask Macallan 1999** cask no. CM120, dist 99, bott 07 **(83.5) n21 t23 f19 b20.5.** The intensity of the honeycomb on delivery is an absolute treat. 57%. House of Macduff. 283 bottles.

⌁ **Hart Brothers Macallan Aged 15 Years** dist Dec 92, bott Jun 08 **(77.5) n18 t22 f19 b19.5.** What a shame! Loads of sweet juice and for a moment it really takes off with spices in tow. But dries and tightens. 46%. Hart Brothers Limited.

Heiko Thieme's 1974 Macallan 65th Birthday Bottling cask no. 16807 dist 25 Nov 74 bott Jul 08 **(94) n23** the clarity of the sherry takes some believing: this malt has obviously been in a good clean home for the last 34 years: not a single off note and the balance between grape, oak, spice and sweetened tomato puree is exceptional...; **t23** the arrival is sharp, both in terms of barley and grape. At first it looks shocked to have escaped the cask, or is hunting around for the alcohol to tie it together. But soon it finds harmony, helped along the way by a stunning chocolate and raisin middle which leads to some sweetening molasses; **f24** now enters into a class of its own. We all know about the fruitcake cliché: well here it is in glorious roasted raisin brilliance. Melton Hunt cake and trifle combined; the length makes a mockery of the strength. And it looks as though someone forgot to go easy on the burnt cherry. The vanillas are deft, the coffees are medium roast; **b24** this is not whisky because it is 38%abv. It is Scottish spirit. However, this is more of a whisky than a great many samples I have tasted this year. Ageism is outlawed. So is sexism. But alcoholism isn't....!! Try and become a friend of Herr Thieme and grab hold of something a little special. 38% 238 bottles.

Kingsbury "The Selection" Macallan 8 Years Old 1998 (88.5) n23 to die for: delicate, thin citrus mixed with delicate thin vanilla in perfect proportion; **t21.5** gentle barley with a light oily coating; **f22** the barley-vanilla interplay resumes; **b22** simple, delicate and very tasty. 43%. nc ncf. Japan Import System Co. Ltd.

Murray McDavid Macallan Aged 16 Years bourbon/Madeira, dist 90, bott 07 **(84.5) n21.5 t22 f20 b21.** A curious malt: it ticks many boxes yet somehow the overall sum is less than its parts. 46%. nc ncf. 1974 bottles.

⌁ **Norse Cask Selection Macallan 1991 Aged 17 Years** hogshead cask no. CM703, dist May 91, bott Jul 08 **(85) n21.5 t22 f20.5 b21.** Dusty in a few places, but the delivery sparkles bright barley. 57%. Qualityworld for WhiskyOwner.com, Denmark.

Northern Light Macallan 1995 Cask Strength bourbon cask no. Q583 **(83.5) n21 t21.5 f20 b21.** The gristiness on nose and palate leaves little doubt about the age. 57.5%. Qualityworld, Denmark.

Old & Rare Macallan Aged 20 Years sherry cask, dist Sep 87, bott Feb 08 **(89) n21** clipped grape is outgunned by sandalwood and polished floors; **t23** a metallic, small still, coppery intensity succeeds in intensifying the delivery of grape; **f22.5** long, juicy with a delicate fruit persona clinging to the building vanillas; **b22.5** a really fun, intense whisky absolutely bursting with attitude and intent. 54.4%. nc ncf. Douglas Laing. 187 bottles.

Old & Rare Macallan Aged 28 Years dist Oct 78, bott Sep 07 **(84) n19 t22 f21.5 b21.5.** The sun may have set on the nose, but streaming rays of honeyed barley are breaking through the oaky clouds. 52%. Douglas Laing. 219 bottles.

Old & Rare Macallan Aged 30 Years sherry finish **(86) n21 t22 f21.5 b21.5.** Works impressively with some coconut on the nose and buzzing oak-drenched spices on the delivery. The malt remains delightfully intact. 53.2%. Douglas Laing.

⌁ **Old & Rare Macallan Aged 30 Years** bott 09 **(88.5) n22** big oak, but a teasing wisp of smoke on the barley; **t22** juicy barley and a light coppery sheen; **f22.5** the oak bites but there is a lovely spice buzz, too **b22** a creaky old 'un, this. More ancient on the palate than its 30 years but a fair degree of juicy charm, too. *45.1%. Douglas Laing.*

Old Malt Cask Macallan Aged 15 Years rum cask no. 3874, dist Dec 91, bott Sep 07 **(89) n21** surprisingly aggressive oak; **t23** oh yes...!!! Wonderful delivery with a fabulous body and weight comfortably with outer rock-hard grain carrying a soft barley-sugar centre; **f22.5** traces of golden syrup keeps the spiced oak at bay **b22.5** a really classy Macallan showing an usual gait and weight. *50%. nc ncf. Douglas Laing. 346 bottles.*

⁘ **Old Malt Cask Macallan Aged 15 Years** dist Jun 93, bott Jul 09 **(83) n20.5 t22.5 f19 b21.** Far from perfect, but for a while the vivid sweetness of the noble rot grape hinted on the nose shines on the palate, too. *50%. Douglas Laing.*

Old Malt Cask Macallan Aged 16 Years bourbon cask no. 3737, dist Mar 91, bott Aug 07 **(81) n21.5 t20 f19.5 b20.** Firm barley and clear enough to show traces of smoke. *50%. Douglas Laing. 336 bottles.*

⁘ **Old Malt Cask Macallan Aged 18 Years** refill hogshead, dist Aug 90, bott Feb 09 **(84) n20.5 t21 f21.5 b21.** Even with the dab of peat this one carries, it is pleasant and enjoyable rather than inspiring as a Macallan of this vintage hopefully should be. *50%. Douglas Laing. 292 bottles.*

Old Malt Cask Macallan Aged 19 Years (78.5) n19 t19.5 f20 b20. Off key malt, a touch of sweet spice...19-years-old...?!?!?... zzzz...wake me up when something happens... *50%*

⁘ **Old Malt Cask Macallan Aged 19 Years** rum finish refill hogshead, finished in rum cask, dist Nov 89, bott Nov 08 **(89.5) n22.5** clean with barley sugar; **t22.5** sweet delivery; a slow barley encroachment still cannot entirely dislodge the sugary middle, though some building vanilla adds good weight; a fine peppery spice completes the treat; **f22** not a single bitter or off note: just more of the same; **b22.5** classic crisp rum finishing. Excellent. *50%. Douglas Laing. 277 bottles.*

Old Malt Cask Macallan Aged 20 Years rum cask no. 3873, dist Sep 87, bott Sep 07 **(87) n23.5** honey nut Cornflakes with a bourbony edge; **t21** layers of soft sugar and vanilla hints of a young bourbon; **f21.5** gentle vanilla dries with a vaguely spicy flourish; **b21.5** sweet, if confused, on the palate. But some real moments of joy, though bourbon appears to have more weight than rum. *50%.nc ncf. Douglas Laing. 312 bottles.*

⁘ **Old Malt Cask Macallan Aged 20 Years** Wine Finish refill hogshead, finished in wine barrel, dist Jun 88, bott Oct 08 **(85) n21 t21 f21.5 b21.5.** Sweet, grapey, enjoyable. But could have been devised and matured in East Anglia of England rather than the Highlands of Scotland. *50%. Douglas Laing. 274 bottles.*

Old Malt Cask Macallan Aged 21 Years refill hogshead no. 3847, dist Apr 86, bott Aug 07 **(85.5) n21.5 t22.5 f20 b21.** Attractive malt full of intense barley riches but which is denied of greatness at the death as natural toffee goes into overdrive. *50%. Douglas Laing. 319 bottles.*

Old Malt Cask Macallan Aged 22 Years claret wine barrel no. 3800, dist Apr 85, bott Aug 07 **(86.5) n22.5 t22 f21 b21.** Takes off elegantly but never quite makes it into the stratosphere. Big grape and spice early on compensates and the depth to the layering ensures a high quality experience. *50%. Douglas Laing. 292 bottles.*

⁘ **Old Malt Cask Macallan Aged 23 Years** Rum Finish refill hogshead, finished in rum cask, dist Apr 85, bott Oct 08 **(86) n22.5 t21.5 f21 b21.5.** Scented but not quite soapy on the nose and a stirring, almost thirst-quenching juiciness on delivery. *50%. Douglas Laing.*

⁘ **Old Malt Cask Macallan Aged 24 Years** refill hogshead, dist Apr 85, bott Apr 09 **(93.5) n23** a beautiful bourbon come Canadian oaky sweetness; **t24** glorious honey and butterscotch with a few slices of lime for extra liveliness; the background is a demure gooseberry and pecan tart, rounded off by maple syrup; **f23** a little drier – well, it had to be, with a pulsing echo of the previous round, but a drier vanilla exit; **b23.5** how can a whisky be this sweet but not for a second either cloying or over the top? I defy anyone to say a bad word against this classic dram. *50%. Douglas Laing. 281 bottles..*

Old Malt Cask Macallan Aged 30 Years sherry cask no. 3885, dist May 77, bott Sep 07 **(67.5) n17.5 t18 f15.5 b16.5.** Oh dear. I would not expect sulphur from a cask of this vintage. But there it is: indisputably so. Has the cask been finished (in every sense, alas) on a new, tainted, butt, I wonder...? *50%. nc ncf. Douglas Laing. 263 bottles.*

Premier Barrel Macallan Aged 10 Years (78.5) n19 t21.5 f19 b19. Just checking in the dictionary the definition of the word "Premier"... *46%. Douglas Laing.*

⁘ **Premier Barrel Macallan Aged 11 Years (86.5) n21.5 t22 f21.5 b21.5.** A beautiful example of a well used barrel giving the distillery a chance to show its credentials: the barley is gristy-sweet and carried on a coppery-sharp oiliness. *46%. Douglas Laing. 376 bottles.*

Premier Barrel Macallan Aged 16 Years bourbon finish **(80) n21 t20.5 f18.5 b20.** Slightly more Conference North. *46%. Douglas Laing. 335 bottles.*

Premier Barrel Macallan Aged 17 Years dist Apr 85, bott Jan 07 **(87) n23 t22 f21 b21.** Doesn't live up to the early promise, but still a little sweetie. *46%. Douglas Laing. 327 bottles.*

Premier Barrel Macallan Aged 18 Years (89) n22 precise, unruffled barley; **t23** gathers in the complexity stakes as layers of fruity-sweet barley give the vanillas a good thumping; **f22** dries demurely; **b22** Mac at its (apparently) un-sherried best. *46%. 312 btls.*

Private Cellar's Selection Macallan 1987 bott 07 **(84.5) n20.5 t21 f22 b21.** Clean, lush malt. Evidence of small still intensity, sweet, almost sharp barley and serious chewability. *43%*

Provenance Macallan Aged 8 Years hogshead no. 3837-3838, dist autumn 98, bott summer 07 **(85.5) n21 t22 f21.5 b21.** Makes little attempt to blind you with complexity, but it's a clean, fresh, malty number well performed. *46%. Douglas Laing.*

Provenance Macallan Aged 9 Years refill hogshead nos. 4076 & 4077, dist 98, bott 07 **(88) n23** who cannot love the shrill call of the citrus; **t22.5** as mouth-watering as the nose suggests with a light coating of zestiness on the fresh barley; **f20.5** dulls with unexpected rapidity; **b22** spot on nose and delivery. *46%. nc ncf. Douglas Laing.*

Provenance Macallan Aged 9 Years refill barrel nos. 4269 and 4270, dist Autumn 98, bott Spring 08 **(87.5) n21.5** clean, steady barley; **t22.5** fine barley-spice interplay; slow dissolving of gooseberry in the gentle oil; **f21.5** some major treacle toffee at the death; **b22** a playful, teasing complexity. *46%. nc ncf. Douglas Laing.*

⠐⠄ **Provenance Macallan Aged 11 Years** refill hogshead, dist winter 97, bott autumn 08 **(78.5) n20 t21 f18.5 b19.** Low key with the barley working flat out against the bitter oak. *46%. Douglas Laing.*

Provenance Macallan Aged 16 Years rum finished barrel no. 3903, dist spring 91, bott autumn 07 **(79.5) n20 t20.5 f20 b19.** A rum cove, and make no mistake. There appears to be something smoked on the nose, but fails to find a rhythm or balance as the finish appears incomplete. *46%. Douglas Laing.*

Scotch Malt Whisky Society Cask 24.100 Aged 11 Years sherry butt, dist Jun 96 **(73) n18 t19 f18 b18.** A disappointing way to bring up the century. *59.5%*

Scotch Malt Whisky Society Cask 24.101 Aged 23 Years refill hogshead, dist Apr 85 **(90) n21.5 t23.5 f22 b23** High quality mix of suet pudding and farmhouse cake. *52.8%*

⠐⠄ **Scotch Malt Whisky Society Cask 24.104 Aged 18 Years** sherry butt, dist May 90 **(68.5) n17 t18.5 f16 b17.** Nothing more to say than what has already been said on 24.106... *56.9%*

⠐⠄ **Scotch Malt Whisky Society Cask 24.105 Aged 25 Years** refill hogshead, dist Apr 85 **(92) n23.5** a touch of spice on the baked banana; custard cream biscuits and barley sugar; a lovely, semi-bourbony aroma and make no mistake; **t23.5** propels itself around the palate with a feverish fizziness, helped along the way by excellent spices. The barley is crisp yet mouth-watering while some coconut and liquorice reinforce that bourbony feel; **f22** tires after such an energetic display, allowing in the drier oaks; **b23** if this one doesn't keep you amused and charmed in equal measure, nothing will. *58.6%*

⠐⠄ **Scotch Malt Whisky Society Cask 24.106 Aged 12 Years** sherry butt, dist Jun 96 **(64.5) n17 t17.5 f14 b16.** How the hell did such a grotesquely sulphured monster as this blag its way past the tasting panel? A absolute shocker. *58.9%*

⠐⠄ **Scotch Malt Whisky Society Cask 24.107 Aged 12 Years** sherry butt, dist Jun 96 **(77) n20 t19 f19 b19.** Juicy with some green fig sweetness. Remnants of what once must have been a great butt before the sulphur stick got to work. *58.6%*

Scott's Selection Macallan 1989 bott 07 **(78.5) n21 t20.5 f19 b18.** Malty, clean but boring. *48.3%*

The Single Malts of Scotland Macallan 1990 Aged 17 Years bott Sep 07 **(83.5) n19 t22 f21.5 b21.** The butterscotch and barley on the palate compensates for the tired nose. *46%*

⠐⠄ **Speymalt Macallan 1988 (88) n22** seriously citrussy; **t22.5** as light, juicy, grassy and lemon-sharpened as the nose suggests; **f21.5** dulls down as the vanillas move in; **b22** a real Speyside feel to this one. *43%. Gordon & MacPhail.*

Speymalt from Macallan 1988 (88) n23 about as delicate barley will ever get; **t22** the clean lines and soft, buttery barley kiss continue; wonderful bitter-sweet charm **f21** thins out too rapidly; **b22** but for the finish this'd be a Must Have. *40%.*

⠐⠄ **Speymalt Macallan 1999 (72.5) n19 t19.5 f16 b18.** Juicy early on but dulls as the flaws become apparent. *43%. Gordon & MacPhail.*

The Whisky Fair Macallan Aged 14 Years Artist Edition sherry, dist 93, bott 07 **(86.5) n21.5 t22 f21.5 b21.5.** Splendidly gristy, juicy and mouth-watering but seriously underdeveloped for its age. *50%. Germany.*

Wilson & Morgan Barrel Selection Macallan 16 Years Old Cask Strength dist 91, bott 07 **(89.5) n21.5** cold spotted dog...with the emphasis on the spots...; **t23.5** succulent with both fruit and barley showing vividly; the slow burn on the spice is exemplary; **f22** fat and fabulously marbled with veins of barley and fruit; **b22.5** at first an easy one to overlook, such as its outwardly cumbersome nature. But slow reflection repays you handsomely. *58.6%*

⫶⫶⫶ **Wilson & Morgan Barrel Selection Macallan Aged 20 Years** dist 88, bott 08 **(79) n21 t20 f19 b19.** Very tight. *46%. Wilson & Morgan.*

⫶⫶⫶ **Wilson & Morgan Barrel Selection Macallan 1998** Marsala Finish bott 08 **(82) n20.5 t21 f20.5 b20.** Juicy yet dry and restrained. *46%. Wilson & Morgan.*

MACDUFF
Speyside, 1963. Dewar's. Working

Glen Deveron Aged 10 Years dist 95 db **(86) n19 t23 f23 b21.** The enormity of the third and fourth waves on delivery give some idea of the greatness this distillery could achieve perhaps with a little more care with cask selection, upping the strength to 46% and banning caramel. We'd have a malt scoring in the low to mid 90s every time. At the moment we must remain frustrated. *40%* ⊙⊙

⫶⫶⫶ **Berry's Own Selection Macduff 1991** bott 08 **(88) n23** raspberry jam buffeted by an almost pathetic degree of smoke. beautiful... **t22** light textured and major emphasis on juicy barley. Some major oak keeps a distance; again the faintest smoke imaginable; **f21** vanilla led; **b22** quite an unusual type of malt which needs three or four mouthfuls to get the measure of. *46%. Berry Bros & Rudd.*

⫶⫶⫶ **Cärn Mör Vintage Collection Macduff 2005** hogshead, cask no. 23, dist 05, bott 09 **(78) n19 t21 f19 b19.** Sweet malt on delivery, otherwise not picked at the best moment of its early life cycle. *46%. The Scottish Liqueur Centre.*

Duncan Taylor Collection Macduff 1968 cask no. 8546 **(79) n19 t19 f21 b20.** Just a fraction too much oak to win minds as well as hearts. *46.9%*

Duncan Taylor Collection Macduff 1968 cask no. 8544 **(85.5) n22 t21 f21.5 b21.** Diluted maple syrup sweetens enormously in a bid to keep the oak honest. Has served its time well, but not as complex as something of this magnificent age might be. *45.2%*

Duncan Taylor Collection Macduff 1968 cask no. 8550 **(89.5) n21.5** buckling under the oak; **t22.5** an oaky threat initially, then waves of rich barley sugar and spice ride to the rescue; **f22.5** a tad molassed but those deft spices plus mocha work well with the vanilla; **b23** on the nose, it looks as though 8544 will have what it takes, but in this game you never know for certain. Wonderful grace and imagination even after all these years. *49.1%*

⫶⫶⫶ **Duncan Taylor Collection Macduff 1969** cask no. 3668 **(86.5) n22.5 t21 f21.5 b21.5.** Lovely malt showing some knots of age but having the grace and wherewithal to allow the more elegant barley notes to take a bow. *40.8%*

Lonach Macduff 1969 (92) n23 a fruit cocktail with a side dish of cold custard; a teasing herbal note complements beautifully; **t23** how can something this old be so juicy? Like freshly-squeezed barley sugar; **f23** the oak starts gathering forces but such is the depth of the fresh barley it nothing more than complements and balances **b23** uncompromised star quality throughout. One of those malts that makes writing this book so rewarding...!! *40.6% Duncan Taylor.*

⫶⫶⫶ **Old Malt Cask Miltonduff Aged 12 Years** refill hogshead, dist Mar 96, bott Sep 08 **(79.5) n19.5 t19 f21 b20.** Recovers with a malty-vanilla flourish after an uncertain, off-key start. *50%. Douglas Laing. 357 bottles.*

Old Malt Cask Macduff Aged 17 Years rum finished barrel no. 3905, dist Oct 90, bott Oct 07 **(88.5) n22** good grief: if this hasn't been sitting in an old cask of DOK-marked rum from Hampden distillery, Jamaica, then I'll be very surprised: you can't move for jackfruit and esters....; **t23** a car crash of confusion: fruit and barley all over the place, but you can't help but like it... **f22** sharp, eye-watering barley leaves a syrupy-sweet trail; **b21.5** there are rum finishes and then there are rum finishes. Now let me tell you ladies and gentlemen: that was a rum finish... *50%. nc ncf. Douglas Laing. 150 bottles.*

⫶⫶⫶ **Old Malt Cask Macduff Aged 19 Years** dist Mar 90, bott Jul 09 **(69) n17 t18 f17 b17.** MacDuff without the Mac. *50%. Douglas Laing.*

Old Malt Cask Macduff Aged 40 Years bourbon finished barrel no. 3904, dist Jun 67, bott Sep 07 **(85.5) n21.5 t19 f23 b22.** Coffee walnut cake with plenty of coffee and walnuts. Essentially a dram that's absorbed too much oak. But somehow that creamy coffee effect saves the day and makes for a lovely long finish. *50%. Douglas Laing. 227 bottles.*

Old Masters Macduff Aged 17 Years cask no. 1418 dist 90, bott 08 **(68.5) n16 t18 f17 b17.5.** Duff by name and nature. Noses do come worse than this...but not that often. *57.8%. James MacArthur & Co. Ltd.*

Scott's Selection Macduff 1978 bott 07 **(84.5) n20 t21 f22.5 b21.** Macduffed up by oak it may be, but enough honeyed barley clings on to give the odd clout of its own. *44.4%*

The Single Malts of Scotland Macduff 1991 Aged 16 Years (88) n23 custard over rhubarb; **t22** bitter-sweet with juicy barley just in control; **f21** splintery; **b22** a malt on the very edge, but the pervading oily sweetness just guarantees excellence. *59.6%. sc. Speciality Drinks, UK.*

MANNOCHMORE
Speyside, 1971. Diageo. Working.
Mannochmore Aged 12 Years db (84) n22 t21 f20 b21. As usual the mouth arrival fails to live up to the great nose. Quite a greasy dram with sweet malt and bitter oak. *43%.*

Connoisseurs Choice Mannochmore 1990 (85) n20 t22 f21 b22. Perhaps overly sweet and slightly featureless. *46%. Gordon & MacPhail.*

Duncan Taylor The NC2 Range Mannochmore 1996 Aged 10 Years (76.5) n20.5 t19 f18 b19. Mannoch-less. Overly sweet. Otherwise has little or nothing to say. *46%*

The Exclusive Malts Mannochmore Aged 16 Years cask no. 6600, dist May 92 **(84.5) n20.5 t22 f21 b21.** Decent barley sugar but one-dimensional. *53.8%. The Creative Whisky Company. 234 bottles.*

⊹ **Old Malt Cask Mannochmore Aged 18 Years** refill barrel, dist Feb 91, bott Apr 09 **(91) n22.5** just a touch of resin to the grist; refreshing, though, thanks to a citrus sub plot; **t23** sublime melt-in-the-mouth gristy delivery which makes no apology for its big malty theme; a dab of coconut water lightly sweetens the grassy middle; **f22.5** citrus returns, almost apologetically; vanilla intertwines with the barley; **b23** modest in its intentions and delicate, it is never less than charming. *50%. Douglas Laing. 288 bottles.*

Scotch Malt Whisky Society Cask 64.15 Aged 15 Years refill barrel, dist Jun 92 **(88.5) n21.5 t23 f22 b22** Excellent in-your-face delivery; neat touches elsewhere. *57.1%*

⊹ **Scotch Malt Whisky Society Cask 64.18 Aged 24 Years** refill butt, dist Dec 84 **(93.5) n23** subtle floral notes sit wonderfully with the lemon curd tart and butterscotch ...delicate and yummy...; **t24** such a crisp delivery: a surprise, really. The barley is sharp and mouth-watering: simple, but just so right... **f23.5** back to the butterscotch; the barley is right behind. Clear and crystalline to the very end; **b23** rarely are we let down by this distillery. And this is a particular cracker, even if the tale it tells is oft told. *56.3%*

MILLBURN
Highland (Northern), 1807–1985. Closed.
Millburn 1969 Rare Malt db (77) n19 t21 f18 b19. Some lovely bourbon-honey touches but sadly over the hill and declining fast. Nothing like as interesting or entertaining as the massage parlour that was firebombed a few yards from my office twenty minutes ago. Or as smoky... *51.3%.*

Cadenhead's Millburn 31 Years Old (88) n22 an attractive sprinkling of fresh sawdust over the very softest of peats and custard tart; **t23** lush malt coats the mouth before a bombardment of spicy oak keeps the barley at bay; **f21** an oaky echo; **b22** a rumbustuous, red-hot affair which is ensuring the distillery is not disappearing with a whimper. Now a must have cask: decent bottlings of any of the old Inverness distilleries are few and far between. *52.3%*

MILTONDUFF
Speyside, 1824. Chivas. Working.
Miltonduff Aged 15 Years bott code L00/123 db **(86) n23 t22 f20 b21.** Some casks beyond their years have crept in and unsettled this one. But some real big salty moments to savour, too. *46%*

Battlehill Miltonduff 1999 cask no. 807 **(85) n21 t22 f21 b21.** Sturdy malt throughout. *43%.*

Dewar Rattray Miltonduff 1980 cask no. 12499, dist Sep 80, bott Nov 07 **(91) n23** thumping malt bolstered by butterscotch and earthy bluebells...is this really over 25 years old....??? **t23** gripping stuff; in that you find yourself gripping your seat as the malt pile-drives its way around the palate sending out mouth-watering, ultra-juicy shockwaves. Just so clean and dynamic... **f22.5** settles with a fizzing, sharp candy bitter-sweetness and doesn't allow the oak a look in; **b22.5** if there is such a thing as whisky vintages, for the record I always thought that the era around 1982 was about the best MD I ever found. This busy, tight, aggressive little classic helps prove the point. *51.9%*

Duncan Taylor Collection Miltonduff 1999 (86) n22 t22.5 f20.5 b21. A delightful, though more vanilla-accented and curiously underpowered version of the WG '99. *40%*

The Exclusive Malts Miltonduff Aged 11 Years finished in Chateauneuf du Pape wine cask no. 5566, dist Mar 96 **(63) n15 t17 f18 b18.** The only thing created here is another French wine casked nightmare. Where the hell did that nose come from...? *54.1%. The Creative Whisky Company. 327 bottles.*

James MacArthur's Fine Malt Selection Miltonduff Aged 12 Years bott May 08 **(86) n21.5 t21.5 f22 b21.** Clean with big malt surge. Much younger than a 12 in many ways, but no bad habits either. 43%. James MacArthur & Co. Ltd.

Lonach Miltonduff 1966 (79.5) **n22 t19 f19.5 b19.** Both the oak and barley are polished: a malt feeling its age. 40%. Duncan Taylor.

Old Malt Cask Miltonduff Aged 17 Years refill hogshead no. 3890, dist Sep 90, bott Sep 07 **(84.5) n22 t21 f20.5 b21.** Malty with bitterish tendencies. 50%. Douglas Laing. 216 bottles.

⊱ **Old Malt Cask Miltonduff Aged 28 Years** refill hogshead, dist Sep 80, bott Feb 09 **(92) n24** eye-closing, purr-inducing stuff: a stick of very lightly salted celery beside a glass of sweet orange juice. Cut up on the plate is a beetroot sans vinegar. Somewhere else some honey is spread on toast... Captivating, delicate, multi-complex and never less than sublime... **t23** much more oak involvement on delivery than the nose, but the barley is deftly applied and there is a gracious sweetness underpinning it all; **f22** oatcakes and distant vanilla: the oak plays an important but controlled role. **b23** doesn't quite live up to the nose: it is hard to see how it might. Nosing must constitute at least 60% of the experience with this whisky, though it's no disappointment in the glass, either, showing elegance throughout. 44.5%

⊱ **Old Masters Miltonduff Aged 13 Years** cask no. 5563, dist 96, bott 09 **(81) n19 t21 f20.5 b20.5.** Not all the heat is generated by the alcohol. By no means unpleasant but its scope is limited. 57.2%. James MacArthur & Co. Ltd.

Private Cellar's Selection Miltonduff 1987 bott 07 **(86) n21.5 t22 f21 b21.5.** A sturdy yet rotund old stager which fails to quite develop as it might towards the finale. The early fruit-edged barley does have some distinctively attractive elements. 43%

⊱ **Provenance Miltonduff Aged 11 Years** refill hogshead, dist winter 98, bott spring 09 **(74) n19 t19 f18 b18.** Sweetish, but never begins to gel. 46%. Douglas Laing.

⊱ **Scotch Malt Whisky Society Cask 72.21 Aged 11 Years** refill hogshead, dist Oct 97 **(90) n23** easy integration of light barley, vanilla and spiced yam; something of a light, youngish Guyanese pot still rum, too.; **t22.5** soft and bulging with gristy barley freshness and pounding spice, though tires and dries towards the middle; **f22** regains a second wind as a light oiliness helps stretch the sweeter notes over the exposed oak; **b22.5** refined and delicate but makes a big early statement. 56%

⊱ **Scott's Selection Miltonduff 1988** bott 08 **(83) n21 t22 f20 b20.** A pleasing malt with its entire emphasis on the early barley kick. 54.3%. Speyside Distillers.

Whisky-Doris Miltonduff 8 Years Old dist 6 Jun 99, bott 19 Oct 07 **(84.5) n22 t21 f21.5 b21.** Clean, malty, attractive: a mildly fiery up and downer. 55.7%. Whisky-Doris.

Whisky Galore Miltonduff 1999 (87.5) n21.5 grist little troubled by oak; **t22.5** mountainous malt with a fleck here and there of spice; **f21.5** soft oils keeps the barley going; **b22** absolutely top hole MD for this age. Simplistic maybe. But as fresh as a nibble on the ear. 46%. Duncan Taylor.

MORTLACH
Speyside, 1824. Diageo. Working.

Mortlach Aged 16 Years db **(87) n20** big, big sherry, but not exactly without a blemish or two; **t23** sumptuous fruit and then a really outstanding malt and melon mouthwatering rush; **f22** returns to heavier duty with a touch of spice, too; **b22** once it gets past the bold if very mildly sulphured nose, the rest of the journey is superb. Earlier Mortlachs in this range had a slightly unclean feel to them and the nose here doesn't inspire confidence. But from arrival on the palate onwards, it's sure-footed, fruity and even refreshing ... and always delicious. 43%. Flora and Fauna range.

Mortlach 32 Years Old dist 71 db **(88) n22 t22 f22 b22.** Big and with attitude.... 50.1%

Adelphi Mortlach 1990 Aged 17 Years sherry butt, cask no. 5945, dist 90, bott 08 **(86.5) n21 t21.5 f22.5 b21.5.** Competent and attractive for this distillery during this less than glorious period. A touch of smoke on the nose, lively spice and a lid kept on the sweetness makes for a lovely dram. 57.5%. 516 bottles.

Berrys' Own Selection Mortlach 1991 cask no. 4227, bott 07 **(66) n17 t16 f15 b16.** A classic example of the old United Distillers wine-treated casks. I need say no more. 56.4%. Berry Bros & Rudd.

Cadenhead's Mortlach Aged 19 Years sherry butt, dist 88, bott Feb 08 **(78.5) n19 t21.5 f19 b19.** Some decent oily grape. 57.6%. 664 bottles.

Chieftain's Mortlach Aged 15 Years sherry wood **(69) n17 t18 f17 b17.** This sweet and sulphurous effort is one 69 I don't like... 46%. Ian Macleod.

Dewar Rattray Mortlach 1991 cask no. 4238, dist May 91, bott Nov 07 **(80) n19 t20 f20.5 b20.5.** Clumsy, sweet, chewy and with a certain brown-sugared charm. 55.5%

Distillery Malt Mortlach Aged 15 Years (69) n16 t18 f18 b17. Fifteen years ago Mortlach was busy churning out some of Speyside's least impressive whisky. Here's some more of it. *43%. Gordon & MacPhail.*

Dun Bheagan Mortlach 10 Years Old dist 96, bott for the Whisky Festival Belgium 07 **(84) n21 t22 f20 b21.** A real malty slugfest with complexity at a premium and the finish little helped by a tired cask. But it's just so great to see this once excellent distillery getting back to being its big, impressive self after so many years in the wilderness. *57.5%. nc ncf.*

Duncan Taylor The NC2 Range Mortlach 1993 (81) n21 t20 f20 b20. A steady, no frills, malty Speysider. *46%*

⋅≫⋅ **Duthies Mortlach 16 Years Old (88.5) n22.5** unusually clean aroma for this distillery with a lovely, intense fruity theme; **t22.5** genuinely juicy with barley concentrate on the rampage; **f21.5** drier, vanilla-led; **b22** easily one of the more enjoyable Mortlachs on the market. *46%. Cadenhead's for Germany.*

⋅≫⋅ **The Golden Cask Mortlach 1994** cask no. CM115 **(76) n19 t20 f18 b19.** Syrupy and though sumptuous and hearty, enough of the mud from the cask sticks...especially on the finish. *55.1%. House of Macduff. 305 bottles.*

Northern Light Mortlach 1988 Cask Strength cask no. Q125 **(86.5) n22 t22 f21 b21.5.** Thoroughly pleasant with some delightful orangey notes on the nose and seriously thick spiced malt on the delivery and middle. Well spiced, complex and the kind of dram that demands a refill. *59.2%. Qualityworld, Denmark.*

Old Malt Cask Mortlach Aged 15 Years sherry butt no. 3934, dist Sep 92, bott Oct 07 **(88) n22.5** almost pot still rum-like in its thick, sugared intensity; **t22** mouth-coatingly beautiful with lashings of demerara sugar and honeycomb; **f21.5** toasty and attractively bitter-sweet; **b22** a bit of a typically cloying pup for this distillery but, untypically, there are no off notes and balance is pretty satisfying. *50%. Douglas Laing. 671 bottles.*

⋅≫⋅ **Old Malt Cask Mortlach Aged 16 Years** sherry cask, dist Sep 92, bott Jan 09 **(81.5) n20.5 t22 f19 b20.** The old-fashioned trifle, grapey nose survives a sulphur scare, as does the initial, fresh delivery. And even for a while we have a bit of a sultana festival. But that dreaded off note can't escape the finale, as is so often the case... *50%. Douglas Laing.*

⋅≫⋅ **Old Malt Cask Mortlach Aged 16 Years** sherry butt, dist Sep 92, bott Dec 08 **(73.5) n18.5 t19 f18 b18.** Grapey, sweet, lush...and flawed. *50%. Douglas Laing. 582 bottles.*

⋅≫⋅ **Old Malt Cask Mortlach Aged 19 Years** Gabriel Meffre red wine cask, dist Mar 89, bott Sep 08 **(85) n22 t21 f21 b21.** Pretty acceptable version of a malt which struggles from bottling to bottling. Here there are an extra few spoonfuls of Demerara on the Dundee cake and the big, fig biscuit chew ends up with a bit of Jammy Dodger. Silky but laid on with a trowel. *50%. Douglas Laing. 359 bottles.*

Old Malt Cask Mortlach Aged 12 Years Sherry Finish dist Jul 94, bott May 07 **(72) n18 t19 f17 b18.** Malt ordinaire. *50%. Douglas Laing. 654 bottles.*

Old Masters Mortlach 1989 Aged 16 Years cask no. 969 **(77) n19 t20 f19 b19.** Furry, bitter, harsh and hot: one of the better Mortlachs from this period... *56.5%. James MacArthur.*

Premier Barrel Mortlach Aged 11 Years Sherry Finish (68) n17 t17 f17 b17. Another victim of the S word. *46%. Douglas Laing. 776 bottles.*

Private Collection Mortlach 1968 (80) n19 t21 f20 b20. An opaque malt with the sherry blotting out all further complexity, oak apart. If you like your sherry enormous and clean, here you go... *45%. Gordon & MacPhail.*

⋅≫⋅ **Provenance Mortlach Aged 12 Years** refill hogshead, dist summer 96, bott spring 09 **(81) n18 t20.5 f22 b20.5.** Treacle-sweet; recovers well with a bit of barley bite and spice, even, after the poor nose. *46%. Douglas Laing.*

⋅≫⋅ **Sassenach's Dram Whisky Club Mortlach 14 Year Old (83.5) n22 t21 f20 b20.5.** Excellent fresh, grassy barley on nose. *46%. Exclusively for members of Sassenach's Dram Whisky Club Ltd.*

Scotch Malt Whisky Society Cask 76.57 Aged 8 Years 1st fill barrel, dist Jun 99 **(81.5) n20 t21 f20.5 b20.** Clumsy, sweet and cloying: must be Mortlach. *60.2%*

Scotch Malt Whisky Society Cask 76.58 Aged 23 Years refill hogshead, dist Apr 85 **(83.5) n22 t20 f21.5 b20.** Wonderful nose, full of intensely malty, slightly fruity possibilities. But hopes of greatness are dashed by the cloying, furry delivery. *60%*

Scotch Malt Whisky Society Cask 76.59 Aged 23 Years refill hogshead, dist Apr 85 **(79) n20 t19 f20 b20.** Seriously hot whisky: and I'm not talking about the strength. Some less than delicate sugar-coated barley bails it out. At Whisky Fairs (usually in German-speaking lands) I am amazed by how many tell me they count Mortlach among their favourites. The fact that the SMWS have bottled three casks of the stuff must mean there is a big demand out there. I am at a loss: I really must be missing something. *61.8%*

⁙ **Scotch Malt Whisky Society Cask 76.62 Aged 9 Years** refill barrel, dist Jun 99 **(85) n21.5 t22.5 f21 b20.** Last week I was at the dentist. Time to go back: it's like sucking on molten barley-flavoured sugar. Decent juiciness, though. 59.4%

⁙ **Scotch Malt Whisky Society Cask 76.63 Aged 12 Years** refill barrel, dist Sep 96 **(84) n21 t21.5 f20.5 b21.** Sweet and moderately hot. But some excellent oak absorbs the worst excesses and allows an attractively malty dram to flourish. 60.3%

Scott's Selection Mortlach 1990 bott 07 **(84.5) n20 t22.5 f21 b21.** A collector's item: a lightly peated Mortlach. Some charm on delivery and the smoke helps disguise an unhelpful cask. 56%

Tanners Mortlach Aged 14 Years (69) n19 t18 f16 b16. Chewy and initially sweet but displaying that furry character so typical of Mortlach at this time when the casks were dreadful and strange things were happening in the still house. Why it is used by so many companies as their own label brand is absolutely beyond me. Tanners are a much better merchant than this. 45%. Tanners Wine Merchants.

Whisky Tales Mortlach 16 Years Old sherry cask, dist 91, bott 07 **(72) n20.5 t22 f16 b17.5.** It's the finish that tells the most telling tale, and as is often the case with this distillery it's a grizzly one involving sulphur. 56.2%. nc ncf. 349 bottles. Germany.

⁙ **Wilson & Morgan Barrel Selection Mortlach Aged 18 Years** Old butt no. 4422, dist 90 **(74.5) n18 t19 f19 b18.5.** A typically mucky, lightly sulphured affair from this distillery. Oddly enough there is a strawberry jam attractiveness late on. 56.8%. Wilson & Morgan.

MOSSTOWIE

Speyside, 1964–1981. Two Lomond stills within Miltonduff Distillery. Now dismantled.

Rarest of the Rare Mosstowie 1975 cask no. 5811 **(94) n25** egg noggin, several squirts of vanilla essence, crumpled rose petals and a stunning mixture of citrus and berry fruit. Whisky of this age just doesn't get better on the nose... **t23.5** soft, almost playful barley thickened slightly by a backbone of diluted maple syrup; very delicate fruit naturally intertwines; **f22** a degree of bitterness reminds you of the great age here; **b23.5** given that these chaps don't happen along too often, I thought it'd be the perfect way to celebrate 999 whiskies for this edition (an even rarer Glencraig is lined up next). And I have been perfectly rewarded: a much better bottling than the last I tasted, this has remained intact from nose to finish and apparently revels in its rarity. The best I have tasted from these lost stills for over a decade. Actually, thinking about it....ever. 48.5% Duncan Taylor.

Rarest of the Rare Mosstowie 1975 cask no. 5814, dist May 75, bott Apr 06 **(88) n22 t22 f22 b22.** A wonderful surprise: the nose at first indicated that it might be beyond greatness. Not a bit of it – a rare treat, indeed! 48.1%. Duncan Taylor. 191 bottles.

⁙ **Rarest of the Rare Mosstowie 1975** cask no. 5816 **(90.5) n23** peaches and custard; a light flicker of mango **t23** soft with the barley dissolving on impact; the vanillas begin with an equally deft touch but show they mean business by the middle; the early soft, peachy fruits dissolve with the barley **f22** thins and spices out but the custard remains **b22.5** talk about getting old gracefully... 48.4%. Duncan Taylor.

⁙ **Rarest of the Rare Mosstowie 1975** cask no. 5817 **(81) n21.5 t21.5 f19 b19.** Pleasant, malty but hot and skeletal. 47.7%. Duncan Taylor.

NORTH PORT

Highland (Eastern), 1820–1983. Demolished.

Brechin 1977 db **(78) n19 t21 f18 b20.** Fire and brimstone was never an unknown quantity with the whisky from this doomed distillery. Some soothing oils are poured on this troubled – and sometimes attractively honeyed – water of life. 54.2%

Cadenhead's Chairman's Stock North Port (Brechin) Aged 29 Years bourbon hogshead, dist 77, bott Sep 06 **(83) n21 t21 f20 b21.** Fishermen's Friend cough sweets by the bag-load. Hints of hotness but pretty good for this usually harsh and unforgiving malt. 51.4%. 174 bottles.

⁙ **Connoisseurs Choice North Port Brechin 1982** bott 08 **(79.5) n21 t21 f18.5 b19.** Although the oak has left a bitter mark, there is a jaunty fruitiness to this on both nose and delivery which speaks well of the barley. 43%. Gordon & MacPhail.

⁙ **Private Cellar North Port 1982** bott 07 **(89.5) n24** anyone old enough to remember Zoom lollies will appreciate this one: a kind of banana-strawberry mix, topped with a delicate sugared sweetness. I have just zoomed back 45 years...; the faintest peat, however, was not something I would have recognised in my most tender years...; **t22** ballooning oak is pricked by a slow advance of thick barley, almost reaching soup-like proportions; **f21.5** the dryness of the oak continues to dominate while the odd sprinkling of barley sugar helps point towards a chocolatey-minty finale....anyone remember Merlin Brew lollies from around the time this whisky was distilled....? **b22** an over-aged malt which, having reached greatness against the odds, has begun a descent. Even so, the fabulous nose and big barley oomph makes this dram a very enjoyable place to be. *43%. Speyside Distillers.*

Rarest of the Rare North Port 1981 cask no. 775 **(93.5) n23** oh, you fruity thing... kumquats and pears with a splash of custard...and even something vaguely smoky; **t24** North Port....??? Really....???? The delivery is sublime; just the right degree of oil and then a slow release of delicate sugars and a build up of intense barley. Wonderful...!!! **f23** wondrous layering of vanilla, lemon and butterscotch. Long, confident and just so classy; **b23.5** Rarest of the Rare all right...!! Easily the finest North Port I have come across in bottled form. This may have been a throat-ripping monster in its youth, but in old age it really has reached a point of true charm and charisma. Stunning – and one hell of a shock! *52.9%. Duncan Taylor.*

⠿ **Rarest of the Rare North Port 1981** cask no. 779 **(95) n24.5** candyfloss, old-fashioned sweetshops, old-fashioned leather handbags; syrup-coated coconut, Niederegger marzipan...mmmmm!!! **t24.5** no less beautiful on delivery: the weight of the softly sugared coating is sublime, but better still there is spice and warmer vanilla notes for contrast; for all this the barley is never lost, is heard early and gets louder towards the middle; **f22.5** still delightful, but by comparison with the just about perfect delivery, the finale is so much thinner with the malt clinging onto the vanilla the best it can; **b23.5** the old Brechin distillery is in danger of getting a good posthumous name for itself...this is what great whisky is all about. *56.5%. Duncan Taylor.*

Scott's Selection North Port 1980 bott 07 **(95) n23.5** firm, banana and malt in pretty equal measures; a speck of peat tops it off with aplomb; **t24.5** superb delivery, not least because, just like the nose, the malt is working on split levels: it is firm, brittle almost and pings around the teeth yet sumptuous enough to mould itself into every crevice; equally, the degree of sweetness switches to sharper, to counter the building vanilla, and soft, to give a background noise; **f23.5** refuses to lie down and just hugs on to the palate with sultry spice, a touch of citrus, malt and a late peat echo; **b23.5** Brechin, the home of North Port, must be where they make London buses: you wait a lifetime for a fantastic bottling...then two come along at once.... The Rarest of the Rare bottling really was the finest I had tasted – until five minutes later when I encountered this. My job never ceases to amaze me. Who knew that east coast malt could be this damned good...???? *48%*

OBAN

Highland (Western), 1794. Diageo. Working.

Oban 14 db **(84) n20 t22 f21 b21.** Slick and fruity, you can close your eyes and think of Jerez. Oban seems a long way away. A very decent dram. But I want my old, bracing, mildly smoky, fruitless Oban back!! Those who prefer malts with a sheen, sweet and with enormous fruit depth won't be disappointed. *43%*

Oban Aged 15 Years The Distiller's Edition db finished in Montilla Fino casks, dist 92, bott 07 **(90) n22.5** splashed on grape offers a lovely bitter-sweet tang – even on the nose! **t23** simplistic delivery: soft, velvety and lush. The grape makes for one of the softest landings buyable; **f22.5** more big sultanas and a stirring of porridge and vanilla for good measure; **b22** this isn't all about complexity and layering. It's about style and effect. And it pulls it off brilliantly. *43%*

⠿ **Oban Aged 15 Years The Distiller's Edition** db finished in Montilla Fino casks, dist 93, bott 08 **(91.5) n22** nutty, tight, a little musty; **t24** much more assured: the dryness of the grape sports beautifully against the obviously more outgoing and sweeter barley: excellent balance between the two; **f22.5** perhaps the Fino wins, as it dries and embraces the oak quite happily; **b23** delicate and sophisticated whisky. *43%*

PITTYVAICH

Speyside 1975–1993. Demolished.

Pittyvaich Aged 12 Years db **(64) n16 t18 f15 b15.** It was hard to imagine this whisky getting worse. But somehow it has achieved it. From fire-water to cloying undrinkability. What amazes me is not that this is such bad whisky: we have long known that Pittyvaich can be as grim as it gets. It's the fact they bother bottling it and inflicting it on the public. Vat this with malt from Fettercairn and neighbouring Dufftown and you'll have the perfect dram for masochists. Or those who have entirely lost the will to live. Jesus.... *43%. Flora and Fauna.*

Cadenhead's Pittyvaich 21 Years Old (68) n18 t17 f16 b17. God help us...any Port in a storm, but little respite from the crashing waves of red-hot barley. *54.3%*

Old Malt Cask Pittyvaich Aged 16 Years refill hogshead no. 3886, dist Oct 90, bott Sep 07 **(71) n17.5 t18 f18 b17.5.** Drinkable. But you'll wonder why you bothered: another nothing dram from Speyside's ugly duckling. *50%. Douglas Laing. 345 bottles.*

❖ **Old Malt Cask Pittyvaich Aged 18 Years** sherry butt, dist Jun 90, bott Jan 09 **(76) n18.5 t21 f17.5 b19.** If you find a more uncompromisingly sweet malt this year, let me know. *50%. Douglas Laing. 703 bottles.*

Provenance Pittyvaich Aged 12 Years refill hogshead no. 4255, dist Autumn 95, bott Spring 08 **(78) n20 t20 f19 b19.** Thin, hot-ish, niggardly barley with minimal development: which means for a Pittyvaich not bad at all... *46%. nc ncf. Douglas Laing.*

❖ **Rarest of the Rare Pittyvaich 1979** cask no. 5635 **(87) n22.5** a delicate Pittyvaich? The barley appears untroubled by the normal gluepot vapours which have taken a day off; **t23** I'm waiting for my throat to be ripped out and it hasn't happened. A bit like Wylie Cyote jumping up and down on the ACME dynamite to see if it works, I take another mouthful and am very pleasantly surprised – no, make that shocked - that the huge malt actually caresses the tastebuds and brings with it a mild sugary edge to the natural caramels. Ye gods...!! This is Pittyvaich and actually very pleasant stuff... **f20** much more like it at the death with a thin, gluey fade; **b21.5** I had to check the bottle for this one. Was this really Pittyvaich? Could it be that this mouth-filling, ultra-delicious beast is the prodigy of one of the world's most hopeless distilleries? It appears it is.....!!!! The finish is up to scratch, though.. *48.3%. Duncan Taylor.*

Rarest of the Rare Pittyvaich 1979 cask no. 5636 **(79) n21 t20 f19 b19.** Just when for a fleeting second you think the beast may have been tamed, you suddenly – and painfully – realise it hasn't. In this case with a momentary spasm of agony through a rear tooth. At moments like that, there is almost a begrudging respect. *54%. Duncan Taylor.*

❖ **Rarest of the Rare Pittyvaich 1979** cask no. 5640 **(81.5) n21 t21 f19 b20.5.** Big, rollocking barley flattened by natural caramels, hot and graceless with a splintering finish. But still much better than the norm. *50.2%. Duncan Taylor.*

❖ **Scotch Malt Whisky Society Cask 90.11 Aged 19 Years** refill barrel, dist Mar 90 **(75.5) n20 t20 f17 b18.5.** Thin and impoverished, though the oak does its level best to beef up the barley: one can only imagine with a horror bordering on morbid fascination what this must have been like 19 years ago.... *54.9%*

PORT ELLEN
Islay, 1825–1983. Closed.

Port Ellen 1979 db **(93) n22** mousy and retiring; a degree of oak fade and fruit on the delicate smoke **t23** non-committal delivery but bursts into stride with a series of sublime, peat-liquorice waves and a few rounds of spices; **f24** a surprising gathering of oils rounds up the last traces of sweet barley and ensures an improbably long – and refined – finish; **b24** takes so long to get out of the traps, you wonder if anything is going to happen. But when it does, my word...it's glorious! *57.5%*

Port Ellen 4th Release Aged 25 Years dist 78, bott 04 db **(95) n22** much less smoky than previous release, with greater emphasis on fruit, especially cinnamon-sprinkled apple. The oak offers perhaps the firmest thread, marginally threatening to dominate; **t25** just so, so stunning! The immaculate balance between the peat-malt and oak hits home from the very first second. Somehow, after 25 years, it has retained the trademark gristiness with the peat being released in controlled waves. Hints of honey help fend off any advancement of oak, and the threat from the nose never materialises. Instead there is a steady throbbing of perfect spices; **f24** honey-vanilla and more lapping waves of peat and spice bring a gentle end to proceedings...eventually. **b24** for those of us who can remember it in its original younger form, this is almost something to give you a lump in the throat and a watery eye: it remains just so true to character and form, cocking the most elegant and contemptuous snook at those who decided to kill the distillery off. When they closed the distillery I remember being told by the decision-makers there was no difference in quality between PE and Caol Ila. I disagreed then, strongly. Today, my argument is mute: the eloquence belongs to the contents of this bottle. *56.2%. 5,100 bottles.*

Port Ellen 27 Years Old special release 06, dist 78 db **(94) n25 t24 f22 b23.** A luxurious malt and worth an hour of anybody's valuable time. *54.2%*

Port Ellen 28 Years Old 7th release, bott 2007 db **(92.5) n22.5** not so much grist these days as ash; some heavy lilac and garden perfume business going on and a touch of lime, too; **t23** an immediate sweet introduction shows the malt in hearty voice and some decent spice shows there is plenty of life left yet; the peats are delicate and staggered rather than staggering while the oak conjures the more caramel-chocolate side of things; **f24** longer than you'd think possible, especially with the oak starting on a short leash but in need of muzzling.

Those cocoa notes linger seemingly forever with just a touch of ginger; **b23** this has now taken about as much oak as it can comfortably absorb. There are splinters in every segment but such is the all round brilliance of this malt, it appears to take it all in its stride, even allowing some citrus strains to be heard. It's the stuff that brings a tear to the eye... *53.8%*

Port Ellen 29 Year Old 8th release, dist 78, bott 08 db **(90.5) n23** plenty of oak ensures the lemon/vanilla aspect outweighs the smoke and barley; **t22.5** barley and butterscotch make a hesitant landing before a huge wave of oak and smoke crashes down upon it; **f22.5** relatively short compared to bygone days. The vanilla remains the main theme, with drying oaky pulses and soft oils developing; a final, defiant trademark gristiness ensures enough sweetness covers the journey...gosh, it's the kind of thing to bring a tear to the eye... **b22.5** all great dynasties come to an end, and Port Ellen, at this kind of vintage, is reaching its. Quite simply, this was a whisky designed for blending but was capable of so much more and in its own distilling lifetime was never recognised as such. Only after its demise was its genius formally acknowledged. Here, in this bottle, we have a whisky crooning to us in much the way that an old great singer might in his or her dotage for one last time to a loving crowd experiencing the full gamut of bitter-sweet emotion. For the glory and charisma is still there to cast you under its spell, but some high notes are missed, the timing not quite what it was; yet still we stand and applaud because we recognise it exactly for what it is: beauty and genius still, but fading beauty; receding genius. Something which only those of us, ourselves now of a certain vintage, can remember as being that unique, almost naked, celebration of Islay malt whisky it once so beautifully and so gloriously was. *55.3%*

Berrys' Own Selection Port Ellen 1982 cask no. 2030/2035, bott 08 **(95.5) n24** when in form like this, easily one of the most seductive of the Islay noses: a curious mixture of sweet grist and dry smoke, with a distant hint of roasted coffee on the wind; **t24** the delivery is almost unique amongst island malts in that both the juiciness of the barley and the dryness of the smoke are apparent, as if being played from two different speakers; **f23.5** that improbable freshness remains until the last; some slightly more bitter oak does make an appearance, but it's minor stuff against the unrelenting charm of the delicate peat; **b24** if you are to never taste a Port Ellen again and remember it in all its deft glory, then you could do a lot worse than this. *46%. Berry Bros & Rudd.*

Dewar Rattray Cask Collection Port Ellen Aged 24 Years cask no. 2488 dist 13 Oct 82 bott 17 Sep 07 **(95.5) n24** citrus and grist...can this really be 24 years old? The evenness of the peat, yet the way it lands randomly like so many snowflakes, is something to behold. Just keep breathing in pure majesty... **t24** ...and like snowflakes, just melts in the mouth. The softness of the smoke despite the thumping strength is almost a paradox; the citrus evident on the nose makes a shy entry while the oaky vanillas keep a respectful distance; **f23.5** sublimely bitter-sweet with all traces of early oil dissipated. The vanillas, naturally, have a louder say but it's as easy as a Sunday afternoon... **b24** of all the Port Ellen bottling this year, this has to be about the best. It is a near faultless example of a great distillery held for a very long time in a near perfect cask. *60.6%. 188 bottles.*

The Golden Cask Port Ellen 1982 cask no. CM105, dist Oct 82, bott Oct 07 **(84.5) n21 t22.5 f20 b21.** A most curious Port Ellen which from nose to finish appears to be giving its all while handcuffed. The oak influence is not the best. But there are some lovely moments, especially as it reached a honey-tipped crescendo; and also briefly as the salty-vanilla searches for those sweeter notes. But it all seems somewhat muted with the peating and overall complexity levels down. *51%. House of Macduff. 355 bottles.*

John Milroy Selection Port Ellen 1982 (85) n21 t22 f21 b21. Camp coffee with no little oak. *56.8%*

Norse Cask Selection Port Ellen 1979 Aged 28 Years hogshead ref no. QW1311, dist 79, bott Dec 07 **(93) n23** distinctive salty, seaweedy character added to the usual gristiness; **t24** full textured with the lightest of oils helping lubricate the peat-fruity effect; plenty of molassed chocolate adds an almost mousse-like feel to the middle; **f22.5** some lime breaks down the peat; a touch of hickory represents the moderate oak incursions; **b23.5** a wonderful bottling which has a dash of something unexpected and previously unspotted each time you taste it. *53.6%. nc ncf. Qualityworld, Denmark. 277 bottles.*

Norse Cask Selection Port Ellen 1983 Aged 24 Years hogshead cask no. CM016, dist 83, bott Jul 08 **(92) n22** pure farmyard – or impure – with the sweetish smoke blanketing some building peppers and hickory; **t23.5** dazzlingly sweet at first, with a sugar candy softening of the tastebuds before the smoke strikes; a burst of peppers is restrained as a light toffee-raisin fills the middle ground; **f23** chewy, a return of spice and a touch of hickory. The smoke is never more than an accompaniment; **b23.5** a very different PE, here in a form I'd say is unique. The story chops and changes from one minute to the next and though perhaps technically challenged from time to time, the result is as intriguingly different as it is enjoyable. 52.5%. Qualityworld for WhiskyOwner.com, Denmark.

⟿ **Old Malt Cask Lochnagar Aged 19 Years** sherry butt, dist May 90, bott Jul 09 **(85) n22.5 t21 f21 b20.5.** certainly no shortage of honey, or chocolate fudge. But it is all rather swimming in natural caramels. 50%. Douglas Laing.

Old Malt Cask Port Ellen Aged 24 Years refill butt no. 3915, dist Nov 82, bott Sep 07 **(94) n23.5** dusty, dry peat, flakes of ground chocolate and some coffee on the go in the next room; **t23.5** massive malt: for its age astonishing in its clean, refined juiciness; the smoke smiles down from a respectful distance; **f23** some citrus notes which had started to make a presence on delivery, now help thin the soft oaks; **b24** enchanting. 50%. Douglas Laing. 476 bottles.

Old Malt Cask Port Ellen Aged 25 Years refill hogshead no. 3651, dist Apr 82, bott Jul 07 **(81.5) n20 t20 f21 b20.5.** Big spices...in fact this one is pretty hot. 50%.

Old Malt Cask Port Ellen Aged 25 Years cask no. 4117, dist Nov 82, bott Jan 08 **(83) n20 t20.5 f21.5 b21.** Oily and full of citrus. 50%. nc ncf. Douglas Laing. 589 bottles.

Old Malt Cask Port Ellen Aged 25 Years refill butt no. 4244, dist Nov 82, bott Apr 08 **(77) n19.5 t20 f18.5 b19.** Great whisky in a poor barrel. 50%. nc ncf. Douglas Laing. 506 bottles.

Old Malt Cask Port Ellen Aged 25 Years sherry cask no. 3639, dist Feb 82, bott Aug 07 **(65.5) n16.5 t17 f16 b16.** Very severe sulphur. Bugger. 50%. nc ncf. Douglas Laing. 594 bottles.

⟿ **Old Malt Cask Port Ellen Aged 26 Years** dist May 82, bott Oct 08 **(87) n23** citrus (and creosote!) is woven throughout the sweet, peaty fabric; **t22** big oaky demeanor, but the lightly sweetened phenols still possess charm and depth; **f20.5** the peat fades as dry vanilla takes over; **b21.5** sees off the oaky challenge. 50%. Douglas Laing.

⟿ **Old Malt Cask Port Ellen Aged 26 Years** refill hogshead, dist May 82, bott Oct 08 **(86) n20 t23 f21 b22.** A bit hot and oily. But this is much better than the slightly murky nose shapes up. The delivery is dense and beautifully peated. 50%. Douglas Laing. 263 bottles.

Old Malt Cask Port Ellen Aged 26 Years sherry cask no. 4447, dist 82, bott Jun 08 **(80) n18 t21.5 f20.5 b20.** Sulphur stained, perhaps. But the gooseberries amid the peat makes for something unique and just about collectable. 50%. Douglas Laing. 721 bottles.

Old Malt Cask Port Ellen Aged 27 Years refill butt no. 3887, dist Dec 79, bott Sep 07 **(84.5) n21.5 t22 f20.5 b21.** Lovely, gentle whisky, but there gets a point, even for malts as outstanding and unique as Port Ellen, where they become too old and begin an inexorable path downwards. 50%. Douglas Laing. 589 bottles.

Old & Rare Port Ellen Aged 25 Years dist Apr 82, bott Sep 07 **(95) n23.5** beautifully evocative of a distillery kiln, complete with coal and peat in about equal portions; **t24.5** how can something be this big in the mouth, and yet offer flavours and nuances in such microscopic detail? The sweetness to oak ratio is near perfect; the gradual build up and climb down of the smoke is near perfect; the layering and structure is near perfect. Only an oaky bleed towards the middle diminishes in any way; **f23** long, but dries as the oaks add a warming touch with late spice and building vanilla; **b24** simply fabulous. 54.8%. Douglas Laing, exclusively for The Whisky Shop, Edinburgh. 226 bottles.

Old & Rare Port Ellen Aged 25 Years dist 82, bott Jan 08 **(95) n24** surprising pear drops in to lighten the peaty load; sublimely weighted; even people claiming not to like peaty whisky might just be teased into submission by this one... **t24** succulent barley, more fruit – probably still pear – and a mounting smoky weight; a touch of mocha and hickory fans out the complexity; **f23** bitter coffee and thumping spice; **b24** were it not for the semi-brittle finale this would have been in the play offs for world whisky of the year. Utter joy. 57.7%. Douglas Laing. 300 bottles.

⟿ **Old & Rare Port Ellen Aged 30 Years** dist Sept 78, bott Jan 09 **(91.5) n21.5** thickset with peat and dusty burnt toast; **t23** the first half dozen or so waves are gorgeously weighted with smoke and molasses and bolstered by a superb sharpness; **f24** long, satisfying, a touch of salt and mocha while a few lime notes thin out the weighty smoke and vanilla; **b23** has stemmed the march of time impressively. 52.5%. Douglas Laing.

Parkers Whisky Port Ellen 1982 "Pert mELLon" Bottling bott 07 **(96) n24** when God invented peaty whisky, I think he had something like this in mind for the nose: the intertwining of smoke and oak is rarely bettered; **t25** early spices, but the star again is the just-so proportioned smoke to oak, then the weighty liquorice surge; a light shower of Demerara sugar ensures balance and charm. Yep: this is as good as it gets! **f23** tannins and vanillins abound as the smoke tires, but that late Demerara does the trick in keeping away any threat of old age; **b24** don't know about "Pert Mellons". But this is so arousing in many other ways. A true classic. 56.8%. Parker's Whisky, UK. 220 bottles.

Platinum Port Ellen Aged 27 Years dist 79, bott 07 **(91) n22** very light with clipped peat; **t23** brittle, sweet barley; **f23** remains juicy with an extra squirt of barley sugar and smokin' grist; **b23** not entirely unlike the style of rum-cask malt. Understated and as delicate as old peated Islay ever gets. *57.1%. Douglas Laing. 258 bottles.*

Port Ellen Aged 25 Years Single Cask Butt No 2036 (87) n24 how, after 25 years, can this still offer so much young grist? Must have been a pretty washed up butt, because there is no sherry evidence whatsoever. The peat manifests itself both as grist and spice. Delicate, erotic stuff. **t22.5** astonishing injection of peaty sweetness from the very go. Just as the story gets into mid stride the buffers are hit and toffee takes over; **f20** dull and lacking the early inspiration; **b20.5** an odd one, this. Starts off like a train, cocking a gristy snook at its age. Then just flattens out under a welter of toffee blows. *58.1% Bottled by Bladnoch Distillery 638 Bottles*

Provenance Port Ellen Aged 23 Years refill butt no. 3402+3403, dist spring 83, bott winter 07 **(88.5) n23** dry, peat cinders and kippers with a curl of salted butter melting; **t21** an unsympathetic cask has left a mark on the sweet barley and smoke; **f22.5** fights to make a balance, but gets there in the end **b22** weird how a malt, which gets a whopping 88-plus mark is a little disappointing. But that just shows the quality we have come to expect from this tragically lost distillery. *46%. nc, ncf. Douglas Laing.*

Provenance Port Ellen Aged 24 Years dist 83, bott 07 **(86.5) n22 t22 f21 b21.5.** Attractive sweet-dry balance; breathtakingly laid-back for its age. *46%. nc ncf. Douglas Laing.*

Provenance Port Ellen Aged 24 Years refill butt no. 4114, dist spring 83, bott winter 08 **(86) n22 t22 f21 b21.** Attractive citrus, lethargic smoke and signs of a slightly tiring cask. *46%. nc, ncf. Douglas Laing.*

Provenance Port Ellen Aged 24 Years refill butt no. 4127, dist spring 83, bott winter 08 **(93) n23.5** quite beautifully layered, and lightened by a splash of kumquat; **t24** the fruity-citrus found on the nose soon makes an impressive appearance here, actually dominating early on before the smoke takes genteel control; like the nose, the layering astounds and though the peat could almost snap, so fragile is it, somehow it makes its presence fully felt; **f22** soft vanilla dark in and out of smoky showers; **b23.5** takes a few mouthfuls to genuinely recognise the grace and suavity on display. *46%. Douglas Laing.*

⋅∷⋅ **Provenance Port Ellen Aged 25 Years** sherry butt, dist winter 83, bott autumn 08 **(90) n23.5** an idyllic rock pool nose: the peat is firm yet restrained in its overall effect; a sprig of mint confirms the antiquity; **t22.5** some intriguing coconut cake amid the medium-layered peat; predominantly sweet, and barley can be found as well as smoke; **f21.5** lightly smoky; just bitters out a little; **b22.5** a lovely cask on the edge of its age range. *46%. Douglas Laing.*

Provenance Port Ellen Aged 25 Years (93.5) n23 uniquley, the fruit appears to galvanise and hardens the smoke: the peat feels almost in solid form; **t23** superb hard-soft delivery with duel personalities seeming to be totally at home with each other; the fruit drapes itself juicily around the peat; **f24** now it really takes off with those same seemingly simple characterisations now breaking off and looking for drier or even juicier tangents; vanilla and mildly overdone toast help create a faintly sawdusty feel, but somehow it works so well with the soft fruit and ashy peat; **b23.5** now this is closer to what I really expect from a Port Ellen 25, though it does have some unusual attributes. A controlled explosion of masterful beauty and a must for Port Elleners. *46%*

The Queen of the Moorlands Rare Cask Port Ellen 1982 bott 07 **(90) n23** a dexterous, highly complex nose, at first seeming flat and graped to death but on warming the slow unravelling of vanilla and peat makes for a heady mixture.. **t22** silky, grape-led delivery with slow evolution of smoke; **f22** sweetens with sultana and gentle gristy peat **b23** one of those whiskies you really have to take your time over and concentrate on. Take straight, without thinking; you might not be too excited. Peruse it, and you might just be very pleasantly surprised... *46%. nc ncf. The Wine Shop, Leek & Congleton, and Islay Whisky Shop.*

Signatory Port Ellen Distilled 1982 Aged 25 Years dist 07.04.82 bott 11.09.07 cask no 1136 **(92.5) n24** at body temperature this opens up like petals before the sun: the peat drifts through on varying levels, some stiff and awkward, others flowing and free and retaining that unique gristy PE character. Some serious citrus here, which would be appreciated by Ardbeg lovers. Delicate to the point of fragile; **t23.5** the big citrus on the nose shows first followed by smoke at first apologetically and then with a little more clout: here some soft spices take effect, as well as molten brown sugar as the oak enters the fray; **f22** minimal smoke as the vanilla and fruits bring down the drying, tad over-aged and fractionally bitter curtain; **b23** after 25 years and sporting such a peaty countenance it is hard to believe a whisky could be quite so elegant and refined. But this is all about charm. And a sense of loss and regret. *46%*

The Whisky Fair Port Ellen Aged 25 Years sherry wood, dist 82, bott 07 **(94) n23** plasticine and peat; coke-smoke, too; **t24** delivery of soft barley first, then a wonderful wave of peat breaks over the palate; the sweetness continues to grow but vanilla keeps it within reason; **f23** long, slightly peppered with some liquorice and hickory adding to the Demerara-sweetened coffee...and the smoke keeps coming... **b24** an enchanting malt which captures many of the delicate – and powerful – facets of this late distillery's personality. *59.6%*

PULTENEY
Highland (Northern), 1826. Inver House. Working.

Old Pulteney Aged 12 Years db **(85) n22 t23 f19 b21.** There are few malts whose finish dies as spectacularly as this. The nose and delivery are spot on with a real buzz and panache. The delivery in particular just bowls you over with its sharp barley integrity: real pulse-racing stuff! Then...toffee...!!! Grrrr!!! If it is caramel causing this, then it can be easily remedied. And in the process we'd have a malt absolutely basking in the low 90s...! *43%*

Old Pulteney Aged 15 Years db **(91) n21** pretty harsh and thin at first but some defter barley notes can be detected; **t24** an attention-grabbing, eye-wateringly sharp delivery with the barley in roasty mood and biting immediately with a salty incision; the barley-sugar effect is mesmerising and the clarity astonishing for its age; **f23** long, with those barley sugars working overtime, a slight salty edge there but the oak behaves impeccably; **b23** only on about the fourth or fifth mouthful do you start getting the picture here: enormously complex with a genuine coastal edge to this. The complexity is awesome. *54.9%*

Old Pulteney Aged 17 Years db **(95) n22** some weaker oak notes that shows signs of fatigue. But these are offset by evidence of praline and the most delicate puff of smoke; **t24** amazingly sweet, as though the barley has ganged up with the oak and pooled its sugars. To balance, drier vanilla and even the odd bourbony liquorice note can be detected; **f25** now this is where this malt comes into its own. In fact, this is one of the finishes of the year thanks to the slow burn with the transition from clear, slightly salted barley with a dollop of maple syrup to something running the gamut of milky chocolate notes. One of the longest finishes to be found with the transformation in flavour taking place in super slow-mo so every single nuance can be captured by the tastebuds. In style, unique. In terms of pleasure, absolutely mind-blowing. This is, quite simply, perfection... **b24** an improvement on last year's wheezy bottling that defies belief: indeed, if there was a Jim Murray Award for Most Improved Whisky of the Year, this would walk it. And confession time: like a Victorian murderer visiting the scene of his crime, I returned to this malt having originally given it 86. However, for some reason – and a reason that became so apparent when the magnitude of this whisky's astonishing finale got through my thick skull – something kept nagging at me that I might have been very wrong about this one. Now, at 11.23pm, I have taken time out I should be spending in bed to see if justice was being done. It wasn't. Hopefully it is now. This truly is a world great whisky. *46%*

Old Pulteney Aged 21 Years db **(90.5) n21.5** salty, chalky and citric; **t24** what a lovely delivery: lemon and lime fused with barley sugar and chocolate caramel; has almost the character of a candy with a soft centre as the flavours spread around the palate; a flavour profile far removed from the dowdy nose; **f22** back to more toffee caramel with a dusting of mildly salted grist; **b23** maybe it's just my imagination, but it appears as though some of these distillery bottlings have been worked on over the last year to 18 months, Here's another example of a so-so bottling not so long ago showing some real zeal and class. Surprisingly light for a malt that can scrap like the best of them, but this really is a lovely surprise dram. *46%*

Old Pulteney Aged 23 Years bourbon db **(84) n20 t22 f21 b21.** For all its great age there is a lethargy to this malt which doesn't quite work on the nose but does on the body. Intense malt, but at this age perhaps the complexity should be higher. *46%*

Old Pulteney Aged 23 Years sherry db **(89) n22** Party Ring biscuits and the softest of crushed raisin; **t22** wonderful bitter-sweet/barley-sherry balance; an unusual style and mouthfeel with spices prominent early on; **f22** again, superbly relaxed delivery of fruit before the coffee cream; dries with aplomb; **b23** highly stylish. Not a single note out of tune. *46%*

Old Pulteney 30 Years Old db **(86.5) n20 t23 f21.5 b22.** Had the nose been stretched any further by the oak, this whisky would have gone twang. As it is, some most un-Pulteney style oil helps bandage over the cracks and we can concentrate on a triumphant delivery on the palate which is full of barley doing the most unlikely of things at this age. Like making your jaws ache with its juicy chewability. The house toffee-chocolate style is evident at the end, but it all seems a whole lot softer than the actual strength. As Pulteney has the fascinating tendency to radically shift style over not too long a period, I can't wait for the next instalment! *45.8%*

➤➤ **Old Pulteney 30 Years Old** db **(92) n23.5** fabulous mix of Jaffa cake and bourbon, seasoned by a pinch of salt; **t23.5** an early, unexpected, wave of light smoke and silkier oak gives immediate depth. But stunning, ultra-juicy citrus and barley ensures this doesn't get all big and brooding; **f22** thinner and oakier with a playful oak-spice tingle; plenty of vanilla controls the drier aspects; **b23** I had to laugh when I tasted this: indeed, it had me scrambling for a copy of the 2009 Bible to check for sure what I had written. And there it was: after bemoaning the over oaking I conjectured, "As Pulteney has the fascinating tendency to radically shift style over not too long a period, I can't wait for the next instalment." And barely a year on, here it is. Pretty far removed from last year's offering and an absolute peach of a dram that laughs in the face of its 30 years.... *45%*

⋯ **A.D. Rattray Old Pulteney 1982** cask no. 502 **(90) n23** any more coastal and you'd expect to see an albatross sitting atop a lighthouse singing sea shanties...salty, with a distant buzz of peat reek being tossed around by the shoreline breeze. Pretty malty, too... **t24** faultless weight to the delivery and the manner in which the barley unfolds in dream-like fashion allows the sweeter notes to flourish, including the most vague smoky, spicy ones; **f21.5** annoyingly bitters out as the timbers begin to shiver.. **b22** you really can't keep an excellent distillery down... *47.7%*

Duncan Taylor Collection Pulteney 1977 cask no. 3976 **(88) n21** quite soupy with thick oak lightened by salted barley; **t23** brilliant recovery with the juicy barley and spice battling for supremacy; extremely rich with a coppery, metallic texture; **f22** the slight saltiness returns; fabulous touches of Blue Mountain; the fade is pure vanilla **b22** no doubting the class on show here. *55.9%*

Duncan Taylor Collection Pulteney 1989 Aged 18 Years cask no. 10259 **(85) n21 t21.5 f21.5 b21.** The oak this excellent spirit was put into was not quite up to the mark. A shame. There is evidence enough that a better cask would have resulted in a belter. As it is, there is enough energy and charisma to make for a genuinely enjoyable dram. *57.1%*

Duncan Taylor Collection Pulteney 1989 cask no. 10260 **(91) n22** punchy, salty barley; **t24** enormous explosion of spicy – almost hot – barley that is sharp and almost ridiculously clean for its age; **f22** remains mouth-watering even as the hickory arrives; **b23** displays all the lucidity and verve missing from the distillery bottling at this age. *58%*

⋯ **Gordon & MacPhail Old Pulteney Aged 15 Years (87.5) n22** lemon cupcakes; **t22** salivating mix of fresh, clean barley and thickening fruit; **f21.5** drier: the lightness of the spirit allows the oak to gain a bitter hand. But the clarity of the malt acts as a healthy buffer; **b22** juicy and zesty. *40%. Gordon & MacPhail.*

⋯ **Kingsbury's 'The Selection' Pulteney 7 Years Old** cask no. 800120 & 800121, dist Jun 01, bott Jun 08 **(83.5) n21 t21.5 f20 b21.** Gristy, sweet and very light. *43%. Japan Import System. 658 bottles.*

Private Collection Old Pulteney Sauterne Wine Finish 1994 (74) n17 t20 f18 b19. Some decent juiciness on arrival. But what is the French for sulphur...? *45%. G&M.*

⋯ **Scotch Malt Whisky Society Cask 52.18 Aged 7 Years** refill barrel, dist Jun 01 **(89) n22** rain-dampened woollen sports jacket; salty; **t23.5** a fabulous riot of fresh, juicy flavours: the barley is spruced up with a salty tang and a light spice buzz helps point towards the sweetish oaks; **f21.5** loses its way slightly as the barley and oak fail to agree terms; some surprisingly chalky vanilla for its age; **b22** I have long been a champion of bottling at this age: this is a good example as to why. *66.3%*

ROSEBANK

Lowland 1840–1993. Closed. (But if there is a God will surely one day re-open.)

Rosebank Aged 12 Years db **(95) n24** strands of honey and honeycomb entwine around a softly herbal, but enormously weighted maltiness: the type of nose you can stick your head in and wallow about for a few minutes; **t24** this has to be near perfection in regard to texture and not far off with the way the honeypolished malt trips around the palate with an almost apologetic spiciness for accompaniment. Just so accomplished and breathtaking; **f23** long, more honeycomb, with hints of liquorice and soft herbs; **b24** infinately better than the last F&F bottling, this is quite legendary stuff, even better than the old 8-y-o version, though probably a point or two down regarding complexity. The kind of whisky that brings a tear to the eye...for many a reason.... *43%. Flora and Fauna.*

Rosebank 22 Years Old Rare Malts 2004 db **(85) n22 t23 f19 b21.** One or two Rosebank moments of joyous complexity but, hand on heart, this is simply too old. *61.1%*

Rosebank 25 Years Old db **(96) n24.5** smoke? From a Rosebank? Well, it's there. My nostrils don't lie to me that much. Grapey fruit? From a Rosebank? Well something is happening in that direction. Either by smoke or mirrors: and there is no question of the smoke...Complex? Don't even start me on that one. The kind if nose that takes 20 minutes of your time. You'll find rose petal and dried dates and chestnut puree...and still you won't be much more in the know... **t23.5** it doesn't just hit the palate, it caresses it with the nubile fingers of young lady and the talons of an eagle: the malt stands erect and proud, yet with a deft smoke and a slight oily complexion; **f24** this is ridiculous; no whisky has the right to be this good at the death. The smoke is now there in terms that can be recognised and appreciated, the soft oils of the body cloak and caress; the exuberance of the malt/fruit fantasy just continues to evolve and not only that with the company of the odd pinch of something cocoa-rich being added; the shifts between sharp barley and softer, more toasty natural sugars become more dramatic: I am almost exhausted just trying to fathom the unfathomable... **b24** I had to sit back, take a deep breath and get my head around this. It was like Highland Park but with a huge injection of sweetened chocolate on the finale and weight – and even smoke – from a Rosebank I had never quite seen before. And believe me, as this distillery's greatest champion, I've tasted a few hundred, possibly thousands, of casks of this stuff over the last 25 years. Is this the greatest of all time? I am beginning to wonder. Is it the most extraordinary since the single malt revolution took off? Certainly, I have just looked at my watch: these tasting notes have taken one hour and 21 minutes to compile....where has the time flown, where have I been? Do I endorse it? My god, yes! 61.4%

Cadenhead's Rosebank Aged 16 Years dist 91, bott Feb 08 **(93) n23.5** wonderful interplay between floral and fruit: evening Surrey gardens with a dab of something vaguely peachy; **t24** light, mouth-watering delivery, yet something a little more substantial – probably on a honey-oak theme – with that late re-emergence of acacia h oney on the tail of the mandarin; **f22** slightly more perfunctory with some of more complex notes dimmed but fades in a pleasingly elegant manner; **b23.5** class never lies.... 55.7%. 230 bottles.

Cadenhead's Rosebank 18 Years Old bourbon hogshead, dist 89, bott May 07 **(84) n21 t22 f20 b21.** Another example of this great distillery bowing too low to the intruding oak. There are moments of indisputable class here. But it's the relentlessness of the oak against the usual magic (and defiant) citrus which persists on the palate here. And as this lost whisky gets older and older, we will have to get used to it. 54.2%. 294 bottles.

⬩⬩⬩ **Cadenhead's Rosebank Aged 20 Years** dist 89, bott 09 **(96) n24.5** pretty close to the perfect nose: not only clean and not an off note from distillate or cask, but the barley shimmers with that vital degree of honey sweetness; salt and lime adds the delicate fizz; **t24** the clarity on the nose is every bit as evident here: the barley appears to be carved from honey and set in golden syrup; **f23.5** sherry trifle...without the sherry... **b24** even at this ridiculous age a distillery which peaked so young, this is legendary whisky for the annals... and to tell your grandchildren you once tasted. 52.1%

⬩⬩⬩ **Chieftain's Rosebank 18 Years Old** sherry butt, dist Feb 90 **(91) n22** complex: a steady stream of discreet oaky-vanilla notes offer differing degrees sweetness and saltiness, occasionally a deeper, dryer gust crowds the barley out altogether; **t23.5** superb delivery with vast amounts more juicy barley concentrate and lightly spiced fudge, natural caramels well up towards the middle; **f23** if anyone remembers that old syrup-treated coconut that passed for kiddies tobacco in the early '60s, you'll appreciate this: funny I never went on to smoke, really...especially as there is the very lightest dab of something phenolic here, too; **b23.5** perhaps not quite in the element of when the malt was a decade younger, but this is unquestionably made of the very finest stuff. Wonderful, and once opened the type of bottle that empties quickly.. 46%. Ian Macleod Distillers Ltd.

Connoisseurs Choice Rosebank 1991 (85.5) n22 t22 f20.5 b21. Disappointing. I visited the distillery in its final days and was aware that something less than the best casks available were being sent there. Here is a typical victim of the United Distillers policy at the time; the malt shows every sign of trying to stretch itself but is thwarted. Promising, but ultimately frustrating malt which still shows enough class on delivery especially to add to any collection. 43%. Gordon & MacPhail.

Connoisseurs Choice Rosebank 1991 (88) n22 lovely interplay between ripe gooseberry and peach. Delicate and subtle; **t23** again the delivery is soft and feather-light: the oaks arrive and dissolve with the gristy barley; the bitter-sweet balance is quite perfect; **f21** much drier with the emphasis on chalky oak; **b22** a shade too old to be a superstar Rosebank, perhaps, but the overall charm beguiles. 40%. Gordon & MacPhail.

⬩⬩⬩ **Hart Brothers Rosebank Aged 17 Years** dist Jun 90, bott Mar 08 **(92) n23.5** delicate, not even slightly over-ambitious fruitiness with deft citrus and pear bonding with the barley; **t23** perfect degree of light oil projects the sweetened citrus beautifully; **f22.5** long, superb cocoa-vanilla input from the oak; **b23** just one of those lovely malts which ticks all the right boxes. And look at the tasting notes for the Montgomerie's 1990 below: tasted a month or two apart and without note comparison...consistent whisky, or what! 46%. Hart Brothers Limited.

Montgomerie's Rosebank 1990 (88.5) n22.5 a touch of grist even after all these years... weak lime livens the custard powder. Everything is gentle and impeccably mannered....; **t22.5**

...and same again on delivery. Mildly custardy, soft hint of tart fruit to the delicate barley; **f22** back to a gristy sweetness with a hint of fudge from the oak; **b22** much fresher than its age might suggest: a gentleman dram. *46%. Montgomery & Co. Ltd.*

⋙ **Montgomerie's Rosebank 1990** cask no. 1756, dist Jul 90, bott Jun 07 **(92.5) n23.5** varied lime-led citrus notes plus lashings of vanilla; **t23.5** mildly more disjointed than the nose; anarchically sweet and sharp; the juiciness is blunted by the vanilla; **f22.5** more sombre with cocoa and vanilla in quiet abundance; b23 busy and beautifully biting. *46%*

Old Malt Cask Rosebank Aged 16 Years Claret Finish dist Jun 90, bott Mar 07 **(85) n22 t23 f19 b21.** I must admit to not being much of a Claret finish man: however this one works, up to a point. The bottlers had recognised that the original oak had probably gone a shade too far, and there is evidence of this on the finish. But the delivery in particular thrusts together, in perfect unison, very fresh fruits with bludgeoning barley. *50%. 263 btls.*

Old Malt Cask Rosebank Aged 17 Years refill hogshead no. 3740, dist Jun 90, bott Jul 07 **(85) n20 t22.5 f21 b21.5.** An up and down Rosebank leaning on its malty weight, but still finding some lively fruit from somewhere. You get the feeling of a solidly-made malt. *50%. Douglas Laing. 283 bottles.*

⋙ **Old Malt Cask Rosebank Aged 18 Years** refill butt, dist Feb 90, bott Sep 08 **(87) n21** gooseberry and marmalade topped with delicate grist; **t22** much younger delivery: not even close to 18 years in stature: but that said, the always mouth-watering, slightly fizzy delivery builds slowly in understated intensity; **f22** longer than expected with the vanilla dissolving into the barley; **b22** outwardly appears a little on the thin and shy side, the victim of a sluggish old cask. Slow investigation reveals something a whole lot more charming, however. *50%.*

⋙ **Old Malt Cask Rosebank Aged 19 Years** refill butt, dist Feb 90, bott Feb 09 **(88) n22** sugar-sprinkled barley-vanilla... enticing; **t22.5** beautifully salivating and lays on the barley sugar thickly, though in a multitude of thin layers; **f21** back to untaxing vanilla; **b22.5** definitely on the simplistic side. But it does clean, sweet maltiness...and does it well!! *50%. Douglas Laing. 374 bottles.*

⋙ **Old Malt Cask Rosebank Aged 19 Years** refill butt, dist Feb 90, bott Mar 09 **(89) n22** light, honey-drizzled barley; **t23** brilliant arrival with an almost Highland Park-style honey and spice beat to the clean malt **f21.5** dries a little too austere, a point, maybe, but loads of chewing on the way; **b22.5** Rosebank doesn't always convert to old age with grace. Here, though, it has embraced a sweet character with relish. *50%. Douglas Laing. 444 bottles.*

Scotch Malt Whisky Society Cask 25.45 Aged 16 Years refill hogshead, dist Jul 91 **(92) n22.5 t23.5 f23 b23** Heavenly malt which tries to out-honey Highland Park...and just about succeeds. Those busy, lively spices, similar to the small grain in certain bourbons means Kenrtucky meets Falkirk. *53.5%*

⋙ **Scotch Malt Whisky Society Cask 25.48 Aged 18 Years** refill hogshead, dist Nov 90 **(77) n19 t20 f18 b19.** A rare very ordinary cask from this distillery. The nose and underlying dull bitterness suggests this was filled into less than excellent wood. *59.9%*

⋙ **Scotch Malt Whisky Society Cask 25.49 Aged 17 Years** refill barrel, dist Jul 91 **(88.5) n21.5** heading towards Kentucky... **t22.5** scrummy mouthfeel with some very early cocoa notes laying the foundation for the gathering malts; juicy but something of a chocolate candy to this one; **f22.5** those bourbony notes are underlined with the big roasty fudge kick and a cascade of drier vanilla; the spices gather pace; **b22** having spent probably twice as long in the cask than it's optimum period, it can be forgiven for its limited complexity. But its character is still without a blemish. *56.1%*

The Single Malts of Scotland Rosebank 1991 Aged 16 Years small batch, bott Sep 07 **(80) n20 t20 f20 b20.** Rosebank in a form I have never seen before: no great notes, no bad ones, little complexity...just thick, enjoyable malt. Weird. *46%. Speciality Drinks.*

The Whisky Society Rosebank 1991 Aged 16 Years bott Sep 07 **(89) n21.5** nipping, niggley..no shortage of character; **t23.5** really lovely malt massages the tastebuds, has real character and depth...and a build up of blood orange and vanilla; **f21.5** oils out and sweetens **b22.5** I must admit, I didn't see Rosebank hang on to its brilliance for quite so may years. Just so alluring. *56.1%. Speciality Drinks.*

ROYAL BRACKLA
Speyside, 1812. Dewar's. Working.

Royal Brackla Aged 10 Years db **(73) n18 t20 f17 b18.** A distinct lowering of the colours since I last tasted this. What on earth is going on? *40%*

Cadenhead's Authentic Collection Royal Brackla Aged 14 Years bourbon barrel, dist 92, bott Feb 07 **(84) n21 t23 f19 b21.** The early delivery of pecan nuts and barley is pretty delicious. The oaky stampede is a surprise. *57.9%. Cadenhead's. 228 bottles.*

Cadenhead's Royal Brackla Aged 15 Years rum barrel, dist 92, bott Feb 08 **(93) n22** something of the perfume bottle about this: something to dab behind your partner's ears... **t24** big, gutsy stuff which makes no attempt at delicate charm: all guns blazing here with a vague rummy, sweet sheen to the bristling barley; **f23** having punched itself out slightly we now go into a repertoire of mildly spiced vanillas; **b23.5** brimming with personality and tension. Really fun, high quality whisky. 57.3%. 232 bottles.

⋰· **Cadenhead's Royal Brackla Aged 16 Years** dist 92, bott 09 **(96.5) n24** just a puff of smoke adds weight to the coconut concerto; **t24.5** simply breathtaking: while the barley fairy melts in the mouth, friendly spices adds complexity to the growing cocoa and coconut; the middle ground begins to take on a cheerful bourbony disposition; **f24** long, very faintly oiled with a light maple syrup massaging the vanilla and delicate liquorice; **b24** another quite awesome cask from Cadenhead's. After tasting the Rosebank, I cannot remember the last time I ever tasted two successive 96-ers: I have been spoiled... 54.7%

⋰· **Premier Barrel Royal Brackla Aged 9 Years** (86) n20 t22.5 f22 b21.5. Deliciously one-dimensional. Excellently made, not a single off-note but the oak has barely made a mark. About as easy-drinking a whisky as you'll ever find. 46%. Douglas Laing. 374 bottles.

⋰· **Provenance Brackla Aged 9 Years** refill hogshead, dist winter 99, bott winter 08 **(84.5) n20 t22 f21 b21.5**. Oily, malty, juicy, refreshing, deftly spiced, Reisling-looking.....and amoebically simple. 46%. Douglas Laing.

Provenance Royal Brackla Aged 12 Years refill hogshead no. 4267, dist Autumn 95, bott Spring 08 **(86) n21.5 t22 f21 b21.5**. Attractively malty and gentle. 46%. nc ncf. Douglas Laing.

ROYAL LOCHNAGAR
Highland (Eastern), 1826. Diageo. Working.

Royal Lochnagar Aged 12 Years db **(84) n21 t22 f20 b21**. More care has been taken with this than some other bottlings from this wonderful distillery. But I still can't understand why it never quite manages to get out of third gear...or is the caramel on the finish the giveaway...? 40% ⊙⊙

Royal Lochnagar Selected Reserve db **(89) n23** superb oloroso, clean and spicy with apples and pears; **t23** stupendous spice lift-off which really starts showing the malts to great effect; **f21** the malts fade as the toffee progresses; **b22** quite brilliant sherry influence. The spices are a treat. 43%

⋰· **The Càrn Mòr Vintage Collection Royal Lochnagar 1986** hogshead, cask no. 1109, dist 86, bott 09 **(77) n20.5 t19 f18.5 b19**. Though this appears to be from the same batch as the Duncan Taylor bottlings, this one isn't in the same league. The slightly lactic nose does offer plenty of small still richness. But the delivery, though malty, errs on the bitter side. 46%. The Scottish Liqueur Centre.

⋰· **Duncan Taylor Collection Royal Lochnagar 1986** cask no. 942 **(87.5) n22.5** soft, clean with a small still metallic note. Attractive; **t22** juicy malt has some real body lurking about; **f21.5** thins, custardy and then a late metallic, malty tang; **b21.5** one of the better Lochnagars on the market, showing elegance. 56.4%. Duncan Taylor.

⋰· **Duncan Taylor Collection Royal Lochnagar 1986** cask no. 948 **(89) n23** a bourbony edge to this one with a dash of honey and salty butter. Pretty understated and sexy; **t22** immediate sweet-tart start with loads of barley shovelled in. Excellent shape and body; **f22** the metallic edge is there but the vanilla and barley adds stature and length; **b22** a more lush, richer version than cask 942 and almost as good as has been seen from this distillery for a while. For the best try cask 951. 56.9%. Duncan Taylor.

⋰· **Duncan Taylor Collection Royal Lochnagar 1986** cask no. 951 **(92) n21.5** light, buttery yet curiously coastal; **t24** much more vim and vigour on delivery with an immediate chalky-barley impact then that small still metallic sharpness you might expect; juicy, with spot-on oils that help spread the just-so sweetness; **f23** fabulous light mocha latches on to the sweet barley and vanilla; **b23.5** the bitter-sweet balance is exemplary. Quite the little star. 53.8%. Duncan Taylor.

⋰· **Harris Whisky Co. Royal Lochnagar Aged 12 Years** cask no. 519, dist Jul 96, bott Sep 08 **(89) n23** gosh! How complex is this...??? Curiously herbal: alongside the more basic citric notes, this is a wonderfully delicate fanfare; **t23** mouth-watering. Although the emphasis is on the fabulous barley and all its varying degrees of sweetness, again there is a herbal infusion which cranks up the complexity meter, **f21** falls flat on its face as the oak bites a little too bitterly after the vanilla takes hold; **b22** big delivery of citrus on the nose and palate paves the way for a really charming malt. A very different Lochnagar. 46%. Harris Whisky Co.

⋰· **Norse Cask Selection Royal Lochnagar Aged 12 Years** Fino sherry butt no. 520, dist Jul 96, bott Nov 08 **(83.5) n20.5 t22.5 f20 b20.5**. An attractive smudge of malty honey through the middle, but the bitter finish unsettles the balance. *576%. Qualityworld for WhiskyOwner.com, Denmark.*

Norse Cask Selection Royal Lochnagar 1977 Aged 29 Years cask no. DL863 **(75)** n20 t19 f18 b18. A touch of soap on the nose and pencil shavings on the palate. But there is still some glossy barley to be had. *50.4%. WhiskyOwner.com, Denmark.*

Old & Rare Lochnagar Aged 21 Years sherry cask **(91)** n24 brilliant! A spoonful or a pinch of everything ranging from grape to bourbon – except smoke. A half hour with your nose poked in this can rarely be better spent...; t22.5 honey and grape arm-wrestle for supremacy.... f22 the sherry wins – just – but is immediately thumped by some bitter-ish oak; b22.5 this little guy has come of age impressively. *53.1%. Douglas Laing.*

⫶ **Old Malt Cask Lochnagar Aged 32 Years** refill hogshead, dist Jan 77, bott Jan 09 **(92.5)** n23.5 well, well...gentle but unmissable smoke on a Lochnagar...if you know where to look!! Mildly leathery and creaking. But for its age...pretty impressive; t23.5 excellent sheen to the barley and even a puff of smoke; melting sugars ward off and perfectly even out the oak; works exceptionally well; genuinely mouth-filling; f22.5 wonderful fade, with lime and figs adding to the vanilla and muscovado; the tell-tale metallic edge is there but blunted by the busy barley; b23 far, far better than I expected: the malt has stayed the course and, perhaps above all other similar distilleries, really does radiate the fact that the stills are circumferentially challenged...Rounds off an above average year for bottled Lochnagars: Great stuff!! *47.7%. Douglas Laing. 74 bottles.*

⫶ **Provenance Lochnagar Aged 9 Years** sherry butt no. 3804, dist winter 98, bott summer 07 **(75.5)** n18.5 t19 f19 b19. Guess what's up with the cask... *46%. Douglas Laing.*

Provenance Lochnagar Aged 11 Years Sherry Finish dist spring 95, bott winter 07 **(68)** n17 t18 f16 b17. Next...! *46%. Douglas Laing.*

⫶ **Wild Scotsman Royal Lochnagar Aged 12 Years** hogshead, cask no. CM118, dist 96, bott 08 **(85)** n21 t21 f21.5 b21.5. An attractively lightweight, refreshing dram with the older cask allowing some of the richer barley notes full scope. *46%. House of Macduff.*

ST MAGDALENE

Lowland, 1798–1983. Closed.

Linlithgow 30 Years Old dist 73 db **(70)** n18 t18 f16 b18. A brave but ultimately futile effort from a malt that is way past its sell-by date. *59.6%*

⫶ **Berry's Own Selection St. Magdalene 1982** bott 08 **(95.5)** n24 not sure honey gets any more subtle than this while the fretwork of the barley against the oaky-vanilla accompaniment is simply astonishing; an insanely teasing smokiness is also just detectable; t22.5 surprisingly, the oak is first to show and it takes a little while before the barley begins to get the upper hand; it does so as the actual mouthfeel changes shape and moves towards a more silky delivery; also a faint smoky weight begins to form; f25 now the oak is fully integrated and the finale is breathtaking in its charm and depth. Like a pastel-coloured sunset, one flavour merges into the next. There is a frappe-mocha signature to the final movements, its glory underlined by the sparing use of muscovado sugar and vanilla: spellbinding and in every way perfect; b24 when you get an old whisky from a dead distillery, you pray for something a little special; those prayers have been answered. Glorious: you have died and St Magdalene is waiting at the gates of heaven... *46%. Berry Bros & Rudd.*

Old Malt Cask Linlithgow Aged 24 Years dist Dec 82, bott May 07 **(90)** n22 ultra clean and grassy; t23 mouth-watering with perfect juiciness and sweet/sharpness from the barley; f22 long, clean barley sugar: benefits from minimum oak presence; b23 this distillery may sound as if it has a lisp, but rarely do you get such malty clarity from the mouth. Best I have tasted from here for a very long time. *50%. Douglas Laing. 303 bottles.*

Old Malt Cask St. Magdalene Aged 25 Years refill butt no. 4282, dist Oct 82, bott May 08 **(83.5)** n22 t20 f21 b20.5. The intriguing aroma has a few scars of battle over the last quarter of a century, and is the highlight of this light and malty dram. *50%. nc ncf. Douglas Laing. 378 bottles.*

⫶ **Old Malt Cask St Magdalene Aged 26 Years** refill butt, dist Sep 82, bott Oct 08 **(90)** n23 the oak is deft and lands on the vibrant citrus notes like snowflakes.... t22.5...and like snowflakes this simply melts on the tongue, such is the delicateness of the barley and gentle lemon; clean, allowing the barley to be seen with no problem; f22 a light fluttering of vanilla adds a chalky dimension; b22.5 simply beautiful. *50%. Douglas Laing. 511 bottles.*

Rare Old St Magdalene 1975 (89) n23 intriguing mix of caramelised and bourbon biscuits; t22 thin maple syrup over an oak-led barley thrust; soft spices enchant; f22 soft cocoa sheen; b22 a noble dram from what appears to be an excellent batch of casks. *43%. G&M.*

SCAPA

Highland (Island–Orkney), 1885. Chivas. Working.

Scapa 12 Years Old db **(88) n23** honeydew melon, soft salt and myriad styles of barley: really complex with a sprinkling of coal dust on the fruit; **t22** truly brilliant mouth arrival: the most complex display of malt and cocoa, the fruit is ripe figs with a thread of honey; **f21** a slight bitterness with some developing toffee, but the malt stays the distance; **b22** always a joy. 40%

Scapa 14 Years Old db **(88) n22** toasted oak, butterscotch and lime; **t22.5** fresh barley for its age, a few bands of light oak but some fruity notes towards the drying middle **f21.5** chalky but some toffee interferes with the usual sweeter finale; **b22** enormous variation from bottling to bottling. In Canada I have tasted one that I gave 94 to: but don't have notes or sample here. This one is a bit of dis-service due to the over-the-top caramel added which appears to douse the usual honeyed balance. Usually, this is one of the truly great malts of the Chivas empire and a classic islander. 40%

❖ **Scapa 16 Years Old** db **(81) n21 t20.5 f19.5 b20.** The label fires the first warning: "A smooth and full bodied single malt". Which is why I am so disappointed. I don't want that from this magnificent, truly great distillery: that is not what Scapa is all about. On the nose, on delivery and finish I get caramel. I should be getting salt and honey. I should be getting petulant, chocolaty oak under a bitter-sweet assault of beguiling complexity. I should be getting, even from my tasting table 700 miles away, the sea-spray and winds of Orkney stabbing into my face. For it to be so tamed and toothless is a crime against a truly great whisky which, handled correctly, would be easily among the finest the world has to offer. Why has this apparently been subjected to such large doses of caramel? It is flat, allowing only a teasing shadow of the massive honey lurking beneath. Due to the cruelly unsympathetic management of Scapa in its benighted days of Allied, there are tragically few casks for Chivas to sell. So, please, can we taste the real Scapa...? It is far too rare and precious to dish out in this toned-down, populist fashion: the whisky lover has moved away from what was acceptable in the 1980s. Uncoloured. Un-chillfiltered and at 46%, these days please. A whisky which will live long in the memories of all those who try it. And, fittingly, at last do the distillery the justice it has long since deserved. 40%

❖ **Gordon & MacPhail Scapa Aged 15 Years** dist 93, bott 08 **(88.5) n22** tangy oak and barley mix: cleaner than you might expect; **t22** a tangle of vanillas and golden syrup with the odd sharp barley note; **f22.5** some late-in-the-fray spices is met by butterscotch and crème brûlée; **b22** oh, had this been a bit nearer natural strength... 40%. Gordon & MacPhail.

Old Malt Cask Scapa Aged 14 Years refill hogshead no. 3888, dist Oct 93, bott Dec 07 **(71.5) n20 t18 f16.5 b17.** Bitter, hot: struggling from a poor cask. 50%. nc ncf. Douglas Laing. 339 bottles.

Old Malt Cask Scapa Aged 14 Years refill hogshead, cask no. 4440, dist Oct 93, bott Jun 08 **(87) n21** Cox's? **t22.5** Pink lady? **f21.5** definitely Crab; **b22** there is a distinct Calvados fruitiness to this which is both enthralling and quite baffling and out of kilter with the distillery style. Can't say it's not unique, though! 50%. nc ncf. Douglas Laing. 370 bottles.

❖ **Old Malt Cask Scapa Aged 15 Years** refill hogshead, dist Sep 93, bott Oct 08 **(87) n22.5** granny's handbags; a pleasant leather-mint mix; **t22** sharp oak delivery, immediate sweet barley counter; juices up well; **f21** back to oaky caramel: burnt fudge and then dries; **b21.5** a curious creature: lighter than its years, yet oaky fingerprints everywhere. 50%. Douglas Laing. 334 bottles.

Old Malt Cask Scapa Aged 16 Years dist Apr 91, bott May 07 **(88) n20** closed: dusty; **t22** takes time to wake up then goes into barley juice overdrive; **f24** now the complexity is cranked up to max as the malt and oak, helped along by a late citrus and honey fling, vie for supremacy. Each blow brings untold joy to the tastebuds; **b22** busy with major spice. The finish is memorable 50%. Douglas Laing. 335 bottles.

Provenance Scapa Aged 11 Years refill hogshead, cask no. 3845, dist winter 95, bott summer 07 **(83.5) n21 t21 f20 b21.5.** Pleasant, malty, suety, but somehow lacking the standard Scapa complexity. 46%. nc ncf. Douglas Laing.

Provenance Scapa Aged 11 Years dist winter 95, bott spring 07 **(84) n20 t22 f21 b21.** Pleasant. A touch syrupy. 46%. Douglas Laing.

Provenance Scapa Aged 12 Years refill hogshead DMG no. 4111 dist Oct 95, bott 08 **(86) n21.5 t23 f20 b21.5.** Beautiful malts make for a superbly nubile and juicy display the dull finish. 46%. nc ncf. Douglas Laing.

Provenance Scapa Aged 12 Years dist spring 94, bott winter 07 **(88) n22 t23 f21 b22** I know some well-respected names in the industry who are less than happy when whiskies from third-filled casks like this one pop up in bottlings. I tend to disagree and here is a wonderful example why: few spirits in the world can offer such delicate joys as this. A genuine lip-smacker. 46%

Provenance Scapa Aged 12 Years refill hogshead no. 3255, dist 94, bott 07 **(91.5) n23** toasted Hovis with a thin spread of honey and marmalade; **t23** lively grain and with a fruity edge; clean and medium-sweet; **f22.5** dries well with the oaks pulsing; **b23** a genuinely classy malt with compartmentalised characteristics each showing to excellent effect. 46%. nc ncf. Douglas Laing.

SPEYBURN
Speyside, 1897. Inver House. Working.

Speyburn 10 Year Old db **(82) n20 t21 f20.5 b20.5.** A tight, sharp dram with slightly more emphasis on the citric. A bit of toffee on the finale. 40%

⫶⫶· **Speyside 12 Years Old** db **(85) n22 t22 f20.5 b21.5** Copious honey and malt on delivery. Simplistic, effective but a tad bitter on finish. 40%

Speyburn Aged 25 Years db **(92) n22** crisp barley sits well with the chalky oak; **t24** beautiful soft honey helps thicken up the malt; exceptional mouth feel as an extra touch of maple syrup helps keeps the oak in check; a real coppery tanginess to this, too; **f23** a thin spread of marmalade on buttered toast; **b23** either they have re-bottled very quickly or I got the diagnosis dreadfully wrong first time round. Last year I wasn't overly impressed; now I'm taken aback by its beauty. Some change. 46%

Speyburn Bradan Orach db **(76.5) n19 t20 f19.5 b18.** Fresh, young, but struggles to find a balance. 40%

Connoisseurs Choice Speyburn 1977 (84) n20 t22 f21 b21. Creaks its way through the oaky gears with enough malty panache to leave you wanting more. 43%.

⫶⫶· **Old Malt Cask Speyburn Aged 18 Years** refill hogshead, finished in rum cask, dist Jan 90, bott Oct 08 **(84) n22.5 t21 f20.5 b20.** Speyburns at this kind of age are pretty rare in bottled form, so it's always a treat to come across a very different character. The green tea characteristic isn't exactly one I have come across in the lab with this distillery at 15 years and onwards, either. Pleasing, but perhaps too many lumps of sugar in it to lift it to greatness. 50%. Douglas Laing. 134 bottles.

SPEYSIDE
Speyside, 1990. Speyside Distillers. Working.

Drumguish db **(71) n17 t19 f17 b18.** This whisky could only improve. And, thankfully, it has. Even so, a long, long way to go on this. The nose is still flawed and, despite an injection of barley early on, it flatlines its way from the fourth taste wave to the end. 40%

Speyside 10 Years Old db **(81) n19 t21 f20 b21.** Plenty of sharp oranges around; the malt is towering and the bite is deep. A weighty Speysider with no shortage of mouth prickle.

Speyside 12 Years Old db **(85) n22 t22 f20.5 b21.5** Copious honey and malt on delivery. Simplistic, effective but a tad bitter on finish. 40% ☉☉

Speyside 15 Years Old db **(75.5) n18 t19.5 f19 b19.** So much malt, so little complexity. Lots of caramel on the finish. 40%

⫶⫶· **Cadenhead's Speyside Aged 15 Years** dist 94, bott 09 **(92.5) n23** almost HP in its lazy-smoked honey; **t24** sweet, mouth-watering barley with a wonderful spice sub plot; **f22.5** the vaguest layer of smoke again before yet more honey and a much drier vanilla sign off; **b23** Speyside as in as fine nick as you've ever seen it. What are Cadenhead's doing...? Tipping honey into the casks...? Seriously, chaps: well done you for finding a classic from its notoriously temperamental distillery. 64.6%

⫶⫶· **The Cärn Mör Vintage Collection Speyside 1995** sherry butt, cask no. 18, dist 95, bott 09 **(85.5) n21.5 t22.5 f20 b21.5.** Some serious biscuity maltiness to this one, even sporting a gentle citrus freshness. Much better than some of what was around at the distillery at the time. 46%. The Scottish Liqueur Centre.

⫶⫶· **Hart Brothers Speyside Aged 13 Years** dist Jun 95, bott Oct 08 **(85) n19 t22.5 f22 b21.5.** Very simple malt. Built entirely around its mega-malty theme there is some serious juiciness. The feints on the nose come to help by adding extra oil and depth to the finish. 46%. Hart Brothers Limited.

Scott's Selection The Speyside 1991 bott 07 **(95) n23.5** just wonderful...as 17-year-old whisky goes: clean, almost bracing with citrus dovetailing with the barley. Not an oaky wobble...it honestly makes the pulse race; **t24** close your eyes and be astounded: the clarity of the barley can only make you sigh; the accord between the sweeter barley and drier oaks could not be more harmonious; the understated enormity of the malt could not be more joyous; **f23.5** long, winding and, somehow, still mouth-watering to degrees that no whisky of this age has a right to even dream; **b24** taste this and weep. This is what Speyside could have tasted like for all these years if the equipment had been run correctly. In whisky terms, tragic. And, gosh. Was it really 14 years ago I drove through the Scottish snow to be there at the warehouses to see the spirit from these new stills turn to whisky on the day of their 3rd birthday? I predicted great things at the time. On this evidence, I was right. And was equally right to feel the   alt's development the greatest disappointment of my whisky career. But when it comes to things mechanical, there is no accounting for human error. And I would be lying if I didn't admit to feeling a pang of vindication. *60.4%*

The Whisky Fair The Speyside Aged 15 Years bourbon hogshead, dist 91, bott 07 **(88) n20** malty, but a bit dirty with the kind of feints that pack a punch on the palate...; **t24** ...bloody hell...and some!! Enormous delivery with tell-tale feints which seems to accentuate every last atom of the richest maltiness imaginable. Outstanding depth to the sweetness; **f22** soft oils, a return to something a little grimy but still OK; **b22** so many faults where do you begin? But the intensity of the delivery is among the best of the year. With this character, I assume this is from the Speyside distillery, rather than just being a Speysider. *53.7%. Germany.*

SPRINGBANK
Campbeltown, 1828. J&A Mitchell & Co. Mothballed.

Hazelburn Aged 8 Years 2nd edition, release 06 db **(90) n22 t23 f22 b23.** I adore this ultra-intense barley style: something you can devour for an age. Wonderful stuff!! *46%. 6000 bottles.*

Hazelburn Aged 8 Years 3rd Edition (triple distilled) bott 07 db **(89) n22** grassy, light, ultra-clean barley; a suggestion of coke smoke and baby oranges; **t22.5** where previously the barley ambushed you, here it makes light, soothing noises: unbelievably clean...; **f22** even for this tender age, vanilla has no problem getting a decent foothold due to the delicate nature of the barley; a vague citric theme blends in attractively; **b22.5** somewhat effete by comparison to last year's big malty number. Here there is a shade more accent on fruit. Very light, indeed. *46%*

Longrow Aged 10 Years db **(78) n19 t20 f19 b20.** Seeing as I was one of the first people alive ever to taste Longrow from its very first bottling and used to track down – in my comparative youth – every expression thereafter (and still have some in my personal collection), you could say I am a fan. But this has completely bemused me: bereft not only of the usual to-die-for smoke, its warts are exposed badly, as this is way too young. Sweet and malty, perhaps, and technically better than the marks I'm giving it – but this is Longrow, dammit! I am astonished. *46%*

Longrow Aged 10 Years 100 Proof db **(86) n20 t23 f22 b21.** Still bizarrely smokeless – well, maybe a flicker of smoke as you may find the involuntary twitching of a leg of a dying fly – but the mouthfeel is much better here and although a bit too oily and dense for complexity to get going, a genuinely decent ride heading towards Hazelburn-esque barley intensity. Love it, because this oozes class. But where's the ruddy peat...? Oi, mister. I want my peat back...!! *57%*

Longrow Aged 14 Years db **(89) n25** a strap-on-to-the-head aroma with so many barley-peat nuances at so many levels it almost defies comprehension; and it wouldn't be a Longrow if there wasn't some salty goings on, too; **t21** mildly tart delivery with the smoke and oak refusing to gel; **f21** where the hell is the peat on the nose? No shortage of natural toffee, though; **b22** hard to get a bearing on this one. The nose, though... *46%. nc ncf.*

Longrow Aged 18 Years db **(94) n23.5** the smoke comes in almost as an afterthought: most un-Longrow like; attractively farmyardy and agricultural; **t23** sharp, raspberry jam mingles with the barley and a puff of something more hickory-like than peat; **f24** long, gentle oils, an indistinct fruit element returns but more barley sugar now and a denouement of vanilla and natural fudgy caramels, **b23.5** determined to hide its light under a bushel...but fails. The most subtle and sophisticated Longrow I've come across in 20 years... *46%*

Longrow C.V db **(95.5) n25** a beautifully balanced smoke alternating between light, top-soil peats and coke; some praline ups the ante; sublime: quite faultless; **t24** dissolves on impact with the peats melting first, followed by molassed barley and mocha; **f22.5** low key, it allows the vanillas to begin to dominate as the smoke drifts off; **b23.5** a master-class in the art of subtle peat use. *46%*

Longrow Gaja Barola Wood Expression Aged 7 Years db **(91.5) n23.5** good grief.....what the bloody hell is this....??? Well, it's a first, I'll say that much. Don't expect any kind of sane or cogent description here. This is whisky insanity, with peat and wine entirely out of control and in need of straight jackets. But there is a morbid curiosity, a rubber-necking need to witness the gruesome that kind of draws you in. And before you know it, you kind of like it...a lot...;

t22.5 again: beyond description. A kind of grape and smoke head on smash with victims everywhere – especially the innocent tastebuds. But it kind of grows on you again... **f23** at last settles down to something approaching structured malt and the degree of molassed and hickory-sharpened sweetness is a delight; **b22.5** taking this on is like running around an asylum claiming you're Napoleon. But I have to admit; it's fun! An accidental classic that is unlikely to be repeated...even if they tried..!! 55.8%

Springbank Society Aged 9 Years Rum Wood bott Mar 07 db **(93.5) n23** wonderful delivery of phenols gives this weight way above the years. The rum adds a dryness to the sweeter barley, which works a treat; **t23.5** biting, nipping, lively: this dram comes with teeth – and pretty sharp ones at that; the rum influence becomes more apparent when the intense barley subsides; **f23** more smoky moments and then a soft cushion of cocoa and vanilla; brown sugars offer the required sweetness; **b24** a mere pup by Springbank standards. For once its comes through as a real winner in these tender years, doubtless aided by the mercurial charms of the rum and even an unexpected touch of smoke to make for one of the most complex and entertaining drams of the year. Don't expect anything too green, though... 60.2%

Springbank 10 Years Old db **(89) n22** a real young and old supershow, with soft, adolescent tones from the barley and something much more brooding from the oak. Intriguing...; **t22.5** ditto the delivery: a slight molassed feel to the juicy barley but the oak is dry and firm; outstanding spices, too; **f22** some shards of citrus and lemon drop gives a lovely contrasting sharpness to the sweet barley; **b22.5** now that's much more like it!! The last bottling I had really was all over the show. This is still slightly Bambi-ish. But there is some real meat here, too. On this showing, I am beginning to change my mind about younger Springbanks.... 46%

Springbank Aged 10 Years (100 Proof) db **(86) n21.5 t22 f21 b21.5.** Trying to map a Springbank demands all the skills required of a young 18th century British naval officer attempting to record the exact form and shape of a newly discovered land just after his sextant had fallen into the sea. There is no exact point on which you can fix...and so it is here. A shifting dram that never quite tastes the same twice, but one constant, sadly, is the bitterness towards the finale. Elsewhere, it's one hell of a journey....! 57%

⚬⚬ **Springbank 11 Years Old Madeira Wood Expression** db **(88) n23** more like a smoked cream sherry: delicious and very different; **t22.5** the lush nose turns into an equally lush delivery with lots of phenols kicking around the medium sweet barley; **f21.5** takes a strange turn, but there again this is strange stuff...struggles to find a relaxed rhythm, though the vanillas do their best; **b21** Madeira perhaps as you've never seen it before: don't go thinking Glenmorangie or Penderyn with this one. As big as the fruit is, the smoke outguns it. 55.8%

Springbank 15 Years Old db **(87.5) n22** furry grape and Oreo biscuit; **t21.5** the silk texture helps move along the grape; a few dry notes perhaps from a less than top butt but the malt regains the moment; **f22** bitter-sweet with a chalky depth to the oak; **b22** pity again about the light sulphur kick which is louder on the palate than nose. Even so, there are so seriously graceful sherry moments. 46%

Springbank Rum Wood Expression 16 Years Old dist Jun 91, bott Aug 07 db **(93.5) n23.5** sharp peppers with a strange sugary sheen; the barley interfolds with the oak beautifully; **t23.5** firm, pepped up malt with varying spice trails; the sharpness on the nose is replicated but the middle fattens out with a gristy-sugared barley; still crisp and brittle in part despite the softer barley sub plot; **f23** medium length with fine bitter-sweet waves; echoes of rum are not lost despite the firm oak presence; **b23.5** a wonderful malt brought to you by the people who actually created the category and described to you by the guy who originally discovered and invented it! Work that out...OK, I'll tell you. In 1991 in a warehouse in Springbank a (then) young whisky writer (one of just five in the world at that time) spotted a couple of strange looking casks. On investigating, it was found they were former rum casks which had been completely forgotten about and overlooked. We opened the casks and I spotted the whisky had turned a shade of green. And so the legend was born. So good was the whisky that Springbank repeated the trick...and from the date of distillation I am assuming this is some of the whisky that was filled into rum to try to recreate this astonishing Green Whisky. However, after eight years it appears these were emptied into bourbon casks. So no green. But brilliant malt, nonetheless. And the meeting of an old friend for whom I'm partly responsible. 54.2%. 6,000 bottles.

⚬⚬ **Springbank 18 Years Old** db **(89.5) n23** another dense offering, but here the fruit is playing a bigger role with blood orange and under-ripe fig adding to the barley. Not perfect but there is so much going on... **t22** cautiously salivating. There is a buzz from the cask, but the barley ignores this and sings its own song, alternating between sharp and juicy; **f22.5** that chocolate mousse finale that appears to not be uncommon from this distillery these days; **b22** it's amazing that even at 18 years of age, you get the overwhelming feeling that this malt has barely cleared its throat.... 46%

Springbank Vintage 1997 refill sherry, batch no. 1, bott Jun 07 db **(85) n21.5 t23 f20.5 b21.** I'm not sure if malt of this age comes much thicker or intense. Not exactly a pristine sherry butt, this, but the grape and spice are graceful enough. 55.2%

⋄⋄ **Springbank 1997 Vintage** batch no. 2 db **(87) n21** so dense it's hard to pick out individual nuances: just one very thick wall of intense malt and oak so heavy it makes a lump of lead look like a helium balloon; **t22.5** taste buds are flattened under the weight of the thick barley; just like on the nose there is a dense oak feel, too but also tons of natural caramels and a shot of cocoa; **f22.5** that cocoa really comes into its own now and sweetens along the way into mousse-like qualities; a little butterscotch is stirred in for extra balance; **b22** less a drink, more of a three course dram. You get the feeling the cut was a little wider here than the norm. Seriously hard work, but ultimately worth it. 54.9%

⋄⋄ **Berry's Own Selection Springbank 1993** bott 09 **(83.5) n22 t21 f20 b20.5.** Doesn't quite live up to the lively, lovely pear drop nose. Emotionless fare. 46%. Berry Bros & Rudd.

Cadenhead's Authentic Collection Springbank Aged 11 Years cream sherry butt, dist 96, bott Sep 07 **(58) n14 t15 f14 b15.** Put it this way: the sulphur is so aggressive on the nose, I decided to make this my last tasting of the day even before I put it to my lips. 56.3%. 640 bottles.

Chieftain's Springbank 37 Years Old cask no. 1343 **(89.5) n21.5** the curious and possibly unique combination of pine and pineapple.... **t23.5** pretty confused and out of kilter at first, then settles in with some waxy sugars which help glaze and protect the powering barley; the oak never lets go; **f22** lots of sturdy oak, but the soft barley notes offer an excellent repost; **b22.5** gripping so tight for life there are splinters everywhere. On nose, delivery and finish are clear signs that this has had a few summers too many. But on the other side of the coin comes a beautifully sweet, still ridiculously well defined barley theme 43%. nc ncf. Ian Macleod Distillers.

Da Mhile Organic "New Born" Springbank dist Jun 92, bott Sep 07 **(95) n24** the type of sherry cask that was common 30 years ago has come back to life for an ultra rare appearance; this is the Melton Hunt fruitcake school, the now lost Saxby's ancient recipe Christmas pudding: knife and fork stuff... **t23** wonderful immediate balance between the dense sherry and thick, molassed sugars; blackberries, too and some vanilla custard makes its play. A bit like one big trifle on steroids... **f24** just so elegant and demure for the enormity which has gone on before: the malt can still be found, the burnt raisins are just that little sweeter...and happy ending to a dramatic story.... **b24** a roaring success on account of the gripping complexity despite the full-on sherry: a rare combination. This is the only whisky I know with a photo of a baby on the label: Danny, the first grandchild of organic whisky producer John Savage Onstwedder, There is absolutely nothing childish about this malt, though, and I think Danny will be a happy chap when he cracks open his bottle on his birthday in 2025. I just hope by then this kind of classic sherry cask will not be a bottled memory. 56.4%. nc ncf. 153 bottles.

Duncan Taylor The NC2 Range Springbank 1993 (82) n22 t21 f19 b20. Some attractive sheen on the barley. But could have done with another eight years in the cask... 46%. nc ncf.

Duncan Taylor The NC2 Range Springbank 1996 (77) n20 t19 f19 b19. Sent enough for only two mouthfuls – so this is first impression only, I'm afraid. Young, flat and lacking grace - typical for this distillery in diapers. 46%. nc ncf.

Glenkeir Treasures Springbank Aged 17 Years dist Dec 89, bott Nov 07 **(84.5) n20 t22 f20.5 b22.** Now this is a bit of a strange one. Yes, the butterscotch is lovely while the honey tones are as good as you'll get on any Springbank....but. Some odd notes from what I presume was not quite the finest cask of all time. 50.1%. Exclusively for The Whisky Shop, Edinburgh. 272 bottles.

⋄⋄ **Founder's Reserve Springbank Aged 17 Years (86) n22 t22 f21 b21.** Another Springbank which sets off at an excellent pace with barley riches galore and then tires towards the end. Delicious in part, but the natural vanillas and caramels are simply too much to take it on to greatness. 46%. Japan Import System.

⋄⋄ **Kingsbury's Single Cask Springbank Aged 14 Years** dist Jun 93, bott Aug 07 **(87) n22** wonderfully clean, grassy barley; a dusting of mallow; **t22** faultlessly intense barley with little deviation until some drier oak notes appear; **f21** spicy but dulls out quickly; **b22** another very even, if undercooked, vanilla-rich offering from this distillery. 46%. Japan Import System.

Old Malt Cask Springbank Aged 10 Years dist Oct 96, bott May 07 **(81) n19 t21 f21 b20.** A barley-fruit rant on the palate. Frustrating how this malt rarely makes the cut at this age. 50%. Douglas Laing. 358 bottles.

Old Malt Cask Springbank Aged 11 Years refill hogshead no. 4245, dist Oct 96, bott Apr 08 **(81.5) n21 t21.5 f20 b19.** In many ways nearer 11 months than 11 years....still, the malt is intense and sweet but don't bother going in search of oak. *50%. nc ncf. Douglas Laing. 358 bottles.*

⋅⋅⋅ **Old Malt Cask Springbank Aged 15 Years** refill hogshead, dist Jun 93, bott Oct 08 **(85.5) n21.5 t21.5 f21 b21.5.** Big, enjoyable malt, sharp and happy to keep sweetness to a minimum. A thorough oaky buzz, too. *50%. Douglas Laing. 365 bottles.*

Old Malt Cask Springbank Aged 18 Years cask no. 3964, dist Dec 89, bott Dec 07 **(84.5) n21.5 t22 f20 b21.** A pleasant, barley-sweet kind of guy, but missing the unspoken salty tang that is part of the distillery's fabric. *50%. Douglas Laing. 353 bottles.*

Old Malt Cask The Argyll Malt (Hazelburn) 1997 Aged 8 Years (82) n20 t21 f21 b20. It's no secret that the malts from this slow-maturing distillery wobble about like Bambi until they get into double figures. This is no exception, though the malt intensity is marked. *58.8%. Exclusively for Vintage House. 296 bottles.*

⋅⋅⋅ **Premium Scotch Importers Springbank 1998** small oak cask **(95) n24.5** a sublimely sexy package: concentrated barley with bourbony concentrated oak. The explosive mix takes you into a land of heady fruit: peaches and guava thickened by toasty molasses, even maybe a hint of PVC phenols; **t24** the tongue-curling effect of the delivery confirms the big oak presence. But the malt has it under control and dishes out plenty of piercingly sharp notes to compensate; spices form in the middle ground, first shyly and then have a freer role; **f23** liquorice and chocolate gives way to chocolate lime; **b23.5** the problem with Springbank is that it is such an enormous malt it needs big age or at least a major reaction with oak to bring the best out of it. So many malts up to the age of about 18 struggle to really be heard: the oak and barley cancel each other out. That has long been my theory and this wonderful, full-throttled bottling from Springbank filled into small casks to maximise the oak influence – a form of premature aging – goes a way to prove it. The best independent Springbank I have tasted in yonks. *53.3%. Premium Scotch Importers Pty Ltd, Australia.*

Scotch Malt Whisky Society Cask 27.67 Aged 12 Years refill butt, dist Dec 95 **(88.5) n21 t23 f22.5 b22** twelve? Twelve...? TWELVE....!!!! You must be bloody kidding me. It's the colour of mahogany – and I mean the antique ultra polished version – it's almost as opaque on the nose as it is in the glass...and this is twelve...? It reminds me in any number of ways of the type of rum produced in Guyana where they pre-caramelise the cask before entering the pot still Demerara into it. Obviously that has not happened here, but if someone told me it had, I'd believe them. A real freak in teak. *54.2%*

Scotch Malt Whisky Society Cask 27.68 Aged 18 Years refill hogshead, dist Dec 89 **(92.5) n23 t23.5 f23 b23** Just so complex!! *52.7%*

Scotch Malt Whisky Society Cask 27.69 Aged 18 Years refill hogshead, dist Dec 89 **(77) n20.5 t19 f19 b18.5.** Entirely out of key and sorts. *52.8%*

⋅⋅⋅ **Scotch Malt Whisky Society Cask 27.73 Aged 12 Years** refill hogshead, dist May 96 **(87.5) n22** I never thought I'd come across a Springbank, that most complex of malts, this clean and uncluttered on the nose: attractive, though; **t21.5** juicy, sharp-ish, thick barley bolstered by one dimensional oak; **f22** medium length with good oil developing sweetness to the barley; **b21.5** dense, simplistic but effective. *55.5%*

⋅⋅⋅ **Scotch Malt Whisky Society Cask 27.74 Aged 12 Years** refill hogshead, dist May 96 **(82.5) n20 t23 f19.5 b20.** decent distillate, and the wave of sweet barley just after initial delivery is superb. But an indifferent cask. *57%*

⋅⋅⋅ **Scotch Malt Whisky Society Cask 126.1 Aged 11 Years** (Hazelburn) sherry butt, dist Jul 97 **(85) n22 t20 f23 b20.** Doubtless some people will be wondering why I haven't given this 96 points and some kind of award. Well, here's the reason: granted, it is wonderful to come across a sherry butt that has not even the slightest trace of sulphur. But when the sherry is this dominant, and from a distillery like Springbank, it needs at least another decade for the oaks to start making a significant contribution and begin to sort out the balance. This is a bit like tasting a 1986 Chateaux Latour just a few years after bottling: it needed time to reach its optimum complexity but wasn't granted it. So we have a grape-soaked malt not without charm and with no little Columbian coffee. And molasses. But no shape or direction. A fantastic cask: but one emptied way, way too soon... *56.7%*

The Whisky Fair Springbank Aged 35 Years sherry wood, dist 71, bott 07 **(96) n24** a must- nose whisky – quite literally: the pressed grape softens the bourbony outline; **t24** a wondrous delivery of fresh, juicy grape and fresh juicy barley: all age is defied here; **f24** the dry Danish marzipan gives a nod to the advancing oak, but a fruit jelly balance is on hand; **b24** a true golden oldie. Quite sensational. *59%. Germany.*

The Whisky Society Springbank 1992 Aged 15 Years bott Sep 07 **(87) n21.5** a tad thin and niggardly; **t22** much more relaxed barley which immediately fills the palate; **f21.5** a touch bitter at first then a more expansive cocoa element arrives; **b22** some big malt moments makes for a big dram, but never quite settles. *52.6%. Speciality Drinks.*

STRATHISLA
Speyside, 1786. Chivas. Working.
Strathisla 12 Years Old db **(87.5) n22.5** the smoke evident on the last few tastings of this has been largely usurped by a heavy fat-sultana grapiness. Back to its old heavyweight self of a few years back, except the malt-fruit balance is kinder to the nose and the merest whiff of smoke is still detectable; **t23.5** thick, sweet barley swamps the tastebuds early on but slowly nudged aside by the trademark sweet sultana; engaging chocolate honeycomb towards the middle; **f20** duller than before with some big caramels kicking in and the unmistakable furry signature of the odd dud sherry butt; **b21.5** still a big, chewy dram which is about as heavy in body as you are likely to find anywhere in Speyside. Very enjoyable, though you know deep down that some fine tuning could take this guy easily into the 90s. *43%* ⊙ ⊙

Strathisla Distillery Edition 15 Years Old db **(94) n23** flawlessly clean and enriched by that silky intensity of fruity malt unique to this distillery; **t23** the malt is lush, sweet and every bit as intense as the nose; a touch of toffeespice does it no harm; **f24** just so long and lingering, again with the malt being of extraordinary enormity: these is simply wave upon wave of pure delight; **b24** what a belter! The distillery is beautiful enough to visit: to take away a bottle of this as well would just be too good to be true! *53.7%*

Cadenhead's Authentic Collection Strathisla Aged 21 Years Port hogshead, matured in oak cask, dist 87, bott Jun 08 **(94.5) n23** a dreamy creaminess: much more Spanish than Portuguese on the grape front. Soft and elegant; **t24** immediate soft spice impact, all couched in juicy grape, a few waves of juicy barley and....there's that creaminess again... **f23.5** medium, but with no oak threat whatsoever; gentle fruit all the way, oh except for the creamy mocha... **b24** quite outstanding. Though, puzzlingly, more Cream Sherry than Port... *57.1%. 216 bottles.*

Duncan Taylor Collection Strathisla 1967 cask no. 1886 **(93) n22.5** barley on the sweet resin; a touch of exotic fruit, but only a hint and some molten brown sugar, too; **t23.5** sugar coated barley takes on the oak; a touch of medium roast Java towards the middle is helped by the molasses being stirred in; **f23** big oaks but the viscosity of the barley, plus a little late spice sees it home comfortably; **b24** in some places a twin to the Lonach of the same age and strength. Just less oak and more barley sheen. But the overall difference is amazing. This is one sexy 40-year-old. *46.4%*

Duncan Taylor Collection Strathisla 1967 cask no. 1894 **(89) n22** pure bourbon... **t23** myriad dark sugars, mostly of the molassed variety, gather to make a juicy statement; **f22** red liquorice, butterscotch on toast; the vaguest honey balancing out vanilla; **b22** Yesiree, Bob... they darn tootin' know how to make great whisky in Kentucky. Errr... I mean, Speyside, ken. *48.8%*

Duncan Taylor Collection Strathisla 1967 cask no. 2716 bott 08 **(86) n21 t21.5 f22 b21.5.** Quite delicious with its waves of natural caramel and honey-tipped barley. But with oak, there is a fine line between excellence and very, very good, as this is. For those who want their first-class whisky to shows its age. *48.6%*

⋰ **Duncan Taylor Collection Strathisla 1967** cask no. 2721 **(88) n24.5** roasted hazelnuts lightened by kumquats and lime; the merest dab of honey is brilliantly balanced by a fleck or two of salt: stunning... **t22** toasted honeycomb splintered with oak; a distinctive old bourbon charm; **f20** tires as the oak is driven home; **b21.5** doesn't live up to the pin-up nose but the bourbony aspects are attractive. *48.3%. Duncan Taylor.*

⋰ **Gordon & MacPhail Distillery Label Strathisla 25 Years Old (89) n22.5** a hickory/ Demerara double bill should point towards a bourbony nose, but it doesn't due to the chalkier, drier oak notes; **t22.5** wonderful presentation of varying dark sugars with enough barley to ensure a mouth-watering middle; the antiquity is told through the sheen; **f22** much drier, spicier and though creaking, by no means decrepit..; **b22** beautifully crafted, the aging process, apparently threatening, has ultimately been kind. *40%. Gordon & MacPhail.*

⋰ **Gordon & MacPhail Distillery Label Strathisla 30 Years Old (91) n23** a forest of oak, but sunlight dapples through thanks to a chocolaty presence; almost old Jamaica rum-like in its estery qualities; **t23.5** too old...too old...? Nope...it survives. The oak really does take you to the precipice, but such is the magnificence of the crystalline Demerara you are hauled back just as the footing gives way; some blood orange and spices further the fun; **f22** a wonderful fade of cappuccino tops off a wonderful experience; **b22.5** old age doesn't equal great whisky – fact. But here, when there is a degree of drama involved, my word: it can be so enjoyable...!! *43%. Gordon & MacPhail.*

⋰⋱ **Gordon & MacPhail Distillery Label Strathisla 40 Years Old (84.5) n23 t21 f20 b20.5.** Excellent exotic fruit nose, but the oak has taken too firm a grip here. 43%. *Gordon & MacPhail.*

Lonach Strathisla 1967 (88) n22 a touch of sweet resin; **t22.5** really pucka delivery of intense, butterscotched barley; **f21.5** shows plenty of splinters from the middle onwards, but the barley does have some attractive stickability; **b22** one of those guys which stands on the oaky precipice, but doesn't jump. 46.4%. *Duncan Taylor.*

Lonach Strathisla 1968 (92) n22.5 butterscotch tart, complete with the salty pasty; burnished oak floors, empty wooden mashtuns and a defying stream of barley essence; **t23.5** brilliant delivery: the sweetness is precise and even, allowing no doubt to the barley's confidence; just so many layers and each one subtly pastel-shaded; **f23** none of the oak on the nose turns up and the modest vanillas are happy to allow the barley to show its clarity; again a speckle of salt from somewhere helps bring out the flavours to their fullest advantage; **b23** age defying stuff. Wonderful. 43.7%. *Duncan Taylor.*

Murray McDavid Mission Strathisla 1967 bourbon/grenache banyuls **(85) n22 t21 f21 b21.** From the school of exotic fruit via bourbon college. Has just about controlled on the oak, but needed a few fruit salad/black Jack nails to help keep the lid on. 43.6%. *300 bottles.*

⋰⋱ **Norse Cask Selection Strathisla 1997 Aged 12 Years** hogshead cask no. 47819, dist 97, bott May 09 **(86) n22 t22 f21 b21.** Malty, juicy and chocolaty. But a bit on the fizzy side, showing a cask not quite on its full game. 57.7%. *Qualityworld for WhiskyOwner.com, Denmark.*

⋰⋱ **Old Malt Cask Strathisla Aged 18 Years** refill hogshead, dist Mar 91, bott Mar 09 **(85) n22 t22 f20 b21.** Juicy, regulation Strathisla in full blending colours. 50%.

Provenance Strathisla Aged 11 Years dist winter 95, bott winter 06 **(84) n21 t22 f20 b21.** Wow!. A syrupy little blighter. Lovely, but hard to find the second dimension. 46%

⋰⋱ **Provenance Strathisla Aged 11 Years** refill hogshead, dist winter 96, bott autumn 08 **(86) n20.5 t22 f21.5 b22.** The nose suggests a flagging cask but the delivery is pure Strathisla with the malt intense and gently sweetened to the point of excellence in part. 46%. *Douglas Laing.*

⋰⋱ **The Whisky Agency Strathisla 42 Year Old** dist 67, bott 09 **(91) n23** when the citrus gets this intense we are talking very serious age...; **t22** the initial oaky wall crashes as the barley piles on the buttery pressure: this is some battle... **f23.5** a peace treaty is signed and the vanillas sweeten, the weight of the oak reduces and the barley shines unmolested...and spices come out to play; **b22.5** this is great whisky on the very edge. Just as much a battle as a dram but the overall effect is startlingly attractive. 44.5%. *The Whisky Agency, Germany.*

Whisky-Doris Strathisla Aged 35 Years sherry cask no. 2516, dist 15 May 69, bott 11 Feb 05 **(97) n25 t24 f23 b25.** May 1969: I was scoring the first run ever in the history of the newly opened Ruskin Junior School, far too young to drink whisky (though by then I had!!), and 500 miles away someone was filling new make into a butt blessed by angels. A dram of sighs... 56.3%. *Germany*

STRATHMILL
Speyside, 1891. Diageo. Working.

Berrys' Own Selection Strathmill 1974 cask no. 1212, bott 07 **(92.5) n23** pear drops at 33 years of age. Now that's what I call confidence in a whisky.... **t21.5** some quick covering up of some major wrinkles with a black of sharp barley....a tad flustered and embarrassed; **f24.5** with its composure back this rather mature lady sweeps along the tastebuds, head held high. The elegance to the rich barley is supreme: a fulsomeness to the body one might expect and the ultra complex vanilla-citrus, all dusted with a light sprinkling of cocoa offering the final, graceful touches; **b23.5** oozes a sensuality that those who are charmed by only the most delicate whiskies will find fatally alluring.... 46%. *Berry Bros & Rudd.*

⋰⋱ **The Cárn Mór Vintage Collection Strathmill 1990** hogshead, cask no. 2400, dist 90, bott 09 **(86) n21.5 t22 f21 b21.5.** So malty and clean it just screams "Speyside" at you... 46%. *The Scottish Liqueur Centre.*

⋰⋱ **Old Malt Cask Strathmill Aged 16 Years** dist Jan 93, bott Jul 09 **(80) n19 t20 f21 b20.** One of the great undiscovered Speysiders. But here it feels pretty restricted and bound in its own natural caramel. 50%. *Douglas Laing.*

Old Malt Cask Strathmill Aged 18 Years cask no. 4071, dist Oct 89, bott Jan 08 **(73) n18 t18.5 f19.5 b18.** A real shame: the whisky has matured from distillate not quite up to scratch for this usually excellent distillery and in a cask which do few favours. 50%. *Douglas Laing. 682 bottles.*

Old Malt Cask Strathmill Aged 30 Years refill hogshead no. 4070, dist Apr 77, bott Dec 07 **(88) n22** the usual sweet barley fanfare which defies both years and logic; and also with the fruity accompaniment; **t21.5** a vague injection of some exotic fruit quickly makes way for a barley-oak duo; **f22.5** as usual, calms down for a lightly oiled barley-rich lullaby; **b22** outstanding old Strathmills appear to be in season. *50%. nc ncf. Douglas Laing. 302 bottles.*

⋅⋅⋅ **Old Malt Cask Strathmill Aged 35 Years** dist May 74, bott Jul 09 **(89) n23** there we have it: geriatric whisky with the heart of a teenager. Plodding exotic fruit gives the age away, but in the heart of it is some years-defying juicy barley; **t21.5** bit of an oaky smack in the kisser. But it doesn't take long for that irrepressible barley to breathe fresh, pulsating life back into the proceedings; **f22.5** a minor oil spillage from somewhere, but it helps the barley and developing cocoa gel happily; **b22** I am astonished how delicate, lightweight malts like these survive 35 years. Well, usually they don't truth be told. And this one's managed it by the skin of its cask. A real gray-haired charmer, though. *474%. Douglas Laing.*

Old Malt Cask Strathmill Aged 45 Years dist Apr 62, bott May 07 **(90) n23** liquorice allsorts – especially the coffee ones. A hint of smoke on the oloroso; **t22** brinkmanship oakiness early on but recovers as the black treacle leaches in; **f22** molassed coffee and liquorice; again the vaguest echo of smoke **b23** quite amazed that such a light malt – even sherry aided – could last this amount of time. One of the surprises of the year. *40.5%. Douglas Laing. 317 bottles.*

TALISKER
Highland (Island–Skye), 1832. Diageo. Working.

Talisker Aged 10 Years db **(93) n23** Cumberland sausage and kipper side by side; **t23** early wisps of smoke that develop into something a little spicier; lively barley that feels a little oak-dried but sweetens out wonderfully; **f24** still not at full throttle with the signature ka-boom spice, but never less than enlivening. Some wonderful chocolate adds to the smoke; **b23** it is wonderful to report that the deadening caramel that had crept into recent bottlings of the 10-y-o has retreated, and although that extraordinary, that wholly unique finale has still to be re-found in its unblemished, explosive entirety, this is much, much closer to the mark and a quite stupendous malt to be enjoyed at any time. But at night especially. *45.8%*

Talisker 12 Years Old Friends of the Classic Malts db **(86) n22 t21.5 f21 b21.5**. Decent, sweet, lightly smoked...but the explosion which made this distillery unique - the old kerpow! - appears kaput. *45.8%*

Talisker Aged 14 Years The Distillers Edition Jerez Amoroso cask, dist 93, bott 07 db **(90.5) n23** lively, spiced and warming; zaps a few white hot holes through the fruit; **t23** a salivating mixture of big fruit and intense barley; although the usual explosiveness has been muted the effect is no less delicious; **f22** a few whimpering spices make their way through the thick crusts of grape and barley; **b22.5** certainly on the nose, one of the more old-fashioned peppery Taliskers I've come across for a while. Still I mourn the loss of the nuclear effect it once had, but the sheer quality of this compensates. *45.8%*

Talisker Aged 20 Years db **(95) n24 t24 f23 b24.** I have been tasting Talisker for 28 years. This is the best bottling ever. Miss this and your life will be incomplete. *62%*

Talisker 25 Years Old db **(92) n23.5** slightly fragmented with the smoke going it alone from the clove-clad oak; a touch of toffee; **t24** hold on tight; It's going in...like a munitions dump going off with spices exploding around every crevice in the palate. Only one distillery in the world is capable of this... **f22.5** strangely lethargic: cream toffee everywhere and dousing the peaty fun; a few strands of honey intertwine with citrus and vanilla, too; **b22.5** fabulous stuff, even though the finish in particular is strangely well behaved. *58.1%*

⋅⋅⋅ **Talisker 25 Year Old** bott 08 db **(92) n23** lazy smoke drifts over a scene of light citrus and slowly forming ancient oaks; **t23.5** soft vanillas arrive first, then a wave of muted peppers stinging only playfully as the sweet barley unfolds just so charmingly; **f22.5** the oaks really are revving up, but the sweet barley provides the balance; peat and citrus provide an unlikely fade; **b23** busy and creaking but a glass or two of this offers some classy entertainment for the evening. *54.2%*

Talisker 30 Years Old db **(84) n21 t22 f20 b21.** Talisker as perhaps never seen before: virtually no peat to make a significant contribution and caramel aplenty on the finish. Some teasing citrus and almost apologetic spice make a decent double act. The oak creaks a bit, but is kept docile enough. Talisker...but very, very different. *50.7%*

⋅⋅⋅ **Talisker 30 Year Old** bott 08 db **(89) n21** very tired oak; **t23.5** who would have believed it....? The delivery shows no woody failings whatsoever, but silky-soft barley, with a touch of toffee, and a slow-motion deployment of half-hearted smoke: just the right degree of sweetness and chewiness; **f22** remains soft with the toffee-vanilla dominant; **b22.5** this malt seriously defies the nose, which gives every indication of a whisky about to peg it. The softness of the experience is memorable; *49%*

⠒∴⠒ **Talisker 57 Degrees North** db **(95) n24** salty, smoky, coastal, breezy. The distillery's location in a nose... **t24.5** peat encased in a muscovado sugar, in the same way a fly might be enveloped in amber, melts to allow the slow blossoming of a quite beautiful and peaty thing...; **f23** some welcome whip and bite; the smoke and vanillas hang in there and even the odd hint of mocha puffs around a bit; **b23.5** a glowing tribute, I hope, for a glowing whisky... 57%

Old Malt Cask Tactical refill hogshead no. 3801, dist Nov 90, bott Aug 07 **(88) n23** unusual grist for a Talisker; **t22.5** bounding spice and a sexy variance to the peat levels; **f21** heaps of vanilla; **b21.5** just holds itself back slightly from its usual full-on assault. Charming. And that's not a word normally associated with this distillery! 50%. Douglas Laing. 317 bottles.

⠒∴⠒ **Old Malt Cask Tactical Aged 18 Years** refill hogshead, dist Dec 90, bott Apr 09 **(96) n24.5** classic ground black peppers: really sneezable stuff. Those peppers have been shaken onto an almost floral salad with that typical old Talisker style of being neither sweet nor dry, heavy nor light...yet smoky and spicy; **t23.5** veerrrroooom...!!!! We have lift off as those spices go into orbit, peppering – in both senses – the tastebuds with pin-prick attacks; the sweetness seems like pure barley concentrate; **f24** some serious subtlety here as the countless strata of barley, pepper, thinned maple syrup and vanilla duck and weave; **b24** talk about taking you back in time. A style lost to the present day distillery bottling, though this one is a tad sweeter than normal. No other distillery can offer this particular, spectacular, package on nose and tastebuds. 50%. Douglas Laing. 152 bottles.

Old Malt Cask Tactical Aged 18 Years dist Apr 85, bott Jan 07 **(94) n23** butterscotch with some telling smoke; **t24** honey-ginger delivery escorted by soft smoke; the trademark spices arrive on about the sixth flavour wave and build in beautiful intensity; **f23** the spices hold sway as the smoked-honey retreats; **b24** I'm amazed: even after 18 years the spices are there in force to dazzle in a glorious expression. 50%. 327 bottles.

Secret Stills Isle of Skye 1955 distillery no. 1 release no. 1, bott 05 **(95) n25 ft23 f23 b24.** Once, G&M would have bottled this at 40% and a lot of the magic would have been lost. Here, we taste a malt that is immeasurably better than it has any right to be and is simply reinforces exactly why tasting truly great whisky is as much an honour as it is a pleasure. 45%. Gordon & MacPhail. 573 bottles.

TAMDHU
Speyside, 1897. Edrington. Working.

Tamdhu db **(84.5) n20 t22.5 f21 b21.** So-so nose, but there is no disputing the fabulous, stylistic honey on delivery. The silkiest Speyside delivery of them all. 40%

⠒∴⠒ **Tamdhu Aged 18 Years** bott code L0602G L12 20/08 db **(74.5) n19 t19 f18 b18.5.** Bitterly disappointing. Literally. 43%.

Tamdhu 25 Years Old db **(88) n22** citrus showing now a more orangey based style to the lemon of its youth; **t22** typically fat and intense; the barley eventually escapes the gravitational pull of the oils to offer a wonderful barley sweetness; **f21** dried dates vanilla; **b23** radiates quality. 43%

⠒∴⠒ **Cadenhead's Tamdhu Aged 18 Years** dist 91, bott 09 **(85) n20 t22.5 f21 b21.5.** A bit of attitude on the nose, but mainly dealt with by the tsunami of sweet barley on delivery. 58.3%

Dewar Rattray Tamdhu 1990 cask no. 10139, dist Jun 90, bott Nov 07 **(84.5) n20 t21 f22 b21.5.** Tamdhu at its maltiest: attacks with all teeth gnashing. This is a wild boy from this usually docile distillery. 62.9%

Harris Whisky Co. Tamdhu Aged 14 Years cask no. 14085, dist Dec 91, bott Jan 06 **(86) n23 t22 f20 b21.** Another desirable malt from this excellent new company, but would have been at optimum ripeness for picking three or four summers earlier. 58.5%. nc ncf. The Harris Whisky Co.

Lonach Tamdhu 1968 (91.5) n23 from the exotic fruit school, but with dollops of honey and butterscotch to ensure balance; **t23.5** fabulous layering; the delivery is typical Tamdhu silk, then a strata of barley – then the inevitable old fruit; more butterscotch, complete with tart; **f22** oiled vanilla and vague nutty tones; **b23** it is strange how some malts displaying the "exotic fruit" style of age just don't work, while others, like this one, just make you roll your eyes in delight. The trick, I think, is that the oak doesn't degenerate to bitterness, and there is not a hint of it here. 40%. Duncan Taylor.

MacPhail's Collection Tamdhu 1962 ref no. 1877 **(87) n20** a dash of creosote to complement the plums and toffee apple; **t23** enormous delivery with the spice hitting the tape alongside the medium roast Java. A teaspoonful of Demerara helps it along. Big... **f22** long, with plenty of coffee and liquorice amid the splinters; **b22** has withstood the years better than some individuals of this vintage I know. Been helped along the way by a pretty sound sherry butt. A long way from perfect, but a grand old timer nonetheless. 43%

MacPhail's Collection Tamdhu 1966 ref no. 1879 **(77) n19 t19 f20 b19.** The odd decent bit of fruit and saving sweetness here and there, but bottled about a decade too late. 43%

⤞ **Old & Rare Tamdhu Aged 19 Years** sherry cask, dist Dec 89, bott Mar 09 **(94) n24** like being tipped head first into a sherry butt in the good old days before sulphur: pristine grape of the noble rot variety and somehow, vitally, some barley makes itself heard; **t24** a wondrous concoction on delivery: that flawless grape is there, but fizzed up by spices and muscovado sugars, and a hint of molasses for good measure; the barley reappears towards the middle; **f22.5** relatively sedate with more dependency on vanillas; **b23.5** Douglas Laing appear to have hit a rich seem of massive, memorable Tamdhus. Just one of those must-have drams. 55.8%. Douglas Laing. 202 bottles.

⤞ **Old Malt Cask Tamdhu Aged 17 Years** refill hogshead, dist Dec 91, bott Apr 09 **(84.5) n22 t21.5 f20 b21.** Good, honest, malty, lightly oily Speyside malt, though showing more like a 10-year-old. 50%. Douglas Laing. 320 bottles.

⤞ **Old Malt Cask Tamdhu Aged 18 Years** sherry hogshead, dist Dec 89, bott Sep 08 **(95) n24** syrupy sherry - oloroso at its bichamin thickest – clogs the nose...but it is all rather wonderful. Can't spot much in the way of barley, though. But when the sherry is this clean and fine, and the oak is making all the right noises, who cares....? **t24** huge toasted raisins still dripping with juice make for an initially one-dimensional, though thanks to the seeping sweetness, enjoyable experience; silky, with a wonderful build up of crystalised muscovado sugars and anciently over-ripened greengages; **f23.5** long, remains silky and then a slow burn of spices as the mocha begins to build and take quiet control. Still those fruits linger **b23.5** a steamroller of a dram, the sherry crushing everything in its path. Initially not a purists' dream, as complexity takes a backseat, but there is a slow dawning of myriad bitter-sweet complexities – though mainly sweet. It's like an old, clean, unsulphured Macallan cask of yesteryear has rolled down the hill and landed in the warehouse of Tamdhu. One for sherry lovers of the original Macallan school...50%. Douglas Laing. 268 bottles.

Provenance Tamdhu Aged 11 Years refill hogshead no. 4253, dist Spring 97, bott Spring 08 **(87) n22** diced apple and marzipan; **t22** double-toned malt with a firmer edge to the softer, sweeter element; **f21.5** waxy honey and more barley layering; **b21.5** so simplistic, but so charming. 46%. nc ncf. Douglas Laing.

TAMNAVULIN
Speyside. 1966. Whyte and Mackay.

Tamnavulin 1966 Aged 35 Years cream sherry butt db **(91) n24** cleanest sherry imaginable: thick, glutinous nose with cream soda and toffee; **t22** enormous delivery of oak and toffee raisin; **f23** thins out to allow complexity to evolve, which it does with a fudgy chewiness; **b22** for those who love great old sherry, this is an absolute. Perhaps too much sherry to ever make it a true great, but there is no denying such quality. 52.6%

⤞ **Connoisseurs Choice Tamnavulin 1990 (82.5) n20 t22 f20.5 b20.** Chugs along pleasantly and maltily enough, but with an annoying lack of enterprise or complexity for a dram normally so good. 43%. Gordon & MacPhail.

The Exclusive Malts Tamnavulin Aged 39 Years cask no. 3665, dist Nov 68 **(81) n21 t20.5 f19.5 b20.** Decent, honest old malt which, frankly, is several summers past its prime. 40.4%. The Creative Whisky Company. 179 bottles.

Master of Malt Tamnavulin 14 Years Old (74) n18 t19 f18 b19. Decidedly below par. 46%. Master of Malt, UK.

Master of Malt Tamnavulin 15 Years Old (93) n23.5 light, breezy, a little coastal with soft salts rubbed into the sweet barley; **t23.5** delicate with a particularly attractive mouthfeel. A mildly boiled candy sweetness surrounds the intense malt backbone; **f23** some bitter oak finds itself outgunned by decent molassed sweetness; **b23** shows a little age at the death but that can be forgiven for its overall beauty. 40%. Master of Malt, UK.

Master of Malt Tamnavulin 16 Years Old Cask Strength (90.5) n22 big'n'grapey: not first class, but it'll do; **t23** big fruit delivery yet the malts don't exactly hang back, either; **f23** loads of chocolate on the go...and so much else, mainly of a honeyed persuasion; **b22.5** at first, not too sure about this one. Then just wears you down with its non-stop enormity. And bloody niceness! 55.1%. Master of Malt, UK.

⤞ **Old Malt Cask Tamnavulin Aged 20 Years** dist May 89, bott Jul 09 **(95.5) n24** just wonderful barley: it comes at you from all directions and in varying degrees and forms of sweetness (and dryness); **t24** oh my gosh...even better on palate where the intensity of that barley defies belief. Arrives in a beautiful mix of lush grassy sharp tones and sweeter, more sugar-tinged higher notes; the tongue simply cannot stop working against the palate, such is the richness and controlled intensity; **f23.5** a few citrus notes creep in before the oak has a chance to establish its vanilla and cocoa-mined territory; **b24** as healthy a specimen of Speyside 20-years-old as you are likely to find. A corker. *50%. Douglas Laing.*

Old Malt Cask Tamnavulin Aged 30 Years bourbon barrel no. 3947, dist Jun 77, bott Oct 07 **(91) n22** the oak is quite forceful here but is heading in a bourbony direction; otherwise floral; **t23.5** the kind of mouthfeel you dream of: just the right amount of rugged barley and firm oak and the oils kept to a minimum; **f22.5** a tad extra vanilla sweetness as the embers fade; **b23** forceful but no violence to the tastebuds. *50%. Douglas Laing. 210 bottles.*

⋰ **Old Malt Cask Tamnavulin Aged 40 Years** refill hogshead, dist Nov 68, bott Mar 09 **(86) n21.5 t21 f22 b21.5.** Not quite in the same league as the formidable OMC 30-y-o of last year. Yet though the oak leaves little doubt about the age there is a melodic sweetness, of the old fashioned boiled sweet school, that ensures the barley gets a good hearing. Pleasantly spiced and in better nick than some 40-year-olds I know....I don't mean whisky. *43.1%. Douglas Laing. 261 bottles.*

Provenance Tamnavulin Aged 12 Years dist winter 94, bott winter 07 **(83) n19 t22 f21 b21.** Wow! If you like your malt green, grassy and salivating then, at last, the dram of your dreams. *46%. Douglas Laing.*

Scott's Selection Tamnavulin 1977 bott 07 **(90) n22.5** citrus, but more lively and fresh than that alone; newly washed clothes and some marzipan on the lemon drizzle cake; **t23** excellent crisp barley radiating a juicy sweetness before some natural oak caramels kick in; **f22** clean and simple with a refreshing metallic tang late on; **b22.5** just beautiful. *50.8%*

TEANINICH
Highland (Northern), 1817. Diageo. Working.

Cadenhead's Authentic Collection Teaninich Aged 12 Years bourbon hogshead, dist 93, bott Sep 06 **(88) n21 t23 f22 b22.** Juicy and attractive throughout. *58.3%. 282 bottles.*

Duncan Taylor The NC2 Range Teaninich 1996 Aged 11 Years (82) n21.5 t21 f20 b20.5. From such an old, well-used cask, this has as much newmake about it as matured whisky. *46%*

Lombard Brands Teaninich 12 Years Old Single Malt (85) n21 t22 f21 b21. An agreeable, chewy malt with some good barley sugar. But it feels as though someone left the hand brake on... *43%. Lombards Brands.*

Old Malt Cask Teaninich Aged 36 Years refill hogshead no. 3914, dist Feb 71, bott Sep 07 **(85.5) n21.5 t22 f21 b21.** Enjoyable, but the oaky wrinkles can't quite be smoothed despite a spirited barley attack. Missing the honey and fruit of the Samorali bottling. *50%. Douglas Laing. 122 bottles.*

The Queen of the Moorlands Rare Cask Teaninich 1993 Edition XIX (93) n23 so complex! Everything geared on the herby/spicy side of the spectrum... **t24** a real touch of the 'Morangies about this one, showing much of its neighbourly trait of massive complexity with the odd orangey fleck that turns up now and again **f23** very long, extremely delicate and goes back over the finer points of the taste but in almost minute detail; **b23** anyone putting forward an argument that there is a Black Isle style of whisky will use this in evidence alongside a standard 10-y-o Glenmorangie. Sometimes the similarities are startling. Truly great whisky. *51.5%. nc ncf. Available at The Wine Shop, Leek.*

⋰ **Scotch Malt Whisky Society Cask 59.38 Aged 25 Years** refill hogshead, dist Nov 83 **(91) n23.5** superb subtle citrus gives the barley and polished wooden floors a lift: a real feel of age and elegance here; **t23** typical Teaninich in all its sugar-barleyed splendour, but somehow keeping the sweetness on acceptable levels; also that strange indefinable, vague oaky hint of something fruity but in underdeveloped form... **f22** putting on its PJs, as this is getting a bit tired. The vanillas are attractive, though, and hang on to enough sweetness to keep the barley active; **b22.5** hard to imagine this one getting through another summer or two without losing some excellence. *54.8%*

TOBERMORY
Highland (Island–Mull), 1795. Burn Stewart. Working.

Ledaig Aged 10 Years db **(63) n14 t17 f15 b17.** What the hell is going on? Even Gulliver on all his weird and wonderful travels would not have come across such a strange world as the one I am on while trying to come to terms with the whisky of Tobermory. Butyric and peat in a ghoulish harmony on nose and palate that is not for the squeamish. *43%*

Ledaig Aged 12 Years db **(90) n23** serious farmyard aromas – and as someone who spent three years living on one, believe me....borderline butyric, but somehow gets away with it, or at least turns it to an advantage; **t23.5** the staggering peat on the nose is no less remarkable here: chunky, clunking, entirely lacking poise and posture. And it obviously doesn't give a damn...; **f21.5** strange gin-type juniper amid the smoke; **b22** it has ever been known that there is the finest of lines between genius and madness. A side-by-side comparison of the Ledaig 10 and 12 will probably be one of whisky's best examples of this of all time... 43%

Tobermory Aged 10 Years db **(67.5) n16 t17 f17.5 b17.** People say to me: "Jim, you must really love your job. It has to be the best in the world." Well, yes I do. And yes it most probably is. But as Newton would tell you: "for every action there is an equal and opposite reaction." Well today I have been a bit lucky, because I have been tasting some nectar, and occasionally where I hadn't expected it. This morning, when planning my day ahead, I had included the tasting of Tobermory as my treat for a tough day. Last time I officially tasted it, it had blown me away with its brilliance. I had tasted the odd so-so bottling in the last six months whilst on my travels, admittedly. But I didn't come prepared for this, a less than brilliantly made malt totally bereft of character or charm. I have no idea what has happened here. I must investigate. Frankly, I'm gutted. 40%

Tobermory Aged 15 Years Limited Edition db **(72.5) n17 t18 f19 b18.5.** Another poorly made whisky: the nose and delivery tells you all you need to know. 46.3%

Berry's Own Selection Tobermorey 1995 casks nos. 486/487, bott 07 **(86) n19 t22 f23 b22.** Marzipan and cherry kernel You'll go nuts for it once your palate acclimatizes... 51.8%

Cadenhead's Authentic Collection Ledaig Aged 11 Years bourbon hogshead, matured in oak cask, dist 97, bott Jun 08 **(81) n19 t21.5 f19.5 b21.** Lovely peat. But, technically, not quite the greatest malt ever made. 57.7%. 234 bottles.

Cadenhead's Tobermory Aged 13 Years sherry butt, dist 94, bott Feb 08 **(65) n15 t19 f18 b19.** No amount of barley bristle and attitude can save this from the cask....and possibly some strange work on the still. 59.6%. 681 bottles.

Chieftain's Ledaig 10 Years Old cask no. 800004, dist Mar 97 **(69.5) n16 t18 f18.5 b17.** Doubtless there will be those who will dance around claiming this to be the best thing since England won the World Cup (No, honest they did...). Well, sorry. But to me this is badly made whisky where only huge peat does a job of making it potable. You can drink it and enjoy it if you don't care about the niceties. But there is something about this which sets my purest nerves on edge. 61.3%. nc ncf. Ian Macleod.

Connoisseurs Choice Ledaig 1990 (85) n21 t21 f22 b21. The smoke is deceptive: there is less than there appears to be. Good honey, though. 43%. Gordon & MacPhail.

Old Malt Cask Tobermory Aged 13 Years refill hogshead no. 4069, dist Apr 94, bott Dec 07 **(86) n20.5 t22 f22 b21.5.** Clean, well made and overflowing with juicy barley. 50%. nc ncf. Douglas Laing. 346 bottles.

Old Malt Cask Tobermory Aged 14 Years (86) n20 t23 f21.5 b21. One of the most enjoyable Tobermorys I have come across for a little while: the nose is naff and the complexity is at a premium. Oh, and it's as hard as nails and has absolutely no give and it's pretty hot whisky, too. But you can't help being rocked by the sheer vibrancy and concentrated form of the barley which gives the tastebuds a rare old work over. Nobody's idea of a classic, but absolutely great fun. 50%

∹ **Private Cellar Tobermory 1995** bott 08 **(86) n21 t22 f21.5 b21.5.** Enjoyable, essentially honeyed and enjoys a coppery richness. 43%. Scott's Selection.

Provenance Ledaig Aged 8 Years (86) n21 t23 f21 b21. Thundering peat but new-makey and a tad feinty. An early juice-fest, though. 46%.

Whisky-Doris Tobermory Aged 34 Years sherry cask, dist Dec 72, bott Feb 07 **(90) n23** a dripping nose...of pure, unruined, old time sherry... **t22** spicy kick on entry then an outrageous, nutty grape attack with every soldier from Jerez; **f23** much better when settled with a toffee apple fade; **b22** I'm sure that once upon-a-time I used not to like this kind of whisky. Now, after so few chances to be merry thanks to poor sherry, I'm beginning to love even the odd OTT classic. 49.5%. ncf. Germany. 96 bottles.

Whisky-Doris Tobermory 35 Years Old dark sherry cask, dist 21 Dec 72, bott 25 Feb 08 **(93) n23.5** oloroso concentrate. Look carefully and below the oloroso you'll find oloroso. Elsewhere an oloroso sub-strata does its grapey worst. Oh, and some peat... **t23** the delivery is pure oloroso; amazingly juicy for its age with oloroso grape oozing around the tastebuds like oloroso on heat. Oh, and some peat... **f23.5** oloroso etc. etc. Oh, and some peat... **b23** this is almost grotesquely over-the-top in terms of its sherry input that it seems almost a parody of the style. But having just tasted a couple of pretty horrendous samples, I am embracing this like a long lost lover and willing, no, demanding, to be seduced. I know this is not the score I'd normally give a whisky like this, but what the hell...I'm only human...! 49.4%. Whisky-Doris.

∹ **Wilson & Morgan Barrel Selection Tobermory 1995** Port Finish bott 08 **(84.5) n21 t21.5 f21 b21.** Eye-wateringly sharp fruit pierces the taste buds. A modicum of smoke confuses the issue further. 46%. Wilson & Morgan.

TOMATIN

Speyside, 1897. Working.

Tomatin 12 Years Old db **(85.5) n21 t21.5 f22 b21.** Reverted back to a delicately sherried style, or at least shows signs of a touch of fruit, as opposed to the single-minded maltfest it had recently been. So, nudge or two closer to the 18-y-o as a style and shows nothing other than good grace and no shortage of barley, either. *40%*

Tomatin 18 Years Old db **(88) n22.5** a real clean sherry statement; **t22** a bit of a finoesque kick to this, then the oily malts grab the fruit and slowly assimilate it into a fruity maltshake **f21.5** unbelievably gentle and demure; **b22** what a well-mannered malt. As though it grew up in a loving, caring family and behaves itself impeccably from first nose to last whimpering finale; *43%*

Tomatin Aged 18 Years db **(85) n22 t21 f21 b21.** I have always held a torch for this distillery and it is good to see some of the official older stuff being released. This one has some serious zing to it, leaving your tastebuds to pucker up - especially as the oak hits. *40%*

Tomatin 25 Years Old db **(89) n22** the trademark Tomatin 25 citrus nose – plus perhaps a dash of exotic fruit - proudly attacks and teases... **t23** but we have a different lad on the palate: starts gently with the citric, mouth-watering maltiness but where once it famously vanished for a while, now a regiment of spices go on the attack; **f21.5** a becalmed finale with the malt having found its voice again; **b22.5** not a nasty bone in its body: understated but significant. *43%*

Tomatin 30 Years Old db **(91) n22** if there was a hint of the exotics in the 25-y-o, it's here, five years on, by the barrel load. Evidence of grape, but the malt won't be outdone, either; **t23** silky and sultry, there is every suggestion that the oak is thinking of going too far. Yet such is the purity and intensity of the malt, damage has been repaired and/or prevented and even at this age one can only salivate as the soft oils kick in; **f23.5** probably my favourite part of the experience because the sheer deliciousness of the chocolaty finale is awesome; **b22.5** malts of this age rarely maintain such a level of viscosity. Soft oils can often be damaging to a whisky, because they often refuse to allow character to flourish. Yet here we have a whisky that has come to terms with its age with great grace. And no little class. *49.3%*

Tomatin 40 Years Old db **(89.5) n21.5** a few oaky yawns because this old guy's feeling a bit tired; **t22** for all the oak intrusion, for all the burntish honeycomb, for all the old aged spices coming through, for all the first-rate impression of a high-class old bourbon, somehow, eventually, it's the malt which really catches the eye; **f23** still oily after all these years and though the oak tries to get a bit tough, it doesn't stand a chance: the sweet malt, and those oils see to that; **b23** not quite sure how it's done it, but somehow it has made it through all those oaky scares to make for one very impressive 40-y-o!! Often it shows the character of a bourbon on a Zimmer. *42.9%*

Tomatin 1962 db **(86) n22** barley sugar, cough drops and sweet pipe tobacco: something of an old-fashioned candy store here; **t23** over-ripe greengages vie with the liquorice and malt for top dog: it's a hard call; **f19** the oak finally gains control; **b22** over-tired on the finish, maybe. But there is no shortage of class and character on the nose and delivery. *40%*

Tomatin 1974 db **(87) n21** dusty but some fruit wafts in from somewhere to offer a certain richness; **t23** salivating first with malt, but as the oak mounts up the fruit returns; a delicate delivery with a pleasing coating of soft oil; **f21** mildly overdone toast but the malt hangs about; **b22** just manages to keep the oak enough at bay to make this a decent late night treat. *40%*

⋯ **Celtic Heartlands Tomatin 1967** bott 08 **(78) n19 t21 f18 b20** Decent malt kick but less than kind cask input. *47.7%. Bruichladdich Ltd. 523 bottles.*

⋯ **Connoisseurs Choice Tomatin 1988** refill American hogshead dist Dec 88, bott Nov 08 **(84.5) n21 t22 f20.5 b21.** Malty and sweetens brightly towards the middle. *43%. Gordon & MacPhail.*

Duncan Taylor Collection Tomatin 1965 cask no. 20942 **(88) n22.5** the plum tart and custard on the nose doused in bourbon doesn't fool anybody: this is a big, bloody oldie!! **t22.5** still the oil!! At first you think: wow!! This is going to make it big time. Then an avalanche of oak puts paid to that. Just enough malt holds sway to ensure the right ticks are made in the correct boxes; **f21.5** the oak has receded and at the very death it is the oily malt which really sings. You feel like applauding...; **b21.5** just so typical of this astonishing distillery. *52.1%*

Duncan Taylor Collection Tomatin 1977 cask no. 1901 **(84) n22 t21 f20 b21.** Plenty of bourbon notes here from nose to finish though the hickory does make for a tight finale. A pleasing experience all the same. *43.3%. Duncan Taylor.*

⋯ **Hart Brothers Tomatin Aged 15 Years** dist Jan 93, bott Jun 08 **(81) n20.5 t21 f19 b20.5.** Malty though it is, every evidence that this one's gone through the top: lactic nose, bitter finish. *46%. Hart Brothers Limited.*

James MacArthur's Fine Malt Selection Tomatin Aged 12 Years cask no. 12391, dist 95, bott 07 **(85.5) n21 t22 f21 b21.5.** Absolutely down the middle, sweet-ish, non-fussy Tomatin at its malty simplistic. And pretty lovely for it, too. *43%. James MacArthur & Co. Ltd.*

⠶ **Mackillop's Choice Tomatin 1978** dist Jan 78, bott May 08 **(84.5) n23.5 t20 f20.5 b20.5** To taste, leaks oak badly. But the nose is something else: dried, pithy tangerine; the grassiest of barleys; the oak is equally gentle, radiating soft cassava; any more delicate and it'd crack. *46%. Iain Mackillop & Co. Ltd.*

Master of Malt Tomatin 19 Years Old (94) n23.5 no shortage of oak, but all entirely at home with the rich, biscuity barley; a wisp of citrus lightens it slightly; **t23** clean, highly intense malt with the most beautiful build in intensity and sweetness; **f24** goes into malty overdrive depite the drier oaks; **b23.5** in this form it out-Cardhus Cardhu in the stunningly clean, ultra-rich malty stakes! Almost stereotypical Speyside at its most magnificent. *40%. Master of Malt, UK.*

Master of Malt Tomatin 19 Years Old Cask Strength (96) n24 very similar to their 40% bottling except here the citrus and the oak have the starring rolls and it takes time for the barley to secure its place; **t24** ooomph...!! For a while you are just speechless but without the power of thought, not so much the alcohol intensity – its pretty pathetic compared to the cask strength rums I work with, for instance – but the sheer thickness of the flavour and mouthfeel. It's a soup of a malt, much reduced, with perhaps some of the most intense barley I have ever had the great fortune to come across; **f24** thins out sufficiently for the brain and tastebuds to make some sense of what is happening in there: the oaks, we learn, have arrived but still can't get much of a word in edgeways against the malt; also, miraculously, a thin seam of citrus has survived; some quaint spices jostle for a place at the very back; **b24** quite simply astounding: this is how 19-year-old whisky should be. *57.6%. Master of Malt, UK.*

Norse Cask Selection Tomatin 1989 Aged 15 Years (85) n21 t21 f22 b21. Exceptionally oily and creamy with massive chewiness to both barley and fruit. Big stuff. *57.7%. Quality World, Denmark.*

Norse Cask Selection Tomatin 1996 Aged 7 Years (79) n20 t21 f19 b19. I must be one of the biggest advocates for young malt going. But this narrowly misses the mark, perhaps by being, despite the obvious youth on the nose, a tad too advanced for its years. The big malt thrust on arrival is wonderful, but it is far flatter than one might otherwise expect. Curious. *50%. Quality World, Denmark.*

Northern Light Tomatin 1990 Cask Strength cask no. Q1324 **(86.5) n21.5 t21.5 f22 b21.5.** Barley delicious, but definitely on the bourbony side of malty. *53.2%. Qualityworld, Denmark.*

Old & Rare Tomatin Aged 31 Years Rioja Finish dist 75, bott 0/ **(86) n21 t22 f21 b22.** Rioja and Tomatin are not usual bed-fellows. But this one appears to work: this isn't a distillery with a track record for excellence at old age, but here the lively fruit really does give a welcome crutch to the big barley. Good stuff!! *55.6%. Douglas Laing. 252 bottles.*

Old & Rare Tomatin Aged 32 Years dist Dec 75, bott May 08 **(91.5) n24** plenty of lively oak and even a hint of smoke here. But not for a second does it show evidence of decay. The degree of variance and complexity on the floral/herbal front defies belief: a 20-minute nosing job if ever there was one; **t23** beautifully constructed with almost a fusion between the barley and oak, **f22** surprisingly, after all these years, it pans out towards the barley; **b22.5** the nose touches genius while the remainder is simply outstanding. *57.7%.*

Old Malt Cask Tomatin Aged 31 Years refill hogshead no. 3923, dist Dec 75, bott Oct 07 **(94) n23.5** the purest, maltiest 31-year-old of all time? Has to be pretty close... **t24** how can something so ancient be this profoundly juicy? The oak is almost arrogantly elegant. But the intensity of the barley reaches almost new levels: astonishingly beautiful! **f23.5** long, long, long! The softest oils carrying with it a wonderful vanilla-latte fade; the Horlicksy malt carries on with its massive symphony; **b23** age just drips off this one. Yet somehow the malty backbone is unbent and the quality undented so there is not a single hint of degeneration. Superb. And about as malty as a malt gets. *50%. Douglas Laing. 296 bottles.*

Private Cellar's Selection Tomatin 1988 bott 0/ **(80.5) n20 t20 f20 b20.5.** Creaky and feeling its age but the honeycomb is superb. *43%*

⠶ **The Scotch Single Malt Circle Tomatin 1976** cask no. 19085, dist Nov 76, bott Jan 08 **(89.5) n23** another quietly extravagant nose with all kinds if bourbony sighs and whimpers blending beautifully with toasted mallows; **t23** gentle, oak-extracted caramels bolt onto the trademark barley and help radiate those docile sugars far and wide; **f21.5** a graceful exit despite the build up of a drier tier; **b22** needs a bit of time in the glass to oxidise and see off some of the worst of the oak. But the low voltage sweetness is simply charming. *49.6%. The Scotch Single Malt Circle. German market.*

⠶ **Scott's Selection Tomatin 1976** bott 08 **(87.5) n23** more than a nod in the direction of bourbon with lemon curd tarts in there, too; **t21.5** the reflex action is too much oak. But there is a wonderful compensating sweet lilt which really does give the malt full power; **f22** pretty long with butterscotch blending with the chalky oak; **b21** the malty notes scream Tomatin and handle the oak sometimes more comfortably than others. *50.9%. Speyside Distillers.*

The Spirit Safe & Cask Tomatin 1989 Aged 17 Years dist 89, bott 07 **(91) n23** find yourself a quiet corner of the house, a spare half hour and indulge: intense barley, but on just how many levels..? **t23** a tsunami of honeycomb barley sweeps over the tastebuds bringing in its wake no shortage of oak. But its all wonderfully integrated, giving a toasty effect to the honey; **f22** beautiful soft coffee, mainly Mysore; **b23** if all 17-y-o Speysiders were like this, the world would be a happier place... *58.6%. nc ncf. Celtic Whisky Compagnie.*

⠐⠂ **Whisky Doris Tomatin 43 Year Old** cask no. 20950, dist Nov 65, bott Mar 09 **(87) n22** carrot cake and marzipan; **t22** a befuddled delivery: the juicy barley tries to take the lead but doesn't quite have the strength or willpower; a few zingy spice and honey notes dive in, then its pretty thick up to and including the middle; **f21.5** lots of oak, but just enough sweetness lends a restraining hand; **b21.5** not a great 43-year-old: far too much oak for that. But the spice and honey intervention makes for a battle royale. *48.2%.*

The Whisky Fair Tomatin Aged 22 Years bourbon hogshead, dist 84, bott 07 **(86.5) n22 t21.5 f22 b21.** Custard tart...and a lot of malt on the nose. Then it's malt all the way. Absolutely minimal attempt at complexity, some vague citrus apart, and here the oils gather sufficiently enough to hinder further development. Delicious, though....!! *48.1%. Germany.*

The Whisky Fair Tomatin Aged 22 Years bourbon hogshead, dist 84, bott 07 **(86.5) n22 t21.5 f22 b21.** Mein got!!! A just about identical dram. Perhaps an extra shake of the sugar spoon and a fraction less oil, but it's pretty minimal. Another lovely dram. *48.9%. Germany.*

⠐⠂ **The Whisky Fair Tomatin 43 Year Old** dist 65, bott 09 **(93) n22.5** soft biscuity-shortbread aroma with just a touch of welcome citrus in the background; **t24** some serious Jaffa Cake to this one: the barley speaks first, and makes a surprisingly juicy fist of it, then a slow move towards orange and spice, with a background grated chocolate balance; **f22.5** soft oils have been conjured from somewhere and they help soften the vanilla and barley fade; **b24** slightly overstretched age-wise for certain, but still has enough charm and sophistication, helped along by soft orange and cocoa, to make for an improbably beautiful dram which defies the ages. *48.1%. The Whisky Fair, Germany.*

TOMINTOUL
Speyside, 1965. Angus Dundee. Working.

Tomintoul Aged 10 Years db **(78) n20 t19 f20 b19.** The true character has been lost under an avalanche of caramel. *40%*

Tomintoul Aged 12 Years Oloroso Sherry Finish Limited Edition db **(95.5) n24** pronounced Oloroso suggests fresh, untainted butts of outstanding quality; some apple juice dovetails with the grape. About the cleanest sherry nose I have seen in a long time; **t24** big malt delivery that perfectly and unexpectedly counters the sherry; at times gloriously bitter-sweet with the accent, rightly, being on the juicy barley; as near as damn-it perfect weight and then a tidal wave of spice; **f23.5** that excellent spice delivery rounds off the malty-sherry marriage beautifully. Wonderfully long and seductive with the finish remaining busy and balanced; **b24** perhaps it is the voluptuousness of the body which works to best effect here: the mouth is filled with a just-so amount of oil to make the soft sherry, firmer oak and balancing sweet barley notes really harmonise. The label claims the sweetness comes from the sherry. It doesn't: the sherry (nose apart) is dry, the barley sweetens. Even so, a huge leap in quality from the standard 10 and a thrilling reminder of just how good an excellent clean-sherry-influenced whisky can be. *40%.*

⠐⠂ **Tomintoul Aged 14 Years** db **(95) n24** curiously, there is a sea-weed saltiness attached to this one: not exactly what you expect to find from a malt made and (I think) matured in the centre of the Scottish Highlands. But it adds a compellingly attractive - if eyebrow raising – element to this delicately framed and gently structured, lightly honeyed malt fest. The oak splendidly keeps within the spirit of the style; **t24** just how many variations on a honeyed theme can you get? Here I count at least five, each wave coming in after the other with just the odd nip and tuck or expansion of its intensity; the very faintest smoke is detectable and just when the natural caramels appear to be getting too excited, the malt re-establishes itself; **f23** medium length, but sheer quality all the way: Bird's custard mixing dreamily with drier, playfully spiced, oaky vanillas. The lightest of oils spreads the grassy, sharper malts to ensure a wonderful lightness of touch; **b24** not a single weakness: no bitterness, no off notes, no caramels other than those naturally from the oak, no sulphur. Just magnificent whisky bottled exactly the way it is meant to be. An absolute corker from this little-known but outstanding distillery and one of the most delicately complex distillery bottlings of the year. *46%*

Tomintoul Aged 14 Years Limited Edition cask no. 1664, dist 02 May 94, bott Jun 08 db **(92.5) n23** sliced cucumber sets the mark for the freshness to this; serious complexity here with a warming spice prickle offset by a light marmalade sweetness; **t23** ripping spices ensure the entry is noticed; the tastebuds are then pummelled by a legion of varying barley tones... **f23** even a hint a vague fruitiness now as the vanillas, gentle spices and crisp barley all lay claim to the finale; **b23.5** "The Gentle Dram" coaxes the label...Yeah, right...!!! 46%. nc ncf. 300 bottles.

⟶ **Tomintoul Aged 16 Years** db **(88.5) n22** beautifully weighted and lightened by a citrus and pear mix; **t23** outstanding control to the sweetness on delivery with the barley really striking home; **f21** chewy and a build up of toffee; **b22** once more has changed shape slightly, but the quality never wavers. 40%

Tomintoul Aged 27 Years db **(87) n22** pretty thick aroma with a decent spread of marmalade and even a hint of something smoky; **t22.5** dullish delivery, perhaps colour-related, but develops slowly, first mouth-wateringly, towards an attractive sweetness that is barley rather than fruit induced; **f21.5** cream toffee and vanilla with some playful spices stirring the pot; **b21** the last time I saw a colour like this was on antique expert David Dickinson's face. Still, lots of charm and character to go round...and on the whisky, too. 40%

Tomintoul 1976 bott 07 db **(93.5) n22.5** double-whammy of exotic fruits and honeyed vanilla points to the unmistakable influence of very old bourbon casks. A vague hint of lavender adds to the potpourri. A malt that reeks of great age from every pore, but with the most subtle dusting of peat on the wind; **t23.5** an immediate statement of ancient classicism with every nuance of controlled antiquity filling the mouth. Wonderfully juicy, yet a languid smokiness adds both weight and helps keep in line the oaky waves. Fabulous interaction between the oak and barley but the great age is driven home by the spicier, drier riches that cling to the understated oiliness so typical of Tomintoul; **f23.5** long and at times improbably lush with the malts having a distinct say before settling below the sea of gentle smoke and oak. Late drying vanilla and cocoa charms and redresses the vaguely fruity sub-plot; **b24** it is in the balance that victory is achieved: malts like this so often topple off the cliff into the oaky forest of age, and this one has clung gamely on to safety. Any understandable worries from the nose that this could be too old are dispelled once the subtlety, charm and unexpected liveliness of the whisky becomes apparent on the palate. Truly great whisky which, paradoxically, both celebrates and belies the years and in the most complex manner imaginable. Supreme stuff! 40%

Tomintoul With A Peaty Tang db **(94) n23** takes me back to my early teens, spending schooldays working on a farm: pure farmyard with an earthy yet fruity punch. The sort of complex nose that almost makes you forget to drink the stuff...almost...; **t24** a gentle coating of vaguely sweet peat that multiplies in intensity; salivating yet chewy. Some liquorice and hickory notes make their drying mark; **f23** distinctly gristy and unusually dry for a smoky malt. Long, luscious and not a little oaky late on; **b24** a bit more than a tang, believe me! Faultlessly clean distillate that revels in its unaccustomed peaty role. The age is confusing and appears mixed, with both young and older traits being evident. 40%

D&M Aficionados' Club Bottling Tomintoul Aged 25 Years cask no. 5964, dist Oct 81 **(89) n21** mild sawdust and butterscotch tart; **t23** seriously delicious barley that gets the saliva gushing: no mean feat for something this ancient; something of the caramelised biscuit, too; **f22** excellent touch of medium roast Java helped along with some mollassed oils; **b23** a quarter centenarian that holds its head high without a single wrinkle to its character. 43%. nc ncf. US by Angus Dundee Distillers.

The Dram Tomintoul Vintage 1989 (80) n22 t21 f18 b19. Disappointingly dull finish defies the promise on nose and early mouth arrival. 43%. nc ncf. Whisky-Doris, Germany. 120 btls.

⟶ **Mackillop's Choice Tominoul 1989** cask no. 5990, dist Aug 89, bott Mar 08 **(94.5) n23** fussy and busy: grassy, salty and a light infusion of honey; **t24.5** stunningly beautiful delivery: then, amazingly, those three major points I picked up on the nose come crashing into the tastebuds with giant, hair-stand-on-end waves. A fabulous spice bites into the middle ground, and you fancy a touch of smoke amid the carnage, too... **f23** long, retains the spice and sweetens with a bourbony, Demerara flourish; **b24** it will take a good five or six mouthfuls to get the measure of this. Once you do, this essay in complexity will be a dangerously hard bottle to put down... 43%. Iain Mackillop & Co. Ltd.

⟶ **Norse Cask Selection Tomintoul 1992 Aged 15 Years** hogshead cask no. CS059, dist Aug 95, bott Jul 08 **(90) n22.5** it's usual rampant self with lots of busy, small, salty – almost curiously coastal – detail, but with oak and citrus leading; **t24** a delivery to savour: absolutely hits the palate at full speed with an almost challenging intensity to the barley; **f21.5** lightly oiled vanilla and malt, but some bitterness from the cask; **b22** though it finishes slightly off course, so much else about this is just so wonderful. *55.5%. Qualityworld for WhiskyOwner.com, Denmark.*

⋇ **Old Malt Cask Tomintoul Aged 33 Years** refill hoghead, dist Sep 75, bott Apr 09 **(86) n22 t21 f22 b21.** The oak is heavy, at times cumbersome, but the greater weight is lifted by a curious molten sugared thread and juniper. The lightest oils all help lessen the burden. Really enjoyable, especially when that late puff of smoke materialises. *43.6%. Douglas Laing. 151 bottles.*

The Peated Malt Old Ballantruan Speyside Glenlivet (88) n21 young, a tad feinty, but with bubbling peat complementing the barley/fruity fudge; **t22** some serious oils where the cut has been so wide. The peat has little coastal quality but instead imparts a delightful sweetness which clamps itself to every corner of the palate; **f23** pretty long, skimping slightly on complexity but the developing spices dovetail sexily with the light muscovado-tinted malt; **b22** I had tasted the new make smoked Tomintoul, but this was my first look at it as the finished article. A Speyside Young Ardbeg, I have heard some day. Hmmm, I think not. The soft feints are still there, as though the stillman has tried to extract every last drop out of the still, but this is malt that ultimately succeeds on its gifts rather than the fortitude of its failings. Worth an investigation. *50%. ncf.*

TORMORE
Speyside, 1960. Chivas. Working.

Tormore 12 Years Old db **(75) n19 t19 f19 b18.** For those who like whisky in their caramel. *40%*

Tormore Aged 15 Years "Special Distillery Bottling" db **(71) n17 t18 f19 b17.** even a supposed pick of choice casks can't save this from its fiery fate. *46%*

Cask Strength Tormore 1994 (68) n18 t17 f16 b17. Better nip down to the hospital to see if any of my torched tastebuds can be saved... *59.9%. G & M.*

Connoisseurs Choice Tormore 1996 (78) n20 t20 f19 b19. Malty, clean but house-style thin. *43%. Gordon & MacPhail.*

D&M Connoisseurs' Club Bottling Tormore Aged 15 Years cask no. 2258, dist Feb 92 **(75.5) n18 t19 f20.5 b18.** Honeyed but also a tad feinty. *43%. nc ncf. US by Angus Dundee.*

Mackillop's Choice Tormore cask no. 2258, dist Feb 92, bott Jul 07 **(79) n19 t21 f20 b19.** No off notes, very good barley, for a Tormore; exceptionally pleasant. But less body than a Burke and Hare dug grave. *43%. Iain Mackillop & Co. Ltd.*

⋇ **Provenance Tormore Aged 12 Years** dist winter 96, bott winter 09 **(82) n20 t21 f21 b20.** Malty, pleasant, clean and entirely untaxing; excellent by Tormore standards. *46%. Douglas Laing.*

TULLIBARDINE
Highland (Perthshire), 1949. Tullibardine Ltd. Working.

Tullibardine 1966 cask no. 3509, bott 08 **(94) n24** toffee apple concentrate. Pot still Demerara at its most ancient and rich; black treacle and further layering of cooked apple. There are some splinters here, but do little or no damage. Dense, immense and slow navigation required: give this at least ten minutes nosing before finally tasting; **t24** silky, immense oloroso and then a soft display of supine spices; layers of black treacle tart as well as manuka Honey; also a coppery edge to this, as though the malt had just had some work done; **f22.5** long and understandably bitter as the 42-y-o oak begins to make some sort of noise; the rich grape and soft honey cushions the worst of this, though; **b23.5** this sister cask of the now legendary '66 World Cup edition has moved on considerably from that '06 bottling. Now we have a malt masquerading as a very old, and it must be said, fine cask of pre-caramelised Demerera rum. Not that there is any caramel, of course: the gushing intensity of the obvious first fill oloroso ensures that such nasty stuff is never needed. No matter how you look at it, this is astonishing whisky, the type of which may be a long time coming round again. Few casks can so majestically endure so many summers, even those as short and minimalist as Scottish ones: this must have been a near perfect sherry butt. For either sherry or Tullibardine lovers, an investigation of the next flight to Calgary will be a must. *49.9%. Exclusively for Willow Park, Calgary.*

Tullibardine 1966 World Cup Edition ex sherry butt cask no. 2132, bott 06 db **(96) n24** one of those gold nugget, pure magic casks with the marks of Hurst and Moore upon it. Forty years on and the sherry is still lashing it out with rich toffee apple, soft natural caramels and moist fruitcake. Not even the hint of an off note to be had; **t24** mouth-watering barley...after all this time!! And then layer upon layer of sherry of varying viscosity and intensity. Lush, lithe and latently spicy; the oak is naturally deep but never gets caught out of position and knows exactly when to pass; **f24** still developing as a touch of Jaffa cake sweetens the vanilla and coating of dark chocolate. After an almost world record number of taste waves for a non-peated cask, very late on even lighter, fresher fruits. There's some peaches running on to the palate. They think it's all over: it is now...; **b24** this cannot be in any way confused with England's bid to win the 2006 World Cup. Because this has style, charisma, shape, purpose, the ability to attack, plenty in reserve and the unmistakable pedigree and aura of something that can not only match just about anything else in the world, but beat it. Ironically, the label says Butt – which sums up to the English France's World Cup comeuppance. And WC, which nutshells to the French (and everyone else) England's quality of management and play...This is one of the great single cask malts of our lifetime. Sven, being a Caol Ila man, would have no idea how to change tactics to understand this. But the rest of us can see what a World Cup winner this is... *48%*

Tullibardine 1975 hogshead cask no. 1009, bott Mar 07 db **(85) n22 t20 f22 b21.** Begins life as a garibaldi biscuit, suddenly overwhelmed by a forest of uncompromising oak and finishes life as a high quality Java/Blue Mountain mix latte. *52.7%*

Tullibardine 1986 John Black Selection ex sherry hogshead cask no. 697 db **(95) n25** blackberries, freshly-made fudge, lichen-covered rocks, fresh grape, mildly burnt raisin. It is all there...and so much more. Some 500 whiskies into the 2007 edition and this is the best nose of the year so far; **t24** dark, intense and slightly foreboding on arrival it lightens with a firm injection of toasted toffee and sweetening, intense barley; **f22** sherry dulls things down but spices form and crème brulee sees us to the end; **b24** there is good reason why John Black has long been one of the most respected distillers in Scotland. Here is liquid, 92 proof why....And though he may not have made it, there's now no doubt he knows what a stunning whisky should nose and taste like. *46%. nc ncf sc. 255 bottles.*

Tullibardine 1988 bott 07 db **(89.5) n23** the beginnings of exotic fruit, which means... serious age; **t23** still big and balls with some huge input, almost as a consortium, of barley and oak with a real grape edge: a super-chewer of magnificent proportions; **f21.5** begins to tire noticeably as the oak really takes hold, but there is enough honeycomb to see it through; **b22** just great whisky which has moved up a noticeable notch in age since it was first brought out as a vintage. What fun! *40%*

Tullibardine 1988 cask no. 556, bott 08 db **(79) n20 t20.5 f19 b19.5.** A steady-as-you-go-Joe, a bit strait-laced and tight and even at full strength refusing to come out of its corner to fully entertain. Lots of early juicy barley, though. *55.1%. Exclusively for Willow Park, Calgary.*

Tullibardine 1992 cask no. 239 bott 08 db **(90.5) n22** engrossing layers of vanilla making a sandwich of softer citrus notes; a faint clarion call to bourbon; **t23.5** beautifully weighted and helped along by the most gentle of oils; the barley is healthy, rich, intact and honeyed, the vanillas are grounded, entirely in sync with what is expected of them at this age and offer the prerequisite degree of balance; further, renegade oak tones offer a soft liquorice bourbon hint; **f22** those oils help the sweetness along considerably, seeing off an oaky threat; **b23** a masterful bottling which outshines another Tully found in the Canadian market, the cask 737. I don't think it is the later bottling which assists: more, this is from a better bourbon cask and the extra degree of alcohol plays to its strengths in every respect. *53.8%. Exclusively for Willow Park, Calgary.*

Tullibardine 1992 cask no. 737, bott Dec 07 db **(88) n22** butterscotch tart meets lemon drizzle cake; **t22.5** a whole raft of lip-smacking vanillas are boosted by an early and surprising surge of spice: considering the cask number, no surprise it should really take off; **f21.5** simplistic layering of barley and vanilla: even a few bourbony tones make themselves present; tiering; **b22** sound malt with a touch of attitude. *46%. 269 bottles for Victoria Whisky Festival 2008.*

Tullibardine 1992 cask no. 18/1 (1st fill Bourbon barrel) db **(93) n24** how do you measure such complexity? Despite the cask type, fruits abound: over-aged apple and simmering citrus plus grassy barley and sultana cake; **t22** light, dusting the palate with barley and gentle vanilla; **f24** gets more into its stride with some raspberry jam playing with the late, mouth-watering barley and drier cocoa. Brilliant; **b23** there are first fill bourbons and first fill bourbons...this one probably came from a cask that held a bourbon for a dozen years or more, so measured is the oaky influence. The nose is whisky heaven. *46%. nc ncf sc. 270 bottles.*

Tullibardine 1993 John Black's Selection 3 sherry cask no. 10022, bott Jun 07 db **(82.5) n21 t21 f20.5 b20.** The odd juicy edge but otherwise surprisingly dull. *57.7%. 259 bottles.*

Tullibardine 1993 Marsala Wood Finish hogshead cask db **(89) n22** a sharp fruitiness: sultanas and under-ripe pears; **t22** a mouthwatering and quite vivid fruit kick adorned with spice; **f22** lush finale with some extra cocoa to the spice; **b23** sophisticated, with enough complexity to keep you quiet for quite a few minutes. *46%. nc ncf.*

Tullibardine 1993 Muscatel Wood Finish hogshead cask db **(91) n23** distinctly grapey in that double-edged Muscat style that seems simultaneously both sweet and dry; **t22** dry and mouth filling with some pounding barley that has somehow had the sweetness removed:

strange but very attractive; **f23** remains bone dry and now some lovely spice begins to tingle the roof of the mouth; **b23** seriously classy whisky which really does exploit a wine finish to the nth degree. And very different. *46%. nc ncf.*

Tullibardine 1993 Rum Finish cask no. 15016, bott Mar 07 db **(81) n21 t20 f20 b20.** Thin and miserly on development. Crisp barley, though. *46%*

Tullibardine 1994 hogshead cask no. 677, dist 94 db **(88) n23** relaxed and floral. Citrus undertones cranks up the complexity; **t22** evenly weighted barley with a delicate flourish; **f21** thins out slightly complexity-wise, perhaps because of the lethargic sherry; **b22** such a fragile thing for something that has spent time in a sherry hogshead. *46%. nc ncf sc. 352 bottles.*

⁘ **Tullibardine PX Finish** dist 93, bott 08 db **(85) n23 t22 f20 b20.** A big, at times bone-hard, whisky which, like many which have spent time in Pedro Xeminez casks, have found it difficult to acquire the kind of balance hoped. The nose offers great promise with a real old-fashioned fruitcake flourish but after the melt-in-the-mouth delivery gets past the barley lead, the degree of bitterness outweighs the growing soft fig notes. For equilibrium, needed less – or more – time in cask: we'll never know. *46%*

⁘ **Tullibardine Vintage Edition Aged 20 Years** dist 88, bott 08 db **(86) n22 t22 f21 b21.** The malt sparkles on the nose and delivery. Fades as caramels kick in. *46%*

Cadenhead's Tullibardine Aged 18 Years sherry butt, dist 89, bott Feb 08 **(78.5) n19 t21 f19 b19.5.** An impressive barley crescendo in there somewhere. *56.8%. 266 bottles.*

⁘ **The Golden Cask Tullibardine 1989** cask no. CM127, dist 89 **(86) n21.5 t22 f21 b21.5.** A thick, lolling malt with some outrageously intense barley and shards of honey. The oak does bite now and again but the soft liquorice sub-plot ensures something to chew over. *56.7%. House of Macduff. 280 bottles.*

The Queen of the Moorlands Rare Cask Tullibardine 1994 Edition XV hogshead no. 676 **(89) n23** different from the Tulli of 20 years ago: a heathery job, this, crisper than the norm and excellent oak involvement; **t21** chaotic barley and oak battle for a foothold; **f23** beautiful simmering of busy barley and earthy oak. The slow cocoa crescendo is a joy; **b22** pretty wild, and it has nothing to do with the strength. The delivery is scrambled but finds a rhythm late on and genuinely impresses. *57.7%. The Wine Shop Leek and Congleton, UK.*

⁘ **Scotch Malt Whisky Society Cask 28.19 Aged 18 Years** refill hogshead, dist Jun 90 **(86) n22 t21 f21.5 b21.5.** Serious, malty top dressing for any well-aged blend. Would add decent oak, too. *53.4%*

⁘ **Scotch Malt Whisky Society Cask 28.21 Aged 18 Years** refill hogshead, dist Jun 90 **(88.5) n21.5** green tea and dried marzipan; **t23** surge of rich, playfully honeyed, biscuity barley on lush but gentle oils; **f22** heaps of toasty vanilla; **b22** thick enough to make a malty milkshake from: a honeyed insertion enriches the still mildly juicy but typically intense barley. *54.8%*

Scott's Selection Tullibardine 1989 bott 07 **(85) n20 t22 f21.5 b21.5.** Wonderful sharp, eye-watering fruit effect to this deliciously salivating version. *55.4%*

⁘ **The Whisky Fair Tullibardine 1976** Dark Sherry hogshead, dist 76, bott Sep 08 **(96) n24** noses like an old Bristol dockyard warehouse of the mid 1970s (and that's bloody good, believe me); **t24.5** spices, as there should be. Grape in prime fruitcake mode, as it should be. Remnants of barley making a brave, lightly juicy, but ultimately futile fight, as it should be. Middle ground occupied by a light coffeeish oakiness, as it should be. Yep, all the excellent bits present and correct; **f23.5** sublimely light, even allowing a delicate Jaffa Cake and fig fade... **b24** you see, when you nose and taste this you get some idea of the unutterable paucity of the indefensible, sulphur-screwed bollocks which passes for an embarrassing percentage of sherry cask whisky today.... *54.1%. The Whisky Fair.*

⁘ **The Whisky Fair Tullibardine 1976** Light Sherry hogshead, dist 76, bott Sep 08 **(94) n24** a lilting golden syrup sweetness is a perfect accompaniment for the grape; **t24** stunning delivery: barley and grape are of equal status, and there's that watered-down syrup again; vanillas just find enough room to squeeze into the middle ground; **f23** wonderfully robust barley refuses to be brow-beaten by the fruit; **b23** absolutely not a single sign of age damage. Superb malt. *54.3%. The Whisky Fair.*

UNSPECIFIED SINGLE MALTS (Campbeltown)

Cadenhead's Campbeltown Malt (92) n22 a touch of cordite to the barley; **t24** as explosive as the nose suggests as the taste bud-ripping barley produces a pyrotechnic display. Gung-ho spices kick in with the advancing oak; **f23** long, enormous depth to the spices while eye-watering orange rind completes the complexity; **b23** on their home turf you'd expect them to get it right...and, my word, so they do!! *59.5%*

Cadenhead's Classic Campbeltown (92) n23 balance at a premium but, my word, the salty liveliness to the malt is worth a few extra minutes to enjoy; **t24** you can drown in your own saliva, so mouth-watering is the barley; a touch of salt accentuates the enormity; **f22** pretty mainstream by comparison, with boring ole salty vanilla tucking in; **b23** what a dram! Must be what they gave Lazarus... *50%*

Chieftain's The Cigar Malt 11 Years Old Chateau la Nethe finish, cask no. 90951, dist Aug 95, bott Jul 07 **(82) n20 t21 f20 b21.** A few spent matches for the cigar evident. Not being a smoker, I'll take their word for this being a Cigar Malt. Mind you, whatever happened to the old Pipe and Slippers dram...? "Splash of soda, dahling?" "Thank you dear." "Let me just get the paper for you to read with your whisky, I've just ironed it for you. Dinner will be ready in 10 minutes. Steak and kidney pie: your favourite, dahling. Is that all right? If not I have some pork chops in the fridge, they wouldn't take a jiffy." "Yes, thank you dear, the pie will be fine. Oh, and Mildred...." "Yes dear?" "You put in a touch too much soda. Top me up with the whisky, there's a good thing." "Of course, dearest. Sorry." Ah... those were the days... *53.5%. nc, ncf. Ian MacLeod. 293 bottles. South African market.*

Wemyss "The Almond Tree" Campbeltown Single Malt Vintage 1970 bott Jan 07 **(88) n22.5** significant age: plenty of marzipan (weirdly enough) amongst the herbs; **t22** stella early delivery for its age with a thin golden syrup coating that just takes the edge off the dry oak; **f21.5** dries considerably with late spice **b22** Absolutely no doubting the age of this one. Indeed, this is one almond tree that is creaking with oak. *46%. Wemyss Vintage Malts. 165 bottles.*

UNSPECIFIED SINGLE MALTS (Highland)

Adelphi Breath of the Highlands 1972 Aged 35 Years bourbon barrel, cask no. 1753, dist 72, bott 07 **(90.5) n22** serious identity crisis. Thinks it's a bourbon...also has a bit of a thing going for gin with a botanical nip supplied by the oak: shall you tell it or I...? **t23** lucky my chair has arm rests...bit of a surge through the body and brain as the tastebuds are thumped almost senseless by a welter of bourbony blows: the oak is on a spree with liquorice and hickory and no end of soft honey; and the spice....!!! **f23** passes the Old Grey Bristle Test as those oaks slam home relentlessly. Again the toasted barley hangs on in there for a good ol' punch up at the death... **b23** fcuking hell...!! Where oh where did they dig this one up from? This is 35 going on 53. Totally over the top, seriously a one-off among the 1500 whiskies I have tasted this year: no other has this type of fingerprint. And you know what...I love it!!! From the last days of psychedelia a bit of a psychedelic dram...Give it to me, baby...yeah, nice 'n' rough... *51.7%. 130 bottles.*

Adelphi Breath of the Highlands 1985 Aged 20 Years cask no. 1065, dist 85, bott Jun 06 **(86) n22 t21 f22 b21.** Loses way in middle but sprightly for its age. *54.8%. Adelphi Distillery. 176 bottles.*

Breath of the Highlands Aged 20 Years Cask no. 1065, dist 1985, bott 06 **(90) n22** some mildly soapy exotic fruit; **t24** beautiful delivery of perfectly weighted barley: just the right amounts of salt to season the malt to imply age and countering sweetness thanks to stunning rays of honey and spice towards the middle **f22** back to a light soapiness and medium toast Blue Mountain; **b22** at times hanging on for grim death so as not be overwhelmed by the oak – lost a few fingernails in the process, but it's survived and with aplomb!! *55.1%. Adelphi Distillery Ltd. 176 bottles*

Cadenhead's Classic Highland (82) n19 t22 f21 b20. The trace of fusel oil on the nose guarantees a big delivery. Highly malty! *50%*

Cadenhead's Highland Malt (90) n22 malt concentrate; **t23** ditto for the delivery; soft oaks and apple develop countering complexity; **f22** hard, fresh barley, vanilla and malt milk-shake all the way; **b23** does barley come any more pure or intense than this...? *60.2%*

Celtique Connexion 1990 Armagnac Finish dist 90, bott 08 **(86) n21.5 t22 f21 b21.5.** Clean, firm, pretty hard-nosed but sweet and never less than enjoyable. *46%*

Celtique Connexion 1990 Sauternes Finish dist 90, bott 07 **(91.5) n22** dextrous and beautifully spiced; clean and compelling; **t23** serious malty weight to the delivery backed sublimely by fruit; superb complexity as the pithy, marmalady notes make their mark; **f23** a touch of soft oil does no harm as the barley really digs in deep; the gentle fruit won't be outdone; **b23** magnifique! *46%. Celtic Whisky Compagnie.*

Celtique Connexion 1992 Quart de Chaume Finish dist 92, bott 07 **(85.5) n19.5 t23 f21 b22.** The nose is less than welcoming and the finish, though offering cocoa aplenty, confirms all is not hunky-dory. However, there is sufficient charm and juiciness on the delivery make for some real fun. *46%. Celtic Whisky Compagnie.*

Celtique Connexion 1994 Monbazillac Finish dist 94, bott 07 **(90) n22.5** soupy fruit – the grapes couldn't be much more succulent: elsewhere almost rum-like in style; **t22** messy delivery with grape and malt tripping over each other; settles towards the middle with a sweet juicy fruit and an attractive bite; **f23** now comes into its own as a few delicate spices intervene and the malts begin to flesh out; pulsing spice and cocoa; **b22.5** takes a bit of getting used to, as flavours are not exactly subtle. But once your taste-buds acclimatise, its pretty damn decent. Impressed! *46%. Celtic Whisky Compagnie.*

Celtique Connexion 1994 Vin de Paille Finish dist 94, bott 07 **(71) n17.5 t18 f17.5 b18.** Ooh-la-la!! La soufrer!!! *46%. Celtic Whisky Compagnie.*

Celtique Connexion Highland Single Malt Aged 14 Years Vin de paille du Jura Finish dist Oct 92, bott Jan 07 **(93) n25** one of the noses of the year: the diffusion of bourbon notes with kumquat, peppery-cinnamon and grape juice is quite divine...; **t23** juicy, barley-topped marriage of green, under-ripe fruits, including Kiwi Fruit – unbelievably salivating; **f22** a much drier prospect thanks to the oak; **b23** fruity, busy...and very different. *46%. nc ncf.*

⋙ **Co-Operative Group Single Highland Malt Aged 12 Years (86.5) n21.5 t22 f21.5 b21.5.** Rich, honeyed and chewy. Overplays the toffee game slightly, but genuinely enjoyable. *40%*

Dun Bheagan Highland 8 Years Old (88) n22.5 lively, energetic, weighty oak for age; **t22** chewy, a wonderful kaleidoscope of sweetness building on the malt and set off by a sharp bite; **f21.5** toffee and honeycomb; **b22** just damned decent drinking. *43%. Ian Macleod Distillers.*

⋙ **Glenandrew Aged 10 Years (83.5) n22 t21 f20 b20.5.** Soft chewy toffee. *40%. Highlands & Islands Scotch Whisky Co. Ltd.*

Glen Burn Single Highland Malt (81) n20 t20 f21 b20. Pleasant, gentle if simplistic pub fodder. *40%. Glen Burn Distillers*

Glenfinnan Highland Scotch Single Malt Over 12 Years Old (84) n22 t23 f19 b20. Starts beautifully with citrus and rose petals among other delights. But then stops dead just as you pass the middle. Damn!! *40%. Celtic Whisky Compagnie, France.*

Glen Torran Highland Single Malt 8 Years Old (75) n17 t21 f18 b19. Sparkles briefly on arrival, helped along the way by lovely spice. But the caramel on the nose and finish does it in. *40%. Roderick & Henderson for London & Scottish International.*

Glen Turner Single Highland Malt Aged 12 Years L616656B **(84) n22 t23 f19 b20.** There's a really lovely malt trying to escape there, but its wings are clipped by some over hefty caramel on the finish. But the nose and delivery sing beautifully and are joyously mouth-watering. I feel a Bible-thumping trip to France coming on....they must realize that because Cognac has spent the last few decades using caramel as a crutch for its own lack-lustre spirit, it doesn't mean to say that Scotch needs it. Absolutely the contrary! Right, down from my soapbox. *40%. Glen Turner Distillery for La Martiniquaise, France.*

⋙ **Glen Turner Single Highland Malt Aged 12 Years (85) n21.5 t22.5 f20 b21.** Pleasant enough. *40%. Glen Turner Distillery for La Martiniquaise, France.*

Glen Turner Single Highland Malt Aged 18 Years L532556A **(87) n21 t23 f21 b22.** A wonderfully clean and characterful malt that lays it on thick with the barley but, again, could do with keeping the caramel at bay. *40%. Glen Turner Distillery for La Martiniquaise, France.*

⋙ **Glen Turner Single Highland Malt Aged 18 Years (83) n19 t23 f20 b21.** Some serious honey doing the rounds here and the fruitiness is at times impressive. But the nose and finish testifies that odd dodgy cask has been tipped into this, too. *40%. Glen Turner Distillery for La Martiniquaise, France.*

⋙ **Matisse Aged 15 Years Highland Single Malt (83.5) n22 t21 f20 b20.5.** Lots of toffee with fruit. Has rather upped the toffee delivery of late. *40%. Matisse Spirits Co. Ltd.*

Matisse Aged 15 Years Highland Single Malt (87) n21 toffee-nougat amid oaky barley **t22** firm malt radiating barley and spice in equal measures; **f22** toffeed yet dies as the oak drives home; **b22** an impressive malt which appears to suffer slightly from some colour adjustment. Even so, superbly weighted and with busy spices and soft oak washing over the barley. Sound. *40%. The Matisse Spirits Co.*

McClelland's Highland Single Malt (80) n21 t20 f19 b20. Easy going – until the bitter finish kicks in. *40%*

Sainsbury's Single Highland Malt Aged 12 Years (82.5) n21.5 t21 f20 b20. Enjoyable, but has lost its old complexity and now displays big cream fudge. *40%. Sainsbury's, UK.*

Secret Stills Highland 6.1 1988 (95) n23.5 from the school of delicacy and subtlety comes a malt that has not a single blemish or lack of grace: oak malt and the very softest fruit in just-so proportions; oh, and for the younger ones amongst us, a nod to Fox's Party Ring biscuits... **t23.5** big, thick barley almost in paste form with a salivating build up of varying sugars from muscovado to a more acacia honeyed via reduced maple syrup; **f24** seriously complex with myriad vanilla and butterscotch notes battling it out with the barley: stunning! **b24** absolutely beautifully made malt which has spent some 20 years in a perfect cask. Truly adorable. *45%. Gordon & MacPhail.*

Tesco Highland Single Malt 12 Years Old (87) n22 t22 f21 b22. A quite lovely malt displaying no shortage of character and charm. *40%. Tesco, UK.*

Wilson & Morgan House Malt cask no. 4082 – 4090 **(85) n21 t21.5 f21 b21.5.** A big-peated, lusty, big-hearted, highly enjoyable chap who eschews subtlety for effect. *43%*

UNSPECIFIED SINGLE MALTS (Island)

Chieftain's The Auld Alliance Flora Macdonald First Edition 15 Year Old Island Malt St. Emilion finish, dist Apr 92 **(83.5) n22 t21 f20 b20.5.** Curious how the fruit barely shows on the smoky nose. Certainly makes up for it once it hits the palate! *50%. Ian Macleod.*

Chieftain's The Auld Alliance Flora Macdonald Second Edition 15 Year Old Island Malt Chateauneuf Du Pape finish, dist Apr 92 **(89) n23** clean, sweet, thumping peat; **t21** if you are wondering where the wine's got to, you soon find out on delivery: a bit of a mess at first begins to find harmony towards the middle; **f23** really finds its feat: the smoke still controls but the grapey undertones are so charming; **b22** normally I find peat and wine a bit like baked beans and eggs or soup and wine: they just weren't meant to be. However, I have to begrudgingly admit that, after a few early pratfalls, it works pretty damn well... *47%. Ian Macleod.*

Dun Bheagan Island Single Malt Aged 8 Years (93) n23 superb honey-smoke combo; **t24** that wonderful promise on the nose is fulfilled twice over: the peat is even bigger than threatened but a rich seam of honey bores deep into it; **f23** the finish demands smoky embers and chocolate and that's just what it gets...in spade-loads; **b23** as beautiful as a Scottish isle. *43%. Ian Macleod Distillers.*

Dun Bheagan Island 8 Years Old (83) n21 t21.5 f19.5 b21. Pleasant and although honeyed, no buzz. *43%. Ian Macleod Distillers.*

Master of Malt Orkney 12 Years Old (91) n23.5 now if you really want to know what heather smells like, invest in a bottle of this: rarely do you come across it in such unabridged form....even if it's Scapa!!; seriously botanical all round; **t23** thick malt, a touch of light honey; **f21.5** long, toffeed, **b23** yet another gem from the Master of Malt (fudgy finish apart). His portfolio is pretty damned impressive, I must say. *40%. Master of Malt, UK.*

UNSPECIFIED SINGLE MALTS (Islay)

Auld Reekie Islay Malt (95) n24 a near-perfect nose with indecipherable complexity, though salt and peat are at the nucleus; **t24** breathtakingly scrummy: bitter-sweetness – perfect; peat-levels – perfect; degree of oak weight – perfect; spice injection – perfect. Perhaps could just do with an addition of a surprise element for true perfection; **f23** long, chewy; Fisherman's Friends dipped in Camp Coffee and hickory; **b24** my last whisky of the day and a dram I shall be tasting all the way to when I clean my teeth. On second thoughts... I'll do them in the morning. Only kidding. But this is a must have dram for Islayphiles: true genius *46%. Duncan Taylor.*

Blackadder Peat Reek (88) n23 dying embers of a peat fire: dry peat soot; **t22** refreshing early on, then dries slightly though a gristy theme plays on; **f21** soft with a touch of jammy fruit; **b22** a clean, very gentle giant. *46%. Blackadder International.*

Breath of Islay Aged 14 Years Cask no. 5347, dist 1992, bott 07 **(86) n21 t23 f22 b20.** Oddly enough this, in some respects, is less Islay-ish than its sister "Breath of the Isles". So much oil on this one the peat, though big, is kept from delivering its full smoky message and complexity really is at a minimum. Extremely Caol Ila-ish in style. Pretty delicious, though! *56.5%. Adelphi Distillery Ltd. 278 bottles.*

Cadenhead's Classic Islay (91) n23 young, light and revealing viperish clarity. The smoky grist is such a delight; **t23** gentle oils and lumbering smoke; the sweetness intensifies and displays a liquorice honeycomb quality; **f22** soft and delicate with gentle smoky brush-strokes; perhaps a tad too bitter for its own good; **b23** I admit: totally baffled by this one. Just can't read the distillery at all: a completely different take on any of them: kind of Ardbegian, but a Lahphraogish blast and a hint of Caol Ila's oils. Yet it is all, yet none of them. Oddly enough, it reminds of Port Ellen when about eight years old. But, obviously, can't be. Classic, indeed! *50%*

Cadenhead's Islay Malt (84) n22 t21 f20 b21. Fat, well enough peated but lacks ambition and complexity. *58%.*

Chieftain's The Auld Alliance Prohibition Wine Cask 16 Year Old Islay Malt Chateauneuf Du Pape finish, dist Dec 90 **(84) n22.5 t20.5 f21 b20.** There are certain aspects here that are impressive, the bothie fire ashes on the nose for a start. But I well remember learning over 25 years ago from an Ardbeg old timer (even then) that you used wine casks only to store the whisky when it came to peat, never to give extra flavour. I'm particularly reminded of those wise words right now... *46%. Ian Macleod.*

Dun Bheagan Islay 8 Years Old (92) n22.5 fresh and clean, the peat taps out a smoky tattoo; **t23.5** again, a certain youthfulness allows the barley to really pulse; some excellent gristy sweetness ensures a wonderful succulence; **f23** drier but layered with the oak offering a butterscotch edge – smoked, of course; **b23** spot on. *43%. Ian Macleod Distillers.*

Dun Bheagan Islay 8 Years Old (Canada Release) (87) n22 silky smoke and something rather fruity and cough candyish; **t21.5** juicy, soft, an amalgam of barley and non-specific fruit candy; **f22** the vanilla helps give a fingerprint; **b21.5** incredibly soft: at times the constituent parts appear to have blurred. *43%. Ian Macleod Distillers.*

Finlaggan Islay Single Malt 10 Years Old (82) n21 t21 f20 b20. Beautiful citrus notes mildly tempered with smoke: an enormous improvement from the caramel-ruined previous "Lightly Peated" bottlings. *40%. The Vintage Malt Whisky Co.*

The Ileach Single Islay Malt Cask Strength (97) n24 t25 f24 b24. Amazingly, my tasting notes for the original weaker version are exactly the same as for this sea-facing monster. Except here the enormity has risen by a significant factor, as has the intensity of each vital cog in its make-up. Perhaps the only change is the honey-thread to the sweetness that pervades throughout. Otherwise, identical. A wondrous, take-it-with-you-when-you-die malt that is easily a contender for whisky of the year. *58%.*

Islay Storm (76) n19 t20 f19 b18. More of a drizzle. *40%. C.S. James & Sons.*

Islay Storm 12 Years Old (81) n20 t21 f20 b20. Some lovely spice emphasis the seaweed kick. Decent oak weight, too. *40%. C.S. James & Sons.*

McClelland's Islay Single Malt (88) n22 delicate yet confident smoke; **t22** light at first then livens as the smoke kicks in; **f22** beautifully long and clean with tapering Fisherman's Friend; **b22** no mistaking which distillery this little beaut is from: Bowmore anyone? *40%.*

Master of Malt Islay 12 Years Old (95) n23.5 huge peat reek, the like of which I've never come across before; **t23.5** a flamboyant marriage of massive peat and soft honey tones; **f24** wave upon wave of extraordinary smoke... **b24** actually, I lie. There is barely any peat at all, save for a gust of peat reek which hovers unspectacular above the stunning honey notes and then muscles in hardly noticed when no-one's looking. Those on the prowl for a massively peated dram will be disappointed. Those hunting a very gently, almost covertly, smoked malt which appears completely relaxed with its honeycomb and barley constitution and its dependency on complexity will be delighted. A treasure of a find. *40%. Master of Malt, UK.*

Milroy's Badger Islay 2001 bourbon cask no. 27, dist Jun 01, bott Jul 07 **(91) n23** young, ultra-clean, nipping smoke with the making of cough sweets... **t22.5** mouth-cleansing, fresh and with a fabulous build up of sweetening smoke; **f23** long, with just the right amount of oak to create a drier balance, yet allowing the barley to lead the way; **b22.5** like a badger, earthy and goes down beautifully... and do you know what? I doubt if this will be significantly better in six or eight years time... *46%. Milroy's of Soho. 398 bottles.*

⋙ **Pibroch Aged 12 Years (92) n23.5** a light, bright gristy nose but a balancing dryness makes for a pretty complex and seductive nose; **t23** much sweeter than the nose foretells: juicy, gristy barley everywhere while the smoke comes in gentle layers, almost as an afterthought; **f22** dry liquorice on the oak; **b22.5** chugs along beautifully... *43%. The Highlands and Islands Scotch Whisky Co.*

⋙ **Port Askaig Aged 17 Years (89) n22** lightly oiled peat reek; **t22.5** a citrussy sharpness for a second or two, then returns to its oily theme; a decent wave of black peppers hits the spot; **f22.5** a touch of liquorice and hickory joins the unerring oily, peaty march; **b22** what it does, it does rather attractively and with minimum fuss. *45.8%. Speciality Drinks.*

⋙ **Port Askaig Aged 25 Years (86) n22 t21.5 f21 b21.5.** Distinctly Caol Ila in style, with big fat oils entirely running the show. The peat is curiously big and modest in the same show, but that has much to do with the sweet citrus and vanilla-enriched oils. Easy dramming. And perfect for keeping the most vicious of midges off you whenever sitting outside the Port Askaig hotel watching the ferry, as indeed I did when this was made 25 years ago... *45.8%.*

The Queen of the Hebrides Islay Single Malt Whisky (85) n22 t22 f20 b21. Big, rolling fat peats: any fatter and it'd be declared obese. *40%. Wine Shop, Leek; Islay Whisky Shop.*

⋙ **Sainsbury's Single Islay Malt Aged 12 Years (90) n23.5** huge, clean peat: almost plastic mach-ish in its phenolic kick; **t22.5** beautiful weight and depth; an uncompromising yet entirely comfortable degree of smoke and chewability with some toffee making the work harder for the jaws; **f21.5** there really is a lot of toffee as its dries; **b22.5** a classic of its type. *40%*

⋙ **Smokehead Extra Black Aged 18 Years (94) n23** what a softie....delicate layers of dry peat ash and oils intermingle; extra oaky-floral life added by gentle hickory and a sprig of prickly lavender; **t24** juicy, rock-hard delivery which is entirely divorced from the nose; almost a bourbony rye-led fruitiness until the peat slowly, methodically and irrevocably takes over in that beautiful dry, ashy style; **f23.5** dry smoked, coffee-stained and with enough molassed sugars to comfortably see off any threat of OTT oak; **b23.5** doubtless some will prefer the in-your-face standard version. This is for those seeking a bit of grey-templed sophistication. *46%.*

Smokehead Islay db **(92) n24** even iodine doesn't come more iodiney than this. Also salty, youngish and bracing; **t23** sweet grist at first, moves into sharp citrus and back into malt; **f22** the complex peats begin to fade as vanilla and caramel kick on; **b23** this company does this kind of whisky so well. A little gem. 43%. Ian Macleod.

The Spirit Safe & Cask Islay Single Malt Vintage 1998 Aged 8 Years Hogshead cask no. 52, dist 1998, bott 07 **(91) n23** wonderful mixture of heavily peated grist and a cold distillery kiln... **t22** a licentious delivery, with the peat pawing each taste bud with wanton abandon; **f23** calms down for a hint of Bowmore-style cough medicine, but heads back to the mill for sweet grist; **b23** for those of us who spent too many years of their adulthood hanging around the south-east coast of Islay, there shouldn't be too many problems spotting this guy. Great to see it so youthful. 58.8%. nc ncf. Celtic Whisky Compagnie. 305 bottles.

Tamifroyg Islay Single Malt Scotch Whisky: The Vaccine to Bird Flu (91) n23 Few Islays so largely depend on dense citrus for the lead role, though the underlying peat possibly stretches back to the ice age. Big, but subtle...sort of; **t23** remains fruity, but massive oils dredge up some serious oak and praline; **f23** succulent oils sweetened by weakened mollased sugar and decent natural caramels; a slight raspberry jam sharpness titillates the tastebuds in the mid of this profound heaviness, **b22** from the guys who brought you the original Papal Ardbeg, another enormous Islay that could – and if not, should - have been named after one of the people most seriously dear to my heart, the Islayphile extraordinaire Tammy Secor (please, darling, say yes to marrying me in my next life). This, very sensibly, has been brought out to ward off bird flu, though several glasses of this would probably mean that you would neither know – or indeed care – if you had it or not. Curiously, after I wrote these notes I was pointed in the direction of the website of the Lindores Whisky Society: a conclave of 12 noble souls in northern Belgium, I think, who have embraced the Jim Murray scoring system with a zeal demanding official blessing. I'm proud to report that they, like me, scored 91, though they have given 23-23-22-23 (as opposed to 23-23-23-22). However, they have spotted on the nose; "sqaushed (sic) strawberries...fine horsemeat..horseleather." Boys, it is nearly 25 years since I lived with a French girl, so I will bow to your Continental in-knowledge. But compared to you, and the amassed genii of Regensburger Whisky Club, I am not worthy... 49%. Regensburger Whisky Club.

Tesco Islay Single Malt 12 Years Old (89) n23 mottled peat vying with a salty, tangy barley and dryish toffee; **t23** sumptuous and mouth coating, the sweetness threatens to overload but holds back. Some toffee notes dig in; **f21** varying degrees of smoke, happily embracing the gathering oak; **b22** timeless whisky: this is like going back 25 years and onto the island when the peat was thick and caramel was thicker!! Had this been at natural colour, I think we'd have a malt closer to about 92: this has come from some wonderful casks. 40%. UK.

Wemyss "Smoked Sausages" Islay Single Malt Vintage 1991 bott Jan 07 **(88) n22.5** dry, dignified and impressively balanced; **t22.5** a disarming citrussy sweetness descends from the very first moment while the peats keep a surprising distance; **f21** bitters out with the oak; **b22** a surprise package with much less peat than the nose suggests. Charming stuff. 46%. Wemyss Vintage Malts. 409 bottles.

Wm Morrison Islay Single Malt Aged 10 Years (84) n21 t22 f21 b20. A uniform Islay which, though pleasant and initially sweet, fails to trouble the imagination or pulse. 40%.

UNSPECIFIED SINGLE MALTS (Lowland)
Cadenhead's Classic Lowland Bourbon wood **(82) n19 t21 f21 b21.** Much juicier and fortified with rich barley than the nose suggests. 50%

Cadenhead's Lowland Malt (90) n22 delightful division between bourbon and citrus; **t23** again the citrus rattles the taste buds with grassy alt not far behind; **f22** soft waves of tidy vanilla sprinkled with demerara; **b23** one of the best lowlanders around. Fabulously fresh! 56.4%

Dun Bheagan Lowland 8 Years Old (81) n19 t20 f21 b21. Recovers from a sweaty armpit nose to offer a bit of bite and juice on the palate. 43%. Ian Macleod Distillers.

Master of Malt Lowland 12 Years Old (78.5) n21 t20 f18.5 b19. Bitter thanks to a pretty poor cask: the malt didn't stand a chance. Unusually off the pace for a MoM bottling. 40%. Master of Malt, UK.

Master of Malt Secret Bottlings Lowland 12 Years Old Collection (83) n20 t22 f20 b21. The nose may be from the sweaty armpit fraternity of casks, but there is enough honey around on the early delivery to compensate. 40%. Master of Malt, UK.

UNSPECIFIED SINGLE MALTS (Speyside)
Apples & Pears Speyside Vintage 1991 Single Malt bott Jan 07 **(71) n16 t19 f18 b18.** How about matchsticks and Rotarua? 46%. Wemyss Vintage Malts.

⋄ **Celtique Connexion Monbazillac Finish Aged 14 Years** dist 94, bott 09 **(88)** n23 good grief....!! Is there any whisky in there? The grape dominates but on careful nosing something spicy and faintly barley-ish raises a white flag... **t22.5** silky delivery, though the grape and spice does all the talking – loudly... **f21** more grape, this time doused in molasses; **b21.5** clean, fabulously sulphur-free and quite substantial whisky, but the Monbazillac has gone Monballistic... *46%. Celtic Whisky Compagnie.*

⋄ **Celtique Connexion Sauternes Finish Aged 13 Years** dist 95, bott 08 **(95)** n23.5 not as sweet as some Sauternes noses: dried orange peel and melted vanilla ice cream; **t24** intriguing firm/soft body makes for a very different start: equally the sharp and sweeter notes also do battle as the spices get wilder; excellent barley for all the obvious fruit; **f23.5** dry, spicy, complex and dignified. **b24** top notch balance between spice and grape. Elegant. *46%.*

⋄ **Celtique Connexion Vin de Paille du Jura Finish Aged 14 Years** dist 94, bott 08 **(71)** n17 **t19 f17 b18.** It seems that many a whisky label with the word Jura on it is accursed: sulphur yet again! *46%. Celtic Whisky Compagnie.*

Chocolate Heaven Speyside Vintage 1991 Single Malt bott Jan 07 **(86)** n22 t21 f22 b21. Lovely gristy stuff at first, then a touch of chocolate sponge. *46%. Wemyss Vintage Malts.*

Coconut Cream Speyside Vintage 1990 Single Malt bott Jan 07 **(87)** n22 does what it says on the label... **t22** beautifully oiled allowing the barley to stick convincingly around the palate; some dried banana towards the middle; **f21** soft vanilla as this gentle malt slowly dries **b22** another good cask choice from Wemyss. *46%. Wemyss Vintage Malts.*

Dun Bheagan Speyside 8 Years Old (85) n22 t22 f21 b20. The fabulous malty-spice surge on delivery is arm-of-seat-gripping stuff! *43%. Ian Macleod Distillers.*

Glace Fruits Speyside Vintage 1994 Single Malt bott Jan 07 **(93)** n23 fabulous nose with all kinds of fresh, juicy intent under a vanilla layer; **t23** after barley-rich cloudburst rich, faultless malt floods the taste buds; **f23** the clean barley intensity shows little sign of abating though deft spices and oak make their appearances as the name of good balance and whisky demands; **b24** perfection for those looking for death by barley. *46%. Wemyss Vintage Malts.*

Master of Malt Speyside 10 Years Old (78) n20 t21 f18 b19. Juicy with plenty of citrus. *40%. Master of Malt, UK.*

⋄ **Master of Malt Speyside 30 Years Old (88.5)** n23 not shy about its age, being happy to wear some oaky creases with pride. But there is more glamourous granny than faded beauty as some sexy citrus tantalize... **t23** a softer, juicier delivery than you have a right to expect; the oaks arrives late and with good manners; **f20.5** back to the fruit you pick up on the nose as light barley mingles with vanilla; a little furry late on; **b22** a character malt, performing all kinds of stunning Speyside tricks, but with the odd one falling flat on its face. Great fun. *40%. Master of Malt, UK.*

Master of Malt Speyside 30 Years Old Special Reserve (87) n22 pine-fresh – which is not normally a great sign: it means the oak is there in force. However, enough barley sneaks through to make a game of it; **t22** again the oak is really churning it out; again honey and molasses this time to the rescue; **f21.5** starts disintegrating but there is character and charisma enough to crank up the charm; the honeycomb is the real saviour, though... **b21.5** shhhh. Stop whatever you are doing. Turn the radio off. And the central heating. Listen. Really listen. Hear that creaking...? It's this whisky... *40%. Master of Malt, UK.*

Master of Malt Speyside 40 Years Old Special Reserve (87.5) n22 dates and walnuts – a style lovers of old Glenfarclas might appreciate; the oak is pretty full on but the grapes hold it in check; **t21.5** silky at first then stringent oak; **f22** settles back down to that date and walnut cake feel, even if a little burned. The mouthfeel remains sensuous; **b22** as the whisky changed in the glass – after 40 years in cask it deserves the longest outing it can possibly get – I was completely bemused by this one. At times it went through phases where it would struggle to get 77, while sometimes it peered into the possibilities of the 90s. But that was fleeting, and this is perhaps a mean score; to some in both senses... *40%. Master of Malt, UK.*

Master of Malt Speyside 50 Years Old Special Reserve (95) n23 the oak may be on the attack but firm malt, aided and abetted by the most docile of smoky backgrounds gives it just the weight and edge it needs; **t24** the delivery is dense and silky and now the smoke really comes into its own, adding weight and seeing off any inquisitive oak; butterscotch and honey add to the brilliance; **f24** long with vanilla and the softest molassed sugar imaginable pitched in the glowing embers of all that has gone before; **b24** a genuine masterpiece of an ancient malt showing improbable integrity and finesse. The only whisky tasted so far this year (and this is number 1,263) that I have not spat a single drop out. I don't know if this was a 1957 cask, or '58. On one hand I hope it was the '57, as that was the year I was born, and on that basis it should be stunning. On the other, a pang of regret that I didn't find this cask first and bottle it for my 50th birthday celebrations... *40%. Master of Malt, UK.*

McClelland's Speyside (77.5) n20 t19 f18.5 b19. Remains stunningly inert. 40%. Morrison Bowmore.

Morrisons The Best Speyside Malt 15 Years Old bott code L6 349 **(79)** n19 t22 f19 b19. Ever been at a dinner party and had someone sitting next to you who is awfully pleasant but a tad dull? Well, if that person was to come back in life as a whisky, it'd probably be as this. The explanation may lie in the colour: "matured in ex-bourbon casks" says the label. Only in Kentucky, and in virgin oak, do you get this depth of bronze. The oppressive hand of caramel can be felt in every mouthful. Shame, because a few moments after the initial entry this has all the hallmarks of a honeyed stunner. 40%

Old Malt Cask Probably Speyside's Finest Aged 40 Years sherry butt no. 3803, dist Dec 66, bott Aug 07 **(88)** n23 I could be in Georgetown looking over some Demerara casks... beautiful, especially with the overdone fruitcake with burnt raisins to match; **t21** too liberal use of oak makes for an uncomfortable landing but the Demerara sugars pave the way for a fruity, spiced recovery; **f22** returns to fruitcake and some accompanying mid-roast Java, **b22** gets away with over-the-top oak thanks to some of the finest rum and raisin coffee I have ever tasted... 50%. nc ncf. Douglas Laing. 329 bottles.

Old Malt Cask Probably Speyside's Finest Aged 41 Years sherry **(94)** n24 outrageously handsome for its age: the fruit is just dribbling with juice and the harmony with the oak defies belief and years; **t22.5** the oak thinks about an over-the-top charge but decides against as the fruit begins its big assault; massively bitter-sweet; **f23.5** back to the Java (actually with a degree of Mysore, honest) again - slightly less high roast than the 40-year-old. No rum but raisins aplenty, most of them burnt. Elsewhere a fresher sultana effect sweetens things and offers a more youthful touch; **b24** my word! You need a bit of a sit down after a whisky like this. A dram to relax with? Hardly. Getting to the bottom of this, fair takes it out of you. But if you can think of a better way to spend an evening with a buxom 41-year-old from Speyside, let me know... 50%. Douglas Laing.

⁑ **Old Malt Cask Speyside's Finest Aged 41 Years** sherry cask **(93)** n23 tart gooseberries with a big vanilla topping; **t24** no less tart barley which really does initially act with extraordinary vim for such an oldie; the oaks compensate by getting pretty heavy; **f23** settles to a degree as some oils evolve and spread a cocoa-ish word; **b23** for all its wrinkles, a malt with great charm and personality 50%. Douglas Laing.

⁑ **Old Malt Cask Speyside's Finest Aged 43 Years** sherry **(83.5)** n20 t22.5 f20 b21. A surprisingly juicy job for its age but not entirely flawless. 50%. Douglas Laing.

Pebble Beach 12 Years Old **(78)** n19 t20 f20 b19. The malt fits with the allusion to something rounded and smooth. But I also presume it's a beach to fall asleep on while sucking a pebble... 43%. Lombard Brands.

⁑ **Sainsbury's Single Speyside Malt Aged 12 Years** **(87)** n22 fruity, fizzy and sharp; **t22** lovely sweet delivery with some light muscovado sprinkled on the fruit; **f21** tangy orange; slightly furry and bitters out; **b22** gosh: behaving just like a Macallan! 40%

Sainsbury's Single Speyside Malt Aged 12 Years **(85.5)** n21.5 t22 f21 b21. Pleasant, toffeed and full-bodied. 40%. Sainsbury's, UK.

Secret Stills Speyside 1966 Distillery No. 2, Release No. 2, Sherry hogshead casks no. 1204, dist 23 Apr 66, 1449 & 1452, dist 21 May 66, bott Jun 06 **(92)** n24 aromas don't come more refined than this: soft, vaguely citrus fruit combined with midnight floral, balanced perfectly with a lightly honey bourbon trait. Astonishing when wet in the glass, stunning when left to dry... **t23** genteel oils, lovely barley sugar and oak that impacts gently; **f22** light brush of softly oiled cocoa; **b23** shows little sign of decay expected for this great age and fruit flies have driven themselves into this malt for a classy death in significant numbers. 45%. Gordon & MacPhail. 600 bottles.

⁑ **Spey Single Malt 1956** **(87.5)** n24 textbook ancient sherry cask single malt from the old school: even now the grape is intense, sweet, profound and yet calm, collected and controlled. Naturally the oaks are having a field day but in a quite acceptable toasty-liquorice manner. Classically beautiful; **t21.5** after the tongue is bathed in soft, magnificent bourbon-tinged sherry the oak tries to run amuck. At first it is thwarted by the raisin, but finally succeeds as the woody waves continue to crash; **f21** seriously burnt toast bitter, though it does move into a more stable cocoa style towards the death; **b21** a case of a dram which has seen too much wood for its own good. Yet, as the magnificence of the nose shows, this cask still has something very special to offer. 45.8%. Harvie's of Edinburgh. Japanese market.

⁑ **Spey Single Malt 1991** **(92)** n23 beautifully presented fruit: clean save a hint of caramel, and some teasing spice; **t24** now that is divine....!! The delivery makes the most of its impressive alcohol content to thump home once again the fruit with some really resounding barley pushing from behind – a further strata of sweetened mocha is just being flash; flattens on the middle; **f22** quietens down towards a coffeed toffee, vanilla finale with the odd raisin here and there; **b23** what a treat of an experience! Layered, complex and very high class. Those who enjoy the Glenfarclas style might enjoy this, too. *63.5%. Harvie's of Edinburgh. Japanese market.*

⌐ **Spey Single Malt Aged 12 Years (80) n20.5 t21 f18.5 b20.** The over-ripe kumquat on the nose warns of some little imperfections to come, especially on the finish. *40%. Harvie's of Edinburgh. Japanese market.*

⌐ **Spey Single Malt Aged 15 Years (84) n22 t21 f20 b21.** Soft and safe, there is not a bump in the tangy-caramel ride. *46%. Harvie's of Edinburgh. Japanese market.*

⌐ **Spey Single Malt Aged 21 Years (92) n24** fabulous!! A controlled fruitfest from the obvious raisiny grape through to fat gooseberries with cooked apples in between; the oak is deep, sympathetic but not for a moment overbearing; **t23** silky sultanas ensure a sweetness to the fruit arrival; the oak makes it mark slowly and with a degree of elegance befitting the overall charm and complexity; **f22** long, delicate and still with fruit but with more toffee arriving and Madeira cake replacing the earlier Dundee style; **b23** oh, had only this wonderful dram been bottled at at least 46%: it is like driving a Mercedes E class with an engine designed for a lawnmower... *40%. Harvie's of Edinburgh. Japanese market.*

⌐ **Spey Single Malt 'Chairman's Choice' (90) n22** firm and oak-framed; a weak golden syrup attachment to barley; **t23.5** brooding OTT oak at first but quickly pans out towards that same barley-golden syrup evident on the nose which morphs into light honey; **f22** regulation vanilla; **b22.5** my experience over the years is that most Chairmen haven't got a clue which end of a barrel is which. This does appear to be an exception, though... *40%. Harvie's of Edinburgh. Japanese market.*

Tesco Speyside Single Malt 12 Years Old (88) n21 some stressed oak is becalmed by subtle smoke and firm barley; **t22** outstanding delivery with a sheen to the barley as it glides over the palate; the spices mass as the oak concentrates; **f22** a gentle return of smoke sits comfortably with the cocoa and barley; **b23** no shrinking violet here: a Speysider with a touch of attitude – and class. *40%. Tesco, UK.*

Wemyss "Chocolate Heaven" Speyside Single Malt Vintage 1995 bott Jan 07 **(86) n21 t22 f21.5 b21.5.** Enjoyable for its fudgy-honey character. But chocolate...? I should cocoa.... *46%. Wemyss Vintage Malts. 341 bottles.*

⌐ **The Whisky Agency Speyside Single Malt 39 Year Old** dist 70, bott 09 **(96) n24.5** as clean and juicy oloroso as the day the cask was filled; toffee apple, but so fresh the apple is still green... **t25** staggering depth to the fruitcake delivery...retains a barley crispness amid the glowing oloroso while the spices are subtle and mount a stealthy attack; remains juicy and mouth-watering right through to the middle; **f22.5** finally bitters out, as surely it had to, as the oak arrives with a certain vengeance yet still retains an overcooked Melton Hunt cake character; **b24** no one has told me what this is. But anyone who knows a Glenfarclas at this age in full flow will understand the type of outstanding whisky this is. In a nutshell: old sherry at its blemish-free olde worlde pre-sulphur ruining finest. *54.4%. The Whisky Agency, Germany.*

UNSPECIFIED SINGLE MALTS (General)

McClelland's 12 Years Old Sherry Finish (86) n22 t21.5 f21 b21.5. Peachy, for once, to find a sherry finish not sulphur-tainted. Attractive, simple, clean and enjoyable for its simplistic charms. Don't expect the pulse to overly quicken but simply enjoy for its intense honesty. *40%. Morrison Bowmore.*

Rossend Castle 15 Years Old bourbon barrels, cask no. 3837 & 3838 **(79) n21 t20 f19 b19.** Malty, but pretty dull fare. *46%. Adelphi. 495 bottles.*

Wilson & Morgan Barrel Selection House Malt cask nos. 8586-8589 **(92) n24** beautifully salted and coastal peats with enough youth to remain refreshing and profound; **t22** lime juice lightens the smoke; **f23** returns to a more gristy sweetness and depth; **b23** a high quality (presumably) Islay of distinctive, compelling clarity. *43%*

Scottish Vatted Malts
(also Pure Malts/Blended Malt Scotch)

100 Pipers Aged 8 Years Blended Malt (74) n19 t20 f17 b18. A better nose, perhaps, and some spice on arrival. But when you consider the Speysiders at their disposal, all those mouth-wateringly grassy possibilities, it is such a shame to find something as bland as this. *40%*

Altore Pure Malt matured in Corsican Muscat cask **(82.5) n21 t21.5 f19 b21.** Rounded with a decent sweetness. Such a short finish, though. *40%. Société Whisky Altore.*

Altore Reserve Moresca Aged 8 Years matured in Cap Corse barrel **(86) n21.5** the odd renegade note here and there but the fruit and gentle phenol win through; **t22.5** intense, highly satisfying delivery with some scrummy over-ripe plum notes; prunes and brown sugar all the way – except for that slight sulphurous hint; **f21** the big burnt raisin edge gets a touch too bitter; **b21** what a shame: evidence of some sulphur in the system here, otherwise this would have been quite a beauty. *40%. Société Whisky Altore.*

Barrogill (90) n22.5 busy and intense there is a coastal tang in the air: not unlike a salty warehouse occasionally battered by the sea. The malt is dense and allows only limited development away from the obvious; **t23** a lusty delivery, again with the barley absolutely in full flight. Darting spices accompany a sharp edge and constrained sweetness. This is all about shape and intensity rather than complex flavour tones; **f22.5** long with a slow, almost sulky, winding down of the intensity until only the spices remain; **b22** Prince Charles, who allows the name to be used for this whisky, is said to enjoy this dram. Hardly surprising, as its pretty hard not to: this is wonderful fun. Curiously, I have just read the back label and noticed they use the word "robust". I have employed "lusty". Either way, I think you might get the message. *40%. Inverhouse for Mey Selections.*

Barrogill North Highland Blended Malt Mey Selections bott code PO12630 **(79) n18 t21 f20 b20.** Recovers attractively – helped by a mighty dose of concentrated maltiness - from the disappointing nose. *40%. Inver House Distillers for North Highland.*

Berrys' Best Islay Vatted Malt Aged 8 Years (82) n20 t21 f20 b21. Smoky, raw, sweet, clean and massive fun! *43%. Berry Bros & Rudd.*

⁙ **Berry's Best 14 Years Old Islay Vatted Malt** bott 09 **(88) n22.5** takes a while for the peat to show – then it takes over; **t22** soft: excellently controlled sweetness and rolling, lightly oiled phenols; **f21.5** duller, a touch of spice but otherwise vanilla-led; **b22** a sleepy, clean vatting which talks in whispers. *43%. Berry Bros & Rudd.*

⁙ **Berry's Own Selection Blue Hanger 4th Release** bott 08 **(87) n22** just so biscuity: German caramelized meets crushed garibaldi; elsewhere the oaks threaten the nostrils with the odd splinter; **t23** a malty dance – in slippers – on arrival then a gradual crescendo of fruit, toasty in part but also balanced by light brown sugars, spice but a nagging bitterness which hints at something just out of kilter; **f21** fruity sugars but the bitter note remains; **b21** its finest notes are very fine, indeed. *45.6%. Berry Bros & Rudd.*

The Big Smoke 40 Islay Malt (83) n20 t21 f21 b21. Keeps it sweet, simple...and very smoky! *40%. Duncan Taylor.*

The Big Smoke 60 Islay Malt (86) n20 t23; f22 b21. Big and bolshy, the peats remorselessly thump anything in their path *60%. Duncan Taylor.*

Carme 10 Years Old (79) n21.5 t20 f18.5 b19. On paper Ardmore and Clynelish should work well together. But vatting is not done on paper and here you have two malts cancelling each other out and some less than great wood sticking its oar in. *43%. The Creative Whisky Company.*

Clan Campbell 8 Years Old Pure Malt (82) n20 t22 f20 b20. Enjoyable, extremely safe whisky that tries to offend nobody. The star quality is all on the complex delivery, then it's toffee. *40%. Chivas Brothers.*

Clan Denny (Bowmore, Bunnahabhain, Caol Ila and Laphroaig) **(94) n24** mildly awesome: a mixing of varying grists – peaty, but on so many planes...; **t23** still on the grist blitz with a powdery smokiness working well with a veiled honey theme; **f23** dries out at first but a smoky butterscotch balances things out; **b24** a very different take on Islay with the heavy peats somehow having a floating quality. Unique. *40%. Douglas Laing.*

Clan Denny Speyside (87) n22 big, big malt: exceptionally clean and soft. Oily, too; **t22** a charming sweetness to the barley helps counter the more bitter aspects of the approaching oak; delicate oils help make for an exceptionally soft delivery **f21** no shortage of vanilla as it bitters out; **b22** a Tamdhu-esque oiliness pervades here and slightly detracts from the complexity. That said, the early freshness is rather lovely. *46%. Douglas Laing.*

Compass Box Canto Cask 6 bott autumn/winter 07 **(86.5) n20.5 t23 f21.5 b21.5.** The busy, rich, intense and honeyed delivery compensates for the surprising dullness elsewhere. The money from the sales of this go to Cancer Research, I hear. *53.1%. nc ncf. Between 200 and 250 bottles.*

Compass Box Canto Cask 15 bott autumn/winter 07 **(75.5) n18.5 t20 f18 b19.** Despite the smear of honey, still something in the curiously sulphurous department appears intent on spoiling things. *46%. nc ncf. Between 200 and 250 bottles.*

Compass Box Canto Cask 17 bott autumn/winter 07 **(87.5) n21** biscuit tins: the home of custard creams; **t23.5** magnificent majesty to the sweet barley which is about as concentrated as it gets; **f21** over-the-top oak bitterness; **b22** gosh, this really is a very strange whisky. The oak never quite finds its comfort zone on the nose, or finish, but there is a wonderful sweet, malty resonance. *53.4%. nc ncf. Between 200 and 250 bottles.*

Compass Box Canto Cask 20 bott autumn/winter 07 **(86) n22.5 t22 f20.5 b21.** Softly oiled, softly spiced, big oaked. 54%. nc ncf. Between 200 and 250 bottles.

Compass Box Canto Cask 27 bott autumn/winter 07 **(83.5) n20 t22 f20.5 b20.** Decent malt explosion on entry, but the natural caramels appear to cancel each other out elsewhere. 52.5%. nc ncf. Between 200 and 250 bottles.

Compass Box Canto Cask 35 bott autumn/winter 07 **(85) n21 t22 f21 b21.** Cream toffee and cocoa. Some major spice, too. 54.4%. nc ncf. Between 200 and 250 bottles.

Compass Box Canto Cask 36 bott autumn/winter 07 **(84.5) n20.5 t21.5 f22 b21.** Delicious malt does its best to beat off some intrusive oak. Settles at the death for some sublime cocoa. 54.3%. nc ncf. Between 200 and 250 bottles

Compass Box Canto Cask 37 bott autumn/winter 07 **(89) n23.5** intense grassy malt sits in the comfort zone despite the close oaky attention; wonderful butterscotch and bourbony-style honey richly entertain; **t22** duller than the nose suggests with a tidal wave of natural caramels; a light degree of juiciness and spice; **f21.5** drier oaks delve into the sweeter caramel; **b22** a much better, richer version where the oak appears to know its place; 53.6%. nc ncf. Between 200 and 250 bottles

Compass Box Canto Cask 46 bott autumn/winter 07 **(88) n22** thickish, belligerent oak but enough fruit barley to work; playfully bourbony; **t22** immediate spice attack and juicy barley; decent sweet edge; **f22** long, soft oils and just the right amount of oaky indulgence; **b22** again, a canto that works, thanks to the oaks staying on a short leash; 53.2%. nc ncf. Between 200 and 250 bottles.

Compass Box Canto Cask 47 bott autumn/winter 07 **(82.5) n20 t22.5 f20 b20.** Another entirely all-over-the-place, scattergun Canto bottling with little rhythm to be found. Musty nose, sensational delivery, muddled middle and then weird finale until the cocoa shines through. Fascinating, if frustrating whisky. 53.7%. nc ncf. Between 200 and 250 bottles.

Compass Box Canto Cask 48 bott autumn/winter 07 **(91.5) n21** some thuggish oak is calmed by a salty, barley thrust. Not exactly in tune; **t24** didn't expect that: after the messy nose, there is immediate harmony as the tastebuds pucker under the sharp, grassy barley attack; the spices are enormous yet precise; **f23** the complexity continues with the cocoa/caramel edge, now a trademark for this brand, working superbly in unison with those drying spices; **b23.5** easily the most beautifully constructed of the Canto range so far. Nose apart, perhaps, not a shred of awkwardness as the malts ignite on the palate. 54.4%. nc ncf. .

Compass Box Canto Cask 50 bott autumn/winter 07 **(86.5) n22.5 t22 f20.5 b21.5.** Sweeter than average with a distinct sugary gloss. 54.4%. nc ncf. Between 200 and 250 bottles.

Compass Box Canto Cask 123 bott autumn/winter 07 **(83) n19 t22 f21.5 b21.5.** Toasty with some major oak contribution. 55.1%. nc ncf. Between 200 and 250 bottles.

Compass Box Canto Cask 124 bott autumn/winter 07 **(85.5) n20.5 t21.5 f22 b21.5.** Plenty of oak, as usual, but the spices sizzle early on, accentuating the more refined finale. 55.1%. nc ncf. Between 200 and 250 bottles.

Compass Box Canto Cask 125 bott autumn/winter 07 **(79.5) n18.5 t22 f19 b20.** And so endeth the first batch of Cantos. Canto, I presume, as in a poem. Too often, though, there were faltering stanzas here, and sometimes neither rhyme nor reason can be found. One or two work stunningly, the majority are good but refusing to show the brilliance normally associated with the Compass Box name. Perhaps this may have something to do with the brave use of Dailuaine, apparently, as one of only three malts to make up these vattings. My own personal feeling is that, especially in such restricted company, you approache malt from this distillery in very much the way you might an unexploded bomb, and a ticking one at that: you prod at your peril. That said, if you are into big-oaked malt then this is the brand for you. 54.9%. nc ncf. Between 200 and 250 bottles.

Compass Box Eleuthera Marriage Married for nine months in an American oak Hogshead **(86) n22 t22 f20 b22.** I'm not sure if it's the name that gets me on edge here, but as big and robust as it is I still can't help feeling that the oak has bitten too deep. Any chance of a Compass Box Divorce...? 49.2%. Compass Box for La Maison du Whisky.

Compass Box Flaming Hart second batch, bottling no. FH16MMVII **(95.5) n23.5** stays on the same idiosyncratic course as batch one with a liquorice theme displaying smoky and lychee fruit tendencies...though in different degrees this time round and with some extra over-ripe greengages and sultanas for good measure. Weird...yet enthrallingly wonderful.. **t24.5** stunning. Fabulous. Clean. Almost too sexy for words. The soft silks only appear to highlight the enormity of the lush smoke-barley theme which twitches with hickory and red licorice. Enormous, controlled, intense and when the middle is reached soft oils are deployed to maximise the effect; the sheer juiciness of the barley flies off any possible scale; **f23** long with a sublime marriage of contrasting barley-smoke notes and that ghostly fruit that appears to be there, yet somehow isn't **b24.5** the Canto range was, I admit, a huge over-oaked disappointment. This, though, fully underlines Compass Box's ability to come up with something approaching genius. This is a whisky that will be remembered by anyone who drinks it for the rest of their lives as just about the perfect study of full-bodied balance and sophistication. And that is not cheap hyperbole. *48.9%. nc ncf. 4,302 bottles.*

Compass Box Juveniles 20th Anniversary Bottling bott autumn/winter 07 **(85) n22 t21 f21 b21.** A Juveniles for Grown Ups: big, lordly with a hollering oaky-fruit theme. For all the fun, nothing like as delicate as the previous, more genteel bottling. As an after-dinner dram designed to blow away the last traces of the crepes suzettes, perfect! *53.9%. nc ncf. For Juveniles restaurant, Paris. 246 bottles.*

Compass Box Morpheus bott autumn/winter 07 **(92.5) n23** fascinating intensity to this: sharp barley with a wisp of smoky bacon. Complete with CB's standard fitting thick oak; **t22** firm barley with an agreeable tartness; flattens midterm thanks to the oak; **f23.5** returns to life: deceptively long with growing toast, a swirl of citrus and that wink-of-an-eye hint of smoke again; **b24** subtlety and balance the key here: just shows what magic can be performed with understatement. *46%. nc ncf. For Milroy's of Soho, London. 1,056 bottles.*

⬩⬩⬩ **Compass Box Peat Monster Reserve (92) n23** comfortable, thickish smoke and a dusting of peppers: complex and well balanced; **t23.5** silky soft malty oils cleverly disguise the big punchy peat which is to follow; lovely touch of golden syrup here and there, but mainly towards the delivery; **f22.5** smoky sweetened mocha; **b23** at times a bit of a Sweet Monster...beautiful stuff! *48.9%*

Compass Box The Spice Tree Inaugural Batch (93) n23 a thick nose, almost offering the botanicals of gin but without the juniper. Oak influence is all-consuming, the barley acting as a thinning agent for the pungent spices and vanilla; **t23** immediately warming yet almost syrupy sweet; the accent is on spiced orange (I think I can see where they are coming from cinnamon-wise, but not cloves); **f23** such is the intensity and enormity, it is hard to pick out individual flavour: we have a marriage of styles in which the key is beautiful, bitter-sweet integration; **b24** the map for flavour distribution had to be drawn for the first time here: an entirely different whisky in shape and flavour emphasis. And it is a map that takes a long time to draw... *46%. 4150 bottles.*

Co-operative Group (CWS) Blended Malt Aged 8 Years (86.5) n22 t22 f21 b21.5. Much, much better! Still a little on the sticky and sweet side, but there is some real body and pace to the changes on the palate. Quite rich, complex and charming. *40%*

Duncan Taylor Regional Malt Collection Islay 10 Years Old (81) n21 t22 f19 b19. Soft citrus cleanses the palate, while gentle peats muddies it up again. *40%.*

The Famous Grouse 10 Years Old Malt (77) n19 t20 f19 b19. The nose and finish headed south in the last winter and landed in the sulphur marshes of Jerez. *40%. Edrington Group.*

The Famous Grouse 15 Years Old Malt (86) n21 t22 f21.5 b21.5. Salty and smoky with a real sharp twang. *43%. Edrington Group.*

The Famous Grouse 15 Years Old Malt (86) n19 t24 f22 b21. There had been a hint of the "s" word on the nose, but it got away with it. Now it has crossed that fine – and fatal – line where the petulance of the sulphur has thrown all else slightly out of kilter. All, that is, apart from the delivery which is a pure symphony of fruit and spice deserving a far better introduction and final movement. Some moving, beautiful moments. Flawed genius or what...? *40%. Edrington Group.*

The Famous Grouse 18 Years Old Malt (82) n19 t21.5 f21 b20.5. Some highly attractive honey outweighs the odd uncomfortable moment. *43%. Edrington Group.*

The Famous Grouse Malt 21 Years Old (91) n22 candy jar spices, green apple and crisp barley. **t24** spot on oak offers a platform for the myriad rich malty notes and now, in the latest bottlings, enlivened further with an injection of exploding spice... wow! **f22** flattens slightly but muscovado sugar keeps it light and sprightly; **b23** a very dangerous dram. the sort where the third or fourth would slip down without noticing. Wonderful scotch! And an object lesson in how vatted malt whisky should be. *43%. Edrington Group.*

The Famous Grouse 30 Years Old Malt (94) n23.5 brain-implodingly busy and complex: labyrinthine depth within a kind of Highland Park frame with extra emphasis on grape and salt; **t24** yesssss!!!! Just so magnificent with the theme being all about honeycomb...but on so many different levels of intensity and toastiness; so juicy, too...; **f23** now the spices dive in as the barley resurfaces again; long, layered with spot on bitter-sweet balance; **b23.5** whisky of this sky-high quality is exactly what vatted malt should be all about. Outrageously good. *43%. Edrington Group.*

⬩⬩⬩ **Glendower 8 Years Old (84) n21.5 t21 f20.5 b21** Nutty and spicy. *43%. John MacLaren & Sons.*

Glen Turner Pure Malt Aged 8 Years L525956A **(84) n**20 **t**22 **f**22 **b**20. A lush and lively vatting annoyingly over dependent on thick toffee but simply brimming with fabulously mouth-watering barley and over-ripe blood oranges. To those who bottle this, I say: let me into your lab. I can help you bring out something sublime!! *40%. Glen Turner Distillery for La Martiniquaise, France.*

Grand Macnish Vatted Malt Scotch Whisky (82) n19 **t**24 **f**19 **b**20. A real shame: a vatting which offered so much has been done to death with caramel. The mouth-watering ultra-intense and beautifully sweet malt which just makes the heart pound on delivery deserves so much more. *40%. MacDuff International. Taiwan.*

Grand Macnish 12 Years Old Vatted Malt Scotch Whisky (78) n18 **t**23 **f**18 **b**19. The oak and caramel carry out a nifty pincer movement on the barley. Dull. *40%. MacDuff International. Taiwan.*

Grand Macnish 21 Years Old Vatted Malt Scotch Whisky (86) n21 **t**23 **f**21 **b**21. After the velvety landing remains firm throughout but a persistent touch of class is there to see. *40%. MacDuff International. Taiwan.*

Glen Orrin Six Year Old (88) n22 a bit sweaty but the oranges delight. Some delicate background smoke is a surprising complement; **t**23 big, chewy and rugged with outstanding soft-oiled lushness which helps to dissipate the youthfulness; **f**21 delicate spice and arousing coffee-cocoa: a bigger age signature than you might expect **b**22 a vatting that has improved in the short time it has been around, now displaying some lovely orangey notes on the nose and a genuinely lushness to the body and spice on the finish. You can almost forgive the caramel, this being such a well balanced, full-bodied ride. A quality show for the price. *40%. Alistair Graham for Aldi Stores, UK.*

Hedges and Butler Special Pure Malt (83) n20 **t**21 **f**22 **b**21. Just so laid back: nosed and tasted blind I'd swear this was a blend (you know, a real blend with grains and stuff) because of the biting lightness and youth. Just love the citrus theme and, err...graininess....!! *40%. Ian Macleod Distillers.*

Imperial Tribute (83) n19.5 **t**21.5 **f**21 **b**21. No, it's not a whisky paying homage to a silent Speysider. It's the first offerings of a new whisky company. It has been praised to the high heavens by others. And I'd like to give it a great mark for as truly fine a fellow as Mike Collings, but I can't. Without doubt a cask that shouldn't be here has snuck in. The result is a good whisky, but one which never quite finds its pitch or level, strains at the high notes and has croaks slightly at the lower. That said, there is enough fabulously intense barley during a purple period towards the very middle of the experience to make for some pleasing moments. And you can just feel the wonderful layering of fruit, barley and oak in clever measures just trying to impress with its sophistication. But that bothersomely bitter, dry residue (the signs of which can be spotted on both nose and delivery) does in some of the good work. I am sure – and sincerely hope – the next bottling will be cleaned up and the true Imperial Tribute can be nosed and tasted. Because this is what should be a very fine malt...but just isn't. *46%. Spencer Collings.*

Islay Trilogy 1969 (Bruichladdich 1966, Bunnahabhain 1968, Bowmore 1969) Bourbon/ Sherry **(91) n**23 sooty embers in a hearth; kiwi fruit and peaches offer sweetness; **t**23 pure silk that melts and moulds into the tastebuds, with the best bit coming about ten seconds in as creamy cocoa tries to usurp the barley-sugar and fruits. And fails...; **f**22 much drier with chalky, salty vanilla and the weakest hint of peat imaginable; **b**23 decided to mark the 700th tasting for the 2007 edition with this highly unusual vatting. And no bad choice. The smoke is as elusive as the Paps of Jura on a dark November morning, but the silky fruits and salty tang tells a story as good as anything you'll hear by a peat fire. Take your time...the whiskies have. *40.3%. Murray McDavid. 1200 bottles.*

J & B Exception Aged 12 Years (80) n20 **t**23 **f**18 **b**19. Very pleasant in so many ways. A charming sweetness develops quickly, with excellent soft honeycomb. But the nose and finish are just so...so....dull...!! For the last 30 years J&B has meant, to me, (and probably within that old company) exceptionally clean, fresh Speysiders offering a crisp, mouth-watering treat. I feel this is off target. *40%. Diageo/ Justerini & Brooks.*

J & B Nox (89) n23 classy Speyside thrust, youthful and crisp with a wonderful strand of honey. Gentle oak balances pleasingly; **t**23 the nose in liquid form: exactly the same characteristics with some extra, gently peppered toast towards the middle; **f**21 dries just a little too much as the barley tires; **b**22 a teasing, pleasing little number that is unmistakably from the J&B stable. *40%. Diageo.*

John Black 8 Years Old Honey (88) n21 vanilla to the fore; **t**22.5 the promised honey arrives on delivery couched by fresh barley; **f**22.5 light, delicate back to vanilla; **b**22 a charming vatting. *40%. Tullibardine Distillery.*

John Black 10 Years Old Peaty (91) n23 salty and peaty; t23 soft and peaty; f22 delicate and peaty; b23 classy and er...peaty. 40%. Tullibardine Distillery.

∴ **John McDougall's Selection Islay Malt 1993** cask no. 103 **(94.5)** n23.5 peek-a-boo peat can barely make itself heard above the honeyed barley and lightly salted oak. 'Delicate' barely covers it... t24.5 seductive beyond belief: the soft rounding off of the honey with a mint-chocolate peatiness, especially as it fills the middle ground, really is one for the collector's corner: unique and simply breathtaking, and with a Bowmore-ish Fisherman's Friend bite hitting for a couple of nano seconds, pretty intriguing, too; f22.5 drier with soft peat embers giving way to the milk coffee and vanilla; b24 complex, superbly weighted and balanced malt which just keeps you wondering what will happen next. 54.7%. House of Macduff. 240 bottles.

Johnnie Walker Green Label 15 Years Old (95) n24 kind of reminds me of a true, traditional Cornish Pasty: it is as though the segments have been compartmentalised, with the oak acting as the edible pastry keeping them apart. Sniff and there is a degree of fruit; nose again and there is the Speyside/Clynelish style of intense, slightly sweet maltiness. Sniff a third time and, at last you can detect just a hint of smoke. Wonderful... t23.5 no compartmentalisation here as the delivery brings all those varying characters together for one magnificently complex maltfest. Weightier than previous Green Label events with the smoke having a bigger say. But the oak really bobs and weaves as the palate is first under a tidal wave of juicy malt and then the fruit and smoke – and no little spice – take hold...; f23.5 soft smoke and grumbling spice latch on to the fruit-stained oak; plenty of cocoa just to top things off; b24 god, I love this stuff...this is exactly how a vatted malt should be and one of the best samples I've come across since its launch. 43%. Diageo.

Jon, Mark and Robbo's The Rich Spicy One (89) n22 a real fruitcake nose; clean and complete with spices and cooked, pithy fruits, t23 pretty rich, again with a raisiny fruit density and excellent bitter-sweet balance; f22 half-hearted spices tag along with the vanilla; b22 so much better without the dodgy casks: a real late night dram of distinction though the spices perhaps a little on the subtle side... 40%. Edrington

Jon, Mark and Robbo's The Smoky Peaty One (92) n23 a faultlessly clean aroma where the reek enjoys a distinctive salty, coastal rock-pool edge; t22 again the peat is delicate yet coastal with a build up of intense barley; f23 beautiful honey tones accompany the peat like a high phenol Highland Park; b24 genuinely high-class whisky where the peat is full-on yet allows impressive complexity and malt development. A malt for those who appreciate the better, more elegant things in life. 40%. Edrington

∴ **Matisse 12 Year Old Blended Malt (93)** n23.5 a wonderful variation of fruit but with the accent on citrus-orangey notes. As astonishing as it is beautiful... t23 soft, delicate, melt-in-the-mouth delivery with those gentle fruits at the fore and the barley tagging on right behind; f22.5 a quieter finale placing the accent on milky custard; b23 succulent, clean-as-a-whistle mixture of malts with zero bitterness and not even a whisper of an off note: easily the best form I have ever seen this brand in. Superb. 40%. Matisse Spirits Co. Ltd.

Matisse Aged 12 Years (79) n17 t21 f20 b21. Not sure if some finishing or re-casking has been going on here to liven it up. Has some genuine buzz on the palate, but intriguing weirdness, too. Don't bother nosing this one. 40%. The Matisse Spirits Co.

"No Age Declared" The Unique Pure Malt Very Limited Edition 16-49 Years (85) n22.5 t19.5 f22 b21. Very drinkable. But this is odd stuff: as the ages are as they are, and as it tastes as it does, I can surmise only that the casks were added together as a matter of necessity rather than any great blending thought or planning. Certainly the malt never finds a rhythm but maybe it's the eclectic style on the finish that finally wins through. 45%. Samaroli.

∴ **Norse Cask Selection Vatted Islay 1992 Aged 16 Years** hogshead cask no. QWVIM3, dist 92, bott 09 **(95)** n24 a unique smorgasbord of dry, peat-reeky smoke and much oilier phenols. The interplay between sweet and dry is as startling and bamboozling is it is beautiful; t24 melts-in-the-mouth – and then explodes into something like phenolic fire: talk about being lulled into a false sense of security...the sugars – mainly muscovado style – go into overdrive while those oils ensure that the palate is fully coated and the tongue keeps smacking around the mouth in enquiry; f23 long, layered, not a single outbreak of anything even remotely bitter from the oak and still the phenols dance to varying tunes; b24 the recipe of 60/35/5 Ardbeg/Laphroaig/Bowmore new make matured in one cask is a surprise: the oiliness here suggests a squirt of Caol Ila somewhere. This hybrid is certainly different, showing that the DNA of Ardbeg is unrecognisable when mixed, like The Fly, with others. Drinkable...? Oh, yes....!! Because this, without a single negative note to its name, is easily one of the whiskies of the year and a collector's and/or Islayphile's absolute must have. 56.7%. Qualityworld for WhiskyOwner.com, Denmark.

Norse Cask Selection Vatted Islay 1995 Aged 10 Years Hogshead no. AR04000008, dist 95, bott 06 **(86) n22 t23 f20 b21.** A spicy beast, this. The oak really does get stuck in just taking the edge off the interplay between the varied malts. Some lovely smoky phases, though and the sweetness helps. *59.4%. nc ncf. WhiskyOwner.com, Denmark. 318 bottles.*

Norse Cask Selection Vatted Islay 1991 Aged 12 Years (89) n24 t23 f21 b21. Fabulous, but not much going in the way of complexity. But if you're a peat freak, I don't think you either notice...or much care...!! *59.5%. Quality World, Denmark.*

Norse Cask Selection Vatted Islay 1992 Aged 15 Years hogshead ref no. QWVIM4, dist 92, bott 07 **(92) n24** well that's my tasting day over: I should just stick my nose in this for the next three or four hours: the peats are intensified by salt, the oaks help along with the spice and the layering.... **t23.5** as thick as the peats are – and believe me, they're thick – there is no difficulty picking out structure and complexity. The Bowmore appears to have a louder say than you'd expect, but the earthy, molassed tones are sublime; **f22** simplifies as the caramels kick in; **b22.5** now that's more like it! Ardbeg 60%, Laphroaig 35%, Bowmore 5%...though that 5% feels two or three times bigger and on the finish especially. Big and serious fun. *57%. nc ncf.*

Norse Cask Selection Vatted Islay 1988 Aged 19 Years hogshead ref no. QWVIM2, dist 88, bott 07 **(84.5) n21.5 t21 f22 b21.** Bowmore 55%, Laphroaig 40%, Caol Ila 5%. With full cough sweet characteristics on show, it seems more than just 555 Bowmore...!! *573%. nc ncf. Qualityworld, Denmark. 348 bottles.*

The Pot Still Scotch Vatted Malt Over 8 Years Old (90) n22 excellent oak sub plot to the ballsy barley; **t24** goes down with all the seductive powers of long fingernails down a chest: the wonderful honey and barley richness is stunning and so beautifully weighted; **f22** a lazier finale, allowing the chalky oaky notes to make folly of those tender years; **b22** such sophistication: the Charlotte Rampling of Scotch. *43.5%. ncf. Celtic Whisky Compagnie, France.*

Prime Blue Pure Malt (83) n21 t21 f21 b20. Steady, with a real chewy toffee middle. Friendly stuff. *40%*

Prime Blue 12 Years Old Pure Malt (78) n20 t20 f19 b19. A touch of fruit but tart. *40%*

Prime Blue 17 Years Old Pure Malt (88) n23 clever weight and a touch of something fruity and exotic, too; **t21** thick malt concentrate; **f22** takes a deliciously latte-style route and would be even better but for the toffee; excellent spicing; **b22** lovely, lively vatting: something to get your teeth into! *40%*

Prime Blue 21 Years Old Pure Malt (77) n21 t20 f18 b18. After the teasing, bourbony nose the remainder disappoints with a caramel-rich flatness. The reprise of a style of whisky I thought had vanished about four of five years ago *40%*

Sainsbury's Malt Whisky Finished in Sherry Casks (70) n18 t19 f16 b17. Never the greatest of the Sainsbury range, it's somehow managed to get worse. Actually, not too difficult when it comes to finishing in sherry, and the odd sulphur butt or three has done its worst here. *40% Sainsbury's, UK.*

Scottish Collie (86.5) n22 t23 f20.5 b21. A really young pup of a vatting. Full of life and fun but muzzled by toffee at the death. *40%. Quality Spirits International.*

Scottish Collie 5 Years Old (90.5) n22.5 teasing interplay between grassy young malts and something just a little more profound and vaguely phenolic; **t23** more of the same on delivery; an engaging sharpness keeps the tastebuds puckered; **f22** long, with the accent on that wonderfully clean ,sweet and sharp barley; even the soft toffee can't get much of a toe-hold; **b23** fabulous mixing here showing just what malt whisky can do at this brilliant and under-rated age. Lively and complex with the malts wonderfully herded and penned. Without colouring and at 50% abv I bet this would have been given a right wolf-whistle. Perfect for one man and his grog. *40%. Quality Spirits International.*

Scottish Collie 8 Years Old (85.5) n22 t21.5 f21 b21. A good boy. But just wants to sleep rather than play. *40%. Quality Spirits International.*

Scottish Collie 12 Years Old (82) n20 t22 f20 b20. For a malt that's aged 84 in Collie years, it understandably smells a bit funny and refuses to do many tricks. If you want some fun you'll need a younger version. *40%. Quality Spirits International.*

Scottish Leader Imperial Blended Malt (77) n20 t20 f18 b19. Now don't be confused here: this isn't Imperial malt from Speyside. And although it says Blended, it is 100% malt. What is clear, though, is that this is pretty average stuff. *40%. Burn Stewart.*

Scottish Leader Aged 14 Years (80) n21 t21 f19 b19. A cleaner, less peaty version than the no-age statement vatting, but still fails to entirely ignite the tastebuds *40%. Burn Stewart.*

Sheep Dip (84) n19 t22 f22 b21. Young and sprightly like a new-born lamb, this enjoys a fresh, mouthwatering grassy style wth a touch of spice. Maligned by some, but to me a clever, accomplished vatting of alluring complexity. *40%*

Vintner's Choice Highland 10 Years Old (88) n22 busy, herbal, with good oak backbone **t22.5** salivating delivery with a big malty accent; a gentle spice tickle; **f21.5** toffees out as the vanilla heads in; **b22** light but with an attractive degree of complexity. *40%.*

Vintner's Choice Island 10 Years Old (95) n24 serious coastal, seaweedy, strata to the smoke, enlivened further by a touch of honey and hickory; **t24** sweet, molassed, softly oiled start; the peat appears to weave in and out with varying intensity and weight; **f23** just so soft, with the sweetness retaining structure and direction, long, with the smoke pulsing and declaring a light, spicy interest; **b24** not hard to guess which island... the complexity and layering of the peats is quite exemplary. An absolute gem of a vatted malt which will blow away any peat lover. *40%. Quality Spirits International.*

Vintner's Choice Lowland 10 Years Old (92.5) n22.5 green, clean and full of lemony promise; **t24** just beautiful: one of the best deliveries of any vatted malt with the harmonization between the lemon sherbet freshness and the subtle oaks touching perfection; **f23** somehow retains its clarity and classy, grassy mouthwatering edge; loses a point for the toffee; **b23** as vatted malts go, this is a joy. As Lowland vatted malts go, it is about as good as I've ever known it. Just so refreshing and complex. It is as if someone has gone out to create a Rosebank. *40%. Quality Spirits International.*

Vintner's Choice Speyside 10 Years Old (84) n21.5 t22 f20 b20.5. Pleasant. But considering the quality of the Speysiders Grants have to play with, the dullness is a bit hard to fathom. *40%. Quality Spirits International.*

Waitrose Pure Highland Malt (86.5) n22 t22 f20.5 b22. Blood orange by the cartload: amazingly tangy and fresh; bitters out at the finish. This is one highly improved malt and great to see a supermarket bottling showing some serious attitude....as well as taste!! Fun, refreshing and enjoyable. *40%*

Wemyss Vintage Malt The Peat Chimney Hand Crafted Blended Malt Whisky (80) n19 t22 f20 b19. The balance is askew here, especially on the bone-dry wallpapery finish. Does have some excellent spicy/coffee moments, though. *43%. Wemyss Vintage Malts Ltd.*

Wemyss Vintage Malt The Smooth Gentleman Hand Crafted Blended Malt Whisky (83) n19 t22 f21 b21. Not sure about the nose: curiously fishy (very gently smoked). But the malts tuck into the tastebuds with aplomb showing some sticky barley sugar along the way. *43%.*

Wemyss Vintage Malt The Spice King Hand Crafted Blended Malt Whisky (84) n22 t22 f20 b20. Funnily enough, I've not a great fan of the word "smooth" when it comes to whisky. But the introduction of oily Caol Ila-style peat here makes it a more of a smooth gentleman than the "Smooth Gentleman." Excellent spices very late on. *43%. Wemyss Vintage Malts.*

Wholly Smoke Aged 10 Years (86.5) n22.5 t22.5 f20 b21.5. A big, peaty, sweat, rumbustuous number with absolutely no nod towards sophistication or balance and the finish virtually disintegrates. The smoke is slapped on and the whole appears seemingly younger than its 10 years. Massive fun, all the same. *Macdonald & Muir Ltd. for Oddbins.*

Wild Scotsman Scotch Malt Whisky (Black Label) batch no. CBV001 **(91) n23.5** smoke hangs moodily in the glass; the atmosphere is heavy and humid with the oak in no mood to give way to the peat and the sugars in sticky, molassed form; even a separate layer of barley is thick and clearly means business...; **t23.5** sublime delivery with those molassed, sugary barley tones seeing to the form. But then the smoke comes crashing through followed shortly by some major oak. Elegant, soft, yet this is not a place for pussycats...; **f21** bitters out slightly as the oaks get a bit too cocky; **b23** the type of dram you drink from a dirty glass. Formidable and entertaining. *47%. House of Macduff.*

Wild Scotsman Aged 15 Years Vatted Malt (95) n23 a seriously attractive marriage between gentle oaky vanilla and preening barley; diluted honey and spiced apple abound; **t24** you really can't ask for more from a malt delivery than this. Soft and vaguely lush, the taste buds are overrun by an enchanting Danish-style moist marzipan in dark chocolate. It is impossible to fault the intensity and beauty of the early barley charge; **f24** settles down to drier marzipan and pistachio oil. The interplay between barley and oak is exceptional and even proffers some very late and welcome spices. One of the longest finishes in the business; **b24** if anyone wants an object lesson as to why you don't screw your whisky with caramel, here it is. Jeff Topping can feel a justifiable sense of pride in his new whisky: for its age, it is an unreconstituted masterpiece... *46% (92 proof). nc ncf. USA.*

Mystery Malts

Chieftain's Limited Edition Aged 40 Years hogshead **(78) n22 t22 f16 b18.** Oak-ravaged and predictably bitter on the death (those of you who enjoy Continental bitters might go for this..!). But the lead up does offer a short, though sublime and intense honey kick. The finish, though... *48.5%. Ian Macleod.*

Scottish Grain

It's a bit weird, really. Many whisky lovers stay clear of blended Scotch, preferring instead single malts. The reason, I am often told, is that the grain included in a blend makes it rough and ready. Yet I wish I had a twenty pound note for each time I have been told in recent years how much someone enjoys a single grain. The ones that the connoisseurs die for are the older versions, usually special independent bottlings displaying great age and more often than not brandishing a lavish Canadian or bourbon style.

Like single malts, grain distilleries produce whisky bearing their own style and signature. And, also, some display characteristics and a richness that can surprise and delight. Most of the grains available in (usually specialist) whisky outlets are pretty elderly. Being made from maize and wheat helps give them either that Canadian or, depending on the freshness of the cask, an unmistakable bourbony style. So older grains display far greater body than is commonly anticipated.

Light whiskies, including some Speysiders, tend to adopt this north American stance when the spirit has absorbed so much oak that the balance has been tipped. So overtly Kentuckian can they be, I once playfully introduced an old single grain Scotch whisky into a bourbon tasting I was conducting and nobody spotted that it was the cuckoo in the nest ... until I revealed all at the end of the evening. And even had to display the bottle to satisfy the disbelievers.

Younger grains may give a hint of oncoming bourbon-ness. But, rather, they tend to celebrate either a softness in taste or, in the case of North British, a certain rigidity. Where many malts have a tendency to pulverise the taste-buds and announce their intent and character at the top of their voice, younger grains are content to stroke and whisper.

Scotch whisky companies have so far had a relaxed attitude to marketing their grains. William Grant has made some inroads with Black Barrel, though with nothing like the enthusiasm they unleash upon us with their blends and malts. And Diageo are apparently content to see their Cameron Brig sell no further than its traditional hunting grounds, just north of Edinburgh, where the locals tend to prefer single grain to any other whisky. And the latest news from that most enormous of distilleries...it is getting bigger. Not only are Diageo planning to up their malt content by building a new Speyside distillery, but Cameronbridge, never a retiring place since the days of the Haigs in the 1820s is set for even grander expansion. Having, with Port Dundas, absorbed the closure of a number of grain distilleries over the last 30 years something had to be done to give it a fighting chance of taking on the expansion into China, Russia and now, most probably, India. It is strange that not more is being done. Cooley in Ireland have in the last year or so forged a healthy following with their introduction of grain whiskies at various ages. They have shown that the interest is there and some fresh thinking and boldness in a marketing department can create niche and often profitable markets. Edrington have entered the market with a vatted grain called Snow Grouse, designed to be consumed chilled and obviously a tilt at the vodka market. The first bottling I received, though, was disappointingly poor and I hope future vattings will be more carefully attended to. All round, then, the news for Scottish grain lovers has not been good of late with the demolition of mighty Dumbarton and now, controversially, the pending closure of Port Dundas itself. With the expansion of Cameronbridge and a 50% stake in North British, Diageo obviously believe they have all the grain capacity they require.

The tastings notes here for grains cover only a few pages, disappointingly, due to their scarcity. However, it is a whisky style growing in stature, helped along the way not just by Cooley but also by Compass Box's recent launching of a vatted grain. And we can even see an organic grain on the market, distilled at the unfashionable Loch Lomond Distillery. Why, though, it has to be asked does it take the relatively little guys to lead the way? Perhaps the answer is in the growing markets in the east: the big distillers are very likely holding on to their stocks to facilitate their expansion there.

At last the message is getting through that the reaction to oak of this relatively lightweight spirit - and please don't for one moment regard it as neutral, for it is most certainly anything but - can throw up some fascinating and sometimes delicious possibilities. Blenders have known that for a long time. Now public interest is growing. And people are willing to admit that they can enjoy an ancient Cambus, Caledonian or Dumbarton in very much the way they might celebrate a single malt. Even if it does go against the grain...

Single Grain Scotch
CALEDONIAN

Clan Denny Caledonian Aged 44 Years dist Jan 65, bott Jul 09 **(94) n23** soft natural caramels caress the nose: toffee wafer with milk chocolate; **t23.5** velvety delivery of corn oil and custard pie; there is almost a bizarre hint of rye from the slightly harder fruity sub plot. Intriguing, if not impossible...; **f24** back to custard cream biscuits dunked in black coffee – and proceeds to melt in the mouth accordingly; **b23.5** I feared that after a gap of four years since last seeing a Clan Denny Caledonian, time might have taken a fatal toll. Not a bit of it! Every bit as gentle as those great drams of yesteryear, even though the oak has, as to be expected, gone up an extra notch. Track a bottle down and cherish it!! *45.8%. Douglas Laing.*

Scotch Malt Whisky Society Cask 93.1 Aged 29 Years refill barrel, dist May 78 **(93.5) n23** cosy spices, a wave of something vaguely fruity and something else definitely floral make for a busy introduction; **t24** brilliantly weighted delivery with the silky corn in almost concentrated form before numerous waves of spice crash over the tastebuds; **f23** softens and sweetens out to calm those battered tastebuds. An effortlessly charming finale; **b23.5** another example of why old grains like these are among the finest whiskies found, not just in Scotland but the world. *60.1%*

CAMERONBRIDGE

Celtic Heartlands Cameronbridge 1974 Aged 33 Years (88) n23 smoky fruit...???? A Grain Whisky, Jim. But not as we know it... **t22** lively fruits appear to have a glimmer of malt about them...what is going on?...then peat...oh, my word...what the hell....??? this is a grain...isn't it..??? **f21** flattens out for a bit of a fruity, smoky grainy mess... **b22** I don't have the benefit of a label or any literature with this: I am nosing as I find....which is one effing weird single grain. Let's just say that if it was an antique, I would point out that there had been some restoration, mainly in the wood department, with oak where there was once walnut. And oak that has carried at various times fruit and peat. Not what you normally come to expect from a grain. It is 21 minutes past midnight and this was going to be the third to last whisky of a long and tiring day. It will instead be the last: my brain, after this assault, can take no more... *48.3%*

Duncan Taylor Collection Cameronbridge 1979 cask no. 46 **(85) n23 t21 f20 b21.** The nose is a celebration of seriously delicate bourbon (not Canadian); a sliver of lime off the soft corn and leathery honeycomb; the delivery shows its age. *50.3%*

Duncan Taylor Collection Cameronbridge 1979 cask no. 3582 **(85) n20 t23 f21 b21.** Almost pure Canadian in style but with the oak perhaps making too many inroads. There is a superb richness to the grain which dovetails wonderfully with the sweetened spices. *52.4%*

Duncan Taylor Collection Cameronbridge 1979 cask no. 3585 **(86) n22.5 t22 f20.5 b21.** Oak pounds into the grain, at first making very little difference on the early sugars but then taking control. *51.9%*

Duncan Taylor Collection Cameronbridge 1979 cask no. 3586 **(84) n22.5 t21 f20 b20.5.** For those who prefer their grain old and dry. *51.2%*

Duncan Taylor Collection Cameronbridge 1979 cask no. 3587 **(82) n22 t22 f18 b20.** The fun and flavour is all front loaded. *51.3%*

Scotch Malt Whisky Society Cask 94.1 Aged 29 Years refill barrel, dist May 79 **(93) n24** absolutely top order grain with a rich corn base and semi-Canadian oak depth: text book for age and type; **t23.5** the balance between the sweet, almost sharp grain and the drier, yolky oaks, as well as the gently oiled texture, just couldn't be better; **f22.5** surprisingly firm with deft spices adding complexity; **b23** a sublime grain which does exactly what it says on the tin. *53%*

CARSEBRIDGE

The Clan Denny Carsebridge Aged 45 Years cask no. HH4132 **(84) n19 t23 f21.5 b20.5.** Though the nose may be crumbling and there may be very shaky balance, the delivery is – almost literally, it seems – pure nectar. Sugary and watery, there is little form to this in true whisky terms. It is something of an old aged freak. Yet the enjoyment and wonderment derived from this ancient dram is unique and entirely priceless. Enjoy for what it is. *45.6%. Douglas Laing. 167 bottles.*

Duncan Taylor Collection Carsebridge 1979 cask no. 32902 **(92) n22** butterscotch tart of the highest order with a dollop of cream and vanilla; **t23** busy yet clean start with oak and grains battling out for early supremacy; stage two sees the palate filled with lush, almost barley-sugar-esque notes dried by an excellent sprinkling of mocha; all through these battles a lively spice bristles playfully **f23** long, with a fruity, mildly sugary edge clinging to the fading oak; **b24** exceptionally well balanced grain getting the emphasis between the spices and bitter-sweet texture absolutely spot on. Fabulous! *60%. Duncan Taylor.*

Duncan Taylor Collection Carsebridge 1979 cask no. 33032 **(84.5) n20 t23 f20 b21.5.** Not quite in the same league as other DT Carsebridges of this run, due in no small measure to tiring, mildly embittered oak. Staggering about a little, not quite sure whether to clout or caress and ends up doing both. The great moments, though, are exactly that. *56%*

⋅∵⋅ **Duncan Taylor Collection Carsebridge 1979** cask no. 33033 **(91) n23** real ye olde candy shop aroma: jars full of boiled fruit sweets and a dusty, wooden floor: takes me back nearly 45 years...; **t23** surprising degree of sugar evident from the kick off: superb gentle fruit and spice interplay; everything controlled and delicate **f22.5** chunky vanilla but its light sugar does a perfect balancing act; **b22.5** a fabulous dram from this lost distillery and about as relaxing as they come. Indeed, I found this Carsebridge the perfect antidote to when my beloved Millwall lost at Wembley against Scunthorpe... *54.9%*

Kingsbury Finest & Rarest Carsebridge 41 Years Old 1964 bourbon cask **(94) n24 t23.5 f23 b23.5.** Strange how some old grains get a Canadian passport, others a US. This is pure Kentucky...Oh, and by the way, it's a real stunner. *476%. nc ncf. Japan Import System Co. Ltd.*

Lonach Carsebridge Aged 43 Years distilled 1963 bottled 07 **(93) n23.5 t23.5 f23 b23.** Not a shred of evidence that the great age has damaged or reduced this in any way. Perhaps the least oak-ruined 40-something whisky you will ever taste. A freaky great and a real treasure for the US market. *43%*

Scotch Malt Whisky Society Cask 92.1 Aged 31 Years refill barrel, dist Nov 76 **(90) n22 t22 f23 b23.** Now here, from beyond the grave, is a wonderful example and object lesson in why it is a sin to add colouring to older blends (well, any blends, if I was to get on my soapbox). Here is a whisky which has extracted from the wood all kinds of natural caramels. It works: it sits well in the scheme of things and balances out beautifully. Add some into the mix and then the balance vanishes. Grab some of this and see what I mean.. *56.6%*

DUMBARTON

Celtic Heartlands Dumbarton 1964 Aged 42 Years (87.5) n20.5 not exactly the best cask Dumbarton was ever filled into; **t23** the arrival on the palate is magic; you are expecting the dark intervention of dodgy wood, instead there is a rich seam of sugar-coated corn; **f21.5** the bitterness reminds you of your earlier cask fears; vanilla, natural toffee and marshmallow more than compensate; **b22.5** defies the odds for a charming dram. *46.7%.*

The Clan Denny Dumbarton Aged 43 Years cask no. HH3829 **(95) n23.5** lilacs? On a grain whisky...? 'Fraid so...Some real fizz and attitude as well as a hint of something from the high quality bourbon front; **t24** a near perfect landing on the palate: forget about spitting this one...the corn has perfect shape and body, the layering of the spice and vanillins – and even a minor blast of tannins; and as for the balance between sweet grist and the slightly, balancing drier oaks...it's off the scale... **f23.5** the vanilla mainstay of the finish is enriched by that continued gristy sweetness and some countering burnt toast bitterness; **b24** so I thought I'd celebrate tasting my 800th whisky for the 2009 Bible by showing an act of solidarity with Dumbarton, a great distillery needlessly lost to us, ritually slaughtered on an accountant's spreadsheet. *51.8%. Douglas Laing. 215 bottles.*

GIRVAN

Berry's Own Selection Girvan 1989 bott 07 **(91) n22** freshly polished wooden floors, gentle bourbon, spiced vanilla; **t23** silky, not entirely un-Canadian in delivery; the sweetness doesn't entirely camouflage the cleverness of the soft-hard duality of the body **f23** long, well oiled and offering a late corn (as opposed to wheated) character; fabulous depth as the soft oaks grow **b23** a Steady-Eddie and eventually beautiful grain with no blemishes or fault-lines giving a good insight into why this make is so popular among blenders. *46%.*

Celtic Heartlands Girvan 1965 Aged 42 Years (83) n21 t22 f20.5 b20.5. I know that around about the time this was made some blenders in Scotland weren't over enamoured with Girvan – which is hardly the case today. Here you get a slight insight as to why some feathers were flying back then, with the sharpness of the firm grain at times biting pretty deep. However, after all these years, it is the oak making the loudest noise and the messages are mixed. Certainly the bitterness is entirely wood related. There is the odd window, though, especially just after initial delivery, through which the grain does show a rich shaft of golden promise. This is not a whisky without moments of great beauty. *45% Bruichladdich Ltd.*

⋅∵⋅ **Scotch Malt Whisky Society Cask G7.1 Aged 18 Years** refill barrel, dist Jul 90 **(86.5) n21 t23 f21 b21.5.** Subtly Canadian and slightly rich. Perhaps over indulges the caramels but weight, mouthfeel, degree of sweetness and spice impact are all very good. *54.2%*

INVERGORDON

⊹ **Berry's Own Selection Invergordon 1971** bott 09 **(88)** n22 just a slight twitch and twinge to an otherwise lifeless bowl of Canadian custard; **t22** melt-in-the-mouth vanilla, dissolving muscovado sugar; vanishing middle; **f22** drier and sharper with all the vicious bite of an enraged butterfly; **b22** steady as a rock; hard as a blancmange...; *48.2%. Berry Bros & Rudd.*

The Clan Denny Invergordon Aged 42 Years cask no. HH4239 **(90)** n23 t22.5 f22 b22.5. How do grain whiskies like this be so effortlessly good? *49.8%. Douglas Laing. 155 bottles.*

Duncan Taylor Collection Invergordon 1965 cask no. 15514 **(86)** n19 t23 f22 b22. Lovely old grain that gets over the flat-ish, faltering, somewhat gluey nose to let loose with a superb display of spices on the otherwise soft and corn-rich arrival. Excellent fade as the oaks integrate with grace. Entirely charming whisky. *50.3%. Duncan Taylor.*

Duncan Taylor Collection Invergordon 1965 cask no. 15516 **(85.5)** n21 t22 f21.5 b21. Lively Lincoln biscuits with an extra sprinkling of sugar. *50.1%*

Duncan Taylor Collection Invergordon 1965 cask no. 15517 **(94)** n23.5 high-class Canadian where the corn and vanilla fit hand in glove, elegant and almost ageless; **t24** the corn shimmers as it hits the palate: sharper grain and deeper honey make for a perfectly proportioned body and then the spice... **f23** spot on spices allow the corn to oil up slightly and bring with it some natural oaky caramels without a single problem. Just so lovely... **b23.5** how strange that two casks can be outwardly so similar, but, on close inspection, so very different. This guy oozes class it has no right to possess after so many years. Perhaps it's the extra spice which does the trick. But just like when you meet two twins of the opposite sex, for one reason or other, one of them just has that special, almost indefinable, thing the other doesn't.... same here. *50.2%*

Duncan Taylor Collection Invergordon 1965 cask no. 15518 **(88.5)** n22.5 crushed biscuits, probably jammy dodgers; **t22.5** wonderful delivery of buttery corn. No honey, but the gentle sprinkling of lightly molassed sugars does the job... **f21.5** quiet, with the accent on the vanilla; **b22** charming, high quality, blemish-free ancient grain. *50.8%*

⊹ **Duncan Taylor Collection Invergordon 1965** cask no. 15519 **(94)** n24.5 textbook complexity: yes it is a bit of a Canadian/bourbon hybrid. But it as if there are small grains at work here breaking up the more dominant vanillas into manageable pieces. A faultless treat of a nose with the bitter-sweet ratio as near as damn-it perfect; **t23** some genuine and surprising blood orange tones amid the regulation vanilla: complex and excellently weighted; small, busy spices prod and jab around the tastebuds, and the sub-plot is a cream-toffee/vanilla mix; **t23** long, relatively simplistic. But not a bad note from the cask and that means the spices and delicate sweet notes continue unsullied; **b23.5** DT obviously have obviously struck upon a rich seam of outstanding Invergordon. 100% must buy whisky. *51.6%*

⊹ **Duncan Taylor Collection Invergordon 1965** cask no. 15532 **(85.5)** n21 t22.5 f20.5 b21.5. Good, simple entirely honest old grain. But here all the accent is on the vanilla and the complexity which wins heart and palate on 15519 is conspicuous by its absence. *52.7%*

LOCH LOMOND

Loch Lomond 2000 Cask No. 37700 Aged in Organic French Wine Hogshead dist 24 Jul 00, bott 27 Apr 07 db **(94)** n23.5 t24 f23 b23.5. A brave decision to mature grain in grape, but this has worked so impressively well. On this evidence, who needs single malt when you can get grain this good....??? *45%. nc ncf. 475 bottles.*

Loch Lomond Cask No. 37697 Single Organic Grain Distillery Select organic French oak, dist 24 Jul 00, bott 27 Apr 07 db **(76)** n18 t21 f18 b19. I wonder if the sulphur is organic.... *45%. 475 bottles.*

Dà Mhile Loch Lomond Organic dist Jul 00, bott Mar 06 **(90)** n23 gentle sweetness that sits well with vanilla; curiously firm yet soft at same time; **t23** beautifully chewy with teasing, subtle vanilla and butter tones; **f21** pretty short but refuses to lose balance; **b23** great to get a chance to see Loch Lomond's high class and complexly bodied grain – organic or not. *46%.*

LOCHSIDE

Clan Denny Grain Lochside Aged 42 Years dist Nov 63, bott Nov 05 **(89)** n23 I'm in deepest Kentucky and just opened up a 17-year-old barrel: it's tired and groaning but the hickory and muscovado sugar are such a treat; nice chestnuts, too; **t23** silky, mesmerising oak with splinters in every direction; lovely heavy roast Java coffee at the very centre; **f21** fades and becomes mildly bitter and tired with the coffee-bourbon theme continuing; **b22** a bit like clapped out bourbon on the nose and even more clapped out bourbon on the finish. My researcher put this under single malts, but as soon as I tasted it, I smelt (and tasted!) a rat. Proof positive that old grain Scotch can produce vintage bourbon!! *44.1%. Douglas Laing.*

NORTH BRITISH

❧ **Berry's Own Selection North British 2000** bott 09 **(78) n19.5 t21 f18.5 b19.** Pock marked by the occasional sulphurous North British house style – this is to do with distillation, not maturation – and for all its brightness on delivery has a bit of problem shaking off the dogged late bitterness. 46%. Berry Bros & Rudd.

Celtic Heartlands North British 1974 Aged 33 Years (93.5) n23.5 low ester Jamaica rum meets Frosties cereal: sweet, lively and Grrreaaattt!! **t23.5** absolutely more of the same on the palate, only with a surprising bite; the acacia honey could not be more delicate; **f23** a glorious soft oil – so unusual in grain whisky – helps coat the corn and honey thickly enough to see off the encroaching oak; instead, soft spices have to make tingling inroads; **b23.5** to be honest, it is rare that you find single malt whisky which stands the test of time with such panache. Women, in particular, are likely to fall for its honeyed charms. 474%. Bruichladdich Ltd.

❧ **Duncan Taylor Collection North British 1978** cask no. 38469 **(89) n21.5** buttery corn oil and lightly sweetened; **t23** melt-in-the-mouth silk: again buttery with a fabulous flutter of golden syrup; **f22** slightly bitter vanilla and a dash of ice cream in cream soda; **b22.5** just charms you to death. 54.9%

❧ **Duncan Taylor Collection North British 1978** cask no. 38472 **(84.5) n21 t22 f20.5 b21.** Many of the usual NB corn characteristics, but evidence of a mildly fatigued cask. 55.2%

Duncan Taylor Collection North British 1978 Aged 29 Years cask no. 39889 **(91) n23 t23.5 f22 b22.5.** There is something about these better old grains which makes you want to applaud. A whisky with a bit of fight, but ends up relaxed and a picture of elegance: surely it is only a matter of time before these grandiose old grains are more widely appreciated. 54.5%

Duncan Taylor Collection North British 1978 cask no. 39890 **(83) n21.5 t20 f21.5 b21.** Pleasantly stays the course. No great statements made, but doesn't veer out of control and crash, either. 55.6%

Duncan Taylor Collection North British 1978 cask no. 239966 **(88) n21 t23 f22 b22.** Pretty complex and always beautifully balanced. 51.6%. Duncan Taylor.

❧ **Duncan Taylor Collection North British 1978** cask no. Q247 **(95) n24** the jackpot..!! Well, nearly. Everything here I look for from this distillery at this kind of age: a complex, softly spiced layering to the usual corn field. Busy and gloriously three dimensional; **t24** what a delivery! Canadian from the top drawer in so many aspects! A real fizz to this as the spices move in and break up any corn mafia that's thinking about dominating proceedings: the starchy backbone also has light banana-vanillas and weak Demerara sugar to contend with; **f23** those soft spices spin on even as the corn oils begin to gain a belated foothold. The vanillas are faultless; **b24** golden proof that great grain is a match for anything. 54.7%

❧ **Norse Cask Selection North British 1997 Aged 11 Years** hogshead cask no. 18278, dist 97, bott 08 **(91) n22.5** crisp, buttery, a Canadian flourish but without the caramel; **t23.5** firm, mouth-watering, on the edge of sweetness but distinctly sharp; **f22.5** long, lingering, excellent oak background to the mildly flinty grain; a bit of spice and mocha at the death **b22.5** an exemplary cask: exactly what you should expect from this distillery at this age. 64.9%. Qualityworld for WhiskyOwner.com, Denmark.

❧ **Private Cellar North British 1992** bott 07 **(86) n21 t22 f21.5 b21.5.** Corn soup with a delightful sweet head and spicy tail. 43%. Speyside Distillers.

❧ **Scotch Malt Whisky Society Cask G1.5 Aged 24 Years** refill barrel, dist Apr 84 **(90.5) n23** starchy corn oil with a dab of maple syrup sweetness...sure this isn't Canadian..? **t23.5** effortless grace on delivery: the soft corn oils envelop the mouth and custard and butterscotch sweetness is dispensed to all corners; better still, there is a fabulous juiciness, too; **f21** long, drying – as it should – but just not quite enough sweetness to counter the late bitter marmalade notes; **b23** even after nearly a quarter of a century, this a powering beauty. 60.7%

NORTH OF SCOTLAND

Private Cellar North of Scotland 1970 bott 07 **(92) n24** stunning mixture of honey and stem ginger; **t23** lush, lusty corn with some amazing notches of honey marked on the softest of oak; **f22** long, vanilla-clad, gently drying, a touch of the Canadians; **b23** this is the way old grain should be: slightly off the wall but radiating charm and class. 43%.

PORT DUNDAS

Duncan Taylor Collection Port Dundas 1973 cask no. 128317 **(96) n24** Christ!!! It's rum!!!! From Demerara. What the bloody hell is going on..? Let me have a look at the bottle. No, it's grain...from Port Dundas. Ah, right the stills...there you go!! Entirely different from any other whisky in the market place. And this is whisky...right? The natural caramelisation from the oak is not dissimilar to the pre-caramelisation in Demerara rum... another confusing point; **t24** makes all the right noises for a supreme corn grain whisky, especially that big corny oiliness. Yet so many aspects of this display a Demerara rum-like sweetness and texture, only with the brilliance of subtlety achieved normally only by corn...my mind, like my tastebuds, is exploding...; **f24** a bitter-sweet balance that you attain normally in your dreams: absolutely zero bitterness or off notes from the cask; the oiliness persists, as does the corn, as does the rum, as do gentle spices **b24** never have I seen a better example of a Coffey still in action: before I actually knew what I was nosing I had, in my mind, been transported back to Guyana and was nosing some Coffey still rum from there: the similarity is extraordinary!! And, believe me, this is one whisky I don't spit whilst working on this book!! A landmark whisky in my long experience. And an award winner of some type. *57.9%*

Duncan Taylor Collection Port Dundas 1973 cask no. 128321 **(77) n19 t20 f19 b19.** A previous bottling of a sister cask was a highlight of the year: in fact, the thing was in my taste offs for World Whisky of the Year. This one, though, might not quite make it that far. I suspect a sherry butt has been employed to liven it up and some sulphur has sneaked in. *54.5%*

⌐ **Scotch Malt Whisky Society Cask G6.1 Aged 28 Years** refill hogshead, dist Dec 80 **(89.5) n23** lavender and citrus head the cast for this most dainty aroma; **t22.5** the grain and vanilla feel inextricably linked: dense with a touch of the eggnog about this; **f22** some serious custard through to the end; **b22** about as friendly a dram as you will ever meet. *51%*

STRATHCLYDE

Duncan Taylor Collection Strathclyde 1973 cask no. 74062 **(78) n20 t21 f18 b19.** Exactly two years after its twin cask was bottled...and just about identical results, except for extra bitters on the finish..!! *56.5%*

Duncan Taylor Collection Strathclyde 1973 cask no. 74063 **(82.5) n20 t21.5 f20 b21.** How can something so old have so many teeth – and bloody sharp ones? Even the citrus stings. *55.5%*

⌐ **Duncan Taylor Collection Strathclyde 1973** cask no. 74067 **(86) n22.5 t22 f20.5 b21.** An infinitely better cask than those previously in this series: the nose is almost identical to the Kentucky Tavern bourbon from the old Barton distillery a decade ago. *55.2%*

Duncan Taylor Collection Strathclyde 1980 cask no. 1496 **(79) n20 t21 f18 b20.** Like an out-of-sorts old Canadian – but with an early, viperish bite. *58.2%*

Vatted Grain

⌐ **Compass Box Hedonism Maximus (93.5) n25** the kind of aroma your nose was invented for: lots of rich bourbony swirls, with butterscotch, liquorice and chocolate-covered honeycomb arriving – big time! – on cue...; oh, and a few gooseberries and greengages tossed in for an extra dimension: it just doesn't get any better... **t22.5** the oak is a bit top heavy on arrival, but lush malt cushions its impact to a degree; still juicy and tongue-teasing; **f23** retains its overtly bourbony character to the end with massive chewy oak extract, but always enough sweetness in reserve to cope; **b23** Bourbon Maximus.... *46%*

Compass Box Hedonism Maximus bottling no. H25 MMVII **(88) n21.5** huge waves of vanilla and natural caramels help cover a wheaty sweetness; **t22.5** almost like dusted icing sugar on bread pudding; **f22** much more sedate with a soft oily lift; the sweetness remains a constant despite the slow oak arousal; **b22** sweet, gentle but with a wicked spice prickle. *50.1%. nc ncf. 2,400 bottles.*

⌐ **Norse Cask Selection Inver Bridge Aged 29 Years** hogshead cask no. QW-gr1108, dist 66 & 79, bott 08 **(88.5) n23** great age is apparent from the first moment: honeycomb/liquorice notes are there in mild, bourbony form, as well as a very light hint of fruit and several layers of vanilla. Yet for all the lightness of shades, the overall feeling is intense; **t23** silky mouthfeel with a touch of natural caramel sweetness, then a dose of something much drier, more boldly oaky; **f21** perhaps too much oaky bitterness – like overly burnt raisin - at the death; **b21.5** hmmm, can't think which two distilleries this will have been made from... *46%. Qualityworld for WhiskyOwner.com, Denmark.*

⌐ **The Snow Grouse (70.5) n17.5 t18 f17 b18.** Served normally, a tedious nonentity of a whisky. What little flavour there is, is toffee-based. On both nose and finish there are distant off notes, but in something so light louder than they might be. Surely...it can't be...? Served chilled as instructed on bottle: **(79) n20 t21 f18 b20.** Much, much better. Very sweet and the 's' word is confined, especially on the vodka-ish nose. The finish is still a give away though. *40%. Edrington.*

Scottish Blends

With a Scottish blend having recently been named Jim Murray's Whisky Bible's Whisky of the Year, the time surely has come for re-evaluating this most misunderstood and undervalued of whiskies. For it really is quite extraordinary how people the world over, with refined palates and a good knowledge of single malts, are so willing to dismiss blends out of hand. Certainly, from the amount of publicity the news received around the world, and some of the shock, horror reactions to it - especially when interviewed by journalists or cornered by malt fundamentalists - it was as if the end of the whisky world was nigh.

Perhaps it is a form of malt snobbery: if you don't drink malts, then you are not a serious Scotch whisky connoisseur ... or so some people think. Perhaps it is the fact that something like 94 out of every 100 bottles of Scotch consumed is a blend that has brought about this rather too common cold-shouldering. Well, not in my books. In fact, perhaps the opposite is true. Until you get to grips with blends you may well be entitled to regard yourself knowledgeable in single malts, but not in Scotch as a whole. Blends should be the best that Scotland can offer, because with a blend you have the ability to create any degree of complexity. And surely balance and complexity are the cornerstones of any great whisky, irrespective of type.

Of course there are some pretty awful blends created simply as a commodity with little thought going into their structure – just young whiskies, sometimes consisting of stock that is of dubious quality and then coloured up to give some impression of age. Yes, you are more likely to find that among blends than malts and for this reason the poorest blends can be pretty nasty. And, yes, they contain grain. Too often, though, grain is regarded as a kind of whisky leper – not to be touched under any circumstances. Some writers dismiss grain as "neutral" and "cheap", thus putting into the minds of the uninitiated the perception of inferiority.

But there really is nothing inferior about blends. In fact, whilst researching The Bible, I have to say that my heart missed more than one beat usually when I received a sample of a blend I had never found before. Why? Well, with single malts each distillery produces a style that can be found within known parameters. With a blend, anything is possible. There are many dozens of styles of malts to choose from and they will react slightly differently with certain grains.

For that reason, perhaps, I have marked blends a little more strictly and tighter than I have single malts. Because blends, by definition, should offer more.

And they do not have to be of any great age to achieve greatness. Look at the brilliance of the likes of Ballantine's Finest, Royal Silk, Black Bottle, Bailie Nicol Jarvie, Grant's and, even the Co-op's own 5-year-old. Look, also, at the diversity of type from crisp and light to peat dominant and myriad styles between. Then you get others where age has also played an astonishing role, not least a 50-years-old, such as Royal Salute. And this year The Last Drop. That picked up any amount of gongs in last year's Jim Murray's Whisky Bible and was on the shortlist for the actual World Whisky of the Year. It feels like a blend with a reasonably high grain content, but years in barrrel has rubbed away any jarring edge like pebbles on a beach. It is always an exciting moment to come across a new and unique whisky type. Had not this been a marriage of grain and malt it is hard to imagine that the character would have been anything like so extraordinary.

Just like malts, blends change in character from time to time. In the case of blends it often has much to do with the running availability of certain malts and grains. The most unforgivable reason is because the marketing guys reckon it needs a bit of extra colour and precious high notes are lost to caramel or sherry. Subtlety and character are the keys for any great blend without fail.

The most exciting blends, like White Horse 12 (why, oh, why is that, like Old Parr 18, restricted mainly to Japan?) Grant's and this year's glorious Ballantine's show bite, character and attitude. Silk and charm are to be appreciated. But after a long, hard day is there anything better than a blend that is young and confident enough to nip and nibble at your throat on its way down and then throw up an array of flavours and shapes to get your taste-buds round? Certainly, I have always found blends ultimately more satisfying than malts. Especially when the balance, like this year's Bible champion, Ballantine's 17, simply caresses your soul.

With Blended Scotch the range and possibilities are limitless. All it takes is for the drinker not just to use his or her nose and taste-buds. But also an open mind.

Scottish Blends

"10 Years and a Bit" Blended Scotch (84) n21.5 t22 f20 b20.5. Matured in oloroso and finished in a Cognac quartercask. Explains why this blend lurches drunkenly all over the palate. Enough honeycomb, though, for a pleasant few minutes *42%. Qualityworld, Denmark.*

100 Pipers (74) n18.5 t18 f19 b18.5. An improved blend, even with a touch of spice to the finish. I get the feeling the grains are a bit less aggressive than they for so long were. I'd let you know for sure, if only I could get through the caramel. *40%. Chivas.*

Aberdour Piper (88.5) n22 green apple and the most delicate smoke imaginable; t23 crisp malt and grain integrate so not a crack shows; juicy and mouth-cleansing; f21.5 vanilla concentrate and late, lethargic smoke; b22 always great to find a blend that appears to have upped the stakes in the quality department. Clean, refreshing with juicy young Speysiders at times simply showing off. *40%. Hayman Distillers.*

Adelphi Private Stock Loyal Old Mature (88) n21 big grain overture; t23 golden syrup notes and bound tightly by firm grain; f22 delightful coffee with just the perfect degree of bite; b22 a very attractive number, especially for those with a slightly sweet tooth. *40%.*

Antiquary 12 Years Old (92) n23.5 by some distance the smokiest delivery I have seen from this blend since my late dear friend Jim Milne got his hands on it. The last time I had hold of this it was Speyside all the way. Now peat rules; t23.5 immediate oils and smoke form a thick layer in almost Caol Ila style, but penetrating grains and juicier Speysiders ensure parity of style; f22 light with vanilla and echoes of peat; b23 a staggering about turn for a blend which, for a very long time, has flown the Speyside flag. I am not convinced that this degree of peatiness was intended. But it works! *40%. Tomatin Distillery.*

Antiquary 21 Years Old (93) n23.5 as dense and brooding as an imminent thunderstorm: just a hint of a less than perfect sherry butt costs a point but manuca honey and crushed leaves, all helped along with a delicate peat-reek, ensure something sultry and wonderful; t23.5 improbably dense with a honeycomb maltiness you have to hack through; the grains offer lighter, bourbony touches; f23 softer vanillas and toffee, topped with the thinnest layer of molassed sugar and further bourbony notes; b23 a huge blend, scoring a magnificent 93 points. But this year I have tasted better, and another sample, direct from the blending lab, came with even greater complexity and, perhaps significantly, less apparent caramel. A top-notch blend of rare distinction. *43%. Tomatin Distillery.*

Antiquary 30 Years Old (86) n22 t23 f20 b21. Decidedly odd fare: not only does the blend offer a greenish tinge, but the late waywardness of the finish suggests something odd has clambered aboard. That said, the endearingly eccentric nose and early delivery are sublime, with silky complexity tumbling all over the palate. *46%. Tomatin Distillery.*

Antiquary Finest (79.5) n20 t21 f19 b19.5. Pleasantly sweet and plump with the accent on the quick early malt delivery. *40%. Tomatin Distillery.*

Arden House Scotch Whisky (86) n19.5 t22 f22.5 b22. Another great bit of fun from the Co-op. Very closely related to their Finest Blend, though this has, for some reason or other, a trace of a slightly fatter, mildly more earthy style. If only they would ditch the caramel and let those sweet malts and grains breathe! *40%. Co-Operative Group.*

Asda Extra Special 12 Years Old (78) n19 t21 f19 b19. Pleasantish but dragged down by the dreaded S word. *40%. Glenmorangie for Asda.*

The Bailie Nicol Jarvie (B.N.J) (95) n24 the sharpest barley has been taken to a barley-sharpening shop and painstakingly sharpened; this is pretty sharp stuff...the citrus gangs together with the fresh grass to form a dew which is pretty well...er... sharp...; t24 mouth-watering, eye-closingly, mouth-puckeringly sharp delivery with the barley pinging off the tautest grain you can imagine; f23 softens with a touch of vanilla and toffee; the late run from the citrus is a masterpiece of whisky closing; b24 I know my criticism of BNJ, historically one of my favourite blends, over the last year or two has been taken to heart by Glenmorangie. Delighted to report that they have responded: the blend has been fixed and is back to its blisteringly brilliant, ultra-mouth-watering self. Someone's sharpened their ideas up. *40%.*

⠿ **Ballantine's Aged 12 Years** (84.5) n22.5 t22 f19 b21. Attractive but odd fellow, this, with a touch of juniper to the nose and furry bitter marmalade on the finish. But some excellent barley-cocoa moments, too. *43%. Chivas.*

Ballantine's 12 Years Old (87) n21 t22 f21 b23. The kind of old-fashioned, mildly moody blend Colonel Farquharson-Smythe (retired) might have recognised when relaxing at the 19th hole back in the early '50s. Too good for a squirt of soda, mind. *40%. Chivas Bros.*

Ballantine's 17 Years Old (96.5) n24 deft grain and honey plus teasing salty peat; ultra high quality with bourbon and pear drops offering the thrust; t24 immediately mouthwatering with maltier tones clambering over the graceful cocoa-enriched grain; the degrees of sweetness are varied but near perfection; just hints of smoke here and there; f23.5 lashings of vanilla and cocoa on the fade; drier with a faint spicey, vaguely smoky buzz; **b25** now only slightly less weighty than of old. After a change of style direction it has comfortably reverted back to its sophisticated, mildly erotic old self. One of the most beautiful, complex and stunningly structured whiskies in the world. Truly the epitome of great Scotch. *43%. Chivas Bros.* ☉☉

Ballantine's Aged 21 Years (93) n24 superbly intrinsic, relying on deft fruit and vanilla notes as the key; **t24** stunningly textured with subtle layers of honey, juicy grasses and refined, slightly subdued, bourbony notes from the grain; **f22** flattens somewhat as the toffee evolves; **b23** one of the reasons I think I have loved the Ballantine's range over the years is because it is a blenders' blend. In other words, you get the feeling that they have made as much, and probably more, as possible from the stocks available and made complexity and balance the keystones to the whisky. That is still the case, except you find now that somehow, although part of a larger concern, it appears that the spectrum of flavours is less wide, though what has been achieved with those available remains absolutely top drawer. This is truly great whisky, but it has changed in style as blends, especially of this age, cannot help but doing. *43%.* ☉

Ballantine's Aged 30 Years (92) n24 ultra ripe peaches, molassed vanilla and nipping spice: rather elegant and high class; **t23** outstanding texture on delivery and early follow through. A tad oily but this appears to really up the malt input; the oaks are firm but non-intrusive and happy to add a nutty texture; **f22.5** gentle, toffeed and works hard to keep the drier, toastier oaks at bay; **b22.5** has impressively ironed out a few kinks and now uses the oak to its advantage far better. *43%. Chivas Bros.* ☉

Ballantine's Finest (96) n24 a playful balance and counter-balance between grains, lighter malts and a gentle smokiness. The upped peat of recent years has given an extra weight and charm that had been missing; **t24** sublime delivery: the mouthfeel couldn't be better had your prayers been answered; velvety and brittle grains combine to get the most out of the juicy malts: a lot of chewing to get through here; **f23.5** soft, gentle, yet retains its weight and shape with a re-emergence of smoke and a gristy sweetness to counter the gentle vanillas and cocoa from the oak **b24.5** as a standard blend this is coming through as a major work of art. Each time I taste this the weight has gone up a notch or two more and the sweetness has increased to balance out with the drier grain elements. Take a mouthful of this and experience the work of a blender very much at the top of his game. *40%. Chivas Bros.* ☉☉

❖ **Ballantine's Limited (89) n22** beautifully clean barley and soft fruits; a touch of vanilla and smoke in the distant background; **t24** a sumptuous delivery of melt-in-the-mouth grain followed by a slow unfurling of complex malt notes, from sweet barley to spicier cocoa-oak. Lovely fruit and a dab of smoke in the middle; **f21** bitters out impatiently; **b22** hadn't tasted this for a little while but maintains its early style and quite glorious delivery. *43%..*

Ballintine's Master's (82) n21 t22 f19 b20. Excellent lively grain and chewy malt, but the always suspect, grain-drizzled finish has become even more nondescript in recent bottlings. *40%.*

Bells 8 Years Old (85) n21.5 t22.5 f20 b21. Some mixed messages here: on one hand it is telling me that it has been faithful to some of the old Bells distilleries – hence a slight dirty note, especially on the finish. On the other, there are some sublime specks of complexity and weight. Quite literally the rough and the smooth. *40%. Diageo.*

Benmore (74) n19 t19 f18 b18. Underwhelming to the point of being nondescript. *40%.*

Ben Nevis "Blended at Birth" 40 Years Old matured in sherry cask, dist 62, bott 02 **(91) n22 t24 f22 b23.** The Ben Nevis distillery manager sent me another bottle of this, as he was a bit miffed I wasn't too impressed by this blend when I first tasted it in 2002. Oddly, I can't find any previous reference in the Bible, so gave it another shot. And am I glad I did. This would have been better called "Married at Birth" because the Ben Nevis grain and Ben Nevis malt were blended as new make and then allowed to mature for 40 years in sherry butts. There is nothing else like it on the market, and there are still some of these to be had at the distillery. *40%. Ben Nevis Distillery.*

Berrys' Blue Hanger 30 Years Old (88) n22 curiously, a touch of the Blue Mouse distillery in Germany about this one, such is the way the bitter-ish oak is grabbed in. Attractive with a tantalizing degree of exotic fruit, but distinctly curious for a blended Scotch; **t22** an unusual, bitter start, despite the near perfect body; then a starburst of malt and kiwi fruit and then back to some oily oak; hard to spot the grain: it must be here somewhere; **f22** an attractive fall out of vanilla and dusty barley; **b22** just a shade too oily for it to blossom to its full potential, perhaps. Stunningly beautiful in part but is it good enough to bear the Blue Hanger badge of brilliance? You decide. *45.6%. Berry Bros & Rudd.*

Berrys' Blue Hanger 30 Years Old 3rd Release bott 07 **(90.5) n23** ye olde oake, as one might expect from this olde companye, manifesting itself in sweet exotic fruit; **t22.5** bitter-sweet and tingly, from the very start the blend radiates fruit and big oak; **f22.5** long, spiced, a dash of something vaguely smoky but never tries to disguise its great age; saved at the death by a lush sweetness which sees off any OTT oak; **b22.5** much improved version on the last, closer to the original in every respect. Excellent. 45.6%. Berry Bros & Rudd.

Big "T" 5 Years Old (75) n19 t20 f18 b18. Big, chunky and bitter. Still doesn't have the finesse of old and clatters about the tastebuds charmlessly. Enormous malt delivery early on, but doesn't compensate for the bitter finish. 40%. Tomatin Distillery.

Black & White (91) n22 firm grin and a softer caramel surround; the second layer hints at smoke and oak; **t23** the crispest of deliveries followed by a radiating softly malted sweetness; the bite is sensational and everything you could demand of a blend; **f22.5** playful peat teases as the oaks gather and the grains carry on their stern, matronly way; **b23.5** this one hasn't gone to the dogs: quite the opposite. I always go a bit misty-eyed when I taste something this traditional: the crisp grains work to maximum effect in reflecting the malts. A classic of its type. 40%. Diageo.

Black Bottle (91) n22 some gnawing grains make the teasingly smoked malt work hard for its money; **t23** a battling fizz reveals some youngsters having fun in there. Like the nose, the grain really does fight its corner and the fault line where it meets the malt is marked by a spicy, smoky sweetness; **f23** the buzz continues and there is a touch of Demerara sweetness and coffee to the chewy smokiness; **b23** it has taken me a bit of time to get used to this slight change in style for this persistently brilliant blend. This one's been reduced in smoke and roughed up a little: the intervening grain which restrain the battling malts has now become a bit of a bruiser in its own right. Ignore the nonsensical claim of "Original Blend" on the label: this is a very old brand that has gone through many changes in its lifetime and will be unrecognisable from the modest whisky concocted over a century ago in an Aberdeen shop. And there are any number of us who are so glad it is nothing like the seething firewater it was 20-30 years ago. But it has kept true-ish to its re-birth under Allied when they turned it into a peaty beast and is probably closer to that in style than Highland's subsequent, lush re-working of it. 40%. Burn Stewart/Gordon Graham & Co.

Black Bottle 10 Years Old (89) n22 so age-weightedly peaty it could almost be a single malt: the grains make little discernible impact; **t23** soft, deft malt and firmer grain. The peat arrives after a short interval; **f22** more vanilla and other oaky tones; **b23** a stupendous blend of weight and poise, but possessing little of the all-round steaming, rampaging sexuality of the younger version...but like the younger version showing a degree less peat: here perhaps even two. Not, I hope, a start of a new trend under the new owners. 40%.

⠸⠆ **Black Bottle Original Blend (93.5) n23** a tad murky and confused, but the grumble of peat is compelling while the grains lighten without dispelling; **t24** brilliant: the delivery appears sweet from a double whammy of barley and young grain then moves off into different flavour spheres, the peat being noticeable but by no means weighty and drier vanillas and nutty toast dig deep; thick stuff, vaguely fruity now and then, chewy, nipping here and there on the tongue and roof of mouth; no end of ballast...and fabulous fun; **f23** the smoke now begins to take a firmer grasp, but the peat element is multi-dimensional, from cough sweet to kippers; predictably furry as it fades; **b23.5** I'll be honest with you, as always. Because of the large number of sulphured Bunnahabhain sherry butts I have seen over the last 25 years, I was a little bit apprehensive as to what I might find with this blend, having not tasted it for the best part of a year. Quite a few blends now have the tell-tale furry buzz of sulphur coming from them these days, a bit like that gray ring of pollution you see above the earth when flying. This has that dull buzz, but is certainly no worse than most other blends these days. Which is a relief, as this is a greatly improved dram where harmony has been restored. A thoroughly enjoyable whisky with just the right amount of bite and aggression when required, and it knows also when to relax and hold its quiet moments. A delight. 40%. Gordon Graham & Co.

Black Dog 12 Years Old batch no. 015, bott Nov 05 **(92) n21** distinctly nutty – especially walnuts – with no more than a hint of citrus lightening the deep vanilla and toffee. Gentle and attractively layered; **t23** soft grains delve gently into the tastebuds offering light oak and a distinct toastiness. The barley sweetness is relaxed and clean; **f24** traces of soft honey and a strand of marmalade welcome the visiting spices which cling to the subtle oils clamped to the roof of the mouth. Almost a near perfect finish for a blend this age. Stunning!; **b24** an altogether thinner style than Century but offering genuine sophistication and élan. This minor classic will probably require two or three glass-fulls before you take the bait... 42.8%.

Black Dog Century (89) n21 a big nose displaying grainy teeth at first but chunky fudge and dried dates weigh in impressively; **t23** mouth-filling and distinctly viscous, chocolate fudge clamps itself to the roof of the mouth allowing a lighter, teasingly spicy pulse to do its work around the back of the tongue while, a well-mannered sweetness lurks around every corner ensuring the oak is on its best behaviour. Big and complex! **f23** brilliantly long and chewy with the chocolate fudge **b22** I adore this style of no-nonsense, full bodied bruising blend which amid the muscle offers exemplary dexterity and finesse. What entertainment in every glass!! 42.8%. McDowell & Co Ltd, India. Blended in Scotland/ Bottled in India.

The Black Douglas bott code 340/06/183 **(84) n19 t20 f23 b22.** Don't expect raptures of mind-bending complexity. But on the other hand, enough chewability and spice buzz here to make for a genuinely decent whisky, especially on the excellent finish. Not dissimilar to a bunch of blends you might have found in the 1950s 40%. Foster's Group, Australia.

The Black Douglas Aged 8 Years bott code 348/06/187 **(79) n20 t21 f19 b19.** Slightly lacking for an 8-y-o: probably duller than its non-age-statement brother because of an extra dollop of caramel. 40%. Foster's Group, Australia.

The Black Douglas Aged 12 Years "The Black Reserve" bott code 347/06/188 **(87) n21** weighty and a bit of sweat from the interesting areas, if you know what I mean.... nice touch of smoke, as well; **t21** thick, soupy-caramel delivery with excellent early grain softness and a slow flowering of barley; **f23** comes into its own for a massive finish with burnt honeycomb and spice making this way above the norm finale. A real treat...; **b22** the toffee does its best to wreck the show – but there sre simply too many good things going on to succeed. The slight smoke to the nose delights and the honeycomb middle really does star. 40%. Foster's Group, Australia.

Black Grouse (94) n23 outwardly a hefty nose, but patience is rewarded with a glorious Demerara edge to the malt and oak: superb, understated stature; **t24** again the smoke appears to be at the fore, but it's not. Rather, a silky sweet delivery also covers excellent cocoa and spice **f23** so gentle, with waves of smoke and oak lapping on an oaky shore. Brilliant... **b24** a superb return to a peaty blend for Edrington for the first time since they sold Black Bottle. Not entirely different from that brand, either, from the Highland Distillers days with the smokiness being superbly couched by sweet malts. A real treasure. 40%. ☉

Black Ram Aged 12 Years (85) n21 t23 f21 b20. An upfront blend that gives its all in the chewy delivery. Some major oak in there but it's all ultra soft toffee and molasses towards the finish. 40%. Vinprom Peshtera, Bulgaria.

Buchanan's De Luxe 12 Years Old (82) n18 t21 f22 b21. Just don't recognize this as the usual ultra-classy blend you could put money on you'd normally get from this brand. The nose shows more than just a single fault and then the character simply refuses to get out of second gear. Certainly pleasant, and some of the chocolate notes towards the end are gorgeous. But just not the normal brilliant show-stopper! 40%. Diageo.

Buchanan's Red Seal (90) n22 clean with almost equal portions of grain, malt and oak; **t23** wonderful malt clarity guarantees a rare charm; the grains are crisp and amplify the barley sweetness; **f22** lovely sweet vanilla complements the persistent barley; **b23** exceptional, no-frills blend whose apparent simplicity paradoxically celebrates its complexity. 40%. Diageo.

Budgen's Scotch Whisky Finely Blended (85) n21 t22 f21 b21. A sweet, chunky blend offering no shortage of dates, walnuts, spice and toffee. A decent one to mull over. 40%..

Campbeltown Loch Aged 15 Years (88) n22.5 deft marzipan and smoke; **t22.5** firm, with ever-increasing oak but never at the cost of the honeyed malt; at times sharp and puckering; **f21** much grainier and firm; dries very slowly; **b22** well weighted with the age in no hurry to arrive. 40%. Springbank Distillers.

⠂⠄⠂ **Catto's Aged 25 Years (87.5) n23** age pours from every molecule, but never in a negative way: teasing exotic fruit states that a significant part is played by the malts; there is toffee (I sincerely hope not from colouring for a 25-year-old whisky!!!) that dulls things a little – and turns it distinctly Canadian in style - but a kind of distant smoked bacon on the wind brings life back into things; **t22.5** a soft, juicy arrival is punctuated by deliciously teasing spice; again there is a caramel kick which flattens things as they get interesting; **f20.5** dull, toffee caramel...we have returned to the tundra of Canada; **b21.5** at once a hugely enjoyable yet immensely frustrating dram. The higher fruit and spice notes are a delight, but it all appears to be played out in a padded cell of cream caramel. One assumes the natural oak caramels have gone into overdrive. Had they not, we would have had a supreme blend scoring well into the 90s. 40%. Inver House.

Catto's Deluxe 12 Years Old (79.5) n20 t21.5 f18 b20. Strange how a standard blend can completely out-manoeuvre its 12-year-old brother. Refreshing and spicy in part, but still a note in there which doesn't quite work. 40%. Inverhouse Distillers.

Catto's Rare Old Scottish (92) n23.5 the young Speysiders leap from the glass with joyous abandon while the grain looks on benevolently; **t23.5** various shades of citrus and juicy grass make for a mouthwatering experience; a soft honey strand adds the slightest touch of weight and the most delicate of spices chime in; **f22** medium length, with gentle vanillas balancing the sweeter notes; remains refreshing to the death; **b23** currently one of my regular blends to drink at home. Astonishingly old-fashioned with a perfect accent on clean Speyside and crisp grain. In the last year or so it has taken on a sublime sparkle on the nose and palate. Of its style, an absolutely masterful whisky which both refreshes and relaxes. Just so understated and classy. 40%. James Catto & Co.

Chequers Deluxe (78.5) n19.5 t20 f19 b20. Charm, elegance, sophistication....not a single sign of any of them. Still if you want a bit of rough and tumble, just the job. And make sure they serve it in a dirty glass... 40%. Diageo.

Chivas Regal Aged 12 Years (83.5) n20.5 t22.5 f20 b20.5. Chewy fruit toffee. Silky grain mouth-feel with a toasty, oaky presence. 40%. Chivas. ⊙⊙

Chivas Regal Aged 18 Years (73.5) n17.5 t20 f17.5 b18.5. The nose is dulled by a whiff of sulphur and confirmation that all is not well comes with the disagreeably dry, bitter finish. Early on in the delivery some apples and spices show promise but it is an unequal battle against the caramel and off notes. I keep being told that this is Chivas' flagship brand. Well, it's been a very long time since I last tasted a good one – and I've tried a few over the years, believe me. Maybe I'm constantly unlucky. Or just maybe it's probable that it ranks among the most over-rated whiskies in the world. 40%

Chivas Regal 25 Years Old (95) n23 exotic fruit of the first order: some pretty serious age here, seemingly older than the 25 years, **t23.5** mesmerisingly two-toned, with a beautiful delivery of velvety grains contrasting stunningly with the much firmer, cleaner malts. Softly chewable, with a gentle spice fizz as the vanilla begins to mount; unbelievably juicy and mouth-watering despite its advanced age; **f24** long, wonderfully textured and deft; some cocoa underlines the oak involvement, but there is not once a single hint of over-aging; **b24.5** unadulterated class where the grain-malt balance is exemplary and the deft intertwining of well-mannered oak and elegant barley leaves you demanding another glass. Brilliant! 40%. ⊙⊙

Clan Campbell (85) n20 t22.5 f21 b21.5. Pleasing and for several exciting moments appears to be returning to its big Speyside roots...before being upended by a toffee surge. Some redeeming coffee notes up the complexity levels again. Always worth a second pour. 40%. ⊙

Clan MacGregor (92) n22 superb grains allow the lemon-fruity malt to ping around: clean, crisp and refreshing; **t24** as mouthwatering as the nose suggests with first clean grain then a succession of fruit and increasingly sweet malty notes. A brilliant mouthful, a tad oilier and spicier than of old; **f23** yielding grain; and now, joy of joys, an extra dollop of spice to jolly it along; **b23** just gets better and better. Now a true classic and getting up there with Grant's. 43%. William Grant & Sons ⊙

Clan Murray Rare Old (84) n18 t23 f21 b22. The wonderful malt delivery on the palate is totally incongruous with the weak, nondescript nose. Glorious, mouth-watering complexity on the arrival, though. Maybe it needs a Murray to bring to perfection... 40%. Benriach Distillery.

The Claymore (85) n19 t22 f22 b22. These days you are run through by spices. The blend is pure Paterson in style with guts etc, which is not something you always like to associate with a Claymore. Even so, a livelier dram than it was with some delightful muscovado sugar at the death. Get the nose sorted (and do away with some toffee) and a very decent and complex whisky is there to be had. 40%. Whyte & Mackay Distillers Ltd.

Compass Box Asyla Marriage married for nine months in an American oak barrel **(88) n22** a soup of a nose, though slightly over oaked for perfect harmony; **t23** a big, sweet cherry tart kick off with custard and spices galooped on top; **f21** warming, spiced vanilla; **b22** a lovely blend, but can't help feeling that this was one marriage that lasted too long. 43.6%. Compass Box Whisky for La Maison du Whisky in commemoration of their 50th Anniversary.

Consulate (89) n22 t22 f22.5 b22.5. One assumes this beautifully balanced dram was designed to accompany Passport in the drinks cabinet. I suggest if buying them, use Visa. 40%.

Co-operative Group (CWS) Finest Blend (93.5) n22.5 indelicate, salty smoke makes for a very traditional blend aroma, the sort a generation back favoured by breweries for their pubs; **t23.5** absolute silk as some top grade grain slithers around the palate, taking with it some hefty traces of smoke; **f24** now really goes to town with the peat becoming solid enough to chew and the sweeter elements balancing with the vanilla and toffee theme. Long, with lapping waves of soft smoke seemingly never ending; **b23.5** on first tasting it is hard to pick that many differences with Arden House. You even wonder if they are opposite ends of the same bottling run. They could be, theoretically; but the depth to the peat and clarity and balance of the sweetness makes this a much more complete dram which, frankly, I could drink any day. Forget about this being a supermarket brand: a must experience for all true whisky lovers out there. A classic is a classic, irrespective of age or label and had only this been caramel free, mostly likely some kind of award winner. Glorious and a cap doffed to tradition: ee, me old 'ostelries of Ancoats wud 'av been proud! What I'd give now for a pint of Chesters'... 40%

Co-operative Group Premium Scotch Aged 5 Years (93.5) n23 no doubt about the malts being present and correct here: good earthy weight; **t24** absolutely brilliant delivery: smoky, thick and lush, but a wonderful molassed sweetness ensures everything stays in harmony; **f23** lightly oiled, a touch of vanilla, but that weighty malt continues to glow... **b23.5** not exactly what you expect from a budget blend: a beautiful whisky fit to grace the home of any connoisseur... 40% ⊙ ☉

Corney & Barrow No. 1 Scotch Whisky 12 Years Old (85) n20 t23 f20 b22. Attractive and beautifully structured, this would be a real classy stunner but for the overuse of caramel. 40%.

Corney & Barrow No. 6 Scotch Whisky (76) n18 t20 f19 b19. A raw, viperish blend that strikes immediately but sooths with an overly sweet, oily fade. 40%

Craigellachie Hotel Quaich Bar Range (81) n20 t21 f20 b20. A delightful malt delivery early on, but doesn't push on with complexity as perhaps it might. 40%

Crawford's (83.5) n19 t21 f22 b21.5. A lovely spice display helps overcome the caramel. 40%.

Cutty Sark (86) n21 t22 f21 b22. The malt bursts around the palate in playful tandem with the crisp grain. Just a strange dull note to the nose and finale on this one. 40%.

Cutty Sark Aged 12 Years (81.5) n18 t21 f21.5 b21. How utterly bizarre. After going a couple of years without tasting this, I thought they'd have ironed out the sulphureous kink by now! Agreeable blend once past it, though. 40%. Berry Bros & Rudd.

Cutty Sark Aged 15 Years (78) n19 t20 f19 b20. A strange case of deja vue! Precisely the same off notes I tasted a year or two back are still there: talk about consistency! 40%.

Cutty Sark Aged 18 Years (88) n22 much oakier output than before with only fragments of sherry; herbal; **t22** a safe delivery of yielding grain with out-reaching fingers of juicier malt; decent spice buzz as a bitter-sweet harmony is reached; **f22** cream toffee and custard creams; **b22** lost the subtle fruitiness which worked so well. Easy-going and attractive. 43%.

Cutty Sark Aged 25 Years (93.5) n23.5 the laziest smoke drifts aimlessly over rich honey-bourbon; **t23.5** for all the weight, a juicy maltiness sets the tone. Like the nose, a degree of bourbony richness pulses a honeycomb sweetness through that wonderfully silky body; **f23** late caramel brings a slightly premature halt but not before the most delicate wisps of smoke reveal themselves; very late cocoa re-lights the fire; **b23.5** outstanding whisky which does much of what you can ask of a 25-y-o blend. 45.7%. Berry Bros & Rudd. ⊙

Demijohn's Finest Blended Scotch Whisky (88) n21 strange, out of shape, but soft; **t22** salivating delivery with a wonderful firmness to the grain; the malts eventually mould into the style; **f23** remains tangy to the end, even with a touch of marmalade thrown in; **b22** a fun, characterful blend that appears to have above the norm malt. Enjoy. 40%. Adelphi

Dew of Ben Nevis Blue Label (82) n19 t22 f20 b21. A busier, lighter blend than the old Millennium one it replaced. The odd off-key note is handsomely outnumbered by deliciously complex, mocha tones with a touch of demerara. Ditch the caramel and you'd have a sizzler! 40%. Ben Nevis Distillery. Replacement for Dew of Ben Nevis Millennium Blend.

Dew of Ben Nevis Special Reserve (85) n19 t21 f23 b22. A much juicier blend than of old, still sporting some bruising and rough patches. But that kind of makes this all the more attractive, with the caramel mixing with some fuller malts to provide a date and nuts effect which makes for a grand finale. 40%. Ben Nevis Distillery.

Dew of Ben Nevis Supreme Selection (77) n18 t20 f20 b19. Some lovely raspberry jam swiss roll moments here. But the grain could be friendlier, especially on the nose. 40%.

Dewar's Special Reserve 12 Years Old (84) n20 t23 f19 b22. Some s... you know what... has crept onboard here and duffed up the nose and finish. A shame because elements of the delivery and background balance shows some serious blending went on here. 40%.

Dewar's 18 Years Old (93) n23 confident and complex, the nose makes no secret that its foundations are solid grain. From it hang a succession of nubile malty notes, weighty and not without a minor degree of smoke. The fruit has a strawberry jam presence, and there are spices, of course... **t24** entirely classical in its delivery: firm grain and rich, sweet malt linked arm in arm. Again the grain is bold and firm but tattooed into it is a buzzing busy maltiness, offering varying degrees of weight, sweetness and depth...; **f22.5** a build up of caramel begins to lessen the degree of complexity, though not the body and weight; **b23.5** here is a classic case of where great blends are not all about the malt. The grain plays in many ways the most significant role here, as it is the perfect backdrop to see the complexity of the malt at its clearest. Simply magnificent blending with the use of flawless whisky. 43%. John Dewar & Sons.

∵ **Dewar's 18 Year Old Founders Reserve (86.5) n22.5 t22 f20.5 b21.5.** A big, blustering dram which doesn't stint on the fruit. A lovely, thin seam of golden syrup runs through the piece, but the dull, aching finale is somewhat out of character. 40%. John Dewar & Son.

∵ **Dewar's Signature (93) n24** a stunning celebration of controlled grape: this is sweet-edged and of a distinctly sauturnes style. Elsewhere the oak offers a light vanilla haze and the barley is clean and relaxed. Just doesn't come much more sultry and elegant than this; **t23.5** as luxuriant a mouthfeel as you could pray for, but with some spicy sparks flying. The fruit continues to dominate while the grain must be distilled satin; **f22** some custard tart is about as aggressive as the oak gets, though there is an unwelcome buzz from a sherry cask or two; **b23.5** a slight departure in style, with the fruit becoming just a little sharper and juicier. Top range blending and if the odd butt could be weeded out, this'd be an award winner for sure. *43%. John Dewar & Son.*

Dimple 12 Years Old (86.5) n22 t22 f21.5 b21. Lots of sultana while the spice adds aggression. *40%. Diageo.*

Dimple 15 Years Old (87.5) n20 simple; **t21** a massive grain lead and with the shy malts all over the place at first, takes its time to get itself into any kind of order... **f24** the late middle shows signs of extraordinary complexity, way above anything that has gone on before. The finish, though, takes it to the next level. All kinds of small flavour explosions with little smoke and barley notes popping about the palate; with so much grain, no surprise about the big cocoa finale; **b22.5** only on the late middle and finish does this particular flower unfurl and to magnificently complex effect. The texture of the grains in particular delight while the strands of barley entwine. A type of treat for the more technically minded of the serious blend drinkers among you. *40%. Diageo.*

⌁ **Drummer Aged 5 Years (83) n19 t22.5 f20.5 b21.** The nose may beat a retreat but it certainly gets on a roll when those fabulous sharp notes hit the palate. However, it deserves some stick as the boring fudge finishes in a cymbal of too much toffee. *40%. Inver House.*

Duncan Taylor Auld Blended Aged 35 Years dist pre 70 **(93) n23** a knife and fork nose appears too oaked but time in the glass allows some excellent marmalade and marzipan to appear; **t24** glorious delivery: amazing silk, lots of gentle, natural caramel but topped with honeycomb; **f22** chocolate malt and burnt toast, **b24** only a handful of companies could come up with something like this. An infinitely better dram than previous bottlings, due mainly to the fact that the dangers of old oak appear to have been compensated for. *46%. 131 bottles.*

Duncan Taylor Auld Aged Blend 38 Years Old (86) n22 t22 f21 b21. Incredibly soft for all those years, but not a patch of the 35-y-o. *40%. 623 bottles.*

Duncan Taylor Auld Blended Aged 35 Years dist pre 70 **(93) n23** a knife and fork nose appears too oaked but time in the glass allows some excellent marmalade and marzipan to appear; **t24** glorious delivery: amazing silk, lots of gentle, natural caramel but topped with honeycomb; **f22** chocolate malt and burnt toast; **b24** only a handful of companies could come up with something like this. An infinitely better dram than previous bottlings, due mainly to the fact that the dangers of old oak appear to have been compensated for. *46%. 131 bottles.*

Duncan Taylor Auld Aged Blend 38 Years Old (86) n22 t22 f21 b21. Incredibly soft for all those years, but not a patch of the 35-y-o. *40%. 623 bottles.*

⌁ **Duncan Taylor Collection Black Bull Deluxe Blend Aged 30 Years (93) n24** fantastically rich: a real mish-mash of fruit, barley, smoke and, of course, oak....really has hit the bullseye; **t24** one of the creamiest-textured deliveries I've come across this year. Again the smoke leads, but there is so much else slushing around in these soft oils; the bourbony liquorice in the middle ground is sublime; **f22** long with a real tapering spiciness amid the molasses and vanilla **b23** this pedigree Black Bull doesn't pull its horns in... *50%. Duncan Taylor.*

Duncan Taylor Collection Rarest of the Rare Deluxe Blend 33 Years Old (94) n24 a heady fusion of rich bourbon and old Canadian characteristics beefed up further with diced exotic fruit and a dash of ancient Demerara rum Uitvlught to be precise; **t24** the bourbon hits the track running, closely followed by some silky barley couched in velvet grain; invariably some spices pitch in to ramp up the complexity even further; **f22** no great length, but no off notes, either. Instead the oak adds an unsweetened custardy grace; **b23** outstanding and astounding blended whisky. An absolute must for blend lovers....especially those with a bourbony bent. *43.4%*

Edinburgh International Festival bott 07, bott code 07/160 **(82.5) n20.5 t21.5 f21 b19.5.** An interesting, curious even, affair with untold grassy freshness and barley-enriched flavour. *40%. J & A Mitchell & Co. Ltd. 2007 bottles.*

The Famous Grouse (89) n22 a weightier aroma than Grouse once was. Not quite so clean and crisp; now a slight smoke can be detected, while honey threads, once audible, have to fight to be heard; once you get used to it, it is quite lovely...; **t23** a real surprise package for a Grouse, as this is no lightweight on delivery: the flavours come thick and fast — literally — though the intensity makes it hard to pick out individual notes; once acclimatised, there are distinct marmalade and custard qualities, but only after a brooding shadow of smoke moves out of the picture taking some honey with it; **f21.5** lots of mocha and cream toffee with the vanilla adding a dusty quality; **b22.5** it almost seems that Grouse is, by degrees, moving from its traditional position of a light blend to something much closer to Grant's as a middle-weighted dram. Again the colouring has been raised a fraction and now the body and depth have been adjusted to follow suit. Have to say that this is one very complex whisky these days: I had spotted slight changes when drinking it socially, but this was the first time I had a chance to sit down and professionally analyse what was happening in the glass. A fascinating and tasty bird, indeed. *40%. Edrington Group*

The Famous Grouse Bourbon Cask Finish (87.5) n21 pretty closed save for the caramel and light oak; **t23** bursts immediately into life with a major Speyside-style juice assault: sweet sugars melt into the malt – almost like a Milky Way candy bar; **f21.5** firm, grainy and finely textured; slow build up of spice; **b22** the extra oak sweetens things up pleasantly. *40%. Edrington Group.*

The Famous Grouse Gold Reserve (90) n23.5 ye gods! What an improvement on the last bottle of this I came across!! Really sexy complexity which, though showing decent weight, including delicate smoke, also celebrates the more citrussy things in life. At body temp the complexity of the structure and degree of layering goes through the roof...; **t23** honeyed to start, then an injection of lime and ground cherry; some caramel tries to interfere and to some extent succeeds; **f21.5** the toffee effect immediately curtails further complexity, but there is a slight spice rumble very late on and even a light sprinkling of barley grist; **b22** great to know the value of the Gold Reserve is going up....as should the strength of this blend. The old-fashioned 40% just ain't enough carats. *40%. Edrington Group*

The Famous Grouse Port Wood Finish (77) n20 t20 f18 b19. If anyone has tasted more different bottlings of Port Wood whisky, then I'd like to shake his hand: the sweaty armpit nose on this one really is unique. Pleasant, but first yawn, and then stupor-inducing as the fruit is lost without trace under the toffee. *40%. Edrington Group.*

The Famous Grouse Scottish Oak Finish bott Nov 05 **(95) n23** not dissimilar to the European oak of Czech whiskies, but better control. This seems to accentuate the smoke slightly and the grain is lost in a fusion of malt and butter. Really lovely – and very different: in fact unique to any blend I've come across; **t24** wow, wow, wow, wow, wow...!!! The mouth arrival is memorable and truly orgasmic: just wave upon wave of something beautiful, seamless and spicy. A kind of half-sweet honeycomb – all roast and chewiness – stars with the grains at last making themselves heard with a string of vanilla thrusts. Those spices pound the sides of the tongue and the roof of the mouth and the bitter-sweet balance is sensational. Just to make things better still, there is just the right degree of bite one desires in a blend; **f23** long, with mounting signs of oak dominance, but those glorious toasted-barley waves, now topped with muscovado sugar keep the blend honest. The final embers offer a surprising hint of juniper. Is that the oak...or the bottling hall?; **b25** what a stunner! What a one off....!!! Sadly, this is a limited edition blend...and once those 7092 bottles have been drunk, that's it! I sincerely hope they are already planting new Caledonian oak to make this a fixture on the whisky shelves for future generations! *44.5%.*

The Formidable Jock of Bennachie (82) n19 t22 f21 b20. "Scotland's best kept secret" claims the label. Hardly. But the silky delivery on the palate is worth investigating. Impressive roastiness to the malt and oak, but the caramel needs thinning. *40%. Bennachie Scotch Whisky.*

Glen Lyon (85) n19 t22.5 f22 b21.5. Works a lot better than the nose suggests: seriously chewy with a rabid spice attack and lots of juices. For those who have just retired as dynamite testers. Unpretentious fun. *43%. Diageo.*

Glenross Blended (83) n20 t22 f20 b21. Decent, easy-drinking whisky with a much sharper delivery than the nose suggests. *40%. Speyside Distillers.*

Glen Simon (77) n20 t19 f19 b19. Simple. Lots of caramel. *40%. Quality Spirits Int.*

The Gordon Highlanders (86) n21 t22 f21 b22. Lush and juicy, there is a distinctive Speysidey feel to this one with the grains doing their best to accentuate the developing spice. Plenty of feel good factor here. *40%. William Grant & Sons.*

Green Plaid 12 Years Old (89) n22 the smoke of old has been doused slightly, though mint comes through with the soft barley; **t23** light oils coat the mouth with a gentle sweetness; **f22** vanilla and a distant rumble of smoke; **b22** a beautifully constructed, mouth-watering blend. *40%. Inverhouse Distillers.*

Haddington House (85.5) n21 t21.5 f22 b21. Mouth-watering and delicate. *40%.*

Haig Gold Label (88) n21 somewhat sparse beyond a vague grapey-graininess; **t23** begins light and unimpressive, but about three flavour waves in begins to offer multi-layered spices and juice aplenty; the sweet-dry ratio as the oak arrives is brilliant; **f22** classy fade with a touch of Cadbury's Fruit and Nut in the mix as the spices persist; **b22** what had before been pretty standard stuff has upped the complexity by an impressive distance. *40%. Diageo.*

Hankey Bannister (84.5) n20.5 t22 f21 b21. Lots of early life and even a malt kick early on. Toffee later. 40%. Inverhouse Distillers. ☉ ☉

Hankey Bannister 12 Years Old (86.5) n22 t21.5 f21 b22. A much improved blend with a nose and early delivery which makes full play of the blending company's Speyside malts. Plenty of toffee on the finish. 40%. Inverhouse Distillers.

Hankey Bannister 21 Years Old (93.5) n22.5 a fruity ensemble, clean, vibrant and loath to show its age; **t23.5** every bit as juicy as the nose suggests, except here there is the odd rumble of distant smoke; mainly a firm, barley-sugar hardness as the grains keep control; **f23.5** the arrival of the oak adds further weight and for the first time begins to behave like a 21-y-o; long, now with decent spice and with some crusty dryness at the very death; **b24** a beautifully balanced blend that takes you on a series of journeys into varying styles and stories. Does the blend movement a great service. 43%. Inverhouse Distillers.

Hankey Bannister 25 Years Old (91) n22.5 a slight bourbony honey-hickory edge, to where the 21-y-o has fruit; **t24** a swooning delivery: just about everything in exactly the right place and showing sympathetic weight to the other. The grains are soft, the malts are sturdier and more energetic, the oak docile...for the time being; **f21.5** some bitter cocoa notes reveal the oak to be a little more militant but the light oils help the grains recover the position and balance; **b23** follows on in style and quality to 21-year-old. Gorgeous. 40%

Hankey Bannister 40 Years Old (89) n22 evidence of high malt levels here: pungent, nippy and lively. No shortage of over-ripe oranges, either.. **t23** juicy, salivating delivery with a silky texture to the grain bringing out the best of the intense, sweet malt; the fruitiness is mixed, rich and blunted only by the toasty oaks; **f22** pretty oak spattered with the grains continuing their soft theme. Enough barley remains to add another cushion against the age; **b22** "This is some of the last whisky produced before England won the World Cup in 1966," Gareth Stanley of Inverhouse gleefully tells me. Yes, Gareth. Thanks for reminding me. But at least I can look Alex Salmond and his brothers straight in the eye and tell him: "Well, at least we once won the bloody thing..." This blend, though, has been put together to mark the 250th anniversary of the forging of the business relations between Messrs. Hankey and Bannister. And although the oak creaks like a ship of its day, there is enough verve and viscosity to ensure a rather delicious toast to the gentlemen. Love it! 44% Inverhouse

Hedges & Butler Royal (92) n22.5 curiously salty and coastal, yet peat-free; the grains couldn't get much crisper; **t23.5** sharp, crisp grain working in complete harmony with the sprightly Speyside-style malts; all kinds of citrus, grassy notes; **f23** a lemon zesty liveliness refreshes and cleanses; some chattering, drier cocoa very late on; **b23** massively improved to become a juicy and charming blend of the very highest order. 40%.

Highland Bird (77) n19 t19 f19 b20. I've has a few of these over the years, I admit. But I can't remember one quite as rough and ready as this... 40%. Quality Spirits International.

Highland Black 8 Years Old Special Reserve (83) n21 t21 f20.5 b20.5. I still maintain that if they stripped out the huge caramel input they would be left with a really stunning blend. Peeling through the murk, there is enough on the nose and delivery to really enjoy, especially the muffled spicy kick. 40%. Aldi

Highland Dream 12 Years Old bott Jan 05 **(94.5) n23.5** all the hallmarks of a married blend, with a genuine silkiness to the nose and absolutely no sign of a suture between the varying smoke, oak and fruit styles and the grain; **t24** lavish and lush, something, possibly the grains, appears a lot older than the minimum 12 years stipulated; wonderfully juicy and chewy at the same time, the smoke gives intermittent pulses; **f23** smoky and softly oiled; plenty of vanilla and butterscotch; **b24** now that is what I call a blend! How comes it has taken me two years to find it? A wet dream, if ever there was one... 43%. J & G Grant. 9000 bottles.

Highland Dream 18 Years Old bott May 07 **(88.5) n22.5** huge sherry input; **t22.5** the silk you expect from this blend is there, as is a soft honey and fruit thread; **f21.5** light with the accent on vanilla and an attractive bourbony sweetness; **b22** perhaps doesn't get the marks on balance that a whisky of this quality might expect. This is due to the slight over egging of the sherry which, while offering a beautiful delivery, masks the complexities one might expect. Lovely whisky, and make no mistake: the type of which you'll find the bottle emptying very quickly during the course of a night before anyone quite realises. But, technically, doesn't match the 12-year-old for balance and brilliance. 43%. J & G Grant. 3000 bottles.

Highland Earl (82) n20 t21 f20.5 b20.5. Much more emphasis on toffee these days but beneath that is a very firm grain. Simple, but attractive. 40%. Aldi

Highland Gathering Blended Scotch Whisky (78) n19 t20 f19 b20. Attractive, juicy stuff, though caramel wins in the end. 40%. Lombards Brands.

Highland Harvest Organic Scotch Whisky (76) n18 t21 f19 b18. A very interesting blend. Great try, but a little bit of a lost opportunity here as I don't think the balance is quite right. But at least I now know what organic caramel tastes like... *40%. London & Scottish International.*

Highland Piper (79) n20 t20 f19 b20. Good quaffing blend – if sweet - of sticky toffee and dates. Some gin on the nose – and finish. *40%.*

Highland Pride (86) n21 t22 f21.5 b21.5. A beefy, weighty thick dram with plenty to chew on. The developing sweetness is a joy. *40%. Whyte & Mackay Distillers Ltd.*

Highland Reserve (82) n20 t21 f20 b21. You'll probably find this just off the Highland Way and incorporating Highland Bird and Monarch of the Glen. Floral and muddy. *40%.*

Highland Warrior (77.8) n19 t19 f19.5 b20. Just like his Scottish Chief, he's on the attack armed with some Dufftown, methinks... *40%. Quality Spirits International.*

Highland Way (84) n19 t20.5 f22.5 b22. This lovely little number takes the High Road with some beautiful light scenery along the way. The finish takes a charming Speyside path. *40%.*

Iona Royale 25 Years Old (89) n22 the rigid grain nails the malt to the glass. Yet there is something attractively of the dank forest about this; t23 hold on to something tight: several tidal waves of oak-spattered malt crash the palate; a second wave of barley remains fresh and salivating before drying with the warming grain; f21 lots of burnt fudge and vanilla softened by an evasive sweetness; b23 a massively malt-rich blend that piles on the complexity early on. *43%. J&G Grant.*

Islay Mist 12 Years Old (90) n22 Bowmore-style cough sweet dominates over the most gentle of grains; t23 decent smoke drive, intense at first then feathering out; remains sweet to the house style f22 long, back to cough sweet and a long fade of gristy, muscovado sugar; b23 adore it: classic bad cop - good cop stuff with an apparent high malt content. *40%.*

Isle of Skye 21 years Old (91) n21 sluggish: trying to work out its own stance; t23.5 sweet chocolate raisin, sumptuously brushed with a layer of soft smoke and demerara; f23 wonderfully deft spices nibble at the tastebuds like tiny fish at your feet in a rock pool; grains at last – soft and silky all the way; b23.5 what an absolute charmer! The malt content appears pretty high, but the overall balance is wonderful. A belter of a blend. *40%. Ian Macleod.*

Isle of Skye 50 Years Old (82.5) n21.5 t21 f20 b20. Drier incarnation than the 50% version. But still the age has yet to be balanced out, towards the end in particular. Early on some distinguished moments involving something vaguely smoked and a sweetened spice. *41.6%.*

James Alexander (85.5) n21 t21.5 f21.5 b21.5. Some lovely spices link the grassier Speysiders to the earthier elements. *40%. Quality Spirits International.*

James King (76.5) n20 t18 f20 b18.5. Young whiskies of a certain rank take their time to find their feet. The finish, though, does generate some pleasant complexity. *43 %.*

James King 8 Years Old (78.5) n18.5 t21.5 f19 b19.5. Charming spices grip at the delivery and fine malt-grain interplay through the middle, even showing a touch of vanilla. But such a delicate blend can't fully survive the caramel. *43 %. Quality Spirits International.*

James King 12 Years Old (81) n19 t23 f19 b20. Caramel dulls the nose and finish. But for some time a quite beautiful blend soars about the taste buds offering exemplary complexity and weight. *40%. Quality Spirits International.*

James King 15 Years Old (89) n22 t23 f21.5 b22.5. Now offers extra spice and zip. 43 %. .

James King 21 Years Old (87.5) n20.5 curiously inferior nose to the 15, thanks to the missing peat. Some dusty fruit atones slightly but mildly off key; t23.5 instant mouthwatering gait and a touch of exotic fruit and spice; the soft malt dovetails elegantly with the gentle vanillas; the starring role, though, goes to the wonderfully velvety grain which offers just enough backbone to help accentuate the malt; f22 dries as the oak and caramel gather intensity. Some very late spice does puncture – and punctuate – the cream caramel; b22 attractive blend, but one that could do with the strength upped to 46% and the caramel reduced if not entirely got rid of. One of those potentially excellent yet underperforming guys I'd love to be let loose on! *43 %. Quality Spirits International.*

James Martin 20 Years Old (93) n21 egg custard; t23.5 massive delivery as per the house style, but now we have a blend working in unison, with the malts having an unusually large say. The silky grains help accentuate the sweetness of the Speysidey barley and the milk chocolate middle holds up a hand of recognition to the oak and age; f24.5 long and exceptionally clever, with the denouement heading in several directions before settling for something a little spicy and continuing on the cocoa theme; b24 I had always regarded this as something of an untamed beast. No longer: still something of a beast, but a beautiful one that is among the most complex found on today's market. *43% Glenmorangie.*

James Martin 30 Years Old (86) n21.5 t22 f21 b21.5. Enjoyable for all its exotic fruitiness. But with just too many creaking joints to take it to the same level as the sublime 20-y-o. Even so, a blend worth treating with a touch of respect and allowing time for it to tell some pretty ancient tales... *43%. Glenmorangie.*

J&B Jet (79.5) n19 t20 f20.5 b20. Never quite gets off the ground due to carrying too heavy a load. Unrecognisable to its pomp in the old J&B days: this one is far too weighty and never properly finds either balance or thrust. *40%. Diageo.*

J&B Reserve Aged 15 Years (78) n23 t19 f18 b18. What a crying shame. The sophisticated and demure nose is just so wonderfully seductive but what follows is an open-eyed, passionless embrace. Coarsely grain-dominant and unbalanced, this is frustrating beyond words and not worthy to be mentioned in the same breath as the old, original J&B 15 which, by vivid contrast, was a malty, salivating fruit-fest and minor classic. *40%. Diageo*

J&B Rare (88.5) n21.5 the most youthful J&B nose ever: young malts and grain integrate well, but those grains really do appear still to have milk teeth; **t22.5** one thing about young whisky: it's packed with flavour. And here you go on salivatory overdrive as the sheer unopposed freshness gives the tastebuds goosebumps; **f22** clean, grain layered with soft vanilla; **b22.5** I have been drinking a lot of J&B from a previous time of late, due to the death of their former blender Jim Milne. I think he would have been pretty taken aback by the youthful zip offered here: whether it is down to a decrease in age or the use of slightly more tired casks – or both – is hard to say. *40%. Diageo.*

John Barr (85.5) n20 t22 f21.5 b22. I assume from the big juicy dates to be found that Fettercairn is at work. Outwardly a big bruiser; given time to state its case and it's a bit of a gentle giant. *40%. Whyte & Mackay Distillers Ltd.* ☉

Johnnie Walker Black Label 12 Years Old (95.5) n23.5 pretty sharp grain: hard and buffeting the nose; a buffer of yielding smoke, apple pie and delicate spice cushions the encounter; **t24.5** if there is a silkier delivery on the market today, I have not seen it: this is sublime stuff with the grains singing the sweetest hymns as they go down, taking with them a near perfection of weighty smoke lightened by brilliantly balanced barley which leans towards both soft apple and crème brûlée; **f23.5** those reassuringly rigid grains re-emerge and with them the most juicy Speysidey malts imaginable; the lovely sheen to the finish underlines the good age of the whiskies used; **b24** here it is: one of the world's most masterful whiskies back in all its complex glory. A bottle like this is like being visited by an old lover. It just warms the heart and excites. *40%. Diageo.* ☉☉

Johnnie Walker Blue Label (88) n21 the old, cleverly peated nose has been lost to us and now the accent falls on fruit though this is hardly as cleanly endearing as it might be; **t24** but the magnificence of the mouth arrival is back with a bang with the most sumptuous marriage of over-ripened figs, volumous malt and lightly sprinkled peat all bound together and then expanded by a brilliant use of firm and soft old grains. Spices also sparkle and tease. Magnificent...; **f21** oh, so disappointing again, with the plot played on the arrival and there being insufficient reserve to see off the broodier elements of the slightly bitter oak; **b22** what a frustrating blend! Just so close to brilliance but the nose and finish are slightly out of kilter. Worth the experience of the mouth arrival alone. *43%. Diageo*

Johnnie Walker Gold Label The Centenary Blend 18 Years Old (96) n24 at first it seems a level nose with little happening. But look again...deeper. Stirring in the glass are diced apples and moist raisins, a squirt of something peaty, and a honey and golden syrup mix. Sweet yet weighty with just enough smoke and oak to anchor; **t24** the silky arrival magnifies the smoky edge to this: some Caol Ila here, I guess, doing what Caol Ila does best – buck up blends. But also that hallmark honey thread is there to savour, linking beautifully with soft grains carrying vanilla and fudge; meanwhile playful spices...play!; **f23** a beautiful denouement in which the vanilla-edged oak refuses to hide, but smoke and barley dovetail in wonderful counterbalance; **b25** at the moment I would say that the blending lab at Diageo is going through a kind of legendary period. In years to come people will look back at it fondly and with a healthy degree of awe and ask: "do you remember when?"; or they will point to this era and say: "that's when it all started." White Horse 12, Old Parr and Johnnie Walker Gold: three blends where the gauntlet has been laid down to all: blenders and drinkers alike. And also where I say to Scotch lovers: well, you might love malts, but just how many can match these for brain-exploding complexity? This is another astonishing whisky which just has to be included in people's must have lists. Some of you I was talking to at a tasting in San Francisco, I think, will remember when I answered a question about age and blends: how I said that Walker's Gold appears to have older whiskies than when it was launched. Well this is because it slipped my radar that it was now a 18-year-old, rather than the original 15. Sorry about that. Age, as I have often argued, is as likely to do a whisky down as improve it. Certainly, though, not in this case... *40%. Diageo/John Walker & Sons.*

Johnnie Walker King George V db (88) n23 delicate smoke and honey with green tea. Unusual, but it works; **t22** good weight and spice buzz on delivery; melting grains help lighten the oak; **f21** gets lost in toffee. Pity... **b22** One assumes that King George V is no relation to King George IV. This has genuine style and breeding, if a tad too much caramel. *43%*

Johnnie Walker Red Label (87.5) n22 such a crisp delivery of grain; toffee apple, too...with young apples...; **t22** juicy and hard delivery, much in keeping with the nose; toffee arrives early, then a welter of malty blows; **f21.5** crisp grain again and the vaguest hint of smoke joins the vanilla; **b22** the ongoing move through the scales quality-wise appears to suggest we have a work still in progress here. This sample has skimped on the smoke, though not quality. Yet a few months back when I was in the BA Business Lounge at Heathrow's new Terminal Five, I nearly keeled from almost being overcome by peat in the earthiest JW Red I had tasted in over three decades. I found another bottle and I'm still not too sure which represents the real Striding Man. *40%. Diageo.* ☉

Kenmore Special Reserve Aged 5 Years bott code L07285 **(75) n18 t20 f19 b18.** Recovers to a degree from the poor nose. A must-have for those who prefer their Scotch big-flavoured and gawky. *40%. Burn Stewart for Marks & Spencer, UK.*

King Robert II (77) n19 t19 f20 b19. A bustier, more bruising batch than the last 40 per cent version. Handles the OTT caramel much better. Enjoyable, agreeably weighty slugging whisky. *43%. Ian MacLeod.*

❖ **Kings Blended 3 Years Old (83) n21 t21.5 f20 b20.5.** A young, chunky blend that you can chew forever. *40%. Speyside Distillers.*

King's Crest Scotch Whisky 25 Years Old (83) n22 t22 f19 b20. A silky middle weight. The toffee-flat finish needs some attention because the softly estered nose and delivery is a honey-rich treat and deserves better. *40%. Speyside Distillers.*

❖ **Label 5 Aged 18 Years (84.5) n20.5 t22 f21 b21.** A big mouthful and mouth-feel. Has changed course since I last had this one. Almost a feel of rum to this with its estery sheen. Sweet, simple, easy dramming. *40%. La Martiniquaise, France.*

Label Five Aged 18 Years L606133A **(87) n22** compare the nose with a fruit smoothie and try and spot the difference....! Some wonderful bourbony notes accentuate the age; **t22** the oils could not have been better placed and the integration of the soft grain and the slowly pulsing malt is a joy: simple but sumptuous; **f21** just loses its sure footedness with an overdose of flattening caramel; **b22** a lovely little blend with a genuinely first-rate mouthfeel. *43%. The First Blending for La Martiniquaise, France.*

Label 5 Classic Black L617456A **(75) n18 t20 f18 b19.** The off-key nose needs some serious re-working. Drop the caramel, though, and you would have a lot more character. Needs some buffing. *40%. The First Blending for La Martiniquaise, France.* ☉

❖ **Lang's Supreme Aged 5 Years (93.5) n23.5** outstanding barley-grain interplay, with the vanillas in fine form; all this underpinned by the most delicate of smoky, mildly seaweedy notes; **t23.5** a gushing early barley delivery confirms the relatively high malt content: Glengoyne's grassy fingers can be felt caressing the tastebuds before the gentle grain vanillas begin to soften things further; **f23** the smoke which made no effort to interfere with the barley-grain love in, reinvents itself as a soft, purring spice; the finale is as deft as it is beautifully weighted though the odd fractious sherry note can be heard and brings the score down a point; **b23.5** every time I taste this the shape and structure has altered slightly. Here there is a fraction more smoke, installing a deeper confidence all round. This is blended whisky as it should be: Supreme in its ability to create shape and harmony. It is the kind of whisky I like to have easily to hand around the home, a blend for every mood. *40%. Ian Macleod Distillers Ltd.*

The Last Drop (96.5) n24 aromas don't get older than this: positively Jurassic yet such is the balance between the sweeter honeycomb and still fertile oak, you can barely bring your nose from the glass. The oak is as old and rounded as an ancient shore-line tree worn smooth by a million waves. The predominant notes are 99.9% bourbony rather than Scotch-style, which is hardly surprising...; **t25** oh my gosh....this blended Scotch has transmogrified into the finest bourbon you can imagine: one assumes the grain content (which was then 100% corn-based) was high. And just as well because you will be hard-pressed to find something this glorious in all Kentucky. The intensity of the liquorice and honey is sublime, as are the lime and kumquat notes; the thinned out Demerara notes ensure just the right degree of sweetness....outright perfection....; **f23.5** miraculously there is not a single hint of bitterness for all the age though a firmness has developed which again points towards a significant grain contribution. Though the complexity may have lessened, there is no let up in overall quality. A touch drier, a hint of spice, a delicious layer of sweetened vanilla... **b24** how do you mark a whisky like this? It is scotch. Yet every molecule of flavour and aroma is pure bourbon. I think I'll have to mark for quality, principally, which simply flies off the graph. I'll dock it a point for not being Scotch-like but I feel a pang of guilt for doing so. This, by the way, is a blend that was discovered by accident. It had been put away many years ago for marrying – and then forgotten about in a warehouse. The chances of finding another whisky quite of this ilk are remote, though I'm sure the hunters are now out. It is a one off and anyone who misses this one will kick themselves forever. Astonishing. Unforgetable. A freak whisky at its very peak. *52%. The Last Drop Distillers Ltd.*

Lochranza (83.5) n21 t21.5 f21 b20. Pleasant, clean, but, thanks to the caramel, goes easy on the complexity. *40%. Isle of Arran.*

Logan (78.5) n19 t19 f20 b19.5. Entirely drinkable but a bit heavy-handed with the grains and caramel. It appears Logan's run continues, despite the fact this was meant to have reached the end of the line. *40%. Diageo.*

Lombard's Gold Label (88) n22 chunky with a good malt depth; **t22** silky and mouth-filling with the malts weaving beautifully into the grains; honeycomb towards the middle; **f22** delicate spice and toffee-nut; **b22** excellently weighted with some wonderful honeycomb and spice making their mark. *40%. Lombards Brands.*

Mackessack Premium Aged 8 Years (87.5) n21.5 orangey, grassy, caramel; **t?3** soft, with an immediate malty impact. Sweetens just as the spice arrives; **f21.5** dulls and dries as the caramel and oak take effect, **b21.5** claims a high Speyside content and the early character confirms it. Shoots itself in the foot, rather, by overdoing the caramel and flattening the finish. *40%. Mackessack Giovenetti. Italian Market*

Mac Na Mara Rum Finish (93) n22 as is often the case, the rum has hardened the aroma; **t24** beautifully crisp with fragile malts clashing with equally crisp barley; the touch of golden syrup works wonders; **f23** serious depth to the malt; the grains soften out with vanilla; **b24** this is high quality blending, and the usage of the rum appears to have retained the old Mac Na Mara style. Sublime. *40%. Praban na Linne.*

MacQueens (89) n21.5 a beautiful and very clever smudge of smoke gives backbone and vibrancy to an otherwise clean and delicate nose; **t22.5** lovely body and weight: voluptuous and silky, again with that delicate smoke intermingling with a caressing grain and sharper Speyside touch; **f22.5** long, beautifully structured with a soft, yielding oiliness that allows those soft sweeter notes to cling; **b22.5** I am long enough in the tooth now to remember blends like this found in quiet country hotels in the furthest-flung reaches of the Highlands beyond a generation ago. A wonderfully old-fashioned, traditional one might say, blend of a type that is getting harder and harder to find. I could drink this all day every day. Well, not really, but you know what I mean... *40%. Quality Spirits International.*

Master of Malt 8 Years Old (88) n22.5 high malt, it appears with the honey and butterscotch zooming in with ease; **t22.5** works exceptionally well with the silky texture early on allowing the malt to again shine ; **f21** toffee aplenty; **b22** understated and refined. *40%.*

Matisse 12 Years Old (90.5) n23 vanilla and citrus make comfortable bedfellows; dry Lubeck marzipan perfects the balance; **t23** mouth-watering with little grain evidence: the malt is clear, almost shrill; **f22** gentle vanillas and caramels; the spices arrive late; **b22.5** moved up yet another notch as this brand continues its development. Much more clean-malt oriented with a Speyside-style to the fore. Majestic and charming. *40%. Matisse Spirits Co Ltd.*

Matisse 21 Years Old (86) n23 t22 f20 b21. Begins breathtakingly on the nose, with a full array of exotic fruit showing the older bourbon casks up to max effect. Nothing wrong with the early delivery, which offers a touch of honeycomb on the grain. But the caramel effect on the finish stops everything in its tracks. Soft and alluring, all the same. *40%.*

Matisse Old (85.5) n20 t23 f21 b21.5. Appears to improve each time I come across it. The nose is a bit on the grimy side and the finish disappears under a sea of caramel. But the delivery works deliciously, with a chewy weight which highlights the sweeter malts. *40%..*

Matisse Royal (81) n19 t22 f20 b20. Pleasant, if a little clumsy. Extra caramel appears to have scuppered the spice. *40%. Matisse Spirits Co Ltd.*

McArthurs (89.5) n22 soft smoke rumbles about like distant thunder on a summer's day: the grains and light barley are bright; **t22.5** silky delivery with a slow injection of peat as the storm moves overhead; the degree of sweetness to the soft vanillas is sublime; **f22** gentle fade with the smoke rumbling though; **b23** one of the most improved blends on the market. The clever use of the peat is exceptional. *40%. Inverhouse Distillers.*

⠿ **Michael Jackson Special Memorial Blend bottled 2009 (89) n24** superb fruit, both grapey and citrussy, controls the shape of the vanilla which is closely tucked in behind; soft but not for a second docile **t22.5** full and fat, but never weighty, again there is a light touch to the juiciness; **f20.5** a touch of bitterness; **b22** whenever Michael and I had a dram together, his would either be massively sherried or equally well endowed with smoke. This is neither, so an odd tribute. Even so, there is more than enough here for him to savour, though I'm not sure what he would have made of the finish. *43%. Berry Bros & Rudd. 1000 bottles*

Mitchell's Glengyle Blend (86.5) n21.5 t22 f21.5 b21.5. A taste of history here, as this is the first blend ever to contain malt from the new Campbeltown distillery, Glengyle. Something of a departure in style from the usual Mitchell blends, which tended to put the accent on a crisper grain. Interestingly, here they have chosen one at least that is soft and voluptuous enough to absorb the sharper malt notes. *40%. Springbank Distillers.*

Monarch of the Glen (83) n20 t20 f22 b21. Elegant young whisky with a sweetish tinge and a lovely mixture of cocoa and barley at the death. *40%. Quality Spirits International.*

Morrisons The Best 8 Years Old bott code L6Q 6995 **(87) n21** a clumsier aroma than last year with the toast, grain and caramel still to the fore, but the vital honey and soft smoke now at a premium. Decent, but no longer great; **t23** weighty stuff with the grains showing a touch of class but the malt really fighting to battle through the toffee; the spices are superb, though **f22** long, pretty thick and chewy in places and at last some hints of oak amid the burnt fudge; some bitter notes where last year there had been none; **b21** I could almost weep: last year this was a blend to delight and win over converts. It was the whisky I was telling everyone to go out and get. This year, some of the traces of its excellence are still there, it remains highly drinkable, but that greatness has been lost in a tide of caramel. Yes, there was caramel used last year, but it had not crossed that fine line: here it has and paid the price and all the high notes have been ruthlessly flattened. When, oh when, are people going to understand that you can't just tip this stuff into whisky to up the colour – even minimally as in the case here – without causing a detrimental effect on the product? Is anybody listening? Does anyone care??? Someone has gone to great lengths to create a sublime blend – to see it wasted. Natural colour and this'd be an experience to die for. *40%*

Muirheads (83) n19 t22 f23 b21. A beautifully compartmentalised dram that integrates superbly, if that makes sense. *40%. MacDonald & Muir.*

Northern Scot (68) n16 t18 f17 b17. Heading South bigtime. *40%. Bruce and Co. for Tesco.*

Old Crofter Special Old Scotch Whisky (83) n18 t22 f21 b22. A very decent blend, much better than the nose suggests thanks to some outstanding, velvety grain and wonderfully controlled sweetness. *40%. Smith & Henderson for London & Scottish International.*

Old Masters "Freemason Whisky" (92) n24 t23 f22 b23 A high quality blend that doesn't stint on the malt. The nose, in particular, is sublime. *40%. Supplied online. Lombard Brands*

Old Mull (84.5) n22 t21 f20.5 b21. With dates and walnuts clambering all over the nose, very much in the house style. But this one is a shade oilier than most – and certainly on how it used to be – and has dropped a degree or two of complexity. That said, enjoyable stuff with the spices performing well, as does the lingering sweetness. *40%.*

Old Parr 12 Years Old (91.5) n21.5 firm and flinty with the grains comfortably in control; **t23.5** no surprise with the mouthwatering juice: the grains help the barley and soft fruit element hit top gear; delicate, light, teasing yet always substantial; **f23** mocha dominates with the vaguest hint of gentle smoke; the weight, length and complexity are stupendous **b23.5** perhaps on about the fourth of fifth mouthful, the penny drops that this is not just exceptionally good whisky: it is blending Parr excellence... *40%. Diageo* ⊙

Old Parr Aged 15 Years (84) n19 t22 f21 b22. Absolutely massive sherry input here. Some of it is of the highest order. The nose, reveals, however, that some isn't... *43%.*

Old Parr Classic 18 Years Old (84.5) n21 t21.5 f21 b21. Decent, yet in the Old Parr scheme of things, just doesn't do it for me. A real jumbled, mixed bag with fruit and barley falling over each other and the grains offering little sympathy. Enough to enjoy, but with Old Parr, one expects a little more... *46%. Diageo.*

Old Parr Superior 18 Years Old batch no. L5171 **(97) n25** here's a nose with just about a touch of everything: especially clever smoke which gives weight but allows apples and bourbon to filter through at will. Perfect weight and harmony while the complexity goes off the scales; **t25** voluptuous body, at times silky but the grains offer enough jagged edges for a degree of bite and bourbon; mouthwatering and spicey with the peats remaining on a slow burner. Toasty and so, so chewy; **f23** the vanilla is gentle and a counter to the firmness of the combined oak and grain. A flinty, almost reedy finish with spices and cocoa very much in evidence; **b24** year in, year out, this blend just gets better and better. This bottling struck me as a possible Whisky of the Year, but perhaps only an outsider. Familiarity, though, bred anything but contempt and over the passing months I have tried to get to the bottom of this truly great whisky. Blended whisky has long needed a champion. This grand old man looks just the chap. This is a worthy, if unexpected (even to me), Jim Murray' Whisky Bible 2007 World Whisky of the Year. *43%. Diageo/MacDonald Greenlees.*

The Original Mackinlay (83) n19 t21 f22 b21. Upped a gear since I last tasted this. Still a hard nose to overcome and the toffee remains in force for those addicted to fudge. But now a degree of bite and ballast appears to have been added, giving more of a story to the experience. Having said that, some 30 years ago this was my daily dram. In style it has moved away significantly. 40%. *Whyte & Mackay Distillers Ltd.*

Passport (83) n22 t19 f21 b21. It looks as though Chivas have decided to take the blend away from its original sophisticated, Business Class J&B/Cutty Sark, style for good now, as they have continued this decently quaffable but steerage quality blend with its big caramel kick and chewy, rather than lithe, body. 40%. *Chivas.*

⋯ v **Passport (91)** n23 crisp and clean, there are Speyside-style malts positively leaping from the glass. Salivating even before it reaches the lips, the grassy character absolutely exudes elegance; **t23.5** spot on grain-barley integration, with the malts always in control; the clarity of the malt allows for a beautiful citrus, mildly strawberry fruitiness to thrive and the oaky vanillas to build into a mildly spiced middle; **f22** drier, a little contribution from the caramel, but the vanillas hold out fine; **b22.5** easily one of the better versions I have come across for a long time and impressively true to its original style. 40%. *Bottled in Brazil.*

⋯ v **Passport (91)** n22.5 classic grain nip; **t22** firm, crisp Speyside-style juiciness, **f23.5** beautiful development of spice and prickle; **b23.5** a lovely version closer to original style with markedly less caramel impact and grittier grain. An old-fashioned treat. 40%. *Ecuador.*

Parkers (78) n17 t22 f20 b19. The nose has regressed, disappearing into ever more caramel, yet the mouth-watering lushness on the palate remains and the finish now holds greater complexity and interest. 40%. *Angus Dundee.*

Prince Charlie Special Reserve (73) n17 t20 f18 b18. Thankfully not as cloyingly sweet as of old, but remains pretty basic. 40%. *Somerfield, UK.*

Prince Charlie Special Reserve 8 Years Old (81) n18 t20 f22 b21. A lumbering bruiser of a dram; keeps its trademark shapelessness but the spices and lush malt ensure an enjoyable experience. 40%. *Somerfield, UK.*

Real Mackenzie (80) n17 t21 f21 b21. As ever, try and ignore the dreadful nose and get cracking with the unsubtle, big bruising delivery. A thug in a glass. 40%. *Diageo.*

Real Mackenzie Extra Smooth (81) n18 dull; **t22** a silk landing with crystal clear grains for a second or two, then the honied malt really takes off, and with it some peppers. A wonderful battle ensues; **f20** Where the battle once played out, the malt and grain become friends and smooch under a toffee umbrella; **b21** once, the only time the terms "Real Mackenzie" and "Extra Smooth" were ever uttered in the same sentence was if someone was talking about the barman. Now it is a genuine descriptor. Which is odd, because when Diageo sent me a sample of their blend last year it was a snarling beast ripping at the leash. This, by contrast, is a whimpering sop. "Killer? Where are you...???" 40%. *Diageo.*

Red Seal 12 Years Old (82) n19 t22 f20 b21. Charming, mouthwatering. But toffee numbs it down towards the finish. 40%. *Charles Wells UK.*

Reliance PL (76) n18 t20 f19 b19. Some of the old spiciness evident. But has flattened out noticeably. 43%. *Diageo.*

Robert Burns (85) n20 t22.5 f21 b21.5. Skeletal and juicy: very little fat and gets to the mouthwatering point pretty quickly. Genuine fun. 40%. *Isle of Arran.*

Robertson's of Pitlochry Rare Old Blended (83) n21 t20 f21 b21. Handsome grain bite with a late malty flourish. Classic light blend available only from Pitlochry's landmark whisky shop. 40%

The Royal & Ancient bott code L19.12.06 **(87)** n20 disappointing, dull toffee; **t23** fat mouthfeel with a beautiful burnished honey follow-through; no shortage of burnt fudge and biting spice; **f22** toffee has replaced the usual Demerara; the grain remains firm and friendly; **b22** what a shame: just a shade of carelessness with the caramel has shaved off the finer points. Last year a staggeringly good blend; this year simply very good, indeed!! 40%. *Cockburn & Campbell.*

Royal Castle 12 Years Old (84.5) n22 t22 f20 b20.5. Busy nose and delivery with much to chew over. Entirely enjoyable, and seems better each time you taste it. Even so, the finish crumbles a bit. 40%. *Quality Spirits International.*

Royal Household (90.5) n21.5 one is joyous of the occasion of the arrival of the smoke and all those other smaller, yet no less important constituents, such as the barley, grain and oak, which make this such a pleasing experience; **t23** my tastebuds and I are entirely delighted with the sophistication shown by the blenders by harmonizing the spices and soft peats to wonderful effect. One finds the sweetness towards the middle entirely to one's satisfaction; **f23** once again one finds the soft sugars a pleasure and it is impossible not to be impressed with the length to which, quite literally, this whisky goes to prove its very good breeding; **b23** we are amused. 43%. *Diageo.*

Royal Salute 21 Years Old (92.5) n23 has persisted with the gentle, exotic fruit but less lush here with much more punch and poke; it even seems that the smoke which had been missing in recent years has returned, but in shadowy form only; **t23.5** yep! Definitely more bite these days with the grains having a much greater input, for all the juiciness, and the vanilla striking home earlier. Makes for a decent sweet/dry middle, the sweetness supplied by boiled sweet candy; **f23** plenty of cocoa and the very lightest dab of something smoky; **b23.5** if you are looking for the velvety character of yore, forget it. This one comes with some real character and is much the better for it. The grain, in particular, excels. *40%. Chivas.*

Royal Salute The Hundred Cask Selection Limited Reserve No. 3 (90) n22 t23 f22 b23 Can a blend be too charming and well behaved? Elegance, or what? *40%. Chivas Brothers.*

Royal Salute The Hundred Cask Selection Limited Release No. 5 (93) n22.5 t23.5 f23 b24 This one reminds me of certain Japanese blends where there is a profound edge to the lighter malts which cut into the oak: a style rarely adopted in Scotland but employed here. A sophisticated blend impossible not to love. *40%. Chivas.*

⫶⫶⫶ **Royal Salute The Hundred Cask Selection Limited Release No. 7 (92) n22** a mixture of Caperdonich-esque exotic fruit and slightly over cooked, lactic oak masquerading as rice pudding; **t23.5** the silky glide onto the palate you'd expect from the nose and previous experience; some groaning oak arrives pretty early on; **f23** sweet, muscovado-sprinkled cocoa; **b23.5** it would be rude to ask how old some of the whiskies that go into making this one up are...As blends go, its entire countenance talks about great age and elegance. And does so with a clipped accent. *40%. Chivas.*

Sainsbury's Finest Old Matured Aged 8 Years bott code L7 109 **(83) n20 t21 f21 b21.** Reasonable fare with firm grain and a juicy depth. Lots of toffee. *40%*

Sainsbury's Scotch Whisky (82) n19 t21 f20 b22. Thinned out significantly over the last year allowing a pleasing degree of complexity amid the agreeable chewability. A great improvement: pretty good, indeed! *40%. Sainsbury's, UK.*

Sandy Mac (76) n18 t20 f19 b19. Basic, decent blend that's chunky and raw. *40%. Diageo.*

Scottish Chief (77) n19 t19 f19 b20. This is one big-bodied chief, and not given to taking prisoners. *40%. Quality Spirits International.*

Scottish Collie (77) n19 t19 f19 b20. Caramel still, but a Collie with a bit more bite. *40%.*

Scottish Collie 12 Years Old (85) n22 t22 f20 b21. On the cusp of a really classy blend here but the bitterness on the finish loses serious Brownie points. *40%. Quality Spirits Int. UK.*

Scottish Collie 18 Years Old (92) n24 the most gentle honey-ginger theme delights; aided and abetted by evidence of some very old grain which radiates succulent, over-ripe exotic fruit amid the drier oaks and gathering spices: a real, rounded charmer; **t23** those sweeter notes apparent on the nose are at the vanguard of a sublime procession of silk-edged barley; myriad sugar-coated notes ranging from acacia honey to maple syrup and brilliantly balanced by the slow march of drier oakier tones; **f22** remains soft and free from the usual Scottish Collie bitterness, though the toffee apparent sits comfortably with the toasty oak; **b23** this, honey-led beaut would be a winner even at Crufts: an absolute master class of how an old, yet light and unpeated blend should be. No discord whatsoever between the major elements and not a single hint of over-aging. Superb. *40%. Quality Spirits International, UK.*

Scottish Glory dist 02, bott 05 **(85) n21 t21 f22 b21.** An improved blend now bursting with vitality. The ability of the grain to lift the barley is very pleasing. *40%. Duncan Taylor. 960 bottles.*

Scottish Leader 3 Years Old (77) n19 t20 f18.5 b19.5. Still absolutely no pretensions about this from nose to finish. A bit rough and ready in places, but there is something attractively old-fashioned about it all. If anything, the toffee element has increased. *40% Burn Stewart.*

Scottish Leader 12 Years Old (82.5) n19.5 t21.5 f20.5 b21. Had a bit of a character makeover of late. The early fruit gets a little lost in the at times sharp, then ultra soft confusion which follows. On about fourth or fifth tasting of this – it needs that many to work out what is happening – it does begin to grow on you *40% Burn Stewart*

Scottish Leader Supreme 3 Years Old (83) n21 t20 f21.5 b20.5. Much spicier and weightier than of old. One of the most characterful, chewable blends around, and not just because of the extra toffee: there is even evidence of some smoke in there. Wonderful mocha at the death: love it! *40% Burn Stewart.*

Scottish Piper (80) n20 t20 f20 b20. A light, mildly- raw, sweet blend with lovely late vanilla intonation. *40%.*

⫶⫶⫶ **Scottish Prince 3 Years Old (83.5) n21 t22 f20 b20.5.** Muscular, but agreeably juicy. *40%. Speyside Distillers.*

Scottish Reel (78.5) n19 t19 f20 b19.5. Non fussy with an attractive bite, as all such blends should boast. *40%. London & Scottish International.*

Scottish Rill (85) n20 t20.5 f22.5 b22. Refreshing yet earthy. *40%. Quality Spirits Int.*

Something Special (85) n21.5 t22 f20.5 b21. The marketing guys missed a trick here. If only they had teamed up with Waddington's and sponsored Cluedo. Colonel Plum. In the

Library. With the Something Special Bottle. Let's face it, the one litre bottle of this has to be one of the most fearsome implements that one can legally buy over the counter today. However, its contents could not be more different if it tried. Mollycoddled by toffee, any murderous tendencies seem to have been fudged away, leaving just the odd moment of attractive complexity. Enough to make you think that there is a hit man in there somewhere just trying to get out... 40%. Chivas. ☉

Something Special Premium Aged 15 Years (89) n22 a vague, distant smokiness sits prettily with some fruity caramel; **t23** boisterous delivery with unshackled malt adding a wonderful, zesty spiciness amid much more mouth-watering Speyside-style fresh grass; the grain offers the desired cut-glass firmness; **f21** lots of vanilla and too much caramel, but remains busy and entertaining; **b23** a hugely enjoyable, fun whisky which pops around the palate like a crackerjack. Fabulous malt thread and some curious raisiny/sultana fruitiness, too. A blend-lover's blend. 40%. Chivas/ Hill Thompson, Venezuela.

Spar Finest Reserve (90.5) n21.5 fabulously clean, young grain offering butterscotch and toffee; elsewhere something earthy rumbles; **t22.5** brilliantly subtle delivery with silky grains ensnared in a sweet shell; towards the middle chocolate fudge and a distinctive smoky rumble forms; **t23.5** one of the best "supermarket" finishes to be found with a stunning array of clean, dapper smoke notes which cling, like softly oiled limpets, to the tastebuds for an improbably long time: lush and beautifully layered, this is masterful blending...; **b23** one of Britain best value for money blends with an honest (or as honest as any whisky with caramel can be) charm which revels in the clean high quality grain and earthier malts which work so well together. The mouthfeel and body are particularly impressive, especially the finish, complete with soft, smoky undertones. Greatly improved even on the last very good sample I came across. Very curiously, the buyer, or whoever, told us quite forcibly that he didn't want this whisky in my book and wouldn't send a sample. In fact he was so adamant about it his tone rather hurt and offended the feelings of my charming and good-natured researcher, Ali. Oh well, Mr. Buyer: isn't life full of disappointments! I'll bang the gong for this lovely whisky even if you won't, so that your customers and shareholders will benefit at least. 40%.

Stewart's Old Blended (93) n22.5 apples and date and walnut cake; clean and more delicate than the early weight suggests; **t24** sublime silky delivery with the slow erection of a fruity platform; the yielding grain cushions the juicy malt aspects; **f23** bitters out as some oak makes its play but firmer malt and molasses compensate superbly; **b23.5** really lovely whisky for those who like to close their eyes, contemplate and have a damned good chew. Voluptuous and as that chunky style goes, absolutely top of its league. 40%.

Swords (78) n20 t21 f18 b19. Beefed up somewhat with some early smoke thrusting through and rapier grains to follow. 40%. Morrison Bowmore.

Talisman 5 Years Old (85.5) n22 t22 f20.5 b21. Unquestionably an earthier, weightier version of what was once a Speyside romp. Soft peats also add extra sweetness. 40%.

Teacher's Highland Cream (90) n23 firm, flinty grain; a tad fruity with gently smoked malt-ensuring weight; **t23** mouth-filling with a tender sweetness; the grains seem softer than the nose suggests; **f22** toffee and lazy smoke; **b22** not yet back to its best but a massive improvement on the 2005 bottlings. So harder grains to accentuate the malt will bring it closer to the classic of old. 40%. Fortune Brands.

⋯ v **Teacher's Highland Cream (90)** n23 grain dominates, but not the old-fashioned sharp Dumbarton style. This is softer, sweeter with a topping of thick vanilla and butterscotch and delicate barley...where's the famous smoke...??? It's there, but the most distant echo; almost a dull background throb – for some Teacher's diehards, it is too well integrated....; **t22.5** as silky a delivery as the nose promises. Again the grain comes through loud and clear with the playful malts hanging on to its coat-tails. Only towards the middle do the two combine, and rather attractively and with style; **f22** much more spiced with a decided vanilla twirl; still virtually no smoke worthy of the name other than a vague oiliness; **b22.5** a very curious, seriously high grade, variant. Although the Ardmore distillery is on the label (though for the life of me I don't recognize it!), it is the only place it can really be seen. Possibly – no, make that certainly - the least smoky Teacher's I've come across in 35 years of drinking the stuff: the smoke is there, but adds only ballast rather than taking any form of lead. But the grain is soft and knits with the malts with ease to make for a sweeter, much more lush version than the rest of the world may recognize. 40%. Bottled in Brazil.

Tesco Scotch Whisky Finest Reserve Aged 12 Years (80) n19 t21 f20 b20. A thumping, thudding blend as hard as the granite rocks over which the waters ran to the Speyside distilleries used in the recipe. Value-for-money-wise, not a bad blend at all but for all the charm and mouth-watering properties of the malt, the grains are seismic. 40%.

Tesco Special Reserve (80) n16 t22 f21 b21. The sweaty armpit nose is relieved by the massively improved, rich, chewy and silky body. *40%. Tesco UK.*

Tesco Value Scotch Whisky (83) n19 t21 f22 b21. Young and genuinely refreshing whisky. Without the caramel this really would be a little darling. *40%*

Ushers Green Stripe (85) n19 t22.5 f21.5 b22. Upped a notch or two in all-round quality. The juicy theme and clever weight is highly impressive and enjoyable. *43%. Diageo.*

VAT 69 (84.5) n20 t22 f21 b21.5. Has thickened up in style: weightier, more macho, much more to say and a long way off that old lightweight. A little cleaning up wouldn't go amiss. *40%. Diageo.*

White Horse (90.5) n22 busy, with a shade more active grain than normal. But the smoky depth is there, as is a gentle hickory, butterscotch and fruity thread; a few bruising malts can be picked up, too; **t23** the usual sensual delivery, at first almost like a young JW Black, thanks to that soft billowing out towards the gentle honeys and juices; as it reaches the middle the clunking, muddied fist of some volumous malts can be easily detected; **f22.5** gets no less complex or more subtle as it develops; playful spices dovetail with vanilla while the smoke reinforces the backbone; **b23** a malt which has subtlety changed shape. Not just the smoke which gives it weight, but you get the feeling that some of Diageo's less delicate malts have been sent in to pack a punch. As long as they are kept in line, as is the case here – just – we can all enjoy a very big blend. *40%. Diageo.*

White Horse Aged 12 Years (86) n21 t23 f21 b21. enjoyable, complex if not always entirely harmonious. For instance, the apples and grapes on the nose appear on a limb from the grain and caramel and nothing like the thoroughbred of old. Lighter, more flaccid and caramel dominated. Just don't recognize it from the glorious beast that so often sat within arm's length of me in my home. *40%. Diageo.*

⁘ **Whyte & Mackay 'The Thirteen' 13 Year Old (92) n22.5** a fruity barley edge to this one; soft and enticing; **t23.5** a silky, mouth-watering delivery with some instant spices ensuring an immediate extra dimension. The sugars are muscovado toned, but with a pinch of molasses as a delicate bourbony sub plot develops below the tingling peppers; **f23** drier with some beautifully integrated vanillas and mocha: clever stuff; **b23** try this and your luck'll be in...easily the pick of the W&M blended range. *40%. Whyte & Mackay Distillers Ltd.*

⁘ **Whyte & Mackay Luxury 19 Year Old (84.5) n21 t22 f20 b21.5.** A pleasant house style chewathon. Nutty, biting but with a tang. *40%. Whyte & Mackay Distillers Ltd.*

⁘ **Whyte & Mackay Supreme 22 Year Old (87) n21** surprisingly rough and ready for a whisky so old; **t23** massive delivery: a real tidal wave of flavours, rather beautifully welded with all kinds of bitter-sweet battles and some spices fizzing around for fun; **f20.5** big caramel kick then a bit furry; **b22.5** ignore the nose and finish and just enjoy the early ride. *43%.*

⁘ **Whyte & Mackay Oldest 30 Year Old (87.5) n23** blackjack candy, punchy vanilla and apples: heavy booted but all rather sexy... **t23** the usual W&M full throttle delivery with fruity flavours galore; **f20** the usual W&M finale which is all a bit flat, tangy and furry; **b21.5** what exasperating whisky this is. So many good things about it, but.... *45%.*

Whyte & Mackay Original Aged Blended 40 Years Old (93) n23 anyone remember fruit fudge? Well, this is it in its toasted form; with burnt raisin and a Melton Hunt Cake. So yummy...!! **t24** appears to have some Fettercairn in there: nonsense malt when young, but when older opens up and delivers the kind of sublime, intense juicy dates to chew on here; also the grains begin to show a gossamer touch and, finally, a soft pastel-shaded barley sweetens the proceedings as the oak arrives; **f22** ultra-light and melt-in-the mouth **b24** I admit, when I nosed and tasted this at room temp, not a lot happened. Pretty, but closed. But once warmed in the hand up to full body temperature, it was obvious that Richard Paterson had created a quite wonderful monster of a blend offering so many avenues to explore that the mind almost explodes. Well done RP for creating something that further proves, and in such magnitude, just how warmth can make an apparently ordinary whisky something bordering genius. *45%* ☉

⁘ **Whyte & Mackay Special (84.5) n20 t23 f20 b21.5.** This has to be the ultimate mood blend. If you are looking for a big-flavoured dram and with something approaching a vicious left uppercut, this might be a useful bottle to have on hand. The nose, I'm afraid, has not improved over the years but there appears to be compensation with the enormity and complexity of the delivery, a veritable orgy of big, oily, juicy, murky flavours and tones if ever there was one. You cannot buy like it, in the same way as you may occasionally like rough sex. But if you are looking for a delicate dram to gently kiss you and caress your fever'd brow, then leave well alone. *40%.*

William Grant's 12 Years Old Bourbon Cask (90.5) n23 lively and floral. The drier notes suggest chalky oak but the sweet spiciness balances beautifully; **t22.5** flinty textured with both malts and grains pinging around the teeth with abandon; **f22** remains light yet with a clever, crisp sweetness keeping the weightier oaks in check; **b23** very clever blending where balance is the key. *40%*

William Grant's 15 Years Old (85) n21 t23 f20 b21. Grain and, later, caramel dominates but the initial delivery reveals the odd moment of sheer genius and complexity on max revs. *43%*.

William Grant's 25 Years Old (95) n23 some serious oak, but chaperoned by top quality oloroso, itself thinned by firm and graceful grain; **t24** sheer quality: complexity by the shovel-load as juicy fruits interact with darting, crisp barley; again the grain shows elegance both sharpening increasingly mouth-watering malt and softening the oak; **f24** medium length, but not a single sign of fatigue: the sweet barley runs and runs and some jammy fruits charm. Just to cap it all, some wonderful spices dazzle and a touch of low roast Java enriches; **b24** absolutely top-rank blending that appears to maximize every last degree of complexity. Most astonishing, though, is its sprightly countenance: even Scottish footballing genius Ally MacLeod struggled to send out Ayr Utd. sides with this kind of brio. And that's saying something! A gem. *43%*.

William Grant's 100 US Proof Superior Strength (92) n23 sublime chocolate lime nose, decent oak; **t24** big mouth arrival, lush and fruity with the excellent extra grain bite you might expect at this strength, just an extra degree of spice takes it into even higher orbit than before; **f22** back to chocolate again with a soft fruit fade; **b23** a fruitier drop now than it was in previous years but no less supremely constructed. *50% (100 US proof)*.

William Grant's Ale Cask Reserve (89) n21 old, peculiar aroma of spilt beer: pretty malty to say the least at this strength; but now with some vivid grain poking through; **t23** enormous complexity with myriad malt notes varying from sweet and chewy to bitter and biting; **f22** quite long with some toffee and hops(??) Yes, I really think so; **b23** a real fun blend that is just jam-packed with jagged malty notes. The hops were around more on earlier bottlings, but watch out for them. Nothing pint-sized about this: this is a big blend and very true in flavour/shape to the original with just a delicious shading of grain to really up the complexity. *40%*.

William Grant's Family Reserve (94) n25 this, to me, is the perfect nose to any blend: harmonious and faultless. There is absolutely everything here in just-so proportions: a bit of snap and bite from the grain, teasing sweet malts, the faintest hint of peat for medium weight, strands of oak for dryness, fruit for lustre. Even Ardbeg doesn't pluck my strings like this glass of genius can; **t23** exceptionally firm grain helps balance the rich, multi-layered malty tones. The sub-plot of burnt raisins and peek-a-boo peat add further to the intrigue and complexity (if it doesn't bubble and nip around the mouth you have a rare sub-standard bottling); **f22** a hint of caramel can be detected amid returning grains and soft cocoa tones: just so clean and complex; **b24** there are those puzzled by my obvious love affair with blended whisky - both Scotch and Japanese - at a time when malts are all the rage. But take a glass of this and carefully nurture and savour it for the best part of half an hour and you may begin to see why I believe this to be the finest art form of whisky. For my money, this brand - brilliantly kept in tip-top shape by probably the world's most naturally gifted blender - is the closest thing to the blends of old and, considering it is pretty ubiquitous, it defies the odds for quality. It is a dram with which you can start the day and end it: one to keep you going at low points in between, or to celebrate the victories. It is the daily dram that has everything. *40%*.

William Grant's Sherry Cask Reserve (82) n20 t22 f20 b20. Raspberry jam and cream from time to time. Attractive, but somewhat plodding dram that's content in second gear. *40%*.

Windsor 12 Years Old (81) n20 t21 f20 b20. Thick, walloped-on blend that you can stand a spoon in. Hard at times to get past the caramel. *40%. Diageo.*

Windsor Aged 17 Years Super Premium (89) n23 a fabulous aroma which bombards the nose with both luxurious grain and a hint of something smoky above the butter-honey theme; **t22** sweet, as is the house style, with a Demerara coating to the crisp malt and gathering vanilla; silky and voluptuous throughout; **f22** a gentle, soft-textured landing with an echo of spice; **b22** still a little on the safe side for all its charm and quality. An extra dose of complexity would lift this onto another level altogether. *40%. Diageo.*

Windsor 21 Years Old (90) n20 fruity and weighty but something a bit lactic and lethargic from some old bourbon casks has crept in; **t23** excellent oils surround the silk to help amplify the intensity of the fruit and drifting smoke; **f24** some spiciness that shows towards the middle really takes off now as drying vanilla counters the sweet grains; **b23** recovers fabulously from the broken nose and envelopes the palate with a silky-sweet style unique to the Windsor scotch brand. Excellent. *40%. Diageo.*

Ye Monks (86) n20 t23 f21.5 b21.5. Just hope they are praying for less caramel to maximize the complexity. Still, a decent spicy chew and outstanding bite which is great fun and worth finding when in South America. *40%. Diageo.*

⋰⋱ **Yokozuna Blended 3 Years Old (79.5) n18.5 t20.5 f20 b20.5.** It appears the Mongols are gaining a passion for thick, sweet, toffeed, oily, slightly feinty whisky. For a nation breastfed on airag, this'll be a doddle... *40%. Speyside Distillers. Mongolian market.*

Irish Whiskey

As is the way with Empires, they grow then blossom and, finally, fall. And so it is now in Ireland.

Until the advent of the Cooley distillery in the late '80s, all Ireland's whiskey was made under the umbrella of Irish Distillers. And for a short period in the '90s it looked like it would be so again when ID tried to consume Cooley whole. But they choked on it and had to spit out when the Irish Government ruled against the move in the interests of competition. Cooley continues to this day as a maverick distiller helping forge new interest and markets in Irish whiskey.

That left Irish Distillers' owners, Pernod Ricard, with Ireland's two other distilleries. In the south they held Midleton, near Cork, where their stupendous pot still whiskey is made. And in the north, just two miles from the cliffs of Antrim, the malt distillery of Old Bushmills dating all the way back to 1784. That was until, as part of Great Whisky Merry-Go-Round following Pernod's acquisition of Allied and all the resultant sell-ons, Diageo parted with the stunning sum of £200 million and in return got The Old Bushmills Distillery (Established 1784) and all its satelite blends and brands.

Forever, it seemed, Irish Distillers' blender Billy Leighton had been travelling to Midleton and back to Bushmills in a dual role as blender for both companies, though of course being an Irish Distillers man through and through but helping Diageo create their own blending team. With job accomplished at his spiritual home of Bushmills he let go of the ties that had held him to the wonderful old distillery for most of his professional life. Though his input at Midleton has already seen some interesting and sometimes quite fabulous developments, with an apparent improvement in Midleton Very Rare and his putting together of the stunning Redbreast 15.....and already a marked improvement in Redbreast 12. Long have I wailed and gnashed my teeth that more was not done with their pot still stocks, as relatively low as I know they are. For 17 years I have been pearching myself on the shoulder of every Irish Distillers executive I can find asking them to bring out pot still (that type of whiskey made from a mixture of malted and unmalted barley unique to Ireland - and now Midleton distillery in particular) as something above the usual Irish Distillers norm of 40abv and at a variation of ages. Yes, I was told. Great idea. It would happen one day, I was reassured. Just needed the stock. And the market.

They at last responded, I am told, to a request from by Le Maison du Whisky in Paris who required something similar to sell. The result was Redbreast 15 and Jim Murray's Whisky Bible 2007 Irish Whiskey of the Year. And a lot of interest from drinkers who before rarely gave Irish a second glance. Or chance. Now, if I can get a result for my constant beseeching them to tone down - and one day remove - colouring from Midleton Very Rare and Powers in particular....

Of course Redbreast is a straight whiskey. The next significant input was with a blend - and what a blend! Jameson Vintage Reserve may have been launched to the improbable sound - or should that be silence? - of Sinead O'Connor forgetting her lines when singing "Nothing Compares 2 U" at Midleton Distillery. Fortunately for Irish Distillers, the Jameson 2007 Vintage Reserve didn't fluff its lines at all, was entirely world perfect and, frankly, nothing compared to it within the Irish whiskey industry for the remainder of the year. Billy Leighton had written a number one. Elsewhere, it has been great to see Cooley recently grabbing the headlines and for all the right reasons. In March 2007 one of the most beautiful whisk(e)y sites in the world, Locke's Distillery at Kilbeggan, changed from being a sealed-in-aspic museum to a working one. Recently a second still has been installed there and is now contentedly making spirit from low wines produced at Cooley's original distillery up north.

This year, though, has been a relatively quiet one in Ireland. The recession has kept heads down and brows furrowed and there has been reports that for the first time in a very long while sales of Jameson have not continued their rocket-like projection upwards. But, there again, it was unlikely they would. New brands from them have been restricted to the wonderfully elegant Jameson Signature, though this has been eclipsed by the marked improvement to Redbreast 12. The most intriguing whisky has to be Writers Tears (sic), a blend I am told of Pot Still and malt from Midleton. Maybe it is, maybe it isn't. I didn't know they had made any malt there in years; and the blend is suspiciously like something I put together using Bushmills some years back. But Irish always did taste better with a little blarney, eh?

Key
- ● **Major Town or City**
- ⛰ Distillery

Pure Pot Still
MIDLETON (old distillery)

Midleton 25-y-o Pot Still db (92) n24 t24 f21 b23. A really enormous whiskey that is in the truest classic Irish style. The un-malted barley really does make the tastebuds hum and the oak has added fabulous depth. Interesting when tasted against an American rye – the closeness of the character is there to be experienced, but also the differences. A subtle mature whiskey of unquestionable quality. Superb. 43%

Midleton 30-y-o Pot Still db (85) n19 t22 f22 b22. A typically brittle, crunchy Irish pot still where the un-malted grains have a telling say. The oak has travelled as far as it can without having an adverse effect. A chewy whiskey which revels in its bitter-sweet balance. An impressively tasty and fascinating insight into yesteryear. 45%

Midleton 1973 Pure Pot Still db (95) n24 t24 f23 b24. The enormous character of true Irish pot still whiskey (a mixture of malted and unmalted barley) appears to absorb age better than most other grain spirits. This one is in its element. But drink at full strength and at body temp (it is pretty closed when cool) for the most startling – and memorable effects. I have no idea how much this costs. But if you can find one and afford it ... then buy it!!

MIDLETON (new distillery)

Green Spot (93) t23 mouthwatering and fresh on one level, honey and menthol on another; t24 crisp, mouthwatering with a fabulous honey burst, alarmingly sensuous; f23 faint coffee intertwines with the pot still. The thumbprint thread of honey remains but a touch more caramel than yore; b23 this honeyed state has remained a few years, and its shar ness has now been regained. Complex throughout. Unquestionably one of the world's greatest branded whiskies. 40%. Irish Distillers for Mitchell & Son, Dublin.

Green Spot 12 Year Old Single Pot Still dist 91 (93) n24 spices and zesty oranges abound, even a distant trace of coriander; uncompromising barley sugar and heather; t24 a stunningly wonderful arrival: layers of sweet malt at first, but that takes a battering from much sharper, more prickly grains and spices. An enormous, vigorous mouthful; f22 a degree of bourbon-style liquorice, vanilla and caramel; **b23** a single cask restricted to exactly 200 bottles to mark the 200th anniversary of the grand old man of Kildare Street, this is the first Middleton pot still I have seen at this strength outside of a lab. A one-off in every sense. *58%.*

Green Spot 10 Year Old Single Pot Still dist 93 **(92) n23** firm barley and orangey fruit with gentle hints of early bourbon: some serious ageing effect on this; **t22** mouthwatering and firm, then a gradual increase in the barley input and spices; **f24** shafts of honey throws a sweetening light on the bitter marmalade; **b23** launched to celebrate the 200th anniversary of this wonderful Dublin landmark, this is bottled from three mixed bourbon casks of Irish Pot Still. The extra age has detracted slightly from the usual vitality of the standard Green Spot (an 8-y-o) but its quality still must be experienced. *40%. Mitchell & Son. 1000 bottles.*

Redbreast 12 Years Old db **(96) n23.5** lively and firm, this one offering a gentle fruity swetness not too dissimilar to a rye, ironic as there is light bourbony kick off the oak, too; **t24.5** wonderfully clipped and correct in delivery: firm at first - very firm!!! - but slowly the barley melts and light muscovado sugars dovetail with a flinty fruitiness and pillow-soft vanilla; incorrigibly mouthwatering and the build up of spices is just showing off; **f24** remains spicy but clean, allowing a clear view of those varying barley tones drifting away; **b24** Yess...!!! Back to its classically classy, brilliant best. No sulphur casks this time (unlike last year). Just juicy pot still all the way. An old loved one has returned...more gorgeous than ever. *40%. Irish Distillers.*

Redbreast 15 Years Old db **(94) n23** seductive soft fruit wrapped in a hard barley shell. A slight soapy blemish, but minor; **t24** such enormity and depth fair takes the breath away; soft hints of citrus amid the pulsing grain. Stunning clarity and delicate spice. Extraordinary; **f23** multi-layered, panning out with barley-edged cocoa; **b24** for years I have been pleading for Irish Distillers to launch a pot still at 46%, natural colour and unchillfiltered. Well, I've got two out of three wishes. And what we have here is a truly great Irish whiskey and my pulse races in the certain knowledge it can get better still... *46%. ncf. France.*

OLD COMBER

Old Comber 30 Years Old Pure Pot Still (88) n23 t24 f20 b21. A classic example of a whiskey spending a few summers too many in wood: increasing age doesn't equal excellence. That said, always very drinkable and early on positively sparkles with a stunning mouthfeel. Out of respect for the old I have made the markings for taste cover the first seven or eight seconds... *40%*

Single Malt
COOLEY

Connemara bott code L5045 db **(85) n22 t20 f22 b21.** Better, but still not quite at its best as its finds balance hard to come by. *40%. Cooley.*

Connemara bott code L7105 **(87.5) n22** earthy and floral; **t22** delicate, soft delivery with the peats building to a muffled crescendo; **f21.5** burnt toast and distant smoke; **b22** another Connemara where the style is very much subdued. *40%. Cooley Distillery.*

Connemara bott code L8065 **(89.5) n22.5** sharper smoke – even a touch of Bowmore-style cough sweet; **t22.5** superb delivery of mollassed sweetness and darker, rumbling smoke; **f22** continues sweet and chewy with a late bite; **b22.5** a superb bottling much closer to its old self with the peats remaining delicate but occasionally having much to say. *40%. Cooley Distillery.*

⟨ **Connemara** bott code L9042 db **(88) n23** a bigger than usual salty, kippery tang; **t22.5** one of the more delicate and mouth-watering deliveries Connemara has given for a while: the peat is at once strident and meek but the subtle gristy sweetness is a constant and first class foil to the vanillas; **f20.5** rather short, toffeed and hurried; **b22** one of the softest smoked whiskies in the world which though quite lovely gives the impression it can't make its mind up about what it wants to be. *40%*

⟨ **Connemara Aged 8 Years** db **(85) n22.5 t21.5 f20 b21.** Another Connemara lacking teeth. The peat charms, especially on the nose, but the sub plot and complexity needs working on. *46%*

Connemara Aged 12 Years bott code L7171 db **(84.5) n21 t22 f21 b20.5.** The uncharacteristically low levels of peating on this one means that some of the oak's more militant notes have a louder say than they might. Delicate, even so. *40%*

∴ **Connemara Aged 12 Years** bott code L9024 db **(85.5) n23 t21.5 f20 b21.** The nose, with its beautiful orange, fruity lilt, puts the shy smoke in the shade. *40%*

∴ **Connemara 1995 Sherry Cask** cask no. V07/08 87, dist Oct 95, bott Oct 08 db **(76) n18 t20 f19 b19** Sulphured butts respect no international boundaries...and particularly love to hide behind peat. *46%*

∴ **Connemara Cask Strength** bott code L9041 db **(90) n21.5** a shrill peatiness fends off a determined, off-key vanilla attack; **t23** fabulous delivery: it's juicy, sharp, eye-watering malt all the way, with the smoke prodding the tastebuds here and there; spices as the smoke becomes a little more hostile; **f22** finally the vanilla gets to have its say; **b22.5** a juicy negative of the standard bottling: does its talking on the palate rather than nose. Maybe an absence of caramel notes might have something to do with that. *57.9%*

Connemara Cask Strength bott code L7016 **(94) t21.5** prickly; the deft smoke is equalled by the oak input; **t24.5** gorgeous, nigh flawless delivery: every aspect from the mouth-watering grassy barley right through to the hickory and forever billowing smoke just melts in the mouth; **f24** long and even, the smoke hits every crevice whilst the bitter-sweet edge is stunningly sharp; **b24** a malt which, since its very first day, has always been at its best when at full strength doesn't disappoint. But for dud-oak nose, this would have been an award-winner. *57.9%. Cooley Distillery.*

Connemara Single Cask cask no. 4086, dist Aug 92, bott Mar 07 db **(88) n22.5** drier smoke than the norm for a Connemara despite the squeeze of citrus, **t22** sharp, chewy, at times tinderbox dry; **f21.5** some thumping oak takes the dryness down to new cocoa powder levels; **b22** a dry, peated Irish, anyone...? *46%*

Locke's Aged 8 Years bott code L8076 **(88) n22** the light citrus and sturdier oak are decent nose-fellows; **t22.5** a sharp, eye-waterer. The malt is profound and as it tries to get all juicy, is brought back to a more sawdusty earth; **f21.5** dry and with more oak around than you might epect for something of such tender years; **b22** a lovely malt that will appease those a drier disposition. *40%*

∴ **Locke's Aged 8 Years** bott code L9005 db **(88) n22.5** excellent, rousing citrus; **t22** begins bright fresh and sharp, clouds over slightly with caramel; **f22** barley loses its toffeed marker from time to time to complete a juicy experience; **b21.5** a beautiful malt at probably this distillery's optimum age. *40%*

Locke's Aged 8 Years Crock (92) n23 pounding, intense, grassy-sweet barley; **t24** excellent mouth arrival and almost immediately a honey-rich delivery of lush, slightly oily malt: wonderful, wonderful stuff! **f22** soft oak tempers the barley and a degree of toffee digs in and flattens the .....; **b23** much, much better cask selection than of old: some real honey casks here. A crock of gold...! *40%*.

∴ **Locke's Aged 9 Years Grand Crew** dist 08/02/00 bott 18/09/09 cask no 696 db **(93.5) n23** distinctly peppery with the odd alternating phrase of celery and citrus; the background, though, is lively – and lovely – barley with a curiously salty edge to the vanilla. Busy or what....? **t24** now that's exactly how a Cooley delivery should be: the malt is juicy enough to show its relative youth. But loads of complexity, triggered by the mixture of incendiary spices – as promised on the nose – and backed up by the big alcohol kick. But the controlled barley sweetness is sovereign while the oak is impeccably behaved and adds no more weight than is required; **f23** those who love chocolaty finishes will be chocoholics by the end of this one.... **b23.5** after a string of some indifferent whiskies (away from Ireland), what a pleasure to be confronted by this near faultless little cracker: fair takes me back to the days when I picked and vatted the Knappogue casks; and I still maintain the malt from this distillery is at its most fascinating and charming at between 7 and 9 years. This excellent bottling, from a cask selected by the new Irish Whisky Society, is to help raise awareness of the pitiful state of the historic canals which surround the old Locke's Distillery at Kilbeggan. Great name, Grand Crew. Mind you, as it is one for the canals, Lock's Grand Crew would have been better still, surely... *59.4%. 216 botts*

The Tyrconnell bott code L8058 db **(86.5) n21.5 t21.5 f22 b21.5.** Weighty, well-oaked malt. *40%*

∴ **The Tyrconnell** bott code L9074 db **(86) n21 t22 f22 b21.** Sweet, soft, chunky and with a finely spice finale. *40%*

∴ **The Tyrconnell Aged 10 Years Madeira Finish** bott code L8136 db **(91) n23** a dull, rumbling marmalade bitter-sweetness, milk toffee and more delicate, twittering marzipan; **t23** lush and fat, the sharpness is confined to the odd exploratory fizz of indeterminate fruit:

purrs along very pleasantly; **f22** toffee raisin; very late spiced apricot; **b23** not quite the award-winning effort of a few years back, as those lilting high notes which so complimented the baser fruit tones haven't turned up here. But remains in the top echelon and still much here to delight the palate. *46%*

The Tyrconnell Aged 10 Years Madeira Finish db **(95) n24** apricots jelly, marzipan and orange-mango hybrid: just about unique; **t24** supreme balance of oil to barley with intense malt spinning around the tastebuds, kept in company by an astonishingly thick oaky-fruity-milkycocoa backdrop; **f23** banana milkshake and vanilla; **b24** this has to be one of the finest Madeira finishes I've ever come across. The balance defies belief while the higher notes make one purr. I am quite astonished. *46%*

⠂⠄ **The Tyrconnell Aged 10 Years Port Finish** bott code L8167 db **(81.5) n21.5 t21 f19 b20.** Toffee all the way. *46%*

The Tyrconnell Aged 10 Years Port Finish db **(93) n23** puckering fruit with a hint of spicy menace; **t23** firm body at first – to the point of shattering; oils out rather beautifully with a touch of raspberry preserve before going all solid again; **f24** very soft spices and lots of fruity cocoa; **b24** Cooley has excelled with its first serious foray into cask finishing. I didn't think this could be topped – until I came across the Madeira version. This, though, is like a fruit and nut chocolate bar – without the nuts. Wonderful. *46%*

The Tyrconnell Aged 10 Years Sherry Finish bott code L8074 db **(78) n20 t21 f18 b19.** One of the great things about Cooley whisky is you know that they hardly ever fill into sherry butt. Therefore you know that sulphur won't be a problem. However, when you see that they have finished a whisky in sherry, your nerves twitch as you know the odds of the whisky improving. Actually, for a few wonderful moments on the palate this one does come alive and sing. But the finish more forcefully confirms what you have already faintly detected on the nose. Boys: you make an exceptional whisky. Why fall into fatal traps? *46%*

⠂⠄ **The Tyrconnell Aged 10 Years Sherry Finish** bott code L8168 db **(84) n22 t21 f21 b20.** Like the Port Cask in this present series we have a thick malt that is friendly, toffeed and generally flat. This one, though, does have the odd peak of grapey richness, but you have to travel through a few plateaux to reach them. *46%*

The Tyrconnell Aged 14 Years cask no. 3179, rotation K92/25 db **(93) n23** apple blossom (no, honestly!), cedar wood and still remnants of ultra clean barley; **t23** refreshingly rich barley offering a shard of golden syrup to its perfectly lush delivery; **f23** long, soft vanilla, a touch of tannin and those continuing gentle oils....sigh, what bliss!! **b24** By rotation, K92 means it was distilled in 1992. Which just proves this distillery really has come of age, because, make no mistake, this is a belter.... *46%*

⠂⠄ **The Tyrconnell Aged 15 Years Single Cask** cask no. 1854/92 db **(92.5) n24** outstanding malt and vanilla interaction: the two poles have met and intertwined to offer maximum complexity; stunning, deft floral notes keep the odd squeak of citrus under control. One of the most beautifully structured Irish noses of the year; **t23** like the nose, the weight is outstanding and the march of the juicy barley a treat; soft vanillas and engagingly shy spices fill in the middle ground; **f22.5** biscuity sweetness before some exhibition cocoa; **b23** infinitely more comfortable in its aging skin a similar malt I tasted in Canada last year. *46%*

The Tyrconnell Single Cask cask no. 351, casked 24 Jan 92, bott 9 May 07 db **(93.5) n23.5** this is just showing off...excellent complexity with the fruity barley shining at so many different levels; **t24** juicy to the point you drown in your own saliva: few 15-year-old malts show this degree of barley clarity, as if every grain has its own edge; **f23** just wonderful spicing to add further structure and polish; soft boiled cooking apples offer an unexpected fruit edge; **b23.5** stunningly juicy with the barley at its most intense and brittle. Bears absolutely no relationship to the average 15-y-o single malt. *46%*

The Tyrconnell Single Cask cask no. 354, casked 24 Jan 92 db **(95.5) n24** that morning-baked custard tart; that morning prepared lemon drizzle; malt shake - with extra malt; **t24.5** you cannot but whimper and sigh on delivery, the tastebuds cannot but pucker; the saliva glands go into overdrive; layer upon layer of acacia honey and mollassed sugar, but all with a bold of barley through them; the overall intensity, even at 46% is near immeasurable; **f23** a slow, rhythmic pulsing of spice, the higher notes of unfettered, ultra clean barley; slow, shuddering jolts of oaky vanilla; **b24** lucky bloody Yanks!! What they have done to deserve a 15-year-old cask of whiskey of such age-defying magnitude, I can only imagine. I'll have to get my PA to book the next flight across The Pond, because this is unmolested Irish malt at its purest and finest. Just timeless brilliance: a classic in every definition. *46%. USA Market.*

The Tyrconnell Single Cask cask no. 356, casked 24 Jan 92, bott 9 May 07 db **(87) n22.5** vanilla and barley in dead equal measures; **t23** a sumptuous fanfare of almost the most intense barley imaginable, all dusted by the most delicate layer of muscovado sugar; **f20** the oaky caramel fights back gamefully; **b21.5** lots of natural caramel amid the massive barley. 46%. For Miniatures.

The Tyrconnell Single Cask cask no. 359, casked 24 Jan 92, bott 9 May 07 db **(84) n21 t22 f20 b21.** Lively and juicy early on with the usual Cooley big malt. Refuses to up the pace complexity-wise, though the gentle spices excel. 46%. For Dugas, France.

The Tyrconnell Single Cask cask no. 360, casked 24 Jan 92, bott 9 May 07 db **(82) n21 t21 f19 b21.** The danger of older malts comes, usually, from within: the cask. This cask has offered lots of natural caramel. Hugely drinkable, even so. 46%

The Tyrconnell Single Cask cask no. 3179, casked 7 Jul 92, bott 29 Nov 06 db **(88) n21.5** slightly off beam for all its grassiness; **t23** whatever oils were interfering with the nose makes amends here with an enormous delivery: you almost swoon with the fabulous intensity of the barley; **f21** annoyingly bitter, but some unravelling spices help; **b22.5** the odd bum note, but a real mouthful of a malt. 46%. For Ireland Market.

The Tyrconnell Single Cask cask no. 9571/1992 db **(85.5) n23 t21 f20.5 b21.** The wonderful citrus notes on the nose are swamped by the oak further down the line. There is no doubting the age of this Cooley! 46%

The Tyrconnell Willow Park Aged 15 Years cask no. 349/92 "The first private bottled single cask in North America" db **(87) n21** showing distinct signs of stress from age, but some excellent banana and barley notes impress; **t22** voluptuous mouth-feel but the oak arrives early straining at the leash; **f22** lots of caramel notes thankfully punctuated by citrus; a late malt surge helps; **b22** a beautiful whisky, in many respects due to the simplicity as the label says, but one on its way down. Remember: we are on a learning curve as regards Cooley. It is a new distillery and we just don't know how the malt will hold up. On this evidence it is reaching its limits and I suspect that had this been bottled two or three years earlier the points would have been considerably higher. That said, enjoy: it is still a delicious experience. 46%

Cadenhead's Cooley Aged 13 Years bott 05 **(93) n24** attractively smoked: orange and mango juice with the kippers; **t23** multi-shaded smoke fighting on varying levels with an influx of natural oaky-caramel and unusual oils; **f23** prickly spices and then a rerun to a semi-gristy sweetness; **b23** absolutely top-rate peaty Irish. 60.6%. 228 bottles.

Cadenhead's Cooley Aged 13 Years bott 05 **(93) n24** attractively smoked: orange and mango juice with the kippers; **t23** multi-shaded smoke fighting on varying levels with an influx of natural oaky-caramel and unusual oils; **f23** prickly spices and then a rerun to a semi-gristy sweetness; **b23** absolutely top-rate peaty Irish. 60.6%. 228 bottles.

Cadenhead's Cooley Aged 14 Years bott May 06 **(80) n20 t21 f19 b20.** Slightly hot and perhaps not from the best bourbon barrel to visit Ireland. 58.7%. 222 btls.

Cadenhead's World Whiskies Cooley Aged 15 Years bourbon barrel, bott May 07 **(94) n23** perhaps as nonchalant a peat delivery as you are likely to find — kilny yet so clean! **t24** soft and silky oils carrying the most sensual, sweet and mildly gristy peat imaginable: sublime.. **f23** long fade with again those perfectly-weighted oily peats callings all the shots... **b24** perhaps the oldest Irish peated single barrel malt to hit the market for over a century, this is nigh on faultless and a revelation... 58.6%. 222 bottles.

Clonmel Peated Aged 8 Years **(86) n22 t23 f20 b21.** Take the toffee away and you have one hell of an Irish. Claims to be "Pure Pot Still". It isn't (in Irish terms): it's malt. 40%. Celtic Whisky Compagnie.

Craoi na Mona Irish Malt Whiskey (68) n16 t18 f17 b17. I'm afraid my Gaelic is slipping these days: I assume Craoi na Mona means "Feinty, badly made smoky malt"... (that's the end of my tasting for the day...) 40%

Glen Dimplex (88) n23 solid malt with a hint of honey; charming, blemish-free; **t22** gentle development of the malts over simple dusty vanilla; **f21** quite dry, spiced and a little toffeed; **b22** overall, clean and classically Cooley. 40%.

Jon, Mark and Robbo's The Smooth Sweeter One Irish Malt (89) n22 a dry, oak-rich vanilla aroma with barley, dried pine nuts and distant honeybourbon to balance; **t23** much more fresh and mouthwatering than the nose suggests with a thick dollop of honey for the main theme: pretty young, almost embryonic, whiskey; **f22** decent spice, nut oils and then more vanilla and late cocoa-caramel; **b22** seriously enjoyable whiskey for all its youth, especially for those with a sweet tooth. 40%. Easy Drinking Whisky Co.

Knappogue Castle 1990 (91) n22 t23 f22 b24. For a light whiskey this shows enormous complexity and depth. Genuine balance from nose to finish; refreshing and dangerously more-ish. Entirely from bourbon cask and personally selected and vatted by a certain Jim Murray. 40%. nc. Great Spirits.

Knappogue Castle 1991 (90) n22 t23 f22 b23. Offers rare complexity for such a youthful malt especially in the subtle battles that rage on the palate between sweet and dry, malt and oak and so on. The spiciness is a great foil for the malt. Each cask picked and vatted by the author. 40%. nc. Great Spirits.

Knappogue Castle 1992 (94) n23 t23 f24 b24. A different Knappogue altogether from the delicate, ultra-refined type. This expression positively revels in its handsome ruggedness and muscular body: a surprisingly bruising yet complex malt that always remains balanced and fresh – the alter-ego of the '90 and '91 vintages. I mean, as the guy who put this whiskey together, what do you expect? But it's not bad if I say so myself and was voted the USA's No. 1 Spirit. Virtually all vanished, but worth getting a bottle if you can find it (I don't receive a penny – I was paid as a consultant!). 40%. nc. Great Spirits.

Knappogue Castle 1993 (see under Bushmills)

Knappogue Castle 1994 (see under Bushmills)

Magilligan Cooley Pure Pot Still Single Malt (91) n22 slightly waxy and honeyed: Cooley at its softest; **t22** beautiful arrival of highly intense, spotlessly clean malt. The sweetness level is near perfect; **f24** spiceless – unlike the previous bottling. Now just the longest fade-out of malt concentrate in Irish whiskey...and with a touch of honey for good measure; **b23** ...or maybe not..!! 43%. Ian MacLeod.

Magilligan Irish Whiskey Peated Malt 8 Years Old (89) n21 old, blackening banana and peat; **t23** lush, sweet barley, wonderfully oiled with the softest injection of smoke; **f22** long, long fade with those oils working wonders. The smoke gathers in intensity considerably before dispersing; **b23** such a different animal from the docile creature that formally passed as Magilligan peated. Quite lovely...and very classy. 43%. Ian Macleod Distillers.

Merry's Single Malt (83) n20 t22 f20 b21. Ultra-clean barley rich nose is found on the early palate. The finish is flat, though. 40%

Michael Collins Irish Whiskey Single Malt db **(76) n20 t19 f19 b18.** The sooner some people in this industry realize that Cooley is far too good and delicate a malt to withstand this insane degree of caramel, the better off everyone will be. 40% (80 proof).

Michael Collins Irish Whiskey Single Malt db **(68) n17 t18 f17 b16.** Bloody hell, I thought. Didn't anyone get my message from last year? Apparently not – and it's our fault as the tasting notes above were accidentally edited out before they went in. Sorry. But the caramel in the latest bottling has been upped to take the whisky from deep gold to bronze. Making this among the most over-coloured single malt I have tasted in years. Please guys. For the love of whiskey. Please let us taste exactly what a great malt this could be. 40% (80 proof).

Milroy's of Soho Cooley 1999 first fill bourbon, cask lot K99/20, dist 13 Jun 99, bott 27 Mar 06 **(85) n21 t22 f21 b21.** You can rest assured that with the exception of Cooley blender Noel Sweeney no other living person has tasted as many different Cooleys from the cask as I have. And I have never yet found a cask like this one: showing the exotic fruit one normally associates with a half clapped-out barrel; the body is oil on silk. I am quite bemused and tasted blind wouldn't have marked this down as a Cooley in about 1,000 million years - give or take the odd 200,000 decades.... Weirdo Whisky of the Year, without doubt. 46%. 289 bottles.

Sainsbury's Single Malt Irish Whiskey bott code L8024/09 **(89) n22.5** brilliant, crisp barley that signals a mouth-watering delivery.... **t23** ...and is duly obliged! The malt is of the juiciest variety with fabulous strata of honeydew melon and eye-watering freshly cut grass; **f21.5** a little vanilla and toffee get in on the act, which remains a pretty classy one; **b22** just a little word to the wise: the back label says: "traditional distilled pot still Irish whiskey." It isn't. This is single malt. To my knowledge this is not a mixture of malted and unmalted barley, which constitutes traditional Irish pot still. Anyway, that apart, this is excellent stuff. 40%

⠿ **Sainsbury's Single Malt Irish Whiskey** bott code L9086/09 **(93.5) n23** beautiful, multi-layered aroma with a soft, lilting barley note, but something more earthy and teasingly smoky forming the anchor; **t24** mouth-watering and absolutely brimming with charm and depth; the clean barley sends the palate into super-salavating mode...and then comes that most delicate of smoky notes...what a darling, this is; **f22.5** shortish, a tad furry and vanilla dried; **b24** a real surprise package: you don't expect smoke on a whisky supplied by Cooley and I even contacted the guys in Ireland to find out where it came from. They don't know

– it shouldn't be there. I am glad it is, if only in trace amounts because it really provides a fabulously balanced malt. 40%

Shannahan's (92) n23 beautifully young, fresh and zesty: this distillery's best style; **t22** refreshing, clean barley that tries to be little else; **f24** excellent late complexity as some first-class soft vanilla appears; more citrus cleans the palate; **b23** Cooley natural and unplugged: quite adorable. 40%

The Spirit Safe & Cask Selection Cooley 1991 12 Years Old dist Sep 91, bott Oct 03 **(89) n22 t23 f22 b22**. Struggles to find a rhythm but the acacia honey holds it together. 43%. nc ncf. Celtique Connexion.

Vom Fass Cooley 4 Years Old (82) n22 t21 f19 b20. Wonderfully clean; for a Cooley, actually has extra sheen and copper richness. Just fades towards the finish and lacks depth. 40%. Austria.

Vom Fass Cooley Peated 8 Years Old (89) n22 gently smoked; lightly cured bacon; **t23** sweet delivery with a wonderful honey shadow to the smoke; **f22** oily liquorice and vanilla; **b22** much more recognisable. This is a treat from an above average cask, though the peating is subtle and subdued. 40%. Austria.

The Whisky Fair Connemara Aged 15 Years bourbon barrel, dist 92, bott 07 **(94) n23.5** fresh ground black pepper nestled in peat ash; **t23** sweeter delivery than nose suggests, with superb layers of smoke. The spices are almost perfectly integrated; **f23.5** now the sweet, clean malts come out to play whilst the vanilla and smoke take a back seat; **b24** superbly balanced. 50.5%. Germany.

The Whisky Fair Cooley Aged 15 Years bourbon barrel, dist 92, bott 07 **(90) n22** intense malt comfortably absorbs the booming oak; **t23** juicy, sweetened barley and puckering spice make for an eventful delivery; the oak tried to get a grip towards the middle but the astonishing freshness of grain, considering its age, comes to the rescue; **f22.5** predictable vanilla and cocoa but the balance with the barley excels; **b22.5** a malty gem. 56.4%. Germany.

The Wild Geese Single Malt (85.5) n21.5 t21 f22 b21. "A Rare Blend of Pure Aged Irish Malt Whiskies" says the front label. Yet it is a single malt. Confusing. And very unhelpful to a whisky public already being totally bamboozled by the bizarre and misguided antics of the Scotch Whisky Association. It is not a blend. It is a mixing of Cooley malt whiskey, as I understand it. The back label's "Smoother Because We Distil it Longer" is also a bit of a blarney. It's made in a pot still and whilst it is true that if you distil faster (by higher temperatures) you could well end up with "hot" whiskey, I am not aware of this being distilled at a significantly slower rate than at either Bushmills or Midleton. Or do they mean the cut of the run from the spirit still is longer, which would impart more oils – not all of them great? Just ignore the Wild Goose chase the labels send you on and enjoy the malt, with all its failings, for what it is (and this is pretty enjoyable in an agreeably rough and ready manner, though not exactly the stiff of Irish whiskey purists): which in this case for all its malt, toffee and delicate smoke, also appears to have more than a slight touch of feints - so maybe they were right all along....!!! 43%. Cooley for Avalon.

OLD BUSHMILLS

Bushmills 10 Years Old matured in two woods db **(90) n22.5** for the first time in living memory there is real grape detectable on the nose; it appears to be of the crushed sultana school of fruitiness with a few minor honeyed notes also around; **t23** a fulsome delivery again with the grape at the vanguard; soft vanilla trundles along at Antrim speed; spices arrive with just a touch of cocoa for company; **f22** soft with the work being done by the grape and toffee; **b22.5** this malt has now changed character enormously....and certainly not for the worse. Until recently it was traditionally a chalky effort, dry-ish with the accent on the barley and oak. Now the sherry is the major shareholder in terms of all round shape and depth. And very good sherry butts they are, too. A great leap forward: this is lush and lovely whiskey. 40% ☉

Bushmills 12 Years Old Distillery Reserve db **(86) n22.5 t22.5 f20 b21**. This version has gone straight for the ultra lush feel. For those who want to take home some 40% abv fruit fudge from the distillery. 40%

Bushmills Select Casks Aged 12 Years married with Caribbean rum cask db **(95) n23** unusual moist rum and raisin cake effect: effective and just enough spice to deliver extra complexity. Just the very slightest hint of bourbon, too; **t24** adorable malt richness; biscuity and stupendously seasoned yet always remains fresh and mouthwatering. The sweetness is very cleverly controlled; **f24** there are just so many layers to this: the oak is a growing force, but restricts itself to a vanilla topping; **b24** one of the most complex Bushmills in living memory, and probably since it was established in 1784. 40%

Bushmills Aged 16 Years db **(90) n24.5** one of the most complex fruit aromas in the world: explodingly ripe greengage and gooseberry; those who love sauternes finishes will appreciate the spiced apricot and layered sweetness. Back to top form with a masterful brilliance; **t22.5** the arrival is pretty two-toned: on one hand is a juicy, sensual, fruit-tinged maltiness. By its side is a more bitter toffee kick; throughout is a fabulous spice rhythm; **f21.5** almost treacle tart toffeeness; **b21.5** a confusing malt: we have a nose that half the blenders of the world would give their right nostril for. And then we have a performance on the palate that promises but does not deliver to its expected potential. Lovely whisky, for sure, and it gets a 90, which means this really is the dbs – and I don't mean distillery bottlings. But I wonder if anything can be done about those duller toffee notes. 40% ☉

Bushmills Rare Aged 21 Years db **(95) n25** one of the cleanest fruit noses of any whiskey in the world and it needs to be: only then can you get a clear enough view and therefore a chance to see what the hell is going on. Grape notes come at you with different intensity in spice and sweetness; barley somehow makes the odd, firm guest appearance and there is a drifting medium roast Java to the oak. But it is the grape which intrigues and entirely seduces... **t23.5** silky, yet charismatic enough to confidently show you the spicier side to its personality early on; the grape ranges from burnt raisin to chocolate sultana; **f23** remains juiced and spiced to the end with a rummy-style bitterness to the sugars; **b23.5** I manage to get round to tasting this, socially, twice a year top whack. But whenever I do, I find myself spending more time nosing this than drinking it. And this sample is absolutely no exception. It almost redefines complexity. But, please, don't forget to taste it. I mean, you can have only so much foreplay.... there again, maybe not. 40% ☉

The Old Bushmills Single Cask 1989 Bourbon Barrel cask 7986 **(88) n22** big vanilla thrust; **t23** quite an outstanding intensity to the buttery malt with the sweetness almost on a precise curve upwards; some oak offers countering dryness; **f21** surprising toffee late on; **b22** perhaps a better malt than the early nose suggests, but very unusual in style for this distillery and would mark higher but for the debilitating toffee. 56.5%. ncf. Specially selected for Canada.

The Old Bushmills Distillery Single Cask Bourbon Barrel 1989 cask 8139 db **(88) n21** fruity, but otherwise languid, with some dry, solid age apparent; **t23** juicy malt that really allows the barley to shine; **f22** long and revelling in its fresh barley richness; some very late, papery and dry oak at the death; **b22** Old Bushmills really springing a surprise with its depth for the age. 56.5%. USA.

The Old Bushmills Distillery Single Cask Bourbon Barrel 1989 cask no 8140 db **(84) n20 t22 f21 b21.** Quite a fiery number, closed early on but with excellent cocoa finale. 56.5%. USA.

The Old Bushmills Distillery Single Cask Bourbon Barrel 1989 cask no 8141 db **(88) n20** dry; soft barley; **t23** pure Bushmills in all its chalky yet oaky barley richness: distinctive and delightful with a bit of a nip; **f23** seriously impressive on the barley front with better balanced cocoa; **b22** the only one of the three bourbon casks to scream "Old Bushmills" at you for its unique style. 56.5%. USA.

The Old Bushmills Distillery Single Cask Rum Barrel 1989 cask no 7110 db **(81) n21 t20 f20 b20.** Big, biting and hot but some serious malt. 53.7%. USA.

The Old Bushmills Distillery Single Cask Rum Barrel 1989 cask no 7112 db **(84) n20 t21 f22 b21.** Sweet and attractively simple with excellent late malt. 53.7%. USA.

The Old Bushmills Single Cask 1989 Rum Barrel cask no. 7115 **(93) n22** delicate coating of sugar over malt; **t24** a uniquely complex series of wonderful, prickly, banana-essence, liquorice-hinting waves of malt and spice: labyrinthine hardly does it justice; **f23** the honied, mildly toffeed richness of the malt seems to multiply in intensity, as does the gentle hint of bourbon: a finish from near the top echelon; **b24** some in Canada may have seen me taste this for the first time with the country's most effortlessly beautiful and charming tv presenter Nancy Sinclair. I said then I thought we had a great malt on our hands, and a later tasting of it under more controlled – and private – conditions confirmed those initial suspicions. A real honey: elegant, deeply desirable, lip-smacking, memorable and something to get your tongue round and experience slowly at least once in your lifetime. And the whiskey's not bad, either.... 53.7%. ncf. Canada.

The Old Bushmills Distillery Single Cask Sherry Butt 1989 db cask no 7429 **(90) n22** passion fruit among the citrus. Sensual and gentle; **t22** gets into a malty stride from go then a slow burning sherry fuse; **f23** delightful finish that is long, vanilla-rich but with the most subtle interwoven fruit and barley and natural caramel; **b23** charismatic, charming, self-confident and supremely elegant. *53.7%. USA.*

The Old Bushmills Distillery Single Cask Sherry Butt 1989 cask no 7430 db **(91) n21** slightly sweaty armpit but a good malt recovery **t23** sweet, enormously malty for a sherry-influenced dram **f24** mildly salty, with many layers of sweet malt and spice that go on almost endlessly **b23** this is a massively complex and striking Bushmills well worth finding: casks 7429 and 7430 could be almost twins...!! *53.7%. USA.*

Clontarf Single Malt (90.5) n23 barley concentrate with a squeeze of orange and distant juniper; **t23** beautifully fresh barley, almost barley sugar, with light sinews of oak; **f22** long, intense barley but with the vanilla standing tallest at the death as welcome spices finally gather; **b22.5** beautiful in its simplicity, this has eschewed complexity for delicious minimalism; *40%. Clontarf Irish Whiskey Co.* ☉☉

The Irishman Single Malt bottle no. E2496 **(83) n20 t21 f21 b21.** Highly pleasant malt but the coffee and toffee on the finish underline a caramel-style whiskey which may, potentially, offer so much more. *40%. Hot Irishman Ltd.*

Knappogue Castle 1990 *(see Cooley)*
Knappogue Castle 1991 *(see Cooley)*
Knappogue Castle 1992 *(see Cooley)*

Knappogue Castle 1993 (91) n22 b22 f23 b24. A malt of exceptional character and charisma. Almost squeaky clean but proudly contains enormous depth and intensity. The chocolate finish is an absolute delight. Quite different and darker than any previous Knappogue but not dwarfed in stature to any of the previous three vintages. Created by yours truly. *40%. nc. Great Spirits.*

Knappogue Castle 1994 lot no. L6 **(89) n23 f20 b22** A wonderful whiskey in the Knappogue tradition, although this one was not done by its creator. That said, it does have an Achilles heel: the finish. This is the most important bit to get right, especially as this is the oldest Knappogue yet. But not enough attention has been paid to getting rid of the oak-induced bitterness. *40%. Castle Brands.*

Knappogue Castle 1995 bott 07 **(88) n23** banana skins and custard; soft barley but drier and dustier than any other Knappogue nose; **t22** early mouthwatering barley fades; a sugary sheen is quickly usurped by an impatient oaky bitterness; **f21** dry-ish and bitter but with a soft barley residue; some ultra late spices; **b22** a charming malt showing Old Bushmills in very unusual colours. Lacking the charisma, clarity and complexity of the first Knappogues simply because they were designed to extol the virtues of young (8 year old) malt. Naturally, extra oak has crept in here, forcing out – as it must – the sharpness and vitality of the barley. A decent effort, but perhaps more should have been done to keep out the aggressive bitterness. *40%. Castle Brands.*

Single Grain
COOLEY

Cooley 1991 16 Years Old 1st fill bourbon cask no. 12441, dist Nov 91, bott Feb 08 **(89.5) n22.5** some solid oak, but a fruity, soft oiliness smooths the ruffled feathers; **t23** a sweet silkiness with bite: love it!! **f22** gentle fade with the corn offering a sweeter edge to the oak; **b22** it hardly makes sense that Cooley grain appears to absorb the years better than their malt! Great stuff. *46%. Milroy's of Soho. 264 bottles.*

⌗ **Greenore 6 Year Old** bott code L9015 db **(89) n23.5** even at such tender age this has more to do with bourbon than Irish: gentle, sweet red liquorice, toffee apple, and hot even the slightest hint of bitterness...; **t22.5**...but tastes of pure Canadian, especially with the over-enthusiastic caramels; sweet with an amazingly yielding texture; **f21** lightly burnt toast and more toffee; **b22** very enjoyable whiskey. But two points: cut the caramel and really see the baby sing. And secondly, as a "Small Batch" bottling, how about putting a batch number on the label...? *40%. Cooley.*

⌗ **Greenore 8 Year Old** bott code L8190 db **(86.5) n20 t22 f23 b21.5.** The vague hint of butyric on the nose is more than amply compensated by the gradual build up to something rather larger on the palate than you might have expected (and don't be surprised if the two events are linked). The corn oil is almost a meal in itself and the degree of accompanying sugar and corn flour is a treat. *40%. Cooley*

Greenore 10 Years Old dist 97, bott 07 db **(87.5) n22** pretty standard Canadian style: plenty of corn digging in, a touch of toffee sweetness and a degree of bite; **t22** lightly oiled corn and vanilla; the oak dips in and out; **f21.5** pleasantly sweet at times yet amazingly docile, knowing what this grain is capable of... **b22** well made grain and always enjoyable but perhaps not brought to its fullest potential due to some less than inspired oak. *40%. 3000 bottles.*

Greenore 15 Years Old bott code L8044 **(90) n23** the depth of ingrained oak mixed with corn heads you in the direction of Canada; a few spicy folds and golden syrup edges ensure a lovely simple elegance; **t22.5** just the right dosage of spice to counter the sugars; **f22** oaky bitterness outgunned by those marauding dark sugars; **b22.5** the advent of the Kilbeggan 15 reminded us that there must be some grain of that age around, and here to prove it is a superb bottling of the stuff which, weirdly, is a lot better than the blend. Beautiful. *43%* ☉

Blends

Bushmills 1608 anniversary edition **(94) n23.5** the grain barely gets a look in as the malt and oak dominates from the first whiff. Toasted oak and bread form a dense background, sweetened by muscovado sugar melting on porridge; **t23.5** now that's different: how many blends do you know kick off with an immediate impact of sweetness that offers about four or five different levels of intensity, and each accompanied by a toasted oakiness? Very, very different, charming, fascinating.....and delicious; **f23** long, mocha with the emphasis on the coffee and then, at the very end some firm grains at last get a toe-hold; **b24** this whiskey is talking an entirely different language to any Irish blend I have come across before, or any blend come to that. Indeed, nosed blind you'd not even regard it a blend: the malt calls to you like a Siren. But perhaps it is the crystal malt they have used here which is sending out such unique signals, helping the whiskey to form a thick cloak of roasty, toasty, burnt toffeed, bitter-sweetness which takes your breath away. What a fabulous whiskey! And whether it be a malt or blend, who cares? Genius whiskey is genius whiskey. *40%*

Bushmills Black Bush (91) n23 a firmer aroma with less evident malt and the spices have also taken a back seat. But the gentle, toffee apple and night garden scent reveal that the malt-grain interaction is still wonderfully alluring; **t23** busy delivery, much softer than the nose indicates with the malt first to show. The oak is no slouch either, offering excellent spices; some burnt, raisiny notes help confirm this is Black Bush on song; **f21.5** still over the top caramel interfering but not before some honeycomb makes a small stand; **b23.5** this famous old blend may be under new management and even blender. But still the high quality, top-notch complexity rolls around the glass and your palate. As beautiful as ever. *40%* ☉

Bushmills Original (80) n19 t21 f20 b20. Remains one of the hardest whiskeys on the circuit with the Midleton grain at its most unflinching. There is a sweeter, faintly maltier edge to this now while the toffee and biscuits qualities remain. *40%*

Cassidy's Distiller's Reserve bott code L8067 **(84.5) n21.5 t22 f20 b21.** Some salivating malt on flavour-exploding delivery, but all else tame and gentle. *40%. Cooley.*

Clancey's bott code L8025 **(87) n22** sweet malt bounces off the firmer grain; young, lively and a touch floral; **t21** early toffeed delivery then a parade of vanilla and varied grains, barley most certainly included; **f22** burnt fudge and some teasing spice; **b22** remains an excellent blend for all the toffee. The spice balance excels. *40%. Cooley for Wm Morrison.*

Clontarf Classic Blend (86) n18 t23 f23 b22. This has to be treated as a new whiskey. Many moons back I created this as a 100% grain from Cooley, a velvet-soft job of real subtlety. These days, with me having no involvement, the whiskies are from Irish Distillers. This is no longer all grain, though the malt content is no more than fractional. And it really underscores the difference in style between Midleton and Cooley grain. For every degree Colley is soft and yielding, Midleton is unremittingly rigid. The nose (though not the taste) is recognizable to devotees of White Bush and Paddy. Which means aroma-wise, with the caramel, it's pretty austere stuff. But you cannot fault the delivery which is crisp, salivating and offering surprising sweetness and big citrus. Not bad once you adapt: in fact, seriously entertaining. *40%.*

Delaney's Special Reserve (84) n21.5 t20.5 f22 b21. An attractive blend with a big late spicy blast. The toffee dominates for long periods. *40%. Cooley for Co-operative Group.*

Feckin Irish Whiskey (81) n20 t21 f20 b20. Tastes just about exactly the feckin same as the Feckin Strangford Gold... *40%. The Feckin Drinks Co.*

Golden Irish bott code L7064 **(93) n23** do I nose before me spice? And syrup-dripping coconut candy tobacco from childhood days? Yep, that and citrussy vanilla; **t23** near perfect mouthfeel helps stoke up the malt intensity. The grain simply moulds into the palate bringing with it an odd twist of cocoa even by the middle; **f23.5** milky chocolate and Demerara make for a long, pleasing, almost breakfast cereal-type finale; **b23.5** by far one of the most enjoyable Irish blends around. Simple, but what it does, it does well – and deliciously well at that...!! *40%. Cooley.*

⌖ **The Irishman Rare Cask Strength** bott 09 **(85.5) n22 t21.5 f21 b21.** A lovely, brawny malt which for all its strength feels that it has never quite slipped out of third gear. A chewy sweetness dominates but the caramel certainly has clipped this whiskey's wings. *56%. Hot Irishman Ltd. 1,800 bottles.*

The Irishman Rare Cask Strength (93.5) n23 a wonderful combination of soft bourbony notes and a light malty sub-plot. No shortage of honey and a lighter spinkling of the ginger which, if memory serves me correctly, is a feature of the mere mortal 40% bottling; **t24** absolutely brilliant! It's not just the strength, although there are few whiskies that are so enormously affected. No, it's the immediate balance with the grains going in strong, but of such high quality and rich character that the gentle bourbon persuasion continues; softly oiled, very lightly malted, the arrival of the drier oak offers the perfect bitter-sweet foil; **f23** long, chocolate rich and sophisticatedly spiced; **b23.5** just so wonderful to come across a full strength blend. Better still when that blend happens to be as quite beautiful and characterful as this. A hot whisky alright: this should be burning a way into most blend lovers' homes. Quite exceptional, to be sure. *56%. Hot Irishman Ltd. 1400 bottles.*

The Irishman Superior Irish Whiskey bott code L6299L059 **(93) n23** chunky caramel perhaps, but the apple is green and inviting; even an inclusion of soft manuka honey and ginger – most un-Irish; **t23** lush, with a distinct malt charge before the caramel and oaky spice arrive; **f23** those spices really tick, accentuated by the contrasting molasses and more honey but doused in vanilla. **b24** what a quite wonderful blend: not of the norm for those that have recently come onto the market and there is much more of the Irish Distillers about this than most. Forget about the smoke promised in the tasting notes on the label...It gives you everything else but. And that is one hell of a lot!! *40%. Hot Irishman Ltd.*

Jameson (95) n24.5 Swoon....bizarrely shows even more Pot Still character than the Redbreast I tasted yesterday. Flinty to the point of cracking. The sherry is there but on reduced terms, allowing the firm grain to amplify the unmalted barley: truly brilliant; **t24** mouth-watering delivery and then wave upon wave of diamond-hard barley and grain; the odd eclectic layer of something sweetish and honeyed, but this is eye-watering stuff; **f22.5** an annoying touch of caramel creeps in, costing points, but even beyond that you still cannot other than be charmed by the layering of cocoa, barley and light grape; **b24** I thought I had detected in bottlings I had found around the world a very slight reduction in the Pot Still character that defines this truly classic whiskey. So I sat down with a fresh bottle in more controlled conditions....and was blown away as usual. The sharpness of the PS is vivid and unique; the supporting grain of the required crispness. Fear not: this very special whiskey remains in stunning, truly wondrous form. *40%.* ☉

Jameson 12 Years Old Special Reserve (88) n22 caramel, lazy sherry, musty; enlivened by a splash of sharper pot still; **t23** the grape shows little sign of shyness, aided by a bitter-sweet element; good body and layering; **f21** dulls out as the caramel arrives; dusty, drying; **b22** much more sherry than of late and the pot still makes inroads, too. Just needs to lose some of the caramel effect; *40%*

Jameson 18 Years Old Limited Reserve eighth batch bott code JJ18-8 **(91) n23** pure bourbon on oak dispenses myriad honey-leather-hickory notes with the Pot Still doing the job of the fruitier "rye"; **t22.5** firm and juicy, gentle spice but a caramel-trimmed middle; **f22.5** the redoubling of the juicier barley notes cuts through the vanilla and caramel to set up a long, delicately weighted finale; **b22.5** the astonishing degree of bourbon on the nose thankfully doesn't make it to the palate where Ireland rather than Kentucky rules. *40%* ☉

Jameson Gold Reserve (88) n22 a touch of menthol has crept into this much weightier nose: creaks with age as bourbony elements drift in and out of the grape; **t23** sweet, sexily spiced delivery; hardens towards the middle but the grains are surprisingly lush and softly oiled; **f20** glutinous and plodding; **b22** enjoyable, but so very different: an absolute re-working with all the lighter, more definitively sweeter elements shaved mercilessly while the thicker oak is on a roll. Some distance from the masterpiece it once was. *40%* ☉

Jameson Rarest 2007 Vintage Reserve (96) n24.5 the crispest, cleanest, most beautifully defined of all the Jameson family: orange peel, hickory, spotted dog pudding, lavender – they're all there mushed around and in near-perfect proportions; **t24** ditto the arrival with the mouth puckering under the onslaught of very old Pot Still: the bitter-sweet sharpness one would expect from this is there in spades; oak present and correct and edged in thin muscovado layer; **f23.5** vanilla by the barrel-load, pithy fruit and softly spiced barley **b24** is this the whiskey where we see a blender truly come of age. Tall green hats off to Billy Leighton who has, as all the better blenders did in the past, worked his way from quality-testing barrels on the dumping room floor to the lab. With this stupendous offering we have a blender in clover for he has earned his Golden Shamrocks. If the blending alone wasn't stellar enough, then making this a 46%, non chill-filtered offering really does put the tin hat on it (so Billy: you really have been listening to me over the years....!!!) This is truly great whiskey, among the pantheon of the world's finest. *46%*

⠿ **Jameson Signature Reserve (93)** n23.5 adore the sharp citrus notes which bore, shrapnel-like, into the firm, though lighter than normal pure Pot Still: supremely balanced; the degree of honey is exemplary....and enticing; **t23.5** gossamer light delivery despite the obvious Pot Still presence. Some caramel momentarily dulls the middle but the flavours return for a beautifully constructed middle with alternating waves of citrus and pot still, occasionally honeyed, much as the nose predicts; the grains are softer than an Irish bog and simply dissolve without fuss: most un-Midleton **f22.5** beautiful: the vanilla does pulse with acacia honey; the Pot still stands firm and lightly fruity; **b23.5** be assured that Signature, with its clever structuring of delicate and inter-weaving flavours, says far more about the blender, Billy Leighton, than it does John Jameson. *40%. Irish Distillers.*

Kilbeggan bott code L7091 **(86)** n21 t22 f21.5 b21.5. A much more confident blend by comparison with that faltering one of the last few years. Here, the malts make a significant drive towards increasing the overall complexity and gentle citrus style. *40%. Cooley.*

Kilbeggan 15 Years Old bott code L7048 **(85.5)** n21.5 t22 f21 b21. My word! 15 years, eh? How time flies! And on the subject of flying, surely I have winged my way back to Canada and am tasting a native blend. No, this is Irish albeit in sweet, deliciously rounded form. However, one cannot help feeling that the dark arts have been performed, as in an injection of caramel, which, as well as giving that Canadian feel has also probably shaved off some of the more complex notes to middle and finish. Even so, a sweet, silky experience. *40%. Cooley.*

Kilgeary bott code L8063 **(79)** n20 t19 f19 b20. There has always, and still proudly is, something strange about this blend. Cold tea on the nose and a bitter bite to the finish, sandwiches a brief flirtation with something sweet. *40%. Cooley.*

Locke's bott code L8056 **(85.5)** n21 t22 f21.5 b21. Now, there you go!! Since I last really got round to analysing this one it has grown from a half-hearted kind of a waif to something altogether more gutsy and muscular. Sweeter, too, as the malts and grains combine harmoniously. A clean and pleasant experience with some decent malt fingerprints. *40%*

Michael Collins A Blend (77) n19 t20 f19 b19. Michael Collins was known as the "big fellow". This pleasant, impressively spiced dram, might have enjoyed the same epithet had it not surrendered to and then been strangled by caramel on the finish. *40% (80 proof). Cooley.*

Midleton Distillery Reserve (85) n22 t22 f20 b21. A whiskey which, for all its muscovado sweetness offers some memorable barley moments. *40%. Irish Distillers Midleton Distillery only. Was once bottled as Jameson Distillery Reserve exclusive to Midleton. Changes character slightly with each new vatting. This one is some departure.*

Midleton Very Rare 1984 (70) n19 t18 f17 b16. Disappointing with little backbone or balance. *40%. Irish Distillers.*

Midleton Very Rare 1985 (77) n20 t20 f18 b19. Medium-bodied and oily, this is a big improvement on the initial vintage. *40%. Irish Distillers.*

Midleton Very Rare 1986 (79) n21 t20 f18 b20. A very malty Midleton richer in character than previous vintages. *40%. Irish Distillers.*

Midleton Very Rare 1987 (77) n20 t19 f19 b19. Quite oaky at first until a late surge of excellent pot still. *40%. Irish Distillers.*

Midleton Very Rare 1988 (86) n23 t21 f21 b21. A landmark MVR as it is the first vintage to celebrate the Irish pot-still style. *40%. Irish Distillers.*

Midleton Very Rare 1989 (87) n22 t22 f22 b21. A real mouthful but has lost balance to achieve the effect. *40%. Irish Distillers.*

Midleton Very Rare 1990 (93) n23 carrying on from where the '89 left off. The pot still doesn't drill itself so far into your sinuses, perhaps: more of a firm massage; **t23** solid pot still again. There is a pattern now: pot still first, sweeter, maltier notes second, pleasant grains third and somewhere, imperceptibly, warming spices fill in the gaps; **f24** long and Redbreast-like in character. Spices seep from the bourbon casks; **b23** astounding whiskey: one of the vintages every true Irish whiskey lover should hunt for. *40%. Irish Distillers.*

Midleton Very Rare 1991 (76) n19 t20 f19 b18. After the Lord Mayor's Show, relatively dull and uninspiring. 40%. Irish Distillers.

Midleton Very Rare 1992 (84) n20 t20 f23 b21. Superb finish with outstanding use of feisty grain. 40%. Irish Distillers.

Midleton Very Rare 1993 (88) n21 pot still with sub plots of honey and pepper; **t22** the pot still makes use of the dry hardness of the grain; **f23** beautiful elevation of the pot still towards something more complex and sharp balancing superbly with malt and bourbony-oak texture; **b22** big, brash and beautiful – the perfect way to celebrate the 10th-ever bottling of MVR. 40%. Irish Distillers.

Midleton Very Rare 1994 (87) n22 pot-still characteristics not unlike the '93 but with extra honey and ginger; **t22** the honeyed theme continues with malt arriving in a lush sweetness; **f21** oily and a spurt of sharper, harder pot still; **b22** another different style of MVR, one of amazing lushness. 40%. Irish Distillers.

Midleton Very Rare 1995 (90) n23 big pot still with fleeting honey; **t24** enormous! Bitter, sweet and tart all together for a chewable battle of apple and barley. Brilliant; **b21** some caramel calms proceedings, but Java coffee goes a little way to restoring complexity; **b22** they don't come much bigger than this. Prepare a knife and fork to battle through this one. Fabulous. 40%. Irish Distillers.

Midleton Very Rare 1996 (82) n21 t22 f19 b20. The grains lead a soft course, hardened by subtle pot still. Just missing a beat on the finish, though. 40%. Irish Distillers.

Midleton Very Rare 1997 (83) n22 t21 f19 b21. The piercing pot still fruitiness of the nose is met by a countering grain of rare softness on the palate. Just dies on the finish when you want it to make a little speech. Very drinkable. 40%. Irish Distillers.

Midleton Very Rare 1999 (89) n21 malt and toffee: as sleepy as a nighttime drink; **t23** stupendous grain, soft enough to absorb some pounding malt; **f22** spices arrive as the blend hardens and some pot still finally battles its way through the swampy grain; **b23** one of the maltiest Midletons of all time: a superb blend. 40%. Irish Distillers.

Midleton Very Rare 2000 (85) n22 t21 f21 b21. An extraordinary departure even by Midleton's eclectic standards. The pot still is like a distant church spire in an hypnotic Fen landscape. 40%. Irish Distillers.

Midleton Very Rare 2001 (79) n21 t20 f18 b20. Extremely light but the finish is slightly on the bitter side. 40%. Irish Distillers.

Midleton Very Rare 2002 (79) n20 t22 f18 b19. The nose is rather subdued and the finish is likewise toffee-quiet and shy. There are some fabulous middle moments, some of flashing genius, when the pot still and grain combine for a spicy kick, but the finish really is lacklustre and disappointing. 40%. Irish Distillers.

Midleton Very Rare 2003 (84) n22 t22 f19 b21. Beautifully fruity on both nose and palate (even some orange blossom on aroma). But the delicious spicy richness that is in mid launch on the tastebuds is cut short by caramel on the middle and finish. A crying shame, but the best Midleton for a year or two. 40%. Irish Distillers.

Midleton Very Rare 2004 (82) n21 t21 f19 b21. Yet again caramel is the dominant feature, though some quite wonderful citrus and spice escape the toffeed blitz. 40%.

Midleton Very Rare 2005 (92) n23 t24 f22 b23. OK, you can take this one only as a rough translation. The sample I have worked from here is from the Irish Distillers blending lab, reduced to 40% in mine but without caramel added. And, as Midleton Very Rares always are at this stage, it's an absolute treat. Never has such a great blend suffered so in the hands of colouring and here the chirpiness of the pot still and élan of the honey (very Jameson Gold Label in part) show just what could be on offer given half the chance. Has wonderful natural colour and surely it is a matter of time before we see this great whiskey in its natural state. 40%

Midleton Very Rare 2006 (92) n22 real punch to the grain, which is there in force and offering a bourbony match for the pot still; **t24** stupendously crisp, then a welter of spices nip and sting ferociously around the palate; the oaky coffee arrives early and with clarity while the barley helps solidify the rock-hard barley; **f23** usually by now caramel intervenes and spoils, but not this time and again it's the grain which really stars; **b23** the best Midleton for some time: as raw as a Dublin rough house and for once not overly swamped with caramel. An uncut diamond. 40%. Irish Distillers.

Midleton Very Rare 2007 (83) n20 t22 f20 b21. Annoyingly buffeted from nose to finish by powering caramel. Some sweeter wisps do escape but the aroma suggests Canadian and insufficient Pot Still gets through to make this a Midleton of distinction. 40%. Irish Distillers

··· **Midleton Very Rare 2008 (88.5) n22** orange peel, pot still and a degree of bourbon... but too much caramel **t23** excellent big honey theme on delivery is augmented by a genuine, rock hard Pot Still juicy sharpness. An unusual coppery-metallic sheen gives the softly fruity proceedings polish; **f21.5** more caramel dulls the persistent pot still; **b22** a dense bottling which offers considerably more than the 2007 Vintage. Attractive, very drinkable and without the caramel it might really have hit the heights. *40%. Irish Distillers.*

Millars Special Reserve bott code L8069 **(86) n21 t22 f21.5 b21.5.** Now that's some improvement on the last bottling of this I found, with spices back with abandon and grains ensuring a fine mouthfeel. Even the chocolate fudge at the death is a treat. *40%. Cooley.*

Paddy (74) n18.5 t20 f17.5 b18. Cleaned its act up a little. Even a touch of attractive citrus on the nose and delivery. But where does that cloying sweetness come from? As bland as an Irish peat bog but, sadly, nothing like so potentially tasty. *40%. Irish Distillers.*

Powers (91) n23 rugged pot still and beefed up by some pretty nippy grain; **t24** brilliant mouth arrival, one of the best in all Ireland: the pot still shrieks and attacks every available tastebud; **f22** pulsing spices and mouthwatering, rock-hard pot still. The sweetness is a bit unusual but you can just chew that barley; **b22** is it any coincidence that in this bottling the influence of the caramel has been significantly reduced and the whiskey is getting back to its old, brilliant self? I think not. Classic stuff. *40%. Irish Distillers.*

Powers Gold Label (87) n22 Powers? Really? I had to look twice and re-pour the sample to ensure this was the right stuff. Where is the clunking pot still? Soft, grainy caramel; **t22** attractively sweet with a distinct candy tobacco golden syrup but a serious departure from the ancient style. It's grain all the way, soft and silky as she goes; **f21** more lightness and caramel; maybe some semblance of pot still but you have to hunt to find it; **b22** the solid pot still, the very DNA of what made Powers, well, Powers is vanishing in front of our very noses. Yes, still some pot still around, but nothing like so pronounced in the way that made this, for decades, a truly one-off Irish and one of the world greats. Still delightful and with many charms but the rock hard pot still effect is sadly missed. What is going on here? *40%. Irish Distillers.* ☉

Redbreast Blend (88) n23 some genuinely telling pot-still hardness sparks like a flint off the no less unyielding grain. Just love this; **t23** very sweet and soft, the grain carrying a massive amount of vanilla. Barley offers some riches, as does spice; **f20** a climbdown from the confrontational beginnings, but pretty delicious all the same; **b22** really impressed with this one-off bottling for Dillons the Irish wine merchants. Must try and get another bottle before they all vanish. *40%. Irish Distillers for Dillone IR (not to be confused with Redbreast 12-y-o Pure Pot Still).*

St Patrick bott code L030907 **(77) n19 t20 f19 b19.** Good grief! No prisoners here as we have either a bitter oakiness or mildly cloying sweetness, rarely working in tandem. A few gremlins for the Kremlin. *40%. Cooley for Russia.*

Strangford Gold (81) n20 t21 f20 b20. A simplistic, exceptionally easy drinking blend with high quality grain offering silk to the countering spice but caramel flattens any malt involvement. *40%. The Feckin Drinks Co.*

Tesco Special Reserve Irish Whiskey bott code L8061 **(89.5) n21.5** gentle caramels try – and fail – to intervene as the vivid malts and seductive grains fuse; **t23.5** Irish blends don't come any softer: Cooley grain is as good as it gets anywhere in the word and here embrace and amplify the malts wonderfully; **f22** gentle, soft, sweet and clean; **b22.5** a cracker of a blend which allows the malts full scope to do their juicy bit. Possibly more malt than usual for a Cooley blend, but as they say: every little bit helps. *40%. Cooley.*

Tullamore Dew (85) n22 t21.5 f20.5 b21. The days of the throat being savaged by this one appear to be over. Much more pot still character from nose to finish and the rough edges remain, attractively, just that. *40%. Campbell & Cochrane Group.* ☉

Tullamore Dew 10 Years Old (81.5) n21 t21.5 f19 b20. A bright start from this new kid on the Tullamore block. Soft fruit and harder pot still make some kind of complexity, but peters out at the death. *40%. Campbell & Cochrane Group.*

Tullamore Dew 12 Years Old (84.5) n21.5 t21.5 f20 b21.5. Silky thanks to some excellent Midleton grain: there are mouthwatering qualities here that make the most of the soft spices and gentle fruit. An improved whiskey, if still somewhat meek and shy. *40%. Campbell & Cochrane Group.*

Tullamore Dew Heritage (78) n20 t21 f18 b19. Tedious going with the caramel finish a real turn off. *40.0%. Campbell & Cochrane Group.*

Walker & Scott Irish Whiskey "Copper Pot Distilled" (83) n20 t22 f20 b21. A collectors' item. This charming, if slightly fudgy-finished blend was made by Cooley as the house Irish for one of Britain's finest breweries. Sadly, someone put "Copper Pot Distilled" on the label, which, as it's a blend, can hardly be the case. And even if it wasn't a blend, would still be confusing in terms of Irish whiskey, there not being any traditional Irish Pot Still, that mixture of malted and unmalted barley. So Sam's, being one of the most traditional brewers in Britain, with the next bottling changed the label by dropping all mention of pot still. Top marks, chaps! The next bottling can be seen below. *40%. Sam Smith's.*

Walker & Scott Irish Whiskey (85) n21 t22 f21 b21. Oddly, sharper grain has helped give his some extra edge through the toffee. A very decent blend. 40%.

⦂⦂⦂∙ **The Whisky Fair Connemara 2001** bott 09 **(90.5) n22** a golden toast dryness to the honeyed smoke; **t23.5** goes into overdrive with some unexpected and unusual oils bulking up the sweetness; the drier points are hammered home with spicy intent; **f22.5** vanilla and butterscotch with a hazelnut oil topping still can't quite master the powering phenols; **b23** not your Irish bog-standard Connemara: extra doses of complexity and oil – not two things which normally go hand-in-hand. *59.2%. The Whisky Fair, Germany.*

The Wild Geese Classic Blend (80.5) n20 t21 f19.5 b19. Easy going, pretty neutral and conservative. If you are looking for zip, zest and charisma you've picked the wrong goose (see below). 40%. Cooley for Avalon.

The Wild Geese Limited Edition Fourth Centennial (93) n23 sensationally clean and with the citrus really taking a starring role; vanillas abound, but in the soft, playful form; light and just so enticing; **t23.5** barley notes peck around the tastebuds entirely unfettered by more tactile and heavier elements; lithe and lean, there is no fat on this goose and the vanilla lives up to its best expectation given on the nose while the mouth is drenched in salivating promises – simply stunning; **f23** just so light, the clarity of the barley sugar and vanilla leaves you purring; **b23.5** a limited edition of unlimited beauty. One of the lightest, subtle, intriguing and quite simply disarming Irish whiskeys on the market. As a bird and whiskey lover, this is one goose that I shall be looking out for. *43%. Cooley for Avalon.*

The Wild Geese Rare Irish (89.5) n22 some toffee, yes, but the excellence of the vanilla is there to behold; just a light layering of barley but the gentle citrus caresses with the more exquisite touch... **t23** superb arrival on the palate; the grain displays nothing other than excellence in both weight and control, and while the oaks and caramels are a tad bitter, the sweeter barley compensates wonderfully; **f22** a silky, almost metallic sheen to the finale which complements the drying vanillins; **b22.5** just love this. The Cooley grain is working sublimely and dovetails with the malt in the same effortless way wild geese fly in perfect formation. A treat. *43%. Cooley for Avalon.*

⦂⦂⦂∙ **Writers Tears (93) n23.5** a glossy Pot Still character: rather than the usual fruity firmness, the recognisable Pot Still traits are shrouded in soft honey tones which dovetail with lightening kumquat-citrus tones. Quite a curious, but always deliciously appealing animal...; **t24** works beautifully well: the arrival is an alternating delivery of hard and soft waves, the former showing a more bitter, almost myopic determination to hammer home its traditional pot still standpoint; the sweeter, more yielding notes dissolve with little or no resistance, leaving an acacia honeyed trail; towards the middle a juicier malt element mingles with soft vanilla but the Pot Still character never goes away; **f22** relatively short with perhaps the Pot Still, with an old-fashioned cough sweet fruitiness, lingering longest, though its does retain its honeyed accompaniment for the most part; **b23.5** now that really was different. The first mix of pure Pot Still and single malt I have knowingly come across in a commercial bottling, but only because I wasn't aware of the make up of last year's Irishman Blend. The malt, like the Pot Still, is, I understand from proprietor Bernard Walsh, from Midleton, but the two styles mixed shows a remarkably similar character to when I carried out an identical experiment with pure pot still and Bushmills the best part of a decade ago. A success and hopefully not a one off. Which is more than I can say for the label, a whiskey collectors – sorry, collector's – item in its own right. There is a wonderfully Irish irony that a whiskey dedicated to Ireland's extraordinary literary heritage should be represented by a label, even a brand name, so punctually inept; it's almost brilliant. The reason for the Writers (sic) Tears, if from the spirits of James Joyce, Samuel Beckett, George Bernard Shaw, Oscar Wilde and perhaps even Maurice Walsh, whose grandson became a legendary blender at Irish Distillers, will be open to debate: we will never know whether they laughed or cried. As far as the actual whiskey is concerned, though, I am sure they, to a man, would have no hesitation but to pen the most luminous and positive critiques possible. *40%. Writers Tears Whiskey Co.*

American Whiskey

Not that long ago American whiskey meant Bourbon. Or perhaps a very close relation called Tennessee. And sometimes it meant rye. Though nothing like often as it did prior to prohibition. Very, very rarely, though, did it ever get called single malt, because virtually none was made on the entire North American continent. That was a specialist - and very expensive - type left to the Scots and, to a lesser extent, the Irish. Or even the Japanese if a soldier or businessman was flying back from Tokyo.

I say "virtually" none was made because, actually, there was the odd batch of malt produced in America and, in my library, I still have some distilled at a rye distillery in Maryland in the early 1970s - indeed, I remember drinking the stuff there back in 1974. But it was hardly a serious commercial concern and the American public were never made greatly aware of it.

Now, though, at last count it appears that there are at least 22 distilleries doing their best to make whiskey mainly from malted barley but sometimes from rye and corn, too. Some still have much to learn, others have shown that they are well on their way to possible greatness. One distillery, Stranahan's in Colorado, has in a very short space of time managed to bring out a series of bottlings which left no doubt that they have joined McCarthy's of Oregon and Anchor of California in achieving it with another Portland distiller, Edgefield, not that far behind.

But as a collective movement it is by far the most exciting in the entire whisky world., despite what is happening in certain parts of Europe, especially German, Austria and Switzerland, where there is an even bigger movement. It appears to me that the better "micro distillers" are just a little more advanced in the US and have a stronger urge to grow. Some new wave American distillers, doubtless, will fall by the wayside while others will take their place. But those at the vanguard are likely to act as the spur to keep the others moving onwards and it is a situation I shall monitor very closely. There are squabbles about whether enzymes should be used for fermentation, a question I have been asked about many times. My view is that they should be avoided, although I can understand the reasons for their employment. However, when you are witnessing the birth of an entirely new whiskey life form it is always fascinating to see how it naturally develops. Usually the strongest live and the weakest die. In this survival of the fittest it will soon become apparent which methods are the ones which succeed - and they tend to be the ones which has served distillers well over the last couple of centuries.

There is no little irony, however, that as we take a closer look at the alternative distilling world within the United States, it is the old order which is now really catching the eye. Doubtless my award to Sazerac Rye 18 Years Old as Jim Murray's Whisky Bible 2010 World Whisky of the Year will bemuse quite a number of whisky lovers because it represents a style of whiskey they have never as much seen, let alone tasted.

Once upon a time, though, rye whiskey was seen as the embodiment of indigenous American spirit and the preferred choice in the country. After falling out of favour following Prohibiton and then World War II the traditional rye distillers in Pennsyslvania and Maryland closed, production of the spirit shrank to a week's fermentation a year, if that, in a few Kentucky distilleries and until recently it was seen only as a rare alternative to bourbon in American liquor stores, often hidden on the end of shelves, or at the bottom. And often, ignominiously, both - with giveaway prices to add insult to injury.

Rye whiskey, where a minimum 51 per cent of the mashbill is made from rye - as opposed to bourbon where 51 per cent must be from corn - has long been my favourite whisk(e)y style. And through the 1990s I made a bit of a pest of myself trying to talk Kentucky distillers to up their rye production, but with only limited success. I genuinely saw it winning hearts in exactly the same way peaty whisky was building an extended cult following around the world. I still do. And, equally, to this day should I ever be talked into building a distillery anywhere in the world it would be either in Maryland, where I discovered this astonishing whiskey style back in 1974, or somewhere around the Monongahela river in Pennsylvania which later became its spiritual home. This Sazerac 18 is the first rye to see off the best rest of the world has to offer; it may be another seven years before rye wins the award again. It would be satisfying to know, then, that the award results in new converts to the original spirit of America.

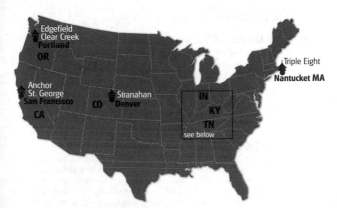

Key

- ● **Major Town or City**
- ⛪ Distillery
- † Dead Distillery

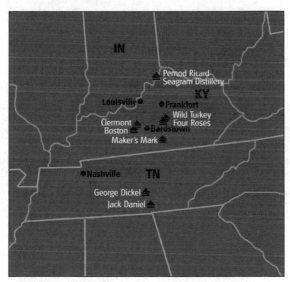

Bardstown
⛪ Heaven Hill†
⛪ Tom Moore
Frankfort
⛪ Buffalo Trace

⛪ Woodford Reserve
Louisville
⛪ Early Times
⛪ Bernheim
⛪ Stitzel Weller

American Single Malt
ANCHOR DISTILLERY (see Rye)

CHARBAY DISTILLERY Napa Valley, California
Charbay Hop Flavoured Whiskey release II, barrels 3-7 **(91)** n22 Sweet, intense barley wine with a rich floral seam; **t22** enormous. The malt is in concentrate form, which makes it sweet. But those hops provide a balancing bitter-sweet fruitiness. All this packed in at full strength. Wow!! **f23** quite bitter as the hops have the final say. The wood, though, forges a bourbon sheen to it all and adds to the all out assault on the tastebuds; **b24** being distilled from beer which includes hops, it can – and will - be argued that this is not beer at all. However, what cannot be disputed is that this is a rich, full-on spirit that has set out to make a statement and has delivered it. Loudspeaker and all. *55%*

CLEAR CREEK DISTILLERY Portland, Oregon
McCarthy's batch W08-01 bottled 3/10/08 **(94.5)** n24 the smokiest of kippers, phenols from the blackest of peat: it has to be McCarthy's! There is something quite farmyardy about this one, and the hog-theme continues with a salty smoked bacon edge. Hook me up to a mask so I can breathe this one in all day....! **t24** for all the posturing on the nose, the delivery is nothing short of gentlemanly and sedate. A coating of muscovado sugar clings to the juicy barley and the oak refuses to interfere other than to add a touch of vanilla; **f23** a long, long fade with the dryness slowly, almost imperceptibly replacing those astonishing sweet themes. Just so delicate, even at the death; **b23.5** the upping of the strength from 40% has done this whisky no harm whatsoever and at 46% it would be better still. Proof that consistent drams can come from small stills. An American masterpiece – and now an institution. *42.5%*

McCarthy's Oregon Single Malt Aged 3 Years (95) n23 kippery but also soft grist and spices and a hint of slightly overdone brown toast; **t24** jackpot hit as the sweetness is controlled and instead we have lush waves of ultra-clean smoke; the oiliness is there but defused enough to allow only a perfect coating of the palate; **f24** not far off the perfect finale. The oak adds a drier element but really it is the Port Ellen-style fresh gristiness that keeps your tongue working overtime as the finish refuses to fade; **b24** this is, unquestionably, the finest bottled whiskey I have tasted anywhere in the world from a small-batch distiller. Only Islay's very finest can out-complex this not so little chap. *40% (80 proof).*

COPPER FOX DISTILLERY Sperryville, Virginia
Wasmund's Rappahannock Single Malt batch 2 **(82.5)** n18 t20 f23.5 b21. There are those who will struggle to get past the apple/cherry wood smoke, especially when it takes on this tobacco-like personality. A mixed bag of a malt, but one that deserves not to be dismissed by the nose alone. And curious, also, as it is the only distillery in the US which malts all its own barley. *48%*

Wasmund's Rappahannock Single Malt batch 3 **(80)** n17 t20 f22 b21. Way more emphasis on the bitter-sweet here but the dry, bitter finale does overcompensate slightly for the gristy start. *48%*

Wasmund's Rappahannock Single Malt batch 7 **(86.5)** n19 t21 f24 b22.5. . The nose is still a bit of a problem to a non-smoker like me but there is no doubting that this is a complex, well-crafted malt the moment it hits the palate. *48%*

Wasmund's Rappahannock Single Malt batch 8 **(81)** n17 t21 f22 b21. Love it or loathe it – and I know whisky drinkers who do both – there is a consistency in style to these bottling which one has to admire. This one, however, suffers from some over indulgence in caramel (either natural or added it is hard to say) which trims the complexity significantly, especially at the finale. *48%*

Wasmund's Rappahannock Single Malt batch 11 **(83.5)** n16 t21 f24 b22.5. Can't help thinking it would be great to see this whisky, made from its own floor malting, naked without any wood-smoke. *48%*

Wasmund's Rappahannock Single Malt batch 13 **(89.5)** n21.5 here's a turn up for the book: little or no smoke and various layers of barley and something on a toffee-vanilla theme; **t23** deliciously soft and velvety textured; spices about, and meet harmoniously with the massively sweet and intense malt; **f22.5** long, chewy with plenty of vanilla and toffee to show the oak's presence; remains silky and melt-in-the-mouth soft from first to last; **b22.5** either someone forgot to smoke the barley or apple and cherrywood was in short supply. Either way, this works genuinely well with tons of character and lucidity. *48%*

Wasmund's Rappahannock Single Malt batch 14 **(87)** n21 for their second batch running, the smoke takes a back seat to allow the barley a good view; **t23** stunning spices make an early entrance; the malt follows slowly behind; **f21.5** way too much caramel on the finish deadens the complexity; **b21.5** exasperating intrusion of caramel – one assumes from the wood chips – spoils what might have been a beautiful story. 48%

Wasmund's Rappahannock Single Malt batch 18 **(84) n18 t21 f23 b22.** Back to original type, with plenty of fruit wood smoke to shape this intriguingly structured malt. I thought I had tasted this one before: I had, while chair judging for the American Distillers' Institute in Kentucky. When I compared my scores, they were exactly identical. Absolutely 96% proof positive what a very distinctive style this whisky is. 48%

Wasmund's Rappahannock Single Malt batch XIX **(84.5) n17 t22 f23 b22.5.** There appears almost to be a dollop of maple syrup to sweeten this one with the wood-smoke really performing a number here. Big, vanilla and caramel charged and even a hint of butterscotch trying to help smooth things over. Controlled spice ensures another layer of complexity. 48%

EDGEFIELD DISTILLERY Troutdale, Oregon

Edgefield Hogshead (94) n23.5 I ordy-me! No compromising or prisoners taken here: the oak and barley are upfront in equal measure and shouting for top attention; **t23.5** salivating to the point of improbability. A touch yeasty in part, but perhaps that accounts for the rolling fruitiness which takes grip as the barleywater intensifies; **f23** long, with a peppery robustness beginning to clobber anything half-hearted or lacking a spine. The enormity of the barley-oak theme takes some comprehending; **b24** this little distillery has very much come of age. This is fabulous malt that makes no attempt to confuse complexity with no-holds-barred enormity. Big, ballsy and just about flawless. No bottling or batch date, but believed to be bottled 2008. 46%

NEW HOLLAND BREWING COMPANY Holland, Michigan

Zeppelin Bend Straight Malt Whisky (87) n19 Intense malt but displaying a curious and disharmonious sweet and sour note; **t22** rare to find a malt with such spell-binding intensity: a sublime coating of grist helps see off some of the oils which should have not made the cut; **f23** much drier with the oak now throwing in liquorice and gentle spice which harmonise sublimely with those gristy/worty tones; **b23** an understandable and forgivable blemish here and there, especially on the nose, from this new distillery. But full marks for intrigue and entertainment! A brand to keep your eye on. 40%.

SAINT JAMES SPIRITS Irwindale, California

Peregrine Rock (83.5) n21 t20.5 f21.5 b20.5. Fruity and friendly, the wine and smoke combo work well ish enough but the thumping oak injection highlights that maybe there isn't quite enough body to take in the aging. Perhaps less time in the barrel will reduce the bitter orange finale. 40%

STRANAHAN DISTILLERY Denver, Colorado

Stranahan's Colorado Whiskey Batch No. 1 dist 9 Apr 04 db **(95) n25 t23 f23 b24.** This is ridiculous. No first-ever bottling has a right to be this good. If any lucky so-and-so still has a bottle of this…sit on it. Or drink it. You win either way. It is America distilling liquid gold and history in a glass. Beautifully distilled and crafted, the average quality of world, let alone American, malt whisky has just gone up a notch or two. 47% (94 proof).

Stranahan's Colorado Whiskey Batch No. 2 dist 29 Apr 04 db **(89.5) n23 t22 f22.5 b22.** A beautiful whisky but lacks the improbable finesse and balance of Batch 1. 47% (94 proof).

Stranahan's Colorado Whiskey Batch No. 3 dist 13 May 04 db **(95.5) n24 t23 f24.5 b24.** Back on song with another stunner. Just how do they get it this good…? 47% (94 proof).

Stranahan's Colorado Whiskey Batch No. 4 dist 7 Jul 04 db **(88) n22.5 t21.5 f22 b22** Less busy than earlier bottlings, emphasising weight rather than dexterity. 47% (94 proof).

Stranahan's Colorado Whiskey Batch No 5 dist 9 Sep 04 **(90) n23 t24 f21 b22** If the Rockies is where east meets west, then this first-ever Colorado whiskey is where bourbon meets single malt. The quality of the distilling is beyond reproach and this 3,608th, and final, whiskey to go into this 2007 Bible really is the perfect way to end six months' solid tasting. But if the whiskey does has a fault it is the enormity of the oak: for a two-year-old only Indian malt whisky matures faster. My instincts tell me that distillers Jake and Jess will benefit in future years from using a mixture of virgin and used casks to maximise the complexity lurking in the obvious riches found in this gold strike. But hey, this is Colorado. Where you don't mess with a man's woman…or his whiskey… 47% (94 proof).

Stranahan's Colorado Whiskey Batch No. 6 dist 6 Oct 04 db **(91) n23 t23 f22.5 b22.5** About as relaxed as you'll ever find this stuff! Also, nothing like as wide a cut as that found on Batch 5, the first from this distillery I tasted a couple of years back. 47% (94 proof).

Stranahan's Colorado Whiskey Batch No. 7 dist 3 Nov 04 db **(90) n23.5 t21.5 f22.5 b22.5** Almost aggressive in its oakiness the manner in which balance is achieved is as fascinating as it is enjoyable on the palate. *47% (94 proof).*

Stranahan's Colorado Whiskey Batch No. 8 db **(94) n23.5 t23.5 f23 b24** Distilled not a million miles away from South Park, this is one Chef of a whiskey. Baby, get on down...! *47% (94 proof).*

Stranahan's Colorado Whiskey Batch No. 9 dist 17 Nov 04 db **(92.5) n23 t24 f22.5 b23** Every bottling of this asks slightly different questions and gives you varying answers. This is such fun....!!! *47% (94 proof)*

Stranahan's Colorado Whiskey Batch No. 10 dist 3 Jan 05 db **(86) n21.5 t22 f21.5 b21.** Even when this fails to get going, still it is very drinkable whiskey. Here we have a thin'un. It never appears to gain its balance or poise and strains at the leash to recover. Some seriously delicate, kumquat-tipped moments which ensure a fine experience. But compared to the others... *47% (94 proof)*

Stranahan's Colorado Whiskey Batch No. 11 dist 12 Jan 05 db **(96) n24 t24 f24 b24.** Like batch 10, a lighter, more thoughtful version. Unlike Batch 10 it appears to hit a stride and rhythm. And as for the complexity....sighhhh. What a way to taste my 812th new whisky for this year, thereby eclipsing the 2008 Bible: it would have been hard to have chosen a finer malt. *47% (94 proof).*

Stranahan's Colorado Whiskey Batch No. 12 db **(89.5) n23 t22.5 f22 b22** A departure from the norm: esters and spices kept to a minimum. *47% (94 proof).*

Stranahan's Colorado Whiskey Batch No. 13 db dist 10 Jan 05 **(88.5) n22.5 t22 f22 b22** The second one on the trot where the natural caramels have played an important part. Here they almost dominate. *47% (94 proof).*

Stranahanís Colorado Whiskey Batch No. 14 dist 10 Oct 05 db **(77) n18 t19 f21 b19.** aggressive sweet bourbon characteristics try to disguise a degree of feintiness which has crept into this batch. The wide cut does ensure some major flavours to develop, though. Big and surly. *47%*

Stranahan's Colorado Whiskey Batch No. 15 dist 3 Mar 05 db **(80) n19 t21 f20 b20.** Fat, enjoyable, caramel-rich. But another wide cut wallah which doesn't quite have the standard Stranahan genius. *47% (94 proof).*

Stranahan's Colorado Whiskey Batch No. 16 dist 14 May 04 db **(92.5) n22** back to better things: honey on toast, cleaner, spicier, some kick-ass attitude; **t24** that's it; my baby's come home to mamma!!! Oh, the elegance, the sheer charisma as those citrus notes coast on a wave of hickory and honey; **f23** long, the caramels have come out to play but are kept in their place, gorgeous, softly oaked, butterscotched, muscovado sugar notes; **b23.5** I was getting worried... *47% (94 proof).*

Stranahan's Colorado Whisky Batch No. 17 **(95.5) n23** whisky styles collide as the big oaky vanillas thump head-first into the healthy malt. The bourbon effect holds bigger sway, but this is never even remotely one dimensional. **t24** hold on to your cowboy hat as your tastebuds go on a Colorado rodeo ride. Liquorish and leather are peppered with honey and spices while soft oils coat the mouth, ensuring a wonderful weight to proceedings. Yee-bloody-harrrr!!! **f23.5** as the liquorish and honey subside the malt ventures out to tango with the softer vanillas. The spices, though, have no intention of relenting and bristle to the end. **b25** how have they done it? How has a distillery come from nowhere and within a couple of years produced one of the best whiskies in the world? The only thing more stunning than the brilliance of their malt is the way in which a new whisky style has not only been invented, but seemingly perfected. For those who love bourbon and single malt, this really is the best of both worlds. *47%*

Stranahan's Colorado Whisky Batch No. 18 **(89.5) n22** drier than the previous batch with the oaks biting deep. **t23** immediate big honey impact. But it is the spices which really begin to take control as the tastebuds sizzle; massively burnt and roasty; **f22** some malt makes an apologetic entry and a slight butterscotch effect also balances the big oak shockwaves; **b22.5** massive oak has tipped this over the edge slightly. Very enjoyable whiskey, but lacking the balance that made the Batch 17 a malt caressed by genius. *47%*

Stranahan's Colorado Whiskey Batch No. 19 db **(90) n21.5** botanicals have turned up on the nose of other Stranahans, a natural by-product of the oak. Here, though there is a strange and not unattractive hint of juniper.... **t23** yep, there's that juniper again, but it rather fits with the Seville orange and honeyed toffee; busy sub-strata of playful oak; **f23** a pussycat finale with claws very much clipped: pretty sweet and tame; **b22.5** very odd, this one: juniper appears on both nose and delivery. Another slightly wider cut here, but does no great harm as the oranges make good. Big and boisterous until the effeminate cowboy of a finish. *47% (94 proof).*

Stranahan's Colorado Whiskey Batch No. 20 dist 14 Dec 05 db **(92) n22** a whole new bunch of characteristics have appeared which are adding to the big whiskey theme: here, for the first time a bitter-sweet fruity edge reminds you of hops (though none are used), as well as tobacco and linseed: it's like sitting in an old English pub with someone oiling their cricket bat... **t23.5** unusually dry delivery with the sweetness growing by degree; towards the middle honeycomb level has been reached; **f23** an afterglow as long as long as a Scandinavian summer sunset; **b23.5** each bottle appears as a test: both for your tastebuds and the fledgling distillery in discovering what it is capable of achieving; 47% (94 proof).

Stranahan's Colorado Whiskey Batch No. 21 dist 12 Apr 05 db **(89) n22.5** now I get curry powder alongside pencil shavings and molten muscovado sugar....I need to lie down for a while... **t22** chocolate lime candy; then several thick layers of natural cream toffee and fudge....oh, and that unique juniper edge, too... **f22** some lazy spice tags onto the vanillins; **b22.5** tasting all these bottlings one after the other...it's kind of like looking at the same tree or building from a slightly different angle, or making love to a new (rather gorgeous) partner at a different pace or position... 47% (94 proof).

Stranahan's Colorado Whiskey Batch No. 22 dist 27 Apr 05 db **(94.5) n23** back to some honeyed basics here...and how...!! **t24** strands of weakened liquorice wrap loosely around the teeth-breakingly firm and crunchy grain: one of the most confident deliveries for a little while with various regiments of brown sugars helping maintain a glorious sheen to the texture; **f23.5** long with spices coming out of hiding as the oaks gather and meet the sweeter, barley-honey notes square in the eye; **b24** returns to something much closer to its original honeyed style sans the heavy natural caramel...and appears much more in tune and complex for it. 47% (94 proof).

Stranahan's Colorado Whiskey Batch No. 23 db **(95) n23.5** curious, intriguing and never less than delicious mix of old bourbon and old single malt, **t23.5** early spices and then a deep, burnt caramel, singed toast affair; a few refreshing citrus notes in there for balance; **f24** any amount of butterscotch and vanilla breathes a sweeter life back into it; caramelised ginger flanked by honeycomb adds a sublime touch; **b24** if you could put a voice to this whiskey, it'd probably be Lee Marvin... 47% (94 proof)

TRIPLE EIGHT DISTILLERY Nantucket, Massachusetts

Triple 8 Notch (94) n22 chalky oaks sit comfortably with the delicate malt. Clean with the softest whisper of fruit; **t24** genuinely pulses with malt that offers both spices and juicy, grassy fruits in equal measure; the barley sugar and Muscovado sugar sweetness is a delight, as are the light peppers; the middle fattens out; **f23** long with a stunning fade with the oak tip-toeing in and trying to overpower the malt: it has only limited success; **b23** this is the malt that was presented at table to the guests at the launch of the distillery's first ever commercial bottling. However, it is likely that a bottle or two has been purloined and will end up at some stage on eBay or an auction somewhere. This was blended by distiller Dean Long and has immediately catapulted this distillery to the top echelons of American malt whisky – and many other countries' besides. What a fabulous and exciting start. 45%

WOODSTONE CREEK DISTILLERY Cincinnatti, Ohio

Woodstone Creek Single Barrel #1 (92) n24 earthy, salty peat much more rendolent of Islay than Cincinnati. Just beautifully constructed with excellent layering of gentle smoke, grapey fruit and toasted oak: glorious! **t23** the silkiness on the palate stuns: all is understated yet the clarity of the riches never fades. Lots of fruit, but the even sweeter peat circles in clouds and dovetails with drier oak-led incursions; a tantalising saltiness gives this a coastal dimension which belie the distillery's position some 1,000 miles inland...; **f22** surprisingly brittle at the finish, but the smoke shows little sign of abating; **b23** what a wonderful whisky! Islayphiles will be confused by this one because it displays so many coastal characters. A massive well done for a first bottling from this new distillery! 47%

Bourbon Distilleries

Bourbon confuses people. Often they don't even realise it is a whiskey, a situation not helped by leading British pub chains, such as Wetherspoon, whose bar menus list "whiskey" and "bourbon" in separate sections. And if I see the liqueur Southern Comfort listed as a bourbon one more time I may not be responsible for my actions.

Bourbon is a whiskey. It is made from grain and matured in oak, so really it can't be much else. To be legally called bourbon it must have been made with a minimum of 51% corn and matured in virgin oak casks for at least two years. Oh, and no colouring can be added other than that which comes naturally from the barrel.

Where it does differ, from, say Scotch, is that the straight whiskey from the distillery may be called by something other than that distillery name. Indeed, the distillery may change its name which has happened to two this year already and two others in the last three or four. So, to make things easy and reference as quick as possible, I shall list the Kentucky-based distilleries first and then their products in alphabetical order along with their owners and operational status.

TOM MOORE Bardstown. Sazerac. Operating.
BUFFALO TRACE Leestown, Frankfort. Sazerac. Operating.
BROWN-FORMAN Shively, Louisville. Brown-Forman. Operating.
FOUR ROSES Lawrenceburg. Kirin. Operating.
HEAVEN HILL BERNHEIM DISTILLERY Louisville. Heaven Hill. Operating.
JIM BEAM Boston and Clermont. Fortune Brands. Operating.
WOODFORD RESERVE Near Millville. Brown-Forman. Operating.
MAKER'S MARK Loretto. Fortune Brands. Operating.
WILD TURKEY Lawrenceburg. Campari Group. Operating.

Bourbon

Ancient Age (72) n18 t19 f17 b18. Pleasant in part: don't go complexity hunting. *40%*

Ancient Ancient Age 10 Star (91.5) n23.5 a different, massively bourbon, world from the standard AAs. Here the oak makes a speech to announce its arrival and there is plenty of rye and honey-coated corn in attendance, too; **t23** a deliciously satisfying delivery: the texture of the rye element almost makes you groan with pleasure whilst the genteel quality of the vanilla simply makes you purr..; **f22** some unexpected spiced coconut notes turn up towards the death, complete with chocolate; **b23** a marked improvement on recent bottling, though this has never been a harbinger of shoddy work. The delicate nature of the rye really does charm. *45%*

Ancient Ancient Age 10 Years Old (95) n24.5 unreal: almost a portrait of how a delicate, well-aged bourbon should be. A basket of mixed fruits, plus sultanas and buttered oatcake, oddly. The vanillas add nothing more than the softest background noise while the most subtle liquorice and hickory confirms the age; **t24** at once delicate and understated, and on another level sharp and mouthwatering; the rye perhaps takes the most significant lead, rounding up honey and Demerara, but the cream toffee allows it to go only so far; **f23** relatively simplistic with a late lemon jelly (I mean the sweet, not the band) surge as those small grains continue to loiter; **b23.5** this was once my standard whiskey when in Kentucky. Then they began using over-matured whiskeys which masked the complexity. Now it is back to its mesmerising best. Bourbon rarely comes more subtle or gentle than this: one to take a good half hour over for each glass. *43%*

Ancient Age Preferred (72.5) n17 t18 f19.5 b18. Curious saccharine sweetness. The oak and corn haven't really forged a partnership here, though some late spices break up the monotony. *40%*

Baker's Aged 7 Years batch B-90-001 **(81.5) n21 t22.5 f18 b20.** Complex, if a little lethargic, with some surprising youthfulness in evidence. The delivery promises untold complexity and then....disappointment for the most part, and, despite the crisp, precise and firm early delivery, there is an overall imbalance with the oak never quite gelling with the grains, especially in the car-crash of a finish. *53.5%*

Barton Two Bobs Kentucky 13 Years Old cask no. 64, dist Jun 94 **(86) n21.5 t22 f21 b21.5.** Seriously odd: the nose was identical to a Glenugie I tasted in the shell of the distillery back on the early 1980s. Must have something to do with Barton's notorious grain character, in this case barley, and the lightness of the Glenugie malt allowing in the oak. Pleasant, though a tad hot. *64%. Ian Macleod Distillers.*

Barton Two Bobs Kentucky 13 Years Old cask no. 65, dist Jun 94 **(93) n23** spot on, classy bourbon of the rich rye variety; enhanced by some hazy fruit and more distinct cocoa powder; **t23** massive delivery but the enormity is couched slightly by the sophisticated layering of the rye, corn and liquorice; **f24** long, near perfectly weighted with the oils deftly gilding a sherry fruitcake depth; strands of honey and lime do the trick balance-wise, as do the late spices; **b23** whether matured in Kentucky or Scotland, Barton rarely reaches 13 years of age. So this is a fascinating brand. Of those I have encountered, though, this captures the busy Barton style in the finest detail. *63.6%. Ian Macleod Distillers.*

Barton Two Bobs Kentucky 13 Years Old cask no. 66, dist Jun 94 **(88.5) n20 t23.5 f22 b23** Unmistakably Barton in style, for all the age. *63.7%. Ian Macleod Distillers.*

Basil Hayden's 8 Years Old (78) n20 t20 f19 b19. A thin bourbon which never quite finds anchor. Certainly one of the most citrusy bourbons around, but, overall, more Basil Fawlty as this is a bit of a strange, mildly neurotic character. *40%*

Benchmark (86) n21 t22 f21.5 b21.5. Unquestionably a better whiskey than once it was with now an entirely well constructed vanilla-sugar depth adding ballast where once there was none. Lovely unexpected spices, too. A real surprise after not having tasted for a couple of years...as, frankly, it hadn't been worth it. Now it is... 40%

Benchmark No. 8 (79) n20 t21 f19 b19. Conspicuously thinner in body and character than the standard Benchmark. Papery aspects to the sweetness, but little of the balancing spice of its stablemate. 40%

Blanton's Gold Single Barrel (93) n23.5 as near as damn it a rye in style, the fruitiness and spice generated by that grain veritably glows in the glass; **t24** big rye again. It absolutely glitters about the palate offering salivating fruit notes against a background of cane juice. Wonderful; **f22.5** softens as the vanilla makes its mark, but the rye still pulses; **b23** looks as though someone tipped a few extra sacks of rye into the recipe by mistake. Not that I'm complaining... (103proof)

Blanton's Red (90) n23 busy, supremely complex with outstanding small grain interaction: classic; **t22** corn oils abound but there is also a pleasant, controlled bitterness as the oaks gain confidence; **f22.5** clever spices ensure life is retained; **b22.5** a bourbon for those who like to think about what it is they are drinking. 40%

Blanton's Silver (85.5) n20.5 t22 f22 b21. Useful spices early on but the development peters out as the sweetness gathers. 49%

Blanton's Single Barrel (77) n18.5 t20 f19.5 b19. Limited in scope. Plenty of corn but otherwise same old, same old from start to finish. Disappointing (93 proof)

Blanton's Single Barrel Green Label barrel 139 dumped 10-1-05 **(89) n23** kumquats and blood orange abound; **t23** a big rye presence on delivery which shows some delicate touches amid the odd punch; **f21** drier vanilla; **b22** deliciously fruity and rye proud. 40%

Blanton's Single Barrel 7 Years Old (86) n22 t22 f21 b21. Enjoyable, but not exactly what I expected. The bourbon and oak haven't quite gelled: a teen beauty with a few unsightly spots. 51.5%. Buffalo Trace. This is one of the single barrels used to make up 1500 bottles for readers of the Suddeutsche Zeitung Magazin, Germany.

⠿ **Blanton's Single Barrel No. 18** warehouse H, rick 14 **(85) n22.5 t20.5 f21 b21.** Delicate, complex tangerines and sawdust on the nose; the delivery, though sweet, feels a little shackled. 40% (80 proof)

⠿ **Blanton's Single Barrel No. 28** warehouse H, rick 50 **(88) n22.5** soft spices enliven an otherwise ultra-soft vanilla and liquorice aroma, **t23** lands without a bump with the liquorice to the fore. Butterscotch and molasses battle it out for the sweet heart, **f21** a little short and vanilla packed; **b21.5** fulsome yet friendly 46.5% (93 proof)

⠿ **Blanton's Single Barrel No. 53** warehouse H, rick 28 **(94) n24** talk about fruity....first we have kumquats and banana and then pure strawberry. Wow!! That is one very different aroma. Somewhere, if you get over the shock, you'll also find red string liquorice and a dab of honey; **t23** typical BT delivery: the mouthfeel has just that spot degree of oils and then a processions of busy, roast-honeyed waves...with a hint of strawberry topping it off; **f23.5** top rate light sugars coating the roastier oaks...and still those rye-induced fruits keep up their good work; **b23.5** when you realise that a score of 94 is pretty average for this particular version of this brand, you are getting some idea of the quality we are talking about here. And as for the strawberries...don't ask....!! (127 proof)

⠿ **Blanton's Single Barrel No. 56** warehouse H, rick 200 **(90.5) n23** molasses and liquorice by sober degree; **t23** bitter-sweet delivery: the bitterness appears to be a rye-packed fruity hardness; the sweetness is the usual molassesed and honey suspects; spices swell the middle ground; **f22** much drier than normal, again with the rye happy to make itself heard; **b22.5** confident and bold. 46.5% (93 proof)

⠿ **Blanton's Single Barrel No. 83** warehouse H, rick 43 **(84.5) n21.5 t21 f21 b21.** Good cocoa and spice 40% (80 proof)

⠿ **Blanton's Single Barrel No. 86** warehouse H, rick 43 **(93.5) n24** classic...the nose trumpets Buffalo Trace like a corny Hollywood blockbuster would fanfare the opening scenes of a Roman games. Stunning honey/molasses mix; salty like sweaty saddle leather; **t23.5** improbably good on the palate also, with those molassed-honeyed notes following through with dexterity, allowing the vanillas all the space they require, **f23** relaxed, light liquorice and still that hint of molasses are happy to ensure not a single trace of bitterness enters the fray from nose to finish; **b23** a big thumbs up. 40% (80 proof)

⠿ **Blanton's Single Barrel No. 183** warehouse H, rick 23 **(88.5) n22.5** unusual hint of sugared carrot cake amid the acacia honey and vanilla; **t22.5** the corn dissolves along with muscovado sugar and honey; **f22** light flecks of vanilla and bitter-free marmalade on toast; **b22** what a sweetie!! 40% (80 proof)

⊰⊱ **Blanton's Single Barrel No. 223** warehouse H, rick 47 **(79.5) n19 t21 f19.5 b20.** Lashings of cream toffee. Emboldened only by minor spice. *46.5% (93 proof)*

⊰⊱ **Blanton's Single Barrel No. 250** warehouse H, rick 1 **(90) n23.5** beautiful rye and small grain lead, the rest falls naturally into place; **t22** juicy, firm, salivating rye – as to be expected from the nose - doused by a delivery of natural caramels; **f22** spices pick up the rye thread; the fade is one of red liquorice; **b22.5** effortlessly beautiful. *46.5% (93 proof)*

⊰⊱ **Blanton's Single Barrel No. 349** warehouse H, rick 33 **(95.5) n24.5** surprisingly fruity and floral in a not dissimilar way to the botanicals found in gin; again the small grains from this batch are busy, at times almost mesmerizingly so; **t23.5** soft delivery with an initial feel of kumquat and pith, then a quiet zap of rye; salivating and lively, the small grains begin to make mischief again towards the delicately-spiced middle; **f24** spices in full flow, but still contained and in sync with those lively rye pulses and now a demarara-sweetened mocha fade; **b24.5** more like Buffalo Treats: stunning...!!! *46.5% (93 proof)*

⊰⊱ **Blanton's Single Barrel No. 368** warehouse H, rick 37 **(86) n21 t22 f21.5 b21.5.** Slightly over emphatic oak makes for good spice but shouts down many of the other notes. *40%*

⊰⊱ **Blanton's Single Barrel No. 477 (94) n23.5** significant degrees of honey and even rye **t24** lordy, lordy: it's as though we have a role call of every flavour value that constitutes excellent bourbon... a delivery and a half: how honeyed and liquoricy can you get....? **f23** drier with the earlier honey fading but more emphasis on liquorice and demerara sugar; **b23.5** the racehorse on the bottle top says it all: a pure thoroughbred... *(129 proof)*

⊰⊱ **Blanton's Single Barrel Barrel Proof No. 7** warehouse H, rick 23 **(93.5) n23** caramelized biscuit, as much liquorice-rimmed rye as you can shake a barrel gauge at; improbably malty in part; **t24** thumping citrus: sexy, bitter-sweet spice-sprinkled corn and again there is an unmistakable and puzzling barley effect towards the middle; **f23** perhaps overdoes the natural caramels and corn oils, which together are immense, but a lovely cocoa thread at the finish does the trick; **b23.5** the massive strength does nothing to hinder the enjoyment. Curiously, this is one that will appeal to single malt lovers yet to be converted to the greatness of bourbon. *65% (130 proof)*

⊰⊱ **Blanton's Single Barrel Gold No. 174** warehouse H, rick 44 **(81) n20 t21 f20 b20.** Fools' gold.... *51.5% (103 proof)*

⊰⊱ **Blanton's Single Barrel Gold No. 201** warehouse H, rick 25 **(93.5) n23** a big rye-liquorice, mildly minty thing; **t24** text-book complexity on delivery: brilliantly layered with those rye tones forming the intermediate backbone while an almost phenolic, cough sweet tang develops around it; **f23** lots of small grain charm **b23.5** distinctly different. *51.5%*

⊰⊱ **Blanton's Single Barrel Gold No. 316** warehouse H, rick 10 **(89) n24** yet another mammoth rye kick on the nose: it feels like a 51/39/10 corn/rye/malted barley mash bill; so firm is the small grains, with their elegant kumquat charm, the oaks actually offer a softening impact with a light, friendly custard tart element; sublime spices completes the score; **t23** a flinty firmness as the rye cuts to the quick; then appears to become entangled with caramel; **f21** big caramel fade: a relative non-finish compared with the might of before; **b21** a superb bourbon on which the curtain comes down all rather too quickly. *51.5% (103 proof)*

⊰⊱ **Blanton's Single Barrel Gold No. 678** warehouse H, rick 44 **(86.5) n22.5 t22 f21 b21.** Juicy, occasionally barbed with sharp rye; natural caramels are out in force, though. *51.5%*

⊰⊱ **Blanton's Single Barrel Silver No. 59** warehouse H, rick 22 **(89) n22** excellent corn-rye interplay; **t23** juicy: a steady stream of almost barley-rich notes surface but not far below if the firmer rye. A light hickory sweetness compliments; **f22** a light flutter of spices return the rye to pole position; **b22** sturdy and sound. *49% (98 proof)*

⊰⊱ **Blanton's Single Barrel Silver No. 316** warehouse H, rick 28 **(96.5) n25** faultless: just so rare to come across a bourbon where the rye sparkles like this on the nose. The corn plays its part, but only as a soft, delicately sweetening buffer between the firm, fruity rye tones and the oak-led butterscotch, fudge candy and custardy vanillins. Just a light sprinkle of muscovado sugar on old-fashioned bitter English marmalade, but the colonel of the sweetness is corn-based; **t24** much sweeter delivery, with the marmalade making an early statement. A real buzz of rye-enriched spice; the liquorice-honey signature of ripe bourbon is there in several strands, but it's that rye firmness which really catches the eye – and tastebuds; **f23.5** long, soft corn oils enforce a never-ending tail. Chewy with shards of firm rye, but the oak plays a greater role now with a coffee-liquorice depth and a playful spice buzz. Elsewhere a gentle, sweet haze ensures nothing the oak can do will get out of hand; **b24** rarely does a bourbon resonate with such astonishing rye tones. I have comes across some straight ryes showing less character and I would not be surprised to learn that this batch was worked from a slightly altered formula. An absolute must for those who love their bourbon the really old-fashioned way. Blanton's Silver? This is pure gold.... *49% (98 proof)*

Blanton's Uncut/Unfiltered (96.5) n25 it's a pity I have only a year to write this book: it could be a lifetime's work to try and explain the depth and myriad nuances of the nose alone. I'm not sure I should even try. Put it this way: if you want to discover exactly, and I mean exactly, what a bourbon should smell like, then stick your nose in this...; **t24** mind-blowingly enormous, yet unravels on the palate with the viciousness of a two-day-old pussycat. It's the rye, you see. It just won't shut up. And the honey. Not your cheap, runny stuff, no: Manuka by the bucketload. And as for spices...phut! You'll have to travel some way to find a deli with spices like these; **f23.5** thins out once the peaches and citrus arrive. But thin here has about three times the body of most other whiskeys...; **b24** uncut. Unfiltered. Unbelievable. 65.9%

Booker's 6 Years 7 Months batch C00-K-15 **(93) n23** wonderfully roasty with Colombian/Java coffee mixing with singed-toast black peppers; older in character than its allotted years; **t23.5** huge delivery, not just in terms of alcohol strength but by that roasty signature chugging through; delightfully bitter-sweet with butterscotch and vanilla playing a useful role; **f23.5** impressive rye signature to the finale with marauding honeycomb and muscovado sugar against darker, oaky forces; **b23** a combative bourbon with all its considerable personality at full volume. Striking stuff. 63.2%

Buffalo Trace (93.5) n23.5 a restrained nose for a BT with the rye hiding behind a curtain of corn. A complex procession of vanillas with the usual citrus presence offering a thin veneer; **t23.5** a series of soft explosions lights up the tastebuds but again it is the corn which dominates, its soft oils acting as a buffer for the rye and spice; **f23** long and improbably elegant with the smaller grains at last finding a coherent voice; the sweeter vanilla is joined by a dry, toasty oakiness. Unquestionably a more easy-going sample than some recent bottlings I have tasted; **b23.5** as an everyday bourbon there is little to match this one. It's all about balance and complexity and injections here and there of the elements that make bourbon unique. 45%

⠂⠺⠂ **Buffalo Trace Experimental Collection Course Grain Oak** rick/row/slot 1/1/2, 62% evaporation, dist Dec 94, bott Jul 09 **(96) n24** almost the burnt raisin aroma of a very old sherry cask, but obviously can't be; also very toasty but here a balancing sweetness hits the oak head on; **t24.5** a commanding yet restrained demerera sweetness is superbly layered between those biting, toasty oak notes: complex and very comfortable with itself; once more the mouth feel is faultless; **f23.5** takes its foot off the pedal, as if having proved just what it can do: everything slows down, but soft liquorice and demerara-sweetened coffee hang around for a while; **b24** just appears to have another gear by comparison to the Fine Grain and ups into it effortlessly. One of the whiskey – and whisky – experiences of the year. 45%

⠂⠺⠂ **Buffalo Trace Experimental Collection Fine Grain Oak** rick/row/slot 1/1/1, 51% evaporation, dist Dec 94, bott Jul 09 **(91.5) n22** toasty, major oak influence but strangely devoid of the usual sweetness one might reasonably associate with a 15-y-0 bourbon. Perhaps a hint of some dried orange peel; **t23** mixed bag on delivery: a minor movement towards fruity sweetness is ruthlessly crushed underfoot by thick oak. This is big and for a while too much. But the middle ground become occupied by varied and complex citrus, some of which was seen on delivery and sublime spices. The body and mouth feel are exceptional; viscous almost; **f23.5** the spices twitter merrily away with the ever-sharpening citrus now on safer ground and unmolested. A charming degree of latte drifts in for the finale; **b23** one of those whiskeys you have to stand up, walk away from the table and start again with. On first tasting you think: woah!! Way too old...!!! Then you look again and suddenly you find that vaguest hint of orange peel on the nose is actually the one things that stands up to the oak in character on the palate. And what's more, fights back.... 45%

Cadenhead's World Whiskies Heaven Hill Aged 15 Years bourbon, bott Sep 07 **(87.5) n22 t21 f22.5 b22** A very odd bourbon in that it doesn't fall into any one distillery's particular character. An attractive, if abrasive, stand-alone bourbon for all that. 57.2%. 150 bottles.

Charter 101 (89) n22 the accent on evening flowers and nose-prickling spices; **t23** big, bold and honeyed. Some glorious sweet oils help transport the busy oaky-vanilla tones to the furthest points. Everything slapped on with a thick brush – but it's great fun...; **f22** settles down to a no less simplistic but much more gentle finale; **b22** a straight as a die bourbon with no interest in veering off its set course. Gathers just enough complexity along the way to make for a delicious, want again experience. 50.5%

⠂⠺⠂ **Corner Creek Reserve (86) n22 t22 f21 b21.** Honeyed with some striking small grain action. 44%. Corner Creek Distilling Company.

Cougar Bourbon Aged 5 Years bott code 038/07/13 **(95) n25** light, fruity rye offers an aroma I have only ever encountered in an Alpine meadow with myriad flowers popping up through the earthy moss; this is probably the best rye in the world diffused to perfection;

t24 soft, sweet delivery with again the rye taking central command, directing fruity, rooty elements in all directions; **f23** dries agreeably with vanilla subduing the fruity freshness **b23** if Karl Kennedy of Neighbours really is the whisky buff he reckons he is, I want to see a bottle of this in his home next to Dahl. By the way: where is Dahl these days...? (And by the way, Karl, the guy who married you and Susan in London is a fan of mine. So you had better listen up...!) *37% (74 proof). Foster's Group, Australia.*

Daniel Stewart 8 Years Old (92.5) n22 bubbling small grains, rye in particular. A hint of celery complements the polished leather; **t23** busy and quite beautifully crafted. The sweetness is a delight, perfectly balanced by rich, marauding ryes. Burned cream toffee acts as delightful ballast; **f23.5** back to the small grains and lashings of muscovado sugar. Long and gloriously elegant, with a late dash of sweetened milked coffee; **b24** stellar sophistication. Real complexity here, and, as 8-year-olds go, probably among the most complex of them all. A deep notch up on the previous bottling I encountered. *45%*

Eagle Rare Aged 10 Years Single Barrel Mac Y 10th Anniversary (93) n23 unmistakable Buffalo Trace whiskey with the vanilla revealed in so many textured layers; **t23** surging oaks on delivery. Then a backing off to allow a more measured, mildly molassed sweetness to interlink with some orangey citrus; **f23** slow spice arrival, a brushing of hickory and some developing rye fruitiness; **b24** beautiful bourbon from the school of complex shades and inferences. *45%. Denmark.*

Eagle Rare Kentucky Straight Bourbon 17 Years Old bott fall 07 **(91) n23.5** just the right amount of honey works wonders; **t22** rich, roasty with a satisfying combination of small grain bite and oaky menace; **f23** long, tons of natural caramels and late liquorice; **b22.5** a bourbon growing old gracefully but not beyond displaying its seniority at crucial moments. Superb. *45%*

❖ **Eagle Rare Kentucky Straight Bourbon 17 Years Old** bott fall 08 **(87.5) n23.5** anyone who has romped in a hayloft will recognize this one: new mown hay; bales of it sweating in the barn. Light, sweet, a dab of acacia honey and lots of natural caramels; **t22** silky, sweet delivery with a quick jolt of rye then a drift towards light oaky sugars; **f21** flattens dramatically as the caramels take command; **b21** attractive, but after the great nose I expected considerably more. *45% (90 proof).*

Eagle Rare Single Barrel (86.5) n21.5 t22 f22 b22. For those who like their bourbons seriously sugary: loads to get the tastebuds round, but the sweetness encroaches on the complexity. *45%*

Elijah Craig 12 Years Old (86) n21 t22 f21 b22. Well, we wondered what would happen when the EC12 switched to a new distillery, following the loss of the mother ship in 1996. Perhaps this is Bardstown bourbon, but older than 12. I don't think so. That slightly yeasty character is in evidence on the nose and a syrupy feel masks the greater complexity. Enjoyable, but.... *47%*

Elijah Craig 18 Years Old Single Barrel barrel no. 2202, barrelled on 8-31-89 **(93.5) n23** riddled with seams of rich rye, a coppery element ensures the honey does not escape the heady atmosphere; **t24** close your eyes and just allow the stunning rich corn and vivid rye to overwhelm the senses. Liberally spiced, but couched in oily shock-absorbers; all the soft liquorice notes you would demand of this vintage are there; **f23.5** long, with wonderful strands of strawberry preserve and other tart fruits. The vanillas cushion the impact; **b23** now this is more like it. Screams Bardstown. Sings lullabies. Sheer class. *45%*

Elmer T Lee Single Barrel (87.5) n22 dense, with a touch of latte coffee, but lightened by a squeeze of something citrusy; **t22** oily, yet busy, with increasing weight towards vanilla; **f21.5** simplistic and sweet at first but with a very late spice arrival; **b22** a steady bottling by ETL's usual standards. *45%*

Evan Williams (76.5) n18 t20 f19 b19.5. Unrelentingly sweet and simplistic. *43.3%*

Evan Williams 12 Years (90) n21.5 a touch of the new HH Character, but compensated by a real old fruitcake kick; **t23.5** brilliant mouth arrival with the spices boldly leading the way. Juicy, fruity rye isn't too far behind and the liquorice notes begin to up the ante at just the right time; **f22.5** varying dark sugar tones are sprinkled over the drier vanillins and chalky oakiness; **b22.5** perhaps not the force it recently was, but enough grunt here to emphasise the important bits. Namely the enormity of the rye and the sharp spices. Much more at home than, say, the 12-year-old Elijah Craig, for so long its match for quality. *50.5%*

Evan Williams 23 Years Old (95.5) n24 unreal: this is really 107 proof? Well, I've just popped open a fresh bottle, so it must be...Not a single harsh or unkind note on the nose: not even spirit attack. Just the patter over the nosebuds of exceptionally well behaved toffee-rye notes, the odd kumquat and kiwifruit and....oh, some liquorice, as befitting its grand age; **t24.5** a sultry delivery....at first. Then a cavalry charge of spices, with rye and demerara at the rear; the fingerprint of the old Bardstown distillery is so firm and clear I could almost weep: glorious! **f23.5** now starts to get a bit flash with the acacia and manuka honey making equal inroads into the drier vanilla. Just works so well with almost effortless grace; **b24** easily the best EW23 I have come across, and by a distance. Sadly not a single marking on the bottle to show which batch this may be. But if I were in commodities, my message would be: buy, buy, buy...!!! 53.5% ☉

Evan Williams 1783 no. 10 brand **(71.5) n17 t18 f18.5 b18.** A struggle to get beyond the nose. 43%

Evan Williams Single Barrel 1993 Vintage barrel no. 001, barrelled Oct 93, bott Oct 02 **(89) n22 t22 f22 b23** Comfortable and complicated. 43.3%

Evan Williams Single Barrel 1994 Vintage barrel no. 511, barrelled Nov 94, bott Oct 04 **(92) n23 t23.5 f22 b23.5** If you demand your bourbon sweet and delicate, track down a bottle of this'un. 43.3%

Evan Williams Single Barrel 1995 Vintage barrel no. 01, barrelled Aug 95, Bott Nov 04 **(87.5) n22 t22 f21 b22.5** A bourbon which is at times too laid back and simplistic for its own good: one oily bottling, this! 43.3%

Evan Williams Single Barrel 1997 barrel no. 1, barreled 20 Feb 97, bott 10 Oct 06 **(87) n22 t24 f20 b21** All the wondrous sugary, toasty notes arrive early on, leaving behind a thinner, more bitter finish. For those of you wondering why this is so removed from the usual EW Single Barrel we have come to know and love over the last decade, the answer, of course, is that it was made at a different distillery following the Great Heaven Hill fire of 1996: in this case the Clermont Distillery of Jim Beam. The recipe may be identical. But the difference is in the glass for all to taste. 43.3%

Evan Williams Single Barrel Vintage 1996 barrel no. 1, bott 4 Oct 05 db **(92) n24 t23 f22 b23** Up to the usual superb standards. 43.3% (86.6 proof).

⋅❖⋅ **Evan Williams Single Barrel 1999** barrel no 1 **(88.5) n24** sensational honeycomb: it just doesn't get more honeyed...or more burnt. It's as though the barrel has spent its entire life at the top of the warehouse and the light eucalyptus note really does suggest a whiskey twice the age it actually is; **t22** initial manuka honey delivery and then roasty oak....big time; **f21** marmalade bitterness and a huge wave of caramels; **b21.5** technically too old: the oak really has got its fingers and thumbs around the neck of the grain. But those moments when it's got it right....boy, oh, boy...!!! 43.3% (86.6 proof)

Fighting Cock Aged 6 Years (85.5) n20 t22 f22.5 b22. The classic old aroma of the first bottling may have been cock-olded, but the arrival on the palate makes for a stunner. Just heaps of small grain bristle around the palate and their combined intensity and assertiveness ensure a chewy, mildly waxed experience. A big cock, indeed... 51.5%

Four Roses Barrel Strength Aged 12 Years 120th Anniversary Limited Edition (88) n21 firm, dry, toasty, **t22** immediate spice explosion, then hickory and fruit; **f22.5** more controlled, corn-rich, chewy and oily; **b22.5** typically understated and charming. 55.4% (110.8 proof).

Four Roses 120th Anniversary 12 Years Old Single Barrel (91.5) n22.5 lots of vanilla; no little spice, **t24** an improbably refined delivery for all the huff and puff of the alcohol: a small grain extravaganza with the rye leading the way, peppering the tastebuds like so much shot; **f22** waves of blunted sweetness crash against an extraordinary French toast finale; **b23** twelve year old bourbons are just so meant to be more in your face than this...An essay in understatement and subtlety. Four Roses is beginning to make its mark as Kentucky's most delicate bourbon. (110.5 proof)

Four Roses Barrel Strength Aged 13.5 Years (86.5) n21 t21.5 f22.5 b21.5. Relatively closed by FR standards with the liquorice and spices on top form. 52.1% (104.2 proof).

Four Roses (Black Label) (88) n20 unhappy, with some off-key lactic moments; **t23** recovers supremely with a fabulous complexity to the rye-oak interchange. Really chewy, with awesome soft oils and spices that pepper the mouth – literally! **f23** a sustained sweetness draws upon the central corn character and is backed by a profusion of late liquorice and honey; **b22** a whiskey which starts falteringly on the nose recovers with a sublime delivery of all things bourbon. 40%

⋅❖⋅ **Four Roses Marriage Collection 2008 (92.5) n23** a trifle pugnacious. The oak is having much to say, throwing down big weight to out punch the evident rye and light botanical (including delicate juniper) feel. Muscular and happy to deliver the odd punch; **t23** as dry as the Single Barrel I tasted was sweet: again it's all about the oak. Very toasty, mild hickory but a subtle coating of molassed sugar ensures there is no oaky excess; **f23** long, complex, with outstanding interweaving between the lightly burned coffee and sweeter liquorice; **b23.5** sophisticated, bourbon lovers' bourbon. 53.9% (107.8 proof)

∴ **Four Roses Marriage Collection 2009 (88.5) n23.5** pretty big by Four Roses standards with an emphasis on caramelized orange-mint; the oak, though, broods; **t22** it's the oak which really makes the impact, ensuring a dry, spicy delivery with a surprising degree of oils; **f21.5** toasty and dry with the caramelized sugars hyper caramelized; **b21.5** not sure of the barrel number for this one, but could do with a little less toastiness if in search of true greatness. Even so, lovely stuff. *58% (116 proof)*

∴ **Four Roses 2009 Limited Edition (88) n22** chunky, perhaps slightly over fried in barrel; **t23** it doesn't take long for spices to make their mark, actually lightening the big oaky delivery along with a few spoon-fulls of molasses and liquorice; **f21** enormous amounts of natural caramels have been let loose, too; **b22** attractive bourbon, but perhaps the nagging feeling that this barrel may have been very slightly over-aged. *58.4% (116.8 proof)*

∴ **Four Roses Single Barrel** warehouse BS, barrel 36-5R **(89) n22** fingers of citrus gently massage the nose buds; floral and delicate; **t22.5** traces of maple syrup throughout; the vanilla alternates between toasty and custardy; **f22** long, still with that distinctive sweet edge but a delicate toastiness; **b22.5** for those who prefer their bourbons soft and very sweet: much more of a sissy than some of the others from this distillery I have tasted of late and, to be honest, much more of the style traditionally associated with Four Roses. *50% (100 proof)*

Four Roses Single Barrel (84) n21 t22 f20 b21. Juicy to the Nth degree early on; perhaps on the flat and oily side at the death. *43%*

Four Roses Single Barrel warehouse KE, barrel no. 9-6A **(93.5) n22 t25 f23 b23.5** A supremely well assembled and deft bourbon of the highest order. The delivery is near enough perfection as damn it. *50%*

Four Roses Small Batch (86.5) n18.5 t22 f24 b22. Lightweight and delicate, this is as juicy and mouth-watering as bourbon gets. A touch tart, perhaps, but a treat for those looking for the ultimate in small gain complexity. The finish, which rumbles like an Evansville earthquake, is nothing short of breathtaking. Such a pity about the off-key nose. *(90 proof)*

Four Roses Super Premium (90.5) n23 Four Roses at its most bruising and macho: real liquorice-led weight here to complement the spices and grainy dexterity; **t23** Ye gods!!! Spices abound as the peppery start leads into something altogether silkier and chewy. Superb balance between well matured virgin oakiness and a cavalry charge of peppery grains; **f22** thins as the vanilla takes hold; **b22.5** this distillery's whiskey is amongst the hardest to judge in the world: on the one hand it is light and sophisticated, on the other it sometimes misses out on the riches and balance that truly great bourbon demands. This bottling, however, successfully accumulates ticks in every department. *(86 proof)*

Four Roses (Yellow Label) (84) n21 t22 f20 b21. A straight as a die bourbon that for all its effete lightness and mannerisms still conjures enough weight and charisma to entertain. On nose and palate, as citrusy as the colour of the label suggests. However, it is the backbone rye that stars early on, though it fades towards the ultra light finish. *40%*

George T Stagg (96.5) n24.5 vanilla concentrate meets rye concentrate meets corn concentrate. But rather than one messy battle the elements ease and slip into each other effortlessly. Really the most gentle of giants; **t24.5** easily one of the most glorious deliveries of any whisky in the world: there is a sheen to this unlike any other on the planet, a crisp edge of rye and indistinct fruits which soon melts and punctures, allowing a tidal wave of honeyed corn to pour through. Simply breathtaking. Literally; **f23.5** much more emphasis on soft brown sugars sprinkled on thick vanilla; liquorice and hickory show the age, but even this is in beautifully rationed portions; **b24** pretty close to perfection with the finale missing a spicy riposte. But that is being churlish: the elegance topples off the scales and the complexity, once the palate adjusts to the powering alcohol, appears to set new standards. One of the whiskeys of the year, easily. *(144.8 proof)*

George T. Stagg (94) n23 t24 f23 b24 Another thundering glass of genius and so complex despite the massive strength. Perhaps a shade oakier, though, than some of its predecessors. *70.6% (141.2 proof). Buffalo Trace.*

George T. Stagg (96) n25 can something this delicate really be 140 proof?? An aroma that drifts like butterflies with no shortage of nectar to feed on; the strands of honey are both deft and deep and balance well with the honeycomb; dulcet rye tones soar on the spirity thermals and oak offers a soft, vanilla-rich cladding. Simply the stuff of whiskey dreams...; **t22** begins sweet but nosedives into something surprisingly dry, mildly compromising the balance for a while until it rediscovers its equilibrium with a wave or ten of Belgian chocolate; **f25** returns to its brilliance once more with those cocoa notes now harmonising with the returning rye; just so long and the late arrival of an orangey, citrus thread doesn't hurt at all; in fact the finish is near perfection; **b24** just one moment or two's madness, where the plot is lost may have cost this one World Whisky of the Year. Another staggering

Stagg, a serious improvement on the previous bottling and a collector's must-have. *70.3% (140.6 Proof). ncf.*

Hancock's Reserve Single Barrel (93.5) n24.5 almost erotic in the way the rye and vanilla tease the senses: a gentle, small-grained attack that is busy, alluring and almost showing off. Changes shape slightly as the temperature alters and the odd orangey note can be detected. But it is the charm of the rye which perhaps excites most; **t23** every bit as busy as the nose with the rye really making itself known. But all done in a casual, relaxed way that allows a custard-cream cream-caramel element to evolve and delight; **f22.5** long, though the vanillas start to take a grip; **b23.5** sticks to its trademark cream caramel signature. But this time far greater emphasis on the firm rye outcrops. Impressively balanced all round: bourbon at its most sophisticated. *44.45% (88.9 Proof)*

Heaven Hill Old Style Bourbon (78) n21 t19 f19 b19. Much better nose but the body thins out dramatically. Decent dose of sweetness, though. *40%*

Heaven Hill Old Style Bourbon Bottled in Bond (81) n20 t21 f20 b20. An entire role reversal from the standard bottling with the shy nose showing absolutely no sign of the rye-led riches that follow. Some decent Demerara cuts in, too. *50%*

Heaven Hill Old Style Bourbon 6 Years Old (66) n17 t17 f16 b16. Very strange bourbon with a weird yeastiness/fermentation residue. Never finds a rhythm or settles. An uncomfortable and very un-Heaven Hill-like ride. *45%*

Heaven Hill 6 Years Old (83) n20 t20 f22 b21. An infinitely more satisfying bourbon than its Old Style stable mate at this age. The battle between crisp rye and compact caramel is intriguing and pretty tasty to boot. *40%*

Heaven Hill Mild and Mellow (80) n18 t20 f21 b21. Also known as the 86 proof, this has changed markedly in recent years. Firm and oily, the corn dominates where once barley had such an unusually large say. Since moving distillery(-ies) the house style has chopped and changed a little and again the nose is the weak spot. Pleasant otherwise. *43%*

Heaven Hill Ultra Deluxe Aged 36 Months (86.5) n20 t22.5 f22 b22. Another Heaven Hill that has changed tack considerably over the last year or so. And possibly age. For all its baby fat, this youngster is something of a beauty in that few bourbons are quite so mouth-watering and fresh. The rye pulses on the tastebuds and there is even an injection of something vaguely of the liquorice family: amazing for its tender years. Simply, pure fun whiskey with zero pretensions but maximum effect. Just love it!! *40%*

Henry McKenna Aged 10 Years Single Barrel bottled in bond barrel no. 327, barrelled Dec 97 **(81.5) n19 t21 f21 b20.5.** Sweet, pleasant, corn-rich, a touch syrupy in parts and never begins to extend itself...or the imbiber. *50%*

Hudson Baby Bourbon bear 08, batch 3 **(71) n15 t17 f19 b18.** Hard to make it past the butyric-riddled nose. Some wonderfully intense fruity notes to ensure a degree of pleasantness. But this is an early attempt from a fledgling distillery and a journey back to the drawing board is required. *46%*

Hudson Four Grain Bourbon bott 08, batch 3 **(78.5) n17 t20 f21.5 b21.** Neither for the feint nor faint hearted. The nose is a problem, but there is no shortage of sharp and puckering complexity to concentrate the mind thanks to the intense and, it has to be said, wonderfully entertaining palate. Sort out a few gremlins and this promises to be a whisky to watch. *46%*

Jefferson's Reserve batch no. 84 **(91) n23** solid as a rock: the rye forms an almost impenetrable barrier to the softer, oilier corn. But not quite..; **t23.5** lush and full bodied, the sweetness gallops off in every direction unmolested until several thick waves of vanilla and spice intervene. Sugar-coated liquorice fills the middle; **f22** much more genteel, with the drier vanillas taking charge; **b23** once a 15-year-old, no age statement here. But this has seen off a few summers, and sweetened with each passing one. *45.1%. 2400 bottles.*

Jim Beam (83) n20 t20 f22 b21. A notch or two lighter than recent years with a noticeably less oaky backbone. A complex finish after a sluggish start, though, with some playful brown sugar stirring things up attractively. *40%*

Jim Beam Black Aged to Perfection (89.5) n22 softer, less pungent than the 8-y-o version; **t23** the accent on the sugars with the usual rye boldness taking a back seat behind the sweeter corn, though by no means invisible; **f22.5** gentle vanilla and more molasses with some puckering liquorice towards the finale; **b22.5** Jim Beam Black. But, teasingly, with no age statement! Does it live in the shadow of the sublime 8-years-old? Well, perhaps not quite. Lacks the lushness and the peaks and troughs of complexity. But, though a lot more even in temperament, it never fails to delight, even if the standard rye kick is conspicuous by its absence. As a bourbon, excellent. As a Jim Beam Black, a little disappointing. *43% (86 proof)*

Jim Beam Black Aged 8 Years (94) n23 the layering here is exemplary: we are talking well aged fruitcakes (of the burnt raisin and cherry on the crust variety) here, not to mention mild ginger cake moistened by subtle oils and a sub layer of fruity rye. Garnish that with the usual leathery liquorice and … mmmmmm….!!! **t24** begins deftly with the corn and oak delivering polished, gentle beats hand in hand; then the sweetness begins to build as do the playful spices. Silky hints of rye on a bed of bitter-sweet oak and a trace of hickory; **f23** mouth-watering rye shows no shyness here and the engrossing dryness never outweighs the Demerara sub-plot. Engrossing, charming and almost hypnotic in its delicacy and balance; **b24** it is if, at last, the guys behind the barrel selection and dumping of this product are now truly believing in what they are doing. As each year comes and goes, so, it seems, this bourbon gets better and better. The jump in quality between this and the standard "white" Beam has shifted from gap to chasm in the last decade, with the pace widening and increasing over the last four years. Unquestionably one of the great bourbons, this is an everyday whiskey with which I win more converts to the bourbon cause than any other. A big whiskey, yet one that openly revels in its finesse and complexity. A Kentucky classic. 43%

Jim Beam Choice Aged 5 Years (89) n22 those who remember the stuttering, faltering nose of the Choice a year or two ago will be taken aback: now firm, almost brooding with a classic red and black liquorice depth; **t22** sweet delivery shows an impressive harmony between corn and oak; **f23** lush, chewy and offering increasing degrees of spice. Superbly structured and layered and improbably confident for its age; **b22** a hugely improved whiskey which is no longer betwixt and between but now strikingly makes its own bold statements. Makes noises on both nose and palate way above its five years. A bourbon to grab whilst in this expansive and impressive mood. 40%

Jim Beam Premium Aged 7 Seven Years Old (White Label) db **(82) n21 t21 f20 b20.** Hard, uncompromising and showing little of what is to come with a stunning 8-years-old. Young in character even to the point of the Old Taylor from the same stable entirely outflanking this for complexity and riches. That said, good crispness and a lovely – and unexpectedly – malty tail- off in middle. Decent but disappointing. 40% (80 proof).

Kentucky Supreme Number 8 Brand (76) n18 t19 f20 b19. Simplistic and undemanding with massive emphasis on a barley sugar-style tartness and sweetness. 40%

Kentucky Tavern (84) n20 t22 f21 b21. Another juicy little number which appears almost to have a young malt feel to it. Clean, with just the right amount of rye sparkle to offer buzz and complexity. 40%

⋰ **Kentucky Vintage (91.5) n23** a slight yeasty kick to the classic honeycomb-liquorice fanfare; **t24** sublime: mouth-watering grains strike a great rapport with copper-sheened molassed notes; light spices keep the tastebuds working overtime; **f22** a lovely amalgamation of dried and juicy dates; **b22.5** damned fine bourbon! 45%

Knob Creek Aged 9 Years (92) n22.5 almost stereotypical of what a chunky and very good bourbon should be: firm yet yielding with excellent honeycomb and cocoa amid vanilla and honey. At times almost old Jamaican pot still rum-like; **t23** sweet delivery – rummy again! – then a delivery of oily corn and spices and wonderful layering of vanilla-fed oak; **f23.5** long and powerful and fabulously lush with a return to honeycomb topped by a sugared rye-spice climax; **b23** no whiskey in the world has a more macho name, and this is not for the faint-hearted. Big, hard in character and expansive, it drives home its point with gusto, celebrating its explosive finish. 50%

Maker's Mark (Red Seal) (88.5) n21 a little spicier than the norm but those fruit and honey strands are tightly bound; a touch of lactose from the oak surprises; **t23.5** the wax is confined not just to the seal as a wonderful coating encrusts every solitary tastebud. A wonderful honey theme plays alongside the busy wheat-induced spices; **f22** thins as the crème brulee gets a grip; **b22** just as the distillery is an official historic landmark of Kentucky, then so too should be the remarkably consistent character of its whisky. By rights, any whisky that boasts no more than 19 casks should jump around pretty spectacularly from bottling to bottling. With MM you do get variance, of course, but the style is so tight and consistent, it is pretty easy to spot even when tasted blind. 45%

Most Wanted Kansas Bourbon Mash Whiskey (83) n18 t20 f23.5 b21.5. A sweaty armpit nose is the unlikely overture for an attractively flavoursome and delicately sweet bourbon. Highly unusual and rather gristy in style, the superb finish offers hugely attractive chocolate. One that really grows on you. 40%

Old 1889 Royal Aged 12 Years (78) n19 t20 f19 b20. A curiously ineffectual and ultimately frustrating bourbon which still needs to feel loved for its small grain complexity but succeeds only in demanding a slap for being so lily-livered. In the end it falls between the delicate and full-blown fruity stools. 43%

Old Charter 8 Years Old (78) n21 t20 f19 b19. Remains dull and overly toffeed. 40% ☉☉

Old Charter 10 Years Old (83) n20.5 t21 f21.5 b21. From having blazed a glorious trail for a brief time in the recent past, it has returned to type. Plods about the palate like a dazed brontosaurus: big, but no serious bite and too unwieldy ever to be a beauty. Pleasant, though, and just the odd busy sugar-vanilla moment helps it along. *43%*

Old Crow Aged 3 Years (85.5) n21 t21.5 f21 b22. Maintained its youthful style solidly with the aroma upping a gear or two. Still a minty freshness to the nose, but now aided and abetted by the first strands of young liquorice. A real surprise package. *40%*

Old Fitzgerald (83.5) n19 t21 f22 b21.5. A greatly improved bourbon that is beginning to feel more at home in its sweet, vaguely spicy surroundings. *43%*

Old Fitzgerald's 1849 (74) n18 t19 f18.5 b18.5. Cloying, shapeless and hugely disappointing: as a corn whiskey it'd do better. "Its quality unchanged since 1849", shrills the label. Well, it's dropped 16 points since 2006 in my book... *45%*

Old Fitzgerald Very Special 12 Years Old (93.5) n23 slightly sluggish and off-colour in parts but some oaky zeal manages to get some spicy banana custard into play; allow the glass to sit for a while, or nose when empty and you get a very clear picture of something very different and beautiful; **t24** soft, entirely melt-in-the-mouth stuff. Sweet, but the sugars are layered, as are the receiving vanillas. Delicate and impressive and the spices genuinely add guile; **f23** many more vanilla-charged layers complete the complexity; **b23.5** in the topsyturvy world of Old Fitz, the 1849 has sunk without trace whilst this has improved beyond all recognition. I suspect some of the bourbon from the old 1849 8-year-old is now making its way into this impressive and highly distinguished little number. The best Old Fitz I've encountered for some 20 years. *45%*

Old Forester Birthday Bourbon distilled spring 93, bottled 05 **(94) n24 t23 f23 b24** One of the most rye-studded stars in the bourbon firmament and wholly in keeping with the fabulous quality for which this brand has now become a byword. *40%*

Old Grand-Dad (90.5) n22 a nose that screams small grains at you, with the rye and even barley having an unusually hefty say. Seriously complex and one that needs a few minutes to get to know; **t23** fabulous marriage of aged weight and grainy complexity. The tastebuds are bombarded with myriad juicy notes as the soft ryes and molassed sugars weave a course through the building vanilla; **f23** light, almost lofty, as those busy grainy notes begin to head towards something a little more traditional in weight and oiliness; not before some mocha creeps in for good measure, though; **b23.5** this one's all about the small grains. A busy, lively bourbon, this offers little to remind me of the original Old Grand-Dad whiskey made out at Frankfort. That said, this is a whisk(e)y-lover's whiskey: in other words the excellence of the structure and complexity outweighs any historical misgivings. Enormously improved and now very much at home with its own busy style. *43%*

Old Grand-Dad Bonded 100 Proof (88) n21.5 t22 f22.5 b22. A punchy, weightier version than the standard Grand-Dad. This appears to have greater age and the encroaching oak manages only to strike out some of the complexity so gloriously relevant in the lighter bottling. Still good whiskey, and with a much more intense cocoa delivery. *50%*

Old Heaven Hill Bottled in Bond (79) n17 t21 f21 b20. A bourbon which grows in stature the longer it stays on the palate with spice/rye/muscovado sugar interplay particularly delightful. The nose, though, does it little justice. *50%*

Old Heaven Hill Very Rare Old Aged 8 Years (84) n20 t22 f21 b21. Fruity and light, there is a decent rye-style surge early on in the delivery which offers a gripping intensity. *43%* ⊙ ⊙

Old Heaven Hill Very Rare Old Aged 10 Years Bottled In Bond (88) n21 Shall we call it the Heaven Hill Character? Certainly an entirely different aroma from the days when distilled back in Bardstown. An amalgam of rye and brown sugars offers something decent and weighty, but a light, fruity sub-stratum undermines the plans. **t22.5** Entirely nonsensical and out of sync, the manner in which the different elements crash blindly about the palate actually makes for serious entertainment. Again it is the rye which totally dominates proceedings, but without ever keeping control. Powering vanillas stir things up like a naughty schoolboy; **f22.5** a degree of sanity is restored and even a touch of finesse injected. The caramel/vanilla/rye trilogy is an intense one; **b22** a mad professor of a bourbon, heading off in every direction without any apparent sense. But then works out beautifully. *50%*

Old Rip Van Winkle 10 Years Old (81.5) n19 t21 f20.5 b21. Oily, soft and slightly effete. *45% Buffalo Trace*

Old Rip Van Winkle Bourbon Aged 13 Years (87) n22 t22 f21 b22 very different: in fact I have never seen a Buffalo Trace whiskey like it. There are restaurants in Stockholm's Old Town whose owners would offer major favours to have a house aquavit like this. *53.3%.*

Old Taylor Aged 6 Years (present bottling) **(89) n23** marzipan and Seville orange offer a delightful lightness of touch and teasing complexity; **t23** almost a hint of single malt about the lightness of touch to the honey here; the arrival is sweet and busy with just enough oaky depth to add ballast; **f21** almost vanishes off the palate though the rye and spice stick around to impress; **b22** the curiously thin finish is in telling contrast to the superbly honeyed middle that simple dances with small-grain charm. So much lighter than the original Old Taylor (see below) of McCracken Pike. But certainly has enough weight and fruit punch to make this better than the cheap brand it is perceived to be. 40%

Old Taylor Aged 6 Years (old bottling) **(94) n24 t23 f23 b24** Just a mile from my home in Kentucky stands, or perhaps I should say stood, the Old Taylor distillery. It may not still be there because the widow of my close and dearly missed friend, Cecil Withrow, finally sold it and the old place where Cecil once worked and, until his untimely death, harboured dreams of distilling again, faces the almost certain prospect of the demolition ball. I thought it fitting, then, that for my 1,000th whiskey tasted from the 2007 edition of the Bible it should be an original Old Taylor six-years-old which I found in a back street liquor store in Verona, Italy. In fact there are still many bottles of this truly classic bourbon to be found in that country and if visiting Italy for its architecture and food isn't enticing enough, then here must be the ultimate reason. And just to put a strange and fitting twist to this tale, how about this: as I was tasting and writing these notes a delivery van turned up. Nothing unusual there: we get four or five deliveries of samples every day. This, though, was a special shipment from Peru: the very first copy of a special edition of the Whisky Bible I produced for the 2006 US Christmas market. And the book had been specially dedicated to... the memory of Cecil Withrow... 40%.

⋯ **Old Virginia Aged 6 Years (79) n20 t21 f18.5 b19.5.** Old Virginia because of the drying tobacco leaf on the aroma? Sweet, but a lot flatter than the state... 40%. La Martiniquaise,

Old Virginia Aged 8 Years L434401A **(85) n22 t21 f21 b21.** Vanilla-rich and never quite lives up to the bold nose. 40%. La Martiniquaise, France.

Pappy Van Winkle's Family Reserve 15 Years Old (93.5) n23.5 classic corn-rye whiskey with a bit of an edge. Blood oranges and something meaty, too; **t24** the mouth puckers under the onslaught of sharp rye and toast-dry vanilla. Yet this is nowhere near over the top and the marmalade fruitiness charms and endears as the spices hit home. Woomphh...!! **f22.5** with the battle over, the waves of juicy rye lap kindly on the palate, though the amount of yield remains minimal; **b23.5** big whiskey making a big statement. Delightful on numerous levels and pappy as it should be. (107proof)

Pappy Van Winkle's Family Reserve 20 Years Old (78.5) n21 t20 f18.5 b19. Flat for the most part and bitter at the end. Just doesn't click as you'd hoped it might. (90.4 proof)

Pappy Van Winkle's Family Reserve 23 Years Old (86.5) n23 t21.5 f21 b21. Massive bourbon but the oak, in true PVW style, has become something of a problem. Lots of lavender hickory, but not even close to being a classic bourbon. (95.6 proof)

Parker's Heritage Collection (94.5) n22.5 huge. Not short of orangey-citrus notes, or the usual leather armchairs, either. Some post Bardstown Character here, but a bourbon aroma with balls... **t24** the thinly disguised rye on the nose absolutely explodes on the palate: we are not talking dynamite – this is nuclear. The big, black cherry fruitiness of the rye is in concentrate form helped along the way by the sweet oils of the thudding corn; the enormity of the entire experience is unforgettable; **f24** long and now finds a voice that is calm, sophisticated and adorably complex. The rye offers almost too many guises to be true, but the oak now kicks on with gentle waves building towards something steeped in cocoa. Improbably long and almost obscenely beautiful; **b24** a bourbon for men – and probably women – with hairs on their chests. The bottle suggests you add water to this. Yeah, if you're a gutless wimp. I have known Parker Beam since before the barrels selected for this was a wicked glint in the old distiller's eye. And I can't believe he didn't pass many a barrel by before he chose those which have given us one of the best new whiskeys of the year. An instant classic. And a new must have bourbon is born. 64.8% (129.6 proof)

Parker's Heritage Collection barrelled 26 Apr 96 **(91.5) n23** a thudding, no holds-barred aroma, full of peppered celery. Leathered armchair stuff: both on nose and countenance. Sophisticated and at times delicate for all its oomph; **t23** boiled apple and soft rye and corn oils combine tactfully; **f22.5** brown sugars and vanillas collide with surprising grace; **b23** big full-on bourbon at first, then simmers down for something unashamedly fragile towards the end. Superb. 122.6 proof. Heaven Hill.

Parker's Heritage Collection Second Edition Aged 27 Years bott 08 **(93)** big and brooding, but nothing to the extent I expected. Still entering unknown territory aroma wise: a vague pine note appears mashed into the thick waxy honey-leather. It is like a wall, or an aroma with no light notes or let up whatsoever: 'dense' doesn't even begin to tell the tale...; **t23** the very first notes are those of exhausted oak. But soon a gamut of livelier, sweeter tones breathe the necessary life back into it and soon we are off with an amazingly rich tapestry of spicy, grainy textures all woven into a burnt fudge background; **f23.5** remarkably long and – even more remarkably - not for one second entering the realms of bitterness I so much expected. All the complex notes orbit a dry, mocha-encrusted world. There is no similar experience to this in bourbon; **b23.5** an improbably excellent bourbon from the oldest commercial bottling I can remember ever seeing. To be honest, I expected the worst and if someone was to ask me prior to tasting this what hope I would have for bourbon of this age hitting the heights, my answer would not have been particularly positive. However, I have now known Parker Beam for more years than I care to admit and am 100% confident in his sound values: he is without a shadow of doubt in the highest echelon of whiskey and whisky men there have been in our generation. It was he who selected the casks so I was intrigued (also in why they didn't bring out 100 single barrel bottlings rather than dump them together for a one-off, but that's another story), to put it mildly. And the result of 27 years in the barrel is an entirely unique experience not even close to being similar to any other whisky in the world. Indeed, it as if it has not so much entered another whisky world but a parallel universe. Normally I'd shudder at the thought of so much oak. However, this works - and some! I hear it's going for 200 bucks a bottle. I don't normally comment on price but, believe me, for its uniqueness of style alone it's a snip. *48% (96 proof)*

⋄⋄ **Parker's Heritage Collection Third Edition 2009 "Golden Anniversary" (96.5)** n24.5 super rich nose with massive orange current riding high on the mountainous oaky waves: almost like controlled anger for having to wait in a barrel for so many decades before being let out; **t24.5** again, absolutely huge: cocoa is normally a characteristic found at the back end of a whisk(e)y as the oaks bite. Here it is the first personally to be heard and is followed close behind by that concentrated, spicy kumquat note you knew would be lurking somewhere and the inevitable honeycomb; yet between the cocoa and kumquat look out for a brief pulse of palma violet. Just so complex and beautifully oiled to (leathery) boot; **f23** the tangy Jaffa gives way to some distant oaky bitterness but there's an assured layer of muscovado sugar to ensure the oaks bow out with grace and natural caramels also help put on the brakes; **b24.5** if you are looking for a quiet whiskey with minimum personality, something which ice actually livens up, then don't waste your time here. This is creaking under the oaky strain, hardly surprising as some of what's in your glass is over 40 years old...or about 80 in Scottish years. But the layering and depth is as monumental as it wondrous. How has old timer Parker Beam managed to restrain so much oak? And, better still, harness it into something radiating such unlikely riches. Probably only he knows: he has a few tricks up his sleeve after 50 years in the game. The best commercially available bourbon I have tasted this year and easily one of the top five whiskies in the world. A whiskey entirely befitting Parker, a quiet colossus not just in the bourbon industry but the world whisky stage. This whiskey, like the man, is the real deal. *50% (100 proof) Heaven Hill.*

Peach Street Bourbon (86) n19 t22 f23 b22. The nose, though the weak link, is not without its charms; the delivery offers excellent spice and a real fruit cake quality, complete with juicy dates. The finish, as the oak finds a home, really is a joy. Impressive stuff from a small batch distiller and a two-year-old bourbon. *43%. Peach Street Distillers, Colorado.*

Pritchard's Double Barrelled 9 Years Old (92) n23 classy, effortless delivery. The corn-rye integration oozes sophistication and the vanilla-themed oak offers the perfect background; **t24** immediate bitter-sweet character celebrates both a raisin-fruity juiciness and a much firmer, burned-honeycombed middle; complex, classy and challenging; **f22** thuddingly firm with limited yield. Spices from the rye try to probe the wall, but this is the metalled hoof of a Kentucky thoroughbred; **b23** a very different bourbon that ticks the boxes as they should but throws in a few curve balls for the palate to negotiate. *45%*

Ridgemont Reserve 1792 8 Years Old (92.5) n23 big, weighty: rye with attitude. From the green tea of the VOB to seriously over-stewed stuff. In a herd of any 30 random bourbons, this one would stand out by nose alone; **t23.5** puckering and mouthwatering, the ryes go ballistic, especially on the spice front. With salivation levels on full blast it is sometimes hard to pick out the more delicate custard-cream and apple nuances; **f22.5** the oak kicks in at the death with a shot of liquorice and coffee. But the ryes refuse to be downbeaten; **b23.5** a shade heavier than when I first tasted this one with the oak showing a burlier attitude. However, the unique rye fizz ensures a delightful and by no means understated degree of charm. Fabulously different and wholly adorable. *(93.7proof)*

Rock Hill Farms Single Barrel (84.5) n20 t22 f21 b21.5. The stodgy, flat nose is rescued by the well-mannered sweetness of the delivery. All just a tad too oily and corn-rich for anything approaching greatness, though. *50%*

Speakeasy Select dist 1/28/93 **(87) n22** honeyed grains with a rye-led fruitiness battling off the encroaching oak; **t22.5** firm, juicy, pleasantly spiced but the corn spends more time fending off the oak than it might; **f21.5** genuinely dry with strands of liquorice and hickory softened by a hint of Demerara; **b21** pleasant, but one or four summers too long for this barrel. *58.1%. Steelbach Hotel, Louisville, Kentucky.*

Ten High (68) n17.5 t16.5 f17 b17. Always one of the lighter bourbons, now sporting a curious sweetness which does little to engage. Still a good mixer, though. *40%*

Tom Moore (83) n19 t21 f22 b21. Gloriously consistent, there is s certain something about the rye attack and the general complexity which I just love. *40%*

Van Winkle Special Reserve 12 Years Old lot B **(77.5)** n21 t19.5 f18 b19. Some ryes make for an interesting interlude. But misfires for the most part. *(90.4 proof)*

Very Old Barton 6 Years Old (90.5) n22.5 the ryes are not shy, displaying their fruity, peppery intent. Fresh, and a hint of Sahara camp fires with green tea on the brew; **t23** darting, firm fruit makes for maximum salivation. You could swear some barley gets in on the action, too; **f22** slightly more imperious in its vanilla delivery than of old but the rye hangs around to the end; **b22.5** a unique style of bourbon with its emphasis on small detail and business around the palate. Always satisfying and fun. *43%*

Virgin Bourbon 7 Years Old (82.5) n19 t21 f21.5 b21. Firm and crisp from the moment it hits the palate. Even a touch of sophistication to the slow unfurling of the vanillas. Not the whiskey it was, but the astonishing chestnut colour stays the same. *50.5%*

Virgin Bourbon 15 Years Old (92.5) n23.5 mesmeric in its copper-rye depth. Some decent honey combined with maple syrup adds only a degree of lustre to the vanilla and red liquorice. Sumptuous. **t23** stately in its elegance and demeanour: this is serious bourbon doing seriously bourbon things. Like pulsing with raisin-rich, spiced honey notes, for instance. **f23.5** long, with clever intermingling of oak-studded vanilla and firm rye. **b23** the kind of bourbon you want to be left in a room with. *50.5%*

Walker's DeLuxe 3 Years Old (86) n22 t22 f21 b21. Excellent by 3-y-o standards. *40%*

Weller Special Reserve 7 Years Old (83) n20 t21 f21 b21. Pleasant stuff which sings a fruity tune and is ably backed by subtle spice. Perhaps a little too sweet, though. *45%*

Weller 12 Years Old (93.5) n23.5 honeydew melon, apple and liquorice are all there in abundance, but with a glossy Demerara (rum and sugar!) coating; **t23.5** the oily corn leads, the honey follows; **f23** drier, as the vanillas try to get a foothold; **b23.5** seismic in its ability to send giant waves of all those rich, honeyed fingerprints one usually associated with old, high quality bourbon. Such an improvement on previous bottlings and a wheated to set the pulse racing. *45%*

Weller Antique (86.5) n21.5 t22 f21.5 b21.5. The firm nose offers dried dates; the palate is the prickly spice that one so often associates with wheated whiskey with a late waxy lustre. Attractive stuff. *53.5%*

Wild Turkey (77) n19 t19 f20 b19. As sweet and simple as bourbon gets. Shows few of the qualities that make it such astonishing whiskey when older. *(80 proof)*

Wild Turkey 101 (88) n20 surprisingly dull; **t23** full bodied from the first with soft oils helping to lift and then maintain the ever-increasing spice assault. Chewy and entirely wonderful! **f22.5** long, with no shortage of deep chocolatey sugar cane notes; **b22.5** a lively bird that has gone up the pecking order over the last year or so. The delivery really does have a genuine lustre to it, which comes as a bit of a shock after the so-so nose. It's the spices, though, that steal the show, together with the long finale. *55.5%*

Wild Turkey American Spirit Aged 15 Years (92) n24 almost the full gambit. The extra year or two on rare Breed means that the oak has subtracted from the overall complexity. But there is enough going on in the fruitcake and custard pie department to know that we have some major complexity and balance here; **t22.5** sharp delivery: the rye appears first but the essence of liquorice that forms a hint on the nose makes a soft landing here; butterscotch is ladled on and the drier oaky and deft honey notes do the rest; a sweeter Turkish delight edge can be located at the death; **f22.5** a touch thinner than might be expected, but the adroitness of the spices is stunning. Vanilla and toffee apple complete the romp; **b23** a delightful Wild Turkey that appears under par for a 100 proofer but offers much when you search those nooks and crannies of your palate. *50.0% (100 proof)*

Wild Turkey Rare Breed bottle no. L8002FH **(96)** n25 one of the wonders of the whisky and whiskey world....the complexity, the brain-exploding perfection of it all is almost frightening. The trick is the understatement of all that's happening on the nose: the apples, the citrus, the lychees, the cherries...All these elements are there, but fusing with the soft rye (or are those fruit notes part of the rye fingerprint?), and then comes the butterscotch, the odd dollop of honey and that glorious hint of the corn fermenting. Just too good to be true and an aroma that has previously non-lovers of bourbon rethinking their whiskey life; **t24** fabulous, yet after the nose almost a letdown....almost. Silkily structured with an immediate spice, corn and vanilla input. The old liquorice of yore has receded on this bottling, replaced by a bitter-sweet rye presence; **f23.5** long, genuinely soft and again playful with so many notes criss-crossing the palate and offering peek-a-boo sightings of all the things you thought you had detected on the nose; **b24.5** a bourbon that almost teases and tortments you with its complexity. A world great. Note: the sample I officially tasted was from a bottle marked at the neck Batch WT-03RB. Every Rare Breed I have ever tasted has boasted this batch number. More relevant is the bottling number. *54.1%*

Wild Turkey Russell's Reserve 10 (94) n23 fascinating layering of diverse aromas: something almost smoky to this one, perhaps from extracting a peculiar, heavy-ish character from the oak; thinned by a delicate gooseberry note (yes, really!) - as opposed to the usual citrus - which itself is sandwiched between subtle Demerara sugar and vanilla; the rye also makes itself heard; **t23** the body flexes muscles enough to compound the rich brown sugar/liquorice background and intense rye fruitiness. Serious chewing required; **f24** excellent depth, with the oaks now offering impressive soft bitter balance; remains long and consistent as the spices amplify; **b24** unquestionably an upgrade on the last bottling I examined and shows the complexity of this world great distillery. But I still cannot even begin to get my head around the fact that a whiskey named after bourbon legend Jimmy Russell is bottled at 90 proof and not his own preferred 101. One of the true wonders of the whiskey world, that... *45%* ⊙⊙

Willett Straight Kentucky Bourbon Aged 11 Years barrel no. 105, bott 08 **(92) n22.5** lively and lovely: a sweet/dry edge to the burgeoning oak, showing that the development was in a state of transition when the whiskey was dumped; pretty light for its age with the vanilla dominating; **t23** that sweet-dry statement now goes into overdrive: the delivery is confident and firm; the liquorice arrives in short, almost hostile bursts; **f23.5** complex as all those elements pulse then fade at varying rates. Remains dry at the death on one level, brimming with crystals of brown sugar on another; **b23** a very different bourbon eschewing the usual honeyed path and offering something that more than borders on deep sophistication. *54.4%. Special bottling for Heinz Taubenheim, Germany. 192 bottles.*

Willett Straight Kentucky Bourbon Aged 15 Years barrel no. 2, bott 08 **(86) n21 t21.5 f22.5 b21.** A crisp bourbon, hard edged and determined to develop certain themes only so far before abandoning them. Deliciously crunchy and the brief honeyed radiance is a winner. At times hot and raw. *50%. Special bottling for Heinz Taubenheim, Germany. 182 bottles.*

Willett Straight Kentucky Bourbon Aged 15 Years barrel no. 84, bott 08 **(92.5) n22** thick: bigger than its 15 years. Polished wooden floors, burnt raisin, almonds and pine. In some respects too old, but alluring, too...; **t23** every bit as aged as the nose suggests. Except now there is a swathe of hickory/Demerara sugar mix which makes for a superbly balanced and gloriously chewable theme; the oak is intense and bites with its puckering intensity; **f23.5** dries as it must from this degree of age but again the balance holds true. Quietly pulsing spice works wonders with the late liquorice and coffee. In its way, classic... **b24** survives the obvious battering it took in the higher parts of the warehouse. The balance is the key and after the threatening nose, it never fails once it hits the tastebuds. Don't expect to enjoy on either first, third or fourth tasting. And don't swallow, either. Remain sober to get and appreciate the full works. Even so, another summer or two and this would have gone down hill very quickly, indeed. *64.7%. Special bottling for Heinz Taubenheim, Germany. 93 bottles.*

William Larue Weller bott 07 **(89) n22.5 t23 f21.5 b22** Just a bit too old and OTT for greatness. The oak has made almost violent inroads into every facet, but there is just enough quality to stand its ground. A pitched battle on the tastebuds – and fun for all that! *(117.9 proof)*

William Larue Weller (92) n22 doughy, spiced but a tad lazy; **t23** hard as nails delivery with as much liquoricey oak as there is small grain; slowly the middle conjures up a much richer backbone and a touch of oil to soften things up. Spices offer a delicate detour; **f24** now goes into overdrive as the right degree of sweetness balances the oak; shades of Demerara here though the threatening spice avalanche never arrive; **b23** lovely and quite different whiskey here – takes about four or five mouthfuls before you start getting the picture - with a clever build up of sugars. Relatively spiceless for a wheated bourbon but its all about structure and form. Even straight, the strength never overwhelms. *60.95%. (121.9 proof). nf*

⋰⋱ **William Larue Weller (93) n23.5** spices often associated with wheat recipe bourbon are here in force and make dazzling inroads into the toasty oaky: complex, sturdy, very well weighted and with impressive bitter marmalade for further balance; **t23** massive arrival with the alcohol playing only a minor part in the intensity. The flavours are already well defined through serious time in the oak. The vanilla forms the background but the backbone has to be thick hickory, with a fabulous interplay between those peppery spices and more playful overcooked plum tart fruit tones; a light dusting of muscovado sugars are present throughout to keep control; **f23.5** much more delicate with strands of mocha overtaking the hickory for lead role. Mild buttery tones to the vanilla; **b23** now that's much more like it. The 2007 version was simply too dependent on the older oaks. Here we have an intelligent balance where the wheat really gets to have a say. Beautiful: a mercurial bourbon that you should track down and bring home dead or alive. Because, as a life-long Millwall supporter, I can tell you there will be a Posse after this Weller.... *62.65% (125.3 proof)*

Woodford Reserve Master's Collection Four Grain (95) n24 highly unusual with a different nose from any other bourbon I know: very light liquorice, kind of Old Forester but with souped up intensity, and extraordinary floral tones; **t24** big and rambling with a quite massive flavour and spice explosion. The small grains are working overtime to provide a deep spicy-fruit texture to the oak. The liquorice comes through, but so does the rye by the spadeful and much softer, oily corn notes. Sensational; **f23** calms down, though it takes its time: very rarely have I experienced the small grains in a bourbon working with such complexity; the oak drives up the intensity as the story unfolds; **b24** Sod's law would have it that the moment we removed this from the 2006 Bible, having appeared in the previous two editions without it ever making the shelves, it should at last be belatedly released. But a whiskey worth waiting for, or what? The tasting notes are not a million miles from the original. But this is better bourbon, one that appears to have received a significant polish in the intervening years. Nothing short of magnificent. *46.2%*

Tennessee Whiskey
GEORGE DICKEL

George Dickel Superior No 12 Brand (90) n21 so floral and perfumy that I actually sneezed! Otherwise a bit lazy and over-relaxed; **t22** varying intensity throughout; sweetened by a barley-sugar richness unusual in American whiskey. However, resonating rye refreshes the palate and steers it back on course; **f24** goes into overdrive with astonishing length and stupendous oak: the complexity has earned its corn, so to speak, with the drying oak offering a get-out clause for the developing sugars; **b23** like watching a sea eagle take to flight after catching a larger fish than anticipated: a lumbering take off that at times looks doomed to failure but finally lift off is achieved with spell-binding grace and beauty. Welcome back to a great whisky after years in the doldrums! *45%*

JACK DANIEL

Gentleman Jack Rare Tennessee Whiskey (77) n19 t20 f18 b19. A Tennessee that appears to have achieved the impossible: it has got even lighter in character in recent years. A whiskey which wilfully refuses to say anything particularly interesting or go anywhere, this is one for those prefer their hard liquor soft. *40%. Brown-Forman.*

Jack Daniel's (Green Label) (84) n20 t21 f22 b21. A light but lively little gem of a whiskey. Starts as a shrinking violet, finishes as a roaring lion with nimble spices ripping into the developing liquorice. A superb session whiskey. *40% (80 proof).*

Jack Daniel's Old No. 7 Brand (Black Label) (87) n21 thick, oily, smoky, dense, corn syrupy ... it's Jack Daniel; **t23** sweet, fat, chewy, various types of burnt notes: tofffee, toast etc. etc; **f21** quite a sweet, fat and toffeed finale; **b22** a quite unique whiskey at which many American whiskey connoisseurs turn up their noses. I always think it's worth the occasional visit; you can't beat roughing it a little. *40% (80 proof). Brown-Forman.*

Jack Daniel's Single Barrel barrel no.7-3915, bott 28 Sep 07 **(87) n21.5** like opening the larder on a warm summer's day: a soft background noise of spices and sugar-sprinkled cookies; **t22** soft and buttery, again with brown sugars at the fore; **f22** creamy corn and thickening vanilla; **b21.5** pleasant, yet perhaps not the most inspiring single cask I have come across from JD. This one refuses to offer up the usual oily weight. *45%. Brown-Forman.*

Corn Whiskey

Dixie Dew (83) n19 t21 f22 b21. A few years back at a New York whisky festival some bore or other buttonholed me. "Hey, Mr Whiskey Expert" he sneeringly greeted me. "You reckon you know everything about whiskey, right? Well, why then in your 'Bi-ble' do you go and say that all them corn whiskies taste different? We all know they are made at the same distillery and taste exactly the same. Fact is, you know shit about whiskey, you limey faggot." When patiently I pointed out to this charmless, dosed-up fan of mine that yes, I was aware that the corn whiskeys were made at the same place and, indeed, bottled at the same strength, he smirked. However this was slowly wiped off his face when I further explained that different bottlings, using different casks at slightly varying ages, carrying different spirit from a different wash, would easily account for the variance in styles – and I had certainly been sent different batches. This time round, though, the Dixie Dew is so similar to the Mellow Corn, they could, indeed, be identical twins. Like my dear friend and his wife. *50%*

Georgia Moon Corn Whiskey aged less than thirty days **(84) n20 t22 f21 b21**. Agreeable, sweet, mildly syrupy white dog. Would love to see this at full strength. *40%. Heaven Hill.*

J W Corn (92) n23 firm, solid base despite the dry, oily surround; even a hint of rye here; easily the most sophisticated corn nose I've yet encountered; **t22.5** initially sweet then a crackerjack delivery of spice; oak and vanilla also make a big effort for centre place; **f23** refuses to buckle under the oily attack and allows the oak to offer wave upon wave of dry, cocoa-crusted depth; **b23.5** appears significantly older than the norm: wouldn't be surprised if the odd very over-aged barrel was added to this dumping. Unusual and complex. Oh, and totally brilliant. Cornutopia! *50%*

Mellow Corn (83) n19 t21 f22 b21. Dull and oily on the nose, though the palate compensates with a scintillating array of sweet and spicy notes. *50%*

Single Malt Rye
ANCHOR DISTILLERY
Old Potrero 18th Century Style Whiskey Essay 10-RW-ARM-3-C (90) n20 t23 f24 b23 Always remember something about wide cuts. The nose will be off beam. But the flavours hitting the tastebuds will be off the Richter scale. After tasting this I need to lie down somewhere and rest. Because so few whiskeys in the world are half as big as this, or more fun. Forget about descriptors: this one writes its own book... *62.55% (125.1 proof).*

Old Potrero Single Malt Hotaling's Whiskey Aged 11 Years Essay MCMVI-MMVI (96) n24 t25 f23 b24 This may sound coarse (and I apologise, but it is relevant), but I belched (twice) whilst tasting this. Oddly enough, that never happens when I taste whisky...only gin.... And I was spitting. I think gin lovers will be converted and whiskey drinkers truly amazed. Let's make no bones here: this is one of the world's true great whiskies, which just shows the quality of Rittenhouse barrel 28. Even so, rarely have I encountered complexity like it. I admit rye whiskey is my favourite genre. And no rye in the world offers anything like this. A must have bottling: there is nothing even close in style. *50% (100 proof).*

Old Potrero Single Malt Hotaling's Whiskey Aged 12 Years Essay MCMVI-MMVII (96) n24 t25 f23 b24. I have tasted this Essay against the previous one, and whilst there are the odd subtle differences, this is the closest in style I have ever found two Potreros to be: their likeness, in general terms, is uncanny. This one has perhaps the slightly drier finish but on the complexity front there is nothing to compare in the whisky world. I am not, remotely, an advocate of whisky and food. But I could murder a beautifully marbled T bone at my third favourite steak joint in the world, Harris's of San Francisco (still has a little way to go to match the incomparable The Ring in Portland and, at a shorter distance, Barbarian's in Toronto), and follow after a delicate pause with a glass of this local super whisky. Life rarely, if ever, gets better than that. *50% (100 proof).*

Old Potrero Single Malt Straight Rye Whiskey Essay 10-SRW-ARM-E (94) n24 t23 f24 b23 The whiskey from this distillery never fails to amaze. *45% (90 proof).*

Straight Rye
Cougar Rye (95) n25 OK. I have died. I have gone to heaven...what next ? **t24** the nose, an impossible jumble of fruity, spicy elements, is nearly perfectly translated onto the palate with the added extra of burnt toast and impressively cindered fruitcake; **f23** the spices prevail as does a liquorice and vanilla dryness; **b23** if I gave World Whisky of the Year to a rye that's 37% I'd be taken out by Malt Extremists who'd have issued a fatwa on me. It's bloody tempting mind... had it been at full strength of about 50% abv, I don't think there would have been much debate. And to think this is from yet another distillery (Lawrenceburg, Indiana) that had been closed and was under threat of extinction is almost beyond belief. However, word reached me this year that the Lawrenceburg distillery will not just continue to produce gin, but also whiskey: some of the most heart-warming intelligence to come from the United States this year. Surely someone will recognise the utter brilliance of both the bourbon and rye - especially the rye - which is produced here and come up with a plan for it to conquer the world. At the moment only Australia and a few pockets in the home market are lucky enough to find whiskey from this distillery on a regular basis. If any distillery should be given a world stage, then this is it. *37%. Foster's Group, Australia.*

Devil's Bit Seven-Year-Old Single Barrel (93.5) n22.5 gloriously floral as well as fruity; the oak dampens the peppery spice but enough only to keep it in harmony; **t24** every bit as juicy and mouth-watering as a great rye should be. The grains are crisp and bounce about the palate brewing up a big spicy storm; the oils are spontaneous and spot on, coating the palate instantly, but never overly so; **f23** oak time as the age plays its part with a switch to sweet fruits to drier vanilla. Chewy and warming to the death; **b24** I am stunned. A few years back I inspected a barrel or two of rye at the distillery and told the guys there that their rye was top quality. This, though, is even better than I remember it: much better, in fact. Brilliantly made, not a single off note or blemish and complexity oozing from every pour. Just hope they start batch-numbering the bottles if they intend to carry on bringing out single cask expressions. This one gives no clue to its age. A must-find rye from one of the most impressive small distilleries in the world. 47.7%. *Edgefield Distillery.*

High West Rendezvous Blend of Straight Rye Whiskies Batch No. 4 (93) n24 brilliant! Unambiguous age here with a compelling mixture of bluebells and cinnamon taking the lead. Muscovado sugar sweetens the pot pourri; **t24** shrieking rye dovetails between fresh, juicy rye and something altogether fuller and more sinister. Complex and demanding full attention; **f22.5** lots of natural caramel again suggests age but the buzzing fruity spices work hard to the end; **b22.5** a very different rye, and no wonder why: it turns out this is a mixture of 6- and 17-year-old, which accounts for the at times bipolar personality. Absolutely seething with character and charisma. 46%

Hudson Manhattan Rye bott 08, batch 1 **(76.5) n16 t20 f21.5 b19.** Fruity rye meets fruity butyric. Unbalanced and ungainly on the nose, it is instantly obvious that there are properties here that perhaps shouldn't be about. Still unmistakably a rye though, and on the palate a real juicy flavour-fest. Again, the oils and properties which make the nose something of a car crash add positively to overall character with the finish having much to celebrate in its spicy demeanour. Batch one and a real juicy work in progress that is very drinkable providing you take on at body temperature. 46%

Jim Beam Rye (88) n23 firm and flowery with lavender amid the cinnamon-encrusted sultanas; **t22** an immediate explosion of almost candy-like tartness and spice. Dulls quickly, though; **f21** soft vanilla begins to outweigh the natural fruity-juiciness; **b22** lost a significant degree of its trademark sharpness and zest for all its charm. 40%

Old Overholt Four Years Old (85) n22 t21 f21 b21. Still little sign of this returning to its old rip-roaring best. Duller and less challenging even than a year back with a frustrating dustiness to the procedings. 40%

Pappy Van Winkle's Family Reserve Rye 13 Years Old (94) n24 outwardly, the aroma basks in a crisp rye flourish; scratch below the surface and there are darker, more sinister oaky forces at work; **t23.5** crisp, almost crackling rye offers both the fruity-clean and burned fruitcake options; **f23** dulls out a bit as the liquorice/toffee oak takes hold but remains alluringly spicy and sensual; **b23.5** uncompromising rye that successfully tells two stories simultaneously. A great improvement on the Winkle rye of old. 47.8%

Pikesville (92.5) n23 one of the liveliest and cleanest rye noses around. Still retains its unique scrumpy and new car interior mix but now the rye is really pitching up with something quite firm, too; **t23.5** sublime clarity in the way the old Jim Beam Yellow Label went about its business until quite recently. The rye is polished and sparkling and helped along by some unrefined sugar; **f22.5** it takes a while for the vanilla to find its range. Even when it does, it is outgunned by the rye; **b23.5** the most improved standard rye on the market place. And none around where the grain is delivered with such unabashed, crystal clarity. 40%

Rathskeller Rye dist 83 **(95) n24** big, firm, with an almost metallic hardness, yet something soft and yielding beneath. Quite beautiful, and, once placed in front of you, is quite impossible not to explore without a degree of excitement. At its very best in the romantic semi-darkness of the uniquely atmospheric Steelbach bar, a whiskey Eden created by the Gods of grain. And in intensity even capable of overcoming the bizarre and daunting polished leather aroma of the hotel's Rathskellar itself where it also reveals itself seductively and memorably; **t24** the tongue cannot help but explore that double layered soft-hard signature. And as the tongue delves into the tempting fruitiness, so everything hardens yet becomes juicier. Absolutely classic Kentucky rye and a lot younger in body than you might be given to think given the label; **f23.5** chewy, chocolate and cherries and brilliantly controlled spice on the oak; **b23.5** a beguiling rye of genuine beauty and charm which electrifies and excites; that complex, yielding hardness so typical of a great rye is something the tongue was invented for. Further exploration needed on my return to the hotel: just hope the bar still has it! 65%. *Steelbach Hotel, Louisville, Kentucky.*

Rittenhouse (86) n21 t23 f21 b21. The only Kentucky rye I know spelt "whisky" has upped its rye character in recent bottlings. However, this one's all about the first few seconds of delivery, which are exquisite. The rest is relatively routine. 40%

Rittenhouse 100 Proof Bottled in Bond (94) n22.5 sampled blind I would swear this to be a mixture of pot and column still rum, with some Barbadian and Guyanan taking the lead; **t24** the tastebuds are left to wave the white flag as they are over-run by marauding rye notes. These are firm, fruity and flighty one moment, duller and weightier the next; always salivating, you are left to drown in your own juices as the spices begin to kick in with aplomb; **f23.5** fantastic marriage between high cocoa chocolate and burnt toffee. Long and chewy until your jaw aches; **b24** staggering whisky. Rye like this, as I predicted long ago, will win a worldwide following which is unlikely to go away: the flavours are delivered with abandon and complexity. No serious whisky lover can be without this guy on his shelf. *50%*

Rittenhouse Rye Single Barrel 23 Year Old barrel no. 8 **(96) n24** singes the nose hairs with its forceful exuberance; the oak tries to dominate totally but there is enough fruit in reserve to stand its ground. Still, strangely phenolic with something of the dental surgery about it all; elsewhere bluebells in the dankest and darkest of Surrey woodlands; brooding honeycomb; **t23.5** the exotic fruit you find in some exceptionally old old Scotch appears to be having a convention of its own here: some of it is the rye, but the massive oak must have some say in this. Wonderfully spiced and lush, the high roast Java towards the middle works rather well; **f24** long, with a viscosity that belies the years; those eye-watering spices stay the distance and then the most bitter of cocoa arrives; throughout, though, the fruity rye adds a consistent and improbably clean voice; **b24.5** it has been 34 years now since I fell in love with rye whiskey. And I can tell you I have never tasted anything quite like this. In most whiskies around the world an injection of oak to this degree would kill it stone dead. Here, however, it survives and somehow appears to turn the very points that should be the whiskey's downfall into its strengths. A freak of a whiskey. But, my God, a fabulous one! *50% (100 proof). Heaven Hill.*

Rittenhouse Very Rare Single Barrel 21 Years Old (91) n25 Incredible. Intriguing. Unique. Such is the punch to the super-ripe fruit, so intense is the oak that has fused into it, that it takes literally hours to try and make sense of what is happening here. There is no other aroma in the whisky or whiskey world that matches, the closest relation being ancient pot still whiskey from Ireland for reasons I will explain later. It perhaps needs a whisky lover with the mind of an archaeologist to understand this one, because the nose is a series of layers built up over time. The key is to dig deeper than the surface spices and burnt honeycomb. In there, in varying strata, are diffused mint and lemon zest and a fruity intensity to the rye grain normally found only when malted. Astonishing and almost too beautiful for words; **t23** impatient oak rampages through the early, oily arrival of rye concentrate. Then waves of spice, of steadily increasing intensity crash lip-smackingly into the tastebuds. But such is the magnitude of the rye it absorbs the oak without too much early damage and only towards the middle does it begin to lose the battle; **f21** a dry finale as the come-of-age oak demands the last say; **b22** I may be wrong, but I would wager quite a large amount that no-one living has tasted more rye from around the world than I. So trust me when I tell you this is different, a genuine one-off in style. By rights such telling oak involvement should have killed the whisky stone dead: this is like someone being struck by lightning and then walking off slightly singed and with a limp, but otherwise OK. The closest style of whisky to rye is Irish pot still, a unique type where unmalted barley is used. And the closest whiskey I have tasted to this has been 35 to 50-year-old pot still Irish. What they have in common is a massive fruit base, so big that it can absorb and adapt to the oak input over many years. This has not escaped unscathed. But it has to be said that the nose alone makes this worthy of discovery, as does the glory of the rye as it first melts into the tastebuds. The term flawed genius could have been coined for this whisky alone. Yet, for all its excellence, I can so easily imagine someone, somewhere, claiming to be an expert on whiskey, bleating about the price tag of $150 a bottle. If they do, ignore them. Because, frankly, rye has been sold far too cheaply for far too long and that very cheapness has sculpted a false perception in people's minds about the quality and standing of the spirit. Well, 21 years in Kentucky equates to about 40 years in Scotland. And you try and find a 40-year-old Scotch for £75. If anything, they are giving this stuff away. The quality of the whiskey does vary from barrel to barrel and therefore bottle to bottle. So below I have given a summary of each individual bottling (averaging (91.1). The two with the highest scores show the least oak interference...yet are quite different in style. That's great whiskey for you. *50% (100 proof). ncf. Heaven Hill.*

Barrel no. 1 (91) n25 t23 f21 b22. As above. *50%*
Barrel no. 2 (89) n24 t23 f20 b22. Dryer, oakier. *50%*
Barrel no. 3 (91) n24 t23 f22 b22. Fruity, soft. *50%*
Barrel no. 4 (90) n25 t22 f21 b22. Enormous. *50%*
Barrel no. 5 (93) n25 t23 f22 b23. Early rye surge. *50%*
Barrel no. 6 (87) n23 t22 f20 b22. Juicy, vanilla. *50%*
Barrel no. 7 (90) n23 t23 f22 b22. Even, soft, honeyed. *50%*
Barrel no. 8 (95) n25 t24 f23 b23. The works: massive rye. *50%*
Barrel no. 9 (91) n24 t23 f22 b22. Sharp rye, salivating. *50%*

Barrel no.10 (93) n25 t24 f22 b22. Complex, sweet. *50%*
Barrel no.11 (93) n24 t24 f22 b23. Rich, juicy, spicy. *50%*
Barrel no.12 (91) n25 t23 f21 b22. Near identical to no.1. *50%*
Barrel no.13 (91) n24 t24 f21 b22. Citrus and toasty. *50%*
Barrel no.14 (94) n25 t24 f22 b23. Big rye and marzipan. *50%*
Barrel no.15 (88) n23 t22 f21 b22. Major oak influence. *50%*
Barrel no.16 (90) n24 t23 f21 b22. Spicy and toffeed. *50%*
Barrel no.17 (90) n23 t23 f22 b22. Flinty, firm, late rye kick. *50%*
Barrel no.18 (91) n24 t24 f21 b22. Big rye delivery. *50%*
Barrel no.19 (87) n23 t22 f21 b21. Major coffee input. *50%*
Barrel no.20 (91) n23 t24 f22 b22. Spicy sugar candy. *50%*
Barrel no.21 (94) n24 t23 f24 b23. Subtle, fruity. *50%*
Barrel no.22 (89) n23 t22 f22 b22. Mollased rye. *50%*
Barrel no.23 (94) n24 t23 f24 b23. Soft fruit, massive rye. *50%*
Barrel no.24 (88) n23 t22 f21 b22. Intense oak and caramel. *50%*
Barrel no.25 (93) n25 t22 f23 b23. Heavy rye and spice. *50%*
Barrel no.26 (92) n23 t23 f23 b23. Subtle, delicate rye. *50%*
Barrel no.27 (94) n25 t23 f23 b23. Delicate rye throughout. *50%*
Barrel no.28 (96) n25 t24 f23 b24. Salivating, roasty, major. *50%*
Barrel no.29 (88) n23 t22 f21 b22. Hot, fruity. *50%*
Barrel no.30 (91) n24 t23 f22 b22. Warming cough sweets. *50%*
Barrel no.31 (90) n25 t22 f21 b22. Aggressive rye. *50%*

Sazarac Rye 6 Years Old (91) n22.5 firm, unambiguous rye with minimum yield and complexity; **t23** much juicier, showing little oak interference. Almost candy-like in its sugar and spice qualities; **f23.5** again the rye dominates with minimal restraint but at least offers several paths, the longest being slightly dry with butterscotch off-shoots; **b22** rye perhaps at its least complicated. But horny stuff, nonetheless. *45%*

Sazarac Rye 18 Years Old bottled fall 07 **(95.5)** n24.5 if you could invent an aroma, it might be something like this: the clarity to the rye is untarnished. Eighteen years in barrel has done nothing to obscure the bitter-sweet perfection. Sheer subtlety and sophistication despite the ultra-juicy black cherries and blackberries running riot; **t24** the framework is firm to the point of brittle; less oily than some other bottlings, offering a degree of austerity amid the spice; **f23** gentle and vanilla-led; the ryes come back in late waves to leave you no doubt as to the pedigree; **b24** remains among the ultimate Kentucky rye experiences with its uncompromising strength and beauty. A true world classic. *45%*

⠿ **Sazarac Rye 18 Years Old** bott fall 08 **(97.5)** n25 simply gorgeous outpouring of clean rye notes: crisp, fruity, saliva-inducing boiled candy. The oak weighs in with a confident but reverently restrained minty sweetness, perhaps with a degree of lavender, too. The overall effect is absolutely perfectly balanced; **t24.5** demi-sec fruit, crisp and brittle as a great rye should be. The oak again take a leading role with a buzzing spice and dry, bitter marmalade on burnt toast qualities which again counter the rye with almost playful panache; a thin layer of molasses provides the balance without ever detracting from the complex battles raging; **f23.5** some inevitable caramels thin out the complexity slightly. But still can't stop those spice pulses or the last juicy remnants of the rye; **b24.5** there are very few greater treats in my life than to see how the latest bottling of Sazarac has turned out. This one, with its cleverly disguised sophistication coupled with its extraordinary maintenance of a unique style, is a classic even by its own Himalayan standards. This radiated possible World Whisky of the Year from the very first nosing: it did not lie. *45% (90 proof)*

Templeton Prohibition Era Recipe Rye batch 2, barrel 122, bott 08 **(93)** n24 huge, unmistakable rye: almost in concentrate or candy form with a dollop of manuka honey for good measure. Different yet familiar in that the style is unique but painted in a way that is familiar to those of us who know the excellence of a certain distillery which, in my humble opinion, pushes out the best rye whisky in the world; **t23.5** rock-hard barley crunches into the taste buds, ricocheting around the palate to astonishing effect. A softer sub-plot involves soft fruits and even a gentle barley grandeur, but that is fleeting and is principally about the ultra-firm rye; **f22.5** a surprising austerity punctured by a very late show of delicate spice; **b23** unique rye that never quite lives up the brilliance of the nose, but offers enough singular entertainment throughout to make this a must have for rye lovers. The mashbill, I have since discovered since writing the notes above is a mixture of rye and malted barley alone. And it is not, as I very much suspected, made at the Templeton distillery in Chicago: I would have been astonished and given up my job as a whisky critic if it had. The actual distillery where it is made, outside Kentucky, is being kept secret by Templeton. But there is no doubt that whoever made this knew exactly what they were doing, and were doing it in stills that needed no proving. Wonderful and truly singular. *40%*

Thomas H Handy Sazerac Straight Rye Whiskey (94.5) n24 any crisper and the glass would shatter: hard as diamond rye, but oh! so much more of a rare and valuable gem! Rye concentrate.... **t24** any crisper and the glass would shatter: hard as diamond rye, but oh! so much more of a rare and valuable gem! Rye concentrate.... **f23** any crisper and the glass would shatter: hard as diamond rye, but oh! so much more of a rare and valuable gem! Rye concentrate.... **b23.5** any crisper and the....I think you may have got the idea...... *674% (134.8 proof). ncf.*

Thomas H. Handy Sazerac Straight Rye Barrel Proof Limited Edition (93) n24 boiled fruit candy. Just so mouth-wateringly firm and sexy; **t21** takes its time to find a rhythm as neither the oak nor rye are sure whether to lead. Settles towards the middle as the salivating rye takes control; a few hickory notes add further depth; **f25** faultless and mesmeric. The tongue is left to wander the mouth involuntarily investigating myriad flavour trails. Early doubts are erased by the majesty of small grain and the perfection of the bittersweet harmony which unravels. Even the late-arriving spices deliver something almost too teasing to be true. One of the greatest finishes in world whiskey, and no mistake; **b23** what a box of tricks! Early on it's as mad a bag of snakes but the finish is something to inspire you to get in the chimney sweep, clean out the hearth and get the ol' log fire going for the first time in 20 years. A fabulous addition to the ever-growing rye family. *66.35% (132.7 Proof). ncf. First-ever bottling.*

Wild Turkey (89) n22 fresh layers of rye topped by a vanilla coating; **t23** sharp, crashing rye blundering into the tastebuds with serious juiciness; a genuine liquorice backbone to this one upping the intensity and weight another degree; **f22** chewy, almost bourbonesque in its fade with a late firm rye resurgence; **b22** true to type but with less natural caramel and more assertiveness from the grain. A grand improvement. *50.5%*

Wild Turkey Russell's Reserve Rye Aged 6 Years (91) n23 rye at its juiciest; a hint of spearmint; sweet, with just enough oak to work beautifully; **t23.5** immediate spice impact, then a spreading of soft brown sugar and honey; **f22.5** soft oils embrace the growing vanilla and soft liquorice; long and luxuriant; **b22.5** a much cleaner, more vibrant version of the standard Turkey rye. Seriously delicious. *45.0% (90 proof)*

Straight Wheat Whiskey

Bernheim Original (91.5) n22 smouldering toast from that-day-baked bread. Mealy, too with a little salt added for effect; **t23** that peculiar salty tang on the nose transfers with little difficulty to the palate. It joins a citrusy throng and a delightful sharpness which counters the sweeter, oilier nature of the beast; **f23** a classy finale where we are back to toast, if a little burned, and dissolving sugars but, mainly, a crackling firmness which appears to be a stand off between the wheat and the oak; **b23.5** by far the driest of the Bernheims I have encountered – and this is about the 10th – showing greater age and perhaps substance. Unique and spellbinding. *45%*

Kentucky Whiskey

Early Times Kentucky Whisky (74) n19 t19 f18 b18. Slightly improved with some extra beefing up, but still light and over sweet. *40% (80 proof). Brown-Forman*

Medley's Kentucky Whiskey bott code L6114 **(81) n21 t21 f19 b20.** Very tight grains. Pleasant, but limited complexity. *40%. Berentzen Distillers.*

American/Kentucky Whiskey Blends

Charter Private Reserve (72.5) n18 t18.5 f19 b17. Molten sugar sprinkled with vanilla. *40%*

Other American Whiskey

Buffalo Trace Experimental Collection Chardonnay After 6 Years Old dist May 92, bott Feb 07 **(77) n21 t19 f18 b19.** A less demanding ride than the 10-y-o and, thanks to the lesser time in Chardonnay, the tastebuds are not so violently pulped by the oak intrusion. Some pleasant chocolate-y notes bring reward and soften the blow. *45% (90 Proof).*

Nor'Easter "Bourbon" (85.5) n22 t22 f20 b21.5. A pretty whiskey with an attractively perfumed nose. The finish is thin and scant but the body delves into sugary recesses in which the odd strip of liquorice can be found. *44.4%. Triple Eight Distillery.*

Old Virginia Extra Rare American Whiskey Aged 12 Years L530133A **(90) n22** molten honeycomb and dark chocolate; almost a Jamaican rummy ester sweetness; **t23** imagine a nubile body contouring a silk gown: that's the shape and texture here as excellent vanillas integrate with honey; **f22** back to the honeycomb again with marmalade as a delightful bitterness creeps in; **b23** Good grief: this is damn good stuff. The most honeyed and high-class non-bourbon on the market. *40%. La Martiniquaise, France.*

Canadian Whisky

It is becoming hard to believe that Canadian was once a giant among the world whisky nations. Dotted all over its enormous land large distilleries pumped out thousands upon thousands of gallons of spirit that after years in barrel became a clean, gentle whisky.

It was cool to be seen drinking Canadian in cocktail bars on both sides of the pond. Now, sadly, Canadian whisky barely raises a beat on the pulse of the average whisky lover. It would not be beyond argument to now call Canadian the forgotten whisky empire with column inches devoted to their column stills measured now in millimetres. It is an entirely sad, almost heartbreaking, state of affairs though hopefully not an irreversible one. The finest Canadian, for me, is still whisky to be cherished and admired. But outside North America it can be painfully hard to find.

Especially seeing how whiskies containing the permitted 9.09% of non-Canadian whisky (or whisky at all) had been barred from the European market. So just to ensure Jim Murray's Whisky Bible remained on the ball I spent last year in Canada tasting every Canadian whisky I could find on the market. The result was illuminating. The latest blitz confirmed there was now a clear divergence of styles between tradionalist whisky like Alberta Premium and a more creamy textured, fruit-enhanced product once

BRITISH COLUMBIA

ALBERTA

MANITOBA

▲Alberta
●Vancouver
Calgary
▲Okanagan
▲Palliser
Gimli ▲

Key
- ● **Major Town or City**
- ▲ Distillery
- + Dead Distillery

confined to the USA but now found in Canada itself. However, there is no doubt that we are seeing a change in the perception of Canadian by drinkers who had previously confined themselves to top quality Scotch malt. Following my award of Jim Murray's Whisky Bible Canadian Whisky of the Year 2006 to Alberta Premium, I had the chance to spend time in televison and radio stations around the country talking about the exceptionally high quality of top Canadian whiskies. It has led to a string of emails from readers telling me they had since tasted Alberta and been somewhat shocked to find a world classic whisky lurking so unobtrusively - and cheaply - on their shelves. For many, this had led to further exploring of Canadian, and uncovering of further gems. The 2010 Award has this gone to another of them: Wiser's Red Letter. It took advantage of a rare blip from Alberta Premium which in my last two tastings was relatively flat by its own extraordinary high standards, especially on the finish.

In last year's search for Canada's finest there were two whiskies which had given Alberta a serious run for its money. And both were new releases. It marked a red letter day for Wiser's, with their Wiser's Red Letter, an astonishing blend which simply radiated complexity. In far too familiar a Canadian style the added caramel did it few favours and probably ensured Alberta Premium then maintained its pole position. Also an upping of the rye content would also have giving a more decisive and traditional sharpness. Even though running out as Canadian Whisky of the Year for the 2010 Bible, it is a whisky just a few tweaks away, you feel, from something ultra special. Meanwhile the Danfield's 21-year-old came from a different angle, managing its great age with improbable ease and this time making no secret of a rye presence which balances sublimely with the oak. Team the two Albertas up with the Danfield's 21 and Wiser's Red Letter and you get the feeling that here you have a representation of Canadian whisky which would give a very tough match to any other four from another distilling nation.

However, the best news to come out of Canada in the last twelve months has to be little Glenora's final humilating victory over the might of the Scotch Whisky Association who had spent no less than nine years fighting the distiller's right to call their tiny single malt brand Glenora Single Malt. Their specious argument had been that it sounded like a Scotch and only Scotch whisky has the right to use the term "Glen" in their brand's title. The actual address of Glenora Distillery is Glenville, Inverness County, Cape Breton. It rather gives the game away regarding the history of the area and who settled it: to this day some locals still speak with a light Scottish burr. In June the Supreme Court of Canada ended the farce by refusing the SWA the right to appeal for a third time. Hurrah for decency and common sence. Now one hopes Glenora will use the money saved in legal costs to improve the quality of their single malt.

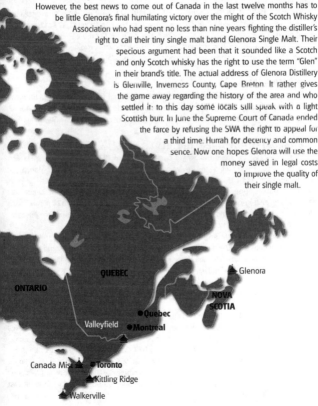

QUEBEC

ONTARIO

NOVA SCOTIA

▲ Glenora

● Quebec

Valleyfield ● Montreal

Canada Mist ▲ ● Toronto

▲ Kittling Ridge

▲ Walkerville

Canadian Single Malts
GLENORA

Glen Breton db **(81)** n19 t21 f20 b21. Enormously sweet malt, in almost concentrated form with a tantalising whiff of smoke hanging around; mildly spiced and slightly oily, soapy finale. *43%*

Glen Breton Rare db **(73)** n14 t21 f19 b19. This is a version – probably a very early one – I had not seen and it makes for exceptionally grim nosing. However, after that very unpleasant, feinty experience, it comes back to life on the palate with remarkable honey and copper input. A right mixed bag. *40%*

Glen Breton Rare db **(80)** n18 t21 f20 b21. Caramel nose a bit soapy but the buttery, sweet malt, with its vanilla fizz, makes for a pleasant experience. *43%*

Glen Breton Rare Aged 10 Years (75) n15 t21 f20 b20. Lashings of butterscotch help put out of the mind the feinty nose (those who tasted the original Sullivan's Cove from Australia will be suffering serious déjà vu here...). Full bodied, as wide-cut whiskies tend to be, and for all the cuts, bruises and plasters, there is enough complexity here to make for an entertaining Canadian - once the nose has been negotiated. *40%*

Glen Breton Ice Aged 10 Years (85.5) n21.5 t21 f22 b22. Tasting both a full strength bottled Canadian, and one that had been matured in Icewine barrels, I was nearly blown through the back of my seat and into the wall. One of the biggest shocks to hit you on the Canadian whisky scene today, there is no denying that this whisky offers sufficient panache and lucidity to genuinely impress. Hardly an exercise in perfect balance, it certainly celebrates the art of surprise and, late on, charm. The cocoa-dusted butterscotch really is a rare treat and, thanks to the fruity world it finds itself in, a truly unique and enjoyable experience. *57.2%*

Glenora 1990 Aged 14 Years Single Cask db **(89)** n22 firm malt but with a distinctive bourbony (or very old Canadian) weight and some attractive natural toffee; **t23** massive malt arrival on the palate buoyed with that dense fudge-caramel; **f22** the oak is distinctive and almost Kentuckian; the malt is profound and the chewy weight is excellent; **b22** by far and away the best Glenora yet bottled. And good to see the distillery use its actual name. *43%*

OKANAGAN

Long Wood 8 Years Old Malt db **(74)** n19 t20 f17 b18. There are no discernable off notes and a pleasant liquorice-spice prevails. But the true life has been strangled out if it by caramel. A tragedy, in whisky terms, as this is very rare malt from a lost distillery. *40%. Germany.*

Canadian Grain Single Barrel

Century Reserve 13 Years Old Single Cask Unblended (92) n22 massive vanilla and toffee but delicately handled and delivered; some very soft prickle helps balance the sweetening grain; **t23** big corn kick from the start with an immediate movement towards sweetness that is stopped in its tracks by developing oak; just so silky despite the natural oak bite; **f23** long, lush in part, with the corn really getting stuck into the oak; **b24** surely "Bush Pilot" by any other name. Those with an affinity with old Scottish grain would recognise this style of corn-led whisky. Very tasty. *40%. Century Distilling Co.*

Century Reserve 15 Years Old 1985 Limited Edition (89) n20 dry oak; mildly burnt toast and red liquorice; **t23** a delicious corn-oil lushness helps keep at bay some bourbony overtures; the degree of Demerara sweetness against the oak is exemplary; **f23** cream toffee that you can chew and chew until subtle spices arrive; **b23** the nose ("smoky, reminiscent of single malt", according to cask selector Nick Bennett; "oaky, reminiscent of Okanagan grain", according to Jim Murray...) reveals little of the joys that are to follow. *40%. Century Distilling Co.*

Forty Creek Single Barrel (93) n23 clean, uncluttered sherry and cherry; **t23** more cherry flanked by gentle spice and silky, mildly oily grain: genuinely complex and classy; **f24** loses balance towards the end, although the sweetness, combined with the bitter cocoa finale, is not entirely unlike a Belgium cherry chocolate; **b23** there are so many things about this whisky that infuriate me...yet I adore it. Perhaps I am a sucker for premier quality liquor chocolates; maybe I get turned on by very clean yet complex distillate. So much of this goes against the purists' grain. Yet it has to be said: this is bloody delicious whisky of the highest magnitude!! *40%. Kittling Ridge.*

Canadian Blended Whisky

Alberta Premium (94.5) n24 throbbing, pulsing rye on a variety of levels: full and juicy, dull and dusty, firm and flinty. Unique and unmistakable; **t25** my first whisky of the day – and it needs to be. The tastebuds are given such a working over that they need to be fully tuned and fit to take this on. Again it is all about the rye: the first, second and third flavours to pound the mouth are all rye-related. The very first are juicy with a minute sweetness. The second, hanging onto the coattails of the first are Rockies hard and brittle, clattering into the tastebuds with zero yield. Next comes a quick follow through of explosive peppers, but again leaving in their wake a semi-sweet juicy, fruitiness, almost certainly from the malted rye. No other whisky in the world unleashes this combination of grainy punches around the palate in this way. Beautiful and complex: just words, and ones that don't even begin to do this whisky justice; **f22** dulls down, probably because of the needless caramel added, but there is slightly more depth than before thanks most probably to the malted rye. The spices continue to fizz as the Demerara-tipped vanillas make their mark; **b23.5** it is 8am and the Vancouver Island sky is one of clear blue. My windows are closed to keep out the honeyed scent of the arbutus tree now in full May bloom, but I can still hear a male house finch singing sweetly and hopefully from its branches. Nearby, violet-green swallows swoop around to celebrate their first day back on the island. On this side of the window my glass sings to me: it is Alberta Premium. Of all the Canadian whiskies I have tasted for this book, so far (and I have only four or five more still to do) not only is it the least changed in style, not just in recent years but, it seems, always. If the weather outside is a rarity for Victoria, then so is what sits in my glass for the entire Canadian whisky scene. It is true rye whisky. Not a misnomer like the rest. The 100% rye grain used, fortified in its mouthwatering delivery by the deployment of a degree of malted rye, offers flavours unlimited. Alberta Premium is no longer just a great Canadian whisky. It has become a national treasure. *40%* ⊙⊙

Alberta Premium 25 Years Old (95) n24 a fabulously weighted nose: diamond couched in silk. It is the vivid hardness which is first to show, with the firmness the rye can muster. Then that softness makes itself felt; a rolling, juicy fruitiness (not dissimilar to an almost lost form of most exquisite Cognac) that has dissolved into it a drier vaguely bourbon-esque oakiness. For complexity few, if any, Canadians are this subtle or sublime. Masterful; **t23** again we have a bipolar story. On one hand the rye takes a rigid course as a hard edge cuts through all else to dominate. Then it fails as it is swamped by that same soft fruit as on the nose and also a crescendo of cocoa. Soft-hard. Sweet-dry. Velvety caresses-playful nips. Whatever you concentrate on dominates: put the tastebuds into neutral and you have a wonderful battle, not fought by fist but wit; **f23** my word: if you are into chocolate you'll love this. Gently sweetened cocoa spreads around the palate, first as a hint then as a full-blown plain chocolate dessert sweetened only by a sprinkling of muscovado. Very long. Improbably gentle; **b25** faultless. Absolutely nothing dominates. Yet every aspect has its moment of conquest and glory. It is neither bitter nor sweet, yet both. It is neither soft nor hard on the palate yet both elements are there. Because of the 100% rye used, this is an entirely new style of whisky to hit the market. No Canadian I know has ever had this uncompromising brilliance, this trueness to style and form. And, frightening to think, it could be improved further by bottling at least 46% and un-chillfiltered. For any whisky lover who ever thought Canadian was incapable of hitting the heights among the world's greats, I have previously recommended Alberta Premium. I still do. But if they want to taste something that will amaze then they can do worse than this. The question will now rage: which is the better of the two? For me, perhaps the Premium, because it also has bite as well as guile and slakes thirsts as well as outrageously entertains. Having made love to a young vixen this, though, is perhaps closer to spending a night in the arms of a sultry lady of greater experience. Passion or elegance? We are back to whisky being a mood thing. And if this doesn't get you in the mood, nothing will. *40%. Alberta Distillers.*

Alberta Springs Aged 10 Years (88) n23 busy and rye rich, there are also icing sugar and green tea elements to this; **t23** voluptuous, mouth-watering and gentle, the rye displays impeccable behaviour choosing only to offer its fruitier element, until the very middle when it hardens out; **f20** a slow development of spices, but the OTT vanilla and caramel really do make things awkward; **b22.5** the intense, disappointing vanilla-toffee fade, plus a curious candy sweetness, robs this otherwise delicious whisky of greatness. *40%*

Barton's Canadian 36 Months Old (78) n19 t20 f19 b20. Sweet, toffeed, easy-going. 40%. Barton.

Black Velvet (78) n18 t20 f20 b20. A distinctly off-key nose is compensated for by a rich corn and vanilla kick on the palate. But that famous spice flourish is a distant memory. Another big caramel number. 40%

Canadian Club 100 Proof (89) n21 an odd biryani note gives an exotic feel to the firm grains which course through this; **t23** one of the sweetest Canadians around with a light Demerara lilt to the intense corn; massive grain assault; **f22** fruit dives in to break up the cornfest; **b23** if you are expecting this to be a high-octane version of the standard CC Premium, you'll be in for a shock. This is a much fruitier dram with an oilier body to absorb the extra strength. An entertaining blend. 50%. Hiram Walker.

Canadian Club Premium (82.5) n20.5 t21 f20 b21. Another Canadian where a fruity element has infiltrated what was once a dryish dram. Lushed up in style some years back and now has an added degree of coppery-honey for good measure. Pleasant. 40% ⊙

Canadian Club Aged 6 Years (88.5) n21.5 interesting if not entirely successful fruit and dry oak mix; **t22** much better, gains impetus with an early fruit imprint, but this gives way as a mild sugary sweetness imposes itself alongside a degree of rye-like sharpness; **f22.5** the cocoa on the finale is something to behold and ensures an improbably long, ever-drying finish. Even before then, the structure is sound and attractive; **b22.5** not at all bad for a Canadian some purists turn their nose up at as it's designed for the American market. Just brimming with mouth-watering enormity and style. Dangerously moreish. 40%

Canadian Club Reserve 10 Years of Age (91) n22.5 no shortage of grapes and apples here; also there is a clear message coming from the oaky vanilla and Java at work; **t22.5** soft, oily laid-back delivery in no hurry to decide which direction to take: corn oil dominates; **f23** now heads back towards a sumptuous mixture of fruits and spices. A tantalising trace of mocha but the softly oily mouthfeel continues with most pathetic of spices and a build up of vanilla and fruit custard; **b23** introduced this into a whisky tasting I gave in Calgary last year and brought the house down. A surprise package for the natives, not least because of the clever interplay between fruit and oak. I suppose the law of averages dictates that one fruited Canadian is going to be pretty damn good: well, this is it! 40% ⊙

Canadian Club Classic Aged 12 Years (92) n22 fruity, firm, a sprinkle of cinnamon yet a touch closed, even with maximum coaxing; **t23.5** beautifully coated with honey and grain oils, allowing for a juicy chewiness to gain momentum before delicate spices strike: they don't come much more luxuriant than this; **f23** long with a similar copper-honey character to the standard CC. Crushed sultana and sharper raisin, but it's not all fruit as some grains deliver some more fiddly, intrinsic notes. Lots of chalky vanilla confirms the age; **b23.5** improved beyond recognition on the previous years. Much, much closer in style to the standard Canadian Club than the idiosyncratic Reserve. From a bit of a dud to one of Canada's finest. 40%

Canadian Club Aged 20 Years (92.5) n24 bread pudding and sherried fruit cake combine. Some real fizzle and entertainment – oh, and some class – make for one of the best Canadian noses around; **t21** a very tame delivery, with soft oils confused by the fruit; pleasant enough but almost a cancelling out of character; **f23.5** readjusts and reinvents itself brilliantly and we are back to the same bread pudding my mum used to make; as those spices settle, some marauding cocoa also goes for it...and then a return to soft corn oil...it's bitter sweet all the way and, as finishes go, this is a bloody long way...!! **b23** in previous years, CC20 has ranked among the worst whiskies I have tasted, not just in Canada, but the world. Their current bottling, though, is not even a distant relation. Sure, it has a big sherry investment. But the sheer elan and clever use of spice make this truly magnificent. Possibly the most pleasant surprise in my latest trawl through all Canada's whiskies. 40%

Canadian Club Sherry Cask batch no. SC-018 **(76) n18 t20 f20 b18.** Question. Am I in my usual suite at the Empress Hotel, Victoria, that emblem of Canada's finest traditions? Or am I in a dusty bodega in Jerez, Spain, sticking my nose into a freshly opened sherry butt? My eyes tells me the sun is setting beyond the flowering arbutus tree and over the ancient, purpling volcanic mountains of British Columbia. My nose sends clear messages of freshly crushed grape, the first part of the wine making process that leads to Portugal's finest export. How do I mark it as a whisky? On the nose where is the grain? Where is the oak? As fruity Canadians go, this has to be the ultimate olfactory experience....In the end I have marked somewhere between the two. Doubtless the blender will be shaking his head, as will the CC execs. But I have to ask them this: what was the point of this whisky? To make it nose and taste like sherry? Then it has succeeded. To make it nose and taste like whisky? Then it has failed. As a fruited Canadian, it is superior because the grape is rich and clean to the point of faultlessness. And anyone into that kind of thing will find the whole thing orgasmic. As a sherry: well, it's twice as strong as you can normally buy it yet somehow has only half the body. As I say, I really don't know what to make of this. Nor do I get the point. 41.3%

Canadian Five Star Rye Whisky (83) n21 t22 f20 b20. An entirely tame, well behaved Canadian which celebrates the inherent sweetness of the species. That said, the immediate impact on the palate is pretty delicious with a quick, flash explosion of something spicy. But it is the deft, satin-soft mouthfeel which may impress most. 40%

Canadian Hunter (83.5) n22 t21.5 f20 b20. Tasted blind you'd spot this as a Canadian 99/100 times. With the vanilla, toffee and oak having such a pleasant say, could it be anything else? 40%

Canadian Mist At least 36 Months old **(73) n18 t18 f17 b18.** Canadian missed. 40% ☉ ☉

Canadian Pure Gold (82) n21.5 t20.5 f20 b20. Full-bodied and still a notably lush whisky. The pure gold may have more to do with the caramel than the years in cask but the meat of this whisky still gives you plenty to chew over. I especially enjoy the gradual building of spices. 40%

Canadian Spirit (78) n20 t20 f19 b19. A real toffee-fest with a touch of hard grain around the edges. 40%. Carrington Distillers (Alberta Distillers).

Centennial 10 Year Limited Edition (86.5) n21.5 t21.5 f22 b21.5. One of Canada's more consistent and slightly improved drams which wholeheartedly embraces the Highwood minimalist house style. The wheat does provoke a lazy but attractive spice buzz throughout and I'm not sure if it is because I am tasting this very early in the morning, but there is an unmistakable honey-edged breakfast cereal element to this one. 40%

Century Reserve 8 Years Old Premium (82) n20 t21 f20 b21. Clean vanilla and caramel. 40%. Century Distillery.

Century Reserve Custom Blend 15 Years Plus (88.5) n21.5 a squeeze of lime makes even lighter the featherweight vanilla; **t22** more astonishing juiciness: one of the few Canadians that appears to hint at something in the direction of barley, though again the vanillas come flying through to muffle that quickly enough; **f23** myriad soft oak noises which delight with their ability to harmonise between sweetish and chalky- and toasty-dry without even missing a beat; **b22** after two days of being ambushed in every direction, or completely steamrollered by Canadian caramel, my tastebuds are in total shock. Caramel kept to an absolute minimum so that it hardly registers at all. Charming and refined drinking. 40%

Corby's Canadian 36 Months Old (85) n20 subtlevariance of vanilla; **t21** sweetcorn to start, oils up and then fills the mouth; **f22** develops into something almost sawdusty. Impressive complexity for one so young; **b22** always attractive with fine bitter-sweet balance and I love the late spice kick-back. 40% Barton. Interesting label: as a keen ornithologist, I had no idea there were parrots in Canada. Must be related to the Norwegian Blue.

Crown Royal (87) n19 dry and grapey, like a puckering fino. The grains, once the fluttering flag of the old CR nose, are hardly anywhere to be seen; **t23.5** credit where due here: CR has taken the fruity route but the delivery is excellent: the mouth-feel is on a par with any of its genre while the layering is boosted by a stunning array of pounding spices; **f22** dries and bitters out; pithy and sharp; **b22.5** it looks as though we have waved goodbye to the old multi-layered rich grained CR for ever: I'll have to pop over to Vancouver and raid the library of Mike Smith for those. But this brand has come a long way in the last year or so and there is now a confidence and shape to the blending that had been badly missing. Still a bit of a shock to us long-time (and I'm talking decades here) CR lovers, but a very decent whisky nonetheless. 40%

Crown Royal Cask No 16 Finished in Cognac Casks (85.5) n21.5 t21 f22 b21. Clean cut and exceptionally grapey. The nose is unique in the whisky world: it is one of Cognac. But otherwise this struggles to really find its shape and rhythm. A perfect Canadian for those who prefer theirs with an air of grace and refinement but very limited depth. In fact, those who prefer a Cognac. 40%

Crown Royal Limited Edition (85.5) n22 t22 f21 b20.5. Decidedly odd mouth texture: creamy, almost like Toffo buttery toffee candy; livens up towards the middle. A whisky that has gone backwards bigtime and where once there was staggering complexity and a whisky vying for Canadian of the year, now there a pleasant, decently spiced highly carameled affair going through the paces. 40%

Crown Royal Special Reserve (94.5) n24 a clean and attractively spiced nose with cinnamon and the faintest pinch of allspice leading the way: rye at work, one presumes; the fruit is clean and precise with weightier grape overshadowing a green apple freshness; **t24** the old rye impact has been lessened by a safety net of cleaner fruits, but something hard and chewy still clings to the palate; the rye really does deliver towards the middle, though; **f23** dries and dusts up; sawdusty in part for all the fruitiness. Vague spices throb, the rye – or is it an echo of rye, like a lost leg – tries to make itself heard; **b23.5** complex, well weighted and simply radiant: it is like looking at a perfectly shaped, gossamer-clad Deb at a ball. The ryes work astonishingly well here (they appear to be of the malted, ultra-fruity variety) and perhaps to best effect after Alberta Premium. 40%

Crown Royal XR Extra Rare bott lot no. L6239 NA2A db **(93) n24** some serious and very varied rye notes; orange peel and bourbon battle it out with marauding vanillas for the sweet-sour supremacy. It's a tie... **t23** those ryes deliver first and do so as part of a breathtaking soft-hard balance. The ryes are hard, the corn and vanilla offer the silky cushion; silver sugar is sprinkled over the mounting vanillins; **f22** medium length, runs out of puff as regards the rye; toffee takes care of the finale; **b24** pretty damn good stuff. This first version of this hen's-teeth bottling may be on the sweet side but makes complexity and balance its be-all and end-all. Wonderful, and another leg up to get people to realise just how good whisky from this country can be. An instant classic. 40%.

Danfield's Limited Edition Aged 21 Years (95) n24 forgive me if I'm wrong, but isn't that rye absolutely pouring from the nose? And probably some malted rye, such is its sweet intensity. God! This is how I dream Canadian whisky should be: rich yet complex and layered, the only discernible fruitiness being rye generated. And if it isn't rye, then well done for finding some fruit that gives it an almost identical character! **t24** fabulously layered with the softer notes proffering rich acacia honey and Demerara, the firmer again accentuating a rye core **f23.5** a busy buzz of spice and building vanillas and tannins; strands of honey soften the burnt-toffee late bitterness; **b23.5** a quite brilliant first-time whisky. The back label claims this to be small batch, but there is no batch number on the bottle, alas. Or even a visible bottling code. But this is a five star performer and one of this year's whiskies of the world. 40%

Danfield's Private Reserve (84.5) n20 t21.5 f22 b21. A curious, non-committal whisky which improves on the palate as it goes along. An overdose of caramel (yawn!!) has done it no favours, but there is character enough for it to pulse out some pretty tasty spice. Seamless and silky, for all the toffee there underlying corn-rich clarity is a bit of a turn on. 40%

Forty Creek Barrel Select (74) n17 t21 f18 b18. A soft but distinct sulphureous note, presumably from a wayward sherry butt, undoes some good work. A real shame as the delivery possesses excellent body. But we all know the dangers of present-day sherry casks... 40%

Forty Creek Small Batch Reserve lot 104 **(91.5) n23.5** seriously chunky with an enticingly complex cereal depth softened by chocolate raisin candy. Charming and charismatic; **t22** initially lighter delivery than the nose suggests. But still mouth-filling and continuing that cereal-fruit theme: liquid breakfast...; **f23** a really excellent panning out of those intense flavours into more easily defined factions. Most delightful has to be the delivery of the spice and the oak-grain balance and a lingering cocoa note; **b23** great stuff, this, not least because the path it follows on the palate is an unusual one with fascinating by-ways and occasional dead-ends. A quality whisky from a distillery now showing obvious self-confidence in its product. 40%

Forty Creek Three Grain (76) n19 t20 f18 b19. Not quite as well assembled as some Three grains I have come across over the last few years. There is a lopsidedness to this one: we know the fruit dominates (and I still haven't a clue why, when surely this of all whiskies, just has to be about the grains!) but the bitterness interferes throughout. If there have been sherry casks used here, I would really have a close look at them. 40%

Gibson's Finest Aged 12 Years (80.5) n20 t20 f20.5 b20. Returned to its irritatingly middle-of-the-road, over-fruited pleasantness which simply refuses to go anywhere beyond the light honey sweetness and soft oils. 40% ☉

Gibson's Finest Rare Aged 18 Years (93) n22.5 genuinely clean grape, but totally in proportion, balance-wise, with the gentle corn weightiness and drying oaks: complex; **t23.5**

mouth cleansing with corn juice and grape and then a wonderful, gradual building of black peppers **f24** long, with varying oak tones fighting with corn-honey and residual spice: near enough perfect weight and mouthfeel for a finale; **b23** changed direction with the input of fruit, but the balance and spices compensate wholly. A Gibson's that really works!! *40%* ⊙⊙

Gibson's Finest Canadian Whisky Bourbon Cask Rare Reserve (89) n23 beautiful bourbon, fruity, kick; **t21** toasty, corn, and light honeyed sugars; **f23** wonderfully long with more golden honey sticking to the corn-rich thread; **b22** a much better version than the first bottling I found, the depth this time being massively greater. *40%*

Gibson's Finest Sterling (70) n18 t18 f17 b17. Frustratingly incoherent, flat, sweet, cloying and, ultimately, bitter. *40%*

Gibson's New Oak (88) n22 decent smattering of spice interrupts the sweet fanfare; **t21** this would be one sensationally lush, almost syrupy, Canadian were it not for sub-strata of light grain and gathering oak; **f23** this is where that new oak does its business with the casks ensuring a delicious counter dryness and spice; **b22** distinctly different from any other Canadian doing the rounds: the oak influence makes a wonderful and clever impact. *40%*

Highwood Pure Canadian (84) n20 t21 f22 b21. A decent, ultra-clean Canadian with markedly more character than before. Certainly the caramel has been seriously reduced in effect and the wheat ensures a rather attractive spice buzz while the cane juice sweetness harmonises well. Perhaps most delightful is the wonderful and distinct lack of fruit. Yippee!! Impressive for all its simplicity. *40%*

Hiram Walker Special Old (91) n22.5 granite-hard with softer, oilier, more citrusy notes being trampled underfoot by almost impermeable grain; **t23** juicy rye and corn fills every crevice medium body at first, then hardens out as some spice develops, though the countering strands of honey work sublimely; **f22.5** not quite the finish of yore, with perhaps an extra serving of caramel dumbing down the citrusy finish. A light coating of muscovado sugar just stays the distance; **b23** in some ways the most solid, uncompromising Canadian of them all. And I love it! Not least because this is the way Special old has been for a very long time with obviously no intentions of joining the fruity bandwagon. Honest, first class Canadian. *40%* ⊙

Lord Calvert (72.5) n19 t18.5 f17 b18. Truly eccentric aristocracy, this. Comes from the most noble of homes, Alberta Distillery, and the pedigree of the rye is evident in patches on both nose and delivery. Then marries something very fruity well beneath its class. *40%*

Lot No. 40 (93) n24 one of the most magnificent and rarest noses in the world: malted rye. Hints of spearmint chewing gum, kumquats, boiled sugar candy, all enveloped in that unique rye fruitiness; **t24** brittle and hard at first, then soft rye-powered fruit arrives, slightly peppery towards the middle, heavy roast cocoa and soft rye oil; **f23** decent oak presence and some straggling fruity rye notes; **b23** this is great whisky, irrespective of whichever country it came from. As for a Canadian, this is true rye whisky, one with which I was very proud to be associated in the early blending days. Elegant stuff. And these notes brought back to you by popular demand!! *43%*

McGuinness Silk Tassel (79.5) n20 t21 f19.5 b19. Silk or satin? The corn oils offer a delightful sheen but still the caramel is over enthusiastic. *40%*

Wm Morrison Imported Canadian Rye (87.5) n22 lavender and still a hint of something in the area of rye. Certainly bold and big; **t22** firm, big and chewy but the caramels deliver much earlier these days; **f21.5** a touch of oak-spice buzz; the toffee dominates the death; **b22** still a lovely Canadian, though the toffee needs toning down. Not sure what "Full Strength" is doing on the label when bottled at 40%, though.... *40%.*

Mountain Rock (87) n22 slightly firmer than of old, but the softer strata oily grain ensures excellent balance; the massive sherry/grape presence is a real surprise; **t20.5** a fruity delivery makes for a slightly puckering early experience, but towards the middle it begins to find its feet; **f22.5** surprisingly long with the fruit-oak combo at last on speaking terms. The result is late spice and fruit chocolate; **b22** still a soft Canadian cocking a melt-in-the-mouth snook at its name. But this time the fruit is just over anxious to be heard and a degree of its old stability has been eroded. *40%. Kittling Ridge.*

Northern Light (82) n20 t21 f20 b21. A young, natural, unpretentious Canadian grain blend with a good, clean character and first-class bite. Very attractive. *40%.*

Pendleton Let'er Buck (91.5) n22.5 firm and dry with the accent on a grain-oak bite; **t23** an immediate grain pinch, then a delicious mouth-watering crescendo; the sweetness is controlled and regulated by spice; **f22.5** some corn oils and building oak make for an excellent bitter-sweet finale of some length and style; **b23.5** a significantly improved whisky from the ultra-sweet, nigh on syrupy concoction of before. Here the surprisingly complex and sensual grains take star billing, despite the caramel: it almost makes a parody of being Canadian, so unmistakable is the style. For those who affectionately remember Canadian Club from 20-30 years ago, this might bring a moistening of the eye. *40% (80 proof). Hood River Distillers.*

Potter's Special Old Rye (90) n23 a busy marriage of hard grain and the shyest of fruit; good vanilla, too; **t23** soft, oily landing then a stunning radiating out of waves of rye. Real rye! A few peppery notes, too; **f21.5** tails off as some caramel and brown sugar digs in; **b22** Potters is one of those whiskies for those of us who cling on to the memory of Canadian whisky as it was 20-30 years ago. Confident and charming. And a treat. *40%*

Potter's Special Old a blend of 5 to 11 year old rye whisky **(91)** n23.5 a genuine rye firmness here sits beautifully with the vanilla; minimum fruit interference; **t23** delicate and beautiful construction to the layered grain; the sweetness works well with the spices; **f22** soft oils and more vanilla...and spice; **b22.5** more Canadian than a hockey punch-up – and, for all the spice, somewhat more gentle, too. *40%*

Rich and Rare (79) n20 t20 f20 b19. Simplistic and soft. One for toffee lovers. *40%*

Royal Canadian (78) n18.5 t19 f21.5 b19. Much better than the nose predicts thanks to an injection of late spice. Some abstract fruitiness dotted around. *40%*

Royal Reserve (79) n20 t19 f20 b20. A noticeable extra injection of caramel has reduced this whisky of late. In this bottling a firmness remains but complexity is at a premium. *40%*

Royal Reserve Gold (92) n23.5 this guy has some attitude! And class. The small pounds away – and remember: size doesn't matter...sensual complexity with one of the best interplays between the pervading dryness and delicate sweet notes. At its best when left in the glass for a short while. Then it becomes a honeypot. And as for an empty glass... quite superb; **t22** again the rye beats a steady, spiced-up rhythm, even though some honeyed caramel tries to take control. No shortage of oak; **f22.5** beautiful spice and chocolate completes a genuinely excellent experience. The lingering acacia honey does a great job in balancing those wonderful drier oaks; **b24** classy, classy Canadian which provides a masterclass in balance. On a different plane to the standard bottling: with the honey and spice, all that is required is a touch of heather for this to go down perfectly. *40%*

Sam Barton Aged 5 Years (83.5) n19 t21.5 f22 b21. Exceptionally sweet session whisky with a lovely maple syrup glow and some complexity on the finish. Friendly, hospitable and impossible not to like. *40%. La Martiniquaise, France.* ☺☺

Schenley Golden Wedding (92) n22 caramel, figs and honey; **t24** now that really is brilliant: full complexity between grains and oak. Still the satin-skinned Canadian of old, but now with the spices more up front and the honey and vanillins enjoying a more confident interplay; a gentle sultana sweetness also adds to the charm; **f22** much drier and its vanilla all the way; **b23** like a rare, solid marriage, this has improved over time. Always been a consistent and pleasant whisky, but now there appears to be a touch of extra age and maturity which has sent the complexity levels up dramatically. Quite sublime. *40%*

Schenley OFC (90) n22 well balanced with drier oaks arriving early. There is a honey thread, though; **t22.5** a sublime viscosity really does ensure that the sweet, softly-spoken corn is amplified: superb texture **f23** long, with some glorious brown sugars tangling with the drier, slightly embittered oak **b22.5** notice anything missing from this whisky? Well the 8-year-old age statement has fallen off the label. But this is still a truly superb whisky which would benefit perhaps from toning down the degree of sweetness, but gets away with it in spectacular fashion thanks to those seductive oils. Not as complex as the magnificent old days, but a whisky that would have you demanding a refill nine time out of ten. *40%*

Seagram's Canadian 83 (86.5) n21 t22 f21.5 b22. A vastly improved blend which, astonishingly, has drastically cut the caramel to reveal a melt-in-the-mouth, slightly crisp grain. There are some citrusy edges but the buttery vanilla and pleasing bite all go to make for a chic little number. *40%*

Seagram's VO (80) n20 t21 f20 b19. The last time I officially tasted this I openly asked what had happened to a once truly great whisky. Where was the old, hugely distinguished rye character? Was it the start of a worrying trend? On this evidence, yes it was. This time there does appear to be rye. But the fruitiness is of a sort where the edges are blurred. Decent whisky? Yes. Fine enough to carry the VO name? Not by a distance. Very Ordinary. *40%*

Tangle Ridge Aged 10 Years (67.5) n17.5 t18 f16 b17. Off-key from nose to finish, cloyingly sweet and curiously dirty at the death. Absolutely dreadful. Yep, it's improved... 40%

Tesco Canadian Whisky (75) n18 t18 f20 b19. Sweet, clean, uninspiring. 40%

Windsor (91.5) n22.5 slightly sharper, tarter rye than usual: a very good sign... t23 the rye comes steaming in with a firm and wonderfully fruity flourish; tones down towards the middle as a custardy sweetness joins in; f22 chocolate toffee, then some longer, oilier grain and spice notes; b24 a whisky that has barely changed over the years: always to be trusted for its big rye statement, this one boasts a bigger one than usual. One of my favourite day-to-day Canadians when in Canada. 40% for Canadian Market.

Windsor (86) n20 t21 f23 b22. Pleasant but with the majority of edges found on the Canadian edition blunted. Some outstanding, almost attritional, spice towards the middle and finale, though. Soft and desirable throughout: a kind of feminine version of the native bottling. 40% for US market.

Wiser's Very Old 18 Years Old (90.5) n24 truly fabulous: one of the great Canadian noses with a stunning tapestry of rye and sherry style fruits combining with maple syrup and green apple: clean, precise and radiating class; t23 that clarity on the nose comes across brilliantly in the rye-studded delivery: firm and crisp with a Demerara coating; f21.5 pleasant but a touch mangled with a bitter note encroaching from some grape or oak – probably both; b22 much better than the last bottling I encountered, which in itself was no slouch. Here, though, the blender has written bolder what he is trying to achieve. 40%

Wiser's De Luxe (83.5) n20.5 t22 f21 b21. I have noticed over the last few years that the shape of this whisky has changed. Once, it was my everyday drinking Canadian: pale coloured though 10 years old and absolutely brimming with grain-oak complexity. Then the age guarantee vanished. And the colour got darker and darker until today it is unrecognisable. Enjoyable, yes: providing you don't remember Wiser's of old. In the place of complexity has arrived fruit. The result is an undeniable softness. There are some decent spices. But as for the old rye character that made this good whisky great? It has vanished under a cartload of fruit. 40%

Wiser's Red Letter (95) n24 the complexity is enough to make you weep: the accent is on elegance, achieved by offering near perfect servings of all you hope to see in a great Canadian. An orangey citrus element is in turn caressed by small grain embedded in a field of soft-oiled corn, which sports a light grape hillside. The toffee-caramel has a flattening effect, sadly: otherwise near perfection in complexity; t24 a wave of soft corn oil spreads over the roof of the mouth; both juicy and chewy in equal measure, the vanilla starts making delightful speeches while the most delicate of rye injections cranks up the complexity further; f23.5 the caramel which builds on the nose does likewise on the finale to form a toffee dam. At least some spices filter through; b23.5 the recent trend with Canadian whisky has been to do away with finesse and cram each bottle with fruit. This returns us to a very old fashioned and traditional Canadian style. And had the rye been upped slightly and the caramel eschewed entirely it might have been a potential world whisky of the year...Even in this form, however, it is certainly good enough to be Jim Murray's Whisky Bible Canadian Whisky of the Year 2010 45% ☉

Wiser's Reserve (75) n19 t20 f18 b18. Something very strange has happened to this. The nose offers curious tobacco while the palate is uneven, with the bitterness out of tandem with the runaway early sweetness. In the confusion the fruit never quite knows which way to turn. A once mighty whisky has fallen. And I now understand it might be the end of the line with the excellent Wiser's Small Batch coming in to replace it. So if you are a reserve fan, buy them up now. 43%

Wiser's Small Batch (92.5) n23 full on, with an outwardly less than subtle nose with fruit in big evidence (including over-ripe fig). But this one, though, has a genuine touch of style thanks not least to a small grain undercurrent which pushes all else into place; t24 mouth-watering, mouth-filling and mouth-teasing: juicy and grapey, but never remotely stodgy; wonderful vanilla sub plot but again there is a bombardment of busy grains, just like the nose; f22.5 slightly overwhelmed by soft fruit, it still has enough in reserve to add some polished cocoa and honey notes; b23 OK it's another fruity one: but this is just so gloriously intrinsic on the nose and delivery. Great stuff and the complete package that's in danger of giving fruity Canadian a good name. 43.4%

Wiser's Special Blend (78) n19 t20 f19 b19. A plodding, pleasant whisky with no great desire to offer much beyond caramel. 40%

Japanese Whisky

Something quite significant happened in the final days of writing Jim Murray's Whisky Bible last year. Of the whiskies which made it to the final five for World Whisky of the Year, two were from Japan. Not only that, they were as far apart in character as you could possibly find.

One was from a sumptuous sherry butt, yet still riddled with all kinds of oaky, malty complexity. The other was single malt from a column still, not much of a looker on first taste, but on second and third simply sent the tastebuds into raptures. Neither in the end got the coveted first place. But one of them did make second - and the other third. It was a glorious vindication of the hard work and attention to detail that Japanese distillers carry out with such pride. Yet still there was a great frustration that these whiskies or at least many like them were most unlikely to be seen outside of Japan, so slow has been the expansion of their whisky empire.

I have met a number of whisky shop owners around the world who will stock only a handful of Japanese simply because they cannot get assurances that what they are being sent does not contain Scotch. Certainly, these mind-blowing single malts which had lorded it with the world's elite were 100% from the land of the rising sun. But until exchanging whiskies within Japanese companies becomes a natural part of their culture it is hard to see how the confidence generated by the excellence of the single malt and grains available as singletons can be extended to the blends.

Part of the problem has been the Japanese custom of refusing to trade with their rivals. Therefore a Japanese whisky, if not made completely from home-distilled spirit, will instead contain a percentage of Scotch rather than whisky from fellow Japanese distillers.

This, ultimately, is doing the industry no favours at all. The practice is partly down to the traditional work ethics of company loyalty and an inherent, and these days false, belief that Scotch whisky is automatically better than Japanese. Back in the late 1990s I planted the first seeds in trying to get rival distillers to discuss with each other the possibility of exchanging whiskies to ensure that their distilleries worked more economically.

In the meantime word is getting round that Japanese whisky is worth finding. It is now not uncommon for me to discuss with whisky lovers at a fair or book signing the merits and differences of Yoichi and Hakushu, two distilleries which are now being correctly recognised for their world-class brilliance. And, increasingly, Yamazaki which has moved away from a

Key
- ● **Major Town or City**
- ▲ Distillery

comfort zone it operated in for many years and is now offering malts of great magnitude: indeed, it was the producer of one of the two Japanese whiskies which was considered as a possible World Whisky of the Year. And I still get a small thrill when I hear Yoichi's name mentioned around the world: I'm proud to have first brought it to the world's attention in 1997 – though these days has to be a little more careful with their use of sherry.

Yoichi's owner, Nikka, though, can take a bow for their continued innovation. Readers of Jim Murray's Whisky Bible will be well aware how good their single grains have been. Last year they eclipsed even a great Yoichi by showing just how good single malt can be when it is distilled through a first-class continuous still - in this case a Coffey Still. My staff know better than to try to get their hands on the samples. But this was the one they hovered around in continued hope: it was a style they had never encountered before and were curious to see why I had rated it the second best whisky in the world. After tasting it, some wondered why it wasn't No 1. As the brand gets better known, I suspect they will not be alone...

Single Malts

CHICHIBU

Golden Horse Chichibu db **(80)** n19 t21 f20 b20. Light, toasty and delicate yet the oak is prominent throughout. Good balancing sweet malt, though. *43%. Toa.*

Golden Horse Chichibu 10 Years Old Single Malt db **(82)** n19 t22 f21 b20. Developing citrus notes lighten the weight as the oak and sweet malt go head to head. *43%. Toa.*

Chichibu 14 Years Old Single Malt db **(89)** n20 tangerine peel and rice: two years older than the 12-y-o, that hint of bourbon has now become a statement; **t23** brilliantly eclectic arrival on the palate with no organisation at all to the flurry of malt and bourbony oak and tangerine-fruity spices that are whizzing around; **f23** pretty long with firm vanilla and a distinctive oiliness. Something approaching a whiff of smoke adds some extra ballast to the oak; **b23** we are talking mega, in-your-face taste explosions here. A malt with a bourbony attitude that is unquestionably superb. *57%. Toa.*

⋅⋰⋅ **Ichiro's Malt Chichibu Newborn** cask no. 127, dist 08, bott 08 **(80)** n18.5 t21 f20.5 b20. A fierce, juicy, fruity, barley-oil intense semi new make which appears to have spent a limited time in cask. Not entirely free of feints, it is not lacking in character for that and while technically challenged, is flavourful fun. *62.5%. Number One Drinks Co.*

FUJI GOTEMBA 1973. Kirin Distillers.

The Fuji Gotemba 15 Years Old db **(92)** n21 diced nuts, especially pistachio with vanilla and a sprinkling of sugar; **t23** mouth watering from the start with a sensational development of sweet malt; **f24** plateaus out with textbook spices binding sweet malt and dry oak. The length is exemplary; **b24** quality malt of great poise. *43%. Kirin.*

The Fuji Gotemba 18 Years Old db **(81)** n20 t19 f21 b21. Jelly-baby fruitiness, complete with powdered sugar. Big, big age apparent. *43%. Kirin.*

Fuji Gotemba 20th Anniversary Pure Malt db **(84)** n21 t20 f22 b21. The nose is a lovely mixture of fruit and mixed oak; the body has a delightful sheen and more fruit with the malt. Handsome stuff. *40%. Kirin.*

HAKUSHU 1973. Suntory.

⋅⋰⋅ **Hakushu Heavily Peated Aged 9 Years** bott 09 db **(92.5)** n22.5 lightly heavily peated with a now lost Port Ellen style gristy sweetness; **t23.5** ultra sweet barley bang on cue and a slow radiation of spice, citrus and sympathetic oak; **f23** drier, oakier but still some sugared lime for balance and freshness. The smoke is distant and barley involved; **b23.5** nothing like as heavily peated as some Hakushus it has been my pleasure to sample over the years. But certainly superbly orchestrated and balanced. *48%*

⋅⋰⋅ **Hakushu Single Malt Whisky Aged 10 Years** bott 09 db **(87.5)** n22 a much more lumbering gait with both barley and oak; **t23** sprightly barley at first, which immediately sweetens deliciously. The oak and toffees become a brooding presence; **f20.5** pretty flat and oak-fuelled; **b22** duller than of old. *40%*

Hakushu Single Malt Whisky Aged 12 Years db **(91.5)** n22.5 t23.5 f22.5 b23. Just about identical to the 43.3% bottling in every respect. Please see those tasting notes for this little beauty. *43.5%*

Hakushu Single Malt Aged 12 Years db **(91)** n22 revitalising barley with smoke as distant as a cloud over Fuji; **t23** multi-layered barley with so many levels of sweetness; the very faintest hint of smoke on the middle; **f23** long with the accent now on vanilla and soft, developing oil and spice; **b23** an even more lightly- peated version of the 40%, with the distillery's fabulous depth on full show. *43.3%.* ⊙

The Hakushu Single Malt Whisky Aged 15 Years Cask Strength db **(95)** n24 pure, unmistakable Hakushu: intense, powering, yet clean and refined. Loads of citrus to lighten matters but the local oak ensures enormity; **t23** big, initially oak-threatened but the barley comes flooding back with light oils helping to soften the early scratchiness; first mouthful is dry, the second shows a much truer picture; **f24** now goes into complexity overdrive as all those fruity-barley-oaky- elements continue to jostle for supremacy, only for late spices and gorgeous milky mocha to come in and steal the thunder; **b24** last time round I lamented the disappointing nose. This time perhaps only a degree of over eagerness from the oak has robbed this as a serious Whisky of the Year contender. No matter how you look at it, though, brilliant!! *56%*

⋅⋰⋅ **Hakushu Single Malt Whisky Aged 18 Years** bott 09 db **(86)** n20 t23.5 f21 b21.5. Wow! Where has all this oak come from? Appears to have gone gray overnight...The delivery, though, makes this a malt worth finding because for 20 seconds or so we have absolutely everything in complete harmony, and the degree of barley sweetness is just about perfect. Then all is lost to the duller oak tones again. *43%*

The Hakushu Single Malt Whisky Aged 25 Years db (93) n23 some blowhard oak is pegged back by an intense barley-fruit mix; thick yet complex; t24 a wonderful combination of silk and barley sheen juxtaposed with busy but light spice; soft fruits adorn the higher places within the palate while a subtle earthiness rumbles below; f23 improbably long. Even though some serious extraction has taken place from the oak, the integrity of the barley makes you sigh with pleasure. Now the spices change in nature to soft and playful to warm and rumbling; **b23** a malt which is impossible not to be blown away by. 43% ☉

Hakushu 1984 db (95) n22 delicate banana and malt with a gentle fly-past of peat. The oak is unbowed but sympathetic; t25 staggeringly beautiful: wave upon wave of astonishing complexity crashes against the tastebuds. The malt is intense but there is plenty of room for oak in varying guises to arrive, make eloquent speeches and retire. The intensity of spice is spot on – perfect; f24 long, more spice and greater malt intensity as the oak fades. Only the softest hints of smoke; mouthwatering to the last as mild coffee appears; **b24** a masterpiece malt of quite sublime complexity and balance. The sort of experience that gives a meaning to life, the universe and everything... 61%

Hakushu 1988 db (92) n21 overtly peaty and dense, pleasant but lacking usual Hakushu complexity; t24 mouthwatering start with massively lively malt and fresh peating hanging on to its coat-tails. Some amazing heather–honey moments that have no right to be there; the peat intensifies then lightens; f23 lots of rich peat and then intense vanilla; crisp and abrupt at the finale with late bitter chocolate; **b24** like all great whiskies this is one that gangs up on you in a way you are not expecting: the limited complexity on the nose is more than compensated for elsewhere. Superb. If this were an Islay malt the world would be drooling over it. 61%

Hakushu Vintage Malt 1990 db (89) n22 firm barley and firmer oak; t23 serious intensity on delivery, this time with all the action being enjoyed by the concentrated, grassy barley; f22 layers of vanilla add balance to the fade; **b22** warming in places with the tastebuds never getting a single moment's peace. 56%. Suntory.

The Cask of Hakushu 1993 Spanish oak Bota Corta, dist 93, bott 08 db (80.5) n20 t22 f18 **b20**. Grape influence rarely gets any bigger than this without taking over entirely. However, this falls on a sulphurous sword which doesn't exactly ruin the experience, but certainly has you looking for a hanky to weep into. 60%. 571 bottles.

The Cask of Hakushu 1993 Heavily Peated Malt cask no 3B40574 white oak hogshead, dist 93, bott 08 db (96) n23.5 subtle smoke is almost – though not quite – out-muscled by the oak; bonfires and rain on warm ash give this an earthy, outdoor feel; t24 brilliant delivery: the peats are pent up but holding back, allowing a really juicy barley theme to develop slowly the smoke is unleashed... f24 long, with a wondrous development of spot on oils which offer almost perfect sweetness and depth to the smoke; spices arrive late to tingle and tease; a slight vegetable feel, too, as if going along with the earthy-garden-allotment feel; **b24.5** it's bottlings like this which underline Hakushu's position as one of the world's great distilleries. I just think they got the title on the label wrong: I think they meant "Heavenly Peated Malt"... 58%. 232 bottles.

Suntory Pure Malt Hakushu Aged 20 Years db (94) n23 fresh, mildly grapey fruit combined with subtle waves of peat; t24 the peat is now less subtle: wave upon wave of it bringing with it flotsam of drifting oak and then a very sharp malt tang; f23 long, sweet spice but the oak forms a chunky alliance with the firm peat. The bitter-sweet compexity almost defies belief; **b24** a hard-to-find malt, but find it you must. Yet another huge nail in the coffin of those who purport Japanese whisky to be automatically inferior to Scotch. 56%

HANYU

Eight of Spades 2000 cask no. 9301, dist 00, bott 08 (66.5) n16 t18 f16 b16.5. The sulphur reduces this to a deuce. 58%. (Ichiro's Malt Card Series).

Full Proof Europe Hanyu 1988 butt no. 9307, bott 08, (74.5) n19 t20.5 f18 b18. Some bright honeyed moments can't quite entirely contain the sulphur. 55%. nc ncf. 534 bottles.

Hanyu 1990 cask no. 9511, dist 90, bott 07 db (91) n23 golden syrup and full on oak; t23 the suppressed sweetness on the nose is on full view from the moment of impact; mega-rich barley, supported by muscovado sugar, heads towards the butterscotch middle; f22 drier and toastier but the barley sugar leaves an excellent sheen; **b23** leaves you in no doubt how outstanding this stuff can be when found nowhere near a sherry butt... 55.5%.

Jack of Clubs 1991 cask no. 9001, dist 91, bott 06 db (87) n22 sweet bourbon-esque notes, except the oak is more European in style; t22 mouth-watering barley sugar with that diffused and powerful oak leading the way; f21 thins out; **b22** an enjoyable malt just missing out on complexity. 56.8%. Ichiro's Malt Card Series.

Jack of Diamonds 1988 cask no. 9103, dist 88, bott 08 db **(92) n22** no going easy on the oak...; the smoke is much more delicate; **t23. 5** brilliant delivery: the spices rage as the barley sings; the oak is definitely of grey-beard persuasion, but there are enough phenols in there to give the weight a certain energy and shape; some citrus lightens matters – but only by a fraction; **f23** exceptionally long with a sublime mocha fade; **b23.5** a malt which takes the oaks to the very limit and somehow comes out as an ancient classic. *56%. Ichiro's Malt Card Series.*

King of Diamonds 1988 cask no. 9003, dist 88, bott 06 db **(96) n25 t23 f24 b24.** This is what whisky should be all about: subtlety and class. And this King of Diamonds has it in Spades.... *56%. Ichiro's Malt Card Series.*

King of Spades 1986 cask no. 9418, dist 86, bott 07 db **(91) n22** various layers of oak – including some from the deepest parts of the stave – embellish the fruity lead; **t23** big barley-fruit delivery; sharp, eye watering, grassy style. Very clean and precise for age; **f23** no less salivating on the finish with some spicier notes now throbbing through and the trademark cocoa trait to tie things off; **b23** another little belter from this excellent distillery showing confidence at this age to the point of arrogance. *57%. Ichiro's Malt Card Series.*

Queen of Clubs 1988 cask no. 7003, dist 88, bott 08 db **(84.5) n20.5 t22 f21 b21.** Is it a rum? Is it a bourbon? No...it's a malt!! Enormous in every respect and a bit of bite and attitude, too; not entirely blemish-free. *56%. Ichiro's Malt Card Series.*

Two of Clubs 2000 cask no. 9500, dist 00, bott 07 db **(92) n22** fruity; what appears a local/European oak hybrid embraces clean barley; **t24** exceptional delivery with outstanding fruity intensity to the barley which is almost too clean and concentrated to be true...wonderful! **f23** simplistic fade, but nothing wrong with luxurious, lightly oiled malt still pulsing a semi-sweet barley residue; **b23** beautifully made and full of malty gusto. A genuine treat – especially for a malt so young. Two of Clubs, maybe. A Full House in anyone's books, though. *57%. Ichiro's Malt Card Series.*

∵ **Ichiro's Card Series Ace of Diamonds Hanyu 1986** cream sherry butt finish, cask no. 9023, dist 86, bott 08 **(94.5) n24** pretty sound sherry: deep, fruitcakey and well spiced; that would normally be enough, but there is a distinct bourbon sub plot here; **t23.5** fine arrival: juicy grape and spice in equal portions and remains clean right through to the barley, muscovado sugars and butterscotch entering the fray; an injection of hickory is respectful nod to the oak; **f23** slightly dry and dusty, but those spices keep coming...; **b24** another big sherry finish. But again sulphur free and here provides sufficient spice to make the whole thing rock. High grade Japanese. And even higher grade finishing... *56.4%. Number One Drinks Co.*

∵ **Ichiro's Card Series Ten of Clubs Hanyu 1990** sherry butt finish, cask no. 9032, dist 90, bott 08 **(85) n22.5 t21.5 f21 b20.** Tempted to give this one extra marks just for finding a non-sulphured cask. But also have to say that the sherry here, though profound and clean, is having too big a say. Some of the grape is formidably beautiful. But there is too much of a good thing, and vital complexity is lost. That said, a whisky worth investigating. *52.4%. Number One Drinks Co.*

KARUIZAWA 1955. Mercian.

Karuizawa 1971 cask no. 6878, dist 71, bott 08 **(94) n24** solid as a rock: firm barley with all kinds of south Pacific fruits plus leather armchairs and honeycomb to underline the age just in case you hadn't got the message; oh and overcooked raisins, just in case you hadn't sussed the barrel type, either... **t23.5** entangled delivery: another bottling where you need some serious time and a brain capable of sorting out Chinese puzzles – or in this case, Japanese. The intensity of the aged oak makes for a puckering start, but beyond that we are into the land of badly burnt raisins (confirming the nose), sultanas that have gone all squidgy and juicy; massive Christmas pudding character with trifle for good measure. Strewth! as they may say a bit further south-east of this distillery; decent esters help give this a slightly rummy edge, too; **f23** long, with some custard powder helping tone things down slightly; the glazed sugar/caramelised biscuit effect is impressive and those toasted raisins remain alluring; **b23.5** it's not just Scotch which goes all exotic fruity on us when it gets towards being an antique malt. By the time you have grappled and overcome this one your tastebuds and brain are pretty knackered. But it's so worth the battle....! *64.1%. Number One Drinks Company.*

Karuizawa 1972 Aged 31 Years cask 5530 db **(78) n19 t18 f21 b20.** Oaky and hot with just a bit too much age.

∵ **Karuizawa 1972** sherry butt finish, cask no. 7290, dist 72, bott 08 **(87.5) n24** ultra clean grape punctuated by even cleaner barley. A nutty colonel offers dry Lubeck marzipan. Almost too beautiful for words... **t20** thin delivery. All spirit and limited malt development... **f22** settles

– kind of - and barley and fruit come through loud and clear; **b21.5** a bizarre whisky, not helped by its strength and spirit-driven punch. But clean and hammers home its finer points if you are able to listen. It's the nose, though, which stars. *65%. Number One Drinks Co.*

Karuizawa 1973 Aged 30 Years cask 6249 db **(84) n20 t21 f22 b21.** Sweet barley and very silky oaky vanilla. Plucked from the cask just in time.

Karuizawa 1974 Aged 29 Years cask 6115 db **(91) n23** brilliant complexity: juicy dates and figs wrapped around a theme of richly oaked barley; **t22** much sweeter arrival on the nose with burnt fudge and toast arriving for the middle; **f23** slightly salty, the barley seems both sweet and roasty. Soft liquorice makes this one you can chew for hours; **b23** an exhibition of bitter-sweet enormity.

Karuizawa 1975 Aged 28 Years cask 4066 db **(85) n20 t21 f23 b21.** Much more relaxed late middle and finish with they honey thread soothing the singed taste buds; loud at first, it sings sweet lullabies at the death. Always complex.

Karuizawa 1976 Aged 27 Years cask 6949 db **(83) n19 t20 f23 b21.** Big, mouthfilling but just a touch too much oak among the honey.

Karuizawa 1977 Aged 26 Years cask 7614 db **(74) n17 t20 f19 b18.** Some decent sweetness but doesn't quite work.

Karuizawa 1978 Aged 25 Years cask 2368 db **(87) n21** seaweedy and shoreline, but without the peat; **t20** almost violent arrival of searing sherry and vicious oak: hang on to your chair; **f23** calms down stupendously with soft smoky peat to be found in the many strata of clean fruit and barley; **b23** extra dry sherry, biting, salty and with a big coastal tang.

Karuizawa 1979 Aged 24 Years cask 8835 db **(94) n23** much more fruit than is usual for this distillery with apples and fresh pear; lots of barley survives despite the age; **t23** the barley is drinking in gentle honey and cocoa-enriched oak; **f24** marvellously long with teasing, toasted caramelised oak adding a glorious repost to the rich, Demerara-sweetened barley; **b24** one of those rare casks that appears to have had a magic wand waved at it and stardust sprinkled liberally.

Karuizawa 1980 Aged 23 Years cask 7614 db **(89) n22** solid age but the softness of the toffee-apple and barley sugar is first class; attractive bourbony notes develop; **t21** gripping, wild and hot at first, then a series of soothing waves of malt and liquorice; **f24** peppery and estery; the honey-malt mouthfeel is long, lush and fabulous; **b22** a classy Japanese malt that relishes the battle against advancing oak.

Karuizawa 1981 Aged 22 Years cask 8280 db **(73) n17 t19 f19 b18.** Sharp redcurrants but too obvious off-notes abound.

Karuizawa 1982 Aged 21 Years cask 8527 db **(85) n21** a forest full of honey bees; **t21** deep honey and toasted fudge; the middle erupts with strangely enjoyable sap; **f22** gentle malt with a pinch of moscavado sugar and liquorice; **b21** a mature whisky showing some sag but just hanging onto its sexy, alluring figure.

Karuizawa 1983 Aged 20 Years cask 8609 db **(88) n20** slightly estery; chocolate honeycomb and a slice of pine; **t24** estery, rich enormous copper presence; **f22** medium length with elegant wisps of honey and toffee, **b22** tasted blind you would bet your own grandmother that this was pot still Jamaican rum. And one probably older than your gran.

Karuizawa 1984 Aged 19 Years cask 2563 db **(78) n17 t20 f21 b20.** Some quality touches of grape against smoky grist, and the mild peat is a redeeming and unexpected surprise, but what a shame that minor sulphury blemish.

Karuizawa 1985 Aged 18 Years cask 6885 db **(90) n22** honey as a side dish on butterscotch tart; **t22** mouth filling, oilier than usual with sumptuous malt and oak; **f23** wonderful tones of butterscotch sweetened over the broadening oak. Just a slight sprinkling of cocoa; **b23** whisky that celebrates its middle age with a show of complex intensity.

Karuizawa 1986 cask no. 7387, dist 86, bott 08 **(82.5) n20 t22 f20 b20.5.** For a malt so obviously trying to overcome a sulphurous handicap it holds its head high with a vivid barley thrust. Lots of caramel on the finish, too. *60.7%. Number One Drinks Company.*

Karuizawa 1986 Aged 17 Years cask 8170 db **(94) n23** full-frontal, naked sherry. And spicy, too; **t23** massive, almost uncontrollable sherry-malt explosion; dried dates and vanilla concentrate form an unlikely but delicious alliance; **f24** long, fruity with hidden spices; the malt ducks in and out playfully; **b24** find a faultless sherry butt and place in it a whisky of the very finest quality and complexity. This is the result.

Karuizawa 1987 Aged 16 Years cask 8694 db **(93) n23** amazingly soft malt with just a touch of far-away, background smoke; **t23** brilliant malt arrival: the barley sings from every direction; **f24** surprising lack of development as the oak remains shy and the barley rules unhindered; just the faintest wisp of smoke here and there; **b23** almost like a malt-shake in its barley intensity. No complaints here, though.

Karuizawa 1988 Aged 15 Years cask 691 db **(88) n20** malty banana and custard; **t22** drying oak at first and then the most teasing build-up of honey imaginable; **f23** this creeping effect continues with a crescendo of acacia honey and green-grassy barley in total control of the oak; **b23** quite fabulous whisky that exudes confidence and charisma.

Karuizawa 1988 Single Cask No. 3397 dist 88, bott 07 db **(90) n21** red liquorice and grist; a soft smokiness helps control some oaky off-notes; **t23** magical delivery with a golden syrup/molassed malt sweetness going head to head with much aggressive oak; **f23** fabulous, pin-pricky spices lengthen the sweet finish; **b23** technically a slightly flawed dram. But there is no denying its drama. *59.8%*

Karuizawa 1991 cask no. 3318, dist 91, bott 07 **(85) n19 t21.5 f22.5 b22.** Aggressive barley tries to help compensate for the over extraction from the oak. Never less than high quality, though, and blessed with delicious molasses all the way. *62.5%.*

Karuizawa 1992 cask no. 3330, dist 92, bott 07 **(92) n23** huge: I think I'm going to be nosing and tasting this for some time...as much rum character as whisky, possibly due to the big esters; seriously fruity but also with a touch of creosote (which is better than it sounds); something of a vaguely sulphury edge, but it is so overwhelmed by all else around it, it hardly seems to matter; **t22.5** no shrinking violet in delivery, either: puckering at times thanks to the oak and possibly something else (three guesses) but towards the middle finds a honeyed seam; **f23.5** now hits the high spots with a fabulous range of rich sugary notes and some marmalade for good measure; **b23.5** flawed, certainly. But in genius, it's just about forgivable.. *61.5%. Number One Drinks Company.*

⸬ **Karuizawa 1995** Japanese wine cask finish no. 5004, dist 95, bott 08 **(93.5) n23.5** a touch of cherry stone brandy: hard, uncompromising, full of nutty fruit...and glorious... **t23** for the enormity of the malt, the salivatory experience goes off the scale as those cherries, now accompanied by liquorice and raspberry jam go into overdrive; **f23.5** much more sedate: but still the mouth-watering barley and fruit carry on regardless of a half-hearted oaky intervention; **b23.5** seatbelts needed for this enormous ride. An unusual malt which doesn't entirely add up....but comes to the right numbers!! *63%. Number One Drinks Co.*

⸬ **Karuizawa Pure Malt Aged 12 Years** **(85) n18 t23 f22 b22.** A recent Gold Medal Winner at the IWSC, but surely not by sporting a fractured nose like this. Thankfully the delivery is quite superb with the emphasis on silky honeycomb. *40%*

Karuizawa Pure Malt 15 Years **(76) n17 t21 f20 b18.** Some vague sulphur notes on the sherry do no favours for what appears to be an otherwise top-quality malt. (Earlier bottlings have been around the 87–88 mark, with the fruit, though clean, not being quite in balance but made up for by an astonishing silkiness with roast chestnut puree and malt). *40%*

⸬ **Karuizawa Single Malt Aged 17 Years** **(87.5) n23** juicy dates in the rich, molassed fruitcake; **t23** almost ridiculously soft on delivery: it's all about fruit, for sure, but the roast coffee and dark molassed sweetness do give it a required dimension; **f20** despite the clarity of grape, still a dry, bitter note develops; **b21.5** a beautiful malt in so many ways, but one less-than-wonderful sherry butt has robbed this of greatness. How many times has this happened this year....? *40%*

Karuizawa Pure Malt Aged 17 Years **(90) n20** bourbony, big oak and pounding fruit; **t24** enormous stuff: the link between malt and fruit is almost without definition; **f23** amazingly long and silky. Natural vanilla melts in with the almost concentrated malt; **b23** brilliant whisky beautifully made and majestically matured. Neither sweetness nor dryness dominates, always the mark of a quality dram. *40%*

The Whisky Fair Karuizawa Aged 19 Years refill sherry, dist 88, bott 07 **(84) n21 t22 f20 b21.** Softly oiled with the accent on barley and caramel. *58.3%. Germany.*

The Whisky Fair Karuizawa Aged 19 Years sherry, dist 88, bott 07 **(89.5) n22.5** earthy grape with the odd sweeter moment; **t23** big spice and fruit delivery; juicy and mouth-watering; **f22** softens with caramel but the spices pulse merrily away; **b22** a fuller, happier malt than the refill version. *60.6%. Germany.*

KIRIN

⸬ **Kirin18 Years Old (86.5) n22 t22 f21.5 b21.** Unquestionably over-aged. Even so, still puts up a decent show with juicy citrus trying to add a lighter touch to the uncompromising, ultra dense oak. As entertaining as it is challenging. *43%. Suntory*

KOMAGATAKE

Komagatake 10 Years Old Single Malt db **(78) n19 t20 f19 b20.** A very simple, malty whisky that's chewy and clean with a slight hint of toffee. *40%. Mars.*

⸬ **Komagatake 10 Years Old Sherry Cask** db **(67) n16.5 t17 f16.5 b17.** Torpedoed by sulphur. Gruesome. *40%. Mars.*

꙰ **Komagatake 1988 Single Cask** sherry cask, cask no. 566, dist 88, bott 09 db **(62.5)** n15 t16.5 f15 b16. I can assume only that this has been "finished" in a relatively recent sherry butt. "Finished" is putting it mildly. A sulphur horror show. *46%. Mars.*

꙰ **Komagatake 1989 Single Cask** American white oak cask, cask no. 617, dist 89, bott 09 db **(88)** n23 candy stores of the 50s and 60s...dentine and waxed floors. Beautiful... t22.5 sugary beginnings, a livid barley scream and then vanilla; f21 bitters out as oak attacks; b21.5 a fine but bitty malt which feels its age at times. *46%. Mars.*

꙰ **Komagatake 1992 Single Cask** American white oak cask, cask no. 1144, dist 92, bott 09 db **(93.5)** n24.5 one of the noses of the year: cartful of apples, some of the toffee apple variety; dentine and molassed rum; t23 firm, teeth-cracking malt which really piles on the malty style; caramel as well, but it appears fresh and breathing - as though extracted from the oak; f22.5 rumbling spice carries on indefinitely; vanilla and walnut oil; b23.5 you know when you've had a glass of this: beautiful and no shrinking violet. *46%. Mars.*

MIYAGIKYO (see Sendai)

SENDAI 1969. Nikka.

꙰ **Miyagikyo** batch 24H20B db **(89)** n22 sweet chestnut and marzipan share the nutty honours; t23.5 beautiful delivery, superbly weighted: the malt really has some backbone and some toffee liquorice makes for a chewy middle ground; f21.5 perhaps a touch too much toffee; b22 another high quality malt from this improving distillery. *43%*

꙰ **Miyagikyo 10 Years Old** batch 06I08C db **(83)** n19 t22 f21 b21. Much better than the sharp nose warns, with some juicy, fruity moments. A little flat, though. *45%*

꙰ **Miyagikyo 12 Years Old** batch 08I28A db **(89)** n22.5 that familiar gooseberry nose with barley and custard; t23 juicy and sweetens superbly mainly with gristy barley, though that oaky vanilla lurks nearby; f21 drier, a hint of bitterness, but that persistent sweet barley compensates; b22.5 in many ways, absolutely 100% recognisable as the distillery house style; in another this has much more confidence and charisma than of old. *45%*

꙰ **Miyagikyo 15 Years Old** batch 02I10D db **(91.5)** n23 fruity, as is the expression's style. But now lighter with much more emphasis on a Sauternes-style sultana; t23.5 pulsing fruit, but the barley is sharp and wonderfully juicy; f22 vanillas balance the barley and still a residual sweet grape can be found; a mild degree of very late bitterness; b23 a much lighter, more refined and elegant creature than before. Despite a minor sherry butt blemish, fabulous. *45%*

Miyagiko Key Malt Aged 12 Years "Fruity & Rich" db **(90)** n22 fruit biscuits with burnt raisin and sugar; t23 wonderful lift-off of sultana and burnt raisin on a sea of chewy barley. Towards the middle, a brief expression of oak and then much sweeter – and oilier – barley. Fruity; f22 rich! b23 a very comfortable whisky, much at home with itself. *55%. Nikka.*

Miyagiko Key Malt Aged 12 Years "Soft & Dry" db **(85)** n22 t21 f21 b21. Perhaps needs a degree of sweetness.... *55%. Nikka.*

Miyagiko 15 Years Old batch 20C44C db **(84)** n20 t21 f22 b21. Very typically Sendai: light body and limited weight even with all the fruit. Clean and gathers in overall enjoyability, though. *45%*

Sendai 12 Years Old code 06C40C db (83) n17 t22 f23 b21. To put it politely, the nose is pretty ordinary; but what goes on afterwards is relative bliss with a wonderful, oily, fruity resonance. For those thinking in Scotch terms, this is very Speysidey with the malt intense and chewy. *45%. Nikka.*

Sendai Miyagikyo Nikka Single Cask Malt Whisky 1986 dist 16 May 86 bott, 5 Dec 03 db **(88)** n22 stewed prunes and oranges; the first rumbles of bourbon and smoke wafting around for extra weight; t20 big fruit kick but a little out of sync; f24 a super nova of a kick back with peat appearing as if from nowhere and the big, booming, bourbony notes and sweetness at the end offering dozens of waves of complexity. A touch of cocoa rounds it off magnificently; b22 little to do with balance, everything about effect. *63.2%*

Sendai Miyagikyo Nikka Single Cask Malt Whisky 1992 dist 22 Apr 92, bott 5 Dec 03 db **(84)** n19 t20 f24 b21. Very strange whisky: I would never have recognised this as Sendai. I don't know if they have used local oak on this but the fruity, off-balance nose and early taste is compensated by an orgy of mouth-watering, softly smoked barley that sends the taste buds into ecstasy. A distinct, at times erratic, whisky that may horrify the purists but really has some perzaz and simply cannot be ignored. *55.3%*

SHIRAKAWA

Shirakawa 32 Years Old Single Malt (94) n23 ripe mango meets a riper, rye-encrusted bourbon. We are talking a major aroma here; t24 the most intense malt you'll ever find explodes and drools all over your tastebuds. To make the flavour bigger still, the oak adds a punchy bourbon quality. Beautiful oils coat the roof of the mouth to amplify the performance; **f23** long, sweet and malty. Some fruitiness does arrive but it is the oak-malt combination that just knocks you out; **b24** just how big can an unpeated malt whisky get? The kind of malt that leaves you in awe, even when you thought you had seen and tasted them all. *55%. Takara.*

WHITE OAK DISTILLERY

⋄⋄⋄ **White Oak Akashi Single Malt Whisky Aged 8 Years** bott 07 db **(74.5) n18.5 t19.5 f17.5 b19.** Always fascinating to find a malt from one of the smaller distilleries in a country. And I look forward to tracking this one down and visiting, something I have yet to do. There is certainly something distinctly small still about his one, with butyric and feintiness causing damage to nose and finish. For all the early malty presence on delivery, some of the off notes are a little on the uncomfortable side. *40%*

YAMAZAKI 1923. Suntory.

Yamazaki Vintage 1979 db **(78) n20 t21 f18 b19.** Spicy and thick malt. But this has plenty of wrinkles and a stoop, too. *56%. Suntory.*

Yamazaki Vintage Malt 1980 db **(75) n19 t19 f18 b19.** Some lovely blood oranges, but no whisky can survive this amount of oak unscathed. *56%*

Yamazaki Vintage 1982 db **(84) n20 t22 f21 b21.** Big, muscly malt with some sexy spices. *56%. Suntory.*

⋄⋄⋄ **Yamazaki 1984** bott 09 db **(94) n24** masive: more dates and walnut – the occasional distillery style - only here in concentrate form; **t24** big. But you'd never know it. Superbly weighted grape is full, buxom and ripe. But gathers in with almost honeycomb-bourbony oak with something approaching tenderness. Juicy and weaving between bourbony and sherried channels with aplomb; **f22.5** a slight buzz to the finale shows we don't have perfection, but the vanillas remain intact; **b23.5** if you like your whisky boringly neutral, lifeless and with nothing to say other than that it has been ruined by sulphur, then this will horrify you. Though there is a little blemish at the very death, there is still no taking away from this being a sublime 25-year-old. When this distillery is on form it makes for compelling whisky and here we have a bottling showing Yamazaki at its brightest. *48%*

Yamazaki Sherry Wood Vintage 1986 db **(93) n24** a sherry butt found in heaven: clean, absolutely dripping in grapejuice yet light enough to allow further complexity from bright malt and a touch of smoke; **t23** mouthwatering fruit clings, thanks to the estery malt, to every crevice in the mouth; **f23** exceptionally long fade with a chocolate and sultana finale, topped with a puff of smoke; **b23** something here for everyone; one of the most outstanding "new" sherry casks of the year. *45%. Suntory Whisky.*

Yamazaki Vintage 1991 db **(88) n23** a curious mixture of peat reek and Golden Graham breakfast cereal; **t23** soft smoke at first and then the grain hardens and takes a stranglehold; **f21** honied yet remaining firm; **b21** hard and tough as nails towards the finish: a surprising conclusion after such a yielding start. *56%. Suntory.*

Yamazaki 1991 db **(88) n21** bourbony and light with a substratum of soft malt; **t23** astonishing unfurling of mouthwatering malt tones that spreads over the mouth revealing a subtle hint of smoke and beautifully graceful oak; **f22** long, lashings of cocoa powder and again soft barley hand-in-hand with gentle oak; **b22** closed when cold, improves dramatically when warmed on the hand. But the mouth arrival really does deserve a medal. *61%*

Yamazaki 1993 db **(87) n23** smoky and clean; gristy and Port Ellen-ish with a bit of extra exotic oak; **t23** sweet, spicy, vaguely Islay-ish start with the peats developing but not at the expense of dense malt. The oak is refined and there is something unusually coastal for a non-Scottish peated malt; **f20** rather hard, closed and brittle. Metallic malt scrapes against rock-like peat; **b21** a real surprise package. At times quite Islay-ish in style – Port Ellen in particular – but the finish is more realistic. A really delicious experience nonetheless.

Yamazaki Vintage 1994 db **(91) n23** butterscotch and cedarwood; **t24** intense, ultra-clean malt and honey; soft oak and spice add balance; **f22** drier, toasty with residual malt; **b22** very high quality whisky without a single blemish. *56%. Suntory.*

Yamazaki Vintage Malt 1983 bott 04 db **(89) n20** the malt is tired and oak is threatening to pounce despite a hint of smoke; **t21** uncompromisingly warming and a little thin; **f25** whoomph!!! Earth to Tokyo...we have whisky!!! Having taken off like a rocket, it now circles the tastebuds sending back unbelievable messages. The first is one of unruined barley, that is both refreshing and refined; next comes a spicy subtext with a Demerara sweetness lightening things. The finale is fabulous, with succulent fruits including greengages and dried dates teaming up with the persisting massive malt; **b23** slightly hot at first but then goes into overdrive: the finish is something to be etched on to the memory for life. *56%. Suntory.*

Yamazaki Vintage Malt 1989 bott 04 db **(90) n22** seasoned oak with the saltiness adding a piquancy to the malt, too; **t23** big, unremitting malt with that salty tang transferring to the taste; **f22** sweetened vanilla and dry cocoa enlivened by a dose of Lukec's finest! **b23** this is quite enormous whisky that may not seem like too much at first, but on second or third mouthful leaves you in no doubt about its stupendous depth. *56%. Suntory.*

Yamazaki Vintage Malt 1992 bott 04 **(85) n19** dry parchment; distilled nut kernel; oak; **t23** gushing, concentrated malt makes for a salivating experience, especially with the fruit of barley juiciness; **f22** long, well layered malt with some developing cocoa; **b21** fruity and fractionally fundamental. *56%. Suntory.*

⋰ **The Yamazaki Single Malt Whisky Aged 10 Years** bott 09 db **(87.5) n21.5** a mixed bag of big vanilla, barley and plummy bananas; **t22** whisky doesn't come softer on delivery but there is a price; the toffees seem to flatten any higher notes but there is still a tangible fruitiness drifting on from somewhere which is very attractive; **f22** remains lightly sweet, with raisins and vanilla the softness continues; **b22** returned to some of its fruitier root. But if it's silky whisky you want, look no further. *40%*

The Yamazaki Single Malt Whisky Aged 10 Years db **(89) n22** subtle vanilla; clean, grassy barley – for those into Speyside style malts; **t23** mouth-watering and wonderful display of barley offering a golden syrup counter to the drier oaks; **f22** more strands of syrup but never over the top as the vanilla pods crank up the intensity **b22** a beautifully improved, charismatic malt displaying a voluptuousness and understanding between clean barley and drier oak that had been lacking. Nothing like so fruity and a very charming experience. *40%*

⋰ **The Yamazaki Single Malt Whisky Aged 12 Years** bott 09 db **(93.5) n23** a seriously "married" nose, as though the many styles and riches have had time to mix: a real sherry trifle feel to this, but so clean it almost sparkles; **t24** brilliant arrival: the fruit and barley unite to form an enormous juicy front. Light milky cocoa follows behind while the sugars are on the lightly molassed side. Dazzling.. **f23** long, retains its sweetness and offers chocolate raisin finale; **b23.5** one of the cleanest and most beautifully integrated whiskies I've tasted for a while. Unlike the 10-y-o, nothing so dominates that the more complex notes are trimmed or flattened. One to find. *43%*

The Yamazaki Single Malt Whisky Aged 12 Years db **(83) n21 t21 f20 b21.** The flattest Yamazaki 12 I have ever tasted. Partly due, I'd say, to an increase in oak and caramel levels, as the toffee is a driving force. Also, perhaps to a degree of extra oil. Some butterscotch around, but it's an uphill battle. *43%*

The Yamazaki Single Malt Whisky Aged 15 Years Cask Strength db **(94) n23** just a hint that its gone OTT oak-wise, but there is a wisp of smoke to this, too. All in all, wonderful brinkmanship that pays off, **t24** stunning: a massive injection of bourbon-style liquorice and honeycomb plays perfectly against the softer malts. The most controlled of malty explosions... **f23** long, lascivious, the tastebuds are debauched by ingots of honeycomb, molasses and dark sugary notes balanced by the drier oaks; **b24** an extraordinary bottling that far exceeds any previous version I have encountered. Stunning. *56%*

The Yamazaki Single Malt Whisky Aged 18 Years db **(88.9) n22** from the date and walnut school of bigness; **t23** surprisingly early signs of chocolate: melts in beautifully with the raisin and nuts; **f21.5** dries in rather too sharp a way, meaning that oak alone isn't responsible. But still malty echoes to enjoy; **b22** a towering recovery from last year's disappointing bottling. I certainly wouldn't wager that every sherry butt is unmolested by sulphur, but overall quality shines through like a rising sun. *43%* ☉

The Yamazaki Single Malt Whisky Aged 25 Years db **(87) n23** no sulphur here – just sherry...and more sherry....!! Once you get below the grapey surface the degree of complexity is bewitching, with the bitter sweet spices and bourbons really going to town; **t22** good grief; the tastebuds are flattened by the oak and sherry-weighted steamroller; **f20** pretty bitter as what seems like highly aged oloroso and extremely old oak kick in with a vengeance; **b22** it has taken me over an hour to taste this. And still I don't know if I have marked it too high. You'll either love it or hate it – but you'll find nothing else like it..!! *43%*

⋰ **The Yamazaki Sherry Cask Aged 10 Years** bott 09 db **(82.5) n21 t22 f19.5 b20.** Very tight. The grape, initially impressive, is domineering leaving the malt's wings clipped. There are those who will adore this. But, technically and balance-wise, not quite right. *48%*

The Cask of Yamazaki 1990 hogshead cask 0W70223, dist Nov 90, bott Apr 05 **(89) n21** dried fruits and dry in general; **t23** a thousand battles for supremacy between insurgent oak and the controlling barley: the barley holds the fort; **f22** the oak begins to win more and more of the skirmishes and a waft of smoke hangs over the battle scene; some lovely roast Santos completes the job; **b23** not too many elements involved here, but the effect on the tastebuds is wonderful: pure sophistication...for warriors! *55%. Suntory.*

The Cask of Yamazaki 1990 Sherry Butt cask no. 0N70646, dist Feb 90, bott Jun 08 db **(97) n24.5** massive, elegantly spiced, sherry. Huge almost Demerara rum molasses, pithy apples, liquorice and hickory, too. Ye olde Macallan lovers – and I mean those of us who used to worship the stuff over 30 years ago – will weep at its flawless beauty and enormity....; **t24** fills the mouth with successive layers of spiced brilliance. Seriously bitter-sweet with a sharp, piercing sugar-coated edge to the malt. The grape crashes into the rock-firm body to produce a juicy element; **f24** just so much coffee – or is it mocha? – with a light sprinkling of Demerara sugar. Long, silky yet crisp; **b24.5** such is the state of sherry butts today – including in Japan – that the first thing to report is that it is entirely sulphur-free....and some!! Without blemish, this is a rare treat. Once, slightly over the top grape-wise. These days a joyous relief! Beyond that, it is gargantuan. Few whiskies this year have covered such a wide variety of flavours and aromas with such panache: the structure and complexity for its type are close to perfection. Even more telling, is the fact that it is hard to believe that one of this company's Scottish distilleries could have come up with something quite so brilliant. *61%. 506 bottles.*

The Cask of Yamazaki 1993 hogshead cask 3P70277, dist Apr 93, bott Apr 05 **(91) n24** attractive, light smoke and citrus; the oak well developed yet adding only a required dryness; **t22** mouthwatering malt and then a relaxed development of something smoky; **f23** wonderful waves of spice and thickening peat balanced perfectly by fresh barley. The oak, again, adds just the right amount of dryness; **b22** a fascinating bottling showing Yamazaki at its most stylishly demure despite all the peat. *54%. Suntory.*

The Cask of Yamazaki 1993 Heavily Peated Malt white oak puncheon cask, dist May 93, bott Oct 07 db **(95) n23.5** the nosebuds are thwacked with a ball and chain of a peatiness. You can pick out other aromas – just – but your brain keeps coming back to the peat. It's like when you meet someone who has an enormous proboscis and you try and look at their eyes, their mouth, ears, anywhere...but, inevitably... **t25** oooomph! The spices....the spices....!! Peat comes at you from all angles and levels: sweet peat, dry peat, heavy peat, slightly less heavy peat, earthy peat, cocoa-powdered peat, oaky peat...they're all there... **f23** the oaks do make their mark and vanilla pods bust into action. Yet still the smoke rumbles and rumbles...a bit like when you are cleaning out the ash from a peat fire and the wind blows some in your face. It's that kind of dryness... **b23.5** when they say "Heavily Peated" they mean heavily. Like some kind of new phenol isotope, this is heavy peat whisky. Like probably twice as thick as the average peaty whisky you come across. It is, shall we say....peaty. Strap yourself in for the ride: only the fittest will survive... *62%. 574 bottles.*

The Cask of Yamazaki 1993 Heavily Peated Malt white oak puncheon cask no. 3Q70048, dist May 93, bott Jun 08 db **(89) n22** dry, peat cinders blowing in the wind; **t21.5** oily, thick delivery reveals little early on; blossoms out with some welcome lemon thinning out the peat until the maltiness is juicy and lively; **f23** long with crashing waves of peat and citrus – easily the best phrase of the story. Glorious bitter-sweet notes, including cocoa (by the spadeful) and chocolate lime candy (by the bagful); **b22.5** takes a long time to get going thanks to an initially unattractive oily coating. But on finding its feet becomes a cracker. *62%. 503 bottles.*

Suntory Pure Malt Yamazaki 25 Years Old db **(91) n23** quite intoxicating marriage between grapey fruitiness and rich oak: supremely spiced and balanced with a wave of pure bourbon following through; **t23** big, big oloroso character then an entrancing molassed, burnt raisin, malty richness; **f22** subtle spices, poppy seed with some late bitter oak; **b23** being matured in Japan, the 25 years doesn't have quite the same value as Scotland. So perhaps in some ways this can lay claim to be one of the most enormously aged, oak-laden whiskies that has somehow kept its grace and star quality. *43%*

Suntory Single Malt Yamazaki Aged 12 Years db **(87) n22** delicate, chalky vanilla with a squeeze of kiwifruit and butterscotch; **t23** a wonderfully light touch with fresh house-style mouth-watering barley and transparent fruit setting up the busy middle spice; **f20** pretty dry with oak and toffee; **b22** this was the 2006 bottling which somehow missed entry into the Bible, although tasted. A fruity little babe. *43%*

YOICHI 1934. Nikka.

Hokkaido 12 Years Old db **(87) n23 t22 f21 b21.** Full-flavoured malt with absolutely zero yield. Just ricochets around the palate. *43%. Nikka.*

Yoichi batch 04H10D **(87.5) n22.5** pineapple candy and caramel; **t22** clean, juiced-up barley delivery; toffee appears early but is initially seen off by more juice and candy – this time barley sugar; **f21.5** succumbs to the toffee; **b21.5** very drinkable, though you get the feeling it is performing well within itself. *43%*

⁖ **Yoichi** batch 04I10D db **(81.5) n21.5 t21.5 f18.5 b20**. A very hard malt: crisp, sweet at first but with limited yield. The apparent sulphur on the finish doesn't help. *43%*

⁖ **Yoichi 10 Years Old** batch 08I16C db **(83.5) n21.5 t21 f20.5 b20.5**. Good grief! What has happened to this whisky? Actually, I think I can tell you: too much sherry and caramel makes for a dull malt. Pleasant. Drinkable. But dull. *45%*

Yoichi 10 Years Old batch 12I32, old Hokkaido "Yoichi" distillery label db **(91) n22** the peat brushes the nose like a feather over skin: just so delicate; **t23** immediate flinty malt, amazingly hard and tooth-cracking then softened slowly by a salty, peaty edge; **f23** peaty, delicate and now as soft, thanks to vanilla, as it was previously uncompromisingly hard. Some toffee and coffee aid the finale; **b23** yet another teasing, unpredictable dram from Yoichi. *43%. Nikka.*

Yoichi 10 Years Old batch 14I16A db **(75) n19 t19 f18 b19**. Proof that sulphur can detract even from a great like Yoichi. *45%*

Yoichi 10 Years Old batch 14B22, new "Yoichi" distillery label db **(88) n18 t23 f23 b24**. Typical Yoichi. Even when it shows a flaw it recovers to an unbelievable degree: like a champion ice skater who falls at the first leap and then dances on as if nothing happened. Keeps you guessing to the very last about what is to happen next. Fabulous verve and complexity. *45%. Nikka.*

Yoichi 10 Years Old batch 14H62A, old Hokkaido "Yoichi" distillery label db **(91) n23** big malt but it is the delicate quality of the peat that is most remarkable. Oak is present, but this is almost too clean to be true; **t23** sweet and soft, then that Yoichi trademark gradual build-up of peat; **f22** hard and brittle despite the softness of the peat, long and chewy with a hint of liquorice and honey; **b23** the crispness and bite of this whisky makes it almost blend like in style – which goes to underline the complexity. *43%. Nikka.*

Yoichi 10 Years Old batch 14H62B, old Hokkaido "Yoichi" distillery label db **(89) n23 t21 f22 b23**. Soft and delicate with beautifully chewy peat throughout. *43%. Nikka.*

Yoichi 10 Years Old batch 24G48C, old Hokkaido "Yoichi" distillery label db **(93) n23** for an aroma carrying smoke this is almost austere: but this is an illusion. Some crisp malty, softly peated notes give it a delicate depth and massive sophistication; **t23** enormous malt, absolutely brimming with lusty barley. Refreshing and mouthwatering, yet all the time that soft peat is present; **f24** a quite brilliant marriage between rich barley and soft oak. No more than the slightest hint of very distant smoke; **b23** a Yoichi in its "Old Speyside" phase, with just a waft of peat-reek to add some ballast to the enormous, clean malt. The fade is nothing short of fabulous. A Japanese version of Ardmore: whisky for grown-ups. *43%. Nikka.*

Yoichi 10 Years Old batch 24H18C, old Hokkaido "Yoichi" distillery label db **(89) n20 t23 f23 b23**. Another bottle of understated genius. *43%. Nikka.*

Yoichi Single Malt 10 Years Old batch 12F04C db **(89) n21** vague echo of oak sappiness rescued by top-notch, weighty barley; **t24** the tongue is forced to inspect the roof of the mouth countless times as wave upon wave of complex barley-honey notes rocket around the palate; **f21** long with a tangy, coppery richness that counters perfectly the barley, golden syrup and toffee; **b23** mildly dodgy nose, overly toffeed finish... and still it's a lightweight treat! *45%*

Yoichi 12 Years Old batch 06C14, new Yoichi label with distillery drawing db **(91) n21** spicy fresh oloroso; **t24** big, clean sultana-fruit with a gathering intensity of ripe dates and sweet, gently smoked malt, **f22** dies slightly, but the dates remain, as does the smoke. The oak kicks in with a late bitter finale; **b24** absolutely magnificent malt with a no-holds-barred intensity of fruit and malt. *45%. Nikka.*

⁖ **Yoichi 12 Years Old** batch 08I18B db **(75.5) n19 t19 f18.5 b19**. fruity but flat and sulphury; some smoke perhaps, but all rather hush-hush...and very disappointing, though had you been at the distillery some dozen years ago not entirely surprising. One feared this day might come....and it has. *45%*

Yoichi 12 Years Old batch 16J32, new Yoichi label with distillery drawing db **(87) n20 t22 f23 b22**. A pretty light Yoichi almost devoid of peat. After getting over a toffee-led lull the malt comes to life with impressive results. *45%. Yoichi.*

Yoichi Key Malt Aged 12 Years "Peaty & Salty" db **(95) n23** the peat rumbles like distant thunder, difficult to pinpoint but letting you know that it is there. The oaky tones suggest a mixing of Kentucky and something local; soft fruits make an almost apologetic appearance; **t25** there is perfect distribution of peat. It rumbles around the palate offering bitter-sweet depth, and a salty, coastal tang emphasises the richness of the malt; **f23** waves of vanilla begin to outflank the soft peat: the finish is long and there is no victor between the sweet malt and the more bitter, salty oak; **b24** of all the peated whiskies of the world, only Ardbeg can stand shoulder to shoulder with Yoichi when it comes to sheer complexity. Here is an astonishing example of why I rate Yoichi in the best five whiskies in the world. Forget the odd sulphur-tarnished bottling. Get Yoichi in its natural state with perfect balance between oak and malt and it delivers something approaching perfection. And this is just such a bottling. 55%. Nikka.

Yoichi Key Malt Aged 12 Years "Sherry & Sweet" db **(80) n19 t22 f19 b20.** Sad to report that this should be called "Very Slight Sulphur and Sweet". A real pity because it is obvious that had the Spaniards not molested these butts, they would have been absolutely top-of-the-range. And probably would have scored in the low to mid 90s. I could weep. 55%. Nikka.

Yoichi Key Malt Aged 12 Years "Woody & Vanillic" db **(83) n21 t22 f20 b20.** Pretty decent whisky. Not sure about creating one that sets out to be woody: that means balance has been sacrificed to concentrate on a particular essence to the whisky that should be used only as a component of complexity. Still, there is enough sweet malt on arrival to make this a dram to be enjoyed. 55%

Yoichi Single Malt 12 Years Old batch 14F36A db **(91) n22** soft smoke and under-ripe fruit; **t23** profound, chewy barley; lots of small still coppery sharpness and then a gentle awakening of peat; **f23** sweet peats dusted with demerara; it takes some time for the chalky oak to finally have a say; **b23** best when left in the glass for 10-15 minutes: only then does the true story emerge. 45%

⋙ **Yoichi 15 Years Old** batch 06I08B db **(91.5) n22** surprisingly quiet and well behaved considering the light smokiness drifting about; **t23.5** nutty, chewy and with lots of early toffee. Juices up to puckering effect as the barley and phenols strikes home; **f23** sweet and spicy in the right places as the malt begins to find its legs and goes up a notch or two **b23** for an early moment or two possibly one of the most salivating whiskies you'll get your kisser around this year. Wonderfully entertaining yet you still suspect that this is another Yoichi reduced in effect somewhat by either caramel and/or sherry. When it hits its stride, though, becomes a really busy whisky that gets tastebuds in a right lather. But I'm being picky as I know that this is one of the world's top five distilleries and am aware as anyone on this planet of its extraordinary capabilities. Great fun; great whisky – could be better still, but so much better than its siblings... 45%

Yoichi Single Malt 15 Years Old batch 04F44D db **(86) n22 t22 f20 b22.** Zesty and tangy; most peculiar by Yoichi standards. But still big, rich and lip-smacking. 45%

⋙ **Yoichi 20 Years Old** batch 06I06A db **(87) n21** an enormous statement from the glass. Immediately the odd sulphur note is detected, but the grape and high roast Java (possibly with medium Mysore) comes to its aid. The result is thick and very warehousy; **t22.5** much lighter delivery than nose: the barley actually shows first and juices up. Soon after though, the dark coffee clouds form; spicy in part, but something niggles away... **f20.5** that off key note gains strength amid a mocha recovery; **b22** bitter-sweet experience, both in taste and perception. Not unusual to find sulphur on this guy, but a shame when it alters the course of the mail. 52%

Yoichi 20 Years Old db **(95) n23** magnificently intense oloroso (a tiny fleck of sulphur burns off in about 10 minutes when warmed), the background malt oak-laden; **t23** again it's oloroso that leads the way, apparently too intensely at first but quickly settling to allow some stupendous spices to unravel and create balance. Fabulous bitter-sweet harmony; **f25** Okay, guys, help me out here. Spot the fault. I can't. The fruit is now spotlessly clean and displaying a grapey complexity, the spices are warming but not entirely engulfing, the oak is firm and adds no more than a hint of dryness and at last the malt comes into full play to offer both mouthwatering barley and something slightly smoky. If you can pick a defect, let me know; **b24** I don't know how much they charge for this stuff but either alone or with mates get some for one hell of an experience. What makes it all the more remarkable is that there is a slight sulphury note on the nose: once you taste the stuff that becomes of little consequence. 52%. Nikka.

Yoichi 1987 batch 113200, dist 87, bott 27 Jul 06 db **(87) n20** heavy duty, orangey but slightly flawed sherry; **t24** juicy grape, concentrated barley then, slowly, the peat delivers by degree; **f21** dries significantly as the sulphur takes a grip; **b22** dense and desirable at times: just so easily could have been a great dram but undone by a poor butt. 63%. France.

Yoichi 1987 batch 22G26B **(89.5) n22** juicy grape somehow outperforms the delicate peats; **t23.5** again the grape is first to show: sweet and juicy and then gives way slightly as some peated chocolate arrives – almost like a smoked fruit chocolate bar: delicious... **f21.5** a few signs of the cask tiring, but the fruit and smoke provide the required sticking plaster; **b23** having tasted from quite a number of casks from this year at the distillery itself, I was a bit worried when I saw that sherry butts had been used. However, no great signs of sulphurous ruination here and the marriage of the varying styles of peat and grape has created the desired degree of complexity. 55%

Yoichi Single Cask 1987 no. 3 dist 27 Apr 87, bott 1 Feb 05 db **(87) n22** throbbing oak; marmalade on toast; **t23** the malt is just so intense, offering at first a charismatic, mouthwatering depth and then something more deeply oaky; **f20** dry, tannin heavy and chewy; **b22** hints here of old age and over-exposure to oak. But the overall thrust remains delightfully rich. 52%. Nikka.

Yoichi Single Cask 1988 no. 29 dist 7 May 88, bott 3 Feb 05 db **(89) n21** a distinct bourbony style to this, with citrus abounding; **t23** light and bourbony at first, then intensifies as a fruity maltiness digs deep into the tastebuds; **f22** spices and vanilla; **b23** effortless to the point of arrogantly beautiful. 60%. Nikka.

Yoichi Nikka Single Cask Malt Whisky 1990 db dist 4 Aug 90, bott 17 Oct 03 **(84) n21 t20 f22 b21.** Most probably a dry sherry cask set the tone for this: astringent by Yoichi standards and although the finish offers a complex vanilla and liquorice counter, this isn't an Hokkaido great. 60.8%

Yoichi Nikka Single Cask Malt Whisky 1991 db dist 25 Feb 91, bott 12 Dec 03 **(95) n24 t24 f23 b24.** It was because I managed to taste many casks like this while tramping through Yoichi's warehouses over the years that I declared the distillery in the world's top six. Taste this, then e-mail me to disagree. 64.5%

Nikka Whisky Yoichi (78) n18 t20 f21 b19. Not often I'm lost for words...but this one left me stunned. Nothing like I expected. Not least because it seems either very young. Or not remotely short of feints. Or both. And the whole thing is propped up by caramel. The best bit is the late spice attack....but this is like nothing I would have expected from one of the top five distilleries in the world. As my one time Japanese girlfriend would have said: "I am shocked..." 43%

Nikka Whisky Yoichi 1986 20 Years Old (94) n23 age, the salty sea air of Hokkaido and sweet oak have accounted for the more excessive possibilities of the peat: weighty but restrained; **t24** no holding back here, though, as the delivery is one first of juicy fruit and then silky waves of peat; chunky heavy-duty stuff which, for some reason, appears to float about the palate; the spices shoot on sight; **f23** a sweeter, more sober finale with liquorice and molasses joining forces with the salty oakiness to keep the lid on the smoke; **b24** now this is unambiguous Yoichi :exactly how I have come to know and adore this distillery. 55.0%

Scotch Malt Whisky Society Cask 116.12 Aged 21 Years refill hogshead, dist Jul 86 **(87.5) n22** soft smoke and cocoa; **t22** the peat is thinly spread around the sweet barley; gentle oils and Party Ring biscuits; **f21** bitters out with the cask, **b22.5** attractive and works to the limitations of the cask itself. 54.2%

-:::- **Scotch Malt Whisky Society Cask 116.14 Aged 25 Years** 1st fill hogshead, dist Sep 83 **(96.5) n23.5** very big, indeed; the oak is creaking yet somehow doesn't make even a hint of threat. Some really dank, floral notes – bluebells in a dark forest – earthy but not peaty. Weighty stuff... **t24.5** very, very big...!!! The delivery, helped along by the big alcohols, really is monumental with, in the space of three of four tsunami-size waves, we cover barley at its most heavy and concentrated, oak at its bourbony sweetest yet controlled by a sprinkling of cocoa, and a disingenuous fruitiness, that is one minute there...then not. The middle is all the above points to greater or lesser degrees. This is whisky and a half; **f24** big, but very, very, very discreet: perhaps more emphasis on the chocolate, though some muscovado has got into the mix. Not a single note of bitterness, or a groan against so many years in the cask...awe inspiring... **b24.5** what a bloody whisky....!!! There are times, when tasting one sulphur-stuffed whisky after another, I wonder why I do this. Then something as beautiful as this comes along and you remember the exact reason. Whisky can be, and should be, the dark matter of our appreciation of the senses. The reason why so many millions of people worldwide have switched on to whisky is because they have discovered that, if made, matured or mixed the right way, it can bring sensations of joy that we previously thought only possible on a bed, or swinging from a chandelier. So whiskies like this have an exotic and erotic element to them, but to make them sexier still there has to be a cerebral quality, too. In other words, all your senses are being stimulated. Few whiskies stimulate them quite as well as this one. 59.4%

-:::- **Scotch Malt Whisky Society Cask 116.15 Aged 25 Years** Japanese oak, dist Sep 83 **(89) n23.5** denser than a Japanese rain forest. The oak has a slightly different call to normal European oak, and at this age is offering quite another alternative. Sweet chestnut and reduced Jaffa cake make for an interesting combination... **t22** big on the kumquaty citrus, and a roll of thick barley. But this disappears beneath a cloak of uncompromising oak for a few moments before some cocoa appears; **f21.5** powdery dry but the oddly-flavoured vanillas succeed in adding a modicum of sweetness; in the end it is the 90% cocoa chocolate which closes the experience; **b22** one of the problems with Japanese oak is that whilst it can add an extra, and quite unique, zing to a malt at conventional Japanese ages, when it gets to 25 years it has perhaps added a little too much. Here is a case of a Japanese oak not exactly doing Japanese oaky sort of things. All that said....a really delightful whisky and one which takes you into fascinating, unexplored lands...!!! *58.9%*

Unspecified Malts
"Hokuto" Suntory Pure Malt Aged 12 Years (93) n22 trademark delicate lightness; fleeting barley chased by soft vanilla; **t24** melt-in-the-mouth malt arrival; hints of honey work well with the loftier barley and earthier oak; **f23** honey on toast with just a little toffee; **b24** another example of Suntory at its most feminine: just so seductive and beautiful. Although a malt, think Lawson's 12-y-o of a decade ago and you have the picture. *40%*

Nikka Whisky From the Barrel (89) n20 carries some weight; good age and subtle malty sugars; **t23** exemplary mouthfeel: delightful oils and nipping spices but the malt remains clean and very sweet; **f22** some dryer oakiness but the malt keeps its balancing sweetness; **b24** a whisky that requires a bit of time and concentration to get the best out of. You will discover something big and exceptionally well balanced. *51.4%. Nikka.*

Nikka Whisky From the Barrel batch 02F26A **(82) n20 t22 f20 b20.** Some attractive honey notes and caramel, but a bit laboured. *51.4%*

Nikka Whisky From the Barrel batch 12F32C db **(91) n22** date and brazil cake; **t24** monumental delivery with soft smoke melting into the most glorious honeycomb known to man; tingly spices and toffee-apple, too; **f22** caramel kicks in slightly but some butterscotch rounds it off wonderfully; **b23** truly great whisky that mostly overcomes the present Japanese curse of big caramel finishes. *51.4%*

Nikka Whisky Single Coffey Malt 12 Years (97) n23.5 forget all about the malt: it's the big bourbony, hickory and honey sweet oak which wins hands down; **t25** hold on to your hats: it's flavour explosion time....on first tasting it's simply too much to comprehend. Only on third or fourth mouthful do you really get an idea. First, the delivery is pretty close to perfection: the soft oils seem to draw every last nuance from the barley; then when it has done that, it manages to mix it with myriad delicate sweet notes radiating from the oak. This includes some of those allied to bourbon, especially chocolate honeycomb and very deep molassed notes usually associated with Demerara Coffey still rum; a unique combination absolutely perfectly displayed; **f24** long...just so long. One mouthful, especially at 55%, last for about six or seven minutes. So impressive here is the delicacy of the fade: after a delivery so large, the finesse is extraordinary. The flavours in effect mirror the earlier delivery. Except now some vanilla does come in to dry things a little; **b24.5** the Scotch Whisky Association would say that this is not single malt whisky because it is made in a Coffey still. When they can get their members to make whisky this stunning on a regular basis via their own pots and casks, then perhaps they should pipe up as their argument might then have a single atom of weight. *55%.*

Vatted Malts
All Malt (86) n22 t21 f21 b22. The best example by a mile of an almost unique style of vatted whisky: both malt and "grain" are distilled from entirely malted barley, identical to Kasauli malt whisky in India. Stupendous grace and balance. *40%. Nikka.*

All Malt "Pure & Rich" (89) n22 honeycomb and liquorice with some thumping oak; **t24** beautifully mouthfilling, and "rich" is an understatement. Barley sugar and molten brown sugar combine and then there is a soft gristiness. Big...; **f21** vanilla and caramel with some residual malt; **b22** my word, this has changed! Not unlike some bottlings of Highland Park with its emphasis on honey. If they could tone down the caramel it'd really be up there. *40%. Nikka.*

All Malt Pure & Rich batch 14F24A **(77) n19 t20 f19 b19.** My former long term Japanese girlfriend, Makie (hope you enjoyed your 30th birthday in April, by the way), used to have a favourite saying, namely: "I am shocked!" Well, I am shocked by this whisky because it is much blander than the previous bottling (04E16D), with all that ultra-delicate and complex honeycomb lost and lovely gristiness removed. For me, one of the biggest surprises – and disappointments - of the 2007 Bible. But proof that, when using something so potentially dangerous as caramel, it is too easy to accidentally cross that fine line between brilliance and blandness. Because, had they gone the other way, we might have had a challenger for World Whisky of the Year. *40%. Nikka.*

Hokuto Pure Malt Aged 12 Years (86) n20 t22 f22 b22. An oaky threat never materialises: excellent mixing. *40%. Suntory.*

Malt Club "Pure & Clear" (83) n21 t22 f20 b20. Another improved vatting, much heavier and older than before with bigger spice. 40%. Nikka.

Mars Maltage Pure Malt 8 Years Old (84) n20 t21 f21 b22. A very level, intense, clean malt with no peaks or troughs, just a steady variance in the degree of sweetness and oak input. Impossible not to have a second glass. 43%. Mars.

Nikka Malt 100 The Anniversary Aged 12 Years (73) n18 t19 f18 b18. The depressing and deadly fingerprint of sulphur is all over this. Shame, as the spices excel. 40%

⋅⋅⋅ **Nikka Pure Malt Aged 21 Years** batch 08I18D db (89) n23 profound, clean, over-ripe grape with some lovely nip and prickle; weighty with a liquorice bourbony element, too; t22.5 soft at first then a steady build up of malt and spice. The fruit is never far away; f21.5 toasty vanilla and a light buzz from the sherry; b22 by far the best of the set. 43%

⋅⋅⋅ **Nikka Pure Malt Aged 17 Years** batch 08I30B db (83) n21 t21 f20 b21. A very similar shape to the 12-years-old, but older - obviously. Certainly the sherry butts have a big say and don't always do great favours to the high quality spirit. 43%

⋅⋅⋅ **Nikka Pure Malt Aged 12 Years** batch 10I24C db (84) n21.5 t21 f20 b21.5. The nose may be molassed, sticky treacle pudding, but it spices up on the palate. The dull buzz on the finish also tells a tale. 40%

Pure Malt Black batch 02C58A (95) n24 an exquisitely crafted nose: studied peat in luxuriant yet deft proportions nestling amid some honeyed malt and oak. The balance between sweet and dry is faultless. There is neither a single off-note nor a ripple of disharmony. The kind of nose you can sink your head into and simply disappear; t23 for all the evident peat, this is medium-weighted, the subtlety encased in a gentle cloak of oil; f23 long, silky, fabulously weighted peat running a sweet course through some surging malt and liquorice tones with a bit of salt in there for zip; b25 well, if anyone can show me a better-balanced whisky than this you know where to get hold of me. You open a bottle of this at your peril: best to do so in the company of friends. Either way, it will be empty before the night is over. 43%. Nikka.

Pure Malt Black batch 06F54B (92) n24 great balance to the nose with a careful sprinkling of barley, honey, peat and oak — but never too much of any; t24 massive, ultra-intense sweet malt with a delicate sub-stratum of smoke; a spiced fruitiness also cranks up the weight and depth; f21 vanilla kicks in as it thins surprisingly fast; b23 not the finish of old, but everything else is present and correct for a cracker! 43%. Nikka.

Pure Malt Red batch 02C30B (86) n21 t21 f22 b22. A light malt that appears heavier than it actually is with an almost imperceptible oiliness. 43%. Nikka.

Pure Malt Red batch 06F54C (84) n21 t22 f20 b21. Oak is the pathfinder here, but the oily vanilla-clad barley is light and mouth-watering. 43%. Nikka.

Pure Malt White batch 02C30C (92) n23 massive, Islay-style peat with a fresh sea kick thanks to brine amid the barley; t24 again, the peat-reek hangs firmly on the tastebuds from the word go, the sweetness of the barley tempered by some drying oaky notes suggesting reasonable age. Lots of subtle oils bind the complexity; f22 liquorice and salt combine to create a powerful malty-oak combo. An oily, kippery smokiness continues to the very end; b23 a big peaty number displaying the most subtle of hands. 43%. Nikka.

Pure Malt White batch 06J26 (91) n22 soft peat interrupted by gentle oak; t23 biting, nippy malt offering a degree of orangey-citrus fruit amid the building smoke; f22 sweet vanilla and light smoke that dries towards a salty, tangy, liquorice finish; b24 a sweet malt, but one with such deft use of peat and oak that one never really notices. Real class. 43%. Nikka.

Pure Malt White batch 10F46C (90) n23 the quality of the delicate peat is beyond reproach; some attractive kumquat juices it up nicely; t23 wonderful balance between silky-soft and nail-hard malts with some tasty local oak getting in on the act; f22 the smoke lessens to allow vanilla and toffee dominance; a sawdusty dryness brings down the curtain; b22 there is a peculiarly Japanese feel to this delicately peated delight. 43%

Southern Alps Pure Malt (93) n24 bananas and freshly peeled lemon skin: one of the world's most refreshing and exhilarating whisky noses; t23 crisp youngish malts, as one might suspect from the nose, mouthwatering and as a clean as an Alpine stream; f22 some vanilla development and a late slightly creamy flourish but finished with a substantial and startling malty rally boasting a very discreet sweetness; b24 this is a bottle I have only to look at to start salivating. Sadly, though, I drink sparingly from it as it is a hard whisky to find, even in Japan. Fresh, clean and totally stunning, the term "pure malt" could not be more apposite. Fabulous whisky: a very personal favourite. 40%. Suntory.

Super Nikka Vatted Pure Malt (76) n20 t19 f19 b18. Decent and chewy but something doesn't quite click with this one. 55.5%. Nikka.

Taketsuru Pure Malt 12 Years Old (80) n19 t22 f19 b20. For its age, heavier than a sumo wrestler. But perhaps a little more agile over the tastebuds. Lovely silkiness impresses, but lots of toffee. *40%. Nikka.*

Taketsuru Pure Malt 17 Years Old (89) n21 firm oak, but compromises sufficiently to allow several layers of malt to battle through with a touch of peat-coffee; **t22** massive: a toasted, honeyed front gives way to really intense and complex malt notes; **f23** superb. Some late marmalade arrives from somewhere: the toast is slightly burnt but the waves of malty complexity are endless; **b23** not a whisky for the squeamish. This is big stuff – about as big as it gets without peat or rye. No bar shelf or whisky club should be without one. *43%. Nikka.*

Taketsuru Pure Malt 21 Years Old (88) n22 middle-aged bourbon with a heavy, vaguely honeyed malt presence; **t21** the oak remains quite fresh and chewy. Again, the malt is massive; **f22** sweet, oily and more honey arrives; **b23** a much more civilised and gracious offering than the 17-y-o: there is certainly nothing linear about the character development from Taketsuru 12 to 21 inclusive. Serious whisky for the serious whisky drinker. *43%. Nikka.*

Zen (84) n19 t22 f22 b21. Sweet, gristy malt; light and clean. *40%. Suntory.*

Japanese Single Grain

Nikka Single Cask Coffey Grain Whisky Aged 12 Years "Woody & Mellow" (93) n22 delicate vanalins and tannins; **t24** sweet and yielding (probably corn) with layers of drying spices. Stupendous; **f23** long, with subtle oils lengthening the grain effect and spice; more vanilla at the very death...eventually. Vague bourbony tones towards the finale; **b24** exceptional grain whisky by any standards – and helps explain why Japanese blends are so damn good!! *55%. Nikka.*

Nikka Single Cask Coffey Grain 12 Years Old 70th Anniversary (85) n20 biting, nose, tingling oak; **t22** massive oak delivery sweetened and soothed by the rich grain; lush and brilliantly weighted throughout; **f22** long liquorice and cocoa tones are met by some bitter, zesty, oaky notes; **b21** more woody than the "woody and mellow". *58%. Nikka.*

Nikka Single Cask Coffey Grain Aged Over 13 Years batch 20 116399, dist 31.1.92, bott 30.5.05 db **(85) n22 t23 f20 b20.** Distinctly subdued by this brand's normal high standards, though the early bourbon riches are mesmerizing. The finish, though attractive, is too simplistic. *62%. sc.*

Nikka Single Cask Coffey Grain Whisky 1991 dist 1 Oct 91, bott 12 May 03 db **(93) n22 t24 f23 b24.** I have tasted much Japanese straight grain over the years but this is the first time in bottled form for public consumption. And Nikka have exceeded themselves. Forget the word "grain" and its inferior connotations. This is a monster whisky from the bourbon family you are unlikely ever to forget. Use the first couple of mouthfuls for a marker: once you get the idea, life will never quite be the same again. Track down...and be consumed. *61.9%*

Nikka Single Cask Coffey Grain 1992 dist 31.2.92, bott 25.7.06 db **(95) n24** a curious mixture with hints of Japanese oak (from the cask heads?) and a bourbony, hickory edge. Rich and rousing; **t24** sweet, flushed with maize and a silky body, almost verging on demerara. Honeyed and revelling in its bourbon theme; **f23** vanilla layers, again with a deep, delicious touch of molasses; **b24** make no mistake: this grain is as entertaining as any malt. Those loving high-class bourbon will be thrilled. *57%. France.*

Blends

Ajiwai Kakubin *(see Kakubin Ajiwai)*

Black Nikka Aged 8 Years (82) n20 t21 f21 b20. Beautifully bourbony, especially on the nose. Lush, silky and great fun. Love it! *40%. Nikka.*

The Blend of Nikka (90) n21 a dry, oaky buzz infiltrates some firm grain and sweeter malt; **t23** brilliant! Absolutely outstanding explosion of clean grassy malts thudding into the tastebuds with confidence and precision: mouthwatering and breath-catching; **f22** delightful grain bite to follow the malt; **b24** an adorable blend that makes you sit up and take notice of every enormous mouthful. Classy, complex, charismatic and brilliantly balanced. *45%. Nikka.*

Evermore (90) n22 big age, salt and outstanding malt riches to counter the oak; **t23** more massive oak wrapped in a bourbony sweetness with glorious malts and a salty, spicy tang; **f22** long, sweet malt and crisp grains: plenty to chew on and savour; **b23** top-grade, well-aged blended whisky with fabulous depth and complexity that never loses its sweet edge despite the oak. *40%. Kirin.*

Ginko (78.5) n20.5 t20 f19 b19. Soft – probably too soft as it could do with some shape and attitude to shrug off the caramel. *46%. Number One Drinks Company.*

Golden Horse Busyuu Deluxe (93) n22 some decent signs of age with some classy oak alongside smoke: sexy stuff; **t24** enormous flavour profile simply because it is so fresh: massive malt presence, some of it peaty, bananas and under-ripe grapes; **f23** clean malt and some sharpish grain with a touch of bite, continuing to tantalise the tastebuds for a long time; **b24** whoever blended this has a genuine feel for whisky: a classic in its own right and one of astonishing complexity and textbook balance. 43%. Toa. To celebrate the year 2000.

Hibiki (82) n20 t19 f23 b20. The grains here are fresh, forceful and merciless, the malts bouncing off them meekly. Lovely cocoa finale. A blend that brings a tear to the eye. Hard stuff – perfect after a hard day! Love it! 43%. Suntory.

⬩⬩⬩ **Hibiki 12 Years Old (89)** n21.5 lots of vanilla and boiled yam; **t22** a fizzing delivery with an impressive, slightly juicy marriage between barley and oak. The grains offer a light oily diversion; **f22.5** the spices begun in the middle ground begin to really take effect and work well with the lightly sugared oaks; **b23** a thoughtful blend which improves greatly and develops a rhythm the longer it goes on. 43%. Suntory.

Hibiki 17 Years Old (85.5) n22 t22 f20 b21.5. Much richer and honeyed than before: the degree of oak on the nose and molasses half way through are a delight. If they can just inject some life into the toffeed finish, this'd be quite superb. 43%. Suntory. ☉

⬩⬩⬩ **Hibiki 21 Years Old (89.5)** n24 big signature as always. Those big cherry and kumquats I always associate with this blend are there in force, as the sweet richness of the old bourbony character. But the smoke appears to be missing, though no damage done to the balance, though the weight is down slightly; **t23** not surprisingly, it's the bourbon style first out of the traps – and with some grace, too: as soft and silky as you like; **f20.5** buttery cocoa but the sherry involvement is represented by a slight sulphurous buzz; **b22** a change of character from last time; the smoke has drifted away, a bit of extra fruit and although nothing like so great a finish, still a charmer. 43%. Suntory.

Hibiki 50.5 Non Chillfiltered 17 Years Old (84) n22 t22 f20 b20. Pleasant enough in its own right. But against what this particular expression so recently was, hugely disappointing. Last year I lamented the extra use of caramel. This year it has gone through the roof, taking with it all the fineness of complexity that made this blend exceptional. Time for the blending lab to start talking to the bottling hall and sort this out. I want one of the great whiskies back...!! 50.5%. Suntory.

Hibiki 21 Years Old (93) n24 fruitier notes of cherry and sherry with a triumphal triumvirate of intense malt, the subtlest of peat smoke and leathery oak combining for maximum, stupendous complexity, also a dash of kumquats; **t22** fat and oily, like the nose hinting slightly at bourbon but the grains thin the middle out sufficiently to let the malt, mildly peaty and otherwise, through; **f23** long and intense with more lightly orchestrated smoke and lashings of late, grapey fruit and a build-up of, first, sweet malts, then a drier, spicier oak; **b24** when people refer to Yoichi as the exception that proves the rule about Japanese whisky, I tend to point them in the direction of this. If I close my eyes and taste this, cherry blossom really does form in my mind's eye. 43%. Suntory.

Hibiki 30 Years Old (88) n21 less smoky than before, a touch of soap and no shortage of bourbon honeycomb, **t22** sweet delivery with that Kentuckian drawl to the middle; **f22** long, with some extra molasses to the finale; a few extra splinters of oak, too; **b23** still remains a very different animal from most other whiskies you might find: the smoke may have vanished somewhat but the sweet oakiness continues to draw its own unique map. 43%. Suntory.

Hibiki 30 Years Old (87) n21 curious mix of peat and bourbon; **t22** sweet, fat oak: bourbon all the way; **f22** the glorious rich-textured sweetness continues forever; **b22** Kentuckians would really go for this one: the smoke might confuse them a little, though. Pretty unique the world over. 43%. Suntory.

Hokuto (86) n22 t24 f19 b21. a bemusing blend. At its peak, this is quite superb, cleverly blended whisky. The finish, though, suggests a big caramel input. If the caramel is natural, it should be tempered. If it is added for colouring purposes, then I don't see the point of having the whisky non-chillfiltered in the first place. 50.5%. ncf. Suntory.

Imperial (81) n20 t22 f19 b20. Flinty, hard grain softened by malt and vanilla but toffee dulled. 43%. Suntory.

Kakubin (92) n23 lemon zest and refreshing grain: wonderful; **t23** light, mouthwatering, ultra-juicy with soft barley sub-strata; true melt-in-the-mouth stuff, **f22** long, with charming vanilla but touched by toffee; **b24** absolutely brilliant blend of stunningly refreshing and complex character. One of the most improved brands in the world. 40%. Suntory.

Kakubin Ajiwai (82) n20 t21 f20 b21. Usual Kakubin hard grain and mouthwatering malt, with this time a hint of warming stem ginger. 40%. Suntory.

Kakubin Kuro 43° (89) n22 a confusing but sexy mix of what appear to be old oak and burnt toffee; **t23** fabulous weight on arrival with again the oak in the vanguard but controlled by a malty, chewy-toffee arm; **f22** long with soft vanillins and toffee; **b22** big, chewy whisky with ample evidence of old age but such is the intrusion of caramel it's hard to be entirely sure. *43%. Suntory.*

Kakubin New (90) n21 gritty grain with very hard malt to accompany it; **t24** stunning mouth arrival with heaps of mouthwatering young malt and then soft grain and oil. Brilliant stuff; **f21** some beautiful cocoa notes round off the blend perfectly; **b24** seriously divine blending: a refreshing dram of the top order. *40%. Suntory.*

∴ **Kirin Whisky Tarujuku 50° (93) n22.5** some prickly oak and prickly pear; **t24** what a delight...! A delivery from the heavens: the combination of malt, grain and oak all appear to be equally divided here, but rather than arriving in layers they erupt upon the palate together. The shockwaves are sweet ones, with subtle molasses infiltrating the oak; **f23** long, cleverly oiled and still with those lightly sugared vanillas having much to say. The balance isn't for one second compromised; **b23.5** a blend not afraid to make a statement and does so boldly. A sheer joy. *50%. Kirin Distillery Co Ltd.*

Master's Blend Aged 10 Years (87) n21 t23 f22 b21. Chewy, big and satisfying. *40%. Mercian/Karuizawa.*

New Kakubin Suntory *(see Kakubin New)*

Nikka Master Blend Blended Whisky 12 Years Old 70th Anniversary (94) n24 nothing shy or retiring here: big oak, big sherry. A little nervousness with the smoke, maybe; **t23** lush, silky grain arrives and then carries intensely sweet malt and weightier grape; **f24** dries as the oak takes centre stage. But the peripheral fruit malt, gentle smoke and grain combine to offer something not dissimilar to fruit and nut chocolate; **b23** an awesome blend swimming in top quality sherry. Perhaps a fraction too much sweetness on the arrival, but I am nit-picking. A blend for those who like their whiskies to have something to say. And this one just won't shut up. *58%. Nikka.*

The Nikka Whisky Aged 34 Years blended and bottled in 99 **(93) n23 t23 f24 b23.** A Japanese whisky of antiquity that has not only survived many passing years, but has actually achieved something of stature and sophistication. Over time I have come to appreciate this whisky immensely. It is among the world's greatest blends, no question. *43%. Nikka.*

Nikka Whisky Tsuru Aged 17 Years (94) n23 the usual fruity suspects one associates with a Tsuru blend, especially the apple and oranges. But the grains are now making a bourbony impact, too; **t24** advanced level textbook delivery here because the marriage between fruit, grain and oak is about as well integrated as you might wish for; simperingly soft yet enough rigidity for the malts to really count and the palate to fully appreciate all the complexities offered; **f23** brushed with cocoa, a touch of sultana and some gripping spices, too; only the caramel detracts; **b24** unmistakingly Tsuru in character, very much in line, profile-wise, with the original bottling and if the caramel was cut this could challenge as a world whisky of the year. *43%*

∴ **Robert Brown (91) n22.5** the grain really has kicked this one on towards a leathery bourbon; **t23** clean, sweet, brown sugars with a juicy sub plot; **f22.5** lovely spices accompany the custardy vanilla; **b23** just love these clean but full-flavoured blends: a real touch of quality here. *43%. Kirin Brewery Company Ltd.*

Royal 12 Years Old (91) n23 chalky and dry, but malt and oranges - and now some extra juicy grape - add character; just a soupcon of smoke adds the perfect weight; **t23** fabulously complex arrival on the palate with some grainy nip countered by sparkling malt and where once there was smoke there is now ultra clean sherry; **f22** the grains and oak carry on as the spice builds; **b23** a splendidly blended whisky with complexity being the main theme. Beautiful stuff that appears recently to have, nose apart, traded smoke for grape. *43%. Suntory.*

Royal Aged 15 Years (95) n25 soft ribbons of smoke tie themselves to a kumquat and sherry flag; supremely well weighted and balanced with the grains and malts united by invisible strands; **t24** few whiskies achieve such a beautifully soft and rounded delivery: there is no dominance on arrival as the tastebuds are confronted by a silky marriage of all that is found on the nose, aided and abetted by luxurious grain; **f22** a degree of toffee slightly hinders the fade but the lightness of touch is spellbinding; **b24** unquestionably one of the great blends of the world that can be improved only by a reduction of toffee input. Sensual blending that every true whisky lover must experience: a kind of Japanese Old Parr 18. *43%. Suntory.*

Shirokaku (79) n19 t21 f20 b19. Some over-zealous toffee puts a cap on complexity. Good spices, though. *40%. Suntory.*

Special Reserve 10 Years Old (94) n23 magnificent approach of rich fruit buttressed by firm, clear grain. Some further fruity spices reveal some age is evident; t24 complex from the off with a tidal tsunami of malt crashing over the tastebuds. The grain holds firm and supports some budding fruit; f23 a touch of something peaty and pliable begins to take shape with some wonderful malty spices coating the mouth; b24 a beguiling whisky of near faultless complexity. Blending at its peak. *43%. Suntory.*

Special Reserve Aged 12 Years (89) n21 peaches and cream with a dollop of caramel; t24 luxurious delivery of perfect weight and softness to body; the barley sweetness works beautifully with the buzz of oak and yielding grains; f21 caramel-coffee crème from a box of chocs; b23 a tactile, voluptuous malt that wraps itself like a sated lover around the tastebuds, though the complexity is compromised very slightly by bigger caramel than the 10-y-o. *40%. Suntory.*

Suntory Old (87) n21 dusty and fruity. Attractive nip and balance; t24 mouthwatering from the off with a rich array of chewy, clean fresh malt: textbook standard, complete with bite; f20 thins out far quicker than it once did leaving the vanilla to battle it out with toffee; b22 a delicate and comfortable blend that just appears to have over-simplified itself on the finale. Delicious, but can be much better than this. *40%*

Suntory Old Mild and Smooth (84) n19 t22 f21 b22. Chirpy and lively around the palate, the grains soften the crisp malts wonderfully. *40%*

Suntory Old Rich and Mellow (91) n22 very lightly smoked with healthy maltiness; an extra touch of older oaks in the most recent bottling helps the balance and works wonders; t23 complex, fat and chewy, no shortage of deep malty tones, including a touch of smoke; f23 sweeter malts see off the grain, excellent spices; b23 a pretty malt-rich blend with the grains offering a fat base. Impressive blending. *43%*

Super Nikka (93) n23 excellent crisp, grassy malt base bounces off firm grain. A distant hint of peat, maybe, offers a little weighty extra; t23 an immediate starburst of rich, mouthwatering and entirely uncompromising malt that almost over-runs the tastebuds; f23 soft, fabulously intrinsic peaty notes from the Yoichi School give brilliant length and depth. But the cocoa notes from the oak-wrapped grain also offer untold riches; b24 a very, very fine blend which makes no apology whatsoever for the peaty complexity of Yoichi malt. Now, with less caramel, it's pretty classy stuff. However, Nikka being Nikka you might find the occasional bottling that is entirely devoid of peat, more honeyed and lighter in style (21-22-23-23 total 89 = no less a quality turn, obviously). Either way, an absolutely brilliant day-to-day, anytime, any place dram. One of the true 24-carat, super nova commonplace blends not just in Japan, but in the world. *43%. Nikka*

⋰ **Super Nikka Rare Old** batch 07118D **(90.5)** n22 toffeed but no shortage of lively barley bouncing against firm grain; some playful fruit, mainly greengages, ensures extra freshness; t23 superb arrival with a shimmering barley sweetness fending off the drier vanillas: the balance is spot on here. Remains delicately mouth-watering though it is milky mocha which arrives, not the peat I normally find here; f22.5 remains happily on its vanilla course but some soft cocoa and fruit also plays along; b23 beautiful whisky which just sings a lilting malty refrain. Strange, though, to find it peatless. *43%. Nikka.*

Torys (76) n18 t19 f20 b19. Lots of toffee in the middle and at the end of this one. The grain used is top class and chewy. *37%. Suntory.*

Torys Whisky Square (80) n19 t20 f21 b20. At first glance very similar to Torys, but very close scrutiny reveals slightly more "new loaf" nose and a better, spicier and less toffeed finale. *37%. Suntory.*

Tsuru (93) n23 apples, cedar, crushed pine nuts, blood oranges and soft malt, all rather chalky and soft – and unusually peatless for Nikka; t24 fantastic grain bite bringing with it a mouthwateringly clean and fresh attack of sweet and lip-smacking malt; f22 a continuation of untaxing soft malts and gathering oak, a slight "Malteser" candy quality to it, and then some late sultana fruitiness; b24 gentle and beautifully structured, genuinely mouthwatering, more-ish and effortlessly noble. If they had the confidence to cut the caramel, this would be even higher up the charts as one of the great blends of the world. As it is, in my house we pass the ceramic Tsuru bottle as one does the ship's decanter. And it empties very quickly. *43%. Nikka.*

The Whisky (88) n22 t22 f21 b23. A really rich, confident and well-balanced dram. *43% Suntory.*

White (80) n19 t21 f20 b20. Boring nose but explodes on the palate for a fresh, mouth-watering classic blend bite. *40%. Suntory.*

Za (79) n19 t21 f19 b20. Some lively boisterous grain offers a suet-pudding chewiness. A little bitter on the finish. *40%. Suntory.*

European Whisky

Have you ever tasted a European mainland whisky? Probably not. Do you know anyone who has? No? Hardly surprising. For all the new distilleries springing up in so many countries and considering the high quality of a good many, tracking down and drinking them is as much an art form as the whisky actually being made.

The problem is that the vast majority of these whiskies come from such small stills that the limited output rarely gets beyond local bars and restaurants or visitors who make the pilgrimage to whichever of these tiny distilleries they can find. In some ways this is part of the charm. Some of the distilleries you find in Switzerland and Austria in particular are almost throwbacks to the Scottish highlands of 200 years ago, or Virginia, Pennsylvania and Kentucky of the same period, when farms would include a still to make the most of the surplus grain. And just like those embryonic distilleries of the early 19th century, they would make their whisky from whichever grain they could grow. Distilleries where the land and spirit were as one.

Even so it really was a magnificent and heart-warming sight last year when I managed to get over to Mackmyra in Sweden to see how they had turned what had been among the most sub atomic of micro distilleries into something that you would expect to find somewhere in a Scottish glen. It is a distillery which every single small distiller in Europe should take the time to see. And then head on to Norfolk in England to give that fabulous outpost, the St George distillery, a thorough once over; especially after December 2009 when it officially joins the ranks of the European whisky community when its spirit turns three. And keep heading west until they reach Penderyn in Wales where the distillery there has now begun to amass a following around the globe and for good reason thanks to a malt which continues its extraordinary climb into the whisky world's stratosphere. Not only have their standard bottlings upped in quality from their already high standard but their special bottlings in Madeira and Port are themselves singular reasons to rejoice. Even Prince Charles is not slow to admit he is a fan. What these three distilleries have shown, and with some aplomb, is that a bold approach can pay dividends not just in quality but awareness of product.

At the end of the tour some of the distillers may decide to take that extra step and expand. Or they might stick with what they know, keep expenditure and investment down and carry on as they are going. There really is no right or wrong way. The smaller guys have proved that they can carry on making wonderfully idiosyncratic whiskies which in equal measure delight, enthrall, frustrate and, occasionally, appall. Among the finest whiskies from the region I tasted this year was from Germany where Blaue Maus actually managed to produce a 25-year-old - the oldest mainland malt I have ever seen - of sublime quality and again came within a squeak of running off with the European Whisky of the Year.

That title went back to Switzerland. Not to Swissky who, I understand, are thinking of selling up, but to Santis. So another peated whisky gets a gong in Jim Murray's Whisky Bible. But I can assure you than none in the past has shown this type of character: let us just say that anyone who enjoys Rupp smoked cheese will recognise and most probably applaud this distillery's unique style. It really is a whisky worth climbing a few mountains to find. Indeed, such is the growth now of European whisky, the section on it in this year's Bible has been expanded, as you can see. Sadly, I was unable to create time for a grand tour of its ever increasing number of distilleries and I cannot thank my old friend Julia Nourney enough for supervising distillers there to send samples to me as she undertook research of her own book on the subject.

One of the things that is instantly noticable with many of the European whiskies is the amount of feints kicking about the glass after the whisky has been poured. this is usually a result of the cut being too wind, often because the stills are so small. I have marked the whiskies as they have come from the glass. But to enjoy the whiskies at their best you could do worse than leave them in an open glass in a very warm room to allow the higher alcohols to evaporate. You will usually be pleasantly surprised by the results.

We end on a tragically sad note. Literally within days of the 2009 Bible announcing the arrival of Belgium's unique Goldly's whisky, the man behind it, Jan Filliers, was killed in a coach crash in Egypt while on holiday. The Filliers family had made the highest grade of Genever for over 120 years before he turned some of the maturing stock into whisky. The loss to the industry of this most gentle, witty and charming man is inestimable.

AUSTRIA
Single Malt
ACHENSEE'R EDELBRENNEREI

⸪ **Whisky Alpin Grain Whisky Hafer** bott code L1/2005 **(92) n24** one of the firmest, cleanest oat noses I have come across for a year or two: porridge with muscovado sugar melting on top and even gooseberries offering a fruity respite; **t22** a bit too firm and oaky at first, maybe, though the sweetness and spices try to confirm complexity; **f23** even better as the spicy oats and butterscotch tart find a tasty compromise; **b23** if you are looking for a whisky with a personality, you've just found it... 44%

⸪ **Whisky Alpin Rye & Malt** bott code L1/2005 **(87.5) n21.5** the fruity rye dominates; **t23** brilliant delivery where the brain can barely cope with the complexity: sweet, juicy lush rye abounds but there are much darker, spicier notes to contest their dominance; **f21** over bitters out; **b22** despite the feinty sub plot, this is one very impressive distillery. 40%

BRENNEREI EBNER

⸪ **Absamer Whisky** bott code L2305 **(79.5) n23 t17 f21.5 b18.** This job of mine prepares you for most things. But not this. What the bloody hell has just hit me....? It was going so well with the nose: punchy oak, but not a normal oak varietal, it seemed to me. Some kind of rare European species, I wondered? Whatever it was, the balance between sweet and dry was pretty bang on and the complexity levels were falling off the page. And then, on delivery, it seared my tastebuds like a blowtorch. Not from the strength, but simply the sheer viciousness of the oak – which arrives only after a few lovely nanoseconds of sweetness lulls you into a completely false sense of security. A liquorice, walnut oil and maple syrup (more wood) sweetness salvages the job. 50%

BRENNEREI LAGLER

⸪ **Best Korn Burgenland** bott 2007 db **(84) n20 t22 f21 b21.** A strange paprika and hop nose, though the body is fruity and sweet. 43%

⸪ **Pannonia Korn Malt** bott 2007 db **(85.5) n21.5 t21.5 f21 b21.5.** Easy drinking whisky with a charming, stimulating sweetness and light though lush finish. 40%

⸪ **Pannonia Blend** bott 2008 db **(83.5) n19 t22 f21 b21.5.** The strength means this is not actually whisky by native European standards. And you fear the worst with the feinty nose. But pans out pleasantly and sweetly, as is the house style. 38.5%

DESTILLERIE HIEBL

⸪ **George Hiebl Mais Whisky 2004 (93) n23** the corn is unmistakable and the cask must be pretty new oak, too: a few spices flit around whilst the lighter of the varied sweetness looks like a delicate dose of maple syrup; best of all though is the unmistakable aroma of newly bound and laid hay bales...just fabulous...**t23.5** melt-in-the-mouth corn and treacle with a real sheen to the coppery, honey notes; light red liquorice dissolves in with the ascending vanilla; **f23** chewy toffee, a touch of cocoa and molasses...and more small still copper; **b23.5** more bourbon in character than some American bourbons I know...!! Beautifully matured, brilliantly matured and European whisky of the very highest order, Ye..haahhhh!! 43%

⸪ **George No. 1 Aged 5 Years (86) n22 t22 f20 b22.** Much more perfumy and oily with honeycomb rather than honey. 40%

⸪ **George No. 2 Aged 5 Years** bott code L1/09 **(84.5) n21.5 t21 f22 b20.** Very pleasant in part. But much of its bourbony personality seems to be shaped from laying in a bed of caramel....making it rather Canadian 41.8%

DESTILLERIE KAUSL

⸪ **Wachauer Whisky "G" Single Barrel Gerste (Barley)** bott code L6WG **(90.5) n22** sweet, soft, clean, mildly buttery; **t23** impressive mouth-feel: the light oils work superbly, and the arrival of sweet barley is without fanfare...very natural, indeed; **f22.5** long, retains a gristy sweetness as the vanillas build; **b23** absolutely charming and well made malt. 40%

⸪ **Wachauer Whisky "H" Single Barrel Hafer (Oat)** bott code L1WH **(88) n21.5** chunky with good oak but a touch of drying tobacco, too. The oats offer a sweet respite in the strange, smoky atmosphere; **t21.5** a confused delivery, with some very sweet and very bitter notes not quite on talking terms. The bitterness heads towards bitter cherry, the sweetness is rather more molassed. By the middle, they have relaxed delightfully; **f23** the best part of the experience with sweetened liquorice heading towards a slight milky coffee finale; **b22** I can safely say that no whisky in the world has quite this signature. A unique and ultimately very enjoyable whisky. 40%

⋙ **Wachauer Whisky "R"** Single Barrel Roggen (Rye) bott code L2WR **(86.5) n21 t22 f23.5 b21.** A real eyebrow-raiser. Bloody hell!! Where do I start...? OK: butyric nose...not good. Way, way too much oak...not good. Yet...also on the nose: superb fruitiness to the unmistakable rye; ditto the sharp juiciness on delivery. This really is rye whisky with knobs on. Like others from this distillery, there is a lovely mocha-coffee slant to the, frankly, astonishing finish. Technically, an absolute nightmare that should be taken out and shot. In effect – and as much as I hate to say it....bloody delicious...!!! 40%

⋙ **Wachauer Whisky "W"** Single Barrel Weizen (Wheat) bott code L1WW **(76.5) n19 t18.5 f20.5 b18.5.** A feinty heavyweight which has real problems finding its direction and balance. Only when some molasses and cocoa form towards the end does it take shape. 40%

DESTILLERIE ROGNER

⋙ **Rogner Waldviertel Whisky No. 2** db **(86) n21.5 t21 f22 b21.5.** Toasted almonds and light molasses make for enjoyable and oily whisky. I wish more of their whiskies were as good as this. 42.7%

⋙ **Rogner Waldviertel Whisky 3/3** db **(77.5) n17.5 t20 f21 b19.** Once you get past the startling nose, which is more akin to certain forms of Scandinavian aquavit than whisky, the rest of the journey is sweet and easy. Though still pretty unwhisky-ish. 42%

⋙ **Rogner Waldviertel Whisky 3/3 Malz** db **(87.5) n19.5** hmmm. A few technical hiccups here, but if you are fan of chocolate nougat... **t23.5** massive oily delivery with sweet, nutty flavours on full throttle. Loads of mocha comes screeching through early on and you have to admit that this is fun stuff; **f22** all kinds of sharp cherry candy while the milky mocha continues; **b22.5** hang on to your hats: this one plays for shocks. Look forward to visiting this distillery to work out what the hell they are up to there. Absolutely love it! 65%

⋙ **Rogner Waldviertel Rye Whisky No. 13** db **(83) n20 t21.5 f20.5 b21.** Drying tobacco nose and not quite the cleanest delivery. But an attractive rye fruitiness does has something to say, aided and abetted by some toffee and oil. 41%

DESTILLERIE WEUTZ

⋙ **Hot Stone Single Malt** db **(88) n21.5** reminds me of a spiced biscuit I've come across from time to time in Eastern Europe, the name of which, annoyingly, escapes me; **t23** wonderful with burnt honeycomb and fudge all over the place; the bitter-sweet ratio just couldn't be better; **f21.5** technically unsound, but really so much beautiful malt-vanilla-walnut interaction, you have to give it a tick; **b22** the Arnold Schwarzenegger of Austrian whisky: huge, muscle-bound....and a bit of a friendly giant. Technically, the finish needs some attention; and it could do with a tweak here and there from nose onwards, really. But just one of those drams that demands a second glassful – even when you are still like to be in a state of wonder and shock from the very first arrival. Delicious! 67.1%

⋙ **Hot Stone Single Malt Single Cask Gerstenmalz** bott code L 041411/01 **(88.5) n21** forensically flawed, but effectively attractive nougat amid rich barley; **t23** seems to be wrapped in caramel, but this is big malt, expanding forever, moving into sweeter, fatter territory; **f22** really kicks in with a coppery screech that gets young tongue working flat; for a second something slightly smoky kicks in; **b22.5** exhausting to taste, as the brain has to go into overdrive to work out what the hell is going on! 42.1%

REISETBAUER

⋙ **Reisetbauer Single Malt 7 Years Old** Chardonnay and sweet wine cask, bott code LWH 099 db **(85.5) n19 t21 f23.5 b22.** Well it takes some time. But it gets there in the end. A less than impressive nose is followed by a rocky delivery. But the panning out is truly spectacular as harmony is achieved with a rich honey and nougat mix, helped along the way with pecan nuts and figs. The finish is like a top rank trifle and fruitcake mix. A whisky of two halves. 43%

⋙ **Reisetbauer Single Malt 12 Years Old Limited Edition** db **(85) n18.5 t21.5 f23 b22.** A remarkably similar story to the 7-y-o, though a touch silkier, with less sweetness and not quite so much complexity at the death. Even so, a dram to find. 48%

Reisetbauer Single Malt Whisky 1998 Destilliert db **(86.5) n20.5 t21 f22.5 b22.5.** A large, rambling malt bursting at the seams with character and charm. Ten years in the cask appears to have seen off the worst of the odd distilling blemish. Bravo for bottling at full strength, because the spices are seen to best effect, as is the barley which tries to find a sugared course, but narrowly fails. Substantial weight throughout and an excellent length to the finish. The toasty dryness is also a delight. I can't wait to see further bottlings from this obviously polished distillery. Impressive and desirable. 56%

WALDVIERTLER

⁘ **Waldviertler J H Single Malt Selection** L7/02 db **(86) n22 t21 f21.5 b21.5**. A pretty, layered, nose, sporting excellent oak integration. Doesn't quite hit the same heights on the palate where sugars and certain oils, some bitter, dominate. Good biscuity tail off, alternating between caramelized dunking fare and sweet digestive. Molasses abounds. Deceptively enjoyable. 46%

⁘ **Waldviertler J H Original Rye** L2/02 db **(82) n20.5 t21 f20.5 b20**. Some quiet spice and aggression amid the sleepy toffee. 41%

⁘ **Waldviertler J H Pure Rye Malt** L14/02 db **(92) n23** a sprig of lavender bolsters the fruity intensity; **t23.5** clean, intense rye. Mouth-watering firm, hard, flinty — exactly how it should be; **f22.5** grains of brown sugar spike up the rye's fruity finale; **b23** some of the most beautifully made whisky I have come across for a little while. This is absolutely top grade European rye whisky. And all the better when left in the glass for 20 minutes before drinking. 41%

⁘ **Waldviertler J H Pure Special Rye Malt "Nougat"** L13/02 db **(78) n19.5 t20 f20 b19.5**. A little fat. A little feinty. A little bitter. 41%

⁘ **Waldviertler J H Special Single Malt "Karamell"** L15/02 db **(74) n18 t19.5 f17.5 b19**. Just too many feints to work. 41%

⁘ **Waldviertler J H Special Single Malt Selection** L15/02 db **(84.5) n20.5 t22 f21 b21**. Attractively simplistic. The malt has the upper hand throughout and there is extra weight and fizz from the slightly feinty oils. 46%

WEIDENAUER DISTILLERY Kottes. Working.

⁘ **Waldviertler Single Malt (75) n18 t19 f19 b19**. Heavy, lush oily and with a big oak signature. The feel is that the cut taken has been very wide, indeed. 42%

⁘ **Waldviertler Dinkelmalz with 2008** award label on neck **(77.5) n18.5 t21 f19 b19**. A bit rough round the edges from time to time, though the citrus on delivery charms. 42%

⁘ **Waldviertler Dinkelmalz** with A La carte label on neck **(89) n22.5** a clean, fascinating battle between the malt and oak. Vanilla appears to just about win out; **t23** like on the nose, two factions battle it out for supremacy, ensuring a lovely degree of complexity. An adroit sweetness ensures a fresh, gristy feel; **f21.5** bitters out slightly, but there's a touch of chocolate mint chip to compensate; **b22** now that's far more like what I expect from this usually excellent distillery. 42%

⁘ **Waldviertler Dinkel** with 2008 Silber Medaille label on neck **(90) n19.5** ooops. Promises much but the stray butyric note pegs this one back; **t23** a beautiful concoction of pulpy apple, the lightest sprinkling of muscovado sugar all glued together by outstanding oils. While the grain simply pulses in happy tandem with the oak; **f23.5** actually ups the anti complexity-wise and now those extra feints are actually piling on the depth and length: what a treat...!! **b24** the nose apart, the odd feint note here and there can't seriously detract from this majestically attractive whisky and towards the end even helps! Classy, classy whisky...!!! 42%

⁘ **Waldviertler Hafer** with 2007 Silber Medaille label on neck **(83.5) n19 t22 f21 b21.5**. A unique flavor profile from these oats. A touch more bitter than usual, perhaps, but there is a superb mouthwatering quality which counters the woody impact. 42%

⁘ **Waldviertler Hafer-Malz** with 2007 Gold Medaille label on neck **(91) n22** a curious aroma of old steam trains back in the 1960s: a little oily, coal smoky and dank; **t22.5** the palate is greeted with a wonderful luster to the arrival. a distinctive, metallic small still copperiness which is coated with the soft sweetness of the oats; **f23** wonderful finish which is displayed in many layers but always that perfect setting of light sweetness if never altered and the grains the oak gel with amazing ease; **b23.5** one of those whiskies that just gets better the longer it stays on the palate. Also, a master class in achieving near perfection in the degree of sweetness generated. 42%

⁘ **Waldviertler Hafer-Malz** with 2008 label on neck **(76.5) n20 t19.5 f18 b19**. The big oaks do their best to compensate. But the damage has been done by making the cut here a little too wide and flooding the usual complexity with heavy oils. 42%

BELGIUM
THE BELGIAN OWL

⁘ **The Belgian Owl Single Malt** first fill bourbon cask, bott 09 db **(90.5) n22** just a slight catch of feints, but nothing untoward, though it ensures a drier edge to the malt; **t23.5** a real weighty thump to the tastebuds from thick, uncompromising malt which is helped along by the small still, wider cut oiliness. Works blindingly well thanks to the slow but delightful build up of high-grade marzipan, which injects a controlled, delicate, mildly nutty and oily sweetness..., but all the time the malts are singing sweetly in the background; **f22.5** a light, fizzing spice embraces the drier oaks. Still the malt is never far away from the horizon; **b22.5** just one of those malts which are a sheer joy to experience. 46%

The Belgian Owl Single Malt Spirit New Make (90) n22 t22 f23 b23. Beautiful small still spirit where the barley content appears to be in concentrate form towards the finish. Excellent sweetness and just the right degree of soft oil. 46%. nc ncf. ⊙

The Belgian Owl Single Malt Spirit Aged 7 Months cask no. 42759.76 db **(77) n18 t21 f19 b19.** Usual lack of balance at this age. Sweet, intense malt, but a touch feinty as well. 46%. ncf.

The Belgian Owl Single Malt Spirit Aged 12 Months cask no. 427 58 72 **(88) n22 t22 f22 b22.** Remarkably even for its age. The oak has fused well but has not the spirit of its high grade malty style. Entirely charming and eminently drinkable. 46%. nc ncf.

The Belgian Owl Single Malt Spirit Aged 13 Months cask no. 4018741 db **(84.5) n20 t22 f21.5 b21.** Much firmer in style than most. The oak and barley are hacking lumps out of each other. Lots of good sugars and spices, though. 46%. ncf.

The Belgian Owl Single Malt Spirit Aged 18 Months cask no. 4275877 db **(85) n22.5 t21 f21.5 b20.** Another hugely tasty but obviously unstable fledgling. Massive natural caramels are thumping home; the malt tries to get a word in edgeways but fails every time. Even so, this is well made spirit and you help to enjoy the spectacle. 46%. nc ncf.

The Belgian Owl Single Malt Spirit Aged 18 Months cask no. 4276017 db **(89) n21 t23 f22 b23.** A fizzing beauty with salivating barley at every turn. The juices are required to help douse the mental spices. Chewy, delicious – even with a surprising mocha character – and a quite freaky balance for its age. 46%. ncf.

The Belgian Owl Limited Edition Single Malt Aged 36 Months cask no. 4275873 db **(90.5) n21.5** a touch of the Blaue Maus nougat to this, but nothing like so pronounced. Naturally spiced and sweetens in elegant style; **t22.5** immediately packs a malty punch. But on delivery there is much more besides: the spices on the nose translate perfectly and those sugars quickly evolve into a muscovado and manuka mix; improbably juicy and alluring... **f23.5** now goes into overdrive as the malt intensifies at about the same rate as the spice. The sugars remain a delightful constant and cling to the most delicate of oils. The entire thing pulses for an improbable time – brilliant...!! **b23** so here it is: the first-ever dedicated malt whisky produced in Belgium. I first tasted this at the distillery alongside distiller Etienne Bouillon, but decided to mark it in the less romantic environs of my tasting room. Really, it doesn't matter where you drink this malt: absolutely brimming with character and after a short while settling in, announces its brilliance. Magnifique!! 46%. ncf.

DESTILLERIE RADERMACHER
⋅∷⋅ **Lambertus Single Grain Aged 10 Years (44) n12 t12 f10 b10.** This is whisky....? Really???!!!!????? Well, that's what it says on the label, and this is a distillery I haven't got round to seeing in action (nor am I now very likely to be invited...). Let's check the label again.... Ten years old....blah, blah. Single grain... blah, blah. But, frankly, this tastes like a liqueur rather than a whisky: the fruit flavours do not seem even remotely naturally evolved: synthetic is being kind. But apparently, this is whisky: I have re-checked the label. No mention of additives, so it must be. I am stunned. 40%

FILLIERS DISTILLERY
Goldly's Belgian Double Still Whisky Aged 10 Years (88) n21.5 bristling grain and a lovely cameo rye touch. But toffee dictates the overall shape; **t23** beautiful delivery and then explosion of complexity. Three grain types are present here and they each show their paces with the rye having the loudest say; the malt adds the comforting sweetness; **f21.5** again toffee returns, though late spices try to inject extra life; **b22** having actually discovered this whisky before the distillers – I'll explain one day...!! – I know this could be a lot better. The caramel does great damage to the finish in particular, which should dazzle with its complexity. Even so, a lovely, high-class whisky which should be comfortably in the 90s but falls short. 40%.

ENGLAND
THE ENGLISH WHISKY CO. (ST. GEORGES DISTILLERY)
English Malt Spirit New Make dist 20 Jul 08 db **(92) n23 t24 f22 b23.** Exceptionally high quality new make. The peat comes across in coke-ash, cindery terms while the sweetness and clarity of barley ticks every box. Top rate. 46%

English Malt Spirit New Make dist 6 Aug 08 db **(93.5) n22.5 t23 f24 b23.** Even without the peat we have a gloriously characterful new make. Indeed, the lack of smoke lets us see the wonderful juicy qualities of this spirit and the extent of the spice and balance. Naturally, with a new still the copper-richness is there in abundance and this is likely to tone down over time. But providing this has been filled into first class new bourbon (please, god, not sherry!) casks, this first dedicated English distillery for over a century is likely to gain a name for exceptional quality. 46%

English Malt Spirit Cask 30, 31, 32 dist 5 Mar 07 db **(85.5) n22 t22 f21.5 b20.** It is a curious fact of whisky nature that spirit matured for a year or two in cask often tastes a lot inferior to new make. Here is a classic example. Entirely respectable and enjoyable. And clearly well made. But there is a Bambi-like effect as the balance stutters all over the place as the oak makes its first incursions and the barley appears ill-prepared to take it on. This is normal for virtually every malt distillery in the world and in no way reflects on the quality of this distillery's malt. I am tasting this one a month or so ahead of its bottling date in September 2008, so there is room for it to improve...or get worse...!!! 46%

FINLAND
PANIMORAVINTOLA BEER HUNTER'S Pori. Working.

Old Buck first release, cask no. 2, dist 25 Nov 01, bott Nov 04 db **(93.5) n23** Golden Gordon breakfast cereal. The slightly burnt ones with honey; **t24** breathtakingly intense barley concentrate and toasted honeycomb; the brown sugars dissolve in layers: spellbinding... **f23** those neo-bourbon notes continue. Some liquorice, inevitably, gets in on the act. The bitter-sweet balance is textbook: mind you...you'd expect a great Finnish, wouldn't you....; **b23.5** what an unexpected treat! 70.6%. nc ncf sc.

Old Buck second release, cask no. 5, dist 25 Feb 03, bott Jul 07 db **(96) n24** I assume Finland is a part of Kentucky. Pure bourbon: with the nose offering every degree of honeycomb-liquorice imaginable... **t24** I am no longer in my chair...I have been catapulted to the furthest recess of my tasting room...the delivery nigh defies description, other than that we are talking huge — and I mean bloody gargantuan — degrees of manuka honey and oak on its sweetest, toastiest form... **f24** long, so enormously long. Just carries on the bourbon theme with the oak throbbing out waves of liquorice and hickory and the spices just pulse merrily away and never for one moment either losing balance or dredging up unwanted notes from either cask or still... **b24** it's as though they have been distilling George T Stagg...!!! Quite amazing: perhaps the surprise package of the year. I thought the first bottling was a freak. This really does send you not so much into another orbit but an entirely parallel universe. Buck me...!! 70.6%. nc ncf sc.

TEERENPELI

Teerenpeli Single Malt Whisky Aged 5 Years db **(86) n21.5 t22 f21 b21.5.** No shrinking violet, this impressive first bottling from Teerenpeli. It radiates the chunkier qualities often found with smaller stills, yet still manages to harness the richer barley notes to enjoyable effect. Weighty and a touch oily, the sweet barley which is briefly announced on arrival soon makes way for a more rumbustious combination of oak and higher oils. I look forward to getting there at last to see how it is done...though I think I can already imagine...!! 43%

FRANCE
Single Malt
DISTILLERIE BERTRAND

⌐ **Uberach (77) n21 t19 f18 b19.** Big, bitter and booming. Gives the impression something happening between smoke and grape...whatever it is, there are prisoners being taken. 42.2%

DISTILLERIE DES MENHIRS

Eddu Gold (93) n22 greater harmonization than the silver; still a hint of tobacco but now a richer, honeyed tone compensates and flourishes; **t23** big, bulging arrival. There is a real pulse to the grain, a sturdiness which helps intensify the controlled Demerara sweetness. Big yet elegant; **f24** now goes into overdrive as the oak adds further weight and spices. Yet the satin effect remains intact; **b24** rarely do whiskies turn up in the glass so rich in character to the point of idiosyncrasy. Some purists will recoil from the more assertive elements. I simply rejoice. This is so proud to be different. And exceptionally good, to boot!! 43%

DISTILLERIE GLANN AR MOR

⌐ **Glann Ar Mor Aged 3 Years** 1st fill bourbon barrel **(85) n21.5 t22 f20.5 b21.** The slight feints, so typical of European small still whisky, works well in upping the weight, structure and chewability. Juicy barley and cocoa dominate, but tasting after it has sat in an open glass for half an hour works wonders. 46%. Celtic Whisky Compagnie.

⸫ **Glann Ar Mor Taol Esa Ian Gwech 08 (92)** n22 a hint of pear lightens the obvious small still weightiness; barley sugar and gentle vanillas do likewise; **t23** stunning silky delivery. A beautiful interwoven barley and soft fruit lead is supported ably by the distinctive coppery sheen: the mouth-feel is exceptionally good; **f23.5** fabulous mocha and mint fade, still with that lovely coppery richness to the texture; the vanillas do become more compelling but the oaks are always at their most gentle; **b23.5** I have been impressed by this distillery in the past and I am impressed again. This is honest whisky, where its character can be charted and defined needing nothing more than a clear mind and palate. It is entirely appropriate that this distillery faces an old lighthouse: because this is a beacon for those in search of excellent malt. These Bretons are keeping the Celtic tradition of making fine whisky flying from the very highest point they can find... 46%

DISTILLERIE GUILLON

Guillon No. 1 Single Malt de la montagne de Reims db **(87)** n22 slight tobacco kick from, presumably, the still. But the crushed (slightly jaded) orange works well with the malt; **t21** lively malt, not entirely clean, has enough in fruity-doughy reserve genuinely to attract; **f22** dry with a shortcake butteriness; the sugarless custard tart finish is excellent **b22** right. I'm impressed. Not exactly faultless, but enough life here really to keep the tastebuds on full alert; By and large well made and truly enjoyable. Well done, Les Chaps! 46%

DISTILLERIE MEYER

⸫ **Meyer's Whisky Alsacien Blend Superieur (88.5)** n22.5 a complex nose showing excellent distilling technique and clarity to the lightly honeyed grain and even a delicate fruitiness; **t22.5** those fruits on the nose, a kind of light raspberry jam, arrive early and complement the soft vanillas and barley; **f21.5** a parting slight toasty bitterness from the oak; **b22** impressively clean, barley-thick and confident: a delight. 40%

DISTILLERIE WARENGHEM

Armorik db **(91)** n23 alluringly spicy and biting, the oak jabs with limited venom whilst the malt takes the blows with ease. Highly attractive and complex; **t22** sweet, easily recognisable malt glides over the palate charmingly; some serious gristy notes develop early; **f23** a long, exceptionally malty finish, again with the barley in the ascendancy and with few challengers; **b23** I admit it; I blanched, when I first nosed this, so vivid was the memory of the last bottling. This, though ,was the most pleasant of surprises. Fabulous stuff: one of the most improved malts in the world. 40%

DOMAINE MAVELA DISTILLERIE ARTISANALE

P&M Pure Malt Whisky bott 05 db **(91)** n23 an extraordinary injection of kumquats makes for a pleasing – and individualistic – aroma; **t23** amazingly sharp and mouth-watering. There are flavours new to me here – and that doesn't happen often; **f22** almost bitter at times; **b23** an outstanding whisky which, being French, seems to offer a style that is entirely different from anything else around. I have been told there is chestnut within the grist which, strictly speaking, means this is not whisky as we know it. My French is not good enough to discover the truth of this. Between now and the 2008 Bible I shall travel to the distillery in Corsica to get to the bottom of this. In the meantime, though, I shall occasionally enjoy this delicious dram! 42%

WAMBRECHIES DISTILLERY

⸫ **Wambrechies Single Malt Aged 3 Years (78.5)** n19 t19 f21 b19.5. Sweet with a Malteser candy touch. A few feints just dampen the overall effect. There is also an aroma on the nose I kind of recognize, but... 40%

⸫ **Wambrechies Single Malt Aged 8 Years (83)** n20 t21 f21 b21. ....and there's that aroma again, just like the 3-y-o. Except how it kind of takes me back 30 years to when I hitchhiked across the Sahara. Some of the food I ate with the local families in Morocco and Algeria was among the best I have ever tasted. And here is an aroma I recognize from that time, though I can't say specifically what it is (tomatoes, maybe?). Attractive and unique to whisky, that's for sure. I rather like this malt. There is nothing quite comparable to it; there is obviously some kind of feinty note, but nothing disastrous. And the curious malty-fruity bit is charming. One I need to investigate a whole lot more. 40%

Blends

P&M Blend Supérieur (82) n21 t21 f20 b20. Bitter and botanical, though no shortage of complexity. 40%. Mavela Distillerie.

P&M Whisky (89) n22 light, lemony, mildly Canadian wheated in style; **t23** beautiful, sharpish citrus ensures a salivating experience; **f22** soft oak lowers the sweetness levels; **b22** no mistaking this is from a fruit distillery. Still quite North American, though. *40%. Mavela Distillerie.*

GERMANY
BELLERHOF-BRENNEREI Owen. Working.

Schwäbischer Whisky vom Bellerhof db **(88) n21** European-style Kentucky dry tobacco with a vaguely honeyed edge; **t22** soft, entirely melt-in-the-mouth barley with dissolving brown sugars; **f23** the most butterscotchy finish of all time with wonderful elements of the softest oak and honey imaginable; **b22** easy drinking clean and deliciously sweet malt with that indelible touch of class. *43%*

Schwäbischer Whisky vom Bellerhof dh **(88) n23** subtle honey and vanilla: exceptionally clean; **t22** more melt in the mouth malt just as before, **f21** dries until the oak bites; **b22** an entirely different route to the same high quality whisky...! *47.4%*

BLAUE MAUS Eggolshein Neuses. Working.

Austrasier Single Cask Grain fass 3, dist Jun 94, bott Jun 08 db **(89.5) n21** liquorice and hickory amid the nougat; **t22** stunning delivery with a fragility to the grain which counters the sturdier oaks; the honey grows – at times in a manuka style – to ensure extra weight and depth; **f23.5** now goes up a few extra gears as some late honeycomb ensured a long sweet finish. The spices have simmered for a while and now pulse; **b23** beautifully weighted whisky with a glorious liquorice development – some finer bourbon notes at play here. High quality whisky. *40%*

❖ **Blaue Maus Single Cask Malt (84.5) n18 t22 f22.5 b22.** Beautifully molassed with a big burnt fudge finale. *40%*

Blaue Maus Single Malt fass 2, dist Oct 97, bott Jun 08 db **(85.5) n20 t21.5 f22.5 b21.5.** Substantial whisky which, as this distillery's style dictates, just gets better as it goes along. The usual burnt sugar effect is in full flow and the spices evolve with a degree of sophistication. *40%*

Blaue Maus Single Malt Munhner Whiskyfestival 4-6 Februar 2005 fass 1, dist Jul 90 db **(93) n23** minty, lavender, faintly herbal; **t24** dry and toasty at first, there is a mad rush of malt before the soft liquorice, oaky notes begin to arrive in numbers, as does the deep honey; **f22** cream toffee and wonderful honeycomb; **b24** tasted blind this could so easily be mistaken for a bourbon. The oldest European mainland whisky I have ever come across. *40%*

Blaue Maus Single Malt 20 Jahre fass 1, dist Jul 88, bott May 08 db **(91) n22** roasted cherries, roasted banana, roasted mallow; **t23** mouth-filling and....roasty. Some high roast coffee but sweetened by muscovado sugar; **f22.5** spices up as the sugars fan out in the distillery-honoured way; even a touch of copper for a mildly metallic finale; **b23.5** complex and superbly balanced, the age is never in doubt while the management of the old oak is sublime. *40%*

Blaue Maus Single Malt 25 Jahre dist 83, bott 08 db **(95.5) n24** faultless: closer to a big age bourbon than a malt. Go through the big bourbon checklist: honeycomb, hickory, leather, liquorice...all the usual suspects...and they are there not only in abundance but to magnificent effect; **t24** distilled manuka honey: thick, intense, sweet but balanced off by darker, drier notes. Soft spices and towards the middle ultra intense butterscotch; **f23.5** a long, dry fade by never once crosses the over-oaked line; the slowly dissolving of those darker sugars borders on the erotic... **b24** my 1,400th whisky for this year's book. And what better way to celebrate than by tasting Robert Fleischmann's special bottling to mark his 25th anniversary as a whisky distiller. I first tasted it with Robert earlier in the year at the Munich Whisky Festival. Back on neutral territory it tastes no worse than the stunning whisky he poured for me then. Quite dazzling and a magnificent way to mark this momentous anniversary. Because if a better German single malt has ever been bottled, then I have missed it. Which is rather unlikely... *40%*

Blaue Maus Single Cask Malt Fassfullung fass 1, dist Jul 96, bott Jun 08 db **(86.5) n18.5 t22 f23.5 b22.5.** The strange, house-style nougat nose is an unworthy fanfare to a really dogged and eventually sophisticated malt. The way in which it grows on the palate in both style, complexity and overall quality is wonderful. The intensity of the lingering malt at the end is almost worthy of applause. *40%*

Blaue Maus Single Cask Malt Fassstarke fass 1, dist Apr 92, bott May 08 db **(89) n20** burnt nougat; **t23** burnt tastebuds....the enormous spice coupled with the full strength of the whisky makes for a memorable delivery. The big honeycomb is there but it is peppered by white-hot spice and vanilla and butterscotch also pass through..; **f23** still pulses but now even the malt can be heard; sweet and defiantly juicy even as the vanilla digs deep; **b23** a massive experience: The Blaue Max. *58.6%*

⚬ **Blaue Maus Single Cask Malt Fassfullung** fass 1, dist Jun 97, bott Jan 09 **(85) n18.5 t21.5 f23 b22.** A steady-as-she-goes whisky: safe, attractive, a touch drier and with a juicy element to the malt and some genuine sophistication to the vanilla-led finale. *40%*

⚬ **Blaue Maus Single Cask Malt Fassstarke (91.5) n19.5** another nose with all kinds of faults...and yet it somehow carries countless positives especially with that big fruity cocoa signature, a kind of distillery trademark these days... **t24.5** one of the best deliveries found in the world this year: sweet, molassed, plenty of cocoa but also ripe figs and dates getting in on the act....I am salivating so much from this I'm in danger of drowning... **f23.5** exactly the kind of oaky bite I'd want from something of this age. Burnt raisin, traditional fruitcake sweetened with molasses...it's all there in spades... **b24** tasting whisky from this unique distillery is always fun. And it appears distiller Robert Fleischmann is really doing this with a smile on his face. This is really what world whisky is all about: what entertainment...what fantastic bloody fun....!!!! *56.3%*

⚬ **Gruner Hund Single Cask Malt** fass 2, dist Aug 96, bott Jan 09 **(91) n21** chocolate nougat: fat, sweet and nutty; **t23.5** beautiful delivery of toffee raisin again with plenty of cocoa to add to the mix; more juicy fruits abound with fat sultanas, fig and exploding ripe plums at the head; a seam of molten brown sugar appears inexhaustible; **f23.5** goes into complexity overdrive with the cocoa notes mingling with vanilla and molasses; **b23** Blaue Maus at its irrestistable best. *40%*

Gruner Hund Single Cask Malt fass 2, dist Aug 97, bott Jun 08 db **(79) n18 t20 f21 b20.** Some bitter oak arrests the usual malt development. *40%*

Krottentaler Single Cask Malt fass 1, dist Jul 96, bott Jun 08 db **(80.5) n18 t19 f22 b21.5.** Another which struggles to find either a rhythm or style until late on when those stunning sugars come into their own. *40%*

⚬ **Krottentaler Single Cask Malt** fass 1, dist Mar 97, bott Jan 09 **(77.5) n17 t21 f19.5 b20.** Loads of sweet cocoa for all its obvious weaknesses. *40%*

⚬ **Old Fahr Single Cask Malt** fass 1, dist Jul 00, bott Jan 09 **(89) n19.5** delicate hickory and cocoa amid the nougat-feints; **t23.5** plenty of mint chocolate on a whisky very similar in style to the Fassfullung, except with a touch of extra sweetness and a dose of busy spice; **f23** long, with a dramatic build up of rich demerara; **b23** quite simply a beautiful whisky. *40%*

Schwarzer Pirat Single Cask Malt fass 1, dist Mar 97, bott Jun 08 db **(89) n21** nutty, though accompanied by Dundee fruitcake; **t23** immediately embracing with a stunning, Demerara sugar-glossed delivery: the oaks and the malts combine with near faultless balance; **f22.5** very dry by Blaue maus standard – but still a sugary glaze; **b22.5** hugely enjoyable *40%*

⚬ **Schwarzer Pirat Single Cask Malt** fass 2, dist Jun 96, bott Jan 09 **(86.5) n20 t22.5 f22 b22.** Honey and nougat all the way. *40%*

Spinnaker Single Cask Malt fass 1, dist Apr 98, bott Jun 08 db **(84) n18.5 t22 f22.5 b21.** Muscovado sugar on heat. *40%*

⚬ **Spinnaker Single Cask Malt** fass 1, dist Aug 93, bott Jan 09 **(89) n19.5** molassed toffee; **t23** exemplary delivery: pure silk as delicate spices try to make an impact on the marzipan-cocoa theme; **f23.5** brilliant butterscotch and vanilla melt-down, with molasses and cocoa just around the corner...brilliant...!!! **b23** stunning chocolate fudge. *40%*

⚬ **Spinnaker Single Cask Malt Fassfullung** fass 1, dist Jun 95, bott Jan 09 **(86.5) n18 t23.5 f22.5 b22.5.** Ignore the nutty nougat/butyric nose and you have a sublime malt absolutely bursting out of the glass with cocoa-laden barley. Fabulously beautiful in every department, other than the aroma. (Note: all Blaue Maus whiskies can be improved by allowing the whisky to stand in heat for a while to burn off the feints) *40%*

Spinnaker Single Cask Malt Fassstarke fass 1, dist Jul 99, bott Apr 08 db **(80) n17 t19 f23 b21.5.** This one is holed very early on with the nose and delivery being way out. But, as is so often the case with this unique distillery, we have here a malt which somehow manages to bounce back with an irresistible finish that appears to explore previously unknown avenues of sweetness and chewability. *48.2%*

BOSCH EDELBRAND

⚬ **Bosch Edelbrand Schwabischer Whisky** Lot 9105 **(83.5) n19 t22.5 f21 b21.** Needs to make the cut a little more selective: has the promise to become a pretty high quality whisky. This shows some outstanding depth and honey for some time after the first, impressive delivery. *40%*

BRANNTWEINBRENNEREI WEINBAU

➤ **Weinbau Keller (89.5) n22** a beautiful Sauternes-style sweetness picks up some extra spices and overcomes a hint of feints; **t23** a very sweet whisky, yet somehow doesn't cross the point of no return: still a slight distilling blemish can be detected, but that appears to offer slightly extra oil for the grape and grain to intensify their battle; **f22** much more emphasis on the dull, throbbing spice, but still that Sauternes/noble rot lushness holds sway, despite a real custardy-vanilla arrival; **b22.5** hardly faultless from a technical point of view. But if you can't enjoy something as raunchy and ribald as this, you might as well stop drinking whisky. 40%

BRENNEREI ANDREAS VALLENDAR

➤ **Threeland Single Malt 2006 (93) n23** green, newly mown grass and hay: beautifully fresh, enticing and with that juicy, just-so degree of sweetness; **t23.5** mouthwatering, slightly sweeter than the nose suggests; gristy but always intense; **f23** an elegant vanilla and barley fade; **b23.5** on this evidence, one of the technically best distillers of malt on mainland Europe. Sensational...!!! 46%

BRENNEREI ERICH SIGEL

➤ **Original Dettinger Schwabischer Whisky (88) n21.5** sharp; egg-custard tart and a supine touch of pine; **t22.5** sugared almonds; body is silky and sweetens gently; **f22** heaps of vanilla and a slow build up of juicy barley notes and spice **b22** softly sophisticated. 40%

BRENNEREI HÖHLER

➤ **Whesskey Special Blend (77) n17.5 t21 f19.5 b20.** One of those odd creatures which surface from time to time in this part of the world. The flavor profile – even taking into account the massive cream toffee caramel style – isn't quite like anything you've encountered before. You kind of like it, admire the deft spice delivery, but..... 41%

BRENNEREI HÜBNER

➤ **Frankischer Whisky (67.5) n15 t17.5 f18 b17.** Well, that was different. Can't really give you tasting notes as such, as I don't really have a reference point as to where to start. Quite simply, a bunch of bizarre aromas and flavours, the vast majority of which I have never encountered before. Another distillery I must seek and visit to find out what all this is about... 40%

➤ **Hubner Los Nr 3 (80.5) n20 t22.5 f18 b20.** Overwhelmed by fruit as far as complexity is concerned, but there is a distinctive smoky, salivating theme to this nonetheless. The balance has been trashed and if it were a novel, you'd have to read it three times...and still make no sense of it. A David Lynch film of a whisky...and I love it, though I have no idea why. 40%

BRENNEREI LOBMÜLLER

➤ **Lobmüller Single Grain Schwäbischer Whisky** fass no. 6 **(83) n20 t22 f20.5 b20.5.** A big toffee presence softens the impact and helps steer this towards a gentle, pleasantly sweet whisky. 41%

BRENNEREI MARTIN ZIEGLER

➤ **Esslinger Single Malt Aged 8 Years** db **(85) n20.5 t22 f21 b21.5.** Malty, nutty, a decent degree of sweetness and toffee marzipan. A well-made malt which you appreciate more as you acclimatise to its compact style. 42%

BRENNEREI RABEL

➤ **Rabel Schwarbischer Whisky (72.5) n15 t20 f18.5 b19.** Only for the feints-hearted. A bit of oily cocoa around, though. 40%

BRENNEREI SCHRAML

➤ **Stonewood 1818 (91) n22.5** delicious lemon curd tart and egg custard tart mix; **t23** sharp as a knife citrus cuts through any oak trying to make a showing: refreshing and with a spot-on degree of sweetness to balance; **f22.5** a touch of spice kicks in, as does a mild degree of oily feints on which the vanillas thrive; **b23** consistant throughout with a superb and endearing degree of sweetness. High quality stuff. 45%

BRENNEREI VOLKER THEURER Tübingen-Unterjesingen. Working.

➤ **Blackhorse Ammertal (83) n21 t21.5 f20 b20.5.** A big puncher, this, with a coastal saline, phenolic uppercut amid the sugary jabs. 40%

BRENNEREI ZAISER

- **Zaiser Schwabischer Whisky (83)** n23 t21.5 f19 b19.5. Surprisingly dry and constricted in development considering the beautiful soft sugars on the nose which also boast excellent clarity. 40%

COILLMOR

- **Coillmor Bavarian Single Malt** American white oak cask, distilled Mar 06 **(82)** n17.5 t22 f21 b21.5. The superb honey delivery on the palate goes some way to make up for the drying tobacco aroma. 43%

- **Coillmor Bavarian Single Malt** Bordeux cask, dist 18 Mar 06, bott code LB0109 **(40)** n10 t10 f10 b10. The French wine industry should never be let anywhere near any country's whisky, unless under the strictest supervision. Absolutely appalling degree of sulphur...about as bad as it gets... 43%. 380 bottles.

- **Coillmor Bavarian Single Malt** sherry cask, dist 05 May 06, bott code LB0109 **(89)** n21 a slight feinty note does its best to knock the superb grape off course...and fails; t22.5 silky barley copes with the feints efficiently, leaving the grape to move in for the juicy kill; f23 a beautiful sweetness to the finale, with gristy malt and sultanas hand-in-hand while the spices seep in from the oak and feints; b23 far from flawless. But you can't ignore the beauty of much of what happens here. 43%. 900 bottles.

- **Coillmor Bavarian Single Malt** sherry cask, dist May 06 **(90)** n21.5 the flawless richness of the grape does all that is possible to overcome the poor nose to the distillate; a strange kind of oily praline cocoa note is the very acceptable hybrid... t23.5 sweet and oily delivery blossoms out into a real old-fashioned fruitcake complete with seriously burnt raisin; beautiful weight and mouth-feel and the gathering spice is a perfect compliment; f22 those slight flaws from the distillate gather at the back of the throat but elsewhere the fruit remains luxurious and high class; b23 excellent: that seriously works....!!! Oh, if only the Scots could come up with a sherry butt of such faultless beauty... 55%

DESTILLERIE HERMANN MÜHLHAUSER

- **Muhlhauser Scwabischer Whisky aus Korn (90)** n22.5 good grief: distilled haystacks... the closest aroma to working on a farm stacking bales since my early youth...; t23 gorgeous gristy wholemeal liberally sugared; f22 some slight feinty oils mix with a light saltiness and drying oak b22.5 so different! If you are into this, it'll be pastoral perfection. 40%

DESTILLERIE WARTMANNSROTH

- **Bischof's Rhoner Whisky (75.5)** n18 t19.5 f19 b19. Rich and chewy, especially the toffee, but all a tad too feinty. 40%

FEINDISTILLERIE GASTHOF-REST

- **Feindistillerie Schwabischer Whisky** Lot 120705 **(78.5)** n19 t20 f19 b19.5. Heavy, oily and with much nougat to chew on. 40%

GUTSBRENNEREI

- **HFG Gutsbrennerei Aglishardt (86.5)** n22 t21 f22 b21.5. Clean, fruity and not entirely without some Fisherman's Friend phenol. A real juicy job. 40%

PRIVATBRENNEREI SONNENSCHEIN

- **Sonnenschein 15 (79.5)** n19.5 t21 f19 b20. So, it's back!! In its youth, this was a tough whisky to entertain. Many years on and some of the old faults remain, but it has picked up a touch of elegance along the way. 41%

SLYRS

Slyrs Bavarian Single Malt 2004 L26143 **(92.5)** n22.5 really expansive oak leaning enticingly towards floral; t23 the oaks stake their claim on delivery but soon allow malty and then honeyed settlers to flourish; the early middle becomes wondrously juicy for a malt which starts so dry – real class at work...; f23.5 now really hits top gear as both oak and barley scuttle off into varying degrees of bitter-sweet complexity; for a while the juicy barley stays the course but fades as the vanillas thicken; b23.5 by far the best malt I have encountered in bottled form from this distillery. Also probably the driest as oak and barley form a happy alliance to create maximum balance. This is the bottling which announced this distillery's greatness. A German treasure. 43%

Slyrs Bavarian Single Malt 2005 L13157 **(80.5)** n20 t20 f21.5 b19. Oily and off centre, an injudicious cut at the stills has taken away any chance of repeating the elegance and excellence of the previous bottling. Big barley ensures it remains drinkable and towards the finish is particularly enjoyable. *43%*

Slyrs Edition Dallmayr 2004 bott 07 **(92) n22** spicy and floral, the barley sub-plot offers a gently oiled edge; **t23.5** quite massive delivery: the barley is, literally, in concentrate form and the blistering spices zapping into the roof of the mouth towards the middle and onwards are a delight; amid all that comes legions of **f23.5** evidence of cocoa butter amid the vanilla and butterscotch. The barley really does take some shaking off. of medium sweetness, you never do.... **b23** another quite stunning offering from this distillery found in the heart of Bavaria. The spices, aided by the full strength, really are majestic. But it's not all about Wagnerian drama: the charm, subtlety and near romance of barley is pure Richard Strauss. *55%*

SPREEWALDBRENNEREI

⬩⬩ **Sloupisti 4 Years (88.5) n22** some kind of wine cask – gloriously unsulphured!! – is working overtime to outdo the grain for the cleanest hit on the nose; **t22** mouthwatering and chewy, there is an immense, clean fruitiness to this which is accompanied by sympathetic spices **f22** a cherry-chocolate finale; **b22.5** very much grows on you: it is obvious the distillers have worked very hard to get both distillation and maturation right. *40%*

⬩⬩ **Sloupisti 4 Years (cask strength) (94) n23** huge...some of you who were tasting whisky over 20 years ago might remember a sherry cask Glengarioch showing just this kind of massive and compelling personality; **t24** the enormity of this whisky hints towards almost something vaguely phenolic mixing in with the lush grape (Glengarioch again!) **f23** chocolate and raisins in concentrated form; **b24** a mind-blowing fruitfest. Just love the clarity in the flavours. This is such great fun....!! *64.8%*

UNIVERSITÄT HOHENHEIM

Hohenheim Universität Single Malt (82) n21 t20 f20 b21. The aroma is atractively nutty, marzipan even, and clean; the taste offers gentle oak, adding some weight to an otherwise light, refreshing maltiness. Pleasant if unspectacular. *40%. Made at the university as an experiment. Later sold!*

LATVIA

L B Lavijas Belzams (83) n20 t22 f20 b21. Soft and yielding on the palate, this is said to be made from Latvian rye, though of all the world's rye whiskies this really does have to be the softest and least fruity. I'll be astonished if there isn't a fair degree of thinning grain in there, too. *40%*

LIECHTENSTEIN
TELSER

⬩⬩ **Telsington (94) n23** rarely are Pinot Noirs particularly salty. And never, in my experience, smoky. Yet salt and light iodine abound in a seaweedy coastal romp. The fruity does turn up, but only once the nose has accustomed itself to the massive onslaught it has faced. Welcome to whisky from Lichtenstein...and it has not arrived quietly... **t23.5** the tastebuds are immediately enveloped in the most slinky of fruity gloves – and yet at the same time a fruit rock-hard one...Pinot at play..!! To complicate matters, the vague smokiness drifts around, landing feeble slaps and punches. And on another layer altogether a juicier barley note abounds: what a delight... **f23.5** although a certain bitterness from the oak comes into play, it is supremely controlled by the deft fruit and barley which play a similar tune to earlier, except now more softly **b24** now here's a conundrum if not irony. The first ever whisky from probably the most land-locked country in the whole of Europe, and it has the aroma of a rock pool found on a Hebridean island of about the same, tiny size. As for the whisky? What can I say? The last time I stayed in this beautiful, idiosyncratic country I had no option other than to spend the night in the worst hotel I have encountered in the western world. Thankfully the new distillery does not perform to such pitiful standards. This is not just good whisky, it is outstanding: far, far better than it has any right to be at first attempt. Obviously a fourth visit to Vaduz is now called for: this whisky is worth another night of misery and rudeness. I seriously need to shake the hand of the distiller...this is the most entertainingly delicious whisky I have tasted from mainland Europe this year. *40%*

THE NETHERLANDS
US HEIT DISTILLERY Bolsward. Working.

Frysk Hynder Frisian Single Malt Whisky dist 05 Nov 03, bott 01 Dec 06 **(87) n22.5** elegantly malty and delicately oaked; **t21.5** again the malts pack the punch and after a rather off-balanced delivery, it steadies itself for a wonderfully rich middle; **f22** back to the same malt-oak mix as on the nose, though the oak has the bigger say here; **b21.5** doesn't even begin to try to be complex. Almost opulently simplistic with its thick barley-oak theme. But well made and perhaps too easily quaffable. *40%.*

SPAIN

∴ **DYC Aged 8 Years (90) n22** a charming meeting of delicate barley and equally light vanilla; **t23** more of the same, with a silky soft grain element totally in tune with the clean juiciness of the malt; **f22.5** more of the same, with a Victoria sponge creamy strawberry note; **b22.5** I really am a sucker for clean, cleverly constructed blends like this. Just so enjoyable! *40%*

∴ **DYC Pure Malt (84.5) n20 t21 f21.5 b21.** I admit it's been a few years since I visited the distillery, but from what I then tasted in their warehouses I am surprised that they have not brought out their own single malt to mark the 50th anniversary of the place. This, which contains a percentage of Scotch, I believe, is OK. But no better than what I remember sampling. *40%*

∴ **DYC Selected Blend (86) n21.5 t22 f21 b21.5.** Although still a bantamweight and remains its old refreshing self, has definitely muscled out slightly on nose, delivery and finish....with a distinct hint of smoke. Unquestionably a bigger DYC than before. *40%*

SWEDEN

Mackmyra Preludium 04 Svensk Single Malt Whisky bott 11 Apr 07 db **(91) n22** heavy oils of the small pot but more of a Lubec marzipan to this guy, rather than the usual curious smoky aromas; **t23** enormous body with the barley showing a thickness of character that requires a gently oiled oakiness to penetrate; the bitter-sweet ration is again spot on; **f23** no shortage of cocoa oils and delicate maple syrup sweetness to the retreating barley; **b23** most distilleries have a trademark character, but Mackmyra's is entirely unique. What is becoming clear now is a density to the malt matched nowhere else. I admit: I adore it...! *53.3%*

Mackmyra Preludium 05 Svensk Single Malt Whisky bott 08 Aug 07 db **(87) n22** thick, mildly burnt honeycomb and chocolate and that peculiarly attractive Mackmyra oil; **t21** very odd delivery, with those coppery oils just having too big a say, though the barley returns to restore parity with a deftly sweet touch; **f22** much better, with the vanilla siding with the barley to up the complexity; **b22** a thinner, more metallic beast but still an enormous mouthful that never seems to taste the same twice. *48.4%*

Mackmyra Preludium 06 Svensk Single Malt Whisky bott 06 Nov 07 db **(87.5) n22** soft honey and a touch of wallpaper paste fixing it to the barley; **t22.5** light, molten muscovado sugars and maple syrup; good spice to liven things up; **f21** dries a tad too energetically as the oak engulfs; **b22** always pleasant, always showing a good mouthfeel yet somehow – by Mackmyra standards – doesn't quite get out of third gear. *50.5%*

Mackmyra Privus 01 Topp Tunnor bott 06 Mar 07 db **(91) n24** astonishing array of herbal and fruity tones: plum pudding and creamed rice but the complexity heightened by astonishing oaky-woody notes like no other whisky on earth; bitter-sweet ration: near perfection... **t24** no less fantastic delivery, again with the controlled explosion of sweetness totally in sync with more aggressive,drier herbal tones; there is one enormous wave of oak which is met by countering soft oils; **f21** just loses the balance slightly as the dryness takes control as those strange and varied herbal/woody tones take greater weight; **b22** no other whisky on the planet matches this in style. It takes some getting used to....but it's worth it! *54.5%*

Mackmyra Privus 02 Näsa För Sprit bott 07 Mar 07 db **(94) n23** nutty on several levels, from dry, barely sweetened marzipan to diced hazelnut; some of the famous Mackmyra oils are present but so is a dull malty sweetness; all balanced by an injection of orange peel; **t24** mouth-filling and mouth-watering, this is simply a pantone book of delicate sugars, though the nutty ones are there in greater numbers; there is even a gristy streak to this; **f23** a gentleman of a finale, dying by degrees over a long period with each sweet nutty note bidding its adieu.. **b24** excellent balance from first to last, poise, charm and idiosyncrasy are there in equal measures. Quite simply makes my whisky tasting year complete to find something so unique – and astonishing. *54.5%*

Mackmyra Privus 03 Rökning Tillåten bott 08 Mar 07 db **(96) n24** peat – Mackmyra style! That means both boldness and delicate tones moulded together – and something herbal just to offer a unique slant; **t24** unusual dryness to the smoke; soft oils help spread the phenols and varied herbal oaky notes in equal measure; but there has to be balance and that comes in ample waves of manuka honey **f24** remains dry and long with the smoke prevailing, a vaguely gristy barley providing sufficient sweetness for balance. Every single flavour wave offers something different from any other whisky's end: the marriage between oak and smoke has an organic bond matched nowhere else; **b24** previously at Mackmyra: fruity, then nutty. Now this. Sensational. Because this is no "me too" whisky. It challenges, asks questions, makes statements. Every expression appears to further and expand my own experience and expectations of whisky, which really is saying something. 56%

⌐ **Mackmyra Privus 04 Ratta Virket** bott 28 Jan 08 db **(95) n24** here we go again.... hang on to your bonfire hats: we're in for another big ride! The smoke is sharp and purposeful: it is busy with things to do and noses to attack. No shrinking violet, this one; one moment offers butter on Arbroath Smokies, the next we are talking dank, earthy forests. And then distant bonfires...wonderful and just so evocative; **t24** attacks almost like a heavily-smoked blended Scotch with a first class bite. The peat wells and swells and offers degrees of oil and hickory; the bitter-sweet resonance almost shakes the body; just the odd dab of citrus lightens matters; **f23** a hugely enjoyable laying down of arms as the earlier welter of blows to the tastebuds give ways to a series of caresses. The citrus is toned up and the smoke down while soft vanillins continue the bitter-sweet theme; **b24** wonderfully raw, almost untamed, around the edges and quite impossible not to love. 55%

Mackmyra Privus 05 Reserve Svensk Single Cask Malt Whisky bodas gruvlager, flask nr. 17/49 db **(93) n22.5** honeycomb and chocolate with some gorgeous spice prickle and a touch of kumquat: being Mackmyra, none of the notes are what you'd normally find – there's an earthier touch here; also being Mackmyra there is a superb herbal chapter to this tale; **t23** beautifully rich delivery with a just-so intensity to the barley, the oak gives an early onslaught of spice and cocoa, again with an orangey-citrus sub strata – like a Jaffa Cake on steroids; **f23.5** the early finish really is the highlight of this dram: like an autumn fall on the palate with a spectacular changing of tones as its life begins to end. The complexity goes through the roof, the various strands and degrees of intensity of the oak is both sexy and compelling; **b24** it is entirely impossible not to be head over heals in love with this whisky. This is a malt which makes one bold statement after another: the only thing it has in common with sitting on the fence is the degree of splinters you get. Big oak, yes. But even bigger flavour development from elsewhere. 54%

Mackmyra Privus 06 I Bergakungens Sal bott 28 Jan 08 db **(93.5) n22.5** a complex interweaving of fruity and salty notes: something wonderfully coastal about this in the manner old, peatless Bunnhabhain so often used to be; **t23.5** juicy at first then a bombardment of spices (including a brief puff of smoke), again pepped by salt, followed by several layers of rich barley of varying degrees of sweetness; the degree of soft oils is exemplary; **f23** long with a withering vanilla kick showing some age coming through; light mocha in this most delicate finale... **b24.5** sober and sultry by Mackmyra standards. No grand statements, no sweeping aromas or flavours taking all before it. Thoughtful, sophisticated and very high class whisky. 54.5%

Mackmyra Reserve "The Smokey Duck" cask no 36/48, dist Sep 03, bott Sep 07 db **(93) n22.5** the smoke is browbeaten by the chunky oak; even so citrus makes waves as does soft barley; **t23.5** massive delivery making no apology for its startling oak theme: lazy oils help spread the weight about but the slow build up of spices is simply dazzling, seeming to magnify, somehow, the thick marmalade/citrus strands; **f24** drier oaks now, as to be expected, but the build up of the cocoa is simply brilliant. Very unusually the sweetness appears to re-enter the mix with a smoky farewell that stokes up the brown sugars and honeyed bourbon; **b23.5** back in my own tasting rooms this comes across as a far better dram than when I first tasted it in Sweden. This is a private bottling to be found in Avesta, Sweden: on first taste (as in Sweden) the oak appears simply too inelegant, almost brutal. However, twenty minutes alone with this one with no other distractions other than a spittoon and you'll be amazed how the complexity crystalises and it all makes sense. Superb. 57%

Mackmyra Whisky Svensk Single Malt Den Forsta Utgavan bodas gruva, batch no. 08-01 db **(91) n22.5** salted buttered toast, a diced, wet vanilla pod and a non-specific sweetness – not quite honey, not quite syrup, not quite honey, not quite barley (well, maybe a touch of barley)....just sweet; **t23** gentle, well-mannered, barley driven...just so un-Mackmya...!! **f22.5** light, mainly oak oriented with the accent of delicate barley edging towards a late, surprising juiciness – all with a touch of cocoa; **b23** how ironic that after all the Privus (or should that be Previ...?) and Preludiums, each howling wolves which blew your socks off, the first whisky to be produced for relative mass market by Mackmyra standards should be pure, playful pussy. That said, when it comes this elegant and demure, and just sings and purrs prettily to you - is there anything more sexy....? 46.1%

Mackmyra Whisky Svensk Single Malt Den Forsta Utgavan bodas gruva, batch no. 08-02 db **(90) n21.5** unusual tobacco smoke amid the malt and vanilla: small still character yet surprisingly light for the distillery; **t23** returns to heart-winning ways with a genuinely juicy delivery bordered by the vaguest smoke and a marmalade sharpness; the honey notes are thick and barley rich; **f23.5** magnificently well weighted and balanced with stunning bitter-sweet echoes. Loads of cocoa dust which just puts the perfect cap on the rich barley, which has to be among the most intense I have tasted this year. The oak also offers a lively chewiness and vanilla depth; **b23** taste two or three times before getting into the rhythm of this malt. Once there, you'll be hooked. More greatness from Mackmyra. 46.1%

SWITZERLAND
BRAUEREI LOCHER Appenzell. Working.

◌ **Säntis Malt Swiss Highlander Edition Dreifaltigkeit (96.5) n24** fantastic mixture of apple-wood style smoke (this is very similar, almost identical in fact, to the smell from the bonfires burned by my late father at his Surrey allotment in the early 60s, and, yes, I think old branches from our apple tree often went up in smoke) and something a bit earthier – obviously the peat. Like a Rupp Cheese of malty heat; **t24.5** this is truly astonishing: the weight of oil on the palate is gentle but sufficient to coat the mouth; next comes a layer of mixed smoke, both woody and earthy; this is followed by a layering of caramelized molasses; an indecipherable fruitiness makes itself heard, while spices pepper the palate like so many small asteroids hitting a small planet.... **f24** a near faultless finale (perhaps a degree of overenthusiastic bitterness), though the experience is so long and seamless, it is hard to know where the main body of the flavours are and when the finish begins... **b24** this is one of the whiskies of the year, without question. Such is the controlled enormity, the sheer magnitude of what we have here, one cannot help taste the whisky with a blend of pleasure and total awe. 52%

◌ **Säntis Malt Swiss Highlander Edition Säntis** oak beer casks **(88) n22.5** charming, delicate, smoked apple wood; **t23** clean, mouthwateringly fresh. A hint of green fig on the silky texture, sweetened slightly by diluted golden syrup; a light touch of phenols hang in the background; **f20.5** a touch of oaky, toasty bitterness; **b22** light, fruity and impressive. 40%

◌ **Säntis Malt Swiss Highlander Edition Sigel** oak beer casks **(91.5) n23.5** though matured in oak beer casks, this appears to be screaming grape from the glass: one sniff of this cleanest of aromas and you simply can't stop salivating **t23** beautiful again: clean, melt-in-the-mouth malt combined with a juicy fruitiness and light spice; **f22** lots of vanillas represents the oak in the friendliest manner; the spice has intensified and now adds some welcome prickle; **b23** high quality whisky which balances with aplomb. 40%

BRENNEREI HOLLEN Lauwil. Working.

◌ **Hollen Single Malt Aged Over 6 Years** matured in red wine casks db **(89) n23** another sublime fruit-riddled number. Not a single degree of sulphur or off-note from the distillate makes this a joy. The most distant echo of something vaguely smoky; **t22.5** stunning delivery on the palate again with a vague phenol to be detected with the ultra-clean grape; a soft spice buzz delivers into the middle ground **f21.5** some natural caramel kicks in to blot out the juices; **b22** perhaps the fruit is rather too emphatic and, a late show of spice apart, some of the other forms of character development you might wish to see are lacking. Apparently peatless. Possibly, but not entirely convinced. 42%

◌ **Hollen Single Malt Aged Over 6 Years** smoke malt, matured in white wine casks db **(92) n23.5** highly complex: the faintest of peaty touches wrestles for a leading spot amid the vanilla and crisp barley...and if that wasn't enough a soft grape presence muddies the waters further; **t23** this must have been one very juicy bunch of casks they found: sweet grape abounds, though a bit of tannin bitterness present, too; a light smokiness on delivery vanishes under the grapey onslaught; **f22.5** pretty long with a butterscotch-truffle fade; **b23** you just can't really fault this stuff. 42%

◌ **Hollen Single Malt Aged Over 6 Years** matured in white wine casks db **(90.5) n23** rum, anyone? Especially if you fancy a Jamaican pot still; **t23.5** be prepared to drown in your own saliva...one of the juiciest whiskies ever. And I mean ever...the fruit is so ridiculously clean, it could be some fruit candy **f21.5** to many a purist so clean and flat; almost a chewy fruit toffee element; **b22.5** many facets to its personality, the nose especially, shows more rum characteristics than malt. A won't-say-no glassful if ever there was one, though, and made and matured to the highest order. Indeed, as I taste and write this, my BlackBerry informs me that Roger Federer is on his way to another Wimbledon title: the similarities in the quiet dignity, elegance and class of both Swiss sportsman and whisky is not such a corny comparison. 42%

◌ **Hollen Single Grain Aged Over 6 Years** db **(86.5) n22.5 t21.5 f21 b21.5.** Big, sharp and bruising. The odd feint kick here and there, but there is a pleasing chocolate fruit and nut touch to this one, too. 51.6%

❖ **Hollen Single Wheat Malt Aged Over 6 Years** db **(74) n18 t19.5 f18 b18.5.** Oooops! Bitter, off-key....Even Federer has his off days....and I've just read that over at Wimbledon Roddick is storming to the fourth set...these things happen. (see Hollen White Wine Cask) 42%

BRENNEREI SCHWAB Oberwil. Working.

❖ **Bucheggberger Single Malt** cask no. 23, bott no. 10 **(74) n17 t21 f17 b19.** Decent malty lead, but the intensely bitter finish makes hard work of it. 42%

BRENNEREI URS LÜTHY

❖ **Dinkel Whisky** pinot noir cask **(92.5) n23** lusty, clean fruit: the grapes appear to be sultana-sweet and beautifully spiced; clean and complex **t24** lush, warmingly-spiced grape – as promised on the nose – medium-thick oils and a wonderful transformation into a coffee and fruit cake mix; the barley scuttles out from this enormous mix to make its mark near the middle ground, **f22** a touch of bitterness creeps in, but some mocha-grape holds firm; **b23.5** a big, striking malt which is not afraid to at times make compellingly beautiful statements. 61.5%

❖ **Wyna Whisky Original No. 2** dist Apr 06, bott Apr 09 **(79) n21 t21 f18 b19.** Fruity, but seriously overcooks the bitterness. 43%. 489 bottles.

BURGDORFER GASTHAUSBRAUEREI

❖ **Reiner Burgdorfer 5 Years Old** cask no. 4 **(82.5) n18 t22 f21 b21.5.** Recovers from the mildly feinty nose to register some wonderfully lush cocoa notes throughout the coppery, small still development on the palate. 43%

DESTILLERIE EGNACH

❖ **Thursky** lot no. 019857 K03 **(93) n24** all kinds of big fruit-edged bourbon notes; liquorice and honeydew melon; some lychee and marzipan add wonderfully to the mix; even a slightly rummy style to this; **t23.5** silky, estery with a controlled sweetness; again there is a lovely bourbon-fruit interaction, perhaps more on the red liquorice honeycomb bourbon style; **f22.5** some oak begins to bite but the honeyed sheen and light mint-cocoa dusting keeps the whisky honest; **b23** what a clean, beautifully even whisky! I am such a sucker for that clean fruity-spice style. Brilliant! 40%

BRENNEREI-ZENTRUM BAUERNHOF Zug. Working.

Swissky db **(91) n23** young, clean, fresh malt which sparkles with a hint of apple: one of the best noses on the European scene; **t23** stunningly clean arrival and then the most delicate of malty displays that all hinges around a juicy youth to the barley. The sweetness is controlled, refined and evenly distributed; a soft oiliness helps to lubricate the tastebuds; **f22** no less soft and simple with the oak offering the kind of weight that can barely be detected; **b23** while retaining a distinct character, this is the cleanest, most refreshing malt yet to come from mainland Europe. Hats off to Edi Bieri for this work of art. Moving stuff. 42%

Swissky Exklusiv Abfüllung L3365 **(94) n23** more intrinsic barley than previous years; the oak offers the perfect frame for the diced, slightly spiced apples and pears; **t23** mouthwatering, beautifully clean barley in Swissky's classic style; **f24** drier, vanilla-led but the waves of rich barley and delicate oak seem endless; **b24** a supremely distilled whisky with the most subtle oak involvement yet. Year after year this distillery bottles truly great single malt, a benchmark for Europe's growing band of small whisky distillers. 40%

HAGEN DISTILLERY Huettwilen. 1919. Working.

❖ **Hagen's Best Whisky No. 2** Lot 00403/04-03-08.08 **(87) n19** heavy, toffee; **t23.5** rich textured malt with a delightful touch of muscovado sugar and a main theme of chocolate nougat; purposeful and confident; **f22** a slight bitterness, but competently handled by those delicate sugars and gristy malt; **b22.5** much more Swiss, small still style than previous bottling and although the nose isn't quite the most enticing, the delivery and follow through are a delight. Lovely whisky. 42%

❖ **Hagen's Best Whisky Oak Special** Lot 3031/03.03 -12.07 **(84) n21 t21.5 f20.5 b21.** A very well made, sweet, uncomplicated malt matured in a thoroughly used bourbon barrel – or so it seems. Not sure if this is a compliment or not, but could easily be mistaken for some kind of Speyside single malt whisky destined for a young blend. 42%

HR Distillery lott no. 10099, dist Dec 99, bott Jan 05 db **(88) n21** clean, fine malt. Crisp with a degree of fruit, especially freshly bitten green apple. Some soft dough adds the extra depth; **t23** mouthwatering and deft, this offers a butterfly delivery of sweet young malt backed again by that apple-fresh fruitiness; **f22** lovely delivery of vanilla which balances just so well with the barley; **b22** again we have an enormously impressive whisky from Switzerland. Here we have a classic case of a whisky that has matured for a few years side by side with fruit spirit (probably apple) and has breathed in some of those delicate elements. *42%*

HUMBEL SPEZIALITÄTENBRENNEREI

⸭ **Farmer's Club Finest Blended (85.5) n22 t22 f20.5 b21.** Clean, well made, astonishingly Scotch-like in its style. In fact, possibly the cleanest whisky made on mainland Europe. Lashings of butterscotch and soft honey; even a coppery sheen while the oak makes delightful conversation. But there appears to be lots of caramel which dulls things down somewhat. *40%*

⸭ **Ourbeer Single Malt (84) n21 t20.5 f21.5 b21.** Once more very well made with some entertaining spice. But the caramels have way too much to say for themselves *43%*

SPEZIALITÄTENBRENNEREI ZURCHER Port. Working.

⸭ **Zürcher Single Lakeland 3 Years Old** dist Jul 06, bott Jul 09 db **(88.5) n21.5** thickset and quite handsome in a rugged, yeasty, honeycombed way; **t23** comes into its own with a real red liquorice and nougat middle; oily, nutty with a touch of redcurrant jam towards the middle; **f21.5** mainly vanilla, but the nutty nougat hangs around **b22.5** this distillery never fails to entertain. Not as technically perfect as usual, but none of the blemishes are seriously damaging and even add a touch of extra character. *42%*

Zürcher Single Lakeland Malt Whisky 3 Years Old dist Sep 04, bott Sep 07 **(83) n21 t22 f20 b20.** Enjoys some highly attractive moments when that famous grape-barley gets into full swing. But a sub-standard barrel has done a little damage here. *42%*

Zürcher Single Lakeland Malt Whisky 3 Years Old dist Jun 05, bott Jun 08 **(91.5) n23** complex weights: the much lighter barley and heftier fruit dovetail superbly. Some custard and rhubarb crumble offers a lovely touch; **t23** immediately mouth-watering. Despite the small still clumsiness, the enormity of the barley and grape dexterity just blows you away; **f22.5** long with the grape fading towards a warmer character and the oak injecting a chewy degree of bitter-sweet depth; **b23** stunning clarity to the fruit ensures a malt which simply sings on the palate. The fruit-barley balance is quite exceptional, though not surprising from this highly impressive distillery. *42%*

WHISKY CASTLE Elfingen. Working.

8820 Whisky 1378 tage im fass (days in cask) db **(87) n20** vaguely piny and herbal; **t22** massive malt that sweetens with each crashing wave. The opening is typically European, threatens to turn nasty but in seconds changes direction and goes into malty overdrive; **f23** fabulous oak interaction as vanilla and very dry walnut and date cake; **b22** one of those whiskies that grow on you once you understand that it has a different viewpoint. Hugely entertaining. *55%. For Wadi Brau Wadenswil.*

Castle Hill Whisky nummer 4, 1125 tage im fass **(93) n22** big barley from a small still. There is a copperish element to this, plus a nutty intonation. Something to really get the nose into; **t24** near perfect delivery: the full mouthfeel is stunning. Perfectly weighted, just the right degree of natural sweetness and the most glorious barley development; **f23** a light finale yet the waves of sweet peat and vanilla are almost endless. Long, charming and a magic wand waved over the degree of gristy sweetness; **b24** has someone moved Cardhu to Switzerland??? I am truly astonished. I have missed out on nummers 2&3 (but I'm hunting!), but this is so far removed from nummer 1 that they are hardly worth comparison. One of the cleanest, most malt intense and unerringly delightful whiskies you will find in Europe and would be a title contender but for the slightly more elegant Swissky. Reaffirmation, that Switzerland is the finest producer of malt whisky on mainland Europe. *40%*

⸭ **Double Wood Castle Hill Single Malt** cask no. 400 **(83) n21 t20 f21 b21.** Oily, fruity, a tad feinty. *43%*

⸭ **Edition Käser Castle One Single Malt** cask no. 406 **(94) n23** chocolate nougat, complete with fruit and nuts... and a few green figs thrown in for good measure; **t23.5** big, grapey, quasi-smoky take off, exploding with massive juice and barley on impact with the tastebuds: mind-bogglingly mouthwatering; **f23.5** some cocoa coats the light fruit and soft vanillas; as seemingly unending as a Federer finish at Wimbledon; **b24** another astonishing whisky from this top-rate distillery. *70.6%*

⸭ **Smoke Rye Whisky Castle Single Malt** cask no. 338 **(90.5) n21.5** the apple-fruity ryes take off in the glass as the heavier of the light feints evaporate in the open air; the smoke appears of a woody – as in smoked cheese - rather than peaty type; **t23.5** juicy, lush and crisp rye of the top order: seriously salivating. Its stretching wings are clipped though by the brooding phenols; **f22.5** some serious cocoa notes dig in and an outbreak of vanilla adds a drying balance; **b23** this will not be to everyone's liking: the distinctive nose alone is not entirely blemish free (though leave a glass of it in a very warm room for about half an hour and most of those blemishes will have vanished) but, like the tale which unfurls on the palate, it is very different, never less than fascinating and sometimes hits the point of high deliciousness. *43%*

❖ **Smoke Spelt Whisky Castle Single Malt** cask no. 336 **(71) n16 t19 f18 b18.** Never, ever, have I smelt the countryside so emphatically in a glass than with this whisky. Fusty hay. In concentrate. Amazing: liquid Constable. Also parts of the aroma is pure malting floors. Sadly, though, I am not convinced all this is entirely intentional: it also appears like some kind of infection has got in somewhere during the brewing process. If there is confirmation, it is from the slightly rancid nut oil on the taste. Yet for all the low scores and negatives, I also recognize certain elements on both nose and taste which are beautiful, or at least potentially so. Certainly unique. There again, I can't remember the last time I came across smoked spelt.... I really want to see these guys try this one again and see what happens. Maybe this is the way it does turn out. Or maybe it will prove to be an invaluable and idiosyncratic addition to the whisky lexicon. The earth may or may not move for you with this one. But at least there is proof that it is still going round.... *43%*

WALES

Penderyn bott code Jan 07 db **(88) n21 t23 f22 b22.** The flavour profile is all upfront. Quite charming, though. *46%. ncf.*

Penderyn bott code Feb 07 db **(89) n22 t22 f22 b23.** Elegant and understated all the way. *46%. ncf.*

Penderyn bott code Mar 07 db **(90) n21 t22 f24 b23.** High quality, softly spoken malt. *46%. ncf.*

Penderyn bott code Apr 07 db **(76) n18 t21 f18 b19.** Hmmm. Oily, a touch hot, bitter and even an unusual hint of feint. Hardly your classic Penderyn. *46%. ncf.*

Penderyn bott code May 07 db **(92) n21 t23 f24 b24.** Normal, quite beautiful service has been resumed...! *46%. ncf.*

Penderyn bott code Jun 07 db **(95) n23.5** some seriously cranked up fruitiness here: one of the freshest noses for a while; **t24.5** improbably salivating: the freshness to the fruit is near faultless yet the way it allows the oak to layer itself onboard for balance and complexity is awesome; **f23** long with a real bitter-sweet relationship between the fruit and oak; a few waves of barley can be heard for good measure; **b24** quite simply the best standard bottling yet. An all day every day dram. Welsh gold, indeed. *46%. ncf.*

Penderyn bott code Jul 07 db **(91) n22.5** classic fruity (berries as well as grape)/chalky dry mix. Busy and enticing; **t23** silky delivery with a chocolate mousse touch; **f23** long and juicy; **b23.5** a rich vein of form as well as Welsh Gold. There is a real confidence to this malt. *46%. ncf.*

Penderyn bott code Aug 07 db **(88) n22** impressively oaked; **t22.5** thuds into the tastebuds like an Ian Gough tackle...; softer fruits are nudged out by fudge; **f21.5** cream toffee with the odd raisin; **b22** a bit brooding and sulky. Takes some work to coax out its more gentle nature. *46%. ncf.*

Penderyn bott code Sep 07 db **(88.5) n22** pretty close relation to the previous bottling; **t23** big fruit statement from the first moment and a slow unfurling of pricklier spices: wonderful thrust and counter between the two; **f21.5** a touch of fudge coats the oak; **b22** *46%. ncf.*

Penderyn bott code Oct 07 db **(88.5) n22.5** dry oaked with fruity specks; **t22** the fruit leads, delicately, with toffee and vanilla right behind; **f22** cream toffee and vanilla; **b22** the third of perhaps the three most consistent bottlings in terms of style and quality since the distillery began bottling. *46%. ncf.*

Penderyn bott code Nov 07 db **(87) n21** thin and miserly; **t22.5** a barley fanfare heralds the soft fruit followed by a trufflesque bite; **f22** much silkier and more agreeable than the nose deserves; **b21.5** a bits and pieces rendition which in the end works attractively though it is a bit parsimonious early on when dealing out the complexity. *46%. ncf.*

Penderyn bott code 1 Dec 07 db **(92.5) n23.5** rich in both grape and a bourbony honeyness which dovetail elegantly; **t23.5** wow! Fabulous delivery with the grape fleetingly at its juiciest before being brought to order with vanilla and toffee; before it does, the honey promised on the nose flashes through; **f22.5** big vanilla shake down with a smudge of fudge for company; **b23** this one pulls out the stops to get the Madeira into full swing. *46%. ncf.*

Penderyn bott code 2 Dec 07 db **(92.5) n23** complex, not dissimilar to the small grains of a bourbon teasing away; the strands of fruit refuse to overwhelm and distort the picture; **t24** beautifully lush: one of the softest deliveries by the distillery with the malt cascading on to the tastebuds from the first nanosecond. The spiced Madeira is hanging to its tail; **f22** disappointingly dull by comparison though not with its vanilla-rich charms; **b23.5** truly magnificent in its complexity. *46%. ncf.*

Penderyn bott code 3 Dec 07 db **(85.5) n22 t21.5 f21 b21.** Rounded and soft. But rather too much fudge to make it a great malt. Unless you are fudge dependent... *46%. ncf.*

Penderyn bott code Jan 08 db **(94) n24** it's as easy to get lost in this nose as it is in some of the back roads of North Wales. Just the most delicate mixture of chocolate and gentle fruit. Intriguing, graceful and alluring, this is pure text book stuff. Worth 20 minutes of anyone's time... **t23** well balanced delivery with equal shares in the oak and fruit; the soft oils really do hit the spot; **f23** really goes to town now with the chocolate **b24** just dripping with class. *46%. ncf.*

Penderyn bott code Feb 08 db **(91) n23** first appears generous with the grape, but closer inspection reveals a charming and delicate nature; **t23** lush with a wonderful Jaffa cake sweetness and a touch of Lubec's top of the range; **f22.5** drier, soft vanillas and shovels on the elegance; **b22.5** yet another high performance malt from this distillery, though this one has much more a sherry than Madeira feel. *46%. ncf.*

Penderyn bott code Mar 08 db **(88.5) n23** back to unmistakenly Madeira, with a touch of apricot and lime with prickly spice; **t23** after the initial fruity avalanche much drier and flatter than the nose suggests; a touch of hickory bares its oaky teeth before some burnt fudge arrives; **f21** a slightly oily, toffeed fade; **b21.5** a very pleasant ride, but doesn't offer the scenery promised by the nose. *46%. ncf.*

Penderyn bott code Apr 08 db **(90) n23** so gentle: figs, limes, moist date – all on a bed of vanilla; **t23** gentle curves and soft, squidgy shapes appear on the palate as the rounder fruits hold sway; **f21.5** dries towards vanilla and toffee; **b22.5** such a relaxing dram. You've heard of an Indian Head Massage: well, this is a Welsh one. *46%. ncf.*

Penderyn bott code May 08 db **(92.5) n24** the grape comes exploding out at you: just so beautifully lush and hits that G spot where the grain and grape meet exactly in perfect harmony; **t23** pure silk as the Madeira really makes a game of it. Sweet with just enough bitterness for comfort and again the grain makes its way through the fruity onslaught; **f22.5** traces of toffee as the vanilla and spices dig deep; **b23** there is something about every second or third bottling that just makes you close your eyes and emit an involuntary groan of satisfaction. Here's another one... *46%. ncf.*

⫶⫶ **Penderyn** bott code June 08 db **(86.5) n21 t22.5 f21.5 b21.5.** A touch thinner than usual, allowing a lovely bite amid the blossoming fruity honey. *46%*

⫶⫶ **Penderyn** bott code Jul 08 db **(94.5) n22.5** light cocoa adds a drier texture to the plummy fruit; **t24** lush with a demure, stewed fruit sweetness; no surprise about the milky chocolate found in the middle ground; **f24** lengthy with enough gentle oil to keep those dreamy fruit notes gripped to the roof of the mouth. The butterscotch is lightly laced with cocoa, the complexity actually increasing with time, rather than dropping off; **b24** one of the finest Penderyns of them all: as complex, dark and intriguing as a Christian Bale character. *46%*

⫶⫶ **Penderyn** bott code Aug 08 db **(91) n22** much more of a bourbony statement made; **t23** juicy and salivating; the oaks nip and bite; **f23** more relaxed and positively grapey; the custardy notes are sweet and mildly sticky; **b23** in a month this whisky shows yet another fascinating said of its character. This is really fun stuff. *46%*

⫶⫶ **Penderyn** bott code Sept 08 db **(86) n21.5 t22 f21 b21.5.** Lots of fruity substance, at times lively, with a bigger say from drier vanillins. *46%*

⫶⫶ **Penderyn** bott code Nov 08 db **(89.5) n22** heavy, lush fruit, some of it citrusy, invigorated with the softest sprinkling of Demerara; the vanillas aren't remotely shy; **t23** sublime, mouth-filling delivery: a chewy experience with a distinct candy feel; a delicate throb of spice ups the complexity; **f22** surprisingly bitters out for a while: bitter marmalade softened by cream toffee; **b22.5** a busy, slightly off the wall bottling by Penderyn standards but a belter all the same. *46%*

⫶⫶ **Penderyn** bott code Dec 08 db **(90) n22** the citrus and grape are seen in a clearer perspective than normal; **t23** the influence of the Madeira comes into play from the first nanosecond – and stays right through, despite several gear changes in fruit intensity; a light milky, mocha sweetness towards the middle; **f22** old fashioned English (!) marmalade (sorry, Welsh people) with thick cut fruit, a persistent zesty bitterness and spices; **b23** the perfect breakfast malt... *46%*

⫶⫶ **Penderyn** bott code Jan 09 db **(89.5) n22** pretty sharp with a distinct nip in the air for the fruitier notes; **t23** the usual lushness on delivery, except here the fruit appears to have a wider remit to offer juicier, more bitter-sweet characteristics; an almost cleaner development showing some real fresh barley notes, too; **f22** the developing house style of bitter marmalade is with us again and it remains a treat; **b22.5** a zingy, lively bottling where the fruits really do get a free hand. 46%

⠐⠄ **Penderyn** bott code Feb 09 db **(93) n22.5** vanilla and custard enjoy a surprising dominance: a serious touch of Madeira trifle.. **t24** a fabulous clarity to the fruit: salivating on both a grapey-orangey score and with sublime barley and cocoa making the middle ground a complex place to be; **f23** a buzzy, busy spiciness. Again, the fruit which really impresses with its see-through juiciness over such a long period; **b23.5** a delicious malt which enjoys the clarity you sometimes feel after a heavy downpour. 46%

⠐⠄ **Penderyn** bott code Mar 09 db **(88) n21.5** a touch flatter than recent bottlings, clean but with mildly less definition; **t22.5** zingy for a split second, then one of the softest Penderyn deliveries: pure silk on the lazy fruits; **f22** straggly vanillas amid the late, tangy fruit; **b22** another lovely bottling, but less inclined towards the dazzling complexity of late. 46%

⠐⠄ **Penderyn** bott code May 09 db **(84.5) n20 t21 f22 b21.5.** Pleasant, and softly fruited – like a chewy candy. But the complexity levels are down and relatively ordinary by the outstanding distillery's own high standards. 46%

Penderyn bottle code 0411208 (750ml) db **(89) n23** perhaps for the US market a touch of bubble gum. Fruity, of course... **t23** seriously juicy grape (and even a hint of Kiwi fruit and greengages) but some toffee lurking around; **f21** caramel tart; **b22** a safe version that is performing elegantly but within itself. 46% (92 proof). ncf. Imported by Monsieur Henri Wine Company, New Orleans.

⠐⠄ **Penderyn** bottle code 1131008 (750ml) db **(93.5) n22.5** a dark, baritone undercurrent to this one: the mushy fruit occasionally flies off on a high one but elsewhere there is more persistent deep murmur of beautifully fused grape and cocoa; **t23.5** exactly the same on delivery: not often outside fresh oloroso that the evident fruit offers such deep base; the odd sparkier high notes carrying both grape and vanilla with aplomb. The middle ground fills in beautifully, shaped by soft oils and embracing the lightest of praline chocolate wafers; **f23.5** no high notes at all here: a long, persistent rumble of fruit and praline with a spot-on degree of sweetness. A creaseless experience: a gentle, almost erotic massaging of the tastebuds ...; **b24** the light cocoa infusion just tops this off perfectly. A truly classic Penderyn; more charm than Tom Jones, hitting just as many pure notes...and just being a fraction of his age 46% US Market.

Penderyn Cask Strength Rich Madeira db **(96.5) n24.5 t24 f24 b24.** Sadly, only three bottles of this were produced. Two were presented to directors of the company, the third to Prince Charles on the occasion of his visit to the distillery to officially open the Visitors' Centre. The remainder of this cask will eventually be bottled, though if quite as sublimely balanced as this I'll be surprised: I suspect this was a whisky plucked in full ripeness. Some of you may have seen on television a certain whisky writer enjoying this with Prince Charles and Penderyn blender Dr Jim Swann. I can tell you we were all genuinely stunned by it – even Jim Swann! Now having had time to study it in my own tasting lab, away from the lights, cameras and the principality's most expensive aftershave and perfume....well, it's even better than I remember it. If finer whisky has been bottled in Wales, then I wasn't alive at the time to see it. A prince of a Welsh whisky truly fit for the Prince of Wales. 577%. ncf. nc.

Penderyn Grand Slam 2008 Edition db **(88.5) n23** a real Madeira scrum with apricots and vanilla in the mix; **t23** beautiful harmony between the big fruit and a real bourbony, hickory-rich kick; **f21** toffee apple...with emphasis on the toffee; **b21.5** you'd think that to mark the winning of a Grand Slam, they'd bring out a real hefty, hairy-arsed dram full of spice and vim. But no: It's a gentle giant. Are they trying to suggest the Championship was won by craft, guile and an understated touch of class...? 46%. ncf.

Penderyn Peated Edition bott code Sep 07 db **(92.5) n23** the softest infusion of smoke appears to give a wonderful roof and cellar to the clean-fruited structure; **t24** voluptuous and instantly endearing with a fabulous almost gristy sweetness accentuating the barley and forming the perfect tandem with the grape; the accompanying spices excel; **f22.5** light, softly oiled and chewy to the last; **b23** not one for those who want their peat naked, but rather wearing something that is vaguely see-through in the soft light. 46%. ncf.

Penderyn Peated Edition bott code Dec 07db **(86.5) n21.5 t22.5 f21 b21.5.** Let's all play "Spot the Peat". It is there, of course, but rather than add an extra dimension, it appears to shield some of the usually more complex notes. Or is that the toffee on the finale...? 46%. ncf.

Penderyn Peated Edition bott code Apr 08 db **(78) n18.5 t20 f19.5 b19.** Oily, clanking, thick whisky. Pleasant in part but something here just doesn't add up – on the nose especially. The most unsubtle Penderyn of them all. 46%. ncf.

∵ **Penderyn Peated Edition** bott code May 09 db **(92) n23.5** that distinctive, light, clean coating of peat enjoys an improbable degree of balance between the sweeter and drier, chalky vanilla tones: the kind of aroma that temps you to keep your nose buried in the glass most of the day... **t23** the delivery is one of pure silk; eventually a juicier grassy barley element emerges with an almost apologetic smokiness hanging on to its coat-tail; **f22** that cocoa/mocha note found from time to time with Penderyn can be spotted here, too. Despite the rumble of spiced peat... **b23.5** for those not of a peaty disposition, don't let the nose worry you: it plays only a character rather than leading role on the palate. Beautiful, anytime whisky. 46%

∵ **Penderyn Port Wood Edition** cask no. PORT 13 db **(96.5) n24** dark and intriguing: the Port character is in a form that will not be easily recognised to usual Port Finish lovers. This one has a brooding, though not quite forbidding presence. And seems to work alongside the bourbony subtext with almost arrogant ease. The result is a stunning, almost rummy experience of the highest Guyanese variety.. **t24** the Port batters open the tastebuds almost ruthlessly for a second or two, as if forgetting its own strength. Shortly, though, it has calmed and the layering of softer, juicier fruit and a more bitter oak infusion has begun; **f24** now blithely enters superstar status with an extraordinary complexity that becomes seductively apparent. Again the grape is there, rich textured and fat, but the bourbony notes are not shy, either, and melt into the story with a burnt honeycomb and medium roast Jamaican Blue Mountain coffee signature. The sweeter notes need to be provided by a molassed/ muscovado style for balance - and is, right on cue..... **b24.5** if you have five minutes to try a great whisky, don't bother with this one. This is a full half hour job. At least. One of those malts which never sits still, changing shape and form and refuses to tell quite the same story twice. Classic doesn't quite cover it....I doubt if even Swansea's much vaunted beautiful football is quite as beautiful as this: that was Spanish inspired...this is Portuguese perfection. 60.4%

∵ **Penderyn Rich Madeira Limited Edition** cask no. M3 **(96) n24.5** certain elements here are not dissimilar to an exceptionally fine old Malmsey I keep in my cellar. But, as with all truly great whisky noses, it's not just about the star attraction: it is about complexity, integration and balance. And here we have some major oak influence manifested in finest Niederegger marzipan, liberally doused in dark chocolate as well as fabulous bitter marmalade and a peppery, spicy nip for good measure...and a bit of matching salt, too. And, of course the apricots so resplendent in the Prince Charles bottling are still there, but not quite as sweet as before; **t24.5** the mouth-feel and delivery oozes complexity: in a fraction of a second the tastebuds are encountered by an eye-wateringly dry bite on one level, and juicy, chewy fruits on another. The barley, silent on the nose, is at last heard but only for a few moments before the grapey-marmaladey fruit signature arrives in the silkiest of fashions. The middle ground is filled with fruit and oak playfully squabbling to be top dog, but eventually allowing each other turns; again there is a light sprinkling of salt to the oak; **f23** the fade has shortened slightly, but now we have a weak milky chocolate attaching to the light oils which is pulsed out alongside the returning apricot and mushy grape. Gentle spices represent the oak with a delicate grace. **b24** this whisky has moved on since that extraordinary bottling was presented to Prince Charles. In some ways it has gained, in others lost. But, quality-wise, it is impossible to separate them by anything wider than the width of a grape skin. Unquestionably one of the world whiskies of the year, and if anything crops up better in Europe we will have found something truly exceptional. This is the kind of whisky where if you can only get a bottle by swearing allegiance to the Principality of Wales, I for one would re-name my house Yaki Dah, eat nothing but leak soup and go back to find that girl I knew in Maesteg and have lots of Welsh-born sprogs. Second thought.... giving up my Millwall season ticket for a Swansea one...now you're asking a bit too much... 54.3%

Penderyn Sherrywood Edition bott code Jun 08 db **(91) n22.5** much more spice buzz than the standard Madeira-finished bottlings; **t23** chunky and chewy some cherry and chocolate enliven the middle; **f22.5** busy vanilla and light grape; more cocoa develops; **b23** a beautifully constructed and weighted malt which fills every crevice in the palate 46%. ncf.

Penderyn Welsh Rugby Union 125th Anniversary Edition Madeira finish db **(95) n23** dripping in lightly spiced grape, the vanilla-barley sub-plot adds just the right weight; **t24** My word! There'll be a few people in Madeira surprised that their fortified wine can be quite this good...the spice-fruit balance is now the stuff of Welsh legend; **f24** the accent falls on the oak but so many layers of grape and barley and black-peppered spice wash over it that you wonder if it will ever end. Even a tendency towards bitterness works in its favour as that honeycomb arrives to absorb it. Stunning; **b24** lamb apart, the best thing from Wales I have ever got my lips round... (!) And I say that with full apologies to a young lady from Maesteg, but it's true, you see... 50%. 1250 bottles.

World Whiskies

I have long said that whisky can be made just about anywhere in the world; that it is not writ large in stone that it is the inalienable right for just Scotland, Ireland, Kentucky and Canada to have it all to themselves. And so, it seems, it is increasingly being proved. Perhaps only sandy deserts and fields of ironstone can prevent its make physically and Islam culturally, though even that has not been a barrier to malt whisky being distilled in both Pakistan and Turkey. While not even the world's highest mountains or jungle can prevent the spread of barley and copper pot.

Outside of North America and Europe, whisky's traditional nesting sites, you can head in any direction and find it being made. South America may be well known for its rum, but in the south of Brazil, an area populated by Italian and German settlers many generations back, malt whisky is thriving. In even more lush and tropical climes it can now also be found, with Taiwan and Thailand leading the way.

Japan has long represented Asia with distinction and whisky-making there is in such an advanced state and to such a high standard Jim Murray's Whisky Bible has given it its own section. But while neighbouring South Korea has ended its malt distilling venture, further east, and at a very unlikely altitude, Nepal has forged a small industry to team up, geographically, with fellow malt distillers India and Pakistan. The one malt whisky from this region making inroads in world markets is India's Amrut single malt. Actually, inroads is hardly doing them justice. Full-bloodied trailblazing, more like. So good now is their whisky they have, with their fantastically complex brand, Fusion, deservedly been awarded Jim Murray's Whisky Bible 2010 Third Finest Whisky in the World. This represents a watershed not just for the distillery, but Indian whisky as a whole and in a broader sense the entire world whisky movement: it proves beyond doubt that excellent distilling and maturation wherever you are on this planet will be recognised and rewarded.

Africa is also represented on the whisky stage. There has long been a tradition of blending Scotch malt with South African grain but now there is single malt there, as well. Two malt distilleries, to be precise, with a second being opened at the Drayman's Brewery in Pretoria. I was supposed to have visited it a little while back, but the distiller, obviously not wanting to see me, went to the trouble of falling off his horse and breaking his thigh the actual day before. Wimp.

One relatively new whisky-making region is due immediate study: Australia. From a distance of 12,000 miles, the waters around Australia's distilleries appear to be muddied. Quality appears to range from the very good to extremely poor. And during the back end of 2004 I managed to discover this first hand when I visited three Tasmanian distilleries and Bakery Hill in Melbourne which perhaps leads the way regarding quality malt whisky made south of the Equator. Certainly green shoots are beginning to sprout at the Tasmania Distillery which has now moved its operation away from its Hobart harbour site to an out of town one close to the airport. The first bottlings of that had been so bad that it will take some time and convincing for those who have already tasted it to go back to it again. However, having been to the warehouse – and having tasted samples from every single cask they have on site – I reported in previous Bibles that it was only a matter of time before those first offerings would be little more than distant – though horrific – memories. Well, as predicted, it is now safe to put your head above the parapet. Their cask strength bottling for the 2009 Bible was a bloody beaut.

Still no news here about Whisky Tasmania's malt, though they have now made some heavily peated spirit. Away from Tasmania there is malt distilling – and further plans to distil – all over Australia. On that has already made it into the shops is from Booie Range, which like Sullivan's Cove suffers from a frighteningly unattractive nose, but unlike early bottlings of the Hobart whisky regroups and recovers significantly on the palate. The remaining casks of Wilson's malt from New Zealand are disappearing fast and when in New Zealand I discovered the stills from there were not just making rum in Fiji but whisky as well. We are all aware of the delights of island whisky, but a Pacific Island malt? Which leaves Antarctica as the only continent not making whisky, though what some of those scientists get up to for months on end no one knows.

ARGENTINA
Blends

Breeders Choice (84) n21 t22 f21 b20. A sweet blend using Scottish malt and, at the helm, an unusually lush Argentinian grain. *40%*

AUSTRALIA
BAKERY HILL DISTILLERY 1999. Operating.

⁖ **Bakery Hill Classic Malt** cask no. 2308 db **(87) n22** flaky oak forms a dry layer over the barley; **t22** a lush malt slowly increases the sugary tempo; a touch of cocoa fattens things out; **f21.5** slightly short with the vanillas and cocoa lording it over the barley; **b21.5** enjoyable. But not a patch on its cask strength version. *46%*

Bakery Hill Classic Malt cask no. 2707 db **(84) n19 t22 f21 b22.** Bizarre. Just checked – and found I have given almost identical marks to last year's version – and the tasting notes remain spot on. *46%*

⁖ **Bakery Hill Classic Malt** cask no. 3108 db **(82) n20 t21 f20.5 b20.5** More than a hint of feints amid the oily barley. *46%*

Bakery Hill Classic Malt barrel 2606, bott 06 db **(93) n23** enough citrus to start a Vitamin C factory; beautifully refreshing with pulsing malts; **t23** salivating and fresh with continuous waves of young, clean barley with not all the new make element completely lost; **f24** major complexity here as the oak inches itself in with a vanilla sheen, but malt refuses to fade; **b23** just so beautiful..!!! *46%. ncf.*

Bakery Hill Classic Malt db **(83) n19 t22 f21 b21.** Lots of serious attitude and gristy sweetness, but a tad feinty. *46%*

Bakery Hill Classic Malt Cask Strength db **(86) n20 t22 f23 b21.** A shadow of something feinty, but nothing like the 46% version. The result, though, is about as big a whisky as you'll get for something theoretically unsmoked...! *60.1%*

Bakery Hill Classic Malt Cask Strength cask no. 2707 db **(86) n20 t22 f22 b22.** A big malty march from delivery to finish aided by some enthusiastic oils that slightly undid the nose. *58%*

⁖ **Bakery Hill Classic Malt Cask Strength** cask no. 2308 db **(92) n23** the oak is full and confident but the light liquorice fits in well with the barley; **t23.5** rich barley offers a mouth-watering impact. A drizzle of muscovado sugar links directly in with the growing cocoa; **f22.5** long, softly oiled and daintily spiced. Still the cocoa lingers and tapers towards a chocolate and vanilla ice mix; **b23** here's incontrovertible proof that whisky does not necessarily improve with the addition of water. Where the 46% version of this is bitty and just keeps itself together for a decent innings, this one has all the oils in full flow ensuring something rich and magnificent. Truly a Bakery Hill Classic. *60.2%*

Bakery Hill Classic Malt Cask Strength cask no. 2606 db **(94) n23** a distinct Speyside style with fresh grasses and citric fruits linking with delicate vanilla for a beaut of an aroma; **t24** almost unbelievable barley intensity, but wonderful cocoa background (curiously cocoa can arrive as an effect of new make, slightly under-matured malt, or later from the oak: here it is possibly from all of these); **f24** that wonderful cocoa theme continues but again the barley is spot on; **b23** there are about 20 distilleries in Speyside that would die to be able to make a whisky this stunningly integrated. Young, barely pubescent but sheer, unadulterated, class... *60.1%*

⁖ **Bakery Hill Classic Malt Cask Strength** cask no. 3108 db **(82.5) n20.5 t21 f20.5 b20.5** Cask strength feintiness. *60.2%*

Bakery Hill Double Wood db **(84) n21 t22 f20 b21.** Attractively chewy, juicy in places but ultimately heavy duty and a tad fey on the finish. *46%*

Bakery Hill Double Wood cask no. 2621, bott 06 db **(91) n23** juicy; incredible clarity to the barley; **t23** decent spice peppers the fruity barley; a lovely bitter-sweet tale; **f22** long, lush and light; **b23** does whisky come any more refreshing than this? *46%*

Bakery Hill Double Wood cask no. 2719 db **(92) n22** some major citrus and grape makes inroads into the oaky malt; a wisp of smoke, or my imagination...? **t23** more of the same with a fruitcakey feel now, complete with a slight doughyness to the malt; big, busy middle; **f23** long, classy finish with some chocolate adding to the fruitcake and some smoke ensuring, with the delicate oils, depth, further length and weight; **b24** high class whisky is high class whisky wherever its made. Get up to body temp – and marvel..! *46%*

⁖ **Bakery Hill Double Wood** cask no. 3536 db **(78.5) n21 t20 f18 b19.5** Citrus and feints. *46%*

Bakery Hill Peated Malt db **(89) n21** ultra delicate: the very lightest smoke and vanilla; **t22** delightful barley sugar lead with peat tagging along as a faint shadow; **f23** the peats begin to gather and some spices arrive; **b23** restrained and delicate from first to last. *46%*

Bakery Hill Peated Malt cask no. 1307 db **(90) n22** half Bowmore-half Laphroaig-style kippery, Fisherman's Friend cough sweet element to this – the most Islay style from this distillery yet; **t23** perfect weight on the oils ensure the delivery is soft and, at first malty. The smoke gathers density... **f23** a sharp, citrus kick to the lightly-oiled finish – smoked marmalade on toast... **b22** well made and simply lovely whisky. 46%

Bakery Hill Peated Malt cask no. 2006, bott 06 db **(93) n23** "dry" iodine: nothing coastal, just a tangy, clean peatiness lightened by soft citrus; **t23** sweet, fresh young and then a big bursting out of grassy barley amid the smoke and spices; **f23** pretty long with lashings of late vanilla and butterscotch; remains salivating; **b24** seriously well-made malt with genuine complexity. Textbook balance. 46%

∴ **Bakery Hill Peated Malt** cask no. 2408 db **(86.5) n22 t21.5 f21.5 b21.5.** Very lightly peated, this actually has more of a Cadbury's Whole Nut character than an all out smoky one. Chewy and very enjoyable. 46%

∴ **Bakery Hill Peated Malt** cask no. 2507 db **(83) n21 t22 f19 b21.** Another big mouth filler with the smoke little more than a distant cloud. Pretty bitter at the death. 46%

Bakery Hill Peated Malt Cask Strength db **(89) n23** clean, the usual citrus house-style; the peats are a bit laid-back but charming; **t23** stunningly refreshing with superb soft oils for the sweet peat to melt into; **f21** a minor vanilla fest and some coppery sharpness; **b22** another really lovely malt from this outstanding distillery. 60.1%

Bakery Hill Peated Malt Cask Strength cask no. 1307 db **(93) n23 t24 f23 b24.** No surprise: it is just like the 40% version (being from the same cask), except the bigger notes are huge and there is just a greater degree of harmony to assist the overall balance. More absolutely outstanding distilling from that true master distiller, David Baker....someone so deserving of an overused and lately cheapened nomenclature. 59.8%

Bakery Hill Peated Malt Cask Strength cask no. 2006, bott 06 db **(91) n22** disorganised and wild; a three-day cold peat fire and citrus; **t23** sma' still copperiness, a touch of honeycomb 'n' apple to the metallic sheen; **f23** long, remaining on that coppery theme but now the peats gather for a rich finale; **b23** you get the feeling that this is made in an ancient still. Lush and rich all the way. How long before we see it in the Scarlet Bar? 60.1%

∴ **Bakery Hill Peated Malt Cask Strength** cask no. 2507 db **(84.5) n20.5 t22 f20.5 b21.5.** Again a much more rotund and confident malt at this strength with a sweetness that falls between chocolate-liquorice and light molasses. But the nose, like the finish, has some unresolved issues. 60.7%

BOOIE RANGE DISTILLERY

Booie Range Single Malt db **(72) n14 t20 f19 b19.** Mounts the hurdle of the wildly off-key nose impressively with a distinct, mouth watering barley richness to the palate that really does blossom even on the finish. 40%

LARK DISTILLERY

∴ **The Lark Distillery Single Malt Whisky** cask LD38, bott Apr 09 db (88.5) **n22.5** a few feints, but some sexy mocha is the bait... **t22** oily (no surprise there given the nose) but a real cranking up of intense barley and cocoa; **f22** sweetens with a touch of dry molasses with an oily vanilla-barley fade; **b22** distiller Kristy Lark has taken a liberty or two here with her cut...and somehow got away with it. That's women distillers for you... 43%

The Lark Distillery Single Malt Whisky cask LD46, bott Apr 07 db **(86) n20 t22 f22 b22.** Some serious malty oomph to the middle and latter stages of this one with heaps of natural caramel. 40%. sc.

The Lark Distillery Single Malt Whisky cask LD48, bott Jan 07 db **(88) n21** some slight feints quickly burn off to leave a bit of a fruity monster; **t23** immediate spice prickles from the off; calms down for a fruit salad/blackjack candy combo; **f22** the vanillins arrive for a custard and fruit finale; **b22** knife and fork whisky – and a spoon wouldn't go amiss. 58%. sc.

The Lark Distillery Single Malt Whisky cask LD60, bott 08 db **(86.5) n21 t21.5 f22 b22.** Celebrates all things malty. The odd touch of butterscotch infiltrates, but really it's all about sweet barley almost in mash form. Charming. 43%

The Lark Distillery Single Malt Whisky Cask Strength cask LD31, bott 08 db **(89.5) n22** salted – and peppered! – celery stick; **t23** dry, prickly-spiced and beautifully fruit and barley layered; **f22.5** puckeringly dry in places but a big Demerara and spice statement rekindles the flame just when it appears to be flickering out; **b22** well made, complex whisky which really does take the sweet-dry balance to a new level.... 58%

The Lark Distillery Single Malt Whisky Cask Strength cask LD58, bott 07 db **(90.5) n23.5** a nose for gin as well as whisky lovers: a plethora of botanicals, leading with juniper – as if just picked from a mature tree/bush and crushed between fingers – plus grape enlivened by ground black pepper and bubblegum: complex to put it mildly... **t22** intense delivery...and it barely dies down for the duration. A real small, still thickness to the entire mouthfeel with the barley and fruit at each other's throat; **f22.5** a brief spice buzz for a moment takes you away from that fruit/barley concentrate but the bittersweet balance doesn't err for a moment; **b22.5** a massively enjoyable, beautifully made, in your face dram which never thins out or even remotely takes its foot off the gas. 58%

The Lark Distillery Single Malt Whisky Cask Strength cask LD68 db **(84) n21 t20 f21.5 b21.5.** Another well made malt from Lark's which again really zaps up the barley content. Some major small, still notes here which engineer a hefty weight to the proceedings. 58%

The Lark Distillery Single Malt Whisky Distillers Selection cask LD51, bott May 07 db **(91) n22** a juniper/gin-style aroma; **t23** typical massive delivery, again with a juniper/botanical kick and lovely bitter-sweet fruit/barley/oak threesome; **f23** so long your tongue licks grooves into the roof of your mouth; subtle spice **b23** one very big malt that keeps your tastebuds guessing all the way. A treat of a whisky. 46%. sc.

The Lark Distillery Single Malt Whisky Distillers Selection cask LD59, bott 08 db **(80) n19 t21 f20 b20.** Hmmm. I just hope distiller Kristy Lark's brand new husband is a bit better than this... 46%

∵ **The Lark Distillery Single Malt Whisky Distillers Selection** cask LD99, bott Feb 09 db **(82) n21 t19 f21 b21** Well there's one to get your kisser round! The nose has almost a toothpaste-y, minty edge and though the delivery doesn't seem quite on the button it recovers impressively enough for a real ol' oak and cocoa dust up further down the track. Not quite up to this distillery's usual high standards, though. 46%

SMALL CONCERN DISTILLERY

Cradle Mountain Pure Tasmanian Malt (87) n21 curiously vivid bourbon character; sweet vanilla with hints of tangerine and hazelnut. Really very, very attractive; **t22** an almost perfect translation onto the palate: gloriously sweet and gently nutty. The mouthfeel and body is firm and oily at the same time, the barley sparkles as the oak fades. Exceptionally subtle, clean and well made; **f21** pretty long with some cocoa offering a praline effect; **b23** a knock-out malt from a sadly now lost distillery in Tasmania. Faultlessly clean stuff with lots of new oak character but sufficient body to guarantee complexity. 43%

Cadenhead's World Whiskies Cradle Mountain Aged 10 Years Ex Cabernet Sauvignon barrel, bott Sep 06 **(71) n14 t19 f20 b18.** Entirely baffling whisky. The Cab Sauv cask is horrendous and not helped by some feints, but what happens next is bemusing: it has every hallmark of rum. Had this not been sent to me as a whisky, I'd have never guessed. That said, some decent notes beyond the nose. 57.9%. 270 bottles.

Cadenhead's World Whiskies Cradle Mountain Aged 11 Years bourbon, bott Sep 07 **(72) n16 t18 f20 b18.** If memory serves me correctly, the last sample I had from this distillery was a bit of a weirdo. On that score we have consistency. Without spoiling the fun and looking back on my own notes, the previous one – I think!! – bore all the hallmarks of rum. This one, bizarrely, has some of the traits found on Brazil nuts left a year or two too long...Some surprisingly charming barley does hoist a flag at the finale. 55.3%. 204 bottles.

TASMAN DISTILLERY

Great Outback Rare Old Australian Single Malt (92) n24 I could stick my nose in a glass of this all day. This is sensational: more a question of what we don't have here! The malt is clean, beautifully defined and dovetails with refined, orangey-citrus notes. The oak is near perfection adding only a degree of tempered weight. I don't detect peat, but there is some compensating Blue Mountain coffee; **t24** just so beautifully textured with countless waves of clean, rich malt neither too sweet nor too dry. This is faultless distillate; **f21** lightens considerably with the oak vanilla dominating; **b23** What can you say? An Australian whisky distillery makes a malt to grace the world's stage. But you can't find it outside of Australia. This will have to be rectified. Strength not known.

TASMANIA DISTILLERY

Old Hobart db **(69) n16 t19 f17 b17.** The nose still has some way to go before it can be accepted as a mainstream malt, though there is something more than a little coastal about it this time. However, the arrival on the palate is another matter and I must say I kind of enjoyed its big, oily and increasingly sweet maltiness and crushed sunflower seed nuttiness towards the end. Green (and yellow) shoots are growing. The whisky is unquestionably getting better. 60%

Sullivan's Cove db **(61) n13 t15 f17 b16.** Some malt but typically grim, oily and dirty; awesomely weird. *40%. Australia.*

Sullivans Cove Cask Strength bourbon maturation, barrel no. HH0270, dist 22 Apr 00, bott 22 Jun 07 **(94.5) n23** textbook bourbon cask influence: ultra busy, mildly prickly oak pushing towards faint honey and liquorice but delicate enough for a clear site of the very clean barley; **t24** voluptuous delivery: the barley hangs on the palate as the oaks storm through with that semi-bourbon character which specially involves Demerara sugar; for all the oak the tastebuds are flooded as the salivation levels go through the roof; **f23.5** long, with a hint of cocoa but the interlinking between oak and barley almost makes the heart swell with joy and in the meantime the sweetness persists; **b24** rarely do malts balance out quite this beautifully. Dramtipodean genius. *60%. 167 bottles.*

Sullivans Cove Cask Strength port maturation, barrel no. HH0544, dist 10 Nov 00, bott 25 Jun 07 db **(92) n24** allow to sit in the glass for ten minutes before nosing: this allows the grape to oxidise slightly and allows the many nuances of barley and oak to shine. One of the most delicate wine-shaped whisky noses found outside the warehouses of Glenfarclas... **t22** juicy grape meets juicy barley. The result is, well...juicy. The oak does try to thump its way through and leaves a slightly bitter trail. But the spiced élan of the malt is not for one moment spoiled; **f23** fruit and nut chocolate – with plenty of raisins; the oaks are dry and vanilla-clad but the grape, at time roasty, remains to the end; **b23** one of the best wine-matured whiskies I have tasted for a long while – and simply because the balance and complexity are never lost for a second. *60%. 402 bottles.*

Sullivans Cove Cask Strength port maturation, barrel no. HH0548, dist 14 Nov 00, bott 14 Feb 07 db **(93) n23** thick grape dipped in molasses; chunky oils; **t24** absolutely off the scales delivery-wise: the tastebuds are caked in the almost glutinous fruit offering near perfect bitter-sweet charms, while the roof of the mouth is sprayed with chocolate mousse and raspberry jam; **f23** massively long with more cocoa and cocoa oil; **b23** nosed blind I might have mistaken this for a Demerara rum! Big and ballsy. *60%. 427 bottles.*

Sullivan's Cove Double Cask bourbon & port oak db **(87) n20** off- key oils are rounded off by fruit with chocolate-y results; **t22** excellent body and weight with a malty flourish; **f23** excellent finale, most probably thanks to the oils that shouldn't be there adding chewiness to the fruit and malt. Long, as one might expect; **b22** right: here's a bet – any money you like. Take a glass of this malt. Leave it by a fire/radiator and come back to it in about an hour. I am sure those off notes will have vanished and you'll have a malt in the 90s displaying the honey notes just dying to get out. Not had time to do it myself, but as soon as the Bible's complete... *40%*

Sullivans Cove Single Malt Whisky 6 Years Old bourbon maturation cask no. HH0274 db **(95) n23** rich and intense, there is a lovely jammy fruitiness attached to the big barley; **t24** barley concentrate with a dab of golden syrup and raspberry jam towards the middle. The body and weight are nigh perfect. Sensational!!; **f24** lovely strands of vanilla interplay with the barley and then cocoa to see out the lightly oiled finish; **b24** great on these guys. This must be the biggest Australian comeback since Larwood and Voce taught them how to bowl. A distillery once understandably a byword for less than brilliant whisky has come up with something that is truly beautiful. When I was in their warehouse a few years back, I detected the odd cracking cask, so knew their future could be bright. But perhaps not quite this brilliant...! *60%*

Sullivans Cove Single Malt Whisky 6 Years Old port maturation cask no. HH0571 db **(90) n23** so much grape but enough room for lots of natural caramel and vanilla; **t23** lush, grapey delivery, which is no surprise. Excellent spice burst in the middle, **f22** those caramels begin to spread; **b22** high quality whisky helped by some pretty top dog casks. *60%*

Sullivans Cove Single Malt Whisky 6 Years Old matured in port and bourbon casks db **(88) n22** butterscotch tart, grape juice and barley in just-so portions; **t23** oak-led and dry with just enough clean barley to sweeten the edge; **f21** vanilla and toast breeze through to the finish; **b22** subtle and sensuous. A bit like your average Tasmanian... *40%*

YALUMBA WINERY

Smith's Angaston Whisky Vintage 1997 Aged 7 Years db **(88) n20** an attractive, if not entirely faultless, combination of barley and fruit sewn together by honey; **t22** an almost implausible silkiness to this: the barley and honey tip-toe over the tastebuds using a touch of oil to help them glide as well; **f23** now we have some serious complexity with the fruits showing a berry-like sharpness, but it's all very effete; **b23** easily one of the most delicate whiskies of the year and one that puts Samuel Smith on the map. Perfect for the hipflask for a night at the ballet. *40%*

Smith's Angaston Whisky Vintage 1998 Aged 8 Years db **(86) n20 t22 f22 b22.** Perhaps conscious that their first offering, a genuine touch of culture that it was, wasn't quite Bruce enough to called Australian, this one's showing bit of aggression. And I mean a bit, as this is no tackle from Lucas Neil. Because after the delivery it's back to the girlie stuff with some admittedly delicious Swiss Roll filling fruitiness. Lovely malt from a distillery I'm going to have to keep my eyes on. *40%*

BRAZIL
HEUBLEIN DISTILLERY

Durfee Hall Malt Whisky (81) n18 t22 f20 b21. Superbly made whisky; the intensity of the malt is beautifully layered without ever becoming too sweet. Very light bodied and immaculately clean. Good whisky by any standards. *43%*

UNION DISTILLERY

Barrilete (72) n18 t19 f18 b17. Nothing particularly wrong with it technically; it just lacks vitality. Thin but extremely malt intense. *39.1%*

Blends

Cockland Gold Blended Whisky (73) n18 t18 f19 b18. Silky caramel. Traces of malt there, but never quite gets it up. *38%. Fante.*

⋯ **Drury's Special Reserve (86.5) n21.5 t22 f21 b22** Deceptively attractive, melt-in-the-mouth whisky; at times clean, regulation stuff, but further investigation reveals a honeycomb edge which hits its peak in the middle ground when the spices mix in beautifully. One to seek out and savour when in Brazil. *40%. Campari, Brasil.*

⋯ **Gold Cup Special Reserve (84.5) n21 t22.5 f20 b21** Ultra soft, easily drinkable and, at times, highly impressive blend which is hampered by a dustiness bestowed upon it by the nagging caramels on both nose and finish. Some lovely early honey does help lift it, though, and there is also attractive Swiss roll jam towards the finish. Yet never quite gets out of third gear despite the most delicate hint of smoke. *39%. Campari, Brasil.*

⋯ **Gran Par (77) n19.5 t22 f17.5 b18.** The delivery is eleven seconds of vaguely malty glory. The remainder is thin and caramelled with no age to live up to the name. And with Par in the title and bagpipes and kilt in the motif, how long before the SWA buys a case of it...? *39%*

Green Valley Special Reserve batch 07/01 **(70) n16 t19 f17 b18.** A softly oiled, gently bitter-sweet blend with a half meaty, half boiled sweet nose. An unusual whisky experience. *38.1%. Muraro & Cia.*

Malte Barrilete Blended Whisky batch 001/03 **(76) n18 t20 f19 b19.** This brand has picked up a distinctive apple-fruitiness in recent years and some extra oak, too. *39.1%.*

⋯ **Natu Nobilis (81.5) n22.5 t20 f19 b20** The nose boasts a genuinely clean, Speyside-style malt involvement. But to taste is much more non-committal with the soft grain dominating and the grassy notes restricted the occasional foray over the tastebuds. Pleasant, but don't expect a flavor fest. *39%. Pernod Ricard, Brasil.*

⋯ **Natu Nobilis Celebrity (86) n22.5 t22 f20.5 b21** A classy blend with a decent weight and body, yet never running to fat. Some spice prickle ensures the flavor profile never settles in a neautral zone and the charming, citrus-domiated malt on the nose is immediately found on the juicy delivery. A cut above the standard Natu Nobilis and if the finish could be filled out with extra length and complexity, we'd have an exceptionally impressive blend on our hands. Another blend to seek out whenever in Brazil. *39%. Pernod Ricard, Brasil.*

O Monge batch 02/02 **(69) n17 t18 f17 b17.** Poor nose but it recovers with a malty mouth arrival but the thinness of the grain does few favours. *38.5%. Union Distillery.*

⋯ **Old Eight Special Reserve (85.5) n20 t21 f22.5 b22** Traditionally reviled by many in Brazil, I can assure you that the big bite followed by calming soft grains is exactly what you need after a day's birding in the jungle. *39%. Campari, Brasil.*

Pitt's (84) n21 t20 f22 b21. The pits it certainly aint!! A beautifully malted blend where the barley tries to dominate the exceptionally flinty grain whenever possible. Due to be launched later in 2004, this will be the best Brazil has to offer – though some fine tuning can probably improve the nose and middle even further and up the complexity significantly. I hope, when I visit the distillery early in 2005, I will be able to persuade them to offer a single malt: on this evidence it should, like Pitt's, be an enjoyable experience and perfect company for any World Cup finals. *40%. Busnello Distillery.*

⋯ **Wall Street (84) n23 t22 f19 b20** Fabulous nose with a sexy citrus-light smoke double bill. And the arrival on the palate excels, too, with a rich texture and confident delivery of malt, again with the smoke dominating. But falls away rather too rapidly as the grains throw the balance out of kilter and ensures too much bitter oak late on. *38%. Pernod Ricard, Brasil.*

INDIA
AMRUT DISTILLERY

Amrut Single Malt B-No-06 bott 26.6.07 db **(89) n22** sharp barley, a sprinkle of muscovado sugar and a touch of liquorice and fudge to the powering vanilla; **t23** brilliant arrival with oak and barley in tandem; both take turns at supremacy while the body-feel excels with gentle oils constantly caressing, while balancing spices playfully nip; **f21.5** thins out with pleasant vanillas and toffee; **b22.5** as 40% abv malts go – from any country – this is pretty spot on. *40%*

Amrut Single Malt bott 08 db **(91.5) n22.5** distinctly confidant liquorice-bourbon notes with near perfect bitter-sweet balance; burnt honeycomb and toffee also abound; **t23.5** outstanding richness and sheen to the enormous barley-oak sweetness; again there is a big bourbony cut to the cloth with all the liquorice and molassed sugar normally associated; but the barley adds that extra dimension; **f22.5** long, wonderfully layered oak offering variations of a sweet-dry theme; a touch silky with some cream toffee at the death; **b23** taking it up that extra 6% abv has made a significant difference as this is stupendous stuff. I had a little moan with the distillers about the slight use of caramel here which helps neither the nose nor finish. They called back the next day to tell me they had considered my comments and decided to drop the use of caramel in all future bottlings of Amrut altogether: Power to the Bible! *46%*

Amrut Cask Strength dist 6 May 01, bott May 06 db **(94) n24 t23 f23 b24.** From the moment you take in the aroma, stunningly structured with the citrus overture teasingly overtaken by the near near-perfect harmonization of vanilla and barley, you know you are in for a rare treat. Certainly the best non-peated Indian single malt to hit the international market. *62.8%*

Amrut Cask Strength dist 6 May 02, bott May 06 db **(92) n23 t23 f22 b24.** It is impossible not to be impressed with a sub-continental showstopper like this. Broad brushes here rather than delicate pastels but the balance is awesome. *62.6%*

Amrut Cask Strength bott Dec 06 db **(87) n23 t22 f20 b22.** So intense is the heat in India, so critical the maturation time, that just a matter of weeks, let alone months, can make a life and death difference between the brilliance of previous bottlings and the oaky near-disaster of this. Another couple of months and it would have been curtains: as it is, there is enough – especially on the nose – still to admire. *63.8%. ncf.*

Amrut Cask Strength Limited Edition bott Sep 07 db **(93.5) n23.5** classic house style with glorious bourbon notes fused with the richest of barley statements; not entirely unlike caramelised biscuit dunked in coffee; oh, and a bit of a spicy attitude, too... **t23** there we go with that unique bitter-sweet overture where the oaks and barley appear joined at the hip; lovely soft oils and then a sharp jolt of blood orange citrus, which is removed by something more buttery and delicate; **f23** long, elegant with the most intricate of fades with the oaks showing various bourbon then buttery characteristics; there is a trace of dark sugar and cocoa to help it along its way; **b24** bottlings such as these are beginning to help cement Amrut's position as one of the great and most consistent distilleries of the world. *61.9%*

⠿ **Amrut Fusion** batch no. 01, bott Mar 09 db **(97) n24** heavy, thickly oaked and complex: some curious barley-sugar notes here shrouded in soft smoke. Big, but seductively gentle, too... **t24** the delivery, though controlled at first, is massive! Then more like con-fusion as that smoke on the nose turns into warming, full blown peat, but it far from gets its own way as a vague sherry trifle note (curious, seeing how there are no sherry butts involved) – the custard presumably is oaky vanilla - hammers home that barley-fruitiness to make for a bit of a free-for-all; but for extra food measure the flavours develop into a really intense chocolate fudge middle which absolutely resonates through the palate; **f24** a slight struggle here as the mouthfeel gets a bit puffy here with the dry peat and oak; enough molassed sweetness to see the malt through to a satisfying end, though. Above all the spices, rather than lying down and accepting their fate, rise up and usher this extraordinary whisky to its exit; **b25** one of the most complex and intriguing new whiskies of the year that needs about two days and half a bottle to get even close to fathoming. Not exactly a textbook whisky, with a few edges grinding together like tectonic plates. And there is even odd note, like the fruit and a kind of furry, oaky buzz, which I have never seen before. But that is the point of whiskies like this: to be different, to offer a unique slant. But, ultimately, to entertain and delight. And here it ticks all boxes accordingly. To the extent that this has to be one of the great whiskies found anywhere in the world this year. And the fact it is Indian? Irrelevant: from distillation to maturation this is genius whisky, from whichever continent... *50%*

∴ **Amrut Peated** batch no. 1, bott Sep 08 db **(94) n23** unusually dry peat; not dissimilar to peat reek absorbed by an old leather armchair; a hint of citrus, too; **t24** despite the nose, the immediate sensation is one of being caressed by molassed sugar and then a ratching up of the peat notes. As they get more forceful, so the experience becomes that little bit drier and spicier, though not without the molasses refusing to give way; **f23.5** you can tell the quality of the distillate and the barrels it has been matured in by the crystalline depth to the finish. Everything is clear on the palate and the butterscotch vanillas wrap the phenols for a comfortable and clean finale; **b23.5** absolutely everything you could ask for a peated malt at this strength. The length and complexity are matched only by a train journey through this astonishing country. 46%

Amrut Peated Cask Strength bott Apr 08 db **(92) n22** gristy smoked barley, kippers with a salted butter, peppered bite; **t22.5** the delivery is youthful and barely reaching puberty then suddenly an intensely malty ascendancy followed by a healthy dose of drier oaks; **f24.5** a sublime finale for its sheer delicacy and elegance; the peat no more than oozes, there are cups galore of sugarless medium roast Mysore and finally, as a bourbony trail is discovered, soft liquorice and molassed sugar – easily the highlight of the experience: one of the best finishes of the year... **b23** a touch of youth to this guy but the finish, entirely uncluttered by unnatural caramel or deprived by filtration, confirms a degree of greatness. By the way: if you want to experience something really stunning, trying mixing the 2007 and 2008 peated. When you get the proportions right...well, watch out Islay...!! 62.78%

Amrut Peated Cask Strength Limited Edition bott Sep 07 db **(94) n23.5** peat smoke drifts through in gentle layers; brilliantly confusing young and old notes permeate the smog; **t23.5** superb delivery: the malt is firm with a youthful citric touch, then there are ancient, bourbony notes embedded, too; but the smoke offers both soft comfort and staccato spice; **f23** long, oils out slightly but no apparent loss of complexity as (Mysore?) coffee begins to take effect; **b24** a split personality of a dram which offers drama and serenity in equal measures: a peat whisky lover's dream. 61.2%. 480 bottles.

∴ **Amrut Two Continents Limited Edition** bott Feb 09 db **(95) n23.5** a classy nose: the oak is abundant, but entirely controlled. It allows those blood orange and kumquat notes that are no stranger to this distillery to flourish, as well as a mildly bourbony dry liquorice; **t24** such a soft landing....the barley is intense, sweet yet never overly so while the oaks again have a presence yet keep their distance, being happy to inject a busy spice kick into the middle ground; the oils are soft, lightly sweetened and lingering; **f23.5** delicate. Some over-ripe, dry banana and a light dusting of muscovado sugars; **b24** here we have a malt distilled in India and matured first on the sub-continent and then Scotland. Let's just say that it is a malt which has travelled exceptionally well...and arrived at greatness. This is exactly how I like my whisky to be. 46%. 786 bottles.

∴ **Milroy's of Soho Amrut 2003** cask no. 08/08/30-1 dist Jul 03, bott Jan 09 **(84) n21 t22 f20 b21.** Juicy in part and very malty. But this whisky struggles at this kind of age with the oak, especially through the flattening natural caramels, dumbing the beauty down. 46%. Milroy's of Soho. 210 bottles.

The Ultimate Amrut 2003 Cask Strength cask no. 348, dist 25 Jul 03, bott 11 Jun 08 **(91) n21.5** so gripped by oak, thick orange marmalade (usually a heavy note) lightens things; **t22.5** I feel fastened to the chair, as though impaled on oak. This amount of maturation shouldn't work, yet such is the intensity of the malt – and the compensating heavyweight bourbony sweetness – it just so does...; oh, and a pretty spicy Indian, too; **f24** for seven tenths of the finish you know that the oak is way too OTT. Yet so delicious is that chocolate spread and malt milkshake, well you've just got to love it; **b23** when they say Ultimate, they aren't joking. They have taken this cask to close on five years. And in India that is Gandhi old. The oak is straining and creaking at every turn, yet somehow – and against the odds – it remains intact. Indeed, at times the experience is nigh transcendental. Other times you are searching for the tweezers...a ridiculous whisky which breaks all the rules. And yet is just so outstanding... 61.6%. nc ncf. 275 bottles. Ultimate Whisky Co. Holland.

PONDA DISTILLERY

Stillman's Dram Single Malt Whisky Limited Edition bourbon cask ref. 11186-90 **(94) n23** beautifully soft peats fuse with lime-led citrus notes. At once delicate and enormous; **t23** softly smoked malts dissolve into honeyed pools on the palate. Sexier and more relaxing than a Goan foot massage; **f24** the way the delicate oak washes gently against the palate, the manner in which the soft peats build to a crescendo - and yet still refuse to overpower – the entrancing waves of muscovado-sweetened coffee, all make for a sublime finale; **b24** well, I thought I had tasted it all with the Amrut cask strength. And then this arrived at my lab...!! I predicted many years back that India would dish out some top grade malt before too long. But I'd be stretching the truth if I said I thought it would ever be this good... 42.8%. McDowell & Co Ltd, India.

Blends

Antiquity blend of rare Scotch and matured Indian malts, bott 14.2.06 **(79) n20 t21 f19 b19.** Uncluttered but clever in places with a silky and distinctly malty delivery on the palate; the oak – not noticeable on the nose - dominates the finish intertwined with toffee-caramel. Attractive, but never quite works out which direction it is going. 42.8%. Shaw Wallace Distilleries, India. No added flavours.

Antiquity Blue bott Oct 05 **(85) n19 t23 f21 b22.** A deliciously subtle smoky edge to this guarantees excellent weight and chewability throughout. Hugely enjoyable. 42.8%. Shaw Wallace Distilleries, India. No added flavours.

Blenders Pride blend of imported Scotch malts and select Indian grain spirits, bott Sep 05 **(74) n19 t20 f17 b18.** The rich mouth arrival descends into dullness: don't know too many blenders who would be proud of that! 42.8%. Seagram Distilleries, India.

Peter Scot Malt Whisky (84) n20 t21 f22 b21. Enjoyable balance between sweetness and oak and entertainingly enlivened by what appears to be some young, juicy malt. 42.8%.

Royal Challenge a blend of rare Scotch and matured Indian malt whiskies, batch no. 350, bott 29 Dec 05 **(78) n21 t20 f18 b19.** A clean, exceptionally firm blend that could do with a little lift on the finish. 42.8%. Shaw Wallace Distilleries, India.

Royal Stag a blend of imported Scotch malts and select Indian grain spirits, batch no. 068, 27 Feb 06 **(90) n20** firm, clean good oak and barley presence; **t23** crisp, refreshing Speyside-style malt dominates early; **f24** attractive drying cocoa and spice prickle; gathering sweetness and even a touch of something very vaguely smoky; **b23** thoroughly attractive, well-balanced and rewarding whisky by any standards: the finish is fabulous. Average nose part, just love it! 42.8%. Seagram's/Gemini Distilleries, India.

Signature batch no. 01, bott Dec 05 **(87) n20** very young, Bowmore-esque tint that needs an extra dimension; **t23** superb mouth arrival that luxuriates in an softly oiled and delicate peatiness. Other grassy malts also abound and makes for a mouth-watering experience; **f22** plenty of vanilla and a curious bitter cherry sharpness amid the smoke and cocoa; **b22** there is an appealing youthfulness to this whisky and no little complexity, nose apart. An enjoyable and rewarding journey. 42.8%. McDowell & Co Ltd, India.

Sikkim Shangri-La "Special" Blended Malt bott 06 **(84) n19 t21.5 f22.5 b21.** An unhappy, strangely industrial nose is entirely dwarfed in character by the big malty beast which rises on the palate and finish. A strange mouthfeel, perhaps, but the silky, coppery texture is a treat. 42.8%. Sikkim Distilleries Ltd.

NEW ZEALAND
THE SOUTHERN DISTILLING CO LTD

The Coaster Single Malt Whiskey batch No. 2356 **(85) n20 t22 f21 b22.** Distinctly small batch and sma' still with the accent very much on honey. Nosed blind I might have mistaken as Blue Mouse whisky from Germany: certainly European in style. Recovers well from the wobble on the nose and rewards further investigation. 40%

The MacKenzie Blended Malt Whiskey (85) n20 t22 f21 b22. A vaguely spicier, chalkier, mildly less honeyed version of Coaster. Quite banana-laden nose. I have flown over Timeru many times, half way as it is between Christchurch and Dunedin. By the time you read this, there is more than even chance I shall have driven there and visited this distillery. I'll let you know on the website. 40%

WILSON DISTILLERY

Milford Aged 10 Years batch 321M42, dist 93, bott 04 db **(89) n20** less than impressive with a touch of soap; **t23** fresh, grassy barley with a mildly metallic hardness; **f23** waves of vanilla, soft spices and that continuing grassy, metallic theme; **b23** what a shame that the Wilson distillery is not still extant and rich new make was being filled into some high quality bourbon casks. 43%. 4780 bottles.

Milford Aged 15 Years batch 89M414, dist 88, bott 04 db **(91) n21** battling, lively vanilla with the barley. Even the most distant hint of coal smoke; **t24** beautiful barley delivery that shows remarkable freshness and zest. Lubeck marzipan offers a mild nutty sweetness, bringing with it some soft oaks which cranks up the complexity towards the middle; **f23** light with strands of vanilla and a touch of citrus; **b23** quality whisky though slightly flattened by age but shows enough early on to confirm its class. 43%. 1878 bottles.

Cadenhead's World Whiskies Lammerlaw Aged 10 Years bott May 06 **(90) n 21** very slightly soapy; fabulous citrus tries to lift it; **t22** rich, juicy barley overcomes that soap; **f24** beautiful orangey notes link heavenly with the barley; **b23** not even a sub-standard bourbon cask can ruin this beautiful malt. *47.3%*.

Cadenhead's World Whiskies Lammerlaw Aged 10 Years bourbon, bott Sep 06 **(90) n22** dry oak forms an elegant structure on which the crisp barley hangs; **t23** sensuous and mouth-watering dovetailing of crystal-clear, fruity malt and balancing oak; **f22** as dry as the nose with the usual cocoa-oak suspects; **b23** one could almost weep for the loss of this unique distillery. The malt, in this classy and delicate form, is comparable with Speyside's finest. *47.7%. 222 bottles.*

Cadenhead's World Whiskies Lammerlaw Aged 10 Years bourbon, bott Sep 07 **(91.5) n22** fired up with citrus and intense barley; **t23.5** a malt which is hard to spit out: the texture and intensity of the barley is magnificent, as are the bitter-sweet waves which pound against the tastebuds like huge South Pacific rollers; there is always a citrussy edge which ensures neither barley or malt become too heavy and a certain freshness clings to the tastebuds; **f23** the growing oak gets in with another, quite different, bitter-sweeter performance to compliment that of the barley. Again, citrus appears to be on the tip of the tongue... **b23** stunning bottlings like this can only leave one mourning the loss of this distillery. *48.9%. 198 bottles.*

Blends

Kiwi Whisky (37) n2 t12 f11 b12. Strewth! I mean, what can you say? Perhaps the first whisky containing single malt offering virtually no nose at all and the flavour appears to be grain neutral spirit plus lashings of caramel and (so I am told) some Lammerlaw single malt. The word bland has been redefined. As has whisky. *40%. Ever-Rising Enterprises, NZ, for the Asian market.*

Wilson's Superior Blend (89) n22 stupendously clean and malt rich. Imperiously mouthwatering and enticing; **t23** brilliant, almost dazzling clean malt arrival sharpened even further with mildly though distant crisp grain. One of the world's maltiest, most salivating blends, perhaps a touch simplistic but the charm of the malt endures while the ultra-delicate oak offers a teasing weight; **f21** loses marks only because of a caramel-induced toffee arrival, but still the malt and grain are in perfect sync while the drying oak offers balance; **b23** apparently has a mixed reception in its native New Zealand but I fail to see why: this is unambiguously outstanding blended whisky. On the nose you expect a mouthwatering mouthful and it delivers with aplomb. Despite this being a lower priced blend it is, intriguingly, a marriage of 60% original bottled 10-y-o Lammerlaw and 40% old Wilson's blend, explaining the high malt apparent. Dangerous and delicious and would be better still at a fuller strength... and with less caramel. *37.5%. Continental Wines and Spirits, NZ.*

SOUTH AFRICA
JAMES SEDGWICK DISTILLERY

Three Ships 10 Years Old db **(83) n21 t21 f20 b21.** Seems to have changed character, with more emphasis on sherry and natural toffee. The oak offers a thrusting undercurrent. *43%*

Blends

Drayman's Solera (86) n19 t22 f23 b22. For a change, the label gets it spot on with its description of chocolate orange: it is there in abundance. If they can get this nose sorted they would be on for an all round impressive dram. As it is, luxuriate in the excellent mouthfeel and gentle interplay between malt and oak. Oh and those chocolate oranges... *43%. Drayman's Distillery. South African/ Scotch Whisky.*

Harrier (78) n20 t20 f19 b19. Not sure what has happened to this one. Has bittered to a significant degree while the smoke has vanished. A strange, almost synthetic, feel to this now. *43%. South African/ Scotch Whisky.*

Knights (83) n20.5 t21 f20 b20.5. While the Harrier has crashed, the Knights is now full of promise. Also shows the odd bitter touch but a better all-round richer body not only absorbs the impacts but radiates some malty charm. *43%. South African/ Scotch Whisky.*

Three Ships 5 Years Old (88.5) n21.5 the trademark soft grist peat remains but burnt toast has replaced the Columbian coffee – drat! **t22.5** a curiously soft yet chunky delivery with the smoke not taking too long to make its mark; elsewhere there are attractive sweet layers of vanilla and barley; **f22** soft oils ensure a silky touch to the finish; **b22.5** a more gentle and mildly austere bottling than of old but the clever use of smoke lifts it into a pretty high league. Really delicious stuff! *43%. South African/ Scotch Whisky.*

Three Ships Bourbon Cask Finish (90) n22 unfazed by the big oak, the soft, nutty undertone melts into the even softer grain; **t23** melt-in-the-mouth with strands of juicy barley kissing gently a, presumably, grainy lushness; ice-cream style vanilla begins to fill the middle; **f22.5** delicate and not quite docile, the barley re-emerges with a vague honeyed sheen; the vanillas and the gentlest spice head towards the sunset; **b22.5** a soft, even whisky which enjoys its finest moments on delivery. Clean with a pressing, toasty oakiness to the sweeter malt elements. Always a delight. 43%

Three Ships Original (82) n19 t22 f21 b20. Not sure if this is meant to be the 3-yo. Certainly has different character, being smokeless save perhaps some late, late spice. Great grains, though. 43%

TAIWAN

∴ **Kavalan Concertmaster Single Malt Port** Cask Finish db **(87)** n22 proud, juicy grape spread over some toasty vanilla; a slight, dull hint of a lesser cask; **t23** voluptuous entry: the silkiness of the malt is matched by the salivating, sharper tones of fruit; the middle ground is diminuendo and more introspective; **f20.5** a familiar buzz of an off-key cask; **b21.5** a malt which will split its audience. In Germany, for instance, the light sulphur note will win all kinds of standing ovations; however, to the purist there will be a preference that it was not there. Because this piece has many moments of beauty as the malt and grape mingle and interlink: together they are company, anything else is a crowd. Even so I envisage many an encore for this... 40%

∴ **Kavalan Solist Single Cask Strength ex-Bourbon Cask** cask no. B070319060 db **(90.5)** n23 an unusual array of dry toast, walnut oil, grated chocolate and even dried banana skin: an attractive compilation; **t23** beautiful delivery with a multi-faceted richness. The oils are soft and wonderfully useful for getting the vanilla-driven complexity across. Fabulous, prickly spices abound while the sweet, juicy malts play the perfect foil; **f22** returns to its drier self; the vanillas now really going into an almost chalky overdrive; a vague bitter marmalade on slightly burned toast bites home as a late surprise; **b22.5** wow....!!! The first single cask from this excellent new distillery has much to say for itself. And most is seriously worth listening to. Much more of a soloist than a solist, I'd say. What's more how can you not adore the natural Eastern Cattle Egret breeding colour of the whisky...? 57.3% ncf nc

∴ **Kavalan Solist Single Cask Strength Sherry Cask** cask no. S080871033 db **(92)** n22.5 the grape is massive, virtually exploding from the glass: this is pure bodega. Against a toasty, hickory background the fruits go through the gears, even with an ultra-ripe cherry note: formidable if very slightly flawed; **t24** more of the same on the palate- mountains of grape in varying guises, from freshly picked to long time cooked, but somehow a team of barley-vanilla have no great difficulties scaling it; the spices are genuinely awe-inspiring, as is the slow development of juiciness to the grape; **f22.5** much drier, as the nose suggests it might be. But the burnt raisins are pretty attractive as is the light cocoa note which accompanies it; **b23** one of those fabulous sherry butts marked by a mild sulphury shadow but has so much else going on, that much, if not all, can be forgiven. 57.3%

MISCELLANEOUS

Jaburn & Co Pure Grain & Malt Spirit (53) n14 t13 f13 b13. Tastes like neutral grain and caramel to me. Some shop keepers, I hear, are selling it as whisky though this is not claimed on the label. Trust me. it isn't. 37.5%. Jaburn & Co, Denmark.

House of Westend Blended Whisky (67) n17 t18 f16 b16. No more than OK if you are being generous; some tobacco-dirty notes around. Doesn't mention country of origin anywhere on the label. 40%. Bernkasteler Burghof, Germany.

Prince of Wales Welsh Whisky (69) n17 t18 f17 b17. A syrupy aroma is compounded by an almost liqueurish body. Thin in true Scotch substance, probably because it claims to be Welsh but is really Scotch with herbs diffused in a process that took place in Wales. Interestingly, my "liqueur" tasting notes were written before I knew exactly what it was I was tasting, thus proving the point and confirming that, with these additives, this really isn't whisky at all. 40%

Shepherd's Export Finest Blend (46) n5 t16 f12 b13. A dreadful, illdefined grain-spirit nose is softened on the palate by an early mega-sweet kick. The finish is thin and eventually bitter. Feeble stuff. 37.2%. "A superb blend of Imported Scotch Malt whiskies and Distilled N.Z. grain spirit", claims the label which originally gives the strength as 40%, but has been over-written. Also, the grain, I was told, was from the USA. Southern Grain Spirit, NZ.

CROSS-COUNTRY VATTED MALT

Celtic Nations (Bruichladdich 1994 & Cooley Irish 1999) **(82) n20 t22 f20 b20.** Pleasant enough, very softly smoked, but a degree of inter-country bickering. *46%. Bruichladdich Distillery.*

Cradle Mountain db **(77) n19 t21 f18 b19**. Doesn't quite gel for me, though it has some delicious malty moments. *46%. This is a vatting of Aussie malt from Cradle Mountain and Springbank single malt scotch.*

Cradle Mountain Double db **(88) n20** no shortage of fruit with tangerines and diced green apples to the fore; **t23** in your face malt of almost awesome intensity. Lashings of clean barley, grassy notes showing both age and youth; **f23** lingers at first, then the Cradle Mountain signature of fruit and nuts descends. Also the cocoa is back with some serious oak present but always in control; **b22** this appears to be a different vatting to the 46% *with greater Tasmanian whisky evident – although it isn't! Much more poise and zest and no shortage of charisma. Brilliant stuff. 54.4%. This is a vatting of Aussie malt from Cradle Mountain and single malt scotch from Springbank.*

Jon, Mark and Robbo's The Smooth Sweeter One a vatting of Scottish and Irish malt **(92) n24** a real citrus and grassy kick to this with soft vanilla offering only a background noise. So delicate, you feel it might shatter if you nose too hard; **t22** fresh and fruity; **f23** long with some genuine complexity on the gently-spiced waves;controlled barley sweetness but drier vanillas dominate with those spices at the end; **b23** a beautiful whisky. Intriguing as it may be, claims I have heard of this being the first such whisky of its type are way off mark – not to mention Jon and Robbo. A hundred years ago and more it was not uncommon to find bottled malt whisky being a combination of Scotch and Irish. It would have come under the general title "whisky" and brought together by merchants procuring whiskies at the best prices they could get. In my library somewhere I have old labels of these forebears. That said, those whiskies of a century ago would have been hard pushed to better it. *40%. Edrington.*

Premium Bottlers Pure Malt Whisky Aged 10 Years LINK cask no. 1013 (marriage of Linkwood Single Malt and Canadian Single Malt) **(86) n21 t23 f21 b21.** Gallops off at a brisk, juicy, malty pace but tires as the natural caramels take hold. *46%. nc ncf.*

Premium Bottler Vatted Malt Whisky Aged 10 Years SCAP 101 (99% Scapa Scotch, 1% Glenora Canadian) **(90) n23** stewing apples form the centre ground of this astonishingly young, new make-coated aroma. As refreshing as a face full of driven rain; **t23** that glorious freshness now turns into something so salivating you'll have to drink a pint of water ahead of time to survive. Rarely is barley this concentrated; **f22** layering of intense barley continues, with just a drying coffee to offer the required balance; **b22** absolutely amazing malt. This Scapa, from a third-fill bourbon cask one assumes, appears half its age and simply glories in its natural brilliance. If this doesn't prove what world-great whisky this distillery conjures up in its most simple form, nothing will. *46%. nc ncf.*

Premium Bottler Vatted Malt Whisky Aged 10 Years STRT 101 (99% Strathisla Scotch, 1% Glenora Canadian) **(86) n20 t22 f23 b21.** Early evidence, on the nose particularly, of an over-tired cask but the natural exuberance and lustre of the distillate carries it through. Wonderfully chewy in part. *46%. nc ncf.*

Premium Bottler Vatted Malt Whisky Aged 10 Years ACHN 102 (99% Auchentoshan Scotch, 1% Glenora Canadian) **(84) n21 t22 f20 b21.** Very young, enormously citrussy effort with all the usual Auchtoshan foibles. Coming from a third fill makes for interesting dramming. *46%. nc ncf.*

Premium Bottlers Pure Malt Whisky Aged 11 Years BLAT cask no. 1011 (marriage of Blair Athol Single Malt and Canadian Single malt) **(84) n19 t22 f21 b22.** After a disaster at the first fence, picks itself up for a deliciously malty comeback. *46%. nc ncf.*

Premium Bottlers Pure Malt Whisky Aged 11 Years RLOC cask no. 1015 (marriage of Royal Lochnagar Single Malt and Canadian Single Malt) **(89) n21** heavy barley and firm, metallic notes; **t22** stodgy barley at first but begins to lighten as some honey bursts through; **f23** goes into honey-barley overdrive, again with a sharp metallic bite, but so delicious.... **b23** after a slow, cumbersome start finishes the course with surprising strength and grace. *46%. nc ncf.*

Premium Bottlers Pure Malt Whisky Aged 12 Years BRIN cask no. 1009 (marriage of Benrinnes Single Malt and Canadian Single Malt) **(76) n18 t20 f19 b19.** A tad feinty and falls at the first hurdle. *46%. nc ncf.*

Premium Bottler Vatted Malt Whisky Aged 12 Years GLLS 101 (99% Glen Lossie Scotch, 1% Glenora Canadian) **(86) n21 t22 f22 b21.** Very drinkable, pre-pubescent Lossie. Beware the false finale: it appears to vanish for a short finish and then reappears even more intensely than before. *46%. nc ncf.*

Premium Bottler Vatted Malt Whisky Aged 12 Years MRTL 101 (99% Mortlach Scotch, 1% Glenora Canadian) **(83) n21 t20 f21 b21.** Very decent heavyweight despite the lack of oak involvement. Excellent natural oils. *46%. nc ncf*

Slàinte

It seems that you can't have a Bible without a whole lot of begetting. And without all those listed below - massing flocks of the world's whisky people - this 2010 Bible would never have been begot at all. Whole fermenters-full of thanks to the usual suspects, especially Julia Nourney in Germany, David Croll of Whisk-e Ltd in Japan and super sleuth Duncan Chisholm. I would like to pay tribute to my indefatigable team of David Rankin, Billy Jeffrey, Edna Mycawka, David Wilson, James Murray, Ali Newton and Mike Leaman who, between them, tracked down over 1,000 whiskies and conquered the technology required to put my thoughts on them into book form. Heroes all. And an extra special mention must again go to Heiko Theime and Mike Smith. Thank you sirs. Thank you all.

Tomo Akaike; Esben Andersen; Justin Apthorp; Raymond Armstrong; Paul Aston; Sarah Bailey; David Baker; Duncan Baldwin; Nicola Ball; Melanie Balmer; Kevin Balmforth; Hazel Barnes; Liselle Barnsley; Rachel Barrie; Edward Bates; Michael Beamish; Lars Benjaminsen; Barry Bernstein; Jim Beveridge; Frank Michael Böer; my beautiful Borat, RIP; Birgit Bornemeire; Etienne Bouillon; Neil Boyd; Jens Breede; Stephen Bremner; David Brisset; Marie Broomer; Morag Brotherton; Karen Brown; Kim Brown; Sara Browne; Alex Bruce; Corinne Bucchioni; Mikki Burgers; Andy Burns; Jim Busuttil; Emily Butcher; Bill Caldwell; John Campbell; Jenny Cantrell; Tina Carey; Chris Carlsson; Alex Carnie; Mark Carpenter; Ehrlich Carsten; Ian Chang; Ian Chapman; Candy Charters; Suzanne Chester; Duncan Chisholm; Ashok Chokalingam; Julie Christian; Karen Christie; Ricky Christie; Nick Clark; Margaret Mary Clarke; Melissa Colman; Kris Comstock; Rick Connolly; Andy Cook; Paula Cormack; Andy Cornwall; Silvia Corrieri; Isabel Coughlan; James Cowan; David Cox; Ronnie Cox; Jason Graig; Georgie Crawford; Fergal Crean; Katherine Crisp; David Croll; Andy Crook; Andrew Currie; Peter Curry; Ewa Czernecka; Bob Dalgarno; Andre Dang; Craig Daniels; John Dannerbeck; Jancine Davies; Stephen Davies; Mark Dawkins; Martin Dawson; Zara D'Cotta; Herbert Debbeler; Jürgen Deibel; Alex Delaloye; Nathalie Desmedt; Eve Dewar; Marco DiCiacca; Steve Dobell; Gordon Doctor; Ed Dodson; Chris Donaldson; Jean Donnay; Simon Downs; Lucy Drake; Jonathan Driver; Hayley Dunn; Peter Dunne; Charles Du Pre; Colin Dunn; Peter Dunne; Frances Dupuy; Gavin Durnin; Lucy Egerton; Ben Ellefsen; Brent Elliot; Pat Ellis; Duncan Elphick; Per Eriksson; Richard Evans; Roy Evans; Lucy Fyrington; Lucy Farber; Joanna Fearnside; Bernie Fennerty; Angus Ferguson; Giles Fisher; Alex Fitch; Keira Fitzpatrick; Robert Fleischmann; Sally Forbes; Mary Forest, Angela Forsgren D'Orazio; Seth Fox; Tim French; Barry Frieslander; Alan Galloway; Luis Garcia Burgos; Nick Garland; Keith Geddes; Emma Gill; Fiona Gittus; John Glaser; Gregg Glass; John Glass; Alyson Goodenough; Jim Gordon; Richard Gordon; Jess Graber; Ed Graham; Isabel Graham-Yooll; George Grant; Lynn Grant; Miaochen Gray; Jonathan Greene; Hardus Greyling; Ken Grier; Christian Gruel; Johann Haider; Monika Haider; Olga Haley; Anna Hall; Archie Hamilton; Claudia Hamm; Wendy Harker; Jay Harman; David Harper; Mark Harris; Susan Harris; Alistair Hart; Andy Hart; Donald Hart; Lily Hassan; Julian Haswell; Christopher Hayman; Michael Heals; CJ Hellie; Jim Helsby; Lincon Henderson; Irene Hemmings; Anne Hempstock; John Hempstock; William Henderson; Robert Hicks; Vincent Hill; Aaron Hillman; Sarah-Jane Hodson; Karl-Holger Hoehler; Alexa Hopkins; Gillian Howell; Steve Hoyles; Mark Hunt; Ford Hussain; David Hynes; Sandy Hyslop; Kai Ivalo; Sean Ivers; Ily Jaffa; Vivienne Jawett; Kate Johansen-Berg; Richard Joynson; Sonia Kalia-Sagoo; Naofumi Kamaguchi; Lara Karakasevic; Larry Kass; Caitriona Kavanagh; Halley Kehoe; Jaclyn Kelly; Bob Kennedy; Sheila Kennedy; Keiko Kinoshita; Phillip J. Kirk; Daniel Kissling; Dennis Klindrup; Mana Kondo; Sare Kotze; Lex Kraaijeveld; Peter Krause; Libby Lafferty; Fiona Laing; Fred Laing; Stuart Laing; Hannah Langdon; Dill Lark; Kristy Lark; Lynne Lark; Liske Larsen; David Larsson; Rohna Lawson; Walter Lecocq; Patricia Lee; Harvey Lees; Anne Marie Le Lay; Guy Le Lay; Billy Leighton; Darren Leitch; Gilles Leizour; Graeme Lindsay; Lochy; Andrew Long; Jim Long; Martin Long; Alistair Longwell; Linda Love; Jason Low; Bill Lumsden; Stuart MacDuff; Frank MacHardy; Dominique Mackay; Roderick Mackenzie; Lorne Mackillop; Sharon Maclaughlin; Stephanie Macleod; Grant MacPherson; Rosalyn MacRae; Iseabail Mactaggart; Lesley-Ann Maguire; Patrick Maguire; Chris Maile; Ellen Malinski; Pekka Marjamaa; Tracy Markey; Gillian Marshall; Elaine Masson; Norman Mathison; Larry Mattingly; David Maxwell-Scott; Iain McCallum; Antony McCallum-Caron; Steve McCarthy; Tom McCulloch; Mhairi McDonald; John McDougall; John McDonough; Barbara McEwan; Jim McEwan; Lynne McEwan; Julie McFadden; Sarah McGhee; Paul McGinlay; Helen McGinn; Alister McIntosh; Doug McIvor; Dominic McKay; Anne McKerrow; Thomas McKenzie;

Margaret McKie; Lorne McKillop; Morna McLelland; Kirsty McLeod; Fred McMillan; Janice McMillan; Steven McNeil; Alan McConnachie; Laura McVicar; Lee Medoff; Clare Meikle; Jon Metcalf, Rick Mew; Paul Miles; Robbie Millar; Ann Miller; Ester Miller; Patrick Millet; Tom Mills; Jack Milroy; John Milroy; Tatsuya Minagawa; Andre Miron; Elaine Mitchell; Euan Mitchell; Matthew Mitchell; Jürgen Moeller; Takeshi Mogi; Zubair Mohamed; Dani Dal Molin, Rainer Mönks; Glen Moore; Les Morgan; Chris Morris; Jemma Morris; Ian Morrison; Mary Morton; Edelle Moss; Gordon Motion; Arthur Motley; Malcolm Mullan; Anna Murby; Jayne Murphy; Alison Murray; Andrew Murray; Bert Murray; Charles Murray; David Murray; Karen Murray; Stacey Murray; Elaine Mutch; Alex Mycawka; Edna Mycawka; Arthur Nagale; Kamiguchi Naofumi; Shin Natsuyama; Marc Neilly; Alie Newton; Margaret Nicol; Thrivikram G Nikam; Micke Nilsson; Kate Nimmo; Edel Nørgaard; Johannes Nørgaard; Lis Nørgaard; Søren Nørgaard; Jake Norris; Tom O'Connor; Catherine O'Grady; Deirbhile O'Grady; Aoife O'Sullivan; Barbara Ortner; Wolfram Ortner; Linda Outterson; Bill Owens; Ian Palmer; C R Parker; Richard Parker; Micheal Patterson; Robert Patterson; Richard Paterson; Rupert Patrick; John Peterson; Plamen Petroff; Justin Petszaft; Stefan E. Petszaft; Catharine Pickering; Edi Pierri; Simon Pointon; Alex Polasek; Dorothea Polasek; Nick Pollachi; Steve Poore; Henry Pratt; Amy Preske; Ashley Presser; Warren Preston; Sabina Pringle; Lucy Pritchard; Annie Pugh; Scott Pugh; Roland Puhl; David Radcliffe; John Ramsay; Caroline Randu; David Rankin, Robert Ransom; Aaron Rasmussen; Kaye Rawlings; Kelly Rayney; Alan Reid; Clémence Réveilhac; Mark Reynier; Jeannie Ritchie; Christine Roberts; Allan Robertson; Jennifer Robertson; Pamela Robertson; Maureen Robinson; Geraldine Roche; Jim Rogerson; Johanne Rolland; Claire Ross; Colin Ross; Duncan Ross; Fabio Rossi; Leonard S Russell; Suzy Russell; Jim Rutledge; Caroline Rylance; Richard Salmond; Silvano S. Samaroli, Courtney Sandora; Christine Sandys; Jacqui Sargeant; Trish Savage; John Savage-Onstwedder; Leander Schadler; Gerd Schmerschneider; Kendra Scott; Tara Serafini; Euan Shand; Rubyna Sheikh; Yuko Shimoda; Naomi Shooman; Joy Simpson; Alistair Sinclair; Sukhinder Singh; David Sloan; Ian Smart; Allan Smith; Barbara Smith; Michelle Smith; Mike Smith; Robert Hill Smith; Isa Sneddon; Emanuel Solinsky; Squeak Sparrow; Jeremy Speirs; Sue Stamps; Rory Steel; Barry Stein; Florian Stetter; Tamsin Stevens; David Stewart; Karen Stewart; David Stirk; Kathleen Stirling; Katy Stollery; Kaj Stovring; Derek Strange; Johanna Strasser; Ivar Svensson; Noel Sweeney; Kier Sword; Shoko Takagi; Katsuhiko Tanaka; James Tanner; Michelle Tansley; Graham Taylor; Elizabeth Teape; Jack Teeling; Jo Terry; Celine Tetu; Volker Theurer; Heiko Thieme; Jens Tholstrup; Corinna Thompson; Stuart Thompson; Terry Threlfall; Nick Tilt; Margrat Mary Timson; Una Tomnay; Jeff Topping; Hamish Torrie; Angela Traver; Sarah True; Robin Tucek; Rob Tuer; Ben Upjohn; Ian Urquhart; Mr Vannan; Johan Venter; Stefanu Venturini; Kenneth Vernon; Alistair Viner; Christine von Allwörden; Hans von Essen; Alistair Walker; Billy Walker; Jamie Walker; Karen Walker; Leesa Walker; Barry Walsh; Bernard Walsh; Christopher Watkin; Joanna Watson; Mark Watt; Andy Watts; Susan Webster; Peter Wheeler; Oswald Weidenauer; Ian Weir; Isabella A Wemyss; Jan H Westcott; Kerry White; Sian Whitelock; Jack Wiebers; Lars-Göran Wiebers; Alex Williams; David Williamson; Anthony Wills; Pamela Wils; David Wilson; Lisa Wilson; Arthur Winning; Lance Winters; Tony Wise; David Wood; Léonie Wood; Steve Worrall; Gordon Wright; Graham Wright; Kate Wright; Vanessa Wright; Junko Yaguchi; Venita Young; Daniel & Ursula Zurcher.